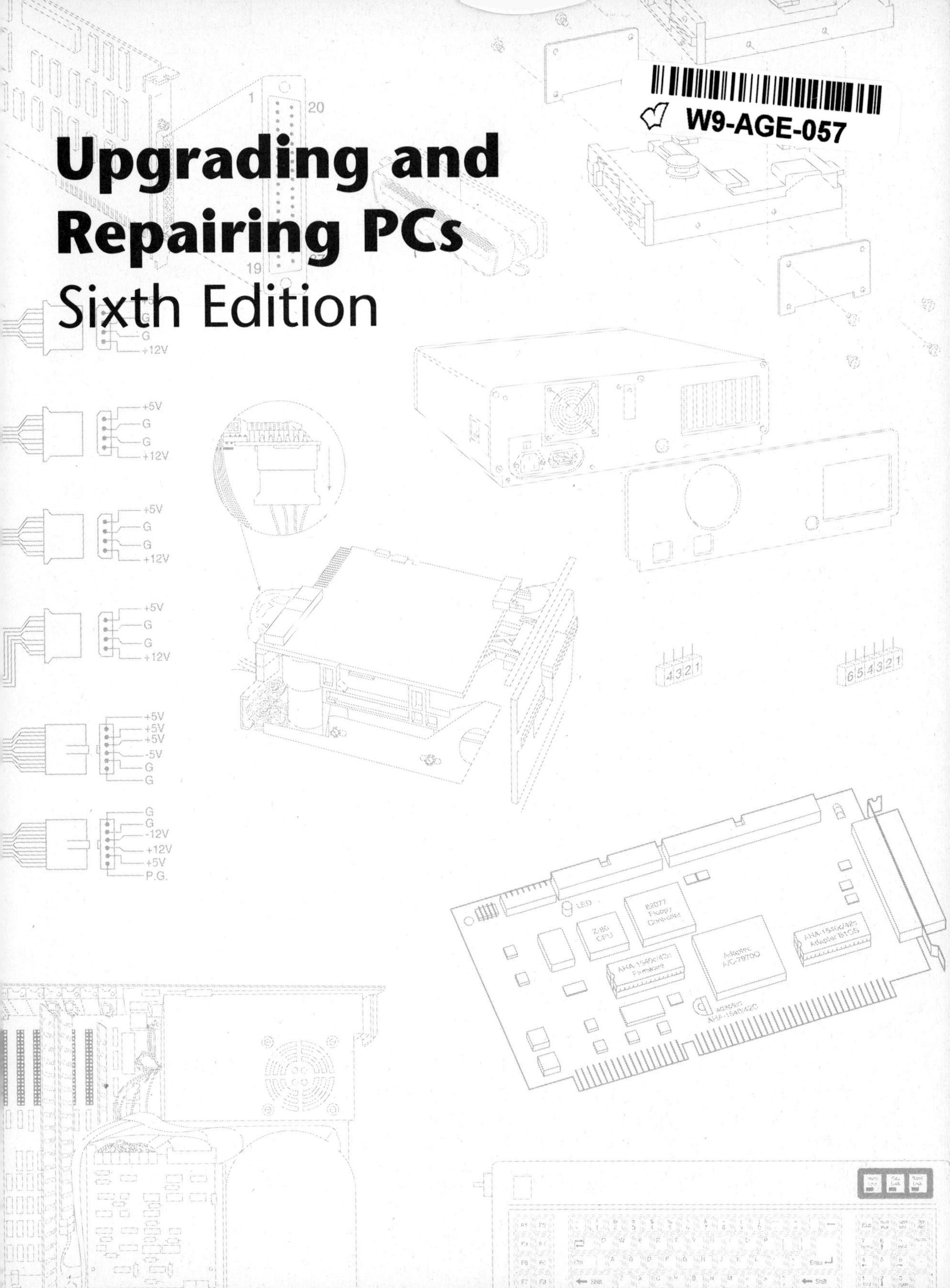
W9-AGE-057
Upgrading and
Repairing PCs
Sixth Edition
1
20
19
+5V
G
G
+12V
+5V
+5V
+5V
-5V
G
G
G
G
-12V
+12V
+5V
P.G.
4 3 2 1
6 5 4 3 2 1
LED
Z-80
CPU
82077
Floppy
Controller
Adaptec
AIC-7970D

Upgrading and Repairing PCs

Sixth Edition

Scott Mueller

Upgrading and Repairing PCs, Sixth Edition

Library of Congress Catalog No.: 96-69951

ISBN: 0-7897-0825-6

98 97 96 6 5 4 3 2 1

Interpretation of the printing code: the rightmost double-digit number is the year of the book's printing; the rightmost single-digit number, the number of the book's printing. For example, a printing code of 96-1 shows that the first printing of the book occurred in 1996.

Screen reproductions in this book were created using Collage Plus from Inner Media, Inc., Hollis, NH.

Credits

President
Roland Elgey

Publishing Director
Brad R. Koch

Editorial Services Director
Elizabeth Keaffaber

Managing Editor
Michael Cunningham

Director of Marketing
Lynn E. Zingraf

Acquisitions Manager
Elizabeth A. South

Product Director
Kevin Kloss

Technical Editor
Jerry Cox

Production Editors
Thomas F. Hayes
Lori A. Lyons

Technical Specialist
Nadeem Muhammed

Acquisitions Coordinator
Tracy Williams

Operations Coordinator
Patty Brooks

Assistant Product Marketing Manager
Christy Miller

Book Designer
Kim Scott

Cover Designer
Dan Armstrong

Production Team
Stephen Adams
Debra Bolhuis
Jason Carr
Erin M. Danielson
Trey Frank
Jason Hand
Daniel Harris
Daryl Kessler
Casey Price
Kaylene Riemen
Laura Robbins
Bobbi Satterfield

Indexer
Ginny Bess

Composed in *Stone Serif* and *MCPdigital* by Que Corporation.

To my family:

Lynn, Amanda, and Emerson

Thanks for your support and patience while yet another edition was completed. This book has become a full-time job.

About the Author

Scott Mueller is president of Mueller Technical Research, an international personal computer research and corporate training firm. Since 1982, MTR has specialized in the industry's most accurate and effective corporate technical training seminars, maintaining a client list that includes Fortune 500 companies, the U.S. and foreign governments, major software and hardware corporations, as well as PC enthusiasts and entrepreneurs. He has logged millions of miles presenting his seminars to thousands of PC professionals throughout North and South America, Europe, and Australia.

As an internationally recognized seminar director and renowned authority in deciphering technical information, Mueller has developed and presented personal computer training courses in all areas of PC hardware and software. He is an expert in PC hardware, data-recovery techniques, local area networks, and major operating systems software, including DOS, Windows, and OS/2. Seminars are available on an on-site contract basis. For more information about a custom computer training seminar for your organization, contact:

Mueller Technical Research
21718 Mayfield Lane
Barrington, IL 60010-9733
(708) 726-0709
(708) 726-0710 FAX
CompuServe ID: **73145,1566**
Internet: **73145.1566@compuserve.com**

Mueller has many popular books, articles, and course materials to his credit, in addition to *Upgrading and Repairing PCs*, which has sold more than 800,000 copies in previous editions. His two hour video, *Your PC—The Inside Story*, is available through LearnKey, Inc. For ordering information, contact:

LearnKey, Inc.
1845 West Sunset Boulevard
St. George, UT 84770
(800) 937-3279
(801) 674-9733
(801) 674-9734 FAX

If you have questions about PC hardware, suggestions for the next version of the book, or any comments in general, send them to Scott via CompuServe or the Internet, if at all possible. Correspondence through standard mail takes him much longer to answer!

When he is not working on books or seminars, Scott can usually be found working in the garage on his soon-to-be LT4-equipped Impala SS as well as various other performance car projects, testing the vehicles at the local drag strip, or showing them off at car shows and the local drive-in scene.

Acknowledgments

This sixth edition is the product of a great deal of additional research and development over the previous editions. Several people have helped me with both the research and production of this book. I would like to thank the following people:

First, a very special thanks to my wife and partner, Lynn. This book continues to be an incredible burden on both our business and family life, and she has put up with a lot! Lynn is excellent at dealing with the many companies we have to contact for product information and research. She is the backbone of MTR.

Thanks to Lisa Carlson of Mueller Technical Research for helping with product research and office management. She has fantastic organizational skills that have been a tremendous help in managing all the information that comes into and goes out of this office.

Thanks to all the companies that have provided hardware, software, and research information that has been helpful in developing this book. Thanks to David Means for feedback from the trenches about various products. Thanks also to Jerry Cox for assistance with updating several of the chapters under intense deadline pressure!

I would like to offer a special thanks to the people at Que who have made this book possible. First off, I would like to extend a special thanks to Elizabeth South, who has been my main contact at Que. Elizabeth oversaw the final deadlines and submissions, and her positive attitude and good nature really helped when the pressure was on. Thanks to Kevin Kloss for his insightful suggestions and queries about PC technology. Thanks also to Tom Hayes and Lori Lyons, who did much of the editing and handling of the text and figures once it was submitted. I have enjoyed working with you all!

Thanks to all the readers who have e-mailed me with suggestions concerning this book, I welcome all of your comments. A special thanks to Paul Reid, who proofread the text and always has many suggestions to offer.

Finally, I would like to thank all the people who have attended the many seminars that I have given; you may not realize how much I learn from each of you and your questions! Thanks also to those of you on the Internet and CompuServe forums with both questions and answers, from which I have also learned a great deal.

We'd Like to Hear from You!

As part of our continuing effort to produce books of the highest possible quality, Que would like to hear your comments. To stay competitive, we *really* want you, as a computer book reader and user, to let us know what you like or dislike most about this book or other Que products.

You can mail comments, ideas, or suggestions for improving future editions to the address below, or send us a fax at (317) 581-4663. For the online inclined, Macmillan Computer Publishing has a forum on CompuServe (type **GO QUEBOOKS** at any prompt) through which our staff and authors are available for questions and comments. The address of our Internet site is **http://www.mcp.com/que** (World Wide Web).

In addition to exploring our forum, please feel free to contact me personally to discuss your opinions of this book: I'm **74201,1064** on CompuServe, and **kkloss@que.mcp.com** on the Internet.

Thanks in advance—your comments will help us to continue publishing the best books available on computer topics in today's market.

Kevin Kloss
Product Director
Que Corporation
201 W. 103rd Street
Indianapolis, Indiana 46290
USA

Note

Although we cannot provide general technical support, we're happy to help you resolve problems you encounter related to our books, discs, or other products. If you need such assistance, please contact our Tech Support department at 800-545-5914 ext. 3833.

To order other Que or Macmillan Computer Publishing books or products, please call our Customer Service department at 800-835-3202 ext. 666.

Contents at a Glance

Appendixes

Contents

II Primary System Components 61

4 Motherboards 63

5 Bus Slots and I/O Cards 81

6 Microprocessor Types and Specifications 145

15 Hard Disk Interfaces 695

16 Hard Disk Drive Installation 763

17 CD-ROM Drives 817

Introduction

Welcome to *Upgrading and Repairing PCs*, Sixth Edition. This book is for people who want to upgrade, repair, maintain, and troubleshoot computers. It covers the full range of PC-compatible systems from the oldest 8-bit machines to the latest in high-end 64-bit workstations.

In addition, this book covers state-of-the-art hardware and accessories that make the most modern personal computers easier, faster, and more productive to use. Hardware coverage includes the 486, Pentium and Pentium Pro CPU chips, new cache and main memory technology, PCI local bus technology, CD-ROM drives, tape backups, sound boards, PCMCIA devices for laptops, IDE and SCSI-interface devices, larger and faster hard drives, and new video adapter and display capabilities.

The comprehensive coverage of the PC-compatible personal computer in this book has consistently won acclaim. With the release of this sixth edition, *Upgrading and Repairing PCs* continues its place as one of the most comprehensive and easily used references on even the most modern system—those based on cutting-edge hardware and software. The book examines PCs in depth, outlines the differences among them, and presents options for configuring each system at the time you purchase it.

Sections of this book provide detailed information about each internal component of a personal computer system, from the processor to the keyboard and video display. The book examines the options available in modern, high-performance PC configurations, and how to use them to your advantage; it focuses on much of the hardware and software available today and specifies the optimum configurations for achieving maximum benefit for the time and money you spend. At a glance, here are the major system components and peripherals covered in this edition of *Upgrading and Repairing PCs*:

- Pentium Pro, Pentium, 486, and earlier central processing unit (CPU) chips.
- The latest processor upgrade socket specifications.
- New motherboard chipsets and designs, including the new ATX form factor.
- Special bus architectures and devices, including high-speed PCI (Peripheral Component Interconnect) and VL-Bus (VESA Local), EISA (Extended Industry Standard Architecture), and MCA (Micro Channel Architecture).
- Bus resources which often conflict such as Interrupt ReQuest (IRQ) lines, Direct Memory Access (DMA) channels, and Input Output (I/O) port addresses.

- Plug and Play architecture.
- Larger, faster hard drives and hard drive interfaces, including IDE and SCSI.
- Floppy drives, including 360K, 1.2M, 1.44M, and 2.88M drives.
- New storage devices such as CD-ROM and Magneto-Optical drives.
- Increasing system memory capacity with SIMM and DIMM modules.
- New types of memory including Synchronous Pipeline Burst cache, EDO RAM, Burst EDO, and Synchronous DRAM.
- Large-screen Super VGA monitors and high-speed graphics adapter cards.
- Peripheral devices such as CD-ROM drives, sound boards, and tape backups.
- PCMCIA devices for laptops.
- Multimedia.

This book also shows you how to troubleshoot the kind of hardware problems that can make PC upgrading and repairing difficult. Troubleshooting coverage includes IRQ, DMA channel and I/O Port addressees, as well as memory address conflicts. This book tells you how to avoid problems with these system resources, and how to make installing a new adapter board in your computer a simple plug-and-play operation. This book also focuses on software problems, starting with the basics of how DOS or another operating system works with your system hardware to start up your system. You also learn how to troubleshoot and avoid problems involving system hardware, the operating system, and applications software such as word processors or spreadsheets.

This book is the result of years of research and development in the production of my PC hardware, operating system, and data recovery seminars. Over the years I have personally taught (and still teach) thousands of people about PC troubleshooting, upgrading, maintenance, repair, and data recovery. This book represents the culmination of many years of field experience as well as knowledge culled from the experiences of thousands of others. What originally started out as a simple course workbook has over the years grown into a complete reference on the subject. Now you can benefit from this experience and research.

What are the Main Objectives of this Book?

Upgrading and Repairing PCs focuses on several objectives. The primary one is to help you learn how to maintain, upgrade, and repair your PC system. To that end, *Upgrading and Repairing PCs* helps you fully understand the family of computers that has grown from the original IBM PC, including all PC-compatible systems. This book discusses all areas of system improvement such as floppy disks, hard disks, central processing units, math coprocessors, and power-supply improvements. The book discusses proper system and component care; it specifies the most failure-prone items in different PC systems, and tells you how to locate and identify a failing component. You'll learn about powerful diagnostics hardware and software that enable a system to help you determine the cause of a problem and how to repair it.

The PC-compatible microcomputer family is moving forward rapidly in power and capabilities. Processor performance increases with every new chip design. *Upgrading and Repairing PCs* helps you gain an understanding of each of the CPU chips used in PC-compatible computer systems.

This book covers the important differences between major system architectures—the original Industry Standard Architecture (ISA), Extended Industry Standard Architecture (EISA), and Micro Channel Architecture (MCA). The most modern systems use special local bus architectures and adapter cards to get top speed from system peripherals like video adapter cards and hard drives. Besides ISA, EISA, and MCA, these local bus architectures include PCI (Peripheral Component Interconnect) and VL-Bus devices. *Upgrading and Repairing PCs* covers each of these system architectures and their adapter boards to help you make decisions about which kind of system you may want to buy in the future, and how to upgrade and troubleshoot such systems.

The amount of storage space available to modern PCs is increasing geometrically. *Upgrading and Repairing PCs* covers storage options ranging from larger, faster hard drives to state-of-the-art storage devices. In addition, this book provides detailed information on upgrading and troubleshooting system RAM.

When you finish reading this book, you should have the knowledge to upgrade as well as troubleshoot and repair almost all systems and components.

Who Should Use this Book?

Upgrading and Repairing PCs is designed for people who want a good understanding of how their PC systems work. Each section fully explains common and not-so-common problems, what causes problems, and how to handle problems when they arise. You will gain an understanding of disk configuration and interfacing, for example, that can improve your diagnostics and troubleshooting skills. You'll develop a feel for what goes on in a system so that you can rely on your own judgment and observations and not some table of canned troubleshooting steps. This book is for people who are truly interested in their systems and how they operate.

Upgrading and Repairing PCs is written for people who will select, install, configure, maintain, and repair systems they or their companies use. To accomplish these tasks, you need a level of knowledge much higher than that of an average system user. You must know exactly which tool to use for a task and how to use the tool correctly. This book can help you achieve this level of knowledge.

What is in this Book?

Part I of this book serves primarily as an introduction. Chapter 1 begins with an introduction to the development of the original IBM PC and PC-compatibles. Chapter 2 provides information about the different types of systems you encounter and what separates one type of system from another, including the types of system bus that differentiate systems. Chapter 2 also provides an overview of the types of PC systems that help build a foundation of knowledge essential for the remainder of the book. Chapter 3 discusses the physical disassembly and reassembly of a system.

Part II covers the primary system components of a PC. Chapter 4 begins this part with a discussion of the components in a PC system by covering the motherboard. Chapter 5 continues this discussion by focusing on the different types of expansion slots and bus types found in PC systems. Chapter 6 goes into detail about the central processing unit (CPU), or main processor, including those from Intel as well as other companies. Chapter 7 gives a detailed discussion of PC memory, from basic architecture to the physical chips and SIMMs themselves. Chapter 8 is a detailed investigation of the power supply, which remains the primary cause for PC system problems and failures.

Part III is about input/output hardware and begins with Chapter 9 on input devices. This chapter includes coverage of keyboards, pointing devices, and the game port. Chapter 10 discusses video display hardware, including video adapters and monitors. Chapter 11 is a detailed discussion of communications and networking hardware, while Chapter 12 focuses on audio hardware including sound boards and speaker systems.

Part IV is about mass storage systems and leads off with Chapter 13 on floppy disk drives and controllers. Chapter 14 is a detailed discussion of hard disk drives and drive technology. Chapter 15 covers hard disk interfaces, including IDE and SCSI, in depth. Chapter 16 details the installation requirements and procedures for a hard disk. This information is invaluable when you install drives as either replacements or upgrades in a system, and if you troubleshoot and repair malfunctioning drives. Chapter 17 is about CD-ROM drives, and Chapter 18 covers tape and other mass storage drives.

Part V covers system assembly and maintenance and starts off with Chapter 19 on buying or building a PC-compatible system as well as system upgrades and improvements. This information is useful especially if you make purchasing decisions, and also serves as a general guideline for features that make a certain compatible computer a good or bad choice. The more adventurous can use this information to assemble their own custom system from scratch. Chapter 20 covers system preventive maintenance, backups, and warranties.

Part VI covers troubleshooting and diagnostics and starts off with Chapter 21 on diagnostic tools. Chapter 22 covers operating system software and troubleshooting as well as data recovery.

Chapter 23 covers in considerable depth the original classic IBM PC, XT, and AT computers. All modern compatibles are based on these systems, so this information can serve as a useful reference. This information is useful not only for supporting actual IBM equipment, but also for PC-compatible systems not supplied with extensive documentation. You learn how to compare systems with the original IBM standard, and see how far we have come since these original cornerstone systems were introduced.

Appendix A provides an extensive PC technical reference section, including a variety of technical information tables. Appendix B provides an extremely well-detailed vendor list useful for finding suppliers and vendors of necessary hardware and software. The last section provides an informative glossary.

I believe that *Upgrading and Repairing PCs* will prove to be the best book of its kind on the market. It offers not only the breadth of PC-compatible equipment, but also much in-depth coverage of each topic. This book is valuable as a reference tool for understanding how various components in a system interact and operate, and as a guide to repairing and servicing problems you encounter. *Upgrading and Repairing PCs* is far more than just a repair manual. I sincerely hope that you enjoy it.

Part I

Introduction

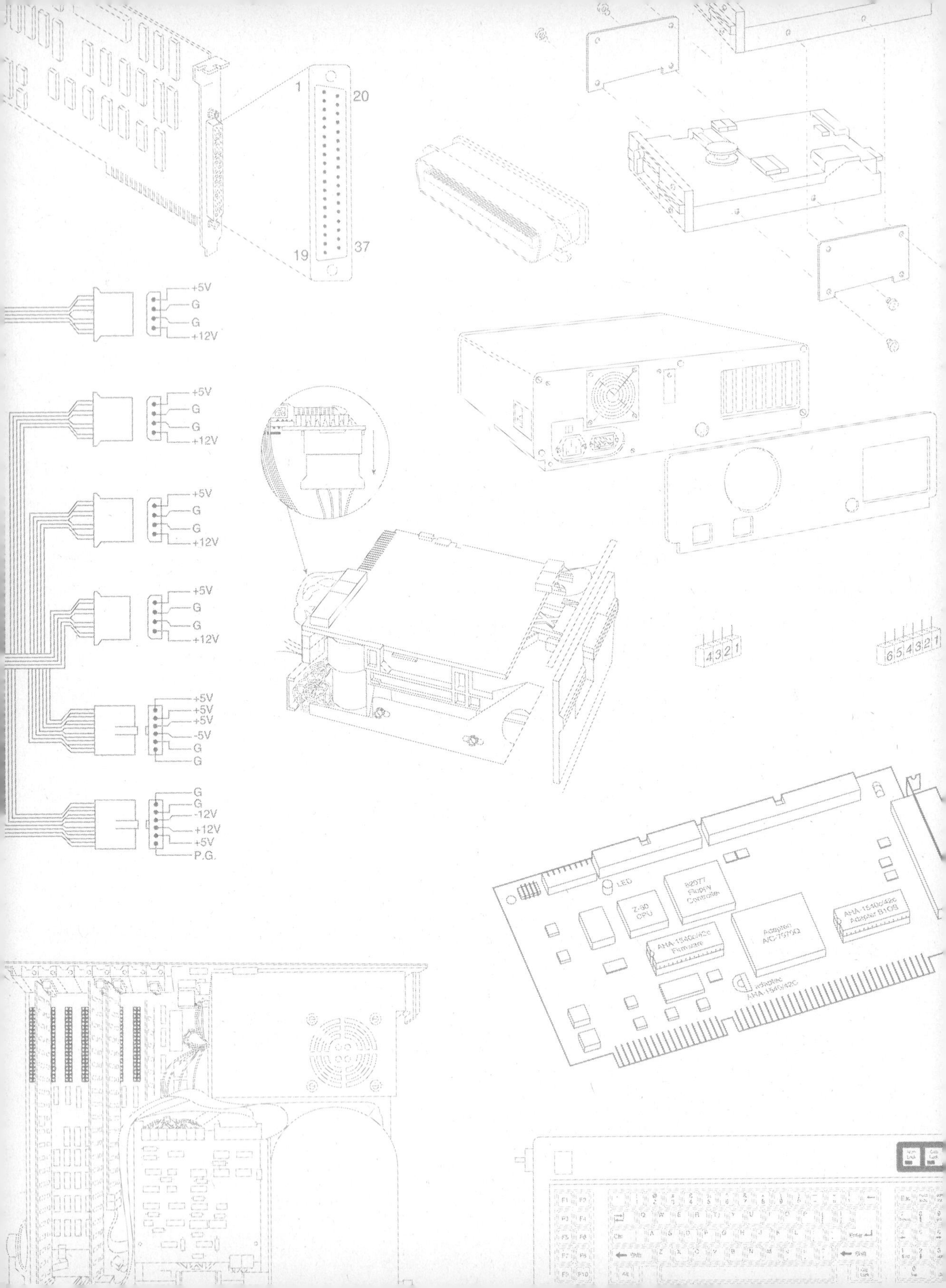

1
20
19
37
+5V
G
G
+12V
+5V
G
G
+12V
+5V
G
G
+12V
+5V
G
G
+12V
+5V
+5V
+5V
-5V
G
G
G
G
-12V
+12V
+5V
P.G.
4 3 2 1
6 5 4 3 2 1
LED
82077 Floppy Controller
Z-80 CPU
Adaptec AIC-7970Q
AHA-1540c/42c Firmware
AHA-1540c/42c Adapter BIOS
adaptec AHA-1540/42C

Chapter 1

Personal Computer Background

Many discoveries and inventions have contributed to the development of the personal computer. Examining a few important developmental landmarks can help bring the entire picture into focus.

Personal Computing History

A modern digital computer is largely a collection of electronic switches. These switches are used to represent, as well as to control, the routing of data elements called *binary digits* (bits). Because of the on or off nature of the binary information and signal routing used by the computer, an efficient electronic switch was required. The first electronic computers used vacuum tubes as switches, and although the tubes worked, they had many problems.

The tube was inefficient as a switch. It consumed a great deal of electrical power and gave off enormous heat—a significant problem in the earlier systems. Primarily because of the heat they generated, tubes were notoriously unreliable—one failed every two hours or so in the larger systems.

The invention of the transistor, or semiconductor, was one of the most important developments leading to the personal computer revolution. The transistor was invented in 1948 by Bell Laboratories engineers John Bardeen, Walter Brattain, and William Shockley. The transistor, which essentially is a solid-state electronic switch, replaced the much less suitable vacuum tube. Because the transistor consumed significantly less power, a computer system built with transistors was much smaller, faster, and more efficient than a computer system built with vacuum tubes.

The conversion to transistors began the trend toward miniaturization that continues to this day. Today's small laptop (or palmtop) PC systems, which run on batteries, have more computing power than many earlier systems that filled rooms and consumed huge amounts of electrical power.

In 1959, engineers at Texas Instruments invented the integrated circuit (IC), a semiconductor circuit that contains more than one transistor on the same base (or substrate material) and connects the transistors without wires. The first IC contained only six transistors. By comparison, the Intel Pentium Pro microprocessor used in many of today's high-end systems has more than 5.5 million transistors, and the integral cache built into some of these chips contains an additional 16 million transistors. Today, many ICs have transistor counts in the multimillion range.

In 1969, Intel introduced a 1K-bit memory chip, which was much larger than anything else available at the time. (1K bits equals 1,024 bits, and a byte equals 8 bits. This chip, therefore, stored only 128 bytes—not much by today's standards.) Because of Intel's success in chip manufacturing and design, Busicomp, a Japanese calculator-manufacturing company, asked Intel to produce 12 different logic chips for one of its calculator designs. Rather than produce 12 separate chips, Intel engineers included all the functions of the chips in a single chip.

In addition to incorporating all the functions and capabilities of the 12-chip design into one multipurpose chip, the engineers designed the chip to be controlled by a program that could alter the function of the chip. The chip then was generic in nature, meaning that it could function in designs other than calculators. Previous designs were hard-wired for one purpose, with built-in instructions; this chip would read from memory a variable set of instructions that would control the function of the chip. The idea was to design almost an entire computing device on a single chip that could perform different functions, depending on what instructions it was given.

The first microprocessor—the Intel 4004, a 4-bit processor—was introduced in 1971. The chip operated on four bits of data at a time. The successor to the 4004 chip was the 8008 8-bit microprocessor, introduced in 1972.

In 1973, some of the first microcomputer kits based on the 8008 chip were developed. These kits were little more than demonstration tools and did little except blink lights. In late 1973, Intel introduced the 8080 microprocessor, which was 10 times faster than the earlier 8008 chip and addressed 64K of memory. This breakthrough was the one that the personal computer industry had been waiting for.

MITS introduced the Altair kit in a cover story in the January 1975 issue of *Popular Electronics* magazine. The Altair kit, considered to be the first personal computer, included an 8080 processor, a power supply, a front panel with a large number of lights, and 256 bytes (not kilobytes) of memory. The kit sold for $395 and had to be assembled. The computer included an open architecture bus (slots) that prompted various add-ons and peripherals from aftermarket companies. The new processor inspired other companies to write programs, including the CP/M (Control Program for Microprocessors) operating system and the first version of the Microsoft BASIC (Beginners All-purpose Symbolic Instruction Code) programming language.

IBM introduced what can be called its first *personal computer* in 1975. The Model 5100 had 16K of memory, a built-in 16-line-by-64-character display, a built-in BASIC language interpreter, and a built-in DC-300 cartridge tape drive for storage. The system's $9,000 price placed it out of the mainstream personal computer marketplace, which was dominated by experimenters (affectionately referred to as *hackers*) who built low-cost kits ($500 or so) as a hobby. The IBM system obviously was not in competition for this low-cost market and did not sell well.

The Model 5100 was succeeded by the 5110 and 5120 before IBM introduced what we know as the IBM Personal Computer (Model 5150). Although the 5100 series preceded the IBM PC, the older systems and the 5150 IBM PC had nothing in common. The PC IBM turned out was closely related to the IBM System/23 DataMaster, an office computer system introduced in 1980.

In 1976, a new company called Apple Computer introduced the Apple I, which sold for $695. This system consisted of a main circuit board screwed to a piece of plywood; a case and power supply were not included. Only a few of these computers were made, and they reportedly have sold to collectors for more than $20,000. The Apple II, introduced in 1977, helped set the standard for nearly all the important microcomputers to follow, including the IBM PC.

The microcomputer world was dominated in 1980 by two types of computer systems. One type, the Apple II, claimed a large following of loyal users and a gigantic software base that was growing at a fantastic rate. The other type, CP/M systems, consisted not of a single system but of all the many systems that evolved from the original MITS Altair. These systems were compatible with one another and were distinguished by their use of the CP/M operating system and expansion slots, which followed the S-100 (for slots with 100 pins) standard. All these systems were built by a variety of companies and sold under various names. For the most part, however, these companies used the same software and plug-in hardware. It is interesting to note that none of these systems were PC-compatible, or Mac-compatible, the two primary standards in place today!

The IBM Personal Computer

At the end of 1980, IBM decided to truly compete in the rapidly growing low-cost personal computer market. The company established what then was called the Entry Systems Division, located in Boca Raton, Florida, to develop the new system. This small group consisted of 12 engineers and designers under the direction of Don Estridge; the team's chief designer was Lewis Eggebrecht. The division developed IBM's first real PC. (IBM considered the 5100 system, developed in 1975, to be an intelligent programmable terminal rather than a genuine computer, even though it truly was a computer.) Nearly all these engineers had been moved to the new division from the System/23 DataMaster project, which in 1980 introduced a small office computer system that was the closest predecessor to the IBM PC.

Much of the PC's design was influenced by the DataMaster's design. In the DataMaster's single-piece design, the display and keyboard were integrated into the unit. Because these features were limiting, they became external units on the PC, although the PC keyboard layout and electrical designs were copied from the DataMaster.

Several other parts of the IBM PC system also were copied from the DataMaster, including the expansion bus (or input/output slots), which included not only the same physical 62-pin connector, but also almost identical pin specifications. This copying was possible because the PC used the same interrupt controller as the DataMaster and a similar direct memory access (DMA) controller. Expansion cards already designed for the DataMaster could then be easily redesigned to function in the PC.

The DataMaster used an Intel 8085 CPU, which had a 64K address limit, as well as an 8-bit internal and external data bus. This arrangement prompted the PC design team to use the Intel 8088 CPU, which offered a much larger (1M) memory address limit, and an internal 16-bit data bus, but only an 8-bit external data bus. The 8-bit external data bus and similar instruction set allowed the 8088 to be easily interfaced into the earlier DataMaster designs.

Estridge and the design team rapidly developed the design and specifications for the new system. In addition to borrowing from the System/23 DataMaster, the team studied the marketplace, which also had enormous influence on the IBM PC's design. The designers looked at the prevailing standards, learned from the success of those systems, and incorporated into the new PC all the features of the popular systems—and more. With the parameters for design made obvious by the market, IBM produced a system that filled its niche in the market perfectly.

IBM brought its system from idea to delivery in one year by using existing designs and purchasing as many components as possible from outside vendors. The Entry Systems Division was granted autonomy from IBM's other divisions and could tap resources outside the company, rather than go through the bureaucratic procedures that required exclusive use of IBM resources. IBM contracted out the PC's languages and operating system, for example, to a small company named Microsoft. (IBM originally contacted Digital Research, which invented CP/M, but that company apparently was not interested in the proposal. Microsoft was interested, however, and today, it is one of the largest software companies in the world.) The use of outside vendors also was an open invitation for the aftermarket to jump in and support the system—and it did.

On Wednesday, August 12, 1981, a new standard took its place in the microcomputer industry with the debut of the IBM PC. Since then, hundreds of millions of PC-compatible systems have been sold, as the original PC has grown into a large family of computers and peripherals. More software has been written for this computer family than for any other system on the market.

The IBM-Compatible Marketplace 15 Years Later

In the more than 15 years since the original IBM PC was introduced, many changes have occurred. The IBM-compatible computer, for example, advanced from a 4.77-MHz 8088-based system to 166-MHz Pentium-based and 200-MHz or faster Pentium Pro-based systems—nearly *1,000 times faster* than the original IBM PC (in actual processing speed, not just clock speed). The original PC had only two single-sided floppy drives that stored 160K each using DOS 1.0, whereas modern systems easily can have several gigabytes of hard disk storage. A rule of thumb in the computer industry is that available processor performance and disk-storage capacity at least double every two to three years. Since the beginning of the PC industry, this pattern has shown no sign of changing.

In addition to performance and storage capacity, another major change since the original IBM PC was introduced is that IBM is not the only manufacturer of "PC-compatible" systems. IBM originated the PC-compatible standard, of course, and it continues to set standards that compatible systems follow, but the company does not dominate the market as it did originally. As often as not, new standards in the PC industry are developed by companies and organizations other than IBM. Hundreds of system manufacturers produce computers that are compatible, not to mention the thousands of peripheral manufacturers whose components expand and enhance PC-compatible systems.

PC-compatible systems have thrived, not only because compatible hardware can be assembled easily, but also because the primary operating system was available not from IBM but from a third party (Microsoft). The core of the system software is the BIOS (Basic Input Output System), and this was also available from third party companies like Phoenix, AMI, and others. This situation allowed other manufacturers to license the operating system and BIOS software and to sell their own compatible systems. The fact that DOS borrowed the best functions from both CP/M and UNIX probably had a lot to do with the amount of software that became available. Later, with the success of Windows and OS/2, there would be even more reasons for software developers to write programs for PC-compatible systems.

One of the reasons why Apple Macintosh systems will likely never enjoy the success of PC-compatibles is that Apple controls all the software (BIOS and OS) and until recently had not licensed any of it to other companies for use in compatible systems. Apple now seems to recognize this flawed stance because it has begun to license this software; however, it seems too late for it to effectively compete with the PC-compatible juggernaut. It is fortunate for the computing public as a whole that IBM did create a more open standard. The competition among manufacturers and vendors of PC-compatible systems is the reason why such systems offer so much performance and so many capabilities for the money compared with non-PC-compatible systems.

The IBM-compatible market continues to thrive and prosper. New technology will be integrated into these systems, enabling them to grow with the times. Because of the high value that these types of systems can offer for the money and the large amount of software that is available to run on them, PC-compatible systems likely will dominate the personal computer marketplace for perhaps the next 10 to 15 years as well.

Summary

This chapter traced the development of personal computing from the transistor to the introduction of the IBM PC. Intel's continuing development of the integrated circuit led to a succession of microprocessors and reached a milestone with the 1973 introduction of the 8080 chip. In 1975, MITS introduced the Altair computer kit, which was based on the 8080 microprocessor. IBM jumped into the personal computer market in 1975 with the Model 5100.

In 1976, Apple sold its first computers, followed in 1977 by the enormously successful Apple II. Because of its success, the Apple II played a major role in setting standards and expectations for all later microcomputers.

Finally, in 1981, IBM introduced its personal computer to a microcomputer world dominated by the Apple II and the computers that evolved from the Altair, which used the CP/M operating system. The IBM PC, designed with the needs of the market in mind and with many of its components produced by outside vendors, immediately set the new standard for the microcomputer industry. This standard has evolved to meet the needs of today's users, with more powerful systems offering performance levels that were not even imagined in 1981.

Chapter 2

Overview of System Features and Components

This chapter discusses the differences in system architecture among PC-compatible systems and also explains memory structure and use. In addition, the chapter discusses how to obtain the documentation necessary for maintaining and upgrading your computer.

Types of Systems

Many types of PC-compatible systems are on the market today. Most systems are similar, but a few important differences in system architecture have become more apparent as operating environments such as Windows and OS/2 have increased in popularity. Operating systems such as OS/2 1.x and Windows 3.1 require at least a 286 CPU platform on which to run. OS/2 2.x, 3.x (Warp), and Windows 95 will run on a 386 system, and Windows NT 4.x requires at least a 486 CPU to run. Knowing and understanding the differences among these hardware platforms will enable you to plan, install, and use modern operating systems and applications so as to use the hardware optimally.

All PC-compatible systems can be broken down into two basic system types, or classes, of hardware:

- 8-bit (PC/XT-class) systems
- 16/32/64-bit (AT-class) systems

The term *PC* stands for Personal Computer, of course; *XT* stands for an eXTended PC; and *AT* stands for an Advanced Technology PC. The terms PC, XT, and AT as used here refer to the original IBM systems of those names. The XT basically was a PC system that included a hard disk for storage in addition to the floppy drive(s) found in the basic PC system. These systems had an 8-bit 8088 processor and an 8-bit Industry Standard Architecture (ISA) Bus for system expansion. The *bus* is the name given to expansion slots in which additional plug-in circuit boards can be installed. The 8-bit designation comes from the fact that the ISA Bus found in the PC/XT class systems can send or receive only eight bits of data in a single cycle. The data in an eight-bit bus is sent along eight wires simultaneously, in parallel.

More advanced systems are said to be *AT-class,* which indicates that they follow certain standards and follow the basic design set forth in the original IBM AT system. *AT* is the designation IBM applied to systems that first included more advanced 16-bit (and later, 32- and 64-bit) processors and expansion slots. AT-class systems must have any processor that is compatible with Intel 286 or higher processors (including the 386, 486, Pentium, and Pentium Pro processors) and must have a 16-bit or greater expansion slot system. The bus architecture is central to AT compatibility; PC/XT-class systems with upgraded processor boards that do not include a 16-bit or greater expansion bus do not qualify as true AT-class systems.

The first AT-class systems had a 16-bit version of the ISA Bus, which is an extension of the original 8-bit ISA Bus found in the PC/XT-class systems. Eventually, several expansion slot or bus designs were developed for AT-class systems, including those in the following list:

- 16-bit ISA Bus
- 16/32-bit Extended ISA (EISA) Bus
- 16/32-bit PS/2 Micro Channel Architecture (MCA) Bus
- 16-bit PC-Card (PCMCIA) Bus
- 32/64-bit VESA Local (VL) Bus
- 32/64-bit Peripheral Component Interconnect (PCI) Bus

A system with any of these types of expansion slots is by definition an AT-class system, regardless of the actual Intel or Intel-compatible processor used. AT-type systems with 386 or higher processors have special capabilities not found in the first generation of 286-based ATs. The 386 and higher systems have distinct capabilities regarding memory addressing, memory management, and possible 32- or 64-bit wide access to data. Most systems with 386DX or higher chips also have 32-bit bus architectures to take full advantage of the 32-bit data transfer capabilities of the processor.

Although 64-bit versions of VL-Bus and PCI have been proposed, it is unlikely a 64-bit VL-Bus will ever actually appear in production because the marketplace has almost entirely shifted in favor of PCI. The proposed 64-bit version of PCI will definitely appear sometime in the future.

The ISA and MCA architectures were developed by IBM and copied by other manufacturers for use in compatible systems. Other expansion bus designs were derived independently by other companies. For years, the ISA Bus dominated the IBM-compatible marketplace. When the 32-bit 386DX processor debuted, however, a need arose for a 32-bit expansion slot design to match. IBM took the high road and developed the Micro Channel Architecture (MCA) Bus, which takes full advantage of the 32-bit data-transfer capabilities.

Unfortunately, IBM has had a difficult time marketing the MCA Bus, due to problems with the high cost of manufacturing MCA motherboards and adapter cards, as well as the perceived notion that MCA is proprietary. Although it is not, IBM has not succeeded in marketing MCA as the new bus of choice, and it has remained largely a feature found only in IBM manufactured systems. The rest of the marketplace has for the most part ignored MCA, although a few companies have produced MCA-compatible systems and many companies produce MCA expansion adapters.

Compaq, on the other hand, was the primary architect of the Extended Industry Standard Architecture (EISA) Bus. Recognizing the difficulty that IBM had in marketing its new MCA Bus, Compaq decided that the best approach would be to give the bus design away rather than keep it as a Compaq-only feature. The company feared a repeat of what IBM was going through in trying to get the MCA Bus accepted throughout the industry. After all, how many companies would market expansion cards for a new bus that was unique to Compaq systems?

Compaq decided that other companies should share in its new design, so it contacted several other system manufacturers to see whether they were interested in participating. These contacts led to the EISA consortium, which in September 1988 introduced the Compaq-designed expansion bus: Extended Industry Standard Architecture (EISA). The system is a 32-bit slot for use with 386DX or higher systems.

Speculators said that EISA was developed to circumvent the royalties that IBM charges competitors who use the ISA or MCA slot design in their systems. This speculation was false, however, because EISA is an extension of the IBM-developed ISA Bus, and manufacturers of EISA systems must pay IBM the same licensing fees that manufacturers of ISA and MCA systems do. EISA was developed not to circumvent licensing fees, but to show technological leadership and to give Compaq and other companies some design freedom and control of their systems. Whether EISA, as an alternative to the IBM-designed MCA, becomes a useful standard depends on the popularity of systems that use the slot.

Unfortunately, EISA never achieved great popularity and sold in far fewer numbers than did MCA systems. There are fewer EISA expansion adapters than MCA adapters as well. This failure in the marketplace occurred for several reasons. One reason is the high cost of integrating the EISA Bus into a system. The special EISA Bus controller chips add several hundred dollars to the cost of a motherboard. In fact, having EISA slots on board can double the cost of the motherboard.

Another reason for the relative failure of EISA was the fact that the performance it offered actually was greater than that of most peripherals to which it could be connected. This incompatibility in performance also was true for MCA. The available hard disks and other peripherals could not transfer data as fast as the 16-bit ISA Bus could handle, so why use EISA, a still faster bus? Memory had already found its way off the standard bus and normally was installed on the motherboard directly, via SIMMs (Single Inline Memory Modules).

EISA complicated system installation and configuration whenever standard ISA boards were mixed with EISA boards. The standard ISA boards could not be controlled by the

EISA configuration program that was required to set up the jumper and switchless EISA cards. In the years following its introduction, EISA found a niche in high-end server systems because of the bus's increased bandwidth. For standard workstations, however, the EISA Bus has been superseded by VL-Bus and PCI. Even for servers, PCI is now the bus of choice over EISA.

The newest trend in expansion slots is the *local bus*. This type of bus is connected closely or directly to the processor. A problem with ISA and EISA is that the bus speed was locked in at a maximum of 8.33 MHz, which was far slower than the processors in most systems today. MCA offered greater performance, but it still was limited compared with the advancements in processors. What was needed were expansion slots that could talk directly to the processor, at processor speed, using all the bits that the processor could handle.

The first of the local buses to achieve popularity was the VESA Local Bus, so named because it was designed by the Video Electronics Standards Association primarily for video adapters. The VL-Bus was designed as an extension to the 486 processor and was essentially an extension of the 486 CPU's own bus. Although the VL-Bus can be used with other processors, this requires a special bridge chip to convert the control signals to those required by the VL-Bus.

VESA was first organized by NEC Corporation, which sought to develop standards for new types of video adapters as well as much faster video adapter functionality. Because NEC Corporation saw strength in numbers, it decided to give away the technology created by them in order to make it an industry standard. The Video Electronics Standards Association was formed and split from NEC to control the new VL-Bus and other VESA standards. The inexpensive design and high performance of the VL-Bus made it a popular addition to the ISA Bus and even to some EISA systems. VL-Bus was defined as an extension connector to the ISA or EISA Bus and could be found only in systems that had those buses.

The Peripheral Component Interconnect (PCI) Bus was created by Intel to be a new-generation bus, offering local bus performance while also offering true processor independence and multiple processor capabilities. Like so many of the other bus creators, Intel formed an independent organization to make the PCI Bus an industry standard in which all manufacturers could participate. The PCI Committee was formed to administer this new bus and to control its destiny. Due to the superior design and performance of PCI, it has rapidly become the bus of choice in the highest-performance systems. PCI has taken over as the dominant high-performance bus architecture.

Chapter 5, "Bus Slots and I/O Cards," contains a great deal of in-depth information on these and other PC system buses, including technical information such as pinouts, performance specifications, and bus operation and theory.

Table 2.1 summarizes the primary differences between a standard PC (or XT) system and an AT system. This information distinguishes between these systems and includes all IBM and compatible models.

Table 2.1 Differences Between PC/XT and AT Systems

System Attributes	(8-bit) PC/XT Type	(16/32/64-bit) AT Type
Supported processors	All x86 or x88	286 or higher
Processor modes	Real	Real or Protected (Virtual Real on 386+)
Expansion slot width	8-bit	16/32/64-bit
Slot type	ISA	ISA, EISA, MCA, PC-Card, VL-Bus, PCI
Hardware interrupts	8	16 or more
DMA channels	4	8 or more
Maximum RAM	1M	16M or 4G
Floppy controller data rates	250 kHz data rate	250/300/500/1,000 kHz data rate
Standard boot drive	360K or 720K	1.2M/1.44M/2.88M
Keyboard interface	Unidirectional	Bidirectional
CMOS memory/clock	No	Yes
Serial-port UART type	8250B	16450/16550A

This table highlights the primary differences between PC/XT and AT architecture. Using this information, you can properly categorize virtually any system as a PC/XT type or an AT type. There really have been no PC/XT type (8-bit) systems manufactured for many years. Unless you are in a computer museum, virtually every system you would encounter today is based on the AT type design.

You usually can identify the older PC and XT types of systems by their Intel-design 8088 or 8086 processors; other choices were also available, however. Some systems used the NEC V-20 or V-30 processors, and these processors are functionally identical to the Intel chips. A few PC and XT systems have a 286 or 386 processor for increased performance. These systems have only 8-bit ISA slots of the same system-bus design featured in the original IBM PC. The design of these slots includes only half the total DMA and hardware interrupts of the 16-bit AT design, which severely limits the use of expansion slots by adapter boards that require the use of these resources.

This type of system can run most software that runs under MS-DOS but is limited in more advanced operating systems, such as newer versions of Windows and any version of OS/2. This type of system cannot run OS/2 or any software designed to run under OS/2; neither can it run Windows 3.1, Windows 95, or Windows NT. These systems also cannot have more than 1M of processor-addressable memory, of which only 640K is available for user programs and data.

You can identify AT systems as any PC compatible with 16-bit or greater (32/64-bit) expansion slots. These systems usually have 8/16-bit ISA slots compatible with the original IBM AT. Other standards—such as EISA, MCA, PC-Card, VL-Bus, and PCI—also would be found only in AT-class systems. Most of these systems today would use 486, Pentium, or the new P6 processors.

PC systems usually have double-density (DD) floppy controllers, but AT systems must have a controller capable of high-density (HD) and double-density operation. Almost all current systems also have a controller capable of extra-high-density (ED) operation. These systems can run the 2.88M floppy drives. Because of the different controller types, the boot drive on a PC system must be the DD, 5 1/4-inch 360K or 3 1/2-inch 720K drive. The AT needs the 5 1/4-inch 1.2M or the 3 1/2-inch 1.44M or 2.88M drive for full compatibility with all software.

You can use a double-density disk drive as the boot drive in an AT system; the problem is that your boot drive is *supposed* to be a high-density drive. Many applications that run only on AT-type systems are packaged on high-density disks. Newer operating systems—such as Windows 95, Windows NT, and OS/2—are packaged on high-density disks and cannot be loaded from double-density disks. The capability to boot and run any of these operating systems is a basic AT-compatibility test.

A subtle difference between PC/XT and AT systems is in the keyboard interface. AT systems use a bidirectional keyboard interface, with an Intel 8042 processor running the show. This processor has built-in ROM and can be considered to be part of the total system ROM package. The PC/XT systems use an 8255 Programmable Peripheral Interface (PPI) chip, which supports only a unidirectional interface. A keyboard can be configured to work with only one of the interface designs. With many keyboards, you can alter the way that the keyboard interfaces by flipping a switch on the bottom of the keyboard. Others, such as IBM's Enhanced 101-key Keyboard, detect which type of system they are plugged into and switch automatically. The older XT and AT keyboards work only with the types of system for which they were designed.

The AT architecture uses CMOS memory and a real-time clock; PC-type systems usually don't. (An exception is the PS/2 Model 30, which has a real-time clock even though it is an XT-class system.) A *real-time clock* is the built-in clock implemented by a special CMOS memory chip on the motherboard in an AT system. You can have a clock added on some expansion adapters in a PC system, but DOS does not recognize the clock unless a special program is run first. The CMOS memory in the AT system also stores the system's basic configuration. In a PC or XT type of system, all these basic configuration options (such as the amount of installed memory, the number and type of floppy drives and hard disks, and the type of video adapter) are set by using switches and jumpers on the motherboard and various adapters.

The serial-port control chip, Universal Asynchronous Receiver/Transmitter (UART), is a National Semiconductor 8250B for PC-type systems; AT systems use the newer NS 16450 or 16550A chips (or compatibles thereof). Because these chips differ in subtle ways, the BIOS software must be designed for a specific chip. In the AT BIOS, which was designed for the 16450 and 16550A chips, using the older 8250B chip can result in strange problems, such as lost characters at high transmission speeds.

Some differences (such as the expansion slots, the hardware interrupts, and the DMA-channel availability) are absolute. Other differences, such as which processors are supported, are less absolute. AT systems, however, must use a 286 or higher processor;

PC systems can use the entire Intel family of chips, from the 8086 on up. Other parameters are less absolute. Your own system may not follow the true standard properly. If your system does not follow all criteria listed for it—especially if it is an AT-type system—you can expect compatibility and operational problems.

Documentation

One of the biggest problems in troubleshooting, servicing, or upgrading a system is having proper documentation. There are several types of documentation available for a given system, from the basic manuals you normally get with the system, to extra cost technical reference or service manuals. Also, because most systems today are made up of components from many different companies, I often recommend obtaining documentation specific to these components from the component manufacturers.

Generally, the type of documentation provided for a system is proportionate to the size of the manufacturing company. (Large companies can afford to produce good documentation.) Some of this documentation, unfortunately, is essential for even the most basic troubleshooting and upgrading tasks. Other documentation is necessary only for software and hardware developers, who have special requirements.

Basic Documentation

When you purchase a system, it should include a minimum set of documentation. There should be a manual covering the motherboard and all other adapters and devices included with the system. For example, if a video card and display are included, manuals for those items should also be present.

The standard manuals included with most systems and peripherals contain basic instructions for system setup, operation, testing, relocation, and option installation. A customer-level basic diagnostics disk (sometimes called a Diagnostics and Setup or Reference Disk) normally is included with a system. Most systems today come with all the software pre-loaded on the hard disk and no floppy disks. In this case, it is important to create images of the install disks should you ever have to recreate the original software installation at a later date. These systems usually include a provision for creating these floppy disk images; if not, then simply perform a complete backup of the hard drive.

These manuals should include listings of all the jumper and switch settings for the motherboard and any of the included expansion cards. For EISA systems, the basic diagnostics disk also has the SETUP routine (used to set the date and time), installed memory, installed disk drives, and installed video adapters. This information is saved by the SETUP program into CMOS battery backed-up memory. For PS/2 systems, the included disk (called the Reference Disk) contains the special Programmable Option-Select (POS) configuration routine and a hidden version of advanced diagnostics.

Technical-Reference Manuals

Technical-Reference manuals provide system-specific hardware and software interface information for the system. The manuals are intended for people who design hardware and software products to operate with these systems, as well as for people who must integrate other hardware and software into a system. On many compatibles, the technical reference manuals and information are included with the purchase of the system and are a part of the standard documentation that comes with the system.

These publications provide basic interface and design information for the system units. The manuals include information about the system board, math coprocessor, power supply, video subsystem, keyboard, instruction sets, and other features of the system. You need this information for integrating and installing aftermarket floppy and hard disk drives, memory boards, keyboards, network adapters, and virtually anything else that you want to plug into your system.

This type of manual often contains schematic diagrams showing the circuit layout of the motherboard and pinouts for the various connectors and jumpers. It also includes listings of the floppy and hard disk drive tables, which show the range of drives that can be installed on a particular system. Power specifications for the power supply are also in this manual. You need these figures in order to determine whether the system has adequate current to power a particular add-on device.

Hardware-Maintenance Manuals

Some larger companies, such as IBM, also provide service manuals for their systems. Each Hardware Maintenance Library consists of two manuals: a Hardware-Maintenance Service manual and a Hardware-Maintenance Reference manual. These are real service manuals that are written for service technicians. Although the intended audience is professional service technicians, the manuals are very easy to follow and useful even for amateur technicians and enthusiasts. IBM and local computer retail outlets use these manuals for diagnosis and service.

The basic Hardware-Maintenance Reference manual IBM has for the PC or PS/2 contains general information about the systems. The manual describes diagnostic procedures and Field-Replaceable Unit (FRU) locations, system adjustments, and component removal and installation. This information is useful primarily to users who have no experience in disassembling and reassembling a system and to users who have difficulty identifying components within the system. Most people do not need this manual after the first time they disassemble a system for service.

Component Documentation

If you really want the ultimate in documentation for your system, I highly recommend getting the documentation for all the components in your system. This would include specific manuals for each of the major components in the system—such as the motherboard, disk drives, and power supply—to individual chips such as the CPU, the ROM BIOS, the motherboard chipset, I/O chipset, and so on.

For example, I often get questions about the Advanced CMOS settings. The people calling seem to assume that these settings would be described in their ROM BIOS documentation, because the ROM based CMOS SETUP program in their system controls these settings. As they quickly find out, the ROM BIOS manufacturer knows little or nothing about these settings. In fact, they have nothing to do with the particular ROM BIOS used, and everything to do with the particular motherboard chipset used. You can find descriptions of all these settings in the documentation for your motherboard chipset, which can be obtained from the chipset manufacturer.

Obtaining Documentation

You cannot troubleshoot or upgrade a system accurately without some type of documentation specific to that system. If your system is from a name-brand manufacturer—such as IBM, Compaq, Hewlett-Packard, and others—then your best bet is to get the technical reference or service manuals direct from that manufacturer. Because of the specific nature of the information in these types of manuals, you most likely will have to obtain it from the manufacturer of the system. An IBM technical-reference manual, for example, is useless to a person who has a Compaq; that person must get the specific manual for that machine from Compaq.

To get this type of hardware-service documentation, contact the system manufacturer. For example, you can easily get IBM manuals direct from IBM. To order the IBM manuals, call this toll-free number:

800-IBM-PCTB (800-426-7282)

TB is the abbreviation for Technical Books. The service is active Monday through Friday from 8 a.m. to 8 p.m. Eastern time. When you call, you can request copies of the Technical Directory, a catalog that lists all part numbers and the prices of available documentation. You also can inquire about the availability of technical-reference or service documentation for newly announced products; this documentation may not be listed in the current directory. Information on how to contact most PC manufacturers can be found in the vendor listing in Appendix B.

The process of obtaining other manufacturers' manuals may (or may not) be so easy. Most large companies run responsible service and support operations that provide technical documentation. Other companies either do not have or are not willing to part with such documentation, in an effort to protect their service departments (and their dealers' service departments) from competition. Contact the manufacturer directly; the manufacturer can direct you to the correct department so that you can inquire about this information.

Summary

Apart from the overall similarity between IBM computers and IBM-compatibles, important differences in system architecture exist. IBM and compatible computers can be broken down into PC/XT and AT categories. This chapter explained the differences among these types of computers. The chapter ended with a discussion about how to obtain the service manuals that you need for maintaining and upgrading your computer.

Chapter 3

System Teardown and Inspection

This chapter examines procedures for tearing down and inspecting a system. The chapter describes the types of tools required, the procedure for disassembling the system, and the various components that make up the system. A special section discusses some of the test equipment you can use when troubleshooting a system; another section covers some problems you may encounter with the hardware (screws, nuts, bolts, and so on).

Using the Proper Tools

To troubleshoot and repair PC systems properly, you need a few basic tools. If you intend to troubleshoot and repair PCs professionally, there are many more specialized tools you will want to purchase. These advanced tools allow you to more accurately diagnose problems and make the jobs easier and faster. The basic tools that should be in every troubleshooter's toolbox are:

- Simple hand tools for basic disassembly and reassembly procedures
- Diagnostics software and hardware for testing components in a system
- Wrap plugs for diagnosing serial- and parallel-port problems
- A Digital Multi-Meter (DMM) that allows accurate measurement of voltage and resistance
- Chemicals, such as contact cleaners, component freeze sprays, and compressed air for cleaning the system

A more advanced troubleshooter's toolbox will likely include the following specialized tools:

- Specialized hand tools, such as PGA (Pin Grid Array), PLCC (Plastic Leaded Chip Carrier), and PQFP (Plastic Quad Flat Pack) chip removal tools

- Logic probes and pulsers, which allow analysis and testing of digital circuits
- Oscilloscopes, which allow accurate display of digital and analog signals for analyzing timing and purity
- Memory testing machines, which are used to evaluate the operation of SIMMs (Single In-line Memory Modules), DIP (Dual In-line Pin) chips, and other memory modules
- Power supply test equipment, such as variable voltage transformers and load testers, which allow verification of power supply performance

In addition, you may need soldering and desoldering tools for problems that require these operations. These tools are discussed in more detail in the following section. Diagnostics software and hardware are discussed in Chapter 21, "Software and Hardware Diagnostic Tools."

Hand Tools

When you work with PC systems, it immediately becomes apparent that the tools required for nearly all service operations are simple and inexpensive. You can carry most of the required tools in a small pouch. Even a top-of-the-line "master mechanic's" set fits inside a briefcase-size container. The cost of these tool kits ranges from about $20 for a small service kit to $500 for one of the briefcase-size deluxe kits. Compare these costs with what might be necessary for an automotive technician. Most automotive service techs spend $5,000 to $10,000 or more for the tools they need. Not only are PC tools much less expensive, but I can tell you from experience that you don't get nearly as dirty working on computers as you do working on cars.

In this section, you learn about the tools required to make up a kit that is capable of performing basic, board-level service on PC systems. One of the best ways to start such a set of tools is a small kit sold especially for servicing PCs.

The following list shows the basic tools that you can find in one of the small PC tool kits that sell for about $20:

3/16-inch nut driver

1/4-inch nut driver

Small Phillips screwdriver

Small flat-blade screwdriver

Medium Phillips screwdriver

Medium flat-blade screwdriver

Chip extractor

Chip inserter

Tweezers

Claw-type parts grabber

T10 and T15 Torx drivers

You use nut drivers to remove the hexagonal-headed screws that secure the system-unit covers, adapter boards, disk drives, power supplies, and speakers in most systems. The nut drivers work much better than conventional screwdrivers.

Because some manufacturers have substituted slotted or Phillips-head screws for the more standard hexagonal-head screws, standard screwdrivers can be used for those systems.

You use the chip-extraction and insertion tools to install or remove memory chips (or other, smaller chips) without bending any pins on the chip. Usually, you pry out larger chips, such as microprocessors or ROMs, with the small screwdriver. Larger processors such as the 486, Pentium or Pentium Pro chips require a chip extractor if they are in a standard socket. These chips have so many pins on them that a large amount of force is required to remove them. The chip extractor tools for removing these chips distributes the force evenly along the chip's underside to minimize the likelihood of breakage.

The tweezers and parts grabber can be used to hold any small screws or jumper blocks that are difficult to hold in your hand. The parts grabber is especially useful when you drop a small part into the interior of a system; usually, you can remove the part without completely disassembling the system.

Finally, the Torx driver is a special, star-shaped driver that matches the special screws found in most Compaq systems and in many other systems as well.

Although this basic set is useful, you should supplement it with some other small hand tools, such as:

Needlenose pliers

Hemostats

Wire cutter or wire stripper

Metric nut drivers

Tamper-proof Torx drivers

Vise or clamp

File

Small Flashlight

Pliers are useful for straightening pins on chips, applying or removing jumpers, crimping cables, or grabbing small parts.

Hemostats are especially useful for grabbing small components, such as jumpers.

The wire cutter or stripper, obviously, is useful for making or repairing cables or wiring.

The metric nut drivers can be used in many clone or compatible systems as well as in the IBM PS/2 systems, all of which use metric hardware.

The tamper-proof Torx drivers can be used to remove Torx screws with the tamper-resistant pin in the center of the screw. A tamper-proof Torx driver has a hole drilled in it to allow clearance for the pin.

You can use a vise to install connectors on cables and to crimp cables to the shape you want, as well as to hold parts during delicate operations.

Finally, you can use the file to smooth rough metal edges on cases and chassis, as well as to trim the faceplates on disk drives for a perfect fit.

The flashlight can be used to illuminate system interiors, especially when the system is cramped and the room lighting is not good. I consider this tool to be essential.

Another consideration for your tool kit is an ESD (electrostatic discharge) protection kit. This kit consists of a wrist strap with a ground wire and a specially conductive mat, also with its own ground wire. Using a kit like this when working on a system will help to ensure that you never accidentally zap any of the components with a static discharge.

The ESD kits, as well as all the other tools and much more, are available from a variety of tool vendors. Specialized Products Company and Jensen Tools are two of the most popular vendors of computer and electronic tools and of service equipment. Their catalogs show an extensive selection of very high-quality tools. (These companies and several others are listed in Appendix B, "Vendor List.") With a simple set of hand tools, you will be equipped for nearly every PC repair or installation situation. The total cost of these tools should be less than $150, which is not much considering the capabilities they give you.

On the Web

The following Web sites are great places to start looking for tools mentioned in this chapter.

http://www.hardwareworld.com/Jensen/products.html

http://www.lfw.com/WWW/CIM/bg/C004402.HTM

Soldering and Desoldering Tools

In certain situations—such as repairing a broken wire, reattaching a component to a circuit board, removing and installing chips that are not in a socket, or adding jumper wires or pins to a board—you must use a soldering iron to make the repair.

Although virtually all repairs these days are done by simply replacing the entire failed board, you may need a soldering iron in some situations. The most common case would be where there was physical damage to a system, such as where somebody had ripped the keyboard connector off of a motherboard by pulling on the cable improperly. Simple soldering skills could save the motherboard in this case.

Most motherboards these days include I/O components such as serial and parallel ports. Many of these ports are fuse protected on the board, however the fuse is usually a small soldered-in component. These fuses are designed to protect the motherboard circuits from damage from an external source. If a short circuit or static charge from an external device blows these fuses, the board can be saved if you can replace them.

To perform minor repairs such as these, you need a low-wattage soldering iron—usually, about 25 watts. More than 30 watts generates too much heat and can damage the components on the board. Even with a low-wattage unit, you must limit the amount of heat to which you subject the board and its components. You can do this with quick and efficient use of the soldering iron, as well as with the use of heat-sinking devices clipped to the leads of the device being soldered. A *heat sink* is a small metal clip-on device designed to absorb excessive heat before it reaches the component that the heat sink is protecting. In some cases, you can use a pair of hemostats as an effective heat sink when you solder a component.

To remove components that originally were soldered into place from a printed circuit board, you can use a soldering iron with a *solder sucker.* This device normally is constructed as a small tube with an air chamber and a plunger-and-spring arrangement. (I do not recommend the squeeze-bulb type of solder sucker.) The unit is "cocked" when you press the spring-loaded plunger into the air chamber. When you want to remove a device from a board, you use the soldering iron from the underside of the board, and heat the point at which one of the component leads joins the circuit board until the solder melts. As soon as melting occurs, move the solder-sucker nozzle into position, and press the actuator. This procedure allows the plunger to retract and creates a momentary suction that inhales the liquid solder from the connection and leaves the component lead dry in the hole.

Always do the heating and suctioning from the underside of a board, not from the component side. Repeat this action for every component lead joined to the circuit board. When you master this technique, you can remove a small component in a minute or two with only a small likelihood of damage to the board or other components. Larger chips that have many pins can be more difficult to remove and resolder without damaging other components or the circuit board.

Tip

These procedures are intended for Through-Hole devices only. These are components whose pins extend all the way through holes in the board to the underside. Surface mount devices are removed with a completely different procedure, and much more expensive tools. Working on surface mounted components is beyond the capabilities of all but the most well-equipped shops.

n the Web

For information about various Weller Soldering Irons and Tips visit

http://www.techni-tool.com/weller.html

If you intend to add soldering and desoldering skills to your arsenal of abilities, you should practice. Take a useless circuit board and practice removing various components from the board; then reinstall the components. Try to remove the components from the board by using the least amount of heat possible. Also, perform the solder-melting operations as quickly as possible, limiting the time that the iron is applied to the joint. Before you install any components, clean out the holes through which the leads must project and mount the component in place. Then apply the solder from the underside of the board, using as little heat and solder as possible.

Attempt to produce joints as clean as the joints that the board manufacturer performed by machine. Soldered joints that do not look clean may keep the component from making a good connection with the rest of the circuit. This "cold-solder joint" normally is created because you have not used enough heat. *Remember that you should not practice your new soldering skills on the motherboard of a system that you are attempting to repair!* Don't attempt to work on real boards until you are sure of your skills. I always keep a few junk boards around for soldering practice and experimentation.

No matter how good you get at soldering and desoldering, some jobs are best left to professionals. Components that are surface-mounted to a circuit board, for example, require special tools for soldering and desoldering, as do other components that have high pin densities.

I upgraded an IBM P75 portable system I had by replacing the 486DX-33 processor with a 486DX2-66 processor. This procedure normally would be simple (especially if the system uses a Zero Insertion Force or ZIF socket), but in this particular system, the 168-pin 486DX chip was soldered into a special processor card. To add to the difficulty, there were surface-mounted components on both sides of the card—even the solder side.

Needless to say, this was a very difficult job that required a special piece of equipment called a *hot air rework station.* The hot air rework station uses blasts of hot air to solder or desolder all of the pins on a chip simultaneously. To perform this replacement job, the components on the solder side of the board were protected with special heat-resistant masking tape, while the hot air was directed at the 168 pins of the 486 chip, allowing it to be removed. Then the replacement chip was inserted into the holes in the board, a special solder paste was applied to the pins, and the hot air was used again to solder all 168 pins simultaneously.

The use of professional equipment such as this resulted in a perfect job that cannot be told from factory original. Attempting a job like this with a conventional soldering iron probably would have damaged the expensive processor chips, as well as the even more expensive multilayer processor card.

Using Proper Test Equipment

In some cases, you must use specialized devices to test a system board or component. This test equipment is not expensive or difficult to use, but it can add much to your troubleshooting abilities. I consider wrap plugs and a voltmeter to be required gear for proper system testing. The wrap plugs allow testing of serial and parallel ports and of their attached cables. A Digital Multi-Meter (DMM) can serve many purposes, including checking for voltage signals at different points in a system, testing the output of the power supply, and checking for continuity in a circuit or cable. An outlet tester is an invaluable accessory that can check the electrical outlet for proper wiring. This capability is useful if you believe that the problem lies outside the computer system itself.

Logic probes and pulsers are not mandatory equipment, but they can add to your troubleshooting proficiency. You use the logic probe to check for the existence and status of digital signals at various points in a circuit. You use the logic pulser to inject signals into a circuit to evaluate the circuit's operation. Using these devices effectively requires a good understanding of the way that the circuit operates.

n the Web

This Web site has more information on Fluke handheld test meters. These are for the more serious troubleshooter.

http://www.fluke.com/handheld/

This Tandy site is loaded with information on most of the test equipment. They sell products for the hobbyist as well as the professional.

http://www.tandy.com/support/2845.html

Wrap Plugs (Loopback Connectors)

For diagnosing serial- and parallel-port problems, you need wrap plugs (also called loopback connectors), which are used to circulate, or wrap, signals. The plugs enable the serial or parallel port to send data to itself for diagnostic purposes.

Several types of wrap plugs are available. You need one for the 25-pin serial port, one for the 9-pin serial port, and one for the 25-pin parallel port (see table 3.1). Many companies, including IBM, sell the plugs separately. IBM also sells a special version that includes all three types in one plug.

Table 3.1 Wrap Plug Types

Description	IBM Part Number
Parallel-port wrap plug	8529228
Serial-port wrap plug, 25-pin	8529280
Serial-port wrap plug, 9-pin (AT)	8286126
Tri-connector wrap plug	72X8546

The handy tri-connector unit contains all commonly needed plugs in one compact unit. The unit costs approximately $30 from IBM. Be aware that most professional diagnostics packages (especially the ones that I recommend) include the three types of wrap plugs in the package; you may not need to purchase them separately. If you're handy, you can even make your own wrap plugs for testing. I include wiring diagrams for the three types of wrap plugs in Chapter 11, "Communications and Networking." In that chapter, you also will find a detailed discussion of serial and parallel ports.

Meters

Many troubleshooting procedures require that you measure voltage and resistance. You take these measurements by using a hand-held Digital Multi-Meter (DMM). The meter can be an analog device (using an actual meter) or a digital-readout device. The DMM has a pair of wires called test leads or probes. The test leads make the connections so that you can take readings. Depending on the meter's setting, the probes measure electrical resistance, direct-current (DC) voltage, or alternating-current (AC) voltage.

Usually, each system-unit measurement setting has several ranges of operation. DC voltage, for example, usually can be read in several scales, to a maximum of 200 millivolts, 2 volts, 20 volts, 200 volts, and 1,000 volts. Because computers use both +5 and +12 volts for various operations, you should use the 20-volt-maximum scale for making your measurements. Making these measurements on the 200-millivolt or 2-volt scale could "peg the meter" and possibly damage it because the voltage would be much higher than expected. Using the 200-volt or 1,000-volt scale works, but the readings at 5 volts and 12 volts are so small in proportion to the maximum that accuracy is low.

If you are taking a measurement and are unsure of the actual voltage, start at the highest scale and work your way down. Most of the better meters have autoranging capability: the meter automatically selects the best range for any measurement. This type of meter is much easier to operate. You just set the meter to the type of reading you want, such as DC volts, and attach the probes to the signal source. The meter selects the correct voltage range and displays the value. Because of their design, these types of meters always have a digital display rather than a meter needle.

I prefer the small digital meters; you can buy them for only slightly more than the analog style, and they're extremely accurate, as well as much safer for digital circuits. Some of these meters are not much bigger than a cassette tape; they fit in a shirt pocket. Radio Shack sells a good unit (made for Radio Shack by Beckman) in the $25 price range; the meter is a half-inch thick, weighs 3 1/2 ounces, and is digital and autoranging as well. This type of meter works well for most, if not all, PC troubleshooting and test uses.

Caution

You should be aware that many analog meters can be dangerous to digital circuits. These meters use a 9-volt battery to power the meter for resistance measurements. If you use this type of meter to measure resistance on some digital circuits, you can damage the electronics, because you essentially are injecting 9 volts into the circuit. The digital meters universally run on 3 to 5 volts or less.

Logic Probes and Logic Pulsers

A logic probe can be useful for diagnosing problems in digital circuits. In a digital circuit, a signal is represented as either high (+5 volts) or low (0 volts). Because these signals are present for only a short time (measured in millionths of a second) or oscillate (switch on and off) rapidly, a simple voltmeter is useless. A logic probe is designed to display these signal conditions easily.

Logic probes are especially useful for troubleshooting a dead system. Using the probe, you can determine whether the basic clock circuitry is operating and whether other signals necessary for system operation are present. In some cases, a probe can help you cross-check the signals at each pin on an IC chip. You can compare the signals present at each pin with the signals that a known-good chip of the same type would show—a comparison that is helpful in isolating a failed component. Logic probes can be useful for troubleshooting some disk drive problems by enabling you to test the signals present on the interface cable or drive-logic board.

A companion tool to the probe is the logic pulser. A pulser is designed to test circuit reaction by delivering into a circuit a logical high (+5 volt) pulse, usually lasting 1 1/2 to 10 millionths of a second. Compare the reaction with that of a known-functional circuit. This type of device normally is used much less frequently than a logic probe, but in some cases, it can be helpful for testing a circuit.

Outlet Testers

Outlet testers are very useful test tools. These simple, inexpensive devices, which are sold at hardware stores, are used to test electrical outlets. You simply plug the device in, and three LEDs light in various combinations, indicating whether the outlet is wired correctly.

Although you may think that badly wired outlets would be a rare problem, I have seen a large number of installations in which the outlets were wired incorrectly. Most of the time, the problem seems to be in the ground wire. An improperly wired outlet can result in flaky system operation, such as random parity checks and lockups. With an improper ground circuit, currents can begin flowing on the electrical ground circuits in the system. Because the system uses the voltage on the ground circuits as a comparative signal to determine whether bits are 0 or 1, a floating ground can cause data errors in the system.

Once, while running one of my PC troubleshooting seminars, I was using a system that I literally could not approach without locking it up. Whenever I walked past the system, the electrostatic field generated by my body interfered with the system, and the PC locked up, displaying a parity-check error message. The problem was that the hotel I was using was very old and had no grounded outlets in the room. The only way I could prevent the system from locking up was to run the class in my stocking feet, because my leather-soled shoes were generating the static charge.

Other symptoms of bad ground wiring in electrical outlets are electrical shocks when you touch the case or chassis of the system. These shocks indicate that voltages are flowing where they should not be. This problem also can be caused by bad or improper grounds within the system itself. By using the simple outlet tester, you can quickly determine whether the outlet is at fault.

SIMM Testers

I now consider a SIMM (Single Inline Memory Module) test machine a virtually mandatory piece of gear for anybody serious about performing PC troubleshooting and repair as a profession. These are basically small test machines designed to evaluate SIMM and other types of memory modules including individual chips such as cache memory as well. They can be somewhat expensive, costing upwards of $1,000 or more, but these types of machines are the only truly accurate way to test memory.

Without one of these testers, you are relegated to testing memory by running a diagnostic program on the PC and testing the memory as it is installed. This can be very problematic, as the memory diagnostic program can only do two things to the memory, write and read. A SIMM tester can do many things that a memory diagnostic running in a PC cannot do such as:

- Identify the type of memory
- Identify the memory speed
- Identify whether the memory has parity, or is using bogus parity emulation
- Vary the refresh timing and access speed timing
- Locate single bit failures
- Detect power and noise related failures
- Detect solder opens and shorts
- Isolate timing related failures
- Detect data retention errors

No conventional memory diagnostic software can do these things because it has to rely on the fixed access parameters set up by the memory controller hardware in the motherboard chipset. This prevents the software from being able to alter the timing and methods used to access the memory. You end up with memory that will fail in one system and work in another, when it is in fact actually bad. This can allow intermittent problems to occur, and be almost impossible to detect.

The bottom line is that there is no way that truly accurate memory testing can be done in a PC, a SIMM tester is required for comprehensive and accurate testing of memory. With the price of a typical 16M memory module at over $500, the price of a SIMM tester can be justified very easily! One of the SIMM testers I recommend the most is the SIGMA LC by Darkhorse Systems. See the vendor list in Appendix B for more information. Also, see Chapter 7, "Memory," for more information on memory in general.

On the Web

The following Web sites provide information on various SIMM testers on the market:

http://www.marshall.com./pub/pub/dsi/test/pddsi04.htm

http://www.simcheck.com/simlpl.mtm

http://www.simmtester.com/

Chemicals

Chemicals can be used to help clean, troubleshoot, and even repair a system. For the most basic function—cleaning components, electrical connectors, and contacts—one of the most useful chemicals was 1,1,1 trichloroethane. This substance was a very effective cleaner. This chemical was used to clean electrical contacts and components, and it will not damage most plastics and board materials. In fact, trichloroethane can be very useful for cleaning stains on the system case and keyboard. Electronic chemical-supply companies are now offering several replacements for trichloroethane because it is being regulated as a chlorinated solvent, along with CFCs (chlorofluorocarbons) such as Freon.

A unique type of contact enhancer and lubricant called Stabilant 22 is on the market. This chemical, which is applied to electrical contacts, greatly enhances the connection and lubricates the contact point; it is much more effective than conventional contact cleaners or lubricants.

Stabilant 22 is a liquid-polymer semiconductor; it behaves like liquid metal and conducts electricity in the presence of an electric current. The substance also fills the air gaps between the mating surfaces of two items that are in contact, making the surface area of the contact larger and also keeping out oxygen and other contaminants that can oxidize and corrode the contact point.

This chemical is available in several forms. Stabilant 22 is the concentrated version, whereas Stabilant 22a is a version diluted with isopropanol in a 4:1 ratio. An even more diluted 8:1-ratio version is sold in many high-end stereo and audio shops under the name Tweek. Just 15 ml of Stabilant 22a sells for about $40, whereas a liter of the concentrate costs about $4,000!

As you can plainly see, Stabilant 22 is fairly expensive, but very little is required in an application, and nothing else has been found to be as effective in preserving electrical contacts. (NASA uses the chemical on spacecraft electronics.) An application of Stabilant can provide protection for up to 16 years, according to the manufacturer, D.W. Electrochemicals. You will find the company's address and phone number in the vendor list in Appendix B.

Stabilant is especially effective on I/O slot connectors, adapter-card edge and pin connectors, disk drive connectors, power-supply connectors, and virtually any connectors in the PC. In addition to enhancing the contact and preventing corrosion, an application of Stabilant lubricates the contacts, making insertion and removal of the connector easier.

Compressed air often is used as an aid in system cleaning. Normally composed of Freon or carbon dioxide (CO2), compressed gas is used as a blower to remove dust and debris from a system or component. Be careful when you use these devices—some of them can generate a tremendous static charge as the compressed gas leaves the nozzle of the can. Be sure that you are using the kind approved for cleaning or dusting computer equipment, and consider wearing a static grounding strap as a precaution. Freon TF is known to generate these large static charges; Freon R12 is less severe.

Of course, because both chemicals damage the ozone layer, most suppliers are phasing them out. Expect to see new versions of these compressed-air devices with carbon dioxide or some other less-harmful propellant.

When using these compressed air products, make sure you hold the can upright so that only gas is ejected from the nozzle. If you tip the can, the raw propellant will come out, which is wasteful. This operation should be performed on equipment that is powered off to minimize any chance of damage through short circuiting or bumping anything.

Caution

If you use any chemical that contains the propellant Freon R12 (dichlorodifluoromethane), *do not expose the gas to an open flame or other heat source.* If you burn this substance, a highly toxic gas called *phosgene* is generated. Phosgene, used as a choking gas in World War I, can be deadly.

Freon R12 is the substance that was used in most automobile air-conditioning systems before 1995. Automobile service technicians are instructed *never* to smoke near air-conditioning systems. By 1996, the manufacture and use of these types of chemicals will have been either banned or closely regulated by the government, and replacements will have to be found. For example, virtually all new car automobile air-conditioning systems have been switched to a chemical called R-134a. The unfortunate side effect of this situation is that all the replacement chemicals are much more expensive than Freon.

Related to compressed-air products are chemical-freeze sprays. These sprays are used to cool a suspected failing component quickly so as to restore it to operation. These substances are not used to repair a device, but to confirm that you have found the failed device. Often, a component's failure is heat-related; cooling it temporarily restores it to normal operation. If the circuit begins operating normally, the device that you are cooling is the suspect device.

On the Web

The following Web sites are great places to start looking for chemicals mentioned in this chapter:

http://www.hardwareworld.com/Jensen/products.html

http://www.lfw.com/WWW/CIM/bg/C004402.HTM

A Word About Hardware

This section discusses some problems that you may encounter with the hardware (screws, nuts, bolts, and so on) used in assembling a system.

Types of Hardware

One of the biggest aggravations that you encounter in dealing with various systems is the different hardware types and designs that hold the units together.

For example, most system hardware types use screws that can be driven with 1/4-inch or 3/16-inch hexagonal drivers. IBM used these screws in all its original PC, XT, and AT systems, and most compatible systems use this standard hardware as well. Some manufacturers use different hardware. Compaq, for example, uses Torx screws extensively in most of its systems. A Torx screw has a star-shape hole driven by the correct-size Torx driver. These drivers carry size designations of T-8, T-9, T-10, T-15, T-20, T-25, T-30, T-40, and so on.

A variation on the Torx screw is the tamper-proof Torx screw, found in power supplies and other assemblies. These screws are identical to the regular Torx screws, except that a pin sticks up from the middle of the star-shape hole in the screw. This pin prevents the standard Torx driver from entering the hole to grip the screw; a special tamper-proof driver, with a corresponding hole for the pin, is required. An alternative is to use a small chisel to knock out the pin in the screw. Usually, a device that is sealed with these types of screws is considered to be a complete, replaceable unit that rarely, if ever, needs to be opened.

Many manufacturers also use the more standard slotted-head and Phillips-head screws. Using tools on these screws is relatively easy, but tools do not grip these fasteners as well as hexagonal head or Torx screws do, and the heads can be rounded off more easily than other types can. Extremely cheap versions tend to lose bits of metal as they're turned with a driver, and the metal bits can fall onto the motherboard. Stay away from cheap fasteners whenever possible; the headaches of dealing with stripped screws aren't worth it.

English versus Metric

Another area of aggravation with hardware is the fact that two types of thread systems are available—English and metric. IBM used mostly English-threaded fasteners in its original line of systems, but many other manufacturers used metric-threaded fasteners in their systems.

The difference becomes apparent especially with disk drives. American-manufactured drives sometimes use English fasteners; drives made in Japan or Taiwan usually use metric fasteners. Whenever you replace a floppy drive in an older PC compatible unit, you encounter this problem. Try to buy the correct screws and any other hardware, such as brackets, with the drive, because they may be difficult to find at a local hardware store. Many of the drive manufacturers offer retail drive kits that include these components. The OEM's drive manual lists the correct data about a specific drive's hole locations and thread size.

Hard disks can use either English or metric fasteners; check your particular drive to see which type it uses. Most drives today seem to use metric hardware.

Caution

Some screws in a system may be length-critical, especially screws that are used to retain hard disk drives. You can destroy some hard disks by using a mounting screw that's too long; such a screw can puncture or dent the sealed disk chamber when you install the drive and fully tighten the screw. When you install a new drive in a system, always make a trial fit of the hardware to see how far the screws can be inserted into the drive before they interfere with components of the drive. When you're in doubt, the drive manufacturer's OEM documentation will tell you precisely what screws are required and how long they should be.

Disassembly Procedures

The process of physically disassembling and reassembling systems isn't difficult. Because of marketplace standardization, only a couple of different types and sizes of screws (with a few exceptions) are used to hold the systems together. Also, the physical arrangement of the major components is similar even among systems from different manufacturers. In addition, a typical system does not contain many components today.

This section covers the disassembly and reassembly procedure in the following sections:

- Case or cover assembly
- Adapter boards
- Disk drives
- Power supply
- Motherboard

This section discusses how to remove and install these components for several different types of system. With regard to assembly and disassembly, it is best to consider each system by the type of case that the system uses. All systems that have AT-type cases, for example, are assembled and disassembled in much the same manner. Tower cases basically are AT-type cases turned sideways, so the same basic instructions apply to those cases as well. Most slim-line and XT style cases are similar; these systems are assembled and disassembled in much the same way.

The following section lists disassembly and reassembly instructions for several case types, including those for all standard IBM-compatible systems.

Disassembly Preparation

Before you begin disassembling any system, you must be aware of several issues. One issue is ESD (electrostatic discharge) protection. The other is recording the configuration of the system, with regard to the physical aspects of the system (such as jumper or switch settings and cable orientations) and to the logical configuration of the system (especially in terms of elements such as CMOS settings).

ESD Protection. When you are working on the internal components of a system, you need to take the necessary precautions to prevent accidental static discharges to the components. At any time, your body can hold a large static voltage charge that can easily damage components of your system. Before I ever put my hands into an open system, I first touch a grounded portion of the chassis, such as the power supply case. This action serves to equalize the charges that the device and I would be carrying. Some people would say that the charge is vented off to ground in this case, but that's not really true.

I never recommend working on a system with the cord plugged in because of the electrical hazard, as well as the simple fact that it is too easy to power the system on at the wrong time or simply forget to turn it off. It also is too easy to drop tools and other things into systems while they are powered on, which would short out and possibly damage circuits. After I destroyed an adapter card by accidentally plugging it in while the system was running, I decided that the only good way to ensure that the system is really off is to unplug it!

I have been told by some people that if the system is not plugged in, the static charges cannot be vented off to ground. That is true, but the problem with static is not whether a device carries a charge relative to ground but whether that charge suddenly flows from one device to another through the delicate logic circuits. By touching the system chassis or any other part of the system's ground circuit, you equalize the charge between you and the system, thereby ensuring that no additional charge will pass from you to the IC chips. No matter what anybody says, you absolutely do not want the system to be plugged in!

A more sophisticated way to equalize the charges between you and any of the system components is to use the ESD protection kit mentioned earlier in this chapter. These kits consist of a wrist strap and mat, with ground wires for attachment to the system chassis. When you are going to work on a system, you place the mat next to or partially below the system unit. Next, you clip ground wire to both the mat and the system's chassis, tying the grounds together. Then you put on the wrist strap and attach that wire to a ground as well. Because the mat and system chassis are already wired together, you can attach the wrist-strap wire to the system chassis or to the mat itself. If you are using a wrist strap without a mat, clip the wrist-strap wire to the system chassis. When clipping these wires to the chassis, be sure to use an area that is free of paint so that a good ground contact can be achieved. This setup ensures that any electrical charges are carried equally by you and any of the components in the system, preventing the sudden flow of static electricity that can damage the circuits.

As you remove disk drives, adapter cards, and especially delicate items such as the entire motherboard, as well as SIMMs or processor chips, you should place these components on the static mat. I see some people putting the system unit on top of the mat, but the unit should be alongside the mat so that you have room to lay out all the components as you remove them. If you are going to remove the motherboard from a system, be sure that you leave enough room for it on the mat.

If you do not have such a mat, simply place the removed circuits and devices on a clean desk or table. Always pick up a loose adapter card by the metal bracket used to secure the card to the system. This bracket is tied into the ground circuitry of the card, so by touching the bracket first, you prevent a discharge from damaging the components of the card. If the circuit board has no metal bracket (a motherboard, for example), handle the board carefully, by the edges, and try not to touch any of the components.

Caution

Some people have recommended placing loose circuit boards and chips on sheets of aluminum foil. *This procedure is absolutely not recommended and can actually result in an explosion!* Many motherboards, adapter cards, and other circuit boards today have built-in lithium or ni-cad batteries. These batteries react violently when they are shorted out, which is exactly what you would be doing by placing such a board on a piece of aluminum foil. The batteries will quickly overheat and possibly explode like a large firecracker (with dangerous shrapnel). Because you will not always be able to tell whether a board has a battery built into it somewhere, the safest practice is to never place any board on any conductive metal surface, such as foil.

Recording Setup and Configuration. Before you power the system off for the last time to remove the case, you should learn, and record, several things about the system. Often, when working on a system, you intentionally or accidentally wipe out the CMOS setup information. Most systems use a special battery-powered CMOS clock and data chip that is used to store the system's configuration information. If the battery is disconnected, or if certain pins are accidentally shorted, you can discharge the CMOS memory and lose the setup. The CMOS memory in most systems is used to store simple things such as how many and what type of floppy drives are connected, how much memory is in the system, and the date and time.

A critical piece of information is the hard disk type settings. Although you or the system easily determine the other settings the next time you power on the system, the hard disk type information is another story. Most modern BIOS software can read the type information directly from most IDE and all SCSI drives. With older BIOS software, however, you have to explicitly tell the system the parameters of the attached hard disk. This means that you need to know the current settings for cylinders, heads, and sectors per track.

Some BIOS software indicates the hard disk only by a type number, usually ranging from 1 through 50. Be aware that most BIOS programs use type 47 or higher for what is called a user-definable type, which means that the cylinder, head, and sector counts for this type were entered manually and are not constant. These user-definable types are especially important to write down, because this information may be very difficult to figure out later, when you need to start the system.

Modern Enhanced IDE drives will also have additional configuration items that should be recorded. These include the translation mode and transfer mode. With drives larger than 528MB it is important to record the translation mode, which will be expressed differently in different BIOS versions. Look for settings like CHS (Cylinder Head Sector), ECHS (Extended CHS), Large (which equals ECHS), or LBA (Logical Block Addressing). If you reconfigure a system and do not set the same drive translation as was used originally with that drive, then all the data may be inaccessible. Most modern BIOS have an autodetect feature that automatically reads the drive's capabilities and sets the CMOS settings appropriately. Even so, there have been some problems with the BIOS not reading the drive settings properly, or where someone had overridden the settings in the previous installation. With translation, you have to match the setting to what the drive was formatted under previously if you want to read the data properly.

The speed setting is a little more straightforward. Older IDE drives can run up a speed of 8.3 MB per second, which is called PIO (Programmed I/O) mode 2. Newer EIDE drives can run PIO Mode 3 (11.1 MB/s) or PIO Mode 4 (16.6 MB/s). Most BIOS today allow you to set the mode specifically, or you can use the autodetect feature to automatically set the speed. For more information on the settings for hard disk drives, see Chapter 15, "Hand Disk Interfaces."

If you do not enter the correct hard disk type information in the CMOS setup program, you will not be able to access the data on the hard disk. I know several people who lost some or all of their data because they did not enter the correct type information when they reconfigured their systems. If this information is incorrect, the usual results are a `Missing operating system` error message when the systems starts and the inability to access the C drive.

Some of you may be thinking that you can just figure out the parameters by looking up the particular hard disk in a table. (I have included a table of popular hard disk drive parameters in Appendix A, and this table has proved to be useful to me time and time again.) Unfortunately, this method works only if the person who set up the system originally entered the correct parameters. I have encountered a large number of systems in which the hard disk parameters were not entered correctly; the only way to regain access to the data is to determine, and then use, the same incorrect parameters that were used originally. As you can see, no matter what, you should record the hard disk information from your setup program.

Most systems have the setup program built right into the ROM BIOS software itself. These built-in setup programs are activated by a hot-key sequence such as Ctrl+Alt+Esc or Ctrl+Alt+S if you have a Phoenix ROM. Other ROMs prompt you for the setup program every time the system boots, such as with the popular AMI BIOS. With the AMI, you simply press the Delete key when the prompt appears on-screen during a reboot.

When you get the setup program running, record all the settings. The easiest way to do this is to print it out. If a printer is connected, press Shift+Print Screen; a copy of the screen display will be sent to the printer. Some setup programs have several pages of information, so you should record the information on each page as well.

Many setup programs, such as those in the AMI BIOS, allow for specialized control of the particular chipset used in the motherboard. These complicated settings can take up several screens of information, all of which should be recorded. Most systems will return all these settings to a default state when the battery is removed, and you lose any custom settings that were made.

MCA and EISA bus systems have a very sophisticated setup program that stores not only the motherboard configuration, but also configurations for all the adapter cards. Fortunately, the setup programs for these systems have the capability to save the settings to a file on a floppy disk so that they can be restored later.

To access the setup program for most of these systems, you need the setup or Reference Diskette for the particular system. Many newer systems such as some of the new PS/2s store a complete copy of the Reference Disk in a hidden partition of the hard disk. When these systems boot up, the cursor jumps to the right side of the screen for a few seconds. During this time, if you press Ctrl+Alt+Ins, the hidden setup programs execute. Other manufacturers will use different keystrokes to activate the setup program or hidden partition, so consult your documentation to find the correct keystrokes for your particular system.

Recording Physical Configuration. While you are disassembling a system, it is a good idea to record all the physical settings and configurations within the system, including jumper and switch settings, cable orientations and placement, ground-wire locations, and even adapter-board placement. Keep a notebook handy for recording these items, and write down all the settings in the book.

It is especially important to record all the jumper and switch settings on every card that you remove from the system, as well as those on the motherboard. If you accidentally disturb these jumpers or switches, you will know how they were originally set. This knowledge is very important if you do not have all the documentation for the system handy. Even if you do, undocumented jumpers and switches often do not appear in the manuals but must be set a certain way for the item to function. It is very embarrassing, to say the least, if you take apart somebody's system and then cannot make it work again because you disturbed something. If you record these settings, you will save yourself the embarrassment.

Also, record all cable orientations. Most name-brand systems use cables and connectors that are keyed so that they cannot be plugged in backward, but most generic compatibles do not have this added feature. In addition, it is possible to mix up hard disk and floppy cables. You should mark or record what each cable was plugged into and its proper orientation. Ribbon cables usually have an odd-colored wire at one end that indicates pin 1. The devices into which the cables are plugged also are marked in some way to indicate the orientation of pin 1; these markings, obviously, should match.

Although cable orientation and placement seem to be very simple, we rarely get through the entire course of my PC troubleshooting seminars without several groups having cable-connection problems. Fortunately, in most cases (excepting power cables), plugging in any of the ribbon cables inside the system backward rarely causes any permanent damage.

Power and battery connections are exceptions to this rule, however; plugging them in backward surely will cause damage. In fact, plugging the motherboard power connectors in backward or in the wrong plug location will put 12 volts where only 5 should be—a situation that can cause components of the board to explode violently. I know people who have facial scars caused by shrapnel from exploding components. I always like to turn my face away from the system when I power it on for the first time.

Plugging the CMOS battery in backward can damage the CMOS chip itself, which usually is soldered into the motherboard; in such a case, the motherboard itself must be replaced.

Finally, it is a good idea to record miscellaneous items such as the placement of any ground wires, adapter cards, and anything else that you may have difficulty remembering later. Some configurations and setups are particular about which slots the adapter cards are located in; it usually is a good idea to put everything back exactly the way it was originally, especially in MCA and EISA bus systems.

Now that you have made the necessary preparations and taken the necessary precautions, you can actually begin working on the systems.

XT and Slim-Line Case Systems

The procedure for disassembling the XT style or Slim Line case systems offered by most manufacturers is very simple. Only two tools are normally required—a 1/4-inch nut driver for the external screws that hold the cover in place, and a 3/16-inch nut driver for all other screws. I almost always prefer to use a nut driver, although most of these screws have a Phillips-type head embedded within the hexagonal head of the screw. Compared with a Phillips screwdriver, the nut driver can get a much better grip on the screw, and you are much less likely to strip it out.

Removing the Cover. To remove the case cover, follow these steps:

1. Turn off the system, and unplug the power cord from the system unit.
2. Turn the system unit around so that the rear of the unit is facing you, and locate the screws that hold the system-unit cover in place (see fig. 3.1).
3. Use the 1/4-inch nut driver to remove the cover screws.
4. Slide the cover toward the front of the system unit until it stops; then lift up the front of the cover and remove it from the chassis.

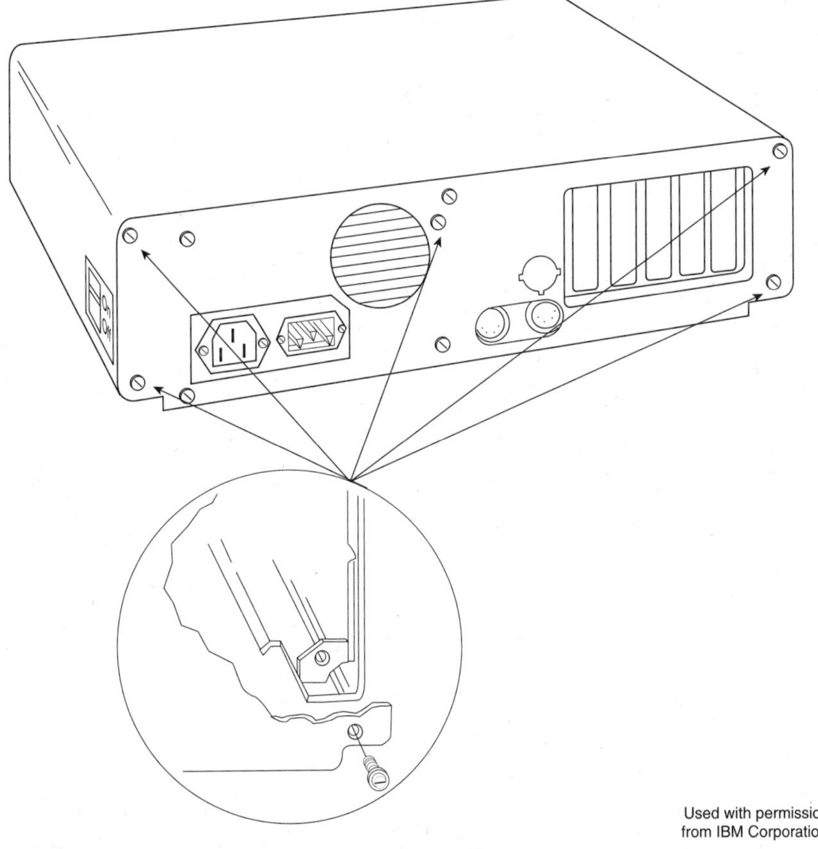

Used with permission from IBM Corporation.

Figure 3.1

The screws that hold the XT-type case cover in place.

To remove all adapter boards from the system unit, first remove the system-unit cover, as described earlier. Proceed as follows for each adapter:

1. Notice which slots all the adapters are in; if possible, make a diagram or drawing.
2. Use the 3/16-inch nut driver to remove the screw that holds the adapter in place (see fig. 3.2).
3. Notice the position of any cables plugged into the adapter before removing them. In a correctly wired system, the colored stripe on one side of the ribbon cable always denotes pin number 1. The power connector normally is shaped so that it can be inserted only the correct way.
4. Remove the adapter by lifting with even force at both ends.
5. Notice the positions of any jumpers or switches on the adapter, especially when documentation for the adapter isn't available. Even when documentation is available, manufacturers often use undocumented jumpers and switches for special purposes, such as testing or unique configurations.

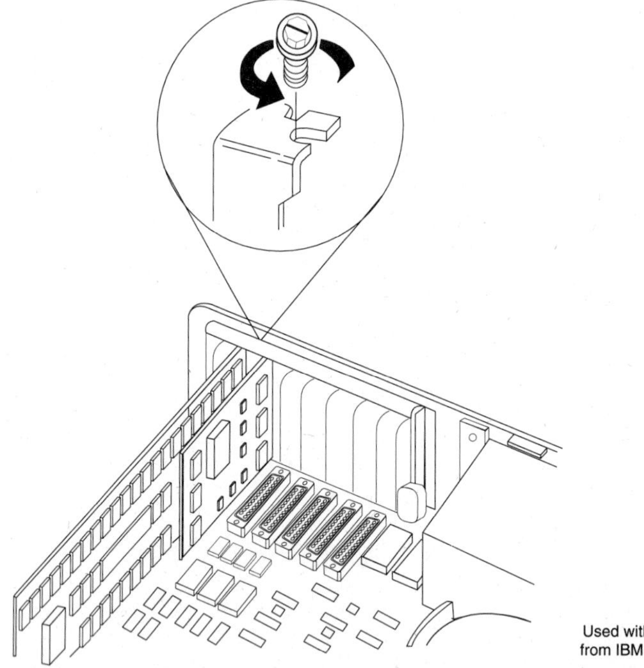

Figure 3.2

Removing the screw that holds the adapter in place.

Jumpers and switches on the circuit board normally are named. SW1 and SW2 are used for switch 1 and switch 2, for example, and J1 and J2 are used for jumper 1 and jumper 2. If these jumpers or switches are disturbed later, you can return to the original configuration—as long as you recorded the configuration the first time that you removed the adapter. The best procedure usually is to make a diagram that shows these features for a particular card.

Removing Disk Drives. Removing drives from XT- or Slim Line-case systems is fairly easy. The procedure is similar for both floppy and hard disk drives.

Before you remove a hard disk from a system, you should back it up. Older drives should have the heads parked as well, but almost all newer drives park the heads automatically when the power is off. The possibility always exists that data will be lost or the drive damaged from rough handling. Hard disks are discussed in more detail in chapters 14 through 16.

First, remove the cover and all adapters, as previously described. Then proceed as follows:

1. Some systems have drive retaining screws on the bottom of the chassis. Lift up the front of the chassis so that the unit stands with the rear of the chassis down and the disk drive facing straight up. Locate any drive retaining screws in the bottom of the chassis, and remove them.

   In IBM equipment, you find these screws in XT systems that have hard disks or half-height floppy drives (see fig. 3.3). These screws may be shorter than others used in the system. You must reinstall a screw of the same length in this location later; using a screw that's too long can damage the drive.

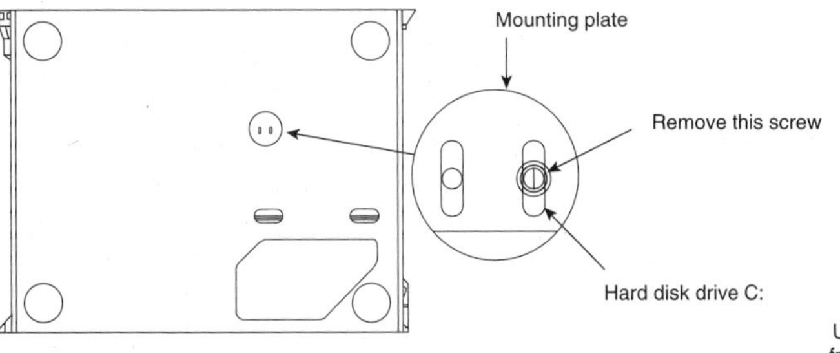

Used with permission from IBM Corporation.

Figure 3.3

Removing the retaining screws from the bottom of the chassis.

2. Set the chassis flat on the table, locate the drive retaining screws on the outboard sides of the drive, and remove them (see figs. 3.4 and 3.5).

3. Slide the disk drive forward about two inches, and then disconnect the power and signal cables from the drive (see figs. 3.6 and 3.7). In a correctly wired system, the odd-colored stripe on one side of the ribbon cable always denotes pin number 1. The power connector is shaped so that it can be inserted only the correct way.

4. Slide the drive completely out of the unit.

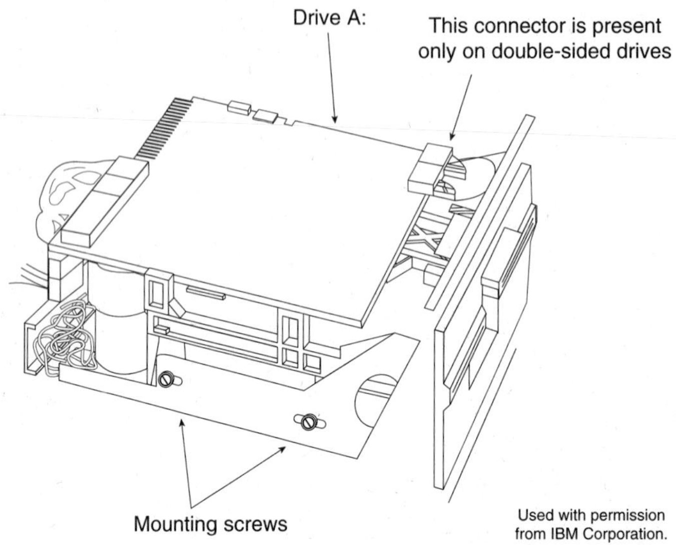

Figure 3.4

Removing the retaining screws from the outboard sides of a floppy disk drive.

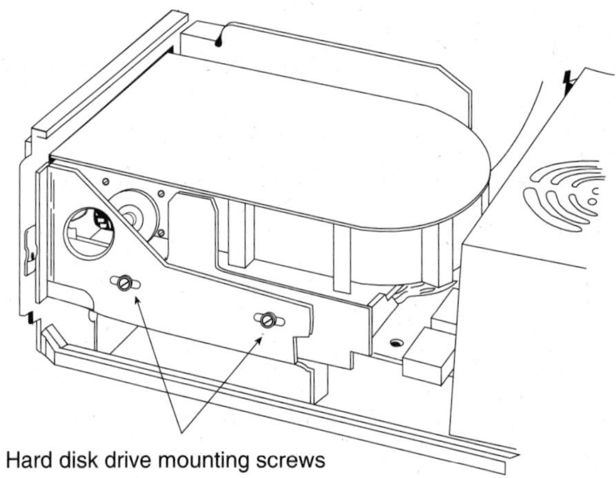

Figure 3.5

Removing the retaining screws from the outboard sides of the hard disk drive.

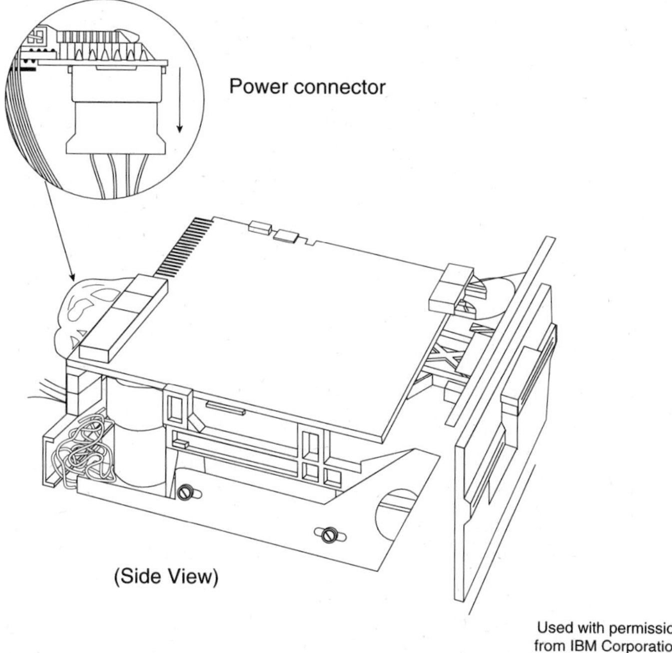

Figure 3.6
The power connector on a floppy disk drive.

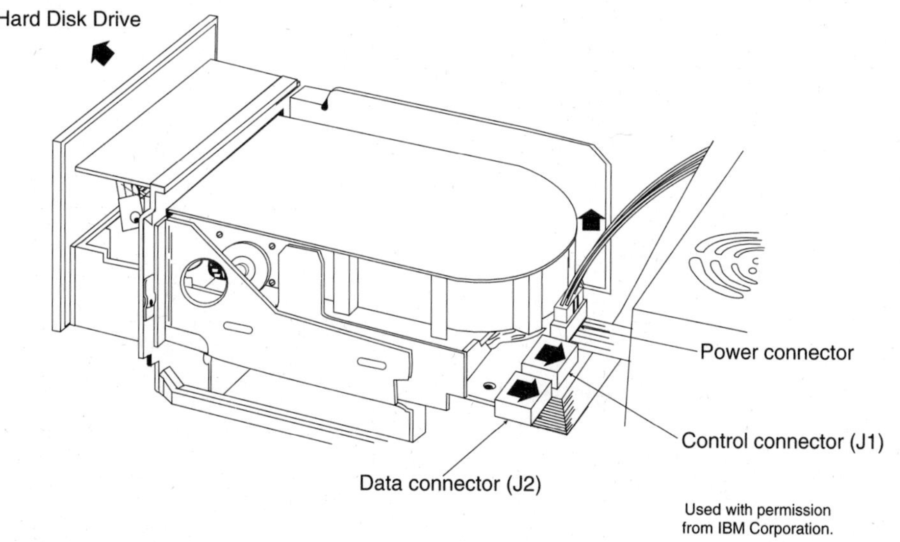

Figure 3.7
Disconnecting the power and signal cables from the hard disk drive.

Removing the Power Supply. In XT- or Slim Line-case systems, the power supply is mounted in the system unit with four screws in the rear and (usually) two interlocking tabs on the bottom. Removing the power supply may require you to remove the disk drives before taking out the power supply. You probably will have to at least loosen the drives to slide them forward for clearance when you remove the supply.

To remove the power supply, first remove the cover, all adapter boards, and the disk drives, as described earlier. (If sufficient clearance exists, you may not have to remove the adapter boards and disk drives.) Then proceed as follows:

1. Remove the four power-supply retaining screws from the rear of the system-unit chassis (see fig. 3.8).
2. Disconnect the cables from the power supply to the motherboard (see fig. 3.9), and then disconnect the power cables from the power supply to the disk drives. Always grasp the connectors themselves; never pull on the wires.
3. Slide the power supply forward about a half-inch to disengage the interlocking tabs on the bottom of the unit, and then lift the power supply out of the unit (see fig. 3.10).

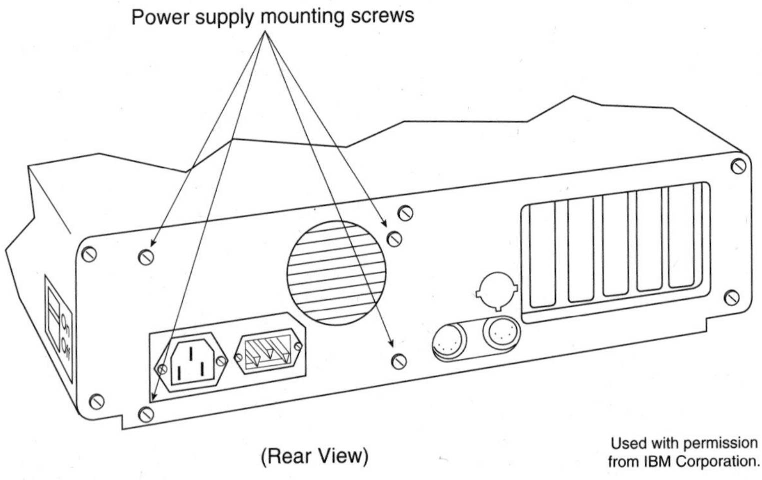

Figure 3.8

Removing the power-supply retaining screws from the rear of the chassis.

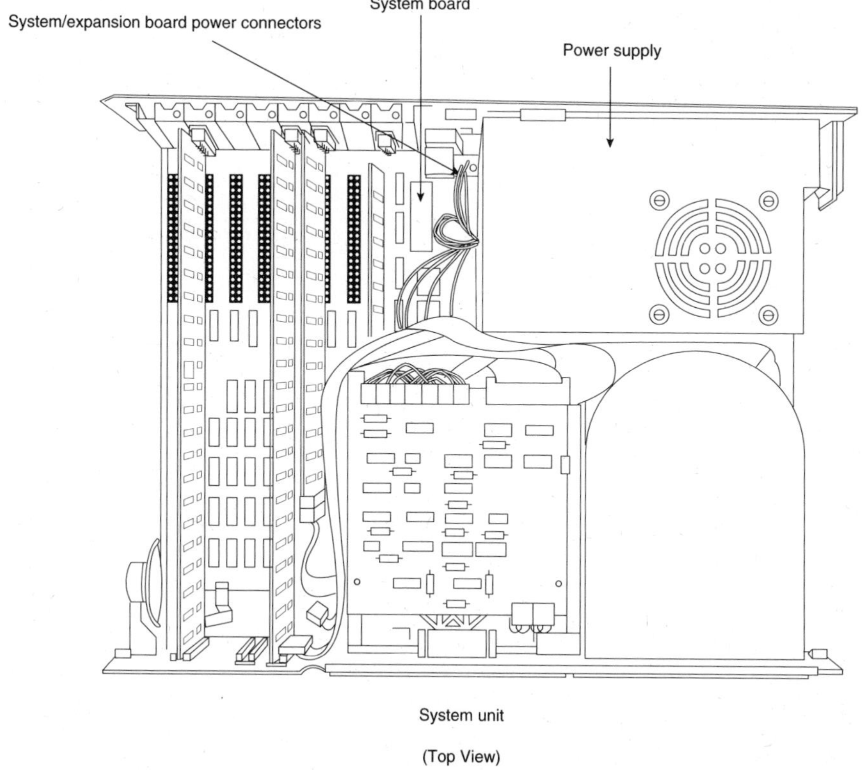

Figure 3.9

Disconnecting the cables from the power supply to the motherboard.

Removing the Motherboard. After all the adapter cards are removed from the unit, you can remove the system board, or *motherboard.* The motherboard in XT- and Slim Line-case systems is held in place by only a few screws and, often, several plastic standoffs that elevate the board from the metal chassis so that it does not touch the chassis and cause a short.

The standoffs slide into slots in the chassis. *These standoffs should remain with the motherboard.* You do not have to extract these standoffs from the motherboard to remove it; just remove the motherboard with the standoffs still attached. When you reinstall the motherboard, make sure that the standoffs slide properly into their slots. If one or more standoffs do not properly engage the chassis, you may crack the motherboard when you tighten the screws or install adapter cards.

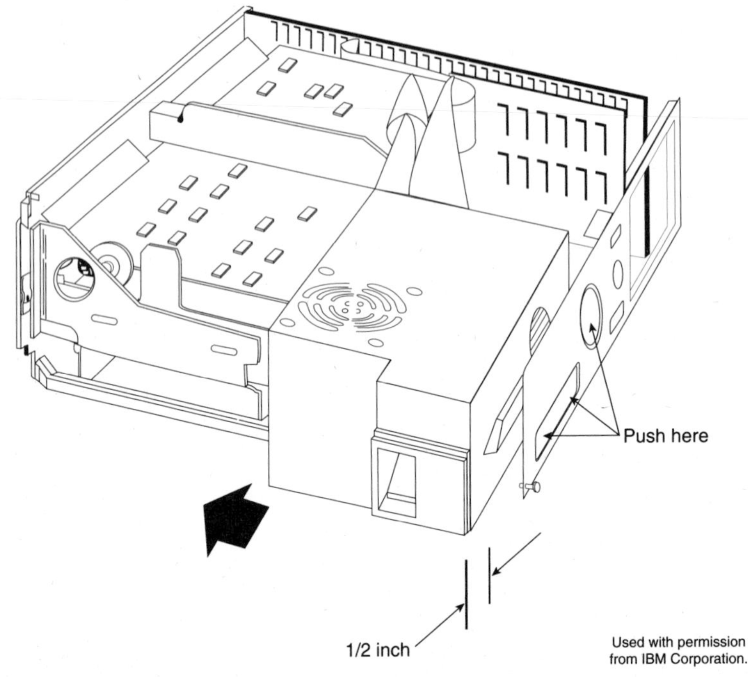

Figure 3.10

Sliding the power supply forward to disengage the interlocking tabs on the unit's bottom.

To remove the motherboard, first remove all adapter boards from the system unit, as described earlier. Then proceed as follows:

1. Disconnect all electrical connectors from the motherboard, including those for the keyboard, power supply, and speaker.
2. Locate and remove the motherboard retaining screws.
3. Slide the motherboard away from the power supply about a half-inch, until the standoffs disengage from their mounting slots (see fig. 3.11).
4. Lift the motherboard up and out of the chassis.

AT- and Tower-Case Systems

Disassembling an AT- or Tower-case system normally requires only two tools—a 1/4-inch nut driver for the external screws that hold the cover in place, and a 3/16-inch nut driver for all the other screws.

Most of the procedures are exactly like those for XT- and Slim Line-case systems. One difference, however, is that many AT-case systems use a different method for mounting the disk drives. Special rails or brackets are attached to the sides of the drives, and the drives slide into the system-unit chassis on these rails or brackets. The chassis has guide tracks for the rails, which enables you to remove the drive from the front of the unit without having to access the side to remove any mounting screws. The rails normally are made of plastic or fiberglass, but they can be made of metal in some systems. A diagram that shows how most of these rails are constructed appears in Chapter 13, "Floppy Disk Drives." It should be noted that any brackets or rails should remain attached to the drive while you are removing or installing it.

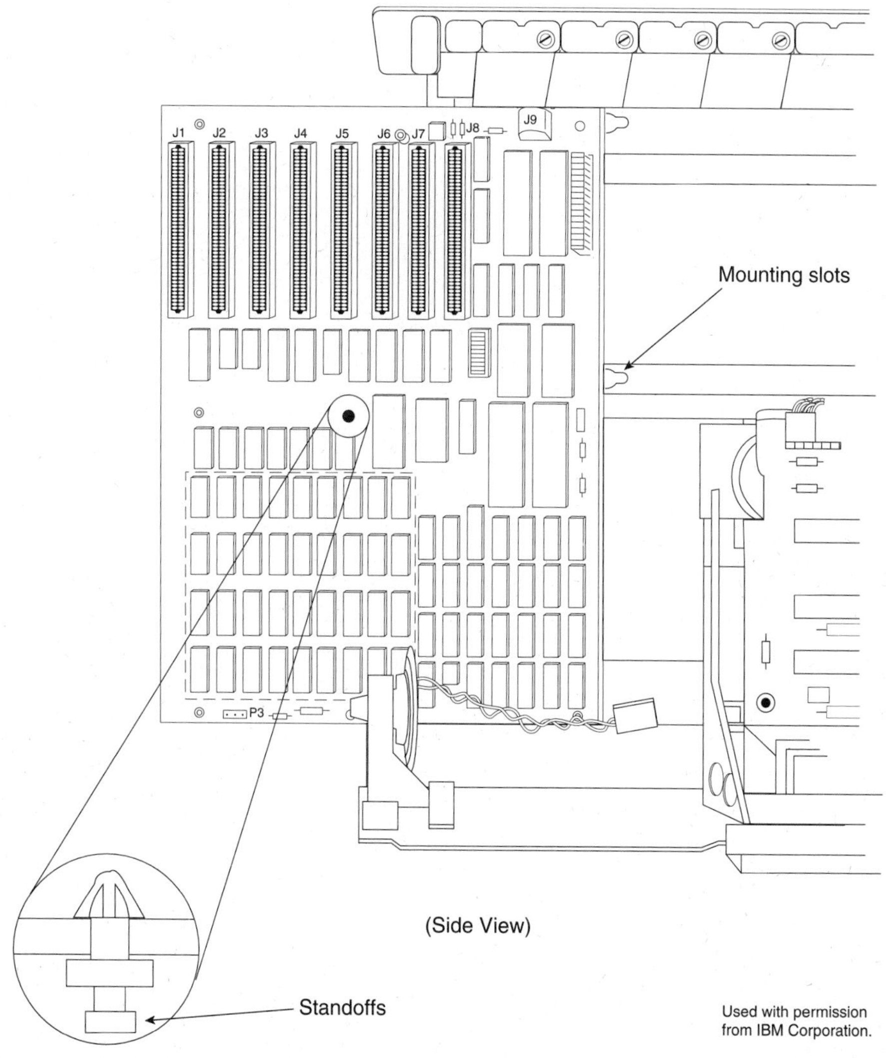

Figure 3.11

Sliding the motherboard away from the power supply until standoffs disengage from mounting slots.

Removing the Cover. To remove the case cover, follow these steps:

1. Turn off the system, and unplug the power cord from the system unit.
2. Turn the system unit around so that you're facing the rear of the unit, and locate the screws that hold the system-unit cover in place (see fig. 3.12).

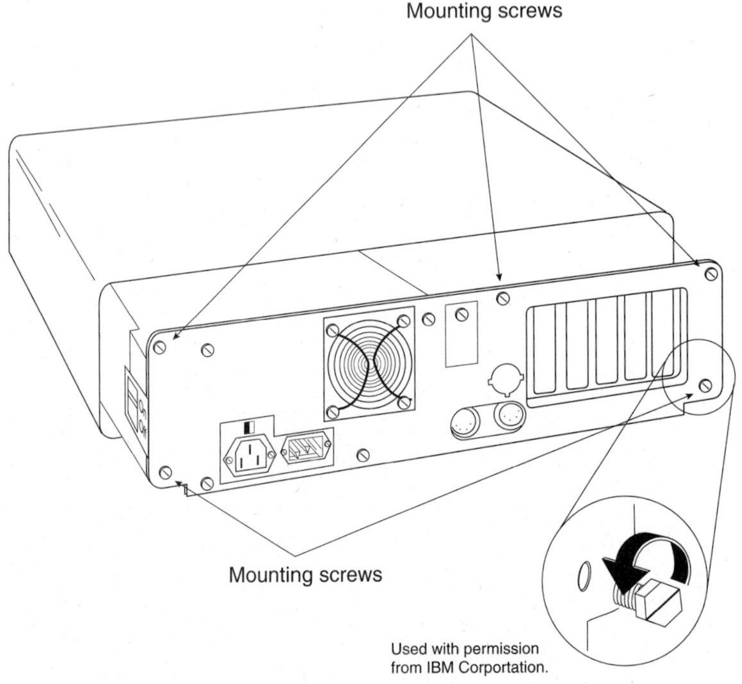

Figure 3.12

Removing the screws that hold the AT-case cover in place.

3. Use the 1/4-inch nut driver to remove the cover screws.
4. Slide the cover toward the front of the system unit until it stops; then lift up the front of the cover and remove it from the chassis.

Removing Adapter Boards. To remove all the adapter boards from the system unit, first remove the system-unit cover, as described earlier. Then proceed as follows for each adapter:

1. Notice which slot each adapter is in; if possible, make a diagram or drawing.
2. Use the 3/16-inch nut driver to remove the screw that holds the adapter in place (refer to fig. 3.2).

3. Notice the positions of any cables that are plugged into the adapter before you remove them. In a correctly wired system, the colored stripe on one side of the ribbon cable always denotes pin number 1. Some connectors have keys that enable them to be inserted only the correct way.

4. Remove the adapter by lifting with even force at both ends.

5. Notice the positions of any jumpers or switches on the adapter, especially when documentation for the adapter is not available. Even when documentation is available, manufacturers often use undocumented jumpers and switches for special purposes, such as testing or unique configurations. It's a good idea to know the existing settings, in case they are disturbed later.

Removing Disk Drives. Removing drives from AT-case systems is very easy. The procedure is similar for both floppy and hard disk drives.

Always back up hard disks completely and park the heads before removing disks from the system. Most newer drives (IDE and SCSI) park the heads automatically when they are powered off. A backup is important, because the possibility always exists that data will be lost or the drive damaged by rough handling.

To remove the drives from an AT-case system, first remove the cover, as described earlier. Then proceed as follows:

1. Depending on whether the drive is a hard disk or floppy disk drive, the drive is retained by a metal keeper bar with two screws or by two small, L-shape metal tabs, each of which held in place by a single screw. Locate these screws and remove them, along with the tabs or keeper bar (see figs. 3.13 and 3.14).

2. Slide the disk drive forward about two inches, and disconnect from the drives the power cables, the signal and data cables, and the ground wire (see figs. 3.15 and 3.16). In a correctly wired system, the colored stripe on one side of the ribbon cable always denotes pin number 1. The power connector is shaped so that it can be inserted only the correct way.

3. Slide the drive completely out of the unit.

Removing the Power Supply. In AT-case systems, the power supply is mounted in the system unit with four screws in the rear and (usually) two interlocking tabs on the bottom. Removing the power supply usually requires that you slide the disk drives forward for clearance when you remove the supply.

To remove the power supply, first remove the cover, loosen the disk-drive mounting screws, and move the disk drive forward about two inches, as described earlier. Then proceed as follows:

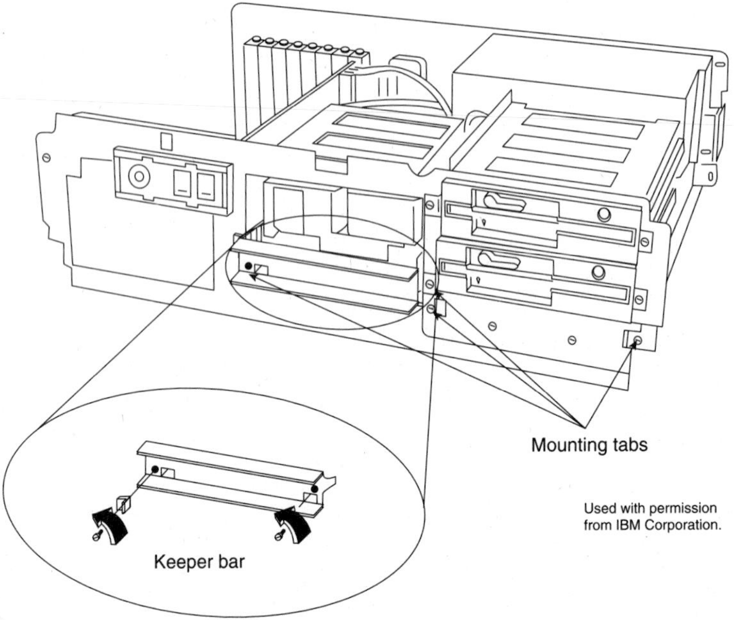

Figure 3.13

Removing mounting tabs and the keeper bar of a hard drive.

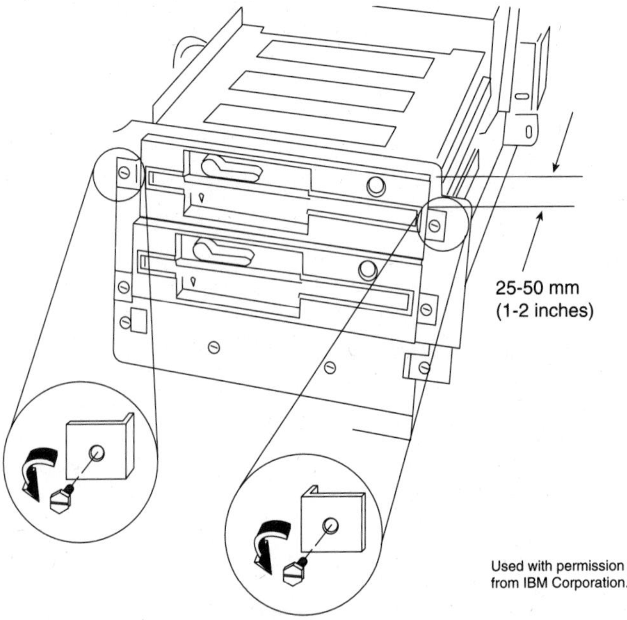

Figure 3.14

Removing the mounting tabs of a floppy drive.

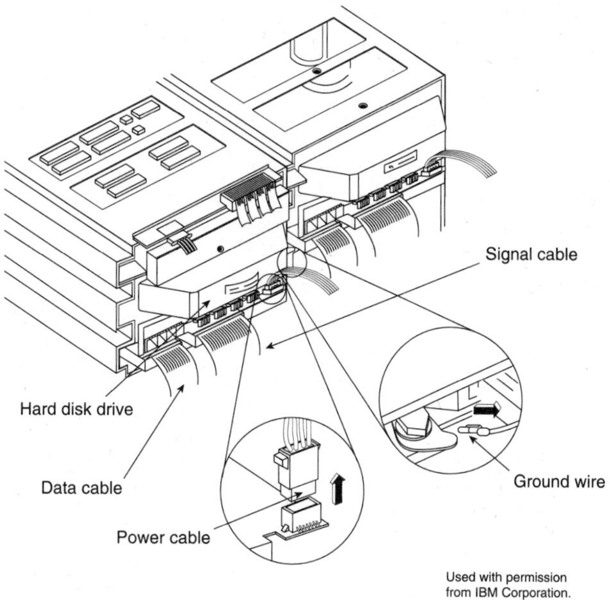

Figure 3.15

Disconnecting the hard drive power cable, signal and data cables, and ground wire.

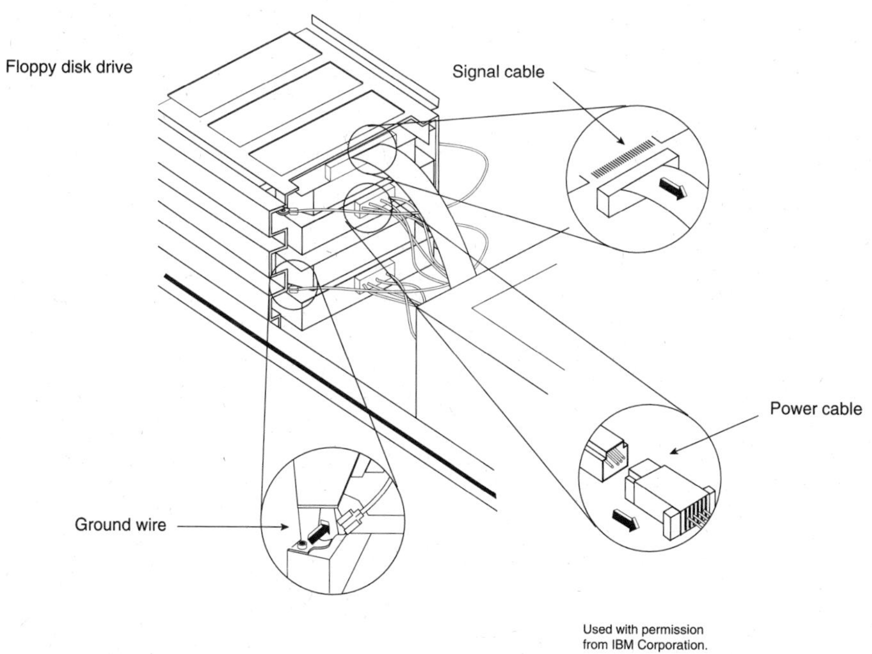

Figure 3.16

Disconnecting the floppy drive power cable, signal cable, and ground wire.

1. Remove the four power-supply retaining screws from the rear of the system-unit chassis (see fig. 3.17).

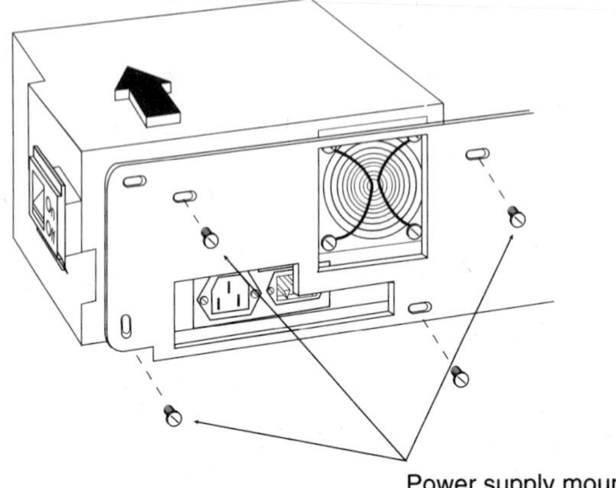

Figure 3.17

Removing the power-supply retaining screws from the rear of the chassis.

2. Disconnect the cables from the power supply to the motherboard (see fig. 3.18), and then disconnect the power cables from the power supply to the disk drive. Always grasp the connectors themselves; never pull on the wires.

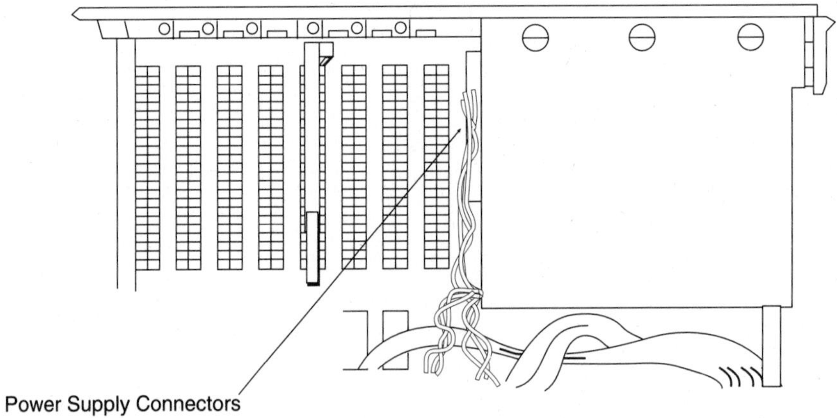

Figure 3.18

Disconnecting the cables from the power supply to the motherboard.

3. Slide the power supply forward about a half-inch to disengage the interlocking tabs on the bottom of the unit; then lift the power supply out of the unit.

Removing the Motherboard. After all adapter cards are removed from the unit, you can remove the motherboard. The motherboard in AT-case systems is held in place by several screws, as well as by plastic standoffs that elevate the board from the metal chassis so that it does not touch the chassis and cause a short.

You should not separate the standoffs from the motherboard; remove the board and the standoffs as a unit. The standoffs slide into slots in the chassis. When you reinstall the motherboard, make sure that the standoffs are located in their slots properly. If one or more standoffs does not engage the chassis properly, you may crack the motherboard when you tighten the screws or install adapter cards.

To remove the motherboard, first remove all adapter boards from the system unit, as described earlier. Then proceed as follows:

1. Disconnect from the motherboard all electrical connectors, including those for the keyboard, power supply, speaker, battery, and keylock.
2. Locate and remove the motherboard retaining screws.
3. Slide the motherboard away from the power supply about a half-inch, until the standoffs have disengaged from their mounting slots (see fig. 3.19).
4. Lift the motherboard up and out of the chassis.

Removing SIMMs (Single In-Line Memory Modules) or DIMMs (Dual In-Line Memory Modules). One benefit of using single or dual in-line memory modules (SIMMs or DIMMs) is that they're easy to remove or install. When you remove memory modules, remember that because of physical interference, you must remove the memory-module package that is closest to the disk drive bus-adapter slot before you remove the package that is closest to the edge of the motherboard. This procedure describes removing a SIMM device, note that a DIMM is also removed in exactly the same way. The only difference is that a DIMM is slightly longer and has more contacts than a SIMM device.

To remove a SIMM (or DIMM) properly, follow this procedure:

1. Gently pull the tabs on each side of the SIMM socket outward.
2. Rotate or pull the SIMM up and out of the socket (see fig. 3.20).

Caution

Be careful not to damage the connector. If you damage the motherboard SIMM connector, you could be looking at an expensive repair. Never force the SIMM; it should come out easily. If it doesn't, you are doing something wrong.

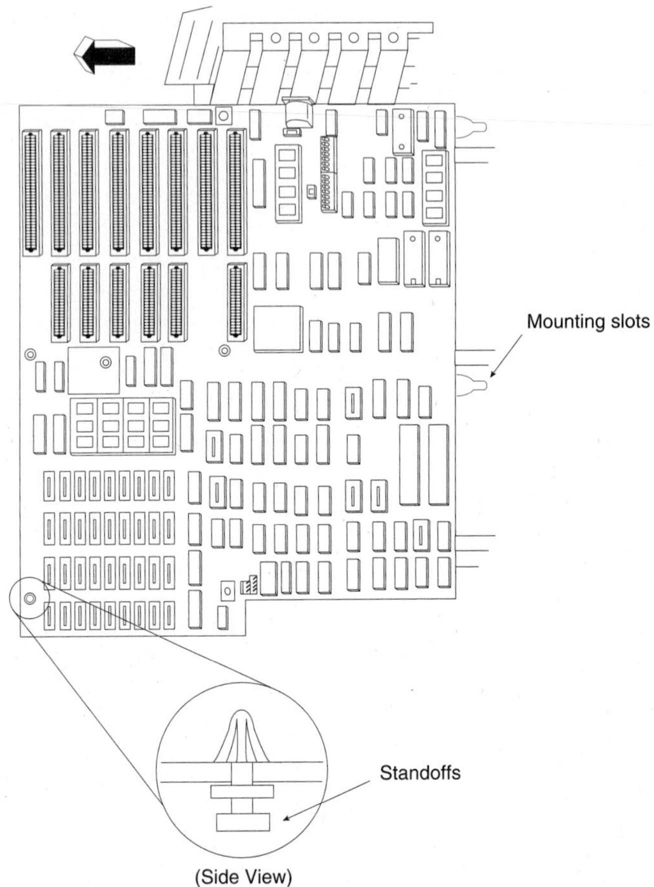

Figure 3.19

Disengaging standoffs from their mounting slots.

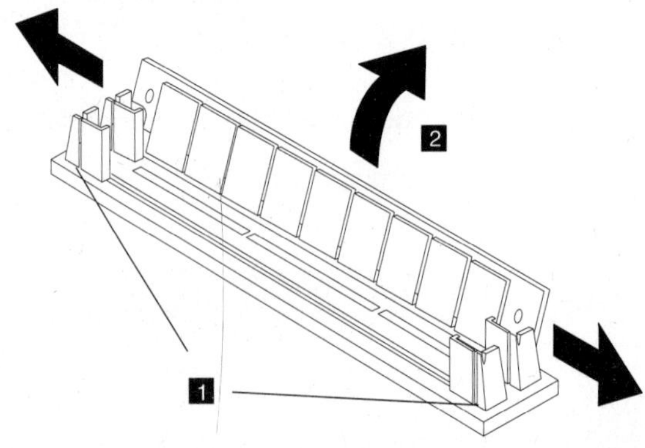

Figure 3.20

Removing a SIMM.

Summary

This chapter discussed the initial teardown and inspection of a system and also examined the types of tools required, ranging from simple hand tools to meters for measuring voltage and resistance. The chapter mentioned some of the problems that you may encounter with the actual hardware (screws, nuts, bolts, and so on) in a system.

The chapter also discussed the physical-disassembly procedure and how to recognize the various components of a system. The chapter emphasized the steps taken before and during disassembly, such as ESD protection, and the recording of system setup information to ensure that the system works properly when it is reassembled.

Different disassembly procedures were discussed, based on the type of case used for the system. Most systems built with a particular-style case (AT and Tower cases, for example) are constructed in a similar fashion. After you work on a system that has a particular case design, you will find that most other systems that have the same type of case are almost identical.

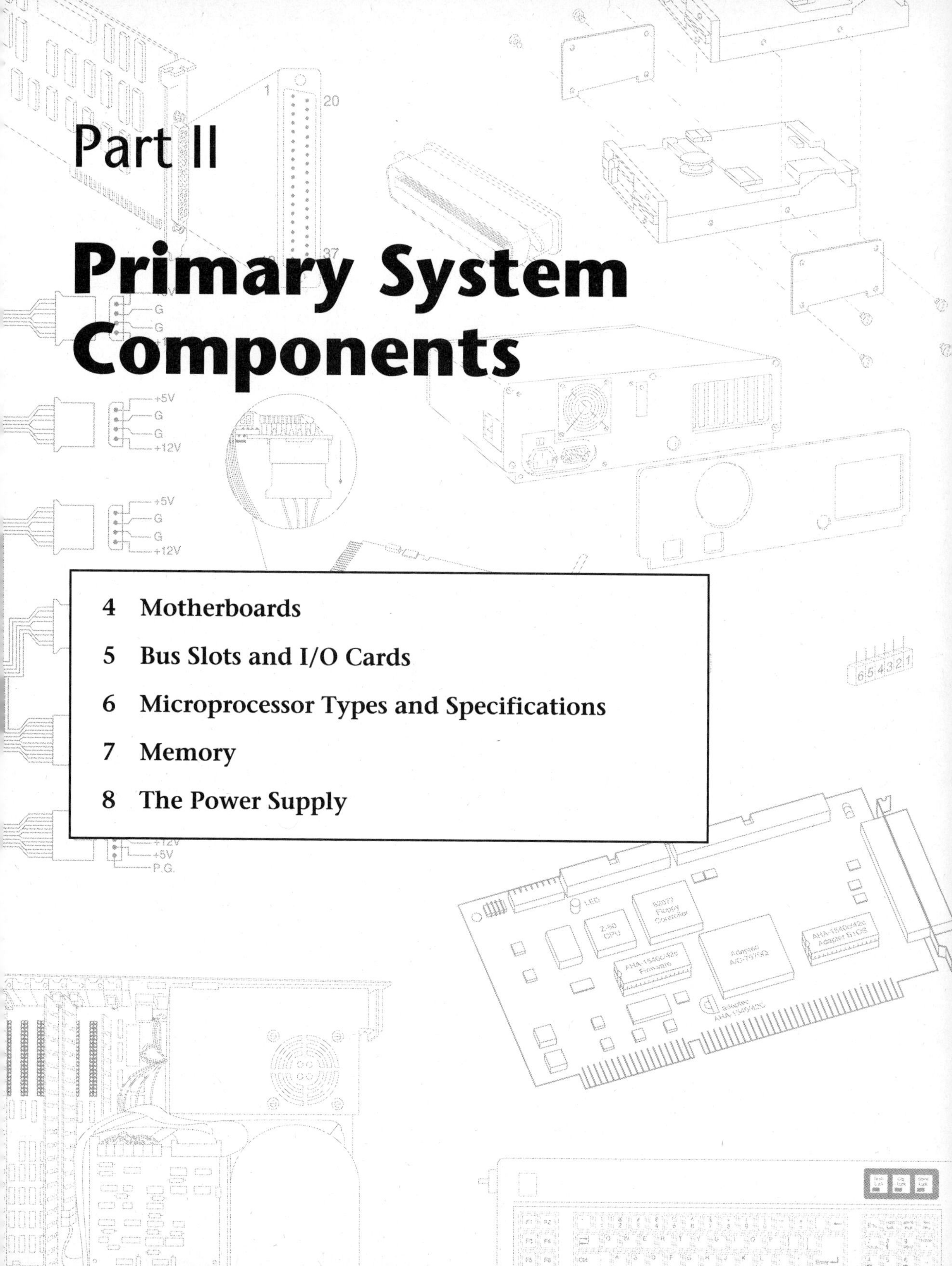

Part II

Primary System Components

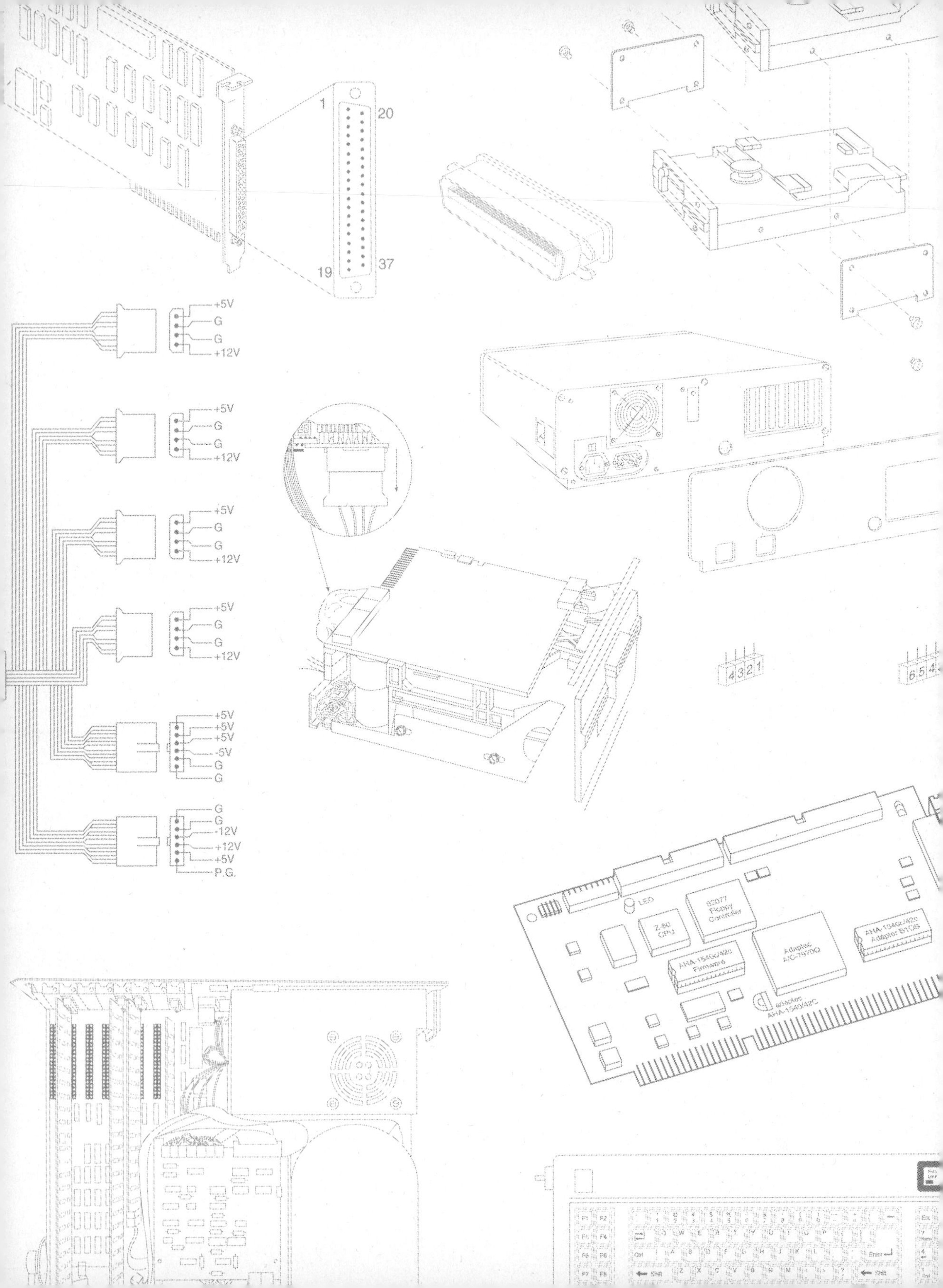
1
20
19
37
+5V
G
G
+12V
+5V
G
G
+12V
+5V
G
G
+12V
+5V
G
G
+12V
+5V
+5V
+5V
-5V
G
G
G
G
-12V
+12V
+5V
P.G.
4321
LED
Z-80
CPU
82077
Floppy
Controller
AHA-1540c/42c
Firmware
Adaptec
AIC-7970Q
AHA-1540c/42c
Adapter BIOS

Chapter 4

Motherboards

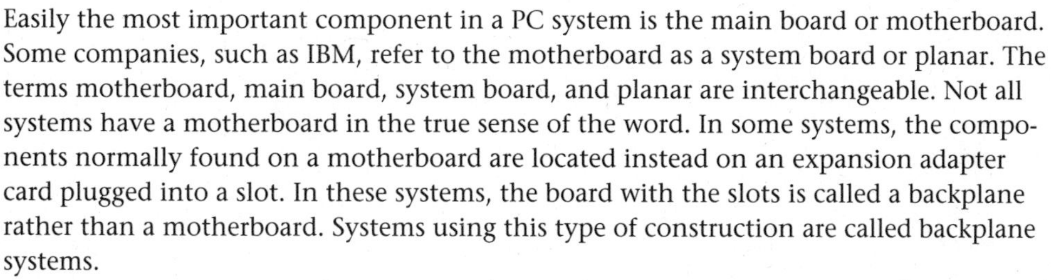

Easily the most important component in a PC system is the main board or motherboard. Some companies, such as IBM, refer to the motherboard as a system board or planar. The terms motherboard, main board, system board, and planar are interchangeable. Not all systems have a motherboard in the true sense of the word. In some systems, the components normally found on a motherboard are located instead on an expansion adapter card plugged into a slot. In these systems, the board with the slots is called a backplane rather than a motherboard. Systems using this type of construction are called backplane systems.

Backplane systems come in two main types, passive and active. A passive backplane means the main backplane board does not contain any circuitry at all except for the bus connectors and maybe some buffer and driver circuits. All the circuitry found on a conventional motherboard is contained on one or more expansion cards installed in slots on the backplane. Some backplane systems use a passive design that incorporates the entire system circuitry into a single mothercard. The mothercard is essentially a complete motherboard that is designed to plug into a slot in the passive backplane. The passive backplane/mothercard concept allows the entire system to be easily upgraded by changing one or more cards. Because of the expense of the high function mothercard, this type of system design is rarely found in PC systems. The passive backplane design does enjoy popularity in industrial systems, which are often rack mounted. Some high-end file servers also feature this design.

An active backplane means the main backplane board contains bus control and usually other circuitry as well. Most active backplane systems contain all the circuitry found on a typical motherboard except for the processor complex. The processor complex is the name of the circuit board that contains the main system processor and any other circuitry directly related to it, such as clock control, cache, and so forth. The processor complex design allows the user to easily upgrade the system later to a new processor type by changing one card. In effect it amounts to a modular motherboard with a replaceable processor section. Most modern PC systems that use a backplane design use an active backplane/processor complex. Both IBM and Compaq have used this type of design in some of their high-end (server class) systems, for example. This allows an easier and generally more affordable upgrade than the passive backplane/mothercard design since the processor complex board is usually much cheaper than a mothercard. Unfortunately, because there are no standards for the processor complex interface to the system, these boards are proprietary and can only be purchased from the system manufacturer. This limited market and availability causes the prices of these boards to be higher than most complete motherboards from other manufacturers.

The motherboard system design and the backplane system design have both advantages and disadvantages. Most original personal computers were designed as backplanes in the late 1970s. Apple and IBM shifted the market to the now traditional motherboard with a slot-type design because this type of system generally is cheaper to mass-produce than one with the backplane design. The theoretical advantage of a backplane system, however, is that you can upgrade it easily to a new processor and new level of performance by changing a single card. For example, you can upgrade a system with a 486-based processor card to a Pentium-based card just by changing the card. In a motherboard-design system, you must change the motherboard itself, a seemingly more formidable task. Unfortunately, the reality of the situation is that a backplane design is often much more expensive to upgrade, and because the bus remains fixed on the backplane, the backplane design precludes more comprehensive upgrades that involve adding local bus slots for example.

Because of the limited availability of the processor complex boards or mothercards, they usually end up being more expensive than a complete new motherboard that uses an industry standard form factor. For this reason, I recommend staying away from any backplane system designs. In most cases a conventional motherboard design makes it much easier to obtain replacement components for repair or upgrade.

Another nail in the coffin of backplane designs is the upgradable processor. Intel has designed all 486, Pentium, and Pentium Pro processors to be upgradable to faster (sometimes called OverDrive) processors in the future by simply swapping (or adding) the new processor chip. Changing only the processor chip for a faster one is the easiest and generally most cost-effective way to upgrade without changing the entire motherboard.

Replacement Motherboards

Some manufacturers go out of their way to make their systems as physically incompatible as possible with any other system. Then replacement parts, repairs, and upgrades are virtually impossible to find—except, of course, from the original system manufacturer, at a significantly higher price than the equivalent part would cost to fit a standard PC-compatible system. For example, if the motherboard in my current AT-chassis system (or any system using a Baby-AT motherboard and case) dies, I can find any number of replacement boards that will bolt directly in, with my choice of processors and clock speeds, at very good prices. If the motherboard dies in a newer IBM, Compaq, Hewlett-Packard, Packard Bell or other proprietary shaped system, you'll pay for a replacement available only from the original manufacturer, and you have little or no opportunity to select a board with a faster or better processor than the one that failed. In other words, upgrading or repairing one of these systems via a motherboard replacement is difficult and usually not cost-effective.

Some of the proprietary systems have become popular enough that at least one company has developed replacement motherboards for them. Reply Corp. (see the vendor list in Appendix B) produces high performance replacement boards for many of the IBM PS/2, Valuepoint, and Compaq models, for example. ALR also makes boards for upgrading Compaq and some other systems.

Knowing What to Look for (Selection Criteria)

As a consultant, I am often asked to make a recommendation for purchases. Making these types of recommendations is one of the most frequent tasks a consultant performs. Many consultants charge a large fee for this advice. Without guidance, many individuals don't have any rhyme or reason to their selections and instead base their choices solely on magazine reviews or, even worse, on some personal bias. To help eliminate this haphazard selection process, I have developed a simple checklist that will help you select a system. This list takes into consideration several important system aspects overlooked by most checklists. The goal is to ensure that the selected system truly is compatible and has a long life of service and upgrades ahead.

It helps to think like an engineer when you make your selection. Consider every aspect and detail of the motherboards in question. For instance, you should consider any future uses and upgrades. Technical support at a professional (as opposed to a user) level is extremely important; what support will be provided? Is there documentation, and does it cover everything else?

In short, a checklist is a good idea. Here is one for you to use in evaluating any PC-compatible system. You might not have to meet every one of these criteria to consider a particular system, but if you miss more than a few of these checks, consider staying away from that system. The items at the top of the list are the most important, and the items at the bottom are perhaps of lesser importance (although I think each item is important). The rest of this chapter discusses in detail the criteria in this checklist.

Processor. A 486 motherboard should be equipped with a DX2 or DX4 type processor—the faster the better. The 486 processor should be an SL Enhanced version, which is standard on the most desirable DX4 based models. A Pentium motherboard should only use the second generation 3.3v Pentium processor, which has a 296-pin Socket 5 or Socket 7 configuration that differs physically from the 273-pin Socket 4 first generation design. All second generation Pentiums (75MHz and up) are fully SL Enhanced.

Processor Sockets. A 486 motherboard should have a ZIF (Zero Insertion Force) processor socket that follows the Intel Socket 3 (237-pin) specifications. A Pentium motherboard should have one or two ZIF sockets that follow the Intel Socket 5 (320-pin) or Socket 7 (321-pin) specification. The Socket 7 with an adjacent VRM (Voltage Regulator Module) socket will allow the best selection of future Pentium processors that will be available at higher speeds. Many of the newer and faster

Pentiums require Socket 7. Pentium Pro motherboards will all have Socket 8, which should be in a ZIF version to allow easy future upgrades.

Motherboard Speed. A 486 motherboard should be speed selectable to run at 33 or 40 MHz for maximum performance and compatibility. These motherboards may allow other speeds to be selected as well. A Pentium or Pentium Pro motherboard should run at 50, 60 or 66 MHz and be speed switchable between these speeds. Notice that most of the 486 and virtually all the Pentium and Pentium Pro processors sold today run at a multiple of the motherboard speed. For example, Pentium 75 runs at a motherboard speed of 50 MHz; Pentium 60, 90, 120, 150, and 180 MHz chips run at a 60MHz base motherboard speed; and the Pentium 66, 100, 133, 166, and 200 run at a 66MHz motherboard speed setting. The Pentium Pro 150, 180, and 200 run at 50, 60, and 66 MHz speeds, respectively. All components on the motherboard (especially cache memory) should be rated to run at the maximum allowable motherboard speed.

Cache Memory. All 486 and Pentium motherboards should have a Level 2 cache onboard. Most Pentium Pro processors have a built in 256K or 512K Level 2 cache, but may also have more Level 2 cache on the motherboard for even better performance. 486 motherboards should have 256K and Pentium motherboards should have 256K to 512K for maximum performance. The Level 2 Cache should be of a Write-Back design, and must be populated with chips that are fast enough to support the maximum motherboard speed, which should be 15ns or faster for 66 MHz maximum motherboard speeds. For Pentium boards, the cache should be a Synchronous SRAM (Static RAM) type, which is also called Pipelined Burst SRAM.

SIMM Memory. 486 motherboards should ideally use 72-pin SIMMs that support a single bank per SIMM. 30-pin SIMMs are acceptable for upgrade boards designed to reuse memory from older motherboards. All Pentium and Pentium Pro motherboards should use either 72-pin SIMMs or 168-pin DIMMs (Dual In-line Memory Modules). Due to the 64-bit design of these boards, the 72-pin SIMMs will be installed in matched pairs, while DIMMs are installed one at a time (one per 64-bit bank). For maximum performance look for systems that support SDRAM (Synchronous DRAM), or EDO (Extended Data Out) type SIMMs. The SIMMs should be rated at 70ns or faster. Mission-critical systems should use Parity SIMMs and ensure that the motherboard fully supports parity checking or even ECC (Error Correcting Code) as well. Note that the popular Intel Triton Pentium chipset (82430FX) does not support parity checked memory at all, but their other Pentium chipsets such as the older Neptune (82430NX) and newer Triton II (82430HX) do indeed offer parity support. Triton II even offers ECC capability using standard parity SIMMs. For this reason, I highly recommend the 82430HX chipset and true Parity memory for mission critical Pentium systems. All the current Pentium Pro chipsets also support Parity memory, and are ideal for file servers and other mission critical use when equipped with parity SIMMs or DIMMs.

Bus Type. 486 motherboards should have an ISA (Industry Standard Architecture) bus with either two or three VL-Bus, or ideally three or four PCI local bus slots.

Pentium and Pentium Pro motherboards should have three or four ISA bus slots and three or four PCI local bus slots.

BIOS. The motherboard should use an industry standard BIOS such as those from AMI, Phoenix, Microid Research or Award. The BIOS should be of a Flash ROM or EEPROM (Electrically Erasable Programmable Read Only Memory) design for easy updating. The BIOS should support the Plug and Play (PnP) specification, Enhanced IDE or Fast ATA, as well as 2.88M floppy drives. APM (Advanced Power Management) support should be built in to the BIOS as well.

Form Factor. For maximum flexibility, the motherboard should come in a Baby-AT form factor. This allows it to be installed in the widest variety of case designs, and be retrofittable in most systems. For the greatest performance and future flexibility, many newer motherboards and systems will incorporate the new ATX form factor, which has distinct performance and functional advantages over Baby-AT. Note that the ATX design will become the form factor of choice over the next few years, replacing the older Baby-AT form factor.

Built-In Interfaces. Ideally a motherboard should contain as many built-in standard controllers and interfaces as possible (except video). A motherboard should have a built-in floppy controller that supports 2.88M drives, built-in primary and secondary local bus (PCI or VL-Bus) Enhanced IDE (also called Fast ATA) connectors, two built-in high speed serial ports (must use 16550A type buffered UARTs), and a built-in high speed parallel port (must be EPP/ECP compliant). A built-in PS/2 type mouse port should be included, although one of the serial ports can be used for a mouse as well. Some newer systems will include a built-in USB (Universal Serial Bus) port, which is a bonus. A built-in SCSI port is a bonus as long as it conforms to ASPI (Advanced SCSI Programming Interface) standards. Built-in network adapters are acceptable, but usually an ISA slot card network adapter is more easily supported via standard drivers and is more easily upgraded as well. Built-in video adapters are also a bonus in some situations, but because there are many different video chipset and adapter designs to choose from, generally there are better choices in external local bus video adapters. The same goes for built-in sound cards; they usually offer basic Sound Blaster compatibility and function, but often do not include other desirable features found on most plug-in soundcards, such as wavetable support.

Plug and Play (PnP). The motherboard should fully support the Intel Plug and Play specification. This will allow automatic configuration of PCI adapters as well as Plug and Play ISA adapters.

Power Management. The motherboard should fully support SL Enhanced processors with APM (Advanced Power Management) and SMM (System Management Mode) protocols that allow for powering down various system components to different levels of readiness and power consumption.

Motherboard Chipset. Pentium motherboards should use a high-performance chipset that allows parity checking, such as the Intel Triton II (82430HX), Opti Viper, ALI

Aladdin, or others with similar specifications. The popular original Intel Triton (82430FX) chipset does not support parity checked memory and should not be used in mission-critical applications. For critical applications using Pentium motherboards where accuracy and data integrity are important, I recommend you use a board based on the newer Triton II (82430HX) chipset or any others like it that support ECC (Error Correcting Code) memory using true parity memory modules.

Pentium Pro motherboards currently do not have many chipsets to choose from, but that is improving. Intel has the high-end Orion (82450KX) chipset, as well as the newer less expensive Natoma (82440FX) chipset. Both chipsets support parity memory and are suitable for critical application use.

Documentation. Good technical documentation is a requirement. Documents should include information on any and all jumpers and switches found on the board, connector pinouts for all connectors, specifications for cache RAM chips, SIMMs, and other plug-in components, and any other applicable technical information. I would also acquire separate documentation from the BIOS manufacturer covering the specific BIOS used in the system, as well as the Data Books covering the specific chipset used in the motherboard. Additional data books for any other controller or I/O chips on-board are a bonus, and may be acquired from the respective chip manufacturers.

You may notice that these selection criteria seem fairly strict, and may disqualify many motherboards on the market, including what you already have in your system! These criteria will, however, guarantee you the highest quality motherboard offering the latest in PC technology that will be upgradable, expandable, and provide good service for many years. Most of the time I recommend purchasing boards from better-known motherboard manufacturers such as Intel, SuperMicro, Micronics, AMI, Acer, Alaris, Asus, and so on. These boards might cost a little more than others that you have never heard of, but there is some safety in the more well known brands. That is, the more boards that they sell, the more likely that any problems will have been discovered by others and solved long before you get yours. Also, if service or support are needed, the larger vendors are more likely to be around in the long run.

Documentation

As mentioned, extensive documentation is an important factor to consider when you're planning to purchase a motherboard. Most motherboard manufacturers design their boards around a particular chipset, which actually counts as the bulk of the motherboard circuitry. There are a number of manufacturers offering chipsets, such as Intel, Opti, ALI, VLSI, UMC, Micronics, Chips & Technologies, and others. I recommend obtaining the data book or other technical documentation on the chipset directly from the chipset manufacturer.

One of the more common questions I hear about a system relates to the BIOS Setup program. People want to know what the "Advanced Chipset Setup" features mean and what will the effects of changing them be. Often they go to the BIOS manufacturer thinking that the BIOS documentation will offer help. Usually, however, people find that there is no real coverage of what the chipset setup features are in the BIOS documentation. You will find this information in the data book provided by the chipset manufacturer. Although these books are meant to be read by the engineers who design the boards, they contain all the detailed information about the chipset's features, especially those that might be adjustable. With the chipset data book, you will have an explanation of all the controls in the Advanced Chipset Setup section of the BIOS Setup program.

Besides the main chipset data books, I also recommend collecting any data books on the other major chips in the system. This would include any floppy or IDE controller chips, "super I/O" chips, and of course the main processor. You will find an incredible amount of information on these components in the data books. A word of warning: Most chipset manufacturers only make a particular chip for a short time, rapidly superseding it with an improved or changed version. The data books are only available during the time the chip is being manufactured so if you wait too long you will find that such documents may no longer be available. The time to collect documentation on your motherboard is NOW!

ROM BIOS Compatibility

The issue of ROM BIOS compatibility is important. If the BIOS is not compatible, any number of problems can result. Several reputable companies that produce compatibles have developed their own proprietary ROM BIOS that works just like IBM's. These companies also frequently update their ROM code to keep in step with the latest changes IBM has incorporated into its ROMs. Because IBM generally does not sell ROM upgrades or provide them for older systems (unless the upgrade is absolutely necessary, and IBM decides if that is the case), keeping current with an actual IBM system is more difficult than with most of the compatible systems on the market. The newer PS/2 systems do use a BIOS that is either stored on the hard disk or contained in a Flash ROM that is easily updated via a floppy disk. If you have one of these systems, BIOS upgrade disks can be obtained via the IBM National Support Center (NSC) BBS. The number is listed in Appendix B. Also, many of the compatibles' OEMs have designed ROMs that work specifically with additional features in their systems while effectively masking the effects of these improvements from any software that would "balk" at the differences.

OEMs. Many OEMs (original equipment manufacturers) have developed their own compatible ROMs independently. Companies such as Compaq, Zenith, and AT&T have developed their own BIOS products, which have proven compatible with IBM's. These companies also offer upgrades to newer versions that often can offer more features and improvements or fix problems with the older versions. If you use a system with a proprietary ROM, make sure that it is from a larger company with a track record and one that will provide updates and fixes as necessary.

Several companies have specialized in the development of a compatible ROM BIOS product. The three major companies that come to mind in discussing ROM BIOS software are American Megatrends, Inc. (AMI), Award Software, and Phoenix Software. Each company licenses its ROM BIOS to a motherboard manufacturer so that the manufacturer can worry about the hardware rather than the software. To obtain one of these ROMs for a motherboard, the OEM must answer many questions about the design of the system so that the proper BIOS can be either developed or selected from those already designed.

Combining a ROM BIOS and a motherboard is not a haphazard task. No single, generic, compatible ROM exists, either. AMI, Award, Microid Research, and Phoenix ship to different manufacturers many variations of their BIOS code, each one custom-tailored to that specific system, much like DOS can be.

AMI. Although AMI customizes the ROM code for a particular system, it does not sell the ROM source code to the OEM. An OEM must obtain each new release as it becomes available. Because many OEMs don't need or want every new version developed, they might skip several version changes before licensing a new one. The AMI BIOS is currently the most popular BIOS in PC systems today. Newer versions of the AMI BIOS are called Hi-Flex due to the high flexibility found in the BIOS configuration program. The AMI Hi-Flex BIOS is used in Intel, AMI, Alaris, and many other manufacturers' motherboards. One special AMI feature is that it is the only third-party BIOS manufacturer to make its own motherboard.

Older versions of the AMI BIOS had a few problems with different keyboards and keyboard controller chips, and very early versions also had some difficulty with certain IDE hard disk drives. To eliminate these types of problems, make sure that your AMI BIOS is dated 04/09/90 or later, and has keyboard controller F or later. You will possibly have keyboard lockups and problems running Windows or OS/2 if you have an older keyboard controller chip.

To locate this information, power on the system and observe the BIOS ID string displayed on the lower left of the screen. The primary BIOS Identification string (ID String 1) is displayed by any AMI BIOS during the POST (Power On Self Test) at the left bottom corner of the screen, below the copyright message. Two additional BIOS ID strings (ID String 2 and 3) can be displayed by the AMI Hi-Flex BIOS by pressing the <Ins> key during POST. These additional ID strings display the options that are installed in the BIOS.

The general BIOS ID String 1 format for older AMI BIOS versions is the following table:

ABBB-NNNN-mmddyy-KK

Position	Description
A	BIOS Options: D = Diagnostics built-in. S = Setup built-in. E = Extended Setup built-in.
BBB	Chipset or Motherboard Identifier: C&T = Chips & Technologies chipset. NET = C&T NEAT 286 chipset. 286 = Standard 286 motherboard. SUN = Suntac chipset. PAQ = Compaq motherboard. INT = Intel motherboard. AMI = AMI motherboard. G23 = G2 chipset 386 motherboard.
NNNN	The manufacturer license code reference number.
mmddyy	The BIOS release date, mm/dd/yy.
KK	The AMI keyboard BIOS version number.

The BIOS ID String 1 format for AMI Hi-Flex BIOS versions is the following:

AB-CCcc-DDDDDD-EFGHIJKL-mmddyy-MMMMMMMM-N

Position	Description
A	Processor Type: 0 = 8086 or 8088. 2 = 286. 3 = 386. 4 = 486. 5 = Pentium. 6 = Pentium Pro.
B	Size of BIOS: 0 = 64K BIOS. 1 = 128K BIOS.
CCcc	Major and Minor BIOS version number.
DDDDDD	Manufacturer license code reference number. 0036xx = AMI 386 motherboard, xx = Series #. 0046xx = AMI 486 motherboard, xx = Series #. 0056xx = AMI Pentium motherboard, xx = Series #. 0066xx = AMI Pentium Pro motherboard, xx = Series #.
E	1 = Halt on Post Error.
F	1 = Initialize CMOS every boot.
G	1 = Block pins 22 and 23 of the keyboard controller.
H	1 = Mouse support in BIOS/keyboard controller.
I	1 = Wait for <F1> key on POST errors.
J	1 = Display floppy error during POST.
K	1 = Display video error during POST.
L	1 = Display keyboard error during POST.
mmddyy	BIOS Date, mm/dd/yy.
MMMMMMMM	Chipset identifier or BIOS name.
N	Keyboard controller version number.

AMI Hi-Flex BIOS ID String 2:

AAB-C-DDDD-EE-FF-GGGG-HH-II-JJJ

Position	Description
AA	Keyboard controller pin number for clock switching.
B	Keyboard controller clock switching pin function: H = High signal switches clock to high speed. L = High signal switches clock to low speed.

(continues)

II System Components

Continued	
Position	**Description**
C	Clock switching through chip set registers: 0 = Disable. 1 = Enable.
DDDD	Port address to switch clock high.
EE	Data value to switch clock high.
FF	Mask value to switch clock high.
GGGG	Port Address to switch clock low.
HH	Data value to switch clock low.
Ii	Mask value to switch clock low.
JJJ	Pin number for Turbo Switch Input.

AMI Hi-Flex BIOS ID String 3:

AAB-C-DDD-EE-FF-GGGG-HH-II-JJ-K-L	
Position	**Description**
AA	Keyboard controller pin number for cache control.
B	Keyboard controller cache control pin function: H = High signal enables the cache. L = High signal disables the cache.
C	1 = High signal is used on the keyboard controller pin.
DDD	Cache control through Chipset registers: 0 = Cache control off. 1 = Cache control on.
EE	Port address to enable cache.
FF	Data value to enable cache.
GGGG	Mask value to enable cache.
HH	Port address to disable cache.
II	Data value to disable cache.
JJ	Mask value to disable cache.
K	Pin number for resetting the 82335 memory controller.
L	BIOS Modification Flag: 0 = The BIOS has not been modified. 1–9, A–Z = Number of times the BIOS has been modified.

The AMI BIOS has many features, including a built-in setup program activated by pressing the Delete or Esc key in the first few seconds of booting up your computer. The BIOS will prompt you briefly as to which key to press and when to press it. The AMI BIOS offers user-definable hard disk types, essential for optimal use of many IDE or ESDI drives. The newer BIOS versions also support Enhanced IDE drives and will autoconfigure the drive parameters. A unique AMI BIOS feature is that, in addition to the setup, it has a built-in, menu-driven, diagnostics package, essentially a very limited version of the stand-alone AMIDIAG product. The internal diagnostics are not a replacement for more comprehensive disk based programs, but they can help in a pinch. The menu-driven diagnostics does not do extensive memory testing, for example, and the hard disk low-level formatter works only at the BIOS level rather than at the controller register level. These limitations often have prevented it from being capable of formatting severely damaged disks.

An excellent feature of AMI is its technical support BBS. You will find the phone number listed in the vendor list in the Appendix. The AMI BIOS is sold through distributors, and any updates to the AMI BIOS or keyboard controller are available through Washburn and Co., also listed in the vendor list in Appendix B.

Award. Award is unique among BIOS manufacturers because it sells its BIOS code to the OEM and allows the OEM to customize the BIOS. Of course, then the BIOS no longer is Award BIOS, but rather a highly customized version. AST uses this approach on its systems, as do other manufacturers, for total control over the BIOS code, without having to write it from scratch. Although AMI and Phoenix customize the ROM code for a particular system, they do not sell the ROM's source code to the OEM. Some OEMs that seem to have developed their own ROM code started with a base of source code licensed to them by Award or some other company.

The Award BIOS has all the normal features you expect, including a built-in setup program activated by pressing Ctrl+Alt+Esc. This setup offers user-definable drive types, required in order to fully utilize IDE or ESDI hard disks. The Power On Self Test is good, and Award runs a technical support BBS. The phone number for the BBS is listed in the vendor list in Appendix B.

In all, the Award BIOS is high quality, has minimal compatibility problems, and offers a high level of support.

Phoenix. The Phoenix BIOS for many years has been a standard of compatibility by which others are judged. It was one of the first third-party companies to legally reverse-engineer the IBM BIOS using a "clean room" approach. In this approach, a group of engineers studied the IBM BIOS and wrote a specification for how that BIOS should work and what features should be incorporated. This information then was passed to a second group of engineers who had never seen the IBM BIOS. They could then legally write a new BIOS to the specifications set forth by the first group. This work would then be unique and not a copy of IBM's BIOS; however, it would function the same way. This code has been refined over the years and has very few compatibility problems compared to some of the other BIOS vendors.

The Phoenix BIOS excels in two areas that put it high on my list of recommendations. One is that the Power On Self Test is excellent. The BIOS outputs an extensive set of beep codes that can be used to diagnose severe motherboard problems that would prevent normal operation of the system. In fact, this POST can isolate memory failures in Bank 0 right down to the individual chip with beep codes alone. The Phoenix BIOS also has an excellent setup program free from unnecessary frills, but that offers all the features one would expect, such as user-definable drive types, and so on. The built-in setup is activated by typing either Ctrl+Alt+S or Ctrl+Alt+Esc, depending on the version of BIOS you have.

The second area in which Phoenix excels is the documentation. Not only are the manuals that you get with the system detailed, but also Phoenix has written a set of BIOS technical-reference manuals that are a standard in the industry. The set consists of three books, titled *System BIOS for IBM PC/XT/AT Computers and Compatibles*, *CBIOS for IBM PS/2 Computers and Compatibles*, and *ABIOS for IBM PS/2 Computers and Compatibles*. Phoenix is one of few vendors who have done extensive research on the PS/2 BIOS and produce virtually all the ROMs in the PS/2 Micro Channel clones on the market. In addition to being an excellent reference for the Phoenix BIOS, these books serve as an outstanding overall reference to any company's IBM-compatible BIOS. Even if you never have a system with a Phoenix BIOS, I highly recommend these books, published by Addison-Wesley and available through most bookstores.

Micronics motherboards have always used the Phoenix BIOS, and these motherboards are used in many of the popular "name brand" compatible systems. Phoenix has been one of the largest OEMs of Microsoft MS-DOS. Many of you who have MS-DOS have the Phoenix OEM version. Phoenix licenses its DOS to other computer manufacturers so long as they use the Phoenix BIOS. Because of its close relationship with Microsoft, it has had access to the DOS source code, which helps in eliminating compatibility problems.

Although Phoenix does not operate a technical support BBS by itself, their largest nationwide distributor does, which is Micro Firmware Inc. The BBS and voice phone numbers are listed in the vendor list in Appendix B. Micro Firmware offers upgrades to many systems with a Phoenix BIOS, including many Packard Bell, Gateway 2000 (with Micronics motherboards), Micron Technologies, and other systems.

Unless the ROM BIOS is a truly compatible, custom OEM version such as Compaq's, you might want to install in the system the ROM BIOS from one of the known quantities, such as AMI, Award, or Phoenix. These companies' products are established as ROM BIOS standards in the industry, and frequent updates and improvements ensure that a system containing these ROMs will have a long life of upgrades and service.

Using Correct Speed-Rated Parts

Some compatible vendors use substandard parts in their systems to save money. Because the CPU is one of the most expensive components on the motherboard, and many motherboards are sold to system assemblers without the CPU installed, it is tempting to the assembler to install a CPU rated for less than the actual operating speed. A system could be sold as a 100 MHz system, for example, but when you look "under the hood," you may find a CPU rated for only 90 MHz. The system does appear to work correctly, but for how long? If the company that manufactures the CPU chip installed in this system had tested the chip to run reliably at 100 MHz, it would have labeled the part accordingly. After all, the company could sell the chip for more money if it worked at the higher clock speed. When a chip is run at a speed higher than it is rated for, it will run hotter than it would normally. This may cause the chip to overheat occasionally, which would appear as random lockups, glitches, and frustration. I highly recommend that you avoid systems whose operation speed exceeds the design of the respective parts.

This practice is easy to fall into since the faster rated chips cost more money, and Intel and other chip manufacturers usually rate their chips very conservatively. I have taken several 25 MHz 486 processors and run them at 33 MHz, and they seemed to work fine. The Pentium 90 chips I have tested seem to run fine at 100 MHz. Although I might purchase a Pentium 90 system and make a decision to run it at 100 MHz, if I were to experience lockups or glitches in operation, I would immediately return it to 90 MHz and retest. If I purchase a 100 MHz system from a vendor, I fully expect it to have 100 MHz parts, not 90 MHz parts running past their rated speed! These days many chips will have some form of heat sink on them, which helps to prevent overheating, but which can also sometimes cover up for a "pushed" chip. If the price is too good to be true, ask before you buy: "Are the parts really manufacturer-rated for the system speed?"

To determine the rated speed of a CPU chip, look at the writing on the chip. Most of the time, the part number will end in a suffix of –xxx where the xxx is a number indicating the maximum speed. For example, a –100 indicates that the chip is rated for 100 MHz operation. Be careful when running software to detect processor speed. Such programs can only tell you at what speed the chip is currently running, not what the true rating is. Also ignore the speed indicator lights on the front of some cases. These digital displays can literally be set via jumpers to read any speed you desire! They have no true relation to actual system speed.

Motherboard Form Factors

There are several compatible form factors used for motherboards. The form factor refers to the physical dimensions and size of the board, and dictates what type of case the board will fit into. The types of motherboard form factors generally available are the following:

- Full-Size AT
- Baby-AT
- LPX
- ATX

Full-Size AT

The full-size AT motherboard is so named because it matches the original IBM AT motherboard design. This allows for a very large board of up to 12 inches wide by 13.8 inches deep. The keyboard connector and slot connectors must conform to specific placement requirements to fit the holes in the case. This type of board will fit into full-size AT or Tower cases only. Because these motherboards will not fit into the popular Baby-AT or Mini-Tower cases, and because of advances in component miniaturization, they are no longer being produced by most motherboard manufacturers.

Baby-AT

The Baby-AT form factor is essentially the same as the original IBM XT motherboard, with modifications in screw hole positions to fit into an AT-style case (see fig. 4.1). These motherboards also have specific placement of the keyboard connector and slot connectors to match the holes in the case. Note that virtually all full size AT and Baby-AT motherboards use the standard 5-pin DIN type connector for the keyboard. Baby-AT motherboards will fit into every type of case except the low profile or slimline cases. Because of their flexibility, this is now the most popular motherboard form factor. Figure 4.1 shows the dimensions and layout of a Baby-AT motherboard.

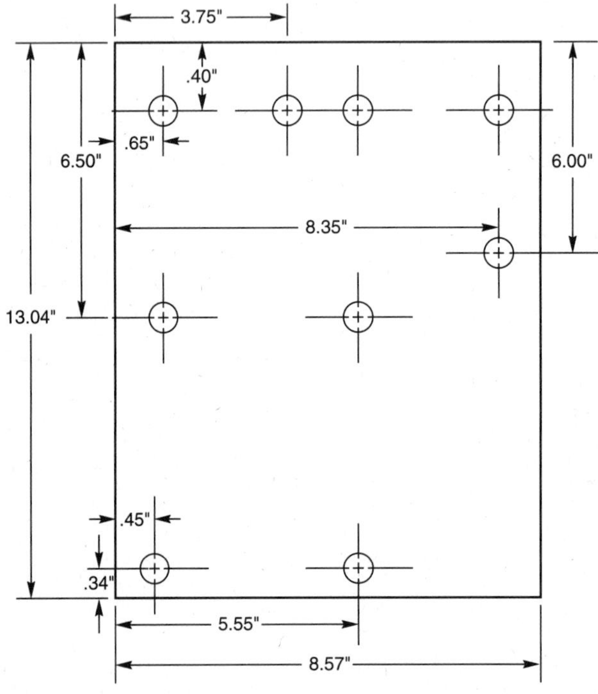

Figure 4.1
Baby-AT motherboard form factor.

LPX

Another popular form factor used in motherboards today is the LPX and Mini-LPX form factors. This form factor was first developed by Western Digital for some of their motherboards. Although they no longer produce PC motherboards, the form factor lives on and has been duplicated by many other motherboard manufacturers. These are used in the Low Profile or slimline case systems sold widely today. The LPX boards are characterized by several distinctive features. The most noticeable is that the expansion slots are mounted on a Bus Riser card that plugs into the motherboard. Expansion cards must plug sideways into the riser card. This sideways placement allows for the low profile case design. Slots will be located on one or both sides of the riser card depending on the system and case design. Another distinguishing feature of the LPX design is the standard placement of connectors on the back of the board. An LPX board will have a row of connectors for video (VGA 15-pin), parallel (25-pin), two serial ports (9-pin each), and mini-DIN PS/2 style Mouse and Keyboard connectors. All of these connectors are mounted across the rear of the motherboard and protrude through a slot in the case. Some LPX motherboards may have additional connectors for other internal ports such as Network or SCSI adapters. Figure 4.2 shows the standard form factors for the LPX and Mini-LPX motherboards used in many systems today.

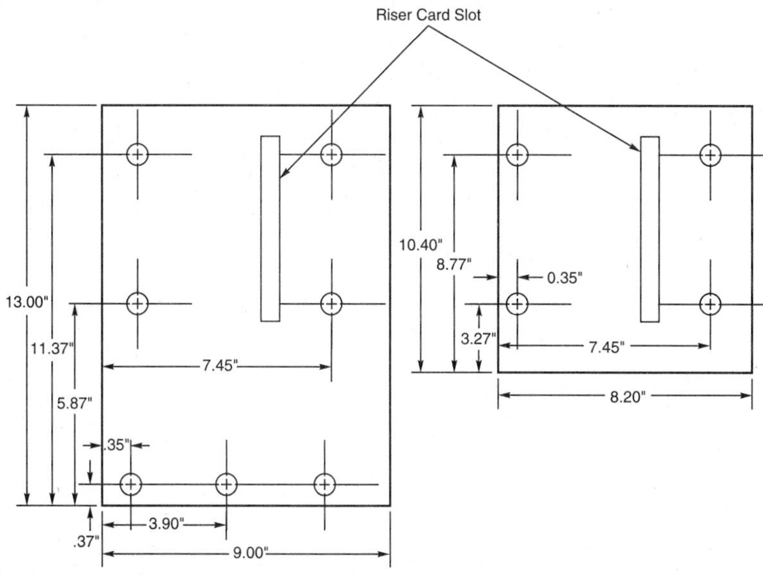

Figure 4.2

LPX and Mini-LPX motherboard form factors.

ATX

The new ATX form factor is a recent evolution in motherboard form factors and looks to be the defacto standard of the future. ATX is a combination of the best features of the Baby-AT and LPX motherboard designs, with many new enhancements and features thrown in. The ATX form factor is essentially a Baby-AT motherboard turned sideways in the chassis, along with a modified power supply location and connector. The most important thing to know initially about the ATX form factor is that it is physically incompatible with either the previous Baby-AT or LPX designs. In other words, a different case and power supply are required to match the ATX motherboard. These new case and power supply designs will become de facto standards as well, and will be found in most of the new systems to come out over the next few years. If you are thinking about maximizing future upgrade potential, then you should look for systems that conform to the new ATX specification.

The official ATX specification was released by Intel in July 1995, and has been written as an open specification for the industry. Intel has published detailed specifications so other manufacturers can use the ATX design in their systems. Intel has truly created a new defacto industry standard with the release of the ATX specification.

ATX improves on the existing Baby-AT and LPX motherboard designs in several major areas:

- *Built-in double high external I/O connector panel.* The rear portion of the motherboard includes a stacked I/O connector area that is 6.25 inches wide by 1.75 inches tall. This allows external connectors to be located directly on the board and negates the need for cables running from internal connectors to the back of the case as with Baby-AT designs.

- *Single keyed internal power supply connector.* This is a boon for the average end user, who always had to worry about interchanging the Baby-AT power supply connectors and subsequently blowing the motherboard! The ATX specification includes a single keyed and shrouded power connector that is easy to plug in, and that cannot be installed incorrectly. This connector also features pins for supplying 3.3 volts to the motherboard, which means that ATX motherboards will not require built-in voltage regulators that are susceptible to failure.

- *Relocated CPU and memory.* The CPU and memory modules are relocated so they cannot interfere with any bus expansion cards, and they can easily be accessed for upgrade without removing any of the installed bus adapters. The CPU and memory are relocated next to the power supply, which has a single fan blowing air across them, thus eliminating the need for inefficient and failure prone CPU cooling fans. There is room for a large passive heatsink above the CPU as well.

- *Relocated internal I/O connectors.* The internal I/O connectors for the floppy and hard disk drives are relocated to be near the drive bays and out from under the expansion board slot and drive bay areas. This means that internal cables to the drives can be much shorter, and accessing the connectors will not require card or drive removal.

- *Improved cooling.* The CPU and main memory are cooled directly by the power supply fan, eliminating the need for separate case or CPU cooling fans. Also the ATX power supply fan blows INTO the system chassis, thus pressurizing it, which greatly minimizes dust and dirt intrusion into the system. If desired, an air filter can be easily added to the air intake vents on the power supply, creating a system that is even more immune to dirt or dust in the environment.

- *Lower cost to manufacture.* The ATX specifications eliminates the need for the rat's nest of cables to external port connectors found on Baby-AT motherboards, eliminates the need for additional CPU or chassis cooling fans, eliminates the need for on-board 3.3v voltage regulators, uses a single power supply connector, and allows for shorter internal drive cables. These all conspire to greatly reduce not only the cost of the motherboard, but also significantly reduces the cost of a complete system including the case and power supply.

Figure 4.3 shows the new ATX system layout and chassis features. Notice how virtually the entire motherboard is clear of the drive bays, and how the devices like CPU, memory, and internal drive connectors are easy to access and do not interfere with the bus slots.

Also notice the power supply orientation and the single power supply fan that blows into the case directly over the high heat, generating items like the CPU and memory.

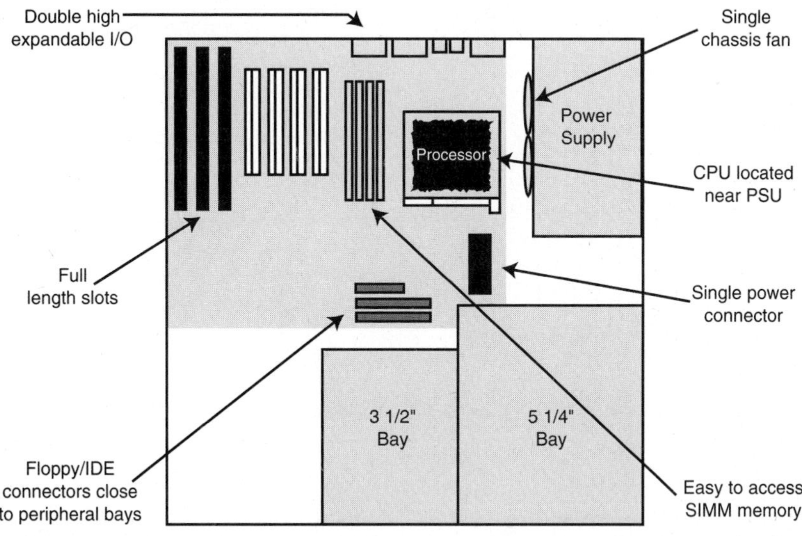

Figure 4.3

ATX system chassis layout and features.

The ATX motherboard is basically a Baby-AT design rotated sideways. The expansion slots are now parallel to the shorter side dimension, and do not interfere with the CPU, memory, or I/O connector sockets. In addition to a full-sized ATX layout, Intel also has specified a mini-ATX design as well, which will fit into the same case. The case holes are similar to the Baby-AT case, and it will be possible for future cases to support either the ATX or Baby AT motherboard designs. The power supplies would require a connector adapter to be interchangeable, but the basic ATX power supply design is similar to the standard Slimline power supply. The ATX and mini-ATX motherboard dimensions are shown in figure 4.4.

Clearly, the advantages of the ATX form factor make it the choice for all future systems. For backwards compatibility, Baby-AT is still hard to beat, and there are still many more Baby-AT motherboards, cases, and power supplies on the market than the ATX versions. Newer cases will be able to support either Baby-AT or ATX motherboards, and it seems clear to me that most future systems will be migrating over to the ATX form factor. Within the next year or so, the ATX form factor will surpass even the Baby-AT in new sold units. As such, I am now leaning towards recommending the ATX form factor for new system purchases.

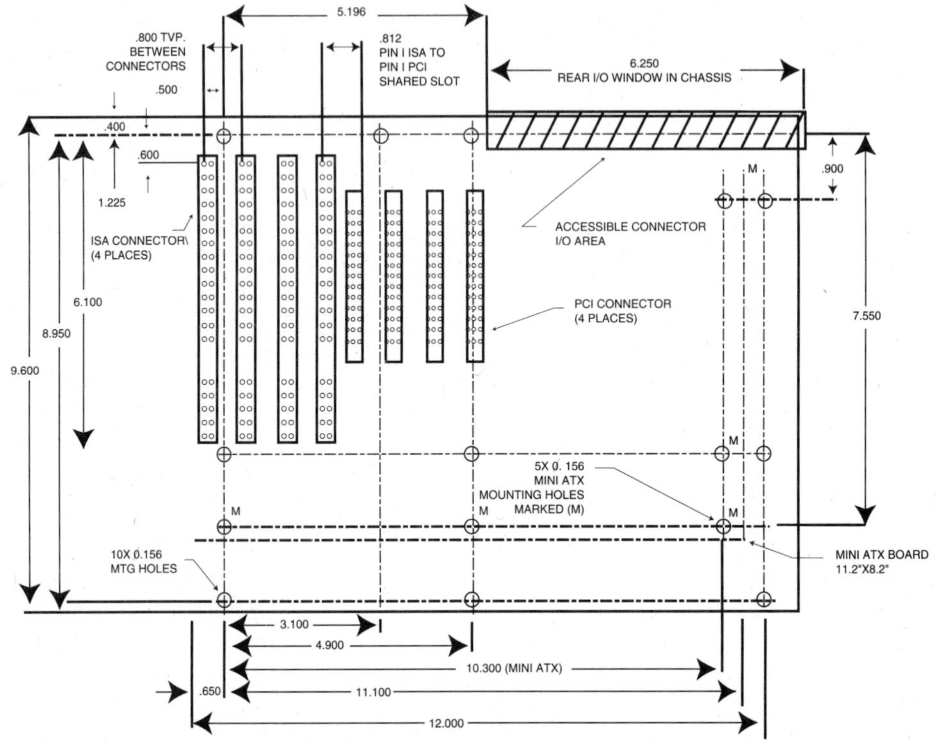

Figure 4.4

ATX and Mini-ATX motherboard form factors.

LPX will still likely be used in the lowest cost systems, such as those often sold through retail electronics superstores. There can be some differences between systems with LPX form factor motherboards, so it is possible to find interchangeability problems between different motherboards and cases. I usually do not recommend LPX style systems if upgradability is a factor because it is not only difficult to locate a new motherboard that will fit, but LPX systems are also limited in expansion slots and drive bays as well. Generally, the Baby AT or newer ATX configurations are the most popular and the most flexible type of systems to consider.

Summary

The motherboard is obviously the core of your system, and is one component that you do not want to take lightly. There are hundreds of versions available, with a variety of different CPUs, speeds, features, and options. This chapter has covered the basics about different motherboards including a list of desirable features. Also discussed was the different form factors you will encounter and how they can affect other system options.

Chapter 5

Bus Slots and I/O Cards

5

At the heart of every system is the motherboard; you learned about various motherboards in a previous chapter. A motherboard is made up of components. The major component that determines how the motherboard actually works is called the bus. In this chapter, you learn about system buses. Specifically, you learn the following:

- What a bus is and what types of buses exist
- Why expansion slots are needed
- What types of I/O buses are used in PC systems
- What system resources are
- How adapter cards use system resources
- How to resolve conflicts among system resources

What is a Bus?

A *bus* is nothing but a common pathway across which data can travel within a computer. This pathway is used for communication and can be established between two or more computer elements. A PC has many kinds of buses, including the following:

- Processor bus
- Address bus
- Memory bus
- I/O bus

If you hear someone talking about the bus in a PC, chances are good that he or she is referring to the I/O bus, which also is called the expansion slot bus. Whatever name it goes by, this bus is the main system bus and the one over which most data flows. The I/O bus is the highway for most data in your system. Anything that goes to or from any device—including your video system, disk drives, and printer—travels over this bus. The busiest I/O pathway typically is to and from your video card.

Because the I/O bus is the primary bus in your computer system, it is the main focus of discussion in this chapter. The other buses deserve some attention, however, and they are covered in the following sections.

The Processor Bus

The processor bus is the communication pathway between the CPU and immediate support chips. These support chips are usually called the "chipset" in modern systems. This bus is used to transfer data between the CPU and the main system bus, for example, or between the CPU and an external memory cache. Figure 5.1 shows how this bus fits into a typical PC system.

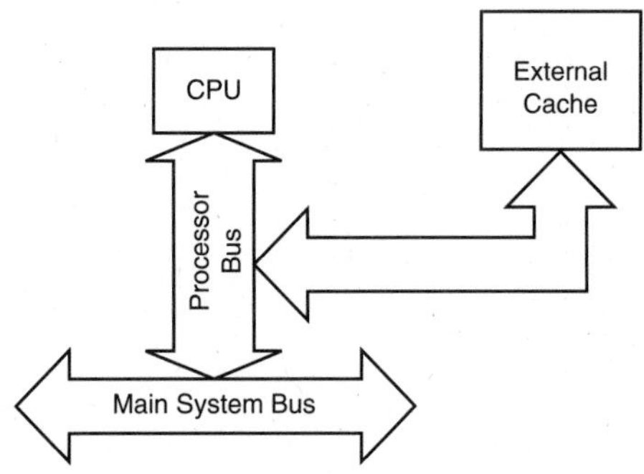

Figure 5.1

The processor bus.

Most systems have an external cache for the CPU; these caches have typically been employed in all systems that use the 486, Pentium, and Pentium-Pro chips.

Becaue the purpose of the processor bus is to get information to and from the CPU at the fastest possible speed, this bus operates at a much faster rate than any other bus in your system; no bottleneck exists here. The bus consists of electrical circuits for data, for addresses (the address bus, which is discussed in the following section), and for control purposes. In a 486-based system, for example, the processor bus consists of 32 address lines, 32 data lines, and a few lines for control purposes. A Pentium system's processor bus has 64 data lines, 32 address lines, and associated control lines. The Pentium Pro has 36 address lines, but otherwise it is the same as the Pentium.

The processor bus operates at the same base clock rate as the CPU does externally. This can be misleading as most CPUs these days run internally at a higher clock rate than they do externally. For example, a Pentium 100 system has a Pentium CPU running at 100MHz internally, but only 66.6MHz externally. A Pentium 133, Pentium 166, and even the Pentium Pro 200 also run the processor external bus at 66.6MHz. In most newer systems, the actual processor speed is some multiple (1.5x, 2x, 2.5x, 3x, and so on) of the processor bus. For more information on this, see Chapter 6 on Processors.

The processor bus is tied to the external processor pin connections and can transfer one bit of data per data line every one or two clock cycles. Thus, a 486-based system can transfer 32 bits of data at a time, whereas a Pentium or Pentium-Pro can transfer 64 bits of data at a time.

To determine the transfer rate for the processor bus, you multiply the data width (32 bits for a 486 or 64 bits for a Pentium or Pentium Pro) by the clock speed of the bus (the same as the base or unmultiplied clock speed of the CPU). If you are using a 66/100/133/166/200 MHz Pentium or Pentium Pro chip that runs at a 66 MHz motherboard speed, and it can transfer a bit of data each clock cycle on each data line, you have a maximum instantaneous transfer rate of 528M per second. You get this result by using the following formula:

66 MHz × 64 bits = 4,224 megabits/second

4,224 megabits/second ÷ 8 = 528M/second

This transfer rate, often called the *bandwidth* of the bus, represents a maximum. Like all maximums, this rate does not represent the normal operating bandwidth; you should expect much lower average throughput. Other limiting factors, such as chipset design, memory design, speed, and so on, conspire to lower the effective average throughput.

The Memory Bus

The memory bus is used to transfer information between the CPU and main memory—the RAM in your system. This bus is either a part of the processor bus itself, or in most cases is implemented separately by a dedicated chipset that is responsible for transferring information between the processor bus and the memory bus. Systems that ran at motherboard clock speeds of 16 MHz or faster cycle at rates that exceed the capabilities of standard Dynamic RAM chips. In virtually all systems that are 16 MHz or faster, there will be a special memory controller chipset that controls the interface between the faster processor bus and the slower main memory. This chipset typically is the same chipset that is responsible for managing the I/O bus. Figure 5.2 shows how the memory bus fits into your PC.

The information that travels over the memory bus is transferred at a much slower rate than the information on the processor bus. The chip sockets or the slots for memory SIMMs are connected to the memory bus in much the same way that expansion slots are connected to the I/O bus.

Caution

Notice that the main memory bus is always the same width as the processor bus. This means that in a system with a 32-bit CPU, for example, you will also have a 32-bit memory bus. Likewise, in a Pentium or Pentium Pro system (which has a 64-bit CPU), you will have a 64-bit memory bus. This will define the size of what is called a "bank" of memory. For example, a 486DX4 processor has a 32-bit bus, so the memory in that system must be added 32-bits at a time for each bank. If you are using 30-pin (8-bit) SIMMs, then four will be required per bank; if the system uses 72-pin (32-bit) SIMMs, then only one has to be added at a time to make up a bank. Pentium systems are 64-bit, and will almost always require two 72-pin (32-bits each) SIMMs to be added at a time. Some newer Pentium and Pentium Pro systems use 168-pin DIMMs (Dual Inline Memory Modules) which are 64-bits each. These compose a single bank in a 64-bit system.

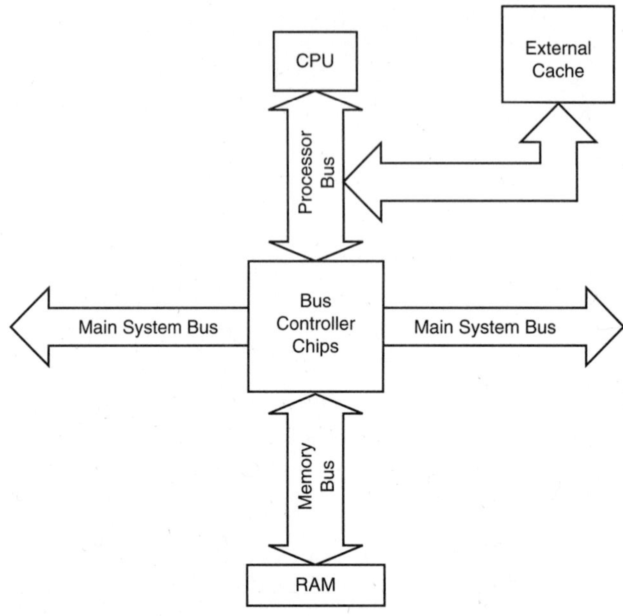

Figure 5.2
The memory bus.

The Address Bus

The address bus actually is a subset of the processor and memory busses. Earlier in this chapter, you learned that the processor bus in a 486 or Pentium system consists of either 32 or 64 data lines, 32 address lines, and a few control lines. These address lines constitute the address bus; in most block diagrams, this bus is actually considered a part of the processor and memory busses.

The address bus is used to indicate what address in memory or what address on the system bus are to be used in a data transfer operation. The address bus indicates precisely where the next bus transfer or memory transfer will occur. The size of the memory bus also controls the amount of memory that the CPU can address directly.

The Need for Expansion Slots

The I/O bus, or expansion slots, are what enables your CPU to communicate with peripheral devices. The bus and its associated expansion slots are needed because basic systems cannot possibly satisfy all the needs of all the people who buy them. The I/O bus enables you to add devices to your computer to expand its capabilities. The most basic computer components, such as sound cards and video cards, can be plugged into expansion slots; you also can plug in more specialized devices, such as network interface cards, SCSI host adapters, and others.

Note

In most modern PC systems, a variety of basic peripheral devices are built into the motherboard. Most systems today have at least dual (primary and secondary) IDE controllers, a floppy controller, two serial ports, and a parallel port directly built-in to the motherboard. This is normally contained on a single chip called a Super I/O chip. Many will even add more items such as an integrated mouse port, Video adapter, SCSI host adapter, or Network Interface also built-in to the motherboard; in such a system, an expansion slot on the I/O bus is probably not even needed. Nevertheless, these built-in controllers and ports still use the I/O bus to communicate with the CPU. In essence even though they are built-in, they act as if they are cards plugged into the system's bus slots.

The number of expansion slots varies among computers. The original IBM PC had five expansion slots, for example, and the PC-XT and later PC-AT had eight slots. To this day, virtually no PC systems have more than eight expansion slots. With few exceptions, the slot spacing has remained the same since the original PC-XT and PC-AT. Slots are spaced 0.8 inches apart in these and virtually all later PC systems; however, the original IBM PC had slots spaced one inch apart.

Some PC systems provide only a single expansion slot on the motherboard. This slot typically is called a riser-card slot. The riser card that plugs into it in turn has expansion slots on its sides. Standard adapter cards are installed in the riser card, meaning that the adapter cards end up being parallel rather than perpendicular to the motherboard.

Riser cards are used when a vendor wants to produce a computer that is shorter in height than normal. These computers usually are called "slimline," "low profile," or sometimes even "pizza-box" systems. Even though this type of configuration may seem to be odd, the actual bus used in these systems is the same kind used in normal computer systems; the only difference is the use of the riser card.

I usually recommend avoiding the low profile or slimline systems because they use a motherboard that has what is called an LPX form factor. This refers to the shape of the board, and replacement LPX motherboards with riser cards that match the case for a given system are difficult to find. This significantly limits the future repair and upgrade capabilities of the system.

Types of I/O Buses

Since the introduction of the first PC, many I/O buses have been introduced. The reason is quite simple: faster I/O speeds are necessary for better system performance. This need for higher performance involves three main areas:

- Faster CPUs
- Increasing software demands
- Greater video requirements

Each of these areas requires the I/O bus to be as fast as possible. Surprisingly, virtually all PC systems shipped today still incorporate the same basic bus architecture as the 1984 vintage IBM PC/AT. However, most of these systems now also include a second high-speed local I/O bus such as VL-Bus or PCI, which offers much greater performance for adapters that need it.

One of the primary reasons why new I/O-bus structures have been slow in coming is compatibility—that old Catch-22 that anchors much of the PC industry to the past. One of the hallmarks of the PC's success is its standardization. This standardization spawned thousands of third-party I/O cards, each originally built for the early bus specifications of the PC. If a new, high-performance bus system was introduced, it often had to be compatible with the older bus systems so that the older I/O cards would not be obsolete. Therefore, bus technologies seem to evolve rather than make quantum leaps forward.

You can identify different types of I/O buses by their architecture. The main types of I/O architecture are:

- ISA
- Micro Channel Architecture (MCA)
- EISA
- VESA Local Bus (VL-Bus)
- PCI Local Bus
- PC-Card (formerly PCMCIA)

The differences among these buses consist primarily of the amount of data that they can transfer at one time and the speed at which they can do it. Each bus architecture is implemented by a chipset that is connected to the processor bus. Typically, this chipset also controls the memory bus (refer to figure 5.2 earlier in this chapter). The following sections describe the different types of PC buses.

The ISA Bus

ISA, which is an acronym for Industry Standard Architecture, is the bus architecture that was introduced as an 8-bit bus with the original IBM PC in 1981 and later expanded to 16-bits with the IBM PC/AT in 1984. ISA is the basis of the modern personal computer and the primary architecture used in the vast majority of PC systems on the market today. It may seem amazing that such a seemingly antiquated architecture is used in today's high-performance systems, but this is true for reasons of reliability, affordability, and compatibility, plus this old bus is still faster than many of the peripherals that we connect to it!

The ISA bus enabled thousands of manufacturers to build systems whose components (except for a few specialized parts) were interchangeable. Serial ports, parallel ports, and video adapters that worked in the original IBM PC, XT, and AT also work in other manufacturer's PC-compatible systems.

Two versions of the ISA bus exist, based on the number of data bits that can be transferred on the bus at a time. The older version is an 8-bit bus; the newer version is a 16-bit bus. The original 8-bit version ran at 4.77 MHz in the PC and XT. The 16-bit version used in the AT ran at 6 MHz and then 8 MHz. Later the industry as a whole agreed on an 8.33 MHz maximum standard speed for 8/16-bit versions of the ISA bus for backward compatibility. Some systems have the ability to run the ISA bus faster than this, but some adapter cards will not function properly at higher speeds. ISA data transfers require anywhere from two to eight cycles. Therefore, the theoretical maximum data rate of the ISA bus is about 8M bytes per second, as the following formula shows:

8 MHz × 16 bits = 128 megabits/second

128 megabits/second ÷ 2 cycles = 64 megabits/second

64 megabits/second ÷ 8 = 8 MBytes/second

The bandwidth of the 8-bit bus would be half this figure (4MB per second). Remember, however, that these figures are theoretical maximums; because of I/O bus protocols, the effective bandwidth is much lower—typically by almost half. Even so, at 8MB per second, the ISA bus is still faster than many of the peripherals we connect to it.

The 8-Bit ISA Bus. This bus architecture is used in the original IBM PC computers. Although virtually nonexistent in new systems today, this architecture still exists in hundreds of thousands of PC systems in the field.

Physically, the 8-bit ISA expansion slot resembles the tongue-and-groove system that furniture makers once used to hold two pieces of wood together. An adapter card with 62 contacts on its bottom edge plugs into a slot on the motherboard that has 62 matching contacts. Electronically, this slot provides 8 data lines and 20 addressing lines, enabling the slot to handle 1M of memory.

Figure 5.3 describes the pinouts for the 8-bit ISA bus. Figure 5.4 shows how these pins are oriented in the expansion slot.

Although the design of the bus is simple, IBM waited until 1987 to publish full specifications for the timings of the data and address lines, so in the early days of PC compatibles, manufacturers had to do their best to figure out how to make adapter boards. This problem was solved, however, as PC-compatible personal computers became more widely accepted as the industry standard and manufacturers had more time and incentive to build adapter boards that worked correctly with the bus.

The dimensions of 8-bit ISA adapter cards are as follows:

4.2 inches (106.68mm) high

13.13 inches (333.5mm) long

0.5 inch (12.7mm) wide

Signal	Pin	Pin	Signal
Ground	B1	A1	-I/O CH CHK
RESET DRV	B2	A2	Data Bit 7
+5 Vdc	B3	A3	Data Bit 6
IRQ 2	B4	A4	Data Bit 5
-5 Vdc	B5	A5	Data Bit 4
DRQ 2	B6	A6	Data Bit 3
-12 Vdc	B7	A7	Data Bit 2
-CARD SLCTD	B8	A8	Data Bit 1
+12 Vdc	B9	A9	Data Bit 0
Ground	B10	A10	-I/O CH RDY
-SMEMW	B11	A11	AEN
-SMEMR	B12	A12	Address 19
-IOW	B13	A13	Address 18
-IOR	B14	A14	Address 17
-DACK 3	B15	A15	Address 16
DRQ 3	B16	A16	Address 15
-DACK 1	B17	A17	Address 14
DRQ 1	B18	A18	Address 13
-Refresh	B19	A19	Address 12
CLK(4.77MHz)	B20	A20	Address 11
IRQ 7	B21	A21	Address 10
IRQ 6	B22	A22	Address 9
IRQ 5	B23	A23	Address 8
IRQ 4	B24	A24	Address 7
IRQ 3	B25	A25	Address 6
-DACK 2	B26	A26	Address 5
T/C	B27	A27	Address 4
BALE	B28	A28	Address 3
+5 Vdc	B29	A29	Address 2
OSC(14.3MHz)	B30	A30	Address 1
Ground	B31	A31	Address 0

Figure 5.3

Pinouts for the 8-bit ISA bus.

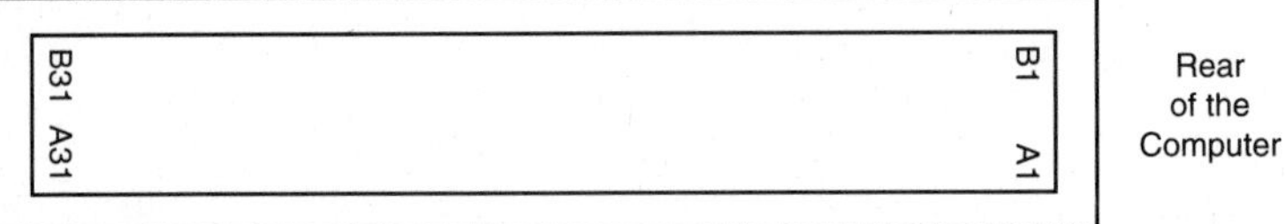

Figure 5.4

The 8-bit ISA bus connector.

In the original XT or Portable PC, the eighth slot—the one closest to the power supply—is a special slot; only certain cards can be installed there. A card installed in the eighth slot must supply to the motherboard, on pin B8, a special card-selected signal, which few cards are designed to do. (The IBM asynchronous adapter card and the keyboard/timer card from a 3270 PC are two examples of cards that fit into the eighth slot.) Additionally, the timing requirements for the eighth slot are stricter.

The reason why this strange slot exists in the XT is that IBM developed the system to support a special configuration called the 3270 PC, which really is an XT with three to six special adapter boards installed. The eighth slot was designed specifically to accept the keyboard/timer adapter from the 3270 PC. This board needed special access to the motherboard because it replaced the motherboard keyboard circuitry. Special timing and the card-selected signal made this access possible.

Contrary to what many users believe, the eighth slot has nothing to do with the IBM expansion chassis, which was popular at the time of the PC-XT. The IBM expansion chassis is a box developed by IBM that looks like another system unit. Because the IBM XT has eight slots, one full-height floppy drive, and one full-height hard drive, the expansion chassis makes room for more expansion slots and for additional floppy and hard drives.

The 16-Bit ISA Bus. IBM threw a bombshell on the PC world when it introduced the AT with the 286 processor in 1984. This processor had a 16-bit data bus, which meant that communications between the processor and the motherboard, as well as memory, would now be 16-bits wide instead of only 8-bits wide. Although this processor could have been installed on a motherboard with only an 8-bit I/O bus, that would have meant a huge sacrifice in the performance of any adapter cards or other devices installed on the bus.

The introduction of the 286 chip posed a problem for IBM in relation to its next generation of PCs. Should the company create a new I/O bus and associated expansion slots, or should it try to come up with a system that could support both 8- and 16-bit cards? IBM opted for the latter solution, and the PC/AT was introduced with a set of expansion slots with 16-bit extension connectors. You can plug an 8-bit card into the forward part of the slot or a 16-bit card into both parts of the slot.

Note

The expansion slots for the 16-bit ISA bus also introduced access keys to the PC environment. An access key is a cutout or notch in an adapter card that fits over a corresponding tab in the connector into which the adapter card is inserted. Access keys typically are used to keep adapter cards from being inserted into a connector improperly.

The extension connector in each 16-bit expansion slot adds 36 connector pins to carry the extra signals necessary to implement the wider data path. In addition, two of the pins in the 8-bit portion of the connector were changed. These two minor changes do not alter the function of 8-bit cards.

Figure 5.5 describes the pinouts for the full 16-bit ISA expansion slot. Figure 5.6 shows the orientation and relation of 8-bit and 16-bit ISA bus slots.

The extended 16-bit slots physically interfere with some 8-bit adapter cards that have a skirt—an extended area of the card that drops down toward the motherboard just after the connector. To handle these cards, IBM left two expansion ports in the PC/AT without the 16-bit extensions. These slots, which are identical to the expansion slots in earlier systems, can handle any skirted PC or XT expansion card. This is not a problem today, as no skirted 8-bit cards have been manufactured for years.

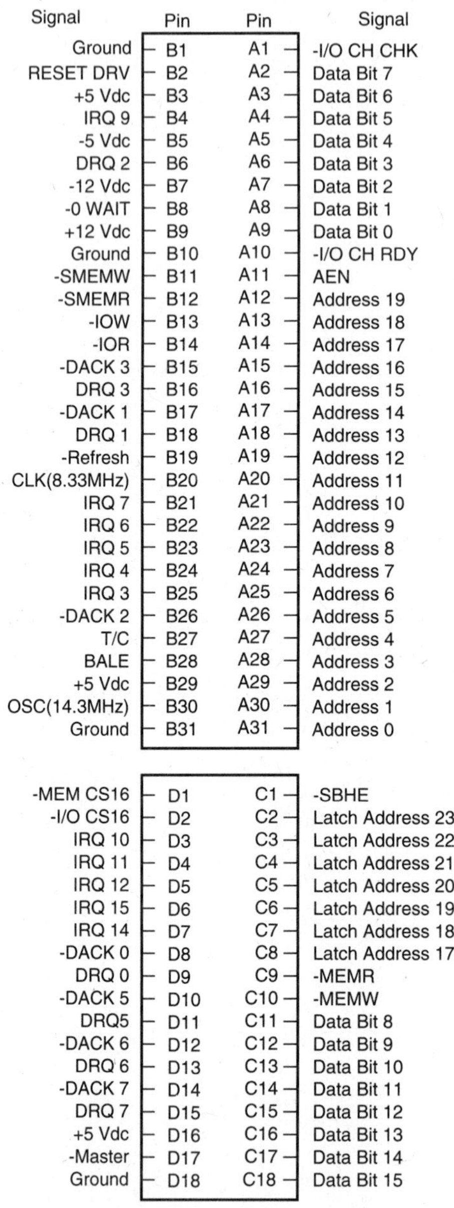
Signal Pin Pin Signal
Ground B1 A1 -I/O CH CHK
RESET DRV B2 A2 Data Bit 7
+5 Vdc B3 A3 Data Bit 6
IRQ 9 B4 A4 Data Bit 5
-5 Vdc B5 A5 Data Bit 4
DRQ 2 B6 A6 Data Bit 3
-12 Vdc B7 A7 Data Bit 2
-0 WAIT B8 A8 Data Bit 1
+12 Vdc B9 A9 Data Bit 0
Ground B10 A10 -I/O CH RDY
-SMEMW B11 A11 AEN
-SMEMR B12 A12 Address 19
-IOW B13 A13 Address 18
-IOR B14 A14 Address 17
-DACK 3 B15 A15 Address 16
DRQ 3 B16 A16 Address 15
-DACK 1 B17 A17 Address 14
DRQ 1 B18 A18 Address 13
-Refresh B19 A19 Address 12
CLK(8.33MHz) B20 A20 Address 11
IRQ 7 B21 A21 Address 10
IRQ 6 B22 A22 Address 9
IRQ 5 B23 A23 Address 8
IRQ 4 B24 A24 Address 7
IRQ 3 B25 A25 Address 6
-DACK 2 B26 A26 Address 5
T/C B27 A27 Address 4
BALE B28 A28 Address 3
+5 Vdc B29 A29 Address 2
OSC(14.3MHz) B30 A30 Address 1
Ground B31 A31 Address 0
-MEM CS16 D1 C1 -SBHE
-I/O CS16 D2 C2 Latch Address 23
IRQ 10 D3 C3 Latch Address 22
IRQ 11 D4 C4 Latch Address 21
IRQ 12 D5 C5 Latch Address 20
IRQ 15 D6 C6 Latch Address 19
IRQ 14 D7 C7 Latch Address 18
-DACK 0 D8 C8 Latch Address 17
DRQ 0 D9 C9 -MEMR
-DACK 5 D10 C10 -MEMW
DRQ5 D11 C11 Data Bit 8
-DACK 6 D12 C12 Data Bit 9
DRQ 6 D13 C13 Data Bit 10
-DACK 7 D14 C14 Data Bit 11
DRQ 7 D15 C15 Data Bit 12
+5 Vdc D16 C16 Data Bit 13
-Master D17 C17 Data Bit 14
Ground D18 C18 Data Bit 15

Figure 5.5

Pinouts for the 16-bit ISA bus.

8/16-bit ISA Bus Pinouts.

8-bit PC/XT Connector:

Signal	Pin Numbers		Signal
GROUND	B1	A1	-I/O CHK
RESET DRV	B2	A2	DATA 7
+5 Vdc	B3	A3	DATA 6
IRQ 2	B4	A4	DATA 5
-5 Vdc	B5	A5	DATA 4
DRQ 2	B6	A6	DATA 3
-12 Vdc	B7	A7	DATA 2
-CARD SLCT	B8	A8	DATA 1
+12 Vdc	B9	A9	DATA 0
GROUND	B10	A10	-I/O RDY
-SMEMW	B11	A11	AEN
-SMEMR	B12	A12	ADDR 19
-IOW	B13	A13	ADDR 18
-IOR	B14	A14	ADDR 17
-DACK 3	B15	A15	ADDR 16
DRQ 3	B16	A16	ADDR 15
-DACK 1	B17	A17	ADDR 14
DRQ 1	B18	A18	ADDR 13
-REFRESH	B19	A19	ADDR 12
CLK (4.77MHz)	B20	A20	ADDR 11
IRQ 7	B21	A21	ADDR 10
IRQ 6	B22	A22	ADDR 9
IRQ 5	B23	A23	ADDR 8
IRQ 4	B24	A24	ADDR 7
IRQ 3	B25	A25	ADDR 6
-DACK 2	B26	A26	ADDR 5
T/C	B27	A27	ADDR 4
BALE	B28	A28	ADDR 3
+5 Vdc	B29	A29	ADDR 2
OSC (14.3MHz)	B30	A30	ADDR 1
GROUND	B31	A31	ADDR 0

16-bit AT Connector:

Signal	Pin Numbers		Signal
GROUND	B1	A1	-I/O CHK
RESET DRV	B2	A2	DATA 7
+5 Vdc	B3	A3	DATA 6
IRQ 9	B4	A4	DATA 5
-5 Vdc	B5	A5	DATA 4
DRQ 2	B6	A6	DATA 3
-12 Vdc	B7	A7	DATA 2
-OWS	B8	A8	DATA 1
+12 Vdc	B9	A9	DATA 0
GROUND	B10	A10	-I/O RDY
-SMEMW	B11	A11	AEN
-SMEMR	B12	A12	ADDR 19
-IOW	B13	A13	ADDR 18
-IOR	B14	A14	ADDR 17
-DACK 3	B15	A15	ADDR 16
DRQ 3	B16	A16	ADDR 15
-DACK 1	B17	A17	ADDR 14
DRQ 1	B18	A18	ADDR 13
-REFRESH	B19	A19	ADDR 12
CLK (8.33MHz)	B20	A20	ADDR 11
IRQ 7	B21	A21	ADDR 10
IRQ 6	B22	A22	ADDR 9
IRQ 5	B23	A23	ADDR 8
IRQ 4	B24	A24	ADDR 7
IRQ 3	B25	A25	ADDR 6
-DACK 2	B26	A26	ADDR 5
T/C	B27	A27	ADDR 4
BALE	B28	A28	ADDR 3
+5 Vdc	B29	A29	ADDR 2
OSC (14.3MHz)	B30	A30	ADDR 1
GROUND	B31	A31	ADDR 0

Signal	Pin Numbers		Signal
-MEM CS16	D1	C1	-SBHE
-I/O CS16	D2	C2	LADDR 23
IRQ 10	D3	C3	LADDR 22
IRQ 11	D4	C4	LADDR 21
IRQ 12	D5	C5	LADDR 20
IRQ 15	D6	C6	LADDR 19
IRQ 14	D7	C7	LADDR 18
-DACK 0	D8	C8	LADDR 17
DRQ 0	D9	C9	-MEMR
-DACK 5	D10	C10	-MEMW
DRQ 5	D11	C11	DATA 8
-DACK 6	D12	C12	DATA 9
DRQ 6	D13	C13	DATA 10
-DACK 7	D14	C14	DATA 11
DRQ 7	D15	C15	DATA 12
+5 Vdc	D16	C16	DATA 13
-MASTER	D17	C17	DATA 14
GROUND	D18	C18	DATA 15

Figure 5.6

The 8-bit and 16-bit ISA bus connectors.

Note

16-bit ISA expansion slots were introduced in 1984. Since then, virtually every manufacturer of 8-bit expansion cards has designed them without drop-down skirts so that they fit properly in 16-bit slots. Most new systems do not have any 8-bit only slots, since a properly designed 8-bit card will work in any 16-bit slot.

The dimensions of a typical AT expansion board are as follows:

4.8 inches (121.92mm) high

13.13 inches (333.5mm) long

0.5 inch (12.7mm) wide

Two heights actually are available for cards that are commonly used in AT systems: 4.8 inches and 4.2 inches (the height of older PC-XT cards). The shorter cards became an issue when IBM introduced the XT Model 286. Because this model has an AT motherboard in an XT case, it needs AT-type boards with the 4.2-inch maximum height. Most board makers trimmed the height of their boards; many manufacturers now make only 4.2-inch-tall (or less) boards so that they will work in systems with either profile.

32-Bit Buses. After 32-bit CPUs became available, it was some time before 32-bit bus standards became available. Before MCA and EISA specs were released, some vendors began creating their own proprietary 32-bit buses, which were extensions of the ISA bus. Although the proprietary buses were few and far between, they do still exist.

The expanded portions of the bus typically are used for proprietary memory expansion or video cards. Because the systems are proprietary (meaning that they are nonstandard), pinouts and specifications are not available.

The Micro Channel Bus

The introduction of 32-bit chips meant that the ISA bus could not handle the power of another new generation of CPUs. The 386DX chips can transfer 32 bits of data at a time, but the ISA bus can handle a maximum 16 bits. Rather than extend the ISA bus again, IBM decided to build a new bus; the result was the MCA bus. MCA (an acronym for micro channel architecture) is completely different from the ISA bus and is technically superior in every way.

IBM not only wanted to replace the old ISA standard, but also to receive royalties on it; the company required vendors that licensed the new MCA bus to pay IBM royalties for using the ISA bus in all previous systems. This requirement led to the development of the competing EISA bus (described later in this chapter) and hindered acceptance of the MCA bus. Another reason why MCA has not been adopted universally for systems with 32-bit slots is that adapter cards designed for ISA systems do not work in MCA systems.

MCA runs asynchronously with the main processor, meaning that fewer possibilities exist for timing problems among adapter cards plugged into the bus.

On the Web

http://www.currents.net/resources/cyclo/tinfo.html?Micro+Channel

Note

The MCA bus is not compatible with the older ISA bus, so cards designed for the ISA bus do not work in an MCA system.

MCA systems produced a new level of ease of use, as anyone who has set up one of these systems can tell you. An MCA system has no jumpers and switches—neither on the motherboard nor on any expansion adapter. You don't need an electrical-engineering degree to plug a card into a PC.

The MCA bus also supports bus mastering. Through implementing bus mastering, the MCA bus provides significant performance improvements over the older ISA buses. (Bus mastering is also implemented in the EISA bus. General information related to bus mastering is discussed in the "Bus Mastering" section later in this chapter.) In the MCA bus mastering implementation, any bus mastering devices can request unobstructed use of the bus in order to communicate with another device on the bus. The request is made through a device known as the Central Arbitration Control Point (CACP). This device arbitrates the competition for the bus, making sure all devices have access and that no single device monopolizes the bus.

Each device is given a priority code to ensure that order is preserved within the system. The main CPU is given the lowest priority code. Memory refresh has the highest priority, followed by the DMA channels, and then the bus masters installed in the I/O slots. One exception to this is when an NMI (non-maskable interrupt) occurs. In this instance, control returns to the CPU immediately.

The MCA specification provides for four adapter sizes, which are described in table 5.1.

Table 5.1 Physical Sizes of MCA Adapter Cards

Adapter Type	Height	Length
Type 3	3.475"	12.3"
Type 3 half	3.475"	6.35"
Type 5	4.825"	13.1"
Type 9	9.0"	13.1"

Four types of slots are involved in the MCA design:

- 16-bit
- 16-bit with video extensions
- 16-bit with memory-matched extensions
- 32-bit

16-Bit MCA Slots. Every MCA slot has a 16-bit connector. This connector is the primary MCA slot design—the one used in all MCA systems. This 16-bit MCA slot has connectors that are smaller than the connectors in an ISA system. The slot itself is divided into two sections; one section handles 8-bit operations, and the other handles 16-bit operations.

Figure 5.7 describes the pinouts for the 16-bit MCA connector. Pins B1/A1 through B45/A45 are responsible for 8-bit operations, and pins B48/A48 through B58/A58 handle 16-bit operations.

Signal	Pin	Pin	Signal
AUDIO GND	B1	A1	-CD SETUP
AUDIO	B2	A2	MADE 24
Ground	B3	A3	Ground
OSC (14.3 MHZ)	B4	A4	Address 11
Ground	B5	A5	Address 10
Address 23	B6	A6	Address 9
Address 22	B7	A7	+5 Vdc
Address 21	B8	A8	Address 8
Ground	B9	A9	Address 7
Address 20	B10	A10	Address 6
Address 19	B11	A11	+5 Vdc
Address 18	B12	A12	Address 5
Ground	B13	A13	Address 4
Address 17	B14	A14	Address 3
Address 16	B15	A15	+5 Vdc
Address 15	B16	A16	Address 2
Ground	B17	A17	Address 1
Address 14	B18	A18	Address 0
Address 13	B19	A19	+12 Vdc
Address 12	B20	A20	-ADL
Ground	B21	A21	-PREEMPT
-IRQ 9	B22	A22	-BURST
-IRQ 3	B23	A23	-12 Vdc
-IRQ 4	B24	A24	ARB 00
Ground	B25	A25	ARB 01
-IRQ 5	B26	A26	ARB 02
-IRQ 6	B27	A27	-12 Vdc
-IRQ 7	B28	A28	ARB 03
Ground	B29	A29	ARB/-GNT
Reserved	B30	A30	-TC
Reserved	B31	A31	+5 Vdc
-CHCK	B32	A32	-SO
Ground	B33	A33	-S1
-CMD	B34	A34	M/-IO
CHRDYRTN	B35	A35	+12 Vdc
-CD SFDBK	B36	A36	CD CHRDY
Ground	B37	A37	Data Bit 0
Data Bit 1	B38	A38	Data Bit 2
Data Bit 3	B39	A39	+5 Vdc
Data Bit 4	B40	A40	Data Bit 5
Ground	B41	A41	Data Bit 6
CHRESET	B42	A42	Data Bit 7
Reserved	B43	A43	Ground
Reserved	B44	A44	-DS 16 RTN
Ground	B45	A45	-REFRESH
KEY	B46	A46	KEY
KEY	B47	A47	KEY
Data Bit 8	B48	A48	+5 Vdc
Data Bit 9	B49	A49	Data Bit 10
Ground	B50	A50	Data Bit 11
Data Bit 12	B51	A51	Data Bit 13
Data Bit 14	B52	A52	+12 Vdc
Data Bit 15	B53	A53	Reserved
Ground	B54	A54	-SBHE
-IRQ 10	B55	A55	-CD DS 16
-IRQ 11	B56	A56	+5 Vdc
-IRQ 12	B57	A57	-IRQ 14
Ground	B58	A58	-IRQ 15
Reserved	B59	A59	Reserved
Reserved	B60	A60	Reserved

Figure 5.7

Pinouts for the 16-bit MCA bus.

Figure 5.8 shows how the connector for this card appears.

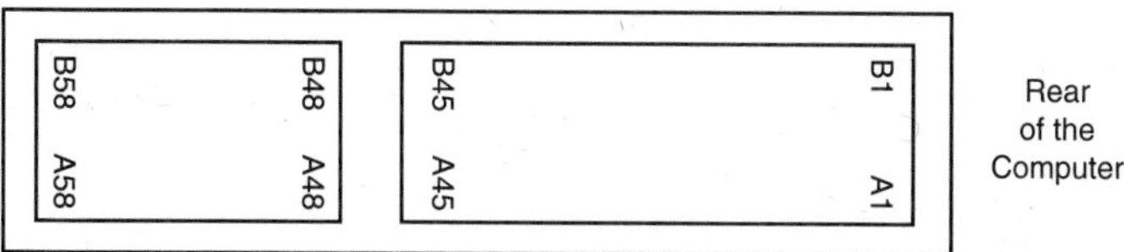

Figure 5.8
A 16-bit MCA connector.

32-Bit MCA Slots. In addition to the basic 16-bit slot, MCA systems based on the 386DX or later CPU have several 32-bit slots that are designed to take advantage of the processors' increased communications and memory-addressing capabilities. Even though the 32-bit slot is an extension of the original MCA connector (as the 16-bit ISA slot is an extension of the 8-bit ISA design), this extension was designed at the same time as the rest of MCA. Therefore, because the extension connector was not an afterthought, the design is more integrated than the 16-bit extension in ISA systems.

Figure 5.9 describes the pinouts for the 32-bit MCA connector. Pins B1/A1 through B58/A58 are exactly the same as in the 16-bit connector. Pins B59/A59 through B89/A89 are the 32-bit section. Figure 5.10 shows how the connector for this card appears.

Memory-Matched Extensions. Certain MCA systems (notably, IBM models 70 and 80) have bus extensions that support the operation of enhanced memory cards and support data transfer to those cards. These extensions are called memory-matched extensions.

The presence of memory-matched extensions varies from system to system. Some systems don't use the extensions at all; other systems include them on only one or a few slots. If one of your slots is equipped with these extensions, it will be on the end of the slot toward the rear of the motherboard (preceding pins B1 and A1 on your main MCA connector). You should refer to your system documentation to determine whether your system uses the extensions.

Figure 5.11 details the additional pin-out specifications for the extensions. Figure 5.12 shows how this connector appears in your system.

MCA Video Extensions. The third type of MCA slot is a standard 16-bit MCA connector with a special video-extension connector. This special slot appears in almost every MCA system. This slot is designed to speed your video subsystem.

The MCA video-extension connector is positioned at the end of the slot toward the rear of the motherboard (before pins B1 and A1 on the main MCA connector). The connector takes advantage of special VGA circuitry built into the motherboard. MCA provides compatible high-resolution video adapters that have special access to this motherboard circuitry, so that the special circuitry does not have to be duplicated on the video card itself.

Signal	Pin	Pin	Signal
AUDIO GND	B1	A1	-CD SETUP
AUDIO	B2	A2	MADE 24
Ground	B3	A3	Ground
OSC (14.3 MHZ)	B4	A4	Address 11
Ground	B5	A5	Address 10
Address 23	B6	A6	Address 9
Address 22	B7	A7	+5 Vdc
Address 21	B8	A8	Address 8
Ground	B9	A9	Address 7
Address 20	B10	A10	Address 6
Address 19	B11	A11	+5 Vdc
Address 18	B12	A12	Address 5
Ground	B13	A13	Address 4
Address 17	B14	A14	Address 3
Address 16	B15	A15	+5 Vdc
Address 15	B16	A16	Address 2
Ground	B17	A17	Address 1
Address 14	B18	A18	Address 0
Address 13	B19	A19	+12 Vdc
Address 12	B20	A20	-ADL
Ground	B21	A21	-PREEMPT
-IRQ 9	B22	A22	-BURST
-IRQ 3	B23	A23	-12 Vdc
-IRQ 4	B24	A24	ARB 00
Ground	B25	A25	ARB 01
-IRQ 5	B26	A26	ARB 02
-IRQ 6	B27	A27	-12 Vdc
-IRQ 7	B28	A28	ARB 03
Ground	B29	A29	ARB/-GNT
Reserved	B30	A30	-TC
Reserved	B31	A31	+5Vdc
-CHCK	B32	A32	-SO
Ground	B33	A33	-S1
-CMD	B34	A34	M/-IO
CHRDYRTN	B35	A35	+12 Vdc
-CD SFDBK	B36	A36	CD CHRDY
Ground	B37	A37	Data Bit 0
Data Bit 1	B38	A38	Data Bit 2
Data Bit 3	B39	A39	+5 Vdc
Data Bit 4	B40	A40	Data Bit 5
Ground	B41	A41	Data Bit 6
CHRESET	B42	A42	Data Bit 7
Reserved	B43	A43	Ground
Reserved	B44	A44	-DS 16 RTN
Ground	B45	A45	-REFRESH
KEY	B46	A46	KEY
KEY	B47	A47	KEY
Data Bit 8	B48	A48	+5 Vdc
Data Bit 9	B49	A49	Data Bit 10
Ground	B50	A50	Data Bit 11
Data Bit 12	B51	A51	Data Bit 13
Data Bit 14	B52	A52	+12 Vdc
Data Bit 15	B53	A53	Reserved
Ground	B54	A54	-SBHE
-IRQ 10	B55	A55	-CD DS 16
-IRQ 11	B56	A56	+5 Vdc
-IRQ 12	B57	A57	-IRQ 14
Ground	B58	A58	-IRQ 15
Reserved	B59	A59	Reserved
Reserved	B60	A60	Reserved

Signal	Pin	Pin	Signal
Reserved	B61	A61	Ground
Reserved	B62	A62	Reserved
Ground	B63	A63	Reserved
Data Bit 16	B64	A64	Reserved
Data Bit 17	B65	A65	+ 12 Vdc
Data Bit 18	B66	A66	Data Bit 19
Ground	B67	A67	Data Bit 20
Data Bit 22	B68	A68	Data Bit 21
Data Bit 23	B69	A69	+ 5 Vdc
Reserved	B70	A70	Data Bit 24
Ground	B71	A71	Data Bit 25
Data Bit 27	B72	A72	Data Bit 26
Data Bit 28	B73	A73	+ 5 Vdc
Data Bit 29	B74	A74	Data Bit 30
Ground	B75	A75	Data Bit 31
-BE 0	B76	A76	Reserved
-BE 1	B77	A77	+ 12 Vdc
-BE 2	B78	A78	-BE 3
Ground	B79	A79	-DS 32 RTN
TR 32	B80	A80	-CD DS 32
Address 24	B81	A81	+ 5 Vdc
Address 25	B82	A82	Address 26
Ground	B83	A83	Address 27
Address 29	B84	A84	Address 28
Address 30	B85	A85	+ 5 Vdc
Address 31	B86	A86	Reserved
Ground	B87	A87	Reserved
Reserved	B88	A88	Reserved
Reserved	B89	A89	Ground

Figure 5.9

Pinouts for the 32-bit MCA bus.

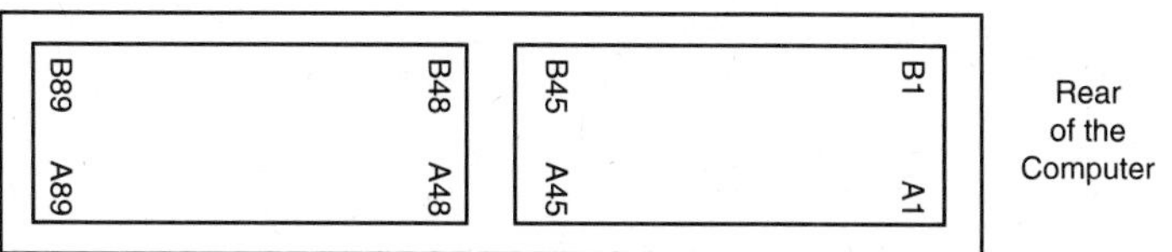

Figure 5.10

The MCA connector.

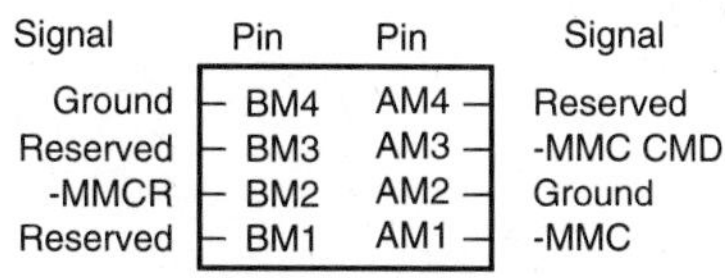

Signal Pin Pin Signal
Ground BM4 AM4 Reserved
Reserved BM3 AM3 -MMC CMD
-MMCR BM2 AM2 Ground
Reserved BM1 AM1 -MMC

Figure 5.11

Additional pinouts for the MCA memory-matched extensions.

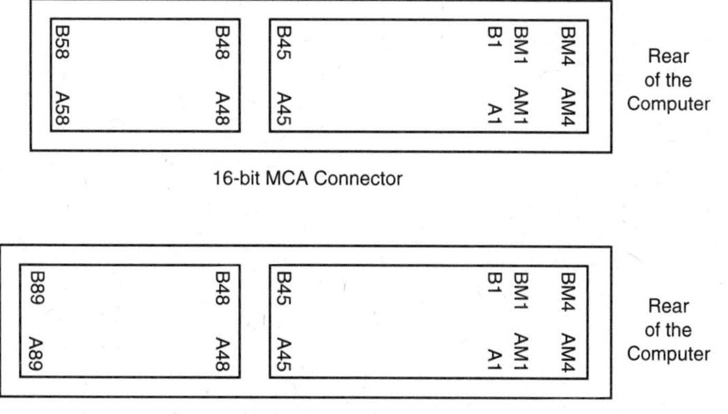

Figure 5.12

The MCA connector with memory-matched extensions.

No matter what new type of video board you add to an MCA system, all your programs will run, because you never lose the built-in VGA circuits. In addition, the built-in VGA circuits do not have to be disabled if you add a newer video card. Your new card can coexist with the VGA circuits and even "borrow" some elements, such as the digital-to-analog converter. This arrangement (in theory) can make the add-on video boards less expensive, because they can rely on motherboard circuitry instead of providing their own.

Typically, only one slot in an MCA system has the video extensions. This arrangement makes sense, because a typical system has only one video card.

Figure 5.13 describes the additional pinout connections for the slot with video extensions.

Signal	Pin	Pin	Signal
ESYNC	BV10	AV10	VSYNC
Ground	BV9	AV9	HSYNC
P5	BV8	AV8	BLSNK
P4	BV7	AV7	Ground
P3	BV6	AV6	P6
Ground	BV5	AV5	EDCLK
P2	BV4	AV4	DCLK
P1	BV3	AV3	Ground
P0	BV2	AV2	P7
Ground	BV1	AV1	EVIDEO
KEY	KEY	KEY	KEY

Figure 5.13

Pinouts for the MCA Auxiliary Video Extension Connector (AVEC).

Figure 5.14 shows what this slot looks like in your system.

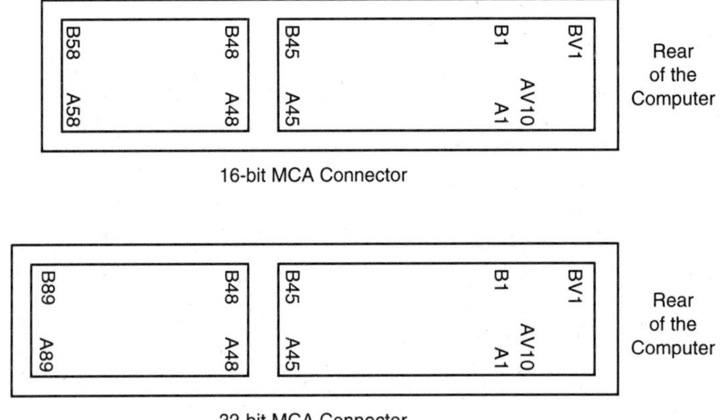

Figure 5.14

The MCA connectors with video extensions.

Although the MCA bus was technically a masterpiece of design and engineering, it was too far ahead of its time. The PC world was not ready for Plug and Play systems in 1987, and seemed willing to fuss with jumpers and switches instead! MCA was deemed too costly, and there was never anywhere near the choice in adapters compared to ISA. MCA had far greater performance potential; in fact the performance of the MCA bus comes close to even the PCI local bus type slots used today, but at the time it came out, most peripherals were even slower than ISA, and the performance advantages of MCA simply could not be exploited.

IBM has discontinued the PS/2 line of computers which were primarily based on the MCA bus, and although some of the newer PCs still being offered by IBM are available with MCA busses, the MCA bus is dead. There are no adapter companies I am aware of that are still actively designing for this bus, although existing cards will be available for several years to come.

If you are in search of MCA cards or peripherals, an organization called the MCDA (Micro Channel Developers Association) is available to assist in supporting MCA systems. It carries virtually every MCA card made, and is an excellent source of information on the MCA bus itself. Check it out in the vendor list in Appendix B.

The EISA Bus

EISA is an acronym for extended industry standard architecture. This standard was announced in September 1988 as a response to IBM's introduction of the MCA bus—more specifically, to the way that IBM wanted to handle licensing of the MCA bus. Vendors did not feel obligated to pay retroactive royalties on the ISA bus, so they turned their backs on IBM and created their own buses.

The EISA standard was developed primarily by Compaq, and was intended to be its way of taking away from IBM future development of the PC bus. Compaq knew that nobody would clone its bus if it was the only company that had it, so it essentially gave the design away to other leading manufacturers. They formed the EISA committee, a nonprofit organization designed specifically to control development of the EISA bus.

Although 95% of it was already done by Compaq by the time the committee was formed, Compaq encouraged at least eight other leading manufacturers to join in to finish the specification. Additionally, the committee would then control all future development of the EISA bus, preventing any one company from dominating. This may sound benevolent on Compaq's part, but it knew the bus structure better than anybody else by this time, and already had chipsets, support chips, adapter cards, and motherboard designs ready to go. It would be the industry leader with this new bus. The ploy backfired, because EISA never even became as popular as MCA, selling in far fewer numbers. The "bus war" that was being touted by the media simply never even really got started. The first EISA machines started appearing on the market in 1989.

Very few EISA adapters were ever developed, and those that were developed centered mainly around disk array controllers and server type network cards. For this reason, EISA systems have found a niche in use as network fileservers. On the desktop, EISA systems were never popular and are definitely not recommended with many better and faster busses available. The saving grace in EISA systems was the fact that they could use existing ISA cards. Unfortunately, most EISA systems only use ISA type cards, and have a significant amount of onboard hardware that simply will never become utilized. The EISA bus was designed as a successor to the ISA bus, although it has not turned out quite that way (as evidenced by the appearance of additional bus specifications). The EISA bus provides 32-bit slots for use with 386DX or higher systems. The EISA slot enables manufacturers to design adapter cards that have many of the capabilities of MCA adapters, but the bus also supports adapter cards created for the older ISA standard.

http://www.surepath.ibm.com/documents/pcs/bioseisa.html

On the Web

EISA provides markedly faster hard-drive throughput when used with devices such as SCSI bus-mastering hard drive controllers. Compared with 16-bit ISA system architecture, EISA permits greater system expansion with fewer adapter conflicts.

The EISA bus adds 90 new connections (55 new signals) without increasing the physical connector size of the 16-bit ISA bus. At first glance, the 32-bit EISA slot looks much like the 16-bit ISA slot. The EISA adapter, however, has two rows of connectors. The first row is the same kind used in 16-bit ISA cards; the other, thinner row extends from the 16-bit connectors.

To visualize the edge connectors on an EISA card, imagine that you are laying a 1'×1' board on a 2'×2' board in a lumberyard. The edge connector on an EISA board is about 0.2 inch longer than the connectors on an 8- or 16-bit ISA adapter board. The longest (and thinnest) connectors on an EISA card pass through the 16-bit part of the slot and make contact with the 32-bit connectors deeper in the slot. Essentially you end up with a double-decker connector with the old ISA bus portion on the top and the new EISA extension connector on the bottom. This connector design solved a potentially disastrous problem with high insertion forces that would have occurred if they had simply extended the ISA connector lengthwise.

The physical specifications of an EISA card are as follows:

5 inches (127mm) high

13.13 inches (333.5mm) long

0.5 inch (12.7mm) wide

The EISA specification calls for more than 45 watts at four different voltages to be available to each slot—a challenge to 200-watt or smaller power supplies, because it takes more than 325 watts to fully power the eight EISA slots in a system. Most EISA adapter cards, however, do not use the full 45 watts available to them; in fact, most cards use about the same amount of power as 8- and 16-bit ISA adapter boards, which is up to about 15 watts. Maximum power consumption for all the different busses is discussed in Chapter 8, "The Power Supply."

The EISA bus can handle up to 32 bits of data at an 8.33 MHz cycle rate. Most data transfers require a minimum of two cycles, although faster cycle rates are possible if an adapter card provides tight timing specifications. The maximum bandwidth on the bus is 33M per second, as the following formula shows:

8.33 MHz × 32 bits = 266.56 megabits/second

266.56 megabits/second ÷ 8 = 33.32M/second

Data transfers through an 8- or 16-bit expansion card across the bus would be reduced appropriately. Remember, however, that these figures represent theoretical maximums. Wait states, interrupts, and other protocol factors can reduce the effective bandwidth—typically, by half. Figure 5.15 describes the pinouts for the EISA bus.

Figure 5.16 shows the locations of the pins.

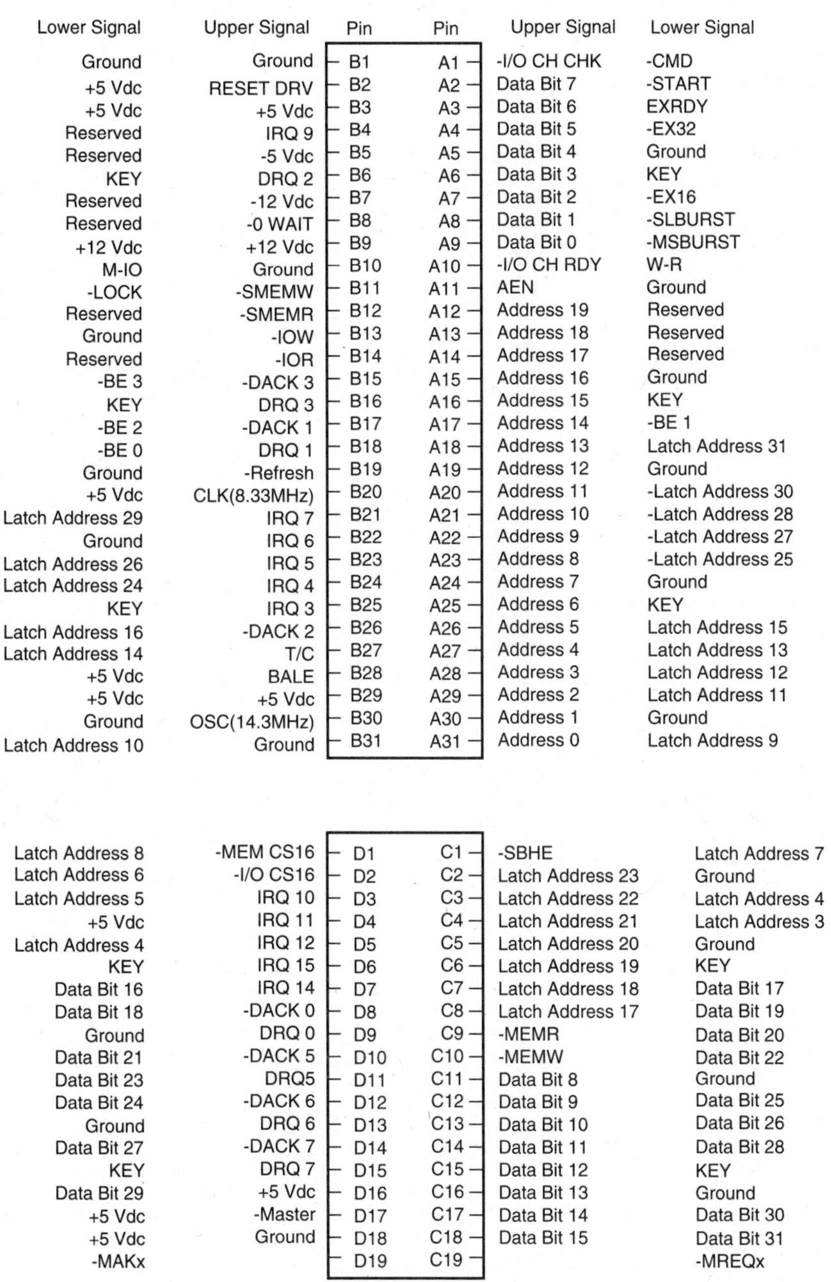
Lower Signal
Upper Signal
Pin
Pin
Upper Signal
Lower Signal
Ground Ground B1 A1 -I/O CH CHK -CMD
+5 Vdc RESET DRV B2 A2 Data Bit 7 -START
+5 Vdc +5 Vdc B3 A3 Data Bit 6 EXRDY
Reserved IRQ 9 B4 A4 Data Bit 5 -EX32
Reserved -5 Vdc B5 A5 Data Bit 4 Ground
KEY DRQ 2 B6 A6 Data Bit 3 KEY
Reserved -12 Vdc B7 A7 Data Bit 2 -EX16
Reserved -0 WAIT B8 A8 Data Bit 1 -SLBURST
+12 Vdc +12 Vdc B9 A9 Data Bit 0 -MSBURST
M-IO Ground B10 A10 -I/O CH RDY W-R
-LOCK -SMEMW B11 A11 AEN Ground
Reserved -SMEMR B12 A12 Address 19 Reserved
Ground -IOW B13 A13 Address 18 Reserved
Reserved -IOR B14 A14 Address 17 Reserved
-BE 3 -DACK 3 B15 A15 Address 16 Ground
KEY DRQ 3 B16 A16 Address 15 KEY
-BE 2 -DACK 1 B17 A17 Address 14 -BE 1
-BE 0 DRQ 1 B18 A18 Address 13 Latch Address 31
Ground -Refresh B19 A19 Address 12 Ground
+5 Vdc CLK(8.33MHz) B20 A20 Address 11 -Latch Address 30
Latch Address 29 IRQ 7 B21 A21 Address 10 -Latch Address 28
Ground IRQ 6 B22 A22 Address 9 -Latch Address 27
Latch Address 26 IRQ 5 B23 A23 Address 8 -Latch Address 25
Latch Address 24 IRQ 4 B24 A24 Address 7 Ground
KEY IRQ 3 B25 A25 Address 6 KEY
Latch Address 16 -DACK 2 B26 A26 Address 5 Latch Address 15
Latch Address 14 T/C B27 A27 Address 4 Latch Address 13
+5 Vdc BALE B28 A28 Address 3 Latch Address 12
+5 Vdc +5 Vdc B29 A29 Address 2 Latch Address 11
Ground OSC(14.3MHz) B30 A30 Address 1 Ground
Latch Address 10 Ground B31 A31 Address 0 Latch Address 9
Latch Address 8 -MEM CS16 D1 C1 -SBHE Latch Address 7
Latch Address 6 -I/O CS16 D2 C2 Latch Address 23 Ground
Latch Address 5 IRQ 10 D3 C3 Latch Address 22 Latch Address 4
+5 Vdc IRQ 11 D4 C4 Latch Address 21 Latch Address 3
Latch Address 4 IRQ 12 D5 C5 Latch Address 20 Ground
KEY IRQ 15 D6 C6 Latch Address 19 KEY
Data Bit 16 IRQ 14 D7 C7 Latch Address 18 Data Bit 17
Data Bit 18 -DACK 0 D8 C8 Latch Address 17 Data Bit 19
Ground DRQ 0 D9 C9 -MEMR Data Bit 20
Data Bit 21 -DACK 5 D10 C10 -MEMW Data Bit 22
Data Bit 23 DRQ5 D11 C11 Data Bit 8 Ground
Data Bit 24 -DACK 6 D12 C12 Data Bit 9 Data Bit 25
Ground DRQ 6 D13 C13 Data Bit 10 Data Bit 26
Data Bit 27 -DACK 7 D14 C14 Data Bit 11 Data Bit 28
KEY DRQ 7 D15 C15 Data Bit 12 KEY
Data Bit 29 +5 Vdc D16 C16 Data Bit 13 Ground
+5 Vdc -Master D17 C17 Data Bit 14 Data Bit 30
+5 Vdc Ground D18 C18 Data Bit 15 Data Bit 31
-MAKx D19 C19 -MREQx

Figure 5.15

Pinouts for the EISA bus.

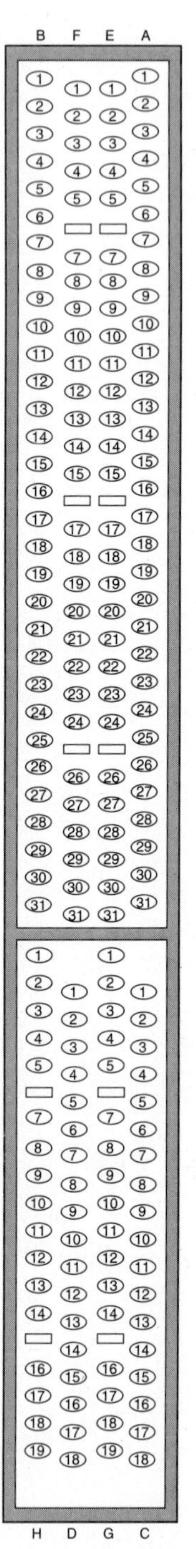

Figure 5.16

The card connector for the EISA bus.

Bus Mastering. EISA use a technology called bus mastering to speed the system. In essence, a bus master is an adapter with its own processor that can execute operations independently of the CPU. To work properly, bus-mastering technology relies on an EISA arbitration unit, most often called an integrated system peripheral (ISP) chip. The ISP enables a bus-mastered board to temporarily take exclusive control of the system, as though the board were the entire system. Because the board has exclusive control of the system, it can perform operations very quickly. A bus-mastering EISA hard drive controller, for example, achieves much greater data throughput with a fast drive than can controller cards that are not bus-mastered.

The ISP determines which device gains control by using a four-level order of priority. That order, in terms of priority, is:

- System-memory refresh
- DMA transfers
- The CPU itself
- Bus masters

A bus-mastering adapter board notifies the ISP when it wants control of the system. At the earliest possible time (after the higher priorities have been satisfied), the ISP hands control over to the bus-mastered board. The boards, in turn, have built-in circuitry to keep them from taking over the system for periods of time that would interfere with first-priority operations, such as memory refresh.

Automated Setup. EISA systems also use an automated setup to deal with adapter-board interrupts and addressing issues. These issues often cause problems when several different adapter boards are installed in an ISA system. EISA setup software recognizes potential conflicts and automatically configures the system to avoid them. EISA does, however, enable you to do your own troubleshooting, as well as to configure the boards through jumpers and switches.

Note

Although automated setup traditionally has not been available in ISA systems, it will be available with the advent of Plug and Play systems and components. Plug and Play systems are discussed toward the end of this chapter in "The Future: Plug and Play Systems."

Local Buses

The I/O buses discussed so far (ISA, MCA, and EISA) have one thing in common: relatively slow speed. This speed limitation is a carryover from the days of the original PC, when the I/O bus operated at the same speed as the processor bus. As the speed of the processor bus increased, the I/O bus realized only nominal speed improvements, primarily from an increase in the bandwidth of the bus. The I/O bus had to remain at a slower speed, because the huge installed base of adapter cards could operate only at slower speeds.

Figure 5.17 shows a conceptual block diagram of the buses in a computer system.

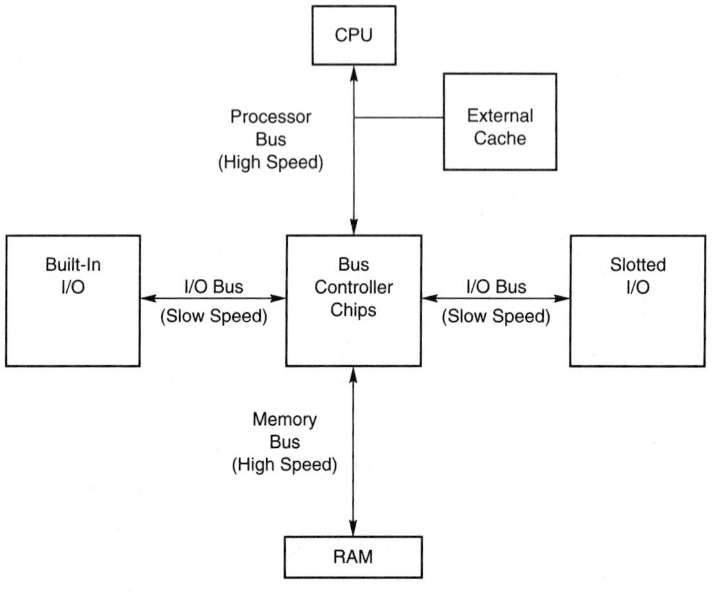

Figure 5.17

Bus layout in a traditional PC.

The thought of a computer system running slower than it could is very bothersome to some computer users. Even so, the slow speed of the I/O bus is nothing more than a nuisance in most cases. You don't need blazing speed to communicate with a keyboard or a mouse, for example; you gain nothing in performance. The real problem occurs in subsystems in which you need the speed, such as video and disk controllers.

The speed problem became acute when graphical user interfaces (such as Windows) became prevalent. These systems required the processing of so much video data that the I/O bus became a literal bottleneck for the entire computer system. In other words, it did little good to have a CPU that was capable of 66 MHz speed if you could put data through the I/O bus at a rate of only 8 MHz.

An obvious solution to this problem is to move some of the slotted I/O to an area where it could access the faster speeds of the processor bus—much the same way as the external cache. Figure 5.18 shows this arrangement.

This arrangement became known as local bus, because external devices (adapter cards) now could access the part of the bus that was local to the CPU—the processor bus. Physically, the slots provided to tap this new configuration would need to be different from existing bus slots, to prevent adapter cards designed for slower buses from being plugged into the higher bus speeds that this design made accessible.

It is interesting to note that the very first 8-bit and 16-bit ISA buses were a form of Local Bus architecture. These systems had the processor bus as the main bus, and everything ran at full processor speeds. When ISA systems ran faster than 8 MHz, the main ISA bus had to be decoupled from the processor bus since expansion cards, memory, and so forth, could not keep up. In 1992, an extension to the ISA bus called the VESA Local Bus started showing up on PC systems, indicating a return to Local Bus architecture.

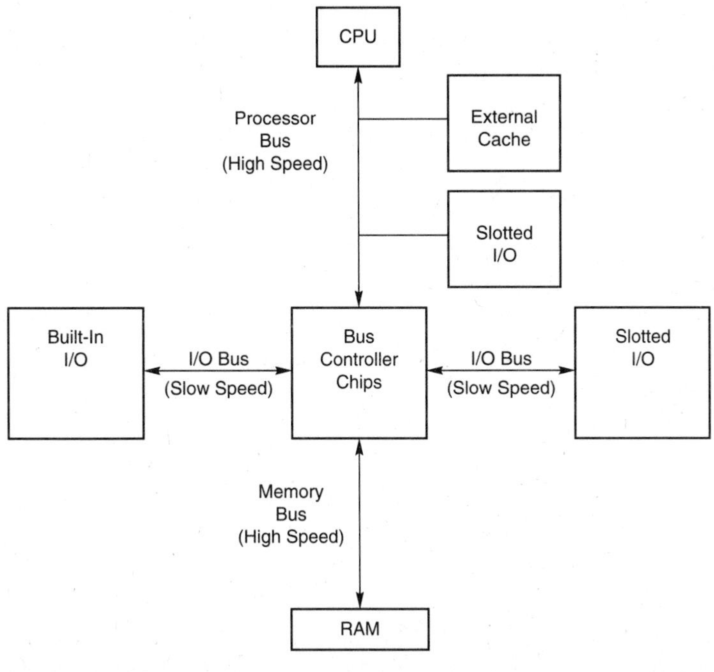

Figure 5.18
How local bus works.

Note

A system does not have to have a local-bus expansion slot to incorporate local-bus technology; instead, the local-bus device can be built directly into the motherboard. (In such a case, the local-bus-slotted I/O shown earlier in fig. 5.11 would in fact be built-in I/O.) This built-in approach to local bus is the way the first local-bus systems were designed.

Local-bus solutions do not replace earlier standards, such as ISA; they are designed as an extension to existing standards. Therefore, a typical system is based on ISA or EISA and has one or more local-bus slots available as well. Older cards still are compatible with the system, but high-speed adapter cards can take advantage of the local-bus slots as well.

Local-bus systems are especially popular with users of Windows and OS/2, because these slots are used for special 32-bit video accelerator cards that greatly speed the repainting of the graphics screens used in those operating systems. The performance of Windows and OS/2 suffers greatly from bottlenecks in even the best VGA cards connected to an ISA or EISA bus.

VESA Local Bus. The VESA Local Bus was the most popular local bus design from its debut in August, 1992 through 1994. It was created by the VESA committee, a nonprofit organization founded by NEC to further development of video display and bus standards. In a similar fashion to how EISA evolved, NEC had done most of the work on the VL-bus (as it would be called), and after founding the nonprofit VESA committee, it turned over future development to VESA. At first, the local-bus slot seemed primarily designed to be used for video cards. Improving video performance was a top priority at NEC to help sell its high-end displays as well as its own PC systems. By 1991, video performance had become a real bottleneck in most PC systems.

The Video Electronics Standards Association (VESA) developed a standardized local-bus specification known as VESA Local Bus or simply VL-Bus. As in earlier local-bus implementations, the VL-Bus slot offers direct access to system memory at the speed of the processor itself. The VL-Bus can move data 32 bits at a time, enabling data to flow between the CPU and a compatible video subsystem or hard drive at the full 32-bit data width of the 486 chip. The maximum rated throughput of the VL-Bus is 128M to 132M per second. In other words, local bus went a long way toward removing the major bottlenecks that existed in earlier bus configurations.

On the Web

This Web site provides a listing for the VESA standards and modifications being considered:

http://www.vesa.org/

Additionally, VL-Bus offers manufacturers of hard-drive interface cards an opportunity to overcome another traditional bottleneck: the rate at which data can flow between the hard drive and the CPU. The average 16-bit IDE drive and interface can achieve throughput of up to 5M per second, whereas VL-Bus hard drive adapters for IDE drives are touted as providing throughput of as much as 8M per second. In real-world situations, the true throughput of VL-Bus hard drive adapters is somewhat less than 8M per second, but VL-Bus still provides a substantial boost in hard-drive performance.

Despite all the benefits of the VL-Bus (and, by extension, of all local buses), this technology has a few drawbacks, which are described in the following list:

- *Dependence on a 486 CPU.* The VL-Bus inherently is tied to the 486 processor bus. This bus is quite different from that used by Pentium processors (and probably from those that will be used by future CPUs). A VL-Bus that operates at the full rated speed of a Pentium has not been developed, although stopgap measures (such as stepping down speed or developing bus bridges) are available. Unfortunately, these result in poor performance. Some systems have been developed with both VL-Bus and PCI slots, but because of design compromises, performance often suffers.

- *Speed limitations.* The VL-Bus specification provides for speeds of up to 66 MHz on the bus, but the electrical characteristics of the VL-Bus connector limit an adapter card to no more than 40 to 50 MHz. In practice running the VL-Bus at speeds over 33 MHz causes many problems, so 33 MHz has become the acceptable speed limit. Systems that use faster processor bus speeds must buffer and step down the clock on the VL-Bus or add wait states. Note that if the main CPU uses a clock modifier (such as the kind that doubles clock speeds), the VL-Bus uses the unmodified CPU clock speed as its bus speed.

- *Electrical limitations.* The processor bus has very tight timing rules, which may vary from CPU to CPU. These timing rules were designed for limited loading on the bus, meaning that the only elements originally intended to be connected to the local bus are elements such as the external cache and the bus controller chips. As you add more circuitry, you increase the electrical load. If the local bus is not implemented correctly, the additional load can lead to problems such as loss of data integrity and timing problems between the CPU and the VL-Bus cards.

- *Card limitations.* Depending on the electrical loading of a system, the number of VL-Bus cards is limited. Although the VL-Bus specification provides for as many as three cards, this can be achieved only at clock rates of up to 40 MHz with an otherwise low system-board load. As the system-board load increases and the clock rate increases, the number of cards supported decreases. Only one VL-Bus card can be supported at 50 MHz with a high system-board load. In practice, these limits could not usually be reached without problems.

The VL-Bus did not seem to be a well-engineered concept. The design was simple indeed; just take the pins from the 486 processor and run them out to a card connector socket. In other words, the VL-Bus is essentially the raw 486 processor bus. This allowed a very inexpensive design, since no additional chipsets or interface chips were required. A motherboard designer could add VL-Bus slots to its 486 motherboards very easily and at a very low cost. This is why these slots appeared on virtually all 486 system designs overnight.

Unfortunately the 486 processor bus was not designed to have multiple devices (called loads) plugged into it at one time. Problems arose with timing glitches caused by the capacitance introduced into the circuit by different cards. Since the VL-Bus ran at the same speed as the processor bus, different processor speeds meant different bus speeds and full compatibility was difficult to achieve. Although the VL-Bus could be adapted to other processors, including the 386 or even the Pentium, it was designed for the 486, and worked best as a 486 solution only. Despite the low cost, after a new bus called PCI (Peripheral Component Interconnect) appeared, VL-Bus fell into disfavor very quickly. It never did catch on with Pentium systems, and there is little or no further development of the VL-Bus in the PC industry. I would not recommend purchasing VL-Bus cards or systems today.

For a used system, or as an inexpensive upgrade for an older system, VL-Bus might be appropriate and can provide an acceptable solution for high-speed computing.

Physically, the VL-Bus slot is an extension of the slots used for whatever type of base system you have. If you have an ISA system, the VL-Bus is positioned as an extension of your existing 16-bit ISA slots. Likewise, if you have an EISA system or MCA system, the VL-Bus slots are extensions of those existing slots. Figure 5.19 shows how the VL-Bus slots could be situated in an ISA system. The VESA extension has 112 contacts and uses the same physical connector as the MCA bus.

The VL-Bus adds a total 116 pin locations to the bus connectors that your system already has. Table 5.2 lists the pinouts for only the VL-Bus connector portion of the total connector.

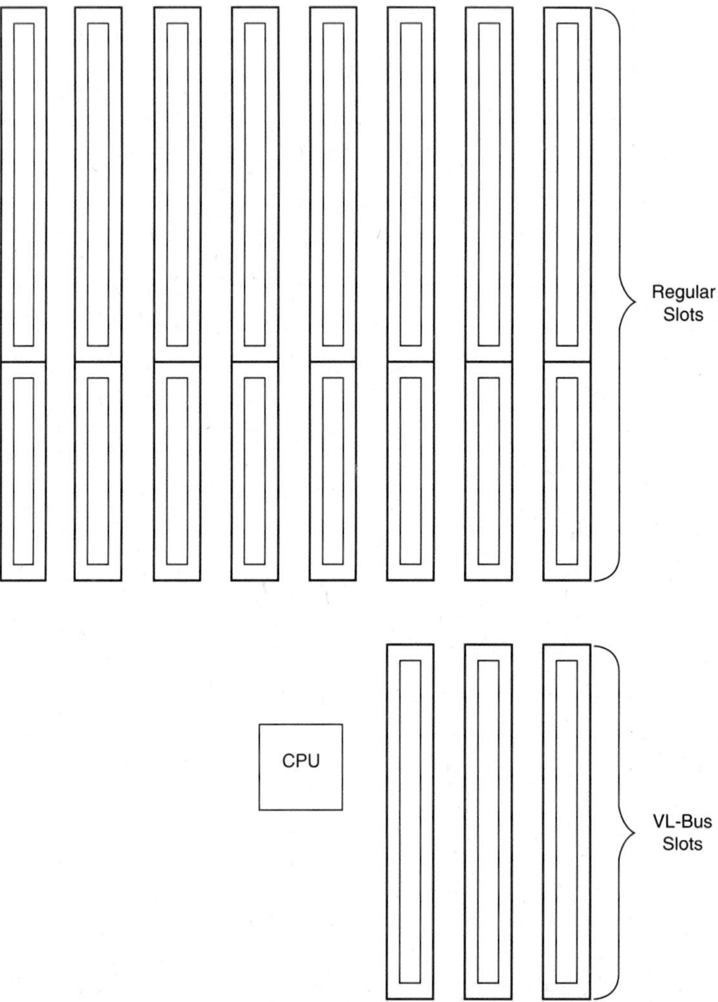

Figure 5.19
An example of VL-Bus slots in an ISA system.

(For pins for which two purposes are listed, the second purpose applies when the card is in 64-bit transfer mode.)

Table 5.2 Pinouts for the VL-Bus

Pin	Signal Name	Pin	Signal Name
B1	Data 0	A1	Data 1
B2	Data 2	A2	Data 3

Pin	Signal Name	Pin	Signal Name
B3	Data 4	A3	Ground
B4	Data 6	A4	Data 5
B5	Data 8	A5	Data 7
B6	Ground	A6	Data 9
B7	Data 10	A7	Data 11
B8	Data 12	A8	Data 13
B9	VCC	A9	Data 15
B10	Data 14	A10	Ground
B11	Data 16	A11	Data 17
B12	Data 18	A12	VCC
B13	Data 20	A13	Data 19
B14	Ground	A14	Data 21
B15	Data 22	A15	Data 23
B16	Data 24	A16	Data 25
B17	Data 26	A17	Ground
B18	Data 28	A18	Data 27
B19	Data 30	A19	Data 29
B20	VCC	A20	Data 31
B21	Address 31 or Data 63	A21	Address 30 or Data 62
B22	Ground	A22	Address 28 or Data 60
B23	Address 29 or Data 61	A23	Address 26 or Data 58
B24	Address 27 or Data 59	A24	Ground
B25	Address 25 or Data 57	A25	Address 24 or Data 56
B26	Address 23 or Data 55	A26	Address 22 or Data 54
B27	Address 21 or Data 53	A27	VCC
B28	Address 19 or Data 51	A28	Address 20 or Data 52
B29	Ground	A29	Address 18 or Data 50
B30	Address 17 or Data 49	A30	Address 16 or Data 48
B31	Address 15 or Data 47	A31	Address 14 or Data 46
B32	VCC	A32	Address 12 or Data 44
B33	Address 13 or Data 45	A33	Address 10 or Data 42
B34	Address 11 or Data 43	A34	Address 8 or Data 40
B35	Address 9 or Data 41	A35	Ground
B36	Address 7 or Data 39	A36	Address 6 or Data 38
B37	Address 5 or Data 37	A37	Address 4 or Data 36
B38	Ground	A38	Write Back
B39	Address 3 or Data 35	A39	Byte Enable 0 or 4
B40	Address 2 or Data 34	A40	VCC
B41	Unused or LBS64#	A41	Byte Enable 1 or 5
B42	Reset	A42	Byte Enable 2 or 6

(continues)

Table 5.2 Continued

Pin	Signal Name	Pin	Signal Name
B43	Data/Code Status	A43	Ground
B44	Memory-I/O Status or Data 33	A44	Byte Enable 3 or 7
B45	Write/Read Status or Data 32	A45	Address Data Strobe
B46	Access key	A46	Access key
B47	Access key	A47	Access key
B48	Ready Return	A48	Local Ready
B49	Ground	A49	Local Device
B50	IRQ 9	A50	Local Request
B51	Burst Ready	A51	Ground
B52	Burst Last	A52	Local Bus Grant
B53	ID0	A53	VCC
B54	ID1	A54	ID2
B55	Ground	A55	ID3
B56	Local Clock	A56	ID4 or ACK64#
B57	VCC	A57	Unused
B58	Local Bus Size 16	A58	Loc/Ext Address Data Strobe

Figure 5.20 shows the locations of the pins.

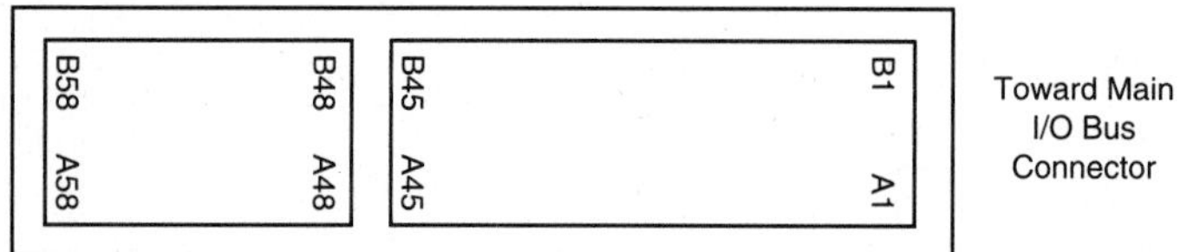

Figure 5.20

The card connector for the VL-Bus.

The PCI Bus. In early 1992, Intel spearheaded the creation of another industry group with the same goals as the VESA group in relation to the PC bus. Recognizing the need to overcome weaknesses in the ISA and EISA buses, the PCI Special Interest Group was formed.

PCI is an acronym for peripheral component interconnect bus. The PCI bus specification, released in June 1992 and updated in April 1993, redesigned the traditional PC bus by inserting another bus between the CPU and the native I/O bus by means of bridges. Rather than tap directly into the processor bus, with its delicate electrical timing (as was done in local bus and VL-Bus), a new set of controller chips was developed to extend the bus, as shown in figure 5.21.

The PCI bus often is called a mezzanine bus because it adds another layer to the traditional bus configuration. PCI bypasses the standard I/O bus; it uses the system bus to increase the bus clock speed and take full advantage of the CPU's data path. Systems that integrate the PCI bus became available in mid-1993 and have since become the mainstay high-end systems.

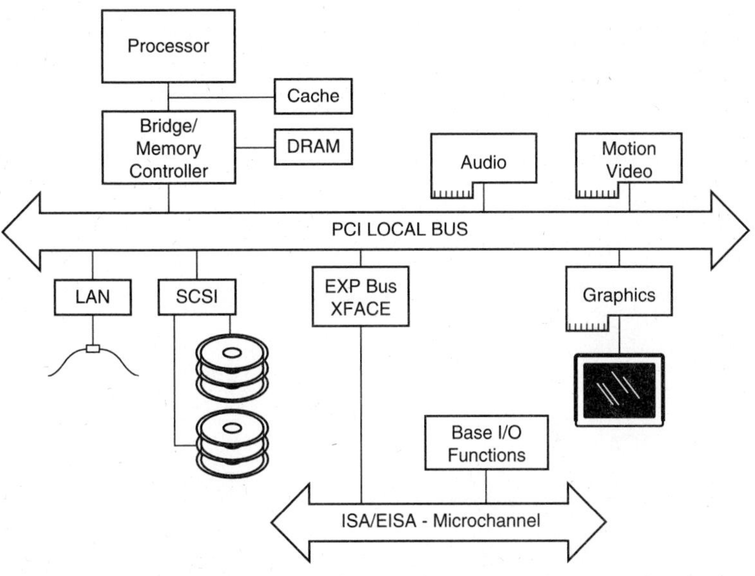

Figure 5.21

Conceptual diagram of the PCI bus.

Although the PCI bus is the clear choice for Pentium-based systems, some critics have contended that for 486 systems, the VL-Bus is better because it is cheaper to implement. These critics base their contention on the fact that extra chips and pins are necessary to implement the mezzanine configuration inherent to PCI. This argument is incomplete, however; in reality, connecting an I/O chip to the VL-Bus requires almost twice as many pins as connecting it to the PCI bus does (88, compared with 47). Therefore, PCI versions of chips (the ones built into the motherboard) should be less expensive than the VL-Bus versions.

Information is transferred across the PCI bus at 33 MHz, at the full data width of the CPU. When the bus is used in conjunction with a 32-bit CPU, the bandwidth is 132M per second, as the following formula shows:

33 MHz × 32 bits = 1,056 megabits/second

1,056 megabits/second ÷ 8 = 132M/second

When the bus is used in future 64-bit implementations, the bandwidth doubles, meaning that you can transfer data at speeds up to 264M per second. Real-life data-transfer speeds necessarily will be lower, but still much faster than anything else that is currently available. Part of the reason for this faster real-life throughput is the fact that the PCI bus can operate concurrently with the processor bus; it does not supplant it. The CPU can be processing data in an external cache while the PCI bus is busy transferring information between other parts of the system—a major design benefit of the PCI bus.

A PCI adapter card uses a standard MCA connector, just like the VL-Bus. This connector can be identified within a computer system because it typically is offset from the normal ISA, MCA, or EISA connectors (see fig. 5.22 for an example). The size of a PCI card can be the same as that of the cards used in the system's normal I/O bus.

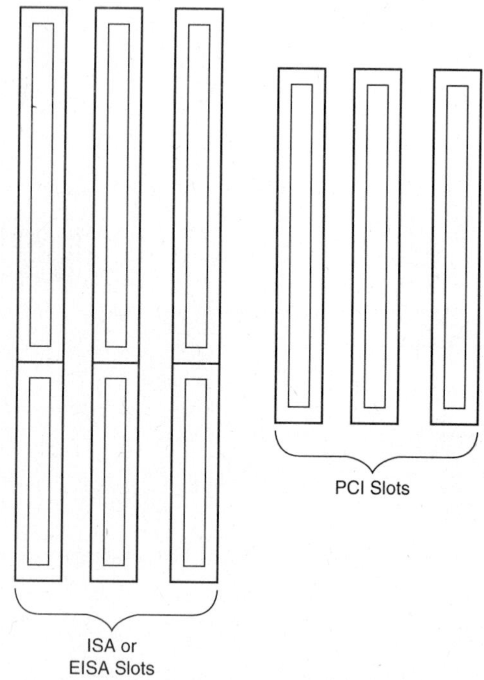

Figure 5.22

Possible configuration of PCI slots in relation to ISA or EISA slots.

The PCI specification identifies three board configurations, each designed for a specific type of system with specific power requirements. The 5-volt specification is for stationary computer systems, the 3.3-volt specification is for portable machines, and the universal specification is for motherboards and cards that work in either type of system.

Table 5.3 shows the 5-volt PCI pinouts, and figure 5.23 shows the pin locations. Table 5.4 shows the 3.3-volt PCI pinouts; the pin locations are indicated in figure 5.24. Finally, table 5.5 shows the pinouts, and figure 5.25 shows the pin locations, for a universal PCI slot and card. Notice that each figure shows both the 32-bit and 64-bit variations on the respective specifications.

Note

If the PCI card supports only 32 data bits, it needs only pins B1/A1 through B62/A62. Pins B63/A63 through B94/A94 are used only if the card supports 64 data bits.

Table 5.3 Pinouts for a 5-Volt PCI Bus

Pin	Signal Name	Pin	Signal Name
B1	–12V	A1	Test Reset
B2	Test Clock	A2	+12V
B3	Ground	A3	Test Mode Select
B4	Test Data Output	A4	Test Data Input
B5	+5V	A5	+5V
B6	+5V	A6	Interrupt A
B7	Interrupt B	A7	Interrupt C
B8	Interrupt D	A8	+5V
B9	PRSNT1#	A9	Reserved
B10	Reserved	A10	+5V I/O
B11	PRSNT2#	A11	Reserved
B12	Ground	A12	Ground
B13	Ground	A13	Ground
B14	Reserved	A14	Reserved
B15	Ground	A15	Reset
B16	Clock	A16	+5V I/O
B17	Ground	A17	Grant
B18	Request	A18	Ground
B19	+5V I/O	A19	Reserved
B20	Address 31	A20	Address 30
B21	Address 29	A21	+3.3V
B22	Ground	A22	Address 28
B23	Address 27	A23	Address 26
B24	Address 25	A24	Ground
B25	+3.3V	A25	Address 24
B26	C/BE 3	A26	Init Device Select
B27	Address 23	A27	+3.3V
B28	Ground	A28	Address 22
B29	Address 21	A29	Address 20
B30	Address 19	A30	Ground
B31	+3.3V	A31	Address 18
B32	Address 17	A32	Address 16
B33	C/BE 2	A33	+3.3V

(continues)

Table 5.3 Continued

Pin	Signal Name	Pin	Signal Name
B34	Ground	A34	Cycle Frame
B35	Initiator Ready	A35	Ground
B36	+3.3V	A36	Target Ready
B37	Device Select	A37	Ground
B38	Ground	A38	Stop
B39	Lock	A39	+3.3V
B40	Parity Error	A40	Snoop Done
B41	+3.3V	A41	Snoop Backoff
B42	System Error	A42	Ground
B43	+3.3V	A43	PAR
B44	C/BE 1	A44	Address 15
B45	Address 14	A45	+3.3V
B46	Ground	A46	Address 13
B47	Address 12	A47	Address 11
B48	Address 10	A48	Ground
B49	Ground	A49	Address 9
B50	Access key	A50	Access key
B51	Access key	A51	Access key
B52	Address 8	A52	C/BE 0
B53	Address 7	A53	+3.3V
B54	+3.3V	A54	Address 6
B55	Address 5	A55	Address 4
B56	Address 3	A56	Ground
B57	Ground	A57	Address 2
B58	Address 1	A58	Address 0
B59	+5V I/O	A59	+5V I/O
B60	Acknowledge 64-bit	A60	Request 64-bit
B61	+5V	A61	+5V
B62	+5V Access key	A62	+5V Access key
B63	Reserved	A63	Ground
B64	Ground	A64	C/BE 7
B65	C/BE 6	A65	C/BE 5
B66	C/BE 4	A66	+5V I/O
B67	Ground	A67	Parity 64-bit
B68	Address 63	A68	Address 62
B69	Address 61	A69	Ground
B70	+5V I/O	A70	Address 60
B71	Address 59	A71	Address 58
B72	Address 57	A72	Ground

Pin	Signal Name	Pin	Signal Name
B73	Ground	A73	Address 56
B74	Address 55	A74	Address 54
B75	Address 53	A75	+5V I/O
B76	Ground	A76	Address 52
B77	Address 51	A77	Address 50
B78	Address 49	A78	Ground
B79	+5V I/O	A79	Address 48
B80	Address 47	A80	Address 46
B81	Address 45	A81	Ground
B82	Ground	A82	Address 44
B83	Address 43	A83	Address 42
B84	Address 41	A84	+5V I/O
B85	Ground	A85	Address 40
B86	Address 39	A86	Address 38
B87	Address 37	A87	Ground
B88	+5V I/O	A88	Address 36
B89	Address 35	A89	Address 34
B90	Address 33	A90	Ground
B91	Ground	A91	Address 32
B92	Reserved	A92	Reserved
B93	Reserved	A93	Ground
B94	Ground	A94	Reserved

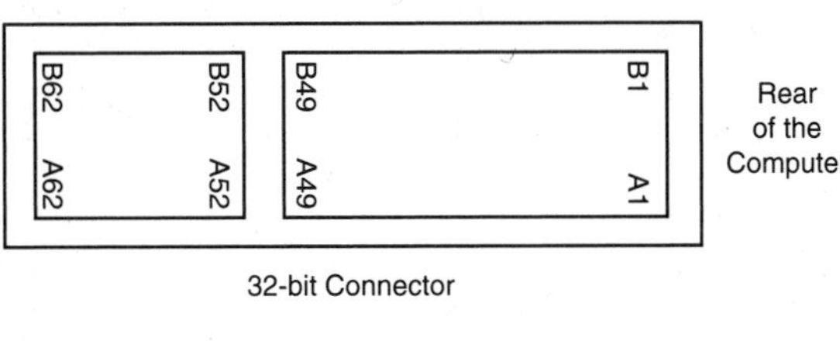

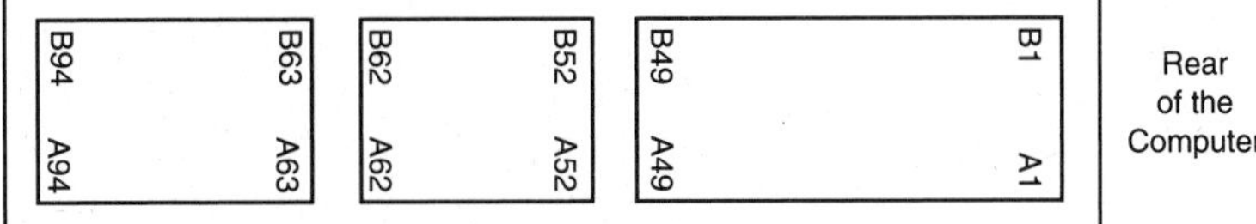

Figure 5.23
The 5-volt PCI slot and card configuration.

Table 5.4 Pinouts for a 3.3-Volt PCI Bus

Pin	Signal Name	Pin	Signal Name
B1	–12V	A1	Test Reset
B2	Test Clock	A2	+12V
B3	Ground	A3	Test Mode Select
B4	Test Data Output	A4	Test Data Input
B5	+5V	A5	+5V
B6	+5V	A6	Interrupt A
B7	Interrupt B	A7	Interrupt C
B8	Interrupt D	A8	+5V
B9	PRSNT1#	A9	Reserved
B10	Reserved	A10	+3.3V
B11	PRSNT2#	A11	Reserved
B12	Access key	A12	Access key
B13	Access key	A13	Access key
B14	Reserved	A14	Reserved
B15	Ground	A15	Reset
B16	Clock	A16	+3.3V
B17	Ground	A17	Grant
B18	Request	A18	Ground
B19	+3.3V	A19	Reserved
B20	Address 31	A20	Address 30
B21	Address 29	A21	+3.3V
B22	Ground	A22	Address 28
B23	Address 27	A23	Address 26
B24	Address 25	A24	Ground
B25	+3.3V	A25	Address 24
B26	C/BE 3	A26	Init Device Select
B27	Address 23	A27	+3.3V
B28	Ground	A28	Address 22
B29	Address 21	A29	Address 20
B30	Address 19	A30	Ground
B31	+3.3V	A31	Address 18
B32	Address 17	A32	Address 16
B33	C/BE 2	A33	+3.3V
B34	Ground	A34	Cycle Frame
B35	Initiator Ready	A35	Ground
B36	+3.3V	A36	Target Ready
B37	Device Select	A37	Ground
B38	Ground	A38	Stop
B39	Lock	A39	+3.3V
B40	Parity Error	A40	Snoop Done

Pin	Signal Name	Pin	Signal Name
B41	+3.3V	A41	Snoop Backoff
B42	System Error	A42	Ground
B43	+3.3V	A43	PAR
B44	C/BE 1	A44	Address 15
B45	Address 14	A45	+3.3V
B46	Ground	A46	Address 13
B47	Address 12	A47	Address 11
B48	Address 10	A48	Ground
B49	Ground	A49	Address 9
B50	Ground	A50	Ground
B51	Ground	A51	Ground
B52	Address 8	A52	C/BE 0
B53	Address 7	A53	+3.3V
B54	+3.3V	A54	Address 6
B55	Address 5	A55	Address 4
B56	Address 3	A56	Ground
B57	Ground	A57	Address 2
B58	Address 1	A58	Address 0
B59	+3.3V	A59	+3.3V
B60	Acknowledge 64-bit	A60	Request 64-bit
B61	+5V	A61	+5V
B62	+5V Access key	A62	+5V Access key
B63	Reserved	A63	Ground
B64	Ground	A64	C/BE 7
B65	C/BE 6	A65	C/BE 5
B66	C/BE 4	A66	+3.3V
B67	Ground	A67	Parity 64-bit
B68	Address 63	A68	Address 62
B69	Address 61	A69	Ground
B70	+3.3V	A70	Address 60
B71	Address 59	A71	Address 58
B72	Address 57	A72	Ground
B73	Ground	A73	Address 56
B74	Address 55	A74	Address 54
B75	Address 53	A75	+3.3V
B76	Ground	A76	Address 52
B77	Address 51	A77	Address 50
B78	Address 49	A78	Ground
B79	+3.3V	A79	Address 48

(continues)

Table 5.4 Continued

Pin	Signal Name	Pin	Signal Name
B80	Address 47	A80	Address 46
B81	Address 45	A81	Ground
B82	Ground	A82	Address 44
B83	Address 43	A83	Address 42
B84	Address 41	A84	+3.3V
B85	Ground	A85	Address 40
B86	Address 39	A86	Address 38
B87	Address 37	A87	Ground
B88	+3.3V	A88	Address 36
B89	Address 35	A89	Address 34
B90	Address 33	A90	Ground
B91	Ground	A91	Address 32
B92	Reserved	A92	Reserved
B93	Reserved	A93	Ground
B94	Ground	A94	Reserved

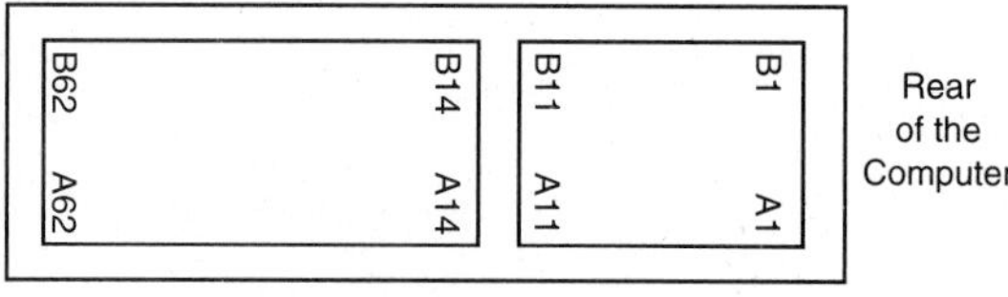

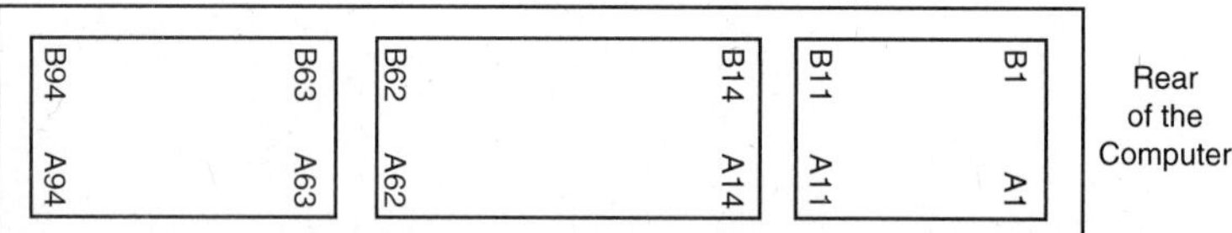

Figure 5.24
The 3.3-volt PCI slot and card configuration.

Table 5.5 Pinouts for a Universal PCI Bus

Pin	Signal Name	Pin	Signal Name
B1	–12V	A1	Test Reset
B2	Test Clock	A2	+12V
B3	Ground	A3	Test Mode Select
B4	Test Data Output	A4	Test Data Input
B5	+5V	A5	+5V

Pin	Signal Name	Pin	Signal Name
B6	+5V	A6	Interrupt A
B7	Interrupt B	A7	Interrupt C
B8	Interrupt D	A8	+5V
B9	PRSNT1#	A9	Reserved
B10	Reserved	A10	+V I/O
B11	PRSNT2#	A11	Reserved
B12	Access key	A12	Access key
B13	Access key	A13	Access key
B14	Reserved	A14	Reserved
B15	Ground	A15	Reset
B16	Clock	A16	+V I/O
B17	Ground	A17	Grant
B18	Request	A18	Ground
B19	+V I/O	A19	Reserved
B20	Address 31	A20	Address 30
B21	Address 29	A21	+3.3V
B22	Ground	A22	Address 28
B23	Address 27	A23	Address 26
B24	Address 25	A24	Ground
B25	+3.3V	A25	Address 24
B26	C/BE 3	A26	Init Device Select
B27	Address 23	A27	+3.3V
B28	Ground	A28	Address 22
B29	Address 21	A29	Address 20
B30	Address 19	A30	Ground
B31	+3.3V	A31	Address 18
B32	Address 17	A32	Address 16
B33	C/BE 2	A33	+3.3V
B34	Ground	A34	Cycle Frame
B35	Initiator Ready	A35	Ground
B36	+3.3V	A36	Target Ready
B37	Device Select	A37	Ground
B38	Ground	A38	Stop
B39	Lock	A39	+3.3V
B40	Parity Error	A40	Snoop Done
B41	+3.3V	A41	Snoop Backoff
B42	System Error	A42	Ground
B43	+3.3V	A43	PAR
B44	C/BE 1	A44	Address 15
B45	Address 14	A45	+3.3V

(continues)

Table 5.5 Continued

Pin	Signal Name	Pin	Signal Name
B46	Ground	A46	Address 13
B47	Address 12	A47	Address 11
B48	Address 10	A48	Ground
B49	Ground	A49	Address 9
B50	Access key	A50	Access key
B51	Access key	A51	Access key
B52	Address 8	A52	C/BE 0
B53	Address 7	A53	+3.3V
B54	+3.3V	A54	Address 6
B55	Address 5	A55	Address 4
B56	Address 3	A56	Ground
B57	Ground	A57	Address 2
B58	Address 1	A58	Address 0
B59	+5 I/O	A59	+V I/O
B60	Acknowledge 64-bit	A60	Request 64-bit
B61	+5V	A61	+5V
B62	+5V Access key	A62	+5V Access key
B63	Reserved	A63	Ground
B64	Ground	A64	C/BE 7
B65	C/BE 6	A65	C/BE 5
B66	C/BE 4	A66	+V I/O
B67	Ground	A67	Parity 64-bit
B68	Address 63	A68	Address 62
B69	Address 61	A69	Ground
B70	+V I/O	A70	Address 60
B71	Address 59	A71	Address 58
B72	Address 57	A72	Ground
B73	Ground	A73	Address 56
B74	Address 55	A74	Address 54
B75	Address 53	A75	+V I/O
B76	Ground	A76	Address 52
B77	Address 51	A77	Address 50
B78	Address 49	A78	Ground
B79	+V I/O	A79	Address 48
B80	Address 47	A80	Address 46
B81	Address 45	A81	Ground
B82	Ground	A82	Address 44
B83	Address 43	A83	Address 42
B84	Address 41	A84	+V I/O

Pin	Signal Name	Pin	Signal Name
B85	Ground	A85	Address 40
B86	Address 39	A86	Address 38
B87	Address 37	A87	Ground
B88	+V I/O	A88	Address 36
B89	Address 35	A89	Address 34
B90	Address 33	A90	Ground
B91	Ground	A91	Address 32
B92	Reserved	A92	Reserved
B93	Reserved	A93	Ground
B94	Ground	A94	Reserved

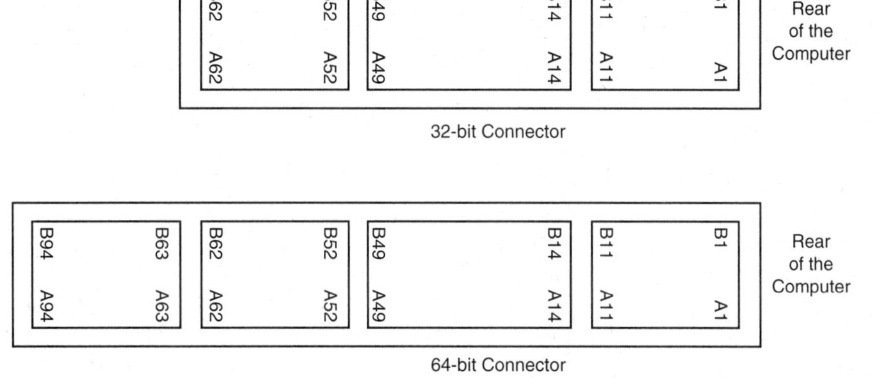

Figure 5.25
The universal PCI slot and card configuration.

Notice that the universal PCI board specifications effectively combine the 5-volt and 3.3-volt specifications. For pins in which the voltage is different, the universal specification labels the pin as V I/O. This type of pin represents a special power pin for defining and driving the PCI signaling rail.

Another important feature of PCI is the fact that it was the model for the Intel Plug and Play (PnP) specification. This means that PCI cards do not have jumpers and switches, and are instead configured through software. True Plug and Play systems will be able to automatically configure the adapters, while non-Plug and Play systems with PCI slots will have to configure the adapters through a program that is usually a part of the system CMOS configuration. Starting in late '95, most PC-compatible systems have included a Plug and Play BIOS that allows the automatic PnP configuration.

The PC-Card (formerly PCMCIA) Bus

In an effort to give laptop and notebook computers the kind of expandability that users have grown used to in desktop systems, the Personal Computer Memory Card

International Association (PCMCIA) has established several standards for credit-card-size expansion boards that fit into a small slot on laptops and notebooks.

http://www.intel.com/product/tech-briefs/pcibus.htm

The PC-Card standards, which were developed by a consortium of more than 300 manufacturers (including IBM, Toshiba, and Apple), have been touted as being a revolutionary advance in mobile computing, because PC-Card laptop and notebook slots enable you to add memory expansion cards, fax/modems, SCSI adapters, local-area-network cards, and many other types of devices. The idea behind PC-Card is to enable you to plug any manufacturer's PC-Card peripheral into your notebook computer.

The promise of the 2.1- by 3.4-inch PC-Card 68-pin cards is enormous. There are not only memory expansion cards, tiny hard drives, and wireless modems, but also wireless LAN connectors, sound cards, CD-ROM controllers, tape backup drives, and a host of other peripherals. Current PC-Card devices cost considerably more than the same devices for ISA desktop systems. In version 2 of the PCMCIA card standard, devices can be longer, which will help manufacturers design some advanced peripheral cards.

PC-Card has just one drawback: the standard has been followed loosely by manufacturers of computers and peripheral devices. If you purchase a laptop or notebook computer with an eye toward expandability, you must do your homework before buying the system; some devices that are advertised as being fully PC-Card-compatible do not work with other systems that advertise themselves as being fully PC-Card-compatible. If you already have a PC-Card-bus computer, the only safe way to buy PC-Card adapters is to contact the device manufacturer and determine whether the device has been tested in your computer. Before you purchase a PC-Card-compatible computer, you should get from the manufacturer a list of devices with which the computer will work.

In an effort to solve these compatibility problems, the PCMCIA has continued to establish standards. At this writing, in fact, four standards exist: PCMCIA Type I through Type IV. Even with all the PC-Card types, compatibility problems remain, mostly because PCMCIA standards are voluntary; some manufacturers do not fully implement these standards before advertising their products as being PCMCIA-compatible. The standards have, however, helped make more and more PCMCIA computers and peripherals compatible with one another, as is the case today.

PC-Card has also been included in the Plug and Play standard. PnP PC-Cards have special drivers that can wake up when their adapter is inserted. To be PnP compatible, a PC-Card should be hot-swappable, which means you can remove it and install a different card without powering down or even rebooting the system.

http://www.sunsetdirect.com/clients/companyinfo/tdk/Industry.html

http://www.toshiba.com/tais/csd/support/files/information/faq/pcmcia.faq

http://www.pc.ibm.com/answerbk/ntu38.html

The following list describes the major features of the PCMCIA standards:

- *PCMCIA Type I.* The original PC-Card standard, now called Type I slots, can handle cards that are 3.3mm thick. These slots work only with memory expansion cards. If you are shopping for a PCMCIA memory expansion card, check with your system manufacturer before buying to ensure that the card you buy will work with your system.

- *PCMCIA Type II.* PCMCIA Type II slots accommodate cards that are 5mm thick but otherwise have the same physical form factor as Type I cards. PCMCIA Type II slots also can be used with Type I cards, because the guides that hold the cards are the same thickness; the center portion of the slot provides more room. Type II cards support virtually any type of expansion device (such as a modem) or LAN adapter.

- *PCMCIA Type III.* In late 1992, PCMCIA Type III was introduced. These slots, intended primarily for computers that have removable hard drives, are 10.5mm thick, but they also are compatible with Type I and Type II cards.

- *PCMCIA Type IV.* PCMCIA Type IV slots are intended to be used with hard drives that are thicker than the 10.5mm Type III slot allows. The exact dimensions of the slot have not yet been determined, but Type IV slots are expected to be compatible with Types I through III.

Table 5.6 shows the PCMCIA pinouts.

Table 5.6 Pinouts for a PCMCIA Card

Pin	Signal Name	Pin	Signal Name
1	Ground	18	Vpp1
2	Data 3	19	Address 16
3	Data 4	20	Address 15
4	Data 5	21	Address 12
5	Data 6	22	Address 7
6	Data 7	23	Address 6
7	–Card Enable 1	24	Address 5
8	Address 10	25	Address 4
9	–Output Enable	26	Address 3
10	Address 11	27	Address 2
11	Address 9	28	Address 1
12	Address 8	29	Address 0
13	Address 13	30	Data 0
14	Address 14	31	Data 1
15	–Write Enable/–Program	32	Data 2
16	Ready/–Busy (IREQ)	33	Write Protect (–IOIS16)
17	+5V	34	Ground

(continues)

Table 5.6 Continued

Pin	Signal Name	Pin	Signal Name
35	Ground	52	Vpp2
36	–Card Detect 1	53	Address 22
37	Data 11	54	Address 23
38	Data 12	55	Address 24
39	Data 13	56	Address 25
40	Data 14	57	RFU
41	Data 15	58	RESET
42	–Card Enable 2	59	–WAIT
43	Refresh	60	RFU (–INPACK)
44	RFU (–IOR)	61	–Register Select
45	RFU (–IOW)	62	Battery Voltage Detect 2 (–SPKR)
46	Address 17	63	Battery Voltage Detect 1 (–STSCHG)
47	Address 18	64	Data 8
48	Address 19	65	Data 9
49	Address 20	66	Data 10
50	Address 21	67	–Card Detect 2
51	+5V	68	Ground

System Resources

System resources are the communications channels, addresses, and other signals used by hardware devices to communicate on the bus. At their lowest level, these resources typically include the following:

- Memory addresses
- IRQ (Interrupt ReQuest) channels
- DMA (Direct Memory Access) channels
- I/O Port addresses

I have listed these roughly in the order you would experience problems with them. Memory conflicts are perhaps the most troublesome of these, certainly the most difficult to fully explain and overcome. These are discussed in Chapter 7 ("Memory"). In this chapter we will focus on the others listed here, and in the order you will likely have problems with them. IRQs cause more problems than DMA; since they are in much higher demand, virtually all cards will use IRQ channels. There are fewer problems with DMA channels since few cards use them, and there are usually more than enough channels to go around. I/O Ports are used by all hardware devices on the bus, but there are technically 64K of them, which means plenty to go around. With all of these resources, you have to make sure that a unique card or hardware function uses each resource—they cannot or should not be shared.

These resources are required and used by many different components of your system. Adapter cards need these resources to communicate with your system and to accomplish their purposes. Not all adapter cards have the same resource requirements. A serial communications port, for example, needs an IRQ channel and I/O port address, whereas a sound board needs these resources and at least one DMA channel as well. Most network cards use a 16K block of memory addresses, an IRQ channel, and an I/O Port address.

As your system increases in complexity, the chance for resource conflicts increases dramatically. Modern systems with sound cards and network cards can really push the envelope and can become a configuration nightmare for the un-initiated. So that you can resolve conflicts, most adapter cards allow you to modify resource assignments by setting jumpers or switches on the cards. Fortunately, in almost all cases there is a logical way to configure the system, once you know the rules.

Interrupts (IRQs)

Interrupt request channels (IRQs), or hardware interrupts, are used by various hardware devices to signal the motherboard that a request must be fulfilled. This procedure is the same as a student raising his hand to indicate that he needs attention.

These interrupt channels are represented by wires on the motherboard and in the slot connectors. When a particular interrupt is invoked, a special routine takes over the system, which first saves all the CPU register contents in a stack and then directs the system to the interrupt vector table. This vector table contains a list of memory addresses that correspond to the interrupt channels. Depending on which interrupt was invoked, the program corresponding to that channel is run.

The pointers in the vector table point to the address of whatever software driver is used to service the card that generated the interrupt. For a network card, for example, the vector may point to the address of the network drivers that have been loaded to operate the card; for a hard disk controller, the vector may point to the BIOS code that operates the controller.

After the particular software routine finishes performing whatever function the card needed, the interrupt-control software returns the stack contents to the CPU registers, and the system then resumes whatever it was doing before the interrupt occurred.

Through the use of interrupts, your system can respond to external events in a timely fashion. Each time that a serial port presents a byte to your system, an interrupt is generated to ensure that the system reads that byte before another comes in.

Hardware interrupts are generally prioritized by their numbers; with some exceptions, the highest-priority interrupts have the lowest numbers. Higher-priority interrupts take precedence over lower-priority interrupts by interrupting them. As a result, several interrupts can occur in your system concurrently, each interrupt nesting within another.

If you overload the system—in this case, by running out of stack resources (too many interrupts were generated too quickly)—an internal stack overflow error occurs, and your system halts. If you experience this type of system error, you can compensate for it by using the STACKS parameter in your CONFIG.SYS file to increase the available stack resources.

The ISA bus uses edge-triggered interrupt sensing, in which an interrupt is sensed by a signal sent on a particular wire located in the slot connector. A different wire corresponds to each possible hardware interrupt. Because the motherboard cannot recognize which slot contains the card that used an interrupt line and therefore generated the interrupt, confusion would result if more than one card were set to use a particular interrupt. Each interrupt, therefore, usually is designated for a single hardware device, and most of the time, interrupts cannot be shared.

A device can be designed to share interrupts, and a few devices allow this; most cannot, however, because of the way interrupts are signaled in the ISA bus. Systems with the MCA bus use level-sensitive interrupts, which allow complete interrupt sharing to occur. In fact, in an MCA system, all boards can be set to the same interrupt with no conflicts or problems. The EISA bus can optionally use level-sensitive interrupts which allow sharing, but only for true EISA cards. For maximum performance, however, interrupts should be staggered as much as possible.

External hardware interrupts often are referred to as maskable interrupts, which simply means that the interrupts can be masked or turned off for a short time while the CPU is used for other critical operations. It is up to the programmer to manage interrupts properly and efficiently for the best system performance.

Because interrupts usually cannot be shared in an ISA bus system, you often run into conflicts and can even run out of interrupts when you are adding boards to a system. If two boards use the same IRQ to signal the system, the resulting conflict prevents either board from operating properly. The following sections discuss the IRQs that any standard devices use, as well as what may be free in your system.

8-Bit ISA Bus Interrupts. The PC and XT (the systems based on the 8-bit 8086 CPU) provide for eight different external hardware interrupts. Table 5.7 shows the typical uses for these interrupts, which are numbered 0 through 7.

Table 5.7 8-Bit ISA Bus Default Interrupt Assignments

IRQ	Function	Bus Slot
0	System Timer	No
1	Keyboard Controller	No
2	Available	Yes (8-bit)
3	Serial Port 2 (COM2:)	Yes (8-bit)
4	Serial Port 1 (COM1:)	Yes (8-bit)
5	Hard Disk Controller	Yes (8-bit)
6	Floppy Disk Controller	Yes (8-bit)
7	Parallel Port 1 (LPT1:)	Yes (8-bit)

If you have a system that has one of the original 8-bit ISA buses, you will find that the IRQ resources provided by the system present a severe limitation. Installing several devices that need the services of system IRQs in a PC/XT-type system can be a study in frustration, because the only way to resolve the interrupt-shortage problem is to remove the adapter board that you need the least.

16-Bit ISA, EISA, and MCA Bus Interrupts. The introduction of the AT, based on the 286 processor, was accompanied by an increase in the number of external hardware interrupts that the bus would support. The number of interrupts was doubled (to 16) by using two Intel 8259 interrupt controllers, piping the interrupts generated by the second one through the unused IRQ 2 in the first controller. This arrangement effectively means that only 15 IRQ assignments are available, and IRQ 2 effectively became inaccessible.

By routing all of the interrupts from the 2nd IRQ controller through IRQ 2 on the first, all of these new interrupts are assigned a nested priority level between IRQ 1 and IRQ 3. Thus IRQ 15 ends up having a higher priority than IRQ 3. Figure 5.26 shows how the two 8259 chips were wired to create the cascade through IRQ 2 on the first chip.

To prevent problems with boards set to use IRQ 2, the AT system designers routed one of the new interrupts (IRQ 9) to fill the slot position left open after removing IRQ 2. This means that any card you install in a modern system that claims to use IRQ 2 is really using IRQ 9 instead. Some cards now label this selection as IRQ 2/9, while others may only call it IRQ 2 or IRQ 9. No matter what the labeling says, you must never set two cards to use that interrupt!

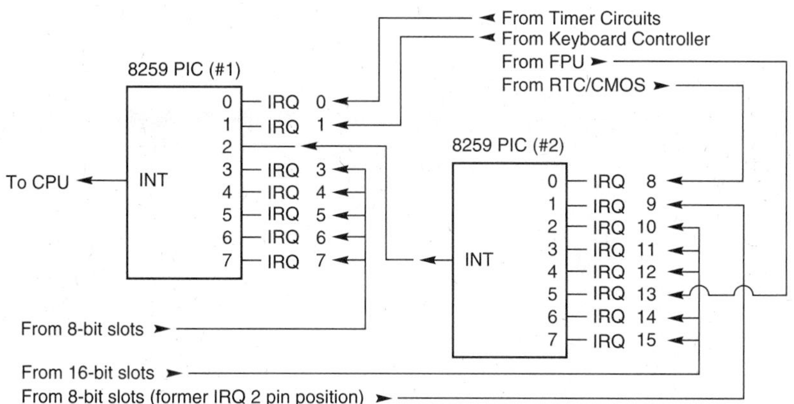

CPU = Central Processing Unit
FPU = Floating Point Unit
PIC = Programmable Interrupt Controller
RTC = Real Time Clock
CMOS = Complimentary Metal Oxide Semiconductor
INT = Interrupt (Prioritized)IRQ = Interrupt ReQuest (from the Bus)

Figure 5.26

Interrupt controller cascade wiring.

Table 5.8 shows the typical uses for interrupts in the 16-bit ISA, EISA, and MCA buses, and lists them in priority order from highest to lowest.

Because IRQ 2 now is used directly by the motherboard, the wire for IRQ 9 has been rerouted to the same position in the slot that IRQ 2 normally would occupy. Therefore, any board you install that is set to IRQ 2 actually is using IRQ 9. The interrupt vector table has been adjusted accordingly to enable this deception to work. This adjustment to the system provides greater compatibility with the PC interrupt structure and enables cards that are set to IRQ 2 to work properly.

Notice that interrupts 0, 1, 2, 8, and 13 are not on the bus connectors and are not accessible to adapter cards. Interrupts 8, 10, 11, 12, 13, 14, and 15 are from the second interrupt controller and are accessible only by boards that use the 16-bit extension connector, because this is where these wires are located. IRQ 9 is rewired to the 8-bit slot connector in place of IRQ 2, which means that IRQ 9 replaces IRQ 2 and therefore is available to 8-bit cards, which treat it as though it were IRQ 2.

Note

Although the 16-bit ISA bus has twice as many interrupts as systems that have the 8-bit ISA bus, you still may run out of available interrupts, because only 16-bit adapters can use most of the newly available interrupts.

Table 5.8 16-Bit ISA, EISA, and MCA Default Interrupt Assignments

IRQ	Standard Function	Bus Slot	Card Type
0	System Timer	No	—
1	Keyboard Controller	No	—
2	2nd IRQ Controller Cascade	No	—
8	Real-Time Clock	No	—
9	Network/Available (Appears as IRQ 2)	Yes	8/16-bit
10	Available	Yes	16-bit
11	SCSI/Available	Yes	16-bit
12	Motherboard Mouse Port/Available	Yes	16-bit
13	Math Coprocessor	No	—
14	Primary IDE	Yes	16-bit
15	Secondary IDE/Available	Yes	16-bit
3	Serial Port 2 (COM2:)	Yes	8/16-bit
4	Serial Port 1 (COM1:)	Yes	8/16-bit
5	Sound/Parallel Port 2 (LPT2:)	Yes	8/16-bit
6	Floppy Disk Controller	Yes	8/16-bit
7	Parallel Port 1 (LPT1:)	Yes	8/16-bit

The extra IRQ lines in a 16-bit ISA system are of little help unless the adapter boards that you plan to use enable you to configure them for one of the unused IRQs. Some devices are hard-wired so that they can use only a particular IRQ. If you have a device that already uses that IRQ, you must resolve the conflict before installing the second adapter. If neither adapter enables you to reconfigure its IRQ use, chances are that you cannot use the two devices in the same system.

IRQ Conflicts. One of the most common areas of IRQ conflict involves serial (COM) ports. You may have noticed in the preceding two sections that two IRQs are set aside for two COM ports. IRQ 3 is used for COM2, and IRQ 4 is used for COM1. The problem occurs when you have more than two serial ports in a system—a situation that is entirely possible, because a PC can support up to four COM ports.

The problems arise here because most people purchase poorly designed COM port boards that do not allow IRQ settings other than 3 or 4. What happens is that they end up setting COM3: to IRQ 4 (sharing it with COM1:), and COM4: to IRQ 3 (sharing it with COM2:). This is not acceptable as it will prevent you from using the two COM ports on any one of the interrupt channels simultaneously. This was somewhat acceptable under plain DOS, since single tasking (running only one program at a time) was the order of the day, but is totally unacceptable with Windows and OS/2.

The proper solution to having more than two COM ports is to purchase COM boards that allow IRQ settings other than just 3 or 4. As a side note, also make sure that the COM board you purchase uses the buffered 16550A type UART (Universal Asynchronous Receiver Transmitter) chip rather than the slow un-buffered 16450 types. One company providing specialized high quality COM boards is ByteRunner Technologies (see the vendor list in Appendix B).

If a device listed in the table is not present, such as the motherboard mouse port (IRQ 12), or parallel port 2 (IRQ 5), then you can consider those interrupts as available. For example, a second parallel port is a rarity, and most systems will have a sound card installed and set for IRQ 5.

DMA Channels

DMA (direct memory access) channels are used by high-speed communications devices that must send and receive information at high speed. A serial or parallel port does not use a DMA channel, but a sound card or SCSI adapter often does. DMA channels sometimes can be shared if the devices are not of the type that would need them simultaneously. For example, you can have a network adapter and a tape backup adapter sharing DMA channel 1, but you cannot back up while the network is running. To back up during network operation, you must ensure that each adapter uses a unique DMA channel.

8-Bit ISA Bus DMA Channels. In the 8-bit ISA bus, four DMA channels support high-speed data transfers between I/O devices and memory. Three of the channels are available to the expansion slots. Table 5.9 shows the typical uses of these DMA channels.

Table 5.9 8-Bit ISA Default DMA-Channel Assignments

DMA	Standard Function	Bus Slot
0	Dynamic RAM Refresh	No
1	Available	Yes (8-bit)
2	Floppy disk controller	Yes (8-bit)
3	Hard disk controller	Yes (8-bit)

Because most systems typically have both a floppy and hard disk drive, only one DMA channel is available in 8-bit ISA systems.

16-Bit ISA DMA Channels. Since the introduction of the 286 CPU, the ISA bus has supported eight DMA channels, with seven channels available to the expansion slots. Like the expanded IRQ lines described earlier in this chapter, the added DMA channels were created by cascading a second DMA controller to the first one. DMA channel 4 is used to cascade channels 0 through 3 to the microprocessor. Channels 0 through 3 are available for 8-bit transfers, and channels 5 through 7 are for 16-bit transfers only. Table 5.10 shows the typical uses for the DMA channels.

The only standard DMA channel used in all systems is DMA 2, which is universally used by the floppy controller. DMA 4 is not usable, and does not appear in the bus slots. DMA channels 1 and 5 are most commonly used by sound cards such as the Sound Blaster 16. These cards use both an 8-bit and a 16-bit DMA channel for high-speed transfers.

Note that although DMA channel 0 appears in a 16-bit slot connector extension, and therefore can only be used by a 16-bit card, it only does 8-bit transfers! You will not see DMA 0 appearing as a choice on most 16-bit cards, since they would not want to be running in an 8-bit mode. Most 16-bit cards (like SCSI host adapters) that use DMA channels will have their choices limited to DMA 5 through 7.

Table 5.10 16-Bit ISA, EISA, and MCA Default DMA-Channel Assignments

DMA	Standard Function	Bus Slot	Card Type	Transfer
0	Available	Yes	16-bit	8-bit
1	Sound/Available	Yes	8/16-bit	8-bit
2	Floppy Disk Controller	Yes	8/16-bit	8-bit
3	ECP Parallel/Available	Yes	8/16-bit	8-bit
4	1st DMA Controller Cascade	No	——	16-bit
5	Sound/Available	Yes	16-bit	16-bit
6	SCSI/Available	Yes	16-bit	16-bit
7	Available	Yes	16-bit	16-bit

EISA. Realizing the shortcomings inherent in the way DMA channels are implemented in the ISA bus, the creators of the EISA specification created a specific DMA controller for their new bus. They increased the number of address lines to include the entire address bus, thus allowing transfers anywhere within the address space of the system. Each DMA channel can be set to run either 8-, 16-, or 32-bit transfers. In addition, each DMA channel can be separately programmed to run any of four types of bus cycles when transferring data:

- *Compatible*. This transfer method is included to match the same DMA timing as used in the ISA bus. This is done for compatibility reasons; all ISA cards can operate in an EISA system in this transfer mode.
- *Type A*. This transfer type compresses the DMA timing by 25 percent over the Compatible method. It was designed to run with most (but not all) ISA cards and still yield a speed increase.
- *Type B*. This transfer type compresses timing by 50 percent over the Compatible method. Using this method, most EISA cards function properly, but only a few ISA cards will be problem-free.
- *Type C*. This transfer method compresses timing by 87.5 percent over the Compatible method; it is the fastest DMA transfer method available under the EISA specification. No ISA cards will work using this transfer method.

EISA DMA also allows for special reading and writing operations referred to as scatter write and gather read. Scattered writes are done by reading a contiguous block of data and writing it to more than one area of memory at the same time. Gathered reads involve reading from more than one place in memory and writing to a device. These functions are often referred to as Buffered Chaining and they increase the throughput of DMA operations.

MCA. It might be assumed that because MCA is a complete rebuilding of the PC Bus structure that DMA in an MCA environment would be better constructed. This is not so. Quite to the contrary, DMA in MCA systems were for the most part all designed around one DMA controller with the following issues:

- It can only connect to two 8-bit data paths. This can only transfer one or two bytes per bus cycle.
- It is only connected to AO:A23 on the address bus. This means it can only make use of the lower 16M of memory.
- It runs at 10MHz.

The inability of the DMA controller to address more than two bytes per transfer severely cripples this otherwise powerful bus.

I/O Port Addresses

Your computer's I/O ports enable you to attach a large number of important devices to your system to expand its capabilities. A printer attached to one of your system's LPT (parallel) ports enables you to make a printout of the work on your system. A modem attached to one of your system's COM (serial) ports enables you to use telephone lines to communicate with computers thousands of miles away. A scanner attached to an LPT port or a SCSI host adapter enables you to convert graphics or text to images and type that you can use with the software installed on your computer.

Most systems come configured with at least two COM (serial) ports and one LPT (parallel printer) ports. The two serial ports are configured as COM1 and COM2, and the parallel port is configured as LPT1. The basic architecture of the PC provides for as many as four COM ports (1 through 4) and three LPT ports (1 through 3). If you use more than two COM ports, make sure that COM3 and COM4 have unique IRQ settings and do not share those with COM1 and COM2. Many older boards do not allow unique IRQ settings for COM3 and COM4 and should be avoided.

Caution

Theoretically, each of the four COM ports in a system can be used to attach a device, such as a mouse or modem, but doing so may lead to resource conflicts. For more information, see the discussion of resolving IRQ conflicts later in this chapter.

Every I/O port in your system uses an I/O address for communication. This address, which is in the lower memory ranges, is reserved for communication between the I/O device and the operating system. If your system has multiple I/O cards, each card must use a different I/O address; if not, your system will not be able to communicate with the devices reliably.

The I/O addresses that your ports use depend on the type of ports. Table 5.11 shows the I/O addresses expected by the various standard ports in a PC system.

Besides your serial and parallel ports, other adapters in your system use I/O addresses. Quite truthfully, the I/O addresses for the serial and parallel ports are fairly standard; it is unlikely that you will run into problems with them. The I/O addresses used by other adapters are not standardized, however, and you may have problems finding a mix of port addresses that works reliably. Later in this chapter, in "Resolving Resource Conflicts," you learn some of the techniques that you can use to solve this problem.

Table 5.11 Standard I/O Addresses for Serial and Parallel Ports

Port	Base I/O Address
COM1	3F8h
COM2	2F8h
COM3	3E8h
COM4	2E8h
LPT1	3BCh or 378h
LPT2	378h or 278h
LPT3	278h only

Resolving Resource Conflicts

The resources in a system are limited. Unfortunately, the demands on those resources seem to be unlimited. As you add more and more adapter cards to your system, you will find that the potential for resource conflicts increases. If your system does not have a bus that resolves conflicts for you (such as an MCA or EISA bus), you need to resolve the conflicts manually.

How do you know whether you have a resource conflict? Typically, one of the devices in your system stops working. Resource conflicts can exhibit themselves in other ways, though. Any of the following events could be diagnosed as a resource conflict:

- A device transfers data inaccurately.
- Your system frequently locks up.
- Your sound card doesn't sound quite right.
- Your mouse doesn't work.
- Garbage appears on your video screen for no apparent reason.
- Your printer prints gibberish.
- You cannot format a floppy disk.
- The PC starts in Safe Mode (Win 95).

In the following sections, you learn some of the steps that you can take to head off resource conflicts or to track them down when they occur.

Caution

Be careful in diagnosing resource conflicts; a problem may not be a resource conflict at all, but a computer virus. Many computer viruses are designed to exhibit themselves as glitches or as periodic problems. If you suspect a resource conflict, it may be worthwhile to run a virus check first to ensure that the system is clean. This procedure could save you hours of work and frustration.

Resolving Conflicts Manually

Unfortunately, the only way to resolve conflicts manually is to take the cover off your system and start changing switches or jumper settings on your adapter cards. Each of these changes then must be accompanied by a system reboot, which implies that they take a great deal of time. This situation brings us to the first rule of resolving conflicts: when you set about ridding your system of resource conflicts, make sure that you allow a good deal of uninterrupted time.

Also make sure that you write down your current system settings before you start making changes. That way, you will know where you began and can go back to the original configuration (if necessary).

Finally, dig out the manuals for all your adapter boards; you will need them. If you cannot find the manuals, contact the manufacturers to determine what the various jumper positions and switch settings mean.

Now you are ready to begin your detective work. As you try various switch settings and jumper positions, keep the following questions in mind; the answers will help you narrow down the conflict areas.

- When did the conflict first become apparent? If the conflict occurred after you installed a new adapter card, that new card probably is causing the conflict. If the conflict occurred after you started using new software, chances are good that the software uses a device that is taxing your system's resources in a new way.
- Are there two similar devices in your system that do not work? If your modem and mouse do not work, for example, chances are good that these devices are conflicting with each other.
- Have other people had the same problem, and if so, how did they resolve it? Public forums—such as those on CompuServe, Internet, and America Online—are great places to find other users who may be able to help you solve the conflict.

Whenever you make changes in your system, reboot and see whether the problem persists. When you believe that you have solved the problem, make sure that you test all your software. Fixing one problem often seems to cause another to crop up. The only way to make sure that all problems are resolved is to test everything in your system.

As you attempt to resolve your resource conflicts, you should work with and update a system-configuration template, as discussed in the following section.

Using a System-Configuration Template

A system-configuration template is helpful, simply because it is easier to remember something that is written down than it is to keep it in your head. To create a configuration template, all you need to do is start writing down what resources are used by which parts of your system. Then, when you need to make a change or add an adapter, you can quickly determine where conflicts may arise.

I like to use a worksheet split into three main areas: one is for Interrupts, another for DMA channels, and a middle area for devices that do not use interrupts. Each section lists the IRQ or DMA channel on the left and the I/O Port device range on the right. This way you get the clearest picture of what resources are used and which ones are available in a given system.

Figure 5.27 shows the system-configuration template I have developed over the years and still use almost daily. This type of configuration sheet is resource based, instead of component based. Each row in the template represents a different resource and lists the component using the resource as well as the resources used. The chart has pre-entered all of the fixed items in a modern PC, whose configuration cannot be changed.

System Resource Worksheet

PC Make and Model: ______________________

Serial Number: ______________________

Date of Last Revision: ______________________

System Interrupts:	I/O Port Addresses:
0 - Timer Circuits....................	040-05F....................
1 - Keyboard Controller....................	060 & 064....................
2 - Second 8259 IRQ Controller....................	0A0-0BF....................
8 - Real-Time Clock / CMOS RAM....................	070-07F....................
9 - ______________________	______________
10 - ______________________	______________
11 - ______________________	______________
12 - ______________________	______________
13 - Math Coprocessor (N/A in Bus Slot)....................	0F0-0FF....................
14 - ______________________	______________
15 - ______________________	______________
3 - ______________________	______________
4 - ______________________	______________
5 - ______________________	______________
6 - ______________________	______________
7 - ______________________	______________

Devices not Using Interrupts:	I/O Port Addresses:
Mono/EGA/VGA Standard Ports....................	3B0-3BB....................
EGA/VGA Standard Ports....................	3C0-3CF....................
CGA/EGA/VGA Standard Ports....................	3D0-3DF....................
______________________	______________
______________________	______________
______________________	______________
______________________	______________
______________________	______________

DMA Channels:

0 - ______________________

1 - ______________________

2 - ______________________

3 - ______________________

4 - Cascade DMA Channels 0-3 (N/A in Bus Slot)...

5 - ______________________

6 - ______________________

7 - ______________________

Figure 5.27

The system-configuration template.

To fill out this type of chart, you would perform the following steps:

1. First enter the default resources used by standard components, such as serial and parallel ports, disk controllers, and video. You can use the filled out example I have provided to see how most standard devices are configured.

2. Then enter the default resources used by additional add-on components such as Sound cards, SCSI cards, Network cards, proprietary cards, and so forth.

3. Finally, change any configuration items that are in conflict. Try to leave built-in devices at their default settings, as well as sound cards. Other installed adapters may have their settings changed, but be sure to document the changes.

Of course a template like this is best used when first installing components, not after. Once you have the template completely filled out to match your system, you can label it and keep it with the system. When you add any more devices, the template will be your guide as to how any new devices should be configured.

Figure 5.28 shows is the same template filled out for a typical modern PC system.

As you can see from this template, only two IRQs and two DMA channels remain available. In this example configuration, the following devices were built-in to the motherboard:

Primary and Secondary IDE connectors

- Floppy controller
- 2 Serial Ports
- 1 Parallel Port

Whether these devices are built-in to the motherboard or on a separate card makes no difference, since the resource allocations are the same in either case. All default settings are normally used for these devices, and are indicated in the completed configuration. Next the accessory cards were configured. In this example, the following cards were installed:

- SVGA Video card (ATI Mach 64)
- Sound card (Creative Labs Sound Blaster 16)
- SCSI host adapter (Adaptec AHA-1542CF)
- Network interface card (SMC EtherEZ)

System Resource Worksheet

PC Make and Model: Intel Advanced ZP

Serial Number: 100000

Date of Last Revision: 7/5/95

System Interrupts:	I/O Port Addresses:
0 - Timer Circuits	040-05F
1 - Keyboard Controller	060 & 064
2 - Second 8259 IRQ Controller	0A0-0BF
8 - Real-Time Clock / CMOS RAM	070-07F
9 - SMC EtherEZ Ethernet card*	340-35F
10 -	
11 - Adaptec 1542CF SCSI adapter (scanner, tape)	334-337*
12 -	
13 - Math Coprocessor (N/A in Bus Slot)	0F0-0FF
14 - Primary IDE (Hard Disk 1 and 2)	1F0-1F7
15 - Secondary IDE (IDE CD-ROM drive)	170-177
3 - Serial Port 2 (COM2: Serial Mouse)	3F8-3FF
4 - Serial Port 1 (COM1: External Modem)	2F8-2FF
5 - Sound Blaster 16 Audio	220-233
6 - Floppy Controller	3F0-3F7
7 - Parallel Port 1 (LPT1: used by Printer)	378-37F

Devices not Using Interrupts:	I/O Port Addresses:
Mono/EGA/VGA Standard Ports	3B0-3BB
EGA/VGA Standard Ports	3C0-3CF
CGA/EGA/VGA Standard Ports	3D0-3DF
ATI Mach 64 SVGA Additional Ports	102,1CE,1CF,2EC-2EF
Sound Blaster 16 MIDI Port	330-331
Sound Blaster 16 Game Port (Joystick connector)	200-207
Sound Blaster 16 FM Synthesizer (Music)	388-38B

DMA Channels:

0 -
1 - Sound Blaster 16 (Low DMA)
2 - Floppy Controller
3 - Parallel Port 1 (EPP/ECP mode)
4 - Cascade DMA Channels 0-3 (N/A in Bus Slot)
5 - Sound Blaster 16 (High DMA)
6 - Adaptec 1542CF SCSI adapter*
7 -

**Represents a resource setting that had to be changed to avoid a conflict.*

Figure 5.28

The same system-configuration template for a typical PC.

It helps to install the cards in this order. Start with the video card, and next add the sound card. Due to problems with software that must be configured to the sound card, it is best to install it early and make sure only default settings are used. It is better to change settings on cards other than the sound card. After the sound card, the SCSI adapter was installed; however, the default I/O Port addresses (330-331) and DMA channel (DMA 5) used were in conflict with other cards (mainly the sound card). These settings were changed to their next logical settings, which did not cause a conflict. Finally the network card was installed, which also had default settings that conflicted with other cards. In this case, the ethernet card came preconfigured to IRQ 3, which was already in use by COM2:. The solution was to change the setting, and IRQ 9 was the next logical choice in the card's configuration settings.

Even though this is a fully loaded configuration, only three individual items among all of the cards had to be changed to achieve an optimum system configuration. As you can see, using a configuration template like the one shown can make what would otherwise be a jumble of settings seem to lay out in an easy-to-follow manner. The only real problems you will run into once you work with these templates are cards that do not allow for enough adjustment in their settings, or cards that are lacking in documentation. As you can imagine, you will need the documentation for each adapter card, as well as the motherboard, in order to accurately complete a configuration table like the one shown.

Do not rely too much on software diagnostics, such as MSD.EXE, that claim to be able to show hardware settings like IRQ and I/O Port settings. While they can be helpful in certain situations, they are often wrong with respect to at least some of the information they are displaying about your system. One or two items shown incorrectly can be very troublesome if you believe the incorrect information and configure your system based on it! Unless your system fully supports Plug and Play (PnP), there is simply no standard way for software to determine resource usage in a PC system. In a non-PnP system, these programs will instead guess at how things are configured and display these guesses with confidence, even though they may be incorrect.

Heading Off Problems: Special Boards

A number of devices that you may want to install in a computer system require IRQ lines or DMA channels, which means that a world of conflict could be waiting in the box that the device comes in. As mentioned in the preceding section, you can save yourself problems if you use a system-configuration template to keep track of the way that your system is configured.

You also can save yourself trouble by carefully reading the documentation for a new adapter board before you attempt to install it. The documentation details the IRQ lines that the board can use, as well as its DMA-channel requirements. In addition, the documentation will detail the adapter's upper-memory needs for ROM and adapter.

The following sections describe some of the conflicts that you may encounter when you install today's most popular adapter boards. Although the list of adapter boards covered in these sections is far from comprehensive, the sections serve as a guide to installing complex hardware with minimum hassle. Included are tips on sound boards, SCSI host adapters, and network adapters.

Sound Boards. Sound cards are probably the biggest single resource hog in your system. They usually use at least one IRQ, two DMA channels, and multiple I/O Port address ranges. This is because a sound card is actually several different pieces of hardware all on one board. Most sound cards are similar to the Sound Blaster 16 from Creative Labs.

Figure 5.29 shows the default resources used by the components on a typical Sound Blaster 16 card.

As you can see, these cards use quite a few resources. If you take the time to read your sound board's documentation and determine its communications-channel needs, compare those needs to the IRQ lines and DMA channels that already are in use in your system, and then change the settings of the other adapters to avoid conflicts with the sound card, your installation will go quickly and smoothly.

Device	Interrupt	I/O Ports	16-bit DMA	8-bit DMA
Audio	IRQ5	220h-233h	DMA 5	DMA 1

Device	Interrupt
MIDI Port	330h-331h
FM Synthesizer	388h-38Bh
Game Port	200h-207h

Figure 5.29

Default resources for Sound Blaster 16 card.

Tip

The greatest single piece of advice I can give you for installing a sound card is to put the sound card in before all other cards, except for video. In other words, let the sound card retain all of its default settings; never change a resource setting to prevent a conflict. Instead, always change the settings of other adapters when a conflict with the sound card arises. The problem here is that many educational and game programs that use sound are very poorly written with respect to supporting alternate resource settings on sound cards. Save yourself some grief and let the sound card have its way!

One example of a potential sound-board conflict is the combination of a Sound Blaster 16 and an Adaptec SCSI adapter. The Sound and SCSI adapters will conflict on DMA 5 as well as on I/O Ports 330-331. Rather than changing the settings of the sound card, it is best to alter the SCSI adapter to the next available settings that will not conflict with the sound card or anything else. The final settings were shown in the previous configuration template.

The cards in question (Sound Blaster 16 and AHA-1542CF) are not singled out here because there is something wrong with them, but instead because they happen to be the most popular cards of their respective types, and as such will often be paired together.

On the Web

http://www.creat.com/wwwnew/complex/products/ps_sound.html

SCSI Adapter Boards. SCSI adapter boards use more resources than just about any other type of add-in device except perhaps a sound card. They will often use resources that are in conflict with sound cards or network cards. A typical SCSI host adapter requires an IRQ line, a DMA channel, a range of I/O Port addresses, and a 16K range of unused upper memory for its ROM and possible scratch-pad RAM use. Fortunately the typical SCSI adapter is also easy to reconfigure, and changing any of these settings should not affect performance or software operation.

Before installing a SCSI adapter, be sure to read the documentation for the card, and make sure that any IRQ lines, DMA channels, I/O Ports, and upper memory that the card needs are available. If the system resources that the card needs are already in use, use your system-configuration template to determine how you can alter the settings on the SCSI card or other cards to prevent any resource conflicts before you attempt to plug in the adapter card.

On the Web

http://www.adaptec.com/

Network Interface Cards (NICs). Networks are becoming more and more popular all the time. A typical network adapter does not require as many resources as some of the other cards discussed here, but will require at least a range of I/O Port addresses and an interrupt. Most NICs will also require a 16K range of free Upper Memory to be used for the RAM transfer buffer on the network card. As with any other cards, make sure that all of these resources are unique to the card, and are not shared with any other devices.

Multiple-COM-Port Adapters. A serial port adapter usually has two or more ports on-board. These COM ports require an interrupt and a range of I/O Ports each. There are not many problems with the I/O Port addresses, since the ranges used by up to four COM ports in a system are fairly well defined. The real problem is with the interrupts. Most older installations of more than two serial ports have any additional ones sharing the same interrupts as the first two. This is incorrect, and will cause nothing but problems with software that runs under Windows or OS/2. Always make sure that each serial port in your system has a unique I/O Port address range, and more importantly, a unique interrupt setting.

Because COM ports are required for so many peripherals that connect to the modern PC, and because the number of COM ports that can be used is strictly limited by the IRQ setup in the basic IBM system design, special COM-port cards are available that enable you to assign a unique IRQ to each of the four COM ports on the card. For example, you can use such a card to leave COM1 and COM2 configured for IRQ 4 and IRQ3, respectively, but to configure COM3 for IRQ 10 and COM4 for IRQ 12 (provided you do not have a motherboard based mouse port in your system).

Although most people have problems incorrectly trying to share interrupts when installing more than two serial ports in a system, there is a fairly common problem with the I/O port addressing that should be mentioned. Many of the newer high performance SVGA (Super VGA) chipsets, such as those from S3 Inc. and ATI, use some additional I/O port addresses that will conflict with the standard I/O port addresses used by COM4.

In the example system configuration just covered, you can see that the ATI video card uses some additional I/O port addresses, specifically 2EC-2EF. This is a problem as COM4 is normally configured as 2E8-2EF, which overlaps with the video card. The video cards that use these addresses are not normally adjustable for this setting, so you will either have to change the address of COM4 to a nonstandard setting, or simply disable COM4 and restrict yourself to using only 3 serial ports in the system. If you do have a serial adapter that supports nonstandard I/O address settings for the serial ports, you must ensure that those settings are not used by other cards, and you must inform any software or drivers, such as those in Windows, of your nonstandard settings.

With a multiple-COM-port adapter card installed and properly configured for your system, you can have devices hooked to four COM ports, and all four devices can be functioning at the same time. For example, you can use a mouse, modem, plotter, and serial printer at the same time.

The Future: Plug and Play Systems

What does the future hold? Perhaps the most exciting development looming on the horizon is Plug and Play systems. The specifications for these systems are available, and the systems themselves started becoming available in 1995. Specifications exist for ISA, PCI, SCSI, IDE CD-ROM, MCA, and PCMCIA systems and components.

Most users of MCA or EISA systems already know what Plug and Play means: it means that your computer senses any new adapter card on the I/O bus and makes the necessary adjustments to share resources without conflict. You never need to worry about I/O address, DMA channels, or IRQ settings.

As mentioned earlier, this sort of capability has been built into EISA and MCA buses for some time; the problem is that these are not the only buses on the market. Other buses (all of which are described earlier in this chapter) enjoy the lion's share of the PC market. As a result, most computer users must use the trial-and-error method of making their systems work properly. The Plug and Play specifications already in existence have perhaps the greatest impact on users of systems that have ISA buses. Their implementation promises a great boon for most PC users.

Plug and Play (PnP) is not only a hardware issue. For Plug and Play to work, three components are required:

- PnP Hardware
- PnP BIOS
- PnP Operating system (optional)

Each of these components needs to be Plug and Play-compatible, meaning that it complies with the Plug and Play specifications.

The Hardware Component. The hardware component refers to both computer systems and adapter cards. The term does not mean, however, that you will not be able to use your older ISA adapter cards (referred to as legacy cards) in a Plug and Play system. You can use these cards; you just won't receive the benefits of automatic configuration, as you would if the cards were compatible.

Plug and Play adapter cards will be able to communicate with the system BIOS and the operating system to convey information about what system resources are needed. The BIOS and operating system, in turn, will resolve conflicts (wherever possible) and inform the adapter cards which specific resources it should use. The adapter card then can modify its configuration to use the specified resources.

The BIOS Component. The BIOS component means that most users of existing PCs will need to update their BIOSs or to purchase new machines that have Plug and Play BIOSs. For a BIOS to be compatible, it must support 13 additional system function calls, which can be used by the operating-system component of a Plug and Play system. The BIOS specification developed for Plug and Play was developed jointly by COMPAQ, Intel, and Phoenix Technologies.

The Plug and Play features of the BIOS are implemented through an expanded power-on self-test (POST). The BIOS is responsible for identification, isolation, and possible configuration of Plug and Play adapter cards. The BIOS accomplishes these tasks by performing the following steps:

1. Disable any configurable devices on the motherboard or on adapter cards.
2. Identify any Plug and Play PCI or ISA devices.
3. Compile an initial resource-allocation map for ports, IRQs, DMAs, and memory.
4. Enable I/O devices.
5. Scan the ROMs of ISA devices.
6. Configure initial-program-load (IPL) devices, which are used later to boot the system.
7. Enable configurable devices by informing them which resources have been assigned to them.
8. Start the bootstrap loader.
9. Transfer control to the operating system.

The Operating-System Component. The operating-system component can be implemented by a brand-new version (such as an update of DOS, OS/2 or Windows, or Windows 95) or through DOS extensions. Extensions of this type should be familiar to most DOS users; extensions have been used for years to provide support for CD-ROM drives. Extension software is available now for existing operating systems, and you can expect all new PC operating systems to have PnP support built-in.

It is the responsibility of the operating system to inform users of conflicts that cannot be resolved by the BIOS. Depending on the sophistication of the operating system, the user then could configure the offending cards manually (on-screen) or turn the system off and set switches on the physical cards. When the system is restarted, the system is checked for remaining (or new) conflicts, any of which are brought to the user's attention. Through this repetitive process, all system conflicts are resolved.

Note that Plug and Play is still going through some revisions. Windows 95 requires at least version 1.0a of the ISA Plug and Play BIOS. If your system does not have the most current BIOS, I suggest that you install a BIOS upgrade. With the Flash ROM used in most Plug and Play systems, all this entails is downloading the new BIOS image from the system vendor or manufacturer and running the supplied BIOS update program.

Summary

This chapter covered a great deal of ground, going from the general to the specific and from the conceptual to the actual. The information in this chapter enables you to understand how your system physically and logically works. You learned the following:

- How buses are used in a computer system.
- What a processor bus, memory bus, address bus, and I/O bus are.
- How expansion slots fit into the architecture of your system.
- How the major types of I/O buses (ISA, MCA, EISA, local bus, VL-Bus, and PCI) compare.
- That system resources (including I/O addresses, IRQ lines, DMA channels, and memory areas) are limited.
- How adapter cards rely on system resources to communicate with your PC and to do their work.
- That system-resource conflicts can stop your adapter cards or your entire system from functioning properly.
- That the MCA bus, the EISA bus, and (in the future) Plug and Play greatly simplify allocation of system resources.
- That if your system does not resolve system-resource conflicts automatically, you must resolve them manually.

Chapter 6

Microprocessor Types and Specifications

6

The brain of the PC is the processor, or *Central Processing Unit* (CPU). The CPU performs the system's calculating and processing—except for special math-intensive processing in systems that have a math coprocessing unit chip. The processor is easily the most expensive chip in the system. All the PC-compatibles use processors that are compatible with the Intel family of chips, although the processors themselves may have been manufactured or designed by various companies, including AMD, IBM, Cyrix, Nexgen, and others.

The following sections cover the processor chips that have been used in personal computers since the first PC was introduced more than a decade ago. These sections provide a great deal of technical detail about these chips and explain why one type of CPU chip can do more work than another in a given period of time. First, however, you learn about two important components of the processor: the data bus and the address bus.

Processor Specifications

Many confusing specifications often are quoted in discussions of processors. The following sections discuss some of these specifications, including the data bus, address bus, and speed. The next section includes a table that lists the specifications of virtually all PC processors.

Data Bus

One of the most common ways to describe a processor is by the size of the processor's data bus and address bus. A *bus* is simply a series of connections that carry common signals. Imagine running a pair of wires from one end of a building to another. If you connect a 110-volt AC power generator to the two wires at any point and place outlets at convenient locations along the wires, you have constructed a power bus. No matter which outlet you plug the wires into, you have access to the same signal, which in this example is 110-volt AC power.

Any transmission medium that has more than one outlet at each end can be called a bus. A typical computer system has several buses, and a typical processor has two important buses for carrying data and memory-addressing information: the data bus and the address bus.

The processor bus discussed most often is the *data bus*–the bundle of wires (or pins) used to send and receive data. The more signals that can be sent at the same time, the more data can be transmitted in a specified interval and, therefore, the faster the bus.

Data in a computer is sent as digital information consisting of a time interval in which a single wire carries 5 volts to signal a 1 data bit or 0 volts to signal a 0 data bit. The more wires you have, the more individual bits you can send in the same time interval. A chip such as the 286, which has 16 wires for transmitting and receiving such data, has a 16-bit data bus. A 32-bit chip, such as the 486, has twice as many wires dedicated to simultaneous data transmission as a 16-bit chip and can send twice as much information in the same time interval as a 16-bit chip.

Table 6.1 Intel Processor Specifications

Processor	CPU Clock	Std. Voltage	Internal Register Size	Data-Bus Width	Address-Bus Width	Maximum Memory
8088	1x	5v	16-bit	8-bit	20-bit	1M
8086	1x	5v	16-bit	16-bit	20-bit	1M
286	1x	5v	16-bit	16-bit	24-bit	16M
386SX	1x	5v	32-bit	16-bit	24-bit	16M
386SL	1x	3.3v	32-bit	16-bit	24-bit	16M
386DX	1x	5v	32-bit	32-bit	32-bit	4G
486SX	1x	5v	32-bit	32-bit	32-bit	4G
486SX2	2x	5v	32-bit	32-bit	32-bit	4G
487SX	1x	5v	32-bit	32-bit	32-bit	4G
486DX	1x	5v	32-bit	32-bit	32-bit	4G
486SL**	1x	3.3v	32-bit	32-bit	32-bit	4G
486DX2	2x	5v	32-bit	32-bit	32-bit	4G
486DX4	2-3x	3.3v	32-bit	32-bit	32-bit	4G
Pentium OD	2.5x	5v	32-bit	32-bit	32-bit	4G
Pentium 60/66	1x	5v	32-bit	64-bit	32-bit	4G
Pentium 75+	1.5-3x	3.3v***	32-bit	64-bit	32-bit	4G
Pentium Pro	2-3x	2.9v	32-bit	64-bit	36-bit	64G

**The 386SL contains an integral-cache controller, but the cache memory must be provided outside the chip.*
***The 486SL processor has been discontinued; instead, Intel now markets SL Enhanced versions of the SX, DX, and DX2 processors. These processors are available in both 5v and 3.3v versions and include power-management capabilities.*
****There are several different voltage variations of Pentium processors, including what Intel calls VRE (3.465v), VR (3.3v), as well as newer 2.9v and 2.5v versions. The Pentium Pro will run at 2.9v or less.*
*****This figure does not include the optional 256K or 512K Level 2 cache chip built in to the CPU package. The L2 cache chip contains an additional 15.5 million or 31 million transistors.*

A good way to understand this flow of information is to consider a highway and the traffic it carries. If a highway has only one lane for each direction of travel, only one car at a time can move in a certain direction. If you want to increase traffic flow, you can add another lane so that twice as many cars pass in a specified time. You can think of an 8-bit chip as being a single-lane highway because with this chip, 1 byte flows through at a time. (1 byte equals 8 individual bits.) The 16-bit chip, with 2 bytes flowing at a time, resembles a two-lane highway. To move a large number of automobiles, you may have four lanes in each direction. This structure corresponds to a 32-bit data bus, which has the capability to move four bytes of information at a time.

Just as you can describe a highway by its lane width, you can describe a chip by the width of its data bus. When you read an advertisement that describes a computer system as being a 16-bit or 32-bit system, the ad usually is referring to the data bus of the CPU. This number provides a rough idea of the performance potential of the chip (and, therefore, the system).

Integral Cache	Cache Type	Burst Mode	Integral FPU	No. of Transistors	Date Introduced
No	-	No	No	29,000	June '79
No	-	No	No	29,000	June '78
No	-	No	No	134,000	Feb. '82
No	-	No	No	275,000	June '88
0K*	WT	No	No	855,000	Oct. '90
No	-	No	No	275,000	Oct. '85
8K	WT	Yes	No	1,185,000	April '91
8K	WT	Yes	No	1,185,000	April '94
8K	WT	Yes	Yes	1,200,000	April '91
8K	WT	Yes	Yes	1,200,000	April '89
8K	WT	Yes	Optional	1,400,000	Nov. '92
8K	WT	Yes	Yes	1,100,000	March '92
16K	WT	Yes	Yes	1,600,000	Feb. '94
2×16K	WB	Yes	Yes	3,100,000	Jan. '95
2×8K	WB	Yes	Yes	3,100,000	March '93
2×8K	WB	Yes	Yes	3,300,000	March '94
2×8K	WB	Yes	Yes	5,500,000	Sept. '95

FPU = Floating-Point Unit (math coprocessor)
WT = Write-Through cache (caches reads only)
WB = Write-Back cache (caches both reads and writes)
Note that the Pentium Pro processor includes 256K of L2 cache in a separate die within the chip.

Table 6.1 lists the specifications, including the data-bus sizes, for the Intel family of processors used in IBM and compatible PCs.

Internal Registers

The size of the internal register is a good indication of how much information the processor can operate on at one time. Most advanced processors today—all the chips from the 386 to the Pentium—use 32-bit internal registers.

Some processors have an internal data bus (made up of data paths and of storage units called *registers*) that is different from the external data bus. The 8088 and 386SX are examples of this structure. Each chip has an internal data bus twice the width of the external bus. These designs, which sometimes are called hybrid designs, usually are low-cost versions of a "pure" chip. The 386SX, for example, can pass data around internally with a full 32-bit register size; for communications with the outside world, however, the chip is restricted to a 16-bit-wide data path. This design enables a systems designer to build a lower-cost motherboard with a 16-bit bus design and still maintain compatibility with the full 32-bit 386.

Internal registers often are larger than the data bus, which means that the chip requires two cycles to fill a register before the register can be operated on. For example, both the 386SX and 386DX have internal 32-bit registers however, the 386SX has to "inhale" twice (figuratively) to fill them, whereas the 386DX can do the job in one "breath." The same thing would happen when the data is passed from the registers back out to the system bus.

The Pentium is an example of the opposite situation. This chip has a 64-bit data bus but only 32-bit registers—a structure that may seem to be a problem until you understand that the Pentium has two internal 32-bit pipelines for processing information. In many ways, the Pentium is like two 32-bit chips in one. The 64-bit data bus provides for very efficient filling of these multiple registers.

Address Bus

The *address bus* is the set of wires that carry the addressing information used to describe the memory location to which the data is being sent or from which the data is being retrieved. As with the data bus, each wire in an address bus carries a single bit of information. This single bit is a single digit in the address. The more wires (digits) used in calculating these addresses, the greater the total number of address locations. The size (or width) of the address bus indicates the maximum amount of RAM that a chip can address.

The highway analogy can be used to show how the address bus fits in. If the data bus is the highway, and if the size of the data bus is equivalent to the number of lanes, the address bus relates to the house number or street address. The size of the address bus is equivalent to the number of digits in the house address number. For example, if you live on a street in which the address is limited to a two-digit (base 10) number, no more than 100 distinct addresses (00 to 99) can exist for that street (10 to the power of 2). Add another digit, and the number of available addresses increases to 1,000 (000 to 999) or 10 to the 3rd power.

Computers use the binary (base 2) numbering system, so a two-digit number provides only four unique addresses (00, 01, 10, and 11) calculated as 2 to the power of 2, and a three-digit number provides only eight addresses (000 to 111) which is 2 to the 3rd power. For example, the 8086 and 8088 processors use a 20-bit address bus that calculates as a maximum of 2 to the 20th power or 1,048,576 bytes (1M) of address locations. Table 6.2 describes the memory-addressing capabilities of Intel processors.

Table 6.2 Intel Processor Memory-Addressing Capabilities

Processor Family	Address Bus	Bytes	Kilobytes	Megabytes	Gigabytes
8088/8086	20-bit	1,048,576	1,024	1	—
286/386SX	24-bit	16,777,216	16,384	16	—
386DX/486/Pentium	32-bit	4,294,967,296	4,194,304	4,096	4
Pentium Pro	36-bit	68,719,476,736	67,108,864	65,536	64

The data bus and address bus are independent, and chip designers can use whatever size they want for each. Usually, however, chips with larger data buses have larger address buses. The sizes of the buses can provide important information about a chip's relative power, measured in two important ways. The size of the data bus is an indication of the information-moving capability of the chip, and the size of the address bus tells you how much memory the chip can handle.

Processor Speed Ratings

A common misunderstanding about processors is their different speed ratings. This section covers processor speed in general and then provides more specific information about Intel processors.

A computer system's clock speed is measured as a frequency, usually expressed as a number of cycles per second. A crystal oscillator controls clock speeds, using a sliver of quartz in a small tin container. As voltage is applied to the quartz, it begins to vibrate (oscillate) at a harmonic rate dictated by the shape and size of the crystal (sliver). The oscillations emanate from the crystal in the form of a current that alternates at the harmonic rate of the crystal. This alternating current is the clock signal. A typical computer system runs millions of these cycles per second, so speed is measured in megahertz (MHz). (One hertz is equal to one cycle per second.)

Note

The hertz was named for the German physicist Heinrich Rudolph Hertz. In 1885, Hertz confirmed through experimentation the electromagnetic theory, which states that light is a form of electromagnetic radiation and is propagated as waves.

A single cycle is the smallest element of time for the processor. Every action requires at least one cycle and usually multiple cycles. To transfer data to and from memory, for example, an 8086 chip needs four cycles plus wait states. (A *wait state* is a clock tick in which nothing happens to ensure that the processor isn't getting ahead of the rest of the computer.) A 286 needs only two cycles plus any wait states for the same transfer.

The time required to execute instructions also varies. The original 8086 and 8088 processors take an average of 12 cycles to execute a single instruction. The 286 and 386 processors improve this rate to about four and one-half cycles per instruction; the 486 drops the rate further, to 2 cycles per instruction. The Pentium includes twin instruction pipelines and other improvements that provide for operation at 1 cycle per average instruction.

Different instruction execution times (in cycles) make it difficult to compare systems based purely on clock speed, or number of cycles per second. One reason why the 486 is so fast is that it has an average instruction-execution time of 2 clock cycles. Therefore, a 100 MHz Pentium is about equal to a 200 MHz 486, which is about equal to a 400 MHz 386 or 286, which is about equal to a 1,000 MHz 8088. As you can see, you have to be careful in comparing systems based on pure MHz alone; many other factors affect system performance.

How can two processors that run at the same clock rate perform differently, with one running "faster" than the other? The answer is simple: efficiency.

Suppose that you are comparing two engines. An engine has a crankshaft revolution, called a cycle. This cycling time is measured in revolutions per minute (RPM). If two engines run the same maximum RPM, they should run the car at the same speed, right?

Wrong! Actually, the car with the higher power output is faster, assuming that the cars weigh the same and are geared the same. As you can see, these types of specification comparisons can be difficult to manage because of all the other variables that can enter in. I would not compare two computer systems based solely on MHz any more than I would compare two cars on the basis of engine RPM.

You can see that comparing the performance of two vehicles based solely on engine RPM is inaccurate. You never would make such a comparison, because you know that many more factors than just engine speed determine vehicle speed and acceleration capability.

Unfortunately, we often make the same type of poor comparison in evaluating computers. Using engine RPM to compare how fast two cars can run is similar to using MHz to compare how fast two computers can run. A better specification to use when you are comparing the two vehicles would be engine horsepower, which is a measurement of the amount of work that each engine can perform. Then you would have to adjust the horsepower figure for the weight of the vehicle, the coefficient of drag, drive-line gearing, parasitic losses, and so on. In effect, too many other variables are involved for you to make any simplistic comparison, even if you first picked a more meaningful specification to compare than engine redline. The best way to evaluate which of the two vehicles is faster is through road testing. In a computer, the equivalent is taking some of your software and running benchmarks, or comparative performance tests.

A big V-8 engine does more work in each crankshaft revolution (or cycle) than a 6-cylinder engine normally can. In the same manner, a Pentium can perform much more work in a single CPU cycle than a 486 can; it's simply more efficient. As you can see, you must be careful in comparing MHz to MHz, because much more is involved in total system performance.

Comparing automobile engines by virtue of their horsepower output is a much more valid comparison than just RPM. What is needed is a sort of horsepower measurement for processors. To compare processors more accurately based on comparative "horsepower," Intel has devised a specific series of benchmarks that can be run against Intel chips to produce a relative gauge of performance. This is called the *ICOMP* (Intel COmparative Microprocessor Performance) index. Table 6.3 shows the relative power, or ICOMP index, for several processors.

Table 6.3 ICOMP Index Ratings

Processor	ICOMP Index
i386 SX-16	22
i386 SX-20	32
i386 SX-25	39
i386 SL-25	41
i386 DX-25	49
i386 SX-33	56
i486 SX-16	63
i386 DX-33	68
i486 SX-20	78
i486 SX-25	100
i486 DX-25	122
i486 SL-25	122
i486 SX-33	136
i486 DX-33	166
i486 SL-33	166
i486 SX2-50	180
i486 DX2-40	182
i486 DX2-50	231
i486 DX-50	249
i486 DX2-66	297
i486 DX4-75	319
i486 Pentium OverDrive-63	380 (443 w/Write-Back Cache)
i486 DX4-100	435
i486 Pentium OverDrive-83	500 (575 w/Write-Back Cache)
Pentium 60	510
Pentium 66	567
Pentium 75	610
Pentium 90	735

(continues)

Table 6.3 Continued

Processor	ICOMP Index
Pentium 100	815
Pentium 120	1000
Pentium 133	1110
Pentium 150	1176
Pentium 166	1308
Pentium Pro 180	N/A
Pentium Pro 200	N/A

The ICOMP index is derived from several independent benchmarks and is a stable indication of relative processor performance. Floating-point calculations are weighed in the ICOMP rating, so processors that have a built-in FPU (Floating-Point Unit) always have some advantage over those that do not.

Another factor in CPU performance is clock speed. Clock speed is a function of a system's design and usually is controlled by an oscillator, which in turn is controlled by a quartz crystal. Typically, the motherboard circuitry divides the crystal-oscillation frequency by some amount to obtain the processor frequency. The divisor amount is determined by the original design of the processor, by related support chips, and by how the motherboard was designed to use these chips together as a system. In the original IBM PC and XT systems, for example, the main crystal frequency is 14.31818 MHz, which is divided by 3 by an 8284 clock generator chip to obtain a 4.77 MHz processor clock speed. In an original IBM AT system, the crystal speeds are 12 or 16 MHz, which is divided by 2 internally inside the 80286 to produce a 6 or 8 MHz processor clock speed, respectively.

Modern systems use a variable frequency synthesizer circuit usually found in the main motherboard chipset to control the motherboard speed. Most 486 and Pentium motherboards will have three or four speed settings. The processors used today are available in a variety of versions that run at different frequencies based on a given motherboard speed. For example, most of the 486 and Pentium chips run at a speed that is some multiple of the true motherboard speed. For example, Pentium processors and motherboards run at the following speeds:

CPU Type/Speed	CPU Clock	Motherboard Speed
Pentium 60	1x	60
Pentium 66	1x	66
Pentium 75	1.5x	50
Pentium 90	1.5x	60
Pentium 100	1.5x	66
Pentium 120	2x	60
Pentium 133	2x	66

CPU Type/Speed	CPU Clock	Motherboard Speed
Pentium 150	2.5x	60
Pentium 166	2.5x	66
Pentium 180	3x	60
Pentium 200	3x	66

If all other variables are equal—including the type of processor, the number of wait states (empty cycles) added to different types of memory accesses, and the width of the data bus—you can compare two systems by their respective clock rates. Be careful with this type of comparison, however; certain variables (such as those influenced by the memory architecture) can greatly influence the speed of a system, causing the unit with a lower clock rate to run faster than you expect, or causing the system with a numerically higher clock rate to run slower than you think it should. The construction and design of the memory subsystem can have an enormous effect on a system's final execution speed.

In building a processor, a manufacturer tests it at different speeds, temperatures, and pressures. After the processor is tested, it receives a stamp indicating the maximum safe speed at which the unit will operate under the wide variation of temperatures and pressures encountered in normal operation. The rating system usually is simple. For example, the top of the processor in one of my systems is marked like this:

A80486DX2-66

The A is Intel's indicator that this chip has a Ceramic Pin Grid Array form factor, which describes the physical packaging of the chip. The 80486DX2 is the part number, which identifies this processor as a clock-doubled 486DX processor. The -66 at the end indicates that this chip is rated to run at a maximum speed of 66 MHz. Because of the clock doubling, the maximum motherboard speed is 33 MHz. This chip would be acceptable for any application in which the chip runs at 66 MHz or slower. For example, you could use this processor in a system with a 25 MHz motherboard, in which case the processor would happily run at 50 MHz.

Most 486 motherboards also have a 40 MHz setting, in which case the DX2 would run at 80 MHz internally. Because this is 14 MHz beyond its rated speed, many would not work, or if they worked at all, it would only be for a short time. On the other hand, I have found that most of the newer chips marked with -66 ratings seem to run fine (albeit somewhat hotter!) at the 40/80 MHz settings. This can end up being a simple, cost effective way to speed up your system. I would not recommend this for mission critical applications where the system reliability is of the utmost importance, because a system pushed beyond specification like this can often exhibit erratic behavior under stress.

Sometimes, however, the markings don't seem to indicate the speed directly. In the older 8086, for example, -3 translates to 6 MHz operation. This marking scheme is more common in some of the older chips manufactured before some of the marking standards used today were standardized.

A manufacturer sometimes places the CPU under a heat sink, which prevents you from reading the rating printed on the chip. (A *heat sink* is a metal device that draws heat away from an electronic device.) Most of the processors running at 50 MHz and higher should have a heat sink installed to prevent the processor from overheating.

Intel Processors

PC-compatible computers use processors manufactured primarily by Intel. Some other companies, such as Cyrix and AMD, have reverse-engineered the Intel processors and have begun making their own compatible versions. IBM also manufactures processors for some of its own systems as well as for installation in boards and modules sold to others. The IBM processors are not reverse-engineered, but are produced in cooperation with and under license from Intel. The terms of IBM's agreement also allow IBM to make modifications and improvements to the basic Intel design. IBM uses these processors in its own systems, but also is allowed to sell the processors in boards it manufactures for other companies. IBM is not allowed to sell these chips raw, but must always install them in some type of board assembly.

Knowing the processors used in a system can be very helpful in understanding the capabilities of the system, as well as in servicing it. To fully understand the capabilities of a system and perform any type of servicing, you must know at least the type of processor that the system uses.

8088 and 8086 Processors

The original IBM PC used an Intel CPU chip called the 8088. The original 8088 CPU chip ran at 4.77 MHz, which means that the computer's circuitry drove the CPU at a rate of 4,770,000 ticks, or computer heartbeats, per second. Each tick represents a small amount of work—the CPU executing an instruction or part of an instruction—rather than a period of elapsed time.

In fact, both the 8088 and 8086 take an average 12 cycles to execute the average instruction. The 8088 has an external data bus 8 bits wide, which means that it can move 8 bits (individual pieces) of information into memory at a time. The 8088 is referred to as a 16-bit processor, however, because it features internal 16-bit-wide registers and data paths. The 8088 also has a 20-bit address bus, which enables the system to access 1M of RAM. Using the 8088, a manufacturer could build a system that would run 16-bit software and have access to 1M of memory while keeping the cost in line with then-current 8-bit designs. Later, IBM used the 8088 chip in the PC/XT computer.

IBM used the 8088 to put together the original IBM PC 5150-001, which sold for $1,355 with 16K of RAM and no drives. A similarly configured Apple II system, the major competition for the original PC, cost about $1,600.

The 8088 eventually was redesigned to run at 8 MHz—nearly double the speed of the original PC. The speed at which the processor operates has a direct effect on the speed of program execution. Later sections of this chapter cover the speeds of the CPU chips that are successors to the 8088.

Note

The real mode of 286 and higher CPU chips refers to the mode that these advanced chips use to imitate the original 8088 chip in the first PC. Real mode is used by 286 and higher CPU chips to run a single DOS program at a time, just as though systems based on these powerful chips are merely faster PCs. The additional modes of 286 and higher CPU chips are covered in subsequent sections of this chapter.

Computer users sometimes wonder why a 640K conventional-memory barrier exists if the 8088 chip can address 1M of memory. The conventional-memory barrier exists because IBM reserved 384K of the upper portion of the 1,024K (1M) address space of the 8088 for use by adapter cards and system BIOS (a computer program permanently "burned into" the ROM chips in the PC). The lower 640K is the conventional memory in which DOS and software applications execute.

In 1976, before the 8088 chip, Intel made a slightly faster chip named the 8086. The 8086, which was one of the first 16-bit chips on the market, addressed 1M of RAM. The design failed to catch on, however, because both the chip and a motherboard designed for the chip were costly. The cost was high because the system needed a 16-bit data bus rather than the less expensive 8-bit bus. Systems available at that time were 8-bit, and users apparently weren't willing to pay for the extra performance of the full 16-bit design. Therefore, Intel introduced the 8088 in 1978. Both the 8086 and the 8088 CPU chips are quite slow by today's standards.

IBM largely ignored the 8086 CPU chip until it manufactured the first PS/2 Models 25 and 30. Systems produced by many other manufacturers, such as the COMPAQ Deskpro and the AT&T 6300, had been using the 8086 for some time. The capability of the 8086 to communicate with the rest of the system at 16 bits gives it about a 20 percent throughput increase over an 8088 with an identical speed (in MHz). This improvement is one reason why IBM can claim that the 8 MHz, 8086-based Model 30 is two and one-half times faster than the 4.77 MHz, 8088-based PC or XT, even though 8 MHz is not more than twice the clock speed. This claim is the first indication of what a CPU chip with a wider data path can mean in terms of speed improvements.

80186 and 80188 Processors

After Intel produced the 8086 and 8088 chips, it turned its sights toward producing a more powerful chip with an increased instruction set. The company's first efforts along this line—the 80186 and 80188—were unsuccessful. But incorporating system components into the CPU chip was an important idea for Intel, because it led to faster, better chips, such as the 286.

The relationship between the 80186 and 80188 is the same as that of the 8086 and 8088; one is a slightly more advanced version of the other. Compared CPU to CPU, the 80186 is almost the same as the 8088 and has a full 16-bit design. The 80188 (like the 8088) is a hybrid chip that compromises the 16-bit design with an 8-bit external communications interface. The advantage of the 80186 and 80188 is that they combine on a single chip 15 to 20 of the 8086–8088 series system components, a fact that can greatly reduce the number of components in a computer design. The 80186 and 80188 chips are used for highly intelligent peripheral adapter cards, such as network adapters.

Although the 80186 and 80188 did provide some new instructions and capabilities, not much in those chips was new compared with the improvements that came later in the 286 and higher chips. The 80186 and 80188 chips were difficult for system designers to use in manufacturing systems that were compatible with the IBM PC. For example, these chips had DMA (Direct Memory Access) and Interrupt controllers built in, but they were incompatible with the external controllers required for a PC-compatible design. Slight differences in the instruction sets also caused problems when the 80186 and 80188 were supposed to emulate 8086 and 8088 chips. In addition to compatibility problems, the chips didn't offer much performance improvement over the earlier 8086 and 8088. In addition, the individual components that the 80186 and 80188 chips were designed to replace had become inexpensive, which made the 80186 and 80188 chips less attractive.

286 Processors

The Intel 80286 (normally abbreviated as 286) processor did not suffer from the compatibility problems that doomed the 80186 and 80188. The 286 chip, introduced in 1981, is the CPU behind the IBM AT. You also can find 286 chips in IBM's original PS/2 Models 50 and 60 (later PS/2s contain 386 or 486 chips). Other computer makers manufactured what came to be known as IBM clones, with many of these manufacturers calling their systems AT compatible or AT-class computers.

When IBM developed the AT, it selected the 286 as the basis for the new system because the chip provided much compatibility with the 8088 used in the PC and the XT, which meant that software written for those chips should run on the 286. The 286 chip is many times faster than the 8088 used in the XT, and it offered a major performance boost to PCs used in businesses. The processing speed, or throughput, of the original AT (which ran at 6 MHz) was five times greater than that of the PC running at 4.77 MHz.

For several reasons, 286 systems are faster than their predecessors. The main reason is that 286 processors are much more efficient in executing instructions. An average instruction takes 12 clock cycles on the 8086 or 8088, but an average 4.5 cycles on the 286 processor. Additionally, the 286 chip can handle up to 16 bits of data at a time through an external data bus twice the size of the 8088.

Another reason why personal computing received a major boost from the 286 chip is clock speed. AT-type systems are based on 6, 8, 10, 12, 16, and 20 MHz versions of the 286 chip. Earlier processors typically are available in versions only up to 8 MHz. Even if the clock speeds are the same—as in comparing a system that has an 8 MHz 8088 with a system that has an 8 MHz 286—the 286-based system operates roughly three times faster.

The 286 chip has two modes of operation: real mode and protected mode. The two modes are distinct enough to make the 286 resemble two chips in one. In real mode, a 286 acts essentially the same as an 8086 chip and is fully object-code-compatible with the 8086 and 8088. (A processor with object-code-compatibility can run programs written for another processor without modification and execute every system instruction in the same manner.)

In the protected mode of operation, the 286 truly was something new. In this mode, a program designed to take advantage of the chip's capabilities believes that it has access to 1G of memory (including virtual memory). The 286 chip, however, can address only 16M of hardware memory. When a program calls for more memory than physically exists in the system, the CPU swaps to disk some of the currently running code and enables the program to use the newly freed physical RAM. The program does not know about this swapping and instead acts as though 1G of actual memory exists. Virtual memory is controlled by the operating system and the chip hardware.

A significant failing of the 286 chip is that it cannot switch from protected mode to real mode without a hardware reset (a warm reboot) of the system. (It can, however, switch from real mode to protected mode without a reset.) A major improvement of the 386 over the 286 is the fact that software can switch the 386 from real mode to protected mode, and vice versa.

When the 286 chip was introduced, Intel said that real mode was created so that much of the 8086- and 8088-based software could run with little or no modification until new software could be written to take advantage of the protected mode of the 286. As with later Intel processors, however, it was a long time before software took advantage of the capabilities of the 286 chip. For example, most 286 systems are used as if they are merely faster PCs. These systems are run in real mode most of the time because the programs were written for DOS, and DOS and DOS programs are limited to real mode. Unfortunately, much of the power of systems based on the 286 chip is unused. In real mode, a 286 chip cannot perform any additional operations or use any extra features designed into the chip.

IBM and Microsoft together began the task of rewriting DOS to run in both real and protected modes. The result was early versions of OS/2, which could run most old DOS programs just as they ran before, in real mode. In protected mode, OS/2 provided true software multitasking and access to the entire 1G of virtual or 16M of physical address space provided by the 286. UNIX and XENIX also were written to take advantage of the 286 chip's protected mode. In terms of mass appeal, however, these operating systems were a limited success.

Little software that took advantage of the 286 chip was sold until Windows 3.0 offered Standard Mode for 286 compatibility, and by that time, the hottest-selling chip was the 386. Still, the 286 was Intel's first attempt to produce a CPU chip that supported *multitasking*, in which multiple programs run at the same time. The 286 is designed so that if one program locks up or fails, the entire system doesn't need a warm boot (reset) or cold boot (power off or on). Theoretically, what happens in one area of memory doesn't affect other programs. Before multitasked programs are "safe" from one another, however, the 286 chip (and subsequent chips) needs an operating system that works cooperatively with the chip to provide such protection.

In a way, this situation leads back to OS/2, which could provide protection but never caught on for the 286 in a big way. Although newer versions of OS/2 offer a graphical user interface (GUI) similar to that of Windows—and although on 386 and newer systems, OS/2 offers full 32-bit processing for software that is designed to take advantage of it—OS/2 is nowhere near replacing DOS as the operating system of choice on PCs and is nowhere near as popular as Windows. One reason why is because few OS/2 applications have been developed, compared with the number of DOS and Windows programs.

Protected mode on a 286 enables multiple programs to run at one time only when those programs are specifically written for the operating system (or operating environment). To run several programs at the same time on a 286 in Windows, for example, each active program must be a Windows program (written specifically to run only under Windows).

Because of the virtual-memory scheme of the 286, the size of programs under operating systems such as OS/2 and UNIX can be extremely large. Even though the 286 does not address more than 16M of physical memory, the 286's virtual-memory scheme enables programs to run as though 1G of memory were available. But programs that require a great deal of swapping run slowly, which is why software manufacturers usually indicate the amount of physical RAM needed to run their programs effectively. The more physical memory you install, the faster 286-based systems running OS/2 or UNIX will work.

Windows 3.0, which is not a true operating system because it uses DOS for its underpinnings, provides only poor protection on a 286. Unruly programs still can crash the entire system. Windows 3.1 does a better job of implementing protection on a 286, but it still is far from perfect.

Although UNIX and XENIX provide support for the 286 chip's protected mode, these operating systems have found a following among a small group of extremely high-end computer users, primarily in academic or scientific settings.

386 Processors

The Intel 80386 (normally abbreviated as 386) caused quite a stir in the PC industry because of the vastly improved performance that it brought to the personal computer. Compared with 8088 and 286 systems, the 386 chip offers greater performance in almost all areas of operation.

The 386 is a full 32-bit processor optimized for high-speed operation and multitasking operating systems. Intel introduced the chip in 1985, but the 386 appeared in the first systems in late 1986 and early 1987. The COMPAQ Deskpro 386 and systems made by several other manufacturers introduced the chip; somewhat later, IBM used the chip in its PS/2 Model 80. For several years, the 386 chip rose in popularity, and peaked around 1991. Since then, the popularity of the 386 has waned; in the past year or so, it has virtually died out due to the availability of inexpensive systems based on the 486 and Pentium CPU chips. The 386 had an extended life in the mainstream due in part to the use of the chip in extremely small, lightweight, and powerful laptop and notebook computers.

The 386 can execute the real-mode instructions of an 8086 or 8088, but in fewer clock cycles. The 386 was as efficient as the 286 in executing instructions, which means that the average instruction takes about four and one-half clock cycles. In raw performance, therefore, the 286 and 386 actually seemed to be about equal at equal clock rates. Many 286-system manufacturers were touting their 16 MHz and 20 MHz 286 systems as being just as fast as 16 MHz and 20 MHz 386 systems, and they were right! The 386 offered greater performance in other ways, mainly due to additional software capability (modes) and a greatly enhanced Memory Management Unit (MMU).

The 386 can switch to and from protected mode under software control without a system reset, a capability that makes using protected mode more practical. In addition, the 386 has a new mode, called *virtual real mode*, which enables several real-mode sessions to run simultaneously under protected mode.

Other than raw speed, probably the most important feature of this chip is its available modes of operation, which are:

- Real mode
- Protected mode
- Virtual real mode (sometimes called virtual 86 mode)

Real mode on a 386 chip, as on a 286 chip, is 8086-compatible mode. In real mode, the 386 essentially is a much faster "turbo PC" with 640K of conventional memory, just like systems based on the 8088 chip. DOS and any software written to run under DOS requires this mode to run.

The protected mode of the 386 is fully compatible with the protected mode of the 286. The protected mode for both chips often is called their *native mode of operation* because these chips are designed for advanced operating systems such as OS/2 and Windows NT, which run only in protected mode. Intel extended the memory-addressing capabilities of 386 protected mode with a new MMU that provides advanced memory paging and program switching. These features are extensions of the 286 type of MMU, so the 386 remains fully compatible with the 286 at system-code level.

The 386 chip's virtual real mode is new. In virtual real mode, the processor can run with hardware memory protection while simulating an 8086's real-mode operation. Multiple copies of DOS and other operating systems, therefore, can run simultaneously on this processor, each in a protected area of memory. If the programs in one segment crash, the rest of the system is protected. Software commands can reboot the blown partition.

In simple terms, a PC with a 386 has the capability to "become" multiple PCs under software control. With appropriate management software, the 386 chip can create several memory partitions, each containing the full services of DOS, and each partition can function as though it were a stand-alone PC. These partitions are often called *virtual machines*.

In 386 virtual real mode under software such as Windows, several DOS programs can be running at the same time as programs designed for Windows. Because the processor can service only a single application at a time by delivering a clock tick, Windows manages the amount of CPU time that each program gets by using a system called *time slices*. Because the 386 chip is so fast and because time slices are tiny fractions of a second, under Windows all applications appear to be running simultaneously.

OS/2 exploits the multitasking capabilities of the 386 chip even more than Windows does. OS/2 2.x can simultaneously manage native OS/2 programs, DOS programs, and most Windows programs. These capabilities aren't available in lesser processors, such as the 286.

The 386 exploits protected mode much more effectively than the 286 does. The 386 can switch to and from protected mode under software control without a system reset. The 286 cannot switch from protected mode without a hardware reset.

Numerous variations of the 386 chip exist, some of which are less powerful and less power-hungry. The following sections cover the members of the 386-chip family and their differences.

386DX Processors

The 386DX chip was the first of the 386-family members that Intel introduced. The 386 is a full 32-bit processor with 32-bit internal registers, a 32-bit internal data bus, and a 32-bit external data bus. The 386 contains 275,000 transistors in a VLSI (Very Large Scale Integration) circuit. The chip comes in a 132-pin package and draws approximately 400 milliamperes (ma), which is less power than even the 8086 requires. The 386 has a smaller power requirement because it is made of CMOS (Complementary Metal Oxide Semiconductor) materials. The CMOS design enables devices to consume extremely low levels of power.

The Intel 386 chip is available in clock speeds ranging from 16 MHz to 33 MHz; other manufacturers offer comparable versions that offer speeds up to 40 MHz.

The 386DX can address 4G of physical memory. Its built-in virtual memory manager enables software designed to take advantage of enormous amounts of memory to act as though a system has 64 terabytes of memory. (A *terabyte* is 1,099,511,627,776 bytes of memory.) Although most 386 systems are built to accept 64M or less in RAM chips on the motherboard, some high-end computer users do take advantage of the 386 chip's capacity for 4G of physical memory, as well as its 64T virtual-memory potential.

386SX Processors

The 386SX, code-named the *P9 chip* during its development, was designed for systems designers who were looking for 386 capabilities at 286-system prices. Like the 286, the 386SX is restricted to only 16 bits when communicating with other system components such as memory. Internally, however, the 386SX is identical to the DX chip; the 386SX has 32-bit internal registers, and can therefore run 32-bit software. The 386SX uses a 24-bit memory-addressing scheme like that of the 286, rather than the full 32-bit memory address bus of the standard 386. The 386SX, therefore, can address a maximum 16M of physical memory rather than the 4G of physical memory that the 386DX can address. The 386SX is available in clock speeds ranging from 16 MHz to 33 MHz.

The 386SX signaled the end of the 286 because of the 386SX chip's superior MMU and the addition of the virtual real mode. Under a software manager such as Windows or OS/2, the 386SX can run numerous DOS programs at the same time. The capability to run 386-specific software is another important advantage of the 386SX over any 286 or older design. For example, Windows 3.1 runs nearly as well on a 386SX as it does on a 386DX.

Note

One common fallacy about the 386SX is that you can plug one into a 286 system and give the system 386 capabilities. This is not true; the 386SX chip is not pin-compatible with the 286 and does not plug into the same socket. Several upgrade products, however, have been designed to adapt the chip to a 286 system. In terms of raw speed, converting a 286 system to a 386 CPU chip results in little performance gain because 286 motherboards are built with a restricted 16-bit interface to memory and peripherals. A 16 MHz 386SX is not markedly faster than a 16 MHz 286, but it does offer improved memory-management capabilities on a motherboard designed for it, as well as the capability to run 386-specific software.

386SL Processors

Another variation on the 386 chip is the 386SL. This low-power CPU has the same capabilities as the 386SX, but it is designed for laptop systems in which low power consumption is needed. The SL chips offer special power-management features that are important to systems that run on batteries. The SL chip offers several sleep modes that conserve power.

The chip includes an extended architecture that includes a System Management Interrupt (SMI), which provides access to the power-management features. Also included in the SL chip is special support for LIM (Lotus Intel Microsoft) expanded memory functions and a cache controller. The cache controller is designed to control a 16–64K external processor cache.

These extra functions account for the higher transistor count in the SL chips (855,000) compared with even the 386DX processor (275,000). The 386SL is available in 25 MHz clock speed.

Intel offers a companion to the 386SL chip for laptops called the 82360SL I/O subsystem. The 82360SL provides many common peripheral functions, such as serial and parallel ports, a direct memory access (DMA) controller, an interrupt controller, and power-management logic for the 386SL processor. This chip subsystem works with the processor to provide an ideal solution for the small size and low power-consumption requirements of portable and laptop systems.

386 Processor Clones

Several manufacturers, including AMD and Cyrix, have developed their own versions of the Intel 386DX and SX processors. These 386-compatible chips are available in speeds up to 40 MHz; Intel produces 386 chips up to only 33 MHz. Intel does not offer a 386 chip faster than 33 MHz because that speed begins to tread on the performance domain of the slowest of its own 486 processors.

In general, these chips are fully function-compatible with the Intel processors, which means that they run all software designed for the Intel 386. Many manufacturers choose these "cloned" 386 chips for their systems because they are faster and less expensive than Intel 386 chips. (Intel developed its "Intel Inside" advertising campaign in hopes of enticing buyers with a promise of getting the real thing.)

The section on IBM processors discusses the Intel-compatible chips designed and sold by IBM. These chips are not quite comparable with the other Intel processor clones because they actually use official masks and microcode licensed directly from Intel. This arrangement essentially gives IBM the full design of the chip to use in its present form or to modify. Thus, the IBM processors are fully compatible with the Intel processors and often offer many enhancements that are not even available in the Intel versions.

486 Processors

In this section, you find information that can dispel any misunderstandings you may have about the 486 chip versions and possible upgrades. The section explains all the available 486 processors, as well as the possible upgrades and interchanges. You learn the differences between items such as the new DX2 and OverDrive CPUs, and you learn which items are appropriate for a given 486-class system. The sections that follow cover the variations on the basic 486 chip.

In the race for more speed, the Intel 80486 (normally abbreviated as 486) was another major leap forward. The additional power available in the 486 fueled tremendous growth in the software industry. Tens of millions of copies of Windows and millions of copies of OS/2 have been sold largely because the 486 finally made the GUI of Windows and OS/2 a realistic option for people who work on their computers every day.

Three main features make a given 486 processor roughly twice as fast as an equivalent MHz 386 chip. These features are:

- *Reduced instruction-execution time.* Instructions in the 486 take an average of only two clock cycles to complete, compared with an average of more than four cycles on the 386.

- *Internal (Level 1) cache.* The built-in cache has a hit ratio of 90–95 percent, which describes how often zero-wait-state read operations will occur. External caches can improve this ratio further.

- *Burst-mode memory cycles.* A standard 32-bit (four-byte) memory transfer takes two clock cycles. After a standard 32-bit transfer, more data up to the next 12 bytes (or three transfers) can be transferred with only one cycle used for each 32-bit (four-byte) transfer. Thus, up to 16 bytes of contiguous, sequential memory data can be transferred in as little as five cycles instead of eight cycles or more. This effect can be even greater when the transfers are only 8 bits or 16 bits each.

- *Built-in (synchronous) enhanced math coprocessor (some versions).* The math coprocessor runs synchronously with the main processor and executes math instructions in fewer cycles than previous designs do. On average, the math coprocessor built in to the DX-series chips provides two to three times greater math performance than an external 387 chip.

The 486 chip is about twice as fast as the 386, which means that a 386DX-40 is about as fast as a 486SX-20. If given a choice between a 40 MHz 386 and a 20 MHz 486, I would go for the 486. The lower-MHz 486 chip not only will be just as fast (or faster), but also can be upgraded easily to a DX2 or DX4 processor—which would be two or three times faster yet. You can see why the arrival of the 486 rapidly killed off the 386 in the marketplace.

Before the 486, many people avoided GUIs because they didn't have time to sit around waiting for the hourglass, which indicates that the system is performing behind-the-scenes operations that the user cannot interrupt. The 486 changed that situation. Many people believe that the 486 CPU chip spawned the widespread acceptance of GUIs.

The 486 chip's capability to handle the GUI prompted sales of pricey hardware: faster and larger hard drives, faster video display boards and larger monitors, faster and better printers, optical storage devices, CD-ROM drives, sound boards, and video capture boards. A fortunate occurrence prompted by all this spending is the fact that hardware (and software) prices have been in a steep decline for several years.

With the release of its faster Pentium CPU chip, Intel began to cut the price of the 486 line to entice the industry to shift over to the 486 as the mainstream system. Now Intel is starting to cut the price of the Pentium as well. The 486 chip is available in numerous versions: with and without math coprocessors, in clock speeds ranging from 16 MHz to 100 MHz, with special power-management capabilities, and with 3.3-volt operation to save even more power.

Besides high performance, one of the best features of the 486 family of chips is upgradability. In most cases, you can enjoy a performance increase in a given 486 system simply by adding or changing to a faster CPU. Unfortunately, Intel has not explained this upgradability well. I have found it difficult to cut through the marketspeak to find out the technical issues behind the different 486 CPU upgrades—specifically, how they work and the ramifications of these upgrades.

The 486 Processor Family. Since the introduction of the original 486DX chip in April 1989, the 486 has spawned an entire family of processors. Although 486 processors share certain features, such as full 32-bit architecture and a built-in memory cache, the various members of the 486 family differ in certain features, as well as in maximum speeds and pin configurations. This section first breaks down the different 486 processors by their major types, speed differences, and physical configuration, and then describes each processor in depth. Following are the current primary versions of the 486:

- 486SX—486 CPU without FPU (Floating-Point Unit)
- 486DX—486 CPU plus FPU
- 486DX2—Double-speed (OverDrive) 486 CPU plus FPU
- 486DX4—Triple-speed 486 CPU plus FPU

In addition, most of these 486 chips are available in a variety of maximum speed ratings, varying from 16 MHz at the low end to 100 MHz for the fastest chips. Table 6.4 shows the maximum speed ratings of the 486 processors.

Table 6.4 486 Processor Maximum Clock Ratings

Processor Type	Clock Speeds in Megahertz (MHz)
486SX	16, 20, 25, 33, 40, 50
486DX	25, 33, 50
486DX2	40, 50, 66, 80
486DX4	75, 100, 120

A processor rated for a given speed always functions at any of the lower speeds. A 100 MHz-rated 486DX4 chip, for example, runs at 75 MHz if it is plugged into a 25 MHz motherboard. Note that the DX2/OverDrive processors operate internally at two times the motherboard clock rate, whereas the DX4 processors operate at two, two and one-half, or three times the motherboard clock rate. Table 6.5 shows the different speed combinations that can result from using the DX2 or DX4 processors with different motherboard clock speeds.

Table 6.5 Intel DX2 and DX4 Operating Speeds Versus Motherboard Clock Speeds

Motherboard Clock Speed	16 MHz	20 MHz	25 MHz	33 MHz	40 MHz	50 MHz
DX2 processor speed	32 MHz	40 MHz	50 MHz	66 MHz	80 MHz	N/A
DX4 (2x mode) speed	32 MHz	40 MHz	50 MHz	66 MHz	80 MHz	100 MHz
DX4 (2.5x mode) speed	40 MHz	50 MHz	63 MHz	83 MHz	100 MHz	N/A
DX4 (3x mode) speed	48 MHz	60 MHz	75 MHz	100 MHz	120 MHz	N/A

The internal core speed of the DX4 processor is controlled by the CLKMUL (Clock Multiplier) signal at pin R-17 (socket 1) or S-18 (socket 2, 3, or 6). The CLKMUL input is sampled only during a reset of the CPU, and defines the ratio of the internal clock to the external bus frequency CLK signal at pin C-3 (socket 1) or D-4 (socket 2, 3, or 6). If CLKMUL is sampled low, the internal core speed will be two times the external bus frequency. If driven high or left floating (most motherboards would leave it floating), triple speed mode is selected. If the CLKMUL signal is connected to the BREQ (Bus Request) output signal at pin Q-15 (socket 1) or R-16 (socket 2, 3, or 6), the CPU internal core speed will be two and one-half times the CLK speed. To summarize, here is how the socket has to be wired for each DX4 speed selection:

CPU Speed	CLKMUL (Sampled Only at CPU Reset)
2x	Low
2.5x	Connected to BREQ
3x	High or Floating

You will have to determine how your particular motherboard is wired and if it can be changed to alter the CPU core speed in relation to the CLK signal. In most cases, this would be one or two jumpers on the board near the processor socket. The motherboard documentation should cover these settings if they can be changed.

One interesting capability here is to run the DX4-100 chip in a doubled mode with a 50 MHz motherboard speed. This would give you a very fast memory bus, along with the same 100 MHz processor speed as if you were running the chip in a 33/100 MHz tripled mode. One caveat is that if your motherboard has VL-Bus slots, they will have to be slowed down to 33 or 40 MHz to operate properly. Many of the newer VL-Bus motherboards can run the VL-Bus slots in a buffered mode, add wait states, or even selectively change the clock only for the VL-Bus slots to keep them compatible. In most cases, they will not run properly at 50 MHz. Consult your motherboard—or even better, your chipset documentation—to see how your board is set up.

Note that PCI slots would be immune to this type of problem because they always run at 33 MHz. This is one of the reasons that the industry is quickly moving away from VL and toward PCI. This is one of the reasons I now only recommend motherboards with PCI slots.

Besides differing in clock speeds, 486 processors have slight differences in overall pin configurations. The DX, DX2, and SX processors have a virtually identical 168-pin configuration, whereas the OverDrive chips sold retail have either the standard 168-pin configuration or a specially modified 169-pin OverDrive (sometimes also called 487SX) configuration. If your motherboard has two sockets, the primary one likely supports the standard 168-pin configuration, and the secondary (OverDrive) socket supports the 169-pin OverDrive configuration. Most newer motherboards with a single ZIF (zero insertion force) socket support any of the 486 processors except the DX4. The DX4 is different because it requires 3.3 volts to operate instead of 5 volts, like most of the other chips.

If you are upgrading an existing system, be sure that your socket will support the chip that you are installing. In particular, if you are putting one of the new DX4 processors in an older system, you need some type of adapter to regulate the voltage down to 3.3 volts. If you put the DX4 in a 5 volt socket, you will destroy the (very expensive) chip!

The 486-processor family is designed for high performance because it integrates formerly external devices, such as cache controllers, cache memory, and math coprocessors. Also, 486 systems are designed for upgradability. Most 486 systems can be upgraded by simple processor additions or swaps that can effectively double the speed of the system. Because of these features, I recommend the 486SX or DX as the ideal entry-level system, especially in a business environment. Your investment will be protected in the future by a universally available, low-cost processor upgrade.

Internal (Level 1) Cache. All members of the 486 family include as a standard feature an integrated (Level 1) cache controller with either 8K or 16K of cache memory included. This cache basically is an area of very fast memory built into the processor that is used to hold some of the current working set of code and data. Cache memory can be accessed with no-wait states because it can fully keep up with the processor. Using cache memory reduces a traditional system bottleneck because system RAM often is much slower than the CPU. This prevents the processor from having to wait for code and data from much slower main memory, therefore improving performance. Without the cache, a 486 frequently would be forced to wait until system memory caught up. If the data that the 486 chip wants is already in the internal cache, the CPU does not have to wait. If the data is not in the cache, the CPU must fetch it from the secondary processor cache or (in less sophisticated system designs) from the system bus.

You do not need special software or programs to take advantage of this cache; it works invisibly inside the chip. Because the cache stores both program instructions (code) and data, it is called a *unified cache.*

The organization of the cache memory in the 486 family technically is called a *4-Way Set Associative Cache,* which means that the cache memory is split into four blocks. Each block also is organized as 128 or 256 lines of 16 bytes each.

To understand how a 4-Way Set Associative Cache works, consider a simple example. In the simplest cache design, the cache is set up as a single block into which you can load the contents of a corresponding block of main memory. This procedure is similar to using a bookmark to locate the current page of a book that you are reading. If main memory equates to all the pages in the book, the bookmark indicates which pages are held in cache memory. This procedure works if the required data is located within the pages marked with the bookmark, but it does not work if you need to refer to a previously read page. In that case, the bookmark is of no use.

An alternative approach is to maintain multiple bookmarks to mark several parts of the book simultaneously. Additional hardware overhead is associated with having multiple bookmarks, and you also have to take time to check all the bookmarks to see which one marks the pages of data that you need. Each additional bookmark adds to the overhead, but also increases your chance of finding the desired pages.

If you settle on marking four areas in the book to limit the overhead involved, you have essentially constructed a 4-Way Set Associative Cache. This technique splits the available cache memory into four blocks, each of which stores different lines of main memory. Multitasking environments, such as OS/2 and Windows, are good examples of environments in which the processor needs to operate on different areas of memory simultaneously and in which a 4-way cache would improve performance greatly.

The contents of the cache must always be in sync with the contents of main memory to ensure that the processor is working with current data. For this reason, the internal cache in the 486 family is a *Write-Through cache. Write-Through* means that when the processor writes information out to the cache, that information is automatically written through to main memory as well.

By comparison, the Pentium chip has an *internal Write-Back cache,* which means that both reads and writes are cached, further improving performance. Even though the internal 486 cache is Write-Through, the system still can employ an external Write-Back cache for increased performance. In addition, the 486 can buffer up to four bytes before actually storing the data in RAM, improving efficiency in case the memory bus is busy.

The cache controller built into the processor also is responsible for watching the memory bus when alternate processors, known as *Bus Masters*, are in control of the system. This process of watching the bus is referred to as *Bus Snooping*. If a Bus Master device writes to an area of memory that also is stored in the processor cache currently, the cache contents and memory no longer agree. The cache controller then marks this data as invalid and reloads the cache during the next memory access, preserving the integrity of the system.

An external secondary cache (Level 2) of up to 512K or more of extremely fast Static RAM (SRAM) chips also is used in most 486-based systems to further reduce the amount of time that the CPU must spend waiting for data from system memory. The function of the secondary processor cache is similar to that of the 486 chip's on-board cache. The secondary processor cache holds information that is moving to the CPU, thereby reducing the time that the CPU spends waiting and increasing the time that the CPU spends performing calculations. Fetching information from the secondary processor cache rather than from system memory is much faster because of the extremely fast speed of the SRAM chips—20 nanoseconds (ns) or less.

The following sections discuss the technical specifications and differences of the various members of the 486-processor family in more detail.

486DX Processors. The original Intel 486DX processor was introduced on April 10, 1989, and systems using this chip first appeared during 1990. The first chips had a maximum speed rating of 25 MHz; later versions of the 486DX were available in 33 MHz- and 50 MHz-rated versions. The 486DX originally was available only in a 5v, 168-pin PGA (Pin Grid Array) version, but now also is available in 5v, 196-pin PQFP (Plastic Quad Flat Pack) and 3.3v, 208-pin SQFP (Small Quad Flat Pack) as well. These latter form factors are available in SL Enhanced versions, which are intended primarily for portable or laptop applications in which saving power is important.

Two main features separate the 486 processor from older processors such as the 386 or 286: integration and upgradability. The 486DX integrates functions such as the math coprocessor, cache controller, and cache memory into the chip. The 486 also was designed with upgradability in mind; double-speed OverDrive are upgrades available for most systems.

The 486DX processor is fabricated with low-power CMOS (Complimentary Metal Oxide Semiconductor) technology. The chip has a 32-bit internal register size, a 32-bit external data bus, and a 32-bit address bus. These dimensions are equal to those of the 386DX processor. The internal register size is where the "32-bit" designation used in advertisements comes from. The 486DX chip contains 1.2 million transistors on a piece of silicon no larger than your thumbnail. This figure is more than four times the number of components on 386 processors and should give you a good indication of the 486 chip's relative power. Table 6.6 shows the technical specifications of the 486DX processor.

Table 6.6 Intel 486DX Processor Specifications

Introduced:	April 10, 1989 (25 MHz) June 24, 1991 (50 MHz)
Maximum rated speeds:	25, 33, 50 MHz
CPU clock multiplier:	1x
Register size:	32-bit
External data bus:	32-bit
Memory address bus:	32-bit
Maximum memory:	4G
Integral-cache size:	8K
Integral-cache type:	4-Way Set Associative, Write-Through
Burst-mode transfers:	Yes
Number of transistors:	1.2 million, 1.4 million (SL Enhanced models)
Circuit size:	1 micron (25, 33 MHz), 0.8 micron (50 MHz and all SL Enhanced models)
External package:	168-pin PGA, 196-pin PQFP*, 208-pin SQFP*
Math coprocessor:	Integral Floating-Point Unit (FPU)
Power management:	SMM (System Management Mode) in SL Enhanced models
Operating voltage:	5v standard, 3.3v optional in 208-pin SQFP models

PGA = Pin Grid Array
PQFP = Plastic Quad Flat Pack
SQFP = Small Quad Flat Pack
**The PQFP and SQFP models are SL Enhanced only.*

The standard 486DX contains a processing unit, a Floating-Point Unit (math coprocessor), a memory-management unit, and a cache controller with 8K of internal-cache RAM. Due to the internal cache and a more efficient internal processing unit, the 486 family of processors can execute individual instructions in an average of only two processor cycles. Compare this figure with the 286 and 386 families, both of which execute an average four and one-half cycles per instruction, or with the original 8086 and 8088 processors, which execute an average 12 cycles per instruction. At a given clock rate (MHz), therefore, a 486 processor is roughly twice as efficient as a 386 processor; a 16 MHz 486SX is roughly equal to a 33 MHz 386DX system; and a 20 MHz 486SX is equal to a 40 MHz 386DX system. Any of the faster 486s are way beyond the 386 in performance.

The 486 is fully instruction-set-compatible with previous Intel processors, such as the 386, but offers several additional instructions (most of which have to do with controlling the internal cache).

Like the 386DX, the 486 can address 4G of physical memory and manage as much as 64 terabytes of virtual memory. The 486 fully supports the three operating modes introduced in the 386: real mode, protected mode, and virtual real mode. In real mode, the 486 (like the 386) runs unmodified 8086-type software. In protected mode, the 486 (like the 386) offers sophisticated memory paging and program switching. In virtual real mode, the 486 (like the 386) can run multiple copies of DOS or other operating systems while simulating an 8086's real-mode operation. Under an operating system such as

Windows or OS/2, therefore, both 16-bit and 32-bit programs can run simultaneously on this processor with hardware memory protection. If one program crashes, the rest of the system is protected, and you can reboot the blown portion through various means depending on the operating software.

Built-In Math Coprocessor. The 486DX series has a built-in math coprocessor that sometimes is called an MCP (math coprocessor) or FPU (Floating-Point Unit). This series is unlike previous Intel CPU chips, which required you to add a math coprocessor if you needed faster calculations for complex mathematics. The FPU in the 486DX series is 100 percent software-compatible with the external 387 math coprocessor used with the 386, but it delivers more than twice the performance because it runs in synchronization with the main processor and executes most instructions in half as many cycles as the 386.

486SL. Intel originally announced a stand-alone chip called the 486SL. Now the SL as a separate chip has been discontinued, and all the SL enhancements and features are available in virtually all the 486 processors (SX, DX, and DX2) in what are called *SL Enhanced versions*. SL Enhancement refers to a special design that incorporates special power-saving features.

The SL Enhanced chips originally were designed to be installed in laptop or notebook systems that run on batteries, but they are finding their way into desktop systems as well. The SL Enhanced chips feature special power-management techniques, such as sleep mode and clock throttling, to reduce power consumption when necessary. These chips are available in 3.3v versions as well. Table 6.7 shows the technical specifications of the 486SL processor.

Table 6.7 Intel 486SL Processor Specifications

Introduced:	November 9, 1992
Maximum rated speeds:	25, 33, 50 MHz
CPU clock multiplier:	1x
Register size:	32-bit
External data bus:	32-bit
Memory address bus:	32-bit
Maximum memory:	4G
Integral-cache size:	8K
Integral-cache type:	4-Way Set Associative, Write-Through
Burst-mode transfers:	Yes
Number of transistors:	1.4 million
Circuit size:	0.8 micron
External package:	168-pin PGA, 196-pin PQFP, 208-pin SQFP, 227-pin LGA*
Math coprocessor:	Integral Floating-Point Unit (FPU), optional in some models
Power management:	System Management Mode (SMM)
Operating voltage:	5v standard, 3.3v optional in 208-pin SQFP models

PGA = Pin Grid Array
PQFP = Plastic Quad Flat Pack
SQFP = Small Quad Flat Pack
LGA = Land Grid Array
**The LGA version has been discontinued.*

Intel has designed a power-management architecture called *System Management Mode* (*SMM*). This new mode of operation is totally isolated and independent from other CPU hardware and software. SMM provides hardware resources such as timers, registers, and other I/O logic that can control and power down mobile-computer components without interfering with any of the other system resources. SMM executes in a dedicated memory space called System Management Memory, which is not visible and does not interfere with operating-system and application software. SMM has an interrupt called *System Management Interrupt* (*SMI*), which services power-management events, and is independent from and higher-priority than any of the other interrupts.

SMM provides power management with flexibility and security that were not available previously. For example, when an application program tries to access a peripheral device that is powered down for battery savings, an SMI occurs, powering up the peripheral device and re-executing the I/O instruction automatically.

Intel also has designed a feature called suspend/resume in the SL processor. The system manufacturer can use this feature to provide the portable-computer user with instant-on-and-off capability. An SL system typically can resume (instant on) in one second from the suspend state (instant off) to exactly where it left off. You do not need to reboot, load the operating system, load the application program, and then load the application data. Simply push the suspend/resume button, and the system is ready to go.

The SL CPU was designed to consume almost no power in the suspend state. This feature means that the system can stay in the suspend state possibly for weeks and yet start up instantly right where it left off. While it is in the suspend state, an SL system can keep working data in normal RAM memory safe for a long time, but saving to a disk still is prudent.

486SX. The 486SX, introduced in April 1991, was designed to be sold as a lower-cost version of the 486. The 486SX is virtually identical to the full DX processor, but the chip does not incorporate the FPU or math coprocessor portion.

As you read earlier in this chapter, the 386SX was a scaled-down (some people would say crippled) 16-bit version of the full-blown 32-bit 386DX. The 386SX even had a completely different pinout and was not interchangeable with the more powerful DX version. The 486SX, however, is a different story. The 486SX is in fact a full-blown 32-bit 486 processor that is basically pin-compatible with the DX. A few pin functions are different or rearranged, but each pin fits into the same socket.

The 486SX chip is more a marketing quirk than new technology. Early versions of the 486SX chip actually were DX chips that showed defects in the math-coprocessor section. Instead of being scrapped, the chips simply were packaged with the FPU section disabled and sold as SX chips. This arrangement lasted for only a short time; thereafter, SX chips got their own mask, which is different from the DX mask. (A *mask* is the photographic blueprint of the processor and is used to etch the intricate signal pathways into a silicon chip.) The transistor count dropped to 1.185 million (from 1.2 million) to reflect this new mask.

The 486SX chip is twice as fast as a 386DX with the same clock speed. Intel has marketed the 486SX as being the ideal chip for new computer buyers, because not much entry-level software uses the math-coprocessor functions. If you use software that does use or require the math coprocessor, you are well advised to stick with the DX series as a minimum.

The 486SX was normally available in 16, 20, 25, and 33 MHz-rated speeds, and there was also a 486 SX/2 which ran at up to 50 or 66 MHz. The 486SX normally comes in a 168-pin version, although other surface-mount versions are available in SL Enhanced models.

Table 6.8 shows the technical specifications of the 486SX processor.

Table 6.8 Intel 486SX Processor Specifications

Introduced:	April 22, 1991
Maximum rated speeds:	16, 20, 25, 33 MHz
CPU clock multiplier:	1x (2x in some SL Enhanced models)
Register size:	32-bit
External data bus:	32-bit
Memory address bus:	32-bit
Maximum memory:	4G
Integral-cache size:	8K
Integral-cache type:	4-Way Set Associative, Write-Through
Burst-mode transfers:	Yes
Number of transistors:	1.185 million, 1.4 million (SL Enhanced models)
Circuit size:	1 micron, 0.8 micron (SL Enhanced models)
External package:	168-pin PGA, 196-pin PQFP*, 208-pin SQFP*
Math coprocessor:	None
Power management:	SMM (System Management Mode) in SL Enhanced models
Operating voltage:	5v standard, 3.3v optional in 208-pin SQFP models

PGA = Pin Grid Array
PQFP = Plastic Quad Flat Pack
SQFP = Small Quad Flat Pack
**The PQFP and SQFP models are SL Enhanced only.*

Despite what Intel's marketing and sales information implies, no provision exists technically for adding a separate math coprocessor to a 486SX system; neither is a separate math coprocessor chip available to plug in. Instead, Intel wants you to add a new 486 processor with a built-in math unit and disable the SX CPU that already is on the motherboard. If this situation sounds confusing, read on, because this topic brings you to the most important aspect of 486 design: upgradability.

487SX. The 487SX math coprocessor, as Intel calls it, really is a complete 25 MHz 486DX CPU with an extra pin added and some other pins rearranged. When the 487SX is installed in the extra socket provided in a 486SX-CPU-based system, the 487SX turns off the existing 486SX via a new signal on one of the pins. The extra key pin actually carries no signal itself and exists only to prevent improper orientation when the chip is installed in a socket.

The 487SX takes over all CPU functions from the 486SX and also provides math coprocessor functionality in the system. At first glance, this setup seems rather strange and wasteful, so perhaps further explanation is in order. Fortunately, the 487SX turned out simply to be a stopgap measure while Intel prepared its real surprise: the OverDrive processor. The DX2/OverDrive speed-doubling chips, which are designed for the 487SX 169-pin socket, have the same pinout as the 487SX. These upgrade chips are installed in exactly the same way as the 487SX; therefore, any system that supports the 487SX also supports the DX2/OverDrive chips.

When the 486SX processor was introduced, Intel told motherboard designers to install an empty 169-pin socket in the motherboard for a 487SX math coprocessor and originally called this socket a Performance Upgrade Socket. At first, the only thing that you could plug into this socket was what Intel called a 487SX math coprocessor. The strange thing was that the 487SX was not really a math coprocessor at all, but a full 486DX processor!

The only difference between a 487SX and a 486DX is the fact that the 487SX uses the 169-pin rearranged pinout. When you plug a 487SX into the upgrade socket, a special signal pin that was not defined before (interestingly, not the extra 169th one) shuts down the original 486SX CPU, and the 487SX takes over. Because the 487SX is functionally a full-blown DX processor, you also get the math coprocessor functions that were left out of the original 486SX CPU. That is one of the reasons why the 487SX is so expensive; you really are buying more than you think. The real crime is that the original CPU sits silently in the system and does nothing!

Even though the 487SX basically is the same as the 486DX, you normally cannot install a "regular" 486DX processor in the OverDrive socket because the pin designations are not the same. (I used the word *normally* because some motherboards have a jumper selection to allow for the different CPU pin configurations.) Because the 486SX actually uses a 168-pin design similar to that of the 486DX (even though it normally is installed in a 169-pin socket), you may be able to install a regular DX chip in the SX socket and have it work, but this capability depends somewhat on the flexibility of your motherboard.

Although in most cases you can upgrade a system by removing the 486SX CPU and replacing it with a 487SX (or even a DX or DX2/OverDrive), Intel originally discouraged this procedure and recommended that PC manufacturers include a dedicated upgrade (OverDrive) socket in their systems, because several risks were involved in removing the original CPU from a standard socket. (The following section elaborates on those risks.) Nowadays, Intel recommends—or even insists on—the use of a single processor socket of a ZIF (zero insertion force) design, which makes upgrading an easy task physically.

DX2/OverDrive Processors. On March 3, 1992, Intel introduced the DX2 speed-doubling processors. On May 26, 1992, Intel announced that the DX2 processors also would be available in a retail version called OverDrive. Originally, the OverDrive versions of the DX2 were available only in 169-pin versions, which meant that they could be used only with 486SX systems that had sockets configured to support the rearranged pin configuration.

On September 14, 1992, Intel introduced 168-pin OverDrive versions for upgrading 486DX systems. These processors can be added to existing 486 (SX or DX) systems as an upgrade, even if those systems do not support the 169-pin configuration. When you use this processor as an upgrade, you simply install the new chip in your system, which subsequently runs twice as fast. (As the guy in *RoboCop* said, "I like it!")

The DX2/OverDrive processors run internally at twice the clock rate of the host system. If the motherboard clock is 25 MHz, for example, the DX2/OverDrive chip runs internally at 50 MHz; likewise, if the motherboard is a 33 MHz design, the DX2/OverDrive runs at 66 MHz. The DX2/OverDrive speed doubling has no effect on the rest of the system; all components on the motherboard run the same as they do with a standard 486 processor. Therefore, you do not have to change other components (such as memory) to accommodate the double-speed chip. In other words, you can achieve a significant performance gain simply by changing the CPU chip; you do not have to use faster (more expensive) motherboard circuitry.

The DX2/OverDrive chips have been available in several speeds. Three different speed-rated versions have been offered:

- 40 MHz DX2/OverDrive for 16 MHz or 20 MHz systems
- 50 MHz DX2/OverDrive for 25 MHz systems
- 66 MHz DX2/OverDrive for 33 MHz systems

Notice that these ratings indicate the maximum speed at which the chip is capable of running. You could use a 66 MHz-rated chip in place of the 50 MHz- or 40 MHz-rated parts with no problem, although the chip will run only at the slower speeds. The actual speed of the chip is double the motherboard clock frequency. When the 40 MHz DX2/OverDrive chip is installed in a 16 MHz 486SX system, for example, the chip will function only at 32 MHz—exactly double the motherboard speed. Intel originally stated that no 100 MHz DX2/OverDrive chip will be available for 50 MHz systems—which technically has not been true because the DX4 can be set to run in a clock doubled mode and used in a 50MHz motherboard (more information on that situation later in the chapter).

The only part of the DX2 chip that doesn't run at double speed is the *bus interface unit*, a region of the chip that handles I/O between the CPU and the outside world. By translating between the differing internal and external clock speeds, the bus interface unit makes speed doubling transparent to the rest of the system. The DX2 appears to the rest of the system to be a regular 486DX chip, but one that seems to execute instructions twice as fast.

DX2/OverDrive chips are based on the 0.8-micron circuit technology that was first used in the 50 MHz 486DX. The DX2 contains 1.1 million transistors in a three-layer form. The internal 8K cache, integer, and Floating-Point Units all run at double speed. External communication with the PC runs at normal speed to maintain compatibility.

Table 6.9 shows the technical specifications of the 486DX2/OverDrive processors.

Table 6.9 486DX2/OverDrive Processor Specifications

Introduced:	March 3, 1992
Maximum rated speeds:	40, 50, 66 MHz
CPU clock multiplier:	2x
Register size:	32-bit
External data bus:	32-bit
Memory address bus:	32-bit
Maximum memory:	4G
Integral-cache size:	8K
Integral-cache type:	4-Way Set Associative, Write-Through
Burst-mode transfers:	Yes
Number of transistors:	1.1 million, 1.4 million (SL Enhanced models)
Circuit size:	0.8 micron
External package:	168-pin PGA, 169-pin PGA, 196-pin PQFP*, 208-pin SQFP*
Math coprocessor:	Integral Floating-Point Unit (FPU)
Power management:	SMM (System Management Mode) in SL Enhanced models
Operating voltage:	5v standard, 3.3v optional in 208-pin SQFP models

PGA = Pin Grid Array
PQFP = Plastic Quad Flat Pack
SQFP = Small Quad Flat Pack
**The PQFP and SQFP models are SL Enhanced only.*

Besides upgrading existing systems, one of the best parts of the DX2 concept is the fact that system designers can introduce very fast systems by using cheaper motherboard designs, rather than the very costly designs that would support a straight high-speed clock. This means that a 50 MHz 486DX2 system is much less expensive than a straight 50 MHz 486DX system. In a 486DX-50 system, the system board operates at a true 50 MHz. In a 486DX2-50 system, the 486DX2 CPU operates internally at 50 MHz, but the motherboard operates at only 25 MHz.

You may be thinking that a true 50 MHz DX-processor-based system still would be faster than a speed-doubled 25 MHz system, and this generally is true, but the differences in speed actually are very slight—a real testament to the integration of the 486 processor and especially to the cache design.

When the processor has to go to system memory for data or instructions, for example, it has to do so at the slower motherboard operating frequency, such as 25 MHz. Because the 8K internal cache of the 486DX2 has a hit rate of 90–95 percent, however, the CPU has to access system memory only 5–10 percent of the time for memory reads. Therefore, the performance of the DX2 system can come very close to that of a true 50 MHz DX system and cost much less. Even though the motherboard runs only at 33.33 MHz, a system with a DX2 66 MHz processor ends up being faster than a true 50 MHz DX system, especially if the DX2 system has a good Level-2 cache.

Because the DX2 66 MHz chips are much cheaper than the straight 50 MHz DX models, the systems are cheaper as well. Additionally, the newer local buses operate best at 33 MHz and do not tolerate 50 MHz speeds without using buffering. All these factors have contributed to the elimination of true 50 MHz DX systems from most manufacturers' inventories.

Many 486 motherboard designs also include a secondary cache that is external to the cache integrated into the 486 chip. This external cache allows for much faster access when the 486 chip calls for external-memory access. The size of this external cache can vary anywhere from 16K to 512K or more. When you add a DX2 processor, an external cache is even more important for achieving the greatest performance gain, because this cache greatly reduces the wait states that the processor will have to add when writing to system memory or when a read causes an internal-cache miss. For this reason, some systems perform better with the DX2/OverDrive processors than others, usually depending on the size and efficiency of the external-memory cache system on the motherboard. Systems that have no external cache will still enjoy a near-doubling of CPU performance, but operations that involve a great deal of memory access will be slower.

At this writing, Intel has stated that it has no plans for a DX2/OverDrive chip for 50 MHz systems. Producing a speed-doubled OverDrive processor for 486DX-50 based systems would mean that the OverDrive chip would have to function internally at 100 MHz. Indirectly, Intel has solved this problem with the introduction of the DX4 processor.

Although the standard DX4 technically is not sold as a retail part, you can indeed purchase it from several vendors, along with the 3.3v adapter that you need to install the chip in a 5v socket. These adapters have jumpers that enable you to select the DX4 clock multiplier and set it to 2x, 2.5x, or 3x mode. In a 50 MHz DX system, you could install a DX4/voltage-regulator combination set in 2x mode for a motherboard speed of 50 MHz and a processor speed of 100 MHz! Although you may not be able to take advantage of the latest local bus peripherals, you will in any case have one of the fastest 486-class PCs available.

Intel also sells a special DX4 OverDrive processor that includes a built-in voltage regulator and heat sink that is specifically designed for the retail market. The DX4 OverDrive chip is essentially the same as the standard 3.3v DX4 with the main exception that it runs on 5v because it includes an on-chip regulator. Also, the DX4 OverDrive chip will only run in the tripled speed mode, and not the 2x or 2.5x modes of the standard DX4 processor.

Differences Between DX2 and OverDrive Processors. One of the most common questions about the DX2/OverDrive processors is, "What's the difference between a DX2 chip and an OverDrive chip?" Although the advertisements are somewhat misleading, the DX2 and OverDrive processor chips actually are the same thing. The real difference is the way that they are sold and in the amenities that are (or are not) included. The simple answer is that if the chip comes installed in a system, it's a DX2; if it comes in an Intel retail upgrade kit, it's an OverDrive processor.

OverDrive processors are DX2 chips that are sold as end-user-installable upgrades. Like math coprocessors, these processors are available at retail outlets and carry either a limited lifetime warranty or a three-year warranty from Intel. Included with OverDrive processors are a user guide, a utilities disk, a chip-extractor tool, and a grounding strap. OverDrive processors for 25 MHz and 33 MHz systems also include a heat sink, which already is attached to the top surface of the chip. Although not all systems have poor-enough air circulation to require the heat sink, its presence increases the number of systems that can use the OverDrive chips. Technical support direct from Intel is provided with each OverDrive processor.

DX2 chips are the raw CPUs, which are sold in quantity only to OEMs (original equipment manufacturers), which install the chips in their systems as the primary microprocessors. The DX2 chips are sold in bulk and do not include the packaging, documentation, software utilities, extractor tool, and other items that are part of the retail package. DX2 chips also do not include a heat sink from Intel; it is up to the system manufacturer to determine whether a heat sink is needed for a particular application and to add one if it is needed.

The raw DX2 CPUs are classified by Intel as OEM products and are warranted only to the OEM or authorized Intel distributor for one year from the ship date. When that OEM or distributor sells the system or the CPU, that company extends the warranty to the purchaser. The warranty and support for a raw 486DX2 come from the company from which you purchase your system or the 486DX2 CPU, not from Intel.

"Vacancy." Perhaps you saw the Intel advertisements—both print and television—that featured a 486SX system with a neon Vacancy sign pointing to an empty socket next to the CPU chip. Unfortunately, these ads were not very informative, and they made it seem that only systems with the extra socket could be upgraded. When I first saw these ads, I was worried because I had just purchased a 486DX system, and the advertisements implied that only 486SX systems with the empty OverDrive socket were upgradable. This, of course, was not true, but the Intel advertisements surely did not communicate that fact very well.

I later found out that upgradability does not depend on having an extra OverDrive socket in the system and that virtually any 486SX or DX system can be upgraded. The secondary OverDrive socket was designed simply to make upgrading easier and more convenient. Even in systems that have the second socket, you can actually remove the primary SX or DX CPU and plug the OverDrive processor directly into the main CPU socket, rather than into the secondary OverDrive socket.

In that case, you would have an upgraded system with a single functioning CPU installed; you could remove the old CPU from the system and sell it or trade it in for a refund. Unfortunately, Intel does not offer a trade-in or core-charge policy; it simply does not want your old chip. For this reason, some people saw the OverDrive socket as being a way for Intel to sell more CPUs. Some valid reasons exist, however, to use the OverDrive socket and leave the original CPU installed.

One reason is that many PC manufacturers void the system warranty if the CPU has been removed from the system. Also, when systems are serviced, most manufacturers require that the system be returned with only the original parts; you must remove all add-in cards, memory modules, upgrade chips, and similar items before sending the system in for servicing. If you replace the original CPU when you install the upgrade, returning the system to its original condition will be much more difficult.

Another reason for using the upgrade socket is that if the main CPU socket is damaged when you remove the original CPU or install the upgrade processor, the system will not function. By contrast, if a secondary upgrade socket is damaged, the system still should work with the original CPU.

If you think that damaging the socket or chip is not a valid concern, you should know that it typically takes 100 pounds of insertion force to install a chip in a standard 169-pin screw machine socket. With this much force involved, you easily could damage either the chip or socket during the removal-and-reinstallation process.

Many motherboard manufacturers began using low-insertion-force (LIF) sockets, which typically require only 60 pounds of insertion force for a 169-pin chip. With the LIF or standard socket, I usually advise removing the motherboard so that you can support the board from behind when you insert the chip. Pressing down on the motherboard with 60 to 100 pounds of force can crack the board if it is not supported properly. A special tool also is required to remove a chip from one of these sockets.

Nowadays, nearly all motherboard manufacturers are using zero-insertion-force (ZIF) sockets. These sockets almost eliminate the risk involved in upgrading because no insertion force is necessary to install the chip. Most ZIF sockets are handle-actuated; you simply lift the handle, drop the chip into the socket, and then close the handle. This design makes replacing the original processor with the upgrade processor an easy task. Because it is so simple to perform the upgrade with a ZIF socket, most motherboards that use such a socket have only one processor socket rather than two. This arrangement is a bonus: the unnecessary second socket does not waste the additional motherboard space, and you are forced to remove the otherwise-dormant original processor, which you then can sell or keep as a spare.

If a ZIF socket is not used, it is usually much easier to install an upgrade processor in an empty OverDrive socket than it is to remove the original CPU and then install the upgrade chip in the CPU socket. For these reasons, Intel now recommends that all 486 systems (SX and DX) use the two-socket approach or (more likely) use a single ZIF socket for the primary CPU as well as for any later upgrades.

Most single-socket systems can take any of the 486-family chips from the 486SX to the DX and the DX2/OverDrive. These boards usually have a set of jumpers or switches that enable you to select the type and speed of CPU that you are installing. In systems that have no second socket or ZIF socket, you may be more restricted in terms of the types of upgrades that you can install.

Some motherboards now include sockets beyond the original 169-pin OverDrive socket (now officially called Socket 1) for use in additional upgrades. These larger sockets can be both primary CPU sockets and OverDrive sockets. This design not only accommodates the original 486DX or DX2 processor, but also allows for an upgrade to the next level of OverDrive CPU based on the Intel Pentium processors.

OverDrive Processors and Sockets

Intel has stated that all its future processors will have OverDrive versions available for upgrading at a later date. As a result, Intel has developed a series of socket designs that will accommodate not only the original processor with which a system is shipped, but also the future OverDrive processor.

In many cases, the future OverDrive unit will be much more than just the same type of processor running at a higher clock rate. Although the original OverDrive series of processors for the 486SX and 486DX chip simply were clock-doubled versions of essentially the same chips, Intel plans OverDrive upgrades that go beyond this level. For example, the company already has designed OverDrive-style single-chip upgrades for DX2, DX4, and Pentium systems.

This new processor will require a larger socket than the original processor does; the additional pins are reserved for the new processor when it is ready. Intel is making available the pin specifications and some functions of the new processors so that motherboard designers can prepare now by installing the proper sockets. Then, when the OverDrive processor becomes available, all the end user will have to do is purchase it and install the new chip in place of the original one. To make the process easy, Intel now requires that all these sockets be of ZIF (zero insertion force) design.

Intel has created a set of socket designs, named Socket 1 through Socket 8. Each socket is designed to support a different range of original and upgrade processors. Table 6.10 shows the specifications of these sockets.

Table 6.10 Intel 486/Pentium CPU Socket Types and Specifications

Socket Number	No. of Pins	Pin Layout	Voltage	Supported Processors
Socket 1	169	17x17 PGA	5v	SX/SX2, DX/DX2*, DX4 OverDrive
Socket 2	238	19x19 PGA	5v	SX/SX2, DX/DX2*, DX4 OverDrive, 486 Pentium OverDrive
Socket 3	237	19x19 PGA	5v/3.3v	SX/SX2, DX/DX2, DX4, 486 Pentium OverDrive
Socket 4	273	21x21 PGA	5v	Pentium 60/66, Pentium 60/66 OverDrive
Socket 5	320	37x37 SPGA	3.3v	Pentium 75-133, Pentium 75+ OverDrive
Socket 6**	235	19x19 PGA	3.3v	DX4, 486 Pentium OverDrive
Socket 7	321	37x37 SPGA	VRM	Pentium 75-200, Pentium 75+ OverDrive
Socket 8	387	dual pattern SPGA	VRM	Pentium Pro

**DX4 also can be supported with the addition of an aftermarket 3.3v-regulator adapter.*
***Socket 6 was a paper standard only and was never actually implemented in any systems.*
PGA = Pin Grid Array
SPGA = Staggered Pin Grid Array
VRM = Voltage Regulator Module

The original OverDrive socket, now officially called Socket 1, is a 169-pin PGA socket. Motherboards that have this socket can support any of the 486SX, DX, and DX2 processors, as well as the DX2/OverDrive versions. This type of socket is found on most 486 systems that originally were designed for OverDrive upgrades. Even if your system has only a 168-pin version (technically not Socket 1), you still can get DX2 chips with the correct pinout that plugs right in. You even can install a DX4 triple-speed processor in this socket by using a voltage-regulator adapter. Figure 6.1 shows the pinout of Socket 1.

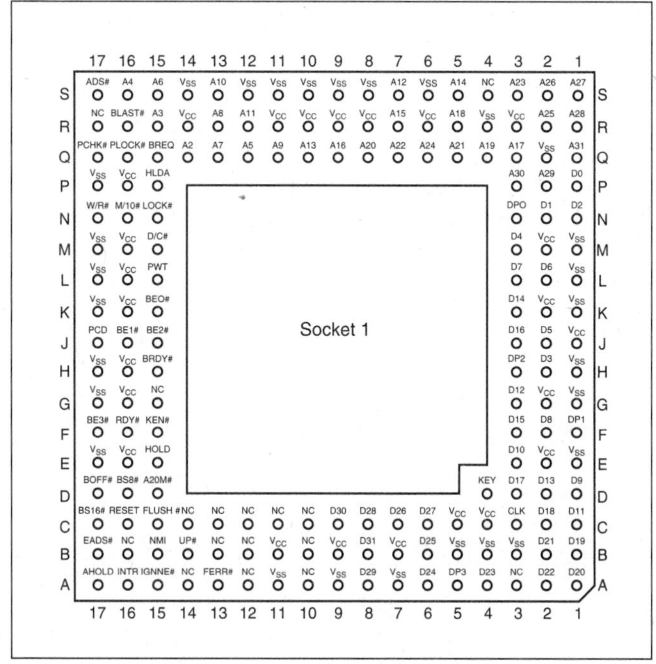

Figure 6.1

Intel Socket 1 pinout.

The original DX processor draws a maximum 0.9 amps of 5v power in 33 MHz form (4.5 watts) and a maximum 1 amp in 50 MHz form (5 watts). The DX2 processor or OverDrive processor draws a maximum 1.2 amps at 66 MHz (6 watts). This minor increase in power requires only a passive heat sink consisting of aluminum fins that are glued to the processor with thermal transfer epoxy. OverDrive processors rated at 40 MHz or less do not have heat sinks.

When the DX2 processor was released, Intel already was working on the new Pentium processor. The company wanted to offer a 32-bit, scaled-down version of the Pentium as an upgrade for systems that originally came with a DX2 processor. Rather than just increasing the clock rate, Intel created an all-new chip with enhanced capabilities derived from the Pentium.

The chip, code-named the P24T and officially called the Pentium OverDrive Processor, will plug into a processor socket with the Socket 2 or Socket 3 design. These sockets will hold any 486 SX, DX, or DX2 processor, as well as the Pentium OverDrive. Because this chip is essentially a 32-bit version of the (normally 64-bit) Pentium chip, many have taken to calling it a *Pentium-SX*. It is available in 25/63 MHz and 33/83 MHz versions. The first number indicates the base motherboard speed, while the second number indicates the actual operating speed of the Pentium OverDrive chip itself. As you can see, it is a clock-multiplied chip that runs at two and one-half times the motherboard speed.

The Pentium OverDrive chip also includes a 32K internal Level 1 cache, and the same superscalar (multiple instruction path) architecture of the real Pentium chip. Because it is hampered by the 32-bit motherboard design, as well as a lower speed than most of the true Pentium chips, the performance gain is not that great. In fact, the 83 MHz version performs only slightly better than a DX4-100 processor, and less than a true Pentium 60 or 75, even though it costs significantly more money. I would not recommend this chip as an upgrade for most 486 systems. Instead, you could get a DX4-100 or DX4-120 for much less, or for a little more money simply upgrade to a true Pentium motherboard and processor.

One interesting feature of the Pentium OverDrive processor that you will likely see on more Intel processors in the future is the built-in active heat sink. This is basically a fan that is clipped right onto the chip. Unlike the poorly implemented aftermarket CPU fan setups, this one draws power directly from the CPU itself, and can be easily unclipped and changed if it ever should fail. Also, if the fan fails while the system is operating, the CPU will automatically detect this condition and drop from a 2.5x multiplication of the motherboard speed to a 1x (non-multiplied) speed. At the 1x speed (25 or 33 MHz in most cases), the chip will not get hot enough to overheat, even with the fan stalled. I expect to see this intelligent heat sink fan setup implemented on more Intel processors in the future.

Figure 6.2 shows the pinout configuration of the official Socket 2 design.

Notice that although the new chip for Socket 2 is called Pentium OverDrive, it is not a full-scale (64-bit) Pentium; the chip is more like a Pentium SX. Most manufacturers that claim to have Pentium-ready systems really mean that their systems have a Socket 2 processor socket that will accommodate the Pentium OverDrive chip in the future.

Intel released the design of Socket 2 a little prematurely and found that the chip ran too hot for many systems. The company solved this problem by adding a special Active Heat Sink to the Pentium OverDrive processor. This active heat sink is a combination of a standard heat sink with a built-in electric fan. Unlike the aftermarket glue-on or clip-on fans for processors that you may have seen, this one actually draws 5v power directly from the socket to drive the fan. No external connection to disk drive cables or the power supply is required. The fan/heat sink assembly clips and plugs directly into the processor, providing for easy replacement should the fan ever fail.

Another requirement of the active heat sink is additional clearance—no obstructions for an area about 1.4 inches off the base of the existing socket to allow for heat-sink clearance. In systems that were not designed with this feature, the Pentium OverDrive upgrade will be difficult or impossible.

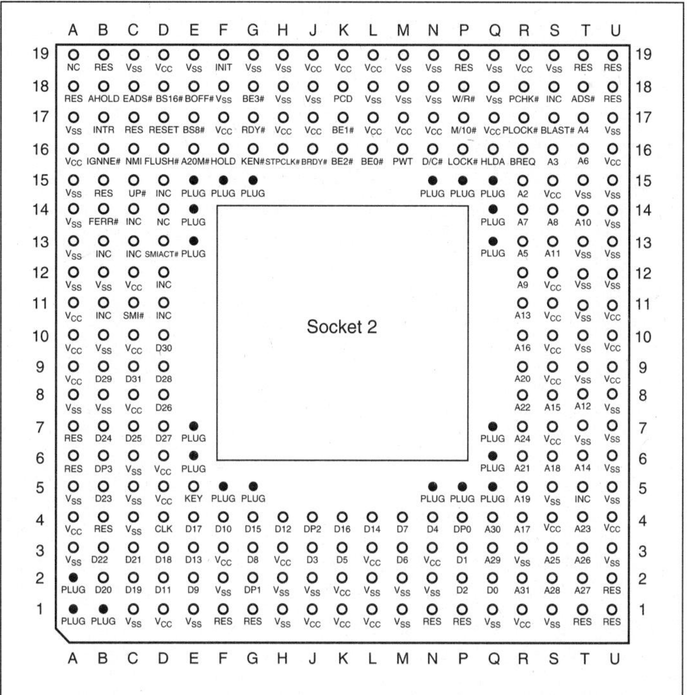

Figure 6.2

238-pin Intel Socket 2 configuration.

Another problem with this particular upgrade is power consumption. The 5v Pentium OverDrive processor will draw up to 2.5 amps at 5v (including the fan) or 12.5 watts, which is more than double the 1.2 amps (6 watts) drawn by the DX2 66 processor. Intel did not provide this information when it established the socket design, so the company set up a testing facility to certify systems for thermal and mechanical compatibility with the Pentium OverDrive upgrade. For the greatest peace of mind, ensure that your system is certified compatible before you attempt this upgrade.

Figure 6.3 shows the dimensions of the Pentium OverDrive processor and active heat sink/fan assembly.

Because of problems with the original Socket 2 specification and the enormous heat the 5v version of the Pentium OverDrive processor generates, Intel came up with an improved design. The new processor, officially called the DX4 OverDrive processor, actually is the same as the Pentium OverDrive processor, with the exception that it runs on 3.3v and draws a maximum 3.0 amps of 3.3v (9.9 watts) and 0.2 amps of 5v (1 watt) to run the fan, for a total 10.9 watts. This configuration provides a slight margin over the 5v version of this processor. The fan will be easy to remove from the OverDrive processor for replacement, should it ever fail.

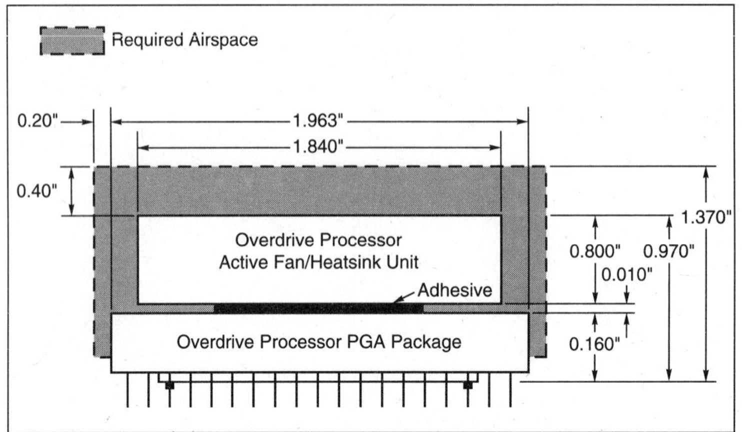

Figure 6.3

Physical dimensions of the Intel Pentium OverDrive processor and active heat sink.

To support both the new DX4 processor, which runs on 3.3v, and the 3.3v DX4 (Pentium) OverDrive processor, Intel had to create a new socket. In addition to the new 3.3v chips, this new socket supports the older 5v SX, DX, DX2, and even the 5v Pentium OverDrive chip. The design, called Socket 3, is the most flexible upgradable 486 design.

Figure 6.4 shows the pinout specification of Socket 3.

Notice that Socket 3 has one additional pin and several others plugged compared with Socket 2. Socket 3 provides for better keying, which prevents an end user from accidentally installing the processor in an improper orientation. One serious problem exists, however: this socket cannot automatically determine the type of voltage that will be provided to it. A jumper is likely to be added on the motherboard near the socket to enable the user to select 5v or 3.3v operation. Because this jumper must be manually set, however, a user could install a 3.3v processor in this socket when it is configured for 5v operation. This installation will instantly destroy a very expensive chip when the system is powered on. It will be up to the end user to make sure that this socket is properly configured for voltage, depending on which type of processor is installed. If the jumper is set in 3.3v configuration and a 5v processor is installed, no harm will occur, but the system will not operate properly unless the jumper is reset for 5v.

The original Pentium processor 60 MHz and 66 MHz versions had 273 pins and would plug into a 273-pin Pentium processor socket—a 5v-only socket, because all the original Pentium processors run on 5v. This socket will accept the original Pentium 60 MHz or 66 MHz processor, as well as the OverDrive processor.

Figure 6.5 shows the pinout specification of Socket 4.

Somewhat amazingly, the original Pentium 66 MHz processor consumes up to 3.2 amps of 5v power (16 watts), not including power for a standard active heat sink (fan), whereas the 66 MHz OverDrive processor that will replace it consumes a maximum 2.7 amps (13.5 watts), including about 1 watt to drive the fan. Even the original 60 MHz Pentium

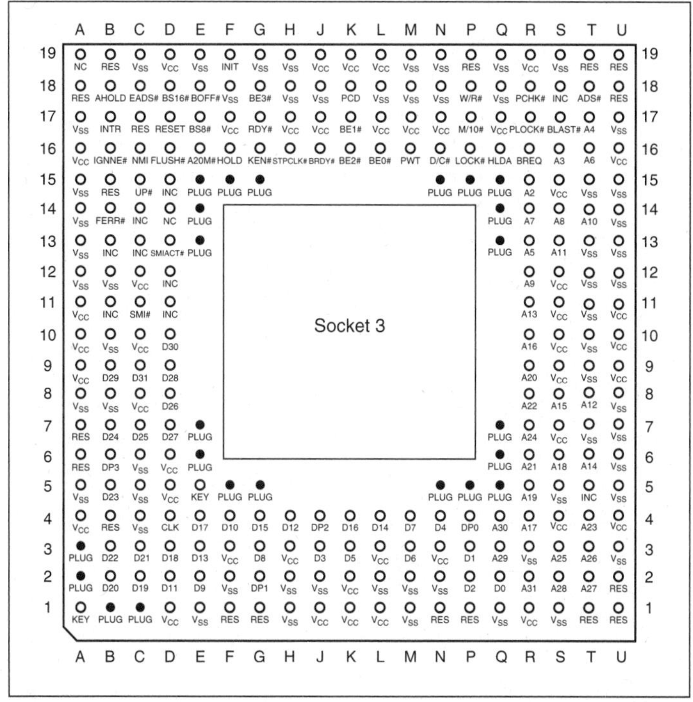

Figure 6.4

237-pin Intel Socket 3 configuration.

processor consumes up to 2.91 amps at 5v (14.55 watts). It may seem strange that the replacement processor, which likely will be twice as fast, will consume less power than the original, but this has to do with the manufacturing processes used for the original and OverDrive processors.

Although both processors will run on 5v, the original Pentium processor was created with a circuit size of 0.8 microns, making that processor much more power-hungry than the newer 0.6-micron circuits used in the OverDrive and the other Pentium processors. Shrinking the circuit size is one of the best ways to decrease power consumption. Although the OverDrive processor for Pentium-based systems indeed will draw less power than the original processor, additional clearance may have to be allowed for the active heat sink (fan) assembly that is mounted on top. As in other OverDrive processors with built-in fans, the power to run the fan will be drawn directly from the chip socket, so no separate power-supply connection is required. Also, the fan will be easy to replace should it ever fail.

When Intel redesigned the Pentium processor to run at 75, 90, and 100 MHz, the company went to a 0.6-micron manufacturing process as well as 3.3v operation. This change resulted in lower power consumption: only 3.25 amps at 3.3v (10.725 watts). Therefore, the 100 MHz Pentium processor can use far less power than even the original 60 MHz version. The newest 120/133 Pentium chips use an even smaller die 0.35-micron

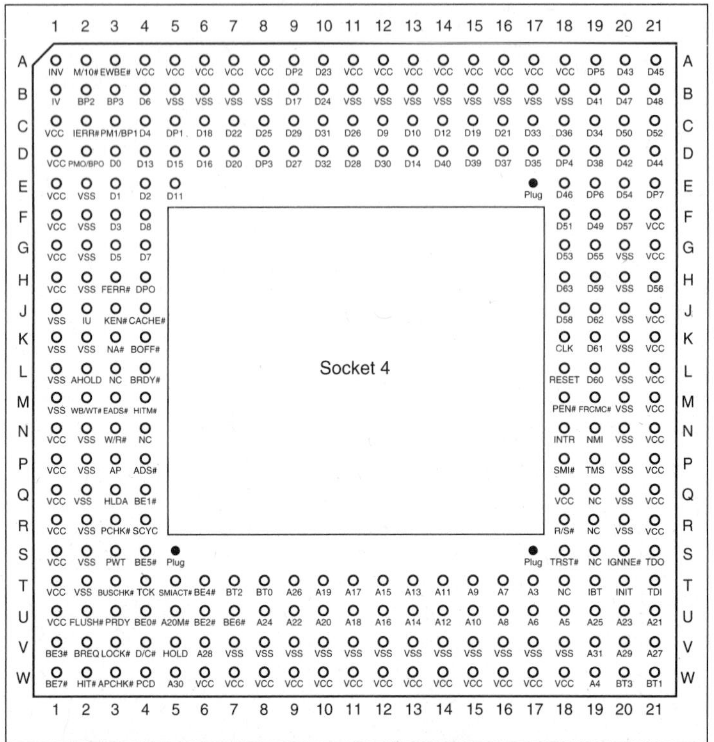

Figure 6.5

273-pin Intel Socket 4 configuration.

process. This results in even lower power consumption and allows the extremely high clock rates without overheating.

The Pentium 75/90/100/120/133 processors actually have 296 pins, although they plug into the official Intel Socket 5 design, which calls for a total 320 pins. The additional pins will be used by what officially is called the Future Pentium OverDrive Processor. This socket has the 320 pins configured in a *Staggered Pin Grid Array* (*SPGA*), in which the individual pins are staggered for tighter clearance.

Figure 6.6 shows the standard pinout for Socket 5.

The Future Pentium OverDrive Processor that eventually will use this socket will have an active heat sink (fan) assembly that will draw power directly from the chip socket. Intel has stated that this chip will require a maximum 4.33 amps of 3.3v to run the chip (14.289 watts) and 0.2 amp of 5v power to run the fan (1 watt), which means total power consumption of 15.289 watts. This amount is less power than the original 66 MHz Pentium processor requires, yet it runs a chip that is likely to be as much as four times faster!

The last 486 socket was created especially for the DX4 and the DX4 (Pentium) OverDrive Processor. Socket 6 basically is a slightly redesigned version of Socket 3, which has an

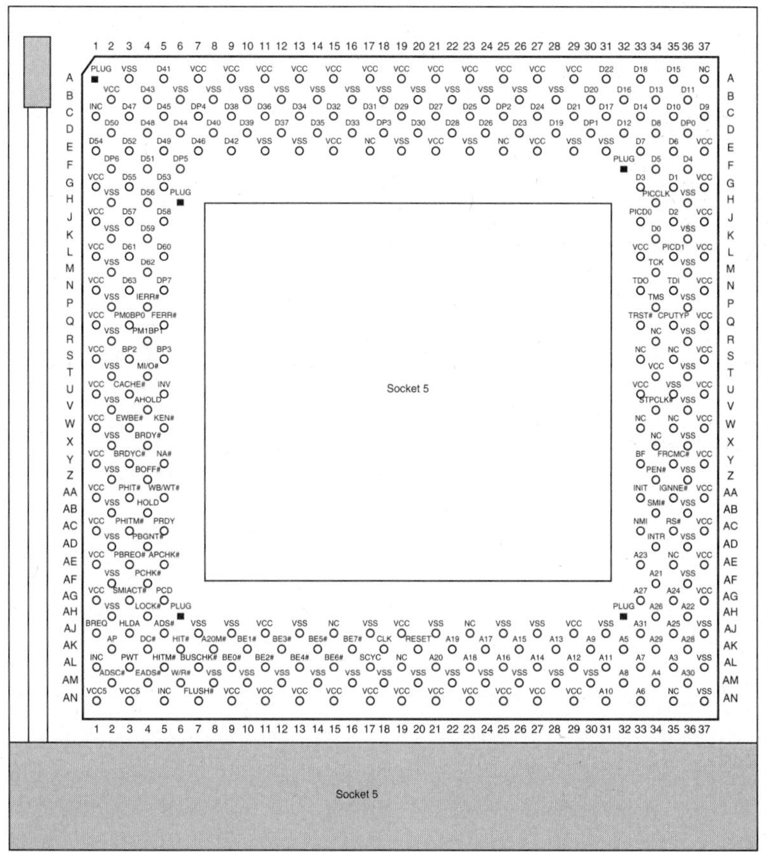

Figure 6.6

320-pin Intel Socket 5 configuration.

additional two pins plugged for proper chip keying. Socket 6 has 235 pins and will accept only 3.3v 486 or OverDrive processors. Currently, this means that Socket 6 will accept only the DX4 and the DX4 (Pentium) OverDrive Processor. Because this socket provides only 3.3v, and because the only processors that plug into it are designed to operate on 3.3v, no chance exists that potentially damaging problems will occur, like those with the Socket 3 design. Most new 486-class systems that come with DX4 chips initially will use Socket 6. Figure 6.7 shows the Socket 6 pinout.

The DX4 100 MHz processor can draw a maximum 1.45 amps of 3.3v (4.785 watts). The DX4 (Pentium) OverDrive Processor that eventually will replace that processor will draw a maximum 3.0 amps at 3.3v (9.9 watts) and 0.2 amp at 5v (1 watt) to run the fan, for a total 10.9 watts. Like all the other OverDrive processors that have active heat sink/fan assemblies, the processor has an easy-to-remove fan that can be replaced should it ever fail.

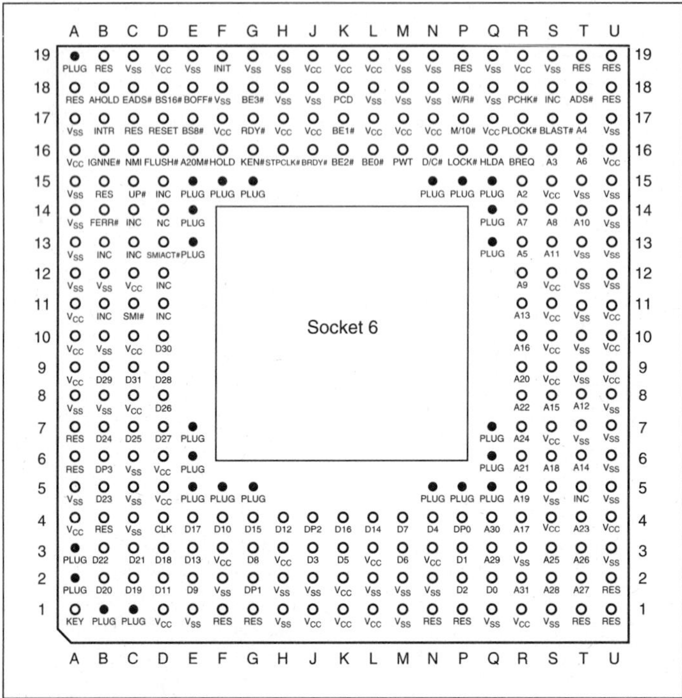

Figure 6.7

235-pin Intel Socket 6 configuration.

The newest socket is Socket 7, which is essentially the same as Socket 5 with one additional key pin in the opposite inside corner of the existing key pin. Socket 7 therefore has 321-pins total in a 21 × 21 SPGA arrangement. The real difference with Socket 7 is not the socket itself, but with the companion VRM (Voltage Regulator Module) that must accompany it.

The *VRM* is a small circuit board that contains all the voltage regulation circuitry used to drop the 5v power supply signal to the correct voltage for the processor. The VRM was implemented for several reasons. One is that voltage regulators tend to run hot and are very failure-prone. By soldering these circuits on the motherboard, as has been done with the Pentium Socket 5 design, you make it very likely that a failure of the regulator will require a complete motherboard replacement. Although technically the regulator could be replaced, many of them are surface-mount soldered, which would make the whole procedure very time-consuming and expensive. Besides, in this day and age, when the top-of-the-line motherboards are only worth $250 (less the processor and any memory), it is just not cost effective to service them. Having a replaceable VRM plugged into a socket will make it easy to replace the regulators should they ever fail.

Although replaceability is nice, the main reason behind the VRM design is that Intel is building new Pentium processors to run on a variety of voltages. Intel has several different versions of the Pentium processors that run on 3.3v (called VR), 3.465v (called VRE), as well as 2.9v, 2.5v, and even lower in the future. Several of the current motherboards support the existing 3.3v or 3.465v processors, but few support the new 2.9v versions. The Pentium processors running at 150 MHz and higher are expected to use the 2.9v or lower settings, which must be supplied via a Socket 7 with VRM adapter.

In other words, if you want to purchase a Pentium board that can be upgraded to the next generation of even higher speed processors—as well as be easily repairable should the voltage regulators fail—look for a system with a Socket 7 and VRM.

OverDrive Processor Installation. You can upgrade almost any system with an OverDrive processor. The most difficult aspect of the installation is simply having the correct OverDrive processor for your system. Currently, 486 OverDrive processors (which really are DX2 processors) are available for replacing 486SX and 486DX processors. The following table lists all the current and future OverDrive processors with their official Intel designations:

Processor Designation	Replaces	Socket	Heat Sink	Max. Power
486SX OverDrive	486SX	Socket 1	Passive	6 watts
486DX OverDrive	486DX	Socket 1	Passive	6 watts
486DX OverDrive	486DX	168-pin*	Passive	6 watts
486 Pentium OverDrive	486DX2	Socket 2 or 3	Active	12.5 watts
60/66 Pentium OverDrive	Pentium 60/66	Socket 4	Active	13.5 watts
75+ Pentium OverDrive	Pentium 90/100	Socket 5/7	Active	15.289 watts

**The 168-pin version is designed for the original 486DX socket, which is slightly different from the official Socket 1 design.*

Three types of system configurations support the original 486 OverDrive (really DX2) processors:

- 486SX (Socket 1)
- 486DX (Socket 1)
- 486DX with standard 168-pin socket

Although Intel labels the OverDrive processors for SX or DX systems with a Socket 1 design, technically, the processors are exactly the same. The 168-pin version was specially created for systems that do not have the Socket 1 design, because it was created after the original 486DX systems were on the market. Many older 486DX systems will need this version of the OverDrive processor, which actually has the same pinout that is sold commercially as the DX2 processor, with the exception of the Intel-applied passive heat sink.

These OverDrive chips also are available in different speed ratings. You must select a version that is rated at least as fast as your motherboard will run. An OverDrive chip rated faster than is necessary will cost more but will work well; an OverDrive chip rated at a speed that is less than your motherboard will run will cause the chip to overheat and fail.

Most motherboards are speed-switchable, which means that if you currently have a 25 MHz 486SX system, you can upgrade to the 66 MHz OverDrive (or DX2) processor by first switching your motherboard to 33 MHz operation. If you leave the motherboard set at 25 MHz, the 66 MHz-rated chip would run at 50 MHz, but you would be missing out on potential performance.

To upgrade any 486SX or DX system that uses dual sockets—and therefore has a vacant Socket 1-type OverDrive Processor socket—you simply turn off the system, plug in the proper 169-pin OverDrive Processor, and turn the system back on. With the 169-pin versions designed for Socket 1, putting the processor in is literally impossible unless it is properly oriented with respect to pin 1. If you are using the 168-pin version that does not feature the key orientation pin, you must match the pin 1 indicator on the chip (usually a dot or a notched corner) with the appropriate designation on the socket (also a dot and/or notched corner). If you install the chip out of orientation, you likely will fry it when you power up the system.

To upgrade a system that has only a single processor socket, remove the existing processor and replace it with either a 169-pin (SX) or a 168-pin (DX) OverDrive Processor. If the system uses a ZIF (zero insertion force) socket, this procedure is very easy; otherwise, you must use a pry tool to remove the old chip.

Intel includes a pry-bar chip-extractor tool for removing the primary CPU, if that is necessary. You simply wedge the tool under one side of the chip and then pull to pry the chip partially out of the socket. You repeat this step for each of the chip's four sides. Then you can lift the loose chip out of the system and store it in a static-protective storage box (included with the OverDrive upgrade kit).

After you plug the OverDrive chip in, some systems require you to change jumper or switch settings on the motherboard to activate the chip. If you have an SX system, you also will have to run your system's setup program, because you must inform the CMOS memory that a math coprocessor is present. (Some DX systems also require you to run the setup program.) Intel provides a utility disk that includes a test program to verify that the new chip is installed and functioning correctly.

After verifying that the installation functions correctly, you have nothing more to do. You do not need to reconfigure any of the software on your system for the new chip. The only difference that you should notice is the fact that everything works nearly twice as fast as it did before the upgrade.

Upgrades that use the newer OverDrive chips for Sockets 2–6 are likely to be much easier because these chips almost always go into a ZIF socket and therefore require no tools. In most cases, special configuration pins in the socket and on the new OverDrive chips take care of any jumper settings for you. In some cases, however, you may have to set some jumpers on the motherboard to configure the socket for the new processor.

OverDrive Compatibility Problems. Although you can upgrade most older 486SX or 486DX systems with the OverDrive processors, some exceptions exist. Four factors can make an OverDrive upgrade difficult or impossible:

- BIOS routines that use CPU-dependent timing loops
- Lack of clearance for the OverDrive heat sink (25 MHz and faster)
- Inadequate system cooling
- A 486 CPU that is soldered in rather than socketed

To start with one of the obvious exceptions, you cannot use a DX2/OverDrive process to upgrade a 50 MHz 486DX system, because Intel does not make a DX2 OverDrive that is rated to run at the 100 MHz internal clock rate. In that case, you can perform an upgrade that is not officially authorized by Intel but that works in most cases: purchase a raw DX4 processor and voltage-regulator adapter to install in the 50 MHz 486DX socket. The voltage regulator will have a jumper for configuring the speed of the DX4 to 2x, 2.5x, or 3x operation. In this case, you need to set the jumper to 2x for 100 MHz operation, which is the maximum for which the DX4 100 chip is rated.

Caution

Because this upgrade is not officially authorized by Intel, and because Intel does not even sell the DX4 chips through retail channels, Intel provides no warranty. Make sure that the vendor from which you purchase the DX4 chip will take it back in case it doesn't work.

If you want a safer upgrade with an Intel warranty, you can use the DX4 OverDrive chip that is sold through retail channels. This chip has a built-in passive heat sink and an integral voltage regulator allowing it to operate in a 5v socket even though the chip runs internally on 3.3v. Unfortunately, this chip will run only in clock-tripled mode, and the heat sink is glued on, preventing the installation of a larger one for even more improved cooling.

Systems that come with DX2, DX4, or Pentium chips installed by the system manufacturer also are eligible for future OverDrive upgrades, which may not yet be available.

In some rare cases, problems may occur in systems that should be upgradable but are not. One of these problems is related to the ROM BIOS. A few 486 systems have a BIOS that regulates hardware operations by using timing loops based on how long it takes the CPU to execute a series of instructions. When the CPU suddenly is running twice as fast, the prescribed timing interval is too short, resulting in improper system operation or even hardware lockups. Fortunately, you usually can solve this problem by upgrading the system's BIOS.

Another problem is related to physical clearance. All OverDrive chips for 25 MHz and faster systems have heat sinks glued or fastened to the top of the chip. The heat sink can add 0.25 to 1.2 inches to the top of the chip. This extra height can interfere with other components in the system, especially in small desktop systems and portables. Solutions to this problem must be determined on a case-by-case basis. You can sometimes relocate an expansion card or disk drive, or even modify the chassis slightly to increase clearance.

In some cases, the interference cannot be resolved, leaving you only the option of running the chip without the heat sink. Needless to say, removing the glued-on heat sink will at best void the warranty provided by Intel and will at worst damage the chip or the system due to overheating. I do not recommend removing the heat sink.

The OverDrive chips can generate up to twice the heat of the chips that they replace. Even with the active heat sink/fan built into the faster OverDrive chips, some systems do not have enough airflow or cooling capability to keep the OverDrive chip within the prescribed safe operating-temperature range. Small desktop systems or portables are most likely to have cooling problems. Unfortunately, only proper testing can indicate whether a system will have a heat problem. For this reason, Intel has been running an extensive test program to certify systems that are properly designed to handle an OverDrive upgrade.

Finally, some systems have the 486SX or DX chip soldered directly into the motherboard rather than in a socket. This method is used sometimes for cost reasons because leaving out the socket is cheaper; in most cases, however, the reason is clearance. The IBM P75 portable that I use, for example, has a credit-card-size CPU board that plugs into the motherboard. Because the CPU card is close to one of the expansion slots, to allow for clearance between the 486 chip and heat sink, IBM soldered the CPU directly into the small card, making an OverDrive upgrade nearly impossible unless IBM offers its own upgrade via a new CPU card with the DX2 chip already installed. This situation did not stop me, of course; I desoldered the DX chip and soldered in a pin-compatible 168-pin DX2 processor in its place. I currently am installing a voltage regulator and DX4 processor.

To clarify which systems are tested to be upgradable without problems, Intel has compiled an extensive list of compatible systems. To determine whether a PC is upgradable with an OverDrive processor, contact Intel via its FaxBACK system (see the vendor list in Appendix B) and ask for the OverDrive Processor Compatibility Data documents. These documents list the systems that have been tested with the OverDrive processors and indicate which other changes you may have to make for the upgrade to work (a newer ROM BIOS or setup program, for example).

One important note about these compatibility lists: if your system is not on the list, the warranty on the OverDrive processor is void. Intel recommends OverDrive upgrades only for systems that are on the compatibility list. The list also includes notes about systems that may require a ROM upgrade, a jumper change, or perhaps a new setup disk.

Some IBM PS/2 486 systems, for example, may require you to use a new Reference disk when you install an OverDrive CPU. You can download the latest version of any PS/2 Reference disk from the IBM National Support Center Bulletin Board System (NSC BBS), which appears in the vendor list. A wise practice is to download the latest version of the Reference and Diagnostics disk(s) for any PS/2 system before attempting a processor upgrade.

Notice that the files on the IBM NSC BBS are compressed Reference and Diagnostics disk images. To decompress and extract the files in the appropriate format, you need one or both of the following files:

FILENAME.EXT	Contents
LDF.COM	".DSK" file-extraction program
TGSFX.COM	".TG0" file-extraction program

These files contain programs that will create the Reference or Diagnostics disk from the compressed DSK or TG0 files.

Pentium OverDrive for DX2 and DX4 Systems. In 1995, the Pentium OverDrive Processor (code-named P24T) became available, while the DX4 (Pentium) OverDrive Processor has yet to be released. These chips are virtually identical, except that the first one will run on 5v, whereas the DX4 version will run on 3.3v and consume slightly less power. Because the Pentium OverDrive chip has not been very successful in the marketplace due to high pricing when compared to the real Pentium processor, it now seems unlikely that Intel will actually ever sell the 3.3v version. Virtually all 486 systems include either the Socket 2 or Socket 3, which is capable of providing the 5v needed by the standard Pentium OverDrive chip.

The Pentium OverDrive Processor is designed for systems that have a processor socket which follows the Intel Socket 2 specification. This processor also will work in systems that have a Socket 3 design, although you should ensure that the voltage is set for 5v rather than 3.3v. Likewise, you should make sure that if you are using any type of 3.3v processor, you have Socket 3 set for 3.3v operation. Plugging the 3.3v version of the OverDrive chip into the Socket 2 design will be impossible; special key pins will prevent improper insertion. If your system has a 3.3v-only Socket 6 design, the only OverDrive processor to get is the DX4 OverDrive Processor.

Besides a 32-bit Pentium core, these processors feature increased clock-speed operation due to internal clock multiplication, and will incorporate an internal Write-Back cache (standard with the Pentium). If the motherboard supports the write-back cache function, increased performance will be realized. Unfortunately, most motherboards out there, especially older ones with the Socket 2 design, only support Write-Through cache.

In essence, these OverDrive processors are Pentium SX chips, because they will have all the features of the real Pentium processors except the 64-bit external data bus; the external data bus of these OverDrive chips will be 32 bits instead. Even so, with the improved Pentium core, separate code and Write-Back data caches, higher clock speeds, and other enhancements, these processors should nearly double the performance of the systems in which they are installed.

Most of the tests of these OverDrive chips show them to be only slightly ahead of the DX4-100 and behind the DX4-120 as well as the true Pentium 60, 66, or 75. Because of their higher price compared to these other solutions, the Pentium OverDrive chip has not turned out to be a very viable upgrade for most 486 systems. A better choice would be a DX4-100 or 120 for a less expensive upgrade, or simply swap out the entire motherboard for a new Pentium board complete with a true Pentium processor, and not the "Pentium-SX" that the Pentium OverDrive chip represents.

Pentium

On October 19, 1992, Intel announced that the fifth generation of its compatible microprocessor line (code-named P5) would be named the Pentium processor rather than the 586, as everybody had been assuming. Calling the new chip the 586 would have been natural, but Intel discovered that it could not trademark a number designation, and the company wanted to prevent other manufacturers from using the same name for any clone chips that they might develop.

The actual Pentium chip shipped on March 22, 1993. Systems that use these chips were only a few months behind.

The Pentium is fully compatible with previous Intel processors, but it also differs from them in many ways. At least one of these differences is revolutionary: the Pentium features twin data pipelines, which enable it to execute two instructions at the same time. The 486 and all preceding chips can perform only a single instruction at a time. Intel calls the capability to execute two instructions at the same time *superscalar technology*. This technology provides additional performance compared with the 486.

The standard 486 chip can execute a single instruction in an average of two clock cycles—cut to an average of one clock cycle with the advent of internal clock multiplication used in the DX2 and DX4 processors. With superscalar technology, the Pentium can execute many instructions at a rate of two instructions per cycle. Superscalar architecture usually is associated with high-output RISC (Reduced Instruction Set Computer) chips. The Pentium is one of the first CISC (Complex Instruction Set Computer) chips to be considered superscalar. The Pentium is almost like having two 486 chips under the hood. Table 6.11 shows the Pentium processor specifications.

Table 6.11 Pentium Processor Specifications

Introduced:	March 22, 1993 (first generation); March 7, 1994 (second generation)
Maximum rated speeds:	60, 66 MHz (first generation); 75, 90, 100 MHz (second generation)
CPU clock multiplier:	1x (first generation); 1.5x–2x (second generation)
Register size:	32-bit
External data bus:	64-bit
Memory address bus:	32-bit
Maximum memory:	4G
Integral-cache size:	8K code, 8K data
Integral-cache type:	2-Way Set Associative, Write-Back Data
Burst-mode transfers:	Yes
Number of transistors:	3.1 million (60/66 MHz), 3.3 million (75 MHz and up)
Circuit size:	0.8 micron (60/66 MHz), 0.6 micron (75-100 MHz), 0.35 micron (120/133 MHz and up)
External package:	273-pin PGA, 296-pin SPGA, Tape Carrier
Math coprocessor:	Built-in FPU (Floating-Point Unit)
Power management:	SMM, enhanced in second generation
Operating voltage:	5v (first generation); 3.465v, 3.3v, 2.9v (second generation)

PGA = Pin Grid Array
SPGA = Staggered Pin Grid Array

The two instruction pipelines within the chip are called the u- and v-pipes. The *u-pipe*, which is the primary pipe, can execute all integer and floating-point instructions. The *v-pipe* is a secondary pipe that can execute only simple integer instructions and certain floating-point instructions. The process of operating on two instructions simultaneously in the different pipes is called *pairing*. Not all sequentially executing instructions can be paired, and when pairing is not possible, only the u-pipe is used. To optimize the Pentium's efficiency, you can recompile software to allow more instructions to be paired.

The Pentium is 100 percent software-compatible with the 386 and 486, and although all current software will run much faster on the Pentium, many software manufacturers want to recompile their applications to exploit even more of the Pentium's true power. Intel has developed new compilers that will take full advantage of the chip; the company will license the technology to compiler firms so that software developers can take advantage of the superscalar (parallel processing) capability of the Pentium. This optimization is starting to appear in some of the newest software on the market. Optimized software should improve performance by allowing more instructions to execute simultaneously in both pipes.

To minimize stalls in one or more of the pipes caused by delays in fetching instructions that branch to nonlinear memory locations, the Pentium processor has a *Branch Target Buffer* (BTB) that employs a technique called *branch prediction*. The BTB attempts to predict whether a program branch will be taken or not and then fetches the appropriate next instructions. The use of branch prediction enables the Pentium to keep both pipelines operating at full speed. Figure 6.8 shows the internal architecture of the Pentium processor.

The Pentium has a 32-bit address-bus width, giving it the same 4G memory-addressing capabilities as the 386DX and 486 processors. But the Pentium expands the data bus to 64 bits, which means that it can move twice as much data into or out of the CPU compared with a 486 of the same clock speed. The 64-bit data bus requires that system memory be accessed 64 bits wide, which means that each bank of memory is 64 bits.

On most motherboards, memory is installed via SIMMs (Single In-Line Memory Modules), which are available in 9-bit-wide and 36-bit-wide versions. Most Pentium systems use the 36-bit-wide (32 data bits plus 4 parity bits) SIMMs—four of these SIMMs per bank of memory. Most Pentium motherboards have four of these 36-bit SIMM sockets, providing for a total two banks of memory.

Even though the Pentium has a 64-bit data bus that transfers information 64 bits at a time into and out of the processor, the Pentium has only 32-bit internal registers. As instructions are being processed internally, they are broken down into 32-bit instructions and data elements, and processed in much the same way as in the 486. Some people thought that Intel was misleading them by calling the Pentium a 64-bit processor, but 64-bit transfers do indeed take place. Internally, however, the Pentium has 32-bit registers that are fully compatible with the 486.

The Pentium has two separate internal 8K caches, compared with a single 8K or 16K cache in the 486. The cache-controller circuitry and the cache memory are embedded in the CPU chip. The cache mirrors the information in normal RAM by keeping a copy of

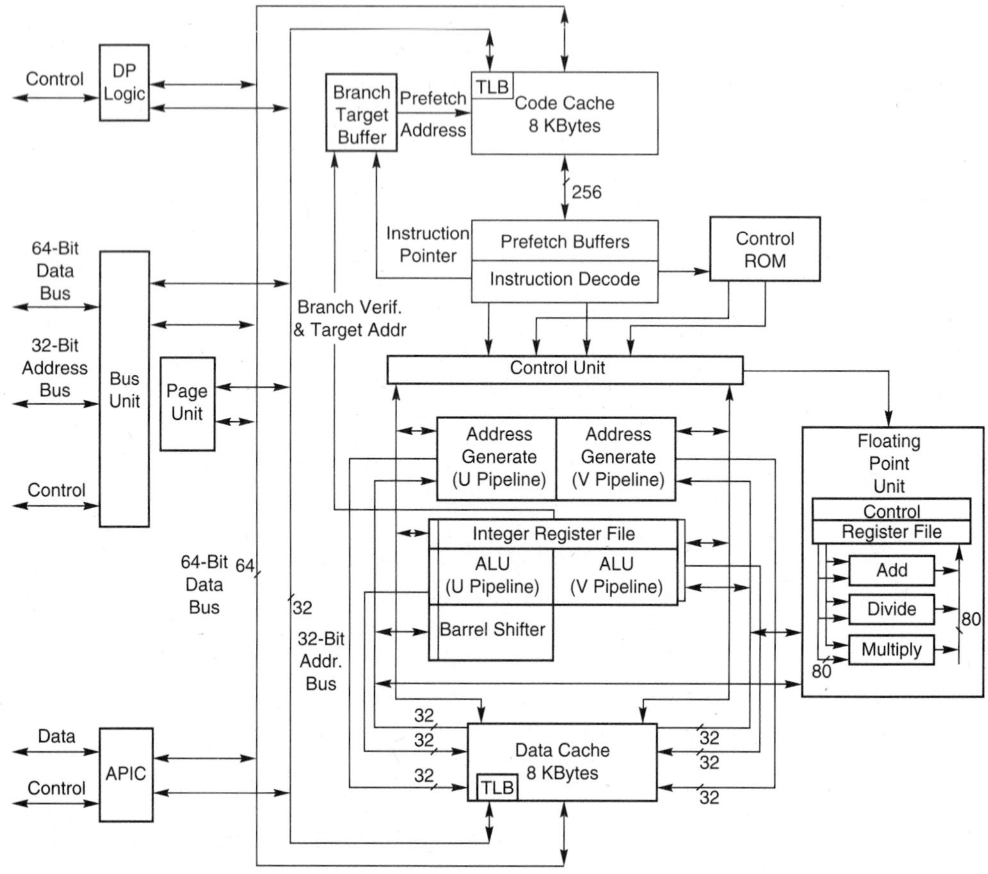

Figure 6.8

Pentium processor internal architecture.

the data and code from different memory locations. The Pentium cache also can hold information to be written to memory when the load on the CPU and other system components is less. (The 486 makes all memory writes immediately.)

The separate code and data caches are organized in a two-way set associative fashion, with each set split into lines of 32 bytes each. Each cache has a dedicated *Translation Lookaside Buffer* (TLB), which translates linear addresses to physical addresses. You can configure the data cache as Write-Back or Write-Through on a line-by-line basis. When you use the Write-Back capability, the cache can store write operations as well as reads, further improving performance over read-only Write-Through mode. Using Write-Back mode results in less activity between the CPU and system memory—an important improvement, because CPU access to system memory is a bottleneck on fast systems. The code cache is an inherently write-protected cache because it contains only execution instructions and not data, which is updated. Because burst cycles are used, the cache data can be read or written very quickly.

Systems based on the Pentium can benefit greatly from secondary processor caches (Level 2), which usually consist of up to 512K or more of extremely fast (15ns or less) Static RAM (SRAM) chips. When the CPU fetches data that is not already available in its internal processor (Level 1) cache, wait states slow the CPU. If the data already is in the secondary processor cache, however, the CPU can go ahead with its work without pausing for wait states.

The Pentium uses a BiCMOS (Bipolar Complementary Metal Oxide Semiconductor) process and superscalar architecture to achieve the level of performance expected from the new chip. BiCMOS adds about 10 percent to the complexity of the chip design, but adds about 30–35 percent better performance without a size or power penalty. Intel will be transitioning back to conventional CMOS designs as the clock speeds of the Pentium and Pentium Pro processor increase. There is no performance advantage to BiCMOS at lower voltages, and some of the new processors will be running on 2.5v or less. Intel uses the BiCMOS process in most of the processors up to 133 MHz, but will use CMOS for any faster ones because they will also run at lower voltages.

All Pentium processors are SL Enhanced, meaning that they incorporate the SMM to provide full control of power-management features, which helps reduce power consumption. The second-generation Pentium processors (75 MHz and faster) incorporate a more advanced form of SMM that includes processor clock control, which allows you to throttle the processor up or down to control power use. With these more advanced Pentium processors, you can even stop the clock, putting the processor in a state of suspension that requires very little power. The second-generation Pentium processors run on 3.3v power (instead of 5v), reducing power requirements and heat generation even further.

For even lower power consumption, Intel has introduced special Mobile Pentium processors in the 75/90/100 MHz family. These do not use a conventional chip package and are instead mounted using a new format called *Tape Carrier Packaging* (*TCP*). The tape carrier packaging does not encase the chip in ceramic or plastic as with a conventional chip package, but instead covers the actual processor die directly with a thin, protective plastic coating. The entire processor is less than 1mm thick, or about half the thickness of a dime, and weighs less than 1 gram. They are sold to system manufacturers in a roll that looks very much like filmstrip. The TCP processor is directly affixed (soldered) to the motherboard by a special machine, resulting in a smaller package, lower height, better thermal transfer, and lower power consumption. Special solder plugs on the circuit board located directly under the processor draw heat away and provide better cooling in the tight confines of a typical notebook or laptop system, and no cooling fans are required.

The Pentium, like the 486, contains an internal math coprocessor or FPU. The FPU in the Pentium has been rewritten and performs significantly better than the FPU in the 486, yet it is fully compatible with the 486 and 387 math coprocessor. The Pentium FPU is estimated to be two to as much as 10 times faster than the FPU in the 486. In addition, the two standard instruction pipelines in the Pentium provide two units to handle standard integer math. (The math coprocessor handles only more complex calculations.) Other processors, such as the 486, have only a single standard execution pipe and one integer-math unit.

First-Generation Pentium Processor. At the time of this writing, the Pentium is available in two basic designs, each with several versions. The first-generation design is available in 60 and 66 MHz processor speeds. This design uses a 273-pin PGA form factor and runs on 5v power. In this design, the processor runs at the same speed as the motherboard—in other words, a 1x clock is used.

The first-generation Pentium was created through an 0.8-micron BiCMOS process. Unfortunately, this process, combined with the 3.1 million transistor count, resulted in a die that was overly large and complicated to manufacture. As a result, reduced yields kept the chip in short supply; Intel could not make them fast enough. The 0.8-micron process was criticized by other manufacturers, including Motorola and IBM, which had been using 0.6-micron technology for their most advanced chips. The huge die and 5v operating voltage caused the 66 MHz versions to consume up to an incredible 3.2 amps or 16 watts of power, resulting in a tremendous amount of heat—and problems in some systems that did not employ conservative design techniques. Often, the system required a separate fan to blow on the processor to keep it cool.

Much of the criticism leveled at Intel for the first-generation Pentium was justified. Some people realized that the first-generation design was just that; they knew that new Pentium versions, made in a more advanced manufacturing process, were coming. Many of those people (including the author of this book) advised against purchasing any Pentium system until the second-generation version became available.

A cardinal rule of computing is never to buy the first generation of any processor. Although you can wait forever because something better always will be on the horizon, a little waiting is worthwhile in some cases.

Second-Generation Pentium Processor. Intel announced the second-generation Pentium (code named P54C) on March 7, 1994. This new processor was introduced in 90 and 100 MHz versions, with a 75 MHz version not far behind. Eventually, 120 and 133 MHz versions were also introduced. The second-generation Pentium uses 0.6-micron (75/90/100 MHz) BiCMOS technology to shrink the die and reduce power consumption. The newer, faster 120 and 133 MHz second-generation versions incorporate an even smaller die built on a 0.35-micron BiCMOS process. These smaller dies are not changed from the 0.6-micron versions; they are basically a photographic reduction of the P54C die. Additionally, these new processors run on 3.3v or even lower power. The 100 MHz version consumes a maximum 3.25 amps of 3.3v power, which equals only 10.725 watts. The slower 90 MHz version uses only 2.95 amps of 3.3v power, which is only 9.735 watts. The 75 MHz uses about 6 watts of power and functions reasonably well in laptop and portable systems that run on batteries.

The P54C second-generation Pentium processors come in a 296-pin SPGA form factor that is physically incompatible with the first-generation versions. The only way to upgrade from the first generation to the second is to replace the motherboard. The second-generation Pentium processors also have 3.3 million transistors—more than the earlier chips. The extra transistors exist because additional clock-control SL enhancements were added, as were an on-chip Advanced Programmable Interrupt Controller (APIC) and dual-processor interface.

The APIC and dual-processor interface are responsible for orchestrating dual-processor configurations in which two second-generation Pentium chips can process on the same motherboard simultaneously. Many of the new Pentium motherboards will come with dual Socket 5 or Socket 7 specification sockets, which fully support the multiprocessing capability of the new chips. Already, software support for what usually is called Symmetric Multi-Processing (SMP) is being integrated into operating systems such as Windows and OS/2.

The second-generation Pentium processors use clock-multiplier circuitry to run the processor at speeds faster than the bus. The 90 MHz Pentium processor can run at 1.5 times the bus frequency, which normally is 60 MHz. The 100 MHz Pentium processor can run at a 1.5x clock in a system using a 66 MHz bus speed or at a 2x clock on a motherboard that is running at 50 MHz. The future 75 MHz version reportedly will also use the 1.5x clock and, therefore, run on 50 MHz motherboards.

Currently, running the motherboard faster than 66 MHz is impractical because of memory and local-bus performance constraints. The fastest Pentium systems would combine the 66 MHz motherboard operation with a 2x internal processor clock and 133 MHz processor operation. If you think that 2 times 66 equals 132 and not 133, you may be right, but in nearly all cases, 66 MHz operation really means 66.6666 MHz actual speed.

Virtually all Pentium motherboards have three speed settings: 50, 60, and 66 MHz. Pentium chips are available with a variety of different internal clock multipliers that cause the processor to operate at various multiples of these motherboard speeds. The following table lists the current and future proposed speeds of Pentium processors and motherboards:

CPU Type/Speed	CPU Clock	Motherboard Speed
Pentium 60	1x	60
Pentium 66	1x	66
Pentium 75	1.5x	50
Pentium 90	1.5x	60
Pentium 100	1.5x	66
Pentium 120	2x	60
Pentium 133	2x	66
Pentium 150	2.5x	60
Pentium 166	2.5x	66
Pentium 180	3x	60
Pentium 200	3x	66

The Core-to-Bus frequency ratio or clock multiplier is controlled in a Pentium processor by two pins on the chip labeled BF1 and BF2. The following table shows how the state of the BFx pins will affect the clock multiplication in the Pentium processor:

BF1	BF2	Clock Multiplier	Bus Speed (MHz)	Core Speed (MHz)
0	1	3x	66	200
0	1	3x	60	180
0	1	3x	50	150
0	0	2.5x	66	166
0	0	2.5x	60	150
0	0	2.5x	50	125
1	0	2x	66	133
1	0	2x	60	120
1	0	2x	50	100
1	1	1.5x	66	100
1	1	1.5x	60	90
1	1	1.5x	50	75

Not all chips support the Bus Frequency (BF) pins. In other words, some of the Pentium processors will operate only at specific combinations of these settings, or maybe even fixed at one particular setting. Many of the newer motherboards will have jumpers or switches that allow you to control the BF pins and therefore alter the clock multiplier ratio within the chip. I have known people who have taken 75 MHz rated Pentium chips and actually got them to run at up to 133 MHz by altering the clock multiplier to 2x, as well as the motherboard bus clock to 66 MHz by simply changing jumpers on the board. This is called *overclocking*, and while it can often work, a chip pushed beyond its rated limits will run much hotter and may not operate properly at the higher speeds. Fortunately, resetting the chip back to its original speed settings almost always returns the chip to normal operation.

Now that the second-generation Pentium processors have arrived in full force, and the next generation Pentium Pro processor is hitting the market at the high end, the time is right to economically purchase Pentium systems. The ideal system today uses the second-generation 133/166/200 MHz processor with a 66 MHz motherboard bus speed.

A new third generation of Pentium processors (code-named P55C) has just been released, which is a minor rework of the second generation. These third-generation Pentiums are available in clock rates of 60/150 MHz, 66/166 MHz, 60/180 MHz, and 66/200 MHz. The 200 MHz version will likely be the fastest Pentium processor Intel will ever make. The P55C processors will have some revisions done on the mask, including additional NSP (Native Signal Processing) support. The main change will be that they will be produced in a 0.25-micron CMOS process, which allows a much smaller die and uses fewer masks in production. These processors can be built using only 16 masks instead of the 20 used in the second-generation BiCMOS versions, and will operate at lower voltage levels. The voltages used will be 2.9v and eventually 2.5v.

Most of the current motherboards can supply only 3.465v or 3.3v. The 3.465v setting is called VRE (Voltage Reduced Extended) by Intel and is required by some versions of the Pentium, particularly some of the 100 MHz versions. The standard 3.3v setting is called STD (Standard), which most of the second-generation Pentiums use. STD-voltage means anything in a range from 3.135v to 3.465v with 3.3v nominal. There is also a special 3.3v setting called VR (Voltage Reduced), which reduces the range from 3.300v to 3.465v with 3.38v nominal. Some of the processors require this narrower specification, which most motherboards provide. Here is a summary:

Voltage Specification	Nominal	Tolerance	Minimum	Maximum
STD (Standard)	3.30v	±0.165	3.135v	3.465v
VR (Voltage Reduced)	3.38v	±0.083	3.300v	3.465v
VRE (VR Extended)	3.50v	±0.100	3.400v	3.600v

In order to use the third-generation Pentiums, the motherboard must be able to supply the new lower voltages these processors will use. Intel has indicated that these new processors will run on 2.9v and 2.5v, but the specifications could vary from those settings. To allow a more universal motherboard solution with respect to these changing voltages, Intel has come up with the Socket 7 with VRM. The VRM is a socketed module that plugs in next to the processor and supplies the correct voltage. Because the module is easily replaced, it will be easy to reconfigure a motherboard to support any of the voltages required by the newer Pentium processors.

If you want the maximum future upgradability to the P55C third-generation Pentiums, make sure that your Pentium motherboard includes 321-pin processor sockets that fully meet the Intel Socket 7 specification. These would also include the VRM socket. If you have dual sockets, you can add a second Pentium processor to take advantage of SMP support in the newer operating systems.

Also make sure that any Pentium motherboard you buy can be jumpered or reconfigured for both 60 and 66 MHz operation, which will enable you to take advantage of future Pentium OverDrive processors that will support the higher motherboard clock speeds.

These simple recommendations will enable you to perform several dramatic upgrades without changing the entire motherboard.

Pentium Pro Processor

Intel's newest chip and successor to the Pentium is called the Pentium Pro. The Pentium Pro was introduced in September of 1995, and became widely available in 1996. The new chip is unique among processors as it is constructed in a Multi-Chip Module (MCM) physical format, which Intel is calling a Dual Cavity PGA (Pin Grid Array) package. Inside the 387-pin chip carrier are two dies: one containing the actual Pentium Pro processor, and the other a 256K or 512K L2 cache. The processor die contains 5.5 million transistors, while the 256K cache die contains 15.5 million transistors, and the 512K cache die has 31 million transistors, for a potential total of 36.5 million transistors in the complete module!

The architecture of the Pentium Pro includes three internal instruction pipes, which can execute multiple instructions in one cycle. The main processor die includes a 16K split L1 cache with an 8K 2-Way Set Associative Cache for primary instructions, and an 8K 4-Way Set Associative Cache for data. The Pentium Pro can execute instructions out of order and has dynamic branch prediction and speculative execution capabilities.

In many ways, the Pentium Pro seems to be more of an evolutionary design compared to the Pentium rather than something totally new. The core of the chip is very RISC-like, while the external instruction interface is classic Intel CISC (Complex Instruction Set Computer). By breaking down the CISC instructions into several different RISC instructions and running them down parallel execution pipelines, the overall performance is increased.

Compared to the Pentium, Intel claims that the Pentium Pro is twice as fast, but it is comparing a 133 MHz Pentium Pro against a 100 MHz Pentium. It claims that this is a fair comparison because the improved design of the Pentium Pro can run on the older 0.6-micron BiCMOS process used by the Pentium 100 rather than the 0.35-micron CMOS process used by the Pentium 150 and higher. Intel has indicated that when the Pentium Pro is migrated to the 0.35-micron and eventually 0.25-micron CMOS process, absolutely incredible speeds will be possible. I gather that speeds of 300 MHz and higher will be possible using these new processes.

Notwithstanding that the Pentium Pro can be manufactured at higher clock speeds on a given process than the Pentium, comparing a 133 MHz operating version of both the Pentium and a Pentium Pro shows that the Pentium Pro has only about a 33 percent advantage in power. This is enhanced further, however, by the fact that Intel has this new chip running at rated speeds of 150, 166, and even 200 MHz. This may improve with future versions of the Pentium Pro—for example, versions with higher speeds and even larger integrated L2 caches have already been proposed.

The integrated L2 cache is one of the really outstanding features of the Pentium Pro. By building the L2 cache into the CPU and getting it off the motherboard, the cache can now run at full processor speed rather than the slower 60 or 66 MHz motherboard bus speeds. In fact, the L2 cache features its own internal 64-bit backside bus, which does not share time with the external 64-bit frontside bus used by the CPU. The internal registers and data paths are still 32-bit as with the Pentium. By building the L2 cache into the system, motherboards will become cheaper because they will no longer require separate cache memory. Some boards may still try to include cache memory in their design, but the general consensus is that Level 3 cache (as it would be called) would offer less improvement with the Pentium Pro than with the Pentium.

One of the features of the built-in L2 cache is that multiprocessing is greatly improved. Rather than just dual processor configurations (SMP) as with the Pentium, the Pentium Pro will support a new type of multiprocessor configuration called the Multi-Processor Specification (MPS 1.1). The Pentium Pro with MPS will allow configurations of up to four processors running together. Unlike other multi-processor configurations, the Pentium Pro will avoid cache coherency problems because each chip maintains a separate L1 and L2 cache internally.

Pentium Pro-based motherboards will be pretty much exclusively PCI and ISA bus based, and Intel is producing its own chipsets for these new motherboards. The first chipset was called Orion, while the newest version is called Natoma. Along with the new chipsets, Intel is proposing a motherboard form factor change for future Pentium Pro boards. The new form factor is called ATX, and will be different from the Baby-AT form factor used by most PC-compatibles. The ATX form factor is about the same 9 × 13-inch size as the Baby-AT, but the board is turned 90 degrees from the way the Baby-AT boards mount. In other words, the long side is now against the back of the case, and the expansion slots will be parallel with the short side of the board. The main reason for the new form factor is to move the CPU to an area where expansion cards will not be located, which should allow much better cooling. Current systems with the CPU under the slots can have problems in this area, sometimes preventing one from using all the available bus slots.

Another benefit of the ATX form factor is that the long edge of the board will be against the back of the case, allowing room for many built-in connectors. ATX boards will be highly integrated, featuring built-in dual serial ports, a parallel port, floppy controller, dual enhanced IDE ports, integrated sound, SVGA video, and optional SCSI and networking interfaces. Of course, this new motherboard form factor will require retooled cases and most likely power supplies, as well. Intel is sharing the specifications of the new ATX form factor, and many other motherboard manufacturers already have designs ready.

Other Pentium Pro system manufacturers intend on sticking with the Baby-AT form factor, at least for the time being. The big problem with the standard Baby-AT form factor will be keeping the CPU properly cooled. The massive Pentium Pro processor will consume 20 watts or more power and generate an appreciable amount of heat.

Initially, the Pentium Pro will be available in 50/150, 60/180, and 66/200 MHz speeds. Eventually, Pentium Pro processors will be available in much higher clock rates beyond 200 MHz.

Intel is already deep into the development of the P7 processor, which should appear sometime in 1997. Not much is known at this early stage, but it would not be too difficult to predict that it should have somewhere around 10 million transistors and will probably debut at speeds up around 200 MHz or greater. Further projecting puts the P8 processor out around 1999 with 20 million transistors at 300 MHz, and possibly a P9 chip during the year 2000 with 40 million transistors and 400 MHz or more! This helps to keep in perspective the fact that whatever you purchase today will be obsolete in two to three years.

IBM (Intel-Licensed) Processors

For many years, IBM and Intel have had a very close relationship, especially considering the fact that IBM is one of Intel's largest customers. The companies often enter into agreements to exchange technology and information. One such agreement involves the licensing of Intel's processors; IBM has a license to produce several of the Intel processors.

In a licensing agreement, Intel shares with IBM the original mask, or design, of the chip. A *CPU chip mask*, which is the photographic blueprint of the processor, is used to etch the intricate signal pathways into a silicon chip. Using this mask, IBM can produce the chip as Intel designed it or make modifications in the basic design. Normally, IBM must also share with Intel any modifications that it makes.

Restrictions often exist in the way that IBM can market these Intel-derived chips. Other manufacturers (such as AMD, Harris, and Siemens) licensed several of the older Intel processors up through the 286, but no manufacturer other than IBM originally licensed the 386 and newer processor masks. The 386 and newer chips produced by companies other than Intel and IBM are often reverse-engineered without Intel's blessing. In fact, Intel has been involved in drawn-out legal battles with several of the clone-processor manufacturers, most of which have been settled.

Several years ago, IBM licensed the 386 processor mask. The company since has produced several variations that include modifications of the basic Intel design, including some versions that also carry a 486 designation. Some of the IBM processors have few design changes; others have major differences that make the chip faster, less power-hungry, or both. Table 6.12 summarizes the IBM processors that are derived from Intel masks.

IBM SLC Processors

The IBM SLC processors are enhanced versions of the Intel 386SX that offer greater performance and lower power consumption. The SLC processors, which are based on the Intel 386SX mask, have the physical form factor and pinout of the 386SX, with some of the unused pins now being used for cache control.

The IBM-enhanced chips have some 486 features (including the internal cache) and perform as well as, or even better than, a 486SX at a much lower cost. IBM states that the 386SLC chip is as much as 80 percent faster than the standard 386SX chip, which means that a 20 MHz 386SLC can outperform a 33 MHz 386DX system. The first system to use any of these custom IBM processors was the PS/2 Model 57. These processors now are used in other manufacturers' systems as well.

The SLC processors are often criticized for having only a 16-bit data bus and a 24-bit address bus. The address bus allows access to only 16M of memory, which is fine for most users. Users who need more memory, however, should look to the IBM Blue

Table 6.12 IBM Processor Specifications

Processor	CPU Clock	Standard Voltage	Internal Register Size	Data-Bus Width	Address-Bus Width
386 SLC	1x	5v	32-bit	16-bit	24-bit
486 SLC	1x	3.3v	32-bit	16-bit	24-bit
486 SLC2	2x	3.3v	32-bit	16-bit	24-bit
486 BL2	2x	3.3v	32-bit	32-bit	32-bit
486 BL3	3x	3.3v	32-bit	32-bit	32-bit

Lightning (BL) or to the Intel 486 processors and beyond, which provide a full 32 bits of memory addressing.

Although the SLC processors have only a 16-bit data bus, these processors still outperform many 32-bit chips because of the large (8K or 16K) internal cache. In fact, the 16K cache in the 486SLC performed so well that the designation of the chip was changed to 486. This chip performs about as well as an Intel 486 chip running at equal clock rates, even though the IBM version is only 16 bits and the Intel version is 32 bits. Because all the SLC chips have the full 486 instruction set, including the cache-control instructions, the designation is accurate.

The SLC2 version runs at twice the system speed (clock-doubled) and yet costs less than the standard Intel 486 chips while providing greater performance. You can find the 486SLC2 processor in many bargain-priced motherboards that offer nearly the performance of the Intel 486SX2 and DX2 processors for much less money. Although the IBM processors do not have a built-in math coprocessor, as some of the Intel processors do, most of the motherboards sold with the IBM processors include an Intel or Intel-compatible 387SX math coprocessor.

Blue Lightning Processors

The IBM Blue Lightning processors are based on the 386DX mask and are full 32-bit processors. These processors also support a full 32-bit memory addressing scheme, which means that they can support the same 4G memory as the Intel 486 processors.

The IBM BL was the first processor to run in clock-tripled mode, which is available in 25/75 MHz and 33/100 MHz versions. Notice that most 33 MHz systems actually run at 33.33 MHz, so a clock-tripled system effectively would run at 100 MHz.

All the IBM processors fully support power-management capabilities, and all of them are considered to be low-power (or green) processors. Due to their low power consumption and low-voltage design, these processors often are used in systems that meet the EPA Energy Star Certification Program, which sets standards for energy conservation and low power consumption in PC systems.

The SLC2 and BL processors are low-power units that run on 3.3v, due in part to IBM's superior chip-fabrication facilities. IBM reduced the die size and power consumption

Maximum Memory	Integral Cache	Burst Mode	Integral FPU	No. of Transistors	Date Introduced
16M	8K	No	No	955,000	October 1991
16M	16K	No	No	1,349,000	1992
16M	16K	No	No	1,349,000	June 1992
4G	16K	No	No	1,400,000	1993
4G	16K	No	No	1,400,000	1993

greatly by going to a 0.6-micron process for these chips. (This figure refers to the minimum individual feature size on the chip mask. Intel did not use the a 0.6-micron process until the DX4 and Pentium chips were introduced.)

The original agreement with Intel was intended to prevent IBM from marketing its processors in the open market in competition with Intel. The agreement specifies that IBM cannot sell processors individually, but only as parts of modules. This restriction essentially means that the chip must be mounted on a circuit board of some type—which actually caused IBM to enter the motherboard and upgrade-board business.

Several companies have designed motherboards and processor upgrade boards that use the low-cost IBM processors. These boards are manufactured by IBM, but they often are designed by the companies for whom IBM makes them. Among the most popular of these motherboards are the Alaris motherboards, which use the IBM processors, and an AMI BIOS. IBM manufactures these boards at its manufacturing plant in Charlotte, NC.

Note

For any of these products, IBM technically is acting as a subcontractor to the company that is considered to be the manufacturer; IBM is not responsible for the design, sales, or support of the products. Support must come from the (so-called) manufacturer, not from IBM.

Intel-Compatible Processors

Several companies—mainly AMD and Cyrix—have developed new processors that are compatible with one or more of the Intel processors. These chips are fully Intel-compatible, which means that they emulate every processor instruction in the Intel chips. Most of the chips are pin-compatible, which means that they can be used in any system designed to accept an Intel processor; others require a custom motherboard design. Any hardware or software that work on Intel-based PCs will work on PCs made with these third-party CPU chips.

AMD and Cyrix have developed their own versions of the Intel 386, 486, and even Pentium processors in a variety of speeds and configurations.

AMD has become a major player in the 486-compatible chip market with its own line of Intel-compatible 486 processors. AMD ran into trouble with Intel because its chips use actual Intel microcode. These differences have been settled and AMD now has a license for the Intel 386 and 486 code. AMD has come out with a variety of 486 processors, focusing on the high end where Intel has left off. For example, AMD makes a 486 DX4 120 and will offer a 133 MHz version as well. Intel has all but discontinued 486 production, and 100 MHz was the fastest version it made. AMD also makes higher speed versions of the DX2 processors as well. The AMD processors are directly interchangeable with the Intel 486 chips and are pin and socket compatible.

AMD chips, including the DX4, have the same 8K internal Level 1 cache as the Intel DX2 processors. The Intel DX4 has 16K of internal L1 cache while the AMD DX4s only have 8K. This results in slightly less performance, with one bonus being that they work with some older BIOSes better than the Intel chips do. Many of the older BIOS versions will not deal properly with the 16K cache in the Intel DX4 chips, requiring a BIOS upgrade before the cache can be used at all. The AMD DX4 chips have the same 8K cache as the standard 486 processors, which is what most older BIOSes were written for.

Unlike Cyrix, Nexgen, and others, AMD has its own foundries and fabrication facilities. In fact, in the past it has often been called on by Intel to manufacture some of the Intel processors. AMD is using this capability to now manufacture a new Pentium class chip called the K5. The new AMD K5 processor has 4.3 million transistors and can execute up to four instructions per cycle compared to two on the Pentium. The K5 includes some of the features of the Intel Pentium Pro processor, including speculative and out-of-order instruction execution. The K5 includes a 24K split cache with 16K for instructions and 8K for data. This chip will be made in AMDs new Fab 25 microprocessor plant in Austin, TX.

Cyrix markets an interesting chip called the 486DRx2, which can be used as a direct replacement for a 386 chip in existing systems. Although the Cyrix chip lacks some of the important features of the Intel 486, it gives a 386-based system many of the benefits of the 486.

Cyrix also markets standard 486DX2 processors in speeds all the way up to 80 MHz. One interesting fact about Cyrix is that IBM Microelectronics is its primary fabrication facility, which means that IBM makes most of the Cyrix processors. Cyrix developed its 486-compatible processors using its own design, which has allowed it to escape many of the legal hassles other companies have had in cloning Intel's designs. For the most part, the Cyrix 486 DX2 processors are pin and socket compatible with the Intel chips, meaning that they can be used interchangeably. Some of the earlier Cyrix 486 processors had less internal Level 1 cache memory than the corresponding Intel chips, but they now use the same size 8K cache as Intel does in the DX2 chips.

Cyrix is now focusing on the Pentium market with a new chip it has designed called the 6x86. This chip offers Pentium level performance in custom design by Cyrix. The M1 has 3.3 million transistors and will initially be manufactured on a 0.65-micron process. The 6x86 has dual internal pipelines and a single unified 16K internal cache. It will offer speculative and out-of-order instruction execution, much like the Intel Pentium Pro processor. The 6x86 will be socket (but not pin) compatible with the Pentium, and will require modified chipsets and new motherboard designs. This means that this chip cannot be installed in older Pentium motherboards, but only in boards designed to accommodate it. Most newer chipsets like the Opti Viper and ALI Aladdin are universal in nature and will support the Pentium, AMD K5, and the Cyrix M1 processors all on the same board. As with the other Cyrix chips, IBM Microelectronics is manufacturing the 686 for Cyrix.

More recently, Cyrix has announced a new 5x86 processor, which is a 486 replacement chip that uses some of the 686 technology. This processor is pin and socket compatible with the 486DX and will be featured in lower-end systems. The 5x86 features an internal 64-bit data path with an external 32-bit 486 interface. It has a 16K unified Write-Back L1 cache and does branch prediction just like the big brother M1. It only has a single instruction pipeline, so it cannot execute more than one instruction per cycle. The chip incorporates built-in power management through SMM and will draw less power than most 486 processors. The 5x86 will be ideal for notebook systems and will be available in 100, 120, and 133 MHz versions.

Note

Texas Instruments formerly manufactured the Cyrix 486 processors. There was a falling out between Cyrix and TI, and in the aftermath TI has retained the rights to some of the Cyrix 486 designs. In other words, the TI 486 processors you see on the market are basically TI-made versions of the Cyrix 486 processors.

Another relative newcomer on the CPU scene is Nexgen. Founded by an ex-Intel engineer who worked on the Pentium processor, Nexgen was the first company actually shipping a Pentium class processor compatible with Intel. The Nexgen Nx586 is a custom-designed RISC-based processor that is not a true clone of the Pentium. The Nx586 is not pin compatible, but will run software designed for the Pentium. It features 3.5 million transistors, a built-in 32K split L1 cache, and has a built-in L2 cache controller. By integrating the L2 controller inside the chip, the L2 cache will be able to run at chip speeds and not the slower motherboard memory bus speed. The Nx586 has only a single internal pipeline, but features out-of-order instruction execution like the Intel Pentium Pro.

Nexgen has recently been purchased by AMD, and all their processor technology is being integrated into upcoming AMD chips. The Nexgen chips will eventually be discontinued.

The Nx586 is designed as a lower-cost alternative to the Pentium, but there are some drawbacks. It is not pin or socket compatible, which means that the motherboards and chipsets will have to be specifically developed around it and may not have future Pentium upgradability. IBM Microelectronics currently manufactures not only the Nx586 chips, but the motherboards as well. The Nx586 is available at several different speeds, including 70, 75, 84, and 93 MHz. Because the chip actually performs somewhat better than a Pentium chip at the same clock rate, the 93 MHz chip is called the Nx586-100, indicating that it performs about as well as a 100 MHz Pentium.

One drawback compared to the Pentium is that the Nx586 chip does not include a floating point unit. This means that floating-point math functions will run much slower, or will require an external math coprocessor. Nexgen has stated that future versions of the chip may include a built-in FPU. Clearly the Nx586 is designed to be marketed as a low-cost alternative to the Pentium.

Math Coprocessors

Each central processing unit designed by Intel (and cloned by other companies) can use a math-coprocessor chip, although the Pentium and 486 chips have a built-in math coprocessor. *Coprocessors* provide hardware for floating-point math, which otherwise would create an excessive drain on the main CPU. Math chips speed your computer's operation only when you are running software designed to take advantage of the coprocessor.

Math chips (as coprocessors sometimes are called) can perform high-level mathematical operations—long division, trigonometric functions, roots, and logarithms, for example—at 10 to 100 times the speed of the corresponding main processor. Math chips also are more accurate in these calculations than are the integer-math units built into the primary CPU. The integer units in the primary CPU work with real numbers, so they perform addition, subtraction, and multiplication operations. The primary CPU is designed to handle such computations; these operations are not offloaded to the math chip.

The instruction set of the math chip is different from that of the primary CPU. A program must detect the existence of the coprocessor and then execute instructions written explicitly for that coprocessor; otherwise, the math coprocessor draws power and does nothing else. Fortunately, most modern programs that can benefit from the use of the coprocessor correctly detect and use the coprocessor. These programs usually are math-intensive: spreadsheet, database applications, statistical, and some graphics, such as computer-aided design (CAD) software. Word processing programs do not benefit from a math chip and therefore are not designed to use one.

Table 6.13 summarizes the coprocessors available for the Intel family of processors.

Table 6.13 Math Coprocessor Summary

Processor	Coprocessor
8086	8087
8088	8087
286	287
386SX	387SX
386SL	387SX
386SLC	387SX
486SLC	387SX
486SLC2	387SX
386DX	387DX
486SX	487SX, DX2/OverDrive*
487SX*	Built-in FPU
486SX2	DX2/OverDrive**
486DX	Built-in FPU
486DX2	Built-in FPU
486DX4	Built-in FPU

Table 6.13 Continued

Processor	Coprocessor
Pentium	Built-in FPU
Pentium Pro	Built-in FPU

FPU = Floating-Point Unit
**The 487SX chip is a modified pinout 486DX chip with the math coprocessor enabled. When you plug in a 487SX chip, it disables the 486SX main processor and takes over all processing. This chip has been discontinued and is replaced by the DX2/OverDrive processor.*
***The DX2/OverDrive is equivalent to the SX2 with the addition of a functional FPU.*

Within each 8087 group, the maximum speed of the math chips varies. A suffix digit after the main number, as shown in table 6.14, indicates the maximum speed at which a system can run a math chip.

Table 6.14 Maximum Math Chip Speeds

Part	Speed
8087	5 MHz
8087-3	5 MHz
8087-2	8 MHz
8087-1	10 MHz
80287	6 MHz
80287-6	6 MHz
80287-8	8 MHz
80287-10	10 MHz

The 387 math coprocessors, as well as the 486 or 487 and Pentium processors, always indicate their maximum speed rating in MHz in the part-number suffix. A 486DX2-66, for example, is rated to run at 66 MHz. Some processors incorporate clock multiplication, which means that they may run at different speeds compared with the rest of the system.

The performance increase in programs that use the math chip can be dramatic—usually, a geometric increase in speed occurs. If the primary applications that you use can take advantage of a math coprocessor, you should upgrade your system to include one.

Most systems that use the 386 or earlier processors are socketed for a math coprocessor as an option, but they do not include a coprocessor as standard equipment. A few systems on the market don't even have a socket for the coprocessor because of cost and size considerations. Usually, these systems are low-cost or portable systems, such as older laptops, the IBM PS/1, and the PCjr. For more specific information about math coprocessors, see the discussions of the specific chips—8087, 287, 387, and 487SX—in the following sections.

Table 6.15 shows some of the specifications of the various math coprocessors.

Table 6.15 Intel Math Coprocessor Specifications

Name	Power Consumption	Case Min. Temp.	Case Max. Temp.	No. of Transistors	Date Introduced
8087	3 watts	0°C, 32°F	85°C, 185°F	45,000	1980
287	3 watts	0°C, 32°F	85°C, 185°F	45,000	1982
287XL	1.5 watts	0°C, 32°F	85°C, 185°F	40,000	1990
387SX	1.5 watts	0°C, 32°F	85°C, 185°F	120,000	1988
387DX	1.5 watts	0°C, 32°F	85°C, 185°F	120,000	1987

Most often, you can learn what CPU and math coprocessor are installed in a particular system by checking the system documentation. The following section examines the Intel family of CPUs and math coprocessors in more detail.

8087 Coprocessor

Intel introduced the 8086 processor in 1976. The math coprocessor that was paired with the chip—the 8087—often was called the *numeric data processor* (*NDP*), the *math coprocessor*, or simply the *math chip*. The 8087 is designed to perform high-level math operations at many times the speed and accuracy of the main processor. The primary advantage of using this chip is the increased execution speed in number-crunching programs such as spreadsheet applications. Using the 8087 has several minor disadvantages, however, including software support, cost, power consumption, and heat production.

The primary disadvantage of installing the 8087 chip is that you notice an increase in speed only in programs written to use this coprocessor—and then not in all operations. Only math-intensive programs such as spreadsheet programs, statistical programs, CAD software, and engineering software support the chip. Even then, the effects vary from application to application, and support is limited to specific areas. For example, versions of Lotus 1-2-3 that support the coprocessor do not use the coprocessor for common operations such as addition, subtraction, multiplication, and division.

Applications that usually do not use the 8087 at all include word processing programs, telecommunications software, database programs, and presentation-graphics programs.

To test the speed capabilities of the 8087 math coprocessor, two spreadsheets were created, each with 8,000 cells. The first spreadsheet used simple math tasks—addition, subtraction, multiplication, and division—split evenly among the 8,000 cells. The second spreadsheet used high-level math operations—including formulas that used SQRT, SIN, COS, and TAN calculations—throughout the 8,000 cells. The following table shows the recalculation times:

Spreadsheet	XT without 8087	XT with 8087
Sheet 1 (standard math)	21 seconds	21 seconds
Sheet 2 (high-level math)	195 seconds	21 seconds

The addition of an 8087 to a standard IBM XT did nothing for the spreadsheet that contained only simple math, but the 8087 calculated the spreadsheet that contained high-level math in one-tenth the time. (This also was the time it took both systems to calculate the spreadsheet that contained only simple math.)

If your spreadsheets consist of nothing but addition, subtraction, multiplication, and division calculations, before buying a math chip, you need to know whether the program that you use takes advantage of the math chip for simple calculations. Many new programs are designed to support the 8087 chip for these operations. Installing an 8087 can extend the useful life of a PC or XT, because the chip closes some of the performance gaps between PC- or XT-type computers and AT-type computers. In short, the chip is an asset whenever the software supports it.

The 8087 chip is inexpensive, costing as little as $50. Remember to purchase a chip with the correct maximum-speed rating; the 8087 must be rated to run at the same rate of speed as the CPU or faster, because the main CPU and the coprocessor must run in synchronization. In an IBM XT, for example, the 8088 and the 8087 run at 4.77 MHz. Look in your system documentation to find the speed at which your system will run the math chip.

Math chips are quite power-hungry because of the number of transistors included. A typical 8088 has only about 29,000 transistors, but the 8087 has about 45,000. (Nearly all the 45,000 transistors are dedicated to math functions, which is why the 8087 can perform math operations so well.) This figure translates to nearly double the calculating horsepower, as well as double the electrical power drain. In a heavily loaded PC, the 8087 could be the straw that breaks the camel's back: the power supply might be insufficient for the increased load. The chip draws nearly 0.5 amp of current.

Another problem is the amount of heat generated: 3 watts. A 75 MHz 486DX4 with 1.6 million transistors uses only 3.63 watts. This heat level generated in such a small chip can raise the temperature to more than 180° Fahrenheit. (The approved maximum temperature for most 8087s is 185°F.) For this reason, math coprocessor chips usually are made of ceramic.

Power and heat are not problems in XT or portable systems because these systems are built to handle these situations. The PC, however, usually requires a higher-watt power supply with a more powerful cooling fan to handle the load. Power supplies are covered later in this chapter.

80287 Coprocessor

Imagine that two company employees have computers. One user has an IBM XT, and the other has a 6 MHz AT. Both employees use Lotus 1-2-3 as their primary application. The AT user delights in being able to outcalculate the XT user by a factor of three. The XT user purchases an 8087 math chip for $50 and installs it. The XT user then finds that the XT calculates many spreadsheets 10 times faster than before—or more than three times as fast as the AT.

This performance frustrates the AT user, who thought that the AT was the faster system. The AT user, therefore, purchases an 80287 for $50 and discovers that the AT is merely equal in speed to the XT for many spreadsheet recalculations. In a few situations, however, the XT may still outrun the AT.

Of course, the AT user wants to know why the 80287 chip did not make the AT superior to the XT, by a significant margin, for spreadsheet recalculations. (For "normal" processing, which does not use the math chip's high-level math functions, the AT holds its performance edge.) The answer is in the 80287 chip. For various design reasons, the 8087 chip has much more effect on the speed of the PC and XT than the 80287 has on the AT.

The 80287, internally, is the same math chip as the 8087, although the pins used to plug them into the motherboard are different. Because the AT has a healthy power supply and generous, thermostatically controlled fan cooling, the heat and power problems mentioned in the discussion of the 8087 generally don't apply to the 287. Internally, however, the 80287 and the 8087 operate as though they were identical.

Another reason is that the 80286 and its math chip are asynchronous, which means that the chips run at different speeds. The 80287 math chip usually runs at two-thirds the speed of the CPU. In most systems, the 80286 internally divides the system clock by 2 to derive the processor clock. The 80287 internally divides the system-clock frequency by 3. For this reason, most AT-type computers run the 80287 at one-third the system clock rate, which also is two-thirds the clock speed of the 80286. Because the 286 and 287 chips are asynchronous, the interface between the 286 and 287 chips is not as efficient as with the 8088 and 8087.

In summary, the 80287 and the 8087 chips perform about the same at equal clock rates. The original 80287 is not better than the 8087 in any real way—unlike the 80286, which is superior to the 8086 and 8088. In most AT systems, the performance gain that you realize by adding the coprocessor is much less substantial than the same type of upgrade for PC- or XT-type systems or for the 80386.

Some systems run the 80287 and the 8087 at the same speed. PS/2 Models 50, 50 Z, and 60 use circuitry that enables both the 80286 and 80287 to run at 10 MHz. The PS/2 Model 25-286 and 30-286, however, follow the standard AT-type design, in which the 286 runs at 10 MHz and the 287 runs at 6.67 MHz.

You must consult the system documentation to learn the speeds at which your system would run a 287 coprocessor because the motherboard designers determine these specifications. Table 6.16 shows 80286 and 80287 clock speeds for most AT-type systems.

Table 6.16 80286 and 80287 Clock Speeds (in MHz)

System Clock	80286 Clock	80287 Clock
12.00	6.00	4.00
16.00	8.00	5.33
20.00	10.00	6.67
24.00	12.00	8.00
32.00	16.00	10.67

How can you improve this differential in performance gain? One method takes advantage of the fact that the 80286 and the 80287 run asynchronously. You can install an add-in board that uses its own clock signal to drive the 80287 chip and therefore can drive the chip at any speed. Some companies have designed a simple speed-up circuit that includes a crystal and an 8284 clock generator chip, all mounted on special boards—some of which are not much bigger than the 287 socket. This special board, called a *daughterboard,* is plugged into the 287 socket; then the 287 is plugged in on top of the special board. Because such boards separate the crystal and clock generator from the motherboard circuitry, the daughterboard can run the 80287 at any speed you want, up to the maximum rating of the chip—8 MHz, 10 MHz, 12 MHz, or more—without affecting the rest of the system.

You could, for example, add one of these daughterboards to your old 6 MHz AT and run a 287 at 10 MHz. Without the daughterboard, the chip would run at only 4 MHz. The boards are available from many math-coprocessor suppliers. Using these boards is highly recommended if you run math-intensive programs. Remember that this type of speed increase does not apply to systems that use 8087 or 80387 chips, because these systems must run the math coprocessor at the same speed as the main CPU.

Intel has introduced new variations of the 80287 called the 287XL and 287XLT. (The original 287 has been discontinued; only the 287XL and XLT are available today.) The XL version is designed to be a replacement for the standard 287 math coprocessor. The XLT version is functionally identical to the XL, but has a plastic leadless chip carrier (PLCC) case, which some laptop systems require.

These redesigned XL chips are patterned after the 387 instead of the 8087. The XL chips consume much less power than the original 287 chips because they are constructed with CMOS technology. The XL chips perform about 20 percent faster than the original 287 at any clock rate as a result of their improved design. The design improvements extend to the instruction set, which includes 387 trigonometric functions not available with older 287 coprocessors.

The XL chips are available at only one speed rating: 12.5 MHz. The chips can be run at lower speeds on slower systems. Unlike the 287 daughterboards, these chips do not increase the clock speed of a math chip.

Many older diagnostics programs incorrectly identify the XL chips because they were designed after the 387 math chips. Some diagnostics simply indicate that the 287XL is a 387; other diagnostics incorrectly show a problem with the math coprocessor if a 287XL is installed. Intel provides a special diagnostics program called CHKCOP (CHecK COProcessor) that can test all its math coprocessors. You can get this program on disk from Intel's customer-support department or download it from the Intel BBS at (503) 645-6275.

After considering all these issues, if you decide to invest in a 287 chip, remember that only the XL or XLT versions are available now and that they are rated for up to 12.5 MHz operation. Adding the 287 to an AT is a good idea if the software that you use supports the chip. You also should consider using one of the math coprocessor-speedup daughterboards, which will run the newer XL chips at the maximum 12 MHz rating regardless of your system's clock speed. Otherwise, the benefits may not be enough to justify the cost.

80387 Coprocessor

Although the 80387 chips run asynchronously, 386 systems are designed so that the math chip runs at the same clock speed as the main CPU. Unlike the 80287 coprocessor, which was merely an 8087 with different pins to plug into the AT motherboard, the 80387 coprocessor is a high-performance math chip designed specifically to work with the 386.

All 387 chips use a low-power-consumption CMOS design. The 387 coprocessor has two basic designs: the 387DX coprocessor, which is designed to work with the 386DX processor; and the 387SX coprocessor, which is designed to work with the 386SX, SL, or SLC processors.

Intel originally offered several speeds for the 387DX coprocessor. But when the company designed the 33 MHz version, a smaller mask was required to reduce the lengths of the signal pathways in the chip. Intel reduced the feature size from 1.5 to 1 micron. This action reduced the size of the silicon chip by 50 percent.

In addition to the size reduction, other design improvements were engineered into the new mask, resulting in a 20 percent improvement in processing efficiency. The 33 MHz version, therefore, outperformed other versions even at slower clock rates.

At the time, purchasing the 33 MHz version of the 387DX was a good idea (even for a 20 MHz 386 system) because the chip would run 20 percent faster than a 20 MHz 387. In October 1990, however, Intel upgraded the entire 387DX line to the improved mask, resulting in a 20 percent performance boost across the board.

You can easily identify these improved 387DX coprocessors by looking at the 10-digit code below the 387 part number. The older (slower) chips begin this line with the letter S, and the improved (faster) chips do not. Recently, Intel discontinued all its 387DX processors except the 33 MHz version, which, of course, always used the new design. (Remember that even though the chip is rated for 33 MHz, it runs at any lower speed.)

The 387SX coprocessors are designed to work specifically with 386SX, SL, or SLC processors. All versions of the 387SX use the improved mask design. When you select a 387SX for your system, be sure to purchase one rated at a speed equal to or higher than that of your CPU. Currently, Intel 387SX chips are available at speeds up to 25 MHz.

Note

Because Intel lagged in developing the 387 coprocessor, some early 386 systems were designed with a socket for a 287 coprocessor. Performance levels associated with that union, however, leave much to be desired.

Installing a 387DX is easy, but you must be careful to orient the chip in its socket properly; otherwise, the chip will be destroyed. The most common cause of burned pins on the 387DX is incorrect installation. In many systems, the 387DX is oriented differently from other large chips. Follow the manufacturer's installation instructions carefully to avoid damaging the 387DX; Intel's warranty does not cover chips that are installed incorrectly.

Several manufacturers have developed their own versions of the Intel 387 coprocessors, some of which are touted as being faster than the original Intel chips. The general compatibility record of these chips is very good. Intel has significantly reduced the prices of its own coprocessors, however, which means that these third-party chips usually are only a few dollars cheaper than the Intel version.

When the 387s were introduced, the Intel 33 MHz 387DX chips listed for more than $2,000. Today, you can buy the chip from various suppliers for as little as $90. The cost is so low that many people should consider making this upgrade. If the software that you run supports the chip, the performance gains can be very impressive.

Weitek Coprocessors

In 1981, several Intel engineers formed Weitek Corporation. Weitek has developed math coprocessors for several systems, including those based on Motorola processor designs. Intel originally contracted Weitek to develop a math coprocessor for the Intel 386 CPU, because Intel was behind in its own development of the 387 math coprocessor. The result was the Weitek 1167, a custom math coprocessor that uses a proprietary Weitek instruction set that is incompatible with the Intel 387.

The Weitek 1167 is not a single chip; it is a daughterboard consisting of several chip elements that plug into a special 112-pin Weitek socket. To use the Weitek processors, your system must have the required socket, which is incompatible with the 387 math coprocessor and 486SX processor enhancement sockets. The daughterboard includes a socket for an Intel 387 coprocessor so that both coprocessors can be installed in a system; as a result, software that runs either Weitek or Intel math instructions will work on such a system.

The 1167 was replaced in April 1988 by a single-chip version called the 3167. Many computers, such as the COMPAQ 386, contain a special socket that enables you to use a Weitek 3167 math coprocessor or an Intel 387DX. This socket has three rows of holes on all four sides. The inner two rows of pins are compatible with the Intel 387DX. If you want to install a 387DX in the special socket, however, you must use extreme caution to orient the chip correctly; otherwise, you could damage both the computer and the 387DX.

Read your system documentation to determine the correct procedure for installing the 387DX in your computer. Some computers, such as the Tandy 4000, use the Weitek socket, but do not support the 387DX. Contact your computer manufacturer or dealer for more specific information.

Unfortunately, even if you have the socket for the Weitek processor, your software probably does not support it. As mentioned, your software must contain programming code that makes use of the specific capabilities of a math coprocessor.

Weitek introduced the 4167 coprocessor chip for 486 systems in November 1989. To use the Weitek coprocessor, your system must have the required additional socket. Before purchasing one of the Weitek coprocessors, you should determine whether your software supports it; then you should contact the software company to determine whether the Weitek has a performance advantage over the Intel coprocessor.

80487 Upgrade

The Intel 80486 processor was introduced in late 1989, and systems using this chip appeared during 1990. The 486DX integrated the math coprocessor into the chip.

The 486SX began life as a full-fledged 486DX chip, but Intel actually disabled the built-in math coprocessor before shipping the chip. As part of this marketing scheme, Intel marketed what it called a 487SX math coprocessor. Motherboard manufacturers installed an Intel-designed socket for this so-called 487 chip. In reality, however, the 487SX math chip was a special 486DX chip with the math coprocessor enabled. When you plugged this chip into your motherboard, it disabled the 486SX chip and gave you the functional equivalent of a full-fledged 486DX system.

Perhaps that somewhat strange marketing scheme is responsible for some of the confusion caused by the Intel advertisements that feature a 486SX system with a neon vacancy sign pointing to an empty socket next to the CPU chip. Unfortunately, these ads do not transmit the message properly. Few people seem to understand that the socket next to the CPU in a 486SX system is not a math-coprocessor socket, but an OverDrive socket.

Essentially, systems that have this extra socket have two processor sockets; however, you can use only one of them at any time. When you install a chip in the secondary socket, that chip takes over from the primary processor and puts the original processor to sleep.

Most newer 486SX systems use a surface-mounted PQFP (Plastic Quad Flat Pack) or SQFP (Small Quad Flat Pack) version that is permanently soldered to the motherboard. These systems still have a conventional processor socket of a specific design for new OverDrive processors. These OverDrive chips will contain all processing functions, including the math-coprocessor functions, and will shut down the 486SX when they are installed. Depending on the type of processor socket on the motherboard, you can install a DX2 or DX4 processor, or even a special version of the Pentium chip.

For more information on this subject, see the section on OverDrive processors earlier in this chapter.

Processor Tests

The processor is easily the most expensive chip in the system. Processor manufacturers use specialized equipment to test their own processors, but you have to settle for a little less. The best processor-testing device to which you have access is a system that you know is functional; you then can use the diagnostics available from IBM and other system manufacturers to test the motherboard and processor functions. Most systems mount processors in a socket for easy replacement.

Landmark offers specialized diagnostics software called Service Diagnostics to test various processors. Special versions are available for each processor in the Intel family. If you don't want to purchase this kind of software, you can perform a quick-and-dirty processor evaluation by using the normal diagnostics program supplied with your system.

Because the processor is the brain of a system, most systems don't function with a defective one. If a system seems to have a dead motherboard, try replacing the processor with one from a functioning motherboard that uses the same CPU chip. You may find that the processor in the original board is the culprit. If the system continues to play dead, however, the problem is elsewhere.

Known Defective Chips

A few system problems are built in at the factory, although these bugs or design defects are rare. By learning to recognize one of these problems, you may avoid unnecessary repairs or replacements. This section describes several known defects in system processors.

Early 8088s. A bug in some early 8088 processors allowed interrupts to occur after a program changed the stack segment register. (An interrupt usually is not allowed until the instruction after the one that changes the stack segment register.) This subtle bug may cause problems in older systems. Most programmers have adopted coding procedures that work around the bug, but you have no guarantee that these procedures exist in all software programs.

Another problem is that the bug may affect the operation of an 8087 math coprocessor. Approximately 200,000 IBM PC units sold during 1981 and 1982 were manufactured with the defective chip.

Originally, in the 8087 math-coprocessor-chip package, IBM always included an 8088 to be installed with the math chip. This practice led to rumors that the parts somehow matched. The rumors were unfounded; IBM had simply found an easy way to prevent machines that used its 8087 chips from using the defective 8088. Because the cost of the chip was negligible, IBM included a bug-free 8088 and eliminated many potential service problems.

You can check the 8088 chip with diagnostics software, or you can identify a good or bad chip by its appearance. If you can open the unit to look at the 8088 chip, the manufacturer and copyright date printed on the chip provide clues about which version you have. An 8088 chip made by a manufacturer other than Intel is bug-free, because Intel began licensing the chip mask to other manufacturers after the bug was corrected. If a chip was manufactured by Intel, older (defective) parts have a 1978 copyright date; newer (good) parts have 1978 and 1981 (or later) copyright dates.

This marking on Intel 8088 chips indicates a chip that has the interrupt bug:

8088

©INTEL 1978

The following markings on Intel 8088 chips indicate chips on which the bug is corrected:

8088	8088
©INTEL '78 '81	©INTEL '78 '83

Many diagnostics programs can identify the chip. You also can identify the chip yourself by using DEBUG, which comes in DOS versions 2.0 and later. Just load DEBUG at the prompt, and enter the commands shown in the following example. The commands that you enter appear in boldface type; the DEBUG screen output is not. XXXX indicates a segment address, which varies from system to system:

```
—A 100
[XXXX:0100] MOV ES,AX
[XXXX:0102] INC AX
[XXXX:0103] NOP
[XXXX:0104]
—T
AX=0001 BX=0000 CX=0000 DX=0000 SP=FFEE BP=0000 SI=0000 DI=0000
DS=XXXX ES=0000 SS=XXXX CS=XXXX IP=0103 NV UP EI PL NZ NA PO NC
XXXX:0103 90 NOP
—Q
```

The `A 100` command tells DEBUG to assemble some instructions, of which three are entered. The `T` command then executes a Trace, which normally executes a single instruction, displays the contents of the 8088's registers, and then stops. The Trace command usually executes only one instruction. However, when the instruction is `MOV` to a segment register, as in this case, the Trace command should execute the second instruction before interrupting the program. The third instruction is a dummy no-operation instruction.

Look at the value shown by DEBUG for the register `AX`. If `AX` is equal to `0000`, the processor has a bug. If `AX` is `0001`, the second instruction in the test was executed properly, and the chip is good. If the second instruction is executed, DEBUG increments the value of the `AX` register by `1`. In this example, after the Trace is executed, `AX` equals `0001`, which indicates a good chip.

Note

If you try this test on a 286 or higher system, the test will fail; it is valid only for 8088s.

If you have an 8087 and a 4.77 MHz 8088 dated 1978 or an 8088 that fails this test, you can get a free replacement 8088. Contact Intel customer support for the replacement. Only 4.77 MHz 8088 chips may need to be upgraded. The 8088-2 and 8088-1 do not require replacement. You also can purchase a replacement 8088 from most chip houses for less than $10. If you suspect that your chip is bad, a replacement is inexpensive insurance.

Early 80386s. Some early 16 MHz Intel 386DX processors had a small bug that you may encounter in troubleshooting what seems to be a software problem. The bug, which apparently is in the chip's 32-bit multiply routine, manifests itself only when you run true 32-bit code in a program such as OS/2 2.x, UNIX/386, or Windows in Enhanced mode. Some specialized 386 memory-management software systems also may invoke this subtle bug, but 16-bit operating systems (such as DOS and OS/2 1.x) probably will not.

The bug usually causes the system to lock up. Diagnosing this problem can be difficult because the problem generally is intermittent and software-related. Running tests to find the bug is difficult; only Intel, with proper test equipment, can determine whether your chip has a bug. Some programs can diagnose the problem and identify a defective chip, but they cannot identify all defective chips. If a program indicates a bad chip, you certainly have a defective one; if the program passes the chip, you still may have a defective one.

Intel requested that its 386 customers return possibly defective chips for screening, but many vendors did not return them. Intel tested returned chips and replaced defective ones. The known-defective chips later were sold to bargain liquidators or systems houses that wanted chips that would not run 32-bit code. The known-defective chips were stamped with a `16-bit SW Only` logo, indicating that they were authorized to run only 16-bit software.

Chips that passed the test, and all subsequent chips produced as bug-free, were marked with a double-sigma ( ) code, which indicates a good chip. 386DX chips that are not marked with either `16-bit SW Only` or the designation have not been tested by Intel and may be defective.

The following marking indicates that a chip has not yet been screened for the defect; it may be either good or bad. Return a chip of this kind to the system manufacturer, which will return the chip for a free replacement:

```
80386-16
```

The following marking indicates that the chip has been tested and has the 32-bit multiply bug. The chip works with 16-bit software (such as DOS) but not with 32-bit, 386-specific software (such as Windows or OS/2):

```
80386-16

16-bit SW Only
```

The following mark on a chip indicates that it has been tested as defect-free. This chip fulfills all the capabilities promised for the 80386:

```
80386-16

ΣΣ
```

This problem was discovered and corrected before Intel officially added DX to the part number. So, if you have a chip labeled `80386DX` or `386DX`, it does not have this problem.

Another problem with the 386DX can be stated more specifically. When 386-based versions of XENIX or other UNIX implementations are run on a computer that contains a 387DX math coprocessor, the computer locks up under certain conditions. The problem does not occur in the DOS environment, however. For the lockup to occur, all the following conditions must be in effect:

- Demand page virtual memory must be active.
- A 387DX must be installed and in use.
- DMA (direct memory access) must occur.
- The 386 must be in a wait state.

When all these conditions are true at the same instant, the 386DX ends up waiting for the 387DX, and vice versa. Both processors will continue to wait for each other indefinitely. The problem is in certain versions of the 386DX, not in the 387DX math coprocessor.

Intel published this problem (Errata 21) immediately after it was discovered to inform its OEM customers. At that point, it became the responsibility of each manufacturer to implement a fix in its hardware or software product. Some manufacturers, such as COMPAQ and IBM, responded by modifying their motherboards to prevent these lockups from occurring.

The Errata 21 problem occurs only in the B Stepping version of the 386DX and not in the later D Stepping version. You can identify the D Stepping version of the 386DX by the letters DX in the part number (for example, 386DX-20). If DX is part of the chip's part number, the chip does not have this problem.

Pentium Defects. In the summer of 1994, more than one year after the Pentium had been introduced, on-going internal testing at Intel finally came upon the floating-point error. At the time, Intel was puzzled as to why neither it nor anyone else had encountered the problem earlier. After months of analysis, Intel concluded that the error was only likely to occur at a frequency of the order of once in 9 billion random floating-point divides, and that this many divides in all the programs it evaluated (which included many scientific programs) would require 27 years to occur. Because Intel thought the error could only happen once in 27 years, that would be longer than the mean time to failure of the physical computer system itself. Unfortunately, this estimate did not take into account the fact that the error itself was not random, and specific sets of numbers could encounter the error very frequently indeed.

The Floating-Point Divide Bug. Probably the most famous processor bug in history is the now legendary flaw in the Pentium FPU. It has often been called the FDIV bug, because it affects primarily the FDIV (Floating-Point Divide) instruction, although several other instructions that use division are also affected. Intel officially refers to this problem as Errata No. 23, titled "Slight precision loss for floating-point divides on specific operand pairs." The bug has been fixed in the D1 or later steppings of the 60/66 MHz Pentium processors, as well as the B5 and later steppings of the 75/90/100 MHz processors. The 120 MHz and higher processors are manufactured from later steppings, which do not include this problem.

This bug caused a tremendous fervor when it first was reported on the Internet by a mathematician on October 30, 1994. Within a few days, news of the defect had spread nationwide, and even people who did not have computers had heard about it! By using certain combinations of numbers, the Pentium would incorrectly perform floating-point division calculations, with errors anywhere from the third digit on up.

By the time the bug was publicly discovered outside of Intel, it had already incorporated the fix into the next stepping of both the 60/66 MHz and the 75/90/100 MHz Pentium processor along with the other corrections it had made.

After the bug was made public and Intel admitted to already knowing about it, a fury erupted. As people began checking their spreadsheets and other math calculations, many discovered that they had also encountered this problem and did not know it. Others who had not really encountered the problem had their faith in the core of their PCs very shaken. People had come to put so much trust in the PC that they had a hard time coming to terms with the fact that it might not even be able to do math correctly!

Intel finally decided that in the best interest of the consumer as well as its public image, it would begin a lifetime replacement warranty on the affected processors. This means that if one ever encounters one of the Pentium processors with the Errata 23 Floating-Point bug, Intel will replace the processor with an equivalent one without this problem. Normally, all you have to do is to call Intel and ask for the replacement. It will ship you a new part matching the ratings of the one you are replacing in an overnight shipping box. The replacement is free, including all shipping charges. You merely remove your old processor, replace it with the new one, and then put the old one back in the box. Then you call the overnight service who will pick it up and send it back. Intel will take a credit card number when you first call for the replacement only to ensure that the original defective chip is returned. As long as Intel gets the original CPU back within a specified amount of time, there will be no charges to you. Intel has indicated that these defective processors will be destroyed and will not be remarketed or resold in another form.

The Discovery. The floating-point problem was first discovered by Dr. Thomas Nicely, Lynchburg College, VA on June 13, 1994 as he was working on a research project in an area of pure mathematics called computational number theory. This involved computations with twin prime numbers and reciprocal sums out to 19 or more digits of accuracy. Cross checks of some test calculations done on a Pentium system turned up errors when compared to known published values.

After thoroughly testing the software for problems (and uncovering other unrelated problems), tests showed that by disabling the FPU, these errors disappeared. Tests on other Pentium systems confirmed the errors; however, when the tests were run on a 486, the errors also disappeared. Tests using other compilers or languages confirmed that the error was not software related.

After testing over a period of more than two months, on October 24, Dr. Nicely contacted Intel tech support. Unfortunately, after waiting for six days, they still had no answer for him concerning the math problems. In an effort to locate other individuals with Pentium systems to test, on October 30 he sent a series of e-mail messages to a number of individuals and organizations who would have access to many other Pentium systems so that they could check for the problem. Because virtually every one of the five million (!) Pentium processors out at the time were flawed, everybody started finding these math errors, and a virtual explosion of e-mail on the subject appeared on the Net. Intel's initial responses were very guarded, which made the topic even more explosive.

The Furor. The negative publicity about this problem practically burned the phone wires across the country as people were sending e-mail back and forth through the Internet about the problem. Intel stock immediately dropped, and news about the bug even hit the prime time news. Estimates of the costs involved with replacing all the five million or so flawed processors ran into the hundreds of millions of dollars.

Rather than jump in to put out the fire, Intel downplayed the problem and indicated that most people would not need a replacement. Instead of soothing the problem, this response was like throwing gas on a fire. People were especially incensed that Intel had discovered the bug before Dr. Nicely had already implemented the fix, but had not told either end users or the manufacturers who use its processors.

Adding even more fuel to the fire was the fact that the Pentium had been the subject of a high-profile advertising campaign by Intel, which was designed to draw attention specifically to the processor in the high-end systems of the time. And although all processors have defects, this one occurs in an elementary, frequently used operation that is easy to demonstrate to those who have little or no computer background.

I'm sure that Intel and many other companies who watched the developing furor surrounding this bug have learned a great deal. Certainly it is important to admit mistakes quickly and directly, and to take all the steps necessary to correct the situation to the customer's satisfaction. Another lesson everybody learned is how important a tool the Internet can be for the disseminating of information, both good and bad.

One interesting result of the fervor surrounding this defect is that people are less likely to implicitly trust their PCs (which is good), and are therefore doing more testing and evaluating of important results. The bottom line is that if your information and calculations are important enough, you should implement some program of checking your results. In looking for problems with math, several programs were found to have problems. For example, a bug was discovered in the yield function of Excel 5.0 that some users were attributing to the Pentium processor. In this case, the problem turned out to be the software, which has been corrected in later versions (5.0c and later).

If you want to read the official Intel account of this problem, Intel has several documents on the problem available through its Faxback network, BBS, CompuServe, or the Internet (see the vendor list in Appendix B).

A Technical Explanation. The Pentium uses a much more aggressive algorithm for hardware floating-point division than did the 486; this is indicated by the fact that it uses only about half as many clock cycles per floating-point division. The difficulty arises from an error in the lookup tables used to implement the hardware division algorithm; the lookup tables are incomplete.

The FPU error can occur in any of the following instructions that use the floating point divide routines in the chip: FDIV, FDIVP, FDIVR, FDIVRP, FIDIV, FIDIVR, FPREM, FPREM1, FPTAN, or FPATAN.

During execution of the affected instructions, the hardware uses a divider circuit that relies on a quotient prediction lookup algorithm. Five entries from the lookup table were accidentally omitted. As a result, a divisor/remainder pair that hits one of these missing entries during the lookup phase of the division algorithm will incorrectly predict an intermediate quotient digit value.

Testing for the FPU Bug. Testing a Pentium for this bug is relatively easy. All you have to do is to execute one of the test division cases cited here and see if your answer compares to the correct result.

The division calculation can be done in a spreadsheet (such as Lotus 1-2-3, Microsoft Excel, or any other), in the Microsoft Windows built-in calculator, or in any other calculating program that uses the FPU. Make sure that for the purposes of this test the FPU has not been disabled. That would normally require some special command or setting specific to the application, and would of course ensure that the test came out correct no matter if the chip is flawed or not.

The most severe Pentium floating-point errors occur as early as the third significant digit of the result. Here is an example of one of the more severe instances of the problem:

962,306,957,033 / 11,010,046 = 87,402.6282027341 (correct answer)

962,306,957,033 / 11,010,046 = 87,399.5805831329 (flawed Pentium)

Note that your particular calculator program may not show the answer to the number of digits shown here. Most spreadsheet programs limit displayed results to 13 or 15 significant digits.

As you can see, in the previous case the error turns up in the third most significant digit of the result. In an examination of more than 5,000 integer pairs in the 5 to 15 digit range found to produce Pentium floating-point division errors, errors beginning in the sixth significant digit were the most likely to occur, although errors occurred anywhere from the third digit on up.

Here is another division problem that will come out incorrectly on a Pentium with this flaw:

4,195,835 / 3,145,727 = 1.33382044913624100 (correct answer)

4,195,835 / 3,145,727 = 1.33373906890203759 (flawed Pentium)

This one shows an error in the fifth significant digit. A variation on the previous calculation can be performed as follows:

x = 4,195,835

y = 3,145,727

z = x - (x/y)*y

4,195,835 - (4,195,835 / 3,145,727) * 3,145,727 = 0 (correct answer)

4,195,835 - (4,195,835 / 3,145,727) * 3,145,727 = 256 (flawed Pentium)

With an exact computation, the answer here should be zero. In fact, you will get zero on most machines, including those using Intel 286, 386, and 486 chips. But, on the Pentium, the answer is 256.

Here is one more calculation you can try:

5,505,001 / 294,911 = 18.66665197 (correct answer)

5,505,001 / 294,911 = 18.66600093 (flawed Pentium)

This one represents an error in the sixth significant digit.

If you don't want to try all these calculations, there are two other ways to determine whether your Pentium has this bug. One way is to run the CPUID program supplied by Intel via its BBS. You can download the file $CPUID.EXE, which is a self-extracting file containing the CPUIDF.EXE program. This program identifies which type of processor you have, and if you have a Pentium, it will tell you whether it has the floating-point bug or not. If the program discovers a bugged chip, it displays on-screen instructions listing where to call and how to get a free replacement.

Another way to determine if your processor is defective or not is to check the stepping level. This will be displayed by the CPUID program or can be determined by looking at the chip itself. Unfortunately, the stepping level is not stamped on the chip, but must be determined by looking up the lot code on the chip in the table at the end of this section.

Workarounds. There are several workarounds for this bug, but they extract a performance penalty. Intel has a software workaround that can be implemented by the compiler companies to produce programs that check for the defective processors, and if necessary, work around the problem. One technique they use is to replace each division by a function call. The function call first performs the division directly, and then tests the answer for correctness (by comparing (x/y)*x to y). If the result is in error due to the Pentium bug, the numerator and denominator are each multiplied by 3 (which changes the number sufficiently to eliminate the problem), and the division is repeated. This process is continued in a loop until the result checks correctly.

The bug can also be temporarily circumvented for some applications by simply locking out the FPU. Check with the documentation for your particular application as to how this can be done. As an example, for most DOS applications, this can be done by means of the DOS SET command. For example,

SET 87=NO

(for executable programs created by Borland compilers) and

SET NO87=NO87

(for executables created by Microsoft compilers). These commands will stop programs created by these compilers from using the floating-point math instructions. Unfortunately, this will significantly hurt performance in any application that uses the FPU. Also, some applications require an FPU, and most Windows programs ignore these environmental variables. Be sure to test the application to ensure that the FPU has been disabled, and that the calculations now come out correct.

The recompiled code workarounds only work for applications whose code has been rewritten, recompiled, and reshipped since the bug appeared. Previously existing programs can only avoid the bug by locking out the FPU. Forcing the application to test each calculation slows the machine down slightly, perhaps 30 percent (dependent on the application). Locking out the FPU may slow the machine down by a factor of ten or more, also depending on the application.

Because Intel has agreed to replace any Pentium processor with this flaw under a lifetime warranty replacement program, if you have a chip with this defect, the best workaround is a free replacement!

Power Management Bugs. Starting with the second-generation Pentium processors, Intel added functions that allow these CPUs to be installed in energy efficient systems. These are usually called Energy Star systems because they meet the specifications imposed by the EPA Energy Star Program, but they are also unofficially called "Green PCs" by many users.

Unfortunately, there have been several bugs with respect to these functions, causing them to either fail or be disabled. These bugs are in some of the functions in the power management capabilities accessed through SMM. These problems are only applicable to the second-generation 75/90/100 MHz processors, because the first-generation 60/66 MHz processors do not have SMM or power management capabilities, and all higher speed (120 MHz and up) processors have the bugs fixed.

Most of the problems are related to the STPCLK# pin and the HALT instruction. If this condition is invoked by the chipset, the system will hang. For most systems, the only workaround for this problem is to simply disable the power-saving modes, such as suspend or sleep. Unfortunately, this means that your "green" PC won't be so green anymore! The best way to repair the problem is to replace the processor with a later stepping version that does not have the bug. These bugs affect the B1 stepping version of the 75/90/100 MHz Pentiums, and were fixed in the B3 and later stepping versions.

Pentium Processor Models and Steppings

It is a sort of dirty little secret in the business that no processor is truly ever perfect. From time to time, the manufacturers will gather up what problems they have found and put into production a new "stepping," which consists of a new set of masks that incorporate the corrections. Each subsequent stepping is better and more refined than the previous ones. Although no microprocessor is ever perfect, manufacturers come closer to perfection with each stepping. In the life of a typical microprocessor, a manufacturer may go through half-dozen or more such steppings.

The following table shows all the versions of the Pentium processor Model 1 (60/66 MHz version) indicating the various steppings that have been available:

Type	Family	Model	Stepping	Mfg. Stepping	Speed	Spec. Number	Comments
0	5	1	3	B1	50	Q0399	ES
0	5	1	3	B1	60	Q0352	
0	5	1	3	B1	60	Q0400	ES
0	5	1	3	B1	60	Q0394	ES,HS
0	5	1	3	B1	66	Q0353	5v1
0	5	1	3	B1	66	Q0395	ES,HS,5v1
0	5	1	3	B1	60	Q0412	
0	5	1	3	B1	60	SX753	
0	5	1	3	B1	66	Q0413	5v2
0	5	1	3	B1	66	SX754	5v2
0	5	1	5	C1	60	Q0466	HS
0	5	1	5	C1	60	SX835	HS
0	5	1	5	C1	60	SZ949	HS,BOX
0	5	1	5	C1	66	Q0467	HS,5v2
0	5	1	5	C1	66	SX837	HS,5v2
0	5	1	5	C1	66	SZ950	HS,BOX,5v2
0	5	1	7	D1	60	Q0625	HS
0	5	1	7	D1	60	SX948	HS
0	5	1	7	D1	60	SX974	HS,5v3
0	5	1	7	D1	60	-*	HS,BOX
0	5	1	7	D1	66	Q0626	HS,5v2
0	5	1	7	D1	66	SX950	HS,5v2
0	5	1	7	D1	66	Q0627	HS,5v3
0	5	1	7	D1	66	SX949	HS,5v3
0	5	1	7	D1	66	-*	HS,BOX,5v2

The following table shows all the versions of the Pentium processor Model 2 and higher (75+ MHz versions) indicating the various steppings that have been available:

Type	Family	Model	Stepping	Mfg. Stepping	Speed	Spec. Number	Comments
0	5	2	1	B1	75	Q0540	ES,HS
2	5	2	1	B1	75	Q0541	ES,HS
0	5	2	1	B1	90	Q0542	HS
0	5	2	1	B1	90	Q0613	VR,HS
2	5	2	1	B1	90	Q0543	DP,HS

(continues)

II System Components

(continued)

Type	Family	Model	Stepping	Mfg. Stepping	Speed	Spec. Number	Comments
0	5	2	1	B1	100	Q0563	HS
0	5	2	1	B1	100	Q0587	VR,HS
0	5	2	1	B1	100	Q0614	VR,HS
0	5	2	1	B1	75	Q0601	TCP
0	5	2	1	B1	90	SX879	HS
0	5	2	1	B1	90	SX885	MD,HS
0	5	2	1	B1	90	SX909	VR,HS
2	5	2	1	B1	90	SX874	DP,HS
0	5	2	1	B1	100	SX886	MD,HS
0	5	2	1	B1	100	SX910	VR,MD,HS
0	5	2	2	B3	90	Q0628	HS
0/2	5	2	2	B3	90	Q0611	HS
0/2	5	2	2	B3	90	Q0612	VR,HS
0	5	2	2	B3	100	Q0677	VRE,MD,HS
0	5	2	2	B3	75	Q0606	TCP
0	5	2	2	B3	75	SX951	TCP
0	5	2	2	B3	90	SX923	HS
0	5	2	2	B3	90	SX922	VR,HS
0	5	2	2	B3	90	SX921	MD,HS
2	5	2	2	B3	90	SX942	DP,HS
2	5	2	2	B3	90	SX943	DP,VR,HS
2	5	2	2	B3	90	SX944	DP,MD,HS
0	5	2	2	B3	90	SZ951	BOX
0	5	2	2	B3	100	SX960	VRE,MD,HS
0/2	5	2	4	B5	75	Q0704	TCP
0/2	5	2	4	B5	75	Q0666	HS
0/2	5	2	4	B5	90	Q0653	HS
0/2	5	2	4	B5	90	Q0654	VR,HS
0/2	5	2	4	B5	90	Q0655	MD,HS
0/2	5	2	4	B5	100	Q0656	MD,HS
0/2	5	2	4	B5	100	Q0657	VR,MD,HS
0/2	5	2	4	B5	100	Q0658	VRE,MD,HS
0	5	2	4	B5	120	Q0707	VRE,MD,HS
0	5	2	4	B5	120	Q0708	HS
0	5	2	4	B5	75	SX975	TCP
0/2	5	2	4	B5	75	SX961	HS
0/2	5	2	4	B5	75	SZ977	HS,BOX
0/2	5	2	4	B5	90	SX957	HS
0/2	5	2	4	B5	90	SX958	VR,HS
0/2	5	2	4	B5	90	SX959	MD,HS

Type	Family	Model	Stepping	Mfg. Stepping	Speed	Spec. Number	Comments
0/2	5	2	4	B5	90	SZ978	HS,BOX
0/2	5	2	4	B5	100	SX962	VRE,MD,HS
0	5	2	5	C2	75	Q0725	TCP
0/2	5	2	5	C2	75	Q0700	
0/2	5	2	5	C2	75	Q0749	MD
0/2	5	2	5	C2	90	Q0699	
0/2	5	2	5	C2	100	Q0698	VRE,MD
0/2	5	2	5	C2	100	Q0697	
0	5	2	5	C2	120	Q0711	VRE,MD
0	5	2	5	C2	120	Q0732	VRE,MD
0	5	2	5	C2	133	Q0733	MD
0	5	2	5	C2	133	Q0751	MD
0	5	2	5	C2	133	Q0775	VRE,MD
0	5	2	5	C2	75	SK079	TCP
0/2	5	2	5	C2	75	SX969	
0/2	5	2	5	C2	75	SX998	MD
0/2	5	2	5	C2	75	SZ994	BOX
0/2	5	2	5	C2	75	SU070	BOXF
0/2	5	2	5	C2	90	SX968	
0/2	5	2	5	C2	90	SZ995	BOX
0/2	5	2	5	C2	90	SU031	BOXF
0/2	5	2	5	C2	100	SX970	VRE,MD
0/2	5	2	5	C2	100	SX963	
0/2	5	2	5	C2	100	SZ996	BOX
0/2	5	2	5	C2	100	SU032	BOXF
0	5	2	5	C2	120	SK086	VRE,MD
0	5	2	5	C2	120	SX994	VRE,MD
0	5	2	5	C2	120	SU033	VRE,MD,BOXF
0	5	2	5	C2	133	SK098	MD
0	5	2	5	mA1	75	Q0686	VRT,TCP
0	5	2	5	mA1	75	Q0689	VRT
0	5	2	5	mA1	90	Q0694	VRT,TCP
0	5	2	5	mA1	90	Q0695	VRT
0	5	2	5	mA1	75	SK089	VRT,TCP
0	5	2	5	mA1	75	SK091	VRT
0	5	2	5	mA1	90	SK090	VRT,TCP
0	5	2	5	mA1	90	SK092	VRT
0/2	5	2	B	cB1	120	Q0776	
0/2	5	2	B	cB1	133	Q0772	
0/2	5	2	B	cB1	133	Q0773	

(continues)

(continued)

Type	Family	Model	Stepping	Mfg. Stepping	Speed	Spec. Number	Comments
0/2	5	2	B	cB1	133	Q0774	VRE,MD
0/2	5	2	B	cB1	120	SK110	
0/2	5	2	B	cB1	133	SK106	
0/2	5	2	B	cB1	133	S106J	
0/2	5	2	B	cB1	133	SK107	
0/2	5	2	B	cB1	133	SU038	BOXF
0	5	2	B	mcB1	100	Q0884	VRT,TCP
0	5	2	B	mcB1	120	Q0779	VRT,TCP
0	5	2	B	mcB1	120	Q0808	
0	5	2	B	mcB1	100	SY029	VRT,TCP
0	5	2	B	mcB1	120	SK113	VRT,TCP
0	5	2	B	mcB1	120	SK118	VRT,TCP
0	5	2	B	mcB1	120	SX999	
0/2	5	2	C	cC0	150	Q0835	
0/2	5	2	C	cC0	150	Q0878	PPGA
0/2	5	2	C	cC0	166	Q0836	VRE
0/2	5	2	C	cC0	166	Q0841	VRE
0/2	5	2	C	cC0	166	Q0886	VRE,PPGA
0/2	5	2	C	cC0	166	Q0890	VRE,PPGA
0	5	2	C	cC0	166	Q0949	VRE,PPGA
0/2	5	2	C	cC0	150	SY015	
0/2	5	2	C	cC0	150	SU071	BOXF
0/2	5	2	C	cC0	166	SY016	VRE
0/2	5	2	C	cC0	166	SY017	VRE
0/2	5	2	C	cC0	166	SU072	VRE,BOXF
0	5	2	C	cC0	166	SY037	VRE,PPGA
0	5	7	0	mA4	75	Q0848	VRT,TCP
0	5	7	0	mA4	75	Q0851	VRT
0	5	7	0	mA4	90	Q0849	VRT,TCP
0	5	7	0	mA4	90	Q0852	VRT
0	5	7	0	mA4	100	Q0850	VRT,TCP
0	5	7	0	mA4	100	Q0853	VRT
0	5	7	0	mA4	75	SK119	VRT,TCP
0	5	7	0	mA4	75	SK122	VRT
0	5	7	0	mA4	90	SK120	VRT,TCP
0	5	7	0	mA4	90	SK123	VRT
0	5	7	0	mA4	100	SK121	VRT,TCP
0	5	7	0	mA4	100	SK124	VRT
0	5	2	C	mcC0	120	Q0879	VRT,TCP
0	5	2	C	mcC0	120	Q0880	3.1v

Type	Family	Model	Stepping	Mfg. Stepping	Speed	Spec. Number	Comments
0	5	2	C	mcC0	133	Q0881	VRT,TCP
0	5	2	C	mcC0	133	Q0882	3.1v
0	5	2	C	mcC0	120	SY021	VRT,TCP
0	5	2	C	mcC0	120	SY027	3.1v
0	5	2	C	mcC0	120	SY030	
0	5	2	C	mcC0	133	SY019	VRT,TCP
0	5	2	C	mcC0	133	SY028	3.1v
0	5	2	6	E0	75	Q0846	TCP
0/2	5	2	6	E0	75	Q0837	
0/2	5	2	6	E0	90	Q0783	
0/2	5	2	6	E0	100	Q0784	
0/2	5	2	6	E0	120	Q0785	VRE
0	5	2	6	E0	75	SY009	TCP
0/2	5	2	6	E0	75	SY005	
0/2	5	2	6	E0	90	SY006	
0/2	5	2	6	E0	100	SY007	
0/2	5	2	6	E0	120	SY033	

The following table shows all the versions of the Pentium OverDrive processors indicating the various steppings that have been available. Note that the Type 1 chips in this table are 486 Pentium OverDrive processors, which are designed to replace 486 chips in systems with Socket 2 or 3. The other OverDrive processors are designed to replace existing Pentium processors in socket 4 or 5/7.

Type	Family	Model	Stepping	Mfg. Stepping	Speed	Spec. Number	Comments
1	5	3	1	B1	63	SZ953	PODP5v63 1.0
1	5	3	1	B2	63	SZ990	PODP5v63 1.1
1	5	3	2	C0	83	SU014	PODP5v83 2.1
0	5	1	A	tA0	133	SU082	PODP5v133 1.0
0	5	2	C	aC0	125	SU081	PODP3v125 1.0
0	5	2	C	aC0	150	SU083	PODP3v150 1.0
0	5	2	C	aC0	166	SU084	PODP3v166 1.0

ES = Engineering Sample. These chips were not sold through normal channels but were designed for development and testing purposes.
HS = Heat Spreader Package. This indicates a chip with a metal plate on the top, which is used to spread heat away from the center part of the chip. The heat spreader helps the chip run cooler; however, most later chips use a smaller, more powerful efficient die, and Intel has been able to eliminate the heat spreader from these.
DP = Dual Processor version where Type 0 is Primary only, Type 2 is Secondary only, and Type 0 or 2 is either.
MD = Minimum Delay timing restrictions on several processor signals.
VR = Voltage Reduced (3.300v to 3.465v)
VRE = VR and Extended (3.45v to 3.60v)

VRT = Voltage Reduction Technology: The processor I/O voltage is 3.3v, but the processor core runs on 2.9v.
TCP = Tape Carrier Package (Mobile Pentium). This is a filmstrip type package intended mainly for laptop or notebook system use. This version is soldered rather than installed in a socket like the others.
BOX = A retail boxed Processor with a standard passive heat sink.
BOXF = A retail boxed processor with an active (fan-cooled) heat sink.
** = These chips have no specification number.*

In these tables, the processor Type heading refers to the dual processor capabilities of the Pentium. Versions indicated with a Type 0 can only be used as a primary processor, while those marked as Type 2 can only be used as the secondary processor in a pair. If the processor is marked as Type 0/2, that means it can serve as either the primary or secondary processor or both.

The Family designation for all Pentiums is "5" (for 586), while the Model indicates the particular revision. Model 1 indicates the first generation 60/66 MHz version while Model 2 or later indicates the second generation 75+ MHz version. The stepping number is the actual revision of the particular model. The family, model, and stepping number can be read by software such as the Intel CPUID program. These also correspond to a particular Manufacturer Stepping code, which is how Intel designates the chips in-house. These are usually an alphanumeric code. For example, stepping 5 of the Model 2 Pentium is also known as the C2 stepping inside Intel.

Manufacturing stepping codes that begin with an "m" indicate a Mobile processor, or one that is designed for laptop or portable systems. These often come in a Tape Carrier Package (TCP), which is a sort of filmstrip package where the raw chip is actually taped and soldered directly to the circuit board. Most Pentium processors come in a standard Ceramic Pin Grid Array (CPGA) package; however, the mobile processors also use the Tape Carrier Package (TCP), and now there is also a Plastic Pin Grid Array (PPGA) package being used to reduce cost.

The specification number is a code that is stamped or printed on the top and often bottom of the chip. This code is the only way externally that you can tell exactly which chip you have. In most systems, there will be a heat sink on the chip that will have to be removed to see the markings on the top; however, most Pentium processors are now marked on the bottom as well. If you cannot easily remove the heat sink, flip the chip over because the specification code may be printed on the bottom, as well.

One interesting item to note is that there are several subtly different voltages required by different Pentium processors. The following table summarizes the different processors and their required voltages:

Model	Stepping	Voltage Specs.	Voltage Range
1	-	Std.	4.75-5.25v
1	-	5v1	4.90-5.25v
1	-	5v2	4.90-5.40v
1	-	5v3	5.15-5.40v
2+	B1-B5	Std.	3.135-3.465v
2+	C2+	Std.	3.135-3.600v

Model	Stepping	Voltage Specs.	Voltage Range
2+	-	VR	3.300-3.465v
2+	B1-B5	VRE	3.45-3.60v
2+	C2+	VRE	3.40-3.60v

Many of the newer Pentium motherboards have jumpers that allow for adjustments to the different voltage ranges. If you are having problems with a particular processor, it may not be matched correctly to your motherboard voltage output.

Many of the Mobile Pentium processors use VRT, which means that they draw the standard 3.3v from the motherboard, but internally they operate on only 2.9 volts. Because the core of the CPU is operating on this lower voltage, it dramatically reduces overall power consumption and heat production, which is ideal for portable or notebook systems where battery life is important. In addition to VRT, some of the Mobile Pentium processors are now designed to run on 3.1v from the system instead of the standard 3.3v.

If I were purchasing a Pentium system today, I would recommend using only Model 2 (second generation) or later version processors that are available in 75 MHz or faster speeds, and I would definitely want stepping C2 or later. Virtually all of the important bugs and problems were fixed in the C2 and later releases.

Other Processor Problems

Some other problems with processors and math coprocessors are worth noting.

After you remove a math coprocessor from an AT-type system, you must rerun your computer's SETUP program. Some AT-compatible SETUP programs do not properly unset the math-coprocessor bit. If you receive a Power-On Self Test (POST) error message because the computer cannot find the math chip, you may have to unplug the battery from the system board temporarily. All SETUP information will be lost, so be sure to write down the hard drive type, floppy drive type, and memory and video configurations before unplugging the battery. This information is critical in reconfiguring your computer correctly.

Another strange problem occurs in some IBM PS/2 Model 80 systems when a 387DX is installed. In the following computers, you may hear crackling or beeping noises from the speaker while the computer is running:

- 8580 Model 111, with serial numbers below 6019000
- 8850 Model 311, with serial numbers below 6502022

If you are experiencing this problem, contact IBM for a motherboard replacement.

Heat and Cooling Problems

Heat can be a problem in any high-performance 486, Pentium, or Pentium Pro system. The higher speed processors normally consume more power and generate correspondingly more heat. If your system is based on any of the 66 MHz or faster processors, you must dissipate the extra thermal energy; the fan inside your computer case may not be able to handle the load.

To cool a system in which processor heat is a problem, you can buy (for less than $5 in most cases) a special attachment for the CPU chip called a heat sink. Many applications may need only a larger standard heat sink with additional or longer fins for a larger cooling area. Several heat sink manufacturers are listed in the vendor list.

Heat sinks come in two basic types: passive and active. The passive type is a simple finned radiator, while the active type includes a small fan. The active designs require power to run the fan, which is normally supplied via a spare disk drive power connector from the power supply.

There are several ways to attach a heat sink to the processor, including clip-on or by using glue or adhesive tape. I prefer clip-on heat sinks, but some are attached with a special adhesive. In many cases, you need to use a thermal transfer paste if the heat sink is clipped on. This paste fills any small air gaps between the processor and the heat sink, providing a more effective transfer of heat.

Most of the OverDrive processors that Intel will be introducing over the next few years will have a built-in active heat sink, which includes a fan. Unlike the aftermarket add-on fans, these built-in fans will draw power directly from the processor itself and will not require additional connections. In addition, these processors are able to detect if the fan fails, and will reduce the clock speed of the processor to prevent overheating in the case of a fan failure.

Aftermarket fan type (active) heat sinks are available for high speed processors; however, if these fail, the processor will quickly overheat. Often the fans used in these heat sinks are cheap sleeve-bearing fans that are designed for an operating life of just about one year. When the bearings finally dry out, the fan will make noise and eventually seize up, causing the processor to overheat and the system to crash. If you must use a processor fan, make sure it is a high-quality unit that uses a long life ball bearing fan. PC Power and Cooling supplies high-quality active heat sinks of this type.

For monitoring the fan operation on a mission critical system, a company called Practical Enhanced Logic (see the vendor list) markets a product called Systo Tek, which is plugged in line between the fan and power supply, and emits an alarm signal in case the fan fails. This alerts you to turn off the system to prevent the processor from overheating, which causes the system to lock up (losing any unsaved data and possibly corrupting files). If the processor overheats severely, it may even be permanently damaged or even damage other components on the motherboard.

Summary

This chapter covered what many people consider to be the primary component of a personal computer: the processor. Sometimes also called the Central Processing Unit (CPU) chip, this is the primary chip in the system. The chapter discussed the variety of processors that are available for PC-compatible systems, including those made by Intel and other vendors. You now should have a much better appreciation of this component, including general functionality and especially how the different processors compare.

Chapter 7

Memory

This chapter looks at memory from both a physical and logical point of view. The chapter discusses the physical chips and SIMMs (Single Inline Memory Modules) that you can purchase and install. The chapter also looks at the logical layout of memory and defines the different areas and uses of these areas from the system's point of view. Because the logical layout and uses are within the "mind" of the processor, memory remains as perhaps the most difficult subject to grasp in the entire PC universe. This chapter contains much useful information that removes the mysteries associated with memory and enables you to get the most out of your system.

The System Logical Memory Layout

The original PC had a total of 1M of addressable memory, and the top 384K of that was reserved for use by the system. Placing this reserved space at the top (between 640K and 1024K instead of at the bottom, between 0K and 640K) led to what today is often called the *conventional memory barrier*. The constant pressures on system and peripheral manufacturers to maintain compatibility by never breaking from the original memory scheme of the first PC has resulted in a system memory structure that is (to put it kindly) a mess. More than a decade after the first PC was introduced, even the newest Pentium Pro-based systems are limited in many important ways by the memory map of the first PCs.

Someone who wants to become knowledgeable about personal computers must at one time or another come to terms with the types of memory installed on their system—the small and large pieces of different kinds of memory, some accessible by software application programs, and some not. The following sections detail the different kinds of memory installed on a modern PC. The kinds of memory covered in the following sections include the following:

- Conventional (Base) memory
- Upper Memory Area (UMA)
- High Memory Area (HMA)
- Extended Memory Specification (XMS)

- Expanded memory (obsolete)
- Video RAM memory (part of UMA)
- Adapter ROM and Special Purpose RAM (part of UMA)
- Motherboard ROM BIOS (part of UMA)

Subsequent sections also cover preventing memory conflicts and overlap, using memory managers to optimize your system's memory, and making better use of memory. In an AT system, the memory map extends beyond the 1M boundary and can continue to 16M on a system based on the 286 or higher processor, or as much as 4G (4,096M) on a 386DX or higher. Any memory past 1M is called *extended memory*.

Figure 7.1 shows the logical address locations for a PC-compatible system. If the processor is running in Real Mode, only the first megabyte is accessible. If the processor is in Protected Mode, the full 16 or 4,096M are accessible. Each symbol is equal to 1K of memory; each line or segment is 64K; this map shows the first 2M of system memory.

Note

To save space, this map is ended after the end of the second megabyte. In reality, this map continues to the maximum of 16M or 4,096M of addressable memory.

Conventional (Base) Memory

The original PC/XT-type system was designed to use 1M of memory workspace, sometimes called *RAM* (Random-Access Memory). This 1M of RAM is divided into several sections, some of which have special uses. DOS can read and write to the entire megabyte, but can manage the loading of programs only in the portion of RAM space called *conventional memory*, which at the time the first PC was introduced was 512K. The other 512K was reserved for use by the system itself, including the motherboard and adapter boards plugged into the system slots.

IBM decided after introducing the system that only 384K was needed for these reserved uses, and the company began marketing PCs with 640K of user memory. Thus, 640K became the standard for memory that can be used by DOS for running programs and is often termed the *640K memory barrier*. The remaining memory after 640K was indicated as reserved for use by the graphics boards, other adapters, and the motherboard ROM BIOS.

Upper Memory Area (UMA)

The term *Upper Memory Area* (UMA) describes the reserved 384K at the top of the first megabyte of system memory on a PC/XT and the first megabyte on an AT-type system. This memory has the addresses from A0000–FFFFF.

```
. = Program-accessible memory (standard RAM)
G = Graphics Mode Video RAM
M = Monochrome Text Mode Video RAM
C = Color Text Mode Video RAM
V = Video ROM BIOS (would be "a" in PS/2)
a = Adapter board ROM and special-purpose RAM (free UMA space)
r = Additional PS/2 Motherboard ROM BIOS (free UMA in non-PS/2 systems)
R = Motherboard ROM BIOS
b = IBM Cassette BASIC ROM (would be "R" in IBM compatibles)
h = High Memory Area (HMA), if HIMEM.SYS is loaded.

Conventional (Base) Memory:

       : 0---1---2---3---4---5---6---7---8---9---A---B---C---D---E---F---
000000: ................................................................
010000: ................................................................
020000: ................................................................
030000: ................................................................
040000: ................................................................
050000: ................................................................
060000: ................................................................
070000: ................................................................
080000: ................................................................
090000: ................................................................

Upper Memory Area (UMA):

       : 0---1---2---3---4---5---6---7---8---9---A---B---C---D---E---F---
0A0000: GGGGGGGGGGGGGGGGGGGGGGGGGGGGGGGGGGGGGGGGGGGGGGGGGGGGGGGGGGGGGGGG
0B0000: MMMMMMMMMMMMMMMMMMMMMMMMMMMMMMMMCCCCCCCCCCCCCCCCCCCCCCCCCCCCCCCC
       : 0---1---2---3---4---5---6---7---8---9---A---B---C---D---E---F---
0C0000: VVVVVVVVVVVVVVVVVVVVVVVVVVVVVVVVaaaaaaaaaaaaaaaaaaaaaaaaaaaaaaaa
0D0000: aaaaaaaaaaaaaaaaaaaaaaaaaaaaaaaaaaaaaaaaaaaaaaaaaaaaaaaaaaaaaaaa
       : 0---1---2---3---4---5---6---7---8---9---A---B---C---D---E---F---
0E0000: rrrrrrrrrrrrrrrrrrrrrrrrrrrrrrrrrrrrrrrrrrrrrrrrrrrrrrrrrrrrrrrr
0F0000: RRRRRRRRRRRRRRRRRRRRRRRRbbbbbbbbbbbbbbbbbbbbbbbbbbbbbbbbRRRRRRRR

Extended Memory:

       : 0---1---2---3---4---5---6---7---8---9---A---B---C---D---E---F---
100000: hhhhhhhhhhhhhhhhhhhhhhhhhhhhhhhhhhhhhhhhhhhhhhhhhhhhhhhhhhhhhhhh

Extended Memory Specification (XMS) Memory:

110000: ................................................................
120000: ................................................................
130000: ................................................................
140000: ................................................................
150000: ................................................................
160000: ................................................................
170000: ................................................................
180000: ................................................................
190000: ................................................................
1A0000: ................................................................
1B0000: ................................................................
1C0000: ................................................................
1D0000: ................................................................
1E0000: ................................................................
1F0000: ................................................................
```

Figure 7.1

The logical memory map of the first 2M.

The way the 384K of upper memory is used breaks down as follows:

- The first 128K after conventional memory is called *Video RAM.* It is reserved for use by video adapters. When text and graphics are displayed on-screen, the electronic impulses that contain their images reside in this space. Video RAM is allotted the address range from A0000–BFFFF.

- The next 128K is reserved for the adapter BIOS that resides in read-only memory chips on some adapter boards plugged into the bus slots. Most VGA-compatible video adapters use the first 32K of this area for their on-board BIOS. The rest can be used by any other adapters installed. Many network adapters also use this area for special purpose RAM called *Shared Memory*. Adapter ROM and special purpose RAM is allotted the address range from C0000–DFFFF.

- The last 128K of memory is reserved for motherboard BIOS, (the basic input-output system, which is stored in read-only RAM chips or ROM). The POST (Power-On Self Test) and bootstrap loader, which handles your system at bootup until DOS takes over, also reside in this space. Most systems only use the last 64K (or less) of this space, leaving the first 64K or more free for remapping with memory managers. Some systems also include the CMOS Setup program in this area. The motherboard BIOS is allotted the address range from E0000–FFFFF.

Not all the 384K of reserved memory is fully used on most AT-type systems. For example, according to IBM's definition of the PC standard, reserved video RAM begins at address A0000, which is right at the 640K boundary. Normally this is used for VGA graphics modes, while the monochrome and color text modes use B0000–B7FFF and B8000–BFFFF respectively. Older non-VGA adapters only used memory in the B0000 segment. Different video adapters use varying amounts of RAM for their operations depending mainly on the mode they are in; however, to the processor, it always appears as the same 128K area no matter how much RAM is really on the video card. This is managed by bank switching areas of memory on the card in and out of the A0000–BFFFF segments.

Although the top 384K of the first megabyte was originally termed *reserved memory*, it is possible to use previously unused regions of this memory to load device drivers (like ANSI.SYS) and memory-resident programs (like MOUSE.COM), which frees up the conventional memory they would otherwise require. The amount of free UMA space varies from system to system depending on the adapter cards installed on the system. For example, most SCSI adapters and network adapters require some of this area for built-in ROMs or special-purpose RAM use.

Segment Addresses and Linear Addresses. One thing that can be confusing is the difference between a segment address and a full linear address. The use of *segmented address numbers* comes from the internal structure of the Intel processors. They use a separate register for the segment information and another for the offset. The concept is very simple. For example, assume that I am staying in a hotel room, and somebody asks for my room number. The hotel has 10 floors, numbered from zero through nine; each floor has 100 rooms, numbered from 00 to 99. A *segment* is defined as any group of 100 rooms starting at a multiple of 10, and indicated by a two-digit number. For example, a segment address of 54 would indicate the actual room 540, and you could have an offset of from 00 to 99 rooms from there.

Thus in this hotel example, each segment is specified as a two-digit number from 00 to 99, and an offset can be specified from any segment start with a number from 00 to 99 as well.

As an example, let's say I am staying in room 541. If the person needs this information in segment:offset form, and each number is two digits, I could say that I am staying at a room segment starting address of 54 (room 540), and an offset of 01 from the start of that segment. I could also say that I am in room segment 50 (room 500), and an offset of 41. You could even come up with other answers, such as that I am at segment 45 (room 450) offset 91 (450+91=541). Here is an example of how this adds up:

```
Segment      54      50      45
 Offset      01      41      91
-------     ---     ---     ---
  Total     541     541     541
```

As you can see, although the particular segment and offset are different, they all add up to the same room address. In the Intel x86 processors, a similar scheme is used where a segment and offset are added internally to produce the actual address. It can be somewhat confusing, especially if you are writing assembly language or machine language software!

This is exactly how segmented memory in an Intel processor works. Notice that the segment and offset numbers essentially overlap on all digits except the first and last. By adding them together with the proper alignment, you can see the linear address total.

A *linear address* is one without segment:offset boundaries, such as saying room 541. It is a single number and not comprised of two numbers added together. For example, a SCSI host adapter might have 16K ROM on the card addressed from D4000 to D7FFF. These numbers expressed in segment:offset form are D400:0000 to D700:0FFF. The segment portion is composed of the most significant four digits, and the offset portion is composed of the least significant four digits. Because each portion overlaps by one digit, the ending address of its ROM can be expressed in four different ways, as follows:

```
D000:7FFF =    D000   segment
             +  7FFF   offset
                -----
             = D7FFF   total

D700:0FFF =    D700   segment
             +  0FFF   offset
                -----
             = D7FFF   total

D7F0:00FF =    D7F0   segment
             +  00FF   offset
                -----
             = D7FFF   total
```

```
D7FF:000F =    D7FF   segment
             +  000F   offset
               -----
             = D7FFF   total
```

As you can see in each case, although the segment and offset differ slightly, the total ends up being the same. Adding together the segment and offset numbers makes possible even more combinations, as in the following examples:

```
D500:2FFF =    D500   segment
             +  2FFF   offset
               -----
             = D7FFF   total

D6EE:111F =    D6EE   segment
             +  111F   offset
               -----
             = D7FFF   total
```

As you can see, several combinations are possible. The correct and generally accepted way to write this address as a linear address is D7FFF, whereas most would write the segment:offset address as D000:7FFF. Keeping the segment mostly zeros makes the segment:offset relationship easier to understand and the number easier to comprehend. If you understand the segment:offset relationship to the linear address, you now know why when a linear address number is discussed it is five digits, whereas a segment number is only four digits.

Video RAM Memory. A video adapter installed in your system uses some of your system's memory to hold graphics or character information for display. Some adapters, like the VGA, also have on-board BIOS mapped into the system's space reserved for such types of adapters. Generally, the higher the resolution and color capabilities of the video adapter, the more system memory the video adapter uses. It is important to note that most VGA or Super VGA adapters have additional on-board memory used to handle the information currently displayed on-screen and to speed screen refresh.

In the standard system-memory map, a total of 128K is reserved for use by the video card to store currently displayed information. The reserved video memory is located in segments A000 and B000. The video adapter ROM uses additional upper memory space in segment C000.

The location of video adapter RAM is responsible for the 640K DOS conventional memory barrier. DOS can use all available contiguous memory in the first megabyte—which means all—of memory until the video adapter RAM is encountered. The use of adapters such as the MDA and CGA allows DOS access to more than 640K of system memory; the video memory *wall* begins at A0000 for the EGA, MCGA, and VGA systems, but the MDA and CGA do not use as much video RAM, which leaves some space that can be used by DOS and programs. The previous segment and offset examples show that the MDA adapter enables DOS to use an additional 64K of memory (all of segment A000), bringing the total for DOS program space to 704K. Similarly, the CGA enables a total of

736K of possible contiguous memory. The EGA, VGA, or MCGA is limited to the normal maximum of 640K of contiguous memory because of the larger amount used by video RAM. The maximum DOS-program memory workspace therefore depends on which video adapter is installed. Table 7.1 shows the maximum amount of memory available to DOS using the referenced video card.

Table 7.1 DOS Memory Limitations Based on Video Adapter Type

Video Adapter Type	Maximum DOS Memory
Monochrome Display Adapter (MDA)	704K
Color Graphics Adapter (CGA)	736K
Enhanced Graphics Adapter (EGA)	640K
Video Graphics Array (VGA)	640K
Super VGA (SVGA)	640K
eXtended Graphics Array (XGA)	640K

Using this memory to 736K might be possible depending on the video adapter, the types of memory boards installed, ROM programs on the motherboard, and the type of system. You can use some of this memory if your system has a 386 or higher processor. With memory manager software, such as EMM386 that comes with DOS, that can operate the 386+ Memory Management Unit (MMU), you can remap extended memory into this space.

The following sections examine how standard video adapters use the system's memory. Figures show where in a system the monochrome, EGA, VGA, and IBM PS/2 adapters use memory. This map is important because it may be possible to recognize some of this as unused in some systems, which may free up more space for software drivers to be loaded.

Monochrome Display Adapter Memory (MDA). Figure 7.2 shows where the original Monochrome Display Adapter (MDA) uses the system's memory. This adapter uses only a 4K portion of the reserved video RAM from B0000–B0FFF. Because the ROM code used to operate this adapter is actually a portion of the motherboard ROM, no additional ROM space is used in segment C000.

```
. = Empty Addresses
M = Original Monochrome Adapter RAM
m = Additional Memory used in VGA Monochrome Text Mode

      : 0---1---2---3---4---5---6---7---8---9---A---B---C---D---E---F---
0A0000: ................................................................
0B0000: MMMMmmmmmmmmmmmmmmmmmmmmmmmmmmmm................................
```

Figure 7.2

The Monochrome Display Adapter memory map.

II System Components

Notice that although the original MDA only used 4K of memory starting at B0000, a VGA adapter running in Monochrome emulation mode (Mono Text Mode) activates 32K of RAM at this address. A true MDA has no on-board BIOS, and instead is operated by driver programs found in the primary motherboard BIOS.

Color Graphics Adapter (CGA) Memory. Figure 7.3 shows where the Color Graphics Adapter (CGA) uses the system's memory. The CGA uses a 16K portion of the reserved video RAM from B8000–BBFFF. Because the ROM code used to operate this adapter is a portion of the motherboard ROM, no additional ROM space is used in segment C000.

```
. = Empty Addresses
C = Original Color Graphics Adapter (CGA) RAM
c = Additional Memory used in VGA Color Text Mode

       : 0---1---2---3---4---5---6---7---8---9---A---B---C---D---E---F---
0A0000: ................................................................
0B0000: ................................CCCCCCCCCCCCCCCCcccccccccccccccc
```

Figure 7.3

The Color Graphics Adapter (CGA) memory map.

The CGA card leaves memory from A0000–B7FFF free, which can be used by memory managers for additional DOS memory space. However, this precludes using any graphics mode software such as Windows. The original CGA card only used 16K of space starting at B8000, whereas a VGA adapter running in CGA emulation (Color Text) mode can activate 32K of RAM at this address. The original CGA card has no on-board BIOS and is instead operated by driver programs found in the primary motherboard BIOS.

Enhanced Graphics Adapter (EGA) Memory. Figure 7.4 shows where the Enhanced Graphics Adapter (EGA) uses the system's memory. This adapter uses all 128K of the video RAM from A0000–BFFFF. The ROM code used to operate this adapter is on the adapter itself and consumes 16K of memory from C0000-C3FFF.

The original IBM EGA card only used 16K ROM at C0000. Aftermarket compatible EGA adapters can use additional ROM space up to 32K total. The most interesting thing to note about EGA (and this applies to VGA adapters as well) is that segments A000 and B000 are not all used at all times. For example, if the card is in a graphics mode, only segment A000 would appear to have RAM installed, whereas segment B000 would appear completely empty. If you switched the mode of the adapter (through software) into Color Text mode, segment A000 would instantly appear empty, and the last half of segment B000 would suddenly "blink on!" The monochrome text mode RAM area would practically never be used on a modern system, because little or no software would ever need to switch the adapter into that mode. Figure 7.4 also shows the standard motherboard ROM BIOS as well so that you can get a picture of the entire UMA.

The EGA card became somewhat popular after it appeared, but this was quickly overshadowed by the VGA card that followed. Most of the VGA characteristics with regard to memory are the same as the EGA because the VGA is backward compatible with EGA.

```
. = Empty Addresses
G = Enhanced Graphics Adapter (EGA) Graphics Mode Video RAM
M = EGA Monochrome Text Mode Video RAM
C = EGA Color Text Mode Video RAM
V = Standard EGA Video ROM BIOS
R = Standard Motherboard ROM BIOS

       : 0---1---2---3---4---5---6---7---8---9---A---B---C---D---E---F---
0A0000: GGGGGGGGGGGGGGGGGGGGGGGGGGGGGGGGGGGGGGGGGGGGGGGGGGGGGGGGGGGGGGGG
0B0000: MMMMMMMMMMMMMMMMMMMMMMMMMMMMMMMMCCCCCCCCCCCCCCCCCCCCCCCCCCCCCCCC
       : 0---1---2---3---4---5---6---7---8---9---A---B---C---D---E---F---
0C0000: VVVVVVVVVVVVVVVV................................................
0D0000: ................................................................
       : 0---1---2---3---4---5---6---7---8---9---A---B---C---D---E---F---
0E0000: ................................................................
0F0000: RRRRRRRRRRRRRRRRRRRRRRRRRRRRRRRRRRRRRRRRRRRRRRRRRRRRRRRRRRRRRRRR
```

Figure 7.4

The Enhanced Graphics Adapter (EGA) memory map.

Video Graphics Array (VGA) Memory. All Video Graphics Array (VGA) compatible cards, including Super VGA cards, are almost identical to the EGA in terms of memory use. Just as with the EGA, they use all 128K of the video RAM from A0000–BFFFF, but not all at once. Again the video RAM area is split into three distinct regions, and each of these regions is used only when the adapter is in the corresponding mode. One minor difference with the EGA cards is that virtually all VGA cards use the full 32K allotted to them for on-board ROM (C0000 to C7FFF). Figure 7.5 shows the VGA adapter memory map.

```
. = Empty Addresses
G = Video Graphics Array (VGA) Adapter Graphics Mode Video RAM
M = VGA Monochrome Text Mode Video RAM
C = VGA Color Text Mode Video RAM
V = Standard VGA Video ROM BIOS
R = Standard Motherboard ROM BIOS

       : 0---1---2---3---4---5---6---7---8---9---A---B---C---D---E---F---
0A0000: GGGGGGGGGGGGGGGGGGGGGGGGGGGGGGGGGGGGGGGGGGGGGGGGGGGGGGGGGGGGGGGG
0B0000: MMMMMMMMMMMMMMMMMMMMMMMMMMMMMMMMCCCCCCCCCCCCCCCCCCCCCCCCCCCCCCCC
       : 0---1---2---3---4---5---6---7---8---9---A---B---C---D---E---F---
0C0000: VVVVVVVVVVVVVVVVVVVVVVVVVVVVVVVV................................
0D0000: ................................................................
       : 0---1---2---3---4---5---6---7---8---9---A---B---C---D---E---F---
0E0000: ................................................................
0F0000: RRRRRRRRRRRRRRRRRRRRRRRRRRRRRRRRRRRRRRRRRRRRRRRRRRRRRRRRRRRRRRRR
```

Figure 7.5

The VGA (and Super VGA) adapter memory map.

You can see that the typical VGA card uses a full 32K of space for the on-board ROM containing driver code. Some VGA cards may use slightly less, but this is rare. Just as with the EGA card, the video RAM areas are only active when the adapter is in the particular mode designated. In other words, when a VGA adapter is in graphics mode, only segment A000 is used; and when it is in color text mode, only the last half of segment B000 is used. Because the VGA adapter is almost never run in monochrome text mode, the first half of segment B000 remains unused (B0000–B7FFF). Figure 7.5 also shows the standard motherboard ROM BIOS so that you can get a picture of how the entire UMA is laid out with this adapter.

IBM created VGA, and the first systems to include VGA adapters were the PS/2 systems introduced in April 1987. These systems had the VGA adapter built directly into the motherboard. Because IBM had written both the video and motherboard BIOS, and they were building the VGA on the motherboard and not as a separate card, they incorporated the VGA BIOS driver code directly into the motherboard BIOS. This meant that segment C000 did not have an on-board video ROM as in most of the compatibles that would follow. Although this may sound like a bonus for the PS/2 systems—they still had the additional ROM code—it was merely located in segment E000 instead! In fact the PS/2 systems used all of segment E000 for additional motherboard ROM BIOS code, whereas segment E000 remains empty in most compatibles.

Many compatibles today have their video adapter built into the motherboard. Systems that use the LPX (Low Profile) motherboard design in an LPX- or Slimline-type case incorporate the video adapter into the motherboard. In these systems, even though the video BIOS and motherboard BIOS may be from the same manufacturer, they are always set up to emulate a standard VGA-type adapter card. In other words, the video BIOS appears in the first 32K of segment C000 just as if a stand-alone VGA-type card were plugged into a slot. The built-in video circuit in these systems can be easily disabled via a switch or jumper, which then allows a conventional VGA-type card to be plugged in. By having the built-in VGA act exactly as if it were a separate card, disabling it allows a new adapter to be installed with no compatibility problems that might arise if the video drivers had been incorporated into the motherboard BIOS.

When the VGA first appeared on the scene, it was built into the PS/2 motherboard. So that you could add VGA to other systems, IBM also introduced at that time the very first VGA card. It was called the PS/2 Display Adapter, which was somewhat confusing at the time because it was designed for standard ISA bus-compatible systems and not for the PS/2s, which mostly used the new Micro Channel Architecture bus and already had VGA built in. Nevertheless, this card was sold to anybody who wanted to add VGA to their ISA bus system. The IBM VGA card (PS/2 Display Adapter) was an 8-bit ISA card that had the same IBM-designed video chip and circuits as were used on the PS/2 motherboard.

If you were involved with the PC industry at that time, you might remember how long it took for clone video card manufacturers to accurately copy the IBM VGA circuits. It took nearly two years (almost to 1989) before you could buy an aftermarket VGA card and expect it to run everything an IBM VGA system would with no problems. Some of my associates who bought some of the early cards inadvertently became members of the video card manufacturer's "ROM of the Week" club! They were constantly finding problems with the operation of these cards, and many updated and patched ROMs were sent to try and fix the problems. Not wanting to pay for the privilege of beta testing the latest attempts at VGA compatibility, I bit the bullet and took the easy way out. I simply bought the IBM VGA card (PS/2 Display Adapter). At that time, the card listed for $595, but I could usually expect a 30 percent discount in purchasing it at the local computer store. That is still about as much as you would pay for the best Local Bus Super VGA cards on the market today. In fact, you can now buy basic VGA clone cards for less than $20 that are actually faster and better than the original IBM VGA card!

I remember well, purchasing the IBM VGA card not only because it was so expensive, but also because the card actually proved somewhat difficult to purchase! When I arrived to buy it at my local IBM authorized retailer (after first calling to see if it had one in stock), I asked for it by name. I said, "I am here to purchase an IBM PS/2 Display Adapter." The salesman asked what type of system I was going to install it in. I replied that I was going to put it in the AT clone I had assembled. Then I met resistance! The salesman told me that I could not use that in my clone because it was designed for PS/2 systems only. I told him he was mistaken and that the card is in fact designed for any IBM-compatible system with an ISA bus, and is supposed to give the system the same graphics capability of the new PS/2s. The salesman maintained that the card was only for PS/2 systems, and I finally had to say, "Look, I have cash, will you sell me the card or not?" Lo and behold I emerged from the store victorious, with the card in hand!

Although the card worked very well, and although I never did find any compatibility problems, I did later run into some interesting problems with the memory use of this card. This was my first introduction to what I call *scratch pad memory* use by an adapter. I found that many different types of adapters may use some areas in the UMA for mapping *scratch pad memory*. This refers to memory on the card that stores status information, configuration data, or any other temporary type information of a variable nature. Most cards keep this scratch pad memory to themselves and do not attempt to map it into the processor's address space, but some cards do place this type of memory in the address space so that the driver programs for the card can use it. Figure 7.6 shows the memory map of the IBM PS/2 Display Adapter (IBM's VGA card).

There is nothing different about this VGA card and any other with respect to the Video RAM area. What is different is that the ROM code that operates this adapter only consumes 24K of memory from C0000–C5FFF. Also strange is the 2K "hole" at C6000, and the 6K of scratch pad memory starting at C6800, as well as the additional 2K of scratch pad memory at CA000. In particular, the 2K "straggler" area really caught me off guard when I installed a SCSI host adapter in this system that had a 16K on-board BIOS with a default starting address of C8000. I immediately ran into a conflict that completely disabled the system. In fact, it would not boot, had no display at all, and could only beep out error codes that indicated that the video card had failed. I first thought that I had somehow "fried" the card, but removing the new SCSI adapter had everything functioning normally. I also could get the system to work with the SCSI adapter and an old CGA card substituting for the VGA, so I immediately knew a conflict was underfoot. This scratch pad memory use was not documented clearly in the technical-reference information for the adapter, so it was something that I had to find out by trial and error. If you have ever had the IBM VGA card and had conflicts with other adapters, now you know why! Needless to say, nothing could be done about this 2K of scratch pad memory hanging out there, and I had to work around it as long as I had this card in the system. I solved my SCSI adapter problem by merely moving the SCSI adapter BIOS to a different address.

```
. = Empty Addresses
G = Video Graphics Array (VGA) Adapter Graphics Mode Video RAM
M = VGA Monochrome Text Mode Video RAM
C = VGA Color Text Mode Video RAM
V = IBM VGA Video ROM BIOS
v = IBM VGA Scratch Pad memory (used by the card)
R = Standard Motherboard ROM BIOS

       : 0---1---2---3---4---5---6---7---8---9---A---B---C---D---E---F---
0A0000: GGGGGGGGGGGGGGGGGGGGGGGGGGGGGGGGGGGGGGGGGGGGGGGGGGGGGGGGGGGGGGGG
0B0000: MMMMMMMMMMMMMMMMMMMMMMMMMMMMMMMMCCCCCCCCCCCCCCCCCCCCCCCCCCCCCCCC
       : 0---1---2---3---4---5---6---7---8---9---A---B---C---D---E---F---
0C0000: VVVVVVVVVVVVVVVVVVVVVVVV..vvvvvv........vv......................
0D0000: ................................................................
       : 0---1---2---3---4---5---6---7---8---9---A---B---C---D---E---F---
0E0000: ................................................................
0F0000: RRRRRRRRRRRRRRRRRRRRRRRRRRRRRRRRRRRRRRRRRRRRRRRRRRRRRRRRRRRRRRRR
```

Figure 7.6

IBM's somewhat strange ISA-bus VGA card (PS/2 Display Adapter) memory map.

As a side note, I have seen other VGA-type video adapters use scratch pad memory, but they have all kept it within the C0000–C7FFF 32K region allotted normally for the video ROM BIOS. By using a 24K BIOS, I have seen other cards with up to 8K of scratch pad area, but none—except for IBM's—in which the scratch pad memory goes beyond C8000.

As you can see in the preceding figures, each type of video adapter on the market uses two types of memory: video RAM, which stores the display information; and ROM code, which controls the adapter; each must exist somewhere in the system's memory. The ROM code built into the motherboard ROM on standard PC and AT systems controls adapters such as the MDA and CGA. All the EGA and VGA adapters for the PC and AT systems use the full 128K of video RAM (not all at once, of course) and up to 32K of ROM space at the beginning of segment C000. IBM's technical-reference manuals say that the memory between C0000 and C7FFF is reserved specifically for ROM on video adapter boards. Note that the VGA and MCGA built into the motherboards of the PS/2 systems have the ROM-control software built into the motherboard ROM in segments E000 and F000 and require no other code space in segment C000. Also note that you can often use your memory manager software (such as what comes with DOS) to map extended memory into the monochrome display area (32K worth), which can get you an extra 32K region for loading drivers and resident programs.

Adapter ROM and Special Purpose RAM Memory. The second 128K of upper memory beginning at segment C000 is reserved for the software programs, or BIOS (basic input-output system), on the adapter boards plugged into the system slots. These BIOS programs are stored on special chips known as *read-only memory (ROM)*, which have fused circuits so that the PC cannot alter them. ROM is useful for permanent programs that always must be present while the system is running. Graphics boards, hard disk controllers, communications boards, and expanded memory boards, for example, are adapter boards that might use some of this memory.

On systems based on the 386 CPU chip or higher, memory managers like the MS-DOS 6 MEMMAKER, IBM DOS RAMBOOST, or aftermarket programs like QEMM by Quarterdeck, can load device drivers and memory-resident programs into unused regions in the UMA.

Video Adapter BIOS. Although 128K of upper memory beginning at segment C000 is reserved for use by the video adapter BIOS, not all this space is used by various video adapters commonly found on PCs. Table 7.2 details the amount of space used by the BIOS on each type of common video adapter card.

Table 7.2 Memory Used by Different Video Cards

Type of Adapter	Adapter BIOS Memory Used
Monochrome Display Adapter (MDA)	None - Drivers in Motherboard BIOS
Color Graphics Adapter (CGA)	None - Drivers in Motherboard BIOS
Enhanced Graphics Adapter (EGA)	16K on-board (C0000-C3FFF)
Video Graphics Array (VGA)	32K on-board (C0000-C7FFF)
Super VGA (SVGA)	32K on-board (C0000-C7FFF)

Some more advanced graphics accelerator cards on the market do use most or all the 128K of upper memory beginning at segment C000 to speed the repainting of graphics displays in Windows, OS/2, or other graphical user interfaces (GUIs). In addition, these graphics cards may contain up to 4M or more of on-board memory in which to store currently displayed data and more quickly fetch new screen data as it is sent to the display by the CPU.

Hard Disk Controller and SCSI Host Adapter BIOS. The upper memory addresses C0000 to DFFFF also are used for the BIOS contained on many hard drive controllers. Table 7.3 details the amount of memory and the addresses commonly used by the BIOS contained on hard drive adapter cards.

Table 7.3 Memory Addresses Used by Different Hard Drive Adapter Cards

Disk Adapter Type	On-Board BIOS Size	BIOS Address Range
IBM XT 10M Controller	8K	C8000-C9FFF
IBM XT 20M Controller	4K	C8000-C8FFF
Most XT Compatible Controllers	8K	C8000-C9FFF
Most AT Controllers	None	Drivers in Motherboard BIOS
Most IDE Adapters	None	Drivers in Motherboard BIOS
Most ESDI Controllers	16K	C8000-CBFFF
Most SCSI Host Adapters	16K	C8000-CBFFF

The hard drive or SCSI adapter card used on a particular system may use a different amount of memory, but it is most likely to use the memory segment beginning at C800 because this address is considered part of the IBM standard for personal computers. Virtually all the disk controller or SCSI adapters today that have an on-board BIOS allow the BIOS starting address to be easily moved in the C000 and D000 segments. The locations listed in table 7.3 are only the default addresses that most of these cards use. If the default address is already in use by another card, you have to consult the documentation for the new card to see how to change the BIOS starting address to avoid any conflicts.

Figure 7.7 shows an example memory map for an Adaptec AHA-1542CF SCSI adapter.

```
. = Empty Addresses
G = Video Graphics Array (VGA) Adapter Graphics Mode Video RAM
M = VGA Monochrome Text Mode Video RAM
C = VGA Color Text Mode Video RAM
V = Standard VGA Video ROM BIOS
S = SCSI Host Adapter ROM BIOS
R = Standard Motherboard ROM BIOS

       : 0---1---2---3---4---5---6---7---8---9---A---B---C---D---E---F---
0A0000: GGGGGGGGGGGGGGGGGGGGGGGGGGGGGGGGGGGGGGGGGGGGGGGGGGGGGGGGGGGGGGGG
0B0000: MMMMMMMMMMMMMMMMMMMMMMMMMMMMMMMMCCCCCCCCCCCCCCCCCCCCCCCCCCCCCCCC
       : 0---1---2---3---4---5---6---7---8---9---A---B---C---D---E---F---
0C0000: VVVVVVVVVVVVVVVVVVVVVVVVVVVVVVVV................................
0D0000: ................................................SSSSSSSSSSSSSSSS
       : 0---1---2---3---4---5---6---7---8---9---A---B---C---D---E---F---
0E0000: ................................................................
0F0000: RRRRRRRRRRRRRRRRRRRRRRRRRRRRRRRRRRRRRRRRRRRRRRRRRRRRRRRRRRRRRRRR
```

Figure 7.7

Adaptec AHA-1542CF SCSI adapter default memory use.

Notice how this SCSI adapter fits in here. Although no conflicts are in the UMA memory, the free regions have been fragmented by the placement of the SCSI BIOS. Because most systems do not have any BIOS in segment E000, that remains as a free 64K region. With no other adapters using memory, this example shows another free UMB (Upper Memory Block) starting at C8000 and continuing through DBFFF, which represents an 80K free region. By using the EMM386 driver that comes with DOS, memory can be mapped into these two regions for loading memory-resident drivers and programs. Unfortunately, because programs cannot be split across regions, the largest program you could load is 80K, which is the size of the largest free region. It would be much better if you could move the SCSI adapter BIOS so that it was next to the VGA BIOS, as this would bring the free UMB space to a single region of 144K. It is much easier and more efficient to use a single 144K region than two regions of 80K and 64K, respectively.

Fortunately, it is possible to move this particular SCSI adapter, although doing so requires that several switches be reset on the card itself. One great thing about this Adaptec card is that a sticker is placed directly on the card detailing all the switch settings! This means that you don't have to go hunting for a manual that may not be nearby. More adapter card manufacturers should place this information right on the card.

After changing the appropriate switches to move the SCSI adapter BIOS to start at C8000, the optimized map would look like figure 7.8.

```
   . = Empty Addresses
   G = Video Graphics Array (VGA) Adapter Graphics Mode Video RAM
   M = VGA Monochrome Text Mode Video RAM
   C = VGA Color Text Mode Video RAM
   V = Standard VGA Video ROM BIOS
   S = SCSI Host Adapter ROM BIOS
   R = Standard Motherboard ROM BIOS

        : 0---1---2---3---4---5---6---7---8---9---A---B---C---D---E---F---
 0A0000: GGGGGGGGGGGGGGGGGGGGGGGGGGGGGGGGGGGGGGGGGGGGGGGGGGGGGGGGGGGGGGG
 0B0000: MMMMMMMMMMMMMMMMMMMMMMMMMMMMMMMMCCCCCCCCCCCCCCCCCCCCCCCCCCCCCCCC
        : 0---1---2---3---4---5---6---7---8---9---A---B---C---D---E---F---
 0C0000: VVVVVVVVVVVVVVVVVVVVVVVVVVVVVVVVSSSSSSSSSSSSSSSS................
 0D0000: ................................................................
        : 0---1---2---3---4---5---6---7---8---9---A---B---C---D---E---F---
 0E0000: ................................................................
 0F0000: RRRRRRRRRRRRRRRRRRRRRRRRRRRRRRRRRRRRRRRRRRRRRRRRRRRRRRRRRRRRRRR
```

Figure 7.8

Adaptec AHA-1542CF SCSI adapter with optimized memory use.

Notice how the free space is now a single contiguous block of 144K. This represents a far more optimum setup than the default settings.

Network Adapters. Network adapter cards also can use upper memory in segments C000 and D000. The exact amount of memory used and the starting address for each network card varies with the type and manufacturer of the card. Some network cards do not use any memory at all. A network card might have two primary uses for memory:

- IPL (Initial Program Load or Boot) ROM
- Shared Memory (RAM)

An *IPL ROM* is usually an 8K ROM that contains a bootstrap loader program that enables the system to boot directly from a file server on the network. This allows the removal of all disk drives from the PC, creating a diskless workstation. Because no floppy or hard disk would be in the system to boot from, the IPL ROM gives the system the instructions necessary to locate an image of the operating system on the file server and load it as if it were on an internal drive. If you are not using your system as a diskless workstation, it would be beneficial to disable any IPL ROM or IPL ROM Socket on the adapter card. Notice that many network adapters do not allow this socket to be disabled, which means that you lose the 8K of address space for other hardware even if the ROM chip is removed from the socket!

Shared memory refers to a small portion of RAM contained on the network card that is mapped into the PC's Upper Memory Area. This region is used as a memory window on the network and offers very fast data transfer from the network card to the system.

IBM pioneered the use of shared memory for its first Token Ring network adapters, and now shared memory is in common use among other companies' network adapters. Shared memory was first devised by IBM because it found transfers using the DMA channels were not fast enough in most systems. This had mainly to do with some quirks in the DMA controller and bus design, which especially affected 16-bit ISA bus systems. Network adapters that do not use shared memory will either use DMA or Programmed I/O (PIO) transfers to move data to and from the network adapter.

Although shared memory is faster than either DMA or PIO for ISA systems, it does require 16K of UMA space to work. Most standard performance network adapters use PIO because this makes them easier to configure, and they require no free UMA space, whereas most high performance adapters will use shared memory. The shared memory region on most network adapters that use one is usually 16K in size and may be located at any user-selected 4K increment of memory in segments C000 or D000.

Figure 7.9 shows the default memory addresses for the IPL ROM and shared memory of an IBM Token Ring network adapter, although other network adapters such as Ethernet adapters would be similar.

```
. = Empty Addresses
G = Video Graphics Array (VGA) Adapter Graphics Mode Video RAM
M = VGA Monochrome Text Mode Video RAM
C = VGA Color Text Mode Video RAM
V = Standard VGA Video ROM BIOS
I = Token Ring Network Adapter IPL ROM
N = Token Ring Network Adapter Shared RAM
R = Standard Motherboard ROM BIOS

       : 0---1---2---3---4---5---6---7---8---9---A---B---C---D---E---F---
0A0000: GGGGGGGGGGGGGGGGGGGGGGGGGGGGGGGGGGGGGGGGGGGGGGGGGGGGGGGGGGGGGGGG
0B0000: MMMMMMMMMMMMMMMMMMMMMMMMMMMMMMMMCCCCCCCCCCCCCCCCCCCCCCCCCCCCCCCC
       : 0---1---2---3---4---5---6---7---8---9---A---B---C---D---E---F---
0C0000: VVVVVVVVVVVVVVVVVVVVVVVVVVVVVVVV................IIIIIIII........
0D0000: ................................NNNNNNNNNNNNNNNN................
       : 0---1---2---3---4---5---6---7---8---9---A---B---C---D---E---F---
0E0000: ................................................................
0F0000: RRRRRRRRRRRRRRRRRRRRRRRRRRRRRRRRRRRRRRRRRRRRRRRRRRRRRRRRRRRRRRRR
```

Figure 7.9

Token Ring network adapter default memory map.

I have also included the standard VGA video BIOS in figure 7.9 because nearly every system would have a VGA-type video adapter as well. Note that these default addresses for the IPL ROM and the shared memory can easily be changed by reconfiguring the adapter. Most other network adapters are similar in that they also would have an IPL ROM and a shared memory address, although the sizes of these areas and the default addresses may be different. Most network adapters that incorporate an IPL ROM option can disable the ROM and socket such that those addresses are not needed at all. This helps to conserve UMA space and prevent possible future conflicts if you are never going to use the function.

Notice in this case that the SCSI adapter used in figure 7.9 would fit both at its default BIOS address of DC000 as well as the optimum address of C8000. The Token Ring shared memory location is not optimum and causes the UMB space to be fragmented. By adjusting the location of the shared memory, this setup can be greatly improved. Figure 7.10 shows an optimum setup with both the Token Ring adapter and the SCSI adapter in the same machine.

To actually move the RAM usage on any given adapter will require that you consult the documentation for the card. Most older cards require that specific switches or jumpers be changed, and the settings will probably not be obvious without the manual. Most newer cards, especially those that are Plug and Play, allow these settings to be changed by software that either comes with the card itself, or the Configuration Manager program that goes with some of the newer operating systems like Windows 95 or OS/2.

```
. = Empty Addresses
G = Video Graphics Array (VGA) Adapter Graphics Mode Video RAM
M = VGA Monochrome Text Mode Video RAM
C = VGA Color Text Mode Video RAM
V = Standard VGA Video ROM BIOS
S = SCSI Host Adapter ROM BIOS
I = Token Ring Network Adapter IPL ROM
N = Token Ring Network Adapter Shared RAM
R = Standard Motherboard ROM BIOS

       : 0---1---2---3---4---5---6---7---8---9---A---B---C---D---E---F---
0A0000: GGGGGGGGGGGGGGGGGGGGGGGGGGGGGGGGGGGGGGGGGGGGGGGGGGGGGGGGGGGGGGGG
0B0000: MMMMMMMMMMMMMMMMMMMMMMMMMMMMMMMMCCCCCCCCCCCCCCCCCCCCCCCCCCCCCCCC
       : 0---1---2---3---4---5---6---7---8---9---A---B---C---D---E---F---
0C0000: VVVVVVVVVVVVVVVVVVVVVVVVVVVVVVVVSSSSSSSSSSSSSSSSNNNNNNNNNNNNNNNN
0D0000: IIIIIIII........................................................
       : 0---1---2---3---4---5---6---7---8---9---A---B---C---D---E---F---
0E0000: ................................................................
0F0000: RRRRRRRRRRRRRRRRRRRRRRRRRRRRRRRRRRRRRRRRRRRRRRRRRRRRRRRRRRRRRRRR
```

Figure 7.10

Adaptec AHA-1542CF SCSI adapter and Network adapter with optimized memory use.

This configuration allows a single 120K Upper Memory Block (UMB) that can be used very efficiently to load software drivers. Notice that the IPL ROM was moved to D0000, which places it as the last item installed before the free memory space. This is because if the IPL function is not needed, it can be disabled and the UMB space would increase to 128K and still be contiguous. If the default settings are used for both the SCSI and network adapters, the UMB memory would be fragmented into three regions of 16K, 40K, and 64K, which would function, but is hardly optimum.

Other ROMs in the Upper Memory Area. In addition to the BIOS for hard drive controllers, SCSI adapters, and network cards, upper memory segments C000 and D000 are used by some terminal emulators, security adapters, memory boards, and various other devices and adapter boards. Some adapters may require memory only for BIOS information, and others may require RAM in these upper memory segments. For information on a specific adapter, consult the manufacturer's documentation.

Motherboard BIOS Memory. The last 128K of reserved memory is used by the motherboard BIOS (which is usually stored in a ROM chip). The BIOS programs in ROM control the system during the boot procedure and remain as drivers for various hardware in the system during normal operation. Because these programs must be available immediately, they cannot be loaded from a device like a disk drive. The main functions of the programs stored in the motherboard ROM are as follows:

- *Power-On Self Test,* the POST, is a set of routines that tests the motherboard, memory, disk controllers, video adapters, keyboard, and other primary system components. This routine is useful when you troubleshoot system failures or problems.
- The *bootstrap loader* routine initiates a search for an operating system on a floppy disk or hard disk. If an operating system is found, it is loaded into memory and given control of the system.
- The *Basic Input-Output System* (BIOS) is the software interface, or master control program, to all the hardware in the system. With the BIOS, a program easily can access features in the system by calling on a standard BIOS program module instead of talking directly to the device.

Both segments E000 and F000 in the memory map are considered reserved for the motherboard BIOS, but only some AT-type systems actually use this entire area. PC/XT-type systems require only segment F000 and enable adapter card ROM or RAM to use segment E000. Most AT systems use all of F000 for the BIOS, and may decode but not use any of segment E000. By decoding an area, the AT motherboard essentially grabs control of the addresses, which precludes installing any other hardware in this region. In other words, it is not possible to install any other adapters to use this area. That is why you will find that most adapters that use memory simply do not allow any choices for memory use in segment E000. Although this may seem like a waste of 64K of memory space, any 386 or higher system can use the powerful MMU in the processor to map RAM from extended memory into segment E000 as an UMB and subsequently use it for loading software. This is a nice solution to what otherwise would be wasted memory. Under DOS, the EMM386 driver controls the MMU remapping functions.

PC/XT System BIOS. Many different ROM-interface programs are in the IBM motherboards, but the location of these programs is mostly consistent. The following figures show the ROM BIOS memory use in segments E000 and F000.

Figure 7.11 shows the memory use in an IBM PC and XT with a Type 1 (256K) motherboard.

```
. = Empty Addresses
b = IBM ROM (Cassette) BASIC Interpreter
R = Motherboard ROM BIOS

       : 0---1---2---3---4---5---6---7---8---9---A---B---C---D---E---F---
0E0000: ................................................................
0F0000: ........................bbbbbbbbbbbbbbbbbbbbbbbbbbbbbbbbRRRRRRRR
```

Figure 7.11

Motherboard ROM BIOS memory use in an original IBM PC and XT.

Figure 7.12 shows the memory use in an XT with a 640K motherboard as well as in the PS/2 Model 25 and Model 30. These systems have additional BIOS code compared to the original PC and XT. Note that Cassette (also called ROM) BASIC remains in the same addresses.

```
. = Empty Addresses
b = IBM ROM (Cassette) BASIC Interpreter
R = Motherboard ROM BIOS

       : 0---1---2---3---4---5---6---7---8---9---A---B---C---D---E---F---
0E0000: ................................................................
0F0000: RRRRRRRRRRRRRRRRRRRRRRRRbbbbbbbbbbbbbbbbbbbbbbbbbbbbbbbbRRRRRRRR
```

Figure 7.12

Motherboard ROM BIOS memory use in IBM XT (Type 2) and PS/2 Models 25 and 30.

Figure 7.13 shows the motherboard ROM BIOS memory use in most PC- or XT-compatible systems. These systems lack the Cassette BASIC Interpreter found in IBM's BIOS.

```
. = Empty Addresses
R = Standard XT Motherboard ROM BIOS

       : 0---1---2---3---4---5---6---7---8---9---A---B---C---D---E---F---
0E0000: ................................................................
0F0000: ................................RRRRRRRRRRRRRRRRRRRRRRRRRRRRRRRR

In compatible XT type systems, the BIOS length may vary, but 32K is common.
```

Figure 7.13

Motherboard ROM BIOS memory use in most PC- or XT-compatibles.

II

System Components

AT System BIOS. Figure 7.14 shows the motherboard BIOS use in an IBM AT or XT-286 system.

```
. = Empty Addresses
b = IBM ROM (Cassette) BASIC Interpreter
R = Motherboard ROM BIOS

       : 0---1---2---3---4---5---6---7---8---9---A---B---C---D---E---F---
0E0000: ................................................................
0F0000: RRRRRRRRRRRRRRRRRRRRRRRRbbbbbbbbbbbbbbbbbbbbbbbbbbbbbbbbRRRRRRRR
```

Figure 7.14

Motherboard ROM BIOS memory use in an IBM AT and XT-286.

Figure 7.15 shows the motherboard ROM BIOS memory use of most AT-compatible systems. These systems lack the IBM Cassette BASIC, but do usually include a built-in Setup program.

```
. = Empty Addresses
R = Standard Motherboard ROM BIOS

       : 0---1---2---3---4---5---6---7---8---9---A---B---C---D---E---F---
0E0000: ................................................................
0F0000: RRRRRRRRRRRRRRRRRRRRRRRRRRRRRRRRRRRRRRRRRRRRRRRRRRRRRRRRRRRRRRRR
```

Figure 7.15

Motherboard ROM BIOS memory use of most AT-compatible systems.

Note that the standard AT-compatible system BIOS uses only segment F000 (64K). In almost every case, the remainder of the BIOS area (segment E000) is completely free and can be used as UMB space.

IBM PS/2 ROM-BIOS. The motherboard BIOS memory use by PS/2 models with a 286 or higher processor, including ISA and MCA systems, is shown in figure 7.16. This shows that PS/2 systems use more of the allocated ROM space for their motherboard ROM BIOS. The extra code contains VGA drivers (PS/2 systems have built-in VGA adapters) and additional code to run the system in protected mode.

Note that some of the newest PS/2 systems no longer have the Cassette BASIC interpreter in ROM. In those systems, additional BIOS code fills that area.

PS/2 Models with 286 and higher processors have additional Advanced BIOS code to be used when the systems are running protected-mode operating systems such as OS/2. Non-PS/2 systems that don't have the Advanced BIOS code can still easily run OS/2, but must load the equivalent of the Advanced BIOS software from disk rather than having it loaded from ROM.

```
 . = Empty Addresses
 b = IBM ROM (Cassette) BASIC Interpreter
 R = Motherboard ROM BIOS

       : 0---1---2---3---4---5---6---7---8---9---A---B---C---D---E---F---
0E0000: RRRRRRRRRRRRRRRRRRRRRRRRRRRRRRRRRRRRRRRRRRRRRRRRRRRRRRRRRRRRRRRR
0F0000: RRRRRRRRRRRRRRRRRRRRRRRRbbbbbbbbbbbbbbbbbbbbbbbbbbbbbbbbRRRRRRRR
```

Figure 7.16

IBM PS/2 motherboard ROM BIOS memory map.

Some compatible systems with a SCSI hard disk and host adapter need a special protected-mode driver for the adapter to work under OS/2 because the on-board BIOS runs only in real mode and not in protected mode. IBM SCSI adapters, however, are unique in that they include both real- and protected-mode BIOS software on-board and operate hard disks under any operating system with no need for drivers. Again, this is not really that much of a bonus or feature because this same type of protected mode operating driver code can simply be loaded from disk (boot-up occurs in real mode) during the OS/2 boot process. In fact, many of the Advanced BIOS routines originally in the PS/2 BIOS have been enhanced, so that many of the built-in BIOS routines are being discarded and superseded by loaded routines anyway. The way things have turned out, there is simply no inherent advantage to the Advanced BIOS code in the PS/2 systems.

IBM Cassette Basic ROM. The ROM maps of most IBM compatibles equal the IBM system with which they are compatible—with the exception of the Cassette BASIC portion. This section examines the origins of Cassette BASIC (also called ROM BASIC) and investigates reasons why you would ever see this in a modern system. A variety of related error messages from compatible systems are explored as well.

It may come as a surprise to some personal computer users, but the original IBM PC actually had a jack on the rear of the system for connecting a cassette tape recorder. This was to be used for loading programs and data to or from a cassette tape. At the time the PC was introduced, the most popular personal computer was the Apple II, which also had the cassette tape connection. Tapes were used at the time because floppy drives were very costly, and hard disks were not even an option yet. Floppy drives came down in price quickly at the time, and the cassette port never appeared on any subsequent IBM systems. The cassette port also never appeared on any compatible system.

The original PC came standard with only 16K of memory in the base configuration. No floppy drives were included, so you could not load or save files from disks. Most computer users at the time would either write their own programs in the BASIC (Beginners All-purpose Symbolic Instruction Code) language or run programs written by others. Various versions of the BASIC language were available, but the Microsoft version had become the most popular. Having a Microsoft BASIC interpreter was essential in the early days of personal computing, yet these interpreters would take 32K of memory when loaded. That meant you would need 32K of RAM just for the language interpreter and additional memory for your program and data. To make the system cheaper and to conserve memory, IBM contacted Microsoft and licensed the MS-BASIC interpreter. It then built the BASIC interpreter directly into the motherboard ROM BIOS, where it occupied the 32K address range F6000-FDFFF. This meant that although the system only came with 16K, you could use all 16K for your own programs and data because no additional memory was required to run the BASIC language interpreter. To save and load programs, this BASIC language was designed to access the cassette port on the back of the system.

If you purchased a floppy drive for your PC system, you would also need DOS (Disk Operating System) to run it. Because the BASIC built into the ROM on the PC motherboard did not have the code required to operate the floppy drive for storing and retrieving files, an extension or overlay to the ROM BASIC interpreter was located on the DOS disk. Called *Advanced BASIC*, or *BASICA.COM*, this program on the DOS disk was actually constructed as an overlay to the ROM BASIC, and would not function independently. Because no compatibles ever had ROM BASIC (no compatibles ever had a cassette tape recorder port, either), the BASICA extensions found on the IBM DOS disks would not run in any compatible. At that time, there was no such thing as a separately available generic MS-DOS as there is today.

Compaq was one of the first to solve this problem. It went to Microsoft and licensed the DOS separately from IBM, thus producing its own version called Compaq DOS. On the Compaq DOS disks, it included a version of the Microsoft BASIC interpreter called *GWBASIC.EXE* (*Graphics Workstation BASIC*) that was complete as a stand-alone program. In other words, it was not constructed as an overlay for the ROM BASIC (which was absent from the Compaq), but was a complete version all by itself. This stand-alone GWBASIC version of the MS-BASIC interpreter would run on any system, IBM or compatible, because it did not depend on the existence of the ROM BASIC, as did IBM's BASICA program. In some strange way, perhaps the reliance of the IBM BASICA on the IBM ROM BASIC was one way to make the IBM PS/2 different from the compatibles. Because any compatible vendor could license the complete BASIC interpreter (and DOS as well) directly from Microsoft, the IBM ROM BASIC became an unimportant feature.

What is really strange is that IBM kept this ROM BASIC and BASICA relationship all the way through most of the PS/2 systems! The portable 486 PS/2 system (IBM P75 Portable) I was using until recently came standard with a built-in SCSI adapter and currently has a 4GB SCSI drive installed, and yet this system still has the ROM BASIC wasting 32K of space! I liken this to humans having an appendix. The ROM BASIC in the IBM systems is a sort of vestigial organ—a leftover that had some use in prehistoric ancestors, but that has no function today!

You can catch a glimpse of this ROM BASIC on IBM systems that have it by disabling all the disk drives in the system. In that case, with nothing to boot from, most IBM systems unceremoniously dump you into the strange (vintage 1981) ROM BASIC screen. When this occurs, the message looks like this:

```
The IBM Personal Computer Basic
Version C1.10 Copyright IBM Corp 1981
62940 Bytes free
```

```
Ok
```

Many people used to dread seeing this because it usually meant that your hard disk had failed to be recognized! Because no compatible systems ever had the Cassette BASIC interpreter in ROM, they had to come up with different messages to display for the same situations in which an IBM system would invoke this BASIC. Compatibles that have an AMI BIOS in fact display a confusing message as follows:

```
NO ROM BASIC - SYSTEM HALTED
```

This message is a BIOS error message that is displayed by the AMI BIOS when the same situations occur that would cause an IBM system to dump into Cassette BASIC, which of course is not present in an AMI BIOS (or any other compatible BIOS for that matter). Other BIOS versions display different messages. For example, under the same circumstances, a Compaq BIOS displays the following:

```
Non-System disk or disk error
replace and strike any key when ready
```

This is somewhat confusing on Compaq's part because this very same (or similar) error message is contained in the DOS Boot Sector, and would normally be displayed if the system files were missing or corrupted.

In the same situations that you would see Cassette BASIC on an IBM system, a system with an Award BIOS would display the following:

```
DISK BOOT FAILURE, INSERT SYSTEM DISK AND PRESS ENTER
```

Phoenix BIOS systems will display either:

```
No boot device available -
strike F1 to retry boot, F2 for setup utility
```

or

```
No boot sector on fixed disk -
strike F1 to retry boot, F2 for setup utility
```

The first or second Phoenix message displays depending on exactly which error actually occurred.

Although the message displayed varies from BIOS to BIOS, the cause is the same for all of them. Two things that can generally cause any of these messages to be displayed, and they both relate to specific bytes in the Master Boot Record, which is the first sector of a hard disk at the physical location Cylinder 0, Head 0, Sector 1.

The first problem relates to a disk that has either never been partitioned or has had the Master Boot Sector corrupted. During the boot process, the BIOS checks the last two bytes in the Master Boot Record (first sector of the drive) for a "signature" value of 55AAh. If the last two bytes are not 55AAh, an Interrupt 18h is invoked, which calls the subroutine that displays the message you received as well as the others indicated, or on an IBM system invokes Cassette (ROM) BASIC itself.

The Master Boot Sector (including the signature bytes) is written to the hard disk by the DOS FDISK program. Immediately after you low level format a hard disk, all the sectors are initialized with a pattern of bytes, and the first sector does *not* contain the 55AAh signature. In other words, these ROM error messages are exactly what you see if you attempt to boot from a hard disk that has been low-level formatted, but has not yet been partitioned.

Now consider the second situation that can cause these messages, and potentially your other problem causing the same message. If the signature bytes are correct, the BIOS executes the Master Partition Boot Record code, which performs a test of the Boot Indicator Bytes in each of the four partition table entries. These bytes are at offset 446 (1BEh), 462 (1CEh), 478 (1DEh), and 494 (1EEh), respectively. They are used to indicate which of the four possible partition table entries contain an active (bootable) partition. A value of 80h in any of these byte offsets indicates that table contains the active partition, whereas all other values must be 00h. If more than one of these bytes is 80h (indicating multiple active partitions), or any of the byte values is anything other than 80h or 00h, you see the following error message:

```
Invalid partition table
```

If all these four Boot Indicator Bytes are 00h, indicating no active (bootable) partitions, you also see Cassette BASIC on an IBM system or the other messages indicated earlier depending on which BIOS you have. This is exactly what occurs if you were to remove the existing partitions from a drive using FDISK, but had not created new partitions on the drive, or had failed to make one of the partitions Active (bootable) with FDISK before rebooting your system.

In the latest PS/2 systems, IBM has finally done away with the ROM BASIC once and for all. DOS versions through 5.x from IBM included the BASICA interpreter; however, with the introduction of DOS 6, IBM eliminated BASICA because the newer systems did not have the ROM portion anyway. Microsoft included GWBASIC in MS-DOS versions up to and including 4.x and eliminated it in later versions. All DOS 5 and higher versions (IBM and MS) have a special crippled version of the Microsoft QuickBASIC Compiler now included rather than GWBASIC or BASICA. The compiler is crippled so that you can compile programs in memory, but cannot create EXE files on disk. The run-time compiler executes virtually all the older interpreted BASIC programs, so newer systems have no need for the old GWBASIC or BASICA interpreters. If you want the full version of QuickBASIC that will compile a program and save it as an EXE file, you must purchase the full version of QuickBASIC.

ROM Versions. Over the years, the BIOS in various PC models has undergone changes almost always associated with either a new system or a new motherboard design for an existing system. There are several reasons for these changes. The introduction of the XT, for example, gave IBM a good opportunity to correct a few things in the system BIOS and also add necessary new features, such as automatic support for a hard disk. IBM retrofitted many of the same changes into the PC's BIOS at the same time.

Because an in-depth knowledge of the types of BIOS is something a programmer might find useful, IBM makes this information available in the technical reference manuals sold for each system. A new ROM BIOS technical reference manual covers all IBM systems in one book. Complete ROM BIOS listings (with comments) accompanied early IBM system documentation, but that information is not supplied for later IBMs.

Even if you aren't a programmer, however, certain things about system BIOS are important to know. IBM has had many different BIOS versions for the PC and PS/2 families. Sometimes a system has different versions of BIOS over the course of a system's availability. For example, at least three versions of BIOS exist for each of the PC, XT, and AT systems. Because a few important changes were made in the software stored in BIOS, knowing which BIOS is in your system can be useful.

To determine which ROM BIOS module is installed in your system, first check your system documentation. If you have a 386 or later system, a few lines of text at the top of your screen during the POST probably identifies the manufacturer, BIOS revision number, and date of manufacture. The BIOS version you have also may be indicated by the manufacturer's name, version number, and date encoded in the chip.

On IBM systems, the ROM BIOS contains an ID byte (the second-to-last byte). The value of the byte at memory location FFFFE (hexadecimal) corresponds to the system type or model. Table 7.4 shows information about the different ROM BIOS versions that have appeared in various IBM systems.

The date that the BIOS module design was completed is important: It has the same meaning as a version number for software. (IBM later began to code an official revision number, as indicated in the last column of table 7.4) You can display the date by entering the following four-statement BASIC program:

```
10 DEF SEG=&HF000
20 For X=&HFFF5 to &HFFFF
30 Print Chr$(Peek(X));
40 Next
```

An easier way to display the date is to use the DOS DEBUG program. First run DEBUG at the DOS prompt by entering the following command:

```
DEBUG
```

Then at the debug "-" prompt, enter the following command to display the ROM BIOS date:

```
D FFFF:5 L 8
```

You also can display the BIOS date with the MSD (Microsoft Diagnostics) program that comes with Windows, or the Device Manager in Windows 95. Most aftermarket diagnostics or utilities also display the BIOS date as well.

If you are interested in a ROM upgrade for your system, you can contact the motherboard or even the BIOS manufacturer, such as Phoenix, Award, or AMI. Occasionally, the BIOS may be updated to fix problems or add support for new peripherals.

Table 7.4 IBM BIOS Model, Submodel, and Revision Codes

System Type	CPU Speed	Clock	Bus Type/ Width
PC	8088	4.77 MHz	ISA/8
PC	8088	4.77 MHz	ISA/8
PC	8088	4.77 MHz	ISA/8
PC-XT	8088	4.77 MHz	ISA/8
PC-XT	8088	4.77 MHz	ISA/8
PC-XT	8088	4.77 MHz	ISA/8
PC*jr*	8088	4.77 MHz	ISA/8
PC Convertible	80C8	4.77 MHz	ISA/8
PS/2 25	8086	8 MHz	ISA/8
PS/2 30	8086	8 MHz	ISA/8
PS/2 30	8086	8 MHz	ISA/8
PS/2 30	8086	8 MHz	ISA/8
PC-AT	286	6 MHz	ISA/16
PC-AT	286	6 MHz	ISA/16
PC-AT	286	8 MHz	ISA/16
PC-XT 286	286	6 MHz	ISA/16
PS/1	286	10 MHz	ISA/16
PS/2 25 286	286	10 MHz	ISA/16
PS/2 30 286	286	10 MHz	ISA/16
PS/2 30 286	286	10 MHz	ISA/16
PS/2 35 SX	386SX	20 MHz	ISA/16
PS/2 35 SX	386SX	20 MHz	ISA/16
PS/2 40 SX	386SX	20 MHz	ISA/16
PS/2 40 SX	386SX	20 MHz	ISA/16
PS/2 L40 SX	386SX	20 MHz	ISA/16
PS/2 50	286	10 MHz	MCA/16
PS/2 50	286	10 MHz	MCA/16
PS/2 50Z	286	10 MHz	MCA/16
PS/2 50Z	286	10 MHz	MCA/16
PS/2 55 SX	386SX	16 MHz	MCA/16
PS/2 55 LS	386SX	16 MHz	MCA/16
PS/2 57 SX	386SX	20 MHz	MCA/16
PS/2 60	286	10 MHz	MCA/16
PS/2 65 SX	386SX	16 MHz	MCA/16
PS/2 70 386	386DX	16 MHz	MCA/32
PS/2 70 386	386DX	16 MHz	MCA/32
PS/2 70 386	386DX	16 MHz	MCA/32

ROM BIOS Date	ID Byte	Submodel Byte	Rev.	ST 506 Drive Types
04/24/81	FF	—	—	—
10/19/81	FF	—	—	—
10/27/82	FF	—	—	—
11/08/82	FE	—	—	—
01/10/86	FB	00	01	—
05/09/86	FB	00	02	—
06/01/83	FD	—	—	—
09/13/85	F9	00	00	—
06/26/87	FA	01	00	26
09/02/86	FA	00	00	26
12/12/86	FA	00	01	26
02/05/87	FA	00	02	26
01/10/84	FC	—	—	15
06/10/85	FC	00	01	23
11/15/85	FC	01	00	23
04/21/86	FC	02	00	24
12/01/89	FC	0B	00	44
06/28/89	FC	09	02	37
08/25/88	FC	09	00	37
06/28/89	FC	09	02	37
03/15/91	F8	19	05	37
04/04/91	F8	19	06	37
03/15/91	F8	19	05	37
04/04/91	F8	19	06	37
02/27/91	F8	23	02	37
02/13/87	FC	04	00	32
05/09/87	FC	04	01	32
01/28/88	FC	04	02	33
04/18/88	FC	04	03	33
11/02/88	F8	0C	00	33
?	F8	1E	00	33
07/03/91	F8	26	02	None
02/13/87	FC	05	00	32
02/08/90	F8	1C	00	33
01/29/88	F8	09	00	33
04/11/88	F8	09	02	33
12/15/89	F8	09	04	33

(continues)

Table 7.4 Continued

System Type	CPU Speed	Clock	Bus Type/ Width
32	01/29/88	F8	04
PS/2 70 386	386DX	20 MHz	MCA/32
PS/2 70 386	386DX	20 MHz	MCA/32
PS/2 70 386	386DX	25 MHz	MCA/32
PS/2 70 386	386DX	25 MHz	MCA/32
PS/2 70 486	486DX	25 MHz	MCA/32
PS/2 70 486	486DX	25 MHz	MCA/32
PS/2 P70 386	386DX	16 MHz	MCA/32
PS/2 P70 386	386DX	20 MHz	MCA/32
PS/2 P75 486	486DX	33 MHz	MCA/32
PS/2 80 386	386DX	16 MHz	MCA/32
PS/2 80 386	386DX	20 MHz	MCA/32
PS/2 80 386	386DX	25 MHz	MCA/32
PS/2 90 XP 486	486SX	20 MHz	MCA/32
PS/2 90 XP 486	487SX	20 MHz	MCA/32
PS/2 90 XP 486	486DX	25 MHz	MCA/32
PS/2 90 XP 486	486DX	33 MHz	MCA/32
PS/2 90 XP 486	486DX	50 MHz	MCA/32
PS/2 95 XP 486	486SX	20 MHz	MCA/32
PS/2 95 XP 486	487SX	20 MHz	MCA/32
PS/2 95 XP 486	486DX	25 MHz	MCA/32
PS/2 95 XP 486	486DX	33 MHz	MCA/32
PS/2 95 XP 486	486DX	50 MHz	MCA/32

The ID byte, Submodel byte, and Revision numbers are in hexadecimal.
— = This feature is not supported.
None = Only SCSI drives are supported.
? = Information is unavailable.

Extended Memory

As mentioned previously in this chapter, the memory map on a system based on the 286 or higher processor can extend beyond the 1M boundary that exists when the processor is in real mode. On a 286 or 386SX system, the extended memory limit is 16M; on a 386DX, 486, or Pentium system, the extended memory limit is 4G (4,096M). Systems based on the new P6 processor will have a limit of 64G (65,536M).

For an AT system to address memory beyond the first megabyte, the processor must be in *protected mode*—the native mode of these newer processors. On a 286, only programs designed to run in protected mode can take advantage of extended memory. 386 and higher processors offer another mode, called *virtual real mode,* which enables extended memory to be, in effect, chopped into 1M pieces (each its own real mode session) and for

ROM BIOS Date	ID Byte	Submodel Byte	Rev.	ST 506 Drive Types
00	33			
04/11/88	F8	04	02	33
12/15/89	F8	04	04	33
06/08/88	F8	0D	00	33
02/20/89	F8	0D	01	33
12/01/89	F8	0D	?	?
09/29/89	F8	1B	00	?
?	F8	50	00	?
01/18/89	F8	0B	00	33
10/05/90	F8	52	00	33
03/30/87	F8	00	00	32
10/07/87	F8	01	00	32
11/21/89	F8	80	01	?
?	F8	2D	00	?
?	F8	2F	00	?
?	F8	11	00	?
?	F8	13	00	?
?	F8	2B	00	?
?	F8	2C	00	?
?	F8	2E	00	?
?	F8	14	00	?
?	F8	16	00	?
?	F8	2A	00	?

several of these sessions to be running simultaneously in protected areas of memory. Although several DOS programs can be running at once, each still is limited to a maximum of 640K of memory because each session simulates a real mode environment, right down to the BIOS and Upper Memory Area. Running several programs at once in virtual real mode, which is termed *multitasking,* requires software that can manage each program and keep them from crashing into one another. OS/2 does this now, and Windows 95 allows this as well.

The 286 and higher CPU chips also run in what is termed *real mode,* which enables full compatibility with the 8088 CPU chip installed on the PC/XT-type computer. Real mode enables you to run DOS programs one at a time on an AT-type system just like you would on a PC/XT. However, an AT-type system running in real mode, particularly a 386-, 486-, Pentium-, or P6-based system, is really functioning as little more than a turbo PC. In real mode, these processors can emulate the 8086 or 8088, but they cannot operate in protected mode at the same time. For that reason the 386 and above also provide a virtual real mode that operates under protected mode. This allows the execution of real mode programs under the control of a protected mode operating system like OS/2 or Windows NT.

Extended memory is basically all memory past the first megabyte, which can only be accessed while the processor is in protected mode.

XMS Memory. The Extended Memory Specification (XMS) was developed in 1987 by Microsoft, Intel, AST Corp., and Lotus Development to specify how programs would use extended memory. The XMS functions on systems based on the 286 or higher and allows real-mode programs (those designed to run in DOS) to use extended memory and another block of memory usually out of the reach of DOS.

Before XMS, there was no way to ensure cooperation between programs that switched the processor into protected mode and used extended memory. There was no way for one program to know what another had been doing with the extended memory because none of them could see that memory while in real mode. HIMEM.SYS becomes an arbitrator of sorts that first grabs all the extended memory for itself and then doles it out to programs that know the XMS protocols. In this manner, several programs that use XMS memory can operate together under DOS on the same system, switching the processor into and out of protected mode to access the memory. XMS rules prevent one program from accessing memory that another has in use. Because Windows 3.x is a program manager that switches the system to and from protected mode in running several programs at once, it has been set up to require XMS memory to function. Windows 95 operates mostly in protected mode, but still calls on real mode for access to many system components. Windows NT is a true protected mode operating system, as is OS/2. In Windows 3.x, HIMEM.SYS must be loaded for Windows to function.

Extended memory can be made to conform to the XMS specification by installing a device driver in the CONFIG.SYS file. The most common XMS driver is HIMEM.SYS, which is included with Windows and recent versions of DOS, starting with 4.0 and up. Other memory managers, like QEMM, also convert extended memory into XMS memory when you add their device drivers to CONFIG.SYS.

High Memory Area (HMA) and the A20 line. The *High Memory Area* (*HMA*) is an area of memory 16 bytes short of 64K in size starting at the beginning of the first megabyte of extended memory. It can be used to load device drivers and memory-resident programs to free up conventional memory for use by real-mode programs. Only one device driver or memory-resident program can be loaded into HMA at one time, no matter what its size. Originally this could be any program, but Microsoft decided that DOS could get there first, and built capability into DOS 5 and newer versions.

The HMA area is extremely important to those who use DOS 5 or higher because these DOS versions can move their own kernel (about 45K of program instructions) into this area. This is accomplished simply by first loading an XMS driver (such as HIMEM.SYS) and adding the line **DOS=HIGH** to your CONFIG.SYS file. Taking advantage of this DOS capability frees another 45K or so of conventional memory for use by real-mode programs by essentially moving 45K of program code into the first segment of extended memory. Although this memory was supposed to be accessible in protected mode only, it turns out that a defect in the design of the original 286 (which fortunately has been propagated forward to the more recent processors as a "feature") accidentally allows access to most of the first segment of extended memory while still in real mode.

The use of the HMA is controlled by the HIMEM.SYS or equivalent driver. The origins of this memory usage are interesting because they are based on a bug in the original 286 processor carried forward to the 386, 486, and Pentium.

The problem started from the fact that memory addresses in Intel processors are dictated by an overlapping segment and offset address. By setting the segment address to FFFF, which itself specifies an actual address of FFFF0 that is 16 bytes from the end of the first megabyte, and then specifies an offset of FFFF, which is equal to 64K, you can create a memory address as follows:

```
   FFFF   segment
+   FFFF  offset
  ------
= 10FFEF  total
```

This type of address is impossible on 8088 or an 8086 system that has only 20 address lines and therefore cannot calculate an address that large. By leaving off the leading digit, these processors interpret the address as 0FFEF, in essence causing the address to "wrap around" and end up 16 bytes from the end of the first 64K segment of the first megabyte. The problem with the 286 and higher was that when they were in real mode, they were supposed to operate the same way, and the address should wrap around to the beginning of the first megabyte also. Unfortunately, a bug in the chip left the 21st address line active (called the *A20 line*), which allowed the address to end up 16 bytes from the end of the first 64K segment in the second megabyte. This memory was supposed to be addressable only in protected mode, but this bug allowed all but 16 bytes of the first 64K of extended memory to be addressable in real mode.

Because this bug caused problems with many real-mode programs that relied on the wrap to take place, when IBM engineers designed the AT, they had to find a way to disable the A20 line while in real mode, but then re-enable it when in protected mode. They did this by using some unused pins on the 8042 keyboard controller chip on the motherboard. The 8042 keyboard controller was designed to accept scan codes from the keyboard and transmit them to the processor, but there were unused pins not needed strictly for this function. So IBM came up with a way to command the keyboard controller to turn on and off the A20 line, thus enabling the "defective" 286 to truly emulate an 8088 and 8086 while in real mode.

Microsoft realized that you could command the 8042 keyboard controller to turn back on the A20 line strictly for the purpose of using this bug as a feature that enabled you to access the first 64K of extended memory (less 16 bytes) without having to go through the lengthy and complicated process of switching into protected mode. Thus HIMEM.SYS and the HMA was born! HIMEM.SYS has to watch the system to see if the A20 line should be off for compatibility, or on to enable access to the HMA or while in protected mode. In essence, HIMEM becomes a control program that manipulates the A20 line through the 8042 keyboard controller chip.

Expanded Memory

Some older programs can use a type of memory called *Expanded Memory Specification* or EMS memory. Unlike conventional (the first megabyte) or extended (the second through 16th or 4,096th megabytes) memory, expanded memory is *not* directly addressable by the processor. Instead, it can only be accessed through a small 64K window established in the UMA. Expanded memory is a segment or bank-switching scheme in which a custom memory adapter has a large number of 64K segments on-board combined with special switching and mapping hardware. The system uses a free segment in the UMA as the home address for the EMS board. After this 64K is filled with data, the board rotates the filled segment out and a new, empty segment appears to take its place. In this fashion, you have a board that can keep on rotating in new segments to be filled with data. Because only one segment can be seen or operated on at one time, EMS is very inefficient for program code and is normally only used for data.

Segment D000 in the first megabyte usually is used for mapping. Lotus, Intel, and Microsoft—founders of the LIM specification for expanded memory (LIM EMS)—decided to use this segment because it is largely unused by most adapters. Programs must be written specially to take advantage of this segment-swapping scheme, and then only data normally can be placed in this segment because it is above the area of contiguous memory (640K) that DOS can use. For example, a program cannot run while it is swapped out and therefore not visible by the processor. This type of memory generally is useful only in systems that do not have extended (processor-addressable) memory available to them.

Figure 7.17 shows how expanded memory fits with conventional and extended memory.

Intel originally created a custom purpose memory board that had the necessary EMS bank switching hardware. It called these boards *Above Boards*, and they were sold widely many years ago. EMS was designed with 8-bit systems in mind and was appropriate for them because they had no capability to access extended memory. 286 and newer systems, however, have the capability to have 15M or more of extended memory, which is much more efficient than the goofy (and slow) bank switching EMS scheme. The Above Boards are no longer being manufactured, and EMS memory—as a concept as well as functionally—is extremely obsolete. If you have any antique software that still requires EMS memory, you are advised to upgrade to newer versions that can use extended memory directly. It is also possible to use the powerful MMU of the 386 and higher processors to convert extended memory to function like LIM EMS, but this should only be done if there is no way to use the extended memory directly. EMM386 can convert extended to expanded, and in fact was originally designed for this purpose, although today it is more likely being used to map extended memory into the UMA for the purposes of loading drivers and not for EMS. The EMM386 driver is included with DOS versions 5 and newer as well as with Windows. If you have several versions on hand, as a rule, always use the newest one.

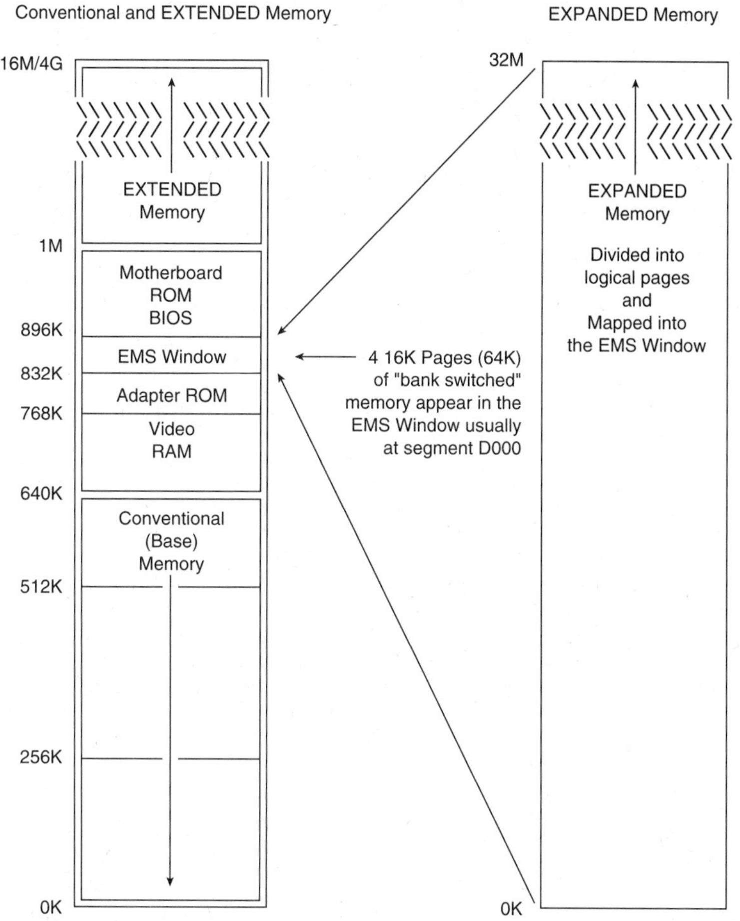

Figure 7.17

Conventional, extended, and expanded memory.

Preventing ROM BIOS Memory Conflicts and Overlap

As detailed in previous sections, C000 and D000 are reserved for use by adapter-board ROM and RAM. If two adapters have overlapping ROM or RAM addresses, usually neither board operates properly. Each board functions if you remove or disable the other one, but they do not work together.

With many adapter boards, you can change the actual memory locations to be used with jumpers, switches, or driver software, which might be necessary to allow two boards to coexist in one system. This type of conflict can cause problems for troubleshooters. You must read the documentation for each adapter to find out what memory addresses the adapter uses and how to change the addresses to allow coexistence with another adapter. Most of the time, you can work around these problems by reconfiguring the board or changing jumpers, switch settings, or software-driver parameters. This change enables the two boards to coexist and stay out of each other's way.

Additionally, you must ensure that adapter boards do not use the same IRQ (interrupt request line), DMA (direct memory access) channel, or I/O Port address. You can easily avoid adapter board memory, IRQ, DMA channel, and I/O Port conflicts by creating a chart or template to mock up the system configuration by penciling on the template the resources already used by each installed adapter. You end up with a picture of the system resources and the relationship of each adapter to the others. This procedure helps you anticipate conflicts and ensures that you configure each adapter board correctly the first time. The template also becomes important documentation when you consider new adapter purchases. New adapters must be configurable to use the available resources in your system.

If your system has Plug and Play capabilities and you use Plug and Play adapters, it will be able to resolve conflicts between the adapters by moving the memory usage on any conflict. Unfortunately, this routine is not intelligent and will still require human intervention, that is, manual specification of addresses in order to achieve the most optimum location for the adapter memory.

ROM Shadowing

Computers based on the 386 or higher CPU chip, which provides memory access on a 32- or 64-bit path, often use a 16-bit data path for system ROM BIOS information. In addition, adapter cards with on-board BIOS may use an 8-bit path to system memory. On these high-end computers, using a 16- or 8-bit path to memory is a significant bottleneck to system performance. In addition to these problems of width, most actual ROM chips are available in maximum speeds far less than what is available for the system's dynamic RAM. For example, the fastest ROMs available are generally 150ns to 200ns, whereas the RAM in a modern system is rated at 60ns. Because ROM is so slow, any system accesses to programs or data in ROM cause many additional wait states to be inserted. These wait states can slow the entire system down tremendously, especially considering that many of the driver programs used constantly by DOS reside in the BIOS chips found on the motherboard and many of the installed adapters. Fortunately, a way was found to transfer the contents of the slow 8- or 16-bit ROM chips into much faster 32-bit main memory. This is called *shadowing the ROMs.*

Virtually all 386 and higher systems enable you to use what is termed *shadow memory* for the motherboard and possibly some adapter ROMs as well. Shadowing essentially moves the programming code from slow ROM chips into fast 32-bit system memory. Shadowing slower ROMs by copying their contents into RAM can greatly speed up these BIOS routines—sometimes making them four to five times faster. The shadowing is accomplished by using the powerful Memory Management Unit (MMU) in the 386 and higher processors. With the appropriate instructions, the MMU can take a copy of the ROM code, place it in RAM, and enable the RAM such that it appears to the system in exactly the same addresses it was originally located at. This actually disables the ROM chips themselves, which are essentially shut down. The system RAM that is now masquerading as ROM is fully write-protected so that it acts in every way just like the real ROM, with the exception of being much faster, of course! Most systems have an option in the system Setup to enable shadowing for the motherboard BIOS (usually segment F000) and the video BIOS (usually the first 32K of segment C000). Some systems will go farther and offer you the capability to enable or disable shadowing in (usually 16K) increments throughout the remainder of the C000 and D000 segments.

The important thing to note about shadowing is that if you enable shadowing for a given set of addresses, anything found there when the system is booting will be copied to RAM and locked in place. If you were to do this to a memory range that had a network adapter's shared memory mapped into it, the network card would cease to function. You must only shadow ranges that contain true ROM and no RAM.

Some systems do not offer shadowing for areas other than the motherboard and video BIOS. In these systems, you can use a memory manager such as EMM386 (which comes with DOS and Windows) to enable shadowing for any range you specify. It is preferable to use the system's own internal shadowing capabilities first because the system shadowing uses memory that would otherwise be discarded. Using an external memory manager such as EMM386 for shadowing costs you a small amount of extended memory, equal to the amount of space you are shadowing.

If you enable shadowing for a range of addresses and one or more adapters or the system in general no longer works properly, you may have scratch pad memory or other RAM within the shadowed area, which is not accessible as long as the shadowing remains active. In this case, you should disable the shadowing for the system to operate properly. If you can figure out precisely which addresses are ROM and which are RAM within the Upper Memory Area, you can selectively shadow only the ROM for maximum system performance.

Total Installed Memory versus Total Usable Memory

One thing that most people don't realize is that not all the SIMM or other RAM memory you purchase and install in a system will be available. Because of some quirks in system design, the system usually has to "throw away" up to 384K of RAM to make way for the Upper Memory Area.

For example, most systems with 4M of RAM (which is 4,096K) installed show a total of only 3,712K installed during the POST or when running Setup. This indicates that 4,096K–3,712K = 384K of missing memory! Some systems may show 3,968K with the same 4M installed, which works out to 4,096K–3,968K = 128K missing.

If you run your Setup program and check out your base and extended memory values, you will find more information than just the single total shown during the POST. In most systems with 4,096K (4M), you have 640K base and 3072K extended. In some systems, Setup reports 640K base and 3328K extended memory, which is a bonus. In other words, most systems come up 384K short, but some come up only 128K short.

This shortfall is not easy to explain, but it is consistent from system to system. I currently take six to nine hours of class time in my seminars to fully explore, explain, and exploit memory, but this explanation must be more brief! Say that you have a 486 system with two installed 72-pin (36-bit) 1M SIMMs. This results in a total installed memory of 2M in two separate banks because the processor has a 32-bit data bus, and one parity bit is required for every eight data bits. Each SIMM is a single bank in this system. Notice that most cheaper 486 systems use the 30-pin (9-bit) SIMMs of which four are required to make a single bank. The first bank (or SIMM in this case) starts at address 000000 (the first meg), and the second starts at 100000 (the second meg).

One of the cardinal rules of memory is that you absolutely cannot have two hardware devices wired to the same address. This means that 384K of the first memory bank in this system would be in direct conflict with the Video RAM (segments A000 and B000), any adapter card ROMs (segments C000 and D000), and of course the motherboard ROM (segments E000 and F000). This means that all SIMM RAM that occupies these addresses must be shut off or the system will not function! Actually, a motherboard designer can do three things with the SIMM memory that would overlap from A0000–FFFFF, as shown in the following list:

- Use the faster RAM to hold a copy of any slow ROMs (shadowing), disabling the ROM in the process.
- Turn off any RAM not used for shadowing, eliminating any UMA conflicts.
- Remap any RAM not used for shadowing, adding to the stack of currently installed extended memory.

Most systems shadow the motherboard ROM (usually 64K), the video ROM (32K), and simply turn off the rest. Some motherboard ROMs allow additional shadowing to be selected between C8000–DFFFF, usually in 16K increments. Note that you can only shadow ROM, never RAM, so if any card (such as a network card for example) has a RAM buffer in the C8000–DFFFF area, you must not shadow the RAM buffer addresses or the card does not function. For the same reason, you cannot shadow the A0000–BFFFF area because this is the video adapter RAM buffer.

Most motherboards do not do any remapping, which means that any of the 384K not shadowed is simply turned off. That is why enabling shadowing does not seem to use any memory. The memory used for shadowing would otherwise be discarded in most systems. These systems would appear to be short by 384K compared to what is physically installed in the system. In my example system with 2M, no remapping would result in 640K of base memory and 1,024K of extended memory, for a total of 1,664K of usable RAM—384K short of the total (2,048K–384K).

More advanced systems shadow what they can and then remap any segments that do not have shadowing into extended memory so as not to waste the non-shadowed RAM. PS/2 systems, for example, shadow the motherboard BIOS area (E0000–FFFFF or 128K in these systems) and remap the rest of the first bank of SIMM memory (256K from A0000–DFFFF) to whatever address follows the last installed bank. Notice that PS/2 systems have the video BIOS integrated with the motherboard BIOS in E0000–FFFFF, so no separate video BIOS exists to shadow as compared to other systems. In my example system with two 1M 36-bit SIMMs, the 256K not used for shadowing would be remapped to 200000–23FFFF, which is the start of the third megabyte. This affects diagnostics because if you had any memory error reported in those addresses (200000–23FFFF), it would indicate a failure in the FIRST SIMM, even though the addresses point to the end of installed extended memory. The addresses from 100000–1FFFFF would be in the second SIMM, and the 640K base memory 000000–09FFFF would be back in the first SIMM. As you can see, figuring out how the SIMMs are mapped into the system is not easy!

Most systems that do remapping can only remap an entire segment if no shadowing is going on within it. The video RAM area in segments A000 and B000 can never contain shadowing, so at least 128K can be remapped to the top of installed extended memory in any system that supports remapping. Because most systems shadow in segments F000 (motherboard ROM) and C000 (Video ROM), these two segments cannot be remapped. This leaves 256K maximum for remapping. Any system remapping the full 384K must not be shadowing at all, which would slow down the system and is not recommended. Shadowing is always preferred over remapping, and remapping what is not shadowed is definitely preferred to simply turning off the RAM.

Systems that have 384K of "missing" memory do not do remapping. If you want to determine if your system has any missing memory, all you need to know are three things. One is the total physical memory actually installed. The other two items can be discovered by running your Setup program. You want to know the total base and extended memory numbers recognized by the system. Then simply subtract the base and extended memory from the total installed to determine the missing memory. You will usually find that your system is "missing" 384K, but you may be lucky and have a system that remaps 256K of what is missing and thus shows only 128K of memory missing. Virtually all systems use some of the missing memory for shadowing ROMs, especially the motherboard and video BIOS; so what is missing is not completely wasted. Systems "missing" 128K will find that it is being used to shadow your motherboard BIOS (64K from F0000–FFFFF) and video BIOS (32K from C0000-C8000). The remainder of segment C0000 (32K from C8000–CFFFF) is simply being turned off. All other segments (128K from A0000-BFFFF and 128K from D0000–EFFFF) are being remapped to the start of the fifth megabyte (400000–43FFFF). Most systems simply disable these remaining segments rather then take the trouble to remap them. Remapping requires additional logic and BIOS routines to accomplish, and many motherboard designers do not feel that it is worth the effort to reclaim 256K. Note that if your system is doing remapping, any errors reported near the end of installed extended memory are likely in the first bank of memory because that is where they are remapped from. The first bank in a 32-bit system would be constructed of either four 30-pin (9-bit) SIMMs or one 72-pin (36-bit) SIMM.

Adapter Memory Configuration and Optimization

Ideally, all adapter boards would be Plug and Play devices that require you to merely plug the adapter into a motherboard slot and then use it. With the new Plug and Play specification, we are moving toward that goal. However, sometimes it almost seems that adapter boards are designed as if they were the only adapter likely to be present on a system. They usually require you to know the upper memory addresses and IRQ and DMA channels already on your system, and then to configure the new adapter so that it does not conflict with your already-installed adapters.

Adapter boards use upper memory for their BIOS and as working RAM. If two boards attempt to use the same BIOS area or RAM area of upper memory, a conflict occurs that can keep your system from booting. The following sections cover ways to avoid these potential conflicts and how to troubleshoot them if they do occur. In addition, these sections discuss moving adapter memory to resolve conflicts and provide some ideas on optimizing adapter memory use.

Adding adapters to EISA and MCA systems is somewhat more simple because these system architectures feature *auto-configure adapter boards*. In other words, EISA and MCA systems work with adapters to determine available upper memory addresses, IRQs, and DMA channels, and automatically configure all adapters to work optimally together.

How to Determine what Adapters Occupy the UMA. You can determine what adapters are using space in upper memory in the following two ways:

- Study the documentation for each adapter on your system to determine the memory addresses they use.
- Use a software utility that can quickly determine for you what upper memory areas your adapters are using.

The simplest way (although by no means always the most foolproof) is to use a software utility to determine the upper memory areas used by the adapters installed on your system. One such utility, MicroSoft Diagnostics (MSD), comes with Windows 3 and DOS 6 or higher versions. You also can download MSD from the Microsoft BBS (see Appendix B for the number). This utility examines your system configuration and determines not only the upper memory used by your adapters, but also the IRQs used by each of these adapters. Many other utilities can accomplish the same task, but most people already have a copy of MSD—whether they know it or not!

After you run MSD or another utility to determine your system's upper memory configuration, make a printout of the memory addresses used. Thereafter, you can quickly refer to the printout when you are adding a new adapter to ensure that the new board does not conflict with any devices already installed on your system.

Moving Adapter Memory to Resolve Conflicts. After you identify a conflict or potential conflict by studying the documentation for the adapter boards installed on your system or using a software diagnostic utility to determine the upper memory addresses used by your adapter boards, you may have to reconfigure one or more of your adapters to move the upper memory space used by a problem adapter.

Most adapter boards make moving adapter memory a somewhat simple process, enabling you to change a few jumpers or switches to reconfigure the board. The following steps help you resolve most conflicts that arise because adapter boards conflict with one another:

1. Determine the upper memory addresses currently used by your adapter boards and write them down.
2. Determine if any of these addresses are overlapping, which results in a conflict.
3. Consult the documentation for your adapter boards to determine which boards can be reconfigured so that all adapters have access to unique memory addresses.
4. Configure the affected adapter boards so that no conflict in memory addresses occurs.

For example, if one adapter uses the upper memory range C8000–CBFFF and another adapter uses the range CA000–CCFFF, you have a potential address conflict. One of these must be changed.

Optimizing Adapter Memory Use. On an ideal PC, adapter boards would always come configured so that the upper memory addresses they use immediately follow the upper memory addresses used by the previous adapter, with no overlap that would cause conflicts. Such an upper memory arrangement would not only be "clean," but would make it much simpler to use available upper memory for loading device drivers and memory-resident programs. However, this is not the case. Adapter boards often leave gaps of unused memory between one another, which is, of course, preferable to an overlap, but still is not the best use of upper memory.

Someone who wanted to make the most of their upper memory might consider studying the documentation for each adapter board installed on their system to determine a way to compact the upper memory used by each of these devices. For example, if it were possible on a particular system using the adapters installed on it, the use of upper memory could be more simple if you configured your adapter boards so that the blocks of memory they use fit together like bricks in a wall, rather than like a slice of Swiss cheese, as is the case on most systems. The more you can reduce your free upper memory to as few contiguous chunks as possible, the more completely and efficiently you can take advantage of the upper memory area.

Taking Advantage of Unused Upper Memory

On systems based on the 386 or higher CPU chip, memory-resident programs and device drivers can be moved into the upper memory area by using a memory manager like the DOS 6.x MEMMAKER utility or Quarterdeck's QEMM. These memory management utilities examine the memory-resident programs and device drivers installed on your system, determine their memory needs, and then calculate the best way to move these drivers and programs into upper memory, thus freeing the conventional memory they used.

Using MEMMAKER and QEMM is quite simple. Make a backup of your CONFIG.SYS and AUTOEXEC.BAT files so that you have usable copies if you need them to restore your system configuration, and then run either MEMMAKER from the DOS prompt or use the installation program on the QEMM disk. Both programs install required device drivers in your CONFIG.SYS file, and then begin optimizing your memory configuration. Both do an outstanding job of freeing up conventional memory, although QEMM can free more conventional memory automatically than most other utilities. With careful fine-tuning, an individual can perform feats of memory management using only the raw DOS HIMEM.SYS and EMM386.EXE drivers that no automatic program can do!

The following sections cover using memory management software to optimize conventional memory, as well as additional ways to configure your system memory to make your system run as efficiently as possible. It is important to note that the DOS HIMEM.SYS and EMM386.EXE play an integral role in MEMMAKER's capability to move device drivers and memory-resident programs into upper memory. The next two sections describe using HIMEM.SYS and EMM386.EXE to configure extended and expanded memory.

Note

Only driver programs that run in the processor's real mode must be loaded within the first megabyte of memory. Because real mode drivers are made up of 16-bit real mode program code, they cannot reside in extended memory, as only the first megabyte (base memory) is accessible when in real mode. DOS and Windows 3.x are 16-bit programs and utilize drivers that run in real mode, hence the need for the base memory optimization. With the number of drivers that people are using today, it can be difficult to fit them all in the available UMA space while leaving enough base memory free to run applications.

Things are changing with the newer operating systems. Windows 95, for example, uses primarily 32-bit protected mode drivers and program code, although there is still a large amount of 16-bit real mode program code left. Windows NT and OS/2 are full 32-bit operating systems, and all their drivers and applications are made up of 32-bit protected mode instruction code. If you are using all 32-bit programs, then virtually no memory optimization is necessary in the first megabyte, as 32-bit programs are free to run in extended memory.

If you are running older 16-bit DOS applications under Windows 95, NT, or OS/2, then you still need to know about base memory optimization. In these cases, you will be running the application in a DOS window, which, using the virtual real mode of the processor, can emulate the first megabyte of real mode workspace. Using these 32-bit operating systems, you can customize how the application running in the DOS window sees the system, and how the system memory appears to be organized.

Using HIMEM.SYS (DOS). The DOS device driver HIMEM.SYS, which has been included with Windows as well as DOS 4.0 and higher, is used to configure extended memory to the XMS specification as well as to enable the use of the first 64K of extended memory as the High Memory Area (HMA). HIMEM.SYS is installed by adding a line invoking the device driver to your CONFIG.SYS file.

The XMS extended memory specification was developed by Microsoft, Intel, AST Corp., and Lotus Development in 1987 and specifies how programs can use memory beyond the first megabyte on systems based on the 286 CPU chip or higher. The XMS specification also allows real mode programs (those designed to run in DOS) to use extended memory in several different ways.

Using EMM386.EXE (DOS). The program EMM386.EXE, which is included with DOS 5.0 and higher, is used primarily to map XMS memory (extended memory managed by HIMEM.SYS) into unused regions of the Upper Memory Area (UMA). This allows programs to be loaded into these regions for use under DOS. EMM386 also has a secondary function of using XMS memory to emulate EMS version 4 memory, which can then be used by programs that need expanded memory. For more information on using EMM386.EXE, refer to Que's *Using MS-DOS 6* or your DOS manual.

MS-DOS 6.x MEMMAKER. You can increase the amount of conventional memory available to software applications on systems based on the 386 chip and above by running the MS DOS 6.x utility MEMMAKER. DOS 5 had the capability, using EMM386, to map extended memory into the Upper Memory Area so that DOS can load memory-resident programs and drivers into the UMA. Unfortunately, this required an extensive knowledge of the upper memory configuration of a particular system, as well as trial and error to see what programs can fit into the available free regions. This process was difficult enough that many people were not effectively using their memory under DOS (and Windows). To make things easier, when DOS 6 was released, Microsoft included a menu driven program called MEMMAKER that determines the system configuration and automatically creates the proper EMM386 statements and inserts them into the CONFIG.SYS file. By manipulating the UMA manually or through MEMMAKER and loading device drivers and memory-resident programs into upper memory, you can have more than 600K of free conventional memory.

Over the course of months or years of use, the installation programs for various software utilities often install so many memory-resident programs and device drivers in your AUTOEXEC.BAT and CONFIG.SYS files that you have too little conventional memory left to start all the programs you want to run. You may want to use MEMMAKER to free up more conventional memory for your programs. When you run the MEMMAKER utility, it automatically performs the following functions to free up more memory:

- Moves a portion of the DOS kernel into the high memory area (HMA).
- Maps free XMS memory into unused regions in the Upper Memory Area (UMA) as *Upper Memory Blocks* (*UMBs*), into which DOS can then load device drivers and memory-resident programs to free up the conventional memory these drivers and programs otherwise use.
- Modifies CONFIG.SYS and AUTOEXEC.BAT to cause DOS to load memory-resident programs and device drivers into UMBs.

Before running MEMMAKER, carefully examine your CONFIG.SYS and AUTOEXEC.BAT files to identify unnecessary device drivers and memory-resident programs. For example, the DOS device driver ANSI.SYS is often loaded in CONFIG.SYS to enable you to use color and other attributes at the DOS prompt as well as to remap the keys on your keyboard. If you are primarily a Windows user and do not spend much time at the DOS prompt, you can eliminate ANSI.SYS from your CONFIG.SYS file to free up the memory the driver is using.

After you strip down CONFIG.SYS and AUTOEXEC.BAT to their bare essentials (it is advisable to make backup copies first), you are ready to run MEMMAKER to optimize your system memory. To run MEMMAKER, exit from any other programs you are running; start your network or any memory-resident programs and device drivers you absolutely need; and at the DOS prompt, type the following:

```
MEMMAKER
```

The MEMMAKER setup runs in two modes—Express and Custom. Express setup is preferable for those who want to enable MEMMAKER to load device drivers and memory-resident programs into high memory with the minimum amount of user input, unless they have an EGA or VGA (but not a Super VGA) monitor. If you have an EGA or VGA monitor, choose Custom Setup and answer Yes in the advanced options screen where it asks whether MEMMAKER should use monochrome region (B0000-B7FFF) for running programs. Use the defaults for the rest of the options in Custom Setup unless you are sure that one of the defaults is not correct for your system. Custom Setup is probably not a good idea unless you are knowledgeable about optimizing system memory, particular device drivers, and memory-resident programs on the system.

When MEMMAKER finishes optimizing the system memory, the following three lines are added to CONFIG.SYS:

```
DEVICE=C:\DOS\HIMEM.SYS
DEVICE=C:\DOS\EMM386.EXE NOEMS
DOS=HIGH,UMB
```

In addition, MEMMAKER modifies each line in CONFIG.SYS and AUTOEXEC.BAT that loads a device driver or memory-resident program now being loaded into UMBs. Various DEVICE= lines in your CONFIG.SYS are changed to DEVICEHIGH=, and various lines in your AUTOEXEC.BAT have the LH (LoadHigh) command inserted in front of them. For example, the line DEVICE=ANSI.SYS is changed to DEVICEHIGH=ANSI.SYS. In your AUTOEXEC.BAT, lines like C:\DOS\DOSKEY are changed to LH C:\DOS\DOSKEY. The DEVICEHIGH and LH commands load the device drivers and memory-resident programs into UMBs. MEMMAKER also adds codes to specify where in upper memory each program will be loaded. For example, after you run MEMMAKER, a statement like this might be added to your AUTOEXEC.BAT:

```
LH /L:1 C:\DOS\DOSKEY
```

The "/L:1" causes the resident program DOSKEY to load into the first UMB region. On many systems, MEMMAKER configures the system to free up 620K of conventional memory.

For detailed information on using the MEMMAKER utility, consult your DOS 6 manual or Que's *Using MS-DOS 6.22, Special Edition*. If you have MS-DOS, you can get help on MEMMAKER by typing **HELP MEMMAKER** at the DOS prompt.

IBM-DOS (6.x and up) RAMBoost. The IBM-DOS 6.x, IBM DOS 7.x, and up RAMBoost utility, licensed from Central Point, which supplies some of the DOS 6 utilities, works much like MEMMAKER to free up additional conventional memory. After you make backup copies of CONFIG.SYS and AUTOEXEC.BAT and strip down these files to only what you need to load, enter the following at the DOS prompt:

```
RAMSETUP
```

RAMBoost calculates the best way to load your memory-resident programs and device drivers into UMBs. RAMBoost gives results roughly equivalent to the MS-DOS 6 MEMMAKER utility. On many systems, it frees up 620K of conventional memory.

Third-Party Memory Managers. Although MEMMAKER and RAMBoost do a good job of freeing-up conventional memory on most systems, memory management utilities like Quarterdeck's QEMM and Qualitas' 386MAX can do a better job on many systems with more complex configurations, and therefore, numerous memory-resident programs and device drivers. The following sections provide information about QEMM and 386MAX.

If you are running the new Windows 95, be aware that these products are available in new versions that are specifically designed for Windows 95.

Quarterdeck QEMM. One of the strengths of QEMM is how simple it is to install and use. Before running the QEMM INSTALL program, make a backup of your CONFIG.SYS and AUTOEXEC.BAT files so that you have usable copies if you need them to restore your system configuration. Then exit any program you are running. At the DOS prompt, log in to the drive where the QEMM install diskette is located and run the INSTALL program. QEMM copies its files to the C:\QEMM directory (or another directory if you want).

Then the INSTALL program loads the Optimize utility, which calculates the upper memory needed for your memory-resident programs and device drivers, and determines the proper region of upper memory for each. During this process, your system is rebooted several times (or when prompted, you may have to turn off your system and then restart it). When Optimize is finished, you can type **MEM** at the DOS prompt to find out how much free conventional memory your system has.

After QEMM is installed and running on your system, each time you add a memory-resident program or device driver, or any time you add or remove an adapter board (which might change the configuration of upper memory), you need to again run OPTIMIZE. For additional information on installing and running QEMM, and for troubleshooting help, consult your QEMM user manual.

One of the best features of QEMM is that it comes with a system configuration diagnostic utility called MANIFEST. This program is much like MSD, but offers more information and detail in many areas.

Qualitas 386MAX. Before running the 386MAX INSTALL program, make a backup copy of your CONFIG.SYS and AUTOEXEC.BAT files in case you need them later to restore your system. Then exit any program you are running, log in to the drive with the 386MAX install disk, and run INSTALL. 386MAX copies its files to the C:\386MAX subdirectory (or any directory you choose). Then the INSTALL program loads the MAXIMIZE utility, which determines where in upper memory to place each memory-resident program and device driver.

When MAXIMIZE finishes, you can type **MEM** at the DOS prompt to find out how much free conventional memory your system has.

As with MEMMAKER and QEMM, 386MAX uses codes to specify which region of upper memory each memory-resident program and device driver is loaded into. Whenever you add a new device driver or memory-resident program to your system, or when you add or remove an adapter, you must again run MAXIMIZE.

Physical Memory

The CPU and motherboard architecture dictates a computer's physical memory capacity. The 8088 and 8086, with 20 address lines, can use as much as 1M (1,024K) of RAM. The

286 and 386SX CPUs have 24 address lines; they can keep track of as much as 16M of memory. The 386DX, 486, and Pentium CPUs have a full set of 32 address lines; they can keep track of a staggering four gigabytes of memory, while the P6 with 36 address lines can manage 64 gigabytes!

When the 286, 386, 486, Pentium, and P6 chips emulate the 8088 chip (as they do when running a single DOS program), they implement a hardware operating mode called *real mode.* Real mode is the only mode available on the 8086 and 8088 chips used in PC and XT systems. In real mode, all Intel processors—even the mighty Pentium—are restricted to using only 1M of memory, just as their 8086 and 8088 ancestors, and the system design reserves 384K of that amount. Only in protected mode can the 286 or better chips use their maximum potential for memory addressing.

Pentium-based systems can address as much as four gigabytes of memory. To put these memory-addressing capabilities into perspective, four gigabytes (4,096M) of memory costing the going rate of about $30 per megabyte for fast (60 nanoseconds or less) RAM chips would total $122,880!! Of course, you could probably negotiate a much better price with a chip vendor if you planned to buy four gigabytes of SIMMs! Even if you could afford all this memory, the largest SIMMs available today are 72-pin versions with 64M capacity. Most Pentium motherboards only have four to eight SIMM sockets, which allows a maximum of 256M to 512M if all four or eight sockets are filled. Not all systems accept all SIMMs, so you might have a limitation of less than this amount for many Pentium and 486 systems.

On many systems, accessing RAM chips installed directly on a motherboard is faster than accessing memory through an expansion slot. Even without considering this speed advantage, you have the advantage of saving slots. The more memory chips you can get on the motherboard, the fewer adapter slots you need to use. A system that does not have a memory expansion slot faces a large reduction in speed if you use a memory expansion board made for a standard 16-bit slot.

Some 386 and 486 motherboards may have problems addressing memory past 16M due to DMA (Direct Memory Access) controller problems. If you install an ISA adapter that uses a DMA channel and you have more than 16M of memory, you have the potential for problems because the ISA bus only allows DMA access to 16M. Attempted transfers beyond 16M cause the system to crash. Most modern 486 motherboards enable you to install a maximum of 64M on the motherboard using four 16M SIMMs.

Because the PC hardware design reserves the top 384K of the first megabyte of system memory for use by the system itself, you have access to 640K for your programs and data. The use of 384K by the system results in the 640K conventional memory limit. The amount of conventional memory you can actually use for programs depends on the memory used by device drivers (such as ANSI.SYS) and memory-resident programs (such as MOUSE.COM) you load in your CONFIG.SYS and AUTOEXEC.BAT files. Device drivers and memory-resident programs usually use conventional memory.

RAM Chips

A *RAM chip* temporarily stores programs when they are running and stores the data being used by those programs. RAM chips are sometimes termed *volatile storage* because when you turn off your computer or an electrical outage occurs, whatever is stored in RAM is lost unless you saved it to your hard drive. Because of the volatile nature of RAM, many computer users make it a habit to save their work frequently. (Some software applications can do timed backups automatically.)

Launching a computer program instructs DOS to bring an EXE or COM disk file into RAM, and as long as they are running, computer programs reside in RAM. The CPU executes programmed instructions in RAM. RAM stores your keystrokes when you use a word processor. RAM stores numbers used in calculations. The CPU also stores results in RAM. Telling a program to save your data instructs the program to store RAM contents on your hard drive as a file.

If you decide to purchase more RAM, you need the information on RAM chips and their speeds presented in the following sections to help ensure that you don't slow down your computer when you add memory.

Physical Storage and Organization

RAM chips can be physically integrated into the motherboard or adapter board in several forms. Older systems used individual memory chips, called *Dual In-line Pin* (DIP) chips, that were plugged into sockets or soldered directly to a board. Most modern systems use a memory package called a *Single In-line Memory Module* (SIMM). These modules combine several chips on a small circuit board plugged into a retaining socket. A SIPP, or *Single In-line Pin Package*, is similar to a SIMM, but it uses pins rather than an edge connector to connect to the motherboard. It would be possible to convert a SIPP to a SIMM by cutting off the pins, or to convert a SIMM to a SIPP by soldering pins on. Also, some companies are making SIPP to SIMM converters that allow the SIPPs to be plugged into conventional 30-pin SIMM sockets.

Many newer Pentium and Pentium Pro systems use 168-pin DIMMs (Dual In-line Memory Modules), which is a newer high-density memory module design suited to 64-bit systems.

Several types of memory chips have been used in PC system motherboards. Most of these chips are single-bit-wide chips, available in several capacities. The following table lists available RAM chips and their capacities:

RAM Chip	Capacity
16K by 1 bit	These devices were used in the original IBM PC with a Type 1 motherboard.
64K by 1 bit	These chips were used in the standard IBM PC Type 2 motherboard and in the XT Type 1 and 2 motherboards. Many memory adapters of the era, such as the popular vintage AST 6-pack boards, also used these chips.
128K by 1 bit	These chips, used in the IBM AT Type 1 motherboard, often were a strange physical combination of two 64K chips stacked on top of one another and soldered together. Single-chip versions also were used for storing the parity bits in the IBM XT 286.
256K by 1 bit (or 64K by 4 bits)	These chips once were very popular in motherboards and memory cards. The IBM XT Type 2 and IBM AT Type 2 motherboards, as well as most compatible systems of that era, used these chips.

(continues)

(continued)

RAM Chip	Capacity
1M by 1 bit (or 256K by 4 bits)	1M chips were very popular for a number of years and were most often used in 256K to 8M SIMMs.
4M by 1 bit (or 1M by 4 bits)	Four-megabit chips are used primarily in SIMMs from 1M to 16M in capacity. They are used primarily in 4M and 8M SIMMs and generally are not sold as individual chips.
16M by 1 bit (or 4M by 4 bits)	16-megabit chips are often used in 72-pin SIMMs of 16M to 32M capacity.
64M by 1 bit (or 16M by 4 bits)	64-megabit chips are popular in high capacity 16M or larger memory modules, especially for notebook systems.
256M by 1 bit (or 64M by 4 bits)	256-megabit chips are the most recent on the market. These chips allow enormous SIMM capacities of 128M or larger! Because of the high expense and limited availability of these chips, you see them only in the most expensive and highest capacity modules on the market.

Figure 7.18 shows a typical memory chip. Each marking on the chip is significant.

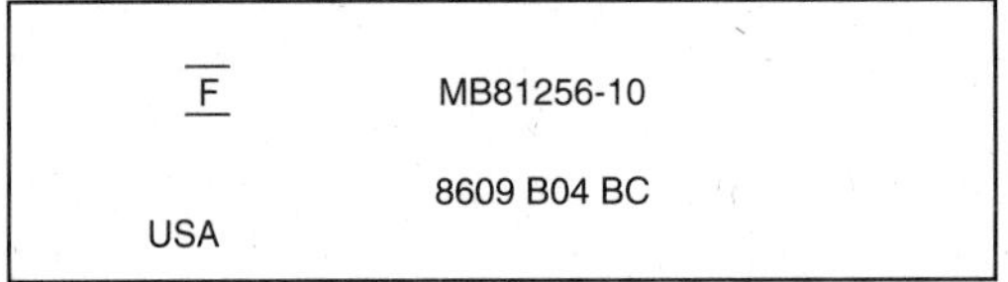

Figure 7.18

The markings on a typical memory chip.

The -10 on the chip corresponds to its speed in nanoseconds (a 100-nanosecond rating). MB81256 is the chip's part number, which usually contains a clue about the chip's capacity. The key digits are 1256, which indicate that this chip is 1 bit wide, and has a depth of 256K. The 1 means that to make a full byte with parity, you need nine of these single-bit-wide chips. A chip with a part number KM4164B-10 indicates a 64K-by-1-bit chip at a speed of 100 nanoseconds. The following list matches common chips with their part numbers:

Part Number	Chip
4164	64K by 1 bit
4464	64K by 4 bits
41128	128K by 1 bit
44128	128K by 4 bits
41256	256K by 1 bit
44256	256K by 4 bits
41000	1M by 1 bit
44000	1M by 4 bits

Chips wider than 1 bit are used to construct banks of less than 9, 18, or 36 chips (depending on the system architecture). For example, in the IBM XT 286, which is an

AT-type 16-bit system, the last 128K bytes of memory on the motherboard consist of a bank with only six chips; four are 64K-by-4 bits wide, and two parity chips are 1 bit wide, storing 18 bits.

In figure 7.18, the "F" symbol centered between two lines is the manufacturer's logo for Fujitsu Microelectronics. The 8609 indicates the date of manufacture (ninth week of 1986). Some manufacturers, however, use a Julian date code. To decode the chip further, contact the manufacturer if you can tell who that is, or perhaps a memory chip vendor.

Memory Banks

Memory chips (DIPs, SIMMs, SIPPs, and DIMMs) are organized in *banks* on motherboards and memory cards. You should know the memory bank layout and position on the motherboard and memory cards.

You need to know the bank layout when adding memory to the system. In addition, memory diagnostics report error locations by byte and bit addresses, and you must use these numbers to locate which bank in your system contains the problem.

The banks usually correspond to the data bus capacity of the system's microprocessor. Table 7.5 shows the widths of individual banks based on the type of PC.

Table 7.5 Memory Bank Widths on Different Systems

Processor	Data Bus	Memory Bank Size (No Parity)	Memory Bank Size (Parity)	30-pin SIMMs per Bank	72-pin SIMMs per Bank	168-pin SIMMs per Bank
8088	8-bit	8-bits	9-bits	1	<1*	<1*
8086	16-bit	16-bits	18-bits	2	<1*	<1*
286	16-bit	16-bits	18-bits	2	<1*	<1*
386SX, SL, SLC	16-bit	16-bits	18-bits	2	<1*	<1*
386DX	32-bit	32-bits	36-bits	4	1	<1*
486SLC, SLC2	16-bit	16-bits	18-bits	2	<1*	<1*
486SX, DX, DX2, DX4	32-bit	32-bits	36-bits	4	1	<1*
Pentium	64-bit	64-bits	72-bits	8	2	1
Pentium Pro	64-bit	64-bits	72-bits	8	2	1

* - *In these cases a single SIMM or DIMM constitutes multiple banks of memory.*

The number of bits for each bank can be made up of single chips, SIMMs, or DIMMs. For example, in a 286 system that would use an 18-bit bank, you could make up a bank of 18 individual 1-bit-wide chips, or you could use four individual 4-bit-wide chips to make up the data bits, and two individual 1-bit-wide chips for the parity bits. Most modern systems do not use chips, but instead use SIMMs. If the system has an 18-bit bank, it likely would use 30-pin SIMMs and have two SIMMs per bank. All the SIMMs in a single bank must be the same size and type. As you can see, the 30-pin SIMMs are less than ideal for

32-bit systems because you must use them in increments of four per bank! Because these SIMMs are available in 1M and 4M capacities today, this means that a single bank has to be 4M or 16M of memory, with no in-between amounts. Using 30-pin SIMMs in 32-bit systems artificially constricts memory configurations and such systems are not recommended. If a 32-bit system uses 72-pin SIMMs, each SIMM represents a separate bank, and the SIMMs can be added or removed on an individual basis rather than in groups of four. This makes memory configuration much easier and more flexible.

Many of the newer systems now use the 168-pin DIMM devices. These are 64 bits without parity, and 72 bits each with parity. The devices are used on Pentium and Pentium Pro systems only, where they function as a single bank.

Older systems often used individual chips. For example, the IBM PC Type 2 and XT Type 1 motherboard contains four banks of memory labeled Bank 0, 1, 2, and 3. Each bank uses nine 64K-by-1-bit chips. The total number of chips present is 4 times 9, or 36 chips, organized as shown in figure 7.19.

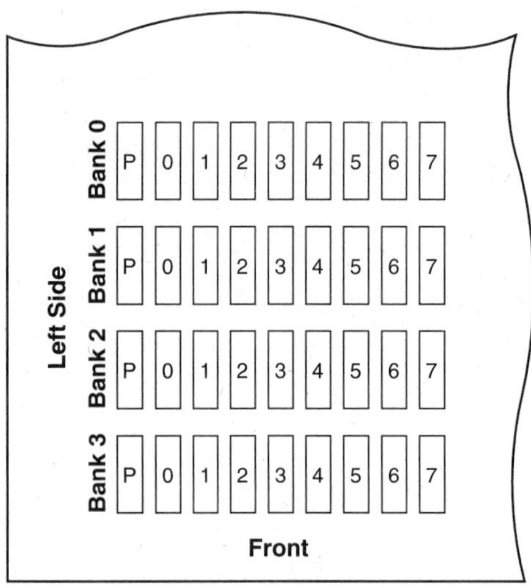

Figure 7.19

A memory bank on a PC Type 2 or XT Type 1 motherboard.

This layout is used in many older 8-bit motherboards, including the Type 1 and 2 PC motherboards and the Type 1 and 2 XT motherboards. Most PC or XT clones also followed this scheme. Note that the parity chip is the leftmost chip in each bank on the XT motherboard.

The physical orientation used on a motherboard or memory card is arbitrary and determined by the board's designers. Documentation covering your system or card comes in very handy. You can determine the layout of a motherboard or adapter card through testing, but this takes time and may be difficult, particularly after you have a problem with a system.

Parity Checking

One standard IBM has set for the industry is that the memory chips in a bank of nine each handle one bit of data: eight bits per character plus one extra bit called the *parity bit*. The parity bit enables memory-control circuitry to keep tabs on the other eight bits—a built-in cross-check for the integrity of each byte in the system. If the circuitry detects an error, the computer stops and displays a message informing you of the malfunction. Some modern SIMMs have only three chips, however, with each chip handling three of the nine bits.

IBM established the *odd parity* standard for error checking. The following explanation may help you understand what is meant by odd parity. As the eight individual bits in a byte are stored in memory, a special chip called a *74LS280 parity generator/checker* on the motherboard (or memory card) evaluates the data bits by counting the number of 1s in the byte. If an even number of 1s is in the byte, the parity generator/checker chip creates a 1 and stores it as the ninth bit (parity bit) in the parity memory chip. That makes the total sum for all nine bits an odd number. If the original sum of the eight data bits is an odd number, the parity bit created is 0, keeping the 9-bit sum an odd number. The value of the parity bit is always chosen so that the sum of all nine bits (eight data bits plus one parity bit) is an odd number. Remember that the eight data bits in a byte are numbered 0 1 2 3 4 5 6 7. The following examples may make it easier to understand:

```
Data bit number:     0 1 2 3 4 5 6 7     Parity bit
 Data bit value:     1 0 1 1 0 0 1 1     0
```

In this example, because the total number of data bits with a value of 1 is an odd number (5), the parity bit must have a value of 0 to ensure an odd sum for all nine bits.

The following is another example:

```
Data bit number:     0 1 2 3 4 5 6 7     Parity bit
 Data bit value:     0 0 1 1 0 0 1 1     1
```

In this example, because the total number of data bits with a value of 1 is an even number (4), the parity bit must have a value of 1 to create an odd sum for all nine bits.

When the system reads memory back from storage, it checks the parity information. If a (9-bit) byte has an even number of bits with a parity bit value of 1, that byte must have an error. The system cannot tell which bit has changed, or if only a single bit has changed. If three bits changed, for example, the byte still flags a parity-check error; if two bits changed, however, the bad byte may pass unnoticed. The following examples show parity-check messages for three types of systems:

```
For the IBM PC:                      PARITY CHECK x
For the IBM XT:                      PARITY CHECK x      yyyyy (z)
For the IBM AT and late model XT:    PARITY CHECK x      yyyyy
```

Where *x* is 1 or 2:

1 = Error occurred on the motherboard

2 = Error occurred in an expansion slot

yyyy represents a number from 00000 through FFFFF that indicates, in hexadecimal notation, the byte in which the error has occurred.

Where *(z)* is (S) or (e):

(S) = Parity error occurred in the system unit

= Parity error occurred in the expansion chassis

Note

An expansion chassis was an option IBM sold for the original PC and XT systems to add more expansion slots. This unit consisted of a backplane motherboard with eight slots, one of which contained a special extender/receiver card cabled to a similar extender/receiver card placed in the main system. Due to the extender/receiver cards in the main system and the expansion chassis, the net gain was six slots.

When a parity-check error is detected, the motherboard parity-checking circuits generate a *non-maskable interrupt* (NMI), which halts processing and diverts the system's attention to the error. The NMI causes a routine in the ROM to be executed. The routine clears the screen and then displays a message in the upper left corner of the screen. The message differs depending on the type of computer system. On some older IBM systems, the ROM parity-check routine halts the CPU. In such a case, the system locks up, and you must perform a hardware reset or a power-off/power-on cycle to restart the system. Unfortunately, all unsaved work is lost in the process. (An NMI is a system warning that software cannot ignore.)

Most systems do not halt the CPU when a parity error is detected; instead, they offer you a choice of either rebooting the system or continuing as though nothing happened. Additionally, these systems may display the parity error message in a different format from IBM, although the information presented is basically the same. For example, many systems with a Phoenix BIOS display these messages:

```
Memory parity interrupt at xxxx:xxxx
Type (S)hut off NMI, Type (R)eboot, other keys to continue
```

or

```
I/O card parity interrupt at xxxx:xxxx
Type (S)hut off NMI, Type (R)eboot, other keys to continue
```

The first of these two messages indicates a motherboard parity error (Parity Check 1), and the second indicates an expansion-slot parity error (Parity Check 2). Notice that the address given in the form *xxxx:xxxx* for the memory error is in a segment:offset form rather than a straight linear address such as with IBM's error messages. The segment:offset address form still gives you the location of the error to a resolution of a single byte.

Note that you have three ways to proceed after viewing this error message. You can press S, which shuts off parity checking and resumes system operation at the point where the parity check first occurred. Pressing R forces the system to reboot, losing any unsaved work. Pressing any other key causes the system to resume operation with parity checking still enabled. If the problem recurs, it is likely to cause another parity-check interruption. In most cases, it is most prudent to press S, which disables the parity checking so that you can then save your work. It would be best in this case to save your work to a floppy disk to prevent the possible corruption of a hard disk. You should also avoid overwriting any previous (still good) versions of whatever file you are saving, because in fact you may be saving a bad file due to the memory corruption. Because parity checking is now disabled, your save operations will not be interrupted. Then you should power the system off, restart it, and run whatever memory diagnostics software you have to try and track down the error. In some cases, the POST finds the error on the next restart, but in most cases you need to run a more sophisticated diagnostics program, perhaps in a continuous mode, to locate the error.

The AMI BIOS displays the parity error messages in the following forms:

```
ON BOARD PARITY ERROR ADDR (HEX) = (xxxxx)
```

or

```
OFF BOARD PARITY ERROR ADDR (HEX) = (xxxxx)
```

These messages indicate that an error in memory has occurred during the POST, and the failure is located at the address indicated. The first one indicates the error occurred on the motherboard, whereas the second message indicates an error in an expansion slot adapter card. The AMI BIOS also can display memory errors in the following manner:

```
Memory Parity Error at xxxxx
```

or

```
I/O Card Parity Error at xxxxx
```

These messages indicate that an error in memory has occurred at the indicated address during normal operation. The first one indicates a motherboard memory error, and the second indicates an expansion slot adapter memory error.

Although many systems enable you to continue processing after a parity error, and even allow for the disabling of further parity checking, continuing to use your system after a parity error is detected can be dangerous if misused. The idea behind letting you continue using either method is to give you time to save any unsaved work before you diagnose and service the computer, but be careful how you do this.

Caution

When you are notified of a memory parity error, remember the parity check is telling you that memory has been corrupted. Do you want to save potentially corrupted data over the good file from the *last* time you saved? Definitely not! Make sure that you save your work to a different file name. In addition, after a parity error, save only to a floppy disk if possible and avoid writing to the hard disk; there is a slight chance that the hard drive could become corrupted if you save the contents of corrupted memory.

After saving your work, determine the cause of the parity error and repair the system. You may be tempted to use an option to shut off further parity checking and simply continue using the system as if nothing were wrong. Doing so resembles unscrewing the oil pressure warning indicator bulb on a car with an oil leak so that the oil pressure light won't bother you anymore!

IBM PS/2 systems have a slightly different way of communicating parity-check errors than the older IBM systems. To indicate motherboard parity errors, the message looks like this:

```
110

xxxxx
```

To indicate parity errors from an expansion slot, the message looks like this:

```
111

xxxxx
```

In these messages, the *xxxxx* indicates the address of the parity error. As with most IBM systems, the system is halted after these messages are displayed, thus eliminating any possibility of saving work.

Single In-Line Memory Modules (SIMMs)

For memory storage, most modern systems have adopted the single in-line memory module (SIMM) as an alternative to individual memory chips. These small boards plug into special connectors on a motherboard or memory card. The individual memory chips are soldered to the SIMM, so removing and replacing individual memory chips is impossible. Instead, you must replace the entire SIMM if any part of it fails. The SIMM is treated as though it were one large memory chip.

IBM compatibles have two main physical types of SIMMs—30-pin (9 bits) and 72-pin (36 bits)—with various capacities and other specifications. The 30-pin SIMMs are smaller than the 72-pin versions, and may have chips on either one or both sides. SIMMs are available both with and without parity bits. Until recently, all IBM-compatible systems used parity checked memory to ensure accuracy. Other non-IBM-compatible systems like the Apple Macintosh have never used parity checked memory. For example, Apple computers use the same 30-pin or 72-pin SIMMs as IBM systems, but Apple computers as a rule do not have parity checking circuitry, so they can use slightly cheaper 30-pin SIMMs that are only eight bits wide instead of nine bits (eight data bits plus one parity bit) as is required on most IBM-compatible systems. They also can use 72-pin SIMMs that are only 32-bits wide rather than 36-bits (32 data bits plus four parity bits) as is required on most IBM compatibles. You can use the parity SIMMs in Apple systems; they will simply ignore the extra bits. If you use non-parity SIMMs in an IBM compatible that requires parity checked memory, you instantly get memory errors, and the system cannot operate. If you service both IBM and Apple systems, you could simply stock only parity SIMMs because they can be used in either system.

Recently, a disturbing trend has developed in the IBM-compatible marketplace. Some of the larger vendors have been shipping systems with parity checking disabled! These systems can use slightly cheaper non-parity SIMMs like the Apple systems. The savings amounts to about $10 per 4M SIMM, which can result in a savings to the manufacturer of about $20 for a typical 8M configuration. Because most buyers have no idea that the parity checking has been taken away (how often have you seen an ad that says "now featuring NO PARITY CHECKING!"), the manufacturer can sell its system that much cheaper. Because several of the big names have started selling systems without parity, most of the others have been forced to follow to remain price competitive. Because nobody wants to announce this information, it has remained as a sort of dirty little secret within the industry! What is amazing is that the 386 and higher processors all contain the parity circuitry within them, so no additional circuits are needed on the mother board. It is solely the cost of the parity chips on the SIMMs that is being saved.

How can they do this? Well, most newer motherboards have a method by which parity checking can be disabled to accommodate non-parity SIMMs. Most older motherboards absolutely required parity SIMMs because there was no way to disable the parity checking. Some newer motherboards have a jumper to enable or disable the parity circuitry. Some include this as a SETUP option, and some systems check the memory for parity bits and if they are not detected in all banks, parity checking is automatically disabled. In these systems, installing a single non-parity SIMM normally causes parity checking to be disabled for all memory. I have often found parity checking to be the first alert to system problems, so I am not thrilled that virtually all newer systems come with non-parity SIMMs. Fortunately, this can be rectified by specifying parity SIMMs when you order a new machine. If you don't specify parity SIMMs, then surely you will get the cheaper non-parity versions. Also make sure that your motherboard has parity checking enabled as well, because most are not coming configured with it enabled.

Unfortunately, there are now many systems that do not even support parity checking at all. In fact, all Pentium systems based on the Intel Triton chipset cannot ever implement parity checking because support for parity is not found in the chipset. That basically rules these systems out for mission critical applications where parity is a necessity. Intel is working on a new Triton II chipset that will not only implement parity, but even better ECC (Error Correcting Code) memory as well.

Figures 7.20 and 7.21 show typical 30-pin (9-bit) and 72-pin (36-bit) SIMMs, respectively. The pins are numbered from left to right and are connected through to both sides of the module. Notice that all dimensions are in inches and millimeters (in parentheses).

A SIMM is extremely compact considering the amount of memory it holds. SIMMs are available in several capacities, depending on the version. Table 7.6 lists the different capacities available for both the 30-pin and 72-pin SIMMs.

Dynamic RAM SIMMs of each type and capacity are available in different speed ratings. These ratings are expressed in nanoseconds (billionths of a second, abbreviated ns). SIMMs have been available in many different speed ratings ranging from 120ns for some of the slowest, to 50ns for some of the fastest available. Many of the first systems to use SIMMs used versions rated at 120ns. These were quickly replaced in the market by 100ns and even faster versions. Today, you can generally purchase SIMMs rated at 80ns, 70ns, or 60ns. Both faster and slower ones are available, but they are not frequently required

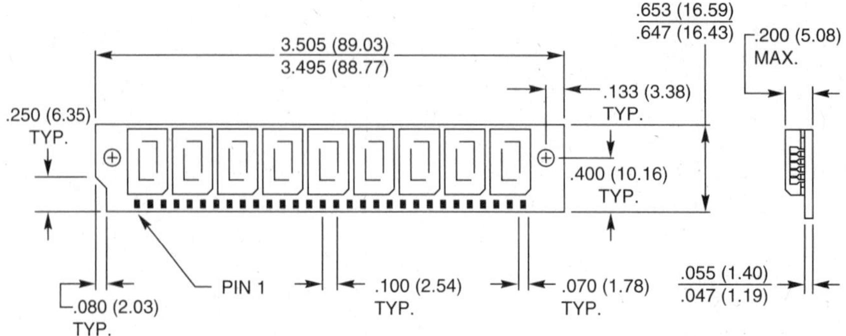

Figure 7.20

A typical 30-pin (9-bit) SIMM.

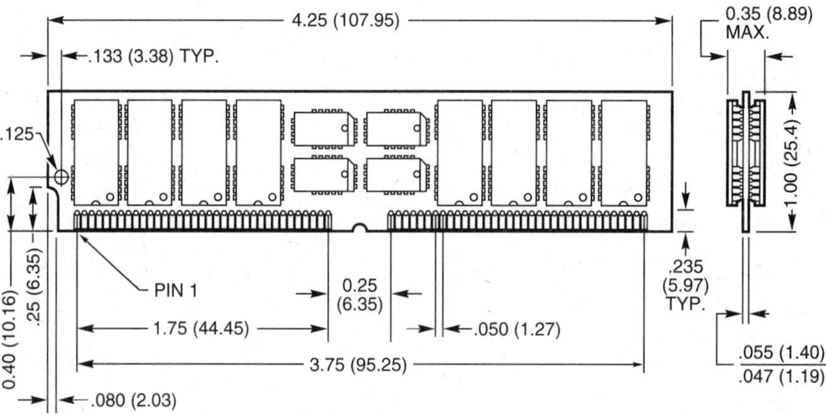

Figure 7.21

A typical 72-pin (36-bit) SIMM.

Table 7.6 SIMM Capacities

30-pin SIMM Capacities

Capacity	Parity SIMM	Non-Parity SIMM
256K	256K × 9	256K × 8
1M	1M × 9	1M × 8
4M	4M × 9	4M × 8
16M	16M × 9	16M × 8

72-pin SIMM Capacities

Capacity	Parity SIMM	Non-Parity SIMM
1M	256K × 36	256K × 32
2M	512K × 36	512K × 32

72-pin SIMM Capacities

Capacity	Parity SIMM	Non-Parity SIMM
4M	1M × 36	1M × 32
8M	2M × 36	2M × 32
16M	4M × 36	4M × 32
32M	8M × 36	8M × 32
64M	16M × 36	16M × 32
128M	32M × 36	32M × 32

and are difficult to obtain. If a system requires a specific speed, you can almost always substitute faster speeds if the one specified is not available. There are no problems in mixing SIMM speeds, as long as you use SIMMs equal to or faster than what the system requires. Because often very little price difference exists between the different speed versions, I usually buy faster SIMMs than are needed for a particular application, as this may make them more usable in a future system that may require the faster speed.

Several variations on the 30-pin SIMMs can affect how they work (if at all) in a particular system. First, there are actually two variations on the pinout configurations. Most systems use a *generic* type of SIMM, which has an industry standard pin configuration. Many older IBM systems used a slightly modified 30-pin SIMM, starting with the XT-286 introduced in 1986 through the PS/2 Model 25, 30, 50, and 60. These systems require a SIMM with different signals on five of the pins. These are known as *IBM-style* 30-pin SIMMs. You can modify a generic 30-pin SIMM to work in the IBM systems and vice versa, but purchasing a SIMM with the correct pinouts is much easier. Be sure you identify to the SIMM vendor if you need the specific IBM-style versions.

Another issue with respect to the 30-pin SIMMs relates to the chip count. The SIMM itself acts as if it were a single chip of 9-bits wide (with parity), and it really does not matter how this total is derived. Older SIMMs were constructed with nine individual 1-bit-wide chips to make up the total, whereas many newer SIMMs use two 4-bit-wide chips and one 1-bit-wide chip for parity, making a total of three chips on the SIMM. Accessing the 3-chip SIMMs can require adjustments to the refresh timing circuits on the motherboard, and many older motherboards cannot cope. Most newer motherboards automatically handle the slightly different refresh timing of both the 3-chip or 9-chip SIMMs, and in this case the 3-chip versions are more reliable, use less power, and generally cost less as well. If you have an older system, most likely it will also work with the 3-chip SIMMs, but some do not. Unfortunately, the only way to know is to try them. To prevent the additional time required to change them for 9-chip versions should the 3-chip versions not work in an older system, it seems prudent to recommend sticking with the 9-chip variety in any older systems.

The 72-pin SIMMs do not have different pinouts and are differentiated only by capacity and speed. These SIMMs are not affected by the number of chips on them. The 72-pin SIMMs are ideal for 32-bit systems like 486 machines because they comprise an entire bank of memory (32 data bits plus 4 parity bits). When you configure a system that uses a 72-pin SIMM, you can usually add or remove memory in single SIMM modules (except on systems that use interleaved memory schemes to reduce wait states). The 30-pin

SIMMs are clumsy when used in a system with a 32-bit memory architecture because these SIMMs must be added or removed in quantities of four to make up a complete bank. A 386SX or a 286 system would require only two 9-bit SIMMs for a single bank of memory so the 30-pin SIMMs are a better match.

Remember that some 486 systems (such as the PS/2 90 and 95 systems) use interleaved memory to reduce wait states. This requires a multiple of two 36-bit SIMMs because interleaved memory accesses are alternated between the SIMMs to improve performance.

Note

A *bank* is the smallest amount of memory that can be addressed by the processor at one time and usually corresponds to the data bus width of the processor. If the memory is interleaved, a virtual bank may be twice the absolute data bus width of the processor.

You cannot always replace a SIMM with a greater capacity unit and expect it to work. For example, the IBM PS/2 Model 70-Axx and Bxx systems accept 72-pin SIMMs of 1M or 2M capacity, which are 80ns or faster. Although an 80ns 4M SIMM is available, it does not work in these systems. The PS/2 Model 55 SX and 65 SX, however, accept 1M, 2M, or 4M 72-pin SIMMs. A larger capacity SIMM works only if the motherboard is designed to accept it in the first place. Consult your system documentation to determine the correct capacity and speed to use.

SIMMs were designed to eliminate chip creep, which plagues systems with memory chips installed in sockets. *Chip creep* occurs when a chip works its way out of its socket, caused by the normal thermal expansion and contraction from powering a system on and off. Eventually, chip creep leads to poor contact between the chip leads and the socket, and memory errors and problems begin.

The original solution for chip creep was to solder all the memory chips to the printed circuit board. This approach, however, was impractical. Memory chips fail more frequently than most other types of chips and soldering chips to the board made the units difficult to service.

The SIMM incorporates the best compromise between socketed and soldered chips. The chips are soldered to the SIMM, but you can replace the socketed SIMM module easily. In addition, the SIMM is held tight to the motherboard by a locking mechanism that does not work loose from contraction and expansion, but is easy for you to loosen. This solution is a good one, but it can increase repair costs. You must replace what amounts to in some cases an entire bank rather than one defective chip.

For example, if you have a 486DX4 with one 60ns 8M SIMM that goes bad, you could replace it for about $250 or less from chip suppliers who advertise in the computer magazines. This is certainly more expensive than replacing a single 256K by 1-bit chip costing about $2 each. Of course, 8M SIMMs are used on systems never designed for single chips. It would take 288 256K-by-1-bit chips to equal the memory storage of one 8M SIMM. Troubleshooting a problem with a single SIMM device is much easier than troubleshooting 288 discrete chips. In addition, one SIMM is more reliable than 288 individual chips!

All systems on the market today use SIMMs. Even Apple Macintosh systems use SIMMs. The SIMM is not a proprietary memory system, but rather an industry-standard device. As mentioned, some SIMMs have slightly different pinouts and specifications other than speed and capacity, so be sure that you obtain the correct SIMMs for your system.

SIMM Pinouts

Tables 7.7 and 7.8 show the interface connector pinouts for both 30-pin SIMM varieties, as well as the standard 72-pin version. Also included is a special presence detect table that shows the configuration of the presence detect pins on various 72-pin SIMMs. The presence detect pins are used by the motherboard to detect exactly what size and speed SIMM is installed. Industry-standard 30-pin SIMMs do not have a presence detect feature, but IBM did add this capability to its modified 30-pin configuration.

Table 7.7 Industry-Standard and IBM 30-Pin SIMM Pinouts

Pin	Standard SIMM Signal Names	IBM SIMM Signal Names
1	+5 Vdc	+5 Vdc
2	Column Address Strobe	Column Address Strobe
3	Data Bit 0	Data Bit 0
4	Address Bit 0	Address Bit 0
5	Address Bit 1	Address Bit 1
6	Data Bit 1	Data Bit 1
7	Address Bit 2	Address Bit 2
8	Address Bit 3	Address Bit 3
9	Ground	Ground
10	Data Bit 2	Data Bit 2
11	Address Bit 4	Address Bit 4
12	Address Bit 5	Address Bit 5
13	Data Bit 3	Data Bit 3
14	Address Bit 6	Address Bit 6
15	Address Bit 7	Address Bit 7
16	Data Bit 4	Data Bit 4
17	Address Bit 8	Address Bit 8
18	Address Bit 9	Address Bit 9
19	Address Bit 10	Row Address Strobe 1
20	Data Bit 5	Data Bit 5
21	Write Enable	Write Enable
22	Ground	Ground
23	Data Bit 6	Data Bit 6
24	No Connection	Presence Detect (Ground)
25	Data Bit 7	Data Bit 7
26	Data Bit 8 (Parity) Out	Presence Detect (1M = Ground)
27	Row Address Strobe	Row Address Strobe

(continues)

Table 7.7 Continued

Pin	Standard SIMM Signal Names	IBM SIMM Signal Names
28	Column Address Strobe Parity	No Connection
29	Data Bit 8 (Parity) In	Data Bit 8 (Parity) I/O
30	+5 Vdc	+5 Vdc

Table 7.8 Standard 72-Pin SIMM Pinout

Pin	SIMM Signal Name
1	Ground
2	Data Bit 0
3	Data Bit 16
4	Data Bit 1
5	Data Bit 17
6	Data Bit 2
7	Data Bit 18
8	Data Bit 3
9	Data Bit 18
10	+5 Vdc
11	Column Address Strobe Parity
12	Address Bit 0
13	Address Bit 1
14	Address Bit 2
15	Address Bit 3
16	Address Bit 4
17	Address Bit 5
18	Address Bit 6
19	Reserved
20	Data Bit 4
21	Data Bit 20
22	Data Bit 5
23	Data Bit 21
24	Data Bit 6
25	Data Bit 22
26	Data Bit 7
27	Data Bit 23
28	Address Bit 7
29	Block Select 0
30	+5 Vdc
31	Address Bit 8
32	Address Bit 9

Pin	SIMM Signal Name
33	Row Address Strobe 3
34	Row Address Strobe 2
35	Parity Data Bit 2
36	Parity Data Bit 0
37	Parity Data Bit 1
38	Parity Data Bit 3
39	Ground
40	Column Address Strobe 0
41	Column Address Strobe 2
42	Column Address Strobe 3
43	Column Address Strobe 1
44	Row Address Strobe 0
45	Row Address Strobe 1
46	Block Select 1
47	Write Enable
48	Reserved
49	Data Bit 8
50	Data Bit 24
51	Data Bit 9
52	Data Bit 25
53	Data Bit 10
54	Data Bit 26
55	Data Bit 11
56	Data Bit 27
57	Data Bit 12
58	Data Bit 28
59	+5 Vdc
60	Data Bit 29
61	Data Bit 13
62	Data Bit 30
63	Data Bit 14
64	Data Bit 31
65	Data Bit 15
66	Block Select 2
67	Presence Detect Bit 0
68	Presence Detect Bit 1
69	Presence Detect Bit 2
70	Presence Detect Bit 3
71	Block Select 3
72	Ground

Notice that the 72-pin SIMMs employ a set of four pins to indicate the type of SIMM to the motherboard. These presence detect pins are either grounded or not connected to indicate the type of SIMM to the motherboard. This is very similar to the industry-standard DX code used on modern 35mm film rolls to indicate the ASA (speed) rating of the film to the camera. Unfortunately, unlike the film standards, the presence detect signaling is not a standard throughout the PC industry. Different system manufacturers sometimes use different configurations for what is expected on these four pins. Table 7.9 shows how IBM defines these pins.

Table 7.9 72-Pin SIMM Presence Detect Pins

70	69	68	67	SIMM Type	IBM Part Number
-	-	-	-	Not a valid SIMM	N/A
-	-	-	Gnd	1MB 120ns	N/A
-	-	Gnd	-	2MB 120ns	N/A
-	-	Gnd	Gnd	2MB 70ns	92F0102
-	Gnd	-	-	8MB 70ns	64F3606
-	Gnd	-	Gnd	Reserved	N/A
-	Gnd	Gnd	-	2MB 80ns	92F0103
-	Gnd	Gnd	Gnd	8MB 80ns	64F3607
Gnd	-	-	-	Reserved	N/A
Gnd	-	-	Gnd	1MB 85ns	90X8624
Gnd	-	Gnd	-	2MB 85ns	92F0104
Gnd	-	Gnd	Gnd	4MB 70ns	92F0105
Gnd	Gnd	-	-	4MB 85ns	79F1003 (square notch) L40-SX
Gnd	Gnd	-	Gnd	1MB 100ns	N/A
Gnd	Gnd	-	Gnd	8MB 80ns	79F1004 (square notch) L40-SX
Gnd	Gnd	Gnd	-	2MB 100ns	N/A
Gnd	Gnd	Gnd	Gnd	4MB 80ns	87F9980
Gnd	Gnd	Gnd	Gnd	2MB 85ns	79F1003 (square notch) L40SX

- = No Connection (open)
Gnd = Ground
Pin 67 = Presence detect bit 0
Pin 68 = Presence detect bit 1
Pin 69 = Presence detect bit 2
Pin 70 = Presence detect bit 3

RAM Chip Speed

Memory-chip speed is reported in nanoseconds (ns). (One *nanosecond* is the time that light takes to travel 11.72 inches.) PC memory speeds vary from about 10ns to 200ns. When you replace a failed memory module, you must install a module of the same type and speed as the failed module. You can substitute a chip with a different speed only if the speed of the replacement chip is equal to or faster than that of the failed chip.

Some people have had problems when "mixing" chips because they used a chip that did not meet the minimum required specifications (for example, refresh timing specifications) or was incompatible in pinout, depth, width, or design. Chip access time always can be less (that is, faster) as long as your chip is the correct type and meets all other specifications.

Substituting faster memory usually doesn't provide improved performance because the system still operates the memory at the same speed. In systems not engineered with a great deal of "forgiveness" in the timing between memory and system, however, substituting faster memory chips might improve reliability.

The same common symptoms result when the system memory has failed or is simply not fast enough for the system's timing. The usual symptoms are frequent parity-check errors or a system that does not operate at all. The POST also might report errors. If you're unsure of what chips to buy for your system, contact the system manufacturer or a reputable chip supplier.

EDO RAM

There is a new type of memory being offered for Pentium systems today called EDO (Extended Data Out) RAM. These are 72-pin SIMMs with specially manufactured chips that allow for a timing overlap between successive accesses. This allows for a tighter coupled access cycle and a performance improvement of 20 percent or so over regular non-EDO SIMMs. EDO RAM is ideal for systems with bus speeds of up to 66 MHz, which fits perfectly with the current and future Pentium and P6 processor architectures.

To actually utilize EDO memory, your motherboard chipset must support it. Currently, chipsets like the Intel Triton, Opti Viper, and ALI Aladdin offer support for EDO. Because these chips cost the same to manufacture as standard chips, the market has jumped on the EDO bandwagon, and virtually all new chipsets will be supporting it. Due to supply constraints, expect to pay more for EDO RAM than standard SIMMs, even though the production costs are not that much higher.

Upgrading by Increasing System Memory

Adding memory to a system is one of the most useful upgrades that you can perform and also one of the least expensive, especially when you consider the increased capabilities of DOS, Microsoft Windows, and OS/2 when you give them access to more memory. In some cases, doubling the memory can virtually double the speed of a computer.

Memory chips come in different shapes and sizes, yet all memory chips in which you are interested are called *DRAM*, or dynamic random-access memory. DRAM chips are the most common type of memory. These chips are considered to be dynamic because they need to be energized hundreds of times per second to hold information. If you shut off the power, the information is lost.

This section discusses adding memory, including selecting memory chips, installing memory chips, and testing the installation.

Upgrade Strategies

Adding memory can be an inexpensive solution; at this writing, the cost of memory has fallen to about $15 per megabyte. A small dose can give your computer's performance a big boost.

How do you add memory to your PC? You have three options, listed in order of convenience and cost:

- Adding memory in vacant slots on your motherboard.
- Replacing your current motherboard's memory with higher-capacity memory.
- Purchasing a memory expansion card.

Adding expanded memory to PC- or XT-type systems is not a good idea, mainly because an expanded memory board with a couple of megabytes of expanded memory installed can cost more than the entire system is worth. Also, this memory does not function for Windows, and a PC- or XT-class system cannot run OS/2. Instead, purchase a more powerful system—for example, an inexpensive 486SX—with greater expansion capabilities.

If you decide to upgrade to a more powerful computer system, you normally cannot salvage the memory from a PC or XT system. The 8-bit memory boards are useless in AT and Micro Channel systems, and the speed of the memory chips usually is inadequate for newer systems. Many new systems use high-speed SIMM modules rather than chips. A pile of 150ns (nanoseconds), 64K or 256K chips is useless if your next system is a high-speed system that uses SIMMs or memory devices faster than 70ns.

Be sure to weigh carefully your future needs for computing speed and for a multitasking operating system (OS/2, for example) with the amount of money that you spend to upgrade current equipment.

Adding Motherboard Memory

This section discusses *motherboard memory*—the memory actually installed on the motherboard—rather than the memory that resides on adapter boards. The first part of this section presents recommendations on selecting and installing chips. The last part of the section provides instructions for modifying an IBM XT Type 1 motherboard. This modification enables you to place a full 640K of memory on the motherboard, eliminating the need for memory-expansion boards. IBM's more recent XT Type 2 motherboards already include this modification.

Selecting and Installing Memory Chips or SIMMs

If you are upgrading a motherboard by adding memory, follow the manufacturer's guidelines on which memory chips or modules to purchase. As you learn in this chapter, memory comes in various form factors, including individual chips known as DIP (dual in-line pin) memory chips, SIMMs (single in-line memory modules), and SIPPs (single in-line pin packages). Your computer may use one or possibly a mixture of these form factors.

The maker of your computer's motherboard determines what type of memory chips are used. The following list describes each chip or module type:

- *DIPs.* Early computers used DIP (dual in-line pin) memory chips. A DIP memory chip is a rectangular chip that has 16 metal legs, eight on each side. To install such a memory chip, you must plug it in place. DIP chips are installed in multiples of nine. For example, you must install 36 separate 256-kilobit chips to acquire 1M of memory. Sometimes, the DIPs are permanently soldered to your motherboard.

- *SIMMs.* Single in-line memory modules are like small circuit boards with chips soldered on them. Different numbers of chips can be mounted on the SIMM, and the chips can be mounted on one or both sides of the SIMM. A SIMM has a row of contacts on one edge of the board. The contacts can be tin- or gold-plated. SIMMs are retained in the system by special sockets with positive latching mechanisms that lock the SIMMs in place. SIMM connectors use a high-force wiping contact that is extremely resistant to corrosion.

  SIMMs are available in two types—30-pin and 72-pin. The 30-pin modules come in 9-bit form with parity or 8-bit form for systems that lack parity checking. The 72-pin SIMMs are 36 bits wide with parity (32 data bits and four parity bits), or 32 bits wide without parity. Notice that the 9-bit and 36-bit SIMMs with parity always can be used in systems that lack parity checking and that the nonparity SIMMs cannot be used in normal systems that require parity bits. Systems that lack parity checking for memory are not recommended.

- *SIPPs.* Single in-line pin packages, sometimes called SIP, really are SIMMs with pins rather than contacts. The pins are designed to be installed in a long connector socket that is much cheaper than the standard SIMM socket. SIPPs are inferior to SIMMs because they lack the positive latching mechanism that retains the module, and the connector lacks the high-force wiping contacts that resist corrosion. SIPPs are rarely used today.

No matter what type of memory chips you have, the chips are installed in memory banks. A *memory bank* is a collection of memory chips that make up a block of memory. Each bank of memory is read by your processor in one pass. A memory bank does not work unless it is filled with memory chips.

Early 8088, 8086, and 286 PCs have four memory banks that are nine chips wide. These memory banks may be labeled 0 through 3 or A through D. The first eight chips are for holding data. The ninth chip is a parity chip meant to ensure that the numbers of the other eight are correct. Each chip is measured in bits, and eight chips make up a byte. Imagine that you had the first two banks full of 256-kilobit chips. How much memory is that? Well, 18 chips (9 chips × 2 banks) of 256-kilobit memory equals 512K.

286 computers usually can take four banks of 256-kilobit chips to make 1,024K (1M). Some 286 computers can handle up to 4M on the motherboard, using 1M chips. In 386SX-based computers, four memory banks are used, requiring 18 chips (16 plus two for parity), or in most cases two 30-pin (8- or 9-bit) SIMMs each. 386DX and 486 computers

often have between two and four memory banks, each bank using four 30-pin (8- or 9-bit) SIMMs or one 72-pin (32- or 36-bit) SIMM. Pentium computers also normally have between two and four banks of memory, but each bank usually requires two 72-pin (32- or 36-bit) SIMMs.

Installing extra memory on your motherboard is an easy way to add memory to your computer. Most systems have at least one vacant memory bank in which you can install extra memory and use it to speed your computer.

RAM-Chip Type (Capacity). Individual RAM chips come in different capacities. The capacity determines the number of data bits that can be stored in a chip of a particular size. For example, RAM chips for the original IBM PC store 16 kilobits of data; these RAM chips are the smallest used in any IBM-compatible system. The RAM chips for the original version of the IBM XT store 64 kilobits of data. The standard chip for Pentium based systems today is the 4M bit or 16M bit chip (usually found in SIMMs).

Before you add RAM to a system (or replace defective RAM chips), you must determine the memory chips required for your system. Your system documentation contains this information.

If you need to replace a defective RAM chip and do not have the system documentation, you can determine the correct chip for your system by inspecting the chips that are already installed. Each chip has markings that indicate the chip's capacity and speed. The following table lists the markings on individual 1M chips produced by various companies:

Markings	Manufacturer
TMS4C1024N/DJ	Texas Instruments
HM511000AP/AJP/AZP	Hitachi
MB81C1000P/PJ/PSZ	Fujitsu

If you do not have the documentation for your system and the manufacturer does not offer technical support, open your system case and carefully write down the markings that appear on your memory chips. Then contact a local computer store or mail-order chip vendor for help in determining the proper RAM chips for your system. Adding the wrong RAM chips to a system can make it as unreliable as leaving a defective chip on the motherboard and trying to use the system in that condition.

RAM-Chip Speed. RAM chips also come in various speeds. For example, 80ns or slower chips are used in older systems, and 60ns or 70ns chips are used in fast 486- and Pentium-based systems.

The motherboard manufacturer determines the correct speed of the memory chips installed in each system. IBM, for example, specifies different speed memory for different systems. Table 7.10 lists the required RAM-chip speeds and wait states for IBM motherboards.

Table 7.10 IBM Motherboard Memory Timing

System	CPU	Clock Speed (MHz)	Wait States	Memory-Access Time (ns)	Notes
PC	8088	4.77	1	200	
XT	8088	4.77	1	200	
AT	286	6	1	150	
AT	286	8	1	150	
XT-286	286	6	0	150	Zero wait
PS/1	286	10	1	120	
25	8086	8	0	150	Zero wait
30	8086	8	0	150	Zero wait
25-286	286	10	1	120	
30-286	286	10	1	120	
35 SX	386SX	20	0-2	85	Paged memory
40 SX	386SX	20	0-2	85	Paged memory
L40	386SX	20	0-2	80	Paged memory
50	286	10	1	150	
50Z	286	10	0	85	Zero wait
53 486SLC2	486SLC2	50	0-2	70	Interleaved memory, internal 16K cache
55 SX	386SX	16	0-2	100	Paged memory
56 486SLC3	486SLC3	75	0-2	70	Interleaved memory, internal 16K cache
57 SX	386SX	20	0-2	70	Paged memory
57 486SLC3	486SLC3	75	0-2	70	Interleaved memory, internal 16K cache
60	286	10	1	150	
65	386SX	16	0-2	100	Paged memory
70	386DX	16	0-2	85	Paged memory
70	386DX	20	0-2	85	Paged memory
70	386DX	25	0-5	80	External 64K cache
70	486DX	25	0-5	80	Internal 8K cache
P70	386DX	16	0-2	85	Paged memory
P70	386DX	20	0-2	85	Paged memory
P75	486DX	33	0-5	70	Internal 8K cache
76	486DX2	66	0-2	70	Interleaved memory, internal 8K cache
76	486SX	33	0-2	70	Interleaved memory, internal 8K cache
76	486DX4	100	0-2	70	Interleaved memory, internal 16K cache

(continues)

Table 7.10 Continued

System	CPU	Clock Speed (MHz)	Wait States	Memory-Access Time (ns)	Notes
77	486DX2	66	0-2	70	Interleaved memory, internal 8K cache
77	486SX	33	0-2	70	Interleaved memory, internal 8K cache
77	486DX4	100	0-2	70	Interleaved memory, internal 16K cache
80	386DX	16	0-2	80	Paged memory
80	386DX	20	0-2	80	Paged memory
80	386DX	25	0-5	80	External 64K cache
90	486SX	20	0-5	70	Interleaved memory, internal 8K cache
90	486SX	25	0-5	70	Interleaved memory, internal 8K cache
90	486DX	25	0-5	70	Interleaved memory, internal 8K cache, optional external 256K cache
90	486DX	33	0-5	70	Interleaved memory, internal 8K cache, optional external 256K cache
90	486DX	50	0-5	70	Interleaved memory, internal 8K cache, optional external 256K cache
95	486SX	20	0-5	70	Interleaved memory, internal 8K cache
95	486SX	25	0-5	70	Interleaved memory, internal 8K cache
95	486DX	25	0-5	70	Interleaved memory, internal 8K cache, optional external 256K cache
95	486DX	33	0-5	70	Interleaved memory, internal 8K cache, optional external 256K cache
95	486DX	50	0-5	70	Interleaved memory, internal 8K cache, optional external 256K cache

It won't hurt to install chips that are faster than required for your motherboard or memory card; buying faster memory chips can be a boon if you intend to transplant them to a faster computer in the future. Unfortunately, the faster memory won't speed your computer; your computer's design anticipates working at a certain speed and no faster.

The speed of a memory chip is printed on the surface of the chip. On the memory chips—whether they are the DIP, SIPP, or SIMM type—you will find an identifying number. The last two digits after the dash (—) are especially important, because they indicate the speed of your memory.

In some systems, the motherboard memory speed can be controlled. Systems with adjustable wait-state settings enable you to choose optimal performance by purchasing the proper high-speed memory or to choose lower performance by purchasing cheaper memory. Many compatibles offer a wait-state jumper or configuration option, which controls whether the motherboard runs with wait states. Running with zero wait states may require faster access speed memory.

Other systems can configure themselves dynamically to the memory installed. The PS/2 Model 90 and 95 system boards check the speeds of the SIMMs installed on the system board and adjust the number of wait states accordingly. Most other PS/2 systems simply check the speed of SIMMs installed on the system board and flag an error condition if the minimum speed requirements are not met.

Systems that use 72-pin SIMMs can detect both the speed and capacity of the installed SIMMs through four special contacts called *presence detect pins*. The motherboard can use these pins to determine the installed SIMM's rated speed and capacity, in much the same way that many cameras can tell what speed film you have loaded by "reading" a series of contacts on the film canister. In the Model 90 and Model 95, if the SIMM is slower than 70ns, the system adds wait states so that the rest of the memory can keep up. In other systems, such as the Model 70, if memory slower than the required 80ns or 85ns is installed, a 225 POST error message appears. If you look up this error code in the IBM error-code list in Appendix A, it says `Wrong-speed memory on system board`. This error message means that the installed memory is too slow for the system.

Systems with 16 MHz or faster clock speeds require extremely fast memory to keep up with the processor. In fact, the speeds that are required are so excessive that standard DRAM typically would be replaced by faster and more expensive static RAM (SRAM). One alternative—adding wait states to reduce the memory-speed requirements—greatly decreases performance, which is not what you want in a fast system.

RAM-Chip Architecture. Some special memory-architecture schemes have been devised to reduce the number of wait states required, boost overall system performance, and keep costs down. The following architecture schemes are most commonly used to increase memory performance:

- Paged memory
- Interleaved memory
- Memory caching

Paged memory is a simple scheme for improving memory performance that divides memory into pages ranging from 512 bytes to a few kilobytes long. The paging circuitry then enables memory locations within a page to be accessed with zero wait states. If the desired memory location is outside the current page, one or more wait states are added while the system selects the new page.

Paged memory has become common in higher-end 286 systems as well as in many 386 systems. For example, many PS/2 systems, such as the Model 70 and Model 80, use paged memory to increase performance so that slower 80ns or 85ns memory can be used.

Interleaved memory offers greater performance than paged memory. This higher-performance scheme combines two banks of memory into one, organized as even and odd bytes. With this combination, an access cycle can begin in the second bank while the first is already processing a previous access, and vice versa. By alternating access to even and odd banks, you can request data from one bank, and while the request is pending, the system can move to the next bank to process another request. The first request becomes available while the second request is still pending, and so on. By interleaving access to memory in this manner, a system can effectively double memory-access performance without using faster memory chips.

Many of the highest-performance systems use interleaved memory to achieve increased performance. Some systems that offer interleaved memory can use the interleaving function only if you install banks in matched-capacity pairs, which usually means adding two 36-bit SIMMs of equal capacity at a time. If you add only a single bank or add two banks of different capacity, the system still functions, but memory interleaving is disabled, and you pay a considerable performance penalty. Consult your system's technical-reference manual for more information.

Memory caching is the most popular and usually the most effective scheme for improving memory performance. This technique relies on a small amount (8K to 512K) of raw, high-speed memory fast enough to keep up with the processor with zero wait states. This small bank of cache memory often is rated at *15ns or less* in access speed. Because this rate is faster than normal DRAM components can handle, a special type of memory is used. This memory is called *SRAM* (static RAM). SRAM devices do not need the constant refresh signals that DRAM devices require. This feature, combined with other design properties, results in extremely fast access times and very high costs.

Although SRAM chips are expensive, only a small number of SRAM chips are required in a caching scheme. SRAM is used by a special cache-controller circuit that stores frequently accessed RAM locations and also is preloaded with the RAM values that the cache controller expects to be accessed next. The cache acts as an intelligent buffer between the CPU and slower dynamic RAM.

A *cache hit* means that the particular data the CPU wanted was available in the cache RAM and that no additional wait states are available for retrieving this data. A *cache miss* means that the data the CPU wanted had not been loaded into the cache RAM and that wait states must be inserted while the data is retrieved. A good cache controller has a hit ratio of 95 percent or more (the system runs with zero wait states 95 percent of the time). The net effect is that the system acts as though nearly all the memory is 15ns or less in speed, although most of the memory really is much slower (and, therefore, much less costly).

Systems based on the 486SX, SL, or DX processors include a cache controller and 8K of internal-cache RAM in the CPU that makes them much faster than earlier systems. The 486SLC CPU has a 1K internal cache, whereas the Pentium CPU includes two 8K internal caches—one for code and the other for data. 486DX4 processors have a 16K internal cache, while both the 486SLC2 and 486SLC3 processors have a 16K cache. Systems with 386SX or DX processors must use an external-cache controller with externally provided cache RAM; these systems have no internal cache. The 386SL provides a built-in cache controller, and the IBM-designed 386SLC incorporates virtually the same cache controller and 8K of built-in cache RAM as the 486 processors. IBM, therefore, can claim an 80 percent performance increase from the regular 386SX or DX chips for systems that use the 386SLC processor.

A CPU internal cache is called a primary or Level 1 (L1) cache, and an external cache is called a secondary or Level 2 (L2) cache. Typically, the larger the memory cache, the better the performance. A larger secondary processor cache, however, is no guarantee; you may find that the system with the least cache RAM can out perform a system with a greater amount of cache RAM. Actual performance depends on the efficiency of the cache controller and the system design; a cache integrated into a CPU, for example, can far out perform an external cache. For example, adding the 256K L2 cache RAM option to a PS/2 Model 90 or 95 with a 486DX processor offers only a small increase in performance relative to the 8K of L1 cache memory built into the 486 CPU chip, because the L1 cache integrated into the CPU can out perform an external (L2) cache. Also, adding cache RAM does not result in a proportional increase in performance. You often gain the best performance by using the middle amount of secondary cache that your computer can accept. A PC that can accommodate a 64K, 128K, or 256K secondary cache provides the most bang for the buck.

To get maximum system performance and reliability, the best recommendation for adding chips or SIMMs to a motherboard is to use memory rated at the speeds recommended by the manufacturer. Faster memory is likely to work in the system, but it creates no performance benefit and therefore is a waste of money.

The minimum access-time specification for motherboard memory in a specific system is listed in the system's technical reference manual. If you have an IBM-compatible system that lacks proper documentation, you can refer to other similar system documentation as a guide, because most compatibles follow the same requirements. Because of the variety of system designs on the market, however, you should try to acquire the proper documentation from the manufacturer.

Adding Adapter Boards

Memory expansion boards typically are a last resort way to add memory. For many systems (such as older models from Compaq) with proprietary local bus memory-expansion connectors, you must purchase all memory-expansion boards from that company. Similarly, IBM used proprietary memory connectors in the PS/2 Model 80 systems. For other industry-standard systems that use nonproprietary memory expansion (such as the IBM PC, XT, and AT) and most IBM-compatible systems, as well as most PS/2 systems, you can purchase from hundreds of vendors memory-expansion boards that plug into the standard bus slots.

Unfortunately, any memory expansion that plugs into a standard bus slot runs at bus speed rather than at full system speed. For this reason, most systems today provide standard SIMM-connector sockets directly on the motherboard so that the memory can be plugged directly into the system's local bus. Using memory adapter cards in these systems only slows them. Other systems use proprietary local bus connectors for memory-expansion adapters, which can cause additional problems and expense when you have to add or service memory.

In some cases, an adapter board can use slower memory than would be required on the system motherboard. (Memory adapters for PS/2 Models 50 and 60, for example, use 120ns memory chips.) Many systems run memory-expansion slots at a fixed slower speed—8 MHz for most ISA bus systems—so that installed adapters function properly. The PS/2 system memory adapters may be able to run more slowly than main memory because of the Micro Channel Architecture (MCA) interface's higher level of controls and capabilities. The MCA's asynchronous design enables adapters to remain independent of the processor's speed and to request additional wait states, as required, to accommodate the slower adapters.

Installing Memory

This section discusses installing memory chips—specifically, new RAM chips or memory modules. The section also covers the problems that you are most likely to encounter and how to avoid them; it also provides information on configuring your system to use new memory.

When you install or remove memory, you are most likely to encounter the following problems:

- Electrostatic discharge
- Broken or bent pins
- Incorrect switch and jumper settings

To prevent electrostatic discharge (ESD) when you install sensitive memory chips or boards, do not wear synthetic-fiber clothing or leather-soled shoes. Remove any static charge that you are carrying by touching the system chassis before you begin, or—better yet—wear a good commercial grounding strap on your wrist. You can order one from an electronics parts store or mail-order house. A grounding strap consists of a conductive wristband grounded at the other end by a wire clipped to the system chassis (usually with an alligator clip). Leave the system unit plugged in, but turned off,to keep it grounded.

Caution

Be sure to use a properly designed commercial grounding strap; *do not make one yourself.* Commercial units have a one-megohm resistor that serves as protection if you accidentally touch live power. The resistor ensures that you do not become the path of least resistance to the ground and therefore become electrocuted. An improperly designed strap can cause the power to conduct through you to the ground, possibly killing you.

Broken or bent leads are another potential problem associated with installing individual memory chips (DIPs) or SIPP modules. Sometimes, the pins on new chips are bent into a *V*, making them difficult to align with the socket holes. If you notice this problem on a DIP chip, place the chip on its side on a table, and press gently to bend the pins so that they are at a 90-degree angle to the chip. For a SIPP module, you may want to use needle-nose pliers to carefully straighten the pins so that they protrude directly down from the edge of the module, with equal amounts of space between pins; then you should install the chips in the sockets one at a time.

Caution

Straightening the pins on a DIP chip or SIPP module is not difficult work, but if you are not careful, you could easily break off one of the pins, rendering the chip or memory module useless. Use great care when you straighten the bent pins on any memory chip or module. You can use chip-insertion and pin-straightening devices to ensure that the pins are straight and aligned with the socket holes. These inexpensive tools can save you a great deal of time.

Each memory chip or module must be installed to point in a certain direction. Each chip has a polarity marking on one end. This marking may be a polarity notch, a circular indentation, or both. The chip socket may have a corresponding notch. Otherwise, the motherboard may have a printed legend that indicates the orientation of the chip. If the socket is not marked, you should use other chips as a guide. The orientation of the notch indicates the location of Pin 1 on the chip. Aligning this notch correctly with the others on the board ensures that you do not install the chip backward. Gently set each chip into a socket, ensuring that every pin is properly aligned with the connector into which it fits, and push the chip in firmly with both thumbs until the chip is fully seated.

SIMM memory is oriented by a notch on one side of the module that is not present on the other side. The socket has a protrusion that must fit into this notched area on one side of the SIMM. This protrusion makes it impossible to install a SIMM backward unless you break the connector. SIPP modules, however, do not plug into a keyed socket; you have to orient them properly. The system documentation can be helpful if the motherboard has no marks to guide you. You also can use existing SIPP modules as a guide.

Before installing memory, make sure that the system power is off. Then remove the PC cover and any installed cards. SIMMs snap easily into place, but chips can be more difficult to install. A chip-installation tool is not required, but it can make inserting the chips into sockets much easier. To remove chips, use a chip extractor or small screwdriver. Never try removing a RAM chip with your fingers, because you can bend the chip's pins or poke a hole in your finger with one of the pins. You remove SIMMs by releasing the locking tabs and either pulling or rolling them out of their sockets.

After adding the memory chips and putting the system back together, you may have to alter motherboard switches or jumper settings. The original PC includes two switch blocks with eight switches per block. Switch positions 1 through 4 of a PC's second switch block must be set to reflect the total installed memory. The XT has only one switch block, which is set to reflect the number of memory banks installed on the system board but not the expansion-card memory. Appendix A provides more detailed information about the PC and XT motherboard switch settings.

IBM AT and PS/2 systems have no switches or jumpers for memory. Rather, you must run a setup program to inform the system of the total amount of memory installed. IBM-compatible AT-type systems usually have a setup program built into the system ROM BIOS, and you must run this program after installing new memory to configure the system properly.

Most memory-expansion cards also have switches or jumpers that must be set. You often must make two settings when you configure a memory card. The first setting—a starting address for the memory on the card—usually enables the memory on the card to begin using system memory addresses higher than those used by any existing memory. The second setting is the total amount of memory installed on the card.

Because of the PS/2's influence in the market, many memory boards, as well as other types of adapter cards, are made without switches. Instead, these boards have a configuration program that is used to set up the card. The configuration is stored in a special nonvolatile memory device contained on the card; after the settings are made, the card can remember the settings permanently. The Intel AboveBoard 286 and Plus versions, for example, have this switchless setup and configuration capability. Following a menu-driven configuration program is much easier than flipping tiny switches or setting jumpers located on a card. Another benefit of software configuration is that you don't even have to open the system to reconfigure a card.

After configuring your system to work properly with the additional memory, you should run a memory-diagnostics program to ensure the proper operation of the new memory. At least two and sometimes three memory-diagnostics programs are available for all systems. In order of accuracy, these programs are:

- POST (Power-On Self Test)
- User diagnostics disk
- Advanced diagnostics disk
- Aftermarket diagnostics software

The POST is used every time you power up the system; you can press Ctrl+A at the opening menu to access the advanced diagnostics on the reference disk.

PS/2 systems include the user diagnostics and advanced diagnostics programs on one reference disk. The disk ensures that PS/2 owners have all three memory-test programs.

Owners of standard IBM PC systems receive (in the guide-to-operations manual) a diagnostics disk that contains a good memory test. PC owners should purchase the advanced diagnostics disk as part of the hardware-maintenance service manual package. If you have purchased this package, you should use the advanced diagnostics program.

Many additional diagnostics programs are available from aftermarket utility software companies. Several companies listed in Appendix B have excellent diagnostics and test software for testing memory and other components of a system. These programs are especially useful when the manufacturer of the system does not provide its own diagnostics.

Installing 640K on an XT Motherboard

This section describes how to install 640K of RAM on the system board in an IBM XT and an IBM Portable. The upgrade essentially changes what IBM calls an XT Type 1 motherboard to a Type 2 motherboard.

The upgrade consists of installing two banks of 256K chips and two banks of 64K chips on the motherboard, and then enabling the memory chips by adding a multiplexer/decoder chip to an empty socket provided for it, as well as jumper wire. The jumper wire enables an existing memory decoder chip (U44) to enable the additional memory. These modifications are relatively easy to perform and can be done with no soldering.

A memory-chip address is selected by two signals called *row-address select* (RAS) and *column-address select* (CAS). These signals determine where a value in a chip is located. You modify the signals by installing the jumper as indicated in this section so that the first two banks can be addressed four times deeper than they originally were, thus using the additional address locations in the 256K chips rather than in the original 64K chips.

To install 640K on an IBM XT motherboard, you must obtain the following parts from a chip vendor or electronics supply store (see Appendix B for sources):

- 18 256K-by-1-bit, 200ns (or faster) memory chips
- One 74LS158 (multiplexer/decoder) chip
- A small length of thin (30-gauge) jumper or wire-wrapping wire

After you have these parts, follow these steps:

1. Remove the motherboard (as explained in Chapter 4, "Motherboards").
2. Plug the 74LS158 chip into the socket labeled U84.

   All motherboard components are identified by an alphanumeric value. The letter usually indicates the type of component, and the number indicates a sequential component ID number for that type of component. The coding can differ among manufacturers, but most use this lettering scheme:

U	Integrated circuit
Q	Transistor
C	Capacitor
R	Resistor
T	Transformer

L Coil

Y Crystal

D Diode

Usually, component numbering follows a pattern in which the numbers increase as you move from left to right along the first row of components. Then the numbers begin again, at the left side and one row lower. You should be able to locate all the IC chips, starting with U1 in the upper-left corner of the board and ending with U90 in the lower-right corner.

3. Remove the IC installed in the socket labeled U44.

4. Install a jumper wire connecting Pin 1 to Pin 8 on the chip removed from position U44. To avoid making changes that you cannot undo later, it is easiest to wrap the ends of the jumper wire around the indicated IC pins. Be sure that the ends of the wire are wrapped securely around pins 1 and 8 and that the connection is good. Route the wire on the underside of the IC so that the wire is held in place when you install the chip. Reinstall the chip with the jumper in place. The IC might sit slightly higher in the socket because of the wire underneath it, so make sure that it is seated as far as it goes.

Caution

Be careful with the U44— it is a unique IBM programmable array logic (PAL) chip that you cannot purchase separately. A PAL chip is burned with a circuit pattern, much as a ROM chip is burned with data values. The only way to obtain the chip is to purchase a new motherboard from IBM. Some chip houses, such as Microprocessors Unlimited (see the vendor list in Appendix B), sell a copy of this PAL chip with the jumper wire modification burned in. Using one of these modified PAL chips is an alternative to adding the jumper wire manually, but be aware that most companies charge $20 for the chip. Adding the wire yourself is much cheaper.

Another alternative to adding the jumper wire to the chip in U44 is soldering two jumper pins into the plated holes numbered 1 and 2 in the jumper pad labeled E2. Using a standard plug-in jumper, you install a jumper across the two added pins. I normally do not recommend this method unless you are experienced with a soldering iron. All IBM XT Type 2 motherboards already have this modification built in.

5. Remove the 18 existing 64K-by-1-bit chips from banks 0 and 1. Reinstall the chips in banks 2 and 3 (if 64K chips are not already in these banks) or store them as spare chips.

6. Install the 18 new 256K-by-1-bit chips in banks 0 and 1.

7. Be sure that switches 3 and 4 of switch block SW1 are set to Off.

8. Replace the motherboard and restore all other system components except memory cards.

Remember that the motherboard now has 640K on it and that no other boards must address that space. If other memory cards were previously configured to supply memory in the first 640K area, you must reconfigure these cards or remove them from the system.

9. Power up the system, and test the installed memory for 640K without other memory-adapter cards.

If all operations are successful, you have performed an inexpensive memory upgrade that matches the capabilities of the Type 2 XT motherboard from IBM.

Upgrading the ROM BIOS

In this section, you learn that ROM BIOS upgrades can improve a system in many ways. You also learn that the upgrades can be difficult and may require much more than plugging in a generic set of ROM chips.

The *ROM BIOS*, or read-only memory basic input-output system, provides the crude brains that get your computer's components working together. A simple $30-to-$90 BIOS replacement can give your computer faster performance and more features.

The BIOS is the reason why DOS can operate on virtually any IBM-compatible system despite hardware differences. Because the BIOS communicates with the hardware, the BIOS must be specific to the hardware and match it completely. Instead of creating their own BIOSes, many computer makers buy a BIOS from specialists such as American Megatrends Inc. (AMI), Award Software, Microid Research, and Phoenix Technologies Ltd. A hardware manufacturer that wants to license a BIOS must undergo a lengthy process of working with the BIOS company to tailor the BIOS code to the hardware. This process is what makes upgrading a BIOS so difficult. BIOS usually resides on ROM chips on the motherboard; some newer PS/2 systems from IBM, however, have a disk-loaded BIOS that is much easier to upgrade.

The BIOS is a collection of small computer programs embedded in an *EPROM* (erasable programmable read-only memory) chip or chips, depending on the design of your computer. That collection of programs is the first thing loaded when you start your computer, even before the operating system. Simply put, the BIOS has three main functions:

- Tests your computer's components when it is turned on. This test is called the Power-On Self Test, or POST. The POST tests your computer's memory, motherboard, video adapter, disk controller, keyboard, and other crucial components.
- Finds the operating system and loads, or boots, it. This operation is called the bootstrap loader routine. If an operating system is found, it is loaded and given control of your computer.
- After an operating system is loaded, the BIOS works with your processor to give software programs easy access to your computer's specific features. For example,

the BIOS tells your computer how to work with your video card and hard disk when a software program requires these devices.

In older systems, you often must upgrade the BIOS to take advantage of some other upgrade. To install some of the newer IDE (Integrated Drive Electronics) hard drives and 1.44M or 2.88M floppy drives in older machines, for example, you may need a BIOS upgrade. Machines still are being sold with older BIOSes that do not support the user-definable drive-type feature required for easy installation of an IDE drive or that may have timing problems associated with IDE drives.

The following list shows the primary functions of a ROM BIOS upgrade:

- Adding 720K, 1.44M, or 2.88M 3 1/2-inch floppy drive support to a system
- Eliminating controller- or device-driver-based hard disk parameter translation for MFM, RLL, IDE, or ESDI drives with 1,024 or fewer cylinders by using a user-definable hard drive type matched to the drive
- Adding support for block-mode Programmed I/O (PIO) transfers for a Fast-ATA (AT Attachment Interface) (Enhanced-IDE) hard disk
- Adding 101-key Enhanced Keyboard support
- Adding compatibility for Novell networks
- Adding compatibility for SVGA displays
- Adding support for additional serial (COM) ports and printer ports
- Adding password protection
- Adding virus protection
- Adding support for additional floppy disk drives
- Correcting known bugs or compatibility problems with certain hardware and software

Because of the variety of motherboard designs on the market, ordering a BIOS upgrade often is more difficult than it sounds. If you have a name-brand system with a well-known design, the process can be simple. For many lesser-known compatible systems, however, you must give the BIOS vendor information about the system, such as the type of manufacturer's chipset that the motherboard uses.

For most BIOS upgrades, you must obtain the following information:

- The make and model of the system unit
- The type of CPU (for example, 286, 386DX, 386SX, 486DX, 486SX, and so on)
- The make and version of the existing BIOS
- The part numbers of the existing ROM chips (you may have to peel back the labels to read this information)

- The make, model, or part numbers of integrated motherboard chipsets, if used (for example, Intel, ALI, Chips & Technologies, VLSI, OPTI, UMC, and others)

An *integrated chipset* is a group of chips on the original AT motherboard that can perform the functions of hundreds of discrete chips. Many chipsets offer customizable features that are available only if you have the correct BIOS. Most differences among systems today lie in the variety of integrated chipsets that are now used to manufacture PCs and in the special initialization required to operate these chips.

The BIOS also must support variations in keyboard-controller programming and in the way that nonstandard features such as speed switching are handled. A computer that uses the Chips & Technologies NEAT chipset, for example, must have a BIOS specifically made for it. The BIOS must initialize the NEAT chipset registers properly; otherwise, the machine does not even boot. The BIOS also must have support for this chipset's special features. Each of the 20 or more popular chipsets for 286, 386, 486, and Pentium machines requires specific BIOS support for proper operation. A generic BIOS may boot some systems, but certain features, such as shifting to and from protected mode and speed switching, may not be possible without the correct BIOS.

Keyboard-Controller Chips

Besides the main system ROM, AT-class computers also have a keyboard controller or keyboard ROM, which is a keyboard-controller microprocessor with its own built-in ROM. The keyboard controller usually is an Intel 8042 microcontroller, which incorporates a microprocessor, RAM, ROM, and I/O ports. The keyboard controller usually is a 40-pin chip, often with a label that has a copyright notice identifying the BIOS code programmed into the chip.

The keyboard controller controls the reset and A20 lines, and also deciphers the keyboard scan codes. The A20 line is used in extended memory and other protected-mode operations. In many systems, one of the unused ports is used to select the CPU clock speed. Because of the tie-in with the keyboard controller and protected-mode operation, many problems with keyboard controllers become evident when you use either Windows or OS/2. If you experience lockups or keyboard problems with either Windows or OS/2 software—or with any software that runs in protected mode, such as Lotus 1-2-3 Release 3.x—get a replacement from your BIOS vendor or system-board vendor.

IBM systems do not need a replacement of the keyboard controller for upgrade purposes. (Replacement is difficult because the chip normally is soldered in.) Most manufacturers of IBM-compatible systems install the keyboard-controller chip in a socket so that you can upgrade or replace it easily. If you upgrade the BIOS in your system, the BIOS vendor often includes a compatible keyboard controller as well. You usually do not have to buy the controller unless your old keyboard controller has a problem with the new BIOS.

BIOS Manufacturers and Vendors

Several BIOS manufacturers have developed ROM BIOS software for use in upgrading IBM or IBM-compatible systems. The following companies are the largest manufacturers of ROM BIOS software:

- Phoenix
- American Megatrends International (AMI)
- Microid Research (MR)
- Award

Phoenix pioneered the IBM-compatible BIOS and the legal means to develop a product that is fully compatible with IBM's BIOS without infringing on the corporation's copyright. Phoenix first introduced many new features, such as user-defined hard drive types and 1.44M drive support. The Phoenix BIOS has a very good Power-On Self Test; this thorough POST presents a complete set of failure codes for diagnosing problems, especially the ones that occur when a system seems to be dead. (Appendix A contains a complete list of Phoenix BIOS POST error codes.)

The Phoenix BIOS documentation, a complete three-volume reference package, is one of the product's most useful features. This documentation includes *System BIOS for IBM PC/XT/AT Computers and Compatibles, CBIOS for IBM PS/2 Computers and Compatibles*, and *ABIOS for IBM PS/2 Computers and Compatibles*. I recommend these excellent reference works, published by Addison-Wesley, even if you do not have the Phoenix BIOS (although some of its specific information does not apply to other systems).

The BIOS produced by AMI is very popular and surpasses even Phoenix in new system installations. The AMI BIOS offers a less comprehensive Power-On Self Test than the Phoenix BIOS does, but it has an extensive diagnostics program in ROM. You even can purchase the program separately, as AMIDIAG. The in-ROM version, however, lacks the capability to test memory—a crucial capability if the failure is in the first bank. On the other hand, the BIOS is very compatible with the PC standard, available for several different chipsets and motherboards, and has been handled responsibly from the support level. When problems have occurred, AMI has fixed them, earning this program full compatibility with OS/2 and other difficult environments.

Because AMI manufactures its own motherboards, it has a distinct advantage over other BIOS companies. If the motherboard and BIOS are made by the same source, the single vendor probably can resolve any interaction problems between the BIOS and motherboard quickly, without shifting blame for the problem to another party. I recommend buying AMI's motherboards, because you generally don't have to worry about compatibility problems between the AMI BIOS and the AMI motherboard. Even if problems occur, AMI corrects them.

Microid Research is newer than some of the other BIOS manufacturers, but its BIOS has proved to be very compatible. The MR BIOS, as it is called, supports several CPU and motherboard chipset combinations. The MR BIOS offers one of the easiest and most informative setup programs available; this program does a good job of explaining the options. Some of you know that setting the advanced chipset functions is not always intuitive with the other BIOS vendors' products. In short, I recommend that you look at the MR BIOS if you are considering a BIOS upgrade or configuring a bare motherboard from scratch.

Award, the third-largest manufacturer of BIOS software, has made a name for itself with many system vendors, because it licenses the BIOS code to them for further modification. AST, for example, purchased the rights to the Award BIOS for its own systems and now can modify the BIOS internally, as though it created the BIOS from scratch. In a sense, AST could develop its own custom BIOS, using the Award code as a starting point. Award also provides precustomized BIOS code for manufacturers. Although Award's BIOS is not yet as popular as the Phoenix and AMI BIOSes, it is very popular, and compatibility even in tough environments such as OS/2 is ensured.

If you want to replace or upgrade your BIOS, you can obtain replacement chips directly from the BIOS manufacturer or from the following recommended distributors:

- *Micro Firmware Inc.* Micro Firmware offers an extensive line of Phoenix BIOS upgrades, with more than 50 common 8088, 286, 386, and 486 versions available. This company develops BIOS upgrades for specific hardware platforms, even when the original motherboard manufacturer is no longer in business. Many other BIOS vendors sell BIOSes developed by Micro Firmware for specific platforms.

- *Washburn & Company Distributors.* This licensed AMI distributor deals exclusively with AMI BIOS upgrades. Washburn has complete AMI motherboard and BIOS packages. A primary distributor for AMI, Washburn has great expertise in dealing with BIOS upgrade problems. The company also sells Second Nature, a disk drive support product that may eliminate the need for a BIOS if all you want is additional hard disk or floppy drive support.

- *Microid Research.* This company manufactures and sells its own MR BIOS direct, and offers technical support as well.

Special ROM BIOS-Related Problems

Some known problems exist in certain ROM BIOS versions as well as in some systems sold during the past few years. Several of these problems have the potential to affect a large number of people, either because the problem is severe or many systems have the problem. This section describes some of the most important known BIOS- and system-interaction problems and also provides solutions for the problems.

Some systems with BIOSes even as recent as 1992 or 1993 may not start after you upgrade to DOS 6.x. Some of the older BIOSes came on line when DOS 3.3 or earlier was the current operating system. As a result, those older BIOSes often cannot take advantage of the advanced features of DOS 6.x.

If you use an AT&T 6300 system, you will want to use BIOS Version 1.43, which is the most recent one made for the system. This version solves many problems with older 6300 systems and also provides support for a 720K floppy disk drive. You can order BIOS Version 1.43 for about $35 from the AT&T National Parts Sales Center (see Appendix B) under part number 105203780.

Some systems with the AMI BIOS have had problems with IDE hard disk drives. IDE (Integrated Drive Electronics) drives have been touted as being fully port-compatible with existing ST-506/412 (MFM or RLL) and ESDI drives. Some IDE drives, however, take somewhat longer than they should after certain commands to present valid data at their ports. In late 1989, AMI received many reports of problems with IDE drives, especially Conner and Toshiba drives. Because of these timing problems, AMI BIOS versions dated earlier than April 9, 1990 are not recommended for use with IDE drives, and data loss can result if earlier versions are used. You may experience `Drive C not ready` errors with certain IDE drives, such as those from Conner Peripherals. If you have a computer with an IDE drive and an AMI BIOS dated earlier than 04/09/90, you should get a newer BIOS from the system vendor.

To make sure that you have the correct AMI BIOS version, look for this figure in the lower-left corner of the screen when you boot your computer:

```
xxxx-zzzz-040990-Kr
```

The `040990` indicates a BIOS date of April 9, 1990—the minimum version to use. Older versions are OK only if you are *not* using IDE drives. The `xxxx-zzzz` indicates the BIOS type code and an OEM (original equipment manufacturer) ID number. For AMI-manufactured motherboards, for example, the BIOS type code is DAMI-[model code]. The `r` indicates the keyboard-controller chip's revision level, which should be revision F or later to avert problems.

Changes to an Existing BIOS

If you have access to the correct tools and knowledge, you can perform some interesting modifications or upgrades to your system by altering your existing ROM BIOS. This section discusses several modifications that I have performed on my own systems. (These modifications have worked *for me*, and I am not necessarily recommending that anyone else perform them.) If nothing else, the research and development of these modifications taught me much about the way some things work in an IBM-compatible system, and I know that many of you are interested in some of this information.

Note

These types of modifications are for readers who are especially technically astute or extremely adventurous; they are not recommended for everyone, especially for readers for whom system reliability is of crucial importance. But the following information should prove to be interesting even for readers of this book who do not attempt these operations on their systems.

Using EPROM Programming Equipment. You can accomplish some interesting modifications or upgrades and even repairs of a system by using an EPROM programmer (or *burner*, as it is sometimes called). *EPROM* stands for erasable programmable read-only memory—a type of chip that can have a program burned, or fused, into it by way of an EPROM programmer device. These devices cost anywhere from about $100 to several thousands of dollars, depending on the capabilities of the device.

Most cheaper EPROM programmers are more than adequate for burning PC ROMs. Both JDR Microdevices and Jameco Electronics sell various EPROM programmers, as do several other distributors. I currently use and recommend one made by Andromeda Research (see Appendix B). This device is very inexpensive, fast, and will handle most types of chips including the new flash ROMs. These programmers either connect to a slot or use the standard serial or parallel ports for communications. The Andromeda Research EPROM programmer connects to a system parallel port that gives it flexibility and performance that are not equaled in most other units.

To erase an EPROM, you also need an EPROM eraser, an inexpensive device ($30 to $100) that exposes the EPROM chip to intense ultraviolet light for about three to five minutes. I recommend and use a simple unit made by DataRace (see the vendor list). With an EPROM programmer, you can modify or customize your system ROM BIOS, as well as the ROM chips found on many expansion cards. You also can add hard drives to the drive table, change sign-on or error messages, and make specific changes to increase performance or otherwise customize your system. The ability to alter ROMs gives you an extra level of capability in upgrading and repairing systems.

Note

You also can use an EPROM programmer to work with ROMs in other types of computer systems. I have even altered the ROMs that contain the programs and data tables for the electronic control module (ECM) in several General Motors automobiles, giving me total control of turbocharger boost settings, engine-temperature and electric-fan calibrations, vehicle speed governors, torque converter clutch operation, and even fuel-injector and spark-advance curves.

Backing Up Your BIOS. One often overlooked benefit of an EPROM programmer is that you can use it to essentially back up your ROMs in case they are later damaged. Many hardware vendors, such as IBM, do not offer ROM upgrades for their systems, and the only way to repair a motherboard or card with a damaged ROM is to burn a new copy from a backup. The backup can be in the form of another EPROM chip with the original program burned in or even in the form of a disk file. I keep files containing images of the ROMs in each of my motherboards and expansion cards, in case I have to burn a new copy to repair one of my systems.

To create a disk-file copy of your motherboard ROM BIOS, you can place the ROM in an EPROM programmer and use the function provided by the device to read the EPROM into a disk file, or you can use the DOS DEBUG program to read your ROM BIOS from memory and transfer it to disk as a file. To use DEBUG in this manner, follow these instructions:

```
C:\>DEBUG                    ;Run DEBUG
-N SEG-F.ROM                 ;Name the file
-R BX                        ;Change BX register (high-order file size)
BX 0000                      ;  from 0
:1                           ;  to 1 (indicates 64K file)
-M F000:0 FFFF CS:0          ;Move BIOS data to current code segment
-W 0                         ;Write file from offset 0 in code segment
Writing 10000 bytes          ;  10000h = 64K
-Q                           ;Quit DEBUG
```

These instructions save the entire 64K segment range from F000:0000 to 000:FFFF as a file by first setting up the name and size of the file to be saved and then moving (essentially, copying) the ROM BIOS code to the current code segment when DEBUG was loaded. The data then can be written to the disk. IBM AT systems and most compatibles have only 64K of BIOS, but IBM PS/2 systems normally have a full 128K of BIOS code that resides in both segment E000 and F000. For these systems, repeat the procedure, using E000:0 as the starting address in the Move command (rather than F000:0) and, of course, a different file name in the Name command. One important quirk of this procedure is that the commands should be entered in the order indicated here. In particular, the Name command must precede the Move command, or some of the data at the beginning of the current code-segment area will be trashed.

You also can use this routine to back up any adapter-board ROMs installed in your system. To back up the ROM on the IBM SCSI adapter with cache installed in my system, for example, a similar DEBUG session works. You must know the ROM's starting address and ending address or length to continue. My SCSI adapter ROM is located at D400:0 and is 16K, or 4,000H (hex) bytes long, which means that it ends at D400:3FFF. To save this ROM as a file, execute these instructions:

```
C:\>DEBUG                    ;Run DEBUG
-N SCSI.ROM                  ;Name the file
-R CX                        ;Change CX register (low-order file size)
CX 0000                      ;  from 0
:4000                        ;  to 4000 (indicates 16K file)
-M D400:0 3FFF CS:0          ;Move BIOS data to current code segment
-W 0                         ;Write file from offset 0 in code segment
Writing 04000 bytes          ;  4000h = 16K
-Q                           ;Quit DEBUG
```

Most EPROM programmers are supplied with software that runs in your PC and enables you to control the unit. Available functions include the capability to read a ROM and save it as a disk file or write a ROM from a disk file, and the capability to copy or test ROMs. The software also should be capable of splitting a file into even and odd addresses for 16- or 32-bit systems, as well as combining two split files into one. Another requirement is the capability to calculate the proper checksum byte (usually, the last byte) in the ROM so that diagnostics passes it. All the programmers mentioned have these functions and more.

Removing the POST Speed Check. One problem in the IBM AT and XT-286 systems is that the clock speed is checked during the Power-On Self Test (POST). Checking the clock speed probably is a good idea, but it causes problems if you want to take advantage of the socketed clock crystal in these systems for a cheap and easy speedup. Most IBM compatibles do not have this speed check and can run at different clock rates, usually with no modifications of the BIOS required.

In IBM systems, the Verify Speed/Refresh Clock Rates test checks the system refresh rate (clock speed) to ensure that it is 6 or 8 MHz, depending on which IBM system you have. A marginally faster or slower rate causes the test to fail and results in a POST error of one long and one short beep, followed by a halt (`HLT`) instruction.

This test occurs at POST checkpoint 11h, which is sent to the manufacturer's test port 80h. A failure of this test, as indicated by one of the POST-card products that read this port, can be identified by reading 11h as the last value sent to the manufacturer's test port. To eliminate the test and enable a faster-than-normal clock rate, you must patch the instruction at the proper location from a 73h (JAE—Jump if Above or Equal) to an EBh (JMP—Jump unconditionally); this patch causes the test for an abnormally high refresh rate (resulting in a low test value) to pass through the JAE instruction. When this instruction is changed to a JMP instruction, the test never passes through and falls into the error routine, no matter how fast the rate.

Notice that the test for a slow refresh rate still is intact and that it fails if the clock is below 6 or 8 MHz, depending on the system. The JAE instruction occurs at F000:05BC in IBM AT systems with the 06/10/85 or 11/15/85 ROM BIOS versions and at F000:05C0 in XT-286 systems. The original AT system with the 01/10/84 BIOS *does not have this test*. By creating a new set of chips with this value changed by an EPROM programmer, you can eliminate this speed check and enable faster clock rates.

Modifying ROM BIOS Hard Disk Drive Parameter Tables. Probably the most common change made to a BIOS is adding or changing drives in existing hard drive tables. For example, I have added two new drive types to one of my systems. Those types—25 and 26—have these parameters:

Type	Cylinders	Heads	WPC	Ctrl	LZ	S/T	Meg	MB
25	918	15	65535	08h	918	17	114.30	119.85
26	918	15	65535	08h	918	26	174.81	183.31

See Chapter 14, "Hard Disk Drives," for more information about these parameters. In my old AT system, these table entries originally were unused (zeros), as are the remainder of types from 27 through 47. By burning a new set of ROMs with these two new completed entries, I can use my Maxtor XT-1140 drive to maximum capacity with an MFM controller (as type 25) or an RLL controller (as type 26). This setup precludes the need for a controller BIOS to override the motherboard table values and also saves me some memory in the C000 or D000 segments, where a hard disk controller ROM normally would reside. The procedure also makes my system more standard. If you are interested in performing this modification, get the *IBM AT Technical Reference Manual*, which documents the position and format of the drive tables in the BIOS.

Changing the Hard Disk Controller Head Step Rate. Another, more complicated modification that you can perform is to increase the stepping rate of the hard disk controller. The first edition of this book briefly mentioned this modification, and a reader wrote to me to express interest in it. This edition explains the precise nature of this modification and what is being changed, to give you greater insight into how the BIOS and disk controller work together. The performance gain, in fact, is relatively slight; I see making the change as being a learning experience more than anything else.

The Western Digital AT Controllers (1002/1003/1006) used by IBM in the original AT system, as well as in other compatible controllers (such as those from Data Technology Corporation and Adaptec), have a default head-stepping rate of 35μsec (microseconds). The fastest usable step rate is 16μsec—more than twice as fast. Most ST-506/412 hard disks have optimum stepping rates as low as 10μsec. By decreasing the rate to 16μsec, you can improve the seeking performance of the drive, resulting in an improvement of several milliseconds or more during an average seek. Because the standard rate is so slow compared with the optimum rate, many ST-506/412 drives—especially fast-seeking drives—do not perform to their manufacturer-rated seek performance unless the step rate from the controller is optimized in this manner.

You can decrease the step rate to 16μsec in two ways. The easiest and best way is to simply set a jumper on the controller card. Not all cards, however, support this option. In fact, only one of the many Western Digital ST-506/412 controllers—the WD1003-WAH (ST-506/412 MFM, no floppy support)—supports this option. None of the other WD cards for the AT permits you to change the step rate by way of a jumper. Adaptec, on the other hand, has a jumper for selecting the step rate on all its AT ST-506/412 controllers. Other than Adaptec's cards, most cards do not have a jumper and require other means of changing the step rate.

The second method of changing the step rate is universal and works with virtually all AT bus ST-506/412 controllers, regardless of whether they are MFM or RLL or whether they support floppy drives. You make the change by changing two bytes in the ROM BIOS hard disk support code, which alters the way that two specific commands are sent to the controller card.

First, consider a little background on the way that the BIOS and controller operate. When DOS reads or writes data to or from a hard disk, it accesses the disk through the ROM BIOS. Specifically, DOS uses the Int 13h (h = hexadecimal) functions provided in the BIOS. Int 13h functions are commands incorporated into the BIOS of an AT system that enable DOS (or any other software) to perform specific commands in relation to the drive. These Int 13h commands then are translated into direct controller-register-level commands by the BIOS. The direct controller commands are called *command control block* (CCB) commands, because each command must be presented to the controller in the form of a 7-byte command block with the command byte itself being the last (seventh) one. The other six bytes contain information such as the number of sectors on which to operate, as well as the cylinder and head positions where the command operates.

Sixteen Int 13h commands are available for hard disks in the IBM AT BIOS. Some of these commands, such as the Get Disk Type BIOS command, perform functions that do not involve accessing the controller or drive. Most other commands, however, are translated by the BIOS to the required code to send one of eight total CCB commands to the controller.

Table 7.11 shows the Int 13h BIOS commands and the specific CCB commands that the BIOS executes in the process.

Table 7.11 Int 13h AT Hard Disk BIOS and AT Controller CCB Commands

BIOS Command	Description	CCB Command	Description
00h	Reset Disk System	91h 10h	Set Parameters Recalibrate
01h	Get Status of Last Operation	—	—
02h	Read Sectors	20h	Read Sector
03h	Write Sectors	30h	Write Sector
04h	Verify Sectors	40h	Read Verify
05h	Format Track	50h	Format Track
08h	Read Drive Parameters	—	—
09h	Initialize Drive Characteristics	91h	Set Parameters
0Ah	Read Long	22h	Read Sector
0Bh	Write Long	32h	Write Sector
0Ch	Seek	70h	Seek
0Dh	Alternate Hard Disk Reset	10h	Recalibrate
10h	Test for Drive Ready	—	—
11h	Recalibrate Drive	10h	Recalibrate
14h	Controller Internal Diagnostic	80h	Diagnose
15h	Get Disk Type	—	—

Although only eight CCB commands are specific to the standard Western Digital (or compatible) AT hard disk controller, variations of some of the commands exist. Each CCB command consists of a single byte, with the most significant four bits (bits 4–7) of the byte indicating the actual command and the least significant four bits (bits 0–3) indicating various command options. For two of the CCB commands, the option bits indicate—and, in fact, set—the step rate for the controller. By changing these bits, you also change the default step rate.

Table 7.12 shows the eight standard CCB commands.

Table 7.12 WD1002/WD1003/WD1006 AT Hard Disk Controller CCB Commands

CCB Command	Description
10h-1Fh	Recalibrate
20h-23h	Read Sector
30h-33h	Write Sector
40h-41h	Read Verify
50h	Format Track
70h-7Fh	Seek
80h	Diagnose
91h	Set Parameters

In each of these commands, the CCB command byte is sent to the controller as the seventh byte of the total command block. The primary value is the first one listed in the chart. By setting the option bits, you can alter the command function. For example, the Read Sector command is 20h. By adding +1h to the command byte (making it 21h), you disable automatic retries in case of errors. This step prevents the controller from automatically rereading the sector as many as 19 additional times, in some cases; instead, the error is reported immediately. For error-correction code (ECC) errors, the controller simply attempts an immediate ECC correction, rather than rereading the sector as many as eight times in attempting to get a good read before making the ECC correction.

You can disable retries only for the Read Sector, Write Sector, and Read Verify commands. This capability is especially useful during low-level formatting, surface analyzing, or even just Read Verify testing of the drive, because any errors are reported more accurately without automatic retries taking place.

You can set another option for the Read Sector and Write Sector commands. This option involves the ECC bytes (an additional four bytes of data past the data area of the sector); it makes the sector read or write include a total 516 bytes instead of the normal 512. To set the "long" option, add +2h to the Read Sector or Write Sector CCB byte value. To change the standard Read Sector command (20h) to include the ECC bytes, for example, you add +2h, which results in a CCB command byte value of 22h. The option to include the ECC bytes during a read or write is especially useful in testing the ECC circuitry on the controller by specifically writing incorrect values and then reading them back to see the ECC in action.

For the Read Sector and Write Sector CCB commands, you can combine the disable-retries option with the long option by adding the two options (+1h and +2h = +3h), a procedure that results in a CCB command byte value of 23h (Read Sector) or 33h (Write Sector).

The last two commands—Recalibrate and Seek—have options that you can set through the option bits. For these two commands only, the option bits are used to set the stepping rate for subsequent seek commands to the drive. By adding a value from 1h through Fh to the CCB command byte for the Recalibrate or Seek commands, you can change the step rate from the default of 35μsec to something else.

The following table shows the different step rates that you can set by adding the step option to these commands.

Step Option	Step Rate (μsec)
0h	35
1h	500
2h	1,000
3h	1,500
4h	2,000
5h	2,500
6h	3,000
7h	3,500

Step Option	Step Rate (µsec)
8h	4,000
9h	4,500
Ah	5,000
Bh	5,500
Ch	6,000
Dh	6,500
Eh	3.2
Fh	16

In this case, you want to add Fh to change the step rate from the default 35µsec to 16µsec. Notice that the other possible values are much too slow (500 to 6,500µsec) and that the 3.2µsec rate is much too fast for most drives. To change the Recalibrate and Seek commands to use the 16µsec step rate, you must patch the BIOS, changing the 10h and 70h to 1Fh and 7Fh, respectively. You essentially are patching the code that is executed when an Int 13h, Function 11h (Recalibrate Drive), or Function 0Ch (Seek) BIOS command is executed. These BIOS routines contain the code that sends the 10h (Recalibrate) or 70h (Seek) CCB commands to the controllers. Because the other BIOS routines that also execute the CCB Recalibrate command do so by calling the same Int 13h Function 11h code, only one patch is required to change all occurrences of the CCB Recalibrate command.

Because these two commands can be in different positions in different BIOS, the following code shows you how to find them by using the DOS DEBUG command:

```
C:\>DEBUG                      ;Run DEBUG
-S F000:0 L 0 C6 46 FE 10      ;Search ROM for Recalibrate command
F000:30CF                      ; Found it!
-S F000:0 L 0 C6 46 FE 70      ;Search ROM for Seek command
F000:309A                      ; Found it!
-Q                             ;Quit
```

The first Search command locates the code sent to the controller for a CCB Recalibrate command, and the second Search locates the Seek command. The 10h (Recalibrate) command is at F000:30D2h in this example, because the address returned by the Search command points to the beginning of the search string, not to the end.

Remember to add 3 to each location returned for the actual location of the 10h or 70h command. The 70h byte, for example, is at F000:309Dh. These "found" locations vary from system to system; this example used an IBM AT Model 339 with an 11/15/85 BIOS. Therefore, you can change these bytes to 1Fh and 7Fh, respectively. You must have an EPROM programmer to record these changes in another set of chips.

This section examined some simple changes that you can make in a ROM BIOS with the help of an EPROM programmer. The steps involved in modifying or burning the ROMs were not described, because these instructions normally are included with the programmer device that you purchase.

Using a Flash BIOS. Flash ROM is a type of EEPROM chip that is included in several systems today. *EEPROM* (electrically erasable programmable read-only memory) is a type of ROM chip that you can erase and reprogram directly in the system without using ultraviolet light and an EPROM programmer device. Using Flash ROM enables a manufacturer to send out ROM upgrades on disk; you then can load the upgrade into the Flash ROM chip on the motherboard without removing and replacing the chip. This method saves time and money for both the system manufacturer and the end user.

Normally, the Flash ROM in a system is write-protected, and you must disable the protection before performing an update, usually by means of a jumper or switch that controls the lock on the ROM update. Without the lock, any program that knows the right instructions can rewrite the ROM in your system—not a comforting thought. Without the write protection, it is conceivable that virus programs could be written that copy themselves directly into the ROM BIOS code in your system! Fortunately, I have not seen an implementation of Flash that did not have write-protection capability.

Most manufacturers that use the Flash BIOS system notify their customers when they upgrade the BIOS for a particular system line. Usually, the cost of the upgrade is nominal; if your system is new enough, the upgrade may even be free.

Using IML System Partition BIOS. IBM uses a scheme similar to a Flash ROM called *Initial Microcode Load* (*IML*). IML is a technique in which the BIOS code is installed on the hard disk in a special hidden system partition and is loaded every time the system is powered up. Of course, the system still has a core BIOS on the motherboard, but all that BIOS does is locate and load updated BIOS code from the system partition. This technique enables IBM to distribute ROM updates on disk for installation in the system partition. The IML BIOS is loaded every time the system is reset or powered on.

Along with the system BIOS code, the system partition contains a complete copy of the Reference Diskette, which provides the option of running the setup and system-configuration software at any time during a reboot operation. This option eliminates the need to boot from the Reference Diskette to reconfigure the system and gives the impression that the entire Reference Diskette is contained in ROM.

One drawback to this technique is that the BIOS code is installed on the (SCSI) hard disk; the system cannot function properly without the properly set-up hard disk connected. You always can boot from the Reference Diskette floppy, should the hard disk fail or become disconnected, but you cannot boot from a standard floppy disk.

Testing Memory

The best way to test memory is to install and use it, using your PC system as the testing tool. Numerous diagnostics programs are available for testing memory. Many advanced diagnostics programs are discussed in Chapter 21, "Software and Hardware Diagnostic Tools." Many of these programs, such as the Norton Utilities NDIAGS program, are very inexpensive and yet offer very complete memory diagnostics capabilities. One word of advice is that all memory testing should be done on a system booted from a plain DOS disk with no memory managers or other resident programs loaded.

Parity Checking

As mentioned previously, the memory chips handle eight bits per character of data plus an extra bit called the *parity bit*. Memory-control circuitry uses the parity bit to cross-check the integrity of each byte of data. When the circuitry detects an error, the computer stops and displays a message informing you of the malfunction. Parity checking is the first line of defense for memory and other system errors. Notice that many newer systems are coming with non-parity SIMMs to save money. This eliminates parity checking, and increases the likelihood that errors go undetected.

Power-On Self Test

The Power-On Self Test (POST), which is in ROM, can be an effective test for problem memory. When you turn on your system, the POST checks the major hardware components including memory. If the POST detects a bad memory chip, it displays a warning. A more sophisticated disk-based program, however, usually does a better job.

Advanced Diagnostic Tests

A number of diagnostic programs can be used to test RAM chips and other system components. For example, Norton Utilities includes a utility called NDIAGS that tests RAM chips for defects. Other utility packages that can be used to test RAM chips are discussed in Chapter 21, "Software and Hardware Diagnostic Tools." For IBM computers, the Advanced Diagnostics Disk contains utilities that can be used to test your system RAM.

Such programs should be used any time you receive a memory parity error message, or a memory error in the POST (Power-On Self Test). Even if you do not receive error messages, if a properly running system suddenly begins locking up or if strange characters appear on-screen, you should run a good diagnostics program. Software diagnostics can help you spot trouble before a hardware problem destroys data.

Summary

This chapter discussed memory from both a physical and a logical point of view. The types of chips and SIMMs that physically comprise the memory in a PC system were discussed, and the logical arrangement of this memory was examined. The terms used to describe the different regions and the purpose for each region were covered. The chapter also looked at ways of reorganizing the system memory and taking advantage of unused areas.

Chapter 8

The Power Supply

One of the most failure-prone components in any computer system is the power supply. The power supply is a critical component in a PC, as it supplies electrical power to every component in the system. Because of its importance to proper and reliable system operation, you should understand both the function and limitations of a power supply, as well as its potential problems and their solutions.

Power Supply Function and Operation

The basic function of the power supply is to convert the type of electrical power available at the wall socket to that which is usable by the computer circuitry. The power supply in a conventional desktop system is designed to convert the 120-volt, 60Hz, AC current into something the computer can use—specifically, both +5- and +12-volt DC current. Usually, the digital electronic components and circuits in the system (motherboard, adapter cards, and disk drive logic boards) use the +5-volt power, and the motors (disk drive motors and any fans) use the +12-volt power. You must ensure a good, steady supply of both types of current so that the system can operate properly.

If you look at a specification sheet for a typical PC power supply, you see that the supply generates not only +5v and +12v, but also –5v and –12v. Because it would seem that the +5v and +12v signals power everything in the system (logic and motors), what are the negative voltages used for? The answer is not much! In fact, these additional negative voltages are not really used at all in modern systems.

Although –5v and –12v are supplied to the motherboard via the power supply connectors, the motherboard uses only the +5v. The –5v signal is simply routed to the ISA Bus on pin B5 and is not used in any way by the motherboard. It was originally used by the analog data separator circuits found in older floppy controllers, which is why it was supplied to the bus. Because modern controllers do not need the –5v, it is no longer used but is still required because it is part of the ISA Bus standard. Note that power supplies in systems with a Micro Channel Architecture (MCA) Bus do not have –5v. This power signal was never needed in these systems, as they always used a more modern floppy controller design.

Both the +12v and –12v signals also are not used by the motherboard logic and instead are simply routed to pins B9 and B7 of the ISA Bus, respectively. These voltages can be used by any adapter card on the bus, but most notably they are used by serial port driver/receiver circuits. If the motherboard has serial ports built in, the +12v and –12v signals can be used for those ports. Notice that the load placed on these voltages by a serial port would be very small. For example, the PS/2 Dual Async adapter uses only 35mA of +12v and 35mA of –12v (0.035 amps each) to operate two ports.

Most newer serial port circuits no longer use 12v driver/receiver circuits, but instead now use circuits that run on only 5v or even 3.3v. If you have one of these modern design ports in your system, the –12v signal from your power supply is likely to be totally unused by anything in the system.

The main function of the +12v power is to run disk drive motors. Usually a large amount of current is available, especially in systems with a large number of drive bays, such as in a tower configuration. Besides disk drive motors, the +12v supply is used by any cooling fans in the system, which of course should always be running. A single cooling fan can draw between 100mA to 250mA (0.1 to 0.25 amps); however, most newer ones use the lower 100mA figure. Note that although most fans run on +12v, most portable systems use fans that run on +5v or even 3.3v instead.

In addition to supplying power to run the system, the power supply also ensures that the system does not run unless the power being supplied is sufficient to operate the system properly. In other words, the power supply actually prevents the computer from starting up or operating until all the correct power levels are present. Each power supply completes internal checks and tests before allowing the system to start. The power supply sends to the motherboard a special signal, called Power_Good. If this signal is not present, the computer does not run. The effect of this setup is that when the AC voltage dips and the power supply becomes over-stressed or overheated, the Power_Good signal goes down and forces a system reset or complete shutdown. If your system has ever seemed dead when the power switch is on and the fan and hard disks are running, you know the effects of losing the Power_Good signal.

IBM originally used this conservative design with the view that if the power goes low or the supply is overheated or over-stressed, causing output power to falter, the computer should not be allowed to operate. You even can use the Power_Good feature as a method of designing and implementing a reset switch for the PC. The Power_Good line is wired to the clock generator circuit (an 8284 or 82284 chip in the original PC/XT and AT systems), which controls the clock and reset lines to the microprocessor. When you ground the Power_Good line with a switch, the chip and related circuitry stop the processor by killing the clock signal and then reset the processor when the Power_Good signal appears after you release the switch. The result is a full hardware reset of the system.

Instructions for installing such a switch in a system not already equipped can be found later in this chapter.

Power Supply Form Factors

The shape and general physical layout of a component is called the *form factor,* and items that share form factor are generally interchangeable. When a system is designed, the designers can choose to use one of the popular standard form factors, or they can "roll their own." Choosing the former means that a virtually inexhaustible supply of inexpensive replacements is available in a variety of quality and power output levels. Going the custom route means that the supply will be unique to the system and available only from the original manufacturer in only the model or models they produce. If you cannot tell already, I am a fan of the industry-standard form factors!

The form factor of the power supply that a particular system uses is based on the case design. Six popular case and power supply types can be called "industry standard." The different types are

- PC/XT style
- AT/Desk style
- AT/Tower style
- Baby AT style
- Slim style
- ATX style

Each of these supplies are available in numerous different configurations and output levels.

When IBM introduced the XT, it used the same basic power supply shape as the original PC, except that the new XT supply had more than double the power output capability (see fig. 8.1). Because they were identical in both external appearance and the type of connectors used, you could easily install the better XT supply as an upgrade for a PC system. Because of the tremendous popularity of the original PC and XT design, a number of manufacturers began building systems that mimicked their shape and layout. These clones, as they have been called, could interchange virtually all components with the IBM systems, including the power supply. Numerous manufacturers have since begun producing these components, and nearly all follow the form factor of one or more IBM systems.

When IBM later introduced the AT desktop system, it created a larger power supply that had a form factor different from the original PC/XT. This system was rapidly cloned as well, and to this day still represents the basis for most IBM-compatible designs. The power supply used in these systems is called the AT/Desktop style power supply (see fig. 8.2). Hundreds of manufacturers now make motherboards, power supplies, cases, and so on that are physically interchangeable with the original IBM AT. If you are buying a compatible system, I recommend those that have form factors compatible with the IBM AT, because you will have numerous motherboards and power supplies from which to choose.

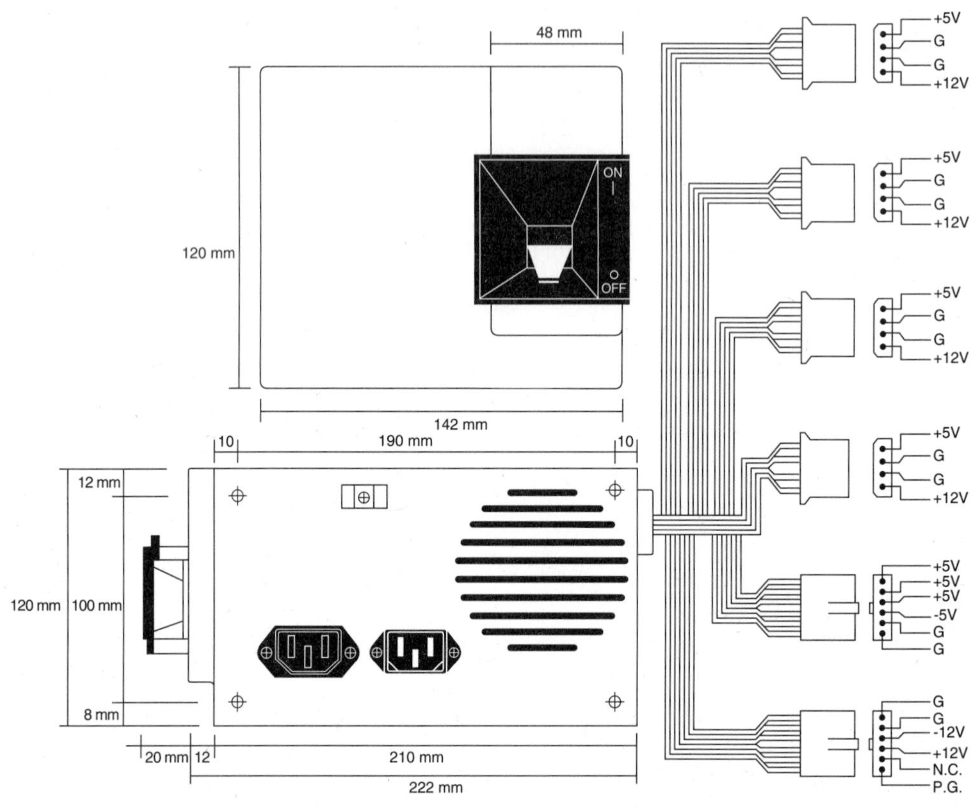

Figure 8.1

PC/XT-form factor power supply.

The compatible market has come up with a couple of other variations on the AT theme that are popular today. Besides the standard AT/Desktop type power supply, we also have the AT/Tower configuration, which is basically a full-sized AT-style desktop system running on its side. The power supply and motherboard form factors are basically the same in the Tower system as in the Desktop. The tower configuration is not new, in fact even IBM's original AT had a specially mounted logo that could be rotated when you ran the system on its side in the tower configuration. The type of power supply used in a tower system is identical to that used in a desktop system, except for the power switch location. Most AT/Desktop systems required that the power switch be located right on the power supply itself, while most AT/Tower systems use an external switch attached to the power supply through a short 4-wire cable. A full sized AT power supply with a remote switch is now called an AT/Tower form-factor supply (see fig. 8.3).

Another type of AT based form factor that has been developed is the so called Baby AT, which is simply a shortened version of the full sized AT system. The power supply in these systems is shortened on one dimension; however, it matches the AT design in all other respects. These Baby AT-style power supplies can be used in both Baby AT chassis and the larger AT-style chassis; however, the full size AT/Tower power supply does not fit in the Baby AT chassis (see fig. 8.4).

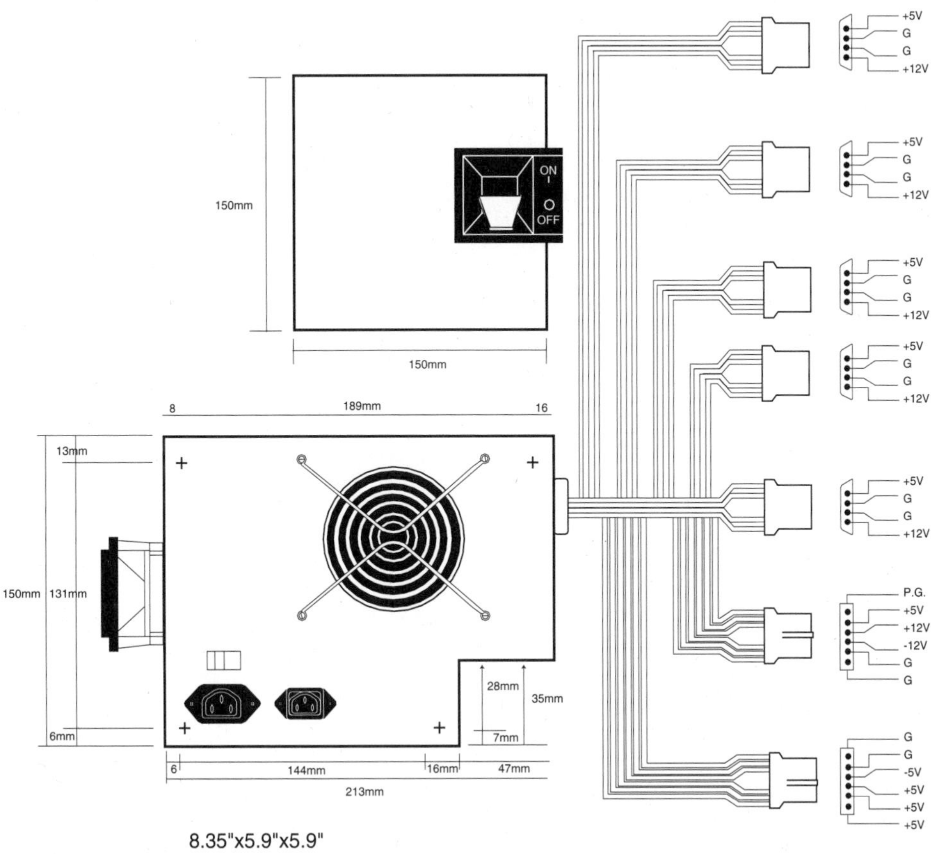

Figure 8.2
AT/Desktop form factor power supply.

The fifth type of form factor that has developed is the Slimline (see fig. 8.5). These systems use a different motherboard configuration that mounts the slots on a "riser" card that plugs into the motherboard. The expansion cards plug into this riser and are mounted sideways in the system. These types of systems are very low in height, hence the name "Slimline." A new power supply was specifically developed for these systems and allows interchangeability between different manufacturers' systems. Some problems with motherboard interchanges occur because of the riser cards, but the Slimline power supply has become a standard in its own right.

The slimline power supply is by far the most popular power supply design in use today. Despite how it might sound, even most full sized AT Desktop and Tower cases today are designed to accept the slimline form factor power supply.

The newest standard on the market today is the ATX form factor (see fig. 8.6). This describes a new motherboard shape, as well as a new case and power supply form factor. The ATX supply is based on the slimline or low-profile design, but has several differences worth noting.

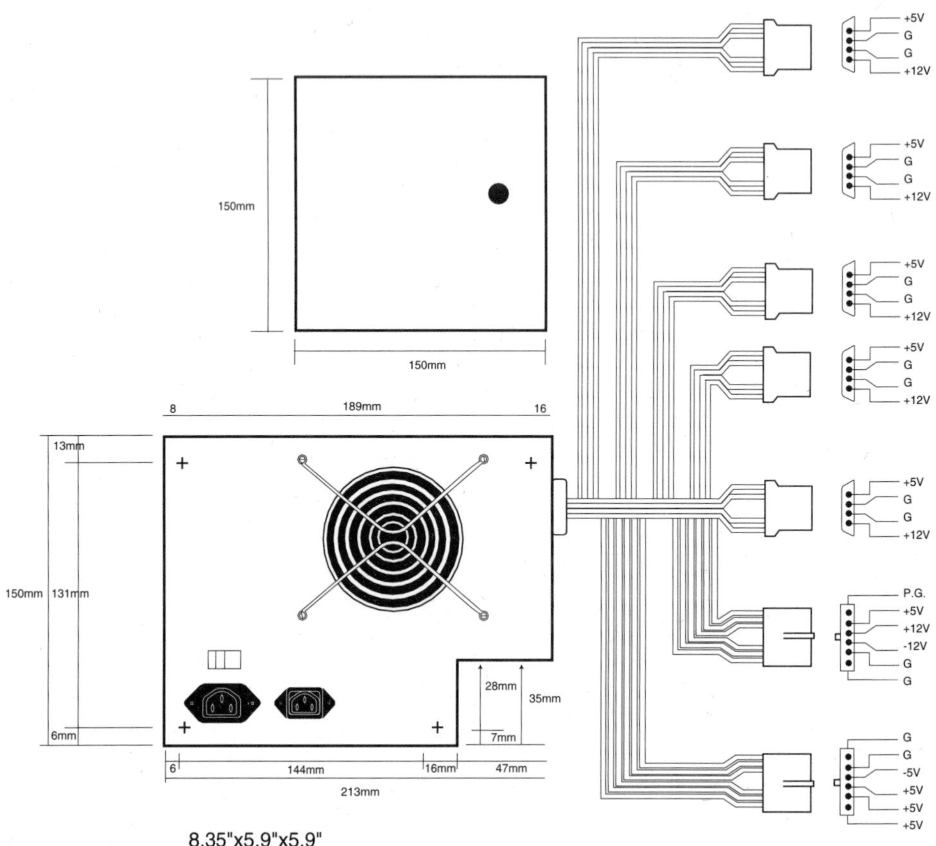

Figure 8.3

AT/Tower form factor power supply.

One difference is that the fan is now mounted along the inner side of the supply, blowing air across the motherboard and drawing it in from the outside at the rear. This flow is opposite most standard supplies, which blow air out the back of the supply and also have the fan positioned at the back. The reverse flow cooling used in the ATX supply forces air over the hottest components of the board, such as the CPU, SIMMs, and expansion slots. This eliminates the need for the notoriously unreliable CPU fans that have unfortunately become common today. Another benefit of the reverse flow cooling is that the system will remain cleaner and free from dust and dirt. The case is essentially pressurized, so air will push out of the cracks in the case, the opposite of what happens in non-ATX systems. For example, if you held a lit cigarette in front of your floppy drive on a normal system, the smoke would be inhaled through the front of the drive and contaminate the heads! On an ATX system with reverse flow cooling, the smoke would be blown out away from the drive because the only air intake is the single fan vent on the power supply at the rear. Systems that operate in extremely harsh environments could add a filter to the fan intake vent, which would ensure even further that all air entering the system is clean and dust free.

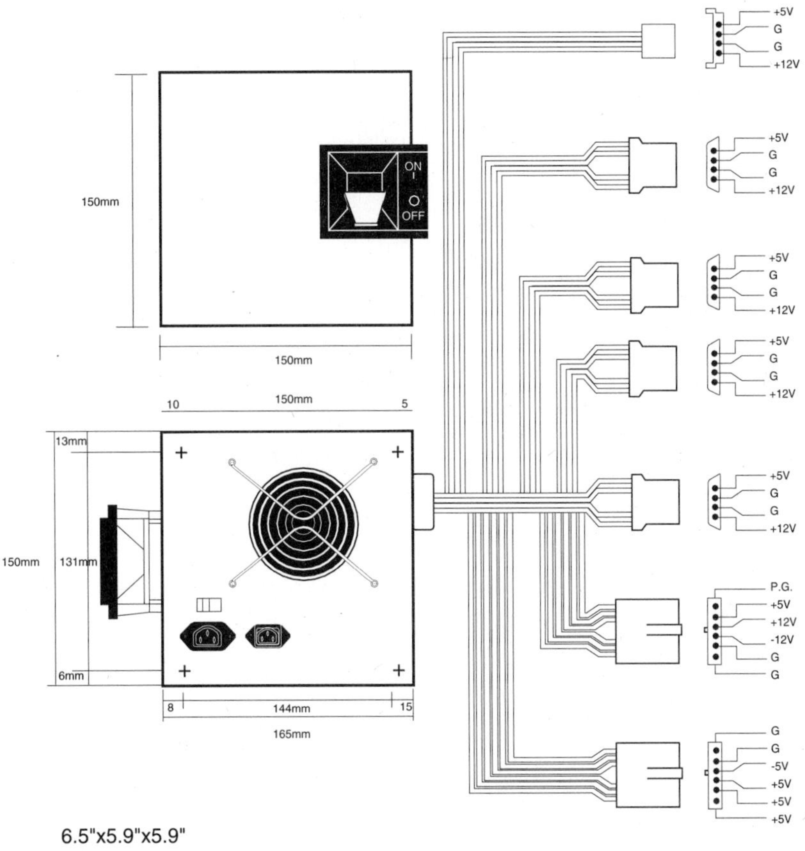

Figure 8.4

Baby-AT form factor power supply.

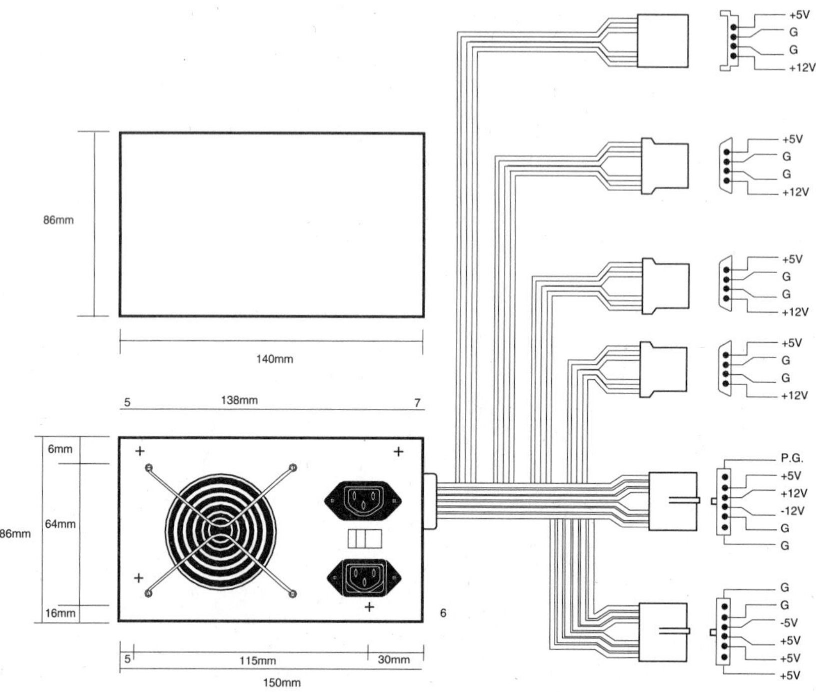

Figure 8.5

Slimline/Low Profile form factor power supply.

The ATX system format was designed by Intel in 1995, but became popular in the new Pentium Pro based PCs in '96. The ATX form factor takes care of several problems with the Baby AT or slimline form factors, and where the power supply is concerned this covers two main problems. One is that the traditional PC power supply since the original one used in the IBM PC has two connectors that plug into the motherboard. The problem is that if you insert these connectors backwards or out of their normal sequence, you will fry the motherboard! Most responsible system manufacturers will have the motherboard and power supply connectors keyed so they cannot be installed backwards or out of sequence, but many of the cheaper system vendors to not feature this keying on the boards or supplies they use.

To solve the potential for disaster that awaits those who might plug their power supply connectors incorrectly, the ATX form factor includes a new power plug for the motherboard. This new connector features 20 pins, and is a single keyed connector. It is virtually impossible to plug it in backwards, and since there is only one connector instead of two almost identical ones, it will be impossible to plug them in out of sequence. The new connector also can optionally supply 3.3v, eliminating the need for voltage regulators on the motherboard to power the CPU and other 3.3v circuits. Although the 3.3v signals are labeled as optional in the ATX specification, they should be considered mandatory in any ATX form factor power supply you purchase. Many systems will require this in the future.

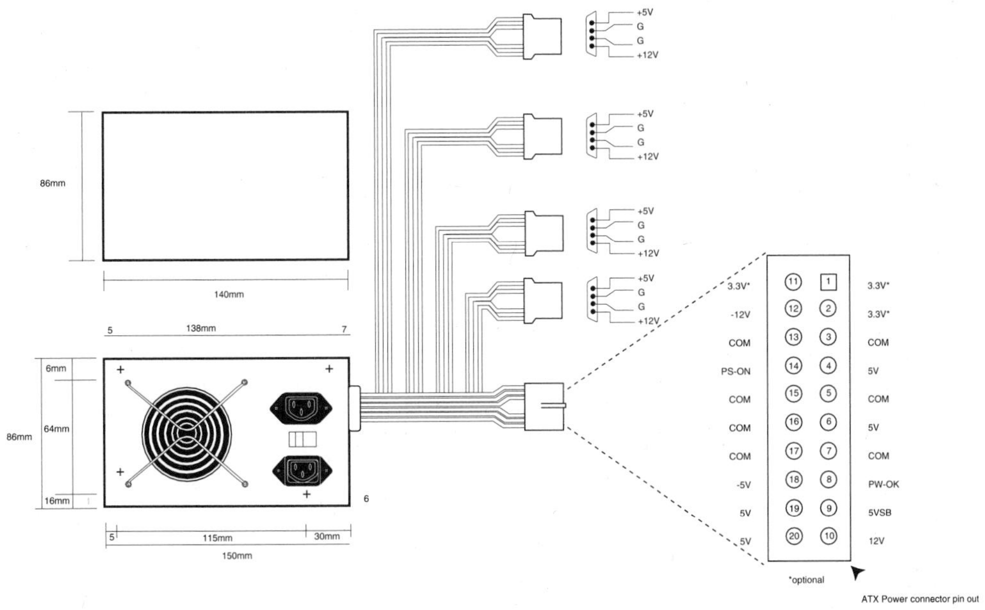

Figure 8.6

ATX form factor power supply.

Besides the new 3.3v signals, there is one other set of signals that will be found on the ATX supply not normally seen on standard supplies. They are the Power_On and 5v_Standby signals, which are also called Soft Power. Power_On is a motherboard signal that can be used with operating systems like Windows 95 or Windows NT, which support the ability to power the system down with software. This will also allow the optional use of the keyboard to power the system back on, exactly like the Apple Macintosh systems. The 5v_Standby signal is always active, giving the motherboard a limited source of power even when off.

The other problem solved by the ATX form factor power supply is that of system cooling. Most of the high end Pentium and Pentium Pro systems have active heat sinks on the processor, which means there is a small fan on the CPU designed to cool it. These small fans are notoriously unreliable, not to mention expensive when compared to standard passive heatsinks. In the ATX design, the CPU fan is eliminated, and the CPU is mounted in a socket right next to the ATX power supply, which has a reverse flow fan blowing onto the CPU. The ATX supply draws air from outside and pressurizes the system case instead of the other way around. Essentially the airflow is backwards from before, which results in far better cooling for the processor and other system components.

You will find it easy to locate supplies that fit these industry-standard form factors. Several vendors who manufacture PC power supplies in all these form factors are listed later in this chapter. For proprietary units, you will likely have to go back to the manufacturer.

Power Supply Connectors

Table 8.1 shows the pinouts for most standard AT or PC/XT-compatible systems. Some systems may have more or fewer drive connectors. For example, IBM's AT system power supplies have only three disk drive power connectors, although most of the currently available AT/Tower type power supplies have four drive connectors. If you are adding drives and need additional disk drive power connectors, "Y" splitter cables are available from many electronics supply houses (including Radio Shack) that can adapt a single power connector to serve two drives. As a precaution, make sure that your total power supply output is capable of supplying the additional power.

Table 8.1 Typical PC/XT and AT Power Supply Connections

Connector	AT Type	PC/XT Type
P8-1	Power_Good (+5v)	Power_Good (+5v)
P8-2	+5v	Key (No connect)
P8-3	+12v	+12v
P8-4	–12v	–12v
P8-5	Ground (0)	Ground (0)
P8-6	Ground (0)	Ground (0)
P9-1	Ground (0)	Ground (0)
P9-2	Ground (0)	Ground (0)
P9-3	–5v	–5v
P9-4	+5v	+5v
P9-5	+5v	+5v
P9-6	+5v	+5v
P10-1	+12v	+12v
P10-2	Ground (0)	Ground (0)
P10-3	Ground (0)	Ground (0)
P10-4	+5v	+5v
P11-1	+12v	+12v
P11-2	Ground (0)	Ground (0)
P11-3	Ground (0)	Ground (0)
P11-4	+5v	+5v
P12-1	+12v	—
P12-2	Ground (0)	—
P12-3	Ground (0)	—
P12-4	+5v	—
P13-1	+12v	—
P13-2	Ground (0)	—
P13-3	Ground (0)	—
P13-4	+5v	—

Notice that the Baby AT and Slimline power supplies also use the AT/Desktop or Tower pin configuration. The only other type of industry standard power supply connector is found on the new ATX form factor power supply. This is a 20-pin keyed connector with pins configured as shown in table 8.2.

Table 8.2 ATX Power Supply Connections

Signal	Pin	Pin	Signal
3.3v*	11	1	3.3v*
-12v	12	2	3.3v*
GND	13	3	GND
Pwr_On	14	4	5v
GND	15	5	GND
GND	16	6	5v
GND	17	7	GND
-5v	18	8	Pwr_Good
5v	19	9	5v_Stby
5v	20	10	12v

* = *Optional signal*

Notice that the ATX supply features several signals not seen before, such as the 3.3v, Power_On, and 5v_Standby signals. Because of this, it will be difficult to adapt a standard slimline or low-profile form factor supply to work properly in an ATX system, although the shapes are virtually identical.

Although the PC/XT power supplies do not have any signal on pin P8-2, you can still use them on AT-type motherboards, or vice versa. The presence or absence of the +5v signal on that pin has little or no effect on system operation. If you are measuring voltages for testing purposes, anything within 10 percent is considered acceptable, although most manufacturers of high-quality power supplies specify a tighter five percent tolerance (see table 8.3). I prefer to go by the five percent tolerance, which is a tougher test to pass.

Table 8.3 Power Supply Acceptable Voltage Ranges

	Loose Tolerance		Tight Tolerance	
Desired Voltage	Min. (–10%)	Max. (+8%)	Min. (–5%)	Max. (+5%)
+/–5.0v	4.5v	5.4v	4.75	5.25
+/–12.0v	10.8v	12.9v	11.4	12.6

The Power_Good signal has tolerances different from the other signals, although it is nominally a +5v signal in most systems. The trigger point for Power_Good is about +2.5v, but most systems require the signal voltage to be within the tolerances listed in table 8.4.

Table 8.4 Power_Good Signal Acceptable Range

Signal	Minimum	Maximum
Power_Good (+5v)	3.0v	6.0v

A power supply should be replaced if the voltages are out of these ranges. A later section in this chapter details how to measure the power supply voltage and where to get replacement supplies.

Power Switch Connectors. The AT/Tower and Slimline power supplies use a remote power switch. This switch is mounted in the front of the system case and is connected to the power supply through a standard type of 4-wire cable. The ends of the cable are fitted with spade connector lugs, which plug onto the spade connectors on the power switch. The switch is usually a part of the case, so the power supply comes with the cable and no switch.

The cable from the power supply to the switch in the case contains four color coded wires. There may also be a 5th wire supplying a ground connection to the case as well. These wires carry 110v wall current, so be careful as you can be electrocuted if you touch them with the power supply plugged in.

Caution

The remote power switch leads carry 110v AC current at all times. You could be electrocuted if you touch the ends of these wires with the power supply plugged in! Always make sure the power supply is unplugged before connecting or disconnecting the remote power switch.

The four or five wires are color coded as follows; the Brown and Blue wires are the live and neutral feed wires from the 110v power cord to the power supply itself. These wires are always hot when the power supply is plugged in. The Black and White wires carry the AC feed from the switch back to the power supply itself. These leads should only be hot when the power supply is plugged in and the switch is turned on. Finally, there is often a green wire or a green wire with a yellow stripe, which is the ground lead. It should be connected somewhere to the PC case, and helps to ground the power supply to the case.

On the switch itself, the tabs for the leads are usually color coded, if not they can still be easily connected. If there is no color coding on the switch, then plug the Blue and Brown wires onto the tabs that are parallel to each other, and the Black and White wires to the tabs that are angled away from each other. See figure 8.7 as a guide.

As long as the Blue and Brown wires are on the one set of tabs, and the Black and White leads are on the other, the switch and supply will work properly. If you incorrectly mix the leads, you will likely blow the circuit breaker for the wall socket, as you can create a direct short circuit.

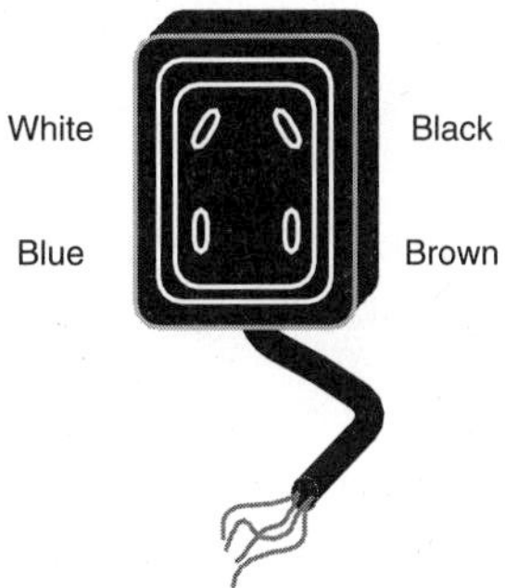

Figure 8.7

Power supply remote switch connections.

Disk Drive Power Connectors. The disk drive connectors are fairly universal with regard to pin configuration and even wire color. Table 8.5 shows the standard disk drive power connector pinout and wire colors.

Table 8.5 Disk Drive Power Connector Pinout

Pin	Wire Color	Signal
1	Yellow	+12v
2	Black	Gnd
3	Black	Gnd
4	Red	+5v

This information applies whether the drive connector is the larger Molex version or the smaller mini-version used on most 3.5-inch floppy drives. In each case, the pinouts and wire colors are the same. To determine the location of pin 1, look at the connector carefully. It is usually embossed in the plastic connector body; however, it is often tiny and difficult to read. Fortunately these connectors are keyed and therefore are difficult to insert incorrectly. The following figure shows the keying with respect to pin numbers on the larger drive power connector.

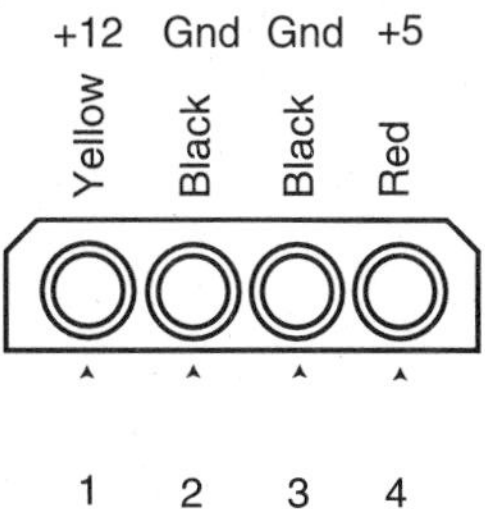

Figure 8.8

A disk drive female power supply cable connector.

Notice that some drive connectors may supply only two wires—usually the +5v and a single ground (Pins 3 and 4)—because the floppy drives in most newer systems run on only +5v and do not use the +12v at all.

Physical Connector Part Numbers. The physical connectors used in industry-standard PC power supplies were originally specified by IBM for the supplies used in the original PC/XT/AT systems. They used a specific type of connector between the power supply and the motherboard (the P8 and P9 connectors), as well as specific connectors for the disk drives. The motherboard connectors used in all the industry-standard power supplies have not changed since 1981 when the IBM PC appeared. With the advent of 3.5-inch floppy drives in 1986, however, a new smaller type of drive power connector appeared on the scene for these drives. Table 8.6 lists the standard connectors used for motherboard and disk drive power.

Table 8.6 Physical Power Connectors

Connector Description	Female (on Power Cable)	Male (on Component)
Motherboard P8/P9	Burndy GTC6P-1	Burndy GTC 6RI
Disk Drive (large style)	AMP 1-480424-0	AMP 1-480426-0
Disk Drive (small style)	AMP 171822-4	AMP 171826-4

You can get these raw connectors through the electronics supply houses (Allied, Newark, Digi-Key, and so on) found in the vendor list. You also can get complete cable assemblies including drive adapters from the large to small connectors, disk drive "Y" splitter cables, and motherboard power extension cables from a number of the cable and miscellaneous supply houses such as Cables To Go, the Cable Connection, Ci Design, and Key Power.

The Power_Good Signal

The Power_Good signal is a +5v signal (+3.0 through +6.0 is generally considered acceptable) generated in the power supply when it has passed its internal self tests and the outputs have stabilized. This normally takes anywhere from 0.1 to 0.5 seconds after you turn on the power supply switch. This signal is sent to the motherboard, where it is received by the processor timer chip, which controls the reset line to the processor.

In the absence of Power_Good, the timer chip continuously resets the processor, which prevents the system from running under bad or unstable power conditions. When the timer chip sees Power_Good, it stops resetting the processor and the processor begins executing whatever code is at address FFFF:0000 (usually the ROM BIOS).

If the power supply cannot maintain proper outputs (such as when a brownout occurs), the Power_Good signal is withdrawn, and the processor is automatically reset. When proper output is restored, the Power_Good signal is regenerated and the system again begins operation (as if you just powered on). By withdrawing Power_Good, the system never "sees" the bad power because it is "stopped" quickly (reset) rather than allowed to operate on unstable or improper power levels, which can cause parity errors and other problems.

In most systems, the Power_Good connection is made via connector P8-1 (P8 Pin 1) from the power supply to the motherboard.

A well-designed power supply delays the arrival of the Power_Good signal until all voltages stabilize after you turn the system on. Badly designed power supplies, which are found in *many* low-cost compatibles, often do not delay the Power_Good signal properly and enable the processor to start too soon. The normal Power_Good delay is from 0.1 to 0.5 seconds. Improper Power_Good timing also causes CMOS memory corruption in some systems. If you find that a system does not boot up properly the first time you turn on the switch but subsequently boots up if you press the reset or Ctrl-Alt-Del warm boot command, you likely have a problem with Power_Good. This happens because the Power_Good signal is tied to the timer chip that generates the reset signal to the processor. What you must do in these cases is find a new high-quality power supply and see whether it solves the problem.

Many cheaper power supplies do not have proper Power_Good circuitry and often just tie any +5v line to that signal. Some motherboards are more sensitive to an improperly designed or improperly functioning Power_Good signal than others. Intermittent startup problems are often caused by improper Power_Good signal timing. A common example occurs when somebody replaces a motherboard in a system and then finds that the system intermittently fails to start properly when the power is turned on. This ends up being very difficult to diagnose, especially for the inexperienced technician, because the problem appears to be caused by the new motherboard. Although it seems that the new motherboard might be defective, it usually turns out to be that the original power supply is poorly designed and either cannot produce stable enough power to properly operate the new board, or more likely has an improperly wired or timed Power_Good signal. In these situations, replacing the supply with a high-quality unit is the proper solution.

Adding a Hardware Reset Switch. A switch that applies a full reset to your system keeps power moving to the system and rescues you from a system lockup. A reset switch saves you much time, as well as some of the wear and tear on your unit from using the power switch as a reset button. IBM and most vendors of compatibles have built reset circuitry into the motherboard and added reset switches to the front of the computer case. If your machine doesn't already have a reset switch, however, the following section teaches you how to add one. (The hardest part of adding a reset switch to your system is figuring out where to mount it.)

Adding a reset button is possible on any system, including all IBM systems, because it has a power supply that provides a Power Good signal. On most IBM-compatible computers, the Power Good signal is on the connector that plugs into the rearmost power-supply connectors. In PC and XT systems, this signal traces through the motherboard to the 8284a chip at Pin 11. When the line is shorted to ground and returned to normal, the 8284a (82284, in an AT) clock-timer chip generates a reset signal on Pin 10. The reset signal is sent to the 8088 at Pin 21, and the boot process begins. In other systems that have different processors and timer chips—for example, AT and PS/2 systems—the Power Good signal also initiates a reset if the signal is grounded and returned to normal, although the wiring details vary.

In all IBM-compatible systems, when the CPU is reset, it begins to execute code at memory location F000:FFF0, which is known as the power-up reset vector. An immediate jump instruction at this location sends the CPU's instruction pointer to the start location for the particular system ROM. The system then begins the POST. The processor and DMA chips are tested first, but before the system initiates the full POST memory test, it compares the memory location 0000:0472 with the value 1234h. If these values are equal, a *warm* start is indicated, and the POST memory tests are skipped. If any other value appears, a *cold* start occurs, forcing all memory to be tested.

This procedure is the basis of an effective reset switch. By setting the flag value at memory location 0000:0472, you can have the system perform either a cold or warm start when you press a reset button. The type of reset—a hardware reset—unfreezes a locked-up machine, unlike the Ctrl-Alt-Del software reset command.

To add a reset switch, you need these parts:

- Six inches of thin (about 20-gauge) insulated wire
- A single-pole, normally open, momentary-contact push-button switch

The idea behind installing a reset switch is to run a momentary-contact switch parallel with the Power Good line and ground. To do so, follow these steps:

1. Remove from the motherboard the power-supply connector that contains the Power Good signal.

> **Note**
>
> Check your technical-reference manual to make sure that you have the right connector and can identify the signal wire that contains the Power Good signal. Sometimes this information is on a sticker attached to the power supply.

2. Poke the stripped end of a wire into the hole in the power-supply connector in which the Power Good signal is carried.
3. Plug the connector, with the wire inserted, back into the motherboard.
4. Run the other end of the wire under one of the screws that secures the motherboard. The screw serves as a ground.
5. Cut the wire in the middle, bare the ends, and attach the stripped wire ends to the normally open, single-pole, momentary-contact push-button switch.
6. Run the wire and the switch outside the case.

You now should have a functioning reset button. You can mount the switch to an available place on the unit (such as an empty card bracket) in which you can drill a small hole to accept the switch. Another idea is to select a blank spot on the front of the case and drill a hole to mount it there. If you do drill through a metal case, make sure that the metal filings do not fall on the motherboard!

A simple button and wire are sufficient for adding a reset switch, but as a safety precaution, you can place a 1/4-watt resistor with a value between 1K ohms and 2.7K ohms inline with the wire from the Power Good line to the switch. The reason for adding the resistor is that the Power Good signal is provided by a PNP transistor inside the power supply, with its emitter connected to the +5 volt signal. Without the resistor, shorting the Power Good signal to ground for a long period can burn out the transistor.

When you press the switch, you initiate the boot sequence. The boot process that occurs (warm or cold) depends on the status of memory location 0000:0472. The value at this location is 0000h when you first power up the system and until you press Ctrl+Alt+Del for the first time. If the last boot operation was a cold boot (an initial power-on), every subsequent time that you press the reset button, a cold boot occurs. After you press Ctrl+Alt+Del once to initiate a manual warm-boot sequence, every subsequent time that you press the reset button you initiate a warm boot that skips the memory tests.

To eliminate the need to press Ctrl+Alt+Del after you start the system every day to "set" the reset button for subsequent warm-boot operations, you can enter a program, using DEBUG, that produces a WARMSET.COM program to run in your AUTOEXEC.BAT file. This simple program quickly sets the memory flag to indicate that a warm boot should be initiated when the reset switch is pressed.

To create WARMSET.COM, make sure that you have the DEBUG program available in the path, and then enter these commands at the DOS prompt:

```
C:\>DEBUG
-N WARMSET.COM
-A 100
xxxx:0100 MOV AX,0040
xxxx:0103 MOV DS,AX
xxxx:0105 MOV WORD PTR [0072],1234
xxxx:010B INT 20
xxxx:010D
-R CX
CX 0000
:D
-W
Writing 0000D bytes
-Q
```

Unlike the Ctrl+Alt+Del combination, the hardware reset cannot be ignored by your system, no matter how locked up the system is.

The Phoenix BIOS sets the warm-boot flag during every boot sequence, regardless of whether the boot is warm or cold. Immediately after power-up, therefore, the flag is zero, which causes the standard POST test to run. Immediately after the POST, the Phoenix BIOS sets the flag for a warm boot, because many compatibles that use the Phoenix BIOS have a reset button integrated into the system. This reset button works the same way as the button that you can construct. Because of the warm-boot flag's automatic setting, a warm boot occurs every time you press the reset button, no matter what the last boot was. If you want a cold boot to occur (including POST), you can create a COLDSET.COM program, also using DEBUG.

To create COLDSET.COM, enter these commands:

```
C:\>DEBUG
-N COLDSET.COM
-A 100
xxxx:0100 MOV AX,0040
xxxx:0103 MOV DS,AX
xxxx:0105 MOV WORD PTR [0072],0000
xxxx:010B INT 20
xxxx:010D
-R CX
CX 0000
:D
-W
Writing 0000D bytes
-Q
```

This procedure causes a reset button to initiate a cold boot with POST tests, no matter which BIOS you have.

An interesting variation on these programs is to produce two additional companion programs called WARMBOOT.COM and COLDBOOT.COM. As their names indicate, these programs go one step further than the WARMSET.COM and COLDSET.COM programs: they not only set the flag, but also cause an immediate boot.

You may wonder why you would need that operation when you can just press Ctrl+Alt+Del or turn the power off and on to reboot the system. The answer is that with these programs, you can initiate the boot you want from a batch file with no operator intervention.

I use the WARMBOOT.COM program in batch files that copy new CONFIG.SYS files to my root directory and then reboot the system automatically to initiate the new configuration. For example, one batch file copies a CONFIG.SYS file, which loads local-area network (LAN) drivers, as well as a new AUTOEXEC.BAT file, to the root directory of the C drive. The AUTOEXEC.BAT file has commands that automatically log on to the network. In seconds, my network is up and running, and I am automatically logged on, with only one command. You probably can come up with other uses for these programs.

Note

If you have DOS 6.x or higher, you can create customized boot menus that replace this whole process. Both CONFIG.SYS and AUTOEXEC.BAT can have configuration blocks that allow you to pick one of several configurations.

To create WARMBOOT.COM, enter these commands:

```
C:\>DEBUG
-N WARMBOOT.COM
-A 100
xxxx:0100 MOV AX,0040
xxxx:0103 MOV DS,AX
```

```
xxxx:0105 MOV WORD PTR [0072],1234
xxxx:010B JMP FFFF:0
xxxx:0110
-R CX
CX 0000
:10
-W
Writing 00010 bytes
-Q
```

To create COLDBOOT.COM, enter these commands:

```
C:\>DEBUG
-N COLDBOOT.COM
-A 100
xxxx:0100 MOV AX,0040
xxxx:0103 MOV DS,AX
xxxx:0105 MOV WORD PTR [0072],0000
xxxx:010B JMP FFFF:0
xxxx:0110
-R CX
CX 0000
:10
-W
Writing 00010 bytes
-Q
```

Whether or not you have a reset button, the WARMBOOT.COM and COLDBOOT.COM programs can be useful.

Power Supply Loading

PC power supplies are of a switching rather than a linear design. The switching type of design uses a high speed oscillator circuit to generate different output voltages, and is very efficient in size, weight and energy compared to the standard linear design, which uses a large internal transformer to generate different outputs.

One characteristic of all switching type power supplies is that they do not run without a load. This means that you must have the supply plugged into something drawing +5v and +12v or the supply does not work. If you simply have the supply on a bench with nothing plugged into it, the supply burns up or protection circuitry shuts it down. Most power supplies are protected from no-load operation and will shut down. Some of the cheap clone supplies, however, lack the protection circuit and relay and are destroyed after a few seconds of no-load operation. A few power supplies have their own built-in load resistors, so that they can run even though no normal load is plugged in.

According to IBM specifications for the standard 192-watt power supply used in the original AT, a minimum load of 7.0 amps was required at +5v and a minimum load of 2.5 amps was required at +12v for the supply to work properly. Because floppy drives present no +12v load unless they are spinning, systems without a hard disk drive often do not operate properly. Most power supplies have a minimum load requirement for both the +5v and +12v sides, and if you fail to meet this minimum load, the supply shuts down.

Because of this characteristic, when IBM used to ship AT systems without a hard disk, they had the hard disk drive power cable plugged into a large 5-Ohm 50-watt sandbar resistor mounted in a little metal cage assembly where the drive would have been. The AT case had screw holes on top of where the hard disk would go specifically designed to mount this resistor cage. Several computer stores I knew in the mid 1980s would order the diskless AT and install their own 20M or 30M drives, which they could get more cheaply from other sources than IBM. They were throwing away the load resistors by the hundreds! I managed to grab a couple at the time, which is how I know the type of resistor they used.

This resistor would be connected between pin 1 (+12v) and pin 2 (Ground) on the hard disk power connector. This placed a 2.4-amp load on the supply's 12-volt output drawing 28.8 watts of power—it would get hot!—thus enabling the supply to operate normally. Note that the cooling fan in most power supplies draws approximately 0.1 to 0.25 amps, bringing the total load to 2.5 amps or more. If the load resistor was missing, the system would intermittently fail to start up or operate properly. The motherboard draws +5v at all times, but +12v is normally used only by motors and the floppy drive motors are off most of the time.

Most of the 200-watt power supplies in use today do not require as much of a load as the original IBM AT power supply. In most cases a minimum load of 2.0 to 4.0 amps at +5v and a minimum load of 0.5 to 1.0 amps at +12v are considered acceptable. Most motherboards will easily draw the minimum +5v current by themselves. The standard power supply cooling fan draws only 0.1 to 0.25 amps, so the +12v minimum load may still be a problem for a diskless workstation. Generally the higher the rating on the supply, the more minimum load is required, however there are exceptions so this is a specification you want to check into.

Some high-quality switching power supplies, like the Astec units used by IBM in all the PS/2 systems, have built-in load resistors and can run under a no-load situation because the supply loads itself. Most of the cheaper clone supplies do not have built-in load resistors, so they must have both +5v and +12v loads to work.

Tip

If you are setting up a "diskless" workstation, it is a good idea to install a load resistor or the power supply may cause intermittent system problems. You can construct the same type of load resistor that IBM originally used by connecting a 5-Ohm, 50-watt sandbar resistor between pins 1 and 2 on a disk drive power connector. You need to worry only about loading the +12v power, because the motherboard places a load on the +5v outputs.

If you want to bench test a power supply, make sure that loads are placed on both the +5v and +12v outputs. This is one reason that it is best to test the supply while it is installed in the system instead of separately on the bench. For impromptu bench testing, you can use a spare motherboard and hard disk drive to load the +5v and +12v outputs, respectively. Information on building your own load resistor network for bench testing power supplies is covered later in this chapter.

Power-Supply Ratings

Most system manufacturers will provide you with the technical specifications of each of their system-unit power supplies. This type of information is usually found in the system's technical-reference manual and also on stickers attached directly to the power supply. Power supply manufacturers can supply this data, which is preferable if you can identify the manufacturer and contact them directly.

Tables 8.6 and 8.7 list power-supply specifications for several of IBM's units, from which most of the compatibles are derived. The PC-system power supplies are the original units that most compatible power supplies have duplicated. The input specifications are listed as voltages, and the output specifications are listed as amps at several voltage levels. IBM reports output wattage level as "specified output wattage." If your manufacturer does not list the total wattage, you can convert amperage to wattage by using the following simple formula:

Wattage = Voltage * Amperage

By multiplying the voltage by the amperage available at each output and then adding them up, you can calculate the total capable output wattage of the supply.

Table 8.7 Power Supply Output Ratings for IBM "Classic" Systems

	PC	Port-PC	XT	XT-286	AT
Minimum Input Voltage	104	90	90	90	90
Maximum Input Voltage	127	137	137	137	137
Worldwide Power(220v)?	No	Yes	No	Yes	Yes
110/220v Switch?	–	Switch	–	Auto	Switch
Output Current (amps):+5v	7.0	11.2	15.0	20.0	19.8
–5v	0.3	0.3	0.3	0.3	0.3
+12v	2.0	4.4	4.2	4.2	7.3
–12v	0.25	0.25	0.25	0.25	0.3
Calculated output wattage	63.5	113.3	129.9	154.9	191.7
Specified output wattage	63.5	114.0	130.0	157.0	192.0

Table 8.8 shows the standard power supply output levels available in industry-standard form factors. Most manufacturers that offer supplies have supplies with different ratings for each type of supply. Supplies are available with ratings from 100 watts to 450 watts or more. Table 8.8 shows the rated outputs at each of the voltage levels for supplies with different manufacturer-specified output ratings. To compile the table, I referred to the specification sheets for supplies from Astec Standard Power and PC Power and Cooling. Although most of the ratings are accurate, as you can see they are somewhat misleading for the higher wattage units.

Table 8.8 Typical Compatible Power Supply Output Ratings

Specified Output Wattage	100W	150W	200W	250W	300W	375W	450W
Output Current (amps):+5v	10.0	15.0	20.0	25.0	32.0	35.0	45.0
–5v	0.3	0.3	0.3	0.5	1.0	0.5	0.5
+12v	3.5	5.5	8.0	10.0	10.0	13.0	15.0
–12v	0.3	0.3	0.3	0.5	1.0	0.5	1.0
Calculated output wattage	97.1	146.1	201.1	253.5	297.0	339.5	419.5

Most compatible power supplies have ratings between 150 to 250 watts output. Although lesser ratings are not usually desirable, it is possible to purchase heavy duty-power supplies for most compatibles that have outputs as high as 500 watts.

The 300-watt and larger units are excellent for enthusiasts who are building a fully optioned desktop or tower system. These supplies run any combination of motherboard and expansion card, as well as a large number of disk drives. In most cases, you cannot exceed the ratings on these power supplies—the system will be out of room for additional items first!

Table 8.9 shows the rated output levels of IBM's PS/2 power supplies. IBM uses high-quality supplies in these systems. They are normally supplied to IBM by Astec, but other manufacturers have made IBM supplies as well.

Table 8.9 Power Supply Output Ratings for PS/2 Systems

Model	Part Number	Worldwide Power (220v)	110/220v Manual/Auto	Output Wattage
25	8525-xx1	Yes	Manual	90
	8525-xx4	Yes	Manual	115
30	8530-0xx	Yes	Auto	70
25 286	8525-xxx	Yes	Manual	124.5
30 286	8530-Exx	Yes	Manual	90
35 SX	8535-xxx	Yes	Auto	118
40 SX	8540-0xx	Yes	Manual	197
50	8550-0xx	Yes	Auto	94
55 SX	8555-xxx	Yes	Manual	90
57 SX	8557-0xx	Yes	Manual	197
60	8560-041	Yes	Auto	207
	8560-071	Yes	Auto	225
65 SX	8565-xxx	Yes	Auto	250
70 386	8570-xxx	Yes	Auto	132
70 486	8570-Bxx	Yes	Auto	132
P70 386	8573-xxx	Yes	Auto	85
P75 486	8573-xxx	Yes	Auto	120

Model	Part Number	Worldwide Power (220v)	110/220v Manual/Auto	Output Wattage
80 386	8580-xxx	Yes	Auto	225
	8580-Axx	Yes	Auto	242
	8580-Axx	Yes	Auto	250
90 XP 486	8590-0xx	Yes	Auto	194
95 XP 486	8595-0xx	Yes	Auto	329

Most power supplies are considered to be *universal,* or *worldwide.* That is, they run on the 220-volt, 50-cycle current used in Europe and many other parts of the world. Most power supplies that can switch to 220-volt input are automatic, but a few require that you set a switch on the back of the power supply to indicate which type of power you will access. (The automatic units sense the current and switch automatically.)

My PS/2 P75, for example, runs on both 110- and 220-volt power. All I have to do is plug it in, and the system automatically recognizes the incoming voltage and switches circuits accordingly. This is different from some other systems that run on both levels of power, but require you to flip a switch manually to select the proper circuits within the power supply.

If your supply does not autoswitch, make sure the voltage setting is correct. If you plug the power supply into a 110v outlet while set in the 220v setting, there will be no damage but it will certainly not operate properly until you correct the setting. On the other hand, if you are in a foreign country with a 220v outlet and have the switch set for 110v, you may cause damage.

Power Supply Specifications

In addition to power output, many other specifications and features go into making a high-quality power supply. I have had many systems over the years. My experience has been that if a brownout occurs in a room with several systems running, the systems with higher-quality power supplies and higher output ratings always make it over power disturbances, whereas others choke. I would not give $5 for many of the cheap, junky power supplies that come in some of the low-end clone systems.

To get an idea of the expected performance from a power supply, you should know the specifications that IBM dictates for all its PS/2 power supplies. This information comes from the PS/2 Hardware Maintenance Manual (#S52G-9971-01) and is an example of what a properly designed power supply should do. Keep in mind that Astec makes virtually all IBM PS/2 supplies. They also make supplies for a number of other high-end system vendors.

PS/2 power supplies operate continuously over two ranges. The first is from 90 to 137 VAC, and the second is from 180 to 265 VAC. The AC signal must be a sine wave and have a maximum of five percent total harmonic distortion. Some units have an automatic voltage range selection feature, whereas others require a switch be set to operate on either the 100v or 200v ranges.

PS/2 power supplies are protected from both input over and under voltages. If the input voltage goes over or under the acceptable range, the power supply shuts down until the power switch is recycled.

All PS/2 supplies have output over-current protection. This means that if more than a safe load is drawn from the supply, it shuts down until the power switch is recycled. This protection extends to short circuits as well. If any short is placed between an output and ground or between any two outputs, the power supply shuts down until the power switch is recycled.

Most PS/2 power supplies have an automatic restart feature that causes the power supply to recycle automatically after an AC power outage. Beginning with products announced in October 1990, a three to six second delay was added to the restart time to give any subsystems or peripherals enough time to reset before the system restarts.

IBM states that the PS/2 supplies sustain operation during the following power line disturbances:

- A 20 percent below nominal voltage (that is, 80 volts) brownout lasting up to two seconds repeated up to 10 times with a 10 percent duty cycle.
- A 30 percent below nominal voltage (70 volts) brownout lasting up to 0.5 seconds repeated up to 10 times with a 10 percent duty cycle.
- A 15 percent above nominal voltage (143 volts) surge lasting up to one second repeated up to 10 times with a 10 percent duty cycle.
- A 400Hz oscillatory (exponentially decaying) disturbance at the peak of the input line voltage that increases the line voltage by two times (200 volts) that occurs up to 100 times at three second intervals.
- A transient pulse of 1.5 times the peak input voltage (150 volts) superimposed at the input voltage peak and repeated up to 100 times at three second intervals.

IBM also states that its PS/2 supplies (or attached systems) are not damaged if any of the following conditions occur:

- A 100 percent power outage of any duration
- A brownout of any kind
- A spike of up to 2,500 volts applied directly to the AC input (for example, a lightning strike or a lightning simulation test)

PS/2 power supplies have an extremely low current leakage to ground of less than 500 microamps. This safety feature is important if your outlet has a missing or improperly wired ground line.

As you can see, these specifications are fairly tough and are certainly representative of a high-quality power supply. Make sure that your supply can meet these specifications. The vendors recommended in this chapter produce supplies that meet or exceed these specifications.

Power-Use Calculations

One way to see whether your system is capable of expansion is to calculate the levels of power drain in the different system components and deduct the total from the maximum power supplied. This calculation might help you decide when to upgrade the power supply to a more capable unit. Unfortunately, these calculations can be difficult to make because many manufacturers do not publish power consumption data for their products.

It is difficult to get power consumption data for most +5v devices including motherboards and adapter cards. Motherboards can consume different power levels, depending on numerous factors. Most 486DX2 motherboards consume about 5 amps or so, but if you can get data on the one you are using, so much the better. For adapter cards, if you can find the actual specifications for the card, use those figures. To be on the conservative side, however, I usually go by the maximum available power levels as set forth in the respective bus standards.

For example, consider the typical power consumption figures for components in a modern PC system. Most standard desktop or slimline PC systems today come with a 200-watt power supply rated for 20 amps at +5v and 8 amps at +12v. The ISA specification calls for a maximum of 2.0 amps of +5v and 0.175 amps of +12v power for each slot in the system. Most systems have eight slots, and you can assume that four of them are filled for the purposes of calculating power draw. The following calculation shows what happens when you subtract the amount of power necessary to run the different system components:

5-Volt Power:		**20.0 Amps**
Less:	Motherboard	–5.0
	4 slots filled at 2.0 each	–8.0
	3.5" and 5.25" floppy drives	–1.5
	3.5" hard disk drive	–0.5
	CD-ROM drive	–1.0
Remaining power		4.0 amps

12-Volt Power:		**8.0 Amps**
Less:	4 slots filled @ 0.175 ea.	–0.7
	3.5" hard disk drive	–1.0
	3.5" & 5.25" floppy drives	–1.0
	Cooling fan	–0.1
	CD-ROM drive	–1.0
Remaining power		4.2 amps

In the preceding example, everything seems all right for now. With half the slots filled, two floppy drives, and one hard disk, the system still has room for more. There might be trouble if this system were expanded to the extreme. With every slot filled and two or more hard disks, there definitely will be problems with the +5v. However, the +12v does seem to have room to spare. You could add a CD-ROM drive or a second hard disk without worrying too much about the +12v power, but the +5v power will be strained. If you anticipate loading up a system to the extreme—as in a high-end multimedia system, for example—you may want to invest in the insurance of a higher output supply. For example, a 250-watt supply usually has 25-amps of +5v and 10-amps of +5v current, whereas a 300-watt unit has 32-amps of +5v power. These supplies would permit a fully expanded system and are likely to be found in full-sized desktop or tower case configurations in which this capability can be fully used.

Motherboards can draw anywhere from 4 to 15 amps or more of +5v power to run. In fact, a single Pentium 66MHz CPU draws up to 3.2 amps of +5v power all by itself. Considering that dual 100MHz Pentium processor systems are now becoming available, you could have 6.4 amps or more drawn by the processors alone. A motherboard like this with 64M of RAM might draw 15 amps or more all by itself. Most 486DX2 motherboards draw approximately 5 to 7 amps of +5v. Bus slots are allotted maximum power in amps as shown in table 8.10.

Table 8.10 Maximum Power Consumption in Amps per Bus Slot

Bus Type	+5v Power	+12v Power	+3.3v Power
ISA	2.0	0.175	N/A
EISA	4.5	1.5	N/A
VL-Bus	2.0	N/A	N/A
16-Bit MCA	1.6	0.175	N/A
32-Bit MCA	2.0	0.175	N/A
PCI	5	0.5	7.6

As you can see from the table, ISA slots are allotted 2.0 amps of +5v and 0.175 amps of +12v power. Note that these are maximum figures and not all cards draw this much power. If the slot has a VL-Bus extension connector, an additional 2.0 amps of +5v power is allowed for the VL-Bus.

Floppy drives can vary in power consumption, but most of the newer 3.5-inch drives have motors that run off +5v in addition to the logic circuits. These drives usually draw 1.0 amps of +5v power and use no +12v at all. Most 5.25-inch drives use standard +12v motors that draw about 1.0 amps. These drives also require about 0.5 amps of +5v for the logic circuits. Most cooling fans draw about 0.1 amps of +12v power, which is almost negligible.

Typical 3.5-inch hard disks today draw about 1 amp of +12v power to run the motors and only about 0.5 amps of +5v power for the logic. The 5.25-inch hard disks, especially those that are full-height, draw much more power. A typical full-height hard drive draws 2.0 amps of +12v power and 1.0 amps of +5v power. Another problem with hard disks is that they require much more power during the spinup phase of operation than during normal operation. In most cases, the drive draws double the +12v power during spinup, which can be 4.0 amps or more for the full-height drives. This tapers off to normal after the drive is spinning.

The figures most manufacturers report for maximum power supply output are full duty-cycle figures, which means that these levels of power can be supplied continuously. You usually can expect a unit that continuously supplies some level of power to supply more power for some noncontinuous amount of time. A supply usually can offer 50 percent greater output than the continuous figure indicates for as long as one minute. This cushion is often used to supply the necessary power to start spinning a hard disk. After the drive has spun to full speed, the power draw drops to a value within the system's continuous supply capabilities. Drawing anything over the rated continuous figure for any long length of time causes the power supply to run hot and fail early, and it can prompt several nasty symptoms in the system.

Tip

If you are using internal SCSI hard drives, this useful tip can ease the startup load on your power supply. The key is to enable the Remote Start option on the SCSI drive, which causes the drive to start spinning only when it receives a startup command over the SCSI bus. The effect is such that the drive remains stationary (drawing very little power) until the very end of the POST and spins up right when the SCSI portion of the POST is begun. If you have multiple SCSI drives, they all spin up sequentially based on their SCSI ID setting. This is designed so that only one drive is spinning up at any one time, and that no drives start spinning until the rest of the system has had time to start. This greatly eases the load on the power supply when you first power the system on. This tip is essential when dealing with portable type systems in which power is at a premium. I burned up a supply in one of my portable systems before resetting the internal drive to Remote Start.

The biggest causes of overload problems are filling up the slots and adding more drives. Multiple hard drives, CD-ROM drives, floppy drives, and so on can exact quite a drain on the system power supply. Make sure that you have enough +12v power to run all the drives you are going to install. Tower systems can be a problem here because they have so many drive bays. Make sure that you have enough +5v power to run all your expansion cards, especially if you are using VL-Bus or EISA cards. It pays to be conservative, but remember that most cards draw less than the maximum allowed.

Many people wait until an existing unit fails before they replace it with an upgraded version. If you are on a tight budget, this "if it ain't broke, don't fix it" attitude works. Power supplies, however, often do not just fail; they can fail in an intermittent fashion or allow fluctuating power levels to reach the system, which results in unstable operation. You might be blaming system lockups on software bugs when the culprit is an overloaded power supply. If you have been running with your original power supply for a long time, you should expect some problems.

Leave It On or Turn It Off?

A frequent question that relates to the discussion of power supplies concerns whether you should turn off a system when it is not in use. You should understand some facts about electrical components and what makes them fail. Combine this knowledge with information on power consumption and cost, not to mention safety, and perhaps you can come to your own conclusion. Because circumstances can vary, the best answer for your own situation might be different depending on your particular needs and application.

Frequently, powering a system on and off does cause deterioration and damage to the components. This seems logical, and the reason is simple but not obvious to most. Many people believe that flipping system power on and off frequently is harmful because it electrically "shocks" the system. The real problem, however, is temperature. In other words, it is not so much electrical shock as thermal shock that damages a system. As the system warms up, the components expand; and as it cools off, the components contract. This alone stresses everything. In addition, various materials in the system have different thermal expansion coefficients, which means that they expand and contract at different rates. Over time, thermal shock causes deterioration in many areas of a system.

From a pure system-reliability point, it is desirable to insulate the system from thermal shock as much as possible. When a system is turned on, the components go from ambient (room) temperature to as high as 185 degrees F (85 degrees C) within 30 minutes or less. When you turn the system off, the same thing happens in reverse and the components cool back to ambient temperature in a short period of time. Each component expands and contracts at slightly different rates, which causes the system an enormous amount of stress.

Thermal expansion and contraction remains the single largest cause of component failure. Chip cases can split, allowing moisture to enter and contaminate them. Delicate internal wires and contacts can break, and circuit boards can develop stress cracks. Surface-mounted components expand and contract at different rates from the circuit board they are mounted on, which causes enormous stress at the solder joints. Solder joints can fail due to the metal hardening from the repeated stress causing cracks in the joint. Components that use heat sinks such as processors, transistors, or voltage regulators can overheat and fail because the thermal cycling causes heat sink adhesives to deteriorate, breaking the thermally conductive bond between the device and the heat sink. Thermal cycling also causes socketed devices and connections to "creep," which can cause a variety of intermittent contact failures.

Thermal expansion and contraction affect not only chips and circuit boards but also things like hard disk drives. Most hard drives today have sophisticated thermal compensation routines that make adjustments in head position relative to the expanding and contracting platters. Most drives perform this thermal compensation routine once every five minutes for the first 30 minutes the drive is running, and then every 30 minutes thereafter. In many drives, this procedure can be heard as a rapid "tick-tick-tick-tick" sound.

In essence, anything you can do to keep the system at a constant temperature prolongs the life of the system, and the best way to accomplish this is to leave the system either permanently on or off. Of course, if the system is never turned on in the first place, it should last a long time indeed!

Now, although it seems like I am saying that you should leave all systems on 24 hours a day, that is not necessarily true. A system powered on and left unattended can be a fire hazard (I have had monitors spontaneously catch fire—luckily I was there at the time), is a data security risk (cleaning crews, other nocturnal visitors, and so on), can be easily damaged if moved while running, and simply wastes electrical energy.

I currently pay $0.11 for a kilowatt-hour of electricity. A typical desktop style PC with display consumes at least 300 watts (0.3 kilowatts) of electricity (and that is a conservative estimate). This means that it would cost 3.3 cents to run this typical PC for an hour. Multiplying by 168 hours in a week means that it would cost $5.54 per week to run this PC continuously. If the PC were turned on at 9:00 a.m. and off at 5:00 p.m., it would only be on 40 hours per week and would cost only $1.32—a savings of $4,22 per week! Multiply this savings by 100 systems, and you are saving $422 per week; multiply this by 1,000 systems, and you are saving $4,220 per week! Using systems certified under the new EPA Energy Star program (that is, "Green" PCs) would account for an additional savings of around $1 per system per week, or $1,000 per week for 1,000 systems. The great thing about Energy Star systems is that the savings are even greater if the systems are left on for long periods of time because the power management routines are automatic.

Based on these facts, my recommendations are that you power the systems on at the beginning of the work day, and off at the end of the work day. Do not power the systems off for lunch, breaks, or any other short duration of time. Servers and the like of course should be left on continuously. This seems to be the best compromise of system longevity with pure economics.

Energy Star Systems

The EPA has started a certification program for energy efficient PCs and peripherals. To be a member of this program, the PC or display must drop to a power draw at the outlet of 30 watts or less during periods of inactivity. Systems that conform to this specification get to wear the Energy Star logo. This is a voluntary program, meaning there is no requirements to meet the specification, however many PC manufacturers are finding that it helps to sell their systems if they can advertise them as energy efficient.

One problem with this type of system is that the motherboard and disk drives literally can "go to sleep," which means they can enter a standby or sleep mode where they draw very little power. This causes havoc with some of the older power supplies, because the low power draw does not provide enough of a load for them to function properly. Most of the newer supplies on the market are designed to work with these systems, and have a very low minimum load specification. I suggest that if you are purchasing a power supply upgrade for a system, ensure that the minimum load will be provided by the equipment in your system, otherwise, when the PC goes to sleep, it may take a power switch cycle to wake it up again! This problem would be most noticeable if you invest in a very high output supply and use it in a system that draws very little power to begin with.

Power Supply Problems

A weak or inadequate power supply can put a damper on your ideas for system expansion. Some systems are designed with beefy power supplies, as if to anticipate a great deal of system add-on or expansion components. Most desktop or tower systems are built in this manner. Some systems have inadequate power supplies from the start, however, and cannot accept the number and types of power-hungry options you might want to add.

In particular, portable systems often have power supply problems because they are designed to fit into a small space. Likewise, many older systems had inadequate power supply capacity for system expansion. For example, the original PC's 63.5-watt supply was inadequate for all but the most basic system. Add a graphics board, hard disk, math coprocessor (8087) chip, and 640K of memory, and you would kill the supply in no time. The total power draw of all the items in the system determines the adequacy of the power supply.

The wattage rating can sometimes be very misleading. Not all 200-watt supplies are created the same. Those who are in to high-end audio systems know that some watts are better than others. Cheap power supplies may in fact put out the rated power, but what about noise and distortion? Some of the supplies are under-engineered to meet their specifications just barely, whereas others may greatly exceed their specifications. Many of the cheaper supplies output noisy or unstable power, which can cause numerous problems with the system. Another problem with under-engineered power supplies is that they run hot and force the system to do so as well. The repeated heating and cooling of solid-state components eventually causes a computer system to fail, and engineering principles dictate that the hotter a PC's temperature, the shorter its life. Many people recommend replacing the original supply in a system with a heavier duty model, which solves the problem. Because power supplies come in common form factors, finding a heavy duty replacement for most systems is easy.

Some of the available replacement supplies have higher capacity cooling fans than the originals, which can greatly prolong system life and minimize overheating problems, especially with some of the newer high-powered processors. If noise is a problem, models with special fans can run quieter than the standard models. These types often use larger diameter fans that spin slower, so that they run quiet while moving the same amount of air as the smaller fans. A company called PC Power and Cooling specializes in heavy-duty and quiet supplies. Another company called Astec has several heavy-duty models as well. Astec supplies are found as original equipment in many high-end systems, such as those from IBM and Hewlett Packard.

Ventilation in a system can be important. You must ensure adequate air flow to cool the hotter items in the system. Most processors have heat sinks today that require a steady stream of air to cool the processor. If the processor heat sink has its own fan, this is not much of a concern. If you have free slots, space the boards out in your system to allow air flow between them. Place the hottest running boards nearest the fan or ventilation holes in the system. Make sure that there is adequate air flow around the hard disk drive, especially those that spin at higher rates of speed. Some hard disks can generate quite a bit of heat during operation. If the hard disks overheat, data is lost.

Always make sure that you run with the lid on, especially if you have a loaded system. Removing the lid can actually cause a system to overheat. With the lid off, the power supply fan no longer draws air through the system. Instead, the fan ends up cooling the supply only, and the rest of the system must be cooled by simple convection. Although most systems do not immediately overheat because of this, several of my own systems, especially those that are fully expanded, have overheated within 15 to 30 minutes when run with the case lid off.

If you experience intermittent problems that you suspect are related to overheating, a higher capacity replacement power supply is usually the best cure. Specially designed supplies with additional cooling fan capacity also can help as well. At least one company sells a device called a *fan card,* but I am not convinced these are a good idea. Unless the fan is positioned to draw air to or from outside the case, all the fan does is blow hot air around inside the system and provide a spot cooling effect for anything it is blowing on. In fact, adding fans in this manner contributes to the overall heat inside the system because each fan consumes power and generates heat.

The CPU-mounted fans are an exception to this because they are designed only for spot cooling of the CPU. Many of the newer processors run so much hotter than the other components in the system that a conventional finned aluminum heat sink cannot do the job. In this case a small fan placed directly over the processor can provide a spot cooling effect that keeps the processor temperatures down. One drawback to these active processor cooling fans is that if they fail, the processor overheats instantly and can even be damaged. Whenever possible, I try to use the biggest passive (finned aluminum) heat sink and stay away from more fans.

Tip

If you seal the ventilation holes on the bottom of the original IBM PC chassis, starting from where the disk drive bays begin and all the way to the right side of the PC, you drop the interior temperature some 10 to 20 degrees Fahrenheit—not bad for two cents' worth of electrical tape. IBM "factory-applied" this tape on every XT and XT-286 it sold. The result is greatly improved interior aerodynamics and airflow over the heat-generating components.

For other PC compatible systems, this may not apply because their case designs may be different.

No matter what system you have, be sure that any empty slot positions have the filler brackets installed. If you leave these brackets off after removing a card, the resultant hole will disrupt the internal airflow and may cause higher internal temperatures.

Power Supply Troubleshooting

Troubleshooting the power supply basically means isolating the supply as the cause of problems within a system. Rarely is it recommended to go inside the power supply to make repairs because of the dangerous high voltages present. Such internal repairs are beyond the scope of this book and are specifically not recommended unless the technician knows what he or she is doing.

Many symptoms would lead me to suspect that the power supply in a system is failing. This can sometimes be difficult for an inexperienced technician to see, because at times little connection appears between the symptom and the cause—the power supply.

For example, in many cases a "parity check" type of error message or problem indicates a problem with the supply. This may seem strange because the parity check message itself specifically refers to memory that has failed. The connection is that the power supply is what powers the memory, and memory with inadequate power fails. It takes some experience to know when these failures are not caused by the memory and are in fact power-related. One clue is the repeatability of the problem. If the parity check message (or other problem) appears frequently and identifies the same memory location each time, I suspect defective memory as the problem. However, if the problem seems random, or the memory location given as failed seems random or wandering, I suspect improper power as the culprit. The following is a list of PC problems that often are power supply related:

- Any power-on or system startup failures or lockups
- Spontaneous rebooting or intermittent lockups during normal operation
- Intermittent parity check or other memory type errors
- Hard disk and fan simultaneously fail to spin (no +12v)
- Overheating due to fan failure
- Small brownouts cause the system to reset
- Electric shocks felt on the system case or connectors
- Slight static discharges disrupt system operation

In fact, just about any intermittent system problem can be caused by the power supply. I always suspect the supply when flaky system operation is a symptom. Of course, the following fairly obvious symptoms point right to the power supply as a possible cause:

- System is completely dead (no fan, no cursor)
- Smoke
- Blown circuit breakers

If you suspect a power-supply problem, some simple measurements as well as more sophisticated tests outlined in this section can help you determine whether the power supply is at fault. Because these measurements may not detect some intermittent failures, you might have to use a spare power supply for a long-term evaluation. If the symptoms and problems disappear when a "known good" spare unit is installed, you have found the source of your problem.

Digital Multi-Meters

A simple test that can be done to a power supply is to check the output voltage. This shows if a power supply is operating correctly and whether the output voltages are within the correct tolerance range. Note that all voltage measurements must be made with the power supply connected to a proper load, which usually means testing while the power supply is still installed in the system.

Selecting a Meter. You need a simple Digital Multi-Meter (DMM) or Digital Volt-Ohm Meter (DVOM) to make voltage and resistance checks in electronic circuits (see fig. 8.9). You should use only a DMM rather than the older needle type multi-meters because the older meters work by injecting a 9v signal into the circuit when measuring resistance. This will damage most computer circuits. A DMM uses a much smaller voltage (usually 1.5v) when making resistance measurements, which is safe for electronic equipment. You can get a good DMM from many sources and with many different features. I prefer the small pocket-sized meters for computer work because they are easy to carry around. Some features to look for in a good DMM are

- *Pocket size.* This is self-explanatory, but small meters are available that have many if not all the features of larger ones. The elaborate features found on some of the larger meters are not really needed for computer work.
- *Overload protection.* This means that if you plug the meter into a voltage or current beyond the capability of the meter to measure, the meter protects itself from damage. Cheaper meters lack this protection and can be easily damaged by reading current or voltage values that are too high.
- *Autoranging.* This means that the meter automatically selects the proper voltage or resistance range when making measurements. This is preferable to the manual range selection, however, really good meters offer both autoranging capability and a manual range override.
- *Detachable probe leads.* The leads can be easily damaged and sometimes a variety of differently shaped probes are required for different tests. Cheaper meters have the leads permanently attached, which means that they cannot easily be replaced. Look for a meter with detachable leads that plug into the meter.
- *Audible continuity test.* Although you can use the Ohm scale for testing continuity (0 ohms indicates continuity), a continuity test function causes a beep noise to be heard when continuity exists between the meter test leads. Using the sound, you can more quickly test cable assemblies and other items for continuity. After you use this feature, you will never want to use the ohms display for this purpose again.
- *Automatic power off.* These meters run on batteries, and the batteries can easily be worn down if the meter is accidentally left on. Good meters have an automatic shutoff that turns off the meter if no readings are sensed for a predetermined period of time.
- *Automatic display hold.* This feature enables the last stable reading to be held on the display even after the reading is taken. This is especially useful if you are trying to work in a difficult-to-reach area single-handedly.
- *Minimum and maximum trap.* This feature enables the lowest and highest readings to be trapped in memory and held for later display. This is especially useful if you have readings that are fluctuating too quickly to see on the display.

Although you can get a basic pocket DMM for about $30, one with all these features is priced in the $200 range. Radio Shack carries some nice inexpensive units, whereas the high-end models can be purchased from electronics supply houses like Allied, Newark, or Digi-Key.

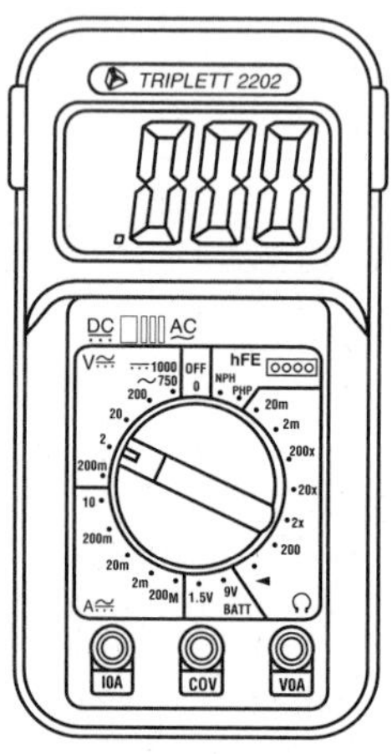

Figure 8.9

A typical Digital Multi-Meter (DMM).

Measuring Voltage. When making measurements on a system that is operating, you must use a technique called *back probing* the connectors. This is because you cannot disconnect any of the connectors while the system is running and instead must measure with everything connected. Nearly all the connectors you need to probe have openings in the back where the wires enter the connector. The meter probes are narrow enough to fit into the connector alongside the wire and make contact with the metal terminal inside. This technique is called back probing because you are probing the connector from the back. Virtually all the following measurements must be made using this back probing technique.

To test a power supply for proper output, check the voltage at the Power_Good pin (P8-1 on most IBM-compatible supplies) for +3v to +6v. If the measurement is not within this range, the system never sees the Power_Good signal and, therefore, does not start or run properly. In most cases, the supply is bad and must be replaced.

Continue by measuring the voltage ranges of the pins on the motherboard and drive power connectors (see Table 8.11). Note that the exact pin specifications and acceptable voltage ranges may vary for different manufacturer's systems; however, they are representative of most IBM-compatibles. Many follow the looser tolerance guidelines of accepting anything approximately 10 percent too low or eight percent too high, especially for the –5v and –12v (negative) signals. I prefer to use tighter tolerances myself and would pass only a supply that is within five percent or less of the correct voltages. Some manufacturers have even tighter tolerances on their systems, and in that case you should go by what the manufacturer specifies. Consult your system's technical reference manual for this information to make sure.

The Power_Good signal has tolerances different from the other signals, although it is nominally a +5v signal in most systems. The trigger point for Power_Good is about +2.5v, but most systems require the signal voltage to be within the tolerances listed in Table 8.12.

Table 8.11 Power Supply Acceptable Voltage Ranges

	Loose Tolerance		Tight Tolerance	
Desired Voltage	**Min. (–10%)**	**Max. (+8%)**	**Min. (–5%)**	**Max. (+5%)**
+/–5.0v	4.5v	5.4v	4.75	5.25
+/–12.0v	10.8v	12.9v	11.4	12.6

Table 8.12 Power_Good Signal Acceptable Range

Signal	Minimum	Maximum
Power_Good (+5v)	3.0v	6.0v

Replace the power supply if the voltages you measure are out of these ranges. Again, it is worth noting that any and all power supply tests and measurements must be made with the power supply properly loaded, which usually means it must be installed in a system and the system must be running.

Specialized Test Equipment

You can use several types of specialized test gear to test power supplies more effectively. Because the power supply is perhaps the most failure-prone item in PCs today, if you service many PC systems, it is wise to have many of these specialized items.

Load Resistors. If you want to bench test a power supply, you must make sure that loads are placed on both the +5v and +12v outputs. This is one reason that it is best to test the supply while it is installed in the system rather than separately on the bench. For impromptu bench testing, you can use a spare motherboard and hard disk drive to load the +5v and +12v outputs, respectively, while you make voltage measurements or check overall system operation.

If you are frequently testing power supplies, you may want to construct your own load resistors to make testing easier. In my shop, I often use one of the +12v load resistors originally installed in AT systems sold without hard disks. Although these are nice, they do not load the +5v signal, and I often want more than a 2.4 amp load on the +12v as well.

You can construct your own power supply load resistor network out of light bulbs. By wiring up a set of light sockets in parallel, you can vary the load by adding or removing bulbs from their sockets. The type of bulb to use for a +12v load is the standard #1156 bulb used in many automobile exterior light assemblies. These bulbs are designed to run on +12v and draw approximately 2.1 amps of current or about 25 watts. Each bulb effectively acts as if it were a 5.7 Ohm resistor. I recommend that you wire up at least four bulb sockets in parallel, mounted on a nonconductive breadboard. For testing high output supplies, you could wire up as many as eight sockets in parallel. It would be wise to have four disk drive connectors also wired in parallel in the same circuit to balance the draw from the supply. A single drive connector cannot handle more than a two-bulb (4 amp) load reliably. To use this load tester, plug the bulb loading network into the disk drive power connectors. By adding or removing bulbs from their sockets, you can control the load. With four bulbs installed, you have approximately an 8 amp load, which is good for maximum load testing of a standard 200-watt PC power supply rated for 8 amps of +12v output.

You will still need a +5v load. Unfortunately, a #1156 type bulb does not work well for a +5v load because each bulb draws only 0.875 amps at +5v (4.4 watts). Even eight of these bulbs would draw only 7 amps, or 35 watts of +5v power. You could substitute a #1493 bulb instead, which draws about 2.75 amps at +5v, or about 14 watts. You would still need eight of these bulbs, which would draw 22 amps at +5v, to perform a maximum load test on a standard 200 watt-rated PC power supply.

Perhaps a better solution than bulbs is to use heavy-duty wirewound resistors to construct a load network. For a +12v load, you could mount a series of 6-Ohm 50-watt resistors in a parallel network with a toggle switch to bring each one into the circuit. Using a 6-Ohm resistor would draw 2 amps, or 24 watts, exactly, so make sure that each switch is rated for 3 amps or more to be safe. As you switch each additional resistor into the circuit, the load increases by 2 amps, or 24 watts. Note that the resistors are rated to handle up to 50 watts, which means we are simply being conservative. I might start this network off with a single #1156 bulb because the visual information from the light is useful. The fact that the light is lit means of course that power is available, and sometimes you can see voltage variations as changes in the brightness of the lamp as you switch in additional loads. This can give you a visual impression of how well the supply is performing.

This same type of setup can be used to create a +5v load network. In this case, I recommend you use 1-Ohm 50-watt wirewound resistors in the same type of parallel network, with a switch for each resistor. You could start the network off with a single #1493 bulb for a visual indicator of power supply output, which would draw 2.75 amps, or about 14 watts of power. Each 1-Ohm 50-watt resistor draws 5 amps of +5v current, or exactly 25 watts. Again, I would specify resistors with a 50-watt rating and a switch with a rating higher than 5 amps to be on the conservative side. A network of four of these resistors alone draws exactly 20 amps of power, which is exactly what the typical 200 watt PC power supply has to offer in +5v. By switching four of these resistors into the load, you could perform a full stress test on the supply. Add more, and you could test higher output supplies as well. Again, it would be prudent to draw this through four disk drive connectors simultaneously so as to balance the load between the connectors. You also could get some motherboard (P8 and P9 type) connectors and draw the load through all the +5v pins on those connectors.

You can purchase all these components, including wirewound resistors, bulbs, sockets, connectors, and breadboard, through electronics parts supply houses such as Allied, Newark, and Digi-Key.

Variable Voltage Transformer. In testing power supplies, it is desirable to simulate different voltage conditions at the wall socket to observe how the supply reacts. A *variable voltage transformer* is a useful test device for checking power supplies because it enables you to have control over the AC line voltage used as input for the power supply (see fig. 8.10). This device consists of a large transformer mounted in a housing with a dial indicator to control the output voltage. You plug the line cord from the transformer into the wall socket and plug the PC power cord into the socket provided on the transformer. The knob on the transformer can be used to adjust the AC line voltage seen by the PC.

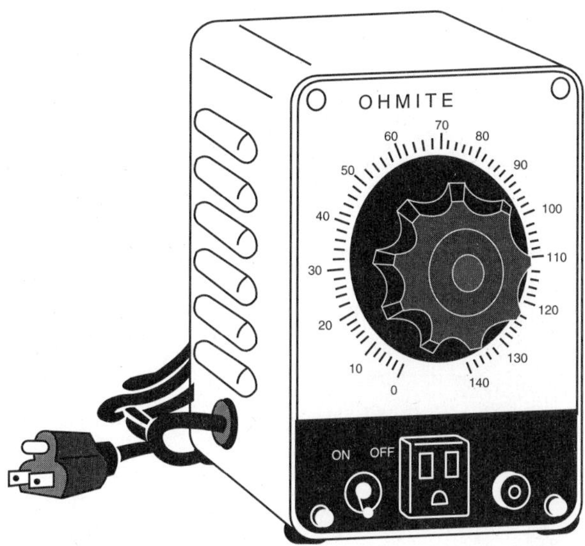

Figure 8.10

A variable voltage transformer.

Most variable transformers can adjust their AC output from 0v to 140v no matter what the AC input (wall socket) voltage is. Some can even cover a range from 0v to 280v as well. You can use the transformer to simulate brownout conditions, enabling you to observe the PC's response. Thus, you can check for proper Power_Good signal operation among other things.

By running the PC and dropping the voltage until the PC shuts down, you can see how much "reserve" is in the power supply for handling a brownout or other voltage fluctuations. If your transformer can output voltages in the 200v range, you can test the capability of the power supply to run on foreign voltage levels as well. A properly functioning supply should operate between 90v to 137v but shut down cleanly if the voltage is outside that range.

An indication of a problem is seeing "parity check" type error messages when you drop the voltage to 80v. This indicates that the Power_Good signal is not being withdrawn before the power supply output to the PC fails. What should happen is that the PC simply stops operating as the Power_Good signal is withdrawn, causing the system to enter a continuous reset loop.

Variable voltage transformers are sold by a number of electronic parts supply houses such as Allied, Newark, and Digi-Key. You should expect to pay anywhere from $100 to $300 for these devices.

PC PowerCheck. The PC PowerCheck card by Data Depot is an ISA bus plug-in card that can be used to test power supplies easily while in the system or on a bench. It has a series of LEDs that indicate over or under voltage conditions, noise, and transient spike occurrences. These indicators can be set up to run in real time, or to trap any anomalies and stay lit.

The PC PowerCheck card can connect to the system in two ways. The easiest way to use it is to plug it directly into a slot like any other adapter card. One caution is to make sure that you plug the card in the correct orientation; if you plug it in backward, serious damage to the card and motherboard can result. No metal bracket is on the card, so it is possible to plug it in either way. You will make that mistake only once!

A second way to use the card is in a bench test mode. In this case, you remove the power supply from the system and plug it directly into the power connectors found on the card. The power connectors on the PC PowerCheck card are not keyed, so if your power supply has keyed connectors, they can be difficult to plug in. Likewise, you must make sure that the power supply connectors are plugged in the proper orientation. If you plug the connectors in backward, you may destroy the card.

In the bench test mode, the card is substituting for the motherboard. The PC PowerCheck card has built-in load resistors; however, they are very small, drawing only 0.5 amps of +5v and 0.1 amps of +12v current. These loads are certainly not enough to stress the supply, and may not be enough in many cases for the supply to operate at all. In this case, additional load can be placed on the supply by plugging in a hard disk or by using custom-made load resistors.

The PC PowerCheck also has an LED to monitor the Power_Good signal, but to monitor that signal the power supply must be plugged in directly in the bench test mode. When plugged into a slot, the same LED monitors the bus Reset line, which is controlled by the Power_Good signal, giving you a secondary indication of Power_Good status.

The PC PowerCheck can be a useful tool in testing PC power supplies as installed in a system, especially for those unwilling to use a digital voltmeter. It is extremely useful for quick pass/fail testing such as on a PC assembly line. Supplies that fail the test can be quickly identified and replaced, and the defective units can be subjected to further testing without holding up the assembly process. The bench test mode is not as useful because additional loads must be placed on the supply for proper stress testing. In any mode, the LED indicators for noise, transients, and Power_Good/Reset are informative, useful, and unique for this product.

PC Power System Analyzer. The most sophisticated power supply test device I have used is the PC Power System Analyzer from TCE. This is a portable toaster-sized piece of gear that comes in a padded case for transport that contains the Analyzer and all its accessories. This device sells for around $750 and performs three main functions, all of which are conducted with the supply still installed in the system unit.

The primary function is to load test the system. The PC Power System Analyzer comes with a bus adapter (for both ISA/EISA and MCA) that probes the power output and adds a few amps of additional load to the +5v and +12v lines. Using this additional load in conjunction with the load of the system, it analyzes the capability of the supply to deliver the proper current.

The unit also performs a Power_Good timing test, which checks whether the Power_Good signal arrives within the proper time span of 100 to 500 ms. Personally, I have seen many supplies that have problems with the Power_Good signal, and some motherboards are more sensitive to this than others. This unit quickly identifies failing or improperly designed supplies.

The other tests are voltage tests. Both the power supply output and line (wall current) voltage are continuously tested, and minimums and maximums are recorded over time. Information from all the tests can be output to a printer via a parallel port on the unit. During voltage measurements, any anomalies are recorded along with the time of the occurrence, actual voltage values, duration of the failure, and additional information. The unit also has several LEDs to indicate failures or proper operation under the different tests.

The printout is excellent especially when you are servicing systems for others. When you have to explain to a customer how their power supply is failing, it gives you documentation to back you up.

The TCE Power System Analyzer is one of the most sophisticated and specialized pieces of test gear for power supplies. It can be used in PC service shops or assembly operations to test and validate power supply function. Because it is portable, it also can be easily carried into the field for testing remote systems. It is more of a professional tool and is probably too expensive for the average end user.

Repairing the Power Supply

Actually repairing a power supply is rarely done anymore, primarily because it is usually cheaper simply to replace the supply with a new one. Even high-quality power supplies are not that expensive relative to the labor required to repair them.

Defective power supplies are usually discarded unless they happen to be one of the higher quality or more expensive units. In that case, it is usually wise to send the supply out to a company that specializes in repairing power supplies and other components. These companies provide what is called *depot repair,* which means you send the supply to them; they repair it and return it to you. If time is of the essence, most of the depot repair companies immediately send you a functional equivalent to your defective supply and take yours in as a core charge. Depot repair is the recommended way to service many PC components such as power supplies, monitors, and printers. If you take your PC in to a conventional service outlet, they often diagnose the problem to the major component and send it out to be depot repaired. You can do that yourself and save the markup that the repair shop normally charges in such cases.

For those with experience around high voltages, it might be possible to repair a failing supply with two relatively simple operations; however, these require opening the supply. I do not recommend this; I mention it only as an alternative to replacement in some cases. Most manufacturers try to prevent you from entering the supply by sealing it with special tamper-proof Torx screws. These screws use the familiar Torx star driver, but also have a tamper prevention pin in the center that prevents a standard driver from working. Most tool companies such as Jensen or Specialized sell sets of TT (tamper-proof Torx) bits, which remove the tamper-resistant screws. Other manufacturers rivet the power supply case shut, which means you must drill out the rivets to gain access. Again, the manufacturers place these obstacles there for a reason—to prevent entry by those who are inexperienced around high voltage. Consider yourself warned!

Most power supplies have an internal fuse that is part of the overload protection. If this fuse is blown, the supply does not operate. It is possible to replace this fuse if you open up the supply. Be aware that in most cases in which an internal power supply problem causes the fuse to blow, replacing it does nothing but cause it to blow again until the root cause of the problem is repaired. In this case, you are better off sending the unit to a professional depot repair company. The vendor list lists several companies that do depot repair on power supplies and other components.

PC power supplies have a voltage adjustment internal to the supply that is calibrated and set when the supply is manufactured. Over time, the values of some of the components in the supply can change, thus altering the output voltages. If this is the case, you often can access the adjustment control and tweak it to bring the voltages back to where they should be. Several adjustable items are in the supply—usually small variable resistors that can be turned with a screwdriver. You should use a nonconductive tool such as a fiberglass or plastic screwdriver designed for this purpose. If you were to drop a metal tool into an operating supply, dangerous sparks and possibly fire could result, not to mention danger of electrocution and damage to the supply. You also have to figure out which of the adjustments are for voltage and which ones are for each voltage signal. This requires some trial and error testing. You can mark the current positions of all the resistors, begin measuring a single voltage signal, and try moving each adjuster slightly until you see the voltage change. If you move an adjuster and nothing changes, put it back to the original position you marked. Through this process, you can locate and adjust each of the voltages to the standard 5v and 12v levels.

Obtaining Replacement Units

There may be times when it is simply easier, safer, or less expensive (considering time and materials) to replace the power supply rather than repair it. As mentioned earlier, replacement power supplies are available from many manufacturers. Before you can shop for a supplier, however, you should consider other purchasing factors.

Deciding on a Power Supply

When looking at getting a new power supply, you should take several things into account. First, consider the power supply's shape, or form factor. For example, the power supply used in the IBM AT differs physically from the one used in the PC or XT. Therefore, AT and PC/XT supplies are not interchangeable.

Differences exist in the size, shape, screw-hole positions, connector type, number of connectors, and switch position in these and other power supplies. Systems that use the same form factor supply can easily interchange. The compatible manufacturers realized this and most began designing systems that mimicked the shape of IBM's AT with regard to motherboard and power supply configuration and mounting. As the clone market evolved, four standard form factors for power supplies became popular: AT/Tower, Baby AT, Slimline, and PC/XT. You can easily interchange any supply with another one of the same form factor. Earlier, this chapter gave complete descriptions of these form factors. When ordering a replacement supply, you need to know which form factor your system requires.

Many systems use proprietary-designed power supplies, which makes replacement difficult. IBM uses a number of designs for the PS/2 systems, and little interchangeability exists between different systems. Some of the supplies do interchange, especially between any that have the same or similar cases, such as the Model 60, 65, and 80. Several different output level power supplies are available for these systems, including 207-, 225-, 242-, and 250-watt versions. The most powerful 250-watt unit was supplied originally for the Model 65 SX and later version Model 80 systems, although it fits perfectly in any Model 60, 65, or 80 system. I have not found any company manufacturing aftermarket supplies for the PS/2 systems, probably because the IBM factory-supplied units are more than adequate for their intended application. Although these supplies are mostly made by Astec, they do not sell them direct because of contractual agreements with IBM. Traditionally, it is too expensive to purchase parts from IBM, so a great number of third-party companies are repairing and even reselling brand new IBM PS/2 power supplies (and other IBM parts) at prices greatly below what IBM charges for the same thing. Scan the vendor list in the back of this book for some recommended vendors of these parts.

One risk with some of the compatibles is that they might not use one of the industry-standard form-factor supplies. If a system uses one of the common form factor power supplies, replacement units are available from hundreds of vendors. An unfortunate user of a system with a nonstandard form factor supply does not have this kind of choice and must get a replacement from the original manufacturer of the system—and usually pay through the nose for the unit. Although you can find AT form factor units for as little as $50, the proprietary units from some manufacturers run as high as $400. When *Popular Mechanics* magazine reviews an automobile, it always lists the replacement costs of the most failure-prone and replacement-prone components, from front bumpers to alternators to taillights. PC buyers often overlook this type of information and discover too late the consequences of having nonstandard components in a system.

An example of IBM-compatible systems with proprietary power supply designs are those from Compaq. None of its systems use the same form factor supply as the IBM systems, which means that Compaq usually is the only place from which you can get a replacement. If the power supply in your Compaq Deskpro system "goes south," you can expect to pay $395 for a replacement, and the replacement unit will be no better or quieter than the one you are replacing. You have little choice in the matter because almost no one offers Compaq form factor power supplies except Compaq. One exception is that PC Power and Cooling offers excellent replacement power supplies for the earlier Compaq Portable systems and for the Deskpro series. These replacement power supplies have higher-output power levels than the original supplies from Compaq and cost much less.

Sources for Replacement Power Supplies

Because one of the most failure-prone items in PC systems is the power supply, I am often called on to recommend a replacement. Literally hundreds of companies manufacture PC power supplies, and I certainly have not tested them all. I can, however, recommend some companies whose products I have come to know and trust.

Although other high-quality manufacturers are out there, at this time I recommend power supplies from either Astec Standard Power or PC Power and Cooling.

Astec makes the power supplies used in most of the high-end systems by IBM, Hewlett-Packard, Apple, and many other name brand systems. They have power supplies available in a number of standard form factors (AT/Tower, Baby AT, and Slimline) and a variety of output levels. They have power supplies with ratings of up to 300 watts and also power supplies especially designed for "green" PCs that meet the EPA Energy Star requirements for low power consumption. Their "green" power supplies are specifically designed to achieve high efficiency at low load conditions. Be aware that high output supplies from other manufacturers may have problems with very low loads. Astec also makes a number of power supplies for laptop and notebook PC systems and has numerous non-PC type supplies.

PC Power and Cooling has the most complete line of power supplies for PC systems. They make supplies in all the standard PC form factors used today (AT/Tower, Baby AT, PC/XT, and Slimline). Versions are available in a variety of different quality and output levels, from inexpensive replacements to very high-quality high-output models with ratings up to 450 watts. They even have versions with built-in battery backup systems and a series of special models with high-volume low-speed (quiet) fan assemblies. Their quiet models are especially welcome to people who cannot take the fan noise that some power supplies emanate.

PC Power and Cooling also has units available to fit some of Compaq's proprietary designs. This can be a real boon if you have to service or repair Compaq systems because the PC Power and Cooling units are available in higher output ratings than Compaq's own. They cost much less than Compaq and bolt in as a direct replacement.

A high-quality power supply from either of these vendors is one of the best cures for intermittent system problems and goes a long way toward ensuring trouble-free operation in the future.

RTC/NVRAM Batteries

All 16-bit and higher systems have a special type of chip in them that combines a Real Time Clock (RTC) with at least 64 bytes (including the clock data) of Non-Volatile RAM (NVRAM) memory. This chip is officially called the RTC/NVRAM chip, but is often referred to as the "CMOS chip" or "CMOS RAM," since the type of chip used is produced using a CMOS (Complimentary Metal Oxide Semiconductor) process. CMOS design chips are known for very low power consumption, and this special RTC/NVRAM chip is designed to run off of a battery for several years.

The original chip of this type used in the original IBM AT was the Motorola 146818 chip. Although the ones used today have different manufacturers and part numbers, they are all designed to be compatible with this original Motorola part.

These chips include a real time clock, and the function there is obvious. The clock is used so that software can read the date and time, and so that the date and time will be preserved even though the system is powered off or unplugged. The NVRAM portion of the chip has another function. It is designed to store the basic system configuration, including the amount of memory installed, types of floppy and hard disk drives, and other information as well. Some of the more modern motherboards use extended NVRAM chips with as much as 2K or more of space to hold this configuration information. This is especially true for the new breed of Plug and Play systems, where the configuration of not only the motherboard, but also of adapter cards is stored. This information can then be read every time the system is powered on.

These chips are normally powered by some type of battery while the system is off to preserve the information in the NVRAM and to power the clock. Most often a lithium type battery is used, because they have a very long life, especially at the low power draw from the typical RTC/NVRAM chip.

Most of the higher quality modern systems sold today have a new type of chip that has the battery embedded within it. These are made by several companies, including Dallas Semiconductor and Benchmarq. These are notable for their long life. Under normal conditions, the battery within these chips will last for 10 years, which is of course longer than the useful life of the system. If your system uses one of the Dallas or Benchmarq modules, the battery and chip must be replaced as a unit because they are integrated. Most of the time these chip/battery combinations will be installed in a socket on the motherboard just in case there is a problem requiring an early replacement. You can get new modules for $18 or less direct from the manufacturers, which is often less than the cost of the older separate battery alone.

Some systems do not use a battery at all. Hewlett-Packard, for example includes a special capacitor in many of their systems that is automatically recharged any time the system is plugged in. Note that the system does not have to be running for the capacitor to charge, it only has to be plugged in. If the system is unplugged, the capacitor will power the RTC/NVRAM chip for up to a week or more. If the system remains unplugged for a duration longer than that, the NVRAM information will be lost. In that case, these systems can reload the NVRAM from a backup kept in a special Flash ROM chip contained on the motherboard. The only information that will actually be missing when you re-power the system is the date and time, which will have to be re-entered. By using the capacitor combined with a NVRAM backup in Flash ROM, they have a very reliable system that will last indefinitely.

Many systems use only a conventional battery, which may be either directly soldered into the motherboard or plugged in via a battery connector. For those systems with the battery soldered in, should it ever fail, they will normally have a spare battery connector on the motherboard where a conventional plug in battery can be used. In most cases you would never have to replace the motherboard battery, even if it were completely dead.

Conventional type batteries come in many forms. The best are of a lithium design because they will last from two to five years or more. I have seen systems with conventional alkaline batteries mounted in a holder, which are much less desirable as they fail more frequently and do not last as long. Also, they can be prone to leak, and if a battery leaks on the motherboard, it may be severely damaged.

Besides the different battery types, there are several different voltages used. The batteries used in PCs are normally either 3.6v, 4.5v, or 6v. If you are replacing the battery, make sure that your replacement is the same voltage as the one you removed from the system. Some motherboards can use batteries of several different voltages, and will have a jumper or switch to select the different settings. If you suspect your motherboard has this capability, consult the documentation for instructions on how to change the settings. Of course the easiest thing to do is to replace the existing battery with another of the same type, in which case the settings would not have to be changed.

When you replace a PC battery, be sure that you get the polarity correct, or you will damage the RTC/NVRAM (CMOS) chip. Because these are soldered into most motherboards, this will be an expensive mistake! The battery connector on the motherboard as well as the battery itself are normally keyed to prevent a backwards connection. The pinout of this connector is in Appendix A, but should also be listed in your system documentation.

When you replace a battery, in most cases the existing data stored in the NVRAM will be lost. Often the data will remain for several minutes (I have observed NVRAM retain information with no power for an hour or more), so if you make the swap quickly the information in the NVRAM will be retained. Just to be sure, it is recommended that you record all the system configuration settings stored in the NVRAM by your system SETUP program. In most cases you would want to run the BIOS SETUP program and print out all the screens showing the different settings. Some SETUP programs offer the ability to save the NVRAM data to a file for later restoration if necessary. That would be a good idea if it is an option in your system.

After replacing a battery, power up the system and use the SETUP program to check the date and time setting as well as any other data that was stored in the NVRAM.

Summary

This chapter examined the power supply in great detail. You should now have an understanding of how the supply functions in the system and the characteristics of power supply operation. You should understand the function of the Power_Good signal and its role in the system. Also covered was troubleshooting power supply problems and using test equipment to check out power supply operation. I have always found that the power supply is the single most failure-prone component in a PC system, and the information presented here should help greatly whether you are building systems from scratch, upgrading existing systems, or repairing a system with a failing power supply.

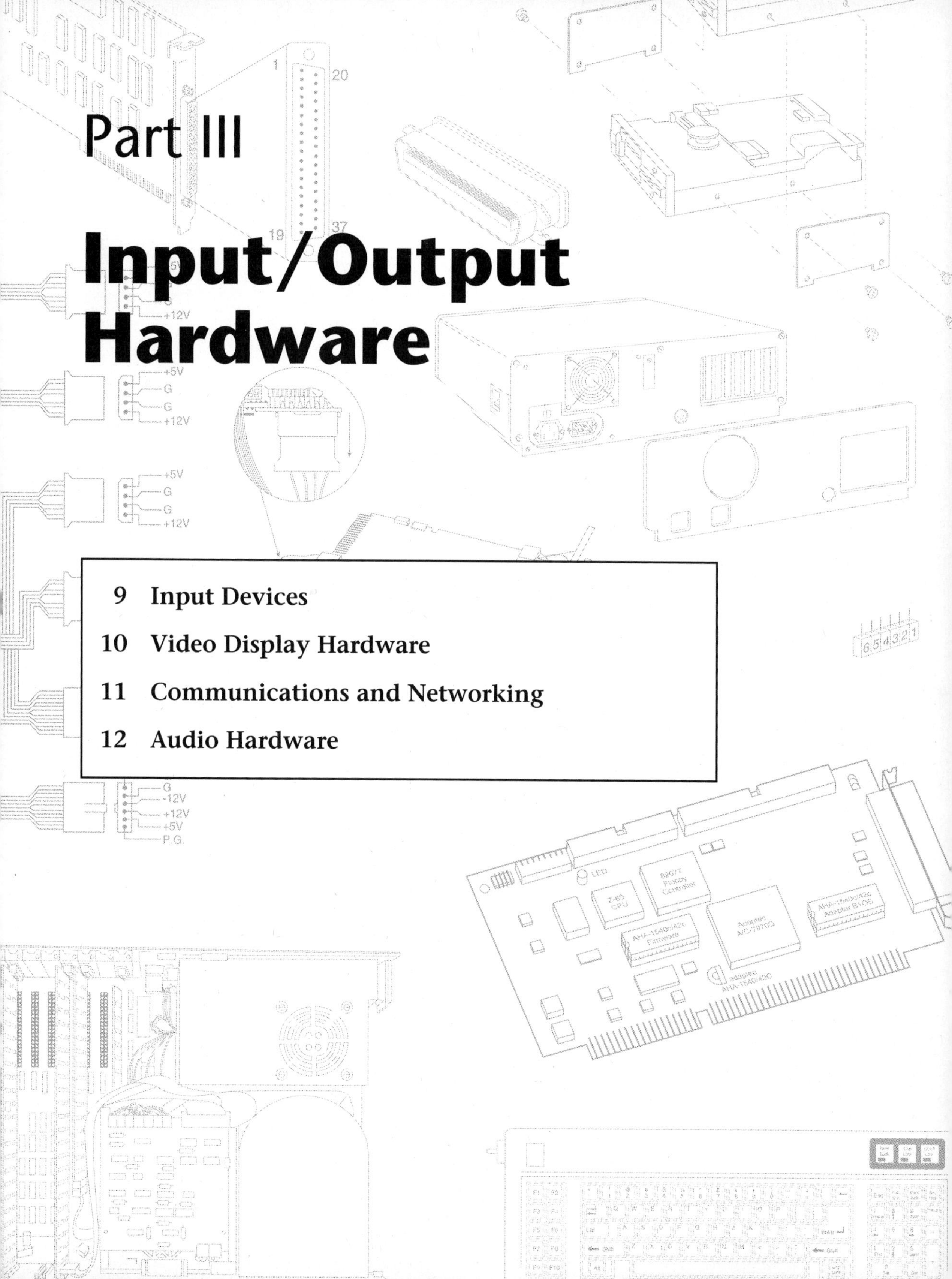

Part III

Input/Output Hardware

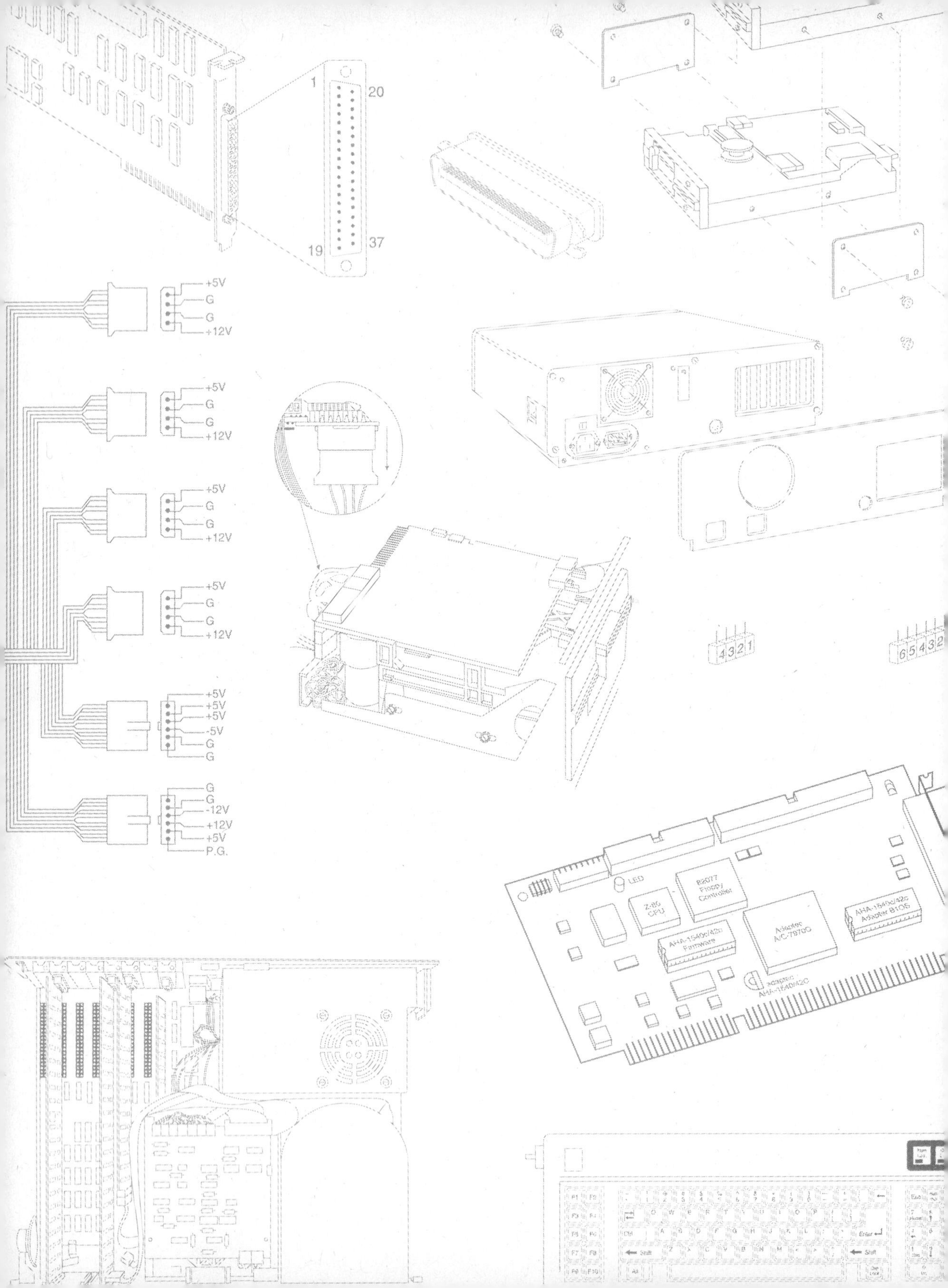
1
20
19
37
+5V
G
G
+12V
+5V
G
G
+12V
+5V
G
G
+12V
+5V
G
G
+12V
+5V
+5V
+5V
-5V
G
G
G
G
-12V
+12V
+5V
P.G.
4321
65432
LED
Z-80
CPU
Floppy
Controller
AHA-1540c/42c
Firmware

Chapter 9

Input Devices

This chapter discusses input devices—the devices used to communicate with the computer. The most common input device is, of course, the keyboard, and this chapter discusses keyboards in depth. It also discusses mice and other pointing device alternatives because they are now a standard requirement for operating a modern PC with a GUI (graphical user interface) such as Windows or OS/2. Finally, this chapter also discusses the game or joystick interface, which is used to input signals from joysticks, paddles, or other game devices.

Keyboards

One of the most basic system components is your keyboard. The keyboard is the primary input device. It is used for entering commands and data into the system. This section looks at the keyboards available for PC compatible systems. It examines the different types of keyboards, how the keyboard functions, the keyboard-to-system interface, and keyboard troubleshooting and repair.

Types of Keyboards

Over the years since the introduction of the original IBM PC, IBM has created three different keyboard designs for PC systems, and Microsoft has augmented one of them. They have become standards in the industry and are shared by virtually all of the PC compatible manufacturers. More recently with the introduction of Windows 95, a modified version of the 101-key design (created by Microsoft) has appeared. The primary keyboard types are

- 83-key PC and XT keyboard
- 84-key AT keyboard
- 101-key enhanced keyboard
- 104-key enhanced Windows keyboard

This section discusses each keyboard type and shows their layout and physical appearance. Because most systems use keyboards based on the 101 and 104-key enhanced keyboard designs, these versions are emphasized.

83-Key PC and XT Keyboard. When the original PC was first introduced, it had something that few other personal computers had at the time: an external detachable keyboard. Most other small personal computers of the time had the keyboard built in, like the Apple II. Although the external design was a good move on IBM's part, the keyboard design was not without its drawbacks. One of the most criticized components of the original 83-key keyboard is the awkward layout (see fig. 9.1). The Shift keys are small and in the wrong place on the left side. The Enter key is also too small. These oversights were especially irritating at the time because IBM had produced the Selectric typewriter, perceived as a standard for good keyboard layout.

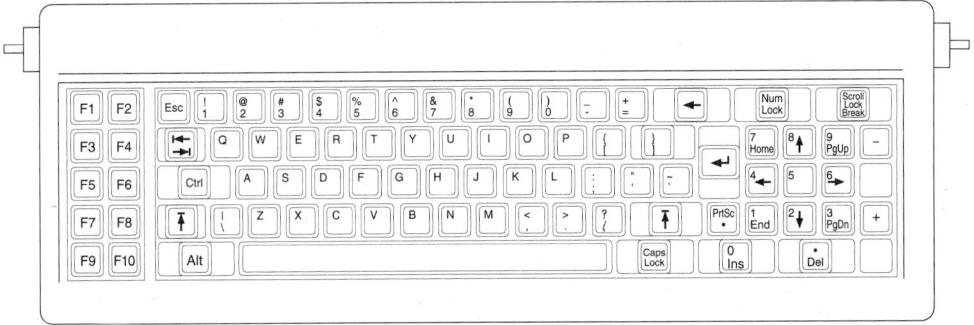

Figure 9.1
PC and XT 83-key keyboard layout.

This keyboard has a built-in processor that communicates with the motherboard via a special serial data link. The communication is one-way, which means that the motherboard cannot send commands or data back to the keyboard. For this reason, IBM 83-key keyboards have no LED indicator lights. Because the status of the Caps Lock, Num Lock, and Scroll Lock are maintained by the motherboard, there is no way to make sure that any LED indicator lights remain in sync with the actual status of the function. Many aftermarket (non-IBM) PC keyboards added the lights, and the keyboard attempted to keep track of the three functions independently of the motherboard. This worked in most situations, but it was entirely possible to see the LEDs become out of sync with the actual function status. Rebooting corrected this temporary problem, but it was annoying nonetheless. By eliminating the lights, IBM keyboards did not have this potential problem.

The original 83-key PC/XT keyboard is no longer used and is not electrically compatible with AT compatible motherboards, although some aftermarket units may be compatible by moving an XT/AT switch usually found on the bottom of the keyboard.

84-Key AT Keyboard. When the AT was introduced in 1984, it included a new keyboard—the 84-key unit (see fig. 9.2). This keyboard corrected many problems of the original PC and XT keyboards. The position and arrangement of the numeric keypad was modified. The Enter key was made much larger, like that of a Selectric typewriter. The Shift key positions and sizes were corrected. IBM also finally added LED indicators for the status of the Caps Lock, Scroll Lock, and Num Lock toggles.

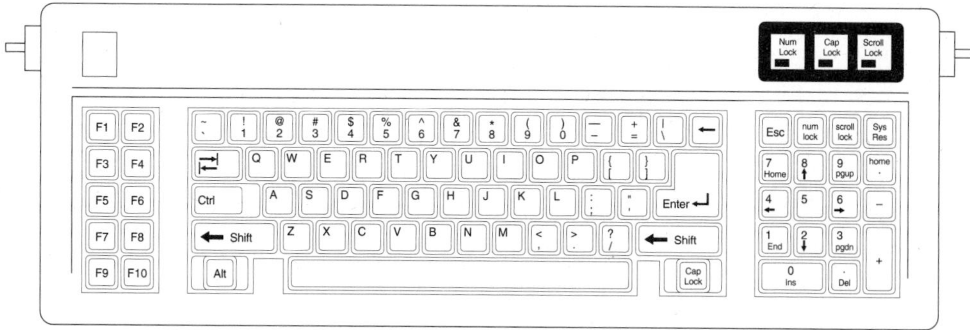

Figure 9.2
AT 84-key keyboard layout.

These keyboards use a slightly modified interface protocol that is bidirectional. This means that the processor built in to the keyboard can talk to another processor (called the *keyboard controller chip*) built in to the motherboard. The keyboard controller on the motherboard can send commands and data to the keyboard, which allows functions such as changing the keyboard typematic (or repeat) rate as well as the delay before repeating begins. The keyboard controller on the motherboard also performs scan code translations, which allows a much easier integration of foreign language keyboards into the system. Scan codes are the names for the hexadecimal codes actually sent by the keyboard to the motherboard. The bi-directional interface can be used to control the LED indicators on the keyboard, thus ensuring that the status of a particular function and the corresponding indicator are always in sync.

The 84-key unit that came with the original AT system is no longer used, although its electrical design is compatible with newer systems. It lacks some of the keys found in the newer keyboards and does not have as nice a numeric keypad section, but many users prefer the more Selectric-style layout of the alphanumeric keys. Likewise, some users prefer to have the 10 function keys arranged on the left-hand side as opposed to the enhanced arrangement in which 12 function keys are lined up along the top.

Enhanced 101-Key (or 102-Key). In 1986, IBM introduced the "corporate" enhanced 101-key keyboard for the newer XT and AT models (see fig. 9.3). I use the word "corporate" because this unit first appeared in IBM's RT PC, which is a RISC (Reduced Instruction Set Computer) system designed for scientific and engineering applications; keyboards with this design are now supplied with virtually every type of system and terminal that IBM sells. Other companies quickly copied this design, and it has been the standard on PC compatible systems ever since. This universal keyboard has a further improved layout over that of the 84-key unit, with perhaps the exception of the Enter key, which reverted to a smaller size. The 101-key enhanced keyboard was designed to conform to international regulations and specifications for keyboards. In fact, other companies such as DEC and TI had already been using designs similar to the IBM 101-key unit. The IBM 101-key units originally came in versions with and without the status indicator LEDs, depending on whether the unit was sold with an XT or AT system. Now there are many other variations to choose from, including some with integrated pointing devices.

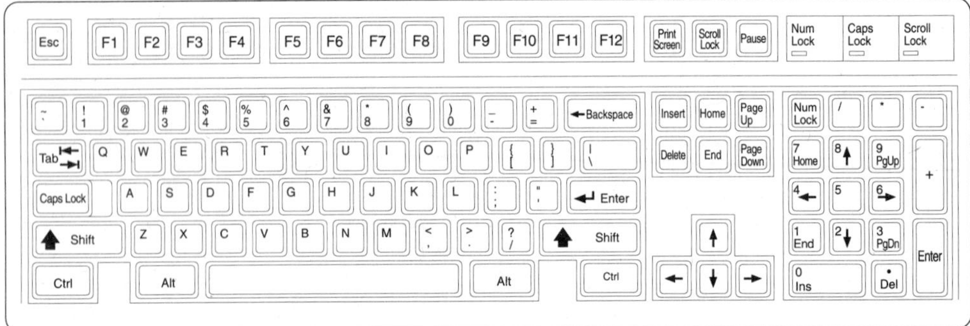

Figure 9.3

101-key enhanced keyboard layout.

The enhanced keyboard is available in several different variations, but all are basically the same electrically and can be interchanged. IBM and its Lexmark keyboard and printer subsidiary have produced a number of versions, including keyboards with built-in pointing devices and new ergonometric layouts. Most of the enhanced keyboards attach to the system via the standard 5-pin DIN connector, but many others come with cables for the 6-pin mini-DIN connector found on many newer systems, including the IBM PS/2s and most Slimline compatibles. Although the connectors may be physically different, the keyboards are not, and you can either interchange the cables or use a cable adapter to plug one type into the other.

Because older PC/XT-style systems lack the bi-directional keyboard interface required to drive the LED indicators found on most enhanced keyboards, IBM even made models without these lights (Caps Lock, Num Lock, and Scroll Lock). These keyboards are the same as the others, but they are missing the small add-on circuit board used to drive the lights. If you use an older XT system with an enhanced keyboard that has the LEDs, they simply remain dark. Some compatible keyboard manufacturers have added circuitry internal to the keyboard that turns the LEDs on and off whenever you press the appropriate keys. In such a case, however, it is possible for the LEDs to get "out of sync" with the actual state of the toggles, which are actually maintained within the computer and not the keyboard.

The 101-key keyboard layout can be divided into the following four sections:

- Typing area
- Numeric keypad
- Cursor and screen controls
- Function keys

The 101-key arrangement is similar to the Selectric keyboard layout with the exception of the Enter key. The Tab, Caps Lock, Shift, and Backspace keys have a larger striking area and are located in the familiar Selectric locations. Ctrl and Alt keys are on each side of the space bar. The typing area and numeric keypad have home-row identifiers for touch typing.

The cursor and screen-control keys have been separated from the numeric keypad, which is reserved for numeric input. (As with other PC keyboards, you can use the numeric keypad for cursor and screen control when the keyboard is not in Num Lock mode.) A division-sign key and an additional Enter key have been added to the numeric keypad.

The cursor-control keys are arranged in the inverted T format. The Insert, Delete, Home, End, Page Up, and Page Down keys, located above the dedicated cursor-control keys, are separate from the numeric keypad. The function keys, spaced in groups of four, are located across the top of the keyboard. The keyboard has two additional function keys—F11 and F12). The Esc key is isolated in the upper-left corner of the keyboard. Dedicated Print Screen/Sys Req, Scroll Lock, and Pause/Break keys are provided for commonly used functions.

Foreign language versions of the enhanced keyboard include 102-keys and a slightly different layout from the 101-key United States versions.

One of the many useful features of the enhanced keyboard is removable keycaps. With clear keycaps and paper inserts, you can customize the keyboard. Keyboard templates are also available to provide specific operator instructions.

The enhanced keyboard will probably come with any PC-compatible desktop system for quite some time. It is currently the most popular design and does not show any signs of being replaced in the future. Because most compatible systems use this same type of keyboard, it is relatively easy to move from one system to another without relearning the layout.

104-Key (Windows keyboard). If you are a touch typist like I am, then you really hate to take your hands off the keyboard to use a mouse. Windows 95 makes this even more of a problem, because it exploits both mouse buttons. Many new keyboards, especially those in portable computers, include a variation of the IBM Trackpoint or the Alps Glidepoint (both of which are discussed later in this chapter) which allow touch typists to keep their hands on the keyboard even while moving the pointer. There is still another alternative that can help. Microsoft has come up with a specification that calls for three new Windows-specific keys to be added to the keyboard. These new keys help with functions that would otherwise require multiple keystrokes or mouse clicks.

Microsoft has released a Windows keyboard specification that outlines a set of new keys and key combinations. The familiar 101-key layout grows to 104 keys, with the addition of left and right Windows keys and an Application key. These keys will be used for operating-system and application-level keyboard combinations, similar to today's Ctrl and Alt combinations. You don't need the new keys to use Windows 95 or NT, but software vendors are starting to add specific functions to their Windows products that will utilize the new Application key (which is the same as the right mouse button).

The standard Windows keyboard layout calls for a shortened space bar, flanked by two Windows Logo keys (called WIN keys), and an Application key on the far right side. The

WIN keys open the Start menu, which then can be navigated with the arrow keys. The Application key simulates the right mouse button; in most applications it brings up context-sensitive pop-up menus. Several WIN key combinations offer preset macro commands as well. For example, you press WIN+E to bring up the Windows Explorer. The following table shows a list of all the new Windows 95 key combinations:

Key Combination	Action
WIN+R	Displays Run dialog box
WIN+M	Minimizes All
Shift+WIN+M	Undoes Minimize All
WIN+F1	Starts Help
WIN+E	Starts Windows Explorer
WIN+F	Finds files or folders
Ctrl+WIN+F	Finds computer
WIN+Tab	Cycles through taskbar buttons
WIN+Break	Displays System properties dialog box

The Windows keyboard specification requires that keyboard makers increase the number of trilograms in their keyboard designs. A *trilogram* is a combination of three rapidly pressed keys that perform a special function, such as Ctrl+Alt+Del. Designing a keyboard so that the switch matrix will correctly register trilograms is expensive, and this plus the additional Windows keys themselves will cause the price of these keyboards to rise. Volume sales should keep the price reasonable, as well as the natural market competition.

Virtually every keyboard manufacturer is now producing keyboards with these Windows-specific keys. Some are also combining these new keys with other features. For example, besides the new Windows keys, the Microsoft Natural Keyboard includes ergonomic features, such as split keypads that are rotated out from the middle to encourage a straight wrist position. It takes some getting used to. Unfortunately, this keyboard (made by Keytronics for Microsoft) does not have nearly the feel of the mechanical switch designs like Alps, Lite-On, or NMB, or the extremely high-quality feel of the Lexmark keyboards.

In addition to the Windows keys, other companies like Lexmark, NMB, and Alps have licensed a new space bar design from Keyboard Enhancements, Inc. called "Erase-Ease." This new design splits the space bar into two parts, using the shorter left (or optionally the right) half as an additional Backspace key. If you see a keyboard advertising 105-keys, then it probably has both the 3 additional Windows keys plus the extra Backspace key next to the space bar.

Although the new Windows keys are not mandatory when running Windows, and certainly not everybody will have them, I do expect more and more new PC systems to include keyboards with these extra keys. They can make it easier for both experienced touch typists as well as novice users to access some of the functions of Windows and their applications.

Compatibility. The 83-key PC/XT type is different from all the others and normally plugs into only 8-bit PC/XT systems that do not use the motherboard based 8042-type keyboard controller chip. This is definitely true for IBM's keyboards and also is true for many compatible units. Some compatibles may be switchable to work with an AT-type motherboard via an XT/AT switch.

The 84-key unit from IBM works on only AT-type 16-bit (or greater) motherboards and does not work at all with PC/XT systems. Again, some aftermarket designs may have an XT/AT switch to allow for compatibility with PC/XT-type systems. If you have the keyboard set in the wrong mode, it will not work, but no damage will occur.

The enhanced keyboards from IBM are universal and auto-switching, which means that they work in virtually any system from the XT to the PS/2 or any PC-compatible by simply plugging them in. Some may require that a switch be moved on the keyboard to make it compatible with PC/XT systems that do not have the 8042-type keyboard controller on the motherboard. In some cases, you may also need to switch to a different cable with the proper system end connector, or use an adapter.

Although the enhanced keyboard is electrically compatible with any AT-type motherboard and even most PC/XT-type motherboards, many older systems will have software problems using these keyboards. IBM changed the ROM on the systems to support the new keyboard properly, and the compatible vendors followed suit. Very old (1986 or earlier) machines may require a ROM upgrade to use properly some of the features on the 101-key enhanced keyboards, such as the F11 and F12 keys. If the individual system ROM BIOS is not capable of operating the 101-key keyboard correctly, the 101-key keyboard may not work at all (as with all three ROM versions of the IBM PC); the additional keys (F11 and F12 function keys) may not work; or you may have problems with keyboard operation in general. In some cases, these compatibility problems cause improper characters to appear when keys are typed (causing the system to beep), and general keyboard operation is a problem. These problems can often be solved by a ROM upgrade to a newer version with proper support for the enhanced keyboard.

If you have an older IBM system, you can tell whether your system has complete ROM BIOS support for the 101-key unit: When you plug in the keyboard and turn on the system unit, the Num Lock light automatically comes on and the numeric keypad portion of the keyboard is enabled. This method of detection is not 100-percent accurate, but if the light goes on, your BIOS generally supports the keyboard. A notable exception is the IBM AT BIOS dated 06/10/85; it turns on the Num Lock light, but still does not properly support the enhanced keyboard. All IBM BIOS versions dated since 11/15/85 have proper support for the enhanced keyboards.

In IBM systems that support the enhanced keyboard, if it is detected on power up, Num Lock is enabled, and the light goes on. If one of the older 84-key AT-type keyboards is detected, the Num Lock function is not enabled because these keyboards do not have arrow keys separate from the numeric keypad. When the enhanced keyboards first appeared in 1986, many users (including me) were irritated on finding that the numeric keypad was automatically enabled every time the system boots. Most compatibles began integrating a function into the system setup that allowed specification of the Num Lock status on boot.

Some thought that the automatic enabling of Num Lock was a function of the enhanced keyboard because none of the earlier keyboards seemed to operate this way. Remember that this function is not really a keyboard function; it is a function of the motherboard ROM BIOS, which identifies an enhanced 101-key unit and turns on the Num Lock as a "favor." In systems that cannot disable the automatic numeric keypad enable feature, you can use the DOS 6.0 or higher version NUMLOCK= parameter in CONFIG.SYS to turn Num Lock on or off as desired. If you are running a version of DOS earlier than 6.0, you can use one of the many public domain programs available for turning off the Num Lock function. Inserting the program command to disable Num Lock in the AUTOEXEC.BAT file turns off the numeric keypad whenever the system reboots.

In an informal test, I plugged the new keyboard into an earlier XT. The keyboard seemed to work well. None of the keys that did not exist previously, such as F11 and F12, were operable, but the new arrow keys and the numeric keypad worked. The enhanced keyboard seems to work on XT or AT systems, but it does not function on the original PC systems because of BIOS and electrical interface problems. Many compatible versions of the 101-key enhanced keyboards have a manual XT/AT switch on the bottom that may allow the keyboard to work in an original PC system.

Keyboard Technology

The technology that makes up a typical PC keyboard is very interesting. This section focuses on all aspects of keyboard technology and design, including the key switches, the interface between the keyboard and the system, scan codes, and the keyboard connectors.

Keyswitch Design. Several types of switches are used in keyboards today. Most keyboards use one of several variations on a mechanical key switch. A mechanical key switch relies on a mechanical momentary contact type switch to make electrical contact in a circuit. Some high-end keyboard designs use a totally different nonmechanical design that relies on capacitive switches. This section discusses these switches and the highlights of each design.

The most common type of key switch is the mechanical type, available in the following variations:

- Pure mechanical
- Foam element
- Rubber dome
- Membrane

The *pure mechanical* type is just that, a simple mechanical switch that features metal contacts in a momentary contact arrangement. Often a tactile feedback mechanism—consisting of a clip and spring arrangement to give a "clickey" feel to the keyboard and offer some resistance to pressing the key—is built in. Several companies, including Alps Electric, Lite-On and NMB Technologies, manufacture this type of keyboard using switches primarily from Alps Electric. Mechanical switches are very durable, usually have self-cleaning contacts, and normally are rated for 20 million keystrokes, which is second only to the capacitive switch. They also offer excellent tactile feedback.

Foam element mechanical switches were a very popular design in some older keyboards. Most of the older compatible keyboards, including those made by Keytronics and many others, use this technology. These switches are characterized by a foam element with an electrical contact on the bottom that is mounted on the bottom of a plunger attached to the key itself (see fig. 9.4).

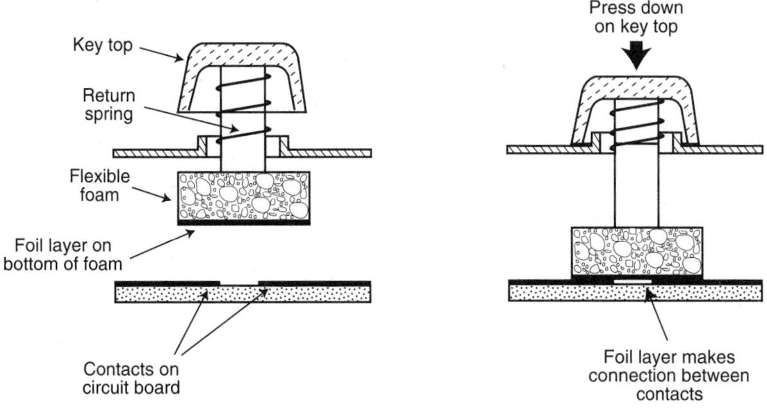

Figure 9.4

Typical foam element mechanical keyswitch.

When the switch is pressed down, a foil conductor on the bottom of the foam element closes a circuit on the printed circuit board below. A return spring pushes the key back up when the pressure is released. The foam dampens the contact, helping to prevent bounce, but unfortunately gives these keyboards a "mushy" feel. The big problem with this type of keyswitch design is that there is often little in the way of tactile feedback, and systems with these keyboards often resort to tricks such as clicking the PC's speaker to signify that contact has been made. Compaq has used keyboards of this type (made by Keytronics) in many of their systems, but perhaps the most popular user today is Packard Bell. Preferences in keyboard feel are somewhat subjective; I personally do not favor the foam element switch design.

Another problem with this type of design is that it is more subject to corrosion on the foil conductor and the circuit board traces below. When this happens, the key strikes may become intermittent, which can be frustrating. Fortunately, these keyboards are among the easiest to clean. By disassembling this type of keyboard completely, you can usually remove the circuit board portion without removing each foam pad separately, and expose the bottoms of all the pads. Then you can easily wipe the corrosion and dirt off the bottom of the foam pads and the circuit board, thus restoring the keyboard to "like new" condition. Unfortunately, over time, the corrosion problem will occur again. I recommend using some Stabilant 22a from D.W. Electrochemicals to improve the switch contact action and to prevent future corrosion. Because of problems like this, the foam element design is not used much anymore and has been superseded in popularity by the rubber dome design.

Rubber dome switches are mechanical switches that are similar to the foam element type but are improved in many ways. Instead of a spring, these switches use a rubber dome that has a carbon button contact on the underside. As you press a key, the key plunger presses down on the rubber dome, causing it to resist and then collapse all at once, much like the top of an oil can. As the rubber dome collapses, the user feels the tactile feedback, and the carbon button makes contact between the circuit board traces below. When the key is released, the rubber dome reforms and pushes the key back up.

The rubber eliminates the need for a spring and provides a reasonable amount of tactile feedback without any special clips or other parts. A carbon button is used because it is resistant to corrosion and also has a self-cleaning action on the metal contacts below. The rubber domes are formed into a sheet that completely protects the contacts below from dirt, dust, and even minor spills. This type of design is the simplest, using the fewest parts. These things make this type of keyswitch very reliable and help make rubber dome type keyboards the most popular in service today.

If rubber dome keyboards have a drawback at all, it is that the tactile feedback is not as good as many users would like. Although it is reasonable for most, some users prefer more tactile feedback than rubber dome keyboards normally provide.

The *membrane* keyboard is a variation on the rubber dome type in which the keys themselves are no longer separate, but are formed together in a sheet that sits on the rubber dome sheet. This severely limits key travel, and membrane keyboards are not considered usable for normal touch typing because of this. They are ideal in extremely harsh environments. Because the sheets can be bonded together and sealed from the elements, membrane keyboards can be used in situations in which no other type could survive. Many industrial applications use membrane keyboards especially for terminals that do not require extensive data entry but are used to operate equipment such as cash registers.

Capacitive switches are the only nonmechanical type of switch in use today (see fig. 9.5). These are the Cadillac of keyswitches. They are much more expensive than the more common mechanical rubber dome, but they also are more resistant to dirt and corrosion and offer the highest-quality tactile feedback of any type of switch.

A capacitive switch does not work by making contact between conductors. Instead, two plates usually made of plastic are connected in a switch matrix designed to detect changes in the capacitance of the circuit.

When the key is pressed, the plunger moves the top plate relative to the fixed bottom plate. Usually a mechanism provides for a distinct over-center tactile feedback with a resounding "click." As the top plate moves, the capacitance between the two plates changes and is detected by the comparator circuitry in the keyboard.

Because this type of switch does not rely on metal contacts, it is nearly immune to corrosion and dirt. These switches are very resistant to key bounce problems that result in multiple characters appearing from a single strike. They are also the most durable in the industry—rated for 25 million or more keystrokes, as opposed to 10 to 20 million for other designs. The tactile feedback is unsurpassed because a relatively loud click and strong over-center feel normally are provided. The only drawback to this design is the cost. Capacitive switch keyboards are among the most expensive designs, but the quality of the feel and their durability are worth it.

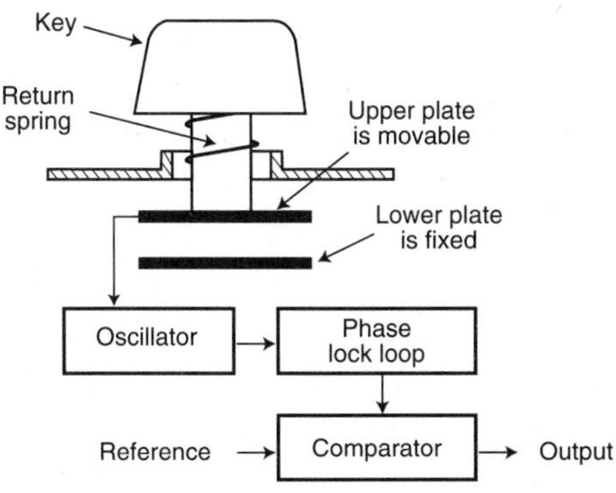

Figure 9.5

A capacitive keyswitch.

Traditionally, the only vendors of capacitive keyswitch keyboards have been IBM and its keyboard division Lexmark, which is why these keyboards have always seemed to stand out as superior from the rest.

The Keyboard Interface. A keyboard consists of a set of switches mounted in a grid or array called the *key matrix*. When a switch is pressed, a processor in the keyboard itself identifies which key is pressed by identifying which grid location in the matrix shows continuity. The keyboard processor also interprets how long the key is pressed and can even handle multiple keypresses at the same time. A 16-byte hardware buffer in the keyboard can handle rapid or multiple keypresses, passing each one in succession to the system.

When you press a key, in most cases the contact actually bounces slightly, meaning that there are several rapid on-off cycles just as the switch makes contact. This is called bounce, and the processor in the keyboard is designed to filter this, or *debounce* the keystroke. The keyboard processor must distinguish bounce from a double keystrike actually intended by the keyboard operator. This is fairly easy because the bouncing is much more rapid than a person could simulate by striking a key quickly several times.

The keyboard in an PC-compatible system is actually a computer itself. It communicates with the main system through a special serial data link that transmits and receives data in 11-bit packets of information consisting of eight data bits in addition to framing and control bits. Although it is indeed a serial (the data flows on one wire) link, it is not compatible with the standard RS-232 serial port commonly used to connect modems. The original PC/XT setup was a one-way connection; however, the AT design is bidirectional, which means that the keyboard can receive as well as send data. In this manner, the AT keyboard could be reprogrammed in several different ways.

The processor in the original PC keyboard was an Intel 8048 microcontroller chip. Newer keyboards often use an 8049 version that has built-in ROM or other microcontroller chips compatible with the 8048 or 8049. For example, in its enhanced keyboards, IBM has always used a custom version of the Motorola 6805 processor, which is compatible with the Intel chips. The keyboard's built-in processor reads the key matrix, debounces the keypress signals, converts the keypress to the appropriate scan code, and transmits the code to the motherboard. The processors built in to the keyboard contain their own RAM, possibly some ROM, and a built-in serial interface.

In the original PC/XT design, the keyboard serial interface is connected to an 8255 Programmable Peripheral Interface (PPI) chip on the motherboard of the PC/XT. This chip is connected to the interrupt controller IRQ1 line, which is used to signal that keyboard data is available. The data itself is sent from the 8255 to the processor via I/O port address 60h. The IRQ1 signal causes the main system processor to run a subroutine (INT 9h) that interprets the keyboard scan code data and decides what to do.

In an AT-type keyboard design, the keyboard serial interface is connected to a special keyboard controller on the motherboard. This is an Intel 8042 Universal Peripheral Interface (UPI) slave microcontroller chip in the original AT design. This microcontroller is essentially another processor that has its own 2K of ROM and 128 bytes of RAM. An 8742 version that uses EPROM (Erasable Programmable Read Only Memory) can be erased and reprogrammed. Often when you get a motherboard ROM upgrade from a motherboard manufacturer, it includes a new keyboard controller chip because it has somewhat dependent and updated ROM code in it as well. Some systems may use the 8041 or 8741 chips, which differ only in the amount of ROM or RAM built in, whereas other systems now have the keyboard controller built into the main system chipset.

In an AT system, the (8048-type) microcontroller in the keyboard sends data to the (8042-type) motherboard keyboard controller on the motherboard. The motherboard-based controller can also send data back to the keyboard. When the keyboard controller on the motherboard receives data from the keyboard, it signals the motherboard with an IRQ1 and sends the data to the main motherboard processor via I/O port address 60h, just as in the PC/XT. Acting as an agent between the keyboard and the main system processor, the 8042-type keyboard controller can translate scan codes and perform several other functions as well. Data also can be sent to the 8042 keyboard controller via port 60h, which is then passed on to the keyboard. Additionally, when the system needs to send commands to or read the status of the keyboard controller on the motherboard, it reads or writes through I/O port 64h. These commands are also usually followed by data sent back and forth via port 60h.

In most older systems the 8042 keyboard controller is also used by the system to control the A20 memory address line, which controls access to system memory over 1 megabyte. More modern motherboards usually incorporate this functionality directly in the motherboard chipset. This aspect of the keyboard controller is discussed in Chapter 7, "Memory" in the section that covers the High Memory Area (HMA).

Typematic Functions. If a key on the keyboard is held down, it becomes *typematic*, which means that the keyboard repeatedly sends the keypress code to the motherboard.

In the AT-style keyboards, the typematic rate is adjustable by sending the keyboard processor the appropriate commands. This is not possible for the earlier PC/XT keyboard types because the keyboard interface is not bi-directional.

AT-style keyboards have a programmable typematic repeat rate and delay parameter. The DOS MODE command in versions 4.0 and later enables you to set the keyboard typematic (repeat) rate as well as the delay before typematic action begins. The default value for the RATE parameter (r) is 20 for PC-compatible systems and 21 for IBM PS/2 systems. The default value for the DELAY parameter (d) is 2. To use the MODE command to set the keyboard typematic rate and delay, use the following command:

```
MODE CON[:] [RATE=r DELAY=d]
```

The acceptable values for the rate "r" and the resultant typematic rate in characters per second (cps) are shown in table 9.1.

Table 9.1 DOS 4.0+ MODE Command Keyboard Typematic Rate Parameters

RATE No.	Rate ± 20%	RATE No.	Rate ± 20%
32	30.0cps	16	7.5cps
31	26.7cps	15	6.7cps
30	24.0cps	14	6.0cps
29	21.8cps	13	5.5cps
28	20.0cps	12	5.0cps
27	18.5cps	11	4.6cps
26	17.1cps	10	4.3cps
25	16.0cps	9	4.0cps
24	15.0cps	8	3.7cps
23	13.3cps	7	3.3cps
22	12.0cps	6	3.0cps
21	10.9cps	5	2.7cps
20	10.0cps	4	2.5cps
19	9.2cps	3	2.3cps
18	8.6cps	2	2.1cps
17	8.0cps	1	2.0cps

Table 9.2 shows the values for DELAY and the resultant delay time in seconds.

Table 9.2 DOS MODE Command Keyboard Typematic Delay Parameters

DELAY No.	Delay Time
1	0.25sec
2	0.50sec
3	0.75sec
4	1.00sec

For example, I always place the following command in my AUTOEXEC.BAT file:

```
MODE CON: RATE=32 DELAY=1
```

This command sets the typematic rate to the maximum speed possible, or 30 characters per second. It also trims the delay to the minimum of 0.25 second before repeating begins. This command "turbocharges" the keyboard and makes operations requiring repeated keystrokes work much faster, such as moving within a file using arrow keys. The quick typematic action and short delay can sometimes be disconcerting to ham-fisted keyboard operators. In that case, slow typists might want to leave their keyboard speed at the default until they become more proficient.

If you have an older system or keyboard, you may receive the following message:

```
Function not supported on this computer
```

This indicates that your system, keyboard, or both do not support the bi-directional interface or commands required to change the typematic rate and delay. Upgrading the BIOS or the keyboard may enable this function, but it is probably not cost-effective to do this on an older system.

Note that many BIOS versions feature keyboard speed selection capability, however not all of them allow full control over the speed and delay.

Keyboard Key Numbers and Scan Codes. When you press a key on the keyboard, the processor built into the keyboard (8048- or 6805-type) reads the keyswitch location in the keyboard matrix. The processor then sends to the motherboard a serial packet of data that contains the scan code for the key that was pressed. In AT-type motherboards that use an 8042-type keyboard controller, the 8042 chip translates the actual keyboard scan code into one of up to three different sets of system scan codes, which are sent to the main processor. It can be useful in some cases to know what these scan codes are, especially when troubleshooting keyboard problems or when reading the keyboard or system scan codes directly in software.

When a keyswitch on the keyboard sticks or otherwise fails, the scan code of the failed keyswitch is usually reported by diagnostics software, including the POST (Power On Self-Test), as well as conventional disk-based diagnostics. This means that you have to identify the particular key by its scan code. Tables 9.3 through 9.7 list all the scan codes for every key on the 83-, 84-, and 101-key keyboards. By looking up the reported scan code on these charts, you can determine which keyswitch is defective or needs to be cleaned.

Note that the 101-key enhanced keyboards are capable of three different scan code sets. Set 1 is the default. Some systems, including some of the PS/2 machines, use one of the other scan code sets during the POST. For example, my P75 uses Scan Code Set 2 during the POST but switches to Set 1 during normal operation. This is rare, but it is useful to know if you are having difficulty interpreting the Scan Code number.

IBM also assigns each key a unique key number to distinguish it from the others. This is important when you are trying to identify keys on foreign keyboards, which may use different symbols or characters from the United States models. In the case of the enhanced keyboard, most foreign models are missing one of the keys (key 29) found on the United States version and have two other additional keys (keys 42 and 45) as well. This accounts for the 102-key total rather than the 101-keys found on the United States version.

Figure 9.6 shows the keyboard numbering and character locations for the original 83-key PC keyboard. Table 9.3 shows the scan codes for each key relative to the key number and character.

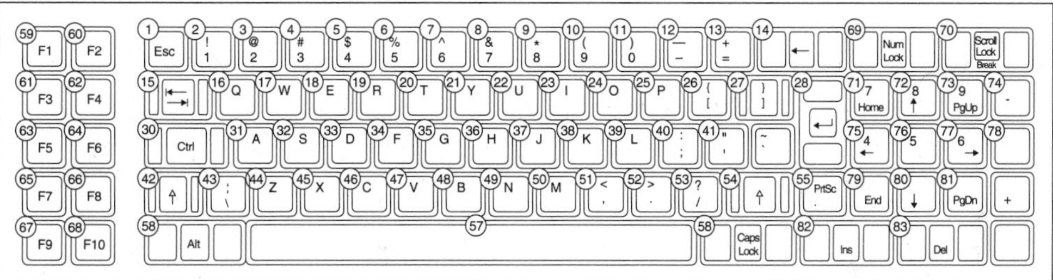

Figure 9.6

83-key PC keyboard key number and character locations.

Table 9.3 83-Key (PC/XT) Keyboard Key Numbers and Scan Codes

Key Number	Scan Code	Key	Key Number	Scan Code	Key
1	01	Escape	19	13	r
2	02	1	20	14	t
3	03	2	21	15	y
4	04	3	22	16	u
5	05	4	23	17	i
6	06	5	24	18	o
7	07	6	25	19	p
8	08	7	26	1A	[
9	09	8	27	1B	]
10	0A	9	28	1C	Enter
11	0B	0	29	1D	Ctrl
12	0C	-	30	1E	a
13	0D	=	31	1F	s
14	0E	Backspace	32	20	d
15	0F	Tab	33	21	f
16	10	q	34	22	g
17	11	w	35	23	h
18	12	e	36	24	j

(continues)

Table 9.3 Continued

Key Number	Scan Code	Key	Key Number	Scan Code	Key
37	25	k	61	3D	F3
38	26	l	62	3E	F4
39	27	;	63	3F	F5
40	28	'	64	40	F6
41	29	'	65	41	F7
42	2A	Left Shift	66	42	F8
43	2B	\	67	43	F9
44	2C	z	68	44	F10
45	2D	x	69	45	Num Lock
46	2E	c	70	46	Scroll Lock
47	2F	v	71	47	Keypad 7 (Home)
48	30	b	72	48	Keypad 8 (Up arrow)
49	31	n	73	49	Keypad 9 (PgUp)
50	32	m	74	4A	Keypad -
51	33	,	75	4B	Keypad 4 (Left arrow)
52	34	.	76	4C	Keypad 5
53	35	/	77	4D	Keypad 6 (Right arrow)
54	36	Right Shift	78	4E	Keypad +
55	37	*	79	4F	Keypad 1 (End)
56	38	Alt	80	50	Keypad 2 (Down arrow)
57	39	Space bar	81	51	Keypad 3 (PgDn)
58	3A	Caps Lock	82	52	Keypad 0 (Ins)
59	3B	F1	83	53	Keypad . (Del)
60	3C	F2			

Figure 9.7 shows the keyboard numbering and character locations for the original 84-key AT keyboard. Table 9.4 shows the scan codes for each key relative to the key number and character.

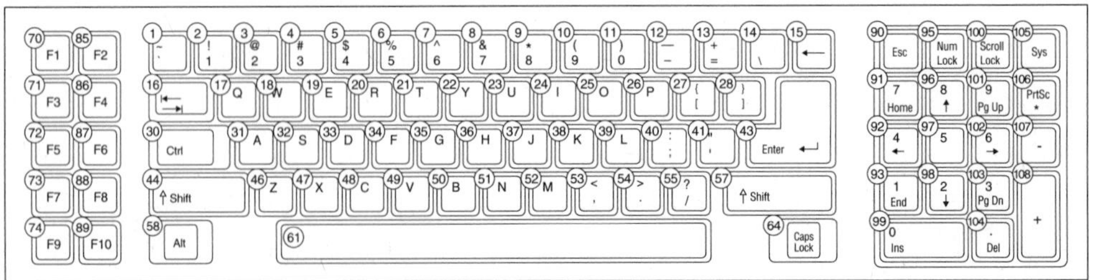

Figure 9.7

84-key AT keyboard key number and character locations.

Table 9.4 84-Key AT Keyboard Key Numbers and Scan Codes

Key Number	Scan Code	Key	Key Number	Scan Code	Key
1	29	'	40	27	;
2	02	1	41	28	'
3	03	2	43	1C	Enter
4	04	3	44	2A	Left Shift
5	05	4	46	2C	z
6	06	5	47	2D	x
7	07	6	48	2E	c
8	08	7	49	2F	v
9	09	8	50	30	b
10	0A	9	51	31	n
11	0B	0	52	32	m
12	0C	-	53	33	,
13	0D	=	54	34	.
14	2B	\	55	35	/
15	0E	Backspace	57	36	Right Shift
16	0F	Tab	58	38	Alt
17	10	q	61	39	Space bar
18	11	w	64	3A	Caps Lock
19	12	e	65	3C	F2
20	13	r	66	3E	F4
21	14	t	67	40	F6
22	15	y	68	42	F8
23	16	u	69	44	F10
24	17	i	70	3B	F1
25	18	o	71	3D	F3
26	19	p	72	3F	F5
27	1A	[	73	41	F7
28	1B	]	74	43	F9
30	1D	Ctrl	90	01	Escape
31	1E	a	91	47	Keypad 7 (Home)
32	1F	s	92	4B	Keypad 4 (Left arrow)
33	20	d	93	4F	Keypad 1 (End)
34	21	f	95	45	Num Lock
35	22	g	96	48	Keypad 8 (Up arrow)
36	23	h	97	4C	Keypad 5
37	24	j	98	50	Keypad 2 (Down arrow)
38	25	k	99	52	Keypad 0 (Ins)
39	26	l	100	46	Scroll Lock

(continues)

Table 9.4 Continued

Key Number	Scan Code	Key	Key Number	Scan Code	Key
101	49	Keypad 9 (PgUp)	105	54	SysRq
102	4D	Keypad 6 (Right arrow)	106	37	Keypad *
			107	4A	Keypad -
103	51	Keypad 3 (PgDn)	108	4E	Keypad +
104	53	Keypad . (Del)			

Figure 9.8 shows the keyboard numbering and character locations for the 101-key enhanced keyboard. Tables 9.5 through 9.7 show each of the three scan code sets for each key relative to the key number and character. Scan Code Set 1 is the default; the other two are rarely used. Figure 9.9 shows the layout of a typical foreign language 102-key version of the enhanced keyboard—in this case, a U.K. version.

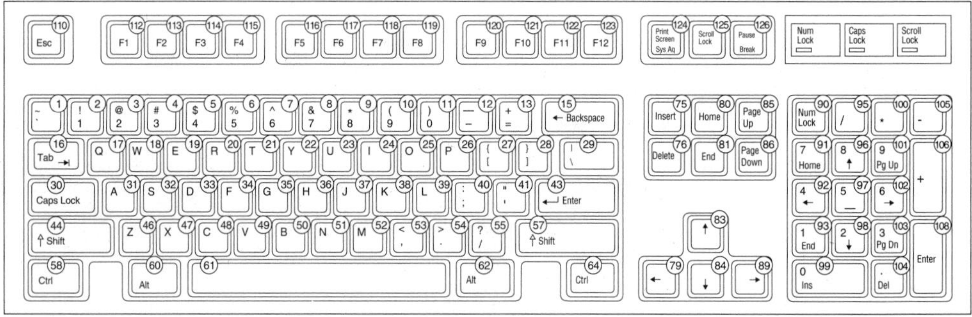

Figure 9.8

101-key enhanced keyboard key number and character locations (U.S. version).

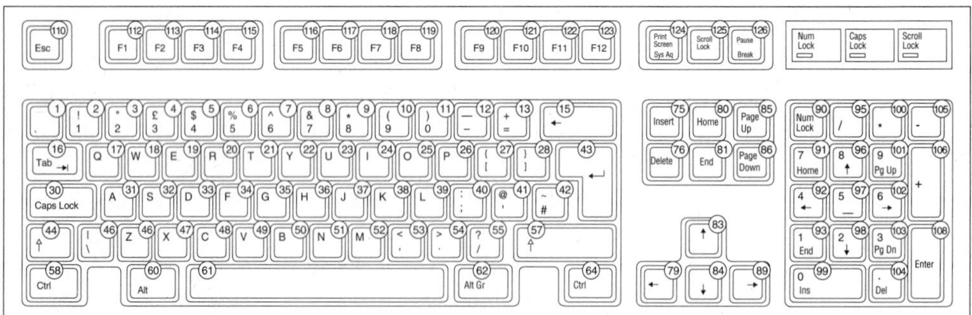

Figure 9.9

102-key enhanced keyboard key number and character locations (U.K. English version).

Table 9.5 101/102-Key (Enhanced) Keyboard Key Numbers and Scan Codes (Set 1)

Key Number	Scan Code	Key	Key Number	Scan Code	Key
1	29	'	39	26	l
2	02	1	40	27	;
3	03	2	41	28	'
4	04	3	42	2B	# (102-key only)
5	05	4	43	1C	Enter
6	06	5	44	2A	Left Shift
7	07	6	45	56	\ (102-key only)
8	08	7	46	2C	z
9	09	8	47	2D	x
10	0A	9	48	2E	c
11	0B	0	49	2F	v
12	0C	-	50	30	b
13	0D	=	51	31	n
15	0E	Backspace	52	32	m
16	0F	Tab	53	33	,
17	10	q	54	34	.
18	11	w	55	35	/
19	12	e	57	36	Right Shift
20	13	r	58	1D	Left Ctrl
21	14	t	60	38	Left Alt
22	15	y	61	39	Space bar
23	16	u	62	E0,38	Right Alt
24	17	i	64	E0,1D	Right Ctrl
25	18	o	75	E0,52	Insert
26	19	p	76	E0,53	Delete
27	1A	[	79	E0,4B	Left arrow
28	1B	]	80	E0,47	Home
29	2B	\ (101-key only)	81	E0,4F	End
30	3A	Caps Lock	83	E0,48	Up arrow
31	1E	a	84	E0,50	Down arrow
32	1F	s	85	E0,49	Page Up
33	20	d	86	E0,51	Page Down
34	21	f	89	E0,4D	Right arrow
35	22	g	90	45	Num Lock
36	23	h	91	47	Keypad 7 (Home)
37	24	j	92	4B	Keypad 4 (Left arrow)
38	25	k	93	4F	Keypad 1 (End)

(continues)

Table 9.5 Continued

Key Number	Scan Code	Key	Key Number	Scan Code	Key
95	E0,35	Keypad /	113	3C	F2
96	48	Keypad 8 (Up arrow)	114	3D	F3
97	4C	Keypad 5	115	3E	F4
98	50	Keypad 2 (Down arrow)	116	3F	F5
99	52	Keypad 0 (Ins)	117	40	F6
100	37	Keypad *	118	41	F7
101	49	Keypad 9 (PgUp)	119	42	F8
102	4D	Keypad 6 (Left arrow)	120	43	F9
103	51	Keypad 3 (PgDn)	121	44	F10
104	53	Keypad . (Del)	122	57	F11
105	4A	Keypad -	123	58	F12
106	4E	Keypad +	124	E0,2A, E0,37	Print Screen
108	E0,1C	Keypad Enter	125	46	Scroll Lock
110	01	Escape	126	E1,1D,45, E1,9D ,C5	Pause
112	3B	F1			

Table 9.6 101/102-Key (Enhanced) Keyboard Key Numbers and Scan Codes (Set 2)

Key Number	Scan Code	Key	Key Number	Scan Code	Key
1	0E	'	17	15	q
2	16	1	18	1D	w
3	1E	2	19	24	e
4	26	3	20	2D	r
5	25	4	21	2C	t
6	2E	5	22	35	y
7	36	6	23	3C	u
8	3D	7	24	43	i
9	3E	8	25	44	o
10	46	9	26	4D	p
11	45	0	27	54	[
12	4E	-	28	5B	]
13	55	=	29	5D	\ (101-key only)
15	66	Backspace	30	58	Caps Lock
16	0D	Tab	31	1C	a

Key Number	Scan Code	Key	Key Number	Scan Code	Key
32	1B	s	86	E0,7A	Page Down
33	23	d	89	E0,74	Right arrow
34	2B	f	90	77	Num Lock
35	34	g	91	6C	Keypad 7 (Home)
36	33	h	92	6B	Keypad 4 (Left arrow)
37	3B	j	93	69	Keypad 1 (End)
38	42	k	95	E0,4A	Keypad /
39	4B	l	96	75	Keypad 8 (Up arrow)
40	4C	;	97	73	Keypad 5
41	52	'	98	72	Keypad 2 (Down arrow)
42	5D	# (102-key only)	99	70	Keypad 0 (Ins)
43	5A	Enter	100	7C	Keypad *
44	12	Left Shift	101	7D	Keypad 9 (PgUp)
45	61	\ (102-key only)	102	74	Keypad 6 (Left arrow)
46	1A	z	103	7A	Keypad 3 (PgDn)
47	22	x	104	71	Keypad . (Del)
48	21	c	105	7B	Keypad -
49	2A	v	106	E0,5A	Keypad +
50	32	b	108	E0,5A	Keypad Enter
51	31	n	110	76	Escape
52	3A	m	112	05	F1
53	41	,	113	06	F2
54	49	.	114	04	F3
55	4A	/	115	0C	F4
57	59	Right Shift	116	03	F5
58	14	Left Ctrl	117	0B	F6
60	11	Left Alt	118	83	F7
61	29	Space bar	119	0A	F8
62	E0,11	Right Alt	120	01	F9
64	E0,14	Right Ctrl	121	09	F10
75	E0,70	Insert	122	78	F11
76	E0,71	Delete	123	07	F12
79	E0,6B	Left arrow	124	E0,12, E0,7C	Print Screen
80	E0,6C	Home			
81	E0,69	End	125	7E	Scroll Lock
83	E0,75	Up arrow	126	E1,14,77, E1,F0,14, F0,77	Pause
84	E0,72	Down arrow			
85	E0,7D	Page Up			

Table 9.7 101/102-Key (Enhanced) Keyboard Key Numbers and Scan Codes (Set 3)

Key Number	Scan Code	Key	Key Number	Scan Code	Key
1	0E	'	40	4C	;
2	16	1	41	52	'
3	1E	2	42	53	# (102-key only)
4	26	3	43	5A	Enter
5	25	4	44	12	Left Shift
6	2E	5	45	13	\ (102-key only)
7	36	6	46	1A	z
8	3D	7	47	22	x
9	3E	8	48	21	c
10	46	9	49	2A	v
11	45	0	50	32	b
12	4E	-	51	31	n
13	55	=	52	3A	m
15	66	Backspace	53	41	,
16	0D	Tab	54	49	.
17	15	q	55	4A	/
18	1D	w	57	59	Right Shift
19	24	e	58	11	Left Ctrl
20	2D	r	60	19	Left Alt
21	2C	t	61	29	Space bar
22	35	y	62	39	Right Alt
23	3C	u	64	58	Right Ctrl
24	43	i	75	67	Insert
25	44	o	76	64	Delete
26	4D	p	79	61	Left arrow
27	54	[	80	6E	Home
28	5B	]	81	65	End
29	5C	\ (101-key only)	83	63	Up arrow
30	14	Caps Lock	84	60	Down arrow
31	1C	a	85	6F	Page Up
32	1B	s	86	6D	Page Down
33	23	d	89	6A	Right arrow
34	2B	f	90	76	Num Lock
35	34	g	91	6C	Keypad 7 (Home)
36	33	h	92	6B	Keypad 4 (Left arrow)
37	3B	j	93	69	Keypad 1 (End)
38	42	k	95	77	Keypad /
39	4B	l	96	75	Keypad 8 (Up arrow)

Key Number	Scan Code	Key
97	73	Keypad 5
98	72	Keypad 2 (Down arrow)
99	70	Keypad 0 (Ins)
100	7E	Keypad *
101	7D	Keypad 9 (PgUp)
102	74	Keypad 6 (Left arrow)
103	7A	Keypad 3 (PgDn)
104	71	Keypad . (Del)
105	84	Keypad -
106	7C	Keypad +
108	79	Keypad Enter
110	08	Escape
112	07	F1
113	0F	F2
114	17	F3
115	1F	F4
116	27	F5
117	2F	F6
118	37	F7
119	3F	F8
120	47	F9
121	4F	F10
122	56	F11
123	5E	F12
124	57	Print Screen
125	5F	Scroll Lock
126	62	Pause

These key number figures and scan code tables are useful when you are troubleshooting stuck or failed keys on a keyboard. Diagnostics can report the defective keyswitch by the scan code, which varies from keyboard to keyboard as to the character it represents and its location.

Keyboard/Mouse Interface Connectors. Keyboards have a cable available with one of two primary types of connectors at the system end. Most aftermarket keyboards have a cable connected inside the keyboard case on the keyboard end and require that you open up the keyboard case to disconnect or test. Actual IBM enhanced keyboards use a unique cable assembly that plugs into both the keyboard as well as the system unit. This makes cable interchange or replacement an easy plug-in affair. A special connector called an SDL (Shielded Data Link) is used at the keyboard end and the appropriate DIN (Deutsche Industrie Norm) connector at the PC end. Any IBM keyboard or cable can be ordered separately as a spare part. The newer enhanced keyboards come with an externally detachable keyboard cable that plugs into the keyboard port with a special connector, much like a telephone connector. The other end of the cable is one of the following two types:

- 5-pin DIN connector—used on most PC compatible systems with Baby-AT form factor motherboards.
- 6-pin mini-DIN connector—used on PS/2 systems and most Low Profile (LPX motherboard) PC compatibles.

Figure 9.10 and table 9.8 show the physical layout and pinouts of all the respective keyboard connector plugs and sockets.

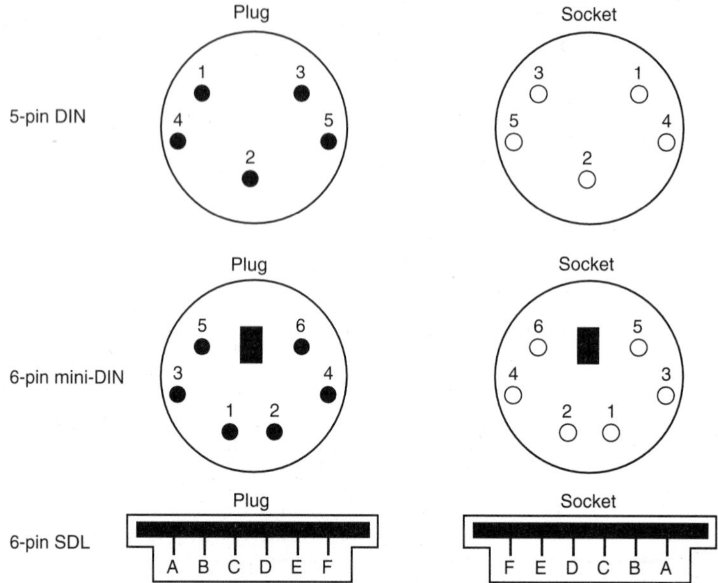

Figure 9.10
Keyboard and mouse connectors.

Table 9.8 Keyboard Connector Signals

Signal Name	5-Pin DIN	6-Pin Mini-DIN	6-Pin SDL
Keyboard Data	2	1	B
Ground	4	3	C
+5v	5	4	E
Keyboard Clock	1	5	D
Not Connected	—	2	A
Not Connected	—	6	F
Not Connected	3	—	—

DIN = German Industrial Norm (Deutsche Industrie Norm), a committee that sets German dimensional standards

SDL = Shielded Data Link, a type of shielded connector created by AMP and used by IBM and others for keyboard cables

Motherboard mouse connectors use the 6-pin mini-DIN connector and have the same pinout and signal descriptions as the keyboard connector; however, the data packets are incompatible. This means that you can easily plug a motherboard mouse (PS/2 style) into a mini-DIN keyboard connector, or plug the mini-DIN type keyboard connector into a motherboard mouse port; however, neither one would work properly in this situation.

Keyboards with Special Features. There are a number of keyboards on the market that have special features not found in the standard designs. These additional features can be simple things such as built-in calculators and clocks, to more complicated features such as integrated pointing devices, special character layouts, shapes, and even programmable keys.

Over the years, many have attempted to change the design of the standard keyboard in an attempt to improve typing speed and ergonomics. Around 1936 August Dvorak and William L. Dealy developed a modified character layout for the keyboard, which replaced the QWERTY layout we are all familiar with today.

The Dvorak-Dealy keyboard design is normally just called the Dvorak design for short. It featured different character positions on the keys designed to promote the alternation of hands during typing. The characters are arranged so that the vowels are in the home row under the left hand, while the consonants used most frequently are placed in the home row under the right hand. The theory was that this would dramatically improve typing speed, however most tests show fairly modest improvements. Being resistant to change, the Dvorak keyboard design has not achieved widespread popularity, and the familiar QWERTY layout is still by far the most common design.

A more recent trend is to change the shape of the keyboard instead of altering the character layout. This has resulted in a number of different so-called ergonometric designs. The goal is to shape the keyboard to better fit the human hand. The most common of these designs split the keyboard in the center, bending the sides back. Some allow the angle between the sides to be adjusted, such as with the Lexmark Select-Ease design, while others are fixed, such as the Microsoft Natural keyboard. These split or bent designs more easily conform to the natural angle of the hands while typing. They can improve productivity and typing speed, as well as help prevent medical problems such as Carpal Tunnel Syndrome (tendon inflammation).

Virtually every keyboard company now has some form of similar ergonometric keyboard, and the same things apply with respect to quality and feel as with the standard keyboard designs. In comparing two of the most popular ergonometric keyboards, the Microsoft Natural Keyboard is manufactured for Microsoft by Keytronics, and uses the inexpensive light-touch keyswitches they are known for. For those who prefer a more rugged keyboard with higher quality switches, I recommend the Lexmark Select-Ease, Alps, NMB Technologies, or Lite-On keyboards. These keyboards use very high quality switches with a positive mechanical tactile feel to them. The Lexmark design, in particular, allows you to adjust the angle between the two sides of the keyboard from fully closed like a standard keyboard, to split at virtually any angle. You can even separate the two halves completely. It also features built-in palm rests, an oversized space bar, and cursor keys on both sides of the keyboard.

Although these ergonometric keyboards sound like a good idea, people are resistant to change, and none of these designs has yet to significantly displace the standard keyboard layout.

Several companies, including Maxi-Switch, have introduced a keyboard that features programmable keys. You can assign different keystrokes to keys, or even reprogram the entire keyboard layout. This type of keyboard has been supplied by some of the PC compatible vendors such as Gateway. I used a number of these keyboards in the seminars I teach, and unfortunately I found the programming functions to be difficult, and accidentally pressing the programming control keys would often put the keyboard into an altered state requiring it to be reset. One other problem was that the extra keys added width to the keyboard, making it wider than most other standard designs. I quickly decided that the programming functions were so rarely used that they were simply not worth the effort, and specified standard keyboards for future purchases.

Keyboard Troubleshooting and Repair

Keyboard errors are usually caused by two simple problems. Other more difficult intermittent problems can arise, but they are also much less likely. The most common problems are

- Defective cables
- Stuck keys

Defective cables are easy to spot if the failure is not intermittent. If the keyboard stops working altogether or every keystroke results in an error or incorrect character, the cable is likely the culprit. Troubleshooting is simple, especially if you have a spare cable on hand. Simply replace the suspected cable with one from a known working keyboard, and verify whether the problem still exists. If it does, the problem must be elsewhere. You also can test the cable for continuity with it removed from the keyboard by using a DMM (Digital Multi-Meter). DMMs that have an audible continuity tester built in make this procedure much easier to perform. Wiggle the ends of the cable as you check each wire to make sure that there are no intermittent connections. If you discover a problem with the continuity in one of the wires, replace the cable or the entire keyboard, if that is cheaper. Because replacement keyboards are so inexpensive, sometimes it can be cheaper to replace the entire unit than to get a new cable.

Many times you first discover a problem with a keyboard because the system has an error during the POST. Most systems use error codes in a 3xx numeric format to distinguish the keyboard. If you have any such errors during the POST, write them down. Some BIOS versions do not use cryptic numeric error codes and simply state something like the following:

```
Keyboard stuck key failure
```

This message normally would be displayed by a system with a Phoenix BIOS if a key were stuck. Unfortunately, that message does not identify which key it is!

If your 3xx (keyboard) error is preceded by a two-digit hexadecimal number, this number is the scan code of a failing or stuck keyswitch. Look up the scan code in the tables provided in this section to determine which keyswitch is the culprit. These charts tell you to which key the scan code refers. By removing the keycap of the offending key and cleaning the switch, you can often solve the problem.

For a simple test of the motherboard keyboard connector, you can check voltages on some of the pins. Use Figure 9.10 in the preceding section as a guide, and measure the voltages on various pins of the keyboard connector. To prevent possible damage to the system or keyboard, first turn off the power before disconnecting the keyboard. Then unplug the keyboard, and turn the power back on. Make measurements between the ground pin and the other pins according to table 9.9. If the voltages are within these specifications, the motherboard keyboard circuitry is probably okay.

Table 9.9 Keyboard Connector Specifications

DIN Connector Pin	Mini-DIN Connector Pin	Signal	Voltage
1	5	Keyboard Clock	+2.0v to +5.5v
2	1	Keyboard Data	+4.8v to +5.5v
3	-	Reserved	—
4	3	Ground	—
5	4	+5v Power	+2.0v to +5.5v

If your measurements do not match these voltages, the motherboard might be defective. Otherwise, the keyboard cable or keyboard might be defective. If you suspect that the cable is the problem, the easiest thing to do is to replace the keyboard cable with a known good one. If the system still does not work normally, you may have to replace either the entire keyboard or the motherboard.

In many newer systems the motherboard keyboard and mouse connectors are protected by a fuse that can be replaced. Look for any type of fuse on the motherboard in the vicinity of the keyboard or mouse connectors. Other systems may have a socketed keyboard controller chip (8042-type). In that case, it may be possible to repair the motherboard keyboard circuit by replacing this chip. Because these chips have ROM code in them, it is best to get the replacement from the motherboard or BIOS manufacturer.

Here is a list of standard POST and diagnostics keyboard error codes:

Error Code	Description
3xx	Keyboard errors
301	Keyboard reset or stuck-key failure (XX 301, XX = scan code in hex)
302	System unit keylock switch is locked
302	User-indicated keyboard test error
303	Keyboard or system-board error; keyboard controller failure
304	Keyboard or system-board error; keyboard clock high
305	Keyboard +5v error; PS/2 keyboard fuse (on motherboard) blown
341	Keyboard error
342	Keyboard cable error
343	Keyboard LED card or cable failure
365	Keyboard LED card or cable failure
366	Keyboard interface cable failure
367	Keyboard LED card or cable failure

Disassembly Procedures and Cautions. Repairing and cleaning a keyboard often requires you to take it apart. When performing this task, you must know when to stop! Some keyboards literally come apart into hundreds of little pieces that are almost impossible to reassemble if you go too far. An IBM keyboard generally has these four major parts:

- Cable
- Case
- Keypad assembly
- Keycaps

You easily can break down a keyboard to these major components and replace any of them, but don't disassemble the keypad assembly or you will be showered with hundreds of tiny springs, clips, and keycaps. Finding all these parts—several hundred of them—and piecing the unit back together is not a fun way to spend your time. You also may not be able to reassemble the keyboard properly. Figure 9.11 shows a typical keyboard with the case opened.

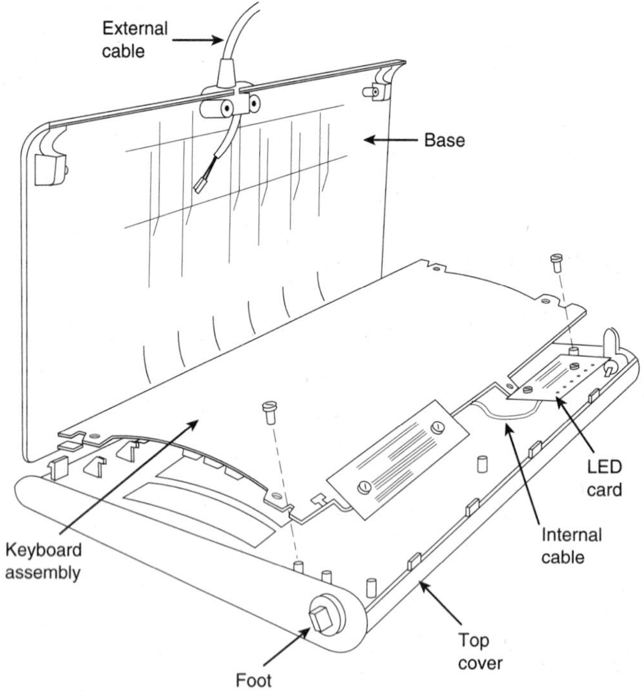

Figure 9.11

Typical keyboard components.

Another problem is that you cannot purchase the smaller parts separately, such as contact clips and springs. The only way to obtain these parts is from another keyboard. If you ever have a keyboard that is beyond repair, keep it around for these parts. They might come in handy some day.

Most repair operations are limited to changing the cable or cleaning some component of the keyboard, from the cable contact ends to the key contact points. The keyboard cable takes quite a lot of abuse and, therefore, can fail easily. The ends are stretched, tugged, pulled, and generally handled roughly. The cable uses strain reliefs, but you still might have problems with the connectors making proper contact at each end or even with wires that have broken inside the cable. You might want to carry a spare cable for every type of keyboard you have.

All keyboard cables plug into the keyboard and PC with connectors, and you can change the cables easily without having to splice wires or solder connections. With the earlier 83-key PC and 84-key AT keyboards, you must open the case to access the connector to which the cable attaches. On the newer 101-key enhanced keyboards from IBM and Lexmark, the cable plugs into the keyboard from the outside of the case, using a modular jack and plug similar to a telephone jack. This design also makes the IBM/Lexmark keyboards universally usable on nearly any system (except the original PC) by easily switching the cable.

The only difference, for example, between the enhanced keyboards for an IBM AT and an IBM PS/2 system is the attached cable. PS/2 systems use a tan cable with a smaller plug on the computer side. The AT cable is black and has the larger DIN-type plug on the computer side. You can interchange the enhanced keyboards as long as you use the correct cable for the system.

The only feasible way to repair a keyboard is to replace the cable and to clean the individual keyswitch assemblies, the entire keypad, or the cable contact ends. The individual spring and keyswitch assemblies are not available as a separate part, and disassembling the unit to that level is not advisable because of the difficulty in reassembling it. Other than cleaning a keyboard, the only thing that you can do is replace the entire keypad assembly (virtually the entire keyboard) or the cable.

Cleaning a Keyboard. One of the best ways to maintain a keyboard in top condition is periodic cleaning. As preventive maintenance, you should vacuum the keyboard weekly or at least monthly. You can also use canned compressed air (available at electronics supply houses) to blow the dust and dirt out instead of using a vacuum. Before you dust a keyboard with the compressed air, turn the keyboard upside down so that the particles of dirt and dust collected inside can fall out.

On all keyboards, each keycap is removable, which can be handy if a key sticks or acts erratically. For example, a common problem is a key that does not work every time you press it. This problem usually results from dirt collecting under the key. An excellent tool for removing keycaps on most any keyboard is the U-shaped chip-puller tool. Simply slip the hooked ends of the tool under the keycap, squeeze the ends together to grip the underside of the keycap, and lift up. IBM sells a tool designed specifically for removing keycaps from its keyboards, but the chip puller works even better. After removing the cap, spray some compressed air into the space under the cap to dislodge the dirt. Then replace the cap and check the action of the key.

When you remove the keycaps, be careful not to remove the space bar on the original 83-key PC and 84-key AT-type keyboards. This bar is very difficult to reinstall. The newer 101-key units use a different wire support that can be removed and replaced much more easily.

Spills also can be a problem. If you tip a soft drink or cup of coffee into a keyboard, you do not necessarily have a disaster. You should immediately (or as soon as possible) flush out the keyboard with distilled water. Partially disassemble the keyboard and use the water to wash the components. (See the following section for disassembly instructions.) If the spilled liquid has dried, soak the keyboard in some of the water for a while. When you are sure that the keyboard is clean, pour another gallon or so of distilled water over it and through the key switches to wash away any residual dirt. After the unit dries completely, it should be perfectly functional. You may be surprised to know that you can drench your keyboard with water, and it will not harm the components. Just make sure that you use distilled water, which is free from residue or mineral content. Also make sure that the keyboard is fully dry before you attempt to use it, or some of the components might short out—water is a conductor of electricity.

Replacement Keyboards. In most cases, it is cheaper or more cost-effective to replace a keyboard rather than to repair it. This is especially true if the keyboard has an internal malfunction or if one of the keyswitches is defective. Replacement parts for keyboards are almost impossible to procure, and in most cases the installation of any repair part is difficult. In addition, many of the keyboards supplied with lower cost compatible machines leave much to be desired. They often have a mushy feel, with little or no tactile feedback. A poor keyboard can make using a system a frustrating experience, especially if you are a touch typist. For all these reasons, it is often a good idea to replace an existing keyboard with something better.

Perhaps the highest quality keyboards in the entire computer industry are those made by IBM, or more accurately, Lexmark. Several years ago IBM spun off its keyboard and printer divisions as a separate company called Lexmark. Lexmark now manufactures most IBM brand keyboards and printers and sells them not only to IBM but also to compatible vendors and end users. This means that if you are lucky, your compatible system comes with a Lexmark keyboard, but if not, you can purchase one separately on your own.

Table 9.10 shows the part numbers of all IBM-labeled keyboards and cables. These numbers can serve as a reference when you are seeking a replacement IBM keyboard from IBM directly or from third-party companies. Many third-party companies sell IBM label keyboards for much less than IBM, in both new and refurbished form. Remember that you can also purchase these same keyboards through Lexmark, although they do not come with an IBM label.

Table 9.10 IBM Keyboard and Cable Part Numbers

Description	Part Number
83-key U.S. PC Keyboard assembly with cable	8529297
Cable assembly for 83-key PC Keyboard	8529168
84-key U.S. AT Keyboard assembly with cable	8286165
Cable assembly for 84-key Keyboard	8286146
101-key U.S. Keyboard without LED panel	1390290
101-key U.S. Keyboard with LED panel	6447033
101-key U.S. Keyboard with LED panel (PS/2 logo)	1392090
6-foot cable for enhanced keyboard (DIN plug)	6447051
6-foot cable for enhanced keyboard (mini-DIN plug)	61X8898
6-foot cable for enhanced keyboard (shielded mini-DIN plug)	27F4984
10-foot cable for enhanced keyboard (mini-DIN plug)	72X8537

Notice that the original 83/84-key IBM keyboards are sold with a cable that has the larger, 5-pin DIN connector already attached. IBM enhanced keyboards are always sold (at least by IBM) without a cable. You must order the proper cable as a separate item. Cables are available to connect the keyboards to either the older system units that use the larger DIN connector or to PS/2 systems (and many compatibles) that use the smaller mini-DIN connector.

Recently, IBM has started selling complete keyboard assemblies under a program called IBM Options. This program is designed to sell these components in the retail channel to end users of both IBM and compatible systems from other vendors. Items under the IBM Options program are sold through normal retail channels such as CompUSA, Elek Tek, and Computer Discount Warehouse (CDW). These items are also priced much cheaper than items purchased as spare parts. They include a full warranty and are sold as complete packages including cables. Table 9.11 lists some of the IBM Options keyboards and part numbers.

Table 9.11 IBM Options Keyboards (Sold Retail)

Description	Part Number
IBM enhanced keyboard (cable w/DIN plug)	92G7454
IBM enhanced keyboard (cable w/mini-DIN plug)	92G7453
IBM enhanced keyboard, built-in Trackball (cable w/DIN plug)	92G7456
IBM enhanced keyboard, built-in Trackball (cable w/mini-DIN plug)	92G7455
IBM enhanced keyboard, integrated Trackpoint II (cable w/mini-DIN plug)	92G7461

The IBM/Lexmark keyboards use capacitive keyswitches, which are the most durable and lowest maintenance. These switches have no electrical contacts and, instead, rely on changing capacitance to signal a keypress within the switch matrix. This type of design does not have wear points, like a mechanical switch, and has no metal electrical contacts, which makes it virtually immune to the dirt and corrosion problems that plague other designs.

The extremely positive tactile feedback of the IBM/Lexmark design is also a benchmark of comparison for the rest of the industry. Although keyboard feel is an issue of personal preference, I have never used a keyboard that feels better than the IBM/Lexmark designs. I now equip every system I use with a Lexmark keyboard, including the many clone or compatible systems I use. You can purchase these keyboards through Lexmark or a Lexmark distributor for very reasonable prices. You can find IBM-labeled models available from advertisers in *Processor* or *Computer Hotline* magazines selling for under $60.

IBM/Lexmark sells other versions for very reasonable prices as well. Many different models are available, including some with a built-in trackball or even the revolutionary Trackpoint pointing device. Trackpoint refers to a small stick mounted between the G, H, and B keys. This device is an IBM/Lexmark exclusive and was first featured on the IBM Thinkpad laptop systems, although the keyboards are now sold for use on compatibles and the technology is being licensed to other firms, including Toshiba. Note that this keyboard comes only with the mini-DIN type connectors for both the keyboard and Trackpoint portions, and it works only with a Motherboard (PS/2 type) mouse port.

Other manufacturers of high-quality keyboards are available. Several companies, such as Alps, Lite-On, or NMB Technologies, manufacture keyboards similar in feel to the IBM/Lexmark units. They have excellent tactile feedback with a positive click sound. They are my second choice, after a Lexmark unit. Maxi-Switch also makes a high-quality aftermarket keyboard used by a number of compatible manufacturers, including Gateway 2000. These also have a good feel and are recommended. Many of these companies can make their keyboards with your own company logo on them (such as the Maxi-Switch models used by Gateway), which is ideal for clone manufacturers looking for name-brand recognition.

Reference Material

If you are interested in more details about keyboard design or interfacing, a company called Annabooks publishes a book/disk package called *PC Keyboard Design*. This document defines the protocol between the keyboard and computer for both XT and AT types and includes schematics and keyboard controller source code. The kit includes a license to use the source code and costs $249.

Other excellent sources of information are the various technical reference manuals put out by IBM. The vendor list contains a list of the important IBM reference manuals in which you can find much valuable information. This information is especially valuable to compatible system manufacturers, because they often do not put out the same level of technical information as IBM, and compatible systems are in many ways similar or even identical to one or more IBM systems. After all, that is why they are called IBM compatible. Much of my personal knowledge and expertise comes from poring over the various IBM technical reference manuals.

Mice

The mouse was invented in 1964 by Douglas Englebart, who at the time was working at the Stanford Research Institute (SRI), a think tank sponsored by Stanford University. The mouse was officially called an "X-Y Position Indicator for a Display System." Xerox later applied the mouse to its revolutionary Alto computer system in 1973. At the time, unfortunately, these systems were experimental and used purely for research.

In 1979, several people from Apple, including Steve Jobs, were invited to see the Alto and the software that ran the system. Steve Jobs was blown away by what he saw as the future of computing, which included the use of the mouse as a pointing device and the graphical user interface it operated. Apple promptly incorporated these features into what was to become the Lisa computer and lured away 15 to 20 Xerox scientists to work on the Apple system.

Although Xerox released the Star 8010 computer that used this technology in 1981, it was expensive, poorly marketed, and perhaps way ahead of its time. Apple released the Lisa computer, which was their first system that used the mouse, in 1983. It also was not a runaway success, largely because of its $10,000 list price, but by then Jobs already had Apple working on the low-cost successor to the Lisa, the Macintosh. The Apple Macintosh was introduced in 1984; although it was not an immediate hit, the Macintosh has grown in popularity since that time.

Many credit the Macintosh with inventing the mouse and GUI, but as you can see, this technology was actually borrowed from others, including SRI and Xerox. Certainly the Macintosh, and now Microsoft Windows and OS/2, have gone on to popularize this interface and bring it to the legion of PC-compatible systems.

Although the mouse did not catch on quickly in the PC-compatible marketplace, today the GUIs for PC systems such as Windows and OS/2 virtually demand the use of a mouse. Because of this, it is common for a mouse to be sold with virtually every new system on the market.

Mice come in many shapes and sizes from many different manufacturers. Some have taken the standard mouse design and turned it upside down, creating the trackball. In the trackball devices, you move the ball with your hand directly rather than the unit itself. IBM even produced a very cool mouse/trackball convertible device called the Trackpoint (p/n 1397040). The Trackpoint could be used as either a mouse (ball side down), or as a track ball (ball side up). In most cases, the dedicated trackballs have a much larger ball than would be found on a standard mouse. Other than the orientation and perhaps the size of the ball, a trackball is identical to a mouse in design, basic function, and electrical interface.

The largest manufacturers of mice are Microsoft and Logitech. Even though mice may come in different varieties, their actual use and care differ very little. The standard mouse consists of several components:

- A housing that you hold in your hand and move around on your desktop
- A roller ball that signals movement to the system

- Buttons (usually two) for making selections
- A cable for connecting the mouse to the system
- An interface connector to attach the mouse to the system

The housing is made of plastic and consists of very few moving parts. On top of the housing, where your fingers normally reside, are buttons. There may be any number of buttons, but in the PC world there are typically only two. If additional buttons are on your mouse, specialized software is required for them to operate. On the bottom of the housing is a small rubber ball that rotates as you move the mouse across the tabletop. The movements of this rubber ball are translated into electrical signals transmitted to the computer across the cable. Some mice use a special optical sensor that detects movement over a grid. These optical mice have fallen into disfavor because they work only if you use a special grid pad underneath them.

The cable can be any length, but is typically between four and six feet long. (If you have a choice on the length of cable to purchase, go for a longer one. This allows easier placement of the mouse in relation to your computer.)

The connector used with your mouse depends on the type of interface you are using. Three basic interfaces are used, with a fourth combination device possible as well.

After the mouse is connected to your computer, it communicates with your system through the use of a device driver, which can be either separately loaded or built into the system software. For example, no separate drivers are needed to use a mouse with Windows or OS/2, but using the mouse with most DOS-based programs requires a separate driver to be loaded. Regardless of whether it is built-in, the driver translates the electrical signals sent from the mouse into positional information and information that indicates the status of the buttons.

Internally, a mouse is very simple as well. The ball usually rests against two rollers, one for translating the X-axis movement and the other for the Y-axis. These rollers are usually connected to small disks with shutters that alternately block and allow the passage of light. Small optical sensors detect movement of the wheels by watching an internal infrared light blink on and off as the shutter wheel rotates and "chops" the light. These blinks are translated into movement along the axes. This type of setup is called an *opto-mechanical mechanism* and is by far the most popular in use today (see fig. 9.12).

The following sections explain the different types of mouse interfaces and how you can care for the mice.

Mouse Interface Types

Mice can be connected to your computer through the following three devices:

- Serial interface
- Dedicated motherboard mouse port
- Bus-card interface

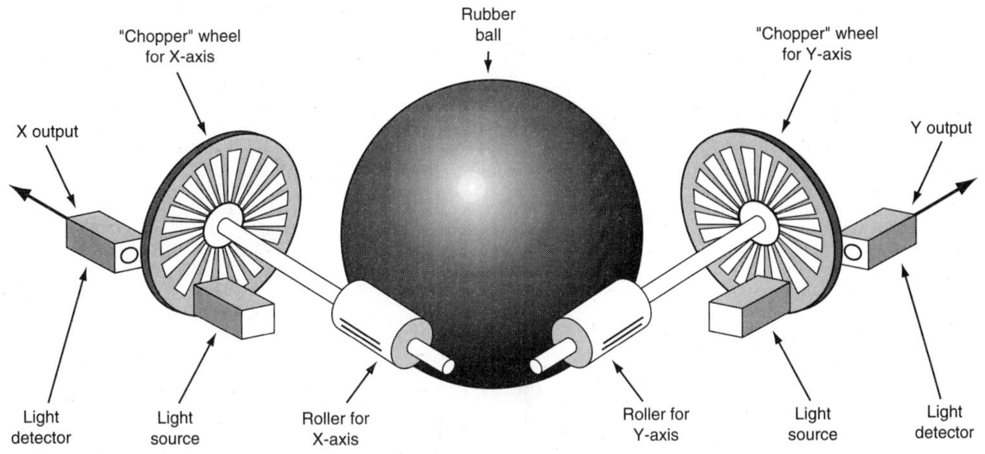

Figure 9.12

Typical opto-mechanical mouse mechanism.

Serial. A popular method of connecting a mouse to most older PC-compatible computers is through a serial interface. As with other serial devices, the connector on the end of the mouse cable is either a 9-pin or 25-pin male connector. Only a couple of pins in the DB-9 or DB-25 connectors are used for communications between the mouse and the device driver, but the mouse connector typically has all 9 or 25 pins present.

Because most PCs come with two serial ports, a serial mouse can be plugged into either COM1: or COM2:. The device driver, when initializing, searches the ports to determine the one to which the mouse is connected.

Because a serial mouse does not connect to the system directly, it does not use system resources by itself. Instead, the resources used are those used by the serial port to which it is connected. For example, if you have a mouse connected to COM2:, it most likely uses IRQ3 and I/O Port Addresses 2F8h-2FFh.

Motherboard Mouse Port (PS/2). Most newer computers now come with a dedicated mouse port built into the motherboard. This was started by IBM with the PS/2 systems in 1987, so this interface is often referred to as a PS/2 mouse interface. This term does not imply that such a mouse can work only with a PS/2; instead, it means that the mouse can connect to any system that has a dedicated mouse port on the motherboard.

A motherboard mouse connector usually is exactly the same as the mini-DIN connector used for newer keyboards. In fact, the motherboard mouse port is connected to the 8042-type keyboard controller found on the motherboard. All the PS/2 computers include mini-DIN keyboard and mouse port connectors on the back. Most compatible Slimline computers also have these same connectors for space reasons. Other motherboards have a pin-header type connector for the mouse port because most standard cases do not have a provision for the mini-DIN mouse connector. In that case, an adapter cable is usually supplied with the system that adapts the pin-header connector on the motherboard to the standard mini-DIN type connector used for the motherboard mouse.

Connecting a mouse to the built-in mouse port is the best method of connection because you do not lose any interface slots or any serial ports, and the performance is not limited by the serial port circuitry. The standard resource usage for a motherboard (or PS/2) mouse port is IRQ 12 and I/O Port Addresses 60h and 64h. Because the motherboard mouse port uses the 8042-type keyboard controller chip, the port addresses are those of this chip. IRQ 12 is an interrupt that is usually free on most systems and, of course, must remain free on any ISA bus systems that have a motherboard mouse port because interrupt sharing is not allowed with the ISA bus.

Serial and Motherboard Mouse Port (PS/2). A hybrid type of mouse can plug into both a serial port or a motherboard mouse port connection. This combination serial-PS/2 mouse is the most popular type because it is more flexible than the single design types. Circuitry in this mouse automatically detects the type of port to which it is connected and configures the mouse automatically. These mice usually come with a mini-DIN connector on the end of their cable and also include an adapter between the mini-DIN to 9- or 25-pin serial port connector.

Sometimes people use adapters to try to connect a serial mouse to a motherboard mouse port, or a motherboard mouse to a serial port. This does not work and is not the fault of the adapter. If the mouse does not explicitly state that it is both a serial-PS/2 type mouse, it does not work on either interface but instead works only on the single interface for which it was designed. Most of the time, you find the designation for what type of mouse you have printed on the bottom of it.

Bus. A bus mouse is typically used in systems that do not have a motherboard mouse port or any available serial ports. The name bus mouse is derived from the fact that the mouse requires a special bus interface board that occupies a slot in your computer and communicates with the device driver across the main motherboard bus. Although the use of a bus mouse is transparent to the user (there is no operational difference between a bus mouse and other types of mice), many people view a bus mouse as less desirable than other types because it occupies a slot that could be used for other peripherals.

Another drawback to the bus mouse is that it is electrically incompatible with the other types of mice. Because it is not very popular, a bus mouse can be hard to find in a pinch. Likewise, the bus adapters are typically available only for ISA slots; because they are always 8-bit cards, you are limited in the choice of nonconflicting hardware interrupts. A bus mouse can also be dangerous because it uses a mini-DIN connector just like the motherboard (PS/2)-type mouse, although they are totally incompatible. I have even heard of people damaging motherboards by plugging a bus mouse into a motherboard mouse connector.

Bus mouse adapter cards usually have a selectable interrupt and I/O port address setting, but the IRQ selection is limited to only 8-bit interrupts. This usually means that you must choose IRQ 5 in most systems that already have two serial ports because all the other 8-bit interrupts will be used. If you also are using another 8-bit-only card that needs an interrupt, like some of the sound cards, you will not be able to run both devices in the same system without conflicts. All in all, I do not recommend bus mice and think they should be avoided.

One thing to note is that Microsoft sometimes calls a bus mouse an *Inport* mouse, which is its proprietary name for a bus mouse connection.

Mouse Troubleshooting

If you are experiencing problems with your mouse, you need to look in only two general places—hardware or software. Because mice are basically simple devices, looking at the hardware takes very little time. Detecting and correcting software problems can take a bit longer, however.

Hardware Problems. Two types of hardware problems can crop up when you are using a mouse. The most common is a dirty mouse, which is fixed by doing some "mouse cleaning." The other relates to interrupt conflicts and is more difficult to solve.

Cleaning Your Mouse. If you notice that the mouse pointer moves across the screen in a jerky fashion, it may be time to clean your mouse. This jerkiness is caused when dirt and dust get trapped around the mouse's ball and roller assembly, thereby restricting its free movement.

From a hardware perspective, the mouse is a simple device, and cleaning it is also very simple. The first step is to turn the mouse housing over so that you can see the ball on the bottom. Notice that surrounding the ball is an access panel that you can open. There may even be some instructions that indicate how the panel is to be opened. (Some off-brand mice may require you to remove some screws to get at the roller ball.) Remove the panel, and you can see more of the roller ball and the socket in which it rests.

If you turn the mouse back over, the rubber roller ball should fall into your hand. Take a look at the ball. It may be gray or black, but it should have no visible dirt or other contamination. If it does, wash it in soapy water or a mild solvent such as contact cleaner solution or alcohol and dry it off.

Now take a look at the socket in which the roller ball normally rests. You will see two or three small wheels or bars against which the ball normally rolls. If you see dust or dirt on or around these wheels or bars, you need to clean them. The best way is to use a compressed air duster to blow out any dust or dirt. You also can use some electrical contact cleaner to clean the rollers. Remember, any remaining dirt or dust impedes the movement of the roller ball and means that the mouse will not work as it should.

Put the mouse back together by inserting the roller ball into the socket and then securely attaching the cover panel. The mouse should look just like it did before you removed the panel except that it will be noticeably cleaner.

Interrupt Conflicts. Interrupts are internal signals used by your computer to indicate when something needs to happen. With a mouse, an interrupt is used whenever the mouse has information to send to the mouse driver. If a conflict occurs and the same interrupt used by the mouse is used by a different device, the mouse will not work properly, if at all.

Interrupt conflicts do not normally occur if your system uses a mouse port, but they can occur with the other types of mouse interfaces. If you are using a serial interface, interrupt conflicts typically occur if you add a third and fourth serial port. This is because in ISA bus systems, odd-numbered serial ports (1 and 3) are often improperly configured to use the same interrupts as the even-numbered ports (2 and 4). Thus, if your mouse is connected to COM2: and an internal modem uses COM4:, they both may use the same interrupt, and you cannot use them at the same time. You may be able to use the mouse and modem at the same time by moving one of them to a different serial port. For instance, if your mouse uses COM1: and the modem still uses COM4:, you can use them both at once because odd and even ports use different interrupts.

The best way around these interrupt conflicts is to make sure that no two devices use the same interrupt. Serial port adapters are available for adding COM3: and COM4: serial ports that do not share the interrupts used by COM1: and COM2:. These boards enable the new COM ports to use other normally available interrupts, such as IRQs 10, 11, 12, 15, or 5. I never recommend configuring a system with shared interrupts; it is a sure way to run into problems later.

If you suspect an interrupt problem with a bus-type mouse, you can use a program such as Microsoft's MSD (MicroSoft Diagnostics) to help you identify what interrupt the mouse is set to. You get MSD free with Windows 3.0 or higher as well as MS-DOS 6.0 or higher. If you use OS/2 and/or PC DOS, you can still get MSD for free by downloading it from the Microsoft BBS (see the vendor list). Beware that programs like MSD that attempt to identify IRQ usage are not always 100-percent accurate—in fact, they are inaccurate in many cases—and usually require that the device driver for the particular device be loaded to work at all. Although these programs can have problems, most will easily identify the mouse IRQ if the mouse driver has been loaded. After the IRQ is identified, you may need to change the IRQ setting of the bus mouse adapter or one or more other devices in your system so that everything works together properly.

If your driver refuses to recognize the mouse at all, regardless of its type, try using a different mouse that you know works. Replacing a defective mouse with a known good one may be the only way to identify if the problem is indeed caused by a bad mouse.

I have had problems in which a bad mouse caused the system to lock as the driver loaded or even when diagnostics such as MSD attempted to access the mouse. You can easily ferret out this type of problem by loading MSD with the /I option, which causes MSD to bypass its initial hardware detection. Then run each of the tests separately, including the mouse test, to see whether the system locks. If the system locks during the mouse test, you have found a problem with either the mouse or the mouse port. Try replacing the mouse to see whether that helps. If it does not, you may need to replace the serial port or bus mouse adapter. If a motherboard-based mouse port goes bad, you can replace the entire motherboard—usually expensive—or you can just disable the motherboard mouse port via jumpers or the system setup program and install a serial or bus mouse instead. This enables you to continue using the system without having to replace the motherboard.

Software Problems. Software problems can be a little trickier than hardware problems. Software problems generally manifest themselves as the mouse "just not working." In such instances, you need to check the driver and your software applications before assuming that the mouse itself has gone bad.

Driver Software. To function properly, the mouse requires the installation of a device driver. I normally recommend using the drivers built into the Windows or OS/2 operating environments. This means that no additional external driver is necessary. The only reason for loading an external driver (via CONFIG.SYS) is if you want the mouse to work with DOS applications.

If you need the mouse to work under standard DOS—in other words, outside Windows or OS/2—you must load a device driver through either your CONFIG.SYS file or your AUTOEXEC.BAT file. This driver, if loaded in the CONFIG.SYS file, is typically called MOUSE.SYS. The version that loads in the AUTOEXEC.BAT file is called MOUSE.COM. (It is possible that your mouse drivers have different names, depending on who manufactured your mouse.) Again, remember that if you only use a mouse under Windows or OS/2, no external drivers are required because the mouse driver is built in.

The first step is to make sure that the proper command to load the driver is in your CONFIG.SYS or AUTOEXEC.BAT file. If it is not, add the proper line, according to the information supplied with your mouse. For instance, the proper command to load the mouse driver through the CONFIG.SYS file for a Microsoft mouse is as follows:

```
DEVICEHIGH=\DOS\MOUSE.SYS
```

The actual working or syntax of the command may vary, depending on whether you are loading the device into upper memory and where the device driver is located on your disk.

One of the biggest problems with the separate mouse driver is getting it loaded into an Upper Memory Block (UMB). The older drivers—9.0 and earlier—require a very large block of 40K to 56K UMB to load into, and upon loading they shrink down to less than 20K. Even though they only take 20K or less after loading, you still need a very large area to get them "in the door."

The best tip I can give you with respect to these separate drivers is to use the newest 9.01 or higher drivers from Microsoft. This new driver is included with the newer Microsoft mice, and is also sold separately as an upgrade. The Microsoft driver works with any type of Microsoft-compatible mouse, which basically means just about any mouse at all. Microsoft requires that you pay about $50 for an upgrade to the newer versions of the mouse driver. You can also get the new driver with a new mouse for $35 or less, which makes the driver-only purchase not very cost effective. Microsoft still includes only the older driver with DOS 6.22 or earlier. IBM included the new driver with PC DOS 6.3 but switched back to the 8.2 driver in PC DOS 7.0.

If you use version 9.01 or later, it will require less memory than previous versions and will automatically load itself into high memory as well. One of the best features is that it first loads itself into low memory; shrinks down to about 24K; and then moves into Upper Memory automatically. Not only that, but the driver seeks out the smallest UMB that can hold it, instead of trying only the largest, as would happen if you use the

DEVICEHIGH, LOADHIGH, or LH commands to load the driver. Previous versions of the driver could not fit into an upper memory block unless that block was at least 40K to 56K or larger in size, and would certainly not do it automatically. The enhanced self-loading capability of the mouse driver 9.01 and higher can save much memory space and is very much worth having. I hope that this type of self-loading and self-optimizing technique will be used in other device drivers. It will make memory management much easier than it currently is.

After placing the proper driver load command in your CONFIG.SYS or AUTOEXEC.BAT file, reboot the system with the mouse connected and observe that the driver loads properly. If the proper command is in place and the driver is not loading, watch your video screen as your system boots. At some point, you should see a message from the mouse driver indicating that it is loaded. If, instead, you see a message indicating that the loading was not done, you must determine why. For example, the driver may not be able to load because not enough memory is available. After you determine why it is not loading, you need to rectify the situation and make sure that the driver loads. Again the new 9.01 or higher driver versions help greatly with memory problems.

It is also possible that some software requires a certain mouse device driver. If you are using an older mouse driver and your application software requires a newer-version mouse driver, the mouse may not work properly. In such cases, contact your mouse vendor directly and request a mouse driver update. Often you can get these through the vendor's BBS or on CompuServe; however, Microsoft charges for its new drivers and does not make them available on its BBS. In that case, it is cheaper to purchase an entire new mouse, which includes the new driver, rather than just the driver upgrade.

Application Software. If your mouse does not work with a specific piece of application software, check the setup information or configuration section of the program. Make sure that you indicated to the program (if necessary) that you are using a mouse. If it still does not work and the mouse works with other software you are using, contact the technical support department of the application software company.

Trackpoint

In April 1992, I attended the spring Comdex computer show in Chicago, and at one of the IBM booths was an enthusiastic gentleman with what looked like some homemade keyboards. These keyboards had a small rubber tipped "stick" that protruded from between the G, H, and B keys. I was invited to play with one of the keyboards, which was connected to a demonstration system. What I found was amazing. By pressing on the stick with my thumb or index finger, I could move the mouse pointer on the screen. The stick itself did not move and is not a joystick. Instead it had a silicone rubber cap that contained pressure transducers that measured the amount of force my finger or thumb was applying and the direction of the force and moved the mouse pointer accordingly. The harder I pressed, the faster the pointer moved. I could move the pointer in any direction smoothly, by slightly changing the direction of push. The silicone rubber gripped my thumb even though I had been sweating from dashing about the show. After playing around with it for just a few minutes, the movements became automatic—almost as if I could just "think" about where I wanted the pointer to go, and it would go there. After reflecting on this for a minute, it really hit me: This had to be the most revolutionary pointing device since the mouse itself!

This device occupies no space on a desk, does not have to be adjusted for left-handed or right-handed use, has no moving parts to fail or become dirty, and—most important—does not require you to move your hands from the home row to use. This is an absolute boon for anybody who touch types.

The gentleman at the booth turned out to be Ted Selker, one of the actual inventors of the device. He and Joseph Rutledge created this amazing integrated pointing device at the IBM T.J. Watson Research Center. When I asked him when such keyboards would become available, he could not answer. At the time, there were apparently no plans for production, and he was only trying to test user reaction to the device. Just over six months later, however, on October 20, 1992, IBM announced the Thinkpad 700, which included this revolutionary device, then called the Trackpoint II integrated pointing device. Since the original version came out, an enhanced version with greater control and sensitivity called the Trackpoint III has been available.

In final production form, the Trackpoint consisted of a small red silicone rubber knob nestled between the G, H, and B keys on the keyboard. Two buttons are placed below the space bar to emulate the LH and RH mouse buttons for making selections. These buttons also can be easily reached without taking your hand off the keyboard. Research done by the inventors found that the act of removing your hand from the keyboard, reaching for a mouse, and replacing the hand on the keyboard takes approximately 1.35 seconds. Almost all this time can be saved each time the track point is used to either move the pointer or make a selection (click or double-click). The combination of the buttons and the positioning knob also enable drag-and-drop functions to be performed easily as well.

By the way, the reason the device was called Trackpoint II is that IBM had previously been selling a convertible mouse/trackball device called the Trackpoint. No relationship exists between the original Trackpoint mouse/trackball, which has since been discontinued, and the Trackpoint II integrated device. Since the original Trackpoint II came out, an improved version called Trackpoint III is now available. It is basically an improved version of the same thing. In the interest of simplicity, I will refer to all of the Trackpoint II, III, and successive devices as just Trackpoint.

Another feature of the Trackpoint is that a mouse can be connected to the system to allow for dual-pointer use. In this case, a single mouse pointer would still be on the screen; however, both the Trackpoint and the simultaneously connected mouse could move the pointer. This allows not only the use of both devices by a single person, but in fact, two people can use both the Trackpoint and the mouse simultaneously to move the pointer on the screen. The first pointing device that moves takes precedence and retains control over the mouse pointer on the screen until it completes a movement action. The second pointing device is automatically locked out until the primary device is stationary. This enables both devices to be used, but prevents each one from interfering with the other.

The Trackpoint is obviously an ideal pointing device for a laptop system where lugging around an external mouse or trackball can be a pain. The trackballs and mini-trackballs built into some laptop keyboards are also very difficult to use and usually require removing your hands from the home row. Mouse and trackball devices are notorious for becoming "sticky" as the ball picks up dirt that affects the internal roller motion. This is especially aggravated with the smaller mini-trackball devices. But the benefits of the Trackpoint are not limited to laptop systems. IBM/Lexmark now manufactures and sells desktop enhanced keyboards with the Trackpoint device built in. These new keyboards are also optional when purchasing a new PS/2 system. One drawback is that the Trackpoint device in these keyboards initially worked only with systems that used a PS/2- or motherboard-type mouse connector. However, the Trackpoint enhanced keyboard is now available in two versions. One interfaces via a motherboard mouse port (mini-DIN connector) and has a mini-DIN type keyboard connector. The other has a standard DIN keyboard connector and a serial connector for the pointing function. I list the part numbers for the IBM enhanced keyboard with the Trackpoint in the section, "Replacement Keyboards," earlier in this chapter. You can also purchase these keyboards directly from Lexmark.

The Trackpoint probably stands as the most important and revolutionary new pointing device since the original invention of the mouse in 1964 by Douglas Englebart at the Stanford Research Institute (SRI). As IBM licenses this technology to other manufacturers, you will see this device show up in many different systems. It is already available built into keyboards, which can upgrade many existing systems, and companies such as Toshiba are using this IBM-developed technology in their own systems. For example, Toshiba is using the Trackpoint in most of their newer portable systems and calls it the "Accupoint" pointing device.

IBM has continued to innovate where laptop or notebook systems are concerned. They have recently introduced models of their Thinkpad line with an expandable automatic fold-out keyboard code-named the butterfly. This allows the system to be much smaller than the competition when folded, yet when opened the keyboard automatically pops out and becomes full-sized. Innovations like this have propelled IBM to the top of the laptop and notebook computer market.

Glidepoint

In response to the Trackpoint, other companies have adopted new pointing device technology as well. For example, Alps Electric has introduced a new pointing device called the Glidepoint. The Glidepoint uses a flat square pad, which senses finger position through body capacitance. This is similar to the capacitance sensitive elevator button controls you sometimes encounter in office buildings or hotels. Instead of sitting in between the keys, the Glidepoint is mounted below the space bar, and detects pressure applied by your thumbs or fingers. Transducers under the pad convert finger movement into pointer movement. Several laptop and notebook manufacturers have licensed this technology from Alps and are incorporating it into their portable systems. Especially for portable systems, new technology like the Trackpoint and Glidepoint have rendered the trackball or mouse totally obsolete!

Game Adapter (Joystick) Interface

The game control or joystick adapter is a special input device that enables up to four paddles or two joysticks to be attached to a PC system. The term paddle is used to refer to a knob that can be rotated to move an object on the screen, and was named after the first popular videogame called Pong, where the knob moved the game paddles.

The game adapter function can be found on a dedicated ISA or MCA bus adapter card, or can be combined with other functions in a multifunction card. The game connector on the card is a female 15-pin D-Shell type socket (see fig. 9.13).

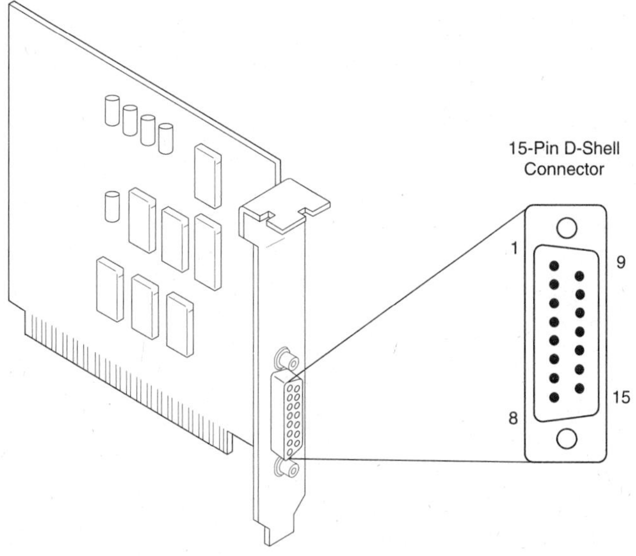

Figure 9.13

Typical game adapter and 15-pin connector.

The game adapter can recognize up to four switches (called buttons) and four resistive inputs. Each paddle normally has one button and one knob that controls a variable resistor, whereas a joystick normally has two buttons and a central stick that controls two variable resistors. In a joystick, the variable resistors are tied to the central stick. One indicates the relative vertical position (or x-coordinate) of the stick, and the other indicates its relative horizontal position (or y-coordinate).

Resistor inputs are variable from 0 to 100K ohms. The adapter converts the resistive value to a digital pulse with a duration proportional to the resistive load. Software can time these pulses to determine the relative resistance value. The game adapter does not use much in the way of system resources. The card does not use an IRQ, DMA channel, or memory and requires only a single I/O address (port) 201h. The adapter is controlled by reading and writing data to and from port 201h.

Table 9.12 shows the interface connector pinout specification for a PC-compatible game adapter.

Table 9.12 PC-Compatible Game Adapter Connector

Pin	Signal	Function	I/O
1	+5v	Paddle 1, Joystick A	Out
2	Button 4	Paddle 1 button, Joystick A button #1	In
3	Position 0	Paddle 1 position, Joystick A x-coordinate	In
4	Ground	—	—
5	Ground	—	—
6	Position 1	Paddle 2 position, Joystick A y-coordinate	In
7	Button 5	Paddle 2 button, Joystick A button #2	In
8	+5v	Paddle 2	Out
9	+5v	Paddle 3 and Joystick B	Out
10	Button 6	Paddle 3 button, Joystick B button #1	In
11	Position 2	Paddle 3 position, Joystick B x-coordinate	In
12	Ground	—	—
13	Position 3	Paddle 4 position, Joystick B y-coordinate	In
14	Button 7	Paddle 4 button, Joystick B button #2	In
15	+5v	Paddle 4	Out

Because this adapter actually reads resistance and can be easily manipulated with standard programming languages, the game adapter serves as a poor man's data acquisition board or real-time interface card. With it, you can hook up to four sensors and four switches and easily read the data in the PC.

Game adapters are available for ISA and MCA bus systems from a number of vendors. Consult the vendor list for some companies that may offer these types of adapters. Generally, the best place to look is one of the larger mail order system and peripheral vendors.

Some manufacturers have produced specialized joysticks that really don't look like joysticks at all. Perhaps the best known of these are the steering wheel and pedal control sets sold for use with driving and flight simulator games. These are really exactly the same as the standard joystick and paddles as far as your system is concerned. Instead of paddle knobs, they have steering wheels and pedals controlling the variable resistors in the circuit. There are a number of these devices on the market for the popular driving and flight simulator games, and they can make these games much more realistic. Because the different controls can be connected to different paddle inputs on the game adapters, make sure that your software will support the particular control device you select.

Summary

This chapter has examined all manner of standard input devices. Keyboards and pointing devices, usually mice, were covered in detail, as was a less known input device, the game interface. The next chapter covers video display hardware.

Chapter 10

Video Display Hardware

Your monitor provides the link between you and your computer. Although you can possibly get rid of your printer, disk drives, and expansion cards, you cannot sacrifice the monitor. Without it, you would be operating blind; you could not see the results of your calculations or the mis-typed words on screen.

The first microcomputers were small boxes that lacked displays. Instead, users observed the information contained in system registers via banks of flashing LEDs and waited for the final output to be printed. All interaction was normally done through a typewriter terminal. When the monitor was finally added as an interface, the computer became more attractive to a wider audience. This trend continues today with graphical user interfaces such as Windows and OS/2.

The video subsystem of a PC consists of two main components:

- Monitor (or video display)
- Video adapter (also called the video card or graphics card)

This chapter explores the range of available PC compatible video adapters and the displays that work with them.

Monitors

The monitor is, of course, the display located on top of, near, or inside your computer. Like any computer device, a monitor requires a source of input. The signals that run from your monitor come from video circuitry inside your computer. Some computers, such as those that use the low profile (LPX) form factor, contain this circuitry on the motherboard. Most systems, though, use a separate circuit board that is plugged into an expansion or bus slot. The expansion cards that produce video signals are called video cards, video adapters, or graphics cards.

Display Technologies

A monitor may use one of several display technologies. By far, the most popular is cathode-ray tube (CRT) technology, the same technology used in television sets. CRTs consist of a vacuum tube enclosed in glass. One end of the tube contains an electron gun; the other end contains a screen with a phosphorous coating.

When heated, the electron gun emits a stream of high-speed electrons that are attracted to the other end of the tube. On the way, a focus control and deflection coil steer the beam to a specific point on the phosphorous screen. When struck by the beam, the phosphor glows. This light is what you see when you watch TV or your computer screen.

The phosphor chemical has a quality called *persistence,* which indicates how long this glow will remain on screen. You should have a good match between persistence and scanning frequency so that the image has less flicker (if the persistence is too low) and no ghosts (if the persistence is too high).

The electron beam moves very quickly, sweeping the screen from left to right in lines from top to bottom, in a pattern called a *raster.* The horizontal scan rate refers to the speed at which the electron beam moves across the screen.

During its sweep, the beam strikes the phosphor wherever an image should appear on screen. The beam also varies by intensity in order to produce different levels of brightness. Because the glow fades almost immediately, the electron beam must continue to sweep the screen to maintain an image—a practice called *redrawing* or *refreshing* the screen.

Most displays have a *refresh rate* (also called a vertical scan rate) of about 70 hertz (Hz), meaning that the screen is refreshed 70 times a second. Low refresh rates cause the screen to flicker, contributing to eyestrain. The higher the refresh rate, the better for your eyes.

It is important that the scan rates expected by your monitor match those produced by your video card. If you have mismatched rates, you cannot see an image and may actually damage your monitor.

Some monitors have a fixed refresh rate. Other monitors may support a range of frequencies; this support provides built-in compatibility with future video standards (described in the "Video Cards" section later in this chapter). A monitor that supports many video standards is called a *multiple-frequency monitor.* Most monitors today are multiple-frequency monitors, which means that they support operation with a variety of popular video signal standards. Different vendors call their multiple-frequency monitors by different names, including multisync, multifrequency, multiscan, autosynchronous, and autotracking.

Phosphor-based screens come in two styles—curved and flat. The typical display screen is curved, meaning that it bulges outward from the middle of the screen. This design is consistent with the vast majority of CRT designs (the same as the tube in your television set).

The traditional screen is curved both vertically and horizontally. Some models use the Trinitron design, which is curved only horizontally and is flat vertically. Many people prefer this flatter screen because it results in less glare and a higher-quality, more accurate image. The disadvantage is that the technology required to produce flat-screen displays is more expensive, resulting in higher prices for the monitors.

Alternative display designs are available. Borrowing technology from laptop manufacturers, some companies provide LCD (liquid-crystal display) displays. LCDs have low-glare flat screens and low power requirements (5 watts versus nearly 100 watts for an ordinary monitor). The color quality of an active-matrix LCD panel actually exceeds that of most CRT displays. At this point, however, LCD screens usually are more limited in resolution than typical CRTs and are much more expensive; for example, a 12.1-inch screen costs several thousand dollars. There are three basic LCD choices: passive-matrix monochrome, passive-matrix color, and active-matrix color. The passive matrix designs are also available in single and dual scan versions.

In an LCD, a polarizing filter creates two separate light waves. In a color LCD, there is an additional filter that has three cells per each pixel, one each for displaying red, green, and blue.

The light wave passes through a liquid-crystal cell, with each color segment having its own cell. The liquid crystals are rod-shaped molecules that flow like a liquid. They enable light to pass straight through, but an electrical charge alters their orientation, as well as the orientation of light passing through them. Although monochrome LCDs do not have color filters, they can have multiple cells per pixel for controlling shades of gray.

In a passive-matrix LCD, each cell is controlled by electrical charges transmitted by transistors according to row and column positions on the screen's edge. As the cell reacts to the pulsing charge, it twists the light wave, with stronger charges twisting the light wave more. Supertwist refers to the orientation of the liquid crystals, comparing on mode to off mode—the greater the twist, the higher the contrast.

Charges in passive-matrix LCDs are pulsed, so the displays lack the brilliance of active-matrix, which provides a constant charge to each cell. To increase the brilliance, some vendors have turned to a new technique called double-scan LCD, which splits passive-matrix screens into a top half and bottom half, cutting the time between each pulse. Besides increasing the brightness, dual scan designs also increase the response time or speed of the display, making this type more usable for video or other applications where the displayed information changes rapidly.

In an active-matrix LCD, each cell has its own transistor to charge it and twist the light wave. This provides a brighter image than passive-matrix displays, because the cell can maintain a constant, rather than momentary, charge. However, active-matrix technology uses more energy than passive-matrix. With a dedicated transistor for every cell, active-matrix displays are more difficult and expensive to produce.

In both active- and passive-matrix LCDs, the second polarizing filter controls how much light passes through each cell. Cells twist the wavelength of light to closely match the filter's allowable wavelength. The more light that passes through the filter at each cell, the brighter the pixel.

Monochrome LCDs achieve gray scales (up to 64) by varying the brightness of a cell or dithering cells in an on-and-off pattern. Color LCDs, on the other hand, dither the three color cells and control their brilliance to achieve different colors on the screen. Double-scan passive-matrix LCDs have recently gained in popularity because they approach the quality of active-matrix displays but do not cost much more to produce than other passive-matrix displays.

The big problem with active-matrix LCDs is that the manufacturing yields are low, forcing higher prices. This means that many of the panels produced have more than a certain maximum number of failed transistors. The resulting low yields limit the production capacity and incurs higher prices.

In the past, several hot cathode ray tubes were needed to light an LCD screen, but portable computer manufacturers now use a single tube the size of a cigarette. Light emitted from a tube gets spread evenly across an entire display using fiber-optic technology.

Thanks to supertwist and triple-supertwist LCDs, today's screens enable you to see the screen clearly from more angles with better contrast and lighting. To improve readability, especially in dim light, some laptops include *backlighting* or *edgelighting* (also called sidelighting). Backlit screens provide light from a panel behind the LCD. Edgelit screens get their light from the small fluorescent tubes mounted along the sides of the screen. Some older laptops excluded such lighting systems to lengthen battery life. Most modern laptops enable you to run the backlight at a reduced power setting that dims the display but allows for longer battery life.

The best color displays are active-matrix or thin-film transistor (TFT) panels in which each pixel is controlled by three transistors (for red, green, and blue). Active-matrix-screen refreshes and redraws are immediate and accurate, with much less ghosting and blurring than in passive-matrix LCDs (which control pixels via rows and columns of transistors along the edges of the screen). Active-matrix displays are also much brighter and can easily be read at an angle.

An alternative to LCD screens is gas-plasma technology, typically known for its black and orange screens in some of the older Toshiba notebook computers. Some companies are incorporating gas-plasma technology for desktop screens and possibly color high-definition television (HDTV) flat-panel screens.

Monochrome versus Color

During the early years of the IBM PC and compatibles, owners had only two video choices—color using a CGA display adapter and monochrome using an MDA display adapter. Since then, many adapter and display options have hit the market.

Monochrome monitors produce images of one color. The most popular is amber, followed by white and green. The color of the monitor is determined by the color of the phosphors on the CRT screen. Some monochrome monitors with white phosphors can support many shades of gray.

Monochrome monitors cost less than color models—typically about one-half the price of color models. A monochrome monitor can be usable for character-based applications—

word processing, spreadsheet analysis, database management, and computer programming. Such monitors, however, may not work as well with Windows because it is usually designed to take advantage of color. In addition, large monochrome monitors designed for specialized applications, such as desktop publishing and CAD/CAM, cost hundreds of dollars more than standard color monitors.

Color monitors use more sophisticated technology than monochrome monitors, which accounts for their higher prices. Whereas a monochrome picture tube contains one electron gun, a color tube contains three guns arranged in a triangular shape referred to as a *delta configuration.* Instead of amber, white, or green phosphors, the monitor screen contains phosphor triads, which consist of one red phosphor, one green phosphor, and one blue phosphor arranged in the same pattern as the electron guns. These three primary colors can be mixed to produce all other colors.

The Right Size

Monitors come in different sizes, ranging from 9-inch to 42-inch diagonal measure. The larger the monitor, the higher the price tag. The most common monitor sizes are 14, 15, 17, and 21 inches. These diagonal measurements, unfortunately, represent not the actual screen that will be displayed but the size of the tube. As a result, comparing one company's 15-inch monitor to that of another may be unfair unless you actually measure the active screen area. This area can vary slightly from monitor to monitor, so one company's 17-inch monitor may display a 15-inch image, and another company's 17-inch monitor may present a 15.5-inch image.

The following table shows the advertised monitor diagonal size along with the approximate diagonal measure of the actual active viewing area for the most common display sizes:

Monitor Size	Viewing Area
12"	10.5"
14"	12"
15"	13"
16"	14"
17"	15"
19"	17"
21"	19"

The size of the actual viewable area varies slightly from manufacturer to manufacturer, but these figures are representative of most monitors. The viewing area refers to the diagonal measure of the lighted area on the screen. In other words, if you are running Windows, the viewing area is the actual diagonal measure of the desktop.

In most cases, the 15-inch monitor is the best bargain in the industry. A 17-inch monitor is most often recommended for new systems and is not much more expensive than a 14-inch display. I recommend a 15-inch monitor as the minimum you should consider for low-end applications, 17-inch or larger displays for a standard full function system, and 21-inch displays for high-end powered systems.

Larger monitors are handy for applications, such as desktop publishing, in which the smallest details must be clearly visible. With a larger 17-inch or 21-inch monitor, you can see an entire 8.5 by 11-inch page in a 100 percent view—in other words, what you see on-screen virtually matches the page that will be printed. This feature is called *WYSIWYG*—short for "what you see is what you get." If you can see the entire page at its actual size, you can save yourself the trouble of printing several drafts before you get it right.

Monitor Resolution

Resolution is the amount of detail that a monitor can render. This quantity is expressed in the number of horizontal and vertical picture elements, or *pixels,* contained in the screen. The greater the number of pixels, the more detailed the images. The resolution required depends on the application. Character-based applications (such as word processing) require little resolution, whereas graphics-intensive applications (such as desktop publishing and Windows software) require a great deal.

There are several standard resolutions available in PC graphics adapters. The following table lists the standard resolutions used in PC video adapters and the term used to commonly describe them:

Resolution	Name
640x480	VGA
800x600	SVGA
1,024x768	XGA
1,280x1,024	UVGA

VGA = Video Graphics Array
SVGA = Super VGA
XGA = eXtended Graphics Array
UVGA = Ultra VGA

In a monochrome monitor, the picture element is a screen phosphor, but in a color monitor, the picture element is a phosphor triad. This difference raises another consideration called *dot pitch,* which applies only to color monitors. Dot pitch is the distance, in millimeters, between phosphor triads. Screens with a small dot pitch contain less distance between the phosphor triads; as a result, the picture elements are closer together, producing a sharper picture. Conversely, screens with a large dot pitch tend to produce images that are less clear.

Another consideration of resolution is the dot pitch of the monitor. Smaller pitch values allow the monitor to produce sharper images. The original IBM PC color monitor had a dot pitch of 0.43mm, which is considered to be poor by almost any standard. The state-of-the-art displays marketed today have a dot pitch of 0.28mm or less. You can save money by picking a smaller monitor or one with a higher dot pitch. The trade-off, of course, is clarity. Don't be too discerning; choosing a monitor with a 0.31mm dot pitch over one with a 0.28mm dot pitch may save you a good deal of money.

Interlaced versus Noninterlaced

Monitors and video adapters may support interlaced or noninterlaced resolution. In *noninterlaced* (conventional) mode, the electron beam sweeps the screen in lines from top to bottom, one line after the other, completing the screen in one pass. In *interlaced* mode, the electron beam also sweeps the screen from top to bottom, but it does so in two passes, sweeping the odd lines first and the even lines second; each pass takes half the time of a full pass in noninterlaced mode. Therefore, both modes refresh the entire screen in the same amount of time. This technique redraws the screen faster and provides more stable images.

Monitors that use interlacing can use lower refresh rates, lessening their cost. The drawback is that interlacing depends on the ability of the eye to combine two nearly identical lines, separated by a gap, into one solid line. If you are looking for high-quality video, however, you want to get a video adapter and monitor that support high-resolution, noninterlaced displays.

Energy and Safety

A properly selected monitor can save energy. Many PC manufacturers are trying to meet the Environmental Protection Agency's Energy Star requirements. Any PC and monitor combination that consumes less than 60 watts (30 watts apiece) during idle periods can use the Energy Star logo. Some research shows that such "green" PCs can save each user about $70 per year in electricity costs.

Monitors, being one of the most power-hungry computer components, can contribute to those savings. Perhaps the best-known energy-saving standard for monitors is VESA's Display Power-Management Signaling (DPMS) spec, which defines the signals that a computer sends to a monitor to indicate idle times. The computer or video card decides when to send these signals.

If you buy a DPMS monitor, you can take advantage of energy savings without remodeling your entire system. If you do not have a DPMS-compatible video adapter, some cards can be upgraded to DPMS with a software utility typically available at no cost. Similarly, some energy-saving monitors include software that works with almost any graphics card to supply DPMS signals.

Another trend in green monitor design is to minimize the user's exposure to potentially harmful electromagnetic fields. Several medical studies indicate that these electromagnetic emissions may cause health problems, such as miscarriages, birth defects, and cancer. The risk may be low, but if you spend a third of your day (or more) in front of a computer monitor, that risk is increased.

The concern is that VLF (very low frequency) and ELF (extremely low frequency) emissions might affect the body. These two emissions come in two forms—electric and magnetic. Some research indicates that ELF magnetic emissions are more threatening than VLF emissions because they interact with the natural electric activity of body cells. Monitors are not the only culprits; significant ELF emissions also come from electric blankets and power lines.

Note

ELF and VLF are a form of electromagnetic radiation; they consist of radio frequencies below those used for normal radio broadcasting.

These two frequencies are covered by the new Swedish monitor-emission standard called SWEDAC, named after the Swedish regulatory agency. In many European countries, government agencies and businesses buy only low-emission monitors. The degree to which emissions are reduced varies from monitor to monitor. The Swedish government's MPR I standard, which dates back to 1987, is the least restrictive. MPR II, established in 1990, is significantly stronger (adding maximums for ELF as well as VLF emissions) and is the level that you will most likely find in low-emission monitors today.

A more stringent 1992 standard called TCO further tightens the MPR II requirements. In addition, it is a more broad-based environmental standard that includes power-saving requirements and emission limits. Nanao is one of the few manufacturers currently offering monitors that meet the TCO standard.

A low-emission monitor costs about $20 to $100 more than a similar regular-emission monitor. When you shop for a low-emission monitor, don't just ask for a low-emission monitor, also find out whether the monitor limits specific types of emission. Use as your guideline the three electromagnetic-emission standards described in this section.

If you decide not to buy a low-emission monitor, you can take other steps to protect yourself. The most important is to stay at arm's length (about 28 inches) from the front of your monitor. When you move a couple of feet away, ELF magnetic emission levels usually drop to those of a typical office with fluorescent lights. Likewise, monitor emissions are weakest at the front of a monitor, so stay at least three feet from the sides and backs of nearby monitors and five feet from any photocopiers, which are also strong sources of ELF.

Electromagnetic emissions should not be your only concern; you also should be concerned about screen glare. In fact, some antiglare screens not only reduce eyestrain but also cut ELF and VLF emissions.

Monitor Buying Criteria

A monitor may account for as much as 50 percent of the price of a computer system. What should you look for when you shop for a monitor?

The trick is to pick a monitor that works with your selected video card. You can save money by purchasing a single-standard (fixed-frequency) monitor and a matching video card; for example, you can order a VGA monitor and a VGA video card. For greatest flexibility, get a multisync monitor that accommodates a range of standards, including those that are not yet standardized.

With multisync monitors, you must match the range of horizontal and vertical frequencies the monitor accepts with those generated by your video card. The wider the range of signals, the more expensive—and more versatile—the monitor. Your video card's vertical and horizontal frequencies must fall within the ranges supported by your monitor. The *vertical frequency* (or refresh/frame rate) determines how stable your image will be. The higher the vertical frequency, the better. Typical vertical frequencies range from 50 to 90 Hz. The *horizontal frequency* (or line rate) ranges between 31.5KHz to 60KHz or more.

To keep the horizontal frequency low, some video cards use interlaced signals, alternately displaying half the lines of the total image. On most monitors, interlacing produces a pronounced flicker in the display, unless the phosphor is designed with a very long persistence. For this reason, you should avoid using interlaced video modes if possible. Some older cards and displays used interlacing as an inexpensive way to attain a higher resolution than otherwise would be possible. For example, the original IBM XGA adapters and monitors used an interlaced vertical frame rate of 43.5Hz in 1,024×768 mode, instead of the 60Hz or higher frame rate that most other adapters and displays use at that resolution.

In my experience, a 60Hz vertical scan frequency (frame rate) is the minimum anybody should use, and even at this frequency, a flicker will be noticed by most people. Especially on a larger display, this can cause eyestrain and fatigue. If you can select a frame rate (vertical scan frequency) of 72Hz or higher, most people will not be able to discern any flicker. Most modern displays easily handle vertical frequencies of up to 85Hz or more, which greatly reduces the flicker seen by the user. Note that increasing the frame rate can slow down the video hardware because it now needs to display each image more times per second. In general, I recommend you set the lowest frame rate you are comfortable with.

When you shop for a VGA monitor, make sure that the monitor supports a horizontal frequency of at least 31.5KHz—the minimum that a VGA card needs to paint a 640-by-480 screen. The VESA super-VGA (800 by 600) or SVGA standard requires a 72Hz vertical frequency and a horizontal frequency of at least 48KHz. The sharper 1,024-by-768 image requires a vertical frequency of 60Hz and a horizontal frequency of 58KHz. If the vertical frequency increases to 72Hz, the horizontal frequency must be 58KHz. For a super crisp display, look for available vertical frequencies of 75Hz or higher and horizontal frequencies of up to 90KHz or more.

Most of the analog monitors produced today are, to one extent or another, multisync. Because literally hundreds of manufacturers produce thousands of monitor models, it is impractical to discuss the technical aspects of each monitor model in detail. Suffice it to say that before investing in a monitor, you should check the technical specifications to make sure that the monitor meets your needs. If you are looking for a place to start, check out some of the different magazines, which periodically feature reviews of monitors. If you cannot wait for a magazine review, investigate monitors at the Web sites run by any of the following vendors:

IBM	Sony
Mitsubishi	Viewsonic
NEC	

Each of these manufacturers creates monitors that set the standards by which other monitors can be judged. Although you typically pay a bit more for these manufacturers' monitors, they offer a known high level of quality and compatibility as well as service and support.

Many inexpensive monitors are curved because it is easier to send an electron beam across them. Flat-screen monitors, which are a bit more expensive, look better to most people. As a general rule, the less curvature a monitor has, the less glare it will reflect.

Consider the size of your desk before you think about a monitor 16 inches or larger. A 16-inch monitor typically is at least a foot and a half deep, and a 20-inch monitor takes up 2 square feet. Typical 14-inch monitors are 16 to 18 inches deep.

You also should check the dot pitch of the monitor. Smaller pitch values indicate sharper images. Most monitors have a dot pitch between 0.25 and 0.52 millimeters. To avoid grainy images, look for a dot pitch of 0.28 millimeters or smaller for 12- and 14-inch monitors, and 0.31mm or smaller for 16-inch and larger monitors. Be wary of monitors with 0.39mm or greater dot pitches; they lack clarity for fine text and graphics.

What resolution do you want for your display? Generally, the higher the resolution, the larger the display you will want. If you are operating at 640-by-480 resolution, for example, you should find a 15-inch monitor to be comfortable. At 1,024 by 768, you probably will find that the display of a 15-inch monitor is too small and therefore will prefer to use a larger one, such as a 17-inch monitor.

Here are the minimum sized monitors I recommend to properly display popular VGA and SVGA resolutions:

Resolution	Recommended Monitor
640x480	13-inch
800x600	15-inch
1,024x768	17-inch
1,280x1,024	21-inch

The minimum recommended display size is the advertised diagonal display dimension of the monitor. Note that this is not what the monitor may be capable of, but is what I recommend. In other words, most 15-inch monitors will display resolutions at least up to 1,024×768, but the characters, icons, and displayed information will be too small and will cause eyestrain if you try to run beyond the 800×600 recommended. In other words, if you plan on spending a lot of time in front of your PC, and you want to run 1,024×768 resolution, I absolutely recommend a 17-inch display. Anything smaller is not considered proper ergonomics, and eyestrain, headaches, and fatigue can result.

One exception to this rule is with the laptop and notebook displays. These are usually an LCD-type display, which is always crisp and perfectly focused by nature. Also, the dimensions advertised for the LCD screens are exactly what you get for display, unlike conventional CRT-based monitors. So the 12.1-inch LCD panels found on many laptop systems today actually have a viewable area that is 12.1-inch diagonal. In other words, 12.1-inch is the size of the Windows desktop or functional area of the screen. This measurement compares to a 14-inch or even 15-inch conventional display in most cases. Not only that, but the LCD is so crisp that you can easily handle resolutions that are higher than otherwise would be acceptable on a CRT. For example, many of the high-end laptop systems now use 12.1-inch LCD panels that feature 1,024×768 resolution. Although this resolution is unacceptable on a 14-inch or 15-inch CRT display, it works well on the 12.1-inch LCD panel.

Get a monitor with positioning and image controls that are easy to reach. Look for more than just basic contrast and brightness controls; some monitors also enable you to adjust the width and height of your screen images. A tilt-swivel stand should be included with your monitor, enabling you to move the monitor to the best angle for your use.

Most of the newer monitors now use digital controls instead of analog controls. This has nothing to do with the signals sent to the monitor but the controls (or lack of them) on the front panel. Monitors with digital controls have a built-in menu system that allows you to set things like brightness, contrast, screen size, vertical and horizontal shifts, and even focus. The menu is brought up on the screen by a button, and you use controls to make menu selections and vary the settings. When done, the monitor saves your settings in NVRAM (Non-Volatile RAM) in the monitor. These settings are permanently stored using no battery, and can be altered at any time in the future. Digital controls give a much higher level of control over the monitor, and are highly recommended.

A monitor is such an important part of your computer that it is not enough to know just its technical specifications. Knowing a monitor has a 0.28mm dot pitch does not necessarily tell you that it is ideal for you. It is best to "kick the tires" of your new monitor at a showroom or (with a liberal return policy) in the privacy of your office. To test your monitor:

- Draw a circle with a graphics program. If the result is an oval, not a circle, this monitor will not serve you well with graphics or design software.
- Type some words in 8- or 10-point type (1 point = 1/72 inch). If the words are fuzzy, or if the black characters are fringed with color, select another monitor.
- Turn the brightness up and down while examining the corner of the screen's image. If the image blooms or swells, it is likely to lose focus at high brightness levels.
- Load Microsoft Windows to check for uniform focus. Are the corner icons as sharp as the rest of the screen? Are the lines in the title bar curved or wavy? Monitors usually are sharply focused at the center, but seriously blurred corners indicate a poor design. Bowed lines may be the result of a poor graphics card, so don't dismiss a monitor that shows those lines without using another card to double-check the effect. A good monitor will be calibrated so that rays of red, green, and blue light hit their targets (individual phosphor dots) precisely. If they don't, you have bad convergence. This is apparent when edges of lines appear to illuminate with a specific color. If you have good convergence, the colors will be crisp, clear, and true, provided that there is not a predominant tint in the phosphor.

Video Cards

A video card provides signals that operate your monitor. With the PS/2 systems introduced in 1987, IBM developed new video standards that have overtaken the older display standards in popularity and support.

Most video cards follow one of several industry standards:

- MDA (Monochrome Display Adapter)
- CGA (Color Graphics Adapter)
- EGA (Enhanced Graphics Adapter)
- VGA (Video Graphics Array)
- SVGA (Super-VGA)
- XGA (eXtended Graphics Array)

These adapters and video standards are supported by virtually every program that runs on IBM or compatible equipment. Other systems are developing into de facto standards as well. For example, super-VGA (SVGA) offers different resolutions from different vendors, but 1,024-by-768 resolution is becoming a standard resolution for doing detailed work.

Most microcomputer monitors support at least one video standard, enabling you to operate them with video cards and software that are compatible with that standard. For example, a monitor that supports VGA may operate with VGA video cards and VGA software.

Obsolete Display Adapters

Although many types of display systems are considered to be standards, not all systems are considered to be viable standards for today's hardware and software. For example, the CGA standard works but is unacceptable for running the graphics-intensive programs on which many users rely. In fact, Microsoft Windows 3.1 does not work with any PC that has less-than-EGA resolution. The next several sections discuss the display adapters that are viewed as being obsolete in today's market.

Monochrome Display Adapter (MDA) and Display. The simplest (and first available) display type is the IBM Monochrome Display Adapter (MDA). (Actually, the MDA card doubles as a video and printer card.) The MDA video card can display text only at a resolution of 720 horizontal by 350 vertical pixels (720 by 350).

A character-only system, the display has no inherent graphics capabilities. The display originally was a top-selling option because it is fairly cost-effective. As a bonus, the MDA provides a printer interface, conserving an expansion slot.

The display is known for clarity and high resolution, making it ideal for business use—especially for businesses that use DOS-based word processing or spreadsheet programs.

Figure 10.1 shows the Monochrome Display Adapter pinouts.

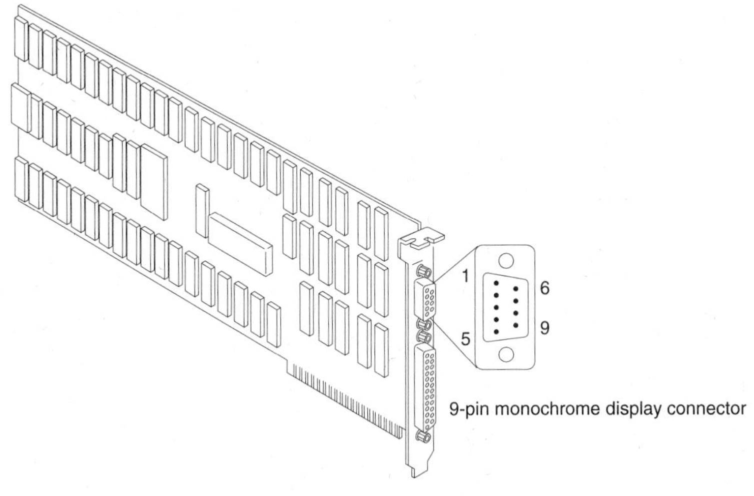

At Standard TTL Levels

IBM Monochrome Display

Signal	Pin
Ground	1
Ground	2
Not Used	3
Not Used	4
Not Used	5
+ Intensity	6
+ Video	7
+ Horizontal	8
- Vertical	9

IBM Monochrome Display and Printer Adapter

Figure 10.1

Monochrome Display Adapter pinouts.

Because the monochrome display is a character-only display, you cannot use it with software that requires graphics. Originally, that drawback only kept the user from playing games on a monochrome display, but today even the most serious business software uses graphics and color to great advantage. With the 9-by-14 dot character box (*matrix*), the IBM monochrome monitor displays attractive characters.

Table 10.1 summarizes the features of the MDA's single mode of operation.

Later, a company named Hercules released a video card called the Hercules Graphics Card (HGC). This card displays sharper text and can handle graphics, such as bar charts.

Color Graphics Adapter (CGA) and Display. For many years, the Color Graphics Adapter (CGA) was the most common display adapter, although its capabilities now leave much to be desired. This adapter has two basic modes of operation—alphanumeric (A/N) or all points addressable (APA). In A/N mode, the card operates in 40-column by 25-line mode or 80-column by 25-line mode with 16 colors. In APA and A/N modes, the character set is formed with a resolution of 8 by 8 pixels. In APA mode, two resolutions are available: medium-resolution color mode (320 by 200), with four colors available from a palette of 16; and two-color high-resolution mode (640 by 200).

Figures 10.2 and 10.3 show the pinouts for the Color Graphics Adapter.

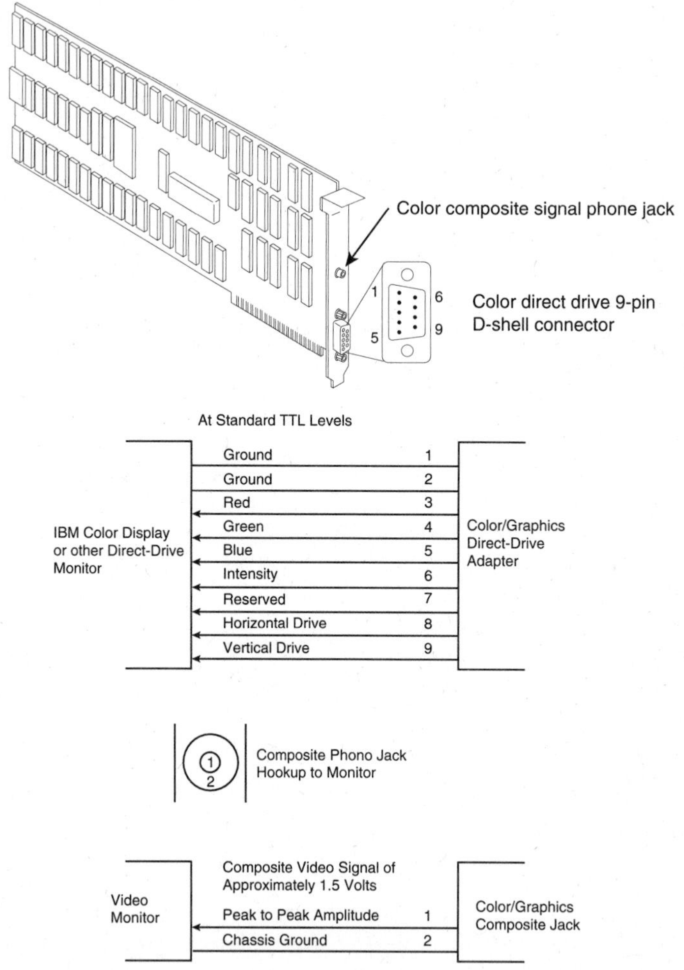

Figure 10.2

CGA display connector specifications.

Table 10.1 IBM Monochrome Display Adapter (MDA) Specifications

Video Standard	Resolution	Number of Colors	Mode Type	BIOS Modes	Character Format
MDA					
(08/12/81)	720 × 350	4	Text	07h	80 × 25

Colors refer to different display attributes such as regular, highlight, reverse video, and underlined.

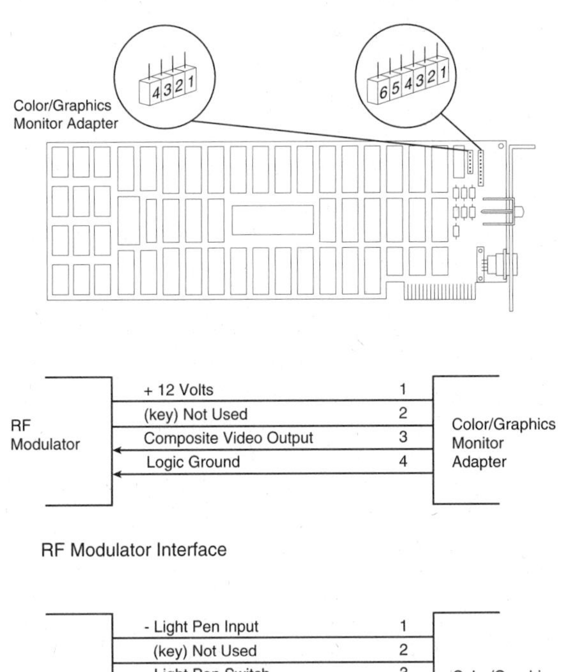

Figure 10.3

CGA RF modulator and light-pen connector specifications.

Most of the monitors sold for the CGA are RGBs, not composite monitors. The color signal of a composite monitor contains a mixture of colors that must be decoded or separated. RGB monitors receive red, green, and blue separately, and combine the colors in different proportions to generate other colors. RGB monitors offer better resolution than composite monitors, and they do a much better job of displaying 80-column text.

One drawback of a CGA video card is the fact that it produces flicker and snow. *Flicker* is the annoying tendency of the text to flash as you move the image up or down. *Snow* is the flurry of bright dots that can appear anywhere on the screen.

Character Box	Scan Frequency Vertical (Hz)	Horizontal (KHz)	Scan Mode
9 × 14	50	18.432	Std

Most companies that sold CGA-type adapters have long since discontinued those products. When many VGA cards cost less than $100, recommending a CGA makes little sense.

Table 10.2 lists the specifications for all CGA modes of operation.

Enhanced Graphics Adapter (EGA) and Display. The IBM Enhanced Graphics Adapter, discontinued when the PS/2 systems were introduced, consists of a graphics board, a graphics memory-expansion board, a graphics memory-module kit, and a high-resolution color monitor. The whole package originally cost about $1,800. The aftermarket gave IBM a great deal of competition in this area; it was possible to put together a similar system from non-IBM vendors for much less money. One advantage of EGA, however, is that you can build your system in modular steps. Because the card works with any of the monitors IBM produced at the time, you can use it with the IBM Monochrome Display, the earlier IBM Color Display, or the IBM Enhanced Color Display.

With the EGA card, the IBM color monitor displays 16 colors in 320-by-200 or 640-by-200 mode and the IBM monochrome monitor shows a resolution of 640 by 350 with a 9-by-14 character box (text mode).

Figures 10.4 and 10.5 show the pinouts and P-2 connector of the Enhanced Graphics Display Adapter.

With the EGA card, the IBM Enhanced Color Display is capable of displaying 640 by 350 pixels in 16 colors from a palette of 64. The character box for text is 8 by 14, compared with 8 by 8 for the earlier CGA board and monitor. The 8 by 8 character box can be used, however, to display 43 lines of text. Through software, the character box can be manipulated up to the size of 8 by 32.

You can enlarge a RAM-resident, 256-member character set to 512 characters by using the IBM memory expansion card. A 1,024-character set is added with the IBM graphics memory-module kit. These character sets are loaded from programs.

Table 10.2 IBM Color Graphics Adapter (CGA) Specifications

Video Standard	Resolution	Number of Colors	Mode Type	BIOS Modes	Character Format
CGA					
(08/12/81)	320 × 200	16	Text	00/01h	40 × 25
	640 × 200	16	Text	02/03h	80 × 25
	160 × 200	16	APA	—	—
	320 × 200	4	APA	04/05h	40 × 25
	640 × 200	2	APA	06h	80 × 25

APA = All points addressable (graphics)
— = Not supported

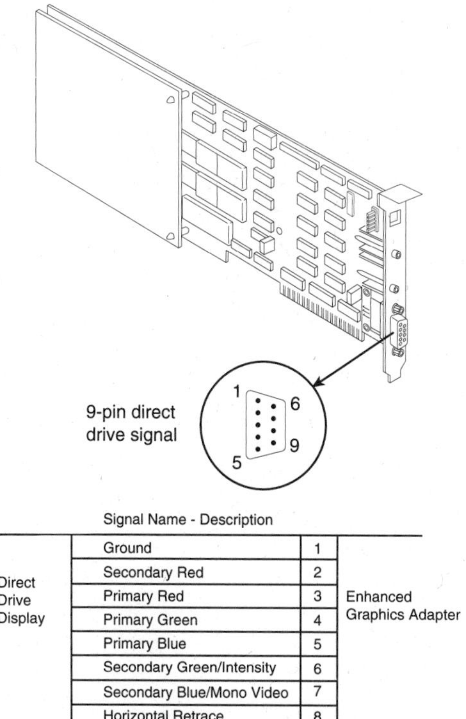

Direct Drive Display	Signal Name - Description		Enhanced Graphics Adapter
	Ground	1	
	Secondary Red	2	
	Primary Red	3	
	Primary Green	4	
	Primary Blue	5	
	Secondary Green/Intensity	6	
	Secondary Blue/Mono Video	7	
	Horizontal Retrace	8	
	Vertical Retrace	9	

Figure 10.4
EGA display connector specifications.

All this memory fits in the unused space between the end of RAM user memory and the current display-adapter memory. The EGA has a maximum 128K of memory that maps into the RAM space just above the 640K boundary. If you install more than 640K, you will probably lose the extra memory after installing the EGA. The graphics memory-expansion card adds 64K to the standard 64K, for a total of 128K. The IBM graphics memory-module kit adds another 128K, for a total of 256K. This second 128K of memory

Character Box	Scan Frequency Vertical (Hz)	Horizontal (KHz)	Scan Mode
8 × 8	60	15.75	Std
8 × 8	60	15.75	Std
—	60	15.75	Std
8 × 8	60	15.75	Std
8 × 8	60	15.75	Std

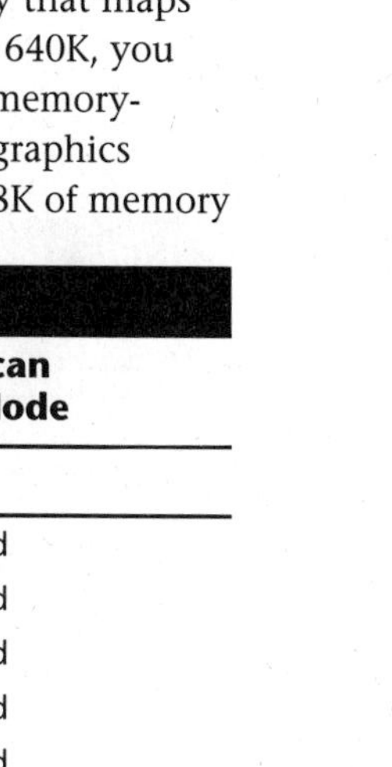

is only on the card and does not consume any of the PC's memory space. (Because almost every aftermarket EGA card comes configured with the full 256K of memory, expansion options are not necessary.)

The VGA system supersedes the EGA in many respects. The EGA has problems emulating the earlier CGA or MDA adapters, and some software that works with the earlier cards will not run on the EGA until the programs are modified.

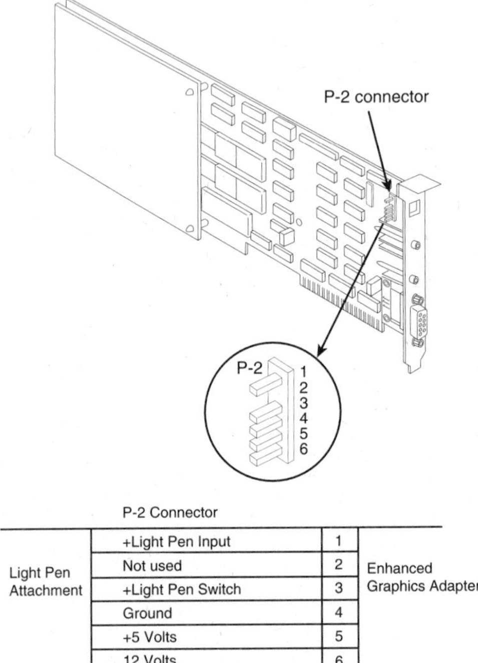

Figure 10.5

EGA light-pen connector specifications.

Table 10.3 IBM Enhanced Graphics Adapter (EGA) Specifications

Video Standard	Resolution	Number of Colors	Mode Type	BIOS Modes	Character Format
EGA					
(09/10/84)	320 × 350	16	Text	00/01h	40 × 25
	640 × 350	16	Text	02/03h	80 × 25
	720 × 350	4	Text	07h	80 × 25
	320 × 200	16	APA	0Dh	40 × 25
	640 × 200	16	APA	0Eh	80 × 25
	640 × 350	4	APA	0Fh	80 × 25
	640 × 350	16	APA	10h	80 × 25

APA = All points addressable (graphics)

Table 10.3 shows the modes supported by the EGA adapter.

Professional Color Display and Adapter. The Professional Graphics Display System is a video display product that IBM introduced in 1984. At $4,290, the system was too expensive to become a mainstream product.

The system consists of a Professional Graphics Monitor and a Professional Graphics Card Set. When fully expanded, this card set uses three slots in an XT or AT system—which is a high price to pay, but the features are impressive. The Professional Graphics Adapter (PGA) offers three-dimensional rotation and clipping as a built-in hardware function. The adapter can run 60 frames of animation per second because the PGA uses a built-in dedicated microcomputer.

The Professional Graphics card and monitor targeted engineering and scientific applications rather than financial or business applications. This system, which was discontinued when the PS/2 was introduced, has been replaced by the VGA and other higher-resolution graphics standards for these newer systems.

Table 10.4 lists all supported PGA modes.

VGA Adapters and Displays

When IBM introduced the PS/2 systems on April 2, 1987, it also introduced the Video Graphics Array display. On that day, in fact, IBM also introduced the lower-resolution MultiColor Graphics Array (MCGA) and higher-resolution 8514 adapters. The MCGA and 8514 adapters did not become popular standards like the VGA, and both were discontinued.

Digital versus Analog Signals. Unlike earlier video standards, which are digital, the VGA is an analog system. Why are displays going from digital to analog when most other electronic systems are going digital? Compact-disc players (digital) have replaced most turntables (analog), and newer VCRs and camcorders have digital picture storage for smooth slow-motion and freeze-frame capability. With a digital television set, you can watch several channels on a single screen by splitting the screen or placing a picture within another picture.

Character	Scan Frequency		Scan
Box	Vertical (Hz)	Horizontal (KHz)	Mode
8 × 14	60	21.8	5td
8 × 14	60	21.8	Std
9 × 14	50	18.432	Std
8 × 8	60	15.75	Std
8 × 8	60	15.75	Std
8 × 14	50	18.432	Std
8 × 14	60	21.85	Std

Table 10.4 IBM Professional Graphics Adapter (PGA) Specifications

Video Standard	Resolution	Number of Colors	Mode Type	BIOS Modes	Character Format
PGA					
(09/10/84)	320 × 200	16	Text	00/01	40 × 25
	640 × 200	16	Text	02/03	80 × 25
	320 × 200	4	APA	04/05	40 × 25
	640 × 200	2	APA	06	80 × 25
	640 × 480	256	APA	—	—

APA = All points addressable (graphics)
— = Not supported

Why, then, did IBM decide to change the video to analog? The answer is color.

Most personal-computer displays introduced before the PS/2 are digital. This type of display generates different colors by firing the red, green, and blue (RGB) electron beams in on-or-off mode. You can display up to eight colors (two to the third power). In the IBM displays and adapters, another signal intensity doubles the number of color combinations from 8 to 16 by displaying each color at one of two intensity levels. This digital display is easy to manufacture and offers simplicity with consistent color combinations from system to system. The real drawback of the digital display system is the limited number of possible colors.

In the PS/2 systems, IBM went to an analog display circuit. Analog displays work like the digital displays that use RGB electron beams to construct various colors, but each color in the analog display system can be displayed at varying levels of intensity—64 levels, in the case of the VGA. This versatility provides 262,144 possible colors (64^3). For realistic computer graphics, color often is more important than high resolution because the human eye perceives a picture that has more colors as being more realistic. IBM moved graphics into analog form to enhance the color capabilities.

Table 10.5 IBM MultiColor Graphics Array (MCGA) Specifications

Video Standard	Resolution	Number of Colors	Mode Type	BIOS Modes
MCGA				
(04/02/87)	320 x 400	16	Text	00/01h
	640 x 400	16	Text	02/03h
	320 x 200	4	APA	04/05h
	640 x 200	2	APA	06h
	640 x 480	2	APA	11h
	320 x 200	256	APA	13h

APA = All points addressable (graphics)
Dbl = Double scan

Character Box	Scan Frequency Vertical (Hz)	Horizontal (KHz)	Scan Mode
8 × 8	60	15.75	Std
8 × 8	60	15.75	Std
8 × 8	60	15.75	Std
8 × 8	60	15.75	Std
—	60	30.48	Std

MultiColor Graphics Array (MCGA). The MultiColor Graphics Array (MCGA) is a graphics adapter that is integrated into the motherboard of the PS/2 Models 25 and 30. The MCGA supports all CGA modes when an IBM analog display is attached, but any previous IBM display is not compatible. In addition to providing existing CGA mode support, the MCGA includes four additional modes.

The MCGA uses as many as 64 shades of gray in converting color modes for display on monochrome displays so that users who prefer a monochrome display still can execute color-based applications.

Table 10.5 lists the MCGA display modes.

Video Graphics Array (VGA). PS/2 systems contain the primary display adapter circuits on the motherboard. The circuits, called the Video Graphics Array, are implemented by a single custom VLSI chip designed and manufactured by IBM. To adapt this new graphics standard to the earlier systems, IBM introduced the PS/2 Display Adapter. Also called a VGA card, this adapter contains the complete VGA circuit on a full-length adapter board

		Scan Frequency		
Character Format	Character Box	Vertical (Hz)	Horizontal (KHz)	Scan Mode
40 x 25	8 x 16	70	31.5	Std
80 x 25	8 x 16	70	31.5	Std
40 x 25	8 x 8	70	31.5	Dbl
80 x 25	8 x 8	70	31.5	Dbl
80 x 30	8 x 16	60	31.5	Std
40 x 25	8 x 8	70	31.5	Dbl

with an 8-bit interface. IBM has since discontinued its VGA card, but many third-party units are available.

The VGA BIOS (basic input/output system) is the control software residing in the system ROM for controlling VGA circuits. With the BIOS, software can initiate commands and functions without having to manipulate the VGA directly. Programs become somewhat hardware-independent and can call a consistent set of commands and functions built into the system's ROM-control software.

Future implementations of the VGA will be different in hardware but will respond to the same BIOS calls and functions. New features will be added as a superset of the existing functions. The VGA, therefore, will be compatible with the graphics and text BIOS functions that were built into the PC systems from the beginning. The VGA can run almost any software that originally was written for the MDA, CGA, or EGA.

In a perfect world, software programmers would write to the BIOS interface rather than directly to the hardware and would promote software interchanges between different types of hardware. More frequently, however, programmers want the software to perform better, so they write the programs to control the hardware directly. As a result, these programmers achieve higher-performance applications that are dependent on the hardware for which they were first written.

When bypassing the BIOS, a programmer must ensure that the hardware is 100-percent compatible with the standard so that software written to a standard piece of hardware runs on the system. Note that just because a manufacturer claims this register level of compatibility does not mean that the product is 100-percent compatible or that all

Table 10.6 IBM Video Graphics Array (VGA) Specifications

Video Standard	Resolution	Number of Colors	Mode Type	BIOS Modes
VGA				
(04/02/87)	360 x 400	16	Text	00/01h
	720 x 400	16	Text	02/03h
	320 x 200	4	APA	04/05h
	640 x 200	2	APA	06h
	720 x 400	16	Text	07h
	320 x 200	16	APA	0Dh
	640 x 200	16	APA	0Eh
	640 x 350	4	APA	0Fh
	640 x 350	16	APA	10h
	640 x 480	2	APA	11h
	640 x 480	16	APA	12h
	320 x 200	256	APA	13h

APA = All points addressable (graphics)
Dbl = Double scan

software runs as it would on a true IBM VGA. Most manufacturers have "cloned" the VGA system at the register level, which means that even applications that write directly to the video registers will function correctly. Also, the VGA circuits themselves emulate the older adapters even to the register level and have an amazing level of compatibility with these earlier standards. This compatibility makes the VGA a truly universal standard.

The VGA displays up to 256 colors on screen from a palette of 262,144 (256K) colors. Because the VGA outputs an analog signal, you must have a monitor that accepts an analog input.

VGA displays come not only in color but also in monochrome VGA models, using color summing. With color summing, 64 gray shades are displayed instead of colors; the translation is performed in the ROM BIOS. The summing routine is initiated if the BIOS detects the monochrome display when the system is booted. This routine uses a formula that takes the desired color and rewrites the formula to involve all three color guns, producing varying intensities of gray. The color that would be displayed, for example, is converted to 30 percent red plus 59 percent green plus 11 percent blue to achieve the desired gray. Users who prefer a monochrome display, therefore, can execute color-based applications.

Table 10.6 lists the VGA display modes.

8514 Display Adapter. The PS/2 Display Adapter 8514/A offers higher resolution and more colors than the standard VGA. This adapter, designed to use the PS/2 Color Display 8514, plugs into a Micro Channel slot in any PS/2 model so equipped.

Character Format	Character Box	Scan Frequency Vertical (Hz)	Horizontal (KHz)	Scan Mode
40 x 25	9 x 16	70	31.5	Std
80 x 25	9 x 16	70	31.5	Std
40 x 25	8 x 8	70	31.5	Dbl
80 x 25	8 x 8	70	31.5	Dbl
80 x 25	9 x 16	70	31.5	Std
40 x 25	8 x 8	70	31.5	Dbl
80 x 25	8 x 8	70	31.5	Dbl
80 x 25	8 x 14	70	31.5	Std
80 x 25	8 x 14	70	31.5	Std
80 x 30	8 x 16	60	31.5	Std
80 x 30	8 x 16	60	31.5	Std
40 x 25	8 x 8	70	31.5	Dbl

All operation modes of the built-in VGA continue to be available. An IBM Personal System/2 8514 memory-expansion kit is available for the IBM Display Adapter 8514/A. This kit provides increased color and grayscale support.

The IBM Display Adapter 8514/A has these advantages:

- Hardware assistance for advanced text, image, and graphics functions
- New high-content display modes
- Increased color and monochrome capability
- Support for the new family of IBM displays
- MDA, CGA, EGA, and VGA modes available
- 256/256K colors and 64/64 grayscales with memory-expansion kit

To take full advantage of this adapter, you should use the 8514 display because it is matched to the capabilities of the adapter. Notice that IBM has discontinued the 8514/A adapter and specifies the XGA in its place. The 8514 display continues to be sold because it works well with the newer XGA.

Table 10.7 shows all 8514 modes.

Super VGA (SVGA)

When IBM's XGA and 8514/A video cards were introduced, competing manufacturers chose not to clone these incremental improvements on VGA. Instead, they began producing lower-cost adapters that offered even higher resolutions. These video cards fall into a category loosely known as Super VGA (SVGA).

SVGA provides capabilities that surpass those offered by the VGA adapter. Unlike the display adapters discussed so far, Super VGA refers not to a card that meets a particular specification but to a group of cards that have different capabilities.

For example, one card may offer several resolutions (such as 800×600 and 1,024×768) that are greater than those achieved with a regular VGA, whereas another card may offer the same or even greater resolutions but also provide more color choices at each

Table 10.7 IBM 8514 Specifications

Video Standard	Resolution	Number of Colors	Mode Type	BIOS Modes	Character Format
8514					
(04/02/87)	1024 × 768	256	APA	H-0h	85 × 38
	640 × 480	256	APA	H-1h	80 × 34
	1024 × 768	256	APA	H-3h	146 × 51

APA = All points addressable (graphics)
IL = Interlaced

resolution. These cards have different capabilities; nonetheless, both are classified as Super VGA.

Unlike the modes offered by IBM's CGA, EGA, and VGA standards, the new graphics modes are more or less proprietary. Because Super VGA cards are a category rather than a specification, the market at this level has been fractured. To take advantage of the enhanced capabilities of each card, you need special video-card drivers. To use an ATI card with Microsoft Windows, for example, you need ATI drivers. You cannot use an ATI driver with a different SVGA card; you can use it only with ATI models. This means that unlike the basic VGA cards—which can have a single driver that works with all VGA cards, regardless of the vendor—each SVGA card must have a corresponding driver for each application you intend to use with it.

If you do not have drivers specific to your card, most SVGA cards will work with a universal driver for 800×600 or 1,024×768 modes. This driver is included with Windows and need not come from the manufacturer. Although this driver will work, it will not exploit the unique features and functions of the particular video chipset you may be using.

The SVGA cards look much like their VGA counterparts. They have the same connectors, including the feature adapter shown in figure 10.6.

Because the technical specifications from different SVGA vendors vary tremendously, it is impossible to provide a definitive technical overview in this book. The pinouts for the standard VGA and SVGA video card connector are shown in the following table:

Pin	Function	Direction
1	Red	Out
2	Green	Out
3	Blue	Out
4	Monitor ID 2	In
5	Digital Ground (monitor self-test)	-_
6	Red Analog Ground	-_
7	Green Analog Ground	-_
8	Blue Analog Ground	-_

(continues)

Character Box	Scan Frequency Vertical (Hz)	Horizontal (KHz)	Scan Mode
12 × 20	43.48	35.52	IL
8 × 14	60	31.5	Std
7 × 15	43.48	35.52	IL

(continued)

Pin	Function	Direction
9	Key (Plugged Hole)	-_
10	Sync Ground	-_
11	Monitor ID 0	In
12	Monitor ID 1	In
13	Horizontal Sync	Out
14	Vertical Sync	Out
15	Monitor ID 3	In

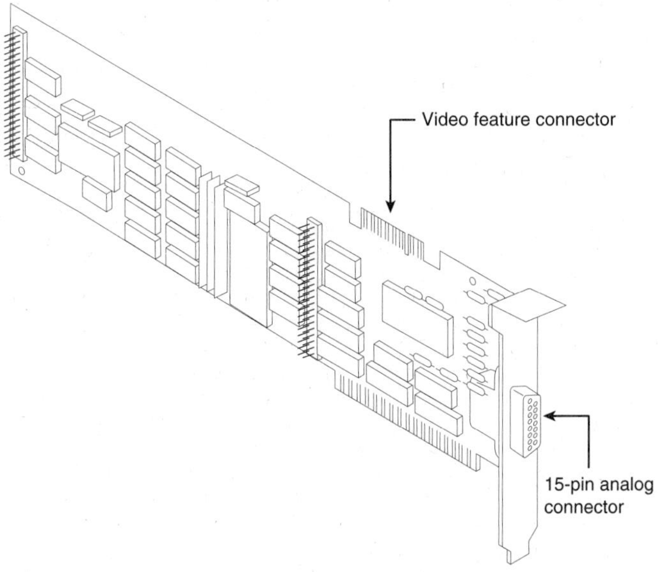

Figure 10.6
The IBM PS/2 Display Adapter (VGA card).

VESA SVGA Standards

In October 1989, the Video Electronics Standards Association (VESA), recognizing that programming for the many SVGA cards on the market is virtually impossible, proposed a standard for a uniform programmer's interface for SVGA cards. This association includes members from various companies associated with PC and computer video products.

The SVGA standard is called the VESA BIOS Extension. If a video card incorporates this standard, a program easily can determine the capabilities of the card and access them. The benefit of the VESA BIOS Extension is that a programmer needs to worry about only one routine or driver to support SVGA. Different cards from different manufacturers are accessible through the common VESA interface.

This concept, when first proposed, met with limited acceptance. Several major SVGA manufacturers started supplying the VESA BIOS Extension as a separate memory-resident program that you could load when you booted your computer. Over the years, however, other vendors started supplying the VESA BIOS Extension as an integral part of their SVGA BIOS. Obviously, from a user's perspective, support for VESA in BIOS is a better solution. You do not have to worry about loading a driver or other memory-resident program whenever you want to use a program that expects the VESA extensions to be present.

Today, most SVGA cards support the VESA BIOS Extensions in one way or another. When you shop for an SVGA card, make sure that it supports the extensions in BIOS. Also, if you are interested in finding out more about programming for the VESA BIOS Extensions, contact the Video Electronics Standards Association for a copy of the VESA Programmer's Toolkit.

The current VESA Super VGA standard covers just about every video resolution and color-depth combination currently available, up to 1,280 by 1,024 with 16,777,216 (24-bit) colors. Even if a SVGA video adapter claims to be VESA-compatible, however, it still may not work with a particular driver, such as the 800-by-600, 256-color, super-VGA driver that comes with Microsoft Windows. In practice, however, manufacturers continue to provide their own driver software.

XGA and XGA-2

IBM announced the PS/2 XGA Display Adapter/A on October 30, 1990, and the XGA-2 in September 1992. Both adapters are high-performance, 32-bit bus-master adapters for Micro Channel-based systems. These video subsystems, evolved from the VGA, provide greater resolution, more colors, and much better performance.

Combine fast VGA, more colors, higher resolution, a graphics coprocessor, and bus-mastering, and you have XGA. Being a bus-master adapter means that the XGA can take control of the system as though it were the motherboard. In essence, a bus master is an adapter with its own processor that can execute operations independent of the motherboard.

The XGA was introduced as the default graphics-display platform with the Model 90 XP 486 and the Model 95 XP 486. In the desktop Model 90, the XGA is on the motherboard; in the Model 95 (a tower unit), it is located on a separate add-in board. This board—the XGA Display Adapter/A—also is available for other 386- and 486-based Micro Channel systems. The XGA adapter can be installed in any MCA systems that have 80386, 80386SX, 80386SLC, 486SLC2, 486SLC3, or 80486 processors, including PS/2 Models 53, 55, 57, 65, 70, and 80.

The XGA comes standard with 512K of graphics memory, which can be upgraded to 1M with an optional video-memory expansion.

Following are some of the XGA adapter's features:

- 1,024 by 768 with 256 colors (16 colors with standard memory)
- 640 by 480 with 256 colors
- DOS XGA adapter interface provides 8514/A compatibility

- Integrates a 16-bit compatible VGA
- Optimized for windowing operating systems
- Includes device drivers for DOS, OS/2, and Windows

In addition to all VGA modes, the XGA adapter offers several new modes of operation, which are listed in table 10.8.

Table 10.8 XGA Unique Modes of Operation

Maximum Resolution	Maximum Colors	Required VRAM
1,024x768	256 colors	1M
1,024x768	64 gray shades	1M
1,024x768	16 colors	512K
1,024x768	16 gray shades	512K
640x480	65,536 colors	1M
640x480	64 gray shades	512K

The reasons for the different memory requirements is explained in the next section. The 65,536-color mode provides almost photographic output. The 16-bit pixel is laid out as 5 bits of red, 6 bits of green, and 5 bits of blue (5-6-5)—in other words, 32 shades of blue, 64 shades of green, and 32 shades of blue. (The eye notices more variations in green than in red or blue.) One major drawback of the current XGA implementation is the interlacing that occurs in the higher-resolution modes. With interlacing, you can use a less expensive monitor, but the display updates more slowly, resulting in a slight flicker.

The XGA-2 improves on the performance of the XGA in several ways. To begin with, the XGA-2 increases the number of colors supported at 1,024-by-768 resolution to 64K. In addition, because of the circuitry of the XGA-2, it can process data at twice the speed of the XGA. The XGA-2 also works in noninterlaced mode, so it produces less flicker than the XGA does.

Both the XGA and XGA-2 support all existing VGA and 8514/A video modes. A large number of popular applications have been developed to support the 8514/A high-resolution 1,024-by-768 mode. These applications are written to the 8514/A Adapter interface which is a software interface between the application and the 8514/A hardware. The XGA's extended graphics function maintains compatibility at the same level. Because of the power of the XGA and XGA-2, current VGA or 8514/A applications run much faster.

Much of the speed of the XGA and XGA-2 also can be attributed to its video RAM (VRAM), a type of dual-ported RAM designed for graphics-display systems. This memory can be accessed by both the processor on the graphics adapter and the system CPU simultaneously, providing almost instant data transfer. The XGA VRAM is mapped into the system's address space. The VRAM normally is located in the top addresses of the 386's 4G address space. Because no other cards normally use this area, conflicts are rare. The adapters also have an 8K ROM BIOS extension that must be mapped somewhere in segments C000 or D000. (The motherboard implementation of the XGA does not require its own ROM because the motherboard BIOS contains all the necessary code.)

Table 10.9 summarizes the XGA modes.

Video Memory

A video card relies on memory in drawing your screen. You can often select how much memory you want on your video card—for example, 256K, 512K, 1M, 2M, or 4M are common choices today. Most cards today come with at least 1M and usually have 2M. Adding more memory does not speed your video card; instead it enables the card to generate more colors and/or higher resolutions.

The amount of memory needed by a video adapter to display a particular resolution and color depth is a mathematical equation. There has to be a memory location used to display every dot (or pixel) on the screen, and the number of total dots is determined by the resolution. For example 1,024×768 resolution represents 786,432 dots on the screen.

If you were to display that resolution with only two colors, you would only need one bit to represent each dot. If the bit were a 0, the dot would be black, and if it were a 1, the dot would be white. If you used 4-bits to control each dot, you could display 16 colors because there are 16 combinations possible with a 4 digit binary number (2 to the 4th power = 16). If you multiplied the number of dots times the number of bits required to represent each dot, you have the amount of memory required to display that resolution. Here is how the calculation would work:

1,024×768 = 786,432 dots × 4-bits per dot = 3,145,728 bits

= 393,216 bytes

= 384 KB

As you can see, to display only 16 colors at 1,024×768 resolution would require exactly 384K of RAM on the video card. Because most cards would normally support only memory amounts of 256K, 512K, 1M, 2M, or 4M, you would have to install 512K to run that resolution. Upping the color depth to 8-bits per pixel results in 256 possible colors and a memory requirement of 786,432 bytes or 768K. Again since no video card can install that exact amount, you would have to install an actual 1M on the video card.

In order to use the higher resolution modes and greater numbers of colors in SVGA cards, they will need more memory than the 256K found on a standard VGA adapter. Table 10.10 shows some of the requirements for SVGA cards based on resolution and color depth.

From table 10.10, you can see that a video adapter with 2M can display 65,536 colors in 1,024x768 resolution mode, but for a true color (16.8M colors) display, you would need to upgrade to 4M. In most cases, unless you are doing photo-realistic editing requiring 24-bit (16.8M color) support, 2M is all you will need on your video adapter.

A 24-bit (or true-color) video card can display photographic images by using 16.8 million colors. If you spend a lot of time working with graphics, you may want to invest in a

Table 10.9 IBM eXtended Graphics Array (XGA) Specifications

Video Standard	Resolution Mode	Number of Colors	Mode Type	BIOS Modes
XGA				
(10/30/90)	360x400	16	Text	00/01h
	720x400	16	Text	02/03h
	320x200	4	APA	04/05h
	640x200	2	APA	06h
	720x400	16	Text	07h
	320x200	16	APA	0Dh
	640x200	16	APA	0Eh
	640x350	4	APA	0Fh
	640x350	16	APA	10h
	640x480	2	APA	11h
	640x480	16	APA	12h
	320x200	256	APA	13h
	1,056x400	16	Text	14h
	1,056x400	16	Text	14h
	1,056x400	16	Text	14h
	1,056x400	16	Text	14h
	1,024x768	256	APA	14h
	640x480	65,536	APA	14h
	1,024x768	256	APA	14h
	1,024x768	256	APA	14h

APA = All points addressable (graphics)
Dbl = Double scan
Il = Interlaced

24-bit video card with up to 4M of RAM. Many of the cards today can easily handle 24-bit color, but you may need to upgrade from 2M to 4M of RAM to get that capability in the higher resolution modes.

Another issue with respect to memory on the graphics adapter is how wide the access is between the graphics chipset and the memory on the adapter. The graphics chipset is usually a single large chip on the card that contains virtually all the adapter's functions. It is wired directly to the memory on the card through a local bus on the card. Most of the high-end adapters use an internal 64-bit or even 128-bit wide memory bus. This jargon is confusing because this does not refer to the kind of bus slot the card plugs into. In other words, when you read about a 64-bit graphics adapter, it is really a 32-bit (PCI or VLB) card that has a 64-bit local memory bus on the card itself.

Character Format	Character Box	Scan Frequency Vertical (Hz)	Horizontal (KHz)	Scan Mode
40x25	9x16	70	31.5	Std
80x25	9x16	70	31.5	Std
40x25	8x8	70	31.5	Dbl
80x25	8x8	70	31.5	Dbl
80x25	9x16	70	31.5	Std
40x25	8x8	70	31.5	Dbl
80x25	8x8	70	31.5	Dbl
80x25	8x14	70	31.5	Std
80x25	8x14	70	31.5	Std
80x30	8x16	60	31.5	Std
80x30	8x16	60	31.5	Std
40x25	8x8	70	31.5	Dbl
132x25	8x16	70	31.5	Std
132x43	8x9	70	31.5	Std
132x56	8x8	70	31.5	Std
132x60	8x6	70	31.5	Std
85x38	12x20	43.48	35.52	Il
80x34	8x14	60	31.5	Std
128x54	8x14	43.48	35.52	Il
146x51	7x15	43.48	35.52	Il

Improving Video Speed

Many efforts have been made recently to improve the speed of video adapters because of the complexity and sheer data of the high-resolution displays used by today's software. The improvements in video speed are occurring along three fronts:

- Processor
- RAM
- Bus

The combination of these three is reducing the video bottleneck caused by the demands of graphical user interface software, such as Microsoft Windows.

Table 10.10 Display Adapter Minimum Memory Requirements

Resolution	Color Depth	No. Colors	Video Memory Required	
640x480	4-bit	16	256KB	153,600 bytes
640x480	8-bit	256	512KB	307,200 bytes
640x480	16-bit	65,536	1MB	614,400 bytes
640x480	24-bit	16,777,216	1MB	921,600 bytes
800x600	4-bit	16	256KB	240,000 bytes
800x600	8-bit	256	512KB	480,000 bytes
800x600	16-bit	65,536	1MB	960,000 bytes
800x600	24-bit	16,777,216	2MB	1,440,000 bytes
1,024x768	4-bit	16	512KB	393,216 bytes
1,024x768	8-bit	256	1MB	786,432 bytes
1,024x768	16-bit	65,536	2MB	1,572,864 bytes
1,024x768	24-bit	16,777,216	4MB	2,359,296 bytes
1,280x1,024	4-bit	16	1MB	655,360 bytes
1,280x1,024	8-bit	256	2MB	1,310,720 bytes
1,280x1,024	16-bit	65,536	4MB	2,621,440 bytes
1,280x1,024	24-bit	16,777,216	4MB	3,932,160 bytes

The Video Processor. Three types of processors, or *chipsets,* can be used in creating a video card. The chipset used is, for the most part, independent of which video specification (VGA, SVGA, or XGA) the adapter follows.

The oldest technology used in creating a video adapter is known as *frame-buffer technology.* In this scheme, the video card is responsible for displaying individual frames of an image. Each frame is maintained by the video card, but the computing necessary to create the frame comes from the CPU of your computer. This arrangement places a heavy burden on the CPU, which could be busy doing other program-related computing.

At the other end of the spectrum is a chip technology known as *coprocessing.* In this scheme, the video card includes its own processor, which performs all video-related computations. This arrangement frees the main CPU to perform other tasks. Short of integrating video functions directly into the CPU, this chipset provides the fastest overall system throughput.

Between these two arrangements is a middle ground: a fixed-function *accelerator chip.* In this scheme, used in many of the graphics accelerator boards on the market today, the circuitry on the video card does many of the more time-consuming video tasks (such as drawing lines, circles, and other objects), but the main CPU still directs the card by passing graphics-primitive commands from applications, such as an instruction to draw a rectangle of a given size and color.

The Video RAM. Historically, most video adapters have used regular dynamic RAM (DRAM) to store video images. This type of RAM, although inexpensive, is rather slow.

The slowness can be attributed to the need constantly to refresh the information contained within the RAM, as well as to the fact that DRAM cannot be read at the same time it is being written.

Modern PC graphics cards need extremely high data transfer rates to and from the video memory. At a resolution of 1,024×768 and a standard refresh rate of 72Hz, the Digital to Analog Converter (DAC) on the card needs to read the contents of the video memory frame buffer 72 times per second. In true color (24-bits per pixel) mode, this means that the video memory must be read at the rate of about 170M per second, which is just about the maximum rate available from a conventional DRAM design. Because of the high bandwidth required, a number of competing memory technologies have emerged over the past several years to meet the performance needs of high-end video memory.

One of the more recent memory designs to be incorporated into video cards is EDO (Extended Data Out) RAM. EDO provides a wider effective bandwidth by offloading memory precharging to separate circuits so that the next access can essentially begin before the last access has finished. As a result, EDO offers a 10% speed boost over DRAM, at a similar cost. EDO RAM was introduced by Micron Technologies. It was originally designed for use in main memories, but it is now also being used in video card applications. EDO chips are constructed using the same dies as conventional DRAM chips, and they differ from DRAMs only in how they are wired up in final production. This method enables EDO chips to be made on the same manufacturing lines and at the same relative costs as DRAM.

VRAM (Video RAM) is a popular type of memory that has been used in video cards for some time now. VRAM is designed to be dual ported, which allows the processor or accelerator chip on the graphics card as well as the Digital to Analog Converter (DAC) or even the PC's own processor to access the RAM simultaneously. This allows for much greater performance than standard DRAM or even EDO, but it comes at a higher price.

WRAM or Window RAM is a modified VRAM type dual-ported memory technology developed by Samsung that is aimed specifically at graphics cards. WRAM offers marginally better performance than standard VRAM at a lower cost. WRAM is now being used in many high-end graphics cards as a replacement for VRAM.

MDRAM (Multibank DRAM) is a new type of memory that is explicitly aimed at graphics and video applications. Developed by MoSys Inc., MDRAMs are constructed of a large number of small (32K) banks. Traditionally, DRAM or VRAM is logically organized as a single, monolithic bank. Being organized into small banks allows MDRAMs to be installed in any size that is an integral multiple of 32K, instead of restricting the size to the traditional binary multiple sizes found in many video cards. This is a significant advantage for the cost-sensitive PC marketplace. For example, a 1,024×768 true color (24-bit) graphics system requires 2.3M for the frame buffer plus some extra memory for off-screen storage. If 256K×16 DRAMs and a 64-bit bus are used, the only workable memory size that accommodates this frame buffer is 4M, constructed of two banks of four chips each. However, with MDRAM, a memory system of 2.5M can be constructed of only two or three individual chips. This eliminates the wasted extra 1.5M, and the total memory cost can be significantly reduced. In addition to the better memory sizing, MDRAM organizes its internal banks off a narrow central bus, which allows access to each bank individually. As such, this design can complete a burst to or from one bank and then begin a burst to or from another, all in a single clock cycle, offering much higher performance than VRAM or WRAM.

SGRAM or Synchronous Graphics RAM is a high-end solution for very fast video card designs. This type of memory can operate at 66MHz or faster and will likely be used in PCI cards when the 66MHz version of PCI begins appearing on PC motherboards. It offers up to four times the speed of conventional DRAM and can run at speeds up to 80MHz. Currently SGRAM is expensive, and until the PCI bus steps up from 33 to 66MHz, you won't see it in many applications.

The Bus. Earlier in this chapter, you learned that certain video cards are designed for certain buses. For example, the VGA was designed for use with an MCA bus, and the XGA and XGA-2 still are intended for use with the MCA. The bus system that you use in your computer (ISA, EISA, or MCA) affects the speed at which your system processes video information. The ISA offers a 16-bit data path at speeds of 8.33 MHz. The EISA or MCA buses can process 32 bits of data at a time, but they also run at speeds up to 10 MHz. (Don't confuse the bus speed with the CPU speed. Even though the CPU currently runs at speeds up to 100 MHz, the bus still can handle only a limited degree of speed.)

One improvement on this frontier was the *VESA local bus* (VL-Bus) standard. The VL-Bus standard typically is an addition to an existing bus technology. For example, you might have an ISA system that also contains a VL-Bus slot. Even if it is used in an ISA system, the VL-Bus processes 32 bits of data at a time and at the full-rated speed of the CPU: up to 40 MHz. Thus, you can achieve blinding speed by using a well implemented VL-Bus in your system.

In July 1992, Intel Corporation introduced Peripheral Component Interconnect (PCI) as a blueprint for directly connecting microprocessors and support circuitry; it then extended the design to a full expansion bus with Release 2 in 1993. Popularly termed a *mezzanine bus,* PCI combines the speed of a local bus with microprocessor independence. PCI video cards, like VL-Bus video cards, can increase video performance dramatically. PCI video cards, by their design, are meant to be plug-and-play, meaning that they require little configuration. The PCI standard has virtually replaced the older VL-Bus standard overnight. From here on, I recommend only PCI-based systems for new purchases and VL-Bus only for upgrading older systems that already have these slots.

VL-Bus and PCI have some important differences, as table 10.11 shows.

The Fastest Speed Possible. Fortunately, you can choose the best of each area—chipset, RAM, and bus—to achieve the fastest speed possible. The faster you want your card to perform, the more money you must spend. It is not unusual to find high-performance video cards that cost more than $1,000. This price does not include the cost of a new motherboard, if you want to implement PCI.

The trick to choosing a video subsystem is making an early decision. As you research specifications for your entire system, you should pay attention to the video and make sure that it performs the way you want it to. The best speeds can be achieved by a PCI card that uses a coprocessor and VRAM.

Table 10.11 Local Bus Specifications

Feature	VL-Bus	PCI
Theoretical maximum throughput	132M/sec	528M/sec*
Slots**	3 (typical)	4 (typical)
Plug-and-play support	No	Yes
Cost	Inexpensive	Slightly higher
Ideal use	Low cost 486	High-end 486, Pentium, P6

**At the maximum 66MHz bus speed and 64-bits*
***More slots are possible through the use of PCI bridge chips.*

Video Card Buying Criteria

One trend is to display higher-resolution images on larger and larger monitors. The growth of multimedia also has encouraged users to invest in 24-bit video cards for photographic-quality images. Both of these trends mean that you may want your video card to produce its 16 million colors at high resolution—at least 1,024 by 768 pixels.

Better cards can produce high color (or 64K colors) at even finer resolutions of 1,280 by 1,024 and 256 colors at very high resolutions of 1,600 by 1,280. To avoid bothersome flickering images, make sure that your card supports at least 72Hz vertical refresh rates at all resolutions; 76Hz is even better. To accomplish such tasks, you need at least 2M of video RAM (VRAM), although 4M is preferable.

True-color cards now appear in both VL-Bus and PCI versions. If you have an older system, plenty of ISA and MCA 24-bit cards are still available.

Whichever card you buy, make sure that it also has on-board VGA support so that you do not need an extra VGA card. Drivers for your particular operating system should be included, as well as a utility for switching resolutions. Look for extras that better cards now include—auto-installation and mode-switching utilities. A Microsoft Windows utility should be provided to ease switching resolutions and colors. Many of these utilities now allow for video mode switching on the fly without having to leave the Windows environment. This capability for changing resolutions (but not color depth) is standard in Windows 95.

If you are shopping for a video card to provide super-VGA resolutions, you need special software drivers for each of your software programs to take advantage of this resolution; otherwise, your video card will act as a typical VGA card. When you shop for a higher-resolution video card, make sure that it has drivers that support the software packages you own.

Video Cards for Multimedia

Multimedia is the result of several different media working together. Video is just one, albeit important, element. Topics not yet discussed include animation, full-motion video (playback and capture), still images, and graphics processing. Still images and video provide dazzling slides, and animation and full-motion video breathe life into any presentation.

A computer can mathematically animate sequences between keyframes. A keyframe identifies specific points. A bouncing ball, for example, can have three keyframes—up, down, and up. Using these frames as a reference point, the computer can create all the images in between. This creates a smooth bouncing ball.

More people are realizing the benefits of 3D animation. Prices are dropping, and technology once available only to high-end workstations is now available on PCs. One example is the 64-bit graphics accelerator offered by Matrox Graphics. What makes this graphics accelerator card unique is the on-board 3D rendering engine. This enables smooth, photo-realistic 3D images to be performed on a PC level at speeds exceeding those of low-end workstations.

Video Feature Connector (VFC). Since IBM first developed the VGA standard in 1987, one often overlooked part of the standard was the Video Feature Connector. This was a 26-pin connector that allowed other video cards to connect to a VGA adapter directly. Unfortunately, this standard was poorly documented by IBM and poorly implemented by most VGA adapter manufacturers. In fact, many VGA cards did not implement this connector at all, basically ignoring the need. That may have been fine in the early days of VGA because there were few multimedia products that would need to tap into the VGA signal. Today, however, there are many types of multimedia add-on boards that have features such as motion video, video capture, television tuners, and so on that need the services of this connector to do their job.

Unfortunately, there was another problem with the VFC besides it not being there or being implemented incorrectly. The problem was one of performance. The original VGA adapter was designed as an 8-bit bus adapter and worked at a resolution of only 640×480 pixels. Thus the VFC had these same limitations, which put a damper on the type of video signal that could be transferred directly from one card to another. In November of 1983 these problems were solved by the Video Electronics Standards Association's (VESA) announcement of the VESA Advanced Feature Connector (VAFC) and the VESA Media Channel (VMC) video bus standards. These new standards would bring about compatibility and performance for interconnected multimedia adapters and video adapters. These standards will ensure rapid growth in the adoption of new applications such as Interactive Video, Video Presentation, Video Conferencing, and Desktop Video Editing.

The VESA Advanced Feature Connector (VAFC) provides a low cost extension of the industry standard Video Feature Connector (VFC) found on many graphics boards. VAFC solves high bandwidth requirements by widening the current feature connector data path from 8 to 16/32-bits and adding additional signals, which provide more reliable operation. The VAFC delivers 75MB/sec throughput in its 16-bit baseline configuration, and up to 150MB/sec in the 32-bit configuration. Other features include multiple pixels per clock, color space data, genlocking, and asynchronous video input.

The VAFC overcomes the current 640×480 pixel 256 color resolution limitations of most video overlay products. New video capture, overlay, compression, and playback products will use the VAFC interface to transfer video pixel data from board to board. This will allow video playback in a window to become a standard feature on PC systems.

The VESA Media Channel (VMC) is a dedicated multimedia bus that provides an independent path for the simultaneous processing of several high bandwidth video streams. The VMC directly addresses the current limitations of running video across a computer's system bus. This design solves the universal bandwidth bottleneck and latency issues that exist in all system or processor bus architectures including ISA, EISA, MicroChannel, VL-Bus, and PCI.

To correct these problems, the VESA Media Channel is designed to allow the transparent integration of video and graphics without the interference of processor interrupts or bus contention. VESA Media Channel provides the option for a 68-pin multi-drop cable allowing multiple devices to be combined in a modular fashion. For example, a graphics system supporting the VESA Media Channel can easily and cost effectively be configured as a capture, decode only, encode only, or a full encode/decode video system. This is important in applications such as video teleconferencing, and it provides flexible, cost effective engineering of a particular system.

For any high performance video adapter, make sure that it supports at least the 80-pin VAFC connector and or the 68-pin VMC connector. If you see only a 26-pin connector on the card, then the card would not be recommended as that is the standard VFC. Most of the higher quality multimedia adapters will require a VAFC connection for high performance video signal transfer.

Video Output Devices. When video technology was first introduced, it was based upon television. There is a difference between the signals that a television uses and the signals used by a computer. In the United States, color TV standards were established in 1953 by the National Television System Committee (NTSC). Some countries, such as Japan, followed this standard. Many countries in Europe developed more sophisticated standards, including Phase Alternate Line (PAL) and SEquential Couleur Avec Memoire (SECAM). Table 10.12 shows the differences among these standards.

Table 10.12 Television versus Computer Monitors

Standard	Yr. Est.	Country	Lines	Rate
Television				
NTSC	1953 (color) 1941 (b&w)	U.S., Japan	525	60Hz
PAL	1941	Europe*	625	50Hz
SECAM	1962	France	625	25Hz
Computer				
VGA			640x480**	72Hz

**England, Holland, West Germany*

***VGA is based upon more lines and uses pixels (480) versus lines; "genlocking" is used to lock pixels into lines and synchronize computers with TV standards.*

A video-output (or VGA-to-NTSC) adapter enables you to show computer screens on a TV set or record them onto videotape for easy distribution. These products fall into two categories—those with *genlocking* (which enables the board to synchronize signals from multiple video sources or video with PC graphics) and those without. Genlocking provides the signal stability needed to obtain adequate results when recording to tape but is not necessary for simply using a video display.

VGA-to-NTSC converters come as both internal boards or external boxes that you can port along with your laptop-based presentation. These latter devices do not replace your VGA adapter but instead connect to your video adapter via an external cable that works with any type of VGA card. In addition to VGA input and output ports, a video-output board has a video output interface for S-Video and composite video.

VGA-to-TV converters support the standard NTSC television format and may also support the European PAL format. The resolution shown on a TV set or recorded on videotape is often limited to straight VGA at 640 by 480 pixels. Such boards may contain an "anti-flicker" circuit to help stabilize the picture, which often suffers from a case of the jitters in VGA-to-TV products.

Still-Image Video Capture Cards. Like a Polaroid camera, you can capture individual screen images for later editing and playback. Some plug into a PC's parallel port. These units capture still images from NTSC video sources like camcorders or VCRs. Although image quality is limited by the input signal, the results are still good enough for presentations and desktop publishing applications. These devices work with 8-, 16-, and 24-bit VGA cards and usually accept video input from VHS, Super VHS, and Hi-8 devices. As you might expect, though, Super VHS and Hi-8 video sources give better results, as do Super VGA modes with more than 256 colors.

You may want to invest in image-processing applications that offer features such as image editing, file conversion, screen capture, and graphics file management.

Desktop Video (DTV) Boards. You can also capture NTSC (television) signals to your computer system for display or editing. When capturing video, you should think in terms of digital versus analog. The biggest convenience of an analog TV signal is efficiency; it is a compact way to transmit video information through a low-bandwidth pipeline. The disadvantage is that although you can control how the video is displayed, you cannot edit it.

Actually capturing and recording video from external sources and saving the files onto your PC requires special technology. What is needed is a *video capture board,* which is also referred to as video digitizer or video grabber.

One of the most common uses for analog video is with interactive CBT programs in which your application sends start, stop, and search commands to a laserdisk player that plays disks you have mastered. The software controls the player via an interface that also converts the laserdisk's NTSC signal into a VGA-compatible signal for display on your computer's monitor. These types of applications require NTSC-to-VGA conversion hardware.

Whereas a computer can display up to 16 million colors, the NTSC standard allows for only approximately 32,000 colors. Affordable video is the Achilles' heel of multimedia. The images are often jerky or less than full-screen. The reason is because full-motion video, such as you see on TV, requires 30 images or frames per second (fps).

The typical computer screen was designed to display mainly static images. The storing and retrieving of these images requires managing huge files. Consider this: A single, full-screen color image requires almost 2M of disk space; a one-second video would require 45M. Likewise, any video transmission that you want to capture for use on your PC must be converted from an analog NTSC signal to a digital signal that your computer can use. On top of that, the video signal must be moved inside your computer at 10 times the speed of the conventional ISA bus structure. You need not only a superior video card and monitor but also an excellent expansion bus, such as VL-Bus or PCI.

Considering the fact that full-motion video can consume massive quantities of disk space (0.5 seconds = 15Meg), it becomes apparent that compression is needed. Compression and decompression (*codec*) applies to both video and audio. Not only does a compressed file take up less space, it also performs better; there is simply less data to process. When you are ready to replay the video/audio, you simply decompress the file during playback. In any case, ensure your hard drive is large enough and has enough performance to handle the huge files that can result in storing video capture files. I would recommend a minimum of a 1 or 2G drive with either an enhanced IDE or SCSI-2 interface.

There are two types of codecs—hardware-dependent codecs and software (or hardware-independent) codecs. Hardware codecs are typically better; however, they require additional hardware. Software codecs do not require hardware for compression or playback, but they typically do not deliver the same quality or compression ratio. Two of the major codec algorithms are:

- *JPEG (Joint Photographic Experts Group).* Originally developed for still images, JPEG can compress and decompress at rates acceptable for nearly full-motion video (30 fps). JPEG still uses a series of still images, which is easier for editing. JPEG is typically lossy, but it can also be lossless. It eliminates redundant data for each individual image (intraframe). Compression efficiency is approximately 30:1 (20:1–40:1).
- *MPEG (Motion Pictures Expert Group).* Because MPEG can compress up to 200:1 at high quality levels, it results in better, faster videos that require less space. MPEG is an interframe compressor. Because MPEG stores only incremental changes, it is not used during editing phases. MPEG decoding can be done in software on high performance Pentium systems.

If you will be capturing, compressing, and playing video, you will need Microsoft Video for Windows (VFW) or Quicktime. Codecs are provided along with VFW:

- *Cinepak.* Although Cinepak can take longer to compress, it can produce better quality and higher compression than Indeo. It is also referred to as Compact Video Coded (CVC).

- *Indeo.* Indeo can outperform Cinepak and is capable of real-time compression. An Intel Smart Video board is required for real-time compression.
- *Microsoft Video 1.* Developed by MediaVision (MotiVE) and renamed MS Video 1, this codec is a DCT based post-processor. A file is compressed after capture.

To play or record video on your multimedia PC (MPC), you will need some extra hardware and software:

- Video system software, such as Apple's QuickTime for Windows or Microsoft's Video for Windows.
- A compression/digitization video card that enables you to digitize and play large video files.
- An NTSC-to-VGA adapter that combines TV signals with computer video signals for output to a VCR. Video can come from a variety of sources: TV, VCR, video camera, or laserdisk player. When an animation file is recorded, it can be saved in a variety of different file formats: AVI (Audio Video Interleave), FLI (a 320-by-200 pixel animation file), and FLC (an animation file of any size).

You can incorporate these files into a multimedia presentation by using authoring software such as Icon Author from AIMTECH, or you can include the animated files as OLE! objects to be used with Microsoft Word, Excel, Access, or other OLE! compliant applications.

When you connect video devices, use the S-Video (S-VHS) connector whenever available. This cable provides the best signal because separate signals are used for color (*chroma*) and brightness (*luma*). Otherwise, you will have to use *composite video,* which mixes luma and chroma. This results in a lower-quality signal. The better your signal, the better your video quality will be.

You can get devices that just display NTSC signals on your computer. Soon, you will not know whether you are using a computer screen or a television. Digital video, in-screen filling, and full-motion color, have arrived on desktop platforms with titles, playback boards, and encoding equipment. Soon, MPEG movie clip libraries will be the next form of clip art on CD-ROM.

Adapter and Display Troubleshooting

Solving most graphics adapter and monitor problems is fairly simple, although costly, because replacing the adapter or display is the usual procedure. A defective or dysfunctional adapter or display usually is replaced as a single unit, rather than repaired. Most of today's cards cost more to service than to replace, and the documentation required to service the adapters or displays properly is not always available. You cannot get schematic diagrams, parts lists, wiring diagrams, and so on for most of the adapters or monitors. Many adapters now are constructed with surface-mount technology that requires a substantial investment in a rework station before you can remove and replace these components by hand. You cannot use a $25 pencil-type soldering iron on these boards!

Servicing monitors is slightly different. Although a display often is replaced as a whole unit, many displays are simply too expensive to replace. Your best bet is to contact the company from which you purchased the display. If your NEC Multisync display goes out, for example, a swap with another monitor can confirm that the display is the problem. After you narrow the problem to the display, call NEC for the location of the nearest factory repair depot. Third-party service companies can repair most displays; their prices often are much lower than factory service.

You usually cannot repair a display yourself. First, opening the case of a color display exposes you to up to 35,000 volts of electricity, and if you do not follow recommended safety precautions, you can easily electrocute yourself. Second, the required documentation is not always available. Without schematic diagrams, board layouts, parts lists, or other documentation, even an experienced service technician may not be able to diagnose and repair the display properly.

Caution

You should not attempt to repair a display yourself. Touching the wrong item can be fatal. The display circuits sometimes hold extremely high voltages for hours, days, or even weeks after the power is shut off. A qualified service person should discharge the tube and power capacitors before proceeding.

For most displays, you are limited to making simple adjustments. For color displays, the adjustments can be quite formidable if you lack experience. Even factory service technicians often lack proper documentation and service information for newer models; they usually exchange your unit for another and repair the defective one later. Never buy a display for which no local factory repair depot is available.

If you have a problem with a display or adapter, it pays to call the manufacturer, who might know about the problem and make repairs available, as occurred with the IBM 8513 display. Large numbers of the IBM 8513 color displays were manufactured with components whose values change over time and may exhibit text or graphics out of focus. This problem haunted my IBM 8513. Opening the monitor and adjusting the focus helped for a while, but the display became fuzzy again. I discovered that IBM replaces these displays at no cost when focusing is a problem. If you have a fuzzy 8513 display, you should contact IBM to learn whether your display qualifies for a free replacement.

You can call IBM at (800) IBM-SERV, or contact an IBM-authorized dealer for assistance. This particular problem is covered under Engineering Change Announcement (ECA) 017.

Remember that most of the problems you have with modern video adapters and displays will be related to the drivers that control these devices rather than the hardware itself.

Contact the manufacturers to ensure that you have the latest and proper drivers; they may have a solution for you that you are unaware of.

Summary

This chapter discussed and examined the video portion of the original PC and its descendants. Monitor technologies and buying criteria were discussed, along with video cards and standards, including techniques used to provide more graphics speed. Lastly, multimedia-related video cards were discussed, including NTSC-to-VGA, still-image capture, and video-in-window adapters and techniques.

Chapter 11

Communications and Networking

Most computer-to-computer connections occur through a serial port, a parallel port, or a network adapter. In this chapter, you explore ways to connect your PC to other computers. Such connections enable you to transfer and share files, send electronic mail, access software on other computers, and generally make two or more computers behave as a team.

Using Communications Ports and Devices

The basic communications ports in any PC system are the serial and parallel ports. The serial ports are used primarily for devices that must communicate bidirectionally with the system. Such devices include modems, mice, scanners, digitizers, and any other devices that "talk to" and receive information from the PC.

Parallel ports are used primarily for printers and operate normally as one-way ports, although sometimes they can be used bidirectionally. Several companies also manufacture communications programs that perform high-speed transfers between PC systems using serial or parallel ports. Several products are currently on the market that make non-traditional use of the parallel port. You can purchase network adapters, floppy disk drives, CD-ROM drives, or tape backup units that attach to the parallel port, for example.

Serial Ports

The asynchronous serial interface is the primary system-to-system communications port. *Asynchronous* means that no synchronization or clocking signal is present, so characters may be sent with any arbitrary time spacing, as when a typist is providing the data.

Each character sent over a serial connection is framed by a standard start and stop signal. A single 0 bit, called the start bit, precedes each character to tell the receiving system that the next eight bits constitute a byte of data. One or two stop bits follow the character to signal that the character has been sent. At the receiving end of the communication, characters are recognized by the start and stop signals instead of by the timing of their arrival. The asynchronous interface is character-oriented and has about a 20 percent overhead for the extra information needed to identify each character.

Serial refers to data sent over a single wire, with each bit lining up in a series as the bits are sent. This type of communication is used over the phone system because this system provides one wire for data in each direction. Add-on serial ports for the PC are available from many manufacturers. You usually can find these ports on one of the multifunction boards available or on a board with at least a parallel port. Figure 11.1 shows the standard 9-pin AT-style serial port, and figure 11.2 shows the 25-pin version.

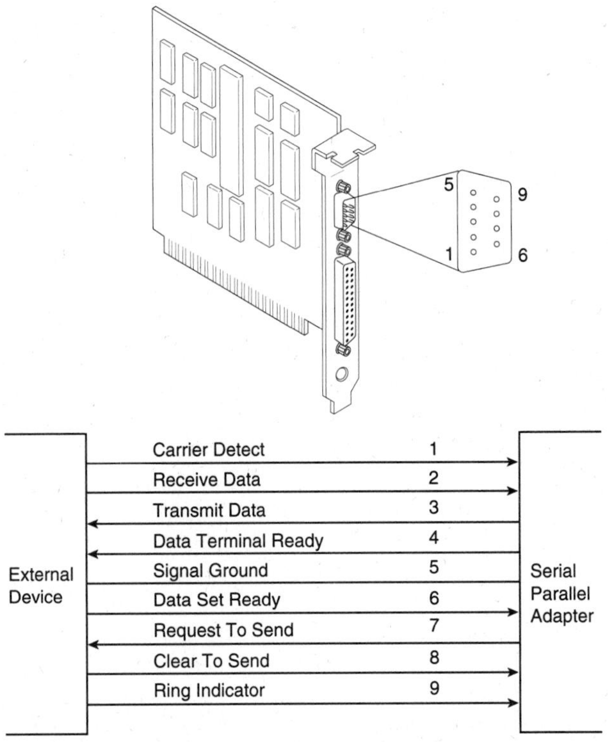

Figure 11.1

AT-style 9-pin serial-port connector specifications.

Serial ports may connect to a variety of devices such as modems, plotters, printers, other computers, bar code readers, scales, and device control circuits. Basically, anything that needs a two-way connection to the PC uses the industry-standard Reference Standard number 232 revision c (RS-232c) serial port. This device enables data transfer between otherwise incompatible devices. Tables 11.1, 11.2, and 11.3 show the pinouts of the 9-pin (AT-style), 25-pin, and 9-pin-to-25-pin serial connectors.

UART Chips. The heart of any serial port is the Universal Asynchronous Receiver/Transmitter (UART) chip. This chip completely controls the process of breaking the native parallel data within the PC into serial format and later converting serial data back into the parallel format.

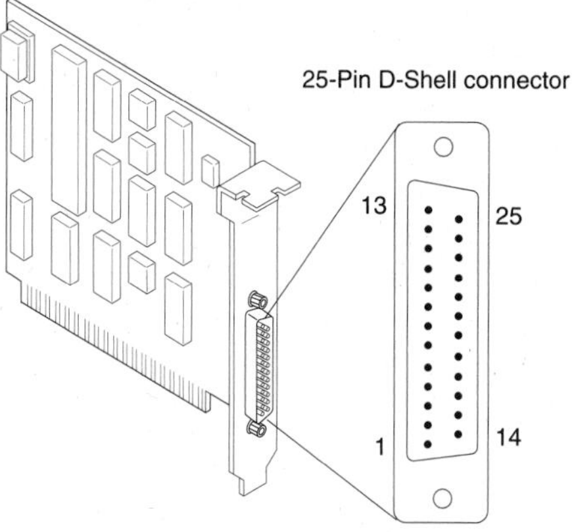

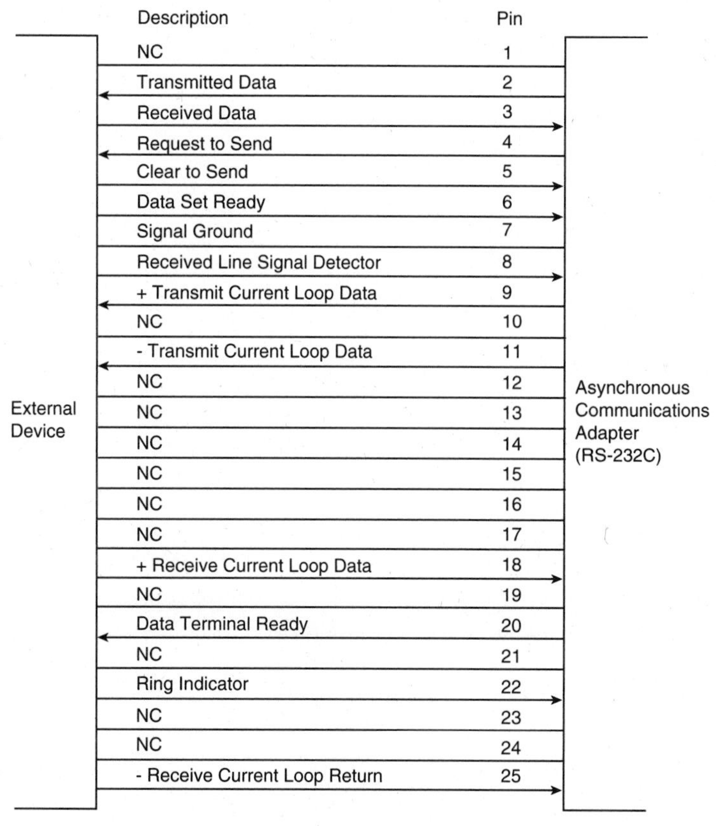

Figure 11.2

Standard 25-pin serial-port connector specifications.

Table 11.1 9-Pin (AT) Serial Port Connector

Pin	Signal	Description	I/O
1	CD	Carrier detect	In
2	RD	Receive data	In
3	TD	Transmit data	Out
4	DTR	Data terminal ready	Out
5	SG	Signal ground	—
6	DSR	Data set ready	In
7	RTS	Request to send	Out
8	CTS	Clear to send	In
9	RI	Ring indicator	In

Table 11.2 25-Pin (PC, XT, and PS/2) Serial Port Connector

Pin	Signal	Description	I/O
1	—	Chassis ground	—
2	TD	Transmit data	Out
3	RD	Receive data	In
4	RTS	Request to send	Out
5	CTS	Clear to send	In
6	DSR	Data set ready	In
7	SG	Signal ground	—
8	CD	Carrier detect	In
9	—	+Transmit current loop return	Out
11	—	-Transmit current loop data	Out
18	—	+Receive current loop data	In
20	DTR	Data terminal ready	Out
22	RI	Ring indicator	In
25	—	-Receive current loop return	In

Table 11.3 9-Pin to 25-Pin Serial Cable Adapter Connections

9-Pin	25-Pin	Signal	Description
1	8	CD	Carrier detect
2	3	RD	Receive data
3	2	TD	Transmit data
4	20	DTR	Data terminal ready
5	7	SG	Signal ground
6	6	DSR	Data set ready
7	4	RTS	Request to send
8	5	CTS	Clear to send
9	22	RI	Ring indicator

There are several types of UART chips on the market. The original PC and XT used the 8250 UART, which is still used in many low-price serial cards on the market. In the PC/AT (or other systems based on at least an 80286 processor), the 16450 UART is used. The only difference between these chips is their suitability for high-speed communications. The 16450 is better suited for high-speed communications than the 8250; otherwise, both chips appear identical to most software.

The 16550 UART was the first serial chip used in the PS/2 line. This chip could function as the earlier 16450 and 8250 chips, but it also included a 16-byte buffer that aided in faster communications. This is sometimes referred to as a FIFO (first in/first out) buffer. Unfortunately, the 16550 also had a few bugs, particularly in the buffer area. These bugs were corrected with the release of the 16550A UART, which is used in all high-performance serial ports.

Because the 16550A is a faster, more reliable chip than its predecessors, it is best to look for serial ports that use it. If you are in doubt about which chip you have in your system, you can use the Microsoft MSD program (provided with Windows, MS DOS 6.X, and Windows 95) to determine the type of UART you have. Another way to tell if you have a 16650 UART in Windows 95 is to right-click on My Computer, and then click on Properties. This brings up the System Properties dialog box. Click on the Device Manager tab, click on Ports, and then double-click on the communications port that you want to check. Choose the Port Settings tab and then choose the Advanced button. This will bring up the Advanced Port Settings box. If you have a 16650 UART, there will be a check mark in the use FIFO Buffers option.

Note that the original designer of these UARTs is National Semiconductor (NS). Many other manufacturers are producing clones of these UARTs, such that you probably don't have an actual NS brand part in your system. Even so, the part you have will be compatible with one of the NS parts, hopefully the 16550. In other words, you should check to see that whatever UART chip you do have does indeed feature the 16-byte FIFO buffer as found in the NS 16550 part.

If you want more information on various chips, check out this Web site:

On the Web

http://www.civil.mtu.edu/chipdir/chipdir.html

High Speed Serial Ports

Some modem manufacturers have gone a step further on improving serial data transfer by introducing Enhanced Serial Ports (ESP) or Super High Speed Serial Ports. These ports enable a 28,800 bps modem to communicate with the computer at data rates up to 921,600 bps. The extra speed on these ports is generated by increasing the buffer size. These ports are usually based on a 16550AF UART or a 16550AF UART emulator with dual 1024 byte buffers and on-board data flow control. These ports can provide great benefit in an environment where both your computer and the "receiving" computer are equipped with these ports. Otherwise, just one of the computers having an ESP doesn't yield any benefit.

Most UART chips used in PC-compatible systems are either made by National Semiconductor or are a clone of one of the National Semiconductor chips. You also can identify the chips by looking for the largest chip on the serial port card and reading the numbers on that chip. Usually the chips are socketed, and replacing only the chip may be possible. Otherwise, you can upgrade the UARTs in your system by purchasing an I/O card or an internal modem that includes the 16550A. Table 11.4 provides a complete list of UART chips that may be in your system.

Note

The interrupt bug referred to in table 11.4 is a spurious interrupt generated by the 8250 at the end of an access. The ROM BIOS code in the PC and XT has been written to work around this bug. If a chip without the bug is installed, random lockups may occur. The 16450 or 16550(A) chips do not have the interrupt bug, and the AT ROM BIOS was written without any of the bug workarounds in PC or XT systems.

Table 11.4 UART Chips in PC or AT Systems

Chip	Description
8250	IBM used this original chip in the PC serial port card. The chip has several bugs, none of which is serious. The PC and XT ROM BIOS are written to anticipate at least one of the bugs. This chip was replaced by the 8250B.
8250A	Do not use the second version of the 8250 in any system. This upgraded chip fixes several bugs in the 8250, including one in the interrupt enable register, but because the PC and XT ROM BIOS expect the bug, this chip does not work properly with those systems. The 8250A should work in an AT system that does not expect the bug, but does not work adequately at 9600 bps.
8250B	The last version of the 8250 fixes bugs from the previous two versions. The interrupt enable bug in the original 8250, expected by the PC and XT ROM BIOS software, has been put back into this chip, making the 8250B the most desirable chip for any non-AT serial port application. The 8250B chip may work in an AT under DOS, but does not run properly at 9600 bps.
16450	IBM selected the higher-speed version of the 8250 for the AT. Because this chip has fixed the interrupt enable bug mentioned earlier, the 16450 does not operate properly in many PC or XT systems because they expect this bug to be present. OS/2 requires this chip as a minimum, or the serial ports do not function properly. It also adds a scratch-pad register as the highest register. The 16450 is used primarily in AT systems because of its increase in throughput over the 8250B.
16550	This newer UART improves on the 16450. This chip cannot be used in a FIFO (first in, first out) buffering mode because of problems with the design, but it does enable a programmer to use multiple DMA channels and thus increase throughput on an AT or higher class computer system. I highly recommend replacing the 16550 UART with the 16550A.
16550A	This chip is a faster 16450 with a built-in 16-character Transmit and Receive FIFO (first in, first out) buffer that works. It also allows multiple DMA channel access. You should install this chip in your AT system serial port cards if you do any serious communications at 9600 bps or higher. If your communications program makes use of the FIFO, which most do today, it can greatly increase communications speed and eliminate lost characters and data at the higher speeds.

Various manufacturers make versions of the 16550A; National Semiconductor was the first. Its full part number for the 40-pin DIP is NS16550AN or NS16550AFN. Make sure that the part you get is the 16550A and not the older 16550. You can contact Fry's Electronics or Jameco Electronics to obtain the NS16550AN, for example.

There are many diagnostic software programs on the market, such as the Norton Utilities, that can identify the type of UART chip you have by testing it. If you have Windows 95, the Device Manager can identify the type of chip you have. Look under "Advanced Port Settings" for the Serial port you want to check. If you see the FIFO (First In First Out) buffers enabled, then you have a 16550A compatible UART. MSD (Microsoft Diagnostics), which is supplied with DOS 6.x and Windows 3.x, can also identify the UART chip, but unfortunately, it has a bug in the UART identification routines. MSD will tell you that you have an 8250 chip when you really have a 16450. It does correctly identify the 16550A type chips, which is what you want to see anyway.

Serial-Port Configuration

Each time a character is received by a serial port, it has to get the attention of the computer by raising an Interrupt Request Line (IRQ). Eight-bit ISA bus systems have eight of these lines, and systems with a 16-bit ISA bus have 16 lines. The 8259 interrupt controller chip usually handles these requests for attention. In a standard configuration, COM1 uses IRQ4, and COM2 uses IRQ3.

When a serial port is installed in a system, it must be configured to use specific I/O addresses (called ports) and interrupts (called IRQs for Interrupt ReQuest). The best plan is to follow the existing standards for how these devices should be set up. For configuring serial ports, you should use the addresses and interrupts indicated in table 11.5.

Table 11.5 Standard Serial I/O Port Addresses and Interrupts

System	COMx	Port	IRQ
All	COM1	3F8h	IRQ4
All	COM2	2F8h	IRQ3
ISA bus	COM3	3E8h	IRQ4*
ISA bus	COM4	2E8h**	IRQ3*
ISA bus	COM5	3E0h	IRQ4*
ISA bus	COM6	2E0h	IRQ3*
ISA bus	COM7	338h	IRQ4*
ISA bus	COM8	238h	IRQ3*
MCA bus	COM3	3220h	IRQ3
MCA bus	COM4	3228h	IRQ3
MCA bus	COM5	4220h	IRQ3
MCA bus	COM6	4228h	IRQ3
MCA bus	COM7	5220h	IRQ3
MCA bus	COM8	5228h	IRQ3

**Note that although many COM3 through COM8 serial ports can be set up to share IRQ 3 and 4 with COM1 and COM2, I absolutely do not recommend this practice. I normally recommend setting COM3 to IRQ 10, and COM4 to IRQ 11 (provided you don't also have a SCSI adapter set to IRQ 11).*

***Note that many newer high-performance accelerated video chipsets or adapters use I/O ports that conflict with the standard I/O port settings for COM4. Since you cannot alter the video I/O port settings, you will either have to re-set the COM4 port to another setting or change to a different video card that does not conflict.*

If you are adding more than the standard COM1 and COM2 serial ports, you should ensure that they use unique and non-conflicting interrupts. If you purchase a serial port adapter card and intend to use it to supply ports beyond the standard COM1 and COM2, be sure that it can use interrupts other than IRQ3 and IRQ4. Most of the time I recommend that you set COM3 to something like IRQ10 and COM4 to IRQ11. Most SCSI adapters would also use IRQ 11, so beware of a potential conflict in this area. A company called Byterunner Technologies (see the vendor list in Appendix B) has a wide variety of high performance serial and parallel adapters that meet these requirements.

On the Web

http://www.byterunner.com/

A problem can occur when the ROM BIOS logs in these ports. If the Power-On Self-Test (POST) does not find a 3F8 serial port but does find a 2F8, then the 2F8 serial port is mistakenly assigned to COM1. The reserved IRQ line for COM1 is IRQ4, but this serial port at 2F8 is using COM2's address, which means that it should be using IRQ3 instead of IRQ4. If you are trying to use BASIC or DOS for COM1 operations, therefore, the serial port or modem cannot work.

Another problem is that IBM never built BIOS support for COM3 and COM4 into its original ISA bus systems. Therefore, the DOS MODE command cannot work with serial ports above COM2 because DOS gets its I/O information from the BIOS, which finds out what is installed in your system and where during the POST. The POST in these older systems checks only for the first two installed ports. PS/2 systems have an improved BIOS that checks for as many as eight serial ports, although DOS is limited to handling only four of them.

To get around this problem, most communications software and some serial peripherals (such as mice) support higher COM ports by addressing them directly, rather than making DOS function calls. The communications program PROCOMM, for example, supports the additional ports even if your BIOS or DOS does not. Of course, if your system or software does not support these extra ports or you need to redirect data using the MODE command, trouble arises.

On the Web

http://www.datastorm.com/

Windows 95 has added the support for up to 128 serial ports, which matches the number of ports now supported by MS-DOS. This allows for the use of multiport boards in the system. Multiport boards give your system the ability to collect or share data with multiple devices while using only one slot and one interrupt.

A couple of utilities enable you to append your COM port information to the BIOS, making the ports DOS-accessible. A program called Port Finder is one of the best and is available in the "general hardware" data library of the PCHW forum on CompuServe.

Port Finder activates the extra ports by giving the BIOS the addresses and providing utilities for swapping the addresses among the different ports. Address-swapping enables programs that don't support COM3 and COM4 to access them. Software that already directly addresses these additional ports usually is unaffected.

Extra ports, however, must use separate interrupts. If you are going to use two COM ports at one time, they should be on non-conflicting interrupts. I do not recommend sharing interrupts among two serial ports, but this practice was common before the advent of multi-tasking operating systems like Windows 95 and OS/2. If you are using more than 2 serial ports and need to share interrupts due to the adapters being inflexible or outdated, try the following possibilities for simultaneous operation:

COM1 (IRQ4) and COM2 (IRQ3)

COM1 (IRQ4) and COM4 (IRQ3)

COM2 (IRQ3) and COM3 (IRQ4)

COM3 (IRQ4) and COM4 (IRQ3)

Divide your COM port inputs into these groups of two, pairing serial devices that will not be used simultaneously on the same interrupt and devices that will be used at the same time on different interrupts. Note again that PS/2 Micro Channel Architecture systems are entirely exempt from these types of problems because they have a BIOS that looks for the additional ports and because the MCA bus can share interrupts without conflicts. EISA bus systems also have the ability to share interrupts.

If you have an ISA, VL-Bus, or PCI based system, I absolutely do not recommend sharing interrupts between the serial ports (even though PCI purports to be able to do so). This will result in numerous problems and conflicts, especially under multitasking operating systems like Windows 95, Windows NT, or OS/2. You should make sure that any COM port adapters you purchase allow the use of IRQs 9-15 so you will be able to utilize some of the free 16-bit interrupts in your system.

Another problem with systems using up to 4 or more COM ports is that many of the newer video chipsets and adapters use the same I/O ports as COM4 does. For example, the standard COM4 setting requires I/O port addresses from 2E8-2EF. The ATI Mach 64 card, as well as many other accelerated video cards (and chipsets), uses 2EC-2EF, which is in direct conflict with the COM4 settings. Because none of the video port address settings are changeable, you must either re-set the port at COM4 to another setting, disable it, or purchase a different video card that does not use these settings.

To configure serial boards in ISA bus systems, you probably will have to set jumpers and switches. Because each board on the market is different, you should always consult the OEM manual for that particular card if you need to know how it is configured.

Modem Standards

Bell Labs and the CCITT have set standards for modem protocols. CCITT is an acronym for a French term that translates into English as the Consultative Committee on International Telephone and Telegraph. The organization was renamed the International Telecommunications Union (ITU) in the early 1990s, but the protocols developed under the old name are often referred to as such. Newly developed protocols are referred to as ITU-T standards. A protocol is a method by which two different entities agree to communicate. Bell Labs no longer sets new standards for modems, although several of its older standards are still used. Most modems built in the last few years conform to the CCITT standards. The ITU is an international body of technical experts responsible for developing data communications standards for the world. The group falls under the organizational umbrella of the United Nations, and its members include representatives from major modem manufacturers, common carriers (such as AT&T), and governmental bodies.

The ITU establishes communications standards and protocols in many areas, so one modem often adheres to several different standards, depending on its various features and capabilities. Modem standards can be grouped into the following three areas:

- Modulation standards

  Bell 103
  Bell 212A
  CCITT V.21
  CCITT V.22bis
  CCITT V.29
  CCITT V.32
  CCITT V.32bis
  CCITT V.34

- Error-correction standards

  CCITT V.42

- Data-compression standards

  V.42bis

Other standards have been developed by different companies (not Bell Labs or the ITU). These are sometimes called proprietary standards, even though most of these companies publish the full specifications of their protocols so that other manufacturers can develop modems to work with them. The following list shows some of the proprietary standards that have become fairly popular:

- Modulation

  HST
  PEP
  DIS

- Error correction

  MNP 1-4
  Hayes V-series

- Data compression

  MNP 5
  CSP

Almost all modems today claim to be Hayes compatible, a phrase which has come to be as meaningless as IBM compatible when referring to PCs. It does not refer to any communication protocol but instead to the commands required to operate the modem. Because almost every modem uses the Hayes command set, this compatibility is a given and should not really affect your purchasing decisions about modems. Table 11.6 lists the command sets for the U.S. Robotics and Hayes brands of modems. Not all modems that function at the same speed have the same functionality. Many modem manufacturers produce modems that have different feature sets at different price points. The more expensive modem usually supports such features as distinctive ring support and caller ID. When purchasing a modem, be sure that it supports all the features that you need.

On the Web

http://www.usrobotics.com/

http://www.hayes.com/

http://www.microcom.com/

http://www.megahertz.com/

Table 11.6 U.S. Robotics and Hayes Modem Commands and Supported Features

Command	Modem Functions and Options	USR Dual	USR 2400	Hayes 2400	Hayes 1200
&	See Extended Command Set	X			
%	See Extended Command Set	X			
A	Force Answer mode when modem has not received an incoming call	X	X	X	X
A/	Re-execute last command once	X	X	X	X
A>	Repeat last command continuously	X			
Any key	Terminate current connection attempt; exit Repeat mode	X	X		
AT	Attention: must precede all other commands, except A/, A>, and +++	X	X	X	X
Bn	Handshake options	X		X	
	B0 CCITT answer sequence	X		X	
	B1 Bell answer tone	X		X	
Cn	Transmitter On/Off	X	X	X	X
	C0 Transmitter Off	X	X	X	X
	C1 Transmitter On-Default	X	X	X	X
Dn	Dial number n and go into originate mode Use any of these options:	X	X	X	X
	P Pulse dial-Default	X	X	X	X
	T Touch-Tone dial	X	X	X	X
	, (Comma) Pause for 2 seconds	X	X	X	X
	; Return to command state after dialing	X	X	X	X

(continues)

Table 11.6 Continued

Command	Modem Functions and Options		USR Dual	USR 2400	Hayes 2400	Hayes 1200
	"...	Dial the letters that follow	X	X		
	!	Flash switch-hook to transfer call	X	X	X	
	W	Wait for 2nd dial tone (if X3 or higher is set)	X	X	X	
	@	Wait for an answer (if X3 or higher is set)	X	X	X	
	R	Reverse frequencies	X	X	X	X
	S	Dial stored number			X	
DL	Dial the last-dialed number		X			
DSn	Dial number stored in NVRAM at position n		X			
En	Command mode local echo; not applicable after a connection has been made		X	X	X	X
	E0	Echo Off	X	X	X	X
	E1	Echo On	X	X	X	X
Fn	Local echo On/Off when a connection has been made		X	X	X	X
	F0	Echo On (Half duplex)	X	X	X	X
	F1	Echo Off (Full duplex)-Default	X	X	X	X
Hn	On/Off hook control		X	X	X	X
	H0	Hang up (go on hook)-Default	X	X	X	X
	H1	Go off hook	X	X	X	X
In	Inquiry		X	X	X	X
	I0	Return product code	X	X	X	X
	I1	Return memory (ROM) checksum	X	X	X	X
	I2	Run memory (RAM) test	X	X	X	
	I3	Return call duration/real time	X	X		
	I4	Return current modem settings	X	X		
	I5	Return NVRAM settings	X			
	I6	Return link diagnostics	X			
	I7	Return product configuration	X			
Kn	Modem clock operation		X			
	K0	ATI3 displays call duration-Default	X			
	K1	ATI3 displays real time; set with ATI3=HH:MM:SSK1	X			
Ln	Loudness of speaker volume;				X	
	L0	Low			X	
	L1	Low			X	
	L2	Medium			X	
	L3	High			X	

Command	Modem Functions and Options	USR Dual	USR 2400	Hayes 2400	Hayes 1200
Mn	Monitor (speaker) control	X	X	X	X
	M0 Speaker always Off	X	X	X	X
	M1 Speaker On until carrier is established-Default	X	X	X	X
	M2 Speaker always On	X	X	X	X
	M3 Speaker On after last digit dialed, Off at carrier detect	X	X	X	X
O	Return on-line after command execution	X	X	X	X
	O0 Return on-line, normal	X	X	X	X
	O1 Return on-line, retrain	X	X	X	X
P	Pulse dial	X	X	X	X
Qn	Result codes display	X	X	X	X
	Q0 Result codes displayed	X	X	X	X
	Q1 Result codes suppressed (quiet mode)	X	X	X	X
	Q2 Quiet in answer mode only	X			
Sr=n	Set Register commands: r is any S-register; n must be a decimal number between 0 and 255.	X	X	X	X
Sr.b=n	Set bit .b of register r to n (0/Off or 1/On)	X			
Sr?	Query register r	X	X	X	X
T	Tone dial	X	X	X	X
Vn	Verbal/Numeric result codes	X	X	X	X
	V0 Numeric mode	X	X	X	X
	V1 Verbal mode	X	X	X	X
Xn	Result code options	X	X	X	X
Yn	Long space disconnect			X	
	Y0 Disabled			X	
	Y1 Enabled; disconnects after 1.5-second break			X	
Z	Software reset	X	X	X	X
+++	Escape code sequence, preceded and followed by at least one second of no data transmission	X	X		
/(Slash)	Pause for 125 msec	X			
>	Repeat command continuously or up to 10 dial attempts Cancel by pressing any key	X	X		
$	Online Help - Basic command summary	X	X		
&$	Online Help - Ampersand command summary	X			
%$	Online Help - Percent command summary	X			

(continues)

Table 11.6 Continued

Command	Modem Functions and Options	USR Dual	USR 2400	Hayes 2400	Hayes 1200
D$	Online Help - Dial command summary	X	X		
S$	Online Help - S-register summary	X	X		
<Ctrl>-S	Stop/restart display of HELP screens		X		
<Ctrl>-C	Cancel display HELP screens		X		
<Ctrl>-K	Cancel display HELP screens		X		
Extended command set					
&An	ARQ result codes 14-17, 19	X			
	&A0 Suppress ARQ result codes	X			
	&A1 Display ARQ result codes-Default	X			
	&A2 Display HST and V.32 result codes	X			
	&A3 Display protocol result codes	X			
&Bn	Data Rate, terminal-to-modem (DTE/DCE)	X			
	&B0 DTE rate follows connection rate-Default	X			
	&B1 Fixed DTE rate	X			
	&B2 Fixed DTE rate in ARQ mode; variable DTE rate in non-ARQ mode	X			
&Cn	Carrier Detect (CD) operations	X		X	
	&C0 CD override	X		X	
	&C1 Normal CD operations	X		X	
&Dn	Data Terminal Ready (DTR) operations	X		X	
	&D0 DTR override	X		X	
	&D1 DTR Off; goes to command state			X	
	&D2 DTR Off; goes to command state and on hook	X		X	
	&D3 DTR Off; resets modem			X	
&F	Load factory settings into RAM	X		X	
&Gn	Guard tone	X		X	
	&G0 No guard tone; U.S., Canada-Default	X		X	
	&G1 Guard tone; some European countries	X		X	
	&G2 Guard tone; U.K., requires B0	X		X	
&Hn	Transmit Data flow control	X			
	&H0 Flow control disabled-Default	X			
	&H1 Hardware (CTS) flow control	X			
	&H2 Software (XON/XOFF) flow control	X			
	&H3 Hardware and software control	X			
&In	Received Data software flow control	X			
	&I0 Flow control disabled-Default	X			
	&I1 XON/XOFF to local modem and remote computer	X			

Command	Modem Functions and Options	USR Dual	USR 2400	Hayes 2400	Hayes 1200
Extended command set					
	&I2 XON/XOFF to local modem only	X			
	&I3 Host mode, Hewlett-Packard protocol	X			
	&I4 Terminal mode, Hewlett-Packard protocol	X			
	&I5 ARQ mode-same as &I2; non-ARQ mode; look for incoming XON/XOFF	X			
&Jn	Telephone jack selection			X	
	&J0 RJ-11/ RJ-41S/ RJ-45S			X	
	&J1 RJ-12/ RJ-13			X	
&Kn	Data compression	X			
	&K0 Disabled	X			
	&K1 Auto enable/disable-Default	X			
	&K2 Enabled	X			
	&K3 V.42bis only	X			
&Ln	Normal/Leased line operation	X		X	
	&L0 Normal phone line-Default	X		X	
	&L1 Leased line	X		X	
&Mn	Error Control/Synchronous Options	X		X	
	&M0 Normal mode, no error control	X		X	
	&M1 Synch mode	X		X	
	&M2 Synch mode 2 - stored number dialing			X	
	&M3 Synch mode 3 - manual dialing	X			
	&M4 Normal/ARQ mode-Normal if ARQ connection cannot be made-Default	X			
	&M5 ARQ mode-hang up if ARQ connection cannot be made	X			
&Nn	Data Rate, data link (DCE/DCE)	X			
	&N0 Normal link operations-Default	X			
	&N1 300 bps	X			
	&N2 1200 bps	X			
	&N3 2400 bps	X			
	&N4 4800 bps	X			
	&N5 7200 bps	X			
	&N6 9600 bps	X			
	&N7 12K bps	X			
	&N8 14.4K bps	X			
&Pn	Pulse dial make/break ratio	X		X	
	&P0 North America-Default	X		X	
	&P1 British Commonwealth	X		X	

(continues)

Table 11.6 Continued

Command	Modem Functions and Options	USR Dual	USR 2400	Hayes 2400	Hayes 1200
Extended command set					
&Rn	Received Data hardware (RTS) flow control	X		X	
	&R0 CTS tracks RTS	X		X	
	&R1 Ignore RTS-Default	X		X	
	&R2 Pass received data on RTS high; used Pass received data on RTS high; used	X			
&Sn	Data Set Ready (DSR) override	X		X	
	&S0 DSR override (always On-Default)	X		X	
	&S1 Modem controls DSR	X		X	
	&S2 Pulsed DSR; CTS follows CD	X			
	&S3 Pulsed DSR	X			
&Tn	Modem Testing	X		X	
	&T0 End testing	X		X	
	&T1 Analog loopback	X		X	
	&T2 Reserved	X			
	&T3 Digital loopback	X		X	
	&T4 Grant remote digital loopback	X		X	
	&T5 Deny remote digital loopback	X		X	
	&T6 Initiate remote digital loopback	X		X	
	&T7 Remote digital loopback with self test	X		X	
	&T8 Analog loopback with self test	X		X	
&W	Write current settings to NVRAM	X		X	
&Xn	Synchronous timing source	X		X	
	&X0 Modem's transmit clock-Default	X		X	
	&X1 Terminal equipment	X		X	
	&X2 Modem's receiver clock	X		X	
&Yn	Break handling. Destructive breaks clear the buffer; expedited Breaks are sent immediately to remote system.	X			
	&Y0 Destructive, but don't send break	X			
	&Y1 Destructive, expedited-Default	X			
	&Y2 Nondestructive, expedited	X			
	&Y3 Nondestructive, unexpedited	X			
&Zn=L	Store last-dialed phone number in NVRAM at position n	X			
&Zn=s	Write phone number(s) to NVRAM at position n (0-3); 36 characters maximum	X			
&Zn?	Display phone number in NVRAM at position n (n=0-3)	X		X	

Command	Modem Functions and Options	USR Dual	USR 2400	Hayes 2400	Hayes 1200
Extended command set					
%Rn	Remote access to Rack Controller Unit (RCU)	X			
	%R0 Disabled	X			
	%R1 Enabled	X			
%T	Enable Touch-Tone recognition	X			
Modem S-Register Functions and Defaults					
S0	Number of rings before automatic answering when DIP switch 5 is UP. Default = 1. S0 = 0 disables Auto Answer, equivalent to DIP switch 5 Down	SW5	SW5	0	SW5
S1	Counts and stores number of rings from incoming call	0	0	0	0
S2	Define escape code character. Default = +	43	43	43	43
S3	Define ASCII carriage return	13	13	13	13
S4	Define ASCII line feed	10	10	10	10
S5	Define ASCII Backspace	8	8	8	8
S6	Number of seconds modem waits before dialing	2	2	2	2
S7	Number of seconds modem waits for a carrier	60	30	30	30
S8	Duration (sec) for pause (,) option in Dial command and pause between command reexecutions for Repeat (>) command	2	2	2	2
S9	Duration (.1 sec units) of remote carrier signal before recognition	6	6	6	6
S10	Duration (.1 sec units) modem waits after loss of carrier before hanging up	7	7	7	7
S11	Duration and spacing (ms) of dialed Touch-Tones	70	70	70	70
S12	Guard time (in .02 sec units) for escape code sequence	50	50	50	50
S13	Bit-mapped register:	0			
	1 Reset when DTR drops				
	2 Auto answer in originate mode				
	4 Disable result code pause				
	8 DS0 on DTR low-to-high				
	16 DS0 on power up, ATZ				
	32 Disable HST modulation				
	64 Disable MNP Level 3				
	128 Watchdog hardware reset				
S15	Bit-mapped register:	0			
	1 Disable high-frequency equalization				
	2 Disable on-line fallback				
	4 Force 300-bps back channel				

(continues)

Table 11.6 Continued

Command	Modem Functions and Options	USR Dual	USR 2400	Hayes 2400	Hayes 1200
Modem S-Register Functions and Defaults					
	8 Set non-ARQ transmit buffer to 128 bytes				
	16 Disable MNP Level 4				
	32 Set Del as Backspace key				
	64 Unusual MNP incompatibility				
	128 Custom applications only				
S16	Bit-mapped register:	0	0	0	
	1 Analog loopback				
	2 Dial test				
	4 Test pattern				
	8 Initiate remote digital loopback				
	16 Reserved				
	32 Reserved				
	64 Reserved				
	128 Reserved				
S18	&Tn Test timer, disabled when set to 0	0		0	
S19	Set inactivity timer in minutes	0			
S21	Length of Break, DCE to DTE, in 10ms units	10		0	
S22	Define ASCII XON	17		17	
S23	Define ASCII XOFF	19		19	
S24	Duration (20ms units) of pulsed DSR when modem is set to &S2 or &S3	150			
S25	Delay to DTR	5			
S26	Duration (10ms units) of delay between RTS and CTS, synchronous mode	1		1	
S27	Bit-mapped register:	0			
	1 Enable V.21 modulation, 300 bps				
	2 Enable unencoded V.32 modulation				
	4 Disable V.32 modulation				
	8 Disable 2100 Hz answer tone				
	16 Disable MNP handshake				
	32 Disable V.42 Detect phase				
	64 Reserved				
	128 Unusual software incompatibility				
S28	Duration (.1 sec units) of V.21/V.23 handshake delay	8			
S32	Voice/Data switch options:	1			
	0 Disabled				
	1 Go off hook in originate mode				

Command	Modem Functions and Options		USR Dual	USR 2400	Hayes 2400	Hayes 1200
Modem S-Register Functions and Defaults						
	2	Go off hook in answer mode				
	3	Redial last-dialed number				
	4	Dial number stored at position 0				
	5	Auto answer toggle On/Off				
	6	Reset modem				
	7	Initiate remote digital loopback				
S34	Bit-mapped register:		0			
	1	Disable V.32bis				
	2	Disable enhanced V.32 mode				
	4	Disable quick V.32 retrain				
	8	Enable V.23 modulation				
	16	Change MR LED to DSR				
	32	Enable MI/MIC				
	64	Reserved				
	128	Reserved				
S38	Duration (sec) before disconnect when DTR drops during an ARQ call		0			

ARQ = Automatic repeat request
ASCII = American Standard Code for Information Interchange
BPS = Bits per second
CCITT = Consultative Committee for International Telephone and Telegraph
CD = Carrier cetect
CRC = Cyclic redundancy check
DCE = Data communications equipment
DTE = Data terminal equipment
EIA = Electronic Industries Association
HDLC = High-level data link control
HST = High-speed technology
Hz = Hertz
LAPM = Link access procedure for modems
MI/MIC = Mode indicate/Mode indicate common
MNP = Microcom networking protocol
NVRAM = Non-volatile memory
RAM = Random-access memory
ROM = Read-only memory
DTR = Data terminal ready
SDLC = Synchronous Data Link Control
MR = Modem ready
LED = Light-emitting diode
CTS = Clear to send
RTS = Ready to send
DSR = Data set ready

Modulation Standards. Modems start with modulation, which is the electronic signaling method used by the modem (from modulator to demodulator). Modems must use the same modulation method to understand each other. Each data rate uses a different modulation method, and sometimes, more than one method exists for a particular rate.

The three most popular modulation methods are frequency-shift keying (FSK), phase-shift keying (PSK), and quadrature-amplitude modulation (QAM). FSK is a form of frequency modulation, otherwise known as FM. By causing and monitoring frequency changes in a signal sent over the phone line, two modems can send information. PSK is a form of phase modulation, in which the timing of the carrier signal wave is altered and the frequency stays the same. QAM is a modulation technique that combines phase changes with signal-amplitude variations, resulting in a signal that can carry more information than the other methods.

Baud versus Bits Per Second (bps). Baud rate and the bit rate often are confused in discussions about modems. Baud rate is the rate at which a signal between two devices changes in one second. If a signal between two modems can change frequency or phase at a rate of 300 times per second, for example, that device is said to communicate at 300 baud. Sometimes a single modulation change is used to carry a single bit. In that case, 300 baud also equals 300 bits per second (bps). If the modem could signal two bit values for each signal change, the bit-per-second rate would be twice the baud rate, or 600 bps at 300 baud. Most modems transmit several bits per baud so that the actual baud rate is much slower than the bit-per-second rate. In fact, people usually use the term baud incorrectly. We normally are not interested in the raw baud rate but in the bit-per-second rate, which is the true gauge of communications speed.

Bell 103. Bell 103 is a U.S. and Canadian 300-bps modulation standard. It uses frequency-shift-keying (FSK) modulation at 300 baud to transmit one bit per baud. Most higher-speed modems will still communicate using this protocol, even though it is obsolete.

Bell 212A. Bell 212A is the U.S. and Canadian 1200-bps modulation standard. It uses differential phase-shift keying (DPSK) at 600 baud to transmit two bits per baud.

V.21. V.21 is an international data-transmission standard for 300-bps communications similar to Bell 103. Because of some differences in the frequencies used, Bell 103 modems are not compatible with V.21 modems. This standard is used primarily outside the United States.

V.22. V.22 is an international 1200-bps data-transmission standard. This standard is similar to the Bell 212A standard but is incompatible in some areas, especially in answering a call. This standard was used primarily outside the United States.

V.22bis. V.22bis is a data-transmission standard for 2400-bps communications. Bis is Latin for second, indicating that this data transmission is an improvement to or follows V.22. This data transmission is an international standard for 2400 bps and is used inside and outside the United States. V.22bis uses quadrature-amplitude modulation (QAM) at 600 baud and transmits four bits per baud to achieve 2400 bps.

V.23. V.23 is a split data-transmission standard, operating at 1200 bps in one direction and 75 bps in the reverse direction. Therefore, the modem is only pseudo-full-duplex, meaning that it can transmit data in both directions simultaneously but not at the maximum data rate. This standard was developed to lower the cost of 1200-bps modem technology, which was expensive in the early 1980s. This standard was used primarily in Europe.

V.29. V.29 is a data-transmission standard at 9600 bps, which defines a half duplex (one-way) modulation technique. This standard generally is used in Group III facsimile (fax) transmissions and only rarely in modems. Because V.29 is a half-duplex method, it is substantially easier to implement this high-speed standard than to implement a high-speed full-duplex standard. As a modem standard, V.29 has not been fully defined, so V.29 modems of different brands seldom can communicate with each other. This does not affect fax machines, which have a fully defined standard.

V.32. V.32 is a full-duplex (two-way) data transmission standard that runs at 9600 bps. It is a full modem standard and also includes forward error-correcting and negotiation standards. V.32 uses TCQAM (trellis coded quadrature amplitude modulation) at 2400 baud to transmit 4 bits per baud, resulting in the 9600-bps transmission speed. The trellis coding is a special forward error-correction technique that creates an additional bit for each packet of 4. This extra check bit is used to allow on-the-fly error correction to take place at the other end. It also greatly increases the resistance of V.32 to noise on the line. In the past, V.32 has been expensive to implement because the technology it requires is complex. Because a one-way, 9600-bps stream uses almost the entire bandwidth of the phone line, V.32 modems implement echo cancellation, meaning that they cancel out the overlapping signal that their own modems transmit and just listen to the other modem's signal. This procedure is complicated and was at one time costly. Advances in lower-cost chipsets then made these modems inexpensive, and they were the de facto 9600-bps standard for some time.

V.32bis. V.32bis is a 14,400-bps extension to V.32. This protocol uses TCQAM modulation at 2400 baud to transmit 6 bits per baud, for an effective rate of 14,400 bits per second. The trellis coding makes the connection more reliable. This protocol is also a full-duplex modulation protocol with a fallback to V.32 if the phone line is impaired. It is the communications standard for dial-up lines because of its excellent performance and resistance to noise. I recommend the V.32bis-type modem.

V.32fast. V.32fast or V.FC (Fast Class) as it is also called, was a new standard being proposed to the CCITT. V.32fast is an extension to V.32 and V.32bis but offers a transmission speed of 28,800 bits per second. It has been superseded by V.34.

V.34. V.34 is the latest in the world of modem standards. It has superseded all the other 28.8 Kbps standards and is the current state of the art in analog modem communications. It has been proven as the most reliable standard of communication at 28,800 bits per second. A recent annex to the V.34 standard also defines optional higher speeds of 31.2 and 33.6 Kbps, which most of the newer V.34 modems will be capable of. Many existing V.34 modems designed using sophisticated Digital Signal Processors (DSPs) can be upgraded to support the new 33.6 Kbps speeds by merely installing a software upgrade in the modem. This is accomplished by downloading the Modem ROM upgrade from the manufacturer and then running a program they supply to "flash" the modem's ROM with the new code.

V.34 is the fastest communication now possible over an analog serial connection. It is also the fastest that analog communications are likely to get. Looming on the horizon is that the phone system eventually will be digital. All further development on analog transmission schemes will end, and new digital modems will be developed.

Error-Correction Protocols. Error correction refers to the capability of some modems to identify errors during a transmission and to automatically resend data that appears to have been damaged in transit. For error correction to work, both modems must adhere to the same correction standard. Fortunately, most modem manufacturers adhere to the same error-correction standards.

V.42. V.42 is an error-correction protocol, with fallback to MNP 4. MNP stands for Microcom Networking Protocol (covered later in this section), and Version 4 is an error-correction protocol as well. Because the V.42 standard includes MNP compatibility through Class 4, all MNP 4 compatible modems can establish error-controlled connections with V.42 modems. This standard uses a protocol called LAPM (Link Access Procedure for Modems). LAPM, like MNP, copes with phone-line impairments by automatically retransmitting data corrupted during transmission, assuring that only error-free data passes between the modems. V.42 is considered to be better than MNP 4 because it offers about a 20 percent higher transfer rate due to its more intelligent algorithms.

Data-Compression Standards. Data compression refers to a built-in capability in some modems to compress the data they're sending, thus saving time and money for long-distance modem users. Depending on the type of files that are sent, data can be compressed to a fourth of its original size, effectively quadrupling the speed of the modem. For example, a 14,400 modem with compression can yield transmission rates of up to 57,600 bps, and a 28,800 can yield up to 115,200 bps.

V.42bis. V.42bis is a CCITT data-compression standard similar to MNP Class 5 but providing about 35 percent better compression. V.42bis is not actually compatible with MNP Class 5, but nearly all V.42bis modems include the MNP 5 data-compression capability as well.

This protocol can sometimes quadruple throughput, depending on the compression technique used. This fact has led to some mildly false advertising: for example, a 2400-bps V.42bis modem might advertise "9600 bps throughput" by including V.42bis as well, but this would be possible in only extremely optimistic cases, such as in sending text files that are very loosely packed. In the same manner, many 9600-bps V.42bis makers now advertise "up to 38.4K bps throughput" by virtue of the compression. Just make sure that you see the truth behind such claims.

V.42bis is superior to MNP 5 because it analyzes the data first and then determines whether compression would be useful. V.42bis only compresses data that needs compression. Files found on bulletin board systems often are compressed already (using PKZIP or a similar program). Further attempts at compressing already compressed data can increase the size of the file and slow things down. MNP 5 always attempts to compress the data, which slows down throughput on previously compressed files. V.42bis, however, compresses only data that will benefit from the compression.

To negotiate a standard connection using V.42bis, V.42 also must be present. Therefore, a modem with V.42bis data compression is assumed to include V.42 error correction. These two protocols, when combined, result in an error-free connection that has the maximum data compression possible.

Proprietary Standards. In addition to the industry-standard protocols for modulation, error correction, and data compression that generally are set forth or approved by the ITU-T, several protocols in these areas were invented by various companies and included in their products without any official endorsement by any standards body. Some of these protocols have been quite popular at times and became pseudo-standards of their own.

The most successful proprietary protocols are the MNP (Microcom Networking Protocols) that were developed by Microcom. These error-correction and data-compression protocols are supported widely by other modem manufacturers as well. Another company that has been successful in establishing proprietary protocols as limited standards is U.S. Robotics with its HST (high speed technology) modulation protocols. Because of an aggressive marketing campaign with bulletin board system operators, it captured a large portion of the market with its products in the 1980s.

This section examines these and other proprietary modem protocols.

HST. The HST is a 14400-bps and 9600-bps modified half-duplex proprietary modulation protocol used by U.S. Robotics. Although common in bulletin board systems, the HST is now all but extinct, due to V.32 modems having become more competitive in price. HST modems run at 9600 bps or 14400 bps in one direction, and 300 or 450 bps in the other direction. This is an ideal protocol for interactive sessions. Because echo-cancellation circuitry is not required, costs are lower.

U.S. Robotics also marketed modems that used the standard protocols as well as their proprietary standard. These dual standard modems incorporated both V.32bis and HST protocols, giving you the best of the standard and proprietary worlds and enabling you to connect to virtually any other system at the maximum communications rate. They were at one time among the best modems available; I used and recommended them for many years.

DIS. The DIS is a 9600-bps proprietary modulation protocol by CompuCom, which uses dynamic impedance stabilization (DIS) with claimed superiority in noise rejection over V.32. Implementation appears to be very inexpensive, but like HST, only one company makes modems with the DIS standard. Because of the lower costs of V.32 and V.32bis, this proprietary standard will likely disappear.

MNP. MNP (Microcom Networking Protocol) offers end-to-end error correction, meaning that the modems are capable of detecting transmission errors and requesting retransmission of corrupted data. Some levels of MNP also provide data compression.

As MNP evolved, different classes of the standard were defined, describing the extent to which a given MNP implementation supports the protocol. Most current implementations support Classes 1 through 5. Higher classes usually are unique to modems manufactured by Microcom, Inc. because they are proprietary.

MNP generally is used for its error-correction capabilities, but MNP Classes 4 and 5 also provide performance increases, with Class 5 offering real-time data compression. The lower classes of MNP usually are not important to you as a modem user, but they are included in the following list for the sake of completeness:

- MNP Class 1 (block mode) uses asynchronous, byte-oriented, half-duplex (one-way) transmission. This method provides about 70 percent efficiency and error correction only, so it's rarely used today.

- MNP Class 2 (stream mode) uses asynchronous, byte-oriented, full-duplex (two-way) transmission. This class also provides error correction only. Because of protocol overhead (the time it takes to establish the protocol and operate it), throughput at Class 2 is only about 84 percent of that for a connection without MNP, delivering about 202 cps (characters per second) at 2400 bps (240 cps is the theoretical maximum). Class 2 is used rarely today.

- MNP Class 3 incorporates Class 2 and is more efficient. It uses a synchronous, bit-oriented, full-duplex method. The improved procedure yields throughput about 108 percent of that of a modem without MNP, delivering about 254 cps at 2400 bps.

- MNP Class 4 is a performance-enhancement class that uses Adaptive Packet Assembly and Optimized Data Phase techniques. Class 4 improves throughput and performance by about 5 percent, although actual increases depend on the type of call and connection and can be as high as 25 percent to 50 percent.

- MNP Class 5 is a data-compression protocol that uses a real-time adaptive algorithm. It can increase throughput up to 50 percent, but the actual performance of Class 5 depends on the type of data being sent. Raw text files allow the highest increase, although program files cannot be compressed as much, and the increase is smaller. On precompressed data (files already compressed with ARC, PKZIP, and so on), MNP 5 decreases performance and, therefore, is often disabled on BBS systems.

V-Series. The Hayes V-series is a proprietary error-correction protocol by Hayes that was used in some of its modems. Since the advent of lower cost V.32 and V.32bis modems (even from Hayes), the V-series has all but become extinct. These modems used a modified V.29 protocol, which is sometimes called a ping-pong protocol because it has one high-speed channel and one low-speed channel that alternate back and forth.

CSP. The CSP (CompuCom Speed Protocol) is an error-correction and data-compression protocol available on CompuCom DIS modems.

FAXModem Standards. Facsimile technology is a science unto itself, although it has many similarities to data communications. These similarities have led to the combination of data and faxes into the same modem. You now can purchase a single board that will send and receive both data and faxes. All of the major modem manufacturers have models that support this capability.

Over the years, the CCITT has set international standards for fax transmission. This has led to the grouping of faxes into one of four groups. Each group (I through IV) uses different technology and standards for transmitting and receiving faxes. Groups I and II are relatively slow and provide results that are unacceptable by today's standards. Group III is the standard in use today by virtually all fax machines, including those combined with modems. Whereas Groups I through III are analog in nature (similar to modems), Group IV is digital and designed for use with ISDN or other digital networks. Because the telephone system has not been converted to a fully digital network yet, there are very few Group IV fax systems available.

Group III Fax. There are two general subdivisions within the Group III fax standard—Class 1 and Class 2. Many times you will hear about a FAXModem supporting Group III, Class 1 fax communications. This simply indicates which protocols the board is able to send and receive. If your FAXModem does this, it can communicate with most of the other fax machines in the world. In FAXModems, the Class 1 specification is implemented by an additional group of modem commands that the modem translates and acts upon.

Earlier you learned about the V.29 modulation standard. As stated in that section, this standard is used for Group III fax transmissions.

Modem Recommendations. Today the cost of 28,800-bps modems has dropped to between $100 and $200, on average, including FAX capabilities. If you want top performance, make sure your V.34 modem conforms to the new V.34 Annex 12, which adds two new higher speeds of 31.2 Kbps and 33.6 Kbps. I would normally recommend that you purchase an internal modem if your computer has space for it; however, I prefer external modems myself, due to the additional troubleshooting capabilities possible by watching the LEDs that indicate the modem's status. Internal modems usually ship with a high speed UART on the modem card, thus eliminating the need to upgrade any older, slower UARTs you may have in your PC. If you don't have an internal slot for a modem, be sure that you have the appropriate UART. Today, most modems come with multiple forms of error correction or data compression. Based on the discussions earlier in this chapter, you should search for the modem that offers the best combination of speed, error correction, and data compression.

Secrets of Modem Negotiation. If you are curious about the complex negotiations that occur when two modems connect, two detailed descriptions of modem handshaking follow. The two examples of connections use V.22bis and V.32. These sequences may differ slightly depending on your modem, and can get more complicated when you combine different modem types into one box. Making a V.22bis connection between two modems involves the following sequence of events:

1. The answering modem detects a ring, goes off-hook, and waits for at least two seconds of billing delay (required by phone company rules so that no data passes before the network recognizes that the call has been connected).

2. The answering modem transmits an answer tone (which is described in CCITT Recommendation V.25, occurs at 2100 Hz, and lasts 3.3 ± 0.7 seconds). The answer tone tells manual-dial originators that they have reached a modem and can put their calling modem in data mode and informs the network that data is going to be transferred so that echo suppressers in the network can be disabled. If the echo suppressers remain enabled, you cannot transmit in both directions at the same time. (The originating modem remains silent throughout this period.)
3. The answering modem goes silent for 75 ± 20 milliseconds (ms) to separate the answer tone from the signals that follow.
4. The answering modem transmits unscrambled binary 1s at 1200 bits per second (USB1), which cause the static, or hash sound, you hear after the answer tone. This sound is slightly higher in pitch than the answer tone because the signal's major components are at 2250 Hz and 2550 Hz.
5. The originating modem detects the USB1 signal in 155 ± 10 ms and remains silent for 456 ± 10 ms.
6. The originating modem transmits unscrambled double-digit 00s and 11s at 1200 bits (S1) for 100 ± 3 ms. A Bell 212 or V.22 modem does not transmit this S1 signal, and it is by the presence or absence of this single 100-ms signal that V.22bis knows whether to fall back to 1200-bps operation.
7. When the answering modem (which is still transmitting the USB1 signal) detects the S1 signal from the originator, it also sends 100 ms of S1 so that the originating modem knows that the answerer is capable of 2400-bps operation.
8. The originating modem then switches to sending scrambled binary 1s at 1200 bits (SB1). Scrambling has nothing to do with encryption or security but is simply a method by which the signal is whitened, or randomized, to even out the power across the entire bandwidth. White noise is a term given by engineers to totally random noise patterns.
9. The answering modem switches to sending SB1 for 500 ms.
10. The answering modem switches to sending scrambled 1s at 2400 bps for 200 ms. After that, it is ready to pass data.
11. 600 ms after the originating modem hears SB1 from the answerer, it switches to sending scrambled 1s at 2400 bps. It does this for 200 ms, and then is ready to pass data.

The signals involved in a V.32 connection are more complicated than V.22bis because of the need to measure the total round-trip delay in the circuit so that the echo cancellers work. Making a V.32 connection involves the following sequence of events:

1. The answering modem detects a ring, goes off-hook, and waits two seconds (the billing delay).

2. The answering modem transmits a V.25 answer tone, but it is different from the preceding example. The phase of the signal is reversed every 450 ms, which sounds like little clicks. These phase reversals inform the network that the modems themselves are going to do echo cancellation, and that any echo cancellers in the network should be disabled so as not to interfere with the modems.

3. The originating V.32 modem does not wait for the end of the answer tone. After one second, it responds with an 1800-Hz tone, which in V.32 is known as signal AA. Sending this signal before the end of the answer tone enables the answering modem to know, very early, that it is talking to another V.32 modem.

4. After the answer tone ends (3.3 ± 0.7 seconds), if the answering modem heard signal AA, it proceeds to try to connect as V.32 immediately. If it did not hear AA, it first tries, for three seconds, to connect as a V.22bis modem (sends signal USB1 and waits for a response). If it does not get a response to USB1, it goes back to trying to connect as a V.32 modem because of the possibility that the calling V.32 modem didn't hear the answer tone, was manually dialed and switched to data mode late, or is an older V.32 model that does not respond to the answer tone.

5. To connect in V.32, the answering modem sends signal AC, which is 600 Hz and 3000 Hz sent together, for at least 64 symbol intervals (1/2400 of a second). It then reverses the phase of the signal, making it into signal CA.

6. When the originating modem detects this phase reversal, in 64 ± 2 symbol intervals, it reverses the phase of its own signal, making AA into CC.

7. When the answer modem detects this phase reversal (in 64 ± 2 symbol intervals), it again reverses the phase of its signal, making CA back into AC. This exchange of phase reversals enables the modems to accurately time the total propagation (round trip) delay of the circuit so that the echo cancellers can be set to properly cancel signal echoes.

8. The modems go into a half-duplex exchange of training signals to train the adaptive equalizers, test the quality of the phone line, and agree on the data rate to be used. The answering modem transmits first, from 650 ms to 3525 ms, and then goes silent.

9. The originating modem responds with a similar signal, but then leaves its signal on while the answering modem responds one more time, establishing the final agreed-on data rate.

10. Both modems then switch to sending scrambled binary 1 (marks) for at least 128 symbol intervals, and then are ready to pass data.

As you can see, these procedures are quite complicated. Although you do not need to understand these communications protocols to use a modem, you can get an idea of what you're hearing when the connection is being established.

Integrated Services Digital Network (ISDN)

ISDN modems are the next step in telecommunications. ISDN modems make the break from the old technology of analog data transfer to the newer digital data transfer. Digital technology allows you to send voice, data, images, and faxes simultaneously over the same pair of wires at up to 128Kbps. ISDN modems required an ISDN service for connection, which is more readily available today. Prices for ISDN service vary widely, depending on your location. U.S. prices—on average—are approximately $130 to $150 for the initial installation and $50 to $60 a month. There is usually a connect-time charge as well that can range from 1 to 6 cents a minute. These are all line charges paid to the telephone company. You will also have to purchase an ISDN modem, and there will be an additional charge from your service provider for Internet Access at ISDN speeds.

ISDN has become extremely popular in Europe, where leased lines are often prohibitively expensive. ISDN modems have also dropped considerably in price; what was once a $1,500 to $2,000 device can now be purchased for as little as $400. As demands for more bandwidth increase and conventional asynchronous modem standards become more inadequate, ISDN should gain in popularity, causing prices to drop further. ISDN modems are far more complex than standard analog modems. ISDN modems have three separate channels. Two of the channels are called B channels; these are the data carrying channels and are 64Kbps each. The third channel is the D channel, which is 16Kbps. The slower D channel is used for routing and handling information. It is this technology that is making it possible for more and more people to participate in video conferencing.

To be technically precise, ISDN devices are not "modems." Modems modulate digital signals so they can be transmitted over an analog phone line and then demodulate the signal back to digital form for the computer. ISDN runs over an entirely digital telephone network (most of the telephone infrastructure in the United States is now digital), so there is no need for the modulation and demodulation processes. The most common type of ISDN device for a PC is called a terminal adapter. ISDN can be implemented as either a serial device or as a network interface. Using a network type interface eliminates the bottleneck at the computer's serial port. This type of ISDN terminal adapter may be the preferred solution for reasons of performance, even if you have only one computer and don't need the other services provided by a network.

ISDN requires additional telephone wiring and service from the telephone company. You will first need to check with your local telephone company to see if ISDN service is available in your area. (It is now available in most parts of the U.S.) In many cases, this can be the most difficult part of the installation. ISDN service, although available for many years, is only beginning to become a popular item. Often, the first hurdle to overcome is finding someone at the telephone company who knows what ISDN is. Then, you will find that prices can vary widely, depending on the distance between your location and the nearest phone company POP (point of presence). You can have the telephone company install the wiring and jacks or install them yourself, if you are so inclined. Que's *Special Edition Using ISDN* has excellent detailed coverage of the wiring process for the ISDN do-it-yourselfer.

Parallel Ports

A parallel port has eight lines for sending all the bits that comprise one byte of data simultaneously across eight wires. This interface is fast and usually is reserved for printers rather than computer-to-computer communications. The only problem with parallel ports is that their cables cannot be extended for any great length without amplifying the signal, or errors occur in the data. Table 11.7 shows the pinout for a standard PC parallel port.

Table 11.7 25-Pin PC-Compatible Parallel Port Connector

Pin	Description	I/O
1	-Strobe	Out
2	+Data Bit 0	Out
3	+Data Bit 1	Out
4	+Data Bit 2	Out
5	+Data Bit 3	Out
6	+Data Bit 4	Out
7	+Data Bit 5	Out
8	+Data Bit 6	Out
9	+Data Bit 7	Out
10	-Acknowledge	In
11	+Busy	In
12	+Paper End	In
13	+Select	In
14	-Auto Feed	Out
15	-Error	In
16	-Initialize Printer	Out
17	-Select Input	Out
18	-Data Bit 0 Return (GND)	In
19	-Data Bit 1 Return (GND)	In
20	-Data Bit 2 Return (GND)	In
21	-Data Bit 3 Return (GND)	In
22	-Data Bit 4 Return (GND)	In
23	-Data Bit 5 Return (GND)	In
24	-Data Bit 6 Return (GND)	In
25	-Data Bit 7 Return (GND)	In

Over the years, several types of parallel ports have evolved. Some of them are IBM specific, while others can be found in any PC compatible system. Here are the primary types of parallel ports found in systems today:

- Unidirectional (4-bit)
- Bidirectional (8-bit)

- Type 1 (standard)
- DMA Type 3 (IBM specific)
- Enhanced Parallel Port (EPP)
- Enhanced Capabilities Port (ECP)

The following sections discuss each of these types of parallel ports.

Unidirectional (4-bit). The original IBM PC did not have different types of parallel ports available. The only port available was the parallel port used to send information from the computer to a device, such as a printer. This is not to say that bidirectional parallel ports were not available; indeed, they were common in other computers on the market and in hobbyist computers at the time.

The unidirectional nature of the original PC parallel port is consistent with its primary use—that is, sending data to a printer. There were times, however, when it was desirable to have a bidirectional port—for example, when you needed feedback from a printer, which is common with PostScript printers. This could not be done with the original unidirectional ports.

Although it was never intended to be used for input, a clever scheme was devised where four of the signal lines could be used as a 4-bit input connection. Thus, these ports can do 8-bit byte output and 4-bit (nibble) input. This is still very common on low-end desktop systems. Systems built after 1993 are likely to have more capable parallel ports, such as 8bit, EPP, or ECP.

4-bit ports are capable of effective transfer rates of about 40-60 KBytes/sec (KB/s) with typical devices and can be pushed to upwards of 140 KB/s with certain design tricks.

Bidirectional (8-bit) Type 1. With the introduction of the PS/2 in 1987, IBM introduced the bidirectional parallel port. These are commonly found in PC compatible systems today and may be designated "PS/2 type," "bidirectional," or "extended" parallel port. This port design opened the way for true communications between the computer and the peripheral across the parallel port. This was done by defining a few of the previously unused pins in the parallel connector and defining a status bit to indicate in which direction information was traveling across the channel.

In IBM documentation, this original PS/2 port became known as a Type 1 parallel port. Other vendors also introduced third-party ports that were compatible with the Type 1 port. These ports can usually be configured in both standard and bidirectional modes, and unless you specifically configure the port for bidirectional use, it will function just like the original unidirectional port. This configuration is normally done with the CMOS SETUP or configuration program that accompanies your system. Most systems built since 1991 have this capability, although many do not enable it as a default setting.

These ports can do both 8-bit input and output using the standard 8 data lines and are considerably faster than the 4-bit ports when used with external devices. 8-bit ports are capable of speeds ranging from 80-300 KB/s, depending on the speed of the attached device, the quality of the driver software, and the port's electrical characteristics.

Bidirectional (8-bit DMA) Type 3. With the introduction of the PS/2 Models 57, 90, and 95, IBM introduced the Type 3 parallel port. This was a special bidirectional port that featured greater throughput through the use of direct memory access (DMA) techniques. This port was specifically used in IBM systems only, and was not found in other PC compatibles.

You may be wondering why IBM skipped from Type 1 to Type 3. In reality, they did not. There is a Type 2 parallel port, and it served as a predecessor to the Type 3. It is only slightly less capable, but was never used widely in any IBM systems.

Enhanced Parallel Port (EPP). This is a newer specification sometimes referred to as the Fast Mode parallel port. The Enhanced Parallel Port (EPP) was developed by Intel, Xircom, and Zenith Data Systems and announced in October 1991. The first products to offer EPP were ZDS laptops, Xircom Pocket LAN Adapters, and the Intel 82360 SL I/O chip.

EPP operates almost at ISA bus speed and offers a 10-fold increase in the raw throughput capability over a conventional parallel port. EPP is especially designed for parallel port peripherals such as LAN adapters, disk drives, and tape backups. EPP has been included in the new IEEE 1284 Parallel Port standard. Transfer rates of 1 to 2 MB/s (Megabytes per second) are possible with EPP.

Since the original Intel 82360 SL I/O chip in 1992, other major chip vendors (such as National Semiconductor, SMC, Western Digital, and VLSI) have also produced I/O chipsets offering some form of EPP capability. One problem is that the procedure for enabling EPP across the various chips differs widely from vendor to vendor, and many vendors offer more than one I/O chip.

EPP version 1.7 (March 1992) identifies the first popular version of the hardware specification. With minor changes, this has since been abandoned and folded into the IEEE 1284 standard. Some technical reference materials have erroneously made reference to "EPP specification version 1.9" causing confusion about the EPP standard. Note that "EPP version 1.9" does not exist, and any EPP specification after the original version 1.7 is technically a part of the IEEE 1284 specification.

Unfortunately this has resulted in two somewhat incompatible standards for EPP parallel ports: the original EPP Standards Committee version 1.7 standard and the IEEE 1284 Committee standard. The two standards are sufficiently similar that new peripherals may be designed in such a way as to support both standards, but existing EPP 1.7 peripherals may not operate with EPP 1284 ports.

Enhanced Capabilities Port (ECP). Another type of high-speed parallel port called the ECP (Enhanced Capabilities Port) was jointly developed by Microsoft and Hewlett-Packard and formally announced in 1992. Like EPP, ECP offers improved performance for the parallel port and requires special hardware logic.

Since the original announcement, ECP is included in IEEE 1284 just like EPP. Unlike EPP, ECP is not tailored to support portable PC's parallel port peripherals; its purpose is to support an inexpensive attachment to a very high-performance printer. Further, ECP mode requires the use of a DMA (direct memory access) channel, which EPP did not define, and which can cause troublesome conflicts with other devices that use DMA. Most PCs with newer "super I/O" chips will be able to support either EPP or ECP mode. In most cases the EPP mode is best for parallel port peripherals. Computer manufacturers are beginning to incorporate EPP BIOS extensions into their systems that comply with the proposed EPP BIOS standards.

IEEE 1284. The IEEE 1284 standard, called "Standard Signaling Method for a Bidirectional Parallel Peripheral Interface for Personal Computers," was approved for final release in March 1994. This standard defines the physical characteristics of the parallel port, including data transfer modes and physical and electrical specifications.

IEEE 1284 defines the electrical signaling behavior external to the PC for a multimodal parallel port which may support 4-bit, 8-bit, EPP, and ECP modes of operation. Not all modes are required by the 1284 specification and the standard makes some provision for additional modes.

The IEEE 1284 specification is targeted at standardizing the behavior between a PC and an attached device, most specifically attached printers, although the specification is of interest to vendors of parallel port peripherals (disks, LAN adapters, etc,).

IEEE 1284 is a hardware-only standard and does not define how software should talk to the port. An offshoot of the original 1284 standard has been created to define the software interface. The IEEE 1284.3 committee was formed to develop a standard for software used with IEEE 1284 compliant hardware. This standard, designed to address the disparity among providers of parallel port chips, contains a specification for supporting EPP mode via the PC's system BIOS.

Upgrading to EPP/ECP Ports. If you are purchasing a system today, I would recommend one that has a so-called "Super I/O" chip that supports both EPP and ECP operation. If you want to test the parallel ports in a system, especially to determine what type they are, I highly recommend a utility called "Parallel". This is a handy parallel port information utility that examines your system's parallel ports and reports the Port Type, IO address, IRQ level, BIOS name, and an assortment of informative notes and warnings in a compact and easy-to-read display. The output may be redirected to a file for tech support purposes. Parallel uses very sophisticated techniques for port and IRQ detection and is aware of a broad range of quirky port features. You can get it from Parallel Technologies (see the Vendor List in Appendix B).

If you have an older system that does not include an EPP/ECP port, and you would like to upgrade, there are several companies now offering boards with the correct super-I/O chips that implement these features. I recommend you check with Farpoint Communications and Byterunner Technologies, they are listed in the Vendor List in Appendix B.

On the Web

http://www.byterunner.com/

http://www.fapo.com/

Parallel Port Configuration

Parallel-port configuration is not as complicated as it is for serial ports. Even the original IBM PC has BIOS support for three LPT ports, and DOS has always had this support. Table 11.8 shows the standard I/O address and interrupt settings for parallel port use.

Table 11.8 Parallel Interface I/O Port Addresses and Interrupts

	LPTx		I/O	
System	Std.	Alt	Port	IRQ
8-bit ISA	LPT1	—	3BCh	IRQ7
8-bit ISA	LPT1	LPT2	378h	IRQ7
8-bit ISA	LPT2	LPT3	278h	None
16-bit ISA	LPT1	—	3BCh	IRQ7
16-bit ISA	LPT1	LPT2	378h	IRQ7
16-bit ISA	LPT2	LPT3	278h	IRQ5
All MCA	LPT1	-	3BCh	IRQ7
All MCA	LPT2	-	378h	IRQ7
All MCA	LPT3	-	278h	IRQ7

Because the BIOS and DOS always have provided three definitions for parallel ports, problems with older systems are infrequent. Problems can arise, however, from the lack of available interrupt-driven ports for ISA bus systems. Normally, an interrupt-driven port is not absolutely required for printing operations; in fact, many programs do not use the interrupt-driven capability. Many programs do use the interrupt, however, such as network print programs and other types of background or spooler-type printer programs. Also, high-speed, laser-printer utility programs often use the interrupt capabilities to allow for printing. If you use these types of applications on a port that is not interrupt driven, you see the printing slow to a crawl, if it works at all. The only solution is to use an interrupt-driven port. Note that because MCA and EISA bus systems can share interrupts, they are completely exempt from this type of problem, and all parallel ports in these systems are interrupt driven on IRQ7. MS-DOS and Windows 95 now support up to 128 parallel ports.

To configure parallel ports in ISA bus systems, you probably will have to set jumpers and switches. Because each board on the market is different, you always should consult the OEM manual for that particular card if you need to know how the card should be configured.

Parallel Port Devices. The original IBM PC designers envisioned that the parallel port would be used only for communicating with a printer. Over the years, the number of devices that can be used with a parallel port has increased tremendously. You now can find everything from tape backup units to LAN adapters to CD-ROMs that connect through your parallel port. Some modem manufacturers now have modems that connect to the parallel port instead of the serial port for faster data transfer.

Perhaps one of the most common uses for bidirectional parallel ports is to transfer data between your system and another, such as a laptop computer. If both systems utilize an EPP/ECP port, you can actually communicate at rates of up to 2M per second, which rivals the speed of some hard disk drives. This capability has led to an increase in software to serve this niche of the market. If you are interested in such software (and the parallel ports necessary to facilitate the software), you should refer to the reviews that periodically appear in sources such as *PC Magazine*.

Connecting two computers via their parallel ports requires a specially wired cable. This is often called an Interlink cable because this type of connection is supported by the INTERNLK utility found in DOS versions 6.0 and higher. This type of connection is also supported by a number of aftermarket utilities such as Fastlynx, Laplink, and others. In addition to the standard Interlink cable wiring, there is an enhanced wiring method that results in even higher performance with the commercial software. They naturally would prefer that you purchase these high performance cables from them, but you can make them yourself. I have included wiring diagrams for both the standard and enhanced Interlink type parallel cables in Appendix A, under "Interlink Cables."

When I run my training seminars, I actually use a 50-foot long (it is high-quality shielded cable!) Interlink cable that I custom made. This allows me to use my main system to download many megabytes of operating systems and utility programs to the student machines. For anybody who has to transfer data between equipment, I highly recommend programs like Fastlynx (Rupp Corp.), Laplink (Travelling Software), and even the Interlink program built into DOS 6.x and higher. Windows 95 has this capability built-in as well. No matter which software you use, you will still need the cable.

Detecting Serial and Parallel Ports with DEBUG

If you cannot tell which ports (parallel and serial) the computer is using, check for the I/O ports by using DEBUG.

To use DEBUG, follow these steps:

1. Run DEBUG.
2. At the DEBUG prompt, type **D 40:0** and press Enter. This step displays the hexadecimal values of the active I/O port addresses—first serial and then parallel. Figure 11.3 shows a sample address.

   The address for each port is shown in the corresponding position. Because addresses are stored as words, the byte values are swapped and should be read backward. This example indicates one serial port installed at 03F8 and one parallel port installed at 03BC.
3. To exit DEBUG, press Q and press Enter.
4. In Windows 95 you can determine what ports you have by going into Device Manager, selecting the port, selecting Properties, and then choosing Resources. The Resources screen shows you the current address and interrupt of the port. The port address and/or interrupt may also be changed from this screen.

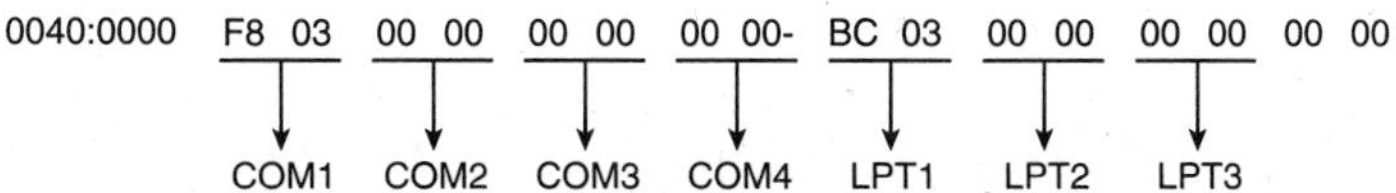

Figure 11.3

DEBUG used to display installed serial and parallel port I/0 port addresses.

Testing Serial Ports

You can perform several tests on serial and parallel ports. The two most common types of tests involve software only, or both hardware and software. The software-only tests are done with diagnostic programs such as Microsoft's MSD, while the hardware and software tests involve using a wrap plug to perform loopback testing.

Microsoft Diagnostics (MSD). MSD is a diagnostic program supplied with MS-DOS 6.X , Microsoft Windows, or Windows 95. Early versions of the program also were shipped with some Microsoft applications such as Microsoft Word for DOS.

To use MSD, switch to the directory in which it is located. This is not necessary, of course, if the directory containing the program is in your search path—which is often the case with the DOS 6.X or Windows-provided versions of MSD. Then simply type **MSD** at the DOS prompt and press Enter. Soon you see the MSD screen.

Choose the Serial Ports option by pressing S. Notice that you are provided information about what type of serial chip you have in your system, as well as information about what ports are available. If any of the ports are in use (for example, a mouse), that information is provided as well.

MSD is helpful in at least determining whether your serial ports are responding. If MSD cannot determine the existence of a port, it does not provide the report indicating that the port exists. This sort of "look and see" test is the first action I usually take to determine why a port is not responding.

Windows 95 also shows whether or not your ports are functioning. To check your ports, right-click on Your Computer and choose Properties. Choose the Device Manager tab. On the Device Manager screen, if a device is not working properly there will be an exclamation point in a yellow circle next to the device on the list. You can also double-click Ports (COM & LPT), and then double-click the desired port to see whether Windows 95 says that the port is functioning or not. In many cases, it tells you what is conflicting with that specific port.

Advanced Diagnostics Using Loopback Testing. One of the most useful tests is the loopback test, which can be used to ensure the correct function of the serial port, as well as any attached cables. Loopback tests basically are internal (digital) or external (analog). Internal tests can be run simply by unplugging any cables from the port and executing the test via a diagnostics program.

The external loopback test is more effective. This test requires that a special loopback connector or wrap plug be attached to the port in question. When the test is run, the port is used to send data out to the loopback plug, which simply routes the data back into the port's receive pins so that the port is transmitting and receiving at the same time. A loopback or wrap plug is nothing more than a cable doubled back on itself. Most diagnostics programs that run this type of test include the loopback plug, and if not, these types of plugs can be purchased easily or even built. See Appendix A, "PC Technical Reference Section," for the necessary diagrams to construct your own wrap plugs.

If you want to purchase a wrap plug, I recommend the IBM tri-connector wrap plug. IBM sells this triple plug, as well as individual wrap plugs, under the following part numbers:

Description	IBM Part Number
Parallel-port wrap plug	8529228
Serial-port wrap plug, 25-pin	8529280
Serial-port wrap plug, 9-pin (AT)	8286126
Tri-connector wrap plug	72X8546

As for the diagnostics software, IBM's own Advanced Diagnostics can be used to test serial ports. If you have a PS/2 system with Micro Channel Architecture, IBM already has given you with the Advanced Diagnostics on the Reference Disk that came with the system. To activate this normally hidden Advanced Diagnostics, press Ctrl+A at the Reference Disk's main menu. For IBM systems that are not MCA, the Advanced Diagnostics must be purchased.

For any system, you can use the serial port tests in the comprehensive diagnostics packages sold by several companies as a replacement for the IBM- (or other manufacturer) supplied Advanced Diagnostics. Programs such as the Norton Utilities, Micro-Scope from Micro 2000, the Troubleshooter from AllMicro, PC Certify from Quarterdeck, or QA-Plus FE from Diagsoft all have this type of test as part of their package. All include or sell as optional the necessary three wrap plugs as well. See Appendix B, "Vendor List" for more information on these programs.

For testing serial ports, as well as any modems that are attached, I highly recommend an inexpensive ($19.95) program called the Modem Doctor by Hank Volpe (see the Vendor List in Appendix B, look under "Volpe, Hank"). This comprehensive serial port and modem test program enables you to go beyond the simple loopback tests and test the complete communications system, including the cable and modem. The program takes command of the modem and runs a variety of tests to determine whether it is functioning correctly.

Testing Parallel Ports

Testing parallel ports is, in most cases, simpler than testing serial ports. The procedures you use are effectively the same as those used for serial ports, except that when you use the diagnostics software, you choose the obvious choices for parallel ports rather than serial ports.

Not only are the software tests similar, but the hardware tests require the proper plugs for the loopback tests on the parallel port. You can use the tri-connector wrap plug recommended earlier, or you can purchase an individual parallel port wrap plug. If you want the individual plug, ask for IBM part number 8529228.

The most comprehensive parallel port testing program I know of is a program called "Parallel," which is available through Parallel Technologies (see the vendor list in Appendix B). I highly recommend this program because it reports the configuration, resource usage, and performance of all types of parallel ports.

Future Serial and Parallel Port Replacements

Two new high-speed serial-bus architectures for desktop and portable are becoming available, called the Universal Serial Bus (USB) and IEEE 1394. These are high-speed communications ports that far outstrip the capabilities of the standard serial and parallel ports most systems contain today. These ports may be used as an alternative to SCSI for high-speed peripheral connections. In addition to performance, these new ports will offer I/O device consolidation, meaning all types of external peripherals will connect to these ports.

The recent trend in high-performance peripheral bus design is to use a serial architecture, where one bit is sent at a time down a wire. Parallel architecture uses 8, 16, or more wires to send bits simultaneously. Although it may seem that at the same clock speed, the parallel bus is faster, what few people realize is that it is much easier to increase the clock speed of a serial connection than a parallel one.

Parallel connections suffer from several problems, the biggest being signal skew and jitter. Skew is the reason that high-speed parallel busses like SCSI are limited to short distances of 3 meters or less. The problem is that although the 8 or 16 bits of data are fired from the transmitter at the same time, by the time they reach the receiver, propagation delays have conspired to allow some bits to arrive before the others. The longer the cable, the longer the time between the arrival of the first and last bits at the other end! This signal skew, as it is called, either prevents you from running a high-speed transfer rate, a longer cable, or both.

With a serial bus, the data is sent one bit at a time. Because there is no worry about when each bit will arrive, the clocking rate can be increased dramatically.

With a high clock rate, parallel signals tend to interfere with each other. Serial again has an advantage in that with only one or two signal wires, crosstalk and interference between the wires in the cable is negligible.

Parallel cables are very expensive. In addition to the many additional wires needed to carry the multiple bits in parallel, the cable also needs to be specially constructed to prevent crosstalk and interference between adjacent data lines. This is one reason external SCSI cables are so expensive. Serial cables, on the other hand, are very inexpensive. For one thing they have very few wires, plus the shielding requirements are far simpler, even at very high speeds.

It is for these reasons, plus the need for new Plug and Play external peripheral interfaces, as well as the elimination of the physical port crowding on portable computers, that these new high-performance serial busses have been developed. Both USB and 1394 will be available on desktop and portable PCs in the near future.

USB (Universal Serial Bus)

The USB was designed as a convenient method to connect a variety of different peripherals to a system. Intel has been the primary proponent of USB, and most of their new PC chipsets, starting with the Triton II (82430HX and VX), will include USB support as standard. Six other companies have worked with Intel in co-developing the USB, including Compaq, Digital, IBM, Microsoft, NEC, and Northern Telecom. Together these companies have established the USB Implementers Forum to develop, support, and promote the USB architecture.

On the Web

For more information on this group, you can contact them at their Web site.

http://www.teleport.com/~usb

The USB is a 12 Mbit/sec (1.5 MByte/sec) interface over a simple 4-wire connection. The bus supports up to 127 devices and uses a tiered star topology built on expansion hubs that can reside in the PC, any USB peripheral, or even stand-alone hub boxes. For low performance peripherals such as pointing devices and keyboards, the USB also has a slower 1.5 Mbit/sec subchannel.

USB also conforms to Intel's Plug and Play (PnP) specification, including hot plugging, which means that devices can be plugged in dynamically without powering down or rebooting the system. Simply plug in the device, and the USB controller in the PC will detect the device and automatically determine and allocate the resources and drivers required. Microsoft has USB drivers developed that will be included in upcoming versions of Windows 95 and NT. USB support will also be required in the BIOS, which will be included in newer systems with USB ports built-in.

Aftermarket USB boards will be available for adding USB to an existing system. Such boards will likely have ROM on-board, which will allow the USB peripherals to function under DOS, while Windows built-in drivers will take care of the USB function under Windows.

USB peripherals will include modems, telephones, joysticks, keyboards, and pointing devices such as mice and trackballs.

One interesting feature of USB is that all attached devices will be powered by the USB bus itself. The PnP aspects of USB allows the system to query the attached peripherals as to their power requirements and issue a warning if available power levels are being exceeded. This will be important for USB when used in portable systems, because battery power to run the external peripherals may be limited.

IEEE 1394

IEEE 1394 is a high-speed local serial bus. 1394 supports speeds of 100, 200, and 400 Mbits/sec (12.5, 25, 50 MBytes/sec), with gigabit per second versions in the works! This bus was derived from the "Firewire" bus originally developed by Apple and Texas Instruments, and it is also a part of the new Serial SCSI (SCSI-3) standard.

1394 uses a simple 6-wire cable with two differential pairs of clock and data lines plus two power lines. Just as with USB, 1394 is fully Plug and Play, including the ability for hot plugging (insertion and removal of components without powering down). Unlike the much more complicated parallel SCSI bus, 1394 does not require complicated termination, and devices connected to the bus can draw up to 1.5 amps of electrical power. 1394 offers equal or greater performance compared to Ultra-Wide SCSI, with a much less expensive and less complicated connection.

1394 is built on a daisy-chained and branched topology and allows up to 63 nodes with a chain of up to 16 devices on each node. If this is not enough, the standard also calls for up to 1,023 bridged busses, which can interconnect more than 64,000 nodes! Additionally, 1394 can support devices with different data rates on the same bus, just as with SCSI.

The types of devices that will be connected to the PC via 1394 include practically anything that might use SCSI today. This includes all forms of disk drives, including hard disk, optical, floppy, CD-ROM, and the new DVD (Digital Video Disc) drives. Also expect to see digital cameras, tape drives, and many other high-speed peripherals also featuring 1394 interfaces built-in. Expect the 1394 bus to be implemented in both desktop as well as portable computers as a replacement for other external high-speed busses like SCSI.

1394 already includes a list of over 200 companies that are members of the 1394 Trade Association.

For more information on the 1394 bus or the 1394 Trade Association, you can contact them on the Web at

On the Web

http://www.firewire.org

Chipsets for the 1394 bus are already available, and PCI adapters allowing 1394 to be added to existing systems should soon follow. Microsoft has indicated that it will be including drivers for 1394 ports in future Windows versions, and we should also see the BIOS companies building support into ROM for bootable devices.

The next section discusses local area network components and concepts.

Understanding the Components of a LAN

A local area network (LAN) enables you to share files, share applications, use client/server software products, send electronic mail, share printers, disk space, modems, faxes, CD-ROM drives, and otherwise make a collection of computers work as a team.

In today's world there are many ways to construct a LAN. A LAN can be as simple as two computers connected together via either their serial or parallel ports. This is the simplest and probably the most common LAN today. Many users connect their laptop to their desktop computer for access to a printer or to transfer files. This type of connection is usually called a direct cable connection, in which one computer is designated as the host computer. The host computer is the machine with the resources you want to access. The guest computer wants to use the resources of the host. You can purchase software that allows you to connect two computers in this manner, but some operating systems such as DOS and Windows 95 have direct cable connection support built in. Although the term network is not often used for this sort of arrangement, it does satisfy the definition.

Peer-to peer-networks have become more popular as the software became more reliable and personal computers became more powerful. Peer-to-peer means computer to computer. In a peer-to-peer network, any computer can access any other computer to which it is connected and has been granted access rights. Essentially, every computer functions as both a server and a client. Peer-to-peer networks can be as small as two computers, or as large as hundreds of units, and they may or may not use a LAN card or network interface card (NIC). For more than two stations, or when higher data transfer speeds are desired, NICs should be used. Peer-to-peer networks are more common in small offices or within a department in a larger organization. The advantage of a peer-to-peer network is that you don't have to dedicate a computer to be a file server. Most peer-to-peer networks allow you to share practically any device attached to any computer. The potential disadvantages to a peer-to-peer network are that there is typically less security and less control.

Windows 95 has built-in peer-to-peer networking. With Windows 95, setting up a peer-to-peer LAN can be accomplished in two ways. The first method is to install the dial-up networking modules. Dial-up networking requires a Windows 95-compatible server, such as Windows 95 dial-up server in the Plus! Package, or Windows NT. Dial-up networking allows the remote system (the one dialing in) to access the server and any peripherals attached to the server to which the remote user has been given rights. These peripherals can be CD-ROM drives, tape drives, removable media drives, hard drives, and even another network as long as it is an IPX/SPX or NetBEUI network. IPX/SPX are the network transport protocols used in NetWare and other networks. NetBEUI is the NetBIOS (Network Basic Input Output System) Extended User Interface; it is the native protocol of Microsoft Windows networks.

The other method of peer-to-peer networking is much like that with which we all became familiar in Windows for Workgroups, but it is much easier to set up in Windows 95. With the new Plug and Play technology incorporated into the operating system, most NICS are automatically detected. Supported NIC manufacturers include 3COM, Digital Equipment Corporation, IBM, Intel, Madge, Novell, Proteon, Racal, SMC, and Thomas-Conrad. Once the NIC is detected, Windows 95 asks for a user name, a computer name, a workgroup name, and a password. Once this is accomplished, your Windows 95 network workstation is ready to go.

A LAN is a combination of computers, LAN cables (usually), network adapter cards, network operating system software, and LAN application software. (You sometimes see network operating system abbreviated as NOS.) On a LAN, each personal computer is called a workstation, except for one or more computers designated as network servers. Each workstation and server contains a network adapter card. LAN cables connect all the workstations and servers, except in less frequent cases when infrared, radio, or microwaves are used.

A network in which the workstations connect only to servers (as opposed to each other, as in a peer-to-peer) is called a *client/server network*. In addition to its local operating system (usually DOS, or one of the Windows operating systems), each workstation runs network software (client software) that enables the workstation to communicate with the servers. Windows 95 itself contains the client software necessary to connect to Novell

NetWare 3.12 and 4.x, IBM OS/2 LAN SERVER, and Windows NT networks. In turn, the servers run network software (server software) that communicates with the workstations and serves up files and other services to those workstations. LAN-aware application software runs at each workstation, communicating with the server when it needs to read and write files. Figure 11.4 illustrates the components that make up a LAN.

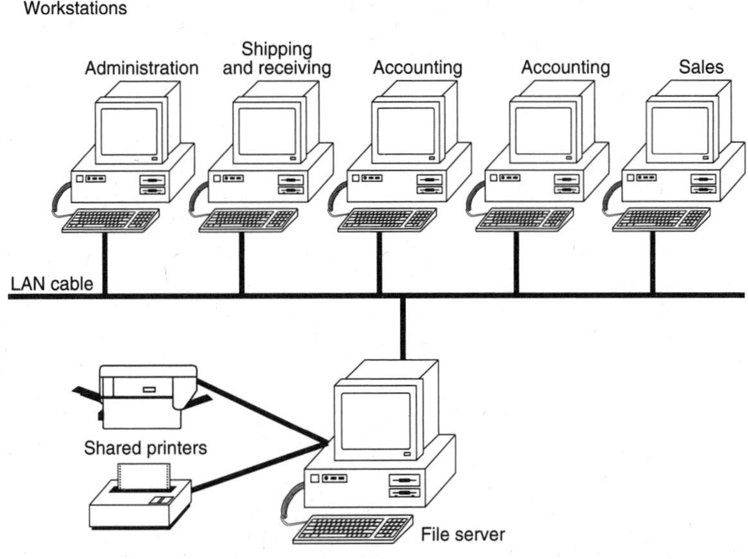

Figure 11.4

The components of a LAN.

Workstations

A LAN is made up of computers. You will usually find two kinds of computers on a LAN: the workstations, usually manned by people on their individual desktops, and the servers, usually located in a secured area, like a separate room or closet. The workstation is used only by the person sitting in front of it, whereas a server allows many people to share its resources. Workstations usually are at least intermediate-speed AT-class machines with an 80286 or better CPU, and they may have 1M to 4M of RAM. Workstations often have good-quality color or grayscale VGA monitors, as well as high-quality keyboards, but these are characteristics that make them easy to use; they are not required to make the LAN work. A workstation also usually has a relatively inexpensive, slow, small hard disk. When constructing a new LAN today, the minimum recommended workstation, for either a client/server or peer-to-peer network, is at least a 486DX2/66 with 8MB of RAM and a 500MB hard drive. The preferred system is a Pentium 75 or greater with 16MB or more of RAM and a 500MB or larger hard drive. As a matter of fact, most of the major suppliers of PCs to the corporate world no longer even carry 486-based machines.

Many existing networks operate very well with older machines, however. Some sites even continue to use diskless workstations—that is, computers that do not have a disk drive of their own. Such workstations rely completely on the LAN for their file access. A diskless workstation requires a NIC card with an auto boot PROM. This type of ROM causes the workstation to boot from files store on a network server.

The advantages to this type of workstation are lower cost for hardware and greater security, which is increased by not having any drives at the local workstation with which to copy files to or from the server. The primary disadvantage is that today's high-performance operating systems will not run efficiently from a network drive. The sheer number of program files opened and closed, as well as the need for frequent swapping of memory to hard disk space, make the practice prohibitive.

File Servers

All the workstations on a peer-to-peer LAN can function as file servers, in that any drive on any peer workstation can be shared with (or, served to) other users.

On a client/server network, however, a file server is a computer that serves all the workstations—primarily by storing and retrieving data from files shared on its disks. Servers usually are fast 486-, Pentium or Pentium Pro-based computers, running at 66 MHz or faster and with 16M or more of RAM. Most servers usually have inexpensive monitors and keyboards, because people do not use the file server console as heavily as that of a workstation. The server normally operates unattended, and it almost always has one or more fast, expensive, large hard disks.

Servers must be high-quality, heavy-duty machines because, in serving the whole network, they do many times the work of an ordinary workstation computer. In particular, the file server's hard disk(s) need to be durable and reliable, and geared to the task of serving multiple users simultaneously. For this reason, SCSI hard drives are usually preferred over IDE drives in today's servers (see Chapter 15, "Hard Disk Interfaces," for more information on IDE versus SCSI).

You will most often see a computer wholly dedicated to the task of being a server. Sometimes, on smaller LANs, the server doubles as a workstation, depending on the network operating system being used. Serving an entire network is a big job that does not leave much spare horsepower to handle workstation duties, however, and if a user locks up the workstation that also serves as the file server, your network also locks up.

Under a heavy load, if there are 20 workstations and one server, each workstation can use only one-twentieth of the server's resources. In practice, though, most workstations are idle most of the time—at least from a network disk-file-access point of view. As long as no other workstation is using the server, your workstation can use 100 percent of the server's resources.

Evaluating File Server Hardware

A typical file server consists of a personal computer that you dedicate to the task of sharing disk space, files, and possibly printers. On a larger network, you may use a personal computer especially built for file server work (a superserver), but the basic components are the same as those of a desktop PC. No matter what sort of computer you choose as a server, it communicates with the workstations through its network adapter cards the LAN cables.

A file server does many times the work of an ordinary workstation. You may type on the server's keyboard only a couple of times a day, and you may glance at its monitor only infrequently. The server's CPU and hard disk drives, however, take the brunt of responding to the file-service requests of all the workstations on the LAN.

If you consider your LAN an important part of your investment in your business (and it is hard to imagine otherwise), you will want to get the highest quality computer you can afford for the file server. If you're going to be running on the Intel platform, the processor should be a Pentium or a Pentium Pro, and it should be one of the faster models. The hard disk drives should be large and fast, although in some cases the highest capacity drive available is not necessarily the best choice. When you consider that the server will be processing the file requests of many users simultaneously, it can be more efficient to have, for example, nine 1-gigabyte SCSI hard drives rather than one 9-gigabyte drive. That way, the requests can be spread across several different units rather than queued up waiting for one device.

Performance is important, of course, but the most crucial consideration in purchasing a server is that the CPU, the motherboard on which the CPU is mounted, and the hard disk drives should be rugged and reliable. Do not skimp on these components. Downtime (periods when the network is not operating) can be expensive because people cannot access their shared files to get their work done. Higher quality components will keep the LAN running without failure for longer periods of time. It is very important that you configure your LAN properly. Be sure that you have enough slots for all your present adapters and any future adapters that you can anticipate. It is also very important that you follow the RAM and hard drive sizing guidelines for your network operating system.

In the same vein, you will want to set up a regular maintenance schedule for your file server. Over the course of a few weeks, the fans within the computer can move great volumes of air through the machine to keep it cool. The air may contain dust and dirt, which accumulates inside the computer. You should clean out the "dust bunnies" in the server every month or two. Many larger network sites house their servers in rooms or closets designed to maintain low dust and static levels as well as constant temperatures.

You do not replace components in the server as part of your regular preventive maintenance, but you will want to know whether a part is beginning to fail. You may want to acquire diagnostic software or hardware products to periodically check the health of your file server. (Chapter 20, "Maintaining Your System: Preventive Maintenance, Backups, and Warranties," discusses the tools you can use to keep your file server fit and trim.)

The electricity the file server gets from the wall outlet may, from time to time, vary considerably in voltage (resulting in sags and spikes). To make your file server as reliable as possible, you should install an uninterruptable power supply between the electric power source and your server. The UPS not only provides electricity in case of a power failure, but it also conditions the line to protect the server from voltage fluctuations.

In general, you want to do whatever you can to make your network reliable, including placing the server away from public access areas.

Evaluating the File Server Hard Disk. The hard disk drives are the most important components of a file server. The hard disks are where the people who use the LAN store their files. To a large extent, the reliability, access speed, and capacity of a server's hard disks determine whether people will be happy with the LAN and will be able to use it productively. The most common bottleneck in the average LAN is disk I/O time at the file server. And the most common complaint voiced by people on the average LAN is that the file server has run out of free disk space. Make sure that your file server's disk drives and hard disk controller are high performance components and that you always have plenty of free disk space on your server's drives.

You also may want to consider enhanced IDE (EIDE) or SCSI host adapters, depending on the number and types of devices you want to connect to the server. Enhanced IDE controllers support up to 4 devices, whereas some of the new dual channel SCSI controllers support up to 14 devices. These devices may be hard drives, removable media, CD-ROMs, or tape drives. There are several other factors to consider when deciding between SCSI or EIDE controllers. EIDE generally has greater performance for single drive installations. This is due to the fact that EIDE is a direct local bus connection while SCSI essentially adds a whole new bus to the system. SCSI shines in multiple drive installations, such as in file servers, and with multi-threaded multi-tasking operating systems such as Windows NT and OS/2. For the ultimate in performance, there are newer SCSI standards such as Ultra-Wide SCSI that is rated at 40 Mbps. SCSI controllers also have the capability to do simultaneous access of multiple drives whereas EIDE is capable only of sequential access. SCSI drives and controllers are slightly more expensive than EIDE drives or controllers. The importance of these issues will be determined by the number of users you must serve and/or the current hardware prices.

If high performance and fault tolerance are key issues in your LAN implementation, you may want to consider a RAID (Redundant Array of Inexpensive Disks) array. RAID drive arrays are SCSI drives usually installed as either a single or double pair. In the single pair configuration the drives are normally mirrored or duplexed. In disk mirroring, two drives connected to a single host adapter contain exactly the same information. If there is a drive problem and one unit cannot be accessed, the replicated data on the good drive can still be used. Duplexing the drives is a similar arrangement, except that each drive has its own host adapter. This configuration is more fault tolerant than mirroring because it can compensate for an adapter as well as a disk drive failure.

When there are double pairs (4 drives), they usually set up as a RAID level 5 array. When the data is stored on a level 5 array, it is written across all three drives. The fourth drive is allocated to the storage of encoded data. This type of data protection is called *data guarding* and requires an operating system that supports it. Data guarding allows for a drive to fail without the loss of any data. The reason the system can continue is because the fourth drive supplies the information that was on the failed drive. Most drive arrays are hot swappable, which means that one drive can be removed without powering down the unit. In a server that is using data guarding on its drive array, the failed drive can be removed and replaced while the system is still acting as a server. The fourth drive will then begin to rebuild the appropriate data from the lost drive on the replacement. This means that a drive failure can be repaired with no down time and no loss of data.

Evaluating the File Server CPU. The file server CPU tells the hard disk drives what to store and retrieve. The CPU is the next most important file server component after the hard disks. Unless your LAN will have only a few users and will never grow, a file server with a fast Pentium or Pentium Pro CPU and plenty of RAM is a wise investment. The next section discusses server RAM.

The CPU chip in a computer executes the instructions given to it by the software you run. If you run an application, that application runs more quickly if the CPU is fast. Likewise, if you run a network operating system, that NOS runs more quickly if the CPU is fast.

Some network operating systems absolutely require certain types of CPU chips. NetWare Version 2, for example, required at least a 286 CPU. NetWare Versions 3 and 4 require at least a 386. IBM LAN Server Version 2 and Microsoft LAN Manager Version 2 require that OS/2 1.3 be running on the server computer; OS/2 1.3 requires an 80286 or later CPU. LAN Server 3.0 requires that the file server use OS/2 2.x, which runs only on 386 or later CPUs. Microsoft Windows NT Advanced Server 3.51 requires a 386DX25 or later CPU and 16MB of RAM. These are, of course, the absolute minimum CPU requirements. Exceeding them is a practice that is highly recommended for any of these products.

Evaluating Server RAM. The network operating system loads into the computer's RAM, just like any other application. You need to have enough RAM in the computer for the NOS to load and run properly. On a peer LAN, the recommended amount of RAM would be whatever it takes to run your applications, whereas on a client/server LAN, you might install 32M, 64M, or more in your file server. Windows 95 in a peer-to-peer environment should have a minimum of 16MB of RAM. Windows NT should have more. The proper amount of RAM for a server-based LAN operating system like NetWare is calculated using a formula that accounts for the software you will be running and the capacity and configuration of your disk drives. Be sure to follow the operating system manufacturer's RAM recommendations carefully, or severe performance problems may result.

You can realize significant performance gains in a NetWare server with a faster CPU and extra RAM because of a process called *file caching*. If the server has sufficient memory installed, it can "remember" those portions of the hard disk that it has accessed previously. When the next user asks for the same file represented by those portions of the hard disk, the server can send it to the next user without having to actually access the hard disk. Because the file server is able to avoid waiting for the hard disk to rotate into position, the server can do its job more quickly. The network operating system merely needs to look in the computer's RAM for the file data that a workstation has requested. Thus, you can be assured that any extra memory installed in your server will be put to beneficial use. Note that the network operating system's caching of file data is distinct from (and in addition to) any caching that might occur due to the hard disk or hard disk controller card having on-board memory.

Evaluating the Network Adapter Card. The server's network adapter card is its link to all the workstations on the LAN. All file requests and other network communications enter and leave the server through the network adapter. Figure 11.5 shows a network adapter you might install in a file server. As you can imagine, the network adapter in a server is a busy component.

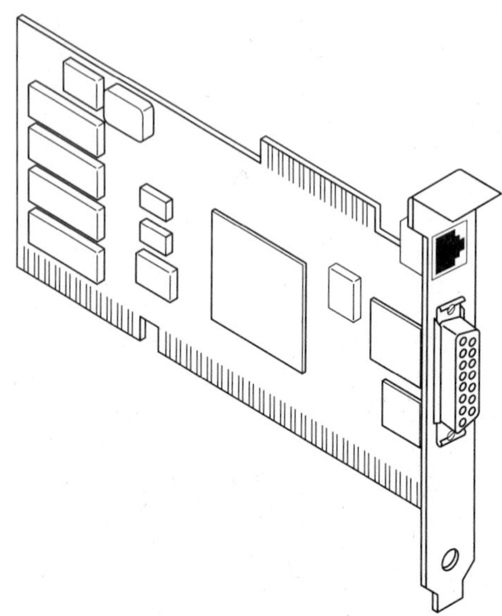

Figure 11.5

The file server's network adapter sends and receives messages to and from all the workstations on the LAN.

All the network adapters on the LAN use Ethernet, Token Ring, ARCnet, or some other low-level protocol. You can find network adapters for each of these protocols, however, that perform better than others. A network adapter may be faster at processing messages because it has a large amount of on-board memory (RAM), because it contains its own microprocessor, or perhaps because the adapter uses a 16-bit or a 32-bit slot instead of an 8-bit slot and thus can transfer more data to and from the CPU at one time. 32-bit slots in server computers could be EISA, VLB, or PCI. PCI is currently the most commonly found 32-bit bus type in the Pentium class machine. A network adapter may also have a newer driver that allows it to transfer data in 32-bit packets instead of 16-bit packets. A faster, more capable network adapter is an ideal candidate for installation in a file server, but be sure to check its compatibility with the network adapters installed in your workstations.

Evaluating the Server's Power Supply. In a file server, the power supply is an important but often overlooked item. Power supply failures and malfunctions can cause problems elsewhere in the computer that are difficult to diagnose. Your file server may display a message indicating that a RAM chip has failed, and then stop; the cause of the problem may indeed be a failed RAM chip, or the problem may be in the power supply.

The fan(s) in the power supply sometimes stop working or become obstructed with dust and dirt. The computer overheats and fails completely or acts strangely. Cleaning the fan(s)—after unplugging the computer from the wall outlet, of course—should be a part of the regular maintenance of your file server. Please keep in mind that some high-end server cabinets may have redundant (multiple) power supplies and fans in them. Most systems today even have fans mounted directly on the CPU. If you have a multiprocessor server, be sure to check for fans on each CPU.

Evaluating the Keyboard, Monitor, and Mouse. The keyboard, monitor, and mouse (if any) are usually not significant components on a file server computer, because they receive far less use than their workstation counterparts. Often you can use lower quality, less-expensive components here. A typical file server runs unattended and may go for hours or days without interaction from you. You can power off the monitor for these long periods.

Note one caution about the keyboard: you should tuck the keyboard away so that falling objects (pencils or coffee mugs, for example) do not harm your network's file server.

Your network server may also have external shared CD-ROM drives, either single or multiple disk and or a network tape drive. If your server has any of these devices, be sure they are easily accessible. When the backup of the server is complete, be sure to remove the tape and store it in a safe place.

Network Interface Cards (NICs)

A network interface card, or NIC, fits into a slot in each workstation and file server. (Some computers now ship with network interface hardware embedded on the motherboard, but most network administrators prefer to select their own.) Your workstation sends requests through the network adapter to the server. The workstation then receives responses through the network adapter when the server delivers all or a portion of a file to that workstation. The sending and receiving of these requests and responses is the LAN equivalent of reading and writing files on your PC's local hard disk. If you're like most people, you probably think of reading and writing files in terms of loading or saving your work.

A typical LAN consists of only a single data channel connecting its various computers. This is called a *baseband* network. As a result of this, only two network adapters can communicate with each other at the same time. If one person's workstation is currently accessing the file server (processing the requests and responses that deliver a file to the workstation), then other users' workstations must wait their turn. Fortunately, such delays are usually not noticeable. The LAN gives the appearance of many workstations accessing the file server simultaneously.

Ethernet adapters have a single BNC connector (for ThinNet), a D-shaped 15-pin connector called a DB15 (for ThickNet), a connector that looks like a large telephone jack called an RJ45 (for 10BaseT), or sometimes a combination of all three. Token Ring adapters can have a 9-pin connector called a DB9 or sometimes an RJ45 telephone jack outlet. Figure 11.6 shows a high-performance Token Ring adapter with both kinds of connectors.

Cards with two or more connectors enable you to choose from a wider variety of LAN cables. A Token Ring card with two connectors, for example, enables you to use shielded twisted pair (STP) or unshielded twisted pair (UTP) cable. You cannot use both connectors at the same time, however, except on special adapters designed specifically for this purpose.

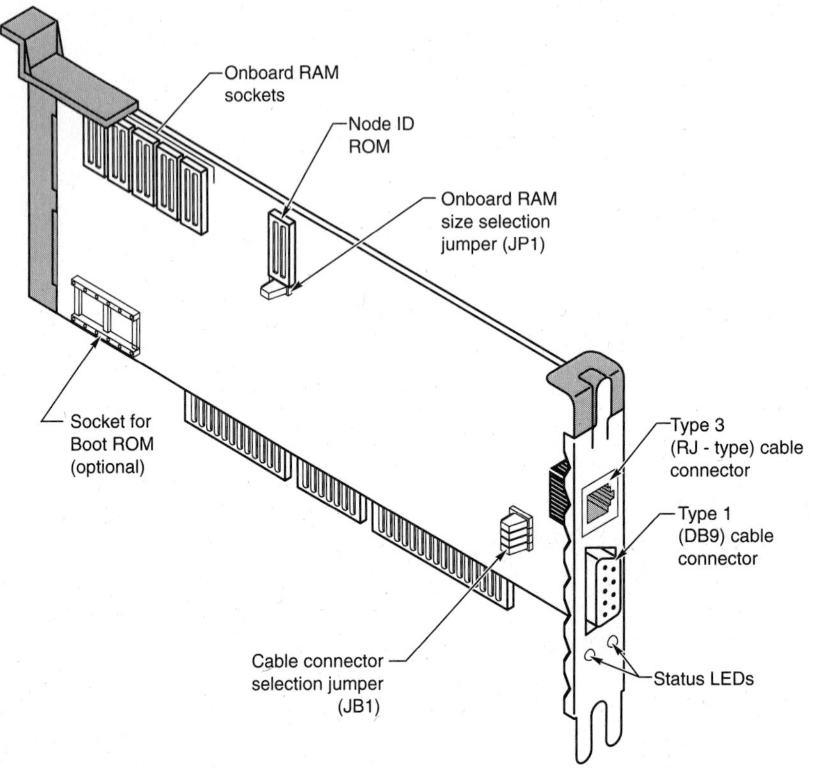

Figure 11.6

The Thomas-Conrad 16/4 Token Ring adapter (with a 9-pin connector and a telephone wire connector).

The LAN adapter card in your PC receives all the traffic going by on the network cable, accepts only the messages destined for your workstation, and passes on the rest to the next machine. The adapter hands these messages over to your workstation when the workstation is ready to attend to them. When the workstation wants to send a request to a server, the adapter card waits for the appropriate time (according to the network type) and inserts your message into the data stream. The workstation is also notified as to whether the message arrived intact and resends the message if it was garbled.

Network adapters range in price from less than $100 to much more than $1,000. What do you get for your money? Primarily, speed. The faster adapters can push data faster onto the cable, which means that the file server gets a request more quickly and sends back a response more quickly.

Data-Transfer Speeds on a LAN

Electrical engineers and technical people measure the speed of a network in megabits per second (Mbps). Because a byte of information consists of 8 bits, you can divide the megabits per second rating by 8 to find out how many millions of characters (bytes) per second the network can handle theoretically. Suppose that you want to transfer an entire 3 1/2-inch 720K floppy disk's worth of information across a LAN. The rated speed of the LAN is 4 megabits per second. Dividing 4 Mbps by 8 tells you that the LAN theoretically can transmit 500 kilobytes (500K) of data per second. This is equivalent to an average hard disk's transfer rate. The data transfer rate for a floppy drive is 500 kilobits per second (500k). The data from the 720K floppy disk takes at least a few seconds to transfer, as you can see from these rough calculations.

In practice, a LAN is slower than its rated speed. In fact, a LAN is no faster than its slowest component. If you were to transfer 720K of data from one workstation's hard disk to the file server, the elapsed time would include not only the transmission time but also the workstation hard disk retrieval time, the workstation processing time, and the file server's hard disk and server CPU processing times. The transfer rate of your hard disk, which in this case is probably the slowest component involved in the copying of the data to the server, governs the rate at which data flows to the file server. Other people's requests interleave with your requests on the LAN, and the total transfer time may be longer because the other people are using the LAN at the same time you are.

If you transfer the data from a 720K floppy disk to the file server, you see that it takes even longer. Floppy disk drives, as you know, are slower than hard disks. Your workstation uses the network in small bursts as it reads the data from the floppy disk. The workstation cannot send data across the LAN in this case any faster than it can read the data from the disk.

ARCnet Adapters. ARCnet is one of the oldest types of LAN hardware. It originally was a proprietary scheme of the Datapoint Corporation, but today many companies make ARCnet-compatible cards. By modern standards, ARCnet is very slow, but it is forgiving of minor errors in installation. It is known for solid reliability, and ARCnet cable/adapter problems are easy to diagnose. ARCnet generally costs less than Ethernet, but hardware prices for Ethernet adapters have plummeted so much in recent years that the difference in price between the two is no longer that great an issue. ARCnet operates something like Token Ring but at the slower rate of 2.5 Mbps. The section on "Token Ring Adapters," later in this chapter, explains the basic principles on which ARCnet and Token Ring work.

Ethernet Adapters. The most widely used type of network adapter is Ethernet. Ethernet-based LANs allow you to interconnect a wide variety of equipment, including UNIX workstations, Apple computers, IBM PCs, and IBM clones. You can buy Ethernet cards from dozens of competing manufacturers. Ethernet comes in three varieties (ThinNet, UTP, and ThickNet), depending on the type of cabling you use. ThickNet cables can span a greater distance, but they are much more expensive. Ethernet traditionally operates at a rate of 10 Mbps, but there are now Ethernet adapters available that operate at a rate of 100 Mbps. These "Fast Ethernet" adapters are manufactured by Intel, Thomas-Conrad, and others. There are even models that run at both 10 and 100 Mbps speeds, allowing you to gradually upgrade your network by installing new NICs and hubs over an extended period of time. 100 Mbps adapters only function at that speed when communicating through a high-speed hub to another 100 Mbps adapter.

Between data transfers (requests and responses to and from the file server), Ethernet LANs remain quiet. After a workstation sends a request across the LAN cable, the cable falls silent again. What happens when two or more workstations (and/or file servers) attempt to use the LAN at the same time?

Suppose that one of the workstations wants to request something from the file server, just as the server is sending a response to another workstation. A collision occurs. (Remember that only two computers can communicate through the cable at a given moment.) Both computers—the file server and the workstation—back off and try again. Ethernet network adapters use an algorithm called Carrier Sense, Multiple Access with Collision Detection (CSMA/CD) to deal with collisions, causing each computer to back off for a random amount of time. This method effectively enables one computer to go first. A certain number of collisions are therefore normal and expected on an Ethernet network, but with higher amounts of traffic, the frequency of collisions rises higher and higher, and response times become worse and worse. A saturated Ethernet network actually can spend more time recovering from collisions than it does sending data. IBM and Texas Instruments, recognizing Ethernet's traffic limitations, designed the Token Ring network to solve the problem.

Token Ring Adapters. Except for fiber optic and some of the new high-speed technologies, Token Ring is the most expensive type of LAN. Token Ring can use shielded or unshielded twisted pair cable. Token Ring's cost is justified, however, when you have a great deal of traffic generated by workstations because under normal conditions, collisions are all but eliminated. You often find Token Ring in large corporations with large LANs, especially if the LANs are attached to mainframe computers. Token Ring can operate at 4 Mbps or 16 Mbps.

Workstations on a Token Ring LAN continuously pass an electronic token among themselves. The token is just a short message indicating that the workstation or server possessing it is allowed to transmit. If a workstation has nothing to send, as soon as it receives the token, it passes it on to the next downstream workstation. Only when a workstation receives the token can it transmit data onto the LAN. After transmitting, the token is again passed down the line. If the LAN is busy, and you want your workstation to send a message to another workstation or server, you must wait patiently for the token to come around. Only then can your workstation send its message. The message circulates through all the workstations and file servers on the LAN and eventually winds its way back to you, the sender. The sender then generates a new token, releasing control of the network to the next workstation. During the circulation of the message around the ring, the workstations or server that is the designated recipient recognizes that the message is addressed to it and begins processing that message, but still passes it on to the next workstation.

Token Ring is not as wasteful of LAN resources as this description makes it sound. An unclaimed token takes almost no time at all to circulate through a LAN, even with 100 or 200 workstations. It is also possible to assign priorities to certain workstations and file servers so that they get more frequent access to the LAN. And the token-passing scheme is much more tolerant of high traffic levels on the LAN than the collision-prone Ethernet.

Early Token Release

On a momentarily idle Token Ring LAN, workstations circulate a token. The LAN becomes busy (carries information) when a workstation receives a token and turns it into a data frame targeted at another computer on the network. After receipt by the target node, the data frame continues circulating around the LAN until it is returned back to its source node. The source node turns the data frame back into a token that circulates until a downstream node needs it. So far, so good—these are just standard Token Ring concepts.

When a workstation sends a file request to a server, it consists of only a few bytes, far fewer than the transmission that actually returns the file to the workstation. If the request packet must go into and out of many workstations to circulate the ring, and if the data frame is small, latency occurs. Latency is the unproductive delay that occurs while the source node waits for its upstream neighbor to return its data frame.

During the latency period, the source node appends idle characters onto the LAN following the data frame until the frame circulates the entire LAN and arrives back at the source node. The typical latency period of a 4-Mbps ring will result in the transmission of about 50 to 100 idle characters. On a 16-Mbps ring, latency may reach 400 or more bytes worth of LAN time.

Early Token Release, available only on 16-Mbps networks, is a feature that allows the originating workstation to transmit a new token immediately after sending its data frame. Downstream nodes pass along the data frame and then receive an opportunity to transmit data themselves—the new token. If you were to perform a protocol analysis of a network using Early Token Release, you would see tokens and other data frames immediately following the file request, instead of a long trail of idle characters.

Sometimes a station fumbles and "drops" the token. LAN stations monitor each other and use a complex procedure called *beaconing* to detect the location of the problem and regenerate a lost token. Token Ring is quite a bit more complicated than Ethernet, and the hardware is correspondingly more expensive.

ARCnet and Token Ring are not compatible with one another, but ARCnet uses a similar token-passing scheme to control workstation and server access to the LAN.

Adapter Functions. As mentioned earlier, network adapters generally are collision-sensing or token-passing. A network adapter's design ties it to one of the low-level protocols—Ethernet, Token Ring, FDDI, ARCnet, or some other protocol.

Collision-sensing and token-passing adapters contain sufficient on-board logic to know when it is permissible to send a frame and to recognize frames intended for the adapters. With the adapter support software, both types of cards perform seven major steps during the process of sending or receiving a frame. Outbound, when data is being sent, the steps are performed in the order presented in the following list. Inbound, as data is received, however, the steps are reversed. Here are the steps:

1. *Data transfer.* Data is transferred from PC memory (RAM) to the adapter card or from the adapter card to PC memory via DMA, shared memory, or programmed I/O.

2. *Buffering.* While being processed by the network adapter card, data is held in a buffer. The buffer gives the card access to an entire frame at once, and the buffer enables the card to manage the difference between the data rate of the network and the rate at which the PC can process data.

3. *Frame formation.* The network adapter has to break up the data into manageable chunks (or, on reception, reassemble it). On an Ethernet network, these chunks are about 1,500 bytes. Token Ring networks generally use a frame size of about 4K. The adapter prefixes the data packet with a frame header and appends a frame trailer to it. The header and trailer are the Physical layer's envelope, which you learned about earlier in this chapter. At this point, a complete, ready-for-transmission frame exists. (Inbound, on reception, the adapter removes the header and trailer at this stage.)

4. *Cable access.* In a CSMA/CD network such as Ethernet, the network adapter ensures that the line is quiet before sending its data (or retransmits its data if a collision occurs). In a token-passing network, the adapter waits until it gets a token it can claim. (These steps are not significant to receiving a message, of course.)

5. *Parallel/serial conversion.* The bytes of data in the buffer are sent or received through the cables in serial fashion, with one bit following the next. The adapter card does this conversion in the split second before transmission (or after reception).

6. *Encoding/decoding.* The electrical signals that represent the data being sent or received are formed. Ethernet adapters use a technique called *Manchester encoding,* while Token Ring adapters use a slightly different scheme called *Differential Manchester.* These techniques have the advantage of incorporating timing information into the data through the use of bit periods. Instead of representing a 0 as the absence of electricity and a 1 as its presence, the 0s and 1s are represented by changes in polarity as they occur in relation to very small time periods.

7. *Sending/receiving impulses.* The electrically encoded impulses making up the data (frame) are amplified and sent through the wire. (On reception, the impulses are handed up to the decoding step.)

Of course, the execution of all of these steps takes only a fraction of a second. While you were reading about these steps, thousands of frames could have been sent across the LAN.

Network Adapter cards and the support software recognize and handle errors, which occur when electrical interference, collisions (in CSMA/CD networks), or malfunctioning equipment cause some portion of a frame to be corrupted. Errors generally are detected through the use of a cyclic redundancy check (CRC) data item in the frame. The CRC is checked by the receiver; if its own calculated CRC doesn't match the value of the CRC in the frame, the receiver tells the sender about the error and requests retransmission of the frame in error. Several products exist that perform network diagnostic and analysis functions on the different types of LANs, should you find yourself in need of such troubleshooting.

The different types of network adapters vary not only in access method and protocol, but also in the following elements:

- Transmission speed
- Amount of on-board memory for buffering frames and data
- Bus design (8-bit, 16-bit, or MicroChannel)
- Bus speed (some fail when run at high speeds)
- Compatibility with various CPU chipsets
- DMA usage
- IRQ and I/O port addressing
- Intelligence (some use an on-board CPU, such as the 80186)
- Connector design

LAN Cables

Generally speaking, the cabling systems described in the next few sections use one of three distinct cable types. These are twisted pair, shielded and unshielded (also known as STP and UTP or 10BaseT), coaxial cable, thin and thick (also known as 10Base2 and 10Base5, respectively), and fiber optic cable.

The kind of cable you use depends mostly on the kind of network layout you select, the conditions at the network site, and of course, your budget.

Using Twisted Pair Cable

Twisted pair cable is just what its name implies: insulated wires within a protective casing, with a specified number of twists per foot. Twisting the wires reduces the effect of electromagnetic interference on the signals being transmitted. Shielded twisted pair refers to the amount of insulation around the cluster of wires and therefore, its noise immunity. You are familiar with unshielded twisted pair; it is often used for telephone wiring. Shielded twisted pair, however, is entirely different in appearance. Shielded twisted pair looks somewhat like the wire used to carry house current (110 volts) throughout your home or apartment. Appearances are deceiving, however, because shielded twisted pair actually carries a relatively low voltage signal. The heavy insulation is for noise reduction, not safety. For modern business LANs, unshielded twisted pair cable is most often used on Ethernet networks (where it's called 10BaseT), while shielded twisted pair is commonly found on Token Ring networks.

Figure 11.7 shows unshielded twisted pair cable; figure 11.8 illustrates shielded twisted pair cable.

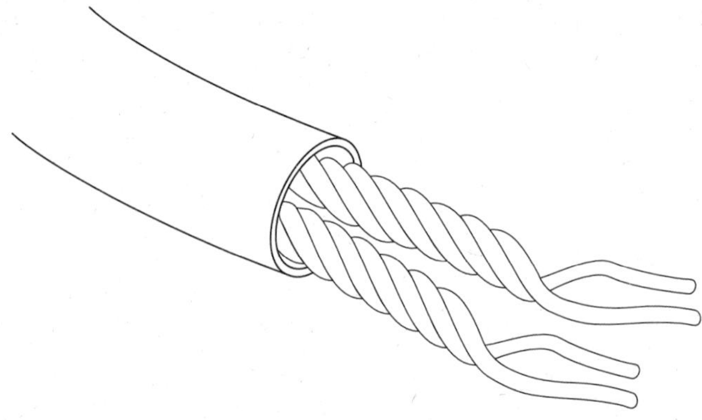

Figure 11.7

An unshielded twisted pair cable.

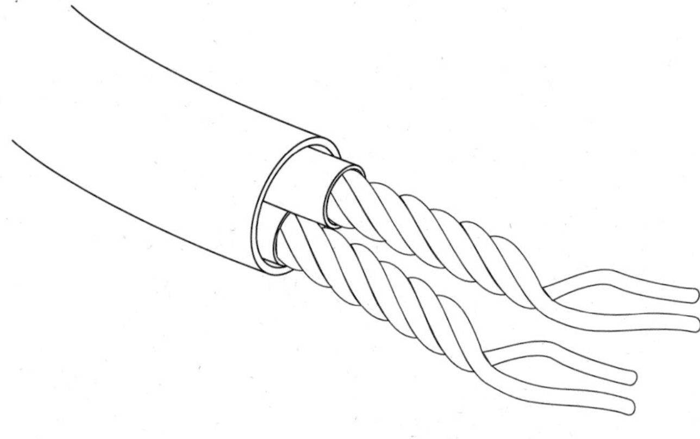

Figure 11.8

A shielded twisted pair cable.

Using Coaxial Cable

Coaxial cable is fairly prevalent in your everyday life; you often find it connected to the backs of television sets and audio equipment. Thin and thick, of course, refer to the diameter of the coaxial cable. Standard Ethernet cable (thick Ethernet) is as thick as your thumb. Thin Ethernet (sometimes called ThinNet or CheaperNet) cable is slightly narrower than your little finger. The thick cable has a greater degree of noise immunity, is more difficult to damage, and requires a vampire tap (a connector with teeth that pierce the tough outer insulation) and a drop cable to connect to a workstation. Although thin cable carries the signal over shorter distances than the thick cable, ThinNet uses a simple BNC (Bayonet-Neill-Concelman) connector (a bayonet-locking connector for thin coaxial cables), is lower in cost, and was at one time the standard in office coaxial cable. ThinNet is wired directly to the back of each computer on the network, and generally installs much more easily than ThickNet, but it is more prone to signal interference and physical connection problems.

Figure 11.9 shows an Ethernet BNC coaxial T-connector, and figure 11.10 illustrates the design of coaxial cable.

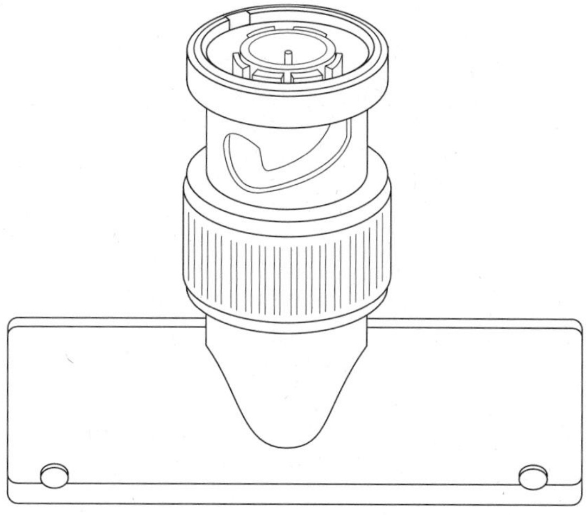

Figure 11.9

An Ethernet coaxial cable T-connector.

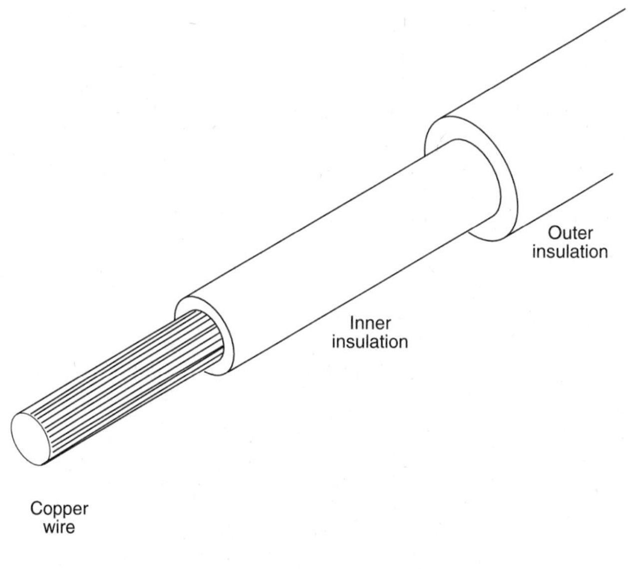

Figure 11.10

Coaxial cable.

Using Fiber Optic Cable

Fiber optic cable uses pulses of light rather than electricity to carry information. It is therefore completely resistant to the electromagnetic interference that limits the length of copper cables. Attenuation (the weakening of a signal as it traverses the cable) is also less of a problem, allowing fiber to send data over huge distances at high speeds. It is, however, very expensive and difficult to work with. Splicing the cable, installing connectors, and using the few available diagnostic tools for finding cable faults are skills that very few people have.

Fiber optic cable is simply designed, but unforgiving of bad connections. Fiber cable usually consists of a core of glass thread, with a diameter measured in microns, surrounded by a solid glass cladding. This, in turn, is covered by a protective sheath. The first fiber optic cables were made of glass, but plastic fibers also have been developed. The light source for fiber optic cable is a light-emitting diode (LED); information usually is encoded by varying the intensity of the light. A detector at the other end of the cable converts the received signal back into electrical impulses. Two types of fiber cable exist: single mode and multimode. Single mode has a smaller diameter, is more expensive, and can carry signals over a greater distance.

Figure 11.11 illustrates fiber optic cables and their connectors.

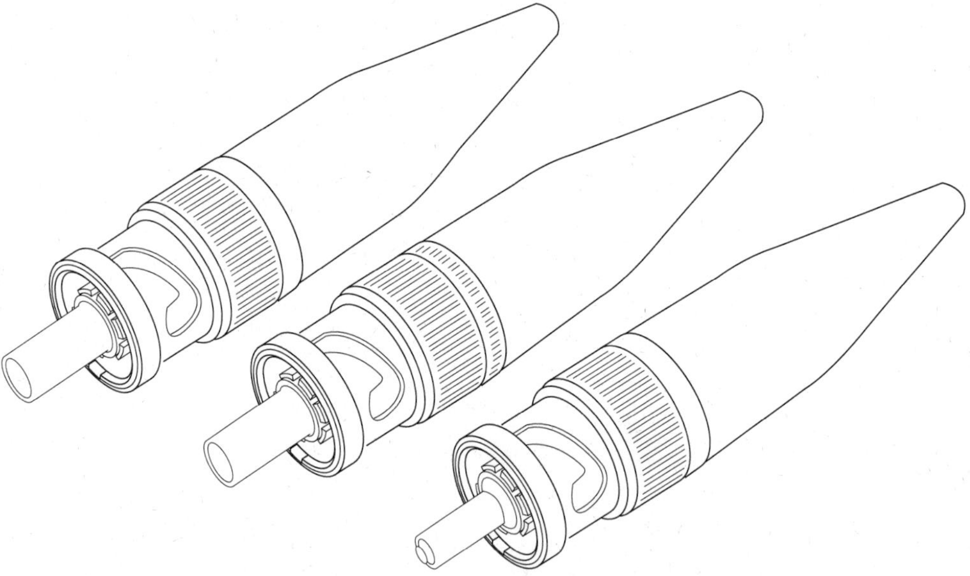

Figure 11.11

Fiber optic cables use light to carry LAN messages. The ST connector is commonly used with fiber optic cables.

Network Topologies

Each workstation on the network is connected with cable (or some other medium) to the other workstations and to one or more servers. Sometimes a single piece of cable winds from station to station, visiting all the servers and workstations along the way. This cabling arrangement is called a *bus topology*, as shown in figure 11.12. (A topology is simply a description of the way the workstations and servers are physically connected.) The potential disadvantage to this type of wiring is that if a workstation has a problem, it can cause all of the stations beyond it on the bus to lose their network connections.

Sometimes separate cables run from a central wiring nexus, often called a hub or a concentrator, to each workstation. Figure 11.13 shows this arrangement, called a star topology. Sometimes the cables branch out repeatedly from a root location, forming the star-wired tree shown in figure 11.14. Bus cabling schemes use the least amount of cable but are the hardest to diagnose or bypass when problems occur.

The other topology often listed in discussions of this type is a ring, in which each workstation is connected to the next, and the last workstation is connected to the first again (essentially a bus topology with the two ends connected). Data travels around a Token Ring network in this fashion, for example. However, the ring is not physically evident in the cabling layout for the network. In fact, the ring exists only within the hub (called a multistation access unit or MSAU on a Token Ring network). Signals generated from one workstation travel back to the hub, are sent out to the next workstation, and then back to the hub again. The data is then passed to each workstation in turn until it arrives back at the computer that originated it, where it is removed from the network. Therefore, although the wiring topology is a star, the data path is theoretically a ring. This is called a *logical ring*.

If you have to run cables (of any type) through walls and ceilings, the cable installation can be the most expensive part of setting up a LAN. At every branching point, special fittings connect the intersecting wires. Sometimes you also need various additional components along the way, such as hubs, repeaters, or access units.

A few companies, such as Motorola, are working on LANs that do not require cables at all. Wireless LAN uses infrared or radio waves to carry network signals from computer to computer, but they have not yet achieved the speed and reliability needed for today's applications.

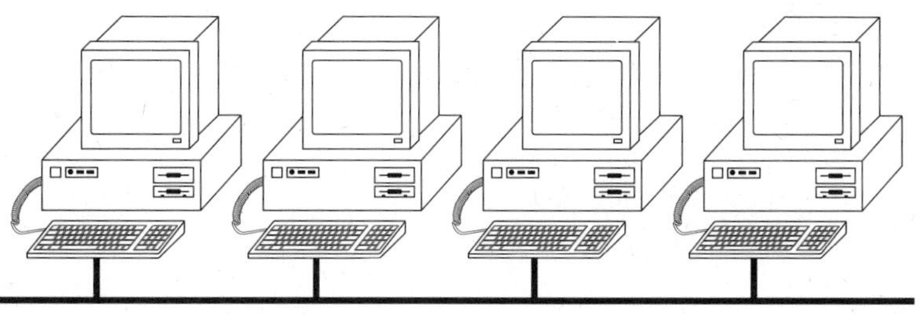

Figure 11.12

The linear bus topology, attaching all network devices to a common cable.

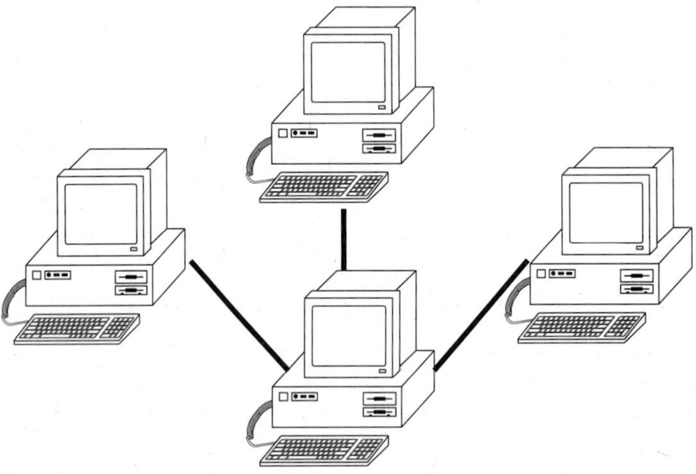

Figure 11.13

The star topology, connecting the LAN's computers and devices with cables that radiate outward, usually from a file server.

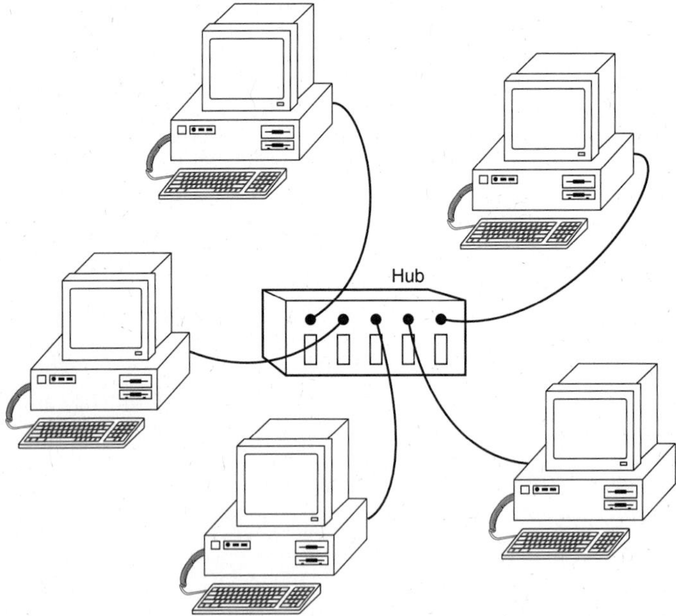

Figure 11.14

The star-wired tree topology, linking the LAN's computers and devices to one or more central hubs, or access units.

Planning the cabling layout, cutting the cable, attaching connectors and installing the cables and fittings are jobs usually best left to experienced workers. If the fittings are not perfect, you may get electronic echoes on the network, which cause transmission errors. There are also a great many physical specifications for each network type that must be observed if the network is to function properly. Coaxial cable costs about 15 cents per foot, whereas shielded twisted pair costs about 25 cents per foot. This may sound like a moderate expense, even for a large LAN, but the cost of installing cable, at about $45 per hour, overshadows the cost of the cable itself. The only time that you might consider installing LAN cable yourself is when you have a group of computers located on adjacent desks, and you do not have to pull cable through the walls or ceiling.

Building codes almost always require you to use fire-proof plenum cables. Plenum cables are more fire-resistant than some other cables. A professional cable installer should be familiar with the building codes in your area. You would be very upset if you installed ordinary cable yourself and were later told by the building inspector to rip out the cable and start over again with the proper kind.

Selecting the Proper Cable

As the demands of network users for ever-increasing amounts of bandwidth continue, and new networking systems are developed to accommodate them, it soon becomes necessary to examine the capabilities of the most fundamental part of the network infrastructure, the cable itself. Ethernet over unshielded twisted pair cable, or 10BaseT, is the medium of choice in the majority of local area network installations today.

The cable used for such networks has traditionally been the same as that used for business telephone wiring. This is known as category 3, or voice grade UTP cable, measured according to a scale that quantifies the cable's data transmission capabilities. The cable itself is 24 AWG (American Wire Gauge, a standard for measuring the diameter of a wire), copper tinned, with solid conductors, 100-105 ohm characteristic impedance, and a minimum of two twists per foot. Category 3 cable is perfectly adequate for networks running at up to 16 Mpbs.

Newer, faster network types require greater performance levels, however. Fast Ethernet technologies that run at 100 Mbps using the same number of wires as standard Ethernet need a greater resistance to signal crosstalk and attenuation; therefore, the use of category 5 cabling is essential. If, when you are building a LAN, you can use category 3 wiring that is already in place, by all means do so. If you are pulling new cable for your network, however, the use of category 5 cable is recommended. Even if you are not running a high-speed network today, you will probably want to consider it in the near future.

Using the IBM Cabling System

IBM, not surprisingly, has its own cabling system designations. Ironically, the cable is not manufactured or sold by IBM. This cabling system consists of a published IBM standard for wiring systems in office buildings that defines cabling system components and different cable types. When it was introduced in 1984, IBM described the IBM cabling system as the intended backbone of its Token Ring network. The first such cables to be manufactured by third-party companies were tested by IBM, verified to IBM specifications, and actually given IBM part numbers. At present, however, cable manufacturers have to rely on the ETL or UL independent testing laboratories or on industry-standard manufacturers (such as AMP) to verify compliance with the specifications published by IBM.

The IBM specification defines workstation faceplates, adapters/connectors, access units, and wiring-closet termination methods. The standard also defines the following cable types:

- *Type 1 data cable.* Copper-based, for data connections only. Available in nonplenum, plenum, and outdoor varieties. It consists of two twisted pairs of 22-gauge solid conductors, shielded with both foil and braid, and covered with a polyvinyl-chloride (PVC) sheath. Type 1 data cable is used for connecting terminal devices located in work areas to distribution panels located in wiring closets and for connecting between wiring closets. The plenum cable is installed in plenums, ducts, and spaces used for environmental air; in case of fire, it gives off less toxic fumes than nonplenum cable. The outdoor cable is protected in a corrugated metallic shield with a polyethylene sheath, and the core is filled with a jellylike compound to prevent moisture from entering.

- *Type 2 data and telephone cable.* For both data and voice (telephone) applications. This cable is similar to Type 1 but has four additional twisted pairs (22-gauge). Type 2 cable comes in plenum and nonplenum varieties.

- *Type 3 telephone twisted pair cable.* Consists of four-pair, 24-gauge wire in polyvinyl-chloride plastic. This cable is equivalent to the IBM Rolm specification and is available in plenum. This cable is unshielded and not as immune to noise as Type 1 cable when used for data.

- *Type 5 fiber optic cable.* Contains two 100/140-micron multimode optical fibers (100-micron core surrounded by 140-micron cladding layer). This cable is not defined by IBM.

- *Type 6 patch panel cable.* For connecting a workstation to a wall faceplate or making connections within a wiring closet. This cable is more flexible than Type 1 cable (hence, its use as patch cable). This cable consists of two twisted pairs of 26-gauge stranded conductors.

- *Type 8 undercarpet cable.* An undercarpet cable useful for open office or workstation areas where there are no permanent walls. Type 8 cable consists of two pairs of 26-gauge solid conductors in a flat sheath.

- *Type 9 low-cost plenum cable.* An economy version of Type 1 plenum cable, with a maximum transmission distance about two-thirds that of Type 1 cable. Type 9 cable consists of two twisted pairs of 26-gauge stranded conductors. This cable is not defined by IBM.

Connecting the Cables

In a token-passing network, the cables from the workstations (or from the wall faceplates) connect centrally to a multistation access unit (abbreviated MSAU, or sometimes just MAU). The MSAU keeps track of which workstations on the LAN are neighbors and which neighbor is upstream or downstream. It is an easy job; the MSAU usually does not even need to be plugged into a electrical power outlet. The exceptions to this need for external power are MSAUs that support longer cable distances, or the use of unshielded twisted pair (Type 3) cable in high-speed LANs. The externally powered MSAU helps the signal along by regenerating it.

An IBM MSAU has eight ports for connecting one to eight Token Ring devices. Each connection is made with a genderless data connector (as specified in the IBM cabling system). The MSAU has two additional ports, labeled RI (Ring-In) and RO (Ring-Out), that daisy-chain several MSAUs together when you have more than eight workstations on the LAN.

It takes several seconds to open the adapter connection on a Token Ring LAN (something you may have noticed). During this time, the MSAU and your Token Ring adapter card perform a small diagnostic check, after which the MSAU establishes you as a new neighbor on the ring. After being established as an active workstation, your computer is linked on both sides to your upstream and downstream neighbors (as defined by your position on the MSAU). In its turn, your Token Ring adapter card accepts the token or frame, regenerates its electrical signals, and gives the token or frame a swift kick to send it through the MSAU in the direction of your downstream neighbor.

In an Ethernet network, the number of connections (taps) and their intervening distances are network's limiting factors. Repeaters regenerate the signal every 500 meters or so. If repeaters were not used, standing waves (additive signal reflections) would distort the signal and cause errors. Because collision detection is highly dependent on timing, only five 500-meter segments and four repeaters can be placed in series before the propagation delay becomes longer than the maximum allowed period for the detection of a collision. Otherwise, the workstations farthest from the sender would be unable to determine whether a collision had occurred.

The people who design computer systems love to find ways to circumvent limitations. Manufacturers of Ethernet products have made it possible to create Ethernet networks in star, branch, and tree designs that overcome the basic limitations already mentioned. You can have thousands of workstations on a complex Ethernet network.

Local area networks are local because the network adapters and other hardware components cannot send LAN messages more than about a few hundred feet. Table 11.9 reveals the distance limitations of different kinds of LAN cable. In addition to the limitations shown in the table, keep in mind that you cannot connect more than 30 computers on a single ThinNet Ethernet segment, more than 100 computers on a ThickNet Ethernet segment, more than 72 computers on unshielded twisted pair Token Ring cable, or more than 260 computers on shielded twisted pair Token Ring cable.

Table 11.9 Network Distance Limitations

Network Adapter	Cable Type	Maximum	Minimum
Ethernet	Thin	607 ft.	20 in.
	Thick (drop cable)	164 ft.	8 ft.
	Thick (backbone)	1,640 ft.	8 ft.
	UTP	328 ft.	8 ft.
Token Ring	STP	328 ft.	8 ft.
	UTP	148 ft.	8 ft.
ARCnet (passive hub)		393 ft.	depends on cable
ARCnet (active hub)		1,988 ft.	depends on cable

Examining Protocols, Frames, and Communications

The network adapter sends and receives messages among the LAN computers, and the network cable carries the messages. It is the less tangible elements, however—the layers of networking protocols in each computer—that turn the individual machines into a local area network.

At the lowest level, networked computers communicate with one another by using message packets, often called *frames*. These frames, so-called because they surround and encapsulate that actual information to be transmitted, are the foundation on which all LAN activity is based. The network adapter, along with its support software, sends and receives these frames. Each computer on the LAN is identified by a unique address to which frames can be sent.

Frames are sent over the network for many different purposes, including the following:

- Opening a communications session with another adapter
- Sending data (perhaps a record from a file) to a PC
- Acknowledging the receipt of a data frame
- Broadcasting a message to all other adapters
- Closing a communications session

Figure 11.15 shows what a typical frame looks like. Different network implementations define frames in very different, highly specific ways, but the following data items are common to all implementations:

- The sender's unique network address
- The destination's unique network address
- An identification of the contents of the frame

- A data record or message
- A checksum or CRC for error-detection purposes

These items are used to perform fundamental tasks that underlie every network transmission: to take the needed information, send it to the proper destination, and ensure that it is received successfully.

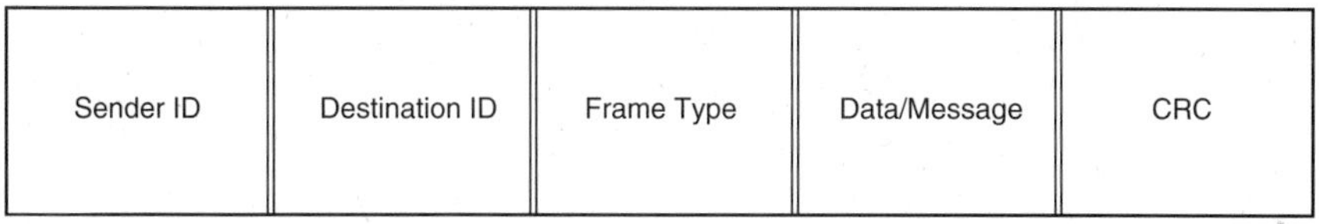

Sender ID	Destination ID	Frame Type	Data/Message	CRC

Figure 11.15

The basic layout of a frame.

Using Frames That Contain Other Frames

The layering of networking protocols within a single frame is a powerful concept that makes network communication possible. The lowest layer knows how to tell the network adapter to send a message, but that layer is ignorant of file servers and file redirection. The highest layer understands file servers and redirection but knows nothing about Ethernet or Token Ring. Together, though, the layers give you the full functionality of a local area network. Frames always are layered (see fig. 11.16).

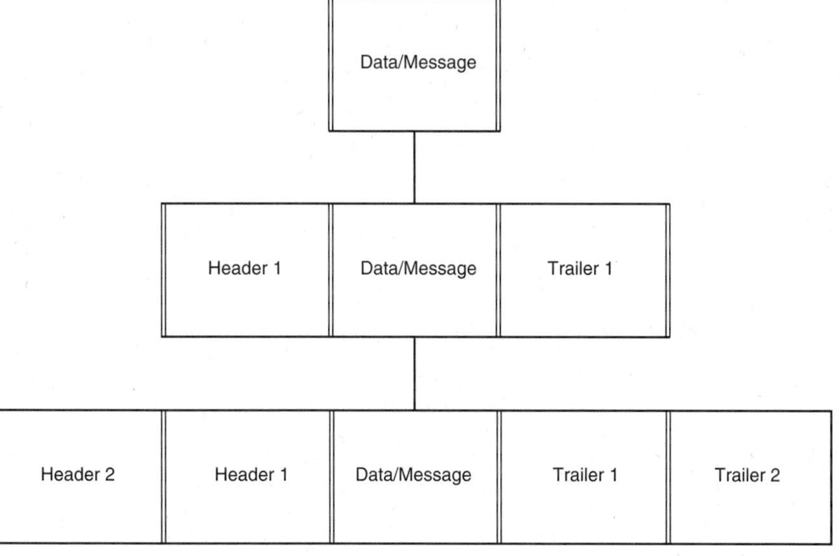

Figure 11.16

Frame layers.

When a higher level file redirection protocol gives a message to a midlevel protocol (such as the Network Basic Input Output System, or NetBIOS, for example), it asks that the message be sent to another PC on the network (probably a file server). The midlevel protocol then puts an envelope around the message packet and hands it to the lowest level protocol, implemented as the network support software and the network adapter card. This lowest layer in turns wraps the (NetBIOS) envelope in an envelope of its own and sends it out across the network. In figure 11.6, you see each envelope labeled header and trailer. On receipt, the network support software on the receiving computer removes the outer envelope and hands the result upward to the next higher level protocol. The midlevel protocol running on the receiver's computer removes its envelope and gives the message—now an exact copy of the sender's message—to the receiving computer's highest-level protocol.

The primary reason for splitting the networking functionality into layers in this manner is that the different hardware and software components of the network are manufactured by different companies. If a single vendor produced every product used on your network, from applications to operating systems to network adapters to cabling, then they could arrange the communications however they wanted, and still be assured of the interoperability of the different parts.

This is not the case, however. Different vendors may split the LAN communications functions in slightly different ways, but they all have to rely on a common diagram of the overall process to ensure that their products will successfully interact with all of the others used on a typical LAN. One such diagram is called the OSI reference model.

Using the OSI Reference Model

The International Organization for Standardization (cryptically abbreviated as the ISO) has published a document called the Open System Interconnection (OSI) model. Most vendors of LAN products endorse the OSI standard but few or none implement it fully. The OSI model divides LAN communications into seven layers. Most network operating system vendors use three or four layers of protocols, overlapping various OSI layers to span the same distance.

The OSI model describes how communications between two computers should occur. It calls for seven layers and specifies that each layer be insulated from the others by a well-defined interface. Figure 11.17 shows the seven layers. Various development projects over the years have attempted to create a networking system that is fully compliant with the OSI architecture, but no practical product has emerged. The OSI model remains a popular reference tool, however, and is a ubiquitous part of the education of any networking professional.

Descriptions of the seven layers follow:

- *Physical.* This part of the OSI model specifies the physical and electrical characteristics of the connections that make up the network (twisted pair cables, fiber optic cables, coaxial cables, connectors, repeaters, and so on). You can think of this layer as the hardware layer. Although the rest of the layers may be implemented as chip-level functions rather than as actual software, the other layers are software in relation to this first layer.

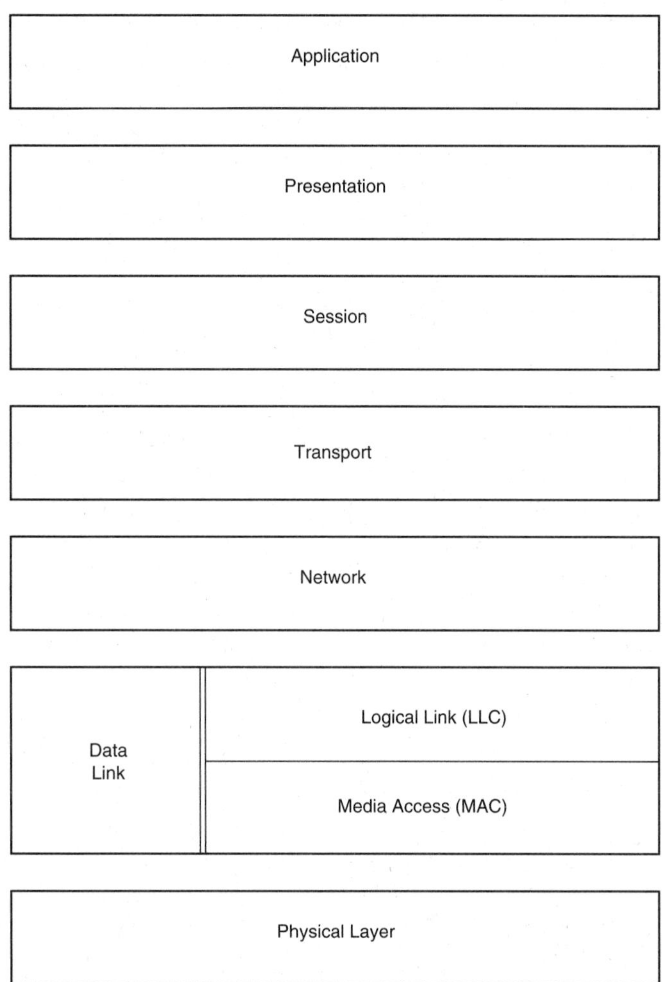

Figure 11.17
The OSI model.

- *Data Link*. At this stage of processing, the electrical impulses enter or leave the network cable. The network's electrical representation of your data (bit patterns, encoding methods, and tokens) is known to this layer, and only to this layer. It is at this point that most errors are detected and corrected (by requesting retransmissions of corrupted packets). Because of its complexity, the Data Link layer often is subdivided into a Media Access Control (MAC) layer and a Logical Link Control (LLC) layer. The MAC layer deals with network access (token-passing or collision-sensing) and network control. The LLC layer, operating at a higher level than the MAC layer, is concerned with sending and receiving the user data messages. Ethernet and Token Ring are Data Link Layer protocols.

- *Network.* This layer switches and routes the packets as necessary to get them to their destinations. This layer is responsible for addressing and delivering message packets. While the Data Link layer is conscious only of the immediately adjacent computers on the network, the Network layer is responsible for the entire route of a packet, from source to destination. IPX and IP are examples of Network layer protocols.
- *Transport.* When more than one packet is in process at any time, such as when a large file must be split into multiple packets for transmission, the Transport layer controls the sequencing of the message components and regulates inbound traffic flow. If a duplicate packet arrives, this layer recognizes it as a duplicate and discards it. SPX and TCP are Transport layer protocols.
- *Session.* The functions in this layer enable applications running at two workstations to coordinate their communications into a single session (which you can think of in terms of a highly structured dialog). The Session layer supports the creation of the session, the management of the packets sent back and forth during the session, and the termination of the session.
- *Presentation.* When IBM, Apple, DEC, NeXT, and Burroughs computers want to talk to one another, obviously a certain amount of translation and byte reordering needs to be done. The Presentation layer converts data into (or from) a machine's native internal numeric format.
- *Application.* This is the layer of the OSI model seen by an application program. A message to be sent across the network enters the OSI model at this point, travels downward toward layer 1 (the Physical layer), zips across to the other workstation, and then travels back up the layers until the message reaches the application on the other computer through its own Application layer.

One of the factors that makes the network operating system of each vendor proprietary (as opposed to having an open architecture) is the vendor's degree and method of noncompliance with the OSI model. Sufficient protocol standardization has been implemented to allow all Ethernet products to function interchangeably (for example), but these standards do not directly comply with the OSI model document.

Using Low-Level Protocols

The Media Access Control (MAC) method for most local area networks (part of the Data Link layer functionality discussed in the preceeding section) works in one of two basic ways: collision-sensing or token-passing. Ethernet is an example of a collision-sensing network; Token Ring is an example of a token-passing network.

The Institute of Electrical and Electronic Engineers (IEEE) has defined and documented a set of standards for the physical characteristics of both collision-sensing and token-passing networks. These standards are known as IEEE 802.3 (Ethernet) and IEEE 802.5 (Token Ring). Be aware, though, that the colloquial names Ethernet and Token Ring actually refer to earlier versions of these protocols, upon which the IEEE standards were based. There are minor differences between the frame definitions for true Ethernet and true IEEE 802.3. In terms of the standards, IBM's 16-Mbps Token Ring adapter card is an 802.5 Token Ring extension.

Some LANs don't conform to IEEE 802.3 or IEEE 802.5, of course. The most well-known of these is ARCnet, available from such vendors as Datapoint Corporation, Standard Microsystems, and Thomas-Conrad. Other types of LANs include StarLan (from AT&T), VistaLan (from Allen-Bradley), LANtastic (from Artisoft), Omninet (from Corvus), PC Net (from IBM), and ProNet (from Proteon). All of these architectures can be considered archaic, however, and are almost never used in the construction of new LANs anymore.

On the Web

http://www.3com.com/0files/products/bguide/index.html

http://www.networks.digital.com/html/products_guide/cat_toc.html

http://www.intel.com/comm-net/sns/showcase/speed/

http://www.proteon.com/products/client-server.html

http://www.smc.com/network/network.html

http://www.artisoft.com/

Fiber Distributed Data Interface (FDDI) is a new physical-layer LAN standard. FDDI uses fiber optic cable and a token-passing scheme similar to IEEE 802.5 to transmit data frames at a snappy 100 Mbps. There are also new standards now on the market designed to upgrade Ethernet networks to 100 Mbps. Some of these, such as 100VG AnyLAN, can no longer be considered as Ethernet and use brand new methods for gaining media access. Some of these new standards are covered in the following section.

Evaluating High-Speed Networking Technologies

If you have fast workstations and a fast file server, you will want a fast network as well. Even the 16Mbps supplied by Token Ring may be too slow if your applications are data-intensive. The explosive growth of multimedia, groupware, and other technologies that require enormous amounts of data has forced network administrators to consider the need for high-speed network connections to individual desktop workstations.

Networking at speeds above 16 Mbps has been around for several years, but it has primarily been limited to high-speed backbone connections between servers, due to its additional expense. Several new technologies are available today, however, that are designed to deliver data at high speeds—up to 100 Mbps and more—to standard user workstations. Real-time data feeds from financial services, videoconferencing, video editing, and high-color graphics processing are just some of the tasks now being performed on PCs that would benefit greatly from an increase in network transmission speed.

Using the Fiber Distributed Data Interface (FDDI)

The Fiber Distributed Data Interface (FDDI) has been available for several years, but it is still a much newer protocol than Ethernet or Token Ring. Designed by the X3T9.5 Task Group of ANSI (the American National Standards Institute), FDDI passes tokens and data frames around a ring of optical fiber at a rate of 100 Mbps. FDDI was designed to be as much like the IEEE 802.5 Token Ring standard as possible, above the Physical layer. Differences occur only where necessary to support the faster speeds and longer transmission distances of FDDI.

If FDDI were to use the same bit-encoding scheme used by Token Ring, every bit would require two optical signals: a pulse of light and then a pause of darkness. This means that FDDI would need to send 200 million signals per second to have a 100 Mbps transmission rate. Instead, the scheme used by FDDI—called NRZI 4B/5B—encodes 4 bits of data into 5 bits for transmission so that fewer signals are needed to send a byte of information. The 5-bit codes (symbols) were chosen carefully to ensure that network timing requirements are met. The 4B/5B scheme, at a 100 Mbps transmission rate, actually causes 125 million signals per second to occur (this is 125 megabaud). Also, because each carefully selected light pattern symbol represents 4 bits (a half byte, or nibble), FDDI hardware can operate at the nibble and byte level rather than at the bit level, making it easier to achieve the high data rate.

Two major differences in the way the token is managed by FDDI and IEEE 802.5 Token Ring exist. In traditional Token Ring, a new token is circulated only after a sending workstation gets back the frame that it sent. In FDDI, a new token is circulated immediately by the sending workstation after it finishes transmitting a frame, a technique that has since been adapted for use in Token Ring networks and called Early Token Release. FDDI classifies attached workstations as asynchronous (workstations that are not rigid about the time periods that occur between network accesses) and synchronous (workstations having very stringent requirements regarding the timing between transmissions). FDDI uses a complex algorithm to allocate network access to the two classes of devices.

Although it provides superior performance, FDDI's acceptance as a desktop network has been hampered by its extremely high installation and maintenance costs (see "Using Fiber Optic Cable," earlier in this chapter).

Using 100 Mbps Ethernet

One of the largest barriers to the implementation of high-speed networking has been the need for a complete replacement of the networking infrastructure. Most companies cannot afford the down time needed to rewire the entire network, replace all the hubs and network interface cards, and then configure everything to operate properly. As a result of this, some of the new 100 Mbps technologies are designed to make the upgrade process easier in several ways. First, they can often use the network cable that is already in place, and second, they are compatible enough with the existing installation to allow a gradual changeover to the new technology, workstation by workstation. Obviously, these factors also serve to minimize the expense associated with such an upgrade.

The two systems that take this approach are 100BaseT, first developed by the Grand Junction Corp., and 100VG AnyLAN, advocated by Hewlett Packard and AT&T. Both of these systems run at 100 Mbps over standard UTP cable, but that is where the similarities end. In fact, of the two, only 100BaseT can truly be called an Ethernet network. 100BaseT uses the same CSMA/CD media access protocol and the same frame layout defined in the IEEE 802.3 standard. In fact, 100BaseT as been ratified as an extension to that standard, called 802.3u.

To accommodate existing cable installations, the 802.3u document defines four different cabling standards, as shown in table 11.10.

Table 11.10 100BaseT Cabling Standards

Standard	Cable Type	Segment Length
100BaseTX	Category 5 (2 pairs)	100 meters
100BaseT4	Category 3, 4, or 5 (4 pairs)	100 meters
100BaseFX	62.6 micrometer Multimode fiber (2 strands)	400 meters

Sites with category 3 cable already installed can therefore use the system without the need for rewiring, as long as the full 4 pairs in a typical run are available.

Note

Despite the apparent wastefulness, in most cases it is not recommended that data and voice traffic be mixed within the same cable, even if sufficient wire pairs are available. Digital phone traffic could possibly coexist, but normal analog voice lines will definitely inhibit the performance of the data network.

100BaseT also requires the installation of new hubs and new network interface cards, but since the frame type used by the new system is identical to that of the old, this replacement can be done gradually, to spread the labor and expense over a protracted period of time. You could replace one hub with a 100BaseT model, and then switch workstations over to it, one at a time, as the users' needs and the networking staff's time permits. You can even purchase NICs that can operate at both 10 and 100 Mbps speeds to make the changeover even easier.

100VG (voice grade) AnyLAN also runs at 100 Mbps and is specifically designed to use existing category 3 UTP cabling. Like 100BaseT4, it requires four pairs of cable strands to affect its communications. There are no separate category 5 or fiber optic options in the standard. Beyond the cabling, 100VG AnyLAN is quite different from 100BaseT and indeed from Ethernet.

While 10 and 100BaseT networks both reserve one pair of wires for collision detection, 100VG AnyLAN is able to transmit over all four pairs simultaneously. This technique is called *quartet signaling*. A different signal encoding scheme called 5B/6B NRZ is also used, sending 2.5 times more bits per cycle than an Ethernet network's Manchester encoding scheme. Multiplied by the four pairs of wires (as compared to 10BaseT's one), you have a tenfold increase in transmission speed.

The fourth pair is made available for transmission because there is no need for collision detection on a 100VG AnyLAN network. Instead of the CSMA/CD media access system that defines an Ethernet network, 100VG AnyLAN uses a brand new technique called *demand priority*. Individual network computers have to request and be granted permission to transmit by the hub before they can send their data.

100VG AnyLAN also used the 802.3 frame type, so its traffic can co-exist on a LAN with regular Ethernet. Like 100BaseT, combination 10/100 NICs are available, and the installation can be gradually migrated to the new technology.

Both of these standards are making a strong bid for market share. Their capabilities are very similar, but the deciding factor may be the proven success of Ethernet technology, versus a very young competitor.

Using ATM

Asynchronous Transfer Mode is one of the newest of the high speed technologies. It has been in an "emerging" state for some time now, without having developed into its full potential. ATM defines a physical layer protocol in which a standard size 53-byte packet (called a cell) can be used to transmit voice, data, and real-time video over the same cable, simultaneously. The cells contain identification information that allow high-speed ATM switches (wiring hubs) to separate the data types and ensure that the cells are re-assembled in the right order.

The basic ATM standard runs at 155 Mbps, but some implementations can go as high as 660 Mbps. Work is also progressing on an ATM desktop standard that runs at 25 Mbps, but this doesn't seem to be enough of a gain over Token Ring's 16 Mbps to be worth the adoption of an entirely new networking technology.

ATM is a radically different concept, and there are no convenient upgrade paths as there are with the 100 Mbps standards described earlier. All the networking hardware must be replaced, and the ATM products currently on the market are still riding the wave of extremely high prices that are common to any new technology. For this reason, ATM is being used primarily for WAN links at this time. When the delivery of real-time video over the network becomes more of a practical reality than it is now, ATM might find its rightful place. For now, it remains a niche technology with very good potential.

TCP/IP and the Internet

TCP/IP stands for Transmission Control Protocol/Internet Protocol. It is the colloquial name given to the suite of networking protocols used by the Internet, as well as by most UNIX operating systems. TCP is primary Transport layer protocol in the suite, and IP defines the Network layer protocol that transmits blocks of data to the host. TCP/IP is an extensive collection of Internet protocol applications and transport protocols and includes File Transfer Protocol (FTP), Terminal Emulation (TELNET), and the Simple Mail

Transfer Protocol (SMTP). TCP/IP was originally developed by the U.S. Department of Defense in the 1970s as platform and hardware-independent medium for communication over what was to become known as the Internet. A good example of this independence is the capability of DOS, Windows, or Windows 95 workstations to access information and transfer files on the Internet, which is a mixed platform environment. The primary advantages of TCP/IP are :

- *Platform Independence.* TCP/IP is not designed for use in any single hardware or software environment. It can and has been used on networks of all types.
- *Absolute Addressing.* TCP/IP provides a means of uniquely identifying every machine on the Internet.
- *Open Standards.* The TCP/IP specifications are publicly available to users and developers alike. Suggestions for changes to the standard can be submitted by anyone.
- *Application Protocols.* TCP/IP allows dissimilar environments to communicate. High-level protocols like FTP and TELNET have become ubiquitous in TCP/IP environments on all platforms.

Although it has been the protocol of choice on UNIX networks for many years, the explosive growth of the Internet has brought the protocols onto all kinds of local area networks as well. Many network administrators are finding that they can adapt their current network operating systems to use TCP/IP, and thus lessen the network traffic problems that can be caused by running several different sets of protocols on the same network.

Connecting to the Internet

You can connect a computer to the Internet through virtually any of the access ports discussed in this chapter thus far. Individual computers can use modems to connect to an Internet Service Provider (ISP), or a network connection can be established, through which all of the users on the LAN gain access. Depending on your organization's degree of Internet involvement, any one of the following access options can be selected.

Asynchronous Modem Connections. Individual computers can use normal asynchronous modems attached to a serial port to connect to the Internet, through the services of an Internet service provider. ISPs provide dial-in capabilities using either the PPP (Point-to-point Protocol) or the SLIP (Serial Line Internet Protocol). Both of these protocols are part of the TCP/IP suite and are now provided by virtually all of the third/-party TCP/IP stacks available for DOS and Windows 3.1. Windows 95 and Windows NT include support for both protocols as part of the operating system. Whichever protocol you use must be supported by the TCP/IP stack on the remote computer, as well as the system to which you are connecting. Your service provider will be able to tell you what protocols are supported by the host system.

SLIP. The SLIP is an extremely simple protocol that provides a mechanism for the packets generated by IP (called *datagrams*) to be transmitted over a serial connection. It sends each datagram sequentially, separating them with a single byte known as the SLIP END character to signify the end of a packet. SLIP provides no means of error correction or data compression, and it was eventually superseded by the PPP.

PPP. The PPP improves the reliability of serial TCP/IP communications with a three-layer protocol that provides the means for implementing the error correction and compression that SLIP lacks. Most TCP/IP stacks provide PPP support, as do most of the ISPs operating today. When given a choice, you should always select PPP over SLIP; it provides superior throughput and reliability.

ISDN Connections. An increasingly popular option for Internet connectivity is the ISDN connection. Providing speeds of 128 Kbps (when both B channels are combined), it is more than four times faster than a 28.8 Kbps modem connection. ISDN can be used to provide Internet access to a network or to an individual computer. The basics of ISDN communications are covered in the "Integrated Services Digital Network" section, earlier in this chapter.

For basic e-mail connectivity and modest use, an ISDN connection could support 10 to 20 users on a network nicely. Giving users a taste of the Internet often leads to a substantial habit, however, and you may find that World Wide Web browsing and FTP transfers cause you to quickly outgrow an ISDN link.

T-1 Connections. For networks that must support a large number of Internet users, and especially for organizations that will be hosting their own Internet services, a T-1 connection to your service provider may be the wise investment. A T-1 is a digital connection running at 1.55 Mbps. This is more than ten times faster than an ISDN link. A T-1 may be split (or *fractioned*), depending on how it is to be used. It can be split into 24 individual 64K lines or left as a single high-capacity pipeline. Some service providers allow you to lease any portion of a T-1 connection that you want (in 64K increments). T-1 links in the United States usually cost several thousand dollars per month, plus a substantial installation fee, but for a large organization that is heavily committed to the Internet, it can be more economical to install a higher capacity service and grow into it, rather than constantly upgrade the link.

T-3 Connections. Equivalent in throughput to approximately 30 T-1 lines, a T-3 connection runs at 45 Mbps and is suitable for use by very large networks, university campuses, and the like. Pricing information falls into the "if you have to ask, you can't afford it" category.

Summary

This chapter gave you an understanding of serial, parallel, and network connectivity methods. You learned about the different types of UART chips, explored ways to diagnose serial and parallel ports, and considered local area network adapters, cables, and protocols.

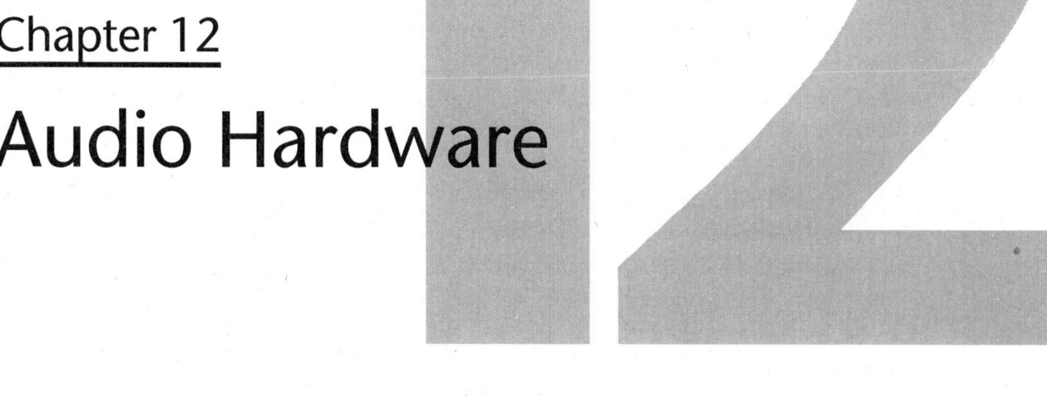

Chapter 12

Audio Hardware

One of the problems with the PC standard is that when it was first created, it did not include audio capabilities other than rudimentary beeping or tone generation. Part of this was due to the fact that the PC standard originated in 1981, and other computers of that time had similar rudimentary capabilities. Systems that were designed later, such as the Macintosh, which debuted in 1984, did include high-quality audio capabilities as an integral part of the system hardware and software. Although there still is no universal audio hardware and software standard for PC compatible systems, the inherent expandability of the PC platform allows audio capability to be easily added and at least one de facto standard has emerged. This chapter will focus on these products and how they are installed and operated.

At first, sound cards were used only for games. Several companies including AdLib, Roland, and Creative Labs had introduced products by the late 1980s. In 1989 Creative Labs introduced the Game Blaster, which provided stereo sound to a handful of computer games. The question for many buyers was "Why spend $100 for a card that adds sound to a $50 game?" More importantly, because no sound standards existed at the time, a sound card might be useless with other games.

A few months after releasing the Game Blaster, Creative Labs announced the Sound Blaster sound card. The Sound Blaster was compatible with the AdLib sound card and Creative Labs' own Game Blaster card. It included a built-in microphone jack and a MIDI (Musical Instrument Digital Interface) for connecting the PC to a musical synthesizer. Finally, the sound card had uses in addition to games.

Sound Card Applications

Unfortunately, there is no single standard for PC compatible sound cards. As in other aspects of the computer industry, standards are often developed by the market leader in a particular segment of the marketplace. These are called defacto standards. For example, Hewlett Packard printers use a command language and graphics language that has become a defacto standard simply because many of their printers have been sold and most software supports them. Other printer manufacturers then strive to make their printers emulate the Hewlett Packard printers so they don't require unique commands and they can use the same commands and drivers as a Hewlett Packard printer. This is how a defacto standard is born. It is essentially based on popularity. While other printer command standards exist, the Hewlett Packard standard is supported by most PC compatible printers.

Over the last few years, several sound card manufacturers have fought for dominance, and there are several popular brands. Although several different companies make audio boards, the ones from Creative Labs have dominated the marketplace and have become the defacto standard. Thus, most audio boards from other companies emulate the Creative Labs "Sound Blaster" boards. Like the Hewlett Packard printer standard, the Creative Labs Sound Blaster interface is the one that most hardware products emulate, and the one that most drivers are written for.

A sound card has many uses, including:

- Adding stereo sound to entertainment (game) software
- Increasing the effectiveness of educational software, particularly for young children
- Adding sound effects to business presentations and training software
- Creating music, using MIDI hardware and software
- Adding voice notes to files
- Adding sound effects to operating system events
- Enabling a PC to read
- Enabling PC use by handicapped individuals
- Playing audio CDs

Games

The sound card was originally designed to play games. In fact, many sound cards include a game adapter interface, which is a connector for adding a game control device (usually a joystick or control paddles). This is a potential area of conflict because other cards such as the multi-I/O type cards used in many PCs that have serial ports, parallel ports, and so on, also have a game interface as well. This will result in an I/O Port address conflict because nearly all game interfaces use the same I/O Port addresses. In these cases, it is usually best to use the game adapter interface on the sound card and disable any other in your system.

By adding a sound card, the game playing takes on a new dimension. The sounds add a level of realism that would otherwise be impossible, even with the best graphics. For example, some games use digitized human voices and dialog. In addition to realistic sounds and effects, games can have musical scores, which add to the excitement and entertainment.

Multimedia

A sound card is a prerequisite if you want to turn your PC into a multimedia PC (MPC). What is multimedia? The term embraces a number of PC technologies, but primarily deals with video, sound, and storage. Basically, multimedia means the ability to merge images, data, and sound on a computer. In a practical sense, multimedia simply means adding a sound card and a CD-ROM drive to your system.

An organization called the Multimedia PC (MPC) Marketing Council was originally formed by Microsoft to generate standards for multimedia PCs. They have created several MPC standards and license their logo and trademark to manufacturers whose hardware and software conform to these standards. This allows compatible hardware and software to be developed for multimedia operation on PC compatible systems.

More recently, the Multimedia PC Marketing Council has formally transferred responsibility for their standards to the Software Publishers Association's Multimedia PC Working Group. This group includes many of the same members as the original MPC and will now be the body governing the MPC specifications. The first thing this group has done is create a new Multimedia PC (MPC) standard.

The MPC Marketing Council originally developed two primary standards for multimedia. They are called the MPC Level 1 and MPC Level 2 standards. Now under the direction of the Software Publishers Association (SPA), these first two standards have been augmented by a third standard called MPC Level 3, which was introduced in June of '95. These standards define the minimum capabilities for a multimedia PC. Table 12.1 shows these standards.

Table 12.1 Multimedia Standards

	MPC Level 1	MPC Level 2	MPC Level 3
Processor	16MHz 386SX	25MHz 486SX	75 MHz Pentium
RAM	2M	4M	8M
Hard Disk	30M	160M	540M
Floppy Disk	1.44M 3.5-inch	1.44M 3.5-inch	1.44M 3.5-inch
CD-ROM Drive	Single-Speed	Double-Speed	Quad-Speed
Audio	8-bit	16-bit	16-bit
VGA Video Resolution	640x480; 16 colors	640x480; 64K colors	640x480; 64K colors
Other I/O	Serial; Parallel ; MIDI; Game	Serial; Parallel; MIDI; Game	Serial; Parallel; MIDI; Game
Software	Microsoft Windows 3.1	Microsoft Windows 3.1	Microsoft Windows 3.1
Date Introduced	May 1993	1990	June 1995

The MPC-3 specifications should be considered the bare minimums for any multimedia system today. In fact, I would normally recommend a system that exceeds the Level 3 standards in several areas, such as RAM, hard disk size, and video capability. Note that although speakers are technically not a part of the MPC specification, they are required for sound reproduction!

MIDI

If you're musically inclined, you'll enjoy MIDI (Musical Instrument Digital Interface). Developed in the early 1980s, MIDI essentially is a powerful programming language that lets your computer store and edit or play back music in tandem with a MIDI-compatible electronic musical instrument, typically a keyboard synthesizer.

The MPC specs mentioned earlier call for MIDI support. With MIDI, you can compose and edit music for presentations, learn about music theory, or turn your PC into a one-stop music mixing studio.

MIDI makes a musical note sound as though it comes from any of a wide array of instruments. The MPC specifications require a sound card to contain an FM MIDI synthesizer chip and be able to play at least six notes simultaneously.

To connect a MIDI device to a PC, you need a sound card that has two round serial ports in back—a MIDI input port and a MIDI output port. In addition to a keyboard, you'll need sequencing software to modify the tempo, sound, and volume of your recordings, or to cut and paste together various prerecorded music sequences.

Unlike other sound files, MIDI messages require little disk space. An hour of stereo music stored in MIDI requires less than 500K. (To contrast, a Microsoft Windows digital sound (WAV) file consumes over 1,000 times that space.) Many games use MIDI sounds to conserve on disk space.

The quality of sound reproduction using MIDI files can vary greatly from card to card. This depends largely on whether your card uses wavetable synthesis or FM synthesis for MIDI reproduction.

Most sound boards generate sounds using FM synthesis, a technology first pioneered in 1976. By using one sine wave operator to modify another, FM synthesis creates an artificial sound that mimics an instrument. Over the years, the technology has progressed (some FM synthesizers now use four operators) to a point where FM synthesis sounds good, but it still sounds artificial.

More realistic, inexpensive sound was pioneered by Ensoniq Corp., the makers of professional keyboards, in 1984. Using a technology that had been theorized at about the same time as FM synthesis, Ensoniq found a way to sample any instrument, including pianos, violins, guitars, flutes, trumpets, and drums, and to store the digitized sound in a wavetable. Stored either in ROM chips or on disk, the wavetable supplies an actual digitized sound of an instrument when called by the application. Soon after Ensoniq's discovery, other keyboard makers replaced their FM synthesizers with wavetable synthesis.

Wavetable synthesis won't make every sound on your PC more realistic—only the MIDI sounds, which are often used in games. Windows WAV files are actual stored sounds and don't benefit from wavetable synthesis.

Presentations

Businesses are discovering that combining graphics, animation, and sound is more impressive, and often less expensive, than a slide show. A sound card adds impact to any presentation or classroom.

A variety of business presentation software and high-end training and authoring packages already exist. And you don't have to be a programmer to get your own show on the road. Even such popular software packages as CorelDRAW! and PowerPoint now include sound and animation features for their presentation files.

Some presentation software packages support MIDI. With these products you can synchronize sounds with objects. When a picture of a new product is displayed, for example, you can play a roaring round of applause. You can even pull in audio from a CD in your CD-ROM drive. Such presentation software programs include clip-media libraries.

A sound card can make tasks (such as learning how to use software) easier. PC software manufacturers have taken an early lead in this area. Many publishers are shipping special CD-ROM versions of some of their products. These versions often include animated online help, replete with music.

You can even take your show on the road. Many laptop and notebook computers today include sound capability and even have built-in CD-ROM drives and speakers. There are also external sound cards and even CD-ROM drives that attach to a laptop computer's parallel port to provide multimedia on the go. Finally, there are several PC-Card (PCMCIA) based sound cards on the market also.

Recording

Virtually all sound cards have an audio input jack. With a microphone, you can record your voice. Using the Microsoft Windows Sound Recorder, you can play, edit, or record a sound file. These files are saved as WAV files, a type of file format. In the Windows Control Panel, you can assign certain Windows events a specific WAV file (see fig. 12.1). I always get a laugh when I exit Windows and hear the sound of a flushing toilet!

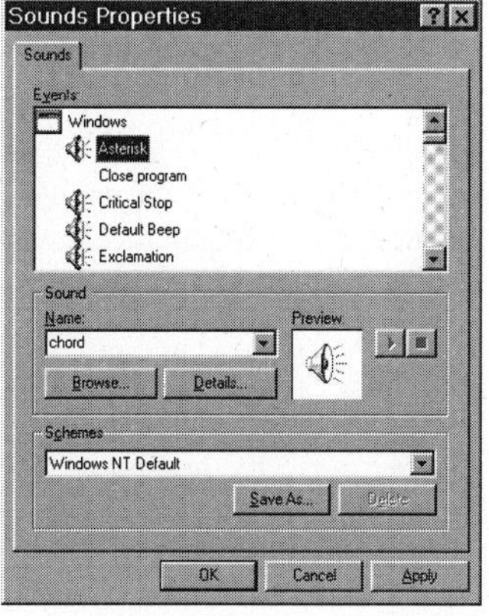

Figure 12.1

The Sound section of the Windows 95 Control Panel adds sound to different Windows events.

By recording your own sounds, you can create your own WAV files. Then you can use them for certain events. These are the standard events:

- Windows Start
- Windows Exit
- Default beep
- Asterisk
- Critical Stop
- Question
- Exclamation

Through the same audio input jack, you can attach your stereo system and record a song to a WAV file. You can also purchase prepackaged WAV files. Prerecorded WAV files can also be found on your local electronic bulletin board or online services such as CompuServe and America Online.

Voice Annotation

Using WAV files, you can record messages into your Windows documents and spreadsheets. For example, a business executive could pick up a microphone and, by embedding a message in a contract, give his or her secretary explicit instructions. This message is called a voice annotation. I like to think of it as a verbal Post-It Note.

With voice annotation you can embed voice messages, suggestions, or questions in a document and send it to a colleague. To leave such messages, your Windows application must support Windows' Object Linking and Embedding (OLE) feature.

Imagine that you're editing a worksheet in Excel and want to insert a voice note next to a total that looks questionable. Place the cursor in the cell next to the total, then select Edit, Insert, Object, Sound to call up Windows' Sound Recorder. Click on the Record button and begin speaking.

Voice Recognition

Some sound cards are capable of voice recognition. You can also get voice recognition for your current sound card in the form of add-on software. Voice-recognition technology is unfortunately still in it's infancy, and you will need a fast computer, such as a Pentium, for quick response times.

Proofreading

Sound cards can be used also as inexpensive proofreaders. Text-to-speech utilities can read back to you a list of numbers or text. This software is included with some sound cards and can be used to read back highlighted words or even an entire file.

This will allow you to more easily spot forgotten words or awkward phrases when you hear a note read back to you. Accountants can double-check numbers, and busy executives can listen to their e-mail while they are doing paperwork.

Audio CDs

One entertaining use of a CD-ROM drive is to play audio CDs while you are working on something else. The music can be piped not only through a pair of speakers but also through a headphone set plugged into the front of your CD-ROM drive. Most sound cards include a CD-player utility, although free versions are available on online services such as CompuServe. These programs usually present a visual display similar to an audio CD player. You operate the controls with a mouse or the keyboard and can listen to audio CDs while you work on other things.

Sound Card Concepts and Terms

To understand sound cards, you need to understand various concepts and terms. Words like 16-bit, CD-quality, and MIDI port are just a few. Concepts such as sampling and digital-to-audio conversion (DAC) are often sprinkled throughout stories about new sound products. The following sections describe some common sound card terms and concepts.

The Nature of Sound

To understand a sound card, you need to understand sound. Every sound is produced by vibrations that compress air or other substances. These sound waves travel in all directions, expanding in balloon-like fashion from the source of the sound. When these waves reach your ear, they cause vibrations that you perceive as sound.

The two basic properties of any sound are its pitch and its intensity.

Pitch is simply the rate at which vibrations are produced. It is measured in the number of hertz (Hz), or cycles per second. One cycle is a complete vibration back and forth. The number of Hz is the frequency of the tone; the higher the frequency, the higher the pitch.

You cannot hear all possible frequencies. Very few people can hear any fewer than 16Hz or any more than about 20KHz (kilohertz; 1KHz equals 1,000Hz). In fact, the lowest note on a piano has a frequency of 27Hz, the highest note, a little more than 4KHz. And frequency-modulation (FM) radio stations broadcast notes up to 15KHz.

The intensity of a sound is called its amplitude. This intensity depends upon the strength of the vibrations producing the sound. A piano string, for example, vibrates gently when the key is struck softly. The string swings back and forth in a narrow arc and the tone it sends out is soft. If the key is struck forcefully, however, the string swings back and forth in a wider arc. The loudness of sounds is measured in decibels (db). The rustle of leaves is rated at 20db, average street noise at 70, and nearby thunder at 120.

Game Standards

Most sound cards support both of the current entertainment audio standards—AdLib and Sound Blaster. The Sound Blaster is a family of sound cards sold by Creative Labs; Ad Lib sells their own cards as well. To play most games, you must tell your game which of these sound card standards your sound card support. Sticking with a popular sound card product (like the Sound Blaster line from Creative Labs) will ensure that you always have software support. Most software supports the Sound Blaster or AdLib cards, and because of this, now most other brand sound cards will emulate one of these popular ones. If you have some off-the-wall brand sound card, and it does not emulate either the Sound Blaster or AdLib cards, then you may find many software products that do not specifically support your card.

Frequency Response

The quality of a sound card is often measured by two criteria—frequency response (or range) and total harmonic distortion.

The frequency response of a sound card is the range in which an audio system can record and/or play at a constant and audible amplitude level. Many cards support 30Hz to 20KHz. The wider the spread, the better the sound card.

The total harmonic distortion measures a sound card's linearity, the straightness of a frequency response curve. In laymen's terms, the harmonic distortion is a measure of accurate sound reproduction. Any nonlinear elements cause distortion in the form of harmonics. The smaller the percentage of distortion, the better.

Sampling

With a sound card, a PC can record Waveform Audio. Waveform audio (also known as sampled or digitized sound) uses the PC as a tape recorder. Small computer chips built into a sound card, called analog-to-digital converters (ADCs), convert analog sound waves into digital bits the computer can understand. Likewise, digital-to-analog converters (DACs) convert the recorded sounds to something audible.

Sampling is the process of turning the original analog sound waves (see fig. 12.2) into digital (on/off) signals that can be saved and later replayed. Snapshots of the analog sounds are taken and saved. For example, at time X the sound may be measured with an amplitude of Y. The higher (or more frequent) the sample rate, the more accurate the digital sound is to its real-life source.

8-Bit versus 16-Bit

The original Multimedia PC (MPC) specifications required 8-bit sound. This doesn't mean the sound card must fit into an 8-bit instead of a 16-bit expansion slot. Rather, 8-bit audio means that the sound card uses eight bits to digitize each sound sample. This translates into 256 possible digital values to which the sample can be pegged (less quality than the 65,536 values possible with a 16-bit sound card). Generally, 8-bit audio is adequate for recorded speech whereas 16-bit sound is best for the demands of music. Figure 12.3 shows the difference between 8 and 16-bit sound.

Many of the older sound cards did 8-bit sound reproduction only. Today, I would not recommend anything less than a 16-bit card, which offers very high resolution.

Besides resolution, the sampling rate or frequency determines how often the sound card measures the level of the sound being recorded or played back. Basically, you have to sample at about two times the highest frequency you want to produce, plus an extra 10 percent to keep out unwanted signals. Humans can hear up to 20,000 cycles per second, or 20KHz. If you double this number and add 10 percent, you get a 44.1KHz sampling rate, the same sampling rate used by high-fidelity audio CDs.

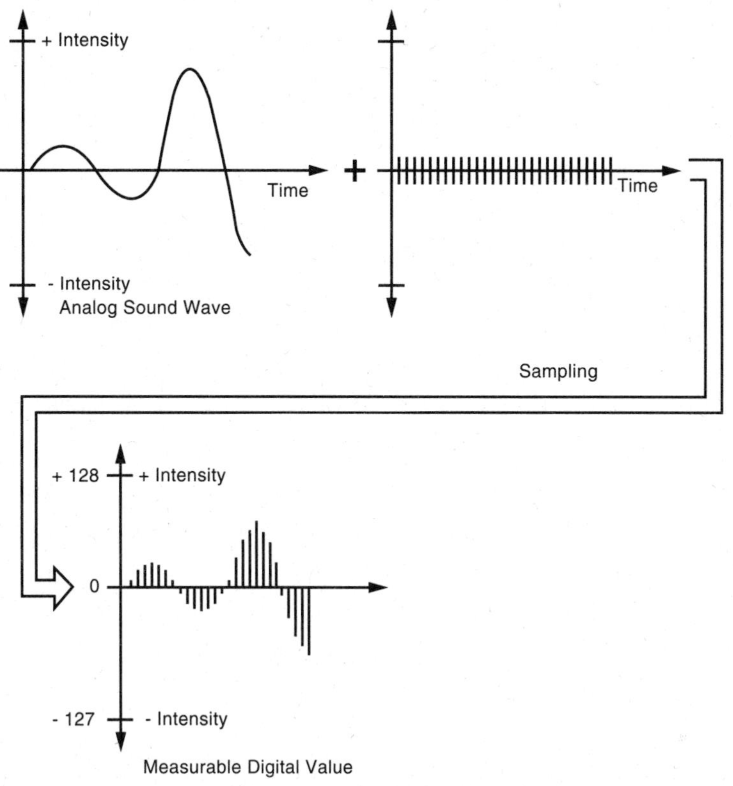

Figure 12.2
Sampling turns a changing sound wave into measurable digital values.

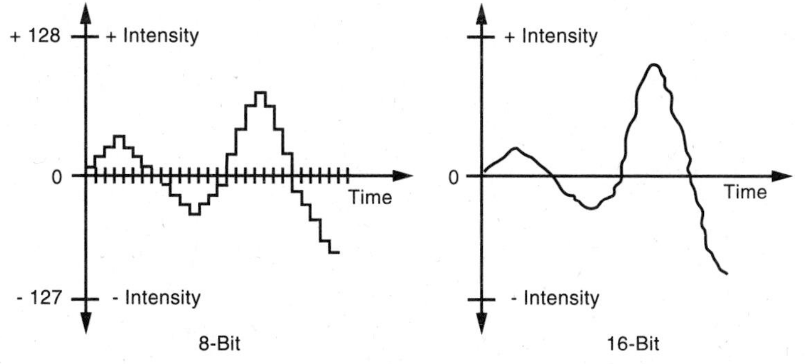

Figure 12.3
16-bit resolution allows more accurate sound reproduction than 8-bit resolution.

Sound recorded at 11KHz (capturing 11,000 samples per second) is fuzzier than sound sampled at 22KHz. A sound sampled in 16-bit stereo (two channel) at 44KHz (CD-audio quality) requires as much as 10.5M per minute of disk space! The same sound sample in 8-bit mono (single channel) at 11KHz takes 1/16th the space. If you were to add a one-minute hi-fi voice annotation to your spreadsheet, you'd find a spreadsheet whose size had at increased by more than 10M.

The CD-ROM Connection

In addition to a sound card, the other foundation of multimedia is a CD-ROM (compact disk read-only memory) drive.

CD-ROM drives provide access to a wealth of text, graphics, sound, video, and animation. Like a sound card, a CD-ROM drive is essential for any multimedia PC.

Many sound cards double as a CD-ROM controller, or interface, card. Some sound cards, however, use a proprietary connection that accommodates only certain proprietary interface CD-ROM drives. For a wider selection of drives, consider a sound card that includes an IDE (Integrated Drive Electronics) or SCSI-2 (Small Computer Systems Interface-2) connector. If you are also going to attach other SCSI devices such as hard disks, tape drives, or scanners, then I recommend staying with a separate stand-alone SCSI-2 adapter. The software driver support and performance will be much better than on the Sound/SCSI combo cards.

All CD-ROM players read all standard CD-ROM disks, just as the CD player in your stereo plays any CD you find in a record store. There's only one caveat—if you eventually want to play CD-ROMs recorded in the extended architecture (XA) format, you may need to upgrade your interface card.

If you want to use multimedia, your CD-ROM drive must also have an extra audio connection to send sound in analog form from the drive to the sound card. This allows you to use the speakers connected to the sound card for CD audio.

Like a hard disk, a CD-ROM drive is measured by two criteria—average access speed and data transfer rate. The average access speed is the length of time the CD-ROM drive takes to find the information you request. This speed is measured in milliseconds (ms), or thousandths of a second. The data transfer rate indicates how fast the information can be sent to your PC after it is located. This rate is measured in kilobytes transferred per second (KBps).

Make sure that the CD-ROM drive you buy meets the MPC (Multimedia PC) specifications for performance. The MPC recipe has changed since its debut: the current MPC Level 3 specification requires a quad-speed drive (capable of a sustained 600KBps data transfer rate). The drive access speed should also be 200ms or less, and the CD-ROM drive should include a built-in memory buffer as well.

Drives are available in single-, double-, triple-, quad-, and even six-speed or faster. I recommend staying away from anything less than the Quad-speed (4X) drives today. The

6X drives are faster, but will likely be quickly passed over in favor of 8X drives in the future, just as the 3X drives were passed over for 4X. It seems that speed jumps come in multiples of two, and the 3X and 6X speeds are therefore not recommended.

When buying a drive, you may be able to trade buffer size for access time or vice versa. If you know you will be using mostly reference materials, such as a magazine text-based database on CD-ROM, then you would prefer a faster access time (under 200 ms) and a minimum of 4X speed. If you will be accessing large sound files, you would also want a buffer of 256K or more. If primarily accessing graphics, such as stock photos on CD, insist on both a 256K or larger buffer, sub 200ns access times, and 4X (quad) speed. In fact I consider these minimum specifications for any CD-ROM purchase.

Sound File Formats

There are several file formats for storing and editing digitized sound. The most notable is the WAV format supported by Windows. (WAV is short for waveform audio.) One audio minute saved to a WAV file requires 2.5M to 10M or more of disk space, depending on the recording options you select. Windows 95 offers recordings at several different rates and bit depths.

The two other types of PC audio are synthesized sound and MIDI music. Synthesized sounds, like synthetic foods, are artificially created. Sound cards typically use one or two FM (frequency modulation) chips, such as those provided by Yamaha, to generate mono or stereo sounds without consuming as much disk space as WAV sound files.

The serious musician may prefer a high-end sound card with wavetable synthesis. These cards use digitized sounds of actual instruments. These sounds are preserved in special ROM (read-only memory) chips. Using this wave-table synthesis technique, the card can play genuine strings and trumpets instead of synthesized music that imitates sounds like strings and trumpets.

MIDI is a step above FM synthesized sound. MIDI, the acronym for Musical Instrument Digital Interface, allows your computer to store, edit, and play back music through a MIDI instrument such as a keyboard synthesizer. MIDI is more like a networking programming language, allowing you to add more instruments, including drum machines and special sound effects generators.

Compression/Decompression

Because one minute of stereo audio can consume up to 11M of disk space, several sound card makers use Adaptive Differential Pulse Code Modulation (ADPCM) compression to reduce file size by over 50 percent. However, a simple fact of audio life is that when you use such compression, you lose sound quality.

Because the sound quality can be degraded, there is no ADPCM standard. Creative Labs uses a proprietary hardware approach, while Microsoft is pushing the Business Audio ADPCM design developed with Compaq.

One emerging compression standard is the Motion Pictures Experts Group (MPEG) standard, which works with both audio and video compression and is gaining support in the non-PC world from products like the Philips CD-I player. With a potential compression ratio of 12:1 and full-motion-video MPEG CD-ROM titles expected soon, this standard may catch on.

Sound Card Characteristics

What are some key features to consider in a sound card? Although some aspects are subjective, the following sections describe some key buying points.

Compatibility

Although there are no official sound card standards, the popular Sound Blaster card has become a de facto standard. The Sound Blaster—the first widely distributed sound card—is supported by the greatest number of software programs. A sound card advertised as Sound Blaster-compatible should run virtually any application that supports sound. Many sound cards also support the Multimedia PC (MPC) Level 2 or Level 3 specifications, allowing you to play sound files in Windows and more. Some sound cards, by excluding a MIDI interface, barely fall short of the MPC specs. Other compatibility standards to look for are AdLib and Pro AudioSpectrum.

Beware of sound cards that require special drivers to be Sound Blaster-compatible. These drivers can cause problems and will take up additional memory that otherwise would be available.

Sampling

The most important sound card quality is its sampling capability. The rate at which the card samples (measured in kilohertz, or KHz) and the size of its sample (expressed in bits) determine the quality of the sound. The standard sampling rates for sound cards are 11.025KHz, 22.050KHz, and 44.1KHZ; sample sizes are 8, 12, and 16 bits.

Inexpensive monophonic cards generally sample at 8 bits up to speeds of 22.050KHz, which is fine for recording voice messages. Some stereo-capable cards sample at 8 bits and run at speeds of 22.050KHz in stereo and up to 44.1KHZ in mono. Other cards can sample 8 bits at 44.1KHZ speeds in both stereo and mono. The latest generation of cards do it all; they can record CD-quality audio of 16 bits at 44.1KHZ.

If you do buy a card that supports 16-bit sampling and plan on doing any recording, make sure you have plenty of hard disk space. The higher the resolution of sampling, the more hard disk space needed to store the file. The sampling rate also affects file size; sampling at the next higher rate doubles the file size.

Stereo versus Mono

You'll also have to consider buying a monophonic or stereophonic sound card. Inexpensive sound cards are monophonic, producing sound from a single source. Still, monophonic cards produce better sound than your PC's speaker.

Stereophonic cards produce many voices, or sounds, concurrently and from two different sources. The more voices a card has, the higher the sound fidelity. Each stereo chip in a sound card is capable of 11 or more voices. To get 20 or more voices, manufacturers had to resort to two FM synthesizer chips. Today, a single chip produces 20 voices, providing truer stereo sound.

The number of voices a stereo card has is especially important for music files because the voices correspond to the individual instruments the card can play.

Most cheaper sound cards use FM synthesis to imitate the musical instruments played. Most use synthesizer chips developed by Yamaha. The least expensive sound cards use the monophonic 11-voice YM3812 or OPL2 chip. Better sound cards use the stereophonic 20-voice YMF262 or OPL3 chip.

Imitated musical instruments are not as impressive as the real thing. Wavetable sound cards often use digital recordings of real instruments and sound effects. Often, several megabytes of these sound clips are embedded in ROM chips on the card. For example, some sound cards use the Ensoniq chip set (a type of circuit design) that does wave-table synthesis of musical instruments. Instead of pretending to play a trombone D flat, the Ensoniq chip set has a little digitized recording of an actual instrument playing that note.

If your primary interest in a sound card is for entertainment or for use in educational or business settings, FM synthesis quality may be good enough.

Stereo sound cards vary in sampling rates and sizes. Some stereo cards do not work in mono mode. Also, moving from mono to stereo sound means an increase in the size of the sound files. As with 16-bit resolution, stereo sound is not supported by most software applications. However, a stereo card playing mono software does generate better sound than a mono card.

Another boon to buying the more expensive stereo cards is that they generally come with additional interfaces, such as connections to a SCSI device (such as a CD-ROM drive) or a MIDI device (such as a keyboard).

CD-ROM Connector

Most stereo sound cards not only provide great sound but also can operate your CD-ROM drive. Although many cards come with a SCSI port for any SCSI device, such as a CD-ROM drive, others support only a proprietary CD-ROM interface, such as Mitsumi or Sony CD-ROM interfaces. If you own a CD-ROM drive, make sure it's compatible with the sound card you plan to buy. If you plan to add a CD-ROM drive or if you expect to upgrade your drive, keep in mind that a proprietary interface will limit your choices, perhaps to a single CD-ROM brand.

If you're seeking to add both a sound card and a CD-ROM drive, consider multimedia upgrade kits. These kits bundle a sound card, CD-ROM drive, CD-ROM titles, software, and cables in an attractively priced package. By buying a multimedia upgrade kit rather than disparate components, you may save some money. And you'll know that the components will work together, especially if the kit includes proper documentation.

Data Compression

The more expensive cards produce CD-quality audio, which is sampled at 44.1KHZ. At this rate, recorded files (even of your own voice) can consume as many as 11M for every minute of recording. To counter this demand for disk space, many sound cards include a data-compression capability. For example, the Sound Blaster ASP 16 includes on-the-fly compression of sound in ratios of 2:1, 3:1, or 4:1.

MIDI Interface

The Musical Instrument Digital Interface (MIDI) is a standard for connecting musical instruments to PCs. Many stereo cards come with MIDI, synthesizer, and sequencing software for composing music. Some cards include only a MIDI interface; you have to purchase the hardware separately to hook up other MIDI devices. Other sound cards may exclude the MIDI.

Bundled Software

Sound cards usually include several sound utilities so that you can begin using your sound card right away. Most of this software is DOS-based, but Windows-based versions are available with some cards. The possibilities include:

- Text-to-speech conversion programs
- Programs for playing, editing, and recording audio files
- Sequencer software, which helps you compose music (generally included with cards with MIDI)
- Various sound clips

Multi-Purpose Digital Signal Processors

One recent addition to many sound boards is the digital signal processor (DSP). DSPs add intelligence to your sound card, freeing your computer from work-intensive tasks, such as filtering noise from recordings or compressing audio on the fly.

About half of most general purpose sound cards use DSPs. The Cardinal Technologies Sound Pro 16 and Sound Pro 16 Plus, for example, use the Analog Devices ADSP2115 digital signal processor. The Sound Blaster AWE32's programmable DSP features compression algorithms for processing text-to-speech data and enables the card's QSound surround-sound 3-D audio, along with reverb and chorus effects. DSPs allow a sound card to be a multi-purpose device. IBM uses its DSP to add a 14.4-kilobit-per-second modem, 9.6-KBps fax, and a digital answering machine to its WindSurfer Communications Adapter.

Are DSPs worth the extra price? On low-powered PCs (those less powerful than a 486SX/25) or in true multitasking environments like Windows 95, Windows NT, or OS/2 Warp, a DSP can make real-time compression possible—a feature valuable for voice annotation. Note that many cards can be purchased without the DSP chip and can have it added later as an upgrade.

Sound Drivers

Most sound cards include universal drivers for DOS and Windows applications. Find out what drivers are included with your card. Windows 3.1 and 95 already includes drivers for the most popular sound cards, such as Sound Blaster. Other drivers are available on a separate driver disk available from Microsoft or from Microsoft's Product Support download service.

Connectors

Most sound cards have the same connectors. These 1/8-inch minijack connectors provide ways to pass sound from the sound card to speakers, headphones, and stereo systems and to receive sound from a microphone, CD player, tape player, or stereo. The four types of connectors your sound card typically could or should have are shown in figure 12.4.

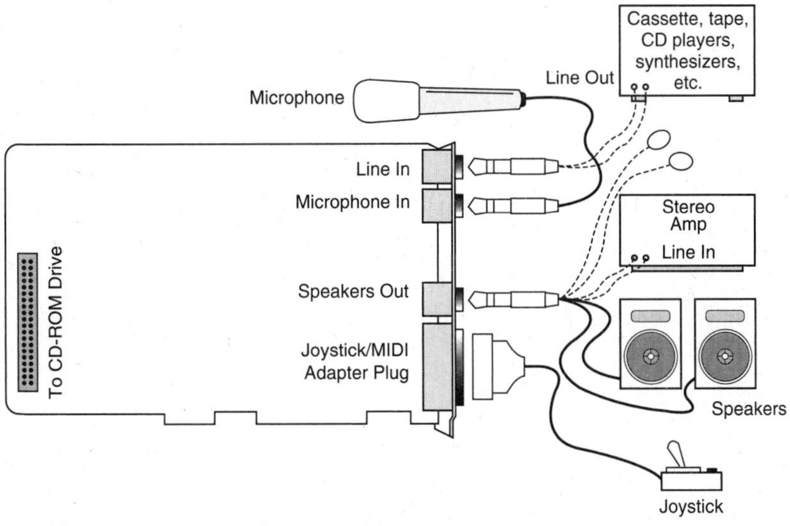

Figure 12.4

The basic features most sound cards have in common.

- *Stereo line, or audio, out connector.* The line out is used to send sound signals from the sound card to a device outside the computer. The cables from the line out connector can be hooked up to stereo speakers, a headphone set, or your stereo system. If you hook up your stereo system, you can have amplified sound. Some sound cards, such as the Microsoft Windows Sound System, provide two jacks for line out. One is for the left channel of the stereo signal; the other is for the right channel.
- *Stereo line, or audio, in connector.* The line in connector is used to record, or mix, sound signals to the computer's hard disk.
- *Speaker/headphone connector.* The speaker/headphone connector is not always provided on a sound card. Instead, the line out (described earlier) doubles as a way to send stereo signals from the sound card to your stereo system or speakers. When both speaker/headphone and line out connectors are provided, the speaker/headphone connector provides an amplified signal that can power your headphones or small bookshelf speakers. Most sound cards can provide up to four watts of power to drive your speakers. Conversely, signals sent through the line out connector are

not amplified. Using the line-out connector provides the best sound reproduction since the stereo system or amplified speakers will amplify the sounds.

Notice that most sound cards have a special pin type connector that plugs directly into an internal CD-ROM drive to allow sound to be played from the drive through the speakers attached to the sound card.

- *Microphone, or mono, in connector.* You connect a microphone to this 1/8-inch minijack to record your voice or other sounds to disk. This microphone jack records in mono, not in stereo. Many sound cards use Automatic Gain Control (AGC) to improve recordings. This feature adjusts the recording levels on the fly. A 600 to 10K ohm dynamic or condenser microphone works best with this jack. Some inexpensive sound cards use the line in connector instead of a separate microphone jack.
- *Joystick/MIDI connector.* The joystick connector is a 15-pin, D-shaped connector. Two of the pins are used to control a MIDI device, such as a keyboard. Many sound card makers offer an optional MIDI connector.

Sometimes the joystick port can accommodate two joysticks if you order the optional Y-adapter. To use this connector as MIDI, you'll need to buy the optional MIDI cable. Some sound cards do not provide MIDI. If you're not interested in making music (and spending a few hundred dollars more for the MIDI keyboard), you may want to consider these models. And don't worry about the lack of a joystick port. These are already found in some PCs as a part of a Multi-I/O card; otherwise, you can buy a separate stand-alone game card.

Volume Control

A thumbwheel volume control is provided on some sound cards, although sophisticated sound cards have no room for such a control. Instead, a combination of keys can be used to adjust the sound. By pressing these key combinations you adjust the volume from within a game, Windows program, or any other application.

Sound Card Options

You'll seldom buy just a sound card. You'll need or want other accessories that raise the cost of your PC sound system. At the very least, you'll have to invest in a set of speakers or headphones. At most, you may want to purchase a MIDI synthesizer keyboard.

Speakers

Successful business presentations, multimedia applications, and MIDI work demand external high-fidelity stereo speakers. Although you can use standard stereo speakers, they are too big to fit on or near your desk. Smaller bookshelf speakers are better.

Sound cards offer little or no power to drive external speakers. Although some sound cards have small 4-watt amplifiers, they are not powerful enough to drive quality speakers. Also, conventional speakers sitting near your display may create magnetic interference, which can distort colors and objects on-screen or jumble the data recorded on your nearby floppy disks.

To solve these problems, computer speakers need to be small, efficient, and self-powered. Also, you need to provide magnetic shielding, either in the form of added layers of insulation in the speaker cabinet or by electronically canceling out the magnetic distortion.

Note

Although most computer speakers are magnetically shielded, do not leave recorded tapes, watches, personal credit cards, or floppy disks in front of the speakers for long periods of time.

Quality sound depends on quality speakers. A 16-bit sound card may provide better sound to computer speakers, but even an 8-bit sound card sounds good from a good speaker. Conversely, an inexpensive speaker makes both 8-bit and 16-bit sound cards sound tinny.

The dozens of models on the market range from less expensive minispeakers from Sony and Koss to larger self-powered models from companies such as Bose. To evaluate speakers, you need to know the lingo. Speakers are measured by three criteria:

- *Frequency response*. A measurement of the range of high and low sounds a speaker can reproduce. The ideal range is from 20Hz to 20KHZ, the range of human hearing. No speaker system reproduces this range perfectly. In fact, few people hear sounds above 18KHz. An exceptional speaker may cover a range of 30Hz to 23,000KHz. Lesser models may cover only 100Hz to 20,000Hz. Frequency response is the most deceptive specification, because identically rated speakers can sound completely different.
- *Total Harmonic Distortion (THD)*. THD, or just distortion, is an expression of the amount of distortion or noise created by amplifying the signal. Simply put, distortion is the difference between the sound sent to the speaker and the sound we hear. The amount of distortion is measured in percentages. An acceptable level of distortion is that below .1 percent (one-tenth of one percent). For some CD-quality recording equipment, a common standard is .05 percent. Some speakers have a distortion of 10 percent or more. Headphones often have a distortion of about two percent or less.
- *Watts*. Usually stated as watts per channel, this is the amount of amplification available to drive the speakers. Check that the company means "per channel" (or RMS) and not total power. Many sound cards have built-in amplifiers, providing up to eight watts per channel. (Most provide four watts.) The wattage is not enough to provide rich sound, however, which is why many speakers have built-in amplifiers. With the flick of a switch or the press of a button, such speakers amplify the signals they receive from the sound card. If you do not want to amplify the sound, you typically leave the speaker switch set to "direct." In most cases, you'll want to amplify the signal.

Two or four "C" batteries are often used to power computer speakers. Because these speakers require so much power, you may want to invest in an AC adapter, although more expensive speakers include one. With an AC adapter, you won't have to buy new batteries every few weeks. If your speakers didn't come with an AC adapter, you can pick one up from your local Radio Shack or hardware store. Be sure that the adapter you purchase matches your speakers in voltage and polarity.

You can control your speakers in various ways, depending on their complexity and cost. Typically, each speaker has a volume knob, although some share one volume control. If one speaker is farther away than the other, you may want to adjust the volume accordingly. Many computer speakers include a dynamic bass boost (DBB) switch. This button provides a more powerful bass and clearer treble, regardless of the volume setting. Other speakers have separate bass and treble boost switches or a three-band equalizer to control low, middle, and high frequencies. When you rely on your sound card's power rather than your speaker's built-in amplifier, the volume and dynamic bass boost controls have no effect. Your speakers are at the mercy of the sound card's power.

A 1/8-inch stereo minijack connects from the sound card output jack to one of the speakers. The signal is then split and fed through a separate cable from the first speaker to the second one.

Before purchasing a set of speakers, check that the cables between the speakers are long enough for your computer setup. For example, a tower case sitting alongside one's desk may require longer speaker wires than a desktop computer.

Beware of speakers that have a tardy built-in "sleep" feature. Such speakers, which save electricity by turning themselves off when they are not in use, may have the annoying habit of clipping the first part of a sound after a period of inactivity.

Headphones are an option when you can't afford a premium set of speakers. Headphones also provide privacy and allow you to play your sound card as loud as you like.

Microphone

Some sound cards do not include a microphone. You'll need one to record your voice to a WAV file. Selecting a microphone is quite simple. You need one that has a 1/8-inch minijack to plug into your sound card's microphone, or audio in, jack. Most have an on/off switch.

Like speakers, microphones are measured by their frequency range. This is not an important buying factor, however, since the human voice has a limited range. If you are recording only voices, consider an inexpensive microphone that covers a limited range of frequencies. An expensive microphone's recording capabilities extend to frequencies outside the voice's range. Why pay for something you won't be needing?

If you are recording music, invest in an expensive microphone, although an 8-bit sound card can record music just as well with an inexpensive microphone.

Your biggest decision is to select a microphone that suits your recording style. If you work in a noisy office, you may want a unidirectional microphone that will prevent extraneous noises from being recorded. An omnidirectional mike is best for recording a group conversation. If you want to leave your hands free, you may want to shun the traditional hand-held microphone for a lapel model.

Most higher priced sound cards include a microphone of some type. This can be a small lapel microphone, a hand-held microphone, or one with a desktop stand. If your sound card does not come with a microphone, see your local stereo or electronics parts store. Be sure that any microphone you purchase has the correct impedance to match the sound card input.

Joysticks

Many sound cards include a joystick, or game port. (This joystick port often doubles as a connection to a MIDI device.) A joystick is ideally meant for game playing, such as simulating flying a Cessna aircraft. Joysticks, like speakers, are best chosen through hands-on experience.

A joystick has a fire button on top of a center wand you move in any of eight directions, with a second button or pair of buttons located on the base.

Good joysticks have resistance that increases the further you move the center wand from dead center. Some joysticks include suction cups that mount the unit on your desk. If you're short on desk space, you may prefer a smaller joystick that fits in your hand. If you are left-handed, look for an ambidextrous joystick, not one that is contoured for right-handers.

Some joysticks are meant especially for flight-simulation or driving games. These simulate an aircraft control yoke or an automobile steering wheel. They often include pedals for other functions as well.

MIDI Connector

If you are interested in MIDI to create synthesized music, you'll need to connect your musical keyboard or other MIDI device to your sound card. The joystick port on sound cards has unused pins that can be used to send and receive MIDI data. By connecting a MIDI cable to the joystick port, you can connect your PC to a MIDI device. The cable has three connectors—a joystick connector and MIDI In and Out connectors.

Synthesizer

If you are considering MIDI, you will also have to get a MIDI keyboard synthesizer. To make MIDI scores, you need sequencer software to record, edit, and play back MIDI files. (Some sound cards include sequencing software.) You also need a sound synthesizer, which is included in the sound card. A MIDI keyboard simplifies the creation of musical scores. A MIDI file contains up to 16 channels of music data, so you can record many different instruments and play them back. Using the keyboard, you can enter the notes for various instruments.

To enhance MIDI sounds for the Sound Blaster 16 ASP sound card, consider the Wave Blaster 2 from Creative Labs. The Wave Blaster attaches to the Sound Blaster ASP 16. When MIDI music is played, it looks to the Wave Blaster for any of 213 CD-quality digitally recorded musical instrument sounds. Without the Wave Blaster, the Sound Blaster 16 ASP would imitate these sounds through FM synthesis. With the Wave Blaster 2, music sounds as though it's being played by real instruments—because it is.

Several MIDI keyboards are available from companies such as Roland, Yamaha, Casio, or others. These keyboards range in price from $100 or less to many thousands of dollars.

Some sound cards have optional memory that can be added to store more sound samples.

Sound Card Installation

Installing a sound card is no more intimidating than installing an internal modem or a VGA card.

Typically, you follow these steps to install a sound card:

1. Open your computer.
2. Configure your sound card.
3. Install the sound card and attach the CD-ROM drive, if present.
4. Close your computer.
5. Install the sound card software.
6. Attach your speakers and other sound accessories.

Once your computer is open, you can install the sound card. Your sound card may be either an 8-bit or 16-bit expansion card. Select a slot that matches the type of card you have. You don't want to put a 16-bit card (one with dual edge connectors) into an 8-bit slot (one with a single edge connector). An 8-bit card, however, can fit in either an 8-bit or 16-bit slot.

If you have several empty slots from which to choose, you may want to place the new card in one as far away as possible from the others. This reduces any possible electromagnetic interference; that is, it reduces stray radio signals from one card that might affect the sound card.

Next, you must remove the screw that holds the metal cover over the empty expansion slot you've chosen. Remove your sound card from its protective packaging. When you open this bag, carefully grab the card by its metal bracket and edges. Do not touch any of the components on the card. Any static electricity you may transmit can damage the card. And do not touch the gold edge connectors. You may want to invest in a grounding wrist strap, which continually drains you of static build-up as you work on your computer.

You may have to set jumpers or DIP switches to configure your sound card to work best with your computer. For example, you may want to turn off your sound card's joystick port because your joystick is already connected elsewhere to your PC. See the instructions that came with your sound card.

If an internal CD-ROM drive is to be connected to the sound card, attach its cables. Attach your CD-ROM's striped ribbon cable to your sound card, placing the red edge of the CD-ROM cable on the side of the connector on which "0" or "1" is printed. The cable must be placed this way for the CD-ROM drive to work.

The CD-ROM drive also may have an audio cable. Connect this cable to the audio connector on the sound card. This connector is keyed so that you can't insert it improperly. Note that there is no true standard for this audio cable, so be sure that you get the right one that matches your drive and sound card.

Next, insert the card in the edge connector. First touch a metal object, such as the inside of the computer's cover, to drain yourself of static electricity. Then, holding the card by its metal bracket and edges, place it in the expansion slot. Attach the screw to hold the expansion card and then reassemble your computer.

You can connect small speakers to the speaker jack. Typically, sound cards provide four watts of power per channel to drive bookshelf speakers. If you are using speakers rated for less than four watts, do not turn up the volume on your sound card to the maximum; your speakers may burn out from the overload. You'll get better results if you plug your sound card into powered speakers, that is, speakers with built-in amplifiers.

Another alternative is to patch your sound card into your stereo system for greatly amplified sound. Check the plugs and jacks at both ends of the connection. Most stereos use pin plugs—also called RCA or phono plugs—for input. Although pin plugs are standard on some sound cards, most use miniature 1/8-inch phono plugs, which require an adapter when connecting to your stereo system. From Radio Shack, for example, you can purchase an audio cable that provides a stereo 1/8-inch miniplug on one end and a phono plug on the other (Cat. No. 42-2481A).

Make sure that you get stereo, not mono, plugs, unless your sound card supports mono only. To ensure that you have enough cable to reach from the back of your PC to your stereo system, get a six-foot long cable.

Hooking up your stereo to a sound card is simply a matter of sliding the plugs into jacks. If your sound card gives you a choice of outputs—speaker/headphone and stereo line out—choose the stereo line out jack for the connection. Choosing it will give you the best sound quality because the signals from the stereo line out jack are not amplified. The amplification is best left to your stereo system.

Connect this output to the auxiliary input of your stereo receiver, preamp, or integrated amplifier. If your stereo doesn't have an auxiliary input, other input options include—in order of preference—tuner, CD, or Tape 2. (Do not use phono inputs, however, because the level of the signals will be uneven.) You can connect the cable's single stereo miniplug to the sound card's Stereo Line Out jack, for example, and then connect the two RCA phono plugs to the stereo's Tape/VCR 2 Playback jacks.

The first time you use your sound card with a stereo system, turn down the volume on your receiver to prevent blown speakers. Barely turn up the volume control and then select the proper input (such as Tape/VCR 2) on your stereo receiver. Finally, start your

PC. Never increase the volume to more than three-fourths of the way up. Any higher and the sound may become distorted.

Troubleshooting Sound Card Problems

To install a sound card, you need to select IRQ numbers, a base I/O address, or DMA channels that don't conflict with other devices. Most cards come already configured to use an otherwise idle set of ports, but problems occasionally arise. Troubleshooting may mean that you have to change board jumpers or switches, or even reconfigure your other cards. No one said life was fair.

Hardware (Resource) Conflicts

The most common problem for sound cards is that they fight with other devices installed in your PC. You may notice that your sound card simply doesn't work (no sound effects or music), repeats the same sounds over and over, or causes your PC to freeze. This situation is called a device, or hardware, conflict. What are they fighting over? Mainly the same bus signal lines or channels (called resources) used for talking to your PC. The sources of conflict in sound card installations are generally threefold:

- Interrupt ReQuests (IRQs). IRQs are used to "interrupt" your PC and get its attention.
- Direct Memory Access (DMA) channels. DMA channels are the way to move information directly to your PC's memory, bypassing your PC's processor. DMA channels allow sound to play while your PC is doing other work.
- Input/Output (I/O) Port addresses. An I/O Port address in your PC is used to channel information between the hardware devices on your sound card and your PC. The addresses usually mentioned in a sound card manual are the starting or base addresses. A sound card has several devices on it, and each one will use a range of addresses starting with a particular base.

Most sound cards include installation software that analyzes your PC and attempts to notify you should any of the standard settings be in use by other devices. Although fairly reliable, this analysis is not complete because unless a device is operating during the analysis, detecting it is not always possible.

Table 12.2 shows the default resources used by the components on a typical Sound Blaster 16 card.

Table 12.2 Default Sound Blaster 16 Resource Assignments

Device	Interrupt	I/O Ports	16-bit DMA	8-bit DMA
Audio	IRQ 5	220h-233h	DMA 5	DMA 1
MIDI Port	-	330h-331h	-	-
FM Synthesizer	-	388h-38Bh	-	-
Game Port	-	200h-207h	-	-

All these resources are used by a *single* sound card in your system. No wonder many people have conflicts and problems with sound card installations! In reality, working out these conflicts is not all that hard as we shall see. Most of these resources used can be changed to alternate settings, should there be conflicts with other devices, or even better, you can change the settings of the other device to eliminate the conflict. Note that some devices on the sound card like the MIDI Port, FM Synthesizer, and Game Port do not use resources like Interrupts (IRQs) or DMA channels.

It is always best to install a sound card using the default settings where possible. This is mainly because of poorly written software that cannot work properly with alternate settings, even it they do not cause conflicts. In other words, if you are having a conflict with another type of adapter, move the settings on the other adapter rather than the sound card. Take this from experience, otherwise you will have to explain to your 5-year old why the new Dinosaur program you just installed does not make any sounds!

If your system is Plug and Play (PnP), you can use the Device Manager in Windows 95 to assist with the configuration of the devices in your system.

Resolving Interrupt Conflicts. The audio portion of a sound card has a default interrupt request (IRQ) setting, but also supports any of several alternate interrupts. As was just stated, you should endeavor to leave the sound card at the default setting (usually IRQ 5) and change other adapters where possible. A typical sound card like the Sound Blaster 16 will support IRQ settings of 2, 5, 7, or 10, although IRQ 5 is the default.

In addition to possible conflicts with other installed adapters, many of the IRQs are reserved for standard components in your PC. If your sound card is set to the same IRQ as another item in your system, you may see symptoms such as skipping, jerky sound, or system lockups. Table 12.3 shows the recommended IRQ assignments for a standard PC compatible system with a Sound Blaster 16 and a normal compliment of other accessories installed.

Table 12.3 Recommended Interrupt (IRQ) Assignments with Sound Blaster Installed

IRQ	Standard Function	Bus Slot	Card Type
0	System Timer	No	-
1	Keyboard Controller	No	-
2	2nd IRQ Controller Cascade	No	-
8	Real-Time Clock	No	-
9	Network card/Available (Appears as IRQ 2)	Yes	8/16-bit
10	Available	Yes	16-bit
11	SCSI adapter/Available	Yes	16-bit
12	Motherboard Mouse Port	Yes	16-bit
13	Math Coprocessor	No	-
14	Primary IDE Controller (Hard Disk)	Yes	16-bit

(continues)

Table 12.3 Continued

IRQ	Standard Function	Bus Slot	Card Type
15	Secondary IDE Controller (CD-ROM)	Yes	16-bit
3	Serial Port 2 (COM2:)	Yes	8/16-bit
4	Serial Port 1 (COM1:)	Yes	8/16-bit
5	Sound Card Audio	Yes	8/16-bit
6	Floppy Disk Controller	Yes	8/16-bit
7	Parallel Port 1 (LPT1:)	Yes	8/16-bit

Notice that the Sound Blaster Audio default setting is located at IRQ 5. This IRQ is normally used by a second Parallel Port (LPT:2), which most systems do not have, making this IRQ available. The alternate settings allowed by the Sound Blaster 16 are 2, 7, or 10. Of those choices, 7 would cause a conflict since normally the first Parallel Port (LPT:1) uses that setting. IRQ 10 is clearly available to any 16-bit adapter card, and could be used by the Sound Blaster if necessary. IRQ 2 also is available, since all motherboards are rewired such that IRQ 9 appears as IRQ 2 for any adapter cards. In other words, you could set the Sound Blaster to IRQ 2, and the system would actually see it as IRQ 9. In most cases, these alternate settings should not be required as the default IRQ 5 should be available.

Resolving DMA Channel Conflicts. A PC compatible system utilizes two DMA controllers, each providing support for four DMA channels. The first DMA controller provides only 8-bit transfers and is connected to the second DMA controller in a cascaded arrangement similar to that used for interrupts. The second controller loses one channel for the cascade, and the other three channels can be used for 16-bit transfers. This leaves a total of seven DMA channels for use by standard and optional system devices.

A typical sound card like the Sound Blaster 16 requires *two* simultaneous DMA channels to be utilized. These are usually split into a requirement for an 8-bit DMA as well as a 16-bit DMA channel. Some of the DMA channels are reserved for standard components in a PC compatible, such as your floppy disk controller (DMA 2). DMA channels 0, 1, 2, and 3 provide only 8-bit transfers, while DMA channels 5, 6, and 7 are used only for 16-bit transfers. The primary symptom of a DMA conflict is that you hear no sound at all.

A typical sound card like the Sound Blaster 16 will use DMA 1 for 8-bit sound (Creative Labs calls this Low DMA), and DMA 5 for 16-bit sound (High DMA). Table 12.4 shows the default DMA usage in a typical PC compatible system with a Sound Blaster installed.

In addition to the default setting of DMA 1 for 8-bit (Low) DMA, the Sound Blaster 16 also allows alternate settings of DMA 0 or 3. Both of these alternates are usually available in a normal PC compatible system. The Sound Blaster also uses a default setting of DMA 5 for 16-bit (High) DMA, and allows alternate settings of DMA 6 or 7. These alternates are also normally available in a standard PC compatible system. Due to inflexibly written software, it is recommended to stick with the default settings wherever possible in all sound card installations.

Table 12.4 Recommended DMA Assignments with Sound Blaster Installed

DMA	Standard Function	Bus Slot	Card Type	Transfer
0	Available	Yes	16-bit	8-bit
1	Sound Card (Low DMA)	Yes	8/16-bit	8-bit
2	Floppy Disk Controller	Yes	8/16-bit	8-bit
3	ECP Parallel/Available	Yes	8/16-bit	8-bit
4	1st DMA Controller Cascade	No	-	16-bit
5	Sound Card (High DMA)	Yes	16-bit	16-bit
6	SCSI adapter/Available	Yes	16-bit	16-bit
7	Available	Yes	16-bit	16-bit

Solving Hardware Conflicts. The best way to find a hardware conflict is to locate all of the documentation for your PC and its various devices, such as a tape backup interface card, CD-ROM drive, etc. This topic is discussed more completely in Chapter 5, "Bus Slots and I/O cards."

The most common causes of system resource conflicts are:

- SCSI host adapters
- Network interface cards
- Bus Mouse adapter cards
- Serial Port adapter cards for COM3: or COM4:
- Parallel Port adapter cards for LPT2:
- Internal Modems
- Tape drive interface cards
- Scanner interface cards

One easy way to find which device is conflicting with your sound card is to temporarily remove all of your expansion cards except the sound card and other essential cards (such as the video card). Then add each of the cards you removed, one at a time, until your sound card no longer works. The last card you added is the troublemaker.

Having found the card that's causing the conflict, you can either switch the settings for the device that is conflicting with your sound card or change the settings of the sound card. In either case, you will have to change the IRQ, DMA, or I/O address. To do this, you must set jumpers or DIP switches or use your sound card's setup software to change its settings.

If you are running Windows 95 and have a Plug and Play (PnP) system, you can use the built-in Device Manager to help locate and resolve conflicts.

Other Sound Card Problems

Sound card problems (like the common cold) have common symptoms. Use the following sections to diagnose your problem.

No Sound. If you don't hear anything from your sound card, consider these solutions:

- Make sure that the sound card is set to use all default resources, and that other devices using these resources are either changed or removed.
- Are the speakers connected? Check that the speakers are plugged into the sound card's Stereo Line Out or speaker jack.
- If you're using amplified speakers, are they powered on? Check the strength of the batteries or the adapter's connection to the electrical outlet.
- Are the speakers stereo? Check that the plug inserted into the jack is a stereo plug, not mono.
- Are mixer settings high enough? Many sound cards include a mixer control for DOS and/or Microsoft Windows. The mixer controls the settings for various sound devices, such as a microphone or CD player. There may be controls for both recording and playback. Increase the master volume or speaker volume when you are in the play mode. In DOS, you can adjust the setting by either modifying your CONFIG.SYS file or pressing keys.
- Use your sound card's setup or diagnostic software to test and adjust the volume of the sound card. Such software usually includes sample sounds that play.
- Turn off your computer for one minute and then turn it back on. Such a hard reset (as opposed to pressing the reset button or pressing Ctrl+Alt+Del) may clear the problem.
- If your computer game lacks sound, check that it works with your sound card. For example, some games may require the exact settings of IRQ 7, DMA 1, and address 220 to be Sound Blaster compatible.

One-Sided Sound. If you hear sound coming from only one speaker, check out these possible causes:

- Are you using a mono plug in the stereo jack? A common mistake is to place a mono plug into the sound card's speaker or stereo out jacks. Seen from the side, a stereo connector has two darker stripes. A mono connector has only one stripe.
- Is the driver loaded? Some sound cards provide only left-channel sound if the driver is not loaded in the CONFIG.SYS file. Again, run your sound card's setup software.

Volume is Low. If you can barely hear your sound card, try these solutions:

- Are the speakers plugged into the proper jack? Speakers require a higher level of drive signal than headphones. Again, adjust the volume level in your DOS or Windows mixer. If your sound card uses keystrokes to adjust the volume, use them.

- Are the mixer settings too low? Again, adjust the volume level in your DOS or Windows mixer. If your sound card uses keystrokes to adjust the volume, use them.
- Is the initial volume too low? Some sound cards provide volume settings as part of the line in CONFIG.SYS that loads the sound card driver. The number for the volume may be set too low.
- Are the speakers too weak? Some speakers may need more power than your sound card can produce. Try other speakers or put a stereo amplifier between your sound card and speakers.

Scratchy Sound.

- Is your sound card near other expansion cards? The sound card may be picking up electrical interference from other expansion cards inside the PC. Move the sound card to an expansion slot as far away as possible from other cards.
- Are your speakers too close to your monitor? The speakers may pick up electrical noise from your monitor. Move them farther away.
- Are you using a cheaper FM synthesis sound card? Most of the cards that use FM synthesis instead of wavetable sound generation have very poor quality output. Many people have been fooled into thinking they had a defective sound card, when in reality it was just a poor quality FM synthesis card that simply does not sound good. I recommend upgrading to a card that does wavetable synthesis so you can get the full benefit if high quality sound.

Your Computer won't Start. If your computer won't start at all, you may not have inserted the sound card completely into its slot. Turn off the PC and then press firmly on the card until it is seated correctly.

Parity Errors or other Lockups. Your computer may display a memory parity error message or simply "crash." This is normally caused by resource conflicts in one of the following areas:

IRQ (Interrupt ReQuest)

DMA (Direct Memory Access)

I/O (Input/Output) Ports

If other devices in your system are using the same resources as your sound card, crashes, lockups, or parity errors can result. You must ensure that multiple devices in your system do not share these resources. Usually it is better to leave the sound card at its default settings and change the other devices to eliminate the conflict. Consult the documentation that comes with all of your other devices to determine which resources they use and how to change them if necessary.

Joystick Troubleshooting. If your joystick won't work, consider the following list of cures:

- Are you using two game ports? If you already have a game port installed in your PC, the game or joystick port provided on your sound card may conflict with it. Usually it is best to disable any other game ports and use the one on the sound card. Many of the Multi-I/O or Super-I/O adapters that come in PC compatible systems feature game ports that should be disabled when a sound card is installed.
- Is your computer too fast? Some fast computers get confused by the inexpensive game ports. During the heat of battle, for example, you may find yourself flying upside down or spiraling out of control. This is one sign that your game port is inadequate. Most of the game adapters built-in to the sound cards work better than the ones on the Multi-I/O adapters. There are also dedicated game cards available, which can work with faster computers. Such game cards include software to calibrate your joystick and dual ports so that you can enjoy a game with a friend. Another solution is to run your computer at a slower speed, which is usually done by pressing some type of "de-turbo" button on your PC.

Other Problems. Sometimes sound problems can be difficult to solve. Due to quirks and problems with the way DMA is implemented in some motherboard chipsets, there can be problems interacting with certain cards or drivers. Sometimes altering the Chipset Setup options in your CMOS settings can resolve problems. These kinds of problems can take a lot of trial and error to solve.

The PC "standard" is based loosely on the cooperation among a handful of companies. Something as simple as one vendor's BIOS or motherboard design can make the standard nonstandard.

Summary

This chapter introduced you to the uses of sound cards, including games, voice annotation, MIDI music-making, and voice recognition. The various facets of a sound card were discussed, such as the nature of sound, analog-to-digital (ADC) and digital-to-analog (DAC) conversion, and sampling. The chapter discussed the differences between 8- and 16-bit sound and how sound cards can double as CD-ROM interfaces. Sound standards such as Sound Blaster and AdLib were discussed as well as various sound file formats, such as WAV (waveform audio), FM and wave-table synthesis, and MIDI.

The chapter discussed the buying criteria for a sound card, such as bundled software, available driver, stereophonic versus monophonic cards, and connectors. Options were discussed, including speakers, MIDI keyboard synthesizers, joysticks, and microphones. Finally, the chapter discussed installing a sound card and troubleshooting installation pitfalls. Most problems result from hardware conflicts involving DMA (direct memory access) channels, IRQs (interrupt request lines), and I/O addresses.

Chapter 13

Floppy Disk Drives

This chapter examines, in detail, floppy disk drives and disks. It explores how floppy disk drives and disks function, how DOS uses a disk, what types of disk drives and disks are available, and how to properly install and service drives and disks. You learn about all the types of drives available for today's personal computer systems, including both the 5 1/4-inch and 3 1/2-inch drives in all different versions. The chapter also discusses the newer, extra-high density (ED) 3 1/2-inch disks. Also discussed are several upgrade options including the addition of the 3 1/2-inch drives to the early PC-family systems, which enables them to be compatible with newer systems, as well as upgrading newer systems to support the ED drives and disks.

Development of the Floppy Disk Drive

Alan Shugart is generally credited with inventing the floppy drive while working for IBM in the late '60s. In 1967, he headed the disk drive development team at IBM's San Jose lab, where and when the floppy drive was created. One of Shugart's senior engineers, David Noble, actually proposed the flexible media (then 8 inches in diameter) and the protective jacket with the fabric lining. Shugart left IBM in 1969 and took more than 100 IBM engineers with him to Memorex. He was nicknamed "The Pied Piper" because of the loyalty exhibited by the many staff members who followed him. In 1973, he left Memorex, again taking with him a number of associates, and started Shugart Associates to develop and manufacture floppy drives. The floppy interface developed by Shugart is still the basis of all PC floppy drives. IBM used this interface in the PC, enabling them to use off-the-shelf third-party drives instead of custom building their own solutions.

Shugart actually wanted to incorporate processors and floppy drives into complete microcomputer systems at that time, but the financial backers of the new Shugart Associates wanted him to concentrate on floppy drives only. He quit (or was forced to quit) Shugart Associates in 1974, right before they introduced the Mini-floppy (5.25-inch) disk drive, which of course became the standard eventually used by personal computers, rapidly replacing the 8-inch drives. Shugart Associates also introduced the Shugart Associates System Interface (SASI), which was later renamed Small Computer Systems Interface (SCSI) when it was formally approved by the ANSI committee in 1986. After being forced to leave, Shugart attempted to legally force Shugart Associates to remove his name from the company, but failed. The remnants of Shugart Associates still operates today as Shugart Corporation.

For the next few years, Shugart took time off, ran a bar, and even dabbled in commercial fishing. In 1979, Finis Conner approached Shugart to create and market 5.25-inch hard disk drives. Together they founded Seagate Technology and by the end of 1979 had announced the ST-506 (6M unformatted, 5M formatted capacity) drive and interface. This drive is known as the father of all PC hard disk drives. Seagate then introduced the ST-412 (12M unformatted, 10M formatted capacity) drive, which was adopted by IBM for the original XT in 1983. IBM was Seagate's largest customer for many years. Today, Seagate Technology is the largest disk drive manufacturer in the world.

When you stop to think about it, Alan Shugart has had a tremendous effect on the PC industry. He (or his companies) has created the floppy, hard disk, and SCSI drive and controller interfaces still used today. All PC floppy drives are still based on (and compatible with) the original Shugart designs. The ST-506/412 interface was the de facto hard disk interface standard for many years and served as the basis for the ESDI and IDE interfaces as well. Shugart also created the SCSI interface, used in both IBM and Apple systems today.

As a side note, in the late 80s Finis Conner left Seagate and founded Conner Peripherals, originally wholly owned and funded by Compaq. Conner became Compaq's exclusive drive supplier, and gradually began selling drives to other system manufacturers as well. Compaq eventually cut Conner Peripherals free, selling off most (if not all) of their ownership of the company.

Drive Components

This section describes the components that make up a typical floppy drive and examines how these components operate together to read and write data—the physical operation of the drive. All floppy drives, regardless of type, consist of several basic common components. To properly install and service a disk drive, you must be able to identify these components and understand their function (see fig. 13.1).

Read/Write Heads

A floppy disk drive normally has two read/write heads, making the modern floppy disk drive a double-sided drive. A head exists for each side of the disk, and both heads are used for reading and writing on their respective disk sides. At one time, single-sided drives were available for PC systems (the original PC had such drives), but today single-sided drives are a fading memory (see fig. 13.2).

Note

Many people do not realize that the first head is the bottom one. Single-sided drives, in fact, use only the bottom head; the top head is replaced by a felt pressure pad (see figure 13.2). Another bit of disk trivia is that the top head (Head 1) is not directly over the bottom head—the top head is located either four or eight tracks inward from the bottom head, depending on the drive type. Therefore, what conventionally are called "cylinders" should more accurately be called "cones."

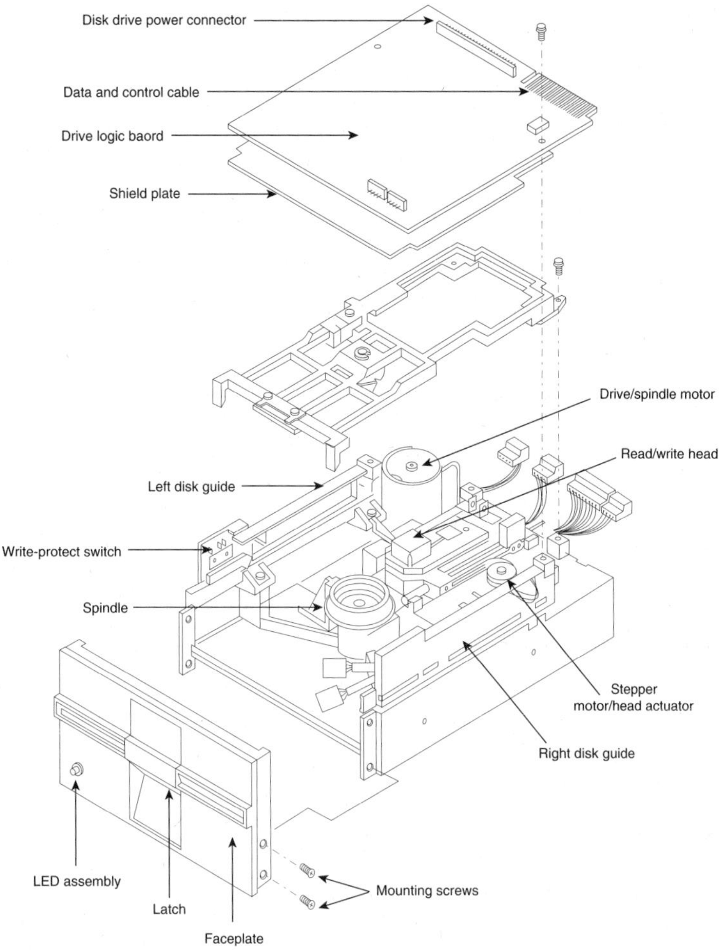

Figure 13.1
A typical full-height disk drive.

The head mechanism is moved by a motor called a head actuator. The heads can move in and out over the surface of the disk in a straight line to position themselves over various tracks. The heads move in and out tangentially to the tracks that they record on the disk. Because the top and bottom heads are mounted on the same rack, or mechanism, they move in unison and cannot move independently of each other. The heads are made of soft ferrous (iron) compounds with electromagnetic coils. Each head is a composite design, with a read/write head centered within two tunnel-erase heads in the same physical assembly (see fig. 13.3).

The recording method is called *tunnel erasure*; as the track is laid down, the trailing tunnel erase heads erase the outer bands of the track, trimming it cleanly on the disk. The heads force the data to be present only within a specified narrow "tunnel" on each track.

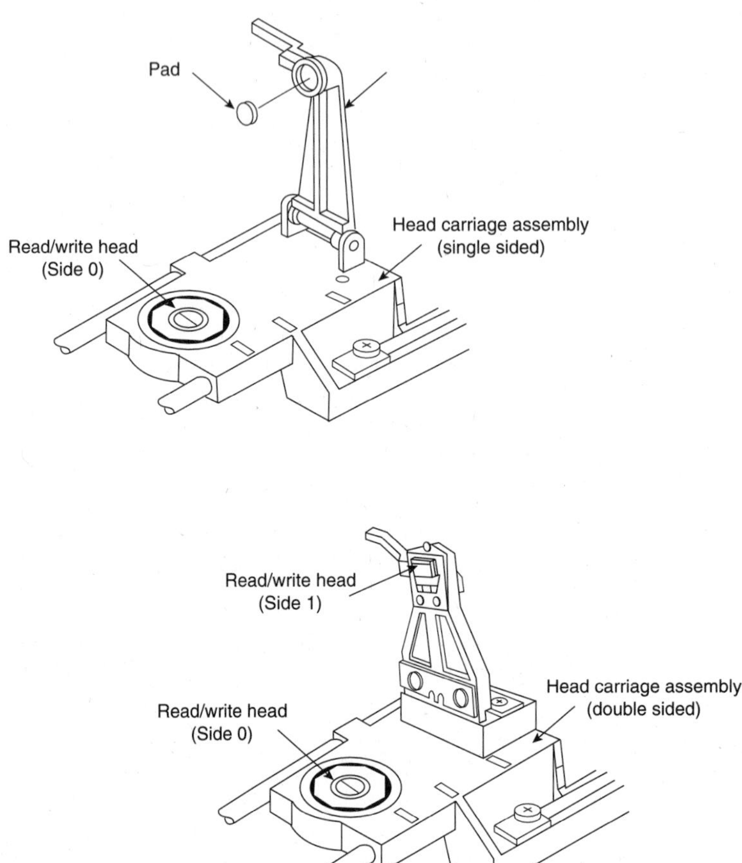

Figure 13.2

Single- and double-sided drive head assemblies.

This process prevents the signal from one track from being confused with the signals from adjacent tracks. If the signal were allowed to "taper off" to each side, problems would occur. The forcibly trimmed track prevents this problem.

Alignment is the placement of the heads with respect to the tracks they must read and write. Head alignment can be checked only against some sort of reference-standard disk recorded by a perfectly aligned machine. These types of disks are available, and you can use one to check your drive's alignment.

The two heads are spring-loaded and physically grip the disk with a small amount of pressure, which means that they are in direct contact with the disk surface while reading and writing to the disk. Because PC-compatible floppy disk drives spin at only 300 or 360 RPM, this pressure does not present an excessive friction problem. Some newer disks are specially coated with Teflon or other compounds to further reduce friction and enable the disk to slide more easily under the heads. Because of the contact between the heads

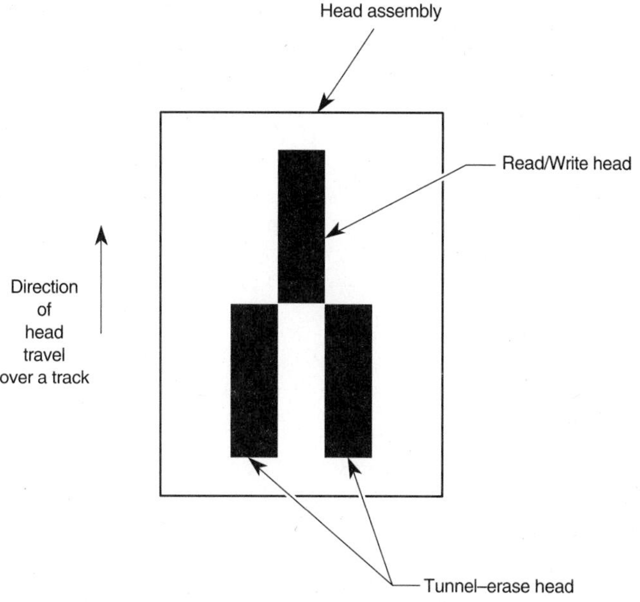

Figure 13.3
Composite construction of a typical floppy drive head.

and the disk, a buildup of the oxide material from the disk eventually forms on the heads. The buildup periodically can be cleaned off the heads as part of a preventive-maintenance or normal service program.

To read and write to the disk properly, the heads must be in direct contact with the media. Very small particles of loose oxide, dust, dirt, smoke, fingerprints, or hair can cause problems with reading and writing the disk. Disk and drive manufacturer's tests have found that a spacing as little as .000032 inches (32 millionths of an inch) between the heads and the media can cause read/write errors. You now can understand why it is important to handle disks carefully and avoid touching or contaminating the surface of the disk media in any way. The rigid jacket and protective shutter for the head access aperture on the 3 1/2-inch disks is excellent for preventing problems with media contamination. 5 1/4-inch disks do not have the same protective elements, therefore more care must be exercised in their handling.

The Head Actuator

The *head actuator* is a mechanical motor device that causes the heads to move in and out over the surface of a disk. These mechanisms for floppy disk drives universally use a special kind of motor, a stepper motor, that moves in both directions in an increment called a step. This type of motor does not spin around continuously; rather, the motor turns a precise specified distance and stops. Stepper motors move in fixed increments, or detents, and must stop at a particular detent position. Stepper motors are not infinitely variable in their positioning. Each increment of motion, or a multiple thereof, defines each track on the disk. The motor can be commanded by the disk controller to position itself according to any relative increment within the range of its travel. To position the heads at track 25, for example, the motor is commanded to go to the 25th detent position.

The stepper motor usually is linked to the head rack by a coiled, split steel band. The band winds and unwinds around the spindle of the stepper motor, translating the rotary motion into linear motion. Some drives use a worm gear arrangement rather than a band. With this type, the head assembly rests on a worm gear driven directly off the stepper motor shaft. Because this arrangement is more compact, you normally find worm gear actuators on the smaller 3 1/2-inch drives.

Most stepper motors used in floppy drives can step in specific increments that relate to the track spacing on the disk. Most 48 Track Per Inch (TPI) drives have a motor that steps in increments of 3.6° (degrees). This means that each 3.6° of stepper motor rotation moves the heads from one track (or cylinder) to the next. Most 96 or 135 TPI drives have a stepper motor that moves in 1.8° increments, which is exactly half of what the 48 TPI drives use. Sometimes you see this information actually printed or stamped right on the stepper motor itself, which is useful if you are trying to figure out what type of drive you have. 5 1/4-inch 360K drives are the only 48 TPI drives available and use the 3.6° increment stepper motor. All other drive types normally use the 1.8° stepper motor. On most drives, the stepper motor is a small cylindrical object near one corner of the drive.

A stepper motor usually has a full travel time of about 1/5 of a second—about 200 milliseconds. On average, a half-stroke is 100 milliseconds and a one-third stroke is 66 milliseconds. The timing of a one-half or one-third stroke of the head-actuator mechanism often is used to determine the reported average-access time for a disk drive. Average-access time is the normal amount of time the heads spend moving at random from one track to another.

The Spindle Motor

The spindle motor spins the disk. The normal speed of rotation is either 300 or 360 RPM, depending on the type of drive. The 5 1/4-inch high-density (HD) drive is the only drive that spins at 360 RPM; all others, including the 5 1/4-inch double-density (DD), 3 1/2-inch DD, 3 1/2-inch HD, and 3 1/2-inch extra-high density (ED) drives, spin at 300 RPM. Most earlier drives used a mechanism on which the spindle motor physically turned the disk spindle with a belt, but all modern drives use a direct-drive system with no belts. The direct-drive systems are more reliable and less expensive to manufacture, as well as smaller in size. The earlier belt-driven systems did have more rotational torque available to turn a sticky disk because of the torque multiplication factor of the belt system. Most newer direct-drive systems use an automatic torque-compensation capability that automatically sets the disk-rotation speed to a fixed 300 or 360 RPM and compensates with additional torque for sticky disks or less torque for slippery ones. This type of drive eliminates the need to adjust the rotational speed of the drive.

Most newer direct-drive systems use this automatic-speed feature, but many earlier systems require that you periodically adjust the speed. Looking at the spindle provides you with one clue to the type of drive you have. If the spindle contains strobe marks for 50 Hz and 60 Hz strobe lights (fluorescent lights), the drive probably has an adjustment for speed somewhere on the drive. Drives without the strobe marks almost always include an automatic tachometer-control circuit that eliminates the need for adjustment. The technique for setting the speed involves operating the drive under fluorescent lighting and adjusting the rotational speed until the strobe marks appear motionless, much like the "wagon wheel effect" you see in old Western movies. The procedure is described later in this chapter, in the "Setting the Floppy Drive Speed Adjustment" section.

To locate the spindle-speed adjustment, you must consult the original equipment manufacturer's (OEM) manual for the drive. IBM provides the information for its drives in the Technical Reference Options and Adapters manual as well as in the hardware-maintenance reference manuals. Even if IBM had sold the drives, they most likely are manufactured by another company, such as Control Data Corporation (CDC), Tandon, YE-Data (C. Itoh), Alps Electric, or Mitsubishi. Contact these manufacturers for the original manuals for your drives.

Circuit Boards

A disk drive always incorporates one or more *logic boards*, which are circuit boards that contain the circuitry used to control the head actuator, read/write heads, spindle motor, disk sensors, and any other components on the drive. The logic board represents the drive's interface to the controller board in the system unit.

The standard interface used by all PC types of floppy disk drives is the Shugart Associates SA-400 interface. The interface, invented by Shugart in the 1970s, has been the basis of most floppy disk interfacing. The selection of this industry-standard interface is the reason that you can purchase "off-the-shelf" drives (raw, or bare, drives) that can plug directly into your controller. (Thanks, IBM, for sticking with industry-standard interfacing; it has been the foundation of the entire PC upgrade and repair industry!)

Some other computer companies making non-PC-compatible systems (especially Apple, for example) have stayed away from industry standards in this and other areas, which can make tasks such as drive repair or upgrades a nightmare—unless, of course, you buy all your parts from them. For example, in both the Apple II series as well as the Mac, Apple used nonstandard proprietary interfaces for the floppy drives.

The Mac uses an interface based on a proprietary chip called either the IWM (Integrated Woz Machine) or the SWIM (Super Woz Integrated Machine) chip, depending on which Mac you have. These interfaces are incompatible with the industry standard SA-400 interface used in PC-compatible systems, which is based on an off the shelf NEC PD765 chip. In fact, the Apple drives use an encoding scheme called GCR (group-coded recording), which is very different from the standard MFM (modified frequency modulation) used in most other systems. The GCR encoding scheme, in fact, cannot be performed by the NEC-type controller chips, which is why it is impossible for PC-compatible systems to read Mac floppy disks. To Apple's credit, the Mac systems with the SWIM chip include drives that can read and write both GCR and MFM schemes, enabling these systems to read and write IBM floppy disks.

Unfortunately, because the electrical interface to the drive is proprietary, you still cannot easily (or cheaply) purchase these drives as bare units from a variety of manufacturers, as you can for PC-compatible systems. IBM uses true industry standards in these and other areas, which is why the PC, XT, AT, and PS/2 systems, as well as most PC-compatible vendors' systems are so open to upgrade and repair.

Logic boards for a drive can fail and usually are difficult to obtain as a spare part. One board often costs more than replacing the entire drive. I recommend keeping failed or misaligned drives that might otherwise be discarded so that they can be used for their remaining good parts—such as logic boards. The parts can be used to restore a failing drive very cost-effectively.

The Faceplate

The faceplate, or *bezel*, is the plastic piece that comprises the front of the drive. These pieces, usually removable, come in different colors and configurations.

Most drives use a bezel slightly wider than the drive. These types of drives must be installed from the front of a system because the faceplate is slightly wider than the hole in the system-unit case. Other drive faceplates are the same width as the drive's chassis; these drives can be installed from the rear—an advantage in some cases. In the later-version XT systems, for example, IBM uses this design in its drives so that two half-height drives can be bolted together as a unit and then slid in from the rear to clear the mounting-bracket and screw hardware. On occasion, I have filed the edges of a drive faceplate to install the drive from the rear of a system—which sometimes can make installation much easier.

Connectors

Nearly all disk drives have at least two connectors—one for power to run the drive and the other to carry the control and data signals to and from the drive. These connectors are fairly standardized in the computer industry; a four-pin in-line connector (called Mate-N-Lock, by AMP), in both a large and small style is used for power (see fig. 13.4); and a 34-pin connector in both edge and pin header designs is used for the data and control signals. 5 1/4-inch drives normally use the large style power connector and the 34-pin edge type connector, whereas most 3 1/2-inch drives use the smaller version of the power connector and the 34-pin header type logic connector. The drive controller and logic connectors and pinouts are detailed later in this chapter as well as in Appendix A.

Both the large and small power connectors from the power supply are female plugs. They plug into the male portion, which is attached to the drive itself. One common problem with upgrading an older system with 3 1/2-inch drives is that your power supply only has the large style connectors, whereas the drive has the small style. An adapter cable is available from Radio Shack (Cat. No. 278-765) and other sources that converts the large style power connector to the proper small style used on most 3 1/2-inch drives.

The following chart shows the definition of the pins on the drive power-cable connectors:

Large Power Connector	Small Power Connector	Signal	Wire Color
Pin 1	Pin 4	+12 Vdc	Yellow
Pin 2	Pin 3	Ground	Black
Pin 3	Pin 2	Ground	Black
Pin 4	Pin 1	+5 Vdc	Red

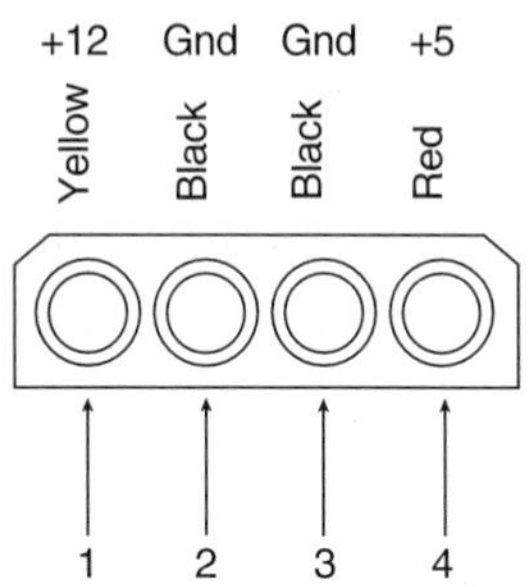

Figure 13.4

A disk drive female power supply cable connector.

Note that the pin designations are reversed between the large and small style power connectors. Also, it is important to know that not all manufacturers follow the wire color coding properly. I have seen instances in which all the wires are a single color (for example, black), or the wire colors are actually reversed from normal! For example, I once purchased the Radio Shack power connector adapter cables just mentioned that had all the wire colors backward. This was not really a problem as the adapter cable was wired correctly from end to end, but it was disconcerting to see the red wire in the power supply connector attach to a yellow wire in the adapter (and vice versa)!

Not all drives use the standard separate power and signal connectors. IBM, for example, uses either a single 34-pin or single 40-pin header connector for both power and floppy controller connections in most of the PS/2 systems. In some older PS/2 systems, for example, IBM used a special version of a Mitsubishi 3 1/2-inch 1.44M drive called the MF-355W-99, which has a single 40-pin power/signal connector. Some newer PS/2 systems use a Mitsubishi 3 1/2-inch 2.88M drive called the MF356C-799MA, which uses a single 34-pin header connector for both power and signal connections.

Most standard IBM clone or compatible systems use 3 1/2-inch drives with a 34-pin signal connector and a separate small style power connector. For older PC- or AT-type systems, many drive manufacturers also sell 3 1/2-inch drives installed in a 5 1/4-inch frame assembly and have a special adapter built in that allows the larger power connector and standard edge type signal connectors to be used. Mitsubishi sold 1.44M drives as the MF-355B-82 (black faceplate) or MF-355B-88 (beige faceplate). These drives included an adapter that enables the standard large style power connector and 34-pin edge type control and data connector to be used. Because no cable adapters are required and they install in a 5 1/4-inch half-height bay, these types of drives are ideal for upgrading earlier systems. Most 3 1/2-inch drive-upgrade kits sold today are similar and include the drive, appropriate adapters for the power and control and data cables, a 5 1/4-inch frame adapter and faceplate, and rails for AT installations. The frame adapter and faceplate enable the drive to be installed where a 5 1/4-inch half-height drive normally would go.

Drive-Configuration Devices

You must locate several items on a drive that you install in a system. These items control the configuration and operation of the drive and must be set correctly depending on which type of system the drive is installed in and exactly where in the system the drive is installed.

You must set or check the following items during installation:

- Drive select jumper
- Terminating resistor
- Disk changeline jumper
- Media sensor jumper

You learn how to configure these items later in this chapter. In this section, you learn what function these devices perform.

Drive Select Jumpers. Each drive in a controller and drive subsystem must have a unique drive number. The drive select jumper is set to indicate to the controller the logical number of a particular drive. The jumper indicates whether the specific drive should respond as drive 0 or 1 (A: or B:). Some idiosyncrasies can be found when you set this jumper in various systems because of strange cable configurations or other differences. Most drives allow four different settings, labeled DS1, DS2, DS3, and DS4. Some drives start with 0, and thus the four settings are labeled DS0, DS1, DS2, and DS3. On some drives, these jumpers are not labeled. If they are not labeled, you have several resources available for information about how to set the drive: the OEM manual, your experience with other similar drives, or simply an educated guess. First check the manual if it is available; if not, then perhaps you can rely on your past experiences and make an educated guess.

You might think that the first drive select position corresponds to A: and that the second position corresponds to B:, but in most cases you would be wrong. The configuration that seems correct is wrong because of some creative rewiring of the cable. IBM, for example, crosses the seven wires numbered 10 through 16 (the drive select, motor enable, and some ground lines) in the floppy interface cable between drives B: and A: to allow both drives to be jumpered the same way, as though they both were drive B:. This type of cable is shown later in this chapter.

When using a floppy cable with lines 10 through 16 twisted, you must set the DS jumper on both drives to the second (same) drive select position. This setup enabled dealers and installers to buy the drives pre-configured by IBM and install them with a minimum of hassle. Sometimes this setup confuses people who attempt to install drives properly without knowing about the twisted-cabling system. With this type of cable design, to swap drive A: and B: positions you can simply swap the cable connections between the drives with no jumper setting changes required. You still probably have to change the terminator resistor settings on the drives, however.

If the cable has a straight-through design, in which lines 10 through 16 are not twisted between the B: and A: connectors, you need to jumper the drives as you might have thought originally—that is, drive A: is set to the first drive select position, and drive B: is set to the second drive select position.

If you install a drive and it either does not respond or responds in unison with the other drive in the system in calling for drive A:, you probably have the drive select jumpers set incorrectly for your application. Check the DS jumpers on both drives as well as the cable for the proper setup.

Terminating Resistors. Any signal carrying electronic media or cable with multiple connections can be thought of as an electrical bus. In almost all cases, a bus must be terminated properly at each end with terminating resistors to allow signals to travel along the bus error free. Terminating resistors are designed to absorb any signals that reach the end of a cabling system or bus so that no reflection of the signal echoes, or bounces, back down the line in the opposite direction. Engineers sometimes call this effect signal ringing. Simply put, noise and distortion can disrupt the original signal and prevent proper communications between the drive and controller. Another function of proper termination is to place the proper resistive load on the output drivers in the controller and drive.

Most floppy disk cabling systems have the controller positioned at one end of the cable, and a terminating resistor network is built in to the controller to properly terminate that end of the bus. IBM and IBM clone or compatible systems use a floppy controller design that normally allows up to two drives on a single cable. To terminate the other end of the bus properly, a terminating resistor must be set, or enabled, on the drive at the end of the cable farthest from the controller. In most systems, this drive also is the lowest-lettered drive (A:) of the pair. The drive plugged into the connector in the center of the cable must have the terminating resistor (or terminator) removed or disabled for proper operation.

Because a terminating resistor is already installed in the controller to terminate the cable at that end; you only need to be concerned with properly terminating the drive end. Sometimes a system operates even with incorrect terminator installation or configuration, but the system might experience sporadic disk errors. Additionally, with the wrong signal load on the controller and drives, you run the risk of damaging them by causing excessive power output because of an improper resistive load.

A terminating resistor usually looks like a memory chip—a 16-pin dual in-line package (DIP) device. The device is actually a group of eight resistors physically wired in parallel with each other to terminate separately each of the eight data lines in the interface subsystem. Normally, this "chip" is a different color from other black chips on the drive.

Orange, yellow, blue, or white are common colors for a terminating resistor. Be aware that not all drives use the same type of terminating resistor, however, and it might be physically located in different places on different manufacturer's drive models. The OEM manual for the drive comes in handy in this situation because it shows the location, physical appearance, enabling and disabling instructions, and even the precise value required for the resistors. Do not lose the terminator if you remove it from a drive; you might need to reinstall it later if you relocate the drive to a different position in a system or even to a different system. Some drives use a resistor network in a single in-line pin (SIP) package, which looks like a slender device with eight or more pins in a line. Most terminating resistors have resistance values of 150 to 330 ohms.

Nearly all 5 1/4-inch floppy drives use a chip style terminator that must be physically installed or removed from the drive as required by the drive's position on the cable. Some 5 1/4-inch drives, especially those made by Toshiba, have a permanently installed terminating resistor enabled or disabled by a jumper labeled TR (Terminating Resistor). I prefer the jumper setup because you never have to actually remove (and possibly lose) the terminating resistor itself. Because some drives use different style and value resistors, if one is lost it can be a hassle to obtain a replacement of the correct type.

Most 3 1/2-inch drives have permanently installed, nonconfigurable terminating resistors. This is the best possible setup because you never have to remove or install them, and there are never any TR jumpers to set. Although some call this automatic termination, technically the 3 1/2-inch drives use a technique called *distributed termination.* With distributed termination, each 3 1/2-inch drive has a much higher value (1,000 to 1,500 ohm) terminating resistor permanently installed, and therefore carries a part of the termination load. These terminating resistors are fixed permanently to the drive and never have to be removed. This feature makes configuring these drives one step simpler. Because each drive is connected in parallel on the floppy cabling system, the total equivalent resistive load is calculated by the following formula:

1/R = 1/R1 + 1/R2 + 1/R3 + etc.

In a typical setup, a 330 ohm terminating resistor is permanently installed on the floppy controller, so the calculations for typical systems with one or two 3 1/2-inch drives (with built-in 1,500 ohm terminating resistors) is as follows:

1/R = 1/330 + 1/1,500 + 1/1,500 so R = 229.17 ohms (two drives)

1/R = 1/330 + 1/1,500 so R = 270.5 ohms (one drive)

Some confusion exists regarding the situation in which you have both 5 1/4-inch and 3 1/2-inch drives installed on a single cable. In this case, the 5 1/4-inch drive must have its terminating resistor configured as appropriate, which is to say either leave it installed or remove it depending on whether the drive is at the end of the cable. Nothing with regards to termination is done with the 3 1/2-inch drive because the terminating resistors are nonconfigurable. Although it sounds like mixing these might cause a problem with the termination, actually it works out quite well as the math shows. In this example, 330 ohm resistors are used both on the floppy controller and the 5 1/4-inch drive:

1/R = 1/330 + 1/1,500 so R = 270.5 ohms (3 1/2-inch drive at cable end)

1/R = 1/330 + 1/330 so R = 165 ohms (5 1/4-inch drive at cable end)

As long as a terminating resistor is at each end of the cable and the total equivalent resistance is between 100 to 300 ohms, the termination is normally considered correct. The drive in the center cable connector should not have a terminating resistor unless it employs distributed termination and has a resistor value of 1,000 ohms or higher. Note that in many cases even if the termination is improper a system seems to work fine, although the likelihood of read and write errors is greatly increased. In some cases, the drives do not work properly at all unless termination is properly configured. I have solved many intermittent floppy drive problems by correcting improper terminating resistor configurations found even in brand new systems.

The Diskette Changeline Jumper. In an XT-type system, pin 34 of the disk drive interface is not used, but in an AT system this pin is used to carry a signal called Diskette Changeline, or DC. Although the XT does not use pin 34, most drives that don't support the DC signal can optionally use the pin to carry a signal called Ready (usually labeled on the drive as RY, RDY, or SR). The Ready signal is actually never used in any IBM or PC-compatible systems and should not be configured, or in most cases, the drive will not work properly.

The AT uses the Diskette Changeline signal to determine whether the disk has been changed, or more accurately, whether the same disk loaded during the previous disk access still is loaded in the floppy drive. Disk Change is a pulsed signal that changes a status register in the controller to let the system know that a disk has been either inserted or ejected. This register is set to indicate that a disk has been inserted or removed (changed) by default. The register is cleared when the controller sends a step pulse to the drive and the drive responds, acknowledging that the heads have moved. At this point, the system knows that a specific disk is in the drive. If the disk change signal is not received before the next access, the system can assume that the same disk is still in the drive. Any information read into memory during the previous access therefore can be reused without rereading the disk.

Because of this process, some systems can buffer or cache the contents of the file allocation table or directory structure of a disk in the system's memory. By eliminating unnecessary rereads of these areas of the disk, the apparent speed of the drive is increased. If you move the door lever or eject button on a drive that supports the disk change signal, the DC pulse is sent to the controller, thus resetting the register indicating that the disk has been changed. This procedure causes the system to purge buffered or cached data that had been read from the disk because the system then cannot be sure that the same disk is still in the drive.

AT-class systems use the DC signal to increase significantly the speed of the floppy interface. Because the AT can detect whether you have changed the disk, the AT can keep a copy of the disk's directory and file allocation table information in RAM buffers. On every subsequent disk access, the operations are much faster because the information does not have to be reread from the disk in every individual access. If the DC signal has been reset (has a value of 1), the AT knows that the disk has been changed and appropriately rereads the information from the disk.

You can observe the effects of the DC signal by trying a simple experiment. Boot DOS on an AT-class system and place a formatted floppy disk with data on it in drive A:. Drive A: can be any type of drive except 5 1/4-inch double-density, although the disk you use can be anything the drive can read, including a double-density 360K disk, if you want. Then type the following command:

```
DIR A:
```

The disk drive lights up, and the directory is displayed. Note the amount of time spent reading the disk before the directory is displayed on-screen. Without touching the drive, enter the DIR A: command again, and watch the drive-access light and screen. Note again the amount of time that passes before the directory is displayed. The drive A: directory should appear almost instantly the second time because virtually no time is spent actually reading the disk. The directory information was simply read back from RAM buffers or cache rather than read again from the disk. Now open and close the drive door and keep the same disk in the drive. Type the DIR A: command again. The disk again takes some time reading the directory before displaying anything because the AT "thinks" that you changed the disk.

The PC and XT controllers (and systems) are not affected by the status of the DC signal. These systems "don't care" about signals on pin 34. The PC and XT systems always operate under the assumption that the disk is changed before every access, and they reread the disk directory and file allocation table each time—one reason that these systems are slower in using the floppy disk drives.

A problem can occur when certain drives are installed in an AT system. As mentioned, some drives use pin 34 for a "Ready" signal. The RDY signal is sent when a disk is installed and rotating in the drive. If you install a drive that has pin 34 set to send RDY, the AT "thinks" that it is continuously receiving a disk change signal, which causes problems. Usually the drive fails with a "Drive not ready" error and is inoperable.

A different but related problem occurs if the drive is not sending the DC signal on pin 34, and it should. If an AT class system is told (through CMOS setup) that the drive is any other type than a 360K (which cannot ever send the DC signal), the system expects the drive to send DC whenever a disk has been ejected. If the drive is not configured properly to send the signal, the system never recognizes that a disk has been changed. Therefore, even if you do change the disk, the AT still acts as though the first disk is in the drive and holds the first disk's directory and file allocation table information in RAM. This can be dangerous as the File Allocation Table (FAT) and directory information from the first disk can be partially written to any subsequent disks written to in the drive.

If you ever have seen an AT-class system with a floppy drive that shows "phantom directories" of the previously installed disk, even after you have changed or removed it, you have experienced this problem firsthand. The negative side effect is that all disks after the first one you place in this system are in extreme danger. You likely will overwrite the directories and file allocation tables of many disks with information from the first disk. Data recovery from such a catastrophe can require quite a bit of work with utility programs such as the Norton Utilities. These problems with Disk Change most often are traced to an incorrectly configured drive. Another possibility is that the disk-eject sensor mechanism no longer operates correctly. A temporary solution to the problem is to press the Ctrl-Break or Ctrl-C key combination every time you change a floppy disk in the drive. These commands cause DOS to flush the RAM buffers manually and reread the directory and file allocation table during the next disk access.

All drives except 5 1/4-inch double-density (360K) drives support the Disk Change signal. Therefore, if your system thinks that one of these drives is installed, the drive is expected to provide the signal. If the system thinks that the installed drive is a 360K drive, no signal is expected on pin 34.

To summarize, PC and XT systems are not affected by pin 34, but on AT systems, non-360K drives must have pin 34 set to send Disk Change. If the drive is a 360K drive and you want to install it in an AT, pin 34 must be disabled (usually preconfigured as such, or set by removing a jumper). Never set a 360K drive (or any other drive for that matter) to send a signal called Ready (RDY) on pin 34 because PC-compatible systems cannot use this signal. The only reason that the Ready signal exists on some drives is that it happens to be a part of the standard Shugart SA-400 disk interface that was not adopted by IBM.

The Media Sensor Jumper. This configuration item exists only on the 3 1/2-inch 1.44M or 2.88M drives. The jumper selection, called the media sensor (MS) jumper, must be set to enable a special media sensor in the disk drive, which senses a media sensor hole found only in the 1.44M high-density and the 2.88M extra-high density floppy disks. The labeling of this jumper (or jumpers) varies greatly between different drives. In many drives, the jumpers are permanently set (enabled) and cannot be changed.

The three types of configurations with regards to media sensing are as follows:

- No media sense (sensor disabled or no sensor present)
- Passive media sense (sensor enabled)
- Active or intelligent media sense (sensor supported by Controller/BIOS)

Most systems use a passive media sensor arrangement. The passive media sensor setup enables the drive to determine the level of recording strength to use and is required for most installations of these drives because of a bug in the design of the Western Digital hard disk and floppy controllers used by IBM in the AT systems. This bug prevents the controller from properly instructing the drive to switch to double-density mode when you write or format double-density disks. With the media sensor enabled, the drive no longer depends on the controller for density mode switching and relies only on the drive's media sensor. Unless you are sure that your disk controller does not have this flaw, make sure that your HD drive includes a media sensor (some older or manufacturer-specific drives do not), and that it is properly enabled. The 2.88M drives universally rely on media sensors to determine the proper mode of operation. The 2.88M drives, in fact, have two separate media sensors because the ED disks include a media sensor hole in a different position than the HD disks.

With only a few exceptions, high-density 3 1/2-inch drives installed in most PC-compatible systems do not operate properly in double-density mode unless the drive has control over the write current (recording level) via an installed and enabled media sensor. Exceptions are found primarily in systems with floppy controllers integrated on the motherboard, including most older IBM PS/2 and Compaq systems as well as most laptop or notebook systems from other manufacturers. These systems have floppy controllers without the bug referred to earlier, and can correctly switch the mode of the drive without the aid of the media sensor. In these systems, it technically does not matter whether you enable the media sensor. If the media sensor is enabled, the drive mode is controlled by the disk you insert, as is the case with most PC-compatible systems. If the media sensor is not enabled, the drive mode is controlled by the floppy controller, which in turn is controlled by DOS.

If a disk is already formatted correctly, DOS reads the volume boot sector to determine the current disk format, and the controller then switches the drive to the appropriate mode. If the disk has not been formatted yet, DOS has no idea what type of disk it is, and the drive remains in its native HD or ED mode.

When you format a disk in systems without an enabled media sensor (such as most PS/2s), the mode of the drive depends entirely on the FORMAT command issued by the user, regardless of the type of disk inserted. For example, if you insert a DD disk into an HD drive in an IBM PS/2 Model 70 and format the disk by entering FORMAT A:, the disk is formatted as though it is an HD disk because you did not issue the correct parameters (/F:720) to cause the FORMAT command to specify a DD format. On a system with the media sensor enabled, this type of incorrect format fails, and you see the Invalid media or Track 0 bad error message from FORMAT. In this case, the media sensor prevents an incorrect format from occurring on the disk, a safety feature most older IBM PS/2 systems lack.

Most of the newer PS/2 systems—including all those that come standard with the 2.88M drives—have what is called an active or intelligent media sensor setup. This means that the sensor not only detects what type of disk is in the drive and changes modes appropriately, but also the drive informs the controller (and the BIOS) about what type of disk is in the drive. Systems with an intelligent media sensor do not need to use the disk type parameters in the FORMAT command. In these systems, the FORMAT command automatically "knows" what type of disk is in the drive and formats it properly. With an intelligent media sensor, you never have to know what the correct format parameters are for a particular type of disk, the system figures it out for you automatically. Many high-end systems such as the newer PS/2 systems as well as high-end Hewlett Packard PCs have this type of intelligent media sensor arrangement.

The Floppy Disk Controller

The floppy disk controller consists of the circuitry either on a separate adapter card or integrated on the motherboard, which acts as the interface between the floppy drives and the system. Most PC- and XT-class systems use a separate controller card that occupied a slot in the system. The AT systems normally have the floppy controller and hard disk controller built into the same adapter card and also plugged into a slot. In most of the more modern systems built since then, the controller is integrated on the motherboard. In any case, the electrical interface to the drives has remained largely static, with only a few exceptions.

The original IBM PC and XT system floppy controller was a 3/4-length card that could drive as many as four floppy disk drives. Two drives could be connected to a cable plugged into a 34-pin edge connector on the card, and two more drives could be plugged into a cable connected to the 37-pin connector on the bracket of this card. Figures 13.5 and 13.6 show these connectors and the pinouts for the controller.

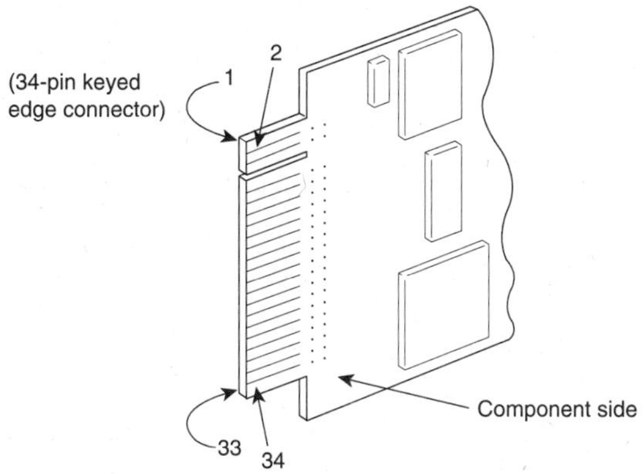

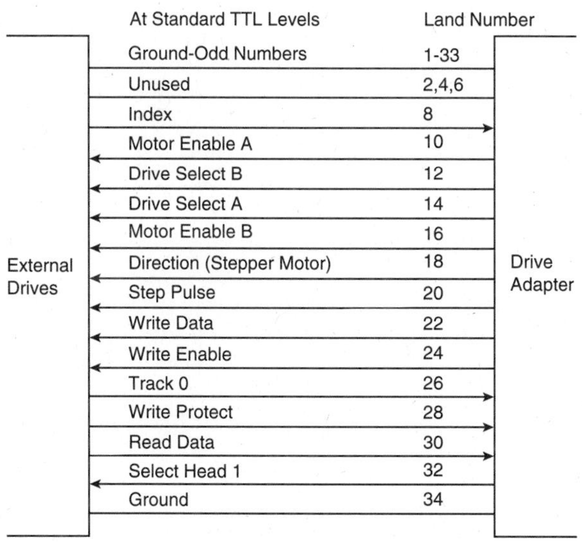

Figure 13.5

A PC and XT floppy controller internal connector.

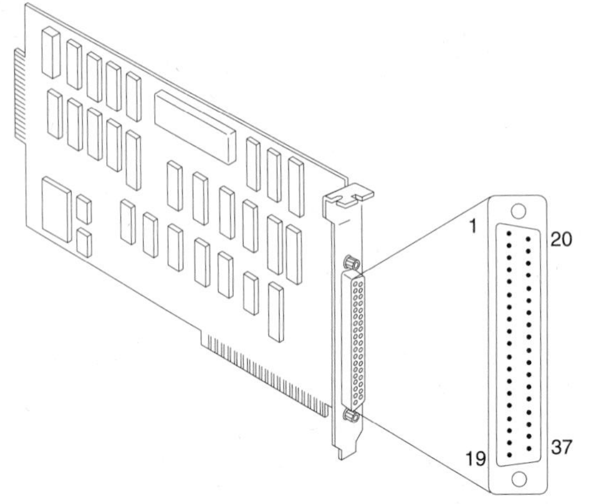

External Drives ↔ Drive Adapter

At Standard TTL Levels	Pin Number
Unused	1-5
Index	6
Motor Enable C	7
Drive Select D	8
Drive Select C	9
Motor Enable D	10
Direction (Stepper Motor)	11
Step Pulse	12
Write Data	13
Write Enable	14
Track 0	15
Write Protect	16
Read Data	17
Select Head 1	18
Ground	20-37

Figure 13.6

A PC and XT floppy controller external connector.

The AT used a board made by Western Digital, which included both the floppy and hard disk controllers in a single adapter. The connector location and pinout for the floppy controller portion of this card is shown in figure 13.7. IBM used two variations of this controller during the life of the AT system. The first one was a full 4.8 inches high, which used all the vertical height possible in the AT case. This board was a variation of the Western Digital WD1002-WA2 controller sold through distributors and dealers. The second-generation card was only 4.2 inches high, which enabled it to fit into the shorter case of the XT-286 as well as the taller AT cases. This card was equivalent to the Western Digital WD1003-WA2, also sold on the open market.

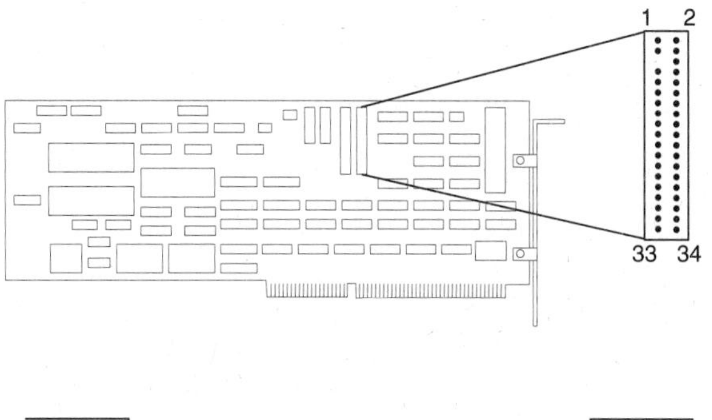

Signal	Pin
Ground – Odd Numbers	1-33
Reduced Write	2
Not Connected	4
Not Connected	6
Index	8
Motor Enable 1	10
Drive Select 2	12
Drive Select 1	14
Motor Enable 2	16
Direction Select	18
Step	20
Write Data	22
Write Enable	24
Track 00	26
Write Protect	28
Read Data	30
Side 1 Select	32
Diskette Change	34

Figure 13.7
An AT floppy controller connector.

Disk Physical Specifications and Operation

PC-compatible systems now use one of as many as five standard types of floppy drives. Also, five types of disks can be used in the drives. This section examines the physical specifications and operations of these drives and disks.

Drives and disks are divided into two classes: 5 1/4-inch and 3 1/2-inch. The physical dimensions and components of a typical 5 1/4-inch disk and a 3 1/2-inch disk are shown later in this chapter.

The physical operation of a disk drive is fairly simple to describe. The disk rotates in the drive at either 300 or 360 RPM. Most drives spin at 300 RPM, only the 5 1/4-inch 1.2M drives spin at 360 RPM (even when reading or writing 360K disks). With the disk spinning, the heads can move in and out approximately one inch and write either 40 or 80 tracks. The tracks are written on both sides of the disk and therefore sometimes are called cylinders. A single cylinder comprises the tracks on the top and bottom of the disk.

The heads record by using a tunnel-erase procedure in which a track is written to a specified width and then the edges of the track are erased to prevent interference with any adjacent tracks.

The tracks are recorded at different widths for different drives. Table 13.1 shows the track widths in both millimeters and inches for the five types of floppy drives supported in PC systems.

Table 13.1 Floppy Drive Track-Width Specifications

Drive Type	No. of Tracks	Track Width	
5 1/4-inch 360K	40 per side	0.300 mm	0.0118 in.
5 1/4-inch 1.2M	80 per side	0.155 mm	0.0061 in.
3 1/2-inch 720K	80 per side	0.115 mm	0.0045 in.
3 1/2-inch 1.44M	80 per side	0.115 mm	0.0045 in.
3 1/2-inch 2.88M	80 per side	0.115 mm	0.0045 in.

The differences in recorded track width can result in data-exchange problems between 5 1/4-inch drives. The 5 1/4-inch drives are affected because the double-density drives record a track width nearly twice that of the high-density drives. A problem occurs, therefore, if a high-density drive is used to update a double-density disk with previously recorded data on it.

Even in 360K mode, the high-density drive cannot completely overwrite the track left by an actual 360K drive. A problem occurs when the disk is returned to the person with the 360K drive: that drive reads the new data as embedded within the remains of the previously written track. Because the drive cannot distinguish either signal, an Abort, Retry, Ignore error message appears on-screen. The problem does not occur if a new disk (one that never has had data recorded on it) is first formatted in a 1.2M drive with the /4 option, which formats the disk as a 360K disk.

Note

You also can format a 360K disk in a 1.2M drive with the /N:9, /T:40, or /F:360 options, depending on the DOS version. The 1.2M drive then can be used to fill the brand-new and newly formatted 360K disk to its capacity, and every file will be readable on the 40-track, 360K drive.

I use this technique all the time to exchange data disks between AT systems that have only the 1.2M drive and XT or PC systems that have only the 360K drive. The key is to start with either a new disk or one wiped clean magnetically by a bulk eraser or degaussing tool. Just reformatting the disk does not work by itself because formatting does not actually erase a disk; instead it records data across the entire disk.

In addition to a track-width specification, specifications exist for the precise placement of tracks on a disk. A 5 1/4-inch DD disk has tracks placed precisely 1/48th of an inch apart. The outermost track on side 0 (the bottom of the disk) is the starting point for measurements, and this track (cylinder 0, head 0) has a radius of exactly 2.25 inches. Because Head 1 (the top of the disk) is offset by four tracks inward from Head 0, the radius of cylinder 0, Head 1 is 2.2500 inches - (1/48 * 4) = 2.1667 inches. Therefore, to calculate the exact track radius R in inches for any specified cylinder C and head position on a 360K disk, use these formulas:

For Head 0 (bottom): R = 2.2500 inches - C/48 inches

For Head 1 (top): R = 2.1667 inches - C/48 inches

That the tracks on top of the disk (Head 1) are offset toward the center of the disk from the tracks on the bottom of the disk (Head 0) might be surprising: in effect, the cylinders are cone shaped. Figure 13.8 shows the physical relationship between the top and bottom heads on a floppy drive. In this figure, both heads are positioned at the same cylinder. You can see that the top track of the cylinder is closer to the center of the disk than is the bottom track, resulting in cylinders shaped more like cones.

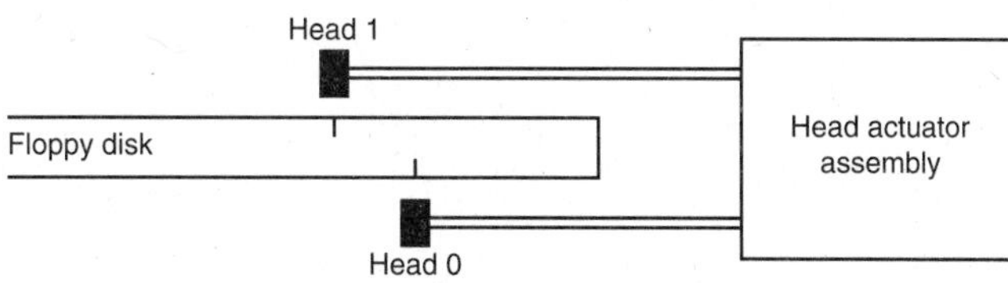

Figure 13.8

Floppy disk drive head offset.

I first saw this track positioning in one of my data-recovery seminars. One of the experiments I perform in these courses is to stick a pin through a disk with data on it. The objective then is to recover as much data as possible from the disk. Normally, I can resolve the damage down to only a few unreadable sectors on either side of the disk and then easily recover all but these damaged sectors. As I was trying to determine the exact location of the hole by its cylinder, head, and sector coordinates, I noticed that I always had what seemed to be two groups of damaged sectors that were always located exactly four or eight (depending on the type of disk) cylinders apart. Because I had stuck the pin straight through the disk, I realized that any offset had to be in the tracks themselves. I then removed the disk from its jacket to look more closely at the holes.

When I want to "see" the tracks on a disk, I use a special type of solution called Magnetic Developer, a fine-powdered iron suspended in a trichloroethane solution. When this developer, which dries very quickly, is sprayed on the disk, the iron particles align themselves directly over magnetized areas of the disk and show very graphically the exact physical appearance and location of the tracks and sectors on the disk. You can see every individual track and sector on the disk "develop" right before your eyes! With a magnifier or low-powered microscope, I can locate the exact sectors and tracks damaged by the hole on either side of the disk. With this technique, it was easy to see that the tracks on top of the disk start and end farther toward the center of the disk. If you want to do similar experiments or simply "see" the magnetic image of your disks, you can obtain the Magnetic Developer solution from Sprague Magnetics (the address and phone number are in the vendor list in Appendix B). By the way, after viewing this magnetic image, the disk "cookie" can be washed with distilled water or pure alcohol, placed back into a new jacket, and reused!

The high-density 5 1/4-inch disk track dimensions are similar to the double-density disk, except that the tracks are spaced precisely 1/96-inch apart, and the top head (Head 1) is offset eight tracks inward from the bottom head (Head 0). The physical head offset between Head 0 and Head 1 is the same as DD disks because twice as many tracks are in the same space as on a DD disk. The calculations for a given track radius R in inches for any cylinder C and head are as follows:

For Head 0 (bottom): R = 2.2500 inches - C/96 inches

For Head 1 (top): R = 2.1667 inches - C/96 inches

All the different 3 1/2-inch disks (DD, HD, ED) are dimensionally the same in track and cylinder spacing. The track and cylinder dimensions of these disks start with the radius of Cylinder 0, Head 0 (the bottom head outer track) defined as 39.5 millimeters. Tracks inward from this track are spaced precisely 0.1875 millimeters apart, and the top head (Head 1) is offset inward by eight tracks from Head 0. The radius, in millimeters, of the outer track on top of the disk (Cylinder 0, Head 1) therefore can be calculated as follows:

39.5 mm – (0.1875 * 8) = 38.0 mm

Now you can calculate the radius R in millimeters of any specified cylinder C and head using these formulas:

For Head 0 (bottom): R = 39.5mm – (0.1875mm * C)

For Head 1 (top): R = 38.0mm – (0.1875mm * C)

An interesting note about the dimensions of the 3 1/2-inch disks is that the dimensional standards all are based in the metric system, unlike the 5 1/4-inch disks. I could have converted these numbers to their English equivalents for comparison with the 5 1/4-inch disk figures, but rounding would have sacrificed some accuracy in the numeric conversion. For example, many texts often give the track spacing for 3 1/2-inch disks as 135 TPI (tracks per inch). This figure is an imprecise result of metric-to-English conversion and rounding. The true spacing of 0.1875 mm between tracks converts to a more precise figure of 135.4667 TPI. The figures presented here are the specifications as governed by the ANSI standards X3.125 and X3.126 for 360K and 1.2M disks, and by Sony, Toshiba, and Accurite, which all are involved in specifying 3 1/2-inch disk standards.

Disk Magnetic Properties

A subtle problem with the way a disk drive works magnetically is that the recording volume varies depending on the type of format you are trying to apply to a disk. The high-density formats use special disks that require a much higher volume level for the recording than do the double-density disks. My classes nearly always are either stumped or incorrect (unless they have read ahead in the book) when they answer this question: "Which type of disk is magnetically more sensitive: a 1.2M disk or a 360K disk?" If you answer that the 1.2M disk is more sensitive, you are wrong! The high-density disks are approximately half as sensitive magnetically as the double-density disks.

The high-density disks are called high-coercivity disks also because they require a magnetic field strength much higher than do the double-density disks. Magnetic field strength is measured in oersteds. The 360K floppy disks require only a 300-oersted field strength to record, and the high-density 1.2M disks require a 600-oersted field strength. Because the high-density disks need double the magnetic field strength for recording, you should not attempt to format a 1.2M high-density disk as though it were a 360K disk, or a 360K disk as though it were a 1.2M high-density disk.

The latter case in particular seems to appeal to people looking for an easy way to save money. They buy inexpensive 360K disks and format them in a 1.2M drive to the full 1.2M capacity. Most of the time, this format seems to work, with perhaps a large amount of bad sectors; otherwise, most of the disk might seem usable. You should not store important data on this incorrectly formatted disk, however, because the data is recorded at twice the recommended strength and density. Eventually, the adjacent magnetic domains on the disk begin to affect each other and can cause each other to change polarity or weaken because of the proximity of these domains, and because the double-density disk is more sensitive to magnetic fields. This process is illustrated later in this chapter, in the "Media Coercivity and Thickness" section. Eventually, the disk begins to erase itself and deteriorates. The process might take weeks, months, or even longer, but the result is inevitable—a loss of the information stored on the disk.

Another problem results from this type of improper formatting: You can imprint the 360K disk magnetically with an image that is difficult to remove. The high-density format places on the disk a recording at twice the strength it should be. How do you remove this recording and correct the problem? If you attempt to reformat the disk in a 360K drive, the drive writes in a reduced write-current mode and in some cases cannot overwrite the higher-volume recorded image you mistakenly placed on the disk. If you attempt to reformat the disk in the high-density drive with the /4 (or equivalent) parameter, which indicates 360K mode, the high-density drive uses a reduced write-current setting and again cannot overwrite the recording.

You can correct the problem in several ways. You can throw away the disk and write it off as a learning experience, or you can use a bulk eraser or degaussing tool to demagnetize the disk. These devices can randomize all the magnetic domains on a disk and return it to an essentially factory-new condition. You can purchase a bulk-erasing device at electronic-supply stores for about $25.

The opposite problem with disk formatting is not as common, but some have tried it anyway: formatting a high-density disk with a double-density format. You should not (and normally cannot) format a 1.2M high-density disk to a 360K capacity. If you attempt to use one, the drive changes to reduced write-current mode and does not create a magnetic field strong enough to record on the "insensitive" 1.2M disk. The result in this case is normally an immediate error message from the FORMAT command: Invalid media or Track 0 bad - disk unusable. Fortunately, the system usually does not allow this particular mistake to be made.

The 3 1/2-inch drives don't have the same problems as the 5 1/4-inch drives—at least for data interchange. Because both the high-density and double-density drives write the same number of tracks and these tracks are always the same width, no problem occurs when one type of drive is used to overwrite data written by another type of drive. A system manufacturer therefore doesn't need to offer a double-density version of the 3 1/2-inch drive for systems equipped with the high-density or extra-high-density drive. The HD and ED drives can perfectly emulate the operations of the 720K DD drive, and the ED drive can perfectly emulate the 1.44M HD drive.

The HD and ED drives can be trouble, however, for inexperienced users who try to format disks to incorrect capacities. Although an ED drive can read, write, and format DD, HD, and ED disks, a disk should be formatted and written at only its specified capacity. An ED disk therefore should be formatted only to 2.88M, and never to 1.44M or 720K. You must always use a disk at its designated format capacity. You are asking for serious problems if you place a 720K disk in the A: drive of a PS/2 Model 50, 60, 70, or 80 and enter FORMAT A:. This step causes a 1.44M format to be written on the 720K disk, which renders it unreliable at best and requires a bulk eraser to reformat it correctly. If you decide to use the resulting incorrectly formatted disk, you will eventually have massive data loss.

This particular problem could have been averted if IBM had used media sensor drives in all PS/2 systems. Drives that use the disk media-sensor hole to control the drive mode are prevented from incorrectly formatting a disk. The hardware causes the FORMAT command to fail with an appropriate error message if you attempt to format the disk to an incorrect capacity.

By knowing how a drive works physically, you can eliminate most of these user "pilot error" problems and distinguish this kind of easily solved problem from a more serious hardware problem. You will be a much better user as well as a troubleshooter of a system if you truly understand how a drive works.

Logical Operation

Each type of drive can create disks with different numbers of sectors and tracks. This section examines how DOS sees a drive. It gives definitions of the drives according to DOS and the definitions of cylinders and clusters.

How the Operating System Uses a Disk. A technical understanding of the way information is stored on your disks is not necessary to use a PC, but you will be a more informed user if you understand the general principles.

To the operating system, data on your PC disks is organized in tracks and sectors. Tracks are narrow, concentric circles on a disk. Sectors are pie-shaped slices of the disk. DOS versions 1.0 and 1.1 read and write 5 1/4-inch double-density disks with 40 tracks (numbered 0 through 39) per side and eight sectors (numbered 1 through 8) per track. DOS versions 2.0 and higher automatically increase the track density from eight to nine sectors for greater capacity on the same disk. On an AT with a 1.2M disk drive, DOS V3.0 supports high-density 5 1/4-inch drives that format 15 sectors per track and 80 tracks per side; DOS V3.2 supports 3 1/2-inch drives that format 9 sectors per track and 80 tracks per side; DOS V3.3 supports 3 1/2-inch drives that format 18 sectors per track and 80 tracks per side. The distance between tracks and, therefore, the number of tracks on a disk, is a built-in mechanical and electronic function of the drive. Tables 13.2 and 13.3 summarize the standard disk formats supported by DOS version 5.0 and higher.

Table 13.2 5 1/4-inch Floppy Disk Drive Formats

5 1/4-Inch Floppy Disks	Double Density 360K (DD)	High Density 1.2M (HD)
Bytes per Sector	512	512
Sectors per Track	9	15
Tracks per Side	40	80
Sides	2	2
Capacity (KBytes)	360	1,200
Capacity (Megabytes)	0.352	1.172
Capacity (Million Bytes)	0.369	1.229

Table 13.3 3 1/2-inch Floppy Disk Drive Formats

3 1/2-Inch Floppy Disks	Double Density 720K (DD)	High Density 1.44M (HD)	Extra-High Density 2.88M (ED)
Bytes per Sector	512	512	512
Sectors per Track	9	18	36
Tracks per Side	80	80	80
Sides	2	2	2
Capacity (KBytes)	720	1,440	2,880
Capacity (Megabytes)	0.703	1.406	2.813
Capacity (Million Bytes)	0.737	1.475	2.949

You can calculate the capacity differences between different formats by multiplying the sectors per track by the number of tracks per side together with the constants of two sides and 512 bytes per sector. Note that the disk capacity can actually be expressed in three different ways. The most common method is to refer to the capacity of a floppy by the number of kilobytes (1,024 bytes equals 1K). This works fine for 360K and 720K disks, but is strange when applied to the 1.44M and 2.88M disks. As you can see, a 1.44M disk is really 1,440K, and not actually 1.44 megabytes. Because a megabyte is 1,024K, what we call a 1.44M disk is actually 1.406 megabytes in capacity. Another way of expressing disk capacity is in millions of bytes. In that case, the 1.44M disk has 1.475 million bytes of capacity. To add to the confusion over capacity expression, both megabyte and millions of bytes are abbreviated as MB or M. No universally accepted standard for the definition of M or MB exists, so throughout this book I will try to be explicit.

Like blank sheets of paper, new disks contain no information. Formatting a disk is similar to adding lines to the paper so that you can write straight across. Formatting places on the disk the information DOS needs to maintain a directory and file table of contents. Using the /S (system) option in the FORMAT command resembles making the paper a title page. FORMAT places on the disk the portions of DOS required to boot the system.

The operating system reserves the track nearest to the outside edge of a disk (track 0) almost entirely for its purposes. Track 0, Sector 1 contains the DOS Boot Record (DBR), or Boot Sector, the system needs to begin operation. The next few sectors contain the File Allocation Tables (FATs), which act as the disk "room reservation clerk" that keeps records of which clusters or allocation units (rooms) on the disk have file information and which are empty. Finally, the next few sectors contain the root directory, in which DOS stores information about the names and starting locations of the files on the disk; you see most of this information when you use the DIR command.

In computer-industry jargon, this process is "transparent to the user," which means that you don't have to (and generally cannot) decide where information is stored on disks. That this process is "transparent," however, doesn't necessarily mean that you shouldn't be aware of the decisions DOS makes for you.

When DOS writes data, it always begins by attempting to use the earliest available data sectors on the disk. Because the file might be larger than the particular block of available sectors selected, DOS then writes the remainder of the file in the next available block of free sectors. In this manner, files can become fragmented as they are written to fill a hole on the disk created by the deletion of some smaller file. The larger file completely fills the hole; then DOS continues to look for more free space across the disk, from the outermost tracks to the innermost tracks. The rest of the file is deposited in the next available free space.

This procedure continues until eventually all the files on your disk are intertwined. This situation is not really a problem for DOS because it was designed to manage files in this way. The problem is a physical one: Retrieving a fragmented file that occupies 50 or 100 separate places across the disk takes much longer than if the file were in one piece. Also, if the files were in one piece, recovering data in the case of a disaster would be much easier. Consider unfragmenting a disk periodically simply because it can make recovery from a disk disaster much easier; many people, however, unfragment disks for the performance benefit in loading and saving files that are in one piece.

How do you unfragment a disk? DOS 6.0 and higher versions include a command called DEFRAG. This utility is actually a limited version of the Norton Utilities Speedisk program. It does not have some of the options of the more powerful Norton version and is not as fast, but it does work well in most cases. Earlier versions of DOS do not provide any easy method for unfragmenting a disk, although by backing up and restoring files, you can accomplish the goal. To unfragment a floppy disk for example, you can copy all the files one by one to an empty disk, delete the original files from the first disk, and then recopy the files. With a hard disk, you can back up all the files, reformat the disk, and restore the files. This procedure is time consuming, to say the least.

Windows 95 also includes a Disk Defragmenter utility that not only works under the Windows graphical environment, but also operates in the background while other applications are running.

Because DOS versions earlier than 6.0 did not provide a good way to unfragment a disk, many software companies have produced utility programs that can easily unfragment disks in a clean and efficient manner. These programs can restore file contiguity without reformat and restore operations. My favorite for an extremely safe, easy, and fast unfragmenting program is the Vopt utility, by Golden Bow. In my opinion, no other unfragmenting utility even comes close to this amazing $50 package. Golden Bow's address and phone number are in Appendix B. If you are using Windows 95 with long file names, be aware that many of the older defragmenter programs do not preserve these file name entries, which can cause many problems. Contact the manufacturer of any disk defragmenting utilities to ensure that they are safe to use on a Windows 95 formatted disk. Many of these programs will require updated versions to work properly.

Caution

These unfragmenting programs, inherently dangerous by nature, do not eliminate the need for a good backup program. Before using an unfragmenting program, make sure that you have a good backup. What shape do you think your disk would be in if the power failed during an unfragmenting session? Also, some programs have bugs or are incompatible with new releases of DOS or Windows 95.

Cylinders. The term cylinder usually is used in place of track. A *cylinder* is all the tracks under read/write heads on a drive at one time. For floppy drives, because a disk cannot have more than two sides and the drive has two heads, normally there are two tracks per cylinder. Hard disks can have many disk platters, each with two (or more) heads, for many tracks per single cylinder.

Clusters or Allocation Units. A cluster also is called an allocation unit in DOS version 4.0 and higher. The term is appropriate because a single cluster is the smallest unit of the disk that DOS can allocate when it writes a file. A cluster or allocation unit consists of one or more sectors—usually two or more. Having more than one sector per cluster reduces the file-allocation table size and enables DOS to run faster because it has fewer individual allocation units of the disk with which to work. The tradeoff is in some wasted disk space. Because DOS can manage space only in the cluster size unit, every file consumes space on the disk in increments of one cluster. Table 13.4 lists the default cluster sizes used by DOS for different floppy disk formats. Chapter 14, "Hard Disk Drives," discusses hard disk cluster or allocation unit sizes.

Table 13.4 DOS Default Cluster and Allocation Unit Sizes

Floppy Disk Capacity	Cluster/Allocation Unit Size		FAT Type
5 1/4-inch, 360K	2 sectors	1,024 bytes	12-bit
5 1/4-inch, 1.2M	1 sector	512 bytes	12-bit
3 1/2-inch, 720K	2 sectors	1,024 bytes	12-bit
3 1/2-inch, 1.44M	1 sector	512 bytes	12-bit
3 1/2-inch, 2.88M	2 sectors	1,024 bytes	12-bit

K = 1,024 bytes
M = 1,048,576 bytes

The high-density disks normally have smaller cluster sizes, which seems strange because these disks have many more individual sectors than do double-density disks. The probable reason is that because these high-density disks are faster than their double-density counterparts, IBM and Microsoft thought that the decrease in wasted disk space cluster size and speed would be welcome. You learn later that the cluster size on hard disks can vary much more between different versions of DOS and different disk sizes. Table 13.5 shows the floppy disk logical parameters.

Types of Floppy Drives

Five types of standard floppy drives are available for a PC-compatible system. The drives can be summarized most easily by their formatting specifications (refer to tables 13.2 and 13.3).

Most drive types can format multiple types of disks. For example, the 3 1/2-inch ED drive can format and write on any 3 1/2-inch disk. The 5 1/4-inch HD drive also can format and write on any 5 1/4-inch disk (although, as mentioned, sometimes track-width problems occur). This drive can even create some older obsolete formats, including single-sided disks and disks with eight sectors per track.

On the Web

http://www.mmm.com/

http://www.compaq.com

As you can see from table 13.5, the different disk capacities are determined by several parameters, some of which seem to remain constant on all drives, whereas others change from drive to drive. For example, all drives use 512-byte physical sectors, which remains true for hard disks as well. Note, however, that DOS treats the sector size as though it could be a changeable parameter, although the BIOS does not.

Note also that now all standard floppy drives are double-sided. IBM has not shipped PC systems with single-sided drives since 1982; these drives are definitely considered obsolete. Also, IBM never has utilized any form of single-sided 3 1/2-inch drives, although that type of drive appeared in the first Apple Macintosh systems in 1984. IBM officially began selling and supporting 3 1/2-inch drives in 1986 and has used only double-sided versions of these drives.

Table 13.5 Floppy Disk Logical DOS-Format Parameters

	Current Formats					Obsolete Formats		
Disk Size (in.)	**3 1/2"**	**3 1/2"**	**3 1/2"**	**5 1/4"**	**5 1/4"**	**5 1/4"**	**5 1/4"**	**5 1/4"**
Disk Capacity (K)	**2,880**	**1,440**	**720**	**1,200**	**360**	**320**	**180**	**160**
Media Descriptor Byte	F0h	F0h	F9h	F9h	FDh	FFh	FCh	FEh
Sides (Heads)	2	2	2	2	2	2	1	1
Tracks per Side	80	80	80	80	40	40	40	40
Sectors per Track	36	18	9	15	9	8	9	8
Bytes per Sector	512	512	512	512	512	512	512	512
Sectors per Cluster	2	1	2	1	2	2	1	1
FAT Length (Sectors)	9	9	3	7	2	1	2	1
Number of FATs	2	2	2	2	2	2	2	2
Root Dir. Length (Sectors)	15	14	7	14	7	7	4	4
Maximum Root Entries	240	224	112	224	112	112	64	64
Total Sectors per Disk	5,760	2,880	1,440	2,400	720	640	360	320
Total Available Sectors	5,726	2,847	1,426	2,371	708	630	351	313
Total Available Clusters	2,863	2,847	713	2,371	354	315	351	313

The 360K 5 1/4-Inch Drive

The 5 1/4-inch low-density drive is designed to create a standard-format disk with 360K capacity. Although I persistently call these low-density drives, the industry term is "double-density." I use "low-density" because I find the term "double-density" to be somewhat misleading, especially when I am trying to define these drives in juxtaposition to the high-density drives.

The term double-density arose from the use of the term single density to indicate a type of drive that used frequency modulation (FM) encoding to store approximately 90 kilobytes on a disk. This type of obsolete drive never was used in any PC-compatible systems, but was used in some older systems such as the original Osborne-1 portable computer. When drive manufacturers changed the drives to use Modified Frequency Modulation (MFM) encoding, they began using the term "double-density" to indicate it, as well as the (approximately doubled) increase in recording capacity realized from this encoding method. All modern floppy disk drives use MFM encoding, including all types listed in this section. Encoding methods such as FM, MFM, and RLL variants are discussed in Chapter 14, "Hard Disk Drives."

The 360K 5 1/4-inch drive normally records 40 cylinders of two tracks each, with each cylinder numbered starting with 0 closest to the outside diameter of the floppy disk. Head position (or side) 0 is recorded on the underside of the floppy disk, and Head 1 records on the top of the disk surface. This drive normally divides each track into nine sectors, but it can optionally format only eight sectors per track to create a floppy disk compatible with DOS versions 1.1 or earlier. This type of format rarely (if ever) is used today.

The 360K 5 1/4-inch drives supplied in the first IBM systems all were full-height units, which means that they were 3.25 inches tall. Full-height drives are obsolete now and have not been manufactured since 1986. Later units used by IBM and most compatible vendors have been the half-height units, which are only 1.6 inches tall. You can install two half-height drives in place of a single full-height unit. These drives, made by different manufacturers, are similar except for some cosmetic differences.

The 360K 5 1/4-inch drives spin at 300 RPM, which equals exactly five revolutions per second, or 200 milliseconds per revolution. All standard floppy controllers support a 1:1 interleave, in which each sector on a specific track is numbered (and read) consecutively. To read and write to a disk at full speed, a controller sends data at a rate of 250,000 bits per second. Because all low-density controllers can support this data rate, virtually any controller supports this type of drive, depending on ROM BIOS code that supports these drives.

All standard PC-compatible systems include ROM BIOS support for these drives; therefore, you usually do not need special software or driver programs to use them. This statement might exclude some aftermarket (non-IBM) 360K drives for PS/2 systems that might require some type of driver in order to work. The IBM-offered units use the built-in ROM support to enable these drives to work. The only requirement usually is to run the Setup program for the machine to enable it to properly recognize these drives.

The 1.2M 5 1/4-Inch Drive

The 1.2M high-density floppy drive first appeared in the IBM AT system introduced in August 1984. The drive required the use of a new type of disk to achieve the 1.2M format capacity, but it still could read and write (although not always reliably) the lower-density 360K disks.

The 1.2M 5 1/4-inch drive normally recorded 80 cylinders of two tracks each, starting with cylinder 0, at the outside of the disk. This situation differs from the low-density 5 1/4-inch drive in its capability to record twice as many cylinders in approximately the same space on the disk. This capability alone suggests that the recording capacity for a disk would double, but that is not all. Each track normally is recorded with 15 sectors of 512 bytes each, increasing the storage capacity even more. In fact, these drives store nearly four times the data of the 360K disks. The density increase for each track required the use of special disks with a modified media designed to handle this type of recording. Because these disks initially were expensive and difficult to obtain, many users attempted incorrectly to use the low-density disks in the 1.2M 5 1/4-inch drives and format them to the higher 1.2M-density format, which results in data loss and unnecessary data-recovery operations.

A compatibility problem with the 360K drives stems from the 1.2M drive's capability to write twice as many cylinders in the same space as the 360K drives. The 1.2M drives position their heads over the same 40 cylinder positions used by the 360K drives through *double stepping*, a procedure in which the heads are moved every two cylinders to arrive at the correct positions for reading and writing the 40 cylinders on the 360K disks. The problem is that because the 1.2M drive normally has to write 80 cylinders in the same space in which the 360K drive writes 40, the heads of the 1.2M units had to be made dimensionally smaller. These narrow heads can have problems overwriting tracks produced by a 360K drive that has a wider head because the narrower heads on the 1.2M drive cannot "cover" the entire track area written by the 360K drive. This problem and possible solutions to it are discussed later in this chapter.

The 1.2M 5 1/4-inch drives spin at 360 RPM, or six revolutions per second, or 166.67 milliseconds per revolution. The drives spin at this rate no matter what type of disk is inserted—either low- or high-density. To send or receive 15 sectors (plus required overhead) six times per second, a controller must use a data-transmission rate of 500,000 bits per second (500 kilohertz, or KHz). All standard high- and low-density controllers support this data rate and, therefore, these drives. This support of course depends also on proper ROM BIOS support of the controller in this mode of operation. When a standard 360K disk is running in a high-density drive, it also is spinning at 360 RPM; a data rate of 300,000 bits per second (300 KHz) therefore is required in order to work properly. All standard AT-style low- and high-density controllers support the 250 KHz, 300 KHz, and 500 KHz data rates. The 300 KHz rate is used only for high-density 5 1/4-inch drives reading or writing to low-density 5 1/4-inch disks.

Virtually all standard AT-style systems have a ROM BIOS that supports the controller's operation of the 1.2M drive, including the 300 KHz data rate.

The 720K 3 1/2-Inch Drive

The 720K, 3 1/2-inch, double-density drives first appeared in an IBM system with the IBM Convertible laptop system introduced in 1986. In fact, all IBM systems introduced since that time have 3 1/2-inch drives as the standard supplied drives. This type of drive also is offered by IBM as an internal or external drive for the AT or XT systems. Note that outside the PC-compatible world, other computer-system vendors (Apple, Hewlett-Packard, and so on) offered 3 1/2-inch drives for their systems well before the PC-compatible world "caught on."

The 720K, 3 1/2-inch, double-density drive normally records 80 cylinders of two tracks each, with nine sectors per track, resulting in the formatted capacity of 720 kilobytes. It is interesting to note that many disk manufacturers label these disks as 1.0-megabyte disks, which is true. The difference between the actual 1.0 megabyte of capacity and the usable 720K after formatting is that some space on each track is occupied by the header and trailer of each sector, the inter-sector gaps, and the index gap at the start of each track before the first sector. These spaces are not usable for data storage and account for the differences between the unformatted and formatted capacities. Most manufacturers report the unformatted capacities because they do not know on which type of system you will format the disk. Apple Macintosh systems, for example, can store 800K of data on the same disk because of a different formatting technique. Note also that the 720K of usable space does not account for the disk areas DOS reserves for managing the disk (boot sectors, FATs, directories, and so on) and that because of these areas, only 713K remains for file data storage.

PC-compatible systems have used 720K, 3 1/2-inch, double-density drives primarily in XT-class systems because the drives operate from any low-density controller. The drives spin at 300 RPM, and therefore require only a 250 KHz data rate from the controller to operate properly. This data rate is the same as the 360K disk drives, which means that any controller that supports a 360K drive also supports the 720K drives.

The only issue to consider in installing a 720K, 3 1/2-inch drive is whether the ROM BIOS offers the necessary support. An IBM system with a ROM BIOS date of 06/10/85 or later has built-in support for 720K drives and requires no driver in order to use them. If your system has an earlier ROM BIOS date, the DRIVER.SYS program from DOS V3.2 or higher—as well as the DRIVPARM CONFIG.SYS command in some OEM DOS versions—is all you need to provide the necessary software support to operate these drives. Of course, a ROM BIOS upgrade to a later version negates the need for "funny" driver software and is usually the preferred option when you add one of these drives to an older system.

The 1.44M 3 1/2-Inch Drive

The 3 1/2-inch, 1.44M, high-density drives first appeared from IBM in the PS/2 product line introduced in 1987. Although IBM has not officially offered this type of drive for any of its older systems, most compatible vendors started offering the drives as options in systems immediately after IBM introduced the PS/2 system.

The drives record 80 cylinders consisting of two tracks each with 18 sectors per track, resulting in the formatted capacity of 1.44 megabytes. Most disk manufacturers label these disks as 2.0-megabyte disks, and the difference between this unformatted capacity and the formatted usable result is lost during the format. Note that the 1,440K of total formatted capacity does not account for the areas DOS reserves for file management, leaving only 1423.5K of actual file-storage area.

These drives spin at 300 RPM, and in fact must spin at that speed to operate properly with your existing high- and low-density controllers. To utilize the 500 KHz data rate, the maximum from most standard high- and low-density floppy controllers, these drives could spin at only 300 RPM. If the drives spun at the faster 360 RPM rate of the 5 1/4-inch drives, they would have to reduce the total number of sectors per track to 15 or else the controller could not keep up. In short, the 1.44M 3 1/2-inch drives store 1.2 times the data of the 5 1/4-inch 1.2M drives, and the 1.2M drives spin exactly 1.2 times faster than the 1.44M drives. The data rates used by both high-density drives are identical and compatible with the same controllers. In fact, because these 3 1/2-inch high-density drives can run at the 500 KHz data rate, a controller that can support a 1.2M 5 1/4-inch drive can support the 1.44M drives also. If you are using a low-density disk in the 3 1/2-inch high-density drive, the data rate is reduced to 250 KHz, and the disk capacity is 720K.

The primary issue in a particular system utilizing a 1.44M 3 1/2-inch drive is one of ROM BIOS support. An IBM system with a ROM BIOS date of 11/15/85 or later has built-in support for these drives and no external driver support program is needed. You might need a generic AT setup program because IBM's setup program doesn't offer the 1.44M drive as an option. Another problem relates to the controller and the way it signals the high-density drive to write to a low-density disk. The problem is discussed in detail in the following section.

The 2.88M 3 1/2-Inch Drive

The new 2.88M drive was developed by Toshiba Corporation in the 1980s, and was officially announced in 1987. Toshiba began production manufacturing of the drives and disks in 1989, and then several vendors began selling the drives as upgrades for systems. IBM officially adopted these drives in the PS/2 systems in 1991, and virtually all PS/2s sold since then have these drives as standard equipment. Because a 2.88M drive can fully read and write 1.44M and 720K disks, the change was an easy one. DOS version 5.0 or higher is required to support the 2.88M drives.

To support the 2.88M drive, modifications to the disk controller circuitry were required because these drives spin at the same 300 RPM but have an astonishing 36 sectors per track. Because all floppy disks are formatted with consecutively numbered sectors (1:1 interleave), these 36 sectors have to be read and written in the same time it takes a 1.44M drive to read and write 18 sectors. This requires that the controller support a much higher data transmission rate of 1 MHz (1 million bits per second). Most of the older floppy controllers either found on an adapter card or built into the motherboard support only the maximum of 500 KHz data rate used by the 1.44M drives. To upgrade to 2.88M drives would require that the controller be changed to one that supports the higher 1 MHz data rate.

An additional support issue is the ROM BIOS. The BIOS must have support for the controller and the capability to specify and accept the 2.88M drive as a CMOS setting. Newer motherboard BIOS sets from companies like Phoenix, AMI, and Award have support for the new extra-high density controllers.

In addition to the newer IBM PS/2 systems, most newer IBM clone and compatible systems now have built-in floppy controllers and ROM BIOS software that fully supports the 2.88M drives. Adding or upgrading to a 2.88M drive in these systems is as easy as plugging in the drive and running the CMOS Setup program. For those systems that do not have this support built-in, this type of upgrade is much more difficult. Several companies offer new controllers and BIOS upgrades as well as the 2.88M drives specifically for upgrading older systems.

Although the 2.88M drives themselves are not much more expensive than the 1.44M drives they replace, the disk media is currently still very expensive. Although you can purchase 1.44M disks for around (or under) 50 cents each, the 2.88M disks can cost more than $2 per disk! As the drives become more generally available, the disk media prices should fall. The 1.44M and even 1.2M disk media also was very expensive when first introduced.

Handling Recording Problems with 1.44M 3 1/2-Inch Drives

A serious problem awaits many users who use the 1.44M 3 1/2-inch drives: If the drive is installed improperly, any write or format operations performed incorrectly on 720K disks can end up trashing data on low-density disks. The problem is caused by the controller's incapability to signal the high-density drive that a low-density recording will take place.

High-density disks require a higher write-current or signal strength when they record than do the low-density disks. A low-density drive can record at only the lower write-current, which is correct for the low-density disks; the high-density drive, however, needs to record at both high and low write-currents depending on which type of disk is inserted in the drive. If a signal is not sent to the high-density drive telling it to lower or reduce the write-current level, the drive stays in its normal high write-current default mode, even when it records on a low-density disk. The signal normally should be sent to the drive by the controller, but many controllers do not provide this signal properly for the 1.44M drives.

The Western Digital controller used by IBM enables the reduced write-current (RWC) signal only if the controller also is sending data at the 300 KHz data rate, indicating the special case of a low-density disk in a high-density drive. The RWC signal is required to tell the high-density drive to lower the head-writing signal strength to be proper for the low-density disks. If the signal is not sent, the drive defaults to the higher write-current, which should be used for only high-density disks. If the controller is transmitting the 250 KHz data rate, the controller knows that the drive must be a low-density drive and therefore no RWC signal is necessary because the low-density drives can write only with reduced current.

This situation presented a serious problem for owners of 1.44M drives using 720K disks because the drives spin the disks at 300 RPM, and in writing to a low-density disk, use the 250 KHz data rate—not the 300 KHz rate. This setup "fools" the controller into "thinking" that it is sending data to a low-density drive, which causes the controller to fail to send the required RWC signal. Without the RWC signal, the drive records improperly on the disk, possibly trashing any data being written or any data already present. Because virtually all compatibles use controllers based on the design of the IBM AT floppy disk controller, most share the same problem as the IBM AT.

Drive and disk manufacturers devised the perfect solution for this problem, short of using a redesigned controller. They built into the drives a media sensor, which, when it is enabled, can override the controller's RWC signal (or lack of it) and properly change the head-current levels within the drive. Essentially, the drive chooses the write-current level independently from the controller when the media sensor is operational.

The sensor is a small, physical or optical sensor designed to feel, or "see," the small hole on the high-density 3 1/2-inch disks located opposite the write-enable hole. The extra hole on these high-density or extra-high density disks is the media sensor's cue that the full write-current should be used in recording. If an ED disk is detected, the ED drive enables the vertical recording heads. Low-density disks do not have these extra holes; therefore, when the sensor cannot see a media-sensor hole, it causes the drive to record in the proper reduced write-current mode for a double-density disk.

Some people, of course, foolishly attempt to override the function of these sensors by needlessly punching an extra hole in a low-density disk to fool the drive's sensor into acting as though an actual high-density disk has been inserted. Several unscrupulous companies have made a fast buck by selling media sensor hole-punchers to unwary or misinformed people. These disk-punch vendors try to mislead you into believing that no difference exists between the low- and high-density disks except for the hole, and that punching the extra hole makes the low-density disk a legitimate high-density disk. This, of course, is absolutely untrue: The high-density disks are very different from low-density disks. The differences between the disks are explained in more detail later in this chapter.

Another reason that this hole-punching is needless is that if you want to record a high-density format on a low-density disk, you only have to remove the jumper from the drive that enables the media sensor. Removing the media sensor jumper still allows the drive to work properly for high-density disks writing at the full write-current level, but unfortunately also allows the higher write-current to be used on low-density disks as well because the drive has no way of knowing the difference. If you really want to risk your data to low-density disks formatted as high-density disks, you can save yourself the cost of the $40 hole-punchers. Note that even if you attempt to format or record properly on a 720K disk, you still will be working at the higher write-current and risk trashing the disk.

Many systems, including the IBM PS/2 series, Compaq, Toshiba laptops, and many others with floppy controllers built into the motherboard, do not need 1.44M drives with media sensors. Their controllers have been fixed to allow the RWC signal to be sent to the drive even when the controller is sending the 250 KHz data rate. This setup allows for proper operation no matter what type of disk or drive is used, as long as the user formats properly. Because these systems do not have a media sensor policing users, they easily can format low-density disks as high-density disks regardless of what holes are on the disk. This has caused problems for users of the older PS/2 systems who have accidentally formatted 720K disks as 1.44M disks. When passed to a system that has an enabled media sensor, the system refuses to read the disks at all because it is not correctly formatted. If you are having disk interchange problems, make sure that you are formatting your disks correctly.

The newer PS/2 and other high-end systems from other manufacturers (Hewlett Packard, for example) use an active media sensor setup in which the user no longer has to enter the correct FORMAT command parameters to format the disk. In these systems the media sensor information is passed through the controller to the BIOS, which properly informs the FORMAT command about which disk is in the drive. With these systems, it is impossible for a user to accidentally format a disk incorrectly, and it eliminates the user from having to know anything about the different disk media types.

Handling Recording Problems with 1.2M and 360K Drives

The 5 1/4-inch drives have their own special problems. One major problem resulting in needless data destruction is that the tracks sometimes are recorded at different widths for different drives. These differences in recorded track width can result in problems with data exchange between different 5 1/4-inch drives.

As shown in Table 13.1, the recorded track-width difference affects only the 5 1/4-inch drives because the 5 1/4-inch low-density drives record a track width more than twice that of the 5 1/4-inch high-density drives. This difference presents a problem if a high-density drive is used to update a low-density disk with previously recorded data on it.

The high-density drive, even in 360K mode, cannot completely overwrite the track left by the 40-track drive. The problem occurs when the disk is returned to the person with the 360K drive because that drive sees the new data as "embedded" within the remains of the previously written track. The 360K drive cannot distinguish either signal, and an Abort, Retry, Ignore error message results.

To avoid this problem, start with a brand-new disk that has never been formatted and format it in the 1.2M drive with the /4 (or equivalent) option. This procedure causes the 1.2M drive to place the proper 360K format on the disk. The 1.2M drive then can be used to fill the disk to its 360K capacity, and every file will be readable on the 40-track 360K drive because no previous wider data tracks exist to confuse the 360K drive. I use this trick all the time to exchange data disks between AT systems that have only a 1.2M drive and XT or PC systems that have only a 360K drive. The key is to start with a brand-new disk or a disk wiped clean magnetically by a bulk eraser. Simply reformatting the disk does not work because formatting actually writes data to the disk.

Note that because all the 3 1/2-inch drives write tracks of the same width, these drives have no disk-interchange problems related to track width.

Analyzing Floppy Disk Construction

The 5 1/4-inch and 3 1/2-inch disks each have unique construction and physical properties.

The flexible (or floppy) disk is contained within a plastic jacket. The 3 1/2-inch disks are covered by a more rigid jacket than are the 5 1/4-inch disks; the disks within the jackets, however, are virtually identical except, of course, for the size.

Differences and similarities exist between these two different-size disks. This section looks at the physical properties and construction of each disk type.

When you look at a typical 5 1/4-inch floppy disk, you see several things (see fig. 13.9). Most prominent is the large, round hole in the center. When you close the disk drive's "door," a cone-shaped clamp grabs and centers the disk through the center hole. Many disks come with hub-ring reinforcements—thin, plastic rings like those used to reinforce three-ring notebook paper—intended to help the disk withstand the mechanical forces of the clamping mechanism. The high-density disks usually lack these reinforcements because the difficulty in accurately placing them on the disk means they will cause alignment problems.

On the right side, just below the center of the hub hole, is a smaller, round hole called the index hole. If you carefully turn the disk within its protective jacket, you see a small hole in the disk. The drive uses the index hole as the starting point for all the sectors on the disk—sort of the "prime meridian" for the disk sectors. A disk with a single index hole is a soft-sectored disk; the software (operating system) decides the actual number of sectors on the disk. Some older equipment, such as Wang word processors, use hard-sectored disks, which have an index hole to demarcate individual sectors. Do not use hard-sectored disks in a PC.

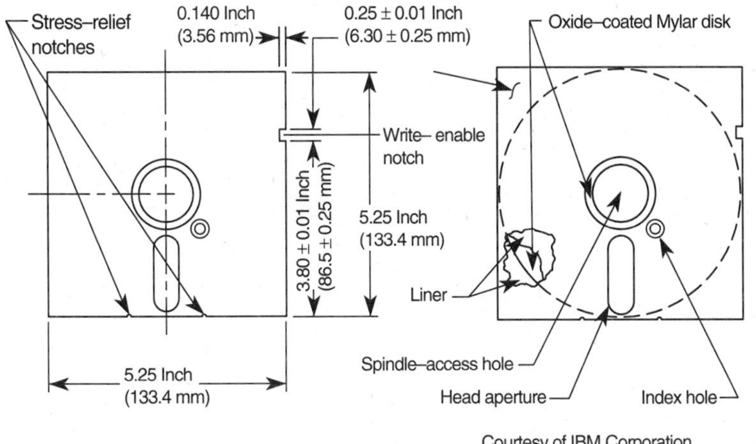

Figure 13.9

Construction of a 5 1/4-inch floppy disk.

Below the hub hole is a slot shaped somewhat like a long racetrack through which you can see the disk surface. Through this media-access hole, the disk drive heads read and write information to the disk surface.

At the right side, about one inch from the top, is a rectangular punch from the side of the disk cover. If this write-enable notch is present, writing to the disk has been enabled. Disks without this notch (or with the notch taped over) are write-protected disks. The notch might not be on all disks, particularly those purchased with programs on them.

On the rear of the disk jacket, at the bottom, two very small, oval notches flank the head slot. The notches relieve stress on the disk and help prevent it from warping. The drive might use these notches also to assist in keeping the disk in the proper position in the drive.

Because the 3 1/2-inch disks use a much more rigid plastic case, which helps stabilize the disk, these disks can record at track and data densities greater than the 5 1/4-inch disks (see fig. 13.10). A metal shutter protects the media-access hole. The shutter is manipulated by the drive and remains closed whenever the disk is not in a drive. The media then is insulated from the environment and from your fingers. The shutter also obviates the need for a disk jacket.

Rather than an index hole in the disk, the 3 1/2-inch disks use a metal center hub with an alignment hole. The drive "grasps" the metal hub, and the hole in the hub enables the drive to position the disk properly.

On the lower-left part of the disk is a hole with a plastic slider—the write-protect/-enable hole (refer to fig. 13.9). When the slider is positioned so that the hole is visible, the disk is write-protected; the drive is prevented from recording on the disk. When the slider is positioned to cover the hole, writing is enabled, and you can record on the disk. For more permanent write-protection, some commercial software programs are supplied on disks with the slider removed so that you cannot easily enable recording on the disk.

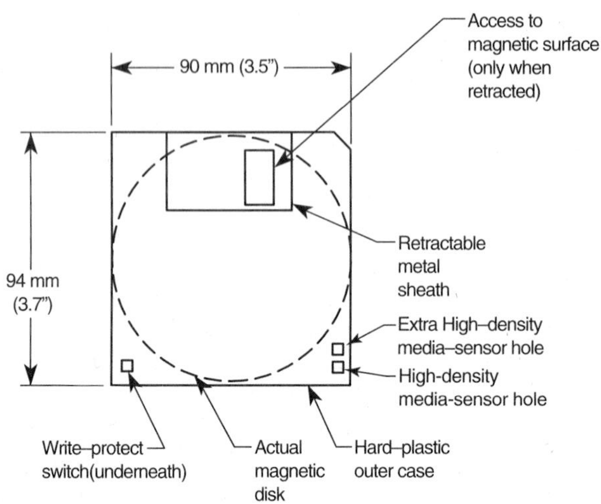

Figure 13.10

Construction of a 3 1/2-inch floppy disk.

On the other (right) side of the disk from the write-protect hole, there might be in the disk jacket another hole called the media-density-selector hole. If this hole is present, the disk is constructed of a special media and is therefore a high-density or extra-high-density disk. If the media-sensor hole is exactly opposite the write-protect hole, it indicates a 1.44M HD disk. If the media-sensor hole is located more toward the top of the disk (the metal shutter is at the top of the disk), it indicates an ED disk. No hole on the right side means that the disk is a low-density disk. Most 3 1/2-inch drives have a media sensor that controls recording capability based on the existence or absence of these holes.

Both the 3 1/2-inch and 5 1/4-inch disks are constructed of the same basic materials. They use a plastic base (usually Mylar) coated with a magnetic compound. The compound is usually a ferric- (iron-) oxide-based compound for the standard density versions; a cobalt-ferric compound usually is used in the higher-coercivity (higher-density) disks. Extended density disks use a barium-ferric media compound. The rigid jacket material on the 3 1/2-inch disks often causes people to believe incorrectly that these disks are some sort of "hard disk" and not really a floppy disk. The disk "cookie" inside the 3 1/2-inch case is just as floppy as the 5 1/4-inch variety.

Floppy Disk Media Types and Specifications

This section examines all the types of disks you can purchase for your system. Especially interesting are the technical specifications that can separate one type of disk from another. This section defines all the specifications used to describe a typical disk.

Single- and Double-Sided Disks. Whether a disk is single- or double-sided is really an issue only for the lower-density disks. Because no single-sided high-density drives are manufactured, no need exists for disks to match the drives. The original IBM PC had single-sided drives, but they were discontinued in 1982.

A single-sided disk is constructed of the same material as a double-sided disk. The difference seems to be that only the single-sided disks are "certified" (whatever that means) on only one side, and the double-sided disks are certified on both sides. Because the single-sided disks are cheaper than the double-sided versions, many PC users quickly determined that they could save some money if they used the single-sided disks even in double-sided drives.

The reason that this reasoning can work is that it is economically impractical for disk manufacturers to make some disks with recording surfaces on one side and other disks with recording surfaces on both sides. Today's single-sided disks look, and usually behave, exactly the same as double-sided disks. The result of this—depending on the brand of disks you buy—is that you can generally format and use "single-sided" disks successfully in double-sided drives, at a savings in disk costs. Unfortunately, the savings now are so small that this practice is obsolete, if not risky.

The danger in this practice is that some manufacturers do not burnish, or polish, the unused (top) side to the same level of smoothness as the used (bottom) side. This practice can cause accelerated wear on the top head. In single-sided drives, because the top head was replaced by a soft, felt pad, the rougher top side caused no problems. For the cost, it is not worth using with the wrong disks. I recommend the conservative route: Spend the small amount of extra money for double-sided disks of the correct density, and you will rarely have to recover damaged data.

Density. *Density*, in simplest terms, is a measure of the amount of information that can be packed reliably into a specific area of a recording surface. The keyword here is reliably.

Disks have two types of densities: longitudinal density and linear density. Longitudinal density is indicated by how many tracks can be recorded on the disk, often expressed as a number of tracks per inch (TPI). Linear density is the capability of an individual track to store data, often indicated as a number of bits per inch (BPI). Unfortunately, both types of densities often are interchanged incorrectly in discussing different disks and drives. Table 13.6 provides a rundown of each available type of disk.

Table 13.6 Floppy Disk Media Specifications

	5 1/4-Inch			3 1/2-Inch		
Media Parameters	**Double Density (DD)**	**Quad Density (QD)**	**High Density (HD)**	**Double Density (DD)**	**High Density (HD)**	**Extra-High Density (ED)**
Tracks Per Inch (TPI)	48	96	96	135	135	135
Bits Per Inch (BPI)	5,876	5,876	9,646	8,717	17,434	34,868
Media Formulation	Ferrite	Ferrite	Cobalt	Cobalt	Cobalt	Barium
Coercivity (Oersteds)	300	300	600	600	720	750
Thickness (Micro-In.)	100	100	50	70	40	100
Recording Polarity	Horiz.	Horiz.	Horiz.	Horiz.	Horiz.	Vert.

It is notable that IBM skipped the quad-density disk type—that is, no IBM system uses a quad-density drive or requires quad-density disks. Don't purchase a quad-density disk unless you just want a better-quality double-density disk.

Both the quad- and double-density disks store the same linear data on each track. They use the same formula for the magnetic coating on the disk, but the quad-density versions represent a more rigorously tested, higher-quality disk. The high-density disks are entirely different, however. To store the increased linear density, an entirely different magnetic coating was required. In both the 5 1/4-inch and 3 1/2-inch high-density disks, a high-coercivity coating is used to allow the tremendous bit density for each track. A high-density disk never can be substituted for a double- or quad-density disk because the write-current must be different for these very different media formulations and thickness.

The extra-high density 3 1/2-inch disk in table 13.6 is newly available in some systems. This type of disk, invented by Toshiba, is available from several other vendors as well. The extra-high density disks use a barium-ferric compound to cover the disk with a thicker coating, which enables a vertical recording technique to be used. In vertical recording, the magnetic domains are recorded vertically rather than flat. The higher density results from their capability to be stacked much more closely together. These types of drives can read and write the other 3 1/2-inch disks because of their similar track dimensions on all formats.

Media Coercivity and Thickness. The coercivity specification of a disk refers to the magnetic-field strength required to make a proper recording on a disk. Coercivity, measured in oersteds, is a value indicating magnetic strength. A disk with a higher coercivity rating requires a stronger magnetic field to make a recording on that disk. With lower ratings, the disk can be recorded with a weaker magnetic field. In other words, the lower the coercivity rating, the more sensitive the disk.

Another factor is the thickness of the disk. The thinner the disk, the less influence a region of the disk has on another adjacent region. The thinner disks therefore can accept many more bits per inch without eventually degrading the recording.

When I ask someone whether the high-density disks are more sensitive or less sensitive than the double-density disks, the answer is almost always "more sensitive." But you can see that this is not true. The high-density disks are in fact as much as half as sensitive as the double-density disks. A high-density drive can record with a much higher volume level at the heads than can the standard double-density drive. For these high-density drives to record properly on a double-density disk, the drive must be capable of using a reduced write-current mode and enable it whenever the lower-density disks are installed. A big problem with users and floppy disks then can occur.

Most users do not like paying more for the high-density disks their drives can use. These users, in an attempt to save money, are tempted to use the lower-density disks as a substitute. Some users attempt to format the "regular" disk at the high-density capacity. This formatting is facilitated by DOS, which always attempts to format a disk to the maximum capacity of the drive's capabilities, unless specifically ordered otherwise through the use of proper parameters in the FORMAT command, or unless your system has an active media sensor. If you use no parameters and simply enter FORMAT A:, however, the disk is formatted as though it were a high-density disk. Many users think that this procedure somehow is equivalent to using the single-sided disks in place of double-sided ones. I can assure you that this is not true—it is much worse. Do not use double-density disks in place of high-density disks, or you will experience severe problems and data loss from improper coercivity, media thickness, and write-current specifications.

The reasons for using the high-coercivity thin disks are simple. In designing the high-density drives, engineers found that the density of magnetic flux reversals caused adjacent flux reversals to begin to affect each other. The effect was that they started to cancel each other out, or cause shifts in the polarity of the domain. Data written at the high densities eventually began to erase itself. As an analogy, imagine a wooden track on which you place magnetic marbles, evenly spaced four inches apart in a specific pattern of magnetic polarity. At this distance, the magnetic forces from each marble are too weak to affect the adjacent marbles. Now imagine that the marbles must be placed only two inches apart. The magnetic attraction and repulsion forces now might start to work on the adjacent marbles so that they begin to rotate on their axis and thus change the direction of polarity and the data they represent.

You could eliminate the interaction of the magnetic domains by either spacing them farther apart or making the domains "weaker," therefore reducing their sphere of influence. If the marbles were made half as strong magnetically as they were before, you could get them twice as close together without any interaction between them. This is the principle behind the high-coercivity, thin media disks. Because they are weaker magnetically, they need a higher recording strength to store an image properly.

Try a simple experiment to verify this principle. Attempt to format a high-density disk in a low-density format. DOS responds with a Track 0 bad, Disk unusable message. The disk did not accept a recording in low-density mode because the low-density recording is also low volume. The drive cannot make a recording on the disk, and therefore the Track 0 bad message is displayed.

It is unfortunate for users that the opposite attempt appears to work: You can format a standard double-density disk as though it were a high-density disk, and the FORMAT command or DOS does not seem to be affected. You might notice a large number of "bad sectors," but DOS allows the format to be completed anyway.

This situation is unfortunate for two reasons. First, you are recording on the (low-density) disk with a density that requires weak magnetic domains to eliminate interaction between the adjacent domains. A low-density disk unfortunately stores magnetic domains twice as strong as they should be, and eventually they interact. You will experience mysterious data losses on this disk over the next few days, weeks, or months.

Second, you have just placed a recording on this disk at twice the signal strength it should be. This "industrial strength" recording might not be removable by a normal disk drive, and the disk might be magnetically saturated. You might not ever be able to reformat it correctly as a double-density disk because a double-density reformat uses reduced write-current. The reduced write-current might not be capable of overwriting the high write-current signal that had been recorded incorrectly. The best way to remove this "burned in" recording is to use a bulk eraser to renew the disk by removing all magnetic information. In most cases, however, a fresh format can overcome the magnetic image of the previous one, even if the write-current had been incorrect.

Soft and Hard Sectors. Floppy disks are either soft sectored or hard sectored. A soft-sectored disk has only one index hole on the disk surface. Once every revolution, the hole is visible through the hole in the protective jacket, and the drive, controller, and DOS use the hole to establish the location and timing of the first sector on a track. Individual sectors are defined by the controller and the software that runs the controller, hence the term soft sectored. Hard-sectored disks have an index hole as well as a separate hole for each sector on the disk marking the beginning of that sector. Hard-sectored disks are not used in IBM compatible PCs, but were used in some dedicated word processing systems and other proprietary computer systems. If you try to use a hard-sectored disk in a PC, the machine will get confused. Sometimes hard-sectored disks are not labeled specifically as hard-sectored, but rather specify "10 sectors" or "16 sectors." Because hard-sectored disks are not used in PC-compatible systems, I have not seen these disks for sale in quite some time.

Formatting and Using High- and Low-Density Disks

This section describes how the different density capabilities of the high- and low-density drives sometimes can cause problems in formatting disks. You must always make sure that a disk initially is formatted to the density in which it is supposed to be run. In some cases, you should have a high-density drive format a low-density disk. You can perform this formatting with the correct format commands. The following section describes how to use DOS correctly so that your disks are formatted properly.

Reading and Writing 360K Disks in 1.2M Drives. Having 1.2M drives read or write to a 360K disk is a simple task. Just place a previously formatted 360K disk in the drive and use it normally. In other words, pretend that the drive is a 360K drive. Nothing special must be done. You can either read or write on the disk with absolutely no problems...yet.

You will have a problem if you decide to return the disk to a 360K drive and attempt to read it. Remember that the recorded track width of the 1.2M drive is half the track width of the 360K drive; therefore, if any tracks have been previously recorded by an actual 360K drive, the tracks are twice as wide as the tracks recorded by the 1.2M drive. If you write to the disk with the 1.2M drive, you cannot overwrite the entire track width—only the center portion of it. When you return this disk to a 360K drive, the wider head system in the 360K drive sees two signals on any overwritten tracks, and the new data is nestled within the image of the old data that could not be completely covered by the 1.2M drive. An immediate Abort, Retry, Ignore error from DOS usually is displayed for any updated portions of the disk. In Windows you would see a dialog box showing a disk read or write error.

To solve this problem easily, if you want to record data in an AT 1.2M drive and later read it properly in a 360K drive, make sure that you use brand-new disks for recording in the 1.2M drive. Because a new disk has no magnetic information on it, the smaller recorded track width can be written on the 1.2M drive and read properly in the 360K drive; the more narrow track is written in "clean space." The 360K drive, therefore, no longer is confused by any "ghost images" of previously recorded wider tracks. Other than starting with a brand-new disk, your only other option is to use a disk erased by a bulk eraser. You cannot erase a disk by reformatting it if has been in use. Formatting records actual data on the disk and causes the track-width problem. The new or bulk-erased disk in fact must be formatted by the 1.2M drive for this procedure to work again. Remember the simple rule: Any track recorded by a 360K drive cannot be overwritten by a 1.2M drive, even in the 360K format.

How do you format a 360K disk in a 1.2M drive? If you just execute the FORMAT command without parameters, DOS attempts to format the disk to its maximum capacity. Because the 1.2M drive has no media-sensing capability, DOS assumes that the disk capability is equal to the maximum capability of the drive and attempts to create a 1.2M format on the disk. The write-current is increased also during a recording in this format, which is incompatible with the 360K media. To format the 360K disk correctly, therefore, look at the alternative command examples in table 13.7.

Table 13.7 Proper Formatting of 5 1/4-inch 360K Disks in a 1.2M Drive

Command	DOS Version 7.x	6.x	5.x	4.x	3.3	3.2	3.1	3.0
FORMAT d: /4	Yes	Yes	Yes	Yes	Yes	Yes	Yes	Yes
FORMAT d: /N:9 /T:40	Yes	Yes	Yes	Yes	Yes	Yes	No	No
FORMAT d: /F:360	Yes	Yes	Yes	Yes	No	No	No	No

d: = The drive to format
N = Number of sectors per track
T = Tracks per side
F = Format capacity

Note that DOS versions prior to 3.0 do not support 1.2M drives, and that DOS 7 is both sold separately by IBM and is also included with Windows 95. Each example command accomplishes the same function, which is to place on a 360K disk a 40-track, nine-sector format using reduced write-current mode.

Reading and Writing 720K Disks in 1.44M and 2.88M Drives. The 3 1/2-inch drives do not have the same problems as the 5 1/4-inch disks—that is, at least not with data interchange. Because both the high- and low-density drives write the same number of tracks and are the same width, one type of drive can be used to overwrite data written by another type of drive. Because of this capability, IBM does not need to offer a low-density version of the 3 1/2-inch drives for the PS/2 systems. These systems (except Models 25 and 30) include only the HD or ED drives, which are capable of imitating perfectly the 720K drives in the Model 25 and Model 30. The high-density drives can be trouble, however, in the hands of an inexperienced (or cheapskate) user. You must make sure that you use only the 1.44M high-density disks in the 1.44M format, and only the 720K disks in the 720K format. You will encounter serious problems if you stick a 720K disk in a drive in a PS/2 without a media sensor drive and enter the command FORMAT A:. If you decide to use the formatted disk anyway, massive data loss eventually will occur.

The 1.44M drives and 720K drives do not have all the same problems as the 5 1/4-inch drives, primarily because all the 3 1/2-inch drives have the same recorded track width. The 1.44M or 2.88M drive has no problem recording 720K disks. For these reasons (and more), I applaud the industry move to the 3 1/2-inch drives. The sooner we stop using 5 1/4-inch disk drives, the better.

The only other problem with formatting, other than incorrectly selecting a drive without a media sensor or failing to enable it during the drive-installation procedure, is naive users attempting to format disks at a capacity for which they were not designed. You must have a 720K (double-density) disk to write a 720K format; a 1.44M (high-density) disk to write a 1.44M format; and a 2.88M (extra-high density) disk to write an extra-high density format. No ifs, ands, or buts. This chapter has explained already that this requirement stems from differences in the coercivity of the media and the levels of recording current used in writing the disks.

When you enter a standard FORMAT command with no parameters, DOS normally attempts to format the disk to the drive's maximum capacity as indicated by the BIOS. If you insert a 720K disk in a 1.44M drive, therefore, and enter the FORMAT command with no parameters, DOS attempts to create a 1.44M format on the disk. If the drive has a passive media sensor, the FORMAT command aborts with an error message. The media sensor does not communicate to DOS the correct information to format the disk—it just prevents incorrect formatting. You still must know the correct commands. If the system supports active media sensing, no FORMAT command parameters are necessary as the BIOS will supply the correct parameters based on the type of disk in the drive. Table 13.8 shows the correct FORMAT command and parameters to use in formatting a 720K disk in a 1.44M drive.

Table 13.8 Proper Formatting of 3 1/2-Inch 720K Disks in a 1.44M or 2.88M Drive

	DOS Version				
Command	**7.x**	**6.x**	**5.x**	**4.x**	**3.3**
FORMAT d: /N:9 /T:80	Yes	Yes	Yes	Yes	Yes
FORMAT d: /F:720	Yes	Yes	Yes	Yes	No

d: = The drive to format
N = Number of sectors per track
T = Tracks per side
F = Format capacity

Note that DOS versions prior to 3.3 do not support 1.44M drives, and versions prior to 5.0 do not support 2.88M drives. Windows 95 includes DOS 7, which is also sold by IBM separately.

Reading and Writing 1.44M Disks in 2.88M Drives. The 2.88M extra-high-density (ED) drive used in some newer systems, such as virtually the entire PS/2 line, is a welcome addition to any system. This drive offers a capacity twice as great as the standard

1.44M HD drive, and also offers full backward compatibility with the 1.44M HD drive and the 720K DD drive.

The 2.88M ED drive uses a technique called vertical recording to achieve its great linear density of 36 sectors per track. This technique increases density by magnetizing the domains perpendicular to the recording surface. By essentially placing the magnetic domains on their ends and stacking them side by side, density increases enormously.

The technology for producing heads that can perform a vertical or perpendicular recording has been around awhile. It is not the heads or even the drives that represent the major breakthrough in technology; rather, it is the media that is special. Standard disks have magnetic particles shaped like tiny needles that lie on the surface of the disk. Orienting these acicular particles in a perpendicular manner to enable vertical recording is very difficult. The particles on a barium-ferrite floppy disk are shaped like tiny, flat, hexagonal platelets that easily can be arranged to have their axis of magnetization perpendicular to the plane of recording. Although barium ferrite has been used as a material in the construction of permanent magnets, no one has been able to reduce the grain size of the platelets enough for high-density recordings.

Toshiba has perfected a glass-crystallization process for manufacturing the ultra fine platelets used in coating the barium-ferrite disks. This technology, patented by Toshiba, is being licensed to a number of disk manufacturers, all of whom are producing barium-ferrite disks using Toshiba's process. Toshiba also made certain modifications to the design of standard disk drive heads to enable them to read and write the new barium-ferrite disks as well as standard cobalt or ferrite disks. This technology is being used not only in floppy drives but also is appearing in a variety of tape drive formats.

The disks are called 4M disks in reference to their unformatted capacity. Actual formatted capacity is 2,880K, or 2.88M. Because of space lost in the formatting process, as well as space occupied by the volume boot sector, file-allocation tables, and root directory, the total usable storage space is 2,863K.

A number of manufacturers are making these drives, including Toshiba, Mitsubishi, Sony, and Panasonic. During the next few years, they should become more popular in higher-end systems. Table 13.9 shows the correct FORMAT command and parameters to use in formatting a 1.44M disk in a 2.88M drive, especially if your system does not support the active media sensor.

Table 13.9 Proper Formatting of 3 1/2-Inch 1.44M Disks in a 2.88M Drive

Command	DOS Version 7.x	6.x	5.x
FORMAT d: /N:18 /T:80	Yes	Yes	Yes
FORMAT d: /F:1.44	Yes	Yes	Yes

d: = The drive to format
N = Number of sectors per track
T = Tracks per side
F = Format capacity

Note that DOS versions prior to 5.0 do not support the 2.88M drive. Also, most 2.88M installations have an active media sensor that automatically formats the disk correctly as determined by the media sensor. With active media sensing, the parameters indicating disk capacity are not necessary, but can be used to override the autodetect capabilities.

FORMAT Command Summary. One basic rule that applies to all drives (except 2.88M) is that a drive always formats in its native mode unless specifically instructed otherwise through the FORMAT command parameters. Therefore, if you insert a 1.44M HD disk in a 1.44M HD A: drive, you can format that disk by simply entering FORMAT A:—no optional parameters are necessary in that case. If you insert any other type of disk (DD, for example), you absolutely must enter the appropriate parameters in the FORMAT command to change the format mode from the default 1.44M mode to the mode appropriate for the inserted disk. Even though the drive might have a media sensor that can detect which type of disk is inserted in the drive, in most cases the sensor does not communicate to the controller or DOS, which does not know which disk it is.

An exception to this is the 2.88M drive installations that support active media sense. Most 2.88M drive installations support this advanced feature, which means that the media sensor will communicate the type of the inserted disk to the controller and DOS. In this case no parameters are ever needed when formatting disks no matter what type is inserted. The FORMAT command will automatically default to the proper type as indicated by the active sensors on the 2.88M drive. I have even seen 1.44M drive installations with active media sensing (certain Hewlett-Packard systems, for example), but this is rare.

In most cases of 1.44M drive installations, the media sensor in the drive is passive, and in effect all the sensor does is force the FORMAT command to fail if you do not enter the correct parameters for the inserted disk type.

Table 13.10 shows the proper format command for all possible variations in drive and disk types. It shows also which DOS versions support the various combinations of drives, disks, and FORMAT parameters.

To use this table, just look up the drive type and disk type you have. You then can see the proper FORMAT command parameters to use as well as the DOS versions that support the combination you want.

Table 13.10 Proper Disk Formatting

Drive Type	Disk Type	DOS Version	Proper FORMAT Command
5 1/4-inch 360K	DD 360K	DOS 2.0+	FORMAT d:
5 1/4-inch 1.2M	HD 1.2M	DOS 3.0+	FORMAT d:
5 1/4-inch 1.2M	DD 360K	DOS 3.0+	FORMAT d: /4
5 1/4-inch 1.2M	DD 360K	DOS 3.2+	FORMAT d: /N:9 /T:40
5 1/4-inch 1.2M	DD 360K	DOS 4.0+	FORMAT d: /F:360
3 1/2-inch 720K	DD 720K	DOS 3.2+	FORMAT d:
3 1/2-inch 1.44M	HD 1.44M	DOS 3.3+	FORMAT d:

Drive Type	Disk Type	DOS Version	Proper FORMAT Command
3 1/2-inch 1.44M	DD 720K	DOS 3.3+	FORMAT d: /N:9 /T:80
3 1/2-inch 1.44M	DD 720K	DOS 4.0+	FORMAT d: /F:720
3 1/2-inch 2.88M	ED 2.88M	DOS 5.0+	FORMAT d:
3 1/2-inch 2.88M	HD 1.44M	DOS 5.0+	FORMAT d: /F:1.44
3 1/2-inch 2.88M	DD 720K	DOS 5.0+	FORMAT d: /F:720

+ = Includes all higher versions
d: = Specifies drive to format
DD = double-density
HD = high-density
ED = extra-high density

Note

If the drive and installation you are using supports active (intelligent) media sense, no diskette type parameters are required. The drive will automatically communicate the type of the installed diskette to the FORMAT program. This is normal for most 2.88M drive installations.

With the advent of DOS 5.0, the FORMAT command has received a number of new functions and capabilities, all expressed through two new parameters: /Q (Quickformat) and /U (Unconditional). Precisely describing the effect of these parameters on the FORMAT command is difficult, especially considering that they have different effects on hard disks and floppy disks. Table 13.11 summarizes the functions of these new parameters and relates the new functions to the older versions of DOS.

From this table you should be able to discern the function of a specific FORMAT command relative to the use of the /Q and /U parameters. For example, suppose that you are using DOS V6.0 and you insert a brand-new 1.44M disk in a 1.44M drive A: on your system. If you enter the command FORMAT A: with no other parameters, what will happen? By looking at table 13.11, you can see that the default operation of the FORMAT command in this case would be as follows:

1. Check the DOS volume boot sector.
2. Perform a read verify (or scan) of the entire disk.
3. Overwrite the DVB, FATs, and the root directory.
4. Overwrite the entire data area of the disk.

These functions do not necessarily happen in this order; in fact, the last three items listed occur simultaneously as the format progresses. Now suppose that you write some files on this disk and reenter the same FORMAT A: command. As you can see from Table 13.11, the functions of the FORMAT command are very different this time. The steps occur something like this:

1. Check the DOS volume boot sector.
2. Save UNFORMAT information.
3. Perform a read verify (or scan) of the entire disk.
4. Overwrite the DVB, FATs, and the root directory.

Table 13.11 DOS FORMAT Command Internal Operations

FORMAT Command Parameters	**Any**	**None**	**None**	**/Q**	**/U**	**/Q/U**
Disk Previously Formatted?	-	**Yes**	**No**	**Yes**	**Yes**	**Yes**
Hard Disk Format Operations:	**DOS 2-4**		**DOS 5 and Higher**			
Check Volume Boot Sector	No	Yes	Yes	Yes	No	Yes
Save UNFORMAT Information	No	Yes	No	Yes	No	No
Read Verify (Scan) Disk	Yes	Yes	Yes	No	Yes	No
Overwrite VBS, FATs & Root Dir.	Yes	Yes	Yes	Yes	Yes	Yes
Overwrite Data Area	No	No	No	No	No	No
Floppy Disk Format Operations:	**DOS 2-4**		**DOS 5 and Higher**			
Check Volume Boot Sector	No	Yes	Yes	Yes	No	Yes
Save UNFORMAT Information	No	Yes	No	Yes	No	No
Read Verify (Scan) Disk	Yes	Yes	Yes	No	Yes	No
Overwrite VBS, FATs & Root Dir.	Yes	Yes	Yes	Yes	Yes	Yes
Overwrite Data Area	Yes	No	Yes	No	Yes	No

/Q = Quick Format
/U = Unconditional Format
"-" = Does Not Matter
VBS = DOS Volume Boot Sector
FAT = File Allocation Table

The default operation of FORMAT on a disk that is already formatted has changed dramatically with DOS V5.0. The biggest difference between this and older versions of DOS is that DOS V5.0 and higher versions (by default) save a backup copy of the disk's DOS volume boot sector, file-allocation tables, and root directory. This information, which is placed in a special format in sectors near the end of the disk, is designed to be utilized by the UNFORMAT command to restore these areas of the disk and therefore undo the work of the FORMAT command. In addition to saving this critical UNFORMAT information, the FORMAT command also defaults to not overwriting the data area of the disk; therefore, the UNFORMAT command can "restore" the disk data. The UNFORMAT does not actually restore the data,—only the saved UNFORMAT information. The disk data is never lost. Older DOS versions do not check the disk to see whether it is formatted and always overwrite the entire floppy disk.

The /Q parameter stands for Quickformat. The basic function of /Q, to eliminate the (sometimes lengthy) read verify scan for disk defects that otherwise would occur, can be performed only on a disk that already is formatted. Any existing defect marks on the disk are preserved by using /Q. The net effect of /Q is to greatly speed up the formatting procedure for disks already formatted. It's a way to delete all the files from a disk quickly and efficiently.

The /U parameter stands for Unconditional. This parameter has two distinctly different effects depending on whether you are formatting a floppy disk or a hard disk. On a floppy disk, the /U parameter instructs the FORMAT command to overwrite the entire disk and skip saving UNFORMAT information because it would be useless anyway if the data were overwritten. On a hard disk, the purpose of /U is only to suppress saving UNFORMAT information. FORMAT on a hard disk never overwrites the data area of the disk, even with the /U parameter! If you have experience with the FORMAT command, you know that FORMAT never has overwritten data on a hard disk, no matter what version of IBM or MS-DOS you are using. (On some older OEM versions, such as COMPAQ and AT&T, DOS did overwrite the entire hard disk.)

When you combine the /Q and /U parameters, you get the fastest reformat possible. /Q prevents the scan for defects, which is the longest operation during formatting, and /U eliminates saving UNFORMAT information. The FORMAT command is restricted to simply erasing the DOS volume boot sector, FATs, and root directory, which it can do very quickly. In fact, a format using the /Q and /U parameters takes only a few seconds to complete no matter how large the disk.

Caring for and Handling Floppy Disks and Drives

Most computer users know the basics of disk care. Disks can be damaged or destroyed easily by the following:

- Touching the recording surface with your fingers or anything else
- Writing on a disk label with a ball-point pen or pencil
- Bending the disk
- Spilling coffee or other substances on the disk
- Overheating a disk (leaving it in the hot sun or near a radiator, for example)
- Exposing a disk to stray magnetic fields

Despite all these cautions, disks are rather hardy storage devices; I can't say that I have ever destroyed one by just writing on it with a pen, because I do so all the time. I am careful, however, not to press too hard, which can put a crease in the disk. Also, simply touching a disk does not necessarily ruin it but rather gets the disk and your drive head dirty with oil and dust. The danger to your disks comes from magnetic fields that, because they are unseen, can sometimes be found in places you never dreamed of.

For example, all color monitors (and color TV sets) have, around the face of the tube, a degaussing coil used to demagnetize the shadow mask inside when the monitor is turned on. The coil is connected to the AC line and controlled by a thermistor that passes a gigantic surge of power to the coil when the tube is powered on, which then tapers off as the tube warms up. The degaussing coil is designed to remove any stray magnetism from the shadow mask at the front area of the tube. Residual magnetism in this mask can bend the electron beams so that the picture appears to have strange colors or be out of focus.

If you keep your disks anywhere near (within one foot) of the front of the color monitor, you expose them to a strong magnetic field every time you turn on the monitor. Keeping disks in this area is not a good idea because the field is designed to demagnetize objects, and indeed works well for demagnetizing disks. The effect is cumulative and irreversible.

Another major disk destructor is the telephone. The mechanical ringer in a typical telephone uses a powerful electromagnet to move the striker into the bell. The ringer circuit uses some 90 volts, and the electromagnetic fields have sufficient power to degauss a disk lying on the desk next to or partially underneath the phone. Keep disks away from the telephone. A telephone with an electronic ringer might not cause this type of damage to a disk, but there are also magnets in the handset, so be careful anyway.

Another source of powerful magnetic fields is an electric motor, found in vacuum cleaners, heaters or air conditioners, fans, electric pencil sharpeners, and so on. Do not place these devices near areas where you store disks.

Airport X-Ray Machines and Metal Detectors. People associate myths with things they cannot see, and we certainly cannot see data as it is stored on a disk, nor the magnetic fields that can alter the data.

One of my favorite myths to dispel is that the airport X-ray machine somehow damages disks. I have a great deal of experience in this area from having traveled around the country for the past 10 years or so with disks and portable computers in hand. I fly about 150,000 miles per year, and my portable computer equipment and disks have been through X-ray machines more than 100 times each year.

Most people commit a fatal mistake when they approach the airport X-ray machines with disks or computers: they don't pass the stuff through! Seriously, X-rays are in essence just a form of light, and disks and computers are just not affected by X-rays at anywhere near the levels found in these machines. What can damage your magnetic media is the metal detector. Time and time again, someone with magnetic media or a portable computer approaches the security check. They freeze and say, "Oh no, I have disks and a computer—they have to be hand inspected." The person then refuses to place the disk and computer on the X-ray belt, and either walks through the metal detector with disks and computer in hand or passes the items over to the security guard, in very close proximity to the metal detector. Metal detectors work by monitoring disruptions in a weak magnetic field. A metal object inserted in the field area causes the field's shape to change, which the detector observes. This principle, which is the reason that the detectors are sensitive to metal objects, can be dangerous to your disks; the X-ray machine, however, is the safest area through which to pass either your disk or computer.

The X-ray machine is not dangerous to magnetic media because it merely exposes the media to electromagnetic radiation at a particular (very high) frequency. Blue light is an example of electromagnetic radiation of a different frequency. The only difference between X-rays and blue light is in the frequency, or wavelength, of the emission.

Electromagnetic radiation is technically a form of wave energy characterized by oscillating electric and magnetic fields perpendicular to one another. An electromagnetic wave is produced by an oscillating electric charge. This wave is not the same thing as a magnetic field. When matter intercepts electromagnetic energy, the energy is converted to thermal, electrical, mechanical, or chemical energy, but not to a magnetic field. Simply put, an electromagnetic wave generates either heat or an electrical alternating current in an object through which the wave passes.

I have been electrically shocked, for example, by touching metal objects in the vicinity of a high-powered amateur-radio transmitter. Your microwave oven induces thermal (kinetic) or even electrical energy in objects because of the same principle. Although a microwave oven is designed to induce kinetic energy in an irradiated substance's molecules, most of you know that when you place conductive (metal) objects in the microwave, an alternating electrical current also is generated, and you might even see sparks. This activity is a generation of electrical or mechanical energy, not of a magnetic field. Because a disk is not a good conductor, the only noticeable effect a high-powered electromagnetic field has on a floppy disk is the generation of kinetic (or thermal) energy. In other words, the only way that X-rays, visible light, or other radiation in these areas of the electromagnetic spectrum can damage a disk is by heating it.

Consider also that if electromagnetic radiation could truly magnetize a disk as a magnetic field can, all magnetic media (disks and tapes) in the world would be in danger. Much electromagnetic radiation is passing through you at this moment, and through all your disks and tapes as well. There is no danger of magnetic damage because the radiation's effect on an object is to impart electrical, thermal, mechanical, or chemical energy—not to magnetize the object. I am not saying that you cannot harm a disk with electromagnetic radiation, because you certainly can; the damage, however, is from the heating effects of the radiation.

You probably know what the sun's extremely powerful electromagnetic radiation can do to a disk. Just leave a disk lying in direct sunlight a while, and you can see the thermal effects of this radiation. A microwave oven would have basically the same cooking effect on a disk, only more intense! Seriously, at the levels of electromagnetic radiation to which we normally are exposed, or which are present in an airport X-ray machine, there is certainly no danger to your disks. The field strength is far too low to raise the temperature of the disk in any perceptible manner, and this radiation has no magnetic effect on a disk.

Some people worry about the effect of X-ray radiation on their system's EPROM (erasable programmable read-only memory) chips. This concern might actually be more valid than worrying about disk damage because EPROMs are erased by certain forms of electromagnetic radiation. In reality, however, you do not need to worry about this effect either.

EPROMs are erased by direct exposure to very intense ultraviolet light. Specifically, to be erased, an EPROM must be exposed to a 12,000 uw/cm2 UV light source with a wavelength of 2,537 angstroms for 15 to 20 minutes, and at a distance of one inch. Increasing the power of the light source or decreasing the distance from the source can shorten the erasure time to a few minutes. The airport X-ray machine is different by a factor of 10,000 in wavelength, and the field strength, duration, and distance from the emitter source are nowhere near what is necessary for EPROM erasure. Be aware that many circuit-board manufacturers use X-ray inspection on circuit boards (with components including EPROMs installed) to test and check quality control during manufacture.

I have conducted my own tests: I passed one disk through different airport X-ray machines for two years, averaging two or three passes a week. The same disk still remains intact with all the original files and data, and never has been reformatted. I also have several portable computers with hard disks installed; one of them has been through the X-ray machines safely every week for more than four years. I prefer to pass computers and disks through the X-ray machine because it offers the best shielding from the magnetic fields produced by the metal detector standing next to it. Doing so also significantly lowers the "hassle factor" with the security guards because if I have it X-rayed, they usually do not require that I plug it in and turn it on.

Now you may not want to take my word for it, but there has been published scientific research that corroborates what I have stated here. A few years ago, a study was published by two scientists, one of whom actually designs X-ray tubes for a major manufacturer. Their study was titled "Airport X-rays and floppy disks: no cause for concern," and was published in 1993 in the Journal "Computer Methods and Programs in Biomedicine." According to the abstract, "A controlled study was done to test the possible effects of X-rays on the integrity of data stored on common sizes of floppy disks. Disks were exposed to doses of X-rays up to seven times that to be expected during airport examination of baggage. The readability of nearly 14 megabytes of data was unaltered by X-irradiation, indicating that floppy disks need not be given special handling during X-ray inspection of baggage." In fact the disks were re-tested after two years of storage, and there has still been no measurable degradation since the exposure.

Drive-Installation Procedures

The procedure for installing floppy drives is simple. You install the drive in two phases. The first phase is to configure the drive for the installation, and the second is to perform the physical installation. Of these two steps, the first one usually is the most difficult to perform, depending on your knowledge of disk interfacing and whether you have access to the correct OEM drive manuals.

Drive Configuration

Configuring a floppy drive consists of setting the jumpers and switches mounted on the drive to match the system in which the drive will be installed, as well as tailoring the function of the drive to the installer's requirements. Every drive has a stable of jumpers and switches, and many drives are different from each other. You will find no standards for what these jumpers and switches are called, where they should be located, or how they should be implemented. There are some general guidelines to follow, but to set up a specific drive correctly and know all the options available, you must have information from the drive's manufacturer, normally found in the original equipment manufacturer's (OEM) manual. The manual is a "must have" item when you purchase a disk drive.

Although additional options might be available, most drives have several configuration features that must be set properly for an installation. These standard options typically need attention during an installation procedure:

- Drive select jumper
- Terminating resistor
- Diskette changeline or ready jumper
- Media sensor jumper

Each configuration item was discussed in more detail earlier in this chapter. The following section describes how these items are to be set for various installations.

Floppy drives are connected by a cabling arrangement called a daisy chain. The name is descriptive because the cable is strung from controller to drive to drive in a single chain. All drives have a drive select (sometimes called DS) jumper that must be set to indicate a certain drive's physical drive number. The point at which the drive is connected on the cable does not matter; the DS jumper indicates how the drive should respond. Most drives allow four settings, but the controllers used in all PC systems support only two on a single daisy-chain cable. The PC and XT floppy controllers, for example, support four drives but only on two separate cables—each one a daisy chain with a maximum of two drives.

Every drive on a particular cable must be set to have unique drive select settings. In a normal configuration, the drive you want to respond as the first drive (A:) is set to the first drive select position, and the drive you want to respond as the second drive (B:) is set to the second drive-select position. On some drives, the DS jumper positions are labeled 0, 1, 2, and 3; other drives use the numbers 1, 2, 3, and 4 to indicate the same positions. For some drives then, a setting of DS0 is drive A:. For others, however, DS1 indicates drive A:. Likewise, some drives use a setting of DS1 for drive B:, and others use a DS2 setting to indicate drive B:. On some drives, the jumpers on the drive circuit board are unlabeled! In this case, consult the drive's manual to find out the descriptions of each jumper setting on the drive.

Make sure that the DS settings for every drive on a single daisy-chain cable are different, or both drives respond to the same signals. If you have incorrect DS settings, both drives respond simultaneously or neither drive responds at all.

The type of cable you use can confuse the drive select configuration. IBM puts in its cables a special twist that electrically changes the DS configuration of the drive plugged in after the twist. This twist causes a drive physically set to the first DS position (A:) to appear to the controller to be set to the second DS position (B:). If the first drive on the cable was before the twist in the cable and was set to the second DS position (B:), the controller would see a conflict. To the controller, both drives would appear to be set to the second DS position (B:), although physically they looked as though they were set differently. In essence, the system would think that two B: drives were installed. The adjustment for this problem is simple: When this type of cable is used, both drives should be set to the second DS position. The drive plugged in to the connector farthest from the controller, which is after the twist in the cable, then would have the physical second-DS-position setting appear to be changed to a first-DS-position setting. Then the system would see this drive as A:, and the drive plugged into the middle cable connector still would appear as B:. A typical daisy-chain drive cable with this included "twist" is connected as shown in figure 13.11.

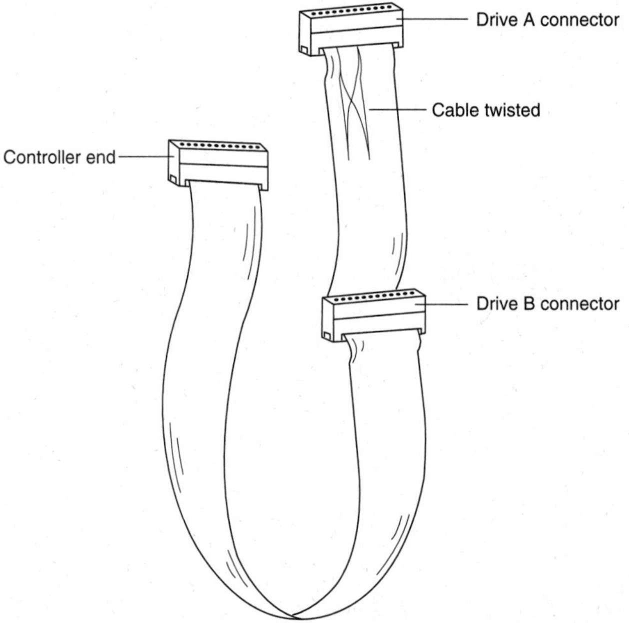

Figure 13.11
A floppy controller cable showing the location of "the twist."

An IBM-style floppy cable is a 34-pin cable with lines 10 through 16 sliced out and cross-wired (twisted) between the drive connectors (refer to figure 13.11). This twisting "cross-wires" the first and second drive-select and motor-enable signals, and therefore inverts the DS setting of the drive following the twist. All the drives in a system using this type of cable, therefore—whether you want them to be A: or B:—are physically jumpered the same way; installation and configuration are simplified because both floppies can be preset to the second DS position. Some drives used by IBM, in fact, have had the DS "jumper" setting permanently soldered into the drive logic board.

Most bare drives you purchase have the DS jumper already set to the second position, which is correct for the majority of systems that use a cable with the twisted lines.

Although this setting is correct for the majority of systems, if you are using a cable with no twist, you will have to alter this setting on at least one of the two drives. Some systems come with only a single floppy drive and no provisions for adding a second one. These types of systems often use a floppy cable with only one drive connector attached. This type of cable does not have any twisted lines, so how do you set up a drive plugged into this cable? Because there is no twist, the DS setting you make on the drive is exactly what the controller sees. You can attach only one drive, and it should appear to the system as A:—therefore, set the drive to the first DS position.

Most PC-compatibles use a floppy cable with the twisted lines between the drive connectors. Drives plugged into this type of cable have their DS jumpers set to the second position. Drives on a single floppy cable or a cable with no twisted lines are set to the first DS position.

A terminating resistor should be placed (or enabled) in any drive plugged into the physical end of a cable. The function of this resistor is to prevent reflections or echoes of signals from reaching the end of the cable. All new drives have this resistor installed by default. The terminating resistor should be removed or disabled for drives that are not the farthest away from the controller. Most 3 1/2-inch floppy drives use the distributed-termination technique, in which the installed terminating resistors are permanently installed, and are nonremovable and cannot be disabled. The resistor value in these drives is adjusted appropriately so that, in effect, the termination is distributed among both drives. When you mix 5 1/4-inch and 3 1/2-inch drives, you should enable or disable the terminators on the 5 1/4-inch drives appropriately, according to their position on the cable and ignore the nonchangeable settings on the 3 1/2-inch drives.

In a typical cabling arrangement for two 5 1/4-inch floppies, for example, the terminating resistor is installed in drive A: (at the end of the cable), and this resistor is removed from the other floppy drive on the same cable (B:). The letter to which the drive responds is not important in relation to terminator settings; the important issue is that the drive at the end of the cable has the resistor installed and functioning and that other drives on the same cable have the resistor disabled or removed.

The terminating resistor usually looks like a memory chip; it might be white, blue, black, gray, or some other color, and memory chips usually are just black. IBM always labels the resistor with a T-RES sticker for easy identification. On some systems, the resistor is a built-in device enabled or disabled by a jumper or series of switches. If you have the removable type, make sure to store the resistor in a safe place because you might need it later. Figure 13.12 shows the location and appearance of the terminating resistor or switches on a typical floppy drive. Because most 3 1/2-inch drives have a form of automatic termination, there is no termination to configure; also, some 5 1/4-inch drives, such as Toshiba drives, have a permanently installed terminating resistor enabled or disabled by a jumper labeled TM.

Table 13.12 explains how a drive should be configured relative to the drive-select jumper and terminating resistor. You can use the table as a universal drive-select and terminating-resistor configuration chart that applies to all types of drives, including floppy disk drives and hard disks.

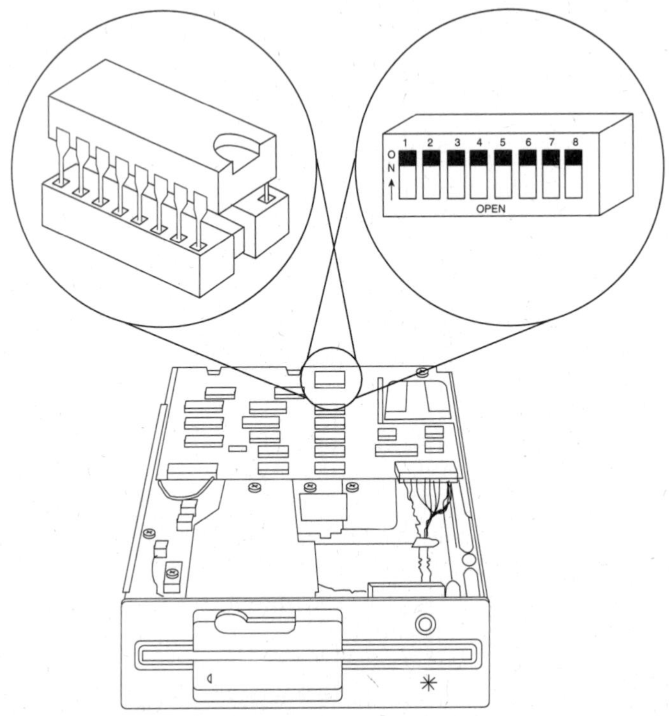

Figure 13.12

A typical floppy drive terminating resistor, or termination switches.

Table 13.12 Configuring Drive-Select Jumpers and Terminating Resistors

Drive	Twisted Cable		Straight Cable	
A: drive (end connector)	DS = second	TR installed	DS = first	TR installed
B: drive (center connector)	DS = second	TR removed	DS = second	TR removed

DS = Drive select position
TR = Terminating resistor

The assumption in table 13.12 is that you always plug drive B: into the center connector on the cable and drive A: into the end connector. This arrangement might seem strange at first, but it is virtually required if you ever assemble a single-drive system. The logical first (A:) drive should be the end, or last, drive on the cable, and should be terminated. The twist in the cable is almost always between the two drive connectors on a cable and not between the controller and a drive.

Two other options might be available for you to set: the status of pin 34 on the drive's connector, and the function of a media-sensor feature. The guidelines for setting these options follow.

If the drive is a 5 1/4-inch 360K drive, set the status of pin 34 to Open (disconnected) regardless of the type of system in which you are installing the drive. The only other option normally found for pin 34 on 360K drives is Ready (RDY), which is incorrect. If you are using only a low-density controller, as in a PC or XT, pin 34 is ignored no matter what is sent on it. If the drive you are installing is a 5 1/4-inch 1.2M or 3 1/2-inch 720K, 1.44M, or 2.88M drive, be sure to set pin 34 to send the Disk Change (DC) signal. The basic rule is simple:

For 360K drives only, pin 34 = Open (disconnected)

For any other drive, pin 34 = Disk Change

The media-sensor setting is the easiest to describe. Only 1.44M and 2.88M drives have a media sensor. The best rule to follow is to set these drives so that the sensor is enabled; this step enables the sensor to control the drive's recording mode and, therefore, the drive's write-current level.

Physical Installation

When you physically install a drive, you plug in the drive. Here, your concerns are using the correct brackets and screws for the system and the drive you are installing.

A special bracket usually is required whenever you install a half-height drive in place of an earlier full-height unit (see fig. 13.13). The brackets enable you to connect the two half-height drives together as a single full-height unit for installation. Remember also that nearly all floppy drives now use metric hardware; only the early, American-manufactured drives use the standard English threads.

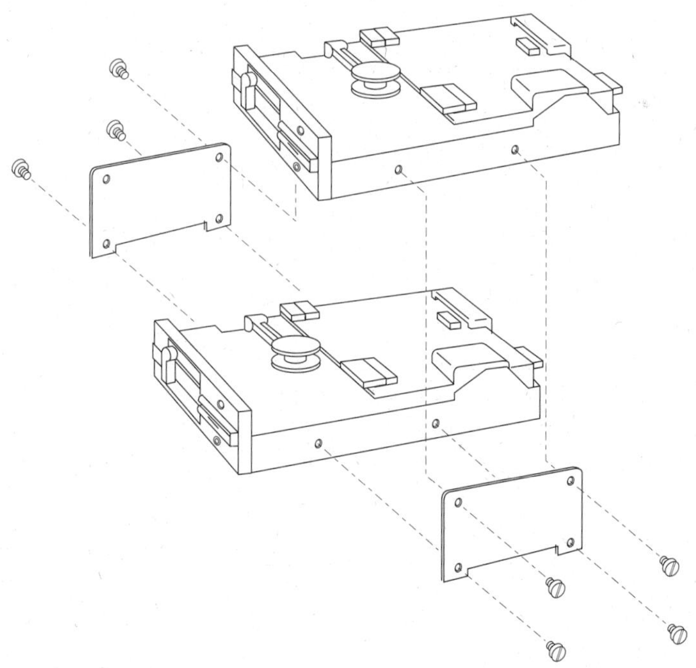

Figure 13.13

Installing half-height drives in a full-height bay with adapter plates.

You can get these adapter plates from most vendors who sell drives, but sometimes they charge as much as $10 for basically a piece of sheet metal with four holes drilled in it! Several companies listed in Appendix B specialize in cables, brackets, screw hardware, and other items useful in assembling systems or installing drives. The template shown in figure 13.14 also will guide you if you want to make your own. I usually use a piece of galvanized sheet metal like that used in ventilation ductwork for the stock, which can be easily obtained at most hardware stores.

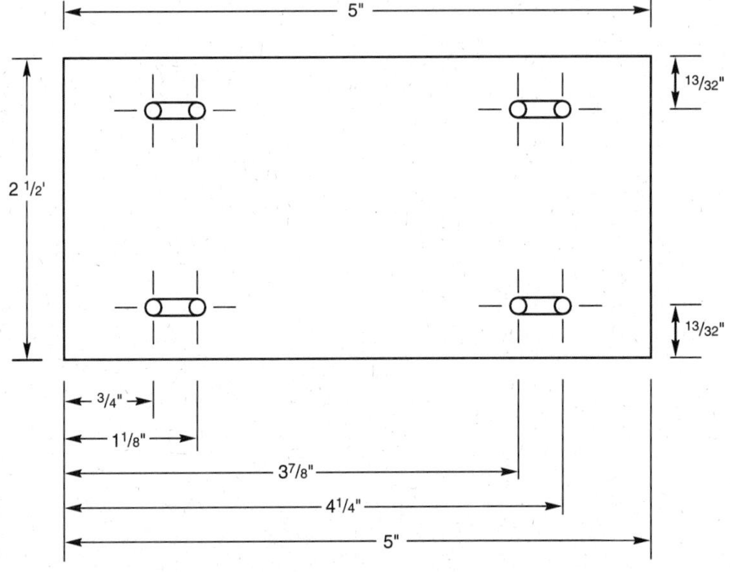

Figure 13.14
The dimensions of a typical drive adapter plate.

Another piece of drive-installation paraphernalia you need is the rails used in installing disk drives in AT systems. Most PC-compatible systems follow the IBM standard for rail design. Again, you can purchase these from some of the vendors listed in Appendix B. If you want to construct your own, figure 13.15 shows the construction of a typical IBM-style drive rail. These rails can be made from metal, but usually are made from plastic. They probably can even be made from wood. Drives installed in an AT are grounded to the system chassis through a separate ground wire and tab, which is why the rails do not need to be made from a conductive material. I find it more cost effective to purchase the rails rather than make them.

As you might expect, Compaq uses a slightly different rail construction. The vendors mentioned in Appendix B that sell cables, brackets, and other installation accessories also carry the Compaq-style rails.

When you connect a drive, make sure that the power cable is installed properly. The cable normally is keyed so that it cannot be plugged in backward. Also, install the data and control cable. If no key is in this cable, which allows only a correct orientation, use

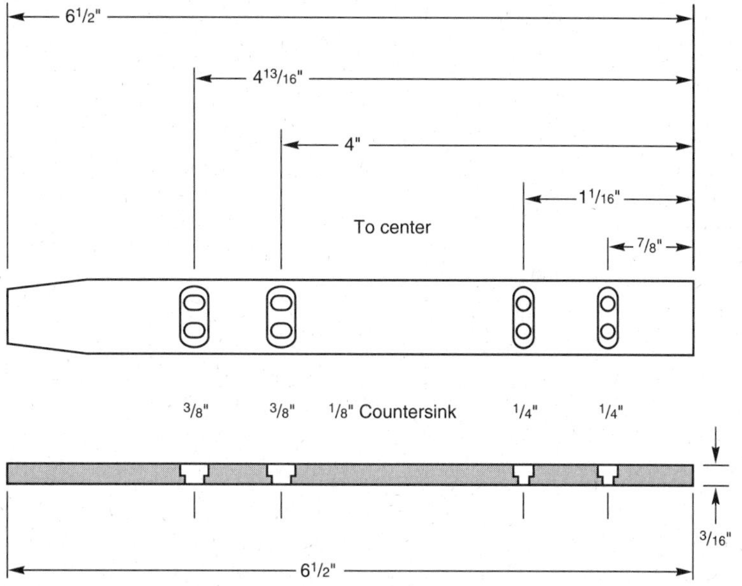

Figure 13.15
A typical AT-drive mounting rail.

the colored wire in the cable as a guide to the position of pin 1. This cable is oriented correctly when you plug it in so that the colored wire is plugged into the disk drive connector toward the cut-out notch in the drive edge connector.

Floppy Drive Installation Summary

To install and set up a floppy drive properly, you must understand and set up primarily four different configuration items on the drive as follows:

- Drive select (DC) jumper setting
- Terminating resistor (TR) enabled or disabled
- Send disk change (DC) or no signal on pin 34
- Enable media sensor

This section explained the proper settings for these items in virtually any installation situation you might encounter.

For more information about configuring and installing a specific drive, you can use several resources. Obviously, this book contains much information about configuring and installing floppy disk drives—make sure that you have read it all! The best source of information about certain drives or controllers is the original equipment manufacturer's (OEM) documentation. These manuals tell you where all configuration items are located on the drive; what they look like; and how to set them. Unfortunately, most of the time you do not receive this detailed documentation when you purchase a drive or controller; instead, you must contact the OEM to obtain it.

Troubleshooting and Correcting Problems

The majority of floppy drive problems are caused primarily by improper drive configuration, installation, or operation. Unfortunately, floppy drive configuration and installation is much more complicated than the average technician seems to realize. Even if you had your drive "professionally" installed, it still might have been done incorrectly.

This section describes some of the most common problems that stem from improperly installing or configuring a drive. Also discussed are several problems that can occur from improperly using drives and disks. Solutions to these problems are presented also.

Handling the "Phantom Directory" (Disk Change)

One of the most common mistakes people make in installing a disk drive is incorrectly setting the signals sent by the drive on pin 34 of the cable to the controller. All drives except the 360K drive must be configured so that a Disk Change (DC) signal is sent along pin 34 to the controller.

If you do not enable the DC signal when the system expects you to, you might end up with trashed disks as a result. For example, a PC user with disk in hand might say to you, "Moments ago, this disk contained my document files, and now it seems as though my entire word processing program disk has mysteriously transferred to it. When I attempt to run the programs that now seem to be on this disk, they crash or lock up my system." Of course, in this case the disk has been damaged, and you will have to perform some data-recovery magic to recover the information for the user. A good thing about this particular kind of problem is that recovering most—if not all—the information on the disk is entirely possible.

You also can observe this installation defect manifested in the "phantom directory" problem. For example, you place a disk with files on it in the A: drive of your AT-compatible system and enter the DIR A: command. The drive starts spinning, the access light on the drive comes on, and after a few seconds of activity, the disk directory scrolls up the screen. Everything seems to be running well. Then you remove the disk and insert in drive A: a different disk with different files on it and repeat the DIR A: command. This time, however, the drive barely (if at all) spins before the disk directory scrolls up the screen. When you look at the directory listing that has appeared, you discover in amazement that it is the same listing as on the first disk you removed from the drive.

Understand that the disk you have inserted in the drive is in danger. If you write on this disk in any way, you will cause the file-allocation tables and root-directory sectors from the first disk (which are stored in your system's memory) to be copied over to the second disk, thereby "blowing away" the information on the second disk. Most AT-compatible systems with high- or low-density controllers utilize a floppy disk caching system that buffers the FATs and directories from the floppy disk that was last read in system RAM. Because this data is kept in memory, these areas of the disk do not have to be reread as frequently. This system greatly speeds access to the disk.

Opening the door lever or pressing the eject button on a drive normally sends the Disk Change signal to the controller, which in turn causes DOS to flush out the floppy cache.

This action causes the next read of the disk drive to reread the FAT and directory areas. If this signal is not sent, the cache is not flushed when you change a disk, and the system acts as though the first disk still is present in the drive. Writing to this newly inserted disk writes not only the new data but also either a full or partial copy of the first disk's FAT and directory areas. Also, the data is written to what was considered free space on the first disk, which might not be free on the subsequent disk and results in damaged files and data.

This problem has several simple solutions. One is temporary; the other is permanent. For a quick, temporary solution, press Ctrl-Break or Ctrl-C immediately after changing any disk, to force DOS to manually flush the floppy I/O buffers. This method is exactly how the old CP/M operating system used to work. After pressing Ctrl-Break or Ctrl-C, the next disk access rereads the FAT and directory areas of the disk and places fresh copies in memory. In other words, you must be sure that every time you change a disk, the buffer gets flushed. Because these commands work only from the DOS prompt (and not in Windows), you must not change a disk while working in an application.

A more permanent and correct solution to the problem is simple—just correct the drive installation. In my experience, incorrect installation is the root cause of this problem nine out of 10 times. Remember this simple rule: If a jumper block is on the disk drive labeled DC, you should install a jumper there. If you are absolutely certain that the installation was correct—for example, the drive has worked perfectly for some time, but then suddenly develops this problem—check the following list of items, all of which can prevent the Disk Change signal from being sent:

- *Bad cable.* Check for continuity on pin 34.
- *Drive configuration/Setup.* Make sure that the DC jumper is enabled; check CMOS Setup for proper drive type.
- *Bad Disk Change sensor.* Clean sensor or replace drive and retest.
- *Bad drive logic board.* Replace drive and retest.
- *Bad controller.* Replace controller and retest.
- *Wrong DOS OEM version.*

The last of these checklist items can stump you because the hardware seems to be functioning correctly. As a rule, you should use only the DOS supplied by the same OEM as the computer system on the system. For example, use IBM DOS on IBM systems, Compaq DOS on Compaq systems, Zenith DOS on Zenith systems, Toshiba DOS on Toshiba systems, Tandy DOS on Tandy systems, and so on. This problem is most noticeable with some laptop systems that apparently have a modified floppy controller design, such as some Toshiba laptops. On many of these systems, you must use the correct (Toshiba, for example) OEM version of DOS.

Handling Incorrect Media-Sensor Operation

Incorrect media-sensor operation occurs on only 1.44M or 2.88M, 3 1/2-inch, high-density drives—the only drives that have a media sensor. Again, this is largely a drive-configuration problem because the installer did not enable the sensor when it should have been enabled. You would think that the sensor would be set correctly when you purchase a drive, but that is not always the case. Never assume that a drive is preconfigured properly for your system. Remember that drive manufacturers sell drives for systems other than PC-compatibles. Sometimes it is hard to remember that many other types of computers exist other than just IBMs or IBM clones.

If the media sensor is not operational, the controller likely will leave the drive in a state in which high write-current always is applied to the heads during write operations. This state is OK for high-density disks, but when low-density disks are used, random and sporadic read and write failures occur, usually ending with the DOS message Abort, Retry, Ignore, Fail?.

Another symptom of incorrect media-sensor operation is generating double-density disks that seem eventually to lose data—perhaps over a few weeks or months. This loss often can be traced back to an improperly configured media sensor on the drive. In some systems, the problem might be more obvious, such as not being capable of formatting or writing successfully on 720K disks. If your system can format a 720K disk to 1.44M without punching any extra holes in the disk, it is an immediate alert that the media sensor is not enabled.

Handling Problems Caused by Using Double-Density Disks at High Density

If you attempt to format a 5 1/4-inch, double-density disk at high-density format, you usually will hear several retries from the drive as DOS finds a large amount of bad sectors on the disk. When the format is completed, hundreds of kilobytes in bad sectors usually are reported. Most people would never use this disk. Because the 5 1/4-inch disks are so radically different from one another in terms of magnetic coercivity and media formulation, the double-density disks do not work well carrying a high-density format.

Problems are seen more often with the 3 1/2-inch disks because the double-density disks are not nearly as different from the high-density disks compared to the 5 1/4-inch versions, although they indeed are different. Because the 3 1/2-inch DD and HD disks differ less, however, a double-density, 3 1/2-inch disk usually accepts a high-density format with no bad sectors reported. This acceptance is unfortunate because it causes most users to feel that they are safe in using the disk for data storage.

A 3 1/2-inch, double-density disk with a 1.44M, high-density format initially seems to work with no problem. If you fill this type of double-density disk with 1.44M of data and store it on a shelf, you will notice that eventually the recording degrades, and the data becomes unreadable. Several months might pass before you can detect the degradation, but then it is too late. From talking to hundreds of my clients, I have found that the average "half life" of such a recording is approximately six months from the time the data is written to the time that one or more files suddenly have unreadable sectors. In six months to a year, much of the rest of the disk rapidly degrades until all the data and files have extensive damage. The recording simply destroys itself during this time. I have substantiated this situation with my own testing and my clients' experiences. If the data is reread and rewritten periodically before any degradation is noticeable, then the recording can be "maintained" for longer periods of time before data is lost.

The technical reasons for this degradation were explained earlier in this chapter. In a sense, the disk eventually performs a self-erasure operation. Again, the time frame for damage seems to be approximately six months to a year from the time the data is written. I certainly expect my disks to hold data for more than six months; in fact, data written properly to your disks should be readable many, many years from now.

If you have been using double-density, 3 1/2-inch disks with high-density formats, you are asking for problems. Using these types of disks for backup, for instance, is highly inappropriate! Many people use double-density disks as high-density disks to save money. You should realize that high-density disks are not very expensive anymore; data-recovery services, however, are very expensive.

If you have a disk that has been formatted improperly and is developing read problems, the first thing to do is DISKCOPY the disk immediately to another proper-density disk. Then you can survey the damage and make repairs to the new copy. For a more detailed investigation of the subject of data recovery, see Que's *Guide to Data Recovery*.

Handling Track-Width Problems from Writing on 360K Disks with a 1.2M Drive

As discussed earlier in this chapter, the 5 1/4-inch, high-density drives usually write a narrower track than the 5 1/4-inch, double-density drives. Therefore, when you use a high-density drive to update a double-density disk originally formatted or written in a double-density drive, the wider tracks written by the double-density drive are not completely overwritten by the high-density drive. Of course, if the double-density disk is newly formatted and subsequently written in only a high-density drive (although at the proper 360K format), there is no problem with overwrites—that is, until you update the disk with a double-density (wide-track) drive and then update it again with a high-density (narrow-track) drive. In that case, you again have a wider track with a narrow-track update embedded within—but not completely covering it.

You must remember never to use a high-density drive to write on a double-density disk previously written by a double-density drive. This procedure makes the disk unreadable by the double-density drive, but usually still readable by the high-density drive. In fact, the best way to recover information from a disk that has been incorrectly overwritten in this manner is to use a high-density disk drive to perform a DISKCOPY operation of the disk to a new, blank, never previously formatted, low-density disk.

Handling Off-Center Disk Clamping

Clamping the disk off-center in the drive has to be absolutely the most frequently encountered cause of problems with floppy drives. In my worldwide troubleshooting seminars, we run the PC systems with the lid off for most of the course. Whenever someone has a problem reading or booting from a floppy disk, I look down at the top of the exposed disk drive on the system while it is spinning to see whether the disk has been clamped by the drive hub in an off-center position. More often than not, that is the problem. I know that the disk is clamped off-center because the disk wobbles while it rotates. Ejecting and reinserting the disk so that it is clamped properly usually makes the disk reading or booting problem disappear immediately. This step might solve the problem in most cases, but it is not much help if you have formatted or written a disk in an off-center position. In that case, all you can do is try to DISKCOPY the improperly written disk to another disk and attempt various data-recovery operations on both disks.

I use a technique for inserting floppy disks that has eliminated this problem for me. After inserting a disk into a drive, I always take an extra half-second to wiggle the drive lever or door, first down, and then up, and then down again to clamp the disk rather than simply push the door or lever down once to clamp it. The reason is that the first partial closing of the lever serves to center the disk in its jacket so that the second motion allows the drive hub to clamp the disk properly in a centered position. If I were in charge of training for a large organization, I would make sure that all the basic PC starter classes taught proper disk handling, including insertion and on-center clamping in the drive.

Note that the 3 1/2-inch drives are virtually immune to this type of problem because of the different type of clamping and centering mechanisms they use. Some 5 1/4-inch drives have adopted a more reliable clamping mechanism similar to the 3 1/2-inch drives. Canon makes some of these new 5 1/4-inch drives, used by IBM and Compaq. The newest version used by IBM in some of its PS/2 systems is totally motorized. You merely slide the disk into the drive slot, and the drive grabs the disk and electrically pulls it in and centers it. These drives also include a motorized eject button.

Realigning Misaligned Drives

If your disk drives are misaligned, you will notice that other drives cannot read disks created in your drive, and you might not be able to read disks created in other drives. This situation can be dangerous if you allow it to progress unchecked. If the alignment is bad enough, you probably will notice it first in the incapability to read original application-program disks, while still being able to read your own created disks. The Drive Probe program from Accurite for checking the alignment and operation of floppy drives is discussed later in this chapter.

To solve this problem, you can have the drive realigned. I don't always recommend realigning drives because of the low cost of simply replacing the drive compared to aligning one. Also, an unforeseen circumstance catches many people off guard: You might find that your newly aligned drive might not be able to read all your backup or data disks created while the drive was out of alignment. If you replace the misaligned drive with a new one and keep the misaligned drive, you can use it for DISKCOPY purposes to transfer the data to newly formatted disks in the new drive.

Repairing Floppy Drives

Attitudes about repairing floppy drives have changed over the years primarily because of the decreasing cost of drives. When drives were more expensive, people often considered repairing the drive rather than replacing it. With the cost of drives decreasing every year, however, certain labor- or parts-intensive repair procedures have become almost as expensive as replacing the drive with a new one.

Because of cost considerations, repairing floppy drives usually is limited to cleaning the drive and heads and lubricating the mechanical mechanisms. On drives that have a speed adjustment, adjusting the speed to within the proper operating range also is common. Note that most newer half-height drives and virtually all 3 1/2-inch drives do not have an adjustment for speed. These drives use a circuit that automatically sets the speed at the required level and compensates for variations with a feedback loop. If such an auto-taching drive is off in speed, the reason usually is that the circuit failed. Replacement of the drive usually is necessary.

Cleaning Floppy Drives

Sometimes read and write problems are caused by dirty drive heads. Cleaning a drive is easy; you can proceed in two ways. In one method, you use one of the simple head-cleaning kits available from computer- or office-supply stores. These devices are easy to operate and don't require the system unit to be open for access to the drive. The other method is the manual method: You use a cleaning swab with a liquid such as pure alcohol, Freon, or trichloroethane. With this method, you must open the system unit to expose the drive and, in many cases (especially in earlier full-height drives), also remove and partially disassemble the drive. The manual method can result in a better overall job, but usually the work required is not worth the difference.

The cleaning kits come in two styles: The wet type uses a liquid squirted on a cleaning disk to wash off the heads; the dry kit relies on abrasive material on the cleaning disk to remove head deposits. I recommend that you never use the dry drive-cleaning kits. Always use a wet system in which a liquid solution is applied to the cleaning disk. The dry disks can prematurely wear the heads if used improperly or too often; wet systems are very safe to use.

The manual drive-cleaning method requires that you have physical access to the heads, in order to swab them manually with a lint-free foam swab soaked in a cleaning solution. This method requires some level of expertise: Simply jabbing at the heads incorrectly with a cleaning swab might knock the drive heads out of alignment. You must use a careful in-and-out motion, and lightly swab the heads. No side-to-side motion (relative to the way the heads travel) should be used; this motion can snag a head and knock it out of alignment. Because of the difficulty and danger of this manual cleaning, for most applications I recommend a simple wet-disk cleaning kit because it is the easiest and safest method.

One question that comes up repeatedly in my seminars is "How often should you clean a disk drive?" Only you can answer that question. What type of environment is the system in? Do you smoke cigarettes near the system? If so, cleaning would be required more often. Usually, a safe rule of thumb is to clean drives about once a year if the system is in a clean office environment in which no smoke or other particulate matter is in the air. In a heavy-smoking environment, you might have to clean every six months or perhaps even more often. In dirty industrial environments, you might have to clean every month or so. Your own experience is your guide in this matter. If DOS reports drive errors in the system by displaying the familiar DOS Abort, Retry, Ignore prompt, you should clean your drive to try to solve the problem. If cleaning does solve the problem, you probably should step up the interval between preventive-maintenance cleanings.

In some cases, you might want to place a (very small) amount of lubricant on the door mechanism or other mechanical contact points inside the drive. Do not use oil; use a pure silicone lubricant. Oil collects dust rapidly after you apply it and usually causes the oiled mechanism to gum up later. Silicone does not attract dust in the same manner and can be used safely. Use very small amounts of silicone; do not drip or spray silicone inside the drive. You must make sure that the lubricant is applied only to the part that needs it. If the lubricant gets all over the inside of the drive, it may cause unnecessary problems.

Setting the Floppy Drive Speed Adjustment

Most older 5 1/4-inch floppy disk drives, especially full-height drives, have a small variable resistor used to adjust the drive's rotational speed. In particular, the Tandon and CDC full-height drives used by IBM in the PC and XT systems have this adjustment. The location of this variable resistor is described in the hardware-maintenance reference manuals IBM sells for these systems.

If you have a Tandon drive, you make the adjustment through a small, brass screw on a variable resistor mounted on the motor control board, attached to the rear of the drive (see fig. 13.16). The resistor is usually blue, and the screw is brass. To gauge the speed, you can use a program such as Drive Probe, by Accurite; IBM's Advanced Diagnostics, supplied with the hardware-maintenance and service manual; or even a purely mechanical method that relies on a fluorescent light to act as a strobe.

The software methods use a disk to evaluate the running speed of the drive. Usually, you turn the screw until the speed reads correctly (300 RPM) according to the program you use. The mechanical method requires you to remove the drive from the system and place it upside down on a bench. Sometimes the drive is set sideways on the power supply so that the drive's case is grounded. Then the underside of the drive is illuminated by a standard fluorescent light. The lights acts as a strobe that flashes 60 times per second because of the cycling speed of the AC line current. On the bottom of the drive spindle are strobe marks for 50 Hz and 60 Hz (see fig. 13.17). Because 60 Hz power is used in the United States, you should use the 60 Hz marks. The 50 Hz marks are used for (50 cycle) European power. While the drive is running, turn the small screw until the strobe marks appear to be stationary, much like the "wagon wheel effect" you see in old western movies. When the marks are completely stationary as viewed under the light, the drive's rotation speed is correct.

With CDC drives, the adjustment resistor is mounted on the logic board, which is on top of the drive. The small, brass screw to the left of the board is the one you want. Other drives also might have an adjustment. The best way to tell whether a drive has a speed adjustment is to look for the telltale strobe marks on the spindle of the drive. If the marks are there, the drive probably has an adjustment; if the marks are not there, the drive probably has an automatic speed circuit and requires no adjustment. The OEM manual for the drive has information about all these adjustments (if any) and where you make them.

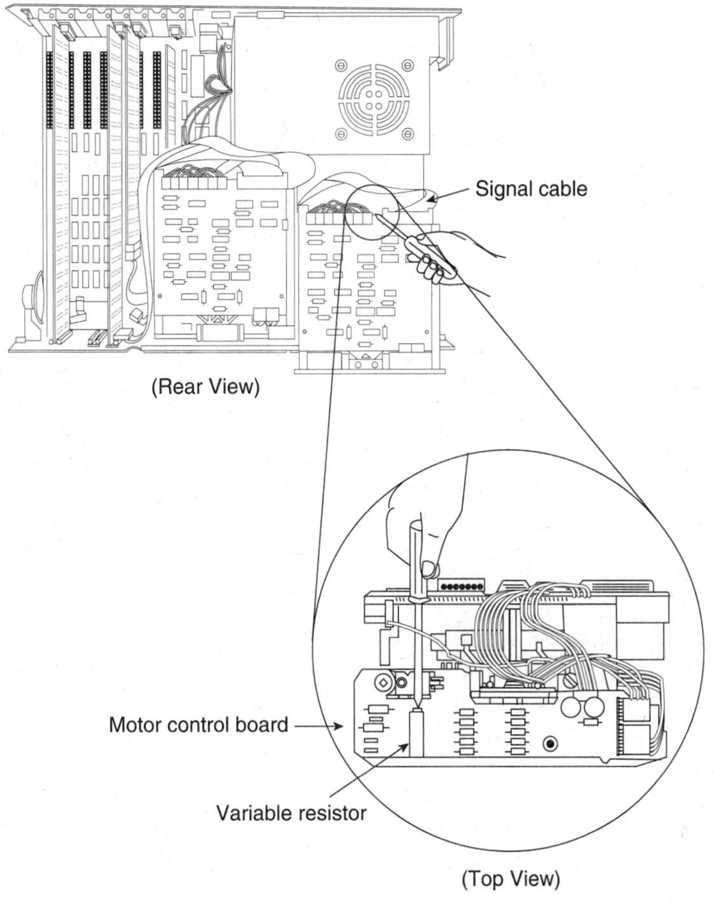

Figure 13.16

The drive-speed adjustment for the Tandom TM-100 series drive.

Aligning Floppy Disk Drives

Aligning disk drives is usually no longer done because of the high relative cost. To align a drive properly requires access to an oscilloscope (for about $500), a special analog-alignment disk ($75), and the OEM service manual for the drive; also, you must spend half an hour to an hour aligning the drive.

A new program, Drive Probe, by Accurite, uses special test disks called High-Resolution Diagnostic (HRD) disks. These disks are as accurate as the analog alignment disks (AAD) and eliminate the need for an oscilloscope to align a drive. You cannot use any program that relies on the older Digital Diagnostic Disk (DDD) or Spiral format test disks because they are not accurate enough to use to align a drive. The Drive Probe and HRD system can make an alignment more cost-effective than before, but it is still a labor-intensive operation.

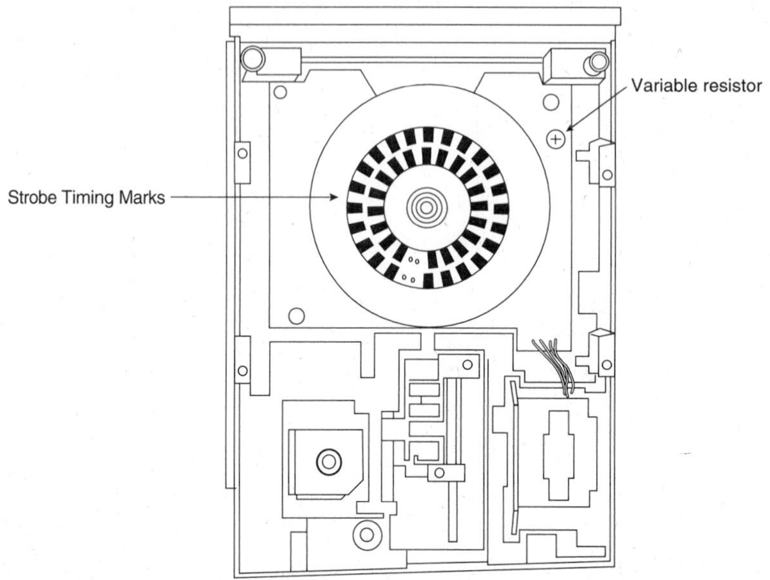

Figure 13.17
Strobe marks and speed adjustment on a typical half-height drive.

With the price of most types of floppy drives hovering at or below the $35 mark, aligning drives usually is not a cost-justified alternative to replacement. One exception exists. In a high-volume situation, drive alignment might pay off. Another alternative is to investigate local organizations that perform drive alignments, usually for $25 to $50. Weigh this cost against the replacement cost and age of the drive. I have purchased brand new 1.44M floppy drives for as low as $25. At these prices, alignment is no longer a viable option.

Summary

This chapter examined floppy drives and floppy media (disks) in great detail. One of the most important things to do when installing a drive in a system is to make sure that the drive is configured correctly. This chapter discussed drive configuration also. With this information, installing drives correctly should be an easy task.

This chapter also discussed many problems that confound floppy drive users, such as reading and writing double-density disks with high-density drives. It discussed thoroughly the differences between high- and double-density drives and disks, and mentioned the consequences of using the wrong type of disk in the wrong drive. Simple drive servicing, such as cleaning and speed adjustment, were explained so that these operations can be performed in-house. After reading this chapter, you should know much about floppy drives.

Chapter 14

Hard Disk Drives

To most users, the hard disk drive is the most important, yet most mysterious, part of a computer system. A *hard disk drive* is a sealed unit that holds the data in a system. When the hard disk fails, the consequences usually are very serious. To maintain, service, and expand a PC system properly, you must fully understand the hard disk unit.

Most computer users want to know how hard disk drives work and what to do when a problem occurs. Few books about hard disks, however, cover the detail necessary for the PC technician or sophisticated user. This chapter corrects that situation.

This chapter thoroughly describes the hard disk drive, from a physical, mechanical, and electrical point of view. In particular, this chapter examines the construction and operation of a hard disk drive in a practical sense.

Definition of a Hard Disk

A hard disk drive contains rigid, disk-shaped platters usually constructed of aluminum or glass. Unlike floppy disks, the platters cannot bend or flex—hence the term *hard disk*. In most hard disk drives, the platters cannot be removed; for that reason, IBM calls them *fixed disk drives*. Although removable-platter hard disk drives are available, their nonstandard nature, higher cost, and reliability problems make them unpopular.

Hard disk drives used to be called *Winchester drives*. This term dates back to the 1960s, when IBM developed a high-speed hard disk drive that had 30M of fixed-platter storage and 30M of removable-platter storage. The drive had platters that spun at high speeds and heads that floated over the platters while they spun in a sealed environment. That drive, the 30-30 drive, soon received the nickname *Winchester* after the famous Winchester 30-30 rifle. After that time, drives that used a high-speed spinning platter with a floating head also became known as Winchester drives. The term has no technical or scientific meaning; it is a slang term and is considered synonymous with *hard disk*.

Hard Drive Advancements

In the 14 or more years that hard disks have commonly been used in PC systems, they have undergone tremendous changes. To give you an idea of how far hard drives have come in that time, following are some of the most profound changes in PC hard disk storage:

- Maximum storage capacities have increased from the 10M 5.25-inch full-height drives available in 1982 to 10G or more for small 3.5-inch half-height drives.
- Data transfer rates from the media have increased from 85 to 102K per second for the original IBM XT in 1983 to nearly 10M per second for some of the fastest drives today.
- Average seek times have decreased from more than 85 ms (milliseconds) for the 10M XT hard disk in 1983 to fewer than 8 ms for some of the fastest drives today.
- In 1982, a 10M drive cost more than $1,500 ($150 per megabyte). Today, the cost of hard drives has dropped to less than $0.20 per megabyte.

Areal Density

Areal density has been used as a primary technology-growth-rate indicator for the hard disk drive industry. *Areal density* is defined as the product of the linear bits per inch (BPI), measured along the length of the tracks around the disk, multiplied by the number of tracks per inch (TPI) measured radially on the disk. The results are expressed in units of Mb/sq-inch and are used as a measure of efficiency in drive recording technology. Current high-end drives record at areal densities of about 160 Megabits per square inch (M/sq-inch). Prototype models with densities as high as several G/sq-inch (Gigabits per square inch) have been constructed, allowing for capacities of more than 2G on a single 2.5-inch platter for notebook drives.

Areal density (and, therefore, drive capacity) has been doubling approximately every two to three years, and disk drives are likely to reach areal densities of 10+ G/sq-inch before the year 2000. A drive built with this technology would be capable of storing up to 20G of data on a single 2.5-inch platter, and the entire drive would fit in the palm of your hand. New media and head technologies, such as ceramic or glass platters, MR (Magneto-Resistive) heads, pseudo-contact recording, and PRML (Partial Response Maximum Likelihood) electronics, are being developed to support these higher areal densities. The primary challenge in achieving higher densities is manufacturing drive heads and disks to operate at closer tolerances.

It seems almost incredible that computer technology improves by doubling performance or capacity every two to three years. If only other industries could match that growth and improvement rate.

Hard Disk Drive Operation

The basic physical operation of a hard disk drive is similar to that of a floppy disk drive: a hard drive uses spinning disks with heads that move over the disks and store data in tracks and sectors. In many other ways, however, hard disk drives are different from floppy disk drives.

Hard disks usually have multiple platters, each with two sides on which data can be stored. Most drives have at least two or three platters, resulting in four or six sides, and some drives have up to 11 or more platters. The identically positioned tracks on each side of every platter together make up a *cylinder.* A hard disk drive has one head per platter side, and all the heads are mounted on a common carrier device, or *rack*. The heads move in and out across the disk in unison; they cannot move independently because they are mounted on the same rack.

Hard disks operate much faster than floppy drives. Most hard disks originally spun at 3,600 RPM—approximately 10 times faster than a floppy drive. Until recently, 3,600 RPM was pretty much a constant among hard drives. Now, however, quite a few hard drives spin even faster. One drive that I have, for example, spins at 4,318 RPM; others spin as fast as 5,400, 5,600, 6,400, and even 7,200 RPM. High rotational speed combined with a fast head-positioning mechanism and more sectors per track make one hard disk faster than another, and all these features combine to make hard drives much faster than floppy drives in storing and retrieving data.

The heads in most hard disks do not (and should not!) touch the platters during normal operation. When the heads are powered off, however, they land on the platters as they stop spinning. While the drive is on, a very thin cushion of air keeps each head suspended a short distance above or below the platter. If the air cushion is disturbed by a particle of dust or a shock, the head may come into contact with the platter spinning at full speed. When contact with the spinning platters is forceful enough to do damage, the event is called a *head crash.* The result of a head crash may be anything from a few lost bytes of data to a totally trashed drive. Most drives have special lubricants on the platters and hardened surfaces that can withstand the daily "takeoffs and landings," as well as more severe abuse.

Because the platter assemblies are sealed and nonremovable, track densities can be very high. Many drives have 3,000 or more tracks per inch of media. Head Disk Assemblies (HDAs), which contain the platters, are assembled and sealed in clean rooms under absolutely sanitary conditions. Because few companies repair HDAs, repair or replacement of items inside a sealed HDA can be expensive. Every hard disk ever made will eventually fail. The only questions are when the hard disk will fail and whether your data is backed up.

Many PC users think that hard disks are fragile, and generally, they are one of the most fragile components in your PC. In my weekly PC Hardware and Troubleshooting or Data Recovery seminars, however, I have run various hard disks for days with the lids off and have even removed and installed the covers while the drives were operating. Those drives continue to store data perfectly to this day with the lids either on or off. Of course, I do not recommend that you try this test with your own drives; neither would I use it on my larger, more expensive drives.

The Ultimate Hard Disk Drive Analogy!

I'm sure that you have heard the traditional analogy that compares the interaction of the head and media in a typical hard disk as being similar in scale to a 747 flying a few feet off the ground at cruising speed (500-plus mph). I have heard this analogy used over and over again for years, and I've even used it in my seminars many times without checking to see whether the analogy is technically accurate with respect to modern hard drives.

One highly inaccurate aspect of the 747 analogy has always bothered me—the use of an airplane of any type to describe the head-and-platter interaction. This analogy implies that the heads fly very low over the surface of the disk—but technically, this is not true. The heads do not fly at all, in the traditional aerodynamic sense; instead, they float on a cushion of air that's being dragged around by the platters.

A much better analogy would use a hovercraft instead of an airplane; the action of a hovercraft much more closely emulates the action of the heads in a hard disk drive. Like a hovercraft, the drive heads rely somewhat on the shape of the bottom of the head to capture and control the cushion of air that keeps them floating over the disk. By nature, the cushion of air on which the heads float forms only in very close proximity to the platter and is often called an *air bearing* by the disk drive industry.

I thought it was time to come up with a new analogy that more correctly describes the dimensions and speeds at which a hard disk operates today. I looked up the specifications on a specific hard disk drive and then, equally magnified and rescaled all the dimensions involved to make the head floating height equal to 1 inch. For my example, I used a Seagate model ST-12550N Barracuda 2 drive, which is a 2GB(formatted capacity), 3.5-inch SCSI-2 drive. In fact, I originally intended to install this drive in the portable system on which I am writing this book, but the technology took another leap and I ended up installing an ST-15230N Hawk 4 drive (4GB) instead. Table 14.1 shows the specifications of the Barracude drive, as listed in the technical documentation:

Table 14.1 Seagate ST-12550N Barracuda 2, 3.5-inch, SCSI-2 Drive Specifications

Specification	Value	Unit of Measure
Linear density	52,187	Bits Per Inch (BPI)
Bit spacing	19.16	micro-inches (μ-in)
Track density	3,047	Tracks Per Inch (TPI)
Track spacing	328.19	micro-inches (μ-in)
Total tracks	2,707	tracks
Rotational speed	7,200	Revolutions Per Minute (RPM)
Average head linear speed	53.55	Miles Per Hour (MPH)
Head slider length	0.08	inches
Head slider height	0.02	inches
Head floating height	5	micro-inches (μ-in)
Average seek time	8	milliseconds (ms)

By interpreting these specifications, you can see that in this drive, the head sliders are about 0.08 inch long and 0.02 inch high. The heads float on a cushion of air about 5 micro-inches (millionths of an inch) from the surface of the disk while traveling at an average speed of 53.55 MPH (figuring an average track diameter of 2.5 inches). These heads read and write individual bits spaced only 19.16 micro-inches apart on tracks separated by only 328.19 micro-inches. The heads can move from one track to any other in only 8 ms during an average seek operation.

To create my analogy, I simply magnified the scale to make the floating height equal to 1 inch. Because 1 inch is 200,000 times greater than 5 micro-inches, I scaled up everything else by the same amount.

Are you ready?

The heads of this "typical" hard disk, magnified to such a scale, would be more than 1,300 feet long and 300 feet high (about the size of the Sears Tower, lying sideways), traveling at a speed of more than 10.7 million MPH (2,975 miles per second) only 1 inch above the ground, and reading data bits spaced a mere 3.83 inches apart on tracks separated by only 5.47 feet.

Additionally, since the average seek of 8 ms (.008 seconds) is defined as the time it takes to move the heads over 1/3 of the total tracks (about 902 in this case) each skyscraper-size head could move sideways to any track within a distance of 0.93 miles (902 tracks × 5.47 feet) which results in an average sideways velocity of over 420,000 MPH (116 miles per second).

The forward speed of this imaginary head is difficult to comprehend, so I'll elaborate. The diameter of the Earth at the equator is 7,926 miles, which means a circumference of about 24,900 miles. At 2,975 miles per second, this imaginary head would circle the Earth about once every 8 seconds.

This analogy should give you a new appreciation of the technological marvel that the modern hard disk drive actually represents. It makes the 747 analogy look rather pathetic (not to mention totally inaccurate) doesn't it?

Magnetic Data Storage

Learning how magnetic data storage works will help you develop a feel for the way that your disk drives operate and can improve the way that you work with disk drives and disks.

Nearly all disk drives in personal computer systems operate on magnetic principles. Purely optical disk drives often are used as a secondary form of storage, but the computer to which they are connected is likely to use a magnetic storage medium for primary disk storage. Due to the high performance and density capabilities of magnetic storage, optical disk drives and media probably never will totally replace magnetic storage in PC systems.

Magnetic drives, such as floppy disk drives and hard disk drives, operate by using *electromagnetism*. This basic principle of physics states that as an electric current flows through a conductor, a magnetic field is generated around the conductor. This magnetic field then can influence magnetic material in the field. When the direction of the flow of electric current is reversed, the magnetic field's polarity also is reversed. An electric motor uses electromagnetism to exert pushing and pulling forces on magnets attached to a rotating shaft.

Another effect of electromagnetism is that if a conductor is passed through a changing magnetic field, an electrical current is generated. As the polarity of the magnetic field changes, so does the direction of the electric current flow. For example, a type of electrical generator used in automobiles, called an alternator, operates by rotating electromagnets past coils of wire conductors in which large amounts of electrical current can be induced. The two-way operation of electromagnetism makes it possible to record data on a disk and read that data back later.

The read/write heads in your disk drives (both floppy and hard disks) are U-shaped pieces of conductive material. This U-shaped object is wrapped with coils of wire, through which an electric current can flow. When the disk drive logic passes a current through these coils, it generates a magnetic field in the drive head. When the polarity of the electric current is reversed, the polarity of the field that is generated also changes. In essence, the heads are electromagnets whose voltage can be switched in polarity very quickly.

When a magnetic field is generated in the head, the field jumps the gap at the end of the U-shaped head. Because a magnetic field passes through a conductor much more easily than through the air, the field bends outward through the medium and actually uses the disk media directly below it as the path of least resistance to the other side of the gap. As the field passes through the media directly under the gap, it polarizes the magnetic particles through which it passes so that they are aligned with the field. The field's polarity and, therefore, the polarity of the magnetic media are based on the direction of the flow of electric current through the coils.

The disk consists of some form of substrate material (such as Mylar for floppy disks or aluminum or glass for hard disks) on which a layer of magnetizable material has been deposited. This material usually is a form of iron oxide with various other elements added. The polarities of the magnetic fields of the individual magnetic particles on an erased disk normally are in a state of random disarray. Because the fields of the individual particles point in random directions, each tiny magnetic field is canceled by one that points in the opposite direction, for a total effect of no observable or cumulative field polarity.

Particles in the area below the head gap are aligned in the same direction as the field emanating from the gap. When the individual magnetic domains are in alignment, they no longer cancel one another, and an observable magnetic field exists in that region of the disk. This local field is generated by the many magnetic particles that now are operating as a team to produce a detectable cumulative field with a unified direction. The term flux describes a magnetic field that has a specific direction.

As the disk surface rotates below the drive head, the head can lay a magnetic flux over a region of the disk. When the electric-current flow through the coils in the head is reversed, so is the magnetic-field polarity in the head gap. This reversal also causes the polarity of the flux being placed on the disk to reverse. The *flux reversal* or *flux transition* is a change in polarity of the alignment of magnetic particles on the disk surface.

A drive head places flux reversals on a disk to record data. For each data bit (or bits) written, a pattern of flux reversals is placed on the disk in specific areas known as bit or transition cells. A *bit cell* or *transition cell* is a specific area of the disk controlled by the time and rotational speed in which flux reversals are placed by a drive head. The particular pattern of flux reversals within the transition cells used to store a given data bit or bits is called the *encoding method.* The drive logic or controller takes the data to be stored and encodes it as a series of flux reversals over a period of time, according to the encoding method used. Modified Frequency Modulation (MFM) and Run Length Limited (RLL) are popular encoding methods. All floppy disk drives use the MFM scheme. Hard disks use MFM or several variations of RLL encoding methods. These encoding methods are described in more detail later in this chapter.

During the write process, voltage is applied to the head, and as the polarity of this voltage changes, the polarity of the magnetic field being recorded also changes. The flux transitions are written precisely at the points where the recording polarity changes. Strange as it may seem, during the read process, a head does not output exactly the same signal that was written; instead, the head generates a voltage pulse or spike only when it crosses a flux transition. When the transition is from positive to negative, the pulse that the head would detect is negative voltage. When the transition changes from negative to positive, the pulse would be a positive voltage spike.

In essence, while reading the disk the head becomes a flux transition detector, emitting voltage pulses whenever it crosses a transition. Areas of no transition generate no pulse. Figure 14.1 shows the relationship between the read and write waveforms and the flux transitions recorded on a disk.

You can think of the write pattern as being a square waveform that is at a positive or negative voltage level and that continuously polarizes the disk media in one direction or another. Where the waveform transitions go from positive to negative voltage, or vice versa, the magnetic flux on the disk also changes polarity. During a read, the head senses the flux transitions and outputs a pulsed waveform. In other words, the signal is zero volts unless a positive or negative transition is being detected, in which case there is a positive or negative pulse. Pulses appear only when the head is passing over flux transitions on the disk media. By knowing the clock timing used, the drive or controller circuitry can determine whether a pulse (and therefore, a flux transition) falls within a given transition cell.

The electrical pulse currents generated in the head while it is passing over a disk in read mode are very weak and can contain significant noise. Sensitive electronics in the drive and controller assembly then can amplify the signal above the noise level and decode the train of weak pulse currents back into data that is (theoretically) identical to the data originally recorded.

So as you now can see, disks are both recorded and read by means of basic electromagnetic principles. Data is recorded on a disk by passing electrical currents through an electromagnet (the drive head) that generates a magnetic field stored on the disk. Data on a disk is read by passing the head back over the surface of the disk; as the head encounters changes in the stored magnetic field, it generates a weak electrical current that indicates the presence or absence of flux transitions in the originally recorded signal.

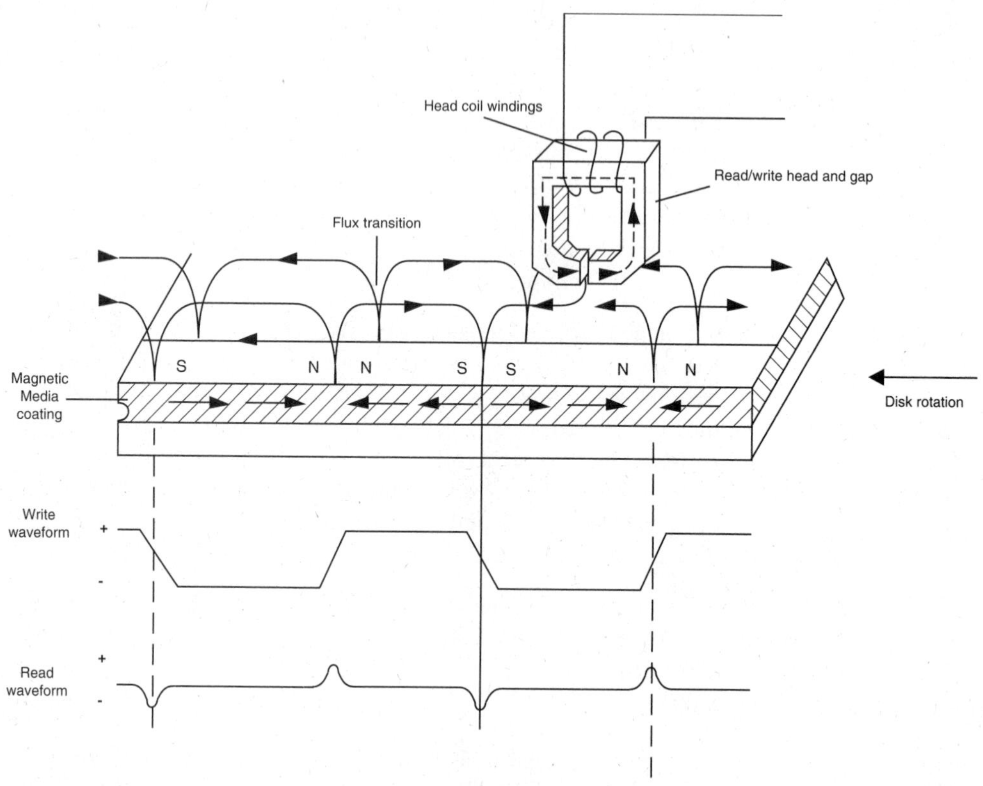

Figure 14.1

Magnetic write and read processes.

Data Encoding Schemes

Magnetic media essentially is an analog storage medium. The data that we store on it, however, is digital information—that is, ones and zeros. When digital information is applied to a magnetic recording head, the head creates magnetic domains on the disk media with specific polarities. When a positive current is applied to the write head, the magnetic domains are polarized in one direction; when negative voltage is applied, the magnetic domains are polarized in the opposite direction. When the digital waveform that is recorded switches from a positive to a negative voltage, the polarity of the magnetic domains is reversed.

During a readback, the head actually generates no voltage signal when it encounters a group of magnetic domains with the same polarity, but it generates a voltage pulse every time it detects a switch in polarity. These magnetic-polarity switches are called *flux reversals*. Each flux reversal generates a voltage pulse in the read head; it is these pulses that the drive detects when reading data. A read head does not generate the same waveform that was written; instead, it generates a series of pulses, each pulse appearing where a magnetic flux transition has occurred.

To optimize the placement of pulses during magnetic storage, the raw digital input data is passed through a device called an *encoder/decoder (Endec)*, which converts the raw binary information to a waveform that is more concerned with the optimum placement of the flux transitions (pulses). During a read operation, the Endec reverses the process and decodes the pulse train back into the original binary data. Over the years, several different schemes for encoding data in this manner have been developed; some are better or more efficient than others.

In any consideration of binary information, the use of timing is important. When interpreting a read or write waveform, the timing of each voltage transition event is critical. If the timing is off, a given voltage transition may be recognized at the wrong time, and bits may be missed, added, or simply misinterpreted. To ensure that the timing is precise, the transmitting and receiving devices must be in sync. This synchronization can be accomplished by adding a separate line for timing, called a *clock signal*, between the two devices. The clock and data signals also can be combined and then transmitted on a single line. This combination of clock and data is used in most magnetic data encoding schemes.

When the clock information is added in with the data, timing accuracy in interpreting the individual bit cells is ensured between any two devices. A *bit cell* is a window in time inside which a voltage transition will be placed to signify a bit. Clock timing is used to determine the start and end of each bit cell. Each bit cell is bounded by two clock cells where the clock transitions can be sent. First, there is a clock transition cell, then the data transition cell, and finally the clock transition cell for the data that follows. By sending clock information along with the data, the clocks will remain in sync, even if a long string of 0 bits are transmitted. Unfortunately, all the transition cells that are used solely for clocking take up space on the media that otherwise could be used for data.

Because the number of flux transitions that can be recorded on a particular medium is limited by the disk media and head technology, disk drive engineers have been trying various ways of encoding the data into a minimum number of flux reversals, taking into consideration the fact that some flux reversals, used solely for clocking, are required. This method permits maximum use of a given drive hardware technology.

Although various encoding schemes have been tried, only a few are popular today. Over the years, these three basic types have been the most popular:

- Frequency Modulation (FM)
- Modified Frequency Modulation (MFM)
- Run Length Limited (RLL)

The following section examines these codes, discusses how they work, where they have been used, and any advantages or disadvantages that apply to them.

FM Encoding. One of the earliest techniques for encoding data for magnetic storage is called *Frequency Modulation (FM)* encoding. This encoding scheme, sometimes called *Single Density* encoding, was used in the earliest floppy disk drives that were installed in

PC systems. The original Osborne portable computer, for example, used these Single Density floppy drives, which stored about 80K of data on a single disk. Although it was popular until the late 1970s, FM encoding no longer is used today.

FM represents one of the simplest ways to encode zeros and ones on a magnetic surface. In each bit cell, a flux reversal is recorded to indicate a 1 bit, and no flux reversal is recorded to indicate a 0 bit. With no other modifications, problems would occur if you were recording a long series of zeros, in which case no flux transitions would be recorded. If no transitions occurred for a long period, the controller easily could get out of sync with the drive, resulting in a possible misinterpretation of the data. To keep the devices in sync, a clock signal is written onto the drive along with the data.

In FM encoding, each bit actually requires two transition cells. A 1 bit is recorded as a clock flux reversal followed by a data flux reversal, which the drive simply would see as two consecutive flux reversals. A 0 bit also is recorded in two transition cells. Only the clock cell, however, contains a flux reversal; the data cell is empty (no reversal). Whether you are recording a 1 or a 0, the initial flux reversal represents the clock signal, and the second transition cell would carry a reversal only if the data were a 1 bit.

Although this method is simple and inexpensive, it has one major disadvantage: each data bit requires two flux reversals, which reduces potential disk capacity by half. Table 14.2 shows how each bit cell is encoded.

Table 14.2 FM Data to Flux Transition Encoding

Data Bit Value	Flux Encoding
1	TT
0	TN

T = flux transition
N = no flux transition

MFM Encoding. *Modified Frequency Modulation (MFM)* encoding was devised to reduce the number of flux reversals used in the original FM encoding scheme and, therefore, to pack more data onto the disk. In MFM encoding, the use of the clock transition cells is minimized, leaving more room for the data. Clock transitions are recorded only if a stored 0 bit is preceded by another 0 bit; in all other cases, a clock transition is not required. Because the use of the clock transitions has been minimized, the actual clock frequency can be doubled from FM encoding, resulting in twice as many data bits being stored in the same number of flux transitions as in FM.

Because it is twice as efficient as FM encoding, MFM encoding also has been called *Double Density* recording. MFM is used in virtually all PC floppy drives today and was used in nearly all PC hard disks for a number of years. Today, most hard disks use RLL (Run Length Limited) encoding, which provides even greater efficiency than MFM.

Because MFM encoding places twice as many data bits in the same number of flux reversals as FM, the clock speed of the data is doubled, so that the drive actually sees the same number of total flux reversals as with FM. This means that data is read and written at twice the speed in MFM encoding, even though the drive sees the flux reversals arriving at the same frequency as in FM. This method allows existing drive technology to store twice the data and deliver it twice as fast.

The only caveat is that MFM encoding requires improved disk controller and drive circuitry because the timing of the flux reversals must be more precise than in FM. As it turned out, these improvements were not difficult to achieve, and MFM encoding became the most popular encoding scheme for many years.

Table 14.3 shows the data bit to flux reversal translation in MFM encoding.

Table 14.3 MFM Data to Flux Transition Encoding

Data Bit Value	Flux Encoding
1	NT
0 preceded by 0	TN
0 preceded by 1	NN

T = flux transition
N = no flux transition

RLL Encoding. Today's most popular encoding scheme, called *RLL (Run Length Limited)*, packs up to 50 percent more information on a given disk than even MFM does and three times as much information as FM. In RLL encoding, groups of bits are taken as a unit and combined to generate specific patterns of flux reversals. By combining the clock and data in these patterns, the clock rate can be further increased while maintaining the same basic distance between the flux transitions on the disk. By optimizing the code to limit the minimum and maximum distance between two flux transitions, the clock rate (and, therefore, storage density) can be increased—typically by 3 times over FM and 1.5 times over MFM encoding.

IBM invented RLL encoding and first used the method in many of its mainframe disk drives. During the late 1980s, the PC hard disk industry began using RLL encoding schemes to increase the storage capabilities of PC hard disks. Today, virtually every drive on the market uses some form of RLL encoding.

Instead of encoding a single bit, RLL normally encodes a group of data bits at a time. The term *Run Length Limited* is derived from the two primary specifications of these codes, which is the minimum number (the run length) and maximum number (the run limit) of transition cells allowed between two actual flux transitions. Several schemes can be achieved by changing the length and limit parameters, but only two have achieved any real popularity—RLL 2,7 and RLL 1,7.

Even FM and MFM encoding can be expressed as a form of RLL. FM can be called RLL 0,1, because there can be as few as zero and as many as one transition cell separating two flux transitions. MFM can be called RLL 1,3, because as few as one and as many as three transition cells can separate two flux transitions. Although these codes can be expressed in RLL form, it is not common to do so.

RLL 2,7 initially was the most popular RLL variation because it offers a high density ratio (1.5 times that of MFM) with a transition detection window the same relative size as that in MFM. This method allows for high storage density with fairly good reliability. In very high-capacity drives, however, RLL 2,7 did not prove to be reliable enough. Most of today's highest-capacity drives use RLL 1,7 encoding, which offers a density ratio 1.27 times that of MFM and a larger transition detection window relative to MFM. Compared with RLL 2,7 the storage density is a little less, but the reliability is much higher. Because of the larger relative window size within which a transition can be detected, RLL 1,7 is a more forgiving and more reliable code, which is required when media and head technology are being pushed to their limits. With the greater need for reliability in high-capacity disk storage, RLL 1,7 is becoming the most popular code used in newer drives.

Another little-used RLL variation called *RLL 3,9*—sometimes called *ARLL (Advanced RLL)*—allowed an even higher density ratio than RLL 2,7. Unfortunately, reliability suffered too greatly under the RLL 3,9 scheme; the method was used by only a few controller companies that have all but disappeared.

It is difficult to understand how RLL codes work without looking at an example. Because RLL 2,7 was the most popular form of RLL encoding used with older controllers, I will use it as an example. Even within a given RLL variation such as RLL 2,7 or 1,7, many different flux transition encoding tables can be constructed to show what groups of bits are encoded as what sets of flux transitions. For RLL 2,7 specifically, thousands of different translation tables could be constructed, but for my examples, I will use the encoder/decoder (Endec) table used by IBM because it is the most popular variation used.

According to the IBM conversion tables, specific groups of data bits 2, 3, and 4 bits long are translated into strings of flux transitions 4, 6, and 8 transition cells long, respectively. The selected transitions coded for a particular bit sequence are designed to ensure that flux transitions do not occur too close together or too far apart.

It is necessary to limit how close two flux transitions can be because of the basically fixed resolution capabilities of the head and disk media. Limiting how far apart these transitions can be ensures that the clocks in the devices remain in sync.

Table 14.4 shows the IBM-developed encoding scheme for RLL 2,7.

Table 14.4 RLL 2,7 (IBM Endec) Data to Flux Transition Encoding

Data Bit Values	Flux Encoding
10	NTNN
11	TNNN
000	NNNTNN
010	TNNTNN
011	NNTNNN
0010	NNTNNTNN
0011	NNNNTNNN

T = flux transition
N = no flux transition

In studying this table, you may think that encoding a byte such as 00000001b would be impossible because no combinations of data bit groups fit this byte. Encoding this type of byte is not a problem, however, because the controller does not transmit individual bytes; instead, the controller sends whole sectors, making it possible to encode such a byte simply by including some of the bits in the following byte. The only real problem occurs in the last byte of a sector if additional bits are needed to complete the final group sequence. In these cases, the encoder/decoder (Endec) in the controller simply adds excess bits to the end of the last byte. These excess bits are truncated during any reads so that the last byte always is correctly decoded.

Encoding Scheme Comparisons

Figure 14.2 shows an example of the waveform written to store an X ASCII character on a hard disk drive under three different encoding schemes.

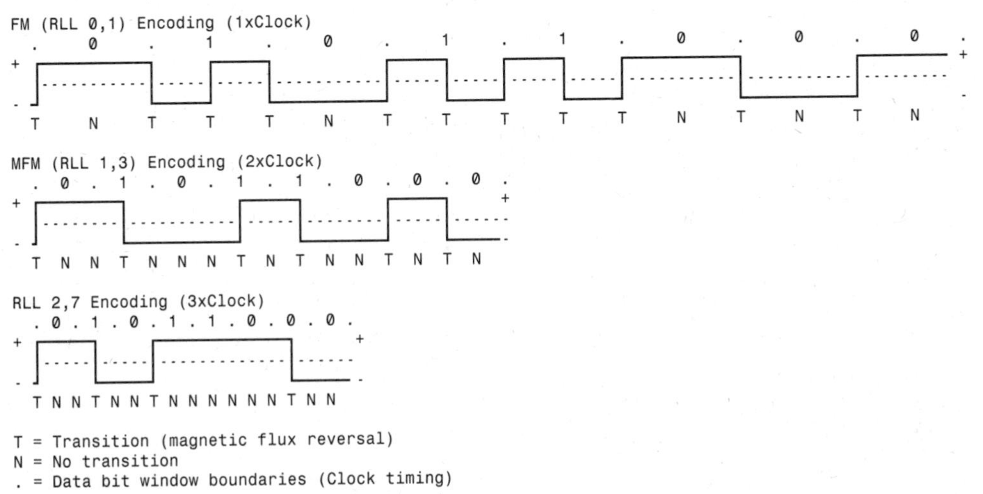

Figure 14.2

ASCII character "X" write waveforms using FM, MFM, and RLL 2,7 encoding.

In each of these encoding-scheme examples, the top line shows the individual data bits (01011000b) in their bit cells separated in time by the clock signal, which is shown as a period (.). Below that line is the actual write waveform, showing the positive and negative voltages as well as voltage transitions that result in the recording of flux transitions. The bottom line shows the transition cells, with T representing a transition cell that contains a flux transition and N representing a transition cell that is empty (no flux transition).

The FM encoding example is easy to explain. Each bit cell has two transition cells: one for the clock information and one for the data itself. All the clock transition cells contain flux transitions, and the data transition cells contain a flux transition only if the data is a 1 bit. No transition at all is used to represent a 0 bit. Starting from the left, the first data bit is 0, which decodes as a flux transition pattern of TN. The next bit is a 1, which decodes as TT. The next bit is 0, which decodes as TN, and so on. Using the FM encoding chart listed earlier, you easily can trace the FM encoding pattern to the end of the byte. Notice that in FM encoding, transitions can be written in adjacent transition cells, with no empty transition cells between them. This method is called a minimum run length of 0. Also, the maximum number of empty transition cells between any two flux transitions is 1, which is why FM encoding can be called RLL 0,1.

The MFM encoding scheme also has clock and data transition cells for each data bit to be recorded. As you can see, however, the clock transition cells carry a flux transition only when a 0 bit is stored after another 0 bit. Starting from the left, the first bit is a 0, and the preceding bit is unknown (assume 0), so the flux transition pattern is TN for that bit. The next bit is a 1, which always decodes to a transition-cell pattern of NT. The next bit is 0, which was preceded by 1, so the pattern stored is NN. Using the MFM encoding table listed earlier, you easily can trace the MFM encoding pattern to the end of the byte. You can see that the minimum and maximum number of transition cells between any two flux transitions is one and three, respectively; hence, MFM encoding also can be called RLL 1,3.

Notice that because half of the total transitions used in FM are required, the clock rate can be doubled, so that the data takes up only half as much space. Also notice that even with the doubled clock rate, the minimum physical distance between any two flux transitions is exactly the same as with FM, meaning that the actual density of the write waveform is the same as with FM even though twice as much data is being encoded.

The RLL 2,7 pattern is more difficult to see because it relies on encoding groups of bits rather than each bit individually. Starting from the left, the first group that matches the groups listed in the encoder/decoder (Endec) table are the first three bits, 010. These bits are translated into a flux transition pattern of TNNTNN. The next two bits, 11, are translated as a group to TNNN; and the final group, 000 bits, is translated to NNNTNN to complete the byte. As you can see in this example, no additional bits were needed to finish the last group.

Notice that the minimum and maximum number of empty transition cells between any two flux transitions in this example are two and six, although a different example could show a maximum of seven empty transition cells. This is where the RLL 2,7 designation comes from. Because even fewer transitions are recorded than in MFM, the clock rate can be further increased to 3 times that of FM or 1.5 times that of MFM, allowing more data to be stored in the same space on the disk. Notice, however, that the resulting write waveform itself looks exactly like a typical FM or MFM waveform in terms of the number and separation of the flux transitions for a given physical portion of the disk. In other words, the physical minimum and maximum distances between any two flux transitions remain the same in all three of these encoding-scheme examples.

Another new feature in high-end drives involves the disk read circuitry. Read channel circuits using Partial-Response, Maximum-Likelihood (PRML) technology allow disk drive manufacturers to increase the amount of data that can be stored on a disk platter by up to 40 percent. PRML replaces the standard "detect one peak at a time" approach of traditional analog peak-detect read/write channels with digital signal processing. In digital signal processing, noise can be digitally filtered out, allowing flux change pulses to be placed closer together on the platter, achieving greater densities.

I hope that the examinations of these different encoding schemes and how they work have taken some of the mystery out of the way data is recorded on a drive. You can see that although schemes such as MFM and RLL can store more data on a drive, the actual density of the flux transitions remains the same as far as the drive is concerned.

Sectors

A disk track is too large to manage effectively as a single storage unit. Many disk tracks can store 50,000 or more bytes of data, which would be very inefficient for storing small files. For that reason, a disk track is divided into several numbered divisions known as sectors. These sectors represent slices of the track.

Different types of disk drives and disks split tracks into different numbers of sectors, depending on the density of the tracks. For example, floppy disk formats use 8 to 36 sectors per track, whereas hard disks usually store data at a higher density and can use 17 to 100 or more sectors per track. Sectors created by standard formatting procedures on PC systems have a capacity of 512 bytes, but this capacity may change in the future.

Sectors are numbered on a track starting with 1, unlike the heads or cylinders, which are numbered starting with 0. For example, a 1.44M floppy disk contains 80 cylinders numbered from 0 to 79 and two heads numbered 0 and 1, and each track on each cylinder has 18 sectors numbered from 1 to 18.

When a disk is formatted, additional areas are created on the disk for the disk controller to use for sector numbering and identifying the start and end of each sector. These areas precede and follow each sector's data area, which accounts for the difference between a disk's unformatted and formatted capacities. For example, a 4M floppy disk (3 1/2-inch) has a capacity of 2.88M when it is formatted, and a 38M hard disk has a capacity of only 32M when it is formatted. All drives use some reserved space for managing the data that can be stored on the drive.

Although I have stated that each disk sector is 512 bytes in size, this statement technically is false. Each sector does allow for the storage of 512 bytes of data, but the data area is only a portion of the sector. Each sector on a disk typically occupies 571 bytes of the disk, of which only 512 bytes are usable for user data. The actual number of bytes required for the sector header and trailer can vary from drive to drive, but this figure is typical.

You may find it helpful to think of each sector as being a page in a book. In a book, each page contains text, but the entire page is not filled with text; rather, each page has top, bottom, left, and right margins. Information such as chapter titles (track and cylinder numbers) and page numbers (sector numbers) is placed in the margins. The "margin" areas of a sector are created and written to during the disk-formatting process. Formatting also fills the data area of each sector with dummy values. After the disk is formatted, the data area can be altered by normal writing to the disk. The sector header and trailer information cannot be altered during normal write operations unless you reformat the disk.

Each sector on a disk has a *prefix portion*, or header that identifies the start of the sector and a sector number, as well as a *suffix portion*, or trailer that contains a *checksum* (which helps ensure the integrity of the data contents). Each sector also contains 512 bytes of data. The data bytes normally are set to some specific value, such as F6h (hex), when the disk is physically (or low-level) formatted. (The following section explains low-level formatting.)

In many cases, a specific pattern of bytes that are considered to be difficult to write are written so as to flush out any marginal sectors. In addition to the gaps within the sectors, gaps exist between sectors on each track and also between tracks; none of these gaps contains usable data space. The prefix, suffix, and gaps account for the lost space between the unformatted capacity of a disk and the formatted capacity.

Table 14.5 shows the format for each track and sector on a typical hard disk with 17 sectors per track.

Table 14.5 Typical 17-Sector/17-Track Disk Sector Format

Bytes	Name	Description
16	POST INDEX GAP	All 4Eh, at the track beginning after the Index mark
The following sector data (shown between the lines in this table) is repeated 17 times for an MFM encoded track.		
13	ID VFO LOCK	All 00h; synchronizes the VFO for the sector ID
1	SYNC BYTE	A1h; notifies the controller that data follows
1	ADDRESS MARK	FEh; defines that ID field data follows
2	CYLINDER NUMBER	A value that defines the actuator position
1	HEAD NUMBER	A value that defines the head selected
1	SECTOR NUMBER	A value that defines the sector
2	CRC	Cyclic Redundancy Check to verify ID data
3	WRITE TURN-ON GAP	00h written by format to isolate the ID from DATA
13	DATA SYNC VFO LOCK	All 00h; synchronizes the VFO for the DATA
1	SYNC BYTE	A1h; notifies the controller that data follows
1	ADDRESS MARK	F8h; defines that user DATA field follows
512	DATA	The area for user DATA
2	CRC	Cyclic Redundancy Check to verify DATA
3	WRITE TURN-OFF GAP	00h; written by DATA update to isolate DATA
15	INTER-RECORD GAP	All 00h; a buffer for spindle speed variation
693	PRE-INDEX GAP	All 4Eh, at track end before Index mark
571	*Total bytes per sector*	
512	*Data bytes per sector*	
10,416	*Total bytes per track*	
8,704	*Data bytes per track*	

This table refers to a hard disk track with 17 sectors. Although this capacity was typical during the mid 1980s, more advanced hard disks place as many as 150 or more sectors per track, and the specific formats of those sectors may vary slightly from the example.

As you can see, the usable space on each track is about 16 percent less than the unformatted capacity. This example is true for most disks, although some may vary slightly.

The Post Index Gap provides a head-switching recovery period so that when switching from one track to another, sequential sectors can be read without waiting for an additional revolution of the disk. In some drives running 1:1 interleave controllers, this time is not enough; additional time can be added by skewing the sectors so that the arrival of the first sector is delayed.

The Sector ID data consists of the Cylinder, Head, and Sector Number fields, as well as a CRC field to allow for verification of the ID data. Most controllers use bit 7 of the Head Number field to mark the sector as bad during a low-level format or surface analysis. This system is not absolute, however; some controllers use other methods to indicate a marked bad sector. Usually, though, the mark involves one of the ID fields.

Write Turn on Gap follows the ID field CRC bytes and provides a pad to ensure a proper recording of the following user data area as well as to allow full recovery of the ID CRC.

The user Data field consists of all 512 bytes of data stored in the sector. This field is followed by a CRC field to verify the data. Although many controllers use two bytes of CRC here, the controller may implement a longer Error Correction Code (ECC) that requires more than two CRC bytes to store. The ECC data stored here provides the possibility of Data-field read correction as well as read error detection. The correction/detection capabilities depend on the ECC code chosen and on the controller implementation. A write turn-off gap is a pad to allow the ECC (CRC) bytes to be fully recovered.

The Inter-Record Gap provides a means to accommodate variances in drive spindle speeds. A track may have been formatted while the disk was running slower than normal and then write updated while the disk was running faster than normal. In such cases, this gap prevents accidental overwriting of any information in the next sector. The actual size of this padding varies, depending on the speed of disk rotation when the track was formatted and each time the Data field is updated.

The Pre-Index Gap allows for speed tolerance over the entire track. This gap varies in size, depending on the variances in disk-rotation speed and write-frequency tolerance at the time of formatting.

This sector prefix information is extremely important because it contains the numbering information that defines the cylinder, head, and sector. All this information except the Data field, Data CRC bytes, and Write Turn-Off Gap is written only during a low-level format. On a typical non-servo-guided (stepper-motor actuator) hard disk on which thermal gradients cause mistracking, the data updates that rewrite the 512-byte Data area and the CRC that follows may not be placed exactly in line with the sector header information. This situation eventually causes read or write failures of the `Abort, Retry, Fail, Ignore` variety. You can often correct this problem by redoing the Low-Level Formatting (LLF) of the disk; this process rewrites the header and data information together at the current track positions. Then, when you restore the data to the disk, the Data areas are written in alignment with the new sector headers.

Disk Formatting. You usually have two types of formats to consider:

- Physical, or *low-level*
- Logical, or *high-level*

When you format a floppy disk, the DOS FORMAT command performs both kinds of formats simultaneously. To format a hard disk, however, you must perform the operations separately. Moreover, a hard disk requires a third step, between the two formats, in which the partitioning information is written to the disk. *Partitioning* is required because a hard disk is designed to be used with more than one operating system. Separating the physical format in a way that is always the same, regardless of the operating system being used and regardless of the high-level format (which would be different for each operating system), makes possible the use of multiple operating systems on one hard drive. The partitioning step allows more than one type of operating system to use a single hard disk or a single DOS to use the disk as several volumes or logical drives. A *volume* or *logical drive* is anything to which DOS assigns a drive letter.

Consequently, formatting a hard disk involves three steps:

1. Low-Level Formatting (LLF)
2. Partitioning
3. High-Level Formatting (HLF)

During a low-level format, the disk's tracks are divided into a specific number of sectors. The sector header and trailer information is recorded, as are intersector and intertrack gaps. Each sector's data area is filled with a dummy byte value or test pattern of values. For floppy disks, the number of sectors recorded on each track depends on the type of disk and drive; for hard disks, the number of sectors per track depends on the drive and controller interface.

The original ST-506/412 MFM controllers always placed 17 sectors per track on a disk. ST-506/412 controllers with RLL encoding increase the number of sectors on a drive to 25 or 26 sectors per track. ESDI drives can have 32 or more sectors per track. IDE drives simply are drives with built-in controllers, and depending on exactly what type of controller design is built in, the number of sectors per track can range from 17 to 100 or more. SCSI drives essentially are IDE drives with an added SCSI Bus Adapter circuit, meaning that they also have some type of built-in controller; and like IDE drives, SCSI drives can have practically any number of sectors per track, depending on what controller design was used.

Virtually all IDE and SCSI drives use a technique called *Zoned Recording*, which writes a variable number of sectors per track. The outermost tracks hold more sectors than the inner tracks do because they are longer. Because of limitations in the PC BIOS, these drives still have to act as though they have a fixed number of sectors per track. This situation is handled by translation algorithms that are implemented in the controller.

Multiple Zone Recording. One way to increase the capacity of a hard drive is to format more sectors on the outer cylinders than on the inner ones. Because they have a larger circumference, the outer cylinders can hold more data. Drives without Zoned Recording store the same amount of data on every cylinder, even though the outer cylinders may be twice as long as the inner cylinders. The result is wasted storage capacity, because the disk media must be capable of storing data reliably at the same density as on the inner cylinders. With ST-506/412 and ESDI controllers, unfortunately, the number of sectors per track was fixed; drive capacity, therefore, was limited by the density capability of the innermost (shortest) track.

In a Zoned Recording, the cylinders are split into groups called *zones*, with each successive zone having more and more sectors per track as you move out from the inner radius of the disk. All the cylinders in a particular zone have the same number of sectors per track. The number of zones varies with specific drives, but most drives have 10 or more zones.

Another effect of Zoned Recording is that transfer speeds vary depending on what zone the heads are in. Because there are more sectors in the outer zones, but the rotational speed is always the same, the transfer rate will be highest.

Drives with separate controllers could not handle zoned recordings because there was no standard way to communicate information about the zones from the drive to the controller. With SCSI and IDE disks, it became possible to format individual tracks with different numbers of sectors, due to the fact that these drives have the disk controller built in. The built-in controllers on these drives can be made fully aware of the zoning that is used. These built-in controllers must then also translate the physical Cylinder, Head, and Sector numbers to logical Cylinder, Head, and Sector numbers so that the drive has the appearance of having the same number of sectors on each track. The PC BIOS was designed to only handle a single number of specific sectors per track throughout the entire drive, meaning that zoned drives always must run under a sector translation scheme.

The use of Zoned Recording has allowed drive manufacturers to increase the capacity of their hard drives by between 20 percent and 50 percent compared with a fixed-sector-per-track arrangement. Nearly all IDE and SCSI drives today use Zoned Recording.

Partitioning. Partitioning segments the drive into areas, called *partitions*, that can hold a particular operating system's file system. Today, PC operating systems use three common file systems:

- *FAT (File Allocation Table)*. This system is the standard file system used by DOS, OS/2, and Windows NT. FAT partitions support file names of 11 characters maximum (8 plus a 3-character extension), and a volume can be as large as 2G in size.
- *HPFS (High Performance File System)*. This UNIX-style file system is accessible only under OS/2 and Windows NT. DOS applications running under OS/2 or Windows NT can access files in HPFS partitions but straight DOS cannot. File names can be 256 characters long, and volume size is limited to 8G.

- *NTFS (Windows NT File System).* This UNIX-style file system currently is accessible only under Windows NT, but drivers should be available for OS/2 to access NTFS as well. DOS cannot access these partitions, but DOS applications running under Windows NT can. File names can be 256 characters long, and volume size is limited to 8G. NTFS capabilities may be added to Windows 95 in the future.

Of these three file systems, the FAT file system still is by far the most popular (and recommended). The main problem with the FAT file system is that disk space is used in groups of sectors called *allocation units* or *clusters.* On large volumes, the larger cluster sizes required cause disk space to be used inefficiently. HPFS and NTFS always manage the disk space in sector increments, so there is no penalty of wasted disk space with large volumes.

The term *cluster* was changed to *allocation unit* in DOS 4.0. The newer term is appropriate because a single cluster is the smallest unit of the disk that DOS can allocate when it writes a file. A cluster is equal to one or more sectors, and although a cluster can be a single sector in some cases (specifically 1.2M and 1.44M floppies), it is usually more than one. Having more than one sector per cluster reduces the size and processing overhead of the FAT and enables DOS to run faster because it has fewer individual units of the disk to manage. The tradeoff is in wasted disk space. Because DOS can manage space only in full cluster units, every file consumes space on the disk in increments of one cluster.

Smaller clusters generate less slack (space wasted between the actual end of each file and the end of the cluster). With larger clusters, the wasted space grows larger. For hard disks, the cluster size varies with the size of the partition. Table 14.6 shows the default cluster sizes DOS selects for a particular partition volume size.

Table 14.6 Default Cluster Sizes

Hard Disk Partition Size	Cluster (Allocation Unit) Size	FAT type
0 to less than 16M	8 sectors or 4,096 (4K) bytes	12-bit
16 through 128M	4 sectors or 2,048 (2K) bytes	16-bit
Over 128 through 256M	8 sectors or 4,096 (4K) bytes	16-bit
Over 256 through 512M	16 sectors or 8,192 (8K) bytes	16-bit
Over 512 through 1,024M	32 sectors or 16,384 (16K) bytes	16-bit
Over 1,024 through 2,048M	64 sectors or 32,768 (32K) bytes	16-bit

In most cases, these cluster sizes, which are selected by the DOS FORMAT command, are the minimum possible for a given partition size. Therefore, 8K clusters are the smallest possible for a partition size greater than 256M. Note that DOS creates a FAT using 12-bit numbers if the partition is 16M or less, while all other FATs are created using 16-bit numbers.

The effect of the larger cluster sizes on larger disk partitions can be substantial. A drive partition over 512M and up to 1G (16K clusters) containing about 5,000 files, with average slack of one-half of the last cluster used for each file (one-half of 16K), wastes about

40M [5000*(.5*16K)] of file space on a disk set up with IBM or MS-DOS. If you were to repartition the drive into two separate partitions of less than or equal to 512M each, then the cluster size would be cut in half, as would the total wasted slack space. After restoring your files, you would end up with approximately 20M more disk space free! The tradeoff is that managing multiple partitions is not as convenient as a single large partition. The only way you can control cluster or allocation unit sizing is by changing the sizes of the partitions.

Because the NTFS, HPFS, and the new FAT32 (32-bit FAT system) offer more allocation unit numbers, the allocation unit sizes are smaller, often a single sector. This dramatically reduces the slack space but increases file management overhead because many more allocation units must be managed.

Despite the problem with slack space, the FAT file system is the most recommended for compatibility reasons. For example, few applications currently are compatible with the longer file names possible in the HPFS and NTFS file systems. All the operating systems can access FAT volumes, and the file structures and data-recovery procedures are well known. Data recovery can be difficult to impossible under the HPFS and NTFS systems; for those systems, good backups are imperative.

During partitioning, no matter what file system is specified, the partitioning software writes a special boot program and partition table to the first sector, called the Master Boot Sector (MBS). Because the term *record* sometimes is used to mean *sector,* this sector can also be called the Master Boot Record (MBR).

High-Level Format. During the high-level format, the operating system (such as DOS, OS/2, or Windows NT) writes the structures necessary for managing files and data. FAT partitions have a Volume Boot Sector (VBS), a file allocation table (FAT), and a root directory on each formatted logical drive. These data structures (discussed in detail in Chapter 17, "CD-ROM Drives") enable the operating system to manage the space on the disk, keep track of files, and even manage defective areas so that they do not cause problems.

High-level formatting is not really formatting, but creating a table of contents for the disk. In low-level formatting, which is the real formatting, tracks and sectors are written on the disk. As mentioned, the DOS FORMAT command can perform both low-level and high-level format operations on a floppy disk, but it performs only the high-level format for a hard disk. Hard disk low-level formats require a special utility, usually supplied by the disk-controller manufacturer.

Basic Hard Disk Drive Components

Many types of hard disks are on the market, but nearly all drives share the same basic physical components. Some differences may exist in the implementation of these components (and in the quality of materials used to make them), but the operational characteristics of most drives are similar. Following are the components of a typical hard disk drive (see fig. 14.3):

- Disk platters
- Read/write heads
- Head actuator mechanism
- Spindle motor
- Logic board
- Cables and connectors
- Configuration items (such as jumpers or switches)
- Bezel (optional)

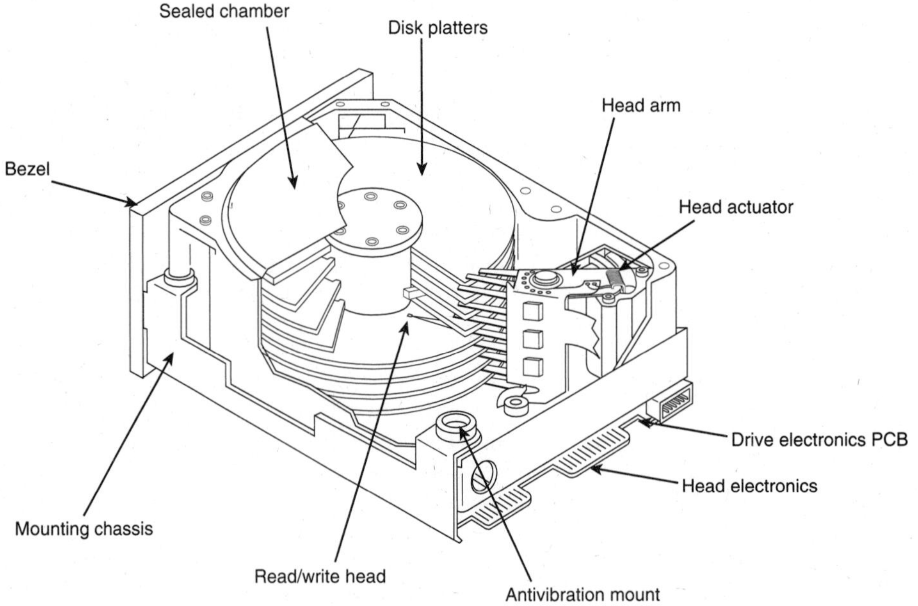

Figure 14.3
Hard disk drive components.

The platters, spindle motor, heads, and head actuator mechanisms usually are contained in a sealed chamber called the *Head Disk Assembly (HDA)*. The HDA usually is treated as a single component; it rarely is opened. Other parts external to the drive's HDA—such as the logic boards, bezel, and other configuration or mounting hardware—can be disassembled from the drive.

Hard Disk Platters (Disks)

A typical hard disk has one or more platters, or *disks*. Hard disks for PC systems have been available in a number of form factors over the years. Normally, the physical size of a drive is expressed as the size of the platters. Following are the most common platter sizes used in PC hard disks today:

- 5.25-inch (actually 130mm, or 5.12 inches)
- 3.5-inch (actually 95mm, or 3.74 inches)
- 2.5-inch
- 1.8-inch

Larger hard drives that have 8-inch, 14-inch, or even larger platters are available, but these drives typically have not been associated with PC systems. Currently, the 3.5-inch drives are the most popular for desktop and some portable systems, whereas the 2.5-inch and smaller drives are very popular in portable or notebook systems. These little drives are fairly amazing, with current capacities of up to 1G or more, and capacities of 20G are expected by the year 2000. Imagine carrying a notebook computer around with a built-in 20G drive—it will happen sooner than you think! Due to their small size, these drives are extremely rugged; they can withstand rough treatment that would have destroyed most desktop drives a few years ago.

I thought it was interesting to note that the 3.5-inch drives actually use platters that are 95mm or 3.74 inches in diameter, whereas the 5.25-inch drives' platters actually are 130mm or 5.12 inches in diameter. (This information could prove to be useful in your next computer trivia contest!)

Most hard drives have two or more platters, although some of the smaller drives have only one. The number of platters that a drive can have is limited by the drive's physical size vertically. So far, the maximum number of platters that I have seen in any 3.5-inch drive is 11.

Platters traditionally have been made from an aluminum alloy, for strength and light weight. With manufacturers' desire for higher and higher densities and smaller drives, many drives now use platters made of glass (or, more technically, a glass-ceramic composite). One such material is called MemCor, which is produced by the Dow Corning glass company. MemCor is composed of glass with ceramic implants, which resists cracking better than pure glass.

Glass platters offer greater rigidity and therefore can be machined to one-half the thickness of conventional aluminum disks, or less. Glass platters also are much more thermally stable than aluminum platters, which means that they do not change dimensions (expand or contract) very much with any changes in temperature. Several hard disks made by companies such as Seagate, Toshiba, Areal Technology, Maxtor, and Hewlett Packard currently use glass or glass-ceramic platters. For most manufacturers, glass disks will replace the standard aluminum substrate over the next few years, especially in high-performance 2.5- and 3.5-inch drives.

Recording Media

No matter what substrate is used, the platters are covered with a thin layer of a magnetically retentive substance called *media* in which magnetic information is stored. Two popular types of media are used on hard disk platters:

- Oxide media
- Thin-film media

Oxide media is made of various compounds, containing iron oxide as the active ingredient. A magnetic layer is created by coating the aluminum platter with a syrup containing iron-oxide particles. This media is spread across the disk by spinning the platters at high speed; centrifugal force causes the material to flow from the center of the platter to the outside, creating an even coating of media material on the platter. The surface then is cured and polished. Finally, a layer of material that protects and lubricates the surface is added and burnished smooth. The oxide media coating normally is about 30 millionths of an inch thick. If you could peer into a drive with oxide-media-coated platters, you would see that the platters are brownish or amber.

As drive density increases, the media needs to be thinner and more perfectly formed. The capabilities of oxide coatings have been exceeded by most higher-capacity drives. Because oxide media is very soft, disks that use this type of media are subject to head-crash damage if the drive is jolted during operation. Most older drives, especially those sold as low-end models, have oxide media on the drive platters. Oxide media, which has been used since 1955, remained popular because of its relatively low cost and ease of application. Today, however, very few drives use oxide media.

Thin-film media is thinner, harder, and more perfectly formed than oxide media. Thin film was developed as a high-performance media that enabled a new generation of drives to have lower head floating heights, which in turn made possible increases in drive density. Originally, thin-film media was used only in higher-capacity or higher-quality drive systems, but today, virtually all drives have thin-film media.

Thin-film media is aptly named. The coating is much thinner than can be achieved by the oxide-coating method. Thin-film media also is known as *plated*, or *sputtered*, media because of the various processes used to place the thin film of media on the platters.

Thin-film plated media is manufactured by placing the media material on the disk with an electroplating mechanism, much the way chrome plating is placed on the bumper of a car. The aluminum platter then is immersed in a series of chemical baths that coat the platter with several layers of metallic film. The media layer is a cobalt alloy about 3 micro-inches (millionths of an inch) thick.

Thin-film sputtered media is created by first coating the aluminum platters with a layer of nickel phosphorus and then applying the cobalt-alloy magnetic material in a continuous vacuum-deposition process called *sputtering*. During this process, magnetic layers as thin as 1 or 2 micro-inches are deposited on the disk, in a fashion similar to the way that silicon wafers are coated with metallic films in the semiconductor industry. The sputtering technique then is used again to lay down an extremely hard, 1 micro-inch protective carbon coating. The need for a near-perfect vacuum makes sputtering the most expensive of the processes described here.

The surface of a sputtered platter contains magnetic layers as thin as 1 millionth of an inch. Because this surface also is very smooth, the head can float closer to the disk surface than was possible previously; floating heights as small as 3 micro-inches above the surface are possible. When the head is closer to the platter, the density of the magnetic flux transitions can be increased to provide greater storage capacity. Additionally, the increased intensity of the magnetic field during a closer-proximity read provides the higher signal amplitudes needed for good signal-to-noise performance.

Both the sputtering and plating processes result in a very thin, very hard film of media on the platters. Because the thin-film media is so hard, it has a better chance of surviving contact with the heads at high speed. In fact, modern thin-film media is virtually uncrashable. Oxide coatings can be scratched or damaged much more easily. If you could open a drive to peek at the platters, you would see that the thin-film media platters look like the silver surfaces of mirrors.

The sputtering process results in the most perfect, thinnest, and hardest disk surface that can be produced commercially. The sputtering process has largely replaced plating as the method of creating thin-film media. Having a thin-film media surface on a drive results in increased storage capacity in a smaller area with fewer head crashes—and in a drive that will provide many years of trouble-free use.

Read/Write Heads

A hard disk drive usually has one read/write head for each platter side, and these heads are connected, or *ganged*, on a single movement mechanism. The heads, therefore, move across the platters in unison.

Mechanically, read/write heads are simple. Each head is on an actuator arm that is spring-loaded to force the head into a platter. Few people realize that each platter actually is "squeezed" by the heads above and below it. If you could open a drive safely and lift the top head with your finger, the head would snap back into the platter when you released it. If you could pull down on one of the heads below a platter, the spring tension would cause it to snap back up into the platter when you released it.

Figure 14.4 shows a typical hard disk head-actuator assembly from a voice coil drive.

When the drive is at rest, the heads are forced into direct contact with the platters by spring tension, but when the drive is spinning at full speed, air pressure develops below the heads and lifts them off the surface of the platter. On a drive spinning at full speed, the distance between the heads and the platter can be anywhere from 3 to 20 or more micro-inches (millionths of an inch).

In the early 1960s, hard disk drive recording heads operated at floating heights as large as 200 to 300 micro-inches; today's drive heads are designed to float as low as 3 to 5 micro-inches above the surface of the disk. To support higher densities in future drives, the physical separation between the head and disk is expected to be as little as 0.5 micro-inch by the end of the century.

Generally speaking, the older the drive and lower its capacity, the higher the heads float above the media. The small size of this gap is why the disk drive's Head Disk Assembly (HDA) should never be opened except in a clean-room environment: any particle of dust or dirt that gets into this mechanism could cause the heads to read improperly, or possibly even to strike the platters while the drive is running at full speed. The latter event could scratch the platter or the head.

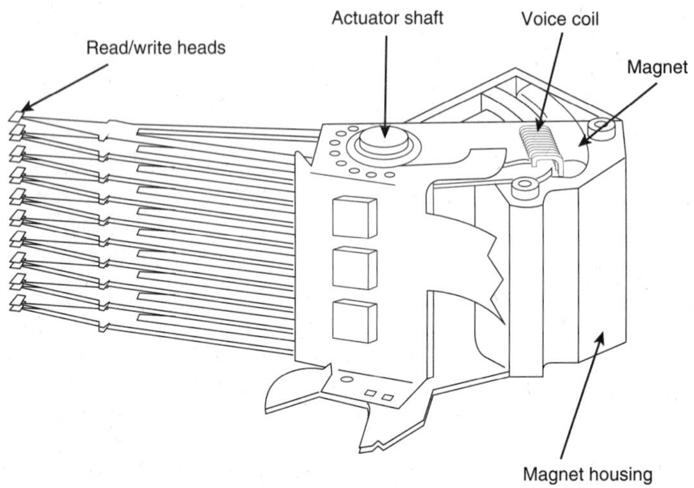

Figure 14.4

Read/write heads and rotary voice coil actuator assembly.

To ensure the cleanliness of the interior of the drive, the HDA is assembled in a class-100 or better clean room. This specification is such that a cubic foot of air cannot contain more than 100 particles that measure up to 0.5 micron (19.7 micro-inch). A single person breathing while standing motionless spews out 500 such particles in a single minute! These rooms contain special air-filtration systems that continuously evacuate and refresh the air. A drive's HDA should not be opened unless it is inside such a room.

Although maintaining such an environment may seem to be expensive, many companies manufacture tabletop or bench-size clean rooms that sell for only a few thousand dollars. Some of these devices operate like a glove box; the operator first inserts the drive and any tools required, and then closes the box and turns on the filtration system. Inside the box, a clean-room environment is maintained, and a technician can use the built-in gloves to work on the drive.

In other clean-room variations, the operator stands at a bench where a forced-air curtain is used to maintain a clean environment on the bench top. The technician can walk in and out of the clean-room field simply by walking through the air curtain. This air curtain is much like the curtain of air used in some stores and warehouses to prevent heat from escaping in the winter while leaving a passage wide open.

Because the clean environment is expensive to produce, few companies except those that manufacture the drives are prepared to service hard disk drives.

Read/Write Head Designs

As disk drive technology has evolved, so has the design of the Read/Write head. The earliest heads were simple iron cores with coil windings (electromagnets). By today's standards, the original head designs were enormous in physical size and operated at very low recording densities. Over the years many different head designs have evolved from the first simple Ferrite Core designs into several types and technologies available today.

This section discusses the different types of heads found in PC type hard disk drives, including the applications and relative strengths and weaknesses of each.

Four types of heads have been used in hard disk drives over the years:

- Ferrite
- Metal-In-Gap (MIG)
- Thin Film (TF)
- Magneto-Resistive (MR)

Ferrite. *Ferrite heads*, the traditional type of magnetic-head design, evolved from the original IBM Winchester drive. These heads have an iron-oxide core wrapped with electromagnetic coils. A magnetic field is produced by energizing the coils; a field also can be induced by passing a magnetic field near the coils. This process gives the heads full read and write capability. Ferrite heads are larger and heavier than thin-film heads and therefore require a larger floating height to prevent contact with the disk.

Many refinements have been made in the original (monolithic) ferrite head design. A type of ferrite head called a *composite ferrite head* has a smaller ferrite core bonded with glass in a ceramic housing. This design permits a smaller head gap, which allows higher track densities. These heads are less susceptible to stray magnetic fields than are heads in the older monolithic design.

During the 1980s, composite ferrite heads were popular in many low-end drives, such as the popular Seagate ST-225. As density demands grew, the competing MIG and thin-film head designs were used in place of ferrite heads, which are virtually obsolete today. Ferrite heads cannot write to the higher coercivity media needed for high-density designs and have poor frequency response with higher noise levels. The main advantage of ferrite heads is that they are the cheapest type available.

Metal-In-Gap. *Metal-In-Gap (MIG) heads* basically are a specially enhanced version of the composite ferrite design. In MIG heads, a metal substance is sputtered into the recording gap on the trailing edge of the head. This material offers increased resistance to magnetic saturation, allowing higher-density recording. MIG heads also produce a sharper gradient in the magnetic field for a better-defined magnetic pulse. These heads permit the use of higher-coercivity thin-film disks and can operate at lower floating heights.

Two versions of MIG heads are available—single-sided and double-sided. Single-sided MIG heads are designed with a layer of magnetic alloy placed along the trailing edge of the gap. Double-sided MIG designs apply the layer to both sides of the gap. The metal alloy is applied through a vacuum-deposition process called *sputtering*. This alloy has twice the magnetization capability of raw ferrite and allows writing to the higher-coercivity thin-film media needed at the higher densities. Double-sided MIG heads offer even higher coercivity capability than the single-sided designs do.

Because of these increases in capabilities through improved designs, MIG heads for a time were the most popular head used in all but very high-capacity drives. Due to market pressures that have demanded higher and higher densities, however, MIG heads have been largely displaced in favor of Thin Film heads.

Thin Film. *Thin Film (TF) heads* are produced in much the same manner as a semiconductor chip—that is, through a photolithographic process. In this manner, many thousands of heads can be created on a single circular wafer. This manufacturing process also results in a very small high-quality product.

TF heads offer an extremely narrow and controlled head gap created by sputtering a hard aluminum material. Because this material completely encloses the gap, this area is very well protected, minimizing the chance of damage from contact with the media. The core is a combination of iron and nickel alloy that is two to four times more powerful magnetically than a ferrite head core.

Thin Film heads produce a sharply defined magnetic pulse that allows extremely high densities to be written. Because they do not have a conventional coil, TF heads are more immune to variations in coil impedance. The small, lightweight heads can float at a much lower height than the ferrite and MIG heads; floating height has been reduced to 2 micro-inches or less in some designs. Because the reduced height enables a much stronger signal to be picked up and transmitted between the head and platters, the signal-to-noise ratio increases, which improves accuracy. At the high track and linear densities of some drives, a standard ferrite head would not be able to pick out the data signal from the background noise. When Thin Film heads are used, their small size enables more platters to be stacked in a drive.

Until the past few years, TF heads were relatively expensive compared with older technologies, such as ferrite and MIG. Better manufacturing techniques and the need for higher densities, however, have driven the market to TF heads. The widespread use of these heads also has made them cost-competitive, if not cheaper than MIG heads.

Thin Film heads currently are used in most high-capacity drives, especially in the smaller form factors. They have displaced MIG heads as the most popular head design being used in drives today. The industry is working on ways to improve TF head efficiency, so Thin Film heads are likely to remain popular for some time, especially in mainstream drives.

Magneto-Resistive. *Magneto-Resistive (MR) heads* are a relatively new technology. Invented and pioneered by IBM, Magneto-Resistive heads currently are the superior head design, offering the highest performance available. Most 3.5-inch drives with capacities in excess of 1GB currently use MR heads. As areal densities continue to increase, the MR head eventually will become the head of choice for nearly all hard drives, displacing the popular MIG and TF head designs.

MR heads rely on the fact that the resistance of a conductor changes slightly when an external magnetic field is present. Rather than put out a voltage by passing through a magnetic-field flux reversal, as a normal head would, the MR head senses the flux reversal and changes resistance. A small current flows through the heads, and the change in resistance is measured by this sense current. This design enables the output to be three or more times more powerful than a Thin Film head during a read. In effect, MR heads are power-read heads, acting more like sensors than generators.

MR heads are more costly and complex to manufacture than other types of heads, because several special features or steps must be added. Among them:

- Additional wires must be run to and from the head to carry the sense current.
- Four to six more masking steps are required.
- Because MR heads are so sensitive, they are very susceptible to stray magnetic fields and must be shielded.

Because the MR principle can only read data and is not used for writing, MR heads really are two heads in one. A standard inductive Thin Film head is used for writing, and a Magneto-Resistive head is used for reading. Because two separate heads are built into one assembly, each head can be optimized for its task. Ferrite, MIG, and Thin Film heads are known as *single-gap heads* because the same gap is used for both reading and writing, whereas the MR head uses a separate gap for each operation.

The problem with single-gap heads is that the gap length always is a compromise between what is best for reading and what is best for writing. The read function needs a thin gap for higher resolution; the write function needs a thicker gap for deeper flux penetration to switch the media. In a dual-gap MR head, the read and write gaps can be optimized for both functions independently. The write (Thin Film) gap writes a wider track than the read (Magneto-Resistive) gap does. The read head then is less likely to pick up stray magnetic information from adjacent tracks.

Although MR heads have many good qualities, they do have some disadvantages. The primary disadvantage is cost. The cost actually is not too limiting, because these heads are primarily used in extremely high-capacity drives, for which cost is not as much of a concern. Another disadvantage is that MR heads are much more delicate than the other head designs. Handling MR heads during manufacturing requires more care due to their greater sensitivity to damage by ESD (Electro-Static Discharge). Finally, drives with MR heads require better shielding from stray magnetic fields, which can affect these heads more easily than they do the other head designs. All in all, however, the drawbacks are minor compared with the advantages that the MR heads offer.

Head Sliders

The term *slider* is used to describe the body of material that supports the actual drive head itself. The slider is what actually floats or slides over the surface of the disk, carrying the head at the correct distance from the media for reading and writing. Most sliders resemble a catamaran with two outboard pods that float along the surface of the disk media and a central "rudder" portion that actually carries the head and read/write gap.

The trend toward smaller and smaller form factor drives has forced a requirement for smaller and smaller sliders as well. The typical mini-Winchester slider design is about .160×.126×.034 inch in size. Most head manufacturers now are shifting to 50 percent smaller nanosliders, which have dimensions of about .08×.063×.017 inch. The nanoslider is being used in both high-capacity and small-form-factor drives. Smaller sliders reduce the mass carried at the end of the head actuator arms, allowing for increased acceleration and deceleration, and leading to faster seek times. The smaller sliders also require less area for a landing zone, thus increasing the usable area of the disk platters. Further, the smaller slider contact area reduces the slight wear on the media surface that occurs during normal startup and spindown of the drive platters.

The newer nanoslider designs also have specially modified surface patterns that are designed to maintain the same floating height above the disk surface whether the slider is above the inner or outer cylinders. Conventional sliders increase or decrease their floating height considerably, according to the velocity of the disk surface traveling below them. Above the outer cylinders, the velocity and floating height are higher. This arrangement is undesirable in newer drives that use Zoned Recording, in which the same bit density is achieved on all the cylinders. Because the same bit density is maintained throughout the drive, the head floating height should be relatively constant as well for maximum performance. Special textured surface patterns and manufacturing techniques allow the nanosliders to float at a much more consistent height, making them ideal for Zoned Recording drives.

Head Actuator Mechanisms

Possibly more important than the heads themselves is the mechanical system that moves them: the *head actuator*. This mechanism moves the heads across the disk and positions them accurately above the desired cylinder. Many variations on head actuator mechanisms are in use, but all of them can be categorized as being one of two basic types:

- Stepper motor actuators
- Voice coil actuators

The use of one or the other type of positioner has profound effects on a drive's performance and reliability. The effect is not limited to speed; it also includes accuracy, sensitivity to temperature, position, vibration, and overall reliability. To put it bluntly, a drive equipped with a stepper motor actuator is much less reliable (by a large factor) than a drive equipped with a voice coil actuator.

The head actuator is the single most important specification in the drive. The type of head actuator mechanism in a drive tells you a great deal about the drive's performance and reliability characteristics. Table 14.7 shows the two types of hard disk drive head actuators and the affected performance parameters.

Table 14.7 Characteristics of Stepper Motor versus Voice Coil Drives

Characteristic	Stepper Motor	Voice Coil
Relative access speed	Slow	Fast
Temperature sensitive	Yes (very)	No
Positionally sensitive	Yes	No
Automatic head parking	Not usually	Yes
Preventive maintenance	Periodic format	None required
Relative reliability	Poor	Excellent

Generally, a stepper motor drive has a slow average access rating, is temperature-sensitive during read and write operations, is sensitive to physical orientation during read and write operations, does not automatically park its heads above a save zone during power-down, and usually requires annual or biannual reformats to realign the sector data with the sector header information due to mistracking. Overall, stepper motor drives are vastly inferior to drives that use voice coil actuators.

Some stepper motor drives feature automatic head parking at power-down. If you have a newer stepper motor drive, refer to the drive's technical reference manual to determine whether your drive has this feature. (Other than removing the lid and watching as you power-off—which is definitely not recommended—reading the documentation is the only reliable way to tell.) Sometimes, you hear a noise after power-down, but that can be deceptive; some drives use a solenoid-activated spindle brake, which makes a noise as the drive is powered off and does not involve head parking.

Floppy disk drives position their heads by using a stepper motor actuator. The accuracy of the stepper mechanism is suited to a floppy drive because the track densities usually are nowhere near those of a hard disk. Many of the less expensive, low-capacity hard disks also use a stepper motor system. Most hard disks with capacities of more than 40MB have voice coil actuators, as do all drives I have seen that have capacities of more than 100MB, which means all drives being manufactured today.

This breakdown does not necessarily apply to other system manufacturers, but it is safe to say that hard disk drives with less than 80MB capacity may have either type of actuator and that virtually all drives with more than 80MB capacity have voice coil actuators. The cost difference between voice coil drives and stepper motor drives of equal capacity is marginal today, so there is little reason not to use a voice coil drive. No new stepper motor drives are being manufactured today.

Stepper Motor. A *stepper motor* is an electrical motor that can "step," or move from position to position, with mechanical detents or click stop positions. If you were to grip the spindle of one of these motors and spin it by hand, you would hear a clicking or buzzing sound as the motor passed each detent position with a soft click. The sensation is much like that of the volume control on some stereo systems which use a detented type control instead of something smooth and purely linear.

Stepper motors cannot position themselves between step positions; they can stop only at the predetermined detent positions. The motors are small (between one and three inches) and can be square, cylindrical, or flat. Stepper motors are outside the sealed HDA, although the spindle of the motor penetrates the HDA through a sealed hole. The stepper motor is located in one of the corners of the hard disk drive and usually is easy to see.

Mechanical Links. The stepper motor is mechanically linked to the head rack by a split-steel band coiled around the motor spindle or by a rack-and-pinion gear mechanism. As the motor steps, each detent, or click-stop position, represents the movement of one track through the mechanical linkage.

Some systems use several motor steps for each track. In positioning the heads, if the drive is told to move from track 0 to 100, the motor begins the stepping motion, proceeds to the 101st detent position, and stops, leaving the heads above the desired cylinder. The fatal flaw in this type of positioning system is that due to dimensional changes in the platter-to-head relationship over the life of a drive, the heads may not be precisely placed above the cylinder location. This type of positioning system is called a *blind system,* because the heads have no true way of determining the exact placement of a given cylinder.

The most widely used stepper motor actuator systems use a *split-metal-band mechanism* to transmit the rotary stepping motion to the in-and-out motion of the head rack. The band is made of special alloys to limit thermal expansion and contraction as well as stretching of the thin band. One end of the band is coiled around the spindle of the stepper motor; the other is connected directly to the head rack. The band is inside the sealed HDA and is not visible from outside the drive.

Some drives use a *rack-and-pinion gear mechanism* to link the stepper motor to the head rack. This procedure involves a small pinion gear on the spindle of the stepper motor that moves a rack gear in and out. The rack gear is connected to the head rack, causing it to move. The rack-and-pinion mechanism is more durable than the split-metal-band mechanism and provides slightly greater physical and thermal stability. One problem, however, is *backlash*: the amount of play in the gears. Backlash increases as the gears wear and eventually renders the mechanism useless.

Temperature Fluctuation Problems. Stepper motor mechanisms are affected by a variety of problems. The greatest problem is temperature. As the drive platters heat and cool, they expand and contract, respectively; the tracks then move in relation to a predetermined track position. The stepper mechanism does not allow the mechanism to move in increments of less than a single track to correct for these temperature-induced errors. The drive positions the heads to a particular cylinder according to a predetermined number of steps from the stepper motor, with no room for nuance.

The low-level formatting of the drive places the initial track and sector marks on the platters at the positions where the heads currently are located, as commanded by the stepper motor. If all subsequent reading and writing occur at the same temperature as during the initial format, the heads always record precisely within the track and sector boundaries.

At different temperatures, however, the head position does not match the track position. When the platters are cold, the heads miss the track location because the platters have shrunk and the tracks have moved toward the center of the disk. When the platters are warmer than the formatted temperature, the platters will have grown larger and the track positions are located outward. Gradually, as the drive is used, the data is written inside, on top of, and outside the track and sector marks. Eventually, the drive fails to read one of these locations, and a DOS `Abort, Retry, Ignore` error message usually appears.

The temperature sensitivity of stepper motor drives also may cause the "Monday morning blues." When the system is powered up cold (on Monday, for example), a 1701, 1790, or 10490 Power-On Self Test (POST) error occurs. If you leave the system on for about 15 minutes, the drive can come up to operating temperature, and the system then may boot normally. This problem sometimes occurs in reverse when the drive gets particularly warm, such as when a system is in direct sunlight or during the afternoon, when room temperature is highest. In that case, the symptom is a DOS error message with the familiar `Abort, Retry, Ignore` prompt.

Temperature-induced mistracking problems can be solved by reformatting the drive and restoring the data. Then the information is placed on the drive at the current head positions for each cylinder. Over time, the mistracking recurs, necessitating another reformat-and-restore operation, which is a form of periodic preventive maintenance for stepper motor drives. An acceptable interval for this maintenance is once a year (or perhaps twice a year, if the drive is extremely temperature-sensitive).

Reformatting a hard drive, because it requires a complete backup-and-restore operation, is inconvenient and time-consuming. To help with these periodic reformats, most low-level-format programs offer a special reformat option that copies the data for a specific track to a spare location, reformats the track, and then copies the data back to the original track. When this type of format operation is finished, you don't have to restore your data, because the program took care of that chore for you one track at a time.

Caution

Never use a so-called nondestructive format program without first making a complete backup. This type of program does wipe out the data as it operates. "Destructive-reconstructive" more accurately describes its operation. If a problem occurs with the power, the system, or the program (maybe a bug that stops the program from finishing), all the data will not be restored properly, and some tracks may be wiped clean. Although such programs save you from having to restore data manually when the format is complete, they do not remove your obligation to perform a backup first.

Beware of programs whose advertising is filled with marketing hype and miracle claims for making a hard disk "better than new." One company even boasted in its advertisements that by using its program, you will "never have any problems" with your hard disk—an outrageous claim indeed! What the ads don't say is that any real low-level-format program performs these same feats of "magic" without the misleading or exaggerated claims and unnecessary hype. Many of these nondestructive formatters really cannot format a large number of drives that are available today. Also, you should note that annual or biannual formatting is not necessary with voice coil actuator drives, because they do not exhibit these types of mistracking errors.

Voice Coil. A *voice coil actuator* is found in all higher-quality hard disk drives, including most drives with capacities greater than 40MB and virtually all drives with capacities exceeding 80MB. Unlike the blind stepper motor positioning system, a voice coil actuator uses a feedback signal from the drive to accurately determine the head positions and to adjust them, if necessary. This system allows for significantly greater performance, accuracy, and reliability than traditional stepper motor actuators offered.

A voice coil actuator works by pure electromagnetic force. The construction of this mechanism is similar to that of a typical audio speaker, from which the term *voice coil* is derived. An audio speaker uses a stationary magnet surrounded by a voice coil connected to the speaker's paper cone. Energizing the coil causes the coil to move relative to the stationary magnet, which produces sound from the speaker cone. In a typical hard disk voice coil system, the electromagnetic coil is attached to the end of the head rack and placed near a stationary magnet. No contact is made between the coil and the magnet; instead, the coil moves by pure magnetic force. As the electromagnetic coils are energized, they attract or repulse the stationary magnet and move the head rack. Such systems are extremely quick and efficient and usually much quieter than systems driven by stepper motors.

Unlike a stepper motor, a voice coil actuator has no click-stops, or detent positions; rather, a special guidance system stops the head rack above a particular cylinder. Because it has no detents, the voice coil actuator can slide the heads in and out smoothly to any position desired, much like the slide of a trombone. Voice coil actuators use a guidance mechanism called a *servo* to tell the actuator where the heads are in relation to the cylinders and to place the heads accurately at the desired positions. This positioning system often is called a *closed loop, servo-controlled mechanism. Closed loop* indicates that the index (or servo) signal is sent to the positioning electronics in a closed-loop system. This loop sometimes is called a *feedback loop,* because the feedback from this information is used to position the heads accurately. *Servo-controlled* refers to this index or the servo information that is used to dictate or control head-positioning accuracy.

A voice coil actuator with servo control is not affected by temperature changes, as a stepper motor is. When the temperature is cold and the platters have shrunk (or when the temperature is hot and the platters have expanded), the voice coil system compensates because it never positions the heads in predetermined track positions. Rather, the voice coil system searches for the specific track, guided by the prewritten servo information, and can position the head rack precisely above the desired track at that track's current position, regardless of the temperature. Because of the continuous feedback of servo information, the heads adjust to the current position of the track at all times. For example, as a drive warms up and the platters expand, the servo information allows the heads to "follow" the track. As a result, a voice coil actuator often is called a *track following system.*

Two main types of voice-coil positioner mechanisms are available:

- Linear voice-coil actuators
- Rotary voice-coil actuators

The types differ only in the physical arrangement of the magnets and coils.

A *linear actuator* (see fig. 14.5) moves the heads in and out over the platters in a straight line, much like a tangential-tracking turntable. The coil moves in and out on a track surrounded by the stationary magnets. The primary advantage of the linear design is that it eliminates the head azimuth variations that occur with rotary positioning systems.

(*Azimuth* refers to the angular measurement of the head position relative to the tangent of a given cylinder.) A linear actuator does not rotate the head as it moves from one cylinder to another, thus eliminating this problem.

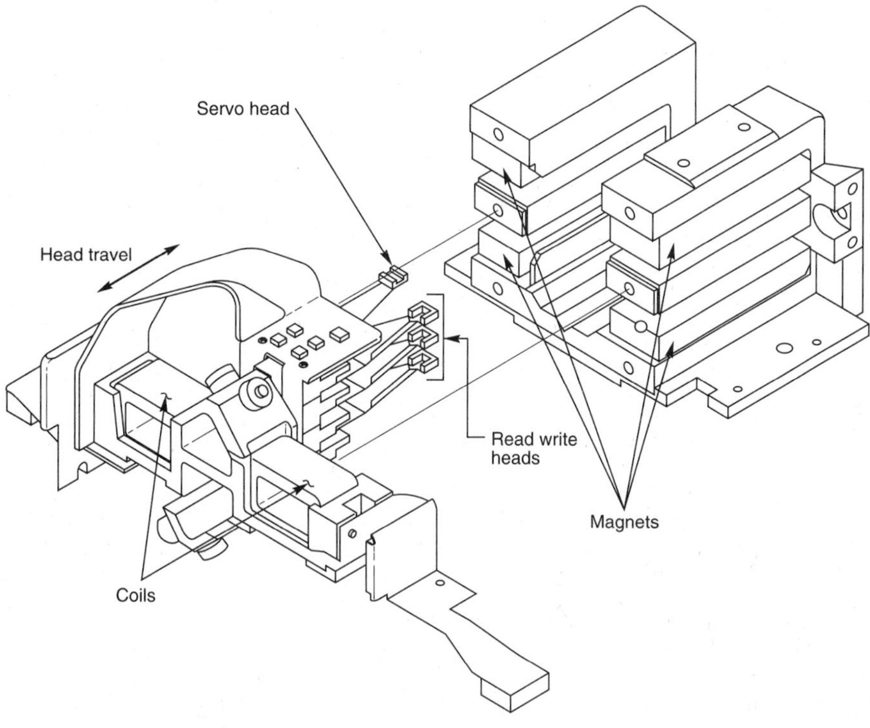

Figure 14.5
A linear voice coil actuator.

Although the linear actuator seems to be a good design, it has one fatal flaw—the devices are much too heavy. As drive performance has increased, the desire for lightweight actuator mechanisms has become very important. The lighter the mechanism, the faster it can be accelerated and decelerated from one cylinder to another. Because they are much heavier than rotary actuators, linear actuators were popular only for a short time; they are virtually nonexistent in drives manufactured today.

Rotary actuators (refer to fig. 14.4) also use stationary magnets and a movable coil, but the coil is attached to the end of an actuator arm, much like that of a turntable's tone arm. As the coil is forced to move relative to the stationary magnet, it swings the head arms in and out over the surface of the disk. The primary advantage of this mechanism is light weight, which means that the heads can be accelerated and decelerated very quickly, resulting in very fast average seek times. Because of the lever effect on the head arm, the heads move faster than the actuator, which also helps to improve access times.

The disadvantage with a rotary system is that as the heads move from the outer to inner cylinders, they are rotated slightly with respect to the tangent of the cylinders. This rotation results in an azimuth error and is one reason why the area of the platter in which the cylinders are located is somewhat limited. By limiting the total motion of the actuator, the azimuth error can be contained to within reasonable specifications. Virtually all voice coil drives today use rotary actuator systems.

Servo Mechanisms. Three servo mechanism designs have been used to control voice coil positioners over the years:

- Wedge servo
- Embedded servo
- Dedicated servo

These designs are slightly different, but they accomplish the same basic task—they enable the head positioner to adjust continuously so that it is precisely placed above a given cylinder in the drive. The main difference among these servo designs is where the gray code information is actually written on the drive.

All servo mechanisms rely on special information that is only written to the disk when the disk is manufactured. This information usually is in the form of a special code called a *Gray code*. A gray code is a special binary notational system in which any two adjacent numbers are represented by a code that differs in only one bit place or column position. This system makes it easy for the head to read the information and quickly determine its precise position. This guidance code can be written only when the drive is manufactured; the code is used over the life of the drive for accurate positional information.

The servo gray code is written at the time of manufacture by a special machine called a *servowriter*: basically, a jig that mechanically moves the heads to a given reference position and then writes the servo information for that position. Many servowriters are themselves guided by a laser-beam reference that calculates its own position by calculating distances in wavelengths of light. Because the servowriter must be capable of moving the heads mechanically, this process is done with the lid of the drive off or through special access ports on the HDA. After the servowriting is complete, these ports usually are covered with sealing tape. You often see these tape-covered holes on the HDA, usually accompanied by warnings that you will void the warranty if you remove the tape. Because servowriting exposes the interior of the drive, it must be done in a clean-room environment.

A servowriter is an expensive piece of machinery, costing up to $50,000 or more, and often must be custom-made for a particular make or model of drive. Some drive-repair companies have *servowriting capability*, which means that they can rewrite the servo information on a drive if it becomes damaged. Lacking a servowriter, a drive with servo-code damage must be sent back to the drive manufacturer for the servo information to be rewritten.

Fortunately, it is impossible to damage the servo information through any normal reading and writing to a hard disk. Drives are designed so that servo information cannot be overwritten, even during low-level formatting of a drive. One myth that has been circulating (especially with respect to IDE drives) is that you can damage the servo information by improper low-level formatting. This is not true. An improper low-level format may compromise the performance of the drive, but the servo information is totally protected and cannot be overwritten.

The track-following capabilities of a servo-controlled voice coil actuator eliminates the positioning errors that occur over time with stepper motor drives. Voice coil drives simply are not affected by conditions such as thermal expansion and contraction of the platters. In fact, many voice coil drives today perform a special thermal-recalibration procedure at predetermined intervals while they run. This procedure usually involves seeking the heads from cylinder 0 to some other cylinder one time for every head on the drive. As this sequence occurs, the control circuitry in the drive monitors how much the track positions have moved since the last time the sequence was performed, and a thermal calibration adjustment is calculated and stored in the drive's memory. This information then is used every time the drive positions to ensure the most accurate positioning possible.

Most drives perform the thermal-recalibration sequence every five minutes for the first half-hour that the drive is powered on and then once every 25 minutes after that. With some drives (such as Quantum, for example), this thermal-calibration sequence is very noticeable; the drive essentially stops what it is doing, and you hear rapid ticking for a second or so. At this time, some people think that their drive is having a problem reading something and perhaps is conducting a read retry, but this is not true. Most of the newer intelligent drives (IDE and SCSI) employ this thermal-recalibration procedure for ultimate positioning accuracy.

As multimedia applications grew, thermal recalibration became a problem with some manufacturer's drives. The thermal recalibration sequence could interrupt a data transfer, which would make audio and video playback jitter. These companies released special A/V (Audio Visual) drives that would hide the thermal recalibration sequences and not let them ever interrupt a transfer. Most of the newer IDE and SCSI drives are A/V capable, which means the thermal recalibration sequences will not interrupt a transfer such as a video playback.

While we are on the subject of automatic drive functions, most of the drives that perform thermal-recalibration sequences also automatically perform a function called a *disk sweep*. This procedure is an automatic head seek that occurs after the drive has been idle for a period of time (for example, nine minutes). The disk-sweep function moves the heads to a random cylinder in the outer portion of the platters, which is considered to be the high float-height area because the head-to-platter velocity is highest. Then, if the drive continues to remain idle for another period, the heads move to another cylinder in this area, and the process continues indefinitely as long as the drive is powered on.

The disk-sweep function is designed to prevent the head from remaining stationary above one cylinder in the drive, where friction between the head and platter eventually would dig a trench in the media. Although the heads are not in direct contact with the media, they are so close that the constant air pressure from the head floating above a single cylinder causes friction and excessive wear.

Wedge Servo. Some early servo-controlled drives used a technique called a *wedge servo*. In these drives, the gray-code guidance information is contained in a "wedge" slice of the drive in each cylinder immediately preceding the index mark. The index mark indicates the beginning of each track, so the wedge-servo information was written in the Pre-Index Gap, which is at the end of each track. This area is provided for speed tolerance and normally is not used by the controller. Figure 14.6 shows the servo-wedge information on a drive.

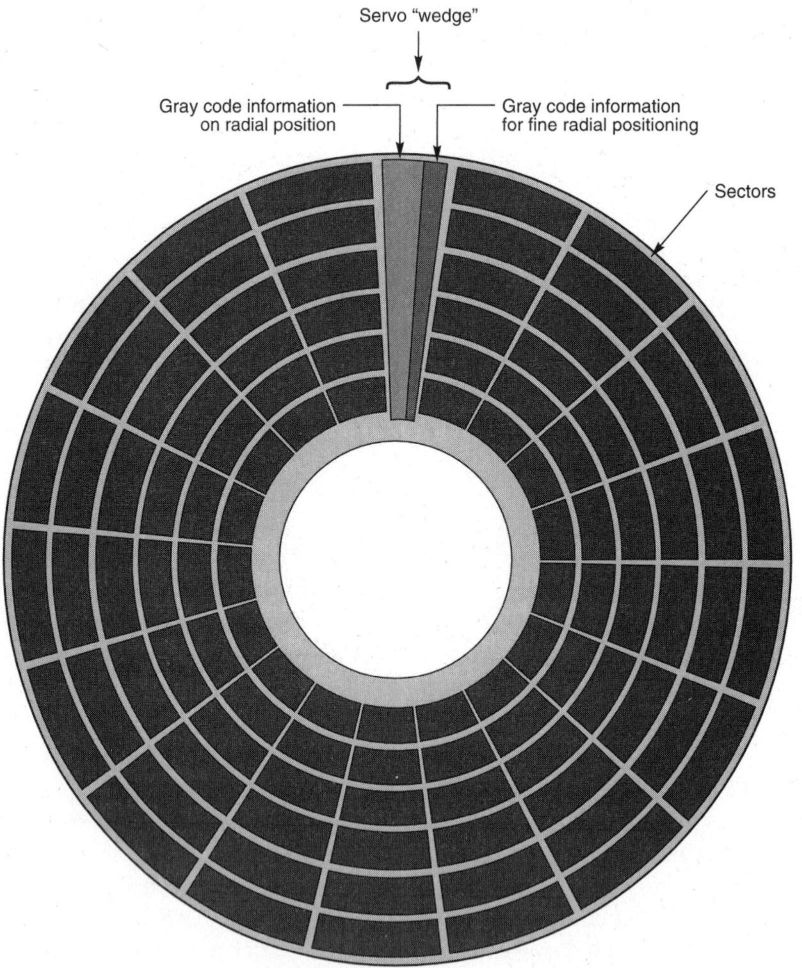

Figure 14.6

A wedge servo.

Some controllers, such as the Xebec 1210 that IBM used in the XT, had to be notified that the drive was using a wedge servo so that they could shorten the sector timing to allow for the wedge-servo area. If they were not correctly configured, these controllers would not work properly with such drives. Many people believed—erroneously—that the wedge-servo information could be overwritten in such cases by an improper low-level format. This is not the case, however; all drives using a wedge servo disable any write commands and take control of the head select lines whenever the heads are above the wedge area. This procedure protects the servo from any possibility of being overwritten, no matter how hard you try. If the controller tried to write over this area, the drive would prevent the write, and the controller would be unable to complete the format. Most controllers simply do not write to the Pre-Index Gap area and do not need to be configured specially for wedge-servo drives.

The only way that the servo information normally could be damaged is by a powerful external magnetic field (or perhaps by a head crash or some other catastrophe). In such a case, the drive would have to be sent in for repair and re-servoing.

One problem is that the servo information appears only one time every revolution, which means that the drive often needs several revolutions before it can accurately determine and adjust the head position. Because of these problems, the wedge servo never was a popular design; it no longer is used in drives.

Embedded Servo. An *embedded servo* (see fig. 14.7) is an enhancement of the wedge servo. Instead of placing the servo code before the beginning of each cylinder, an embedded servo design writes the servo information before the start of each sector. This arrangement enables the positioner circuits to receive feedback many times in a single revolution, making the head positioning much faster and more precise. Another advantage is that every track on the drive has this positioning information, so each head can quickly and efficiently adjust position to compensate for any changes in the platter or head dimensions, especially for changes due to thermal expansion or physical stress.

Most drives today use an embedded servo to control the positioning system. As in the wedge servo design, the embedded-servo information is protected by the drive circuits, and any write operations are blocked whenever the heads are above the servo information. Thus, it is impossible to overwrite the servo information with a low-level format, as many people incorrectly believed.

Although the embedded servo works much better than the wedge servo, because the feedback servo information is available several times in a single disk revolution, a system that offered continuous servo feedback information would be better.

Dedicated Servo. A *dedicated servo* is a design in which the servo information is written continuously throughout the entire track, rather than just one time per track or at the beginning of each sector. Unfortunately, if this procedure were performed on the entire drive, no room would be left for data. For this reason, a dedicated servo uses one side of one of the platters exclusively for the servo-positioning information. The term *dedicated* comes from the fact that this platter side is completely dedicated to the servo information and cannot contain any data. Although the dedicated-servo design may seem to be wasteful, none of the other platter sides carry any servo information, and you end up losing about the same amount of total disk real estate as with the embedded servo.

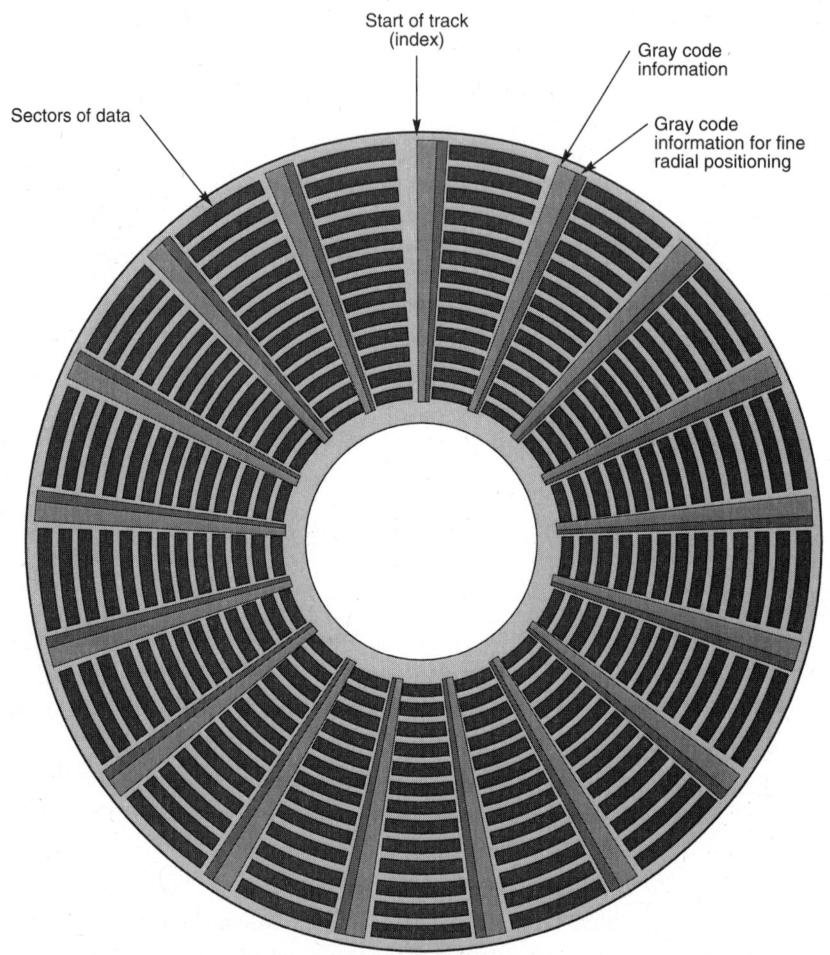

Figure 14.7
An embedded servo.

When a dedicated-servo drive is manufactured, one side of one platter is deducted from normal read/write usage; on this platter is recorded a special set of gray-code data that indicates proper track positions. Because the head that rests above this surface cannot be used for normal reading and writing, these marks can never be erased, and the servo information is protected, as in the other servo designs. No low-level format or other procedure can possibly overwrite the servo information.

When the drive is commanded to move the heads to a specific cylinder, the internal drive electronics use the signals received by the servo head to determine the position of the heads. As the heads are moved, the track counters are read from the dedicated servo surface. When the requested track is detected below the servo head, the actuator is stopped. The servo electronics then fine-tune the position so that before writing is allowed, the heads are positioned precisely above the desired cylinder. Although only one head is used for servo tracking, the other heads are attached to the same rigid rack, so if one head is above the desired cylinder, all the others will be as well.

One noticeable trait of dedicated servo drives is that they usually have an odd number of heads. For example, the Toshiba MK-538FB 1.2G drive on which I am saving this chapter has eight platters but only 15 read/write heads; the drive uses a dedicated-servo positioning system, and the 16th head is the servo head. You will find that virtually all high-end drives use a dedicated servo because such a design offers servo information continuously, no matter where the heads are located. This system offers the greatest possible positioning accuracy. Some drives even combine a dedicated servo with an embedded servo, but this type of hybrid design is rare.

Automatic Head Parking. When a hard disk drive is powered off, the spring tension in each head arm pulls the heads into contact with the platters. The drive is designed to sustain thousands of takeoffs and landings, but it is wise to ensure that the landing occurs at a spot on the platter that contains no data. Some amount of abrasion occurs during the landing and takeoff process, removing just a "micro puff" from the media; but if the drive is jarred during the landing or takeoff process, real damage can occur.

One benefit of using a voice coil actuator is *automatic head parking*. In a drive that has a voice coil actuator, the heads are positioned and held by magnetic force. When power is removed from the drive, the magnetic field that holds the heads stationary over a particular cylinder dissipates, enabling the head rack to skitter across the drive surface and potentially cause damage. In the voice coil design, therefore, the head rack is attached to a weak spring at one end and a head stop at the other end. When the system is powered on, the spring normally is overcome by the magnetic force of the positioner. When the drive is powered off, however, the spring gently drags the head rack to a park-and-lock position before the drive slows down and the heads land. On many drives, you can actually hear the "ting...ting...ting...ting" sound as the heads literally bounce-park themselves, driven by this spring.

On a drive with a voice coil actuator, you can activate the parking mechanism simply by turning off the system; you do not need to run a program to park or retract the heads. In the event of a power outage, the heads park themselves automatically. (The drives unpark automatically when the system is powered on.)

Some stepper motor drives (such as the Seagate ST-251 series drives) park their heads, but this function is rare among stepper motor drives. The stepper motor drives that do park their heads usually use an ingenious system whereby the spindle motor actually is used as a generator after the power to the drive is turned off. The back *EMF (Electro Motive Force)*, as it is called, is used to drive the stepper motor to park the heads.

Air Filters

Nearly all hard disk drives have two air filters. One filter is called the *recirculating filter*, and the other is called either a *barometric* or *breather filter*. These filters are permanently sealed inside the drive and are designed never to be changed for the life of the drive, unlike many older mainframe hard disks that had changeable filters. Many mainframe drives circulate air from outside the drive through a filter that must be changed periodically.

A hard disk on a PC system does not circulate air from inside to outside the HDA, or vice versa. The recirculating filter that is permanently installed inside the HDA is designed to filter only the small particles of media scraped off the platters during head takeoffs and landings (and possibly any other small particles dislodged inside the drive). Because PC hard disk drives are permanently sealed and do not circulate outside air, they can run in extremely dirty environments (see fig. 14.8).

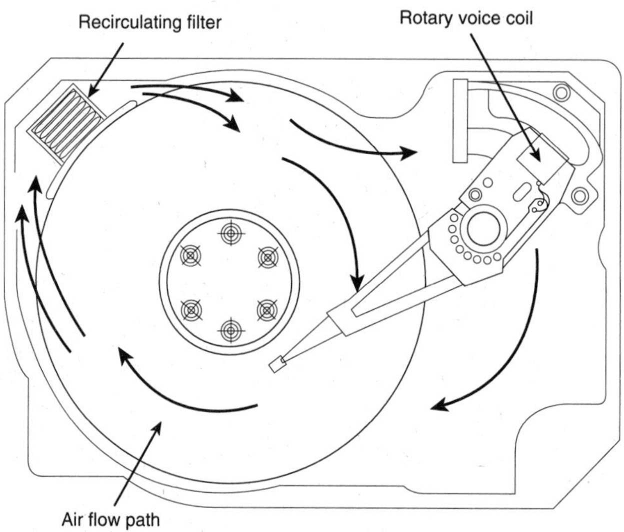

Figure 14.8

Air circulation in a hard disk.

The HDA in a hard disk is sealed but not airtight. The HDA is vented through a barometric or breather filter element that allows for pressure equalization (breathing) between the inside and outside of the drive. For this reason, most hard drives are rated by the drive's manufacturer to run in a specific range of altitudes, usually from –1,000 to +10,000 feet above sea level. In fact, some hard drives are not rated to exceed 7,000 feet while operating because the air pressure would be too low inside the drive to float the heads properly. As the environmental air pressure changes, air bleeds into or out of the drive so that internal and external pressures are identical. Although air does bleed through a vent, contamination usually is not a concern because the barometric filter on this vent is designed to filter out all particles larger than 0.3 micron (about 12 micro-inches) to meet the specifications for cleanliness inside the drive. You can see the vent holes on most drives, which are covered internally by this breather filter. Some drives use even finer-grade filter elements to keep out even smaller particles.

I got a laugh when I read an article in one of the better-known computer magazines, stating not only that hard drives are airtight, but also that the air is evacuated from the interior of the drive, and the heads and platters run in a vacuum! The person who wrote the article obviously does not understand even the most basic principles of hard disk operation. Air is required inside the HDA to float the heads, and this cushion of air (sometimes called an *air bearing*) is the primary principle in Winchester hard disk design.

I conducted a seminar in Hawaii several years ago, and several of the students were from the Mauna Kea astronomical observatory. They indicated that virtually all hard disks they had tried to use at the observatory site had failed very quickly, if they worked at all. This was no surprise, because the observatory is at the 13,800-foot peak of the mountain, and at that altitude, even people don't function very well! At the time, it was suggested that the students investigate solid-state (RAM) disks, tape drives, or even floppy drives as their primary storage medium. Since this time, IBM's Adstar division (which produces all IBM hard drives) introduced a line of rugged 3.5-inch drives that are in fact hermetically sealed (airtight), although they do have air inside the HDA. Because they carry their own internal air under pressure, these drives can operate at any altitude, and also can withstand extremes of shock and temperature. The drives are designed for military and industrial applications, such as aboard aircraft and in extremely harsh environments.

Caution

Airborne particulates such as cigarette smoke normally do not affect a PC hard disk drive, because any air that bleeds into the hard drive is filtered before entering the drive. However, many other components of the system (such as floppy drives, keyboards, connectors, and sockets) will sustain damage from contaminants such as cigarette smoke.

Hard Disk Temperature Acclimation

Although the HDA is sealed, it is not hermetically sealed (except in limited military or aircraft applications), which means that it is not airtight, and that there is air inside. To allow for pressure equalization, hard drives have a filtered port to bleed air into or out of the HDA as necessary.

This breathing also enables moisture to enter the drive, and after some period of time, it must be assumed that the humidity inside any hard disk is similar to that outside the drive. Humidity can become a serious problem if it is allowed to condense—and especially if the drive is powered up while this condensation is present. Most hard disk manufacturers have specified procedures for acclimating a hard drive to a new environment with different temperature and humidity ranges, especially for bringing a drive into a warmer environment in which condensation can form. This situation should be of special concern to users of laptop or portable systems with hard disks. If you leave a portable system in an automobile trunk during the winter, for example, it could be catastrophic to bring the machine inside and power it up without allowing it to acclimate to the temperature indoors.

The following text and table 14.8 are taken from the factory packaging that Control Data Corporation (later Imprimis and eventually Seagate) used to ship its hard drives:

> If you have just received or removed this unit from a climate with temperatures at or below 50°F (10°C) do not open this container until the following conditions are met, otherwise condensation could occur and damage to the device and/or media

may result. Place this package in the operating environment for the time duration according to the temperature chart.

Table 14.8 Hard Disk Drive Environmental Acclimation Table

Previous Climate Temp.	Acclimation Time
+40°F (+4°C)	13 hours
+30°F (–1°C)	15 hours
+20°F (–7°C)	16 hours
+10°F (–12°C)	17 hours
0°F (–18°C)	18 hours
–10°F (–23°C)	20 hours
–20°F (–29°C)	22 hours
–30°F (–34°C) or less	27 hours

As you can see from this chart, a hard disk that has been stored in a colder-than-normal environment must be placed in the normal operating environment for a specified amount of time to allow for acclimation before it is powered on.

Spindle Motors

The motor that spins the platters is called the *spindle motor* because it is connected to the spindle around which the platters revolve. Spindle motors in hard disks always are connected directly; no belts or gears are used. The motors must be free of noise and vibration; otherwise, they transmit to the platters a rumble that could disrupt reading and writing operations.

The motors also must be precisely controlled for speed. The platters on hard disks revolve at speeds ranging from 3,600 to 7,200 RPM or more, and the motor has a control circuit with a feedback loop to monitor and control this speed precisely. Because this speed control must be automatic, hard drives do not have a motor-speed adjustment. Some diagnostics programs claim to measure hard drive rotation speed, but all that these programs do is estimate the rotational speed by the timing at which sectors arrive. There actually is no way for a program to measure hard disk rotational speed; this measurement can be made only with sophisticated test equipment. Don't be alarmed if some diagnostic program tells you that your drive is spinning at an incorrect speed; most likely the program is wrong, not the drive. Platter rotation and timing information is simply not provided through the hard disk controller interface. In the past, software could give approximate rotational speed estimates by performing multiple sector read requests and timing them, but this was valid only when all drives had the same number of sectors per track (17) and they all spun at 3,600 RPM. Zoned Recording combined with a variety of different rotational speeds found in modern drives, not to mention built-in buffers and caches, means that these calculation estimates cannot be performed accurately.

On most drives, the spindle motor is on the bottom of the drive, just below the sealed HDA. Many drives today, however, have the spindle motor built directly into the platter hub inside the HDA. By using an internal hub spindle motor, the manufacturer can stack more platters in the drive, because the spindle motor takes up no vertical space. This method allows for more platters than would be possible if the motor were outside the HDA.

Note

Spindle motors, particularly on the larger form-factor drives, can consume a great deal of 12-volt power. Most drives require two to three times the normal operating power when the motor first spins the platters. This heavy draw lasts only a few seconds, or until the drive platters reach operating speed. If you have more than one drive, you should try to sequence the start of the spindle motors so that the power supply does not receive such a large load from all the drives at the same time. Most SCSI and IDE drives have a delayed spindle-motor start feature.

Spindle Ground Strap

Most drives have a special grounding strap attached to a ground on the drive and resting on the center spindle of the platter spindle motor. This device is the single most likely cause of excessive drive noise.

The *grounding strap* usually is made of copper and often has a carbon or graphite button that contacts the motor or platter spindle. The grounding strap dissipates static generated by the platters as they spin through the air inside the HDA. If the platters generate static due to friction with the air, and if no place exists for this electrical potential to bleed off, static may discharge through the heads or the internal bearings in the motor. When static discharges through the motor bearings, it can burn the lubricants inside the sealed bearings. If the static charge discharges through the read/write heads, the heads can be damaged or data can be corrupted. The grounding strap bleeds off this static buildup to prevent these problems.

Where the spindle of the motor contacts the carbon contact button (at the end of the ground strap) spinning at full speed, the button often wears, creating a flat spot. The flat spot causes the strap to vibrate and produce a high-pitched squeal or whine. The noise may come and go, depending on temperature and humidity. Sometimes, banging the side of the machine can jar the strap so that the noise changes or goes away, but this is not the way to fix the problem. *I am not suggesting that you bang on your system!* (Most people mistake this noise for something much more serious, such as a total drive-motor failure or bearing failure, which rarely occurs.)

If the spindle grounding strap vibrates and causes noise, you can remedy the situation in several ways:

- Dampen the vibration of the strap by attaching some foam tape or rubber to it.
- Lubricate the contact point.
- Tear off the strap (not recommended!).

On some drives, the spindle motor strap is easily accessible. On other drives, you have to partially disassemble the drive by removing the logic board or other external items to get to the strap.

Of these suggested solutions, the first one is the best. The best way to correct this problem is to glue (or otherwise affix) some rubber or foam to the strap. This procedure changes the harmonics of the strap and usually dampens vibrations. Most manufacturers now use this technique on newly manufactured drives. An easy way to do this is to place some foam tape on the back side of the ground strap.

You also can use a dab of silicone RTV (room-temperature vulcanizing) rubber or caulk on the back of the strap. If you try this method, be sure to use low-volatile (noncorrosive) silicone RTV sealer, which commonly is sold at auto-parts stores. The noncorrosive silicone will be listed on the label as being safe for automotive oxygen sensors. This low-volatile silicone also is free from corrosive acids that can damage the copper strap and is described as low-odor because it does not have the vinegar odor usually associated with silicone RTV. Dab a small amount on the back side of the copper strap (do not interfere with the contact location), and the problem should be solved permanently.

Lubricating the strap is an acceptable, but often temporary, solution. You will want to use some sort of conducting lube, such as a graphite-based compound (the kind used on frozen car locks). Any conductive lubricant (such as moly or lithium) will work as long as it is conductive, but do not use standard oil or grease. Simply dab a small amount of lubricant onto the end of a toothpick, and place a small drop directly on the point of contact.

The last solution is not acceptable. Tearing off the strap eliminates the noise, but it has several possible ramifications. Although the drive will work (silently) without the strap, an engineer placed it there for a reason. Imagine those ungrounded static charges leaving the platters through the heads, perhaps in the form of a spark—possibly even damaging the Thin Film heads. You should choose one of the other solutions.

I mention this last solution only because several people have told me that members of the tech-support staff of some of the hard drive vendors, and even of some manufacturers, told them to remove the strap, which—of course—I do not recommend.

Logic Boards

A disk drive, including a hard disk drive, has one or more logic boards mounted on it. The logic boards contain the electronics that control the drive's spindle and head actuator systems and that present data to the controller in some agreed-on form. In some drives, the controller is located on the drive, which can save on a system's total chip count.

Many disk drive failures occur in the logic board, not in the mechanical assembly. (This statement does not seem logical, but it is true.) Therefore, you can repair many failed drives by replacing the logic board, not the entire drive. Replacing the logic board, moreover, enables you to regain access to the data on the failed drive—something that replacing the entire drive precludes.

Logic boards can be removed or replaced because they simply plug into the drive. These boards usually are mounted with standard screw hardware. If a drive is failing and you have a spare, you may be able to verify a logic-board failure by taking the board off the known good drive and mounting it on the bad one. If your suspicions are confirmed, you can order a new logic board from the drive manufacturer. You also may be able to purchase a refurbished unit or even to trade in your old drive or logic board. The drive manufacturer will have details on what services it can offer.

To reduce costs further, many third-party vendors also can supply replacement logic-board assemblies. These companies often charge much less than the drive manufacturers for the same components. (See the Vendor List in Appendix B for vendors of drive components, including logic boards.)

Cables and Connectors

Most hard disk drives have several connectors for interfacing to the system, receiving power, and sometimes grounding to the system chassis. Most drives have at least these three types of connectors:

- Interface connector(s)
- Power connector
- Optional ground connector (tab)

Of these, the *interface connectors* are the most important because they carry the data and command signals from the system to and from the drive. In many drive interfaces, the drive interface cables can be connected in a *daisy chain*, or bus-type configuration. Most interfaces support at least two drives, and SCSI (Small Computer System Interface) supports up to seven in the chain. Some interfaces, such as ST-506/412 or ESDI (Enhanced Small Device Interface), use a separate cable for data and control signals. These drives have two cables from the controller interface to the drive. SCSI and IDE (Integrated Drive Electronics) drives usually have a single data and control connector. With these interfaces, the disk controller is built into the drive (see fig. 14.9).

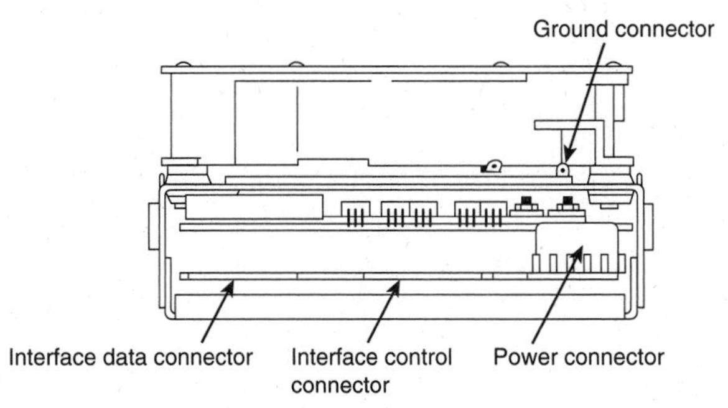

Figure 14.9

Typical hard disk connections (ST-506/412 or ESDI shown).

The different interfaces and cable specifications are covered in the sections on drive interfaces later in this chapter. You also will find connector pinout specifications for virtually all drive interfaces and cable connections in this chapter.

The *power connector* usually is the same type that is used in floppy drives, and the same power-supply connector plugs into it. Most hard disk drives use both 5- and 12-volt power, although some of the smaller drives designed for portable applications use only 5-volt power. In most cases, the 12-volt power runs the spindle motor and head actuator, and the 5-volt power runs the circuitry. Make sure that your power supply can supply adequate power for the hard disk drives installed in your PC system; most hard drives draw quite a bit more power than a floppy drive.

The 12-volt-power consumption of a drive usually varies with the physical size of the unit. The larger the drive is and the more platters there are to spin, the more power is required. Also, the faster the drive spins, the more power will be required. For example, most of the 3.5-inch drives on the market today use roughly one-half to one-fourth the power (in watts) of the full-size 5.25-inch drives. Some of the very small (2.5- or 1.8-inch) hard disks barely sip electrical power and actually use one watt or less!

Ensuring an adequate power supply is particularly important with some systems, such as the original IBM AT. These systems have a power supply with three disk drive power connectors, labeled P10, P11, and P12. The three power connectors may seem to be equal, but the technical-reference manual for these systems indicates that 2.8 amps of 12-volt current is available on P10 and P11 and that only one amp of 12-volt current is available on P12. Because most full-height hard drives draw much more power than 1 amp, especially at startup, the P12 connector can be used only by floppy drives or half-height hard drives. Some 5.25-inch drives draw as much as four amps of current during the first few seconds of startup. These drives also can draw as much as 2.5 amps during normal operation.

Sometimes, you can solve random boot-up failures simply by plugging the hard drive into a suitable power connector (P10 or P11 on the IBM AT). Most IBM-compatible PC systems have a power supply with four or more disk drive power connectors that provide equal power, but some use power supplies designed like those of the IBM AT.

A *grounding tab* provides a positive ground connection between the drive and the system's chassis. In a typical IBM PC or IBM XT system, because the hard disk drive is mounted directly to the chassis of the PC using screws, the ground wire is unnecessary. On AT-type systems from IBM and other manufacturers, the drives are installed on plastic or fiberglass rails, which do not provide proper grounding. These systems must provide a grounding wire, plugged into the drive at this grounding tab. Failure to ground the drive may result in improper operation, intermittent failure, or general read and write errors.

Configuration Items

To configure a hard disk drive for installation in a system, several jumpers (and, possibly, terminating resistors) usually must be set or configured properly. These items will vary from interface to interface and often from drive to drive as well. A complete discussion of the configuration settings for each interface appears in "Hard Disk Installation Procedures" later in this chapter.

The Faceplate or Bezel

Many hard disk drives offer as an option a front faceplate, or *bezel* (see fig. 14.10). A bezel usually is supplied as an option for the drive rather than as a standard item. In most cases today the bezel is a part of the case, and not the drive itself.

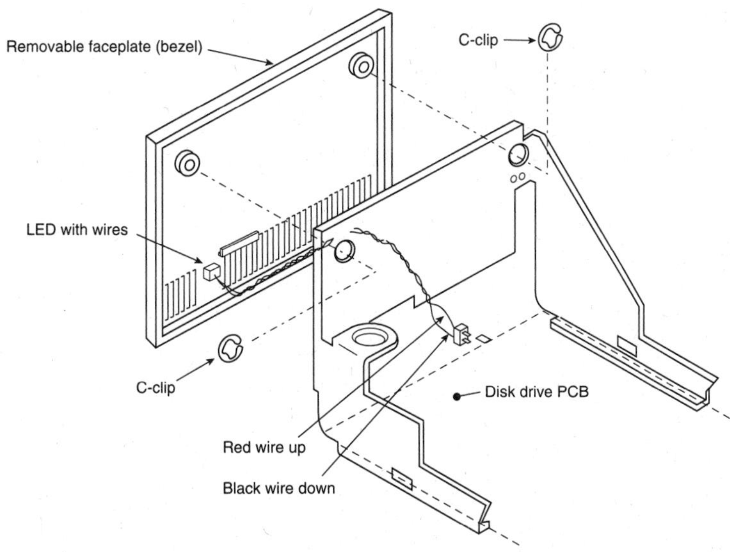

Figure 14.10

A hard drive faceplate (bezel).

Bezels often come in several sizes and colors to match various PC systems. For standard full-height, 5.25-inch, form-factor drives, you have only one choice of bezel. For half-height drives, bezels come in half-height and full-height forms. Using a full-height bezel on a half-height drive enables you to install a single drive in a full-height bay without leaving a hole in the front of the system. To add a second half-height drive, you may want to order the half-height bezels so that you can stack the old and new drives. Many faceplate configurations for 3.5-inch drives are available, including bezels that fit 3.5-inch drive bays as well as 5.25-inch drive bays. You even have a choice of colors (usually, black, cream, or white).

Some bezels feature a light-emitting diode (LED) that flickers when your hard disk is in use. The LED is mounted in the bezel; the wire hanging off the back of the LED plugs into the drive or perhaps the controller. In some drives, the LED is permanently mounted on the drive, and the bezel has a clear or colored window so that you can see the LED flicker while the drive is accessed.

One type of LED problem occurs with some AT-type-system hard disk installations: if the drive has an LED, the LED may remain on continuously, as though it were a "power-on" light rather than an access light. This problem happens because the controller in the AT has a direct connection for the LED, thus altering the drive LED function. Some controllers have a jumper that enables the controller to run the drive in what is called latched or unlatched mode. *Latched mode* means that the drive is selected continuously and that the drive LED remains lighted; in *unlatched mode* (to which we are more accustomed), the LED lights only when the drive is accessed. Check to see whether your controller has a jumper for changing this function; if so, you may be able to control the way that the LED operates.

In systems in which the hard disk is hidden by the unit's cover, a bezel is not needed. In fact, using a bezel may prevent the cover from resting on the chassis properly, in which case the bezel will have to be removed. If you are installing a drive that does not have a proper bezel, frame, or rails to attach to the system, check Appendix B; several listed vendors offer these accessories for a variety of drives.

Hard Disk Features

To make the best decision in purchasing a hard disk for your system, or to understand what differentiates one brand of hard disk from another, you must consider many features. This section examines the issues that you should consider when you evaluate drives:

- Actuator mechanism
- Media
- Head parking
- Reliability
- Speed
- Shock mounting
- Cost

Actuator Mechanism

A drive with high performance and reliability has two basic physical properties:

- Voice coil actuator mechanism
- Thin-film media

Drives with stepper motor actuators should be used only when cost far outweighs other considerations. You should not use these drives in portable systems or in systems that must operate under extreme temperature, noise, or vibration conditions. Don't use these drives where preventive maintenance cannot be provided because they require periodic reformats to maintain data integrity. Finally, you should not use these drives in demanding situations, such as in a network file server. Drives with stepper motor actuators perform adequately in low-volume-usage systems, as long as you provide preventive maintenance at least annually or semiannually and the environment can be controlled. Fortunately, stepper motor drives are virtually out of production today; nearly all new drives use voice coil actuators.

Voice coil actuator drives should be used wherever possible, especially if any real demands are placed on the drive. These drives are ideal for portable systems or for systems that suffer extreme temperatures, noise, or vibration. These drives are ideal when a fast drive is necessary. A voice coil drive requires little or no preventive maintenance, so the first low-level format usually is the only low-level format ever required. Less maintenance (no reformatting) enables this type of drive to be used for high-volume situations in which a single support person maintains many PC systems. Fortunately, virtually all drives manufactured today are voice coil drives, and they should be! Voice coil actuator technology is the only way to build a reliable, high-performance, low-maintenance drive.

Head Parking

Head parking is an often-misunderstood issue with hard disks. When a hard disk comes to a stop (actually, before it stops), the heads land on the media. This contact occurs as the drive slows, and in some drives, the distance that the heads skid before the platters stop may be many linear feet. The same skidding occurs when the drive is powered on and the platters begin to turn. In some drives, the heads land on whatever cylinder they were last positioned above—usually, an area of the disk that contains data.

Most drives today move the heads to a nondata area called the *landing zone* before the platters slow enough for the heads to come into contact with them. This procedure is called *automatic head parking*. Drives that do not park their heads automatically still can be parked, but it requires the manual execution of a program to move the heads before the system is powered down.

Drives with voice coil actuators offer automatic head parking. While the drive is running, an electric coil overcomes the spring tension and moves the head around the disk. When power is lost, the spring automatically pulls the head rack away from data areas of the disk to a special landing zone.

Most stepper motor drives do not have an automatic-parking function; instead they must be parked manually. To find out whether your drive autoparks, contact the drive manufacturer and ask for the technical or specification manual for the drive, which will contain the answer.

Some newer stepper drives do incorporate a parking mechanism. One example is the Seagate ST-251 series. This popular stepper drive autoparks the heads by using an ingenious system in which the drive spindle motor is used as a generator, powering the stepper motor to park the heads. When the drive is powered off, you hear the stepper motor drive the heads to the landing zone. Seagate seems to be using this type of mechanism in many of its newer stepper motor drives as well.

Software is available that enables you to park the heads of drives that lack the automatic-parking feature. The software is not quite as reliable as automatic parking, however, because it does not park the heads if the power goes off unexpectedly. If your system requires a head-parking program, the program usually comes on the configuration or setup utility disk that goes with the system. For example, IBM supplied a head-parking routine on the diagnostics disk supplied with its original XT and AT systems, as well as on the Advanced Diagnostics disk supplied with the hardware-maintenance service manual. Simply boot these disks and select the option Prepare System for Moving. This procedure invokes a program on the disk called SHIPDISK.COM. Different SHIPDISK.COM files exist for XT and AT systems. The heads of all attached disks are parked. Then you shut down the system.

As a note, several years ago IBM issued a warning to its dealers, recommending that they not run SHIPDISK.COM from the DOS prompt. IBM said that a slight chance exists that you can lose data because the program can accidentally write random data on the drive. The memo indicated that SHIPDISK.COM should be run only from the menu. Apparently, the problem was that SHIPDISK.COM parks the disks and then executes a software interrupt to return to the diagnostics-disk menu, and unpredictable things can happen (including stray disk writes) if the program was not run from the diagnostics-disk menu.

For AT systems, IBM supplied a separate program, SHUTDOWN.EXE, that is designed to be run from the DOS prompt. This program is on the AT diagnostics and advanced-diagnostics disks. You can copy this program to the hard disk and enter the SHUTDOWN command at the DOS prompt. You see a graphic of a switch, which turns off as the heads are parked. The program then halts the system, requiring a complete power-down. This program works only on AT-type systems.

Note

It usually is not a good idea to run a hard disk parking program that is not designed for your system. Although no physical harm will occur, the heads may not be parked in the correct landing zone. (Many programs improperly position the heads above Cylinder 0—the last place where you want them!)

If your hard drive is a stepper motor actuator drive without automatic parking, it should come with a parking program. If you have an IBM system, this program comes on the diagnostics and setup disks that came with the system. If you have an IBM-compatible, you probably received such a program on your setup disk. Additionally, some public-domain programs park a stepper motor hard disk.

Should you park the heads every time you shut down the drive? Some people think so, but IBM says that you do not have to park the heads on a drive unless you are moving the drive. My experiences are in line with IBM's recommendations, although a more fail-safe approach is to park the heads at every shutdown. Remember that voice coil drives park their heads automatically every time and require no manual parking operations. I only park a stepper motor drive if I am moving the unit, but there is nothing wrong with parking the heads at every shutdown. The procedure is simple and cannot hurt.

Reliability

When you shop for a drive, you may notice a feature called the *Mean Time Between Failures (MTBF)* described in the brochures. MTBF figures usually range from 20,000 hours to 500,000 hours or more. I usually ignore these figures because they usually are just theoretical—not actual—statistical values. Most drives that boast these figures have not even been manufactured for that length of time. One year of 5-day work weeks with 8-hour days equals 2,080 hours of operation. If you never turn off your system for 365 days and run the full 24 hours per day, you operate your system 8,760 hours each year; a drive with a 500,000-hour MTBF rating is supposed to last (on average) 57 years before failing! Obviously, that figure cannot be derived from actual statistics because the particular drive probably has been on the market for less than a year.

Statistically, for the MTBF figures to have real weight, you must take a sample of drives, measure the failure rate for at least twice the rated figure, and measure how many drives fail in that time. To be really accurate, you would have to wait until all the drives fail and record the operating hours at each failure. Then you would average the running time for all the test samples to arrive at the average time before a drive failure. For a reported MTBF of 500,000 hours (common today), the test sample should be run for at least 1 million hours (114 years) to be truly accurate, yet the drive carries this specification on the day that it is introduced.

Manufacturers and vendors sometimes play with these numbers. For example, several years ago, CDC rated a Wren II half-height drive at 20,000 hours MTBF (this drive was one of the most reliable in the world at the time), but I saw a reseller rate the same unit at 50,000 hours. Some of the worst drives that I have used boasted high MTBF figures, and some of the best drives have lower ones. These figures do not necessarily translate to reliability in the field, and that is why I generally place no importance on them.

Performance

When you select a hard disk, an important feature to consider is the performance (speed) of the drive. Hard disks come in a wide range of performance capabilities. As is true of many things, one of the best indicators of a drive's relative performance is its price. An old saying from the automobile-racing industry is appropriate here: "Speed costs money. How fast do you want to go?"

You can measure the speed of a disk drive in two ways:

- Average seek time
- Transfer rate

Average seek time, normally measured in milliseconds, is the average amount of time it takes to move the heads from one cylinder to another cylinder a random distance away. One way to measure this specification is to run many random track-seek operations and then divide the timed results by the number of seeks performed. This method provides an average time for a single seek.

The standard way to measure average seek time used by many drive manufacturers involves measuring the time that it takes the heads to move across one-third of the total cylinders. Average seek time depends only on the drive; the type of interface or controller has little effect on this specification. (In some cases, the setup of the controller to the drive can affect seek times; this subject is discussed later in this chapter.) The rating is a gauge of the capabilities of the head actuator.

Be wary of benchmarks that claim to measure drive seek performance. Most IDE and SCSI drives use a scheme called sector translation, so any commands to the drive to move the heads to a specific cylinder do not actually cause the intended physical movement. This situation renders such benchmarks meaningless for those types of drives. SCSI drives also require an additional command because the commands first must be sent to the drive over the SCSI bus. Even though these drives can have the fastest access times, because the command overhead is not factored in by most benchmarks, the benchmark programs produce poor performance figures for these drives.

I don't put too much faith in the benchmarks, and the drive manufacturers have been very honest in reporting their true performance figures over the years. The bottom line is that if you want to know the true seek performance of your drive, the most accurate way to find it is simply to look it up in the drive specification manual.

A slightly different measurement, called average access time, involves another element, called latency. *Latency* is the average time (in milliseconds) that it takes for a sector to be available after the heads have reached a track. On average, this figure is half the time that it takes for the disk to rotate one time, which is 8.33 ms at 3,600 RPM. A drive that spins twice as fast would have half the latency. A measurement of average access time is the sum of the average seek time and latency. This number provides the average amount of time required before a randomly requested sector can be accessed.

Latency is a factor in disk read and write performance. Decreasing the latency increases the speed of access to data or files, accomplished only by spinning the drive platters faster. I have a drive that spins at 4,318 RPM, for a latency of 6.95 ms. Some drives spin at 7,200 RPM or faster, resulting in an even shorter latency time of only 4.17 ms. In addition to increasing performance where real-world access to data is concerned, spinning the platters faster also increases the data-transfer rate after the heads arrive at the desired sectors.

The transfer rate probably is more important to overall system performance than any other specification. *Transfer rate* is the rate at which the drive and controller can send data to the system. The transfer rate depends primarily on the drive's HDA and secondarily on the controller. Transfer rate used to be more bound to the limits of the controller, meaning that drives that were connected to older controllers often outperformed those controllers. This situation is where the concept of interleaving sectors came from. *Interleaving* refers to the ordering of the sectors so that they are not sequential, enabling a slow controller to keep up without missing the next sector.

A following section discusses interleaving in more detail. For now, the point I am trying to make is that modern drives with integrated controllers are fully capable of keeping up with the raw drive transfer rate. In other words, they no longer have to interleave the sectors to slow the data for the controller.

Another performance issue is the raw interface performance, which, in IDE or SCSI drives, usually is far higher than any of the drives themselves are able to sustain. Be wary of quoted transfer specifications for the interface, because they may have little effect on what the drive can actually put out. The drive interface simply limits the maximum theoretical transfer rate; the actual drive and controller place the real limits on performance.

In older ST-506/412 interface drives, you sometimes can double or triple the transfer rate by changing the controller because many of the older controllers could not support a 1:1 interleave. When you change the controller to one that does support this interleave, the transfer rate will be equal to the drive's true capability.

To calculate the true transfer rate of a drive, you need to know several important specifications. The two most important specifications are the true rotational speed of the drive (in RPM) and the average number of physical sectors on each track. I say "average" because most drives today use a Zoned Recording technique that places different numbers of sectors on the inner and outer cylinders. The transfer rate on Zoned Recording drives always is fastest in the outermost zone, where the sector per track count is highest. Also be aware that many drives (especially Zoned Recording drives) are configured with sector translation, so that the BIOS reported number of sectors per track has little to do with physical reality. You need to know the true physical parameters, rather than what the BIOS thinks.

When you know these figures, you can use the following formula to determine the maximum transfer rate in millions of bits per second (Mbps):

Maximum Data Transfer Rate (Mbps) = SPT × 512 bytes × RPM / 60 seconds / 1,000,000 bits

For example, the ST-12551N 2GB 3.5-inch drive spins at 7,200 RPM and has an average of 81 sectors per track. The maximum transfer rate for this drive is figured as follows:

81 × 512 × 7,200 / 60 / 1,000,000 = 4.98Mbps

Using this formula, you can calculate the true maximum sustained transfer rate of any drive.

Cache Programs and Caching Controllers. At the software level, disk cache programs, such as SMARTDRV (DOS) or VCACHE (Windows 95) can have a major effect on disk drive performance. These cache programs hook into the BIOS hard drive interrupt and then intercept the read and write calls to the disk BIOS from application programs and the device drivers of DOS.

When an application program wants to read data from a hard drive, the cache program intercepts the read request, passes the read request to the hard drive controller in the usual way, saves the data that was read in its cache buffer, and then passes the data back to the application program. Depending on the size of the cache buffer, numerous sectors are read into and saved in the buffer.

When the application wants to read more data, the cache program again intercepts the request and examines its buffers to see whether the data is still in the cache. If so, the data is passed back to the application immediately, without another hard drive operation. As you can imagine, this method speeds access tremendously and can greatly affect disk drive performance measurements.

Most controllers now have some form of built-in hardware buffer or cache that doesn't intercept or use any BIOS interrupts. Instead, the caching is performed at the hardware level and is invisible to normal performance-measurement software. Track read-ahead buffers originally were included in controllers to allow for 1:1 interleave performance. Some controllers have simply increased the sizes of these read-ahead buffers; others have added intelligence by making them a cache instead of a simple buffer.

Many IDE and SCSI drives have cache memory built directly into the drive. For example, the Seagate Hawk 4G drive on which I am saving this chapter has 512K of built-in cache memory. Other drives have even more built-in caches, such as the Seagate Barracuda 4G with 1M of integral cache memory. I remember when 640K was a lot of memory; now, tiny 3.5-inch hard disk drives have more than that built right in! These integral caches are part of the reason why most IDE and SCSI drives perform so well.

Although software and hardware caches can make a drive faster for routine transfer operations, a cache will not affect the true maximum transfer rate that the drive can sustain.

Interleave Selection. In a discussion of disk performance, the issue of interleave always comes up. Although traditionally this was more a controller performance issue than a drive issue, most modern hard disks now have built-in controllers (IDE and SCSI) that are fully capable of taking the drive data as fast as the drive can send it. In other words, virtually all modern IDE and SCSI drives are formatted with no interleave (sometimes expressed as a 1:1 interleave ratio).

When a disk is low-level formatted, numbers are assigned to the sectors. These numbers are written in the Sector ID fields in the sector header and can be written or updated only by a low-level format. With older drive interfaces that used discrete controllers such as ST-506/412 or ESDI, you often had to calculate the best interleave value for the particular controller and system that you were using so you could low-level format the drive and number the sectors so as to offer optimum performance.

Notice that nearly all IDE and SCSI drives have their interleave ratios fixed at 1:1 and built-in controllers that can handle these ratios with no problem. In these drives, there no longer is a need to calculate or specify an interleave ratio, but knowing about interleaving can give you some further insight into the way that these drives function.

Many older ST-506/412 controllers could not handle the sectors as quickly as the drive could send them. Suppose that you have a standard ST-5096/412 drive with 17 sectors on each track and that you low-level formatted the drive, you specified a 1:1 interleave, which is to say that you numbered the sectors on each track consecutively.

Now suppose that you want to read some data from the drive. The controller commands the drive to position the heads at a specific track and to read all 17 sectors from that track. The heads move and arrive at the desired track. The time it takes for the heads to move is called the *seek time*. When the heads arrive at the desired track, you have to wait for an average half-revolution of the disk for the first sector to arrive. This wait is called *latency*. After an average latency of half of a disk revolution, the sector numbered 1 arrives below the heads. While the disk continues to spin at 3,600 RPM (60 revolutions per second), the data is read from sector 1, and as the data is being transferred from the controller to the system board, the disk continues to spin. Finally, the data is completely moved to the motherboard, and the controller is ready for sector 2. Figure 14.11 shows what is happening.

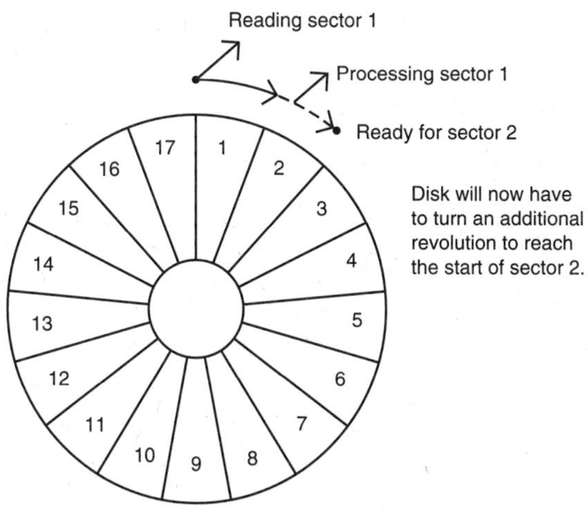

Figure 14.11

A hard disk interleave ratio too low for the controller.

But wait—there's a problem here. Because the disk continues to spin at such a high rate of speed, the sector 2 passed below the head while the controller was working, and by the time the controller is ready again, the heads will be coming to the start of sector 3. Because the controller needs to read sector 2 next, however, the controller must wait for the disk to spin a full revolution, or until the start of sector 2 comes below the heads. After this additional disk revolution, sector 2 arrives below the heads and is read. While the controller is transferring the data from sector 2 to the motherboard, sector 3 passes below the heads. When the controller finally is ready to read sector 3, the heads are coming to the start of sector 4, so another complete revolution is required, and the controller will have to get sector 4 on the next go-around. This scenario continues, with each new revolution allowing only one sector to be read and missing the next sector because that sector passes below the heads before the controller is ready.

As you can see, the timing of this procedure is not working out very well. At this pace, 17 full revolutions of the disk will be required to read all 17 sectors. Because each revolution takes 1/60 of 1 second, it will take 17/60 of 1 second to read this track, or almost one-third of a second—a very long time, by computer standards.

Can this performance be improved? You notice that after reading a specific sector from the disk, the controller takes some time to transfer the sector data to the motherboard. The next sector that the controller can catch in this example is the second sector away from the first one. In other words, the controller seems to be capable of catching every second sector.

I hope that you now can imagine the perfect solution to this problem: simply number the sectors out of order. The new numbering scheme takes into account how fast the controller works; the sectors are numbered so that each time the controller is ready for the next sector, the sector coming below the heads is numbered as the next sector that the controller will want to read. Figure 14.12 shows this new sector numbering scheme.

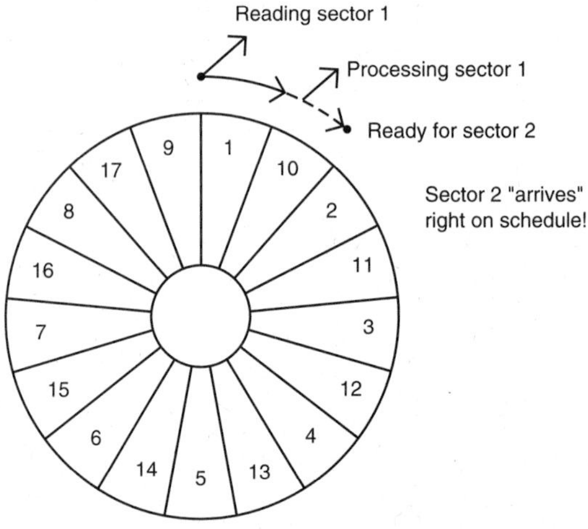

Figure 14.12
A hard disk interleave ratio matching the controller's capabilities.

The new numbering system eliminates the extra disk revolution that previously was required to pick up each sector. Under the new scheme, the controller will read all 17 sectors on the disk in only two complete revolutions. Renumbering the sectors on the disk in this manner is called *interleaving*, which normally is expressed as a ratio. The interleave ratio in this example is 2 to 1 (also written as 2:1), which means that the next numbered sector is 2 sectors away from the preceding one; if the controller is capable of handling this, only two complete revolutions are needed to read an entire track. Thus, reading the track takes only 2/60 of one second at the 2:1 interleave, rather than the 17/60 of one second required to read the disk at the 1:1 interleave—an improvement of 800 percent in the data transfer rate.

This example depicts a system in which the ideal interleave is 2:1. I used this example because most controllers that came in older AT systems worked in exactly this manner. If you set a controller for a 1:1 interleave, you likely would make the drive eight times slower than it should be. This situation, however, has changed with newer controller technology. Most disk controllers sold in the past couple of years support a 1:1 interleave on any AT-class system, even the slowest 6-MHz 286 versions. If you are purchasing or upgrading a system today, consider a disk subsystem with a 1:1 interleave controller to be a standard requirement. Fortunately, this is pretty much a non-issue; virtually all IDE or SCSI drives today have built-in controllers that easily handle a 1:1 interleave, and all these types of drives are preformatted at the factory in that manner. In many of these drives, it is not even possible to change the interleave to any value except 1:1.

The correct interleave for a system depends primarily on the controller and secondarily on the speed of the system into which the controller is plugged. A controller and system that can handle a *consecutive sector interleave* (a 1:1 interleave) must transfer data as fast as the disk drive can present it; this used to be quite a feat but now is commonplace.

Advances in controller technology have made a 1:1 interleave not only possible, but also affordable. Any 286 or faster system easily can handle the 1:1 interleave data transfer rate. The only types of systems that truly are too slow to handle a 1:1 interleave effectively are the original 4.77-MHz PC- and XT-type systems. Those systems have a maximum throughput to the slots of just under 400K per second—not fast enough to support a 1:1 interleave controller.

Even with a 1:1 interleave, however, performance can vary significantly, and this is where the drive itself comes into play. A 1:1 interleave with a 17-sector disk is one thing, but with ESDI or SCSI drives spinning at 7,200 RPM and containing 81 or more sectors per track, the result is nearly 5M of data transfer each second.

The interleave used in standard-issue IBM XT systems with hard drives was 6:1, whereas in IBM AT systems, it was 3:1. The best interleave for these systems actually is one lower than what was set up as standard in each case: In other words, the best interleave for the Xebec 1210 controller in a 4.77-MHz IBM PC or IBM XT is 5:1, and the best interleave for the Western Digital 1002 and 1003 controllers in a 6-MHz or 8-MHz IBM AT system is 2:1. If you redo the low-level format on these systems to the lower interleave number, you gain about 20 to 30 percent in data-transfer performance without changing any hardware and at no cost except some of your time.

Table 14.9 shows data transfer rates that were calculated for a variety of drives at a variety of different interleaves. The rows in this table represent a particular drive-and-controller combination with respect to the speed of revolution and the number of sectors per track. In all but the lowest-end setups, the interleave is 1:1, but I listed the other interleaves to show what the effect would be if they were used.

Compare the 85K-per-second transfer rate of the original IBM XT drive and controller (3,600 RPM, 17 sectors, and a 6:1 interleave standard) with the 4,860K-per-second transfer rate of the Seagate Barracuda 2 drive (7,200 RPM, 81 sectors, and a 1:1 interleave). As you can see, we have come a long way in just over 10 years of disk and controller technology!

Table 14.9 Data-Transfer Rates (in K per Second) at Various Interleaves, Spindle Speeds, and Sector Densities

Speed (RPM)	Sectors /Track	Interleaves 1:1	2:1	3:1	4:1	5:1	6:1
3,600	17	510	255	170	128	102	85
3,600	25	750	375	250	188	150	125
3,600	26	780	390	260	195	156	130
3,600	27	810	405	270	203	162	135
3,600	32	960	480	320	240	192	160
3,600	33	990	495	330	248	198	165
3,600	34	1,020	510	340	255	204	170
3,600	35	1,050	525	350	263	210	175
3,600	36	1,080	540	360	270	216	180
3,600	37	1,110	555	370	278	222	185
3,600	38	1,140	570	380	285	228	190
3,600	39	1,170	585	390	293	234	195
4,500	50	1,875	938	625	469	375	313
3,600	81	2,430	1,215	810	608	486	405
4,500	70	2,625	1,313	875	656	525	438
5,400	70	3,150	1,575	1,050	788	630	525
6,300	90	4,725	2,363	1,575	1,181	945	788
7,200	81	4,860	2,430	1,620	1,215	972	810

If you want to find out the current interleave setting of your drive, I usually recommend using Norton Utilities for performing hard disk drive interleave testing. The Calibrate program included with Norton Utilities can check, and possibly even change, the interleave on ST-506/412 interface drives through a nondestructive low-level format. Notice that in this case, nondestructive actually means that the format is performed one track at a time, with the data for that track being backed up and restored all the while. A full backup of the entire drive beforehand still is recommended because if something goes wrong, one or more tracks can be wiped out.

Calibrate (and other utility programs like it) can change the interleave only on ST-506/412 and possibly some ESDI drives, and there can be problems even on drives that they can handle. If you really want to change the interleave of a drive through a new low-level format, I usually recommend whatever low-level format program the controller manufacturer specifies for the best possible job. In most modern drives (ESDI, IDE, or SCSI), it usually is not possible (or desirable) to change the interleave with a generic low-level format program such as Calibrate. With an ESDI-type drive, for example, you normally would need to use the controller's built-in (or supplied on disk) low-level format (LLF) program to re-set the interleave (most ESDI controllers support 1:1, so there should be little reason to change). IDE and SCSI drives have the disk controller built in, and most have the interleave permanently set (nonchangeable) to the best possible choice, eliminating any reason to change. Virtually all modern drive/controller combinations have a default 1:1 interleave anyway, so changing would not be beneficial.

Head and Cylinder Skewing. Most controllers today are capable of transferring data at a 1:1 sector interleave. This is especially true of controllers that are built in to IDE and SCSI drives. With a 1:1 interleave controller, the maximum data transfer rate can be maintained when reading and writing sectors to the disk. Although it would seem that there is no other way to further improve efficiency and the transfer rate, many people overlook two important factors that are similar to interleave: head and cylinder skewing.

When a drive is reading (or writing) data sequentially, first all of the sectors on a given track are read; then the drive must electronically switch to the next head in the cylinder to continue the operation. If the sectors are not skewed from head to head within the cylinder, no delay occurs after the last sector on one track and before the arrival of the first sector on the next track. Because all drives require some time (although a small amount) to switch from one head to another, and because the controller also adds some overhead to the operation, it is likely that by the time the drive is ready to read the sectors on the newly selected track, the first sector will already have passed by. By skewing the sectors from one head to another—that is, rotating their arrangement on the track so that the arrival of the first sector is delayed relative to the preceding track—you can ensure that no extra disk revolutions will be required when switching heads. This method provides the highest possible transfer rate when head switching is involved.

In a similar fashion, it takes considerable time for the heads to move from one cylinder to another. If the sectors on one cylinder were not skewed from those on the preceding adjacent cylinder, it is likely that by the time the heads arrive, the first sector will already have passed below them, requiring an additional revolution of the disk before reading of the new cylinder can begin. By skewing the sectors from one cylinder to the next, you can account for the cylinder-to-cylinder head-movement time and prevent any additional revolutions of the drive.

Head Skew. *Head skew* is the offset in logical sector numbering between the same physical sectors on two tracks below adjacent heads of the same cylinder. The number of sectors skewed when switching from head to head within a single cylinder is to compensate for head switching and controller overhead time. Think of it as the surface of each platter being rotated as you traverse from head to head. This method permits continuous read or write operation across head boundaries without missing any disk revolutions, thus maximizing system performance.

To understand head skew, you first need to know the order in which tracks and sectors are read from a disk. If you imagine a single-platter (two-head) drive with 10 cylinders and 17 sectors per track, the first sector that will be read on the entire drive is Cylinder 0, Head 0, Sector 1. Following that, all the remaining sectors on that first track (Cylinder 0, Head 0) will be read until Sector 17 is reached. After that, two things could take place—one is that the heads could be moved so that the drive could continue reading the next track on the same side of the platter, or the second head could be selected, and therefore another entire track could be read with no head movement. Because head movement takes much longer than electronically selecting another head, all disk drives will select the subsequent heads on a cylinder before physically moving the heads to the next cylinder. Thus, the next sector to be read would be Cylinder 0, Head 1, Sector 1. Next, all the remaining sectors on that track are read (2 through 17), and then in our single platter example it is time to switch heads. This sequence continues until the last sector on the last track is read—in this example, Cylinder 9, Head 1, Sector 17.

If you could take the tracks off a cylinder in this example and lay them on top of one another, the tracks might look like this:

```
Cyl. 0, Head 0:    1- 2- 3- 4- 5- 6- 7- 8- 9-10-11-12-13-14-15-16-17
Cyl. 0, Head 1:    1- 2- 3- 4- 5- 6- 7- 8- 9-10-11-12-13-14-15-16-17
```

After reading all the sectors on head 0, the controller switches heads to head 1 and continues the read (looping around to the beginning of the track). In this example, the sectors were not skewed at all between the heads, which means that the sectors are directly above and below one another in a given cylinder.

Now the platters in this example are spinning at 3,600 RPM, so one sector is passing below a head once every 980 millionths of a second! This obviously is a very small timing window. It takes some time for the head switch to occur (usually, 15 millionths of a second), plus some overhead time for the controller to pass the head-switch command. By the time the head switch is complete and you are ready to read the new track, sector 1 has already gone by! This problem is similar to interleaving when the interleave is too low. The drive is forced to wait while the platter spins around another revolution so that it can begin to pick up the track, starting with Sector 1.

This problem is easy to solve: simply offset the sector numbering on subsequent tracks from those that precede them sufficiently to account for the head-switching and controller overhead time. That way, when Head 0, Sector 17 finishes and the head switches, Head 1, Sector 1 arrives right on time. The result looks something like this:

```
Cyl. 0, Head 0:    1- 2- 3- 4- 5- 6- 7- 8- 9-10-11-12-13-14-15-16-17
Cyl. 0, Head 1:   16-17- 1- 2- 3- 4- 5- 6- 7- 8- 9-10-11-12-13-14-15
```

Shifting the second track by two sectors provides time to allow for the head-switching overhead and is the equivalent to a head-skew factor of 2. In normal use, a drive switches heads much more often than it switches physical cylinders, which makes head skew more important than cylinder skew. Throughput can rise dramatically when a proper head skew is in place. Different head skews can account for different transfer rates among drives that have the same number of sectors per track and the same interleave.

A nonskewed MFM drive, for example, may have a transfer rate of 380KB per second, whereas the transfer rate of a drive with a head skew of 2 could rise to 425KB per second. Notice that different controllers and drives have different amounts of overhead, so real-world results will be different in each case. In most cases, the head-switch time is very small compared with the controller overhead. As with interleaving, it is better to be on the conservative side to avoid additional disk revolutions.

Cylinder Skew. *Cylinder skew* is the offset in logical sector numbering between the same physical sectors on two adjacent tracks on two adjacent cylinders.

The number of sectors skewed when switching tracks from one cylinder to the next is to compensate for track to track seek time. In essence, all of the sectors on adjacent tracks are rotated with respect to each other. This method permits continuous read or write operations across cylinder boundaries without missing any disk revolutions, thus maximizing system performance.

Cylinder skew is a larger numerical factor than head skew because more overhead exists. It takes much longer to move the heads from one cylinder to another than simply to switch heads. Also, the controller overhead in changing cylinders is higher as well.

Following is a depiction of our example drive with a head-skew factor of 2 but no cylinder skew.

```
Cyl. 0, Head 0:    1- 2- 3- 4- 5- 6- 7- 8- 9-10-11-12-13-14-15-16-17
Cyl. 0, Head 1:    16-17- 1- 2- 3- 4- 5- 6- 7- 8- 9-10-11-12-13-14-15
Cyl. 1, Head 0:    8- 9-10-11-12-13-14-15-16-17- 1- 2- 3- 4- 5- 6- 7
```

In this example, the cylinder-skew factor is 8. Shifting the sectors on the subsequent cylinder by eight sectors gives the drive and controller time to be ready for sector 1 on the next cylinder and eliminates an extra revolution of the disk.

Calculating Skew Factors. You can derive the correct head-skew factor from the following information and formula:

Head skew = (head-switch time/rotational period) × SPT + 2

In other words, the head-switching time of a drive is divided by the time required for a single rotation. The result is multiplied by the number of sectors per track, and 2 is added for controller overhead. The result should then be rounded up to the next whole integer (for example, 2.3 = 2, 2.5 = 3).

You can derive the correct cylinder-skew factor from the following information and formula:

Cylinder skew = (track-to-track seek time/rotational period) × SPT + 4

In other words, the track-to-track seek time of a drive is divided by the time required for a single rotation. The result is multiplied by the number of sectors per track, and 4 is added for controller overhead. Round the result up to a whole integer (for example, 2.3 = 2, 2.5 = 3).

The following example uses typical figures for an ESDI drive and controller. If the head-switching time is 15 us (micro-seconds), the track-to-track seek is 3 ms, the rotational period is 16.67 ms (3,600 RPM), and the drive has 53 physical sectors per track:

Head skew = (0.015/16.67) × 53 +2 = 2 (rounded up)

Cylinder Skew = (3/16.67) × 53 + 4 = 14 (rounded up)

If you do not have the necessary information to make the calculations, contact the drive manufacturer for recommendations. Otherwise, you can make the calculations by using conservative figures for head-switch and track-to-track access times. If you are unsure, just as with interleaving, it is better to be on the conservative side, which minimizes the possibility of additional rotations when reading sequential information on the drive. In most cases, a default head skew of 2 and a cylinder skew of 16 work well.

Because factors such as controller overhead can vary from model to model, sometimes the only way to figure out the best value is to experiment. You can try different skew values and then run data-transfer rate tests to see which value results in the highest performance. Be careful with these tests, however; many disk benchmark programs will only read or write data from one track or one cylinder during testing, which totally eliminates the effect of skewing on the results. The best type of benchmark to use for this testing is one that reads and writes large files on the disk.

Most real (controller register level) low-level format programs are capable of setting skew factors. Those programs that are supplied by a particular controller or drive manufacturer usually already are optimized for their particular drives and controllers, and may not allow you to change the skew. One of the best general-purpose register-level formatters on the market that gives you this flexibility is the Disk Manager program by Ontrack. I highly recommend this program, which you will find listed in Appendix B.

I normally do not recommend programs such as Norton Calibrate and Gibson Spinrite for re-interleaving drives because these programs work only through the BIOS INT 13h functions rather than directly with the disk controller hardware. Thus, these programs cannot set skew factors properly, and using them actually may slow a drive that already has optimum interleave and skew factors.

Notice that most IDE and SCSI drives have their interleave and skew factors set to their optimum values by the manufacturer. In most cases, you cannot even change these values; in the cases in which you can, the most likely result is a slower drive. For this reason, most IDE drive manufacturers recommend against low-level formatting their drives. With some IDE drives, unless you use the right software, you might alter the optimum skew settings and slow the drive. IDE drives that use Zoned Recording cannot ever have the interleave or skew factors changed, and as such, they are fully protected. No matter how you try to format these drives, the interleave and skew factors cannot be altered. The same can be said for SCSI drives.

Shock Mounting

Most hard disks manufactured today have a *shock-mounted* HDA, which means that a rubber cushion is placed between the disk drive body and the mounting chassis. Some drives use more rubber than others, but for the most part, a shock mount is a shock mount. Some drives do not have a shock-isolated HDA due to physical or cost constraints. Be sure that the drive you are using has adequate shock-isolation mounts for the HDA, especially if you are using the drive in a portable PC system or in a system in which environmental conditions are less favorable than in a normal office. I usually never recommend a drive that lacks at least some form of shock mounting.

Cost

The cost of hard disk storage recently has fallen below $0.20 per megabyte. You can purchase 4G drives for under $800. That places the value of the 10M drive that I bought in 1983 at about $2. (Too bad I paid $1,800 for it at the time!)

Of course, the cost of drives continues to fall, and eventually, even $0.20 per megabyte will seem expensive. Because of the low costs of disk storage today, not many drives that are less than 500M are even being manufactured.

Capacity

Four figures commonly are used in advertising drive capacity:

- Unformatted capacity, in millions of bytes (MB)
- Formatted capacity, in millions of bytes (MB)
- Unformatted capacity, in megabytes (Meg or MB)
- Formatted capacity, in megabytes (Meg or MB)

Most manufacturers of IDE and SCSI drives now report only the formatted capacities, because these drives are delivered preformatted. Most of the time, advertisements refer to the unformatted or formatted capacity in millions of bytes (MB) because these figures are larger than the same capacity expressed in megabytes (Meg). This situation generates a great deal of confusion when the user runs FDISK (which reports total drive capacity in megabytes) and wonders where the missing space is. This question ranks as one of the most common questions that I hear during my seminars. Fortunately, the answer is easy; it only involves a little math to figure it out.

Perhaps the most common questions I get are concerning "missing" drive capacity. Consider the following example: "I just installed a new Western Digital AC2200 drive, billed as 212MB. When I entered the drive parameters (989 cylinders, 12 heads, 35 sectors per track), both the BIOS Setup routine and FDISK report the drive as only 203MB! What happened to the other 9MB?"

The answer is only a few calculations away. By multiplying the drive specification parameters, you get this result:

Cylinders:	989
Heads:	12
Sectors per track:	35
Bytes per sector:	512
Total bytes:	212.67MB
Total megabytes:	202.82Meg

The result figures to a capacity of 212.67MB (million bytes) or 202.82Meg. Drive manufacturers usually report drive capacity in millions of bytes, whereas your BIOS and FDISK usually report the capacity in megabytes. 1Meg equals 1,048,576 bytes (or 1,024K, wherein each K is 1,024 bytes). So the bottom line is that this 212.67MB drive also is a 202.82Meg drive! What is really confusing is that there is no industry wide accepted way of differentiating binary Megabytes from decimal ones. Officially they are both abbreviated as "MB", so it is often hard to figure which one is being reported. Usually drive manufacturers will always report metric MBs, since they result in larger, more impressive sounding numbers! One additional item to note about this particular drive is that it is a Zoned Recording drive and that the actual physical parameters are different. Physically, this drive has 1,971 cylinders and 4 heads; however, the total number of sectors on the drive (and, therefore, the capacity) is the same no matter how you translate the parameters.

Although Western Digital does not report the unformatted capacity of this particular drive, unformatted capacity usually works out to be about 19 percent larger than a drive's formatted capacity. The Seagate ST-12550N Barracuda 2G drive, for example, is advertised as having the following capacities:

Unformatted capacity:	2,572.00MB
Unformatted capacity:	2,452.85Meg
Formatted capacity:	2,139.00MB
Formatted capacity:	2,039.91Meg

Each of these four figures is a correct answer to the question "What is the storage capacity of the drive?" As you can see, however, the numbers are very different. In fact, yet another number could be used. Divide the 2,039.91Meg by 1,024, and the drive's capacity is 1.99G! So when you are comparing or discussing drive capacities, make sure that you are working with a consistent unit of measure, or your comparisons will be meaningless.

To eliminate confusion in capacity measurements, I have been using the abbreviation "Meg" in this section, which is not really industry standard. The true industry standard abbreviations for these figures are shown in table 14.10.

Table 14.10 Standard Abbreviations and Meanings

Abbreviation	Description	Decimal Meaning	Binary Meaning
Kb	Kilobit	1,000	1,024
KB	Kilobyte	1,000	1,024
Mb	Megabit	1,000,000	1,048,576
MB	Megabyte	1,000,000	1,048,576
Gb	Gigabit	1,000,000,000	1,073,741,824
GB	Gigabyte	1,000,000,000	1,073,741,824
Tb	Terabit	1,000,000,000,000	1,099,511,627,776
TB	Terabyte	1,000,000,000,000	1,099,511,627,776

Unfortunately there are no differences in the abbreviations when used to indicate metric verses binary values. In other words, MB can be used to indicate both Millions of Bytes and Megabytes. In general, memory values are always computed using the binary derived meanings, while disk capacity goes either way. Unfortunately this often leads to confusion in reporting disk capacities. Note that bits and Bytes are distinguished by a lower- or uppercase *B*. For example, Millions of bits are indicated by using a lowercase *b*, resulting in the abbreviation of Mbps for Million bits per second, while MBps indicates Million Bytes per second.

Specific Recommendations

If you are going to add a hard disk to a system today, I can give you a few recommendations. Starting with the actual, physical hard disk itself, you should demand the following features in a hard disk drive to ensure you that are getting a quality unit:

- Voice coil head actuator
- Thin-film media

For the drive interface, there really are only two types to consider today:

- IDE (Integrated Drive Electronics)
- SCSI (Small Computer System Interface)

SCSI offers great expandability, cross-platform compatibility, high capacity, performance, and flexibility. IDE is less expensive than SCSI and also offers a very high-performance solution, but expansion, compatibility, capacity, and flexibility are more limited compared with SCSI. On the other hand, I usually recommend IDE for most people, since they will not be running more than two hard drives and may not need SCSI for other devices as well. SCSI offers some additional performance potential with a multithreaded OS like NT or OS/2, but IDE offsets this with a lower overhead direct system bus attachment.

Notice that the current IDE standard is ATA-2 (AT Attachment), otherwise called Fast ATA and Enhanced IDE. SCSI-2 is the current SCSI standard, with SCSI-3 on the drawing board.

Summary

This chapter examined hard disks, and explored the physical operations of the hard disk. You learned about how a hard disk operates, and what criteria distinguishes the different models. Now you can use this information to upgrade an existing system with a new hard disk or to troubleshoot and repair an existing configuration. A properly designed and installed hard disk system will give you fewer problems than a haphazardly installed system will.

Chapter 15

Hard Disk Interfaces

This chapter describes the hard disk interface, from the drives to the cables and controllers that run them. You will learn about the various disk interfaces you can select, and the shortcomings and strengths of each type.

Interfaces Choices

A variety of hard disk interfaces are available today. As time has passed, the number of choices has increased, and many of the older designs no longer are viable in newer systems. You need to know about all these interfaces, from the oldest to the newest designs, because you will encounter all of them whenever upgrading or repairing systems is necessary.

The interfaces have different cabling and configuration options, and the setup and format of drives will vary as well. Special problems may arise when you are trying to install more than one drive of a particular interface type or (especially) when you are mixing drives of different interface types in one system.

This section covers the different hard disk drive interfaces, giving you all the technical information you need to deal with them in any way—troubleshooting, servicing, upgrading, and even mixing the different types.

This section also examines the standard controllers and describes how you can work with these controllers, as well as replace them with much faster units. Also discussed are the different types of drive interfaces: ST-506/412, ESDI, IDE, and SCSI. Choosing the proper interface is important, because your choice also affects your disk drive purchase and the ultimate speed of the disk subsystem.

The primary job of the hard disk controller or interface is to transmit and receive data to and from the drive. The different interface types limit how fast data can be moved from the drive to the system and offer different levels of performance. If you are putting together a system in which performance is a primary concern, you need to know how these different interfaces affect performance and what you can expect from them. Many of the statistics that appear in technical literature are not indicative of the real performance figures that you will see in practice. I will separate the myths presented by some of these overoptimistic figures from the reality of what you will actually see.

With regard to disk drives, and especially hard disk drives, the specification on which people seem to focus the most is the drive's reported *average seek time,* the (average) time it takes for the heads to be positioned from one track to another. Unfortunately, the importance of this specification often is overstated, especially in relation to other specifications, such as the data-transfer rate.

The transfer rate of data between the drive and the system is more important than access time because most drives spend more time reading and writing information than they do simply moving the heads around. The speed at which a program or data file is loaded or read is affected most by the data-transfer rate. Specialized operations such as sorting large files, which involve a lot of random access to individual records of the file (and, therefore, many seek operations), are helped greatly by a faster-seeking disk drive, so seeking performance is important in these cases. Most normal file load and save operations, however, are affected most by the rate at which data can be read and written to and from the drive. The data-transfer rate depends on both the drive and the interface.

Several types of hard disk interfaces have been used in PC systems over the years:

- ST-506/412
- ESDI
- IDE
- SCSI

Of these interfaces, only ST-506/412 and ESDI are what you could call true disk-controller-to-drive interfaces. SCSI and IDE are system-level interfaces that usually incorporate a chipset-based variation of one of the other two types of disk controller interfaces internally. For example, most SCSI and IDE drives incorporate the same basic controller circuitry used in separate ESDI controllers. The SCSI interface adds another layer of interface that attaches the controller to the system bus, whereas IDE is a direct bus-attachment interface.

In data recovery, it helps to know the disk interface you are working with because many data-recovery problems involve drive setup and installation problems. Each interface requires a slightly different method of installation and drive configuration. If the installation or configuration is incorrect or accidentally altered by the system user, it may prevent access to data on a drive. Accordingly, anyone who wants to become proficient in data recovery must be an expert on installing and configuring various types of hard disks and controllers.

IBM's reliance on industry-standard interfaces such as those listed here was a boon for everybody in the IBM-compatible industry. These standards allow a great deal of cross-system and cross-manufacturer compatibility. The use of these industry-standard interfaces allows us to pick up a mail-order catalog, purchase a hard disk for the lowest possible price, and be assured that it will work with our system. This plug-and-play capability results in affordable hard disk storage and a variety of options in capacities and speed.

The ST-506/412 Interface

The ST-506/412 interface was developed by Seagate Technologies around 1980. The interface originally appeared in the Seagate ST-506 drive, which was a 5M formatted (or 6M unformatted) drive in a full-height, 5 1/4-inch form factor. By today's standards, this drive is a tank! In 1981 Seagate introduced the ST-412 drive, which added a feature called buffered seek to the interface. This drive was a 10M formatted (12M unformatted) drive that also qualifies as a tank by today's standards. Besides the Seagate ST-412, IBM also used the Miniscribe 1012 as well as the International Memories, Inc. (IMI) model 5012 drive in the XT. IMI and Miniscribe are long gone, but Seagate remains as one of the largest drive manufacturers today. Since the original XT, Seagate has supplied drives for numerous systems made by many different manufacturers.

Most drive manufacturers that made hard disks for PC systems adopted the Seagate ST-506/412 standard, a situation that helped make this interface popular. One important feature is the interface's plug-and-play design. No custom cables or special modifications are needed for the drives, which means that virtually any ST-506/412 drive will work with any ST-506/412 controller. The only real compatibility issue with this interface is the level of BIOS support provided by the system.

When introduced to the PC industry by IBM in 1983, ROM BIOS support for this hard disk interface was provided by a BIOS chip on the controller. Contrary to what most believed, the PC and XT motherboard BIOS had no inherent hard disk support. When the AT system was introduced, IBM placed the ST-506/412 interface support in the motherboard BIOS and eliminated it from the controller. Since then, any system that is compatible with the IBM AT (which includes most systems on the market today) has an enhanced version of the same support in the motherboard BIOS as well. Because this support was somewhat limited, especially in the older BIOS versions, many disk controller manufacturers also placed additional BIOS support for their controllers directly on the controllers themselves. In some cases, you would use the controller BIOS and motherboard BIOS together; in other cases, you would disable the controller or motherboard BIOS and then use one or the other. These issues will be discussed more completely later in this chapter, in the section "System Configuration."

The ST-506/412 interface does not quite make the grade in today's high-performance PC systems. This interface was designed for a 5M drive, and I have not seen any drives larger than 152M (MFM encoding) or 233M (RLL encoding) available for this type of interface. Because the capacity, performance, and expandability of ST-506/412 are so limited, this interface is obsolete and generally unavailable in new systems. However, many older systems still use drives that have this interface.

Encoding Schemes and Problems. As indicated in Chapter 14 in the section "Data Encoding Schemes," encoding schemes are used in communications for converting digital data bits to various tones for transmission over a telephone line. For disk drives, the digital bits are converted, or encoded, in a pattern of magnetic impulses, or flux transitions (also called flux reversals), which are written on the disk. These flux transitions are decoded later, when the data is read from the disk.

A device called an *Endec* (encoder/decoder) accomplishes the conversion to flux transitions for writing on the media and the subsequent reconversion back to digital data during read operations. The function of the Endec is very similar to that of a modem (modulator/demodulator) in that digital data is converted to an analog waveform, which then is converted back to digital data. Sometimes, the Endec is called a data separator because it is designed to separate data and clocking information from the flux-transition pulse stream read from the disk.

One of the biggest problems with ST-506/412 was the fact that this Endec resided on the disk controller (rather than the drive), which resulted in the possibility of corruption of the analog data signal before it reached the media. This problem became especially pronounced when the ST-506/412 controllers switched to using RLL Endecs to store 50 percent more data on the drive. With the RLL encoding scheme, the actual density of magnetic flux transitions on the disk media remains the same as with MFM encoding, but the timing between the transitions must be measured much more precisely.

In RLL encoding, the intervals between flux changes are approximately the same as with MFM, but the actual timing between them is much more critical. As a result, the transition cells in which signals must be recognized are much smaller and more precisely placed than with MFM. RLL encoding places more stringent demands on the timing of the controller and drive electronics. With RLL encoding, accurately reading the timing of the flux changes is paramount. Additionally, because RLL encodes variable-length groups of bits rather than single bits, a single error in one flux transition can corrupt two to four bits of data. For these reasons, an RLL controller usually has a more sophisticated error-detection and error-correction routine than an MFM controller.

Most of the cheaper disk drives on the market did not have data-channel circuits that were designed to be precise enough to handle RLL encoding without problems. RLL encoding also is much more susceptible to noise in the read signal, and the conventional oxide media coatings did not have a sufficient signal-to-noise ratio for reliable RLL encoding. This problem often was compounded by the fact that many drives of the time used stepper motor head positioning systems, which are notoriously inaccurate, further amplifying the signal-to-noise ratio problem.

At this time, manufacturers starting RLL-certifying drives for use with RLL Endec controllers. This stamp of approval essentially meant that the drive had passed tests and was designed to handle the precise timing requirements that RLL encoding required. In some cases, the drive electronics were upgraded between a manufacturer's MFM and RLL drive versions, but the drives are essentially the same. In fact, if any improvements were made in the so-called RLL-certified drives, the same upgrades usually were also applied to the MFM version.

The bottom line is that other than improved precision, there is no real difference between an ST-506/412 drive that is sold as an MFM model and one that is sold as an RLL model. If you want to use a drive that originally was sold as an MFM model with an RLL controller, I suggest that you do so only if the drive uses a voice coil head actuator and thin-film media. Virtually any ST-506/412 drive with these qualities is more than good enough to handle RLL encoding with no problems.

Using MFM encoding, a standard ST-506/412 format specifies that the drive will contain 17 sectors per track, with each sector containing 512 bytes of data. A controller that uses an RLL Endec raises the number of sectors per track to 25 or 26.

The real solution to reliability problems with RLL encoding was to place the Endec directly on the drive rather than on the controller. This method reduces the susceptibility to noise and interference that can plague an ST-506/412 drive system running RLL encoding. ESDI, IDE, and SCSI drives all have the Endec (and, often, the entire controller) built into the drive by default. Because the Endec is attached to the drive without cables and with an extremely short electrical distance, the propensity for timing-and noise-induced errors is greatly reduced or eliminated. This situation is analogous to a local telephone call between the Endec and the disk platters. This local communication makes the ESDI, IDE, and SCSI interfaces much more reliable than the older ST-506/412 interface; they share none of the reliability problems that once were associated with RLL encoding over the ST-506/412 interface. Virtually all ESDI, IDE, and SCSI drives use RLL encoding today with tremendously increased reliability over even MFM ST-506/412 drives.

ST-506/412 Configuration and Installation. The ST-506/412 interface is characterized by a two- or three-cable arrangement, depending on whether one or two drives are connected. One 34-connector control cable is daisy-chained between up to two drives. The daisy-chain arrangement is much like that used for floppy drives. Each drive on the daisy chain is jumped to respond to a particular Drive Select (DS) line. In the controller implementation used in all PC systems, there are two available lines, called Drive Select 1 (DS1) and Drive Select 2 (DS2). Some drives support as many as four DS lines, but only the first two are usable. Although it may appear that you could string four drives on a single daisy-chain cable, the design of the PC system and controllers uses only the first two.

The control cable usually has lines 25 through 29 twisted between the drive D and C connectors. The first drive (drive C) normally is plugged into the last control cable connector at the end of the cable opposite the controller; an optional second drive (D) can be installed in the middle control-cable connector. The twist in the lines serves to reroute the Drive Select lines so that the drive plugged into the last cable position appears to the controller to be attached to Drive Select 1, even though the jumper on the drive is set for DS2. This arrangement is very similar to the one used for floppy drives; if the cable is twisted, both drives must be set to the DS2 jumper position. If the cable does not have the twisted lines, the drive at the end of the cable (C) must be set to DS1.

Another configuration item is the terminating resistor, which must be installed on the drive at the end of the cable (C) and must be removed from the optional second drive (D) attached to the middle control-cable connector. The controller has a permanently installed terminating resistor that never has to be adjusted. Although the control cable is similar in function and appearance to the 34-pin cable used for floppy drives, the cables generally are not interchangeable because different lines are twisted. Whereas pins 25 through 29 are inverted on the hard disk control cable, pins 10 through 16 are inverted on the floppy cable, rendering them incompatible.

The other two cables, called data cables, are 20-connector cables, each of which runs from the controller to a single drive because this cable is not daisy-chained. A two-drive system, therefore, has one control cable from the controller to each of two drives in a daisy chain, plus two separate data cables—one for each drive. The controller has three connectors to support the two-drive maximum limit. As its name suggests, the data cable carries data to and from the drive.

If you are using a single drive, only the data cable connector closest to the control cable connector is used; the other is left unattached. Most ST-506/412 controllers also have an on-board floppy controller, which also will have a 34-pin connector for the floppy drives. Figures 15.1 and 15.2 show the control and data cable connectors on a typical combination ST-506/412 hard disk and floppy disk controller. Notice that some of these combination controllers allow the floppy controller portion to be disabled and others do not, which may cause a conflict if you have any other floppy controller in the system.

ST-506/412 Drive Configuration. With ST-506/412 and ESDI drives, you have to configure the following items on each drive:

- Drive Select (DS) jumpers
- Terminating resistor

These configuration items usually are located near the rear of the drive on the disk drive logic board.

Drive Select Jumpers. The Drive Select jumper selects the Drive Select (DS) signal to which the drive should respond. The drive controller sends control signals on two DS lines, one for each drive. Because each drive must be set to respond to a different DS signal, you can use only two drives per controller.

The DS jumpers must be set so that each drive responds to a different DS line from the controller (DS1 or DS2). If the 34-pin control cable has a twist in lines 25 through 29, both drives should be set to DS2. If the control cable is a straight-through design (no twist), the drive at the end of the cable opposite the controller (C) should be set to DS1, and a second drive attached to the middle control-cable connector (D) should be set to DS2. Notice that some drives label the DS jumpers starting with 0, so that DS1 would be labeled DS0 and DS2 would be labeled DS1.

Terminating Resistors. An ST-506/412 drive is always shipped from the factory with a terminating resistor installed. When you install these drives, you must ensure that the drive plugged into the end of the control-cable daisy chain has this terminator installed. Additionally, this terminator must be removed (or disabled with a jumper, in some cases) from the secondary drive installed in the center control-cable connector.

The functions of the terminating resistor are the same as those discussed for floppy drives. The idea is to provide electrical-signal termination so that the control signals to and from the drive and controller do not reflect back or echo along the cable. The terminating resistor provides the proper signal-to-noise ratio and the proper electrical load for the controller. Improper drive termination results in drives that do not function (or that

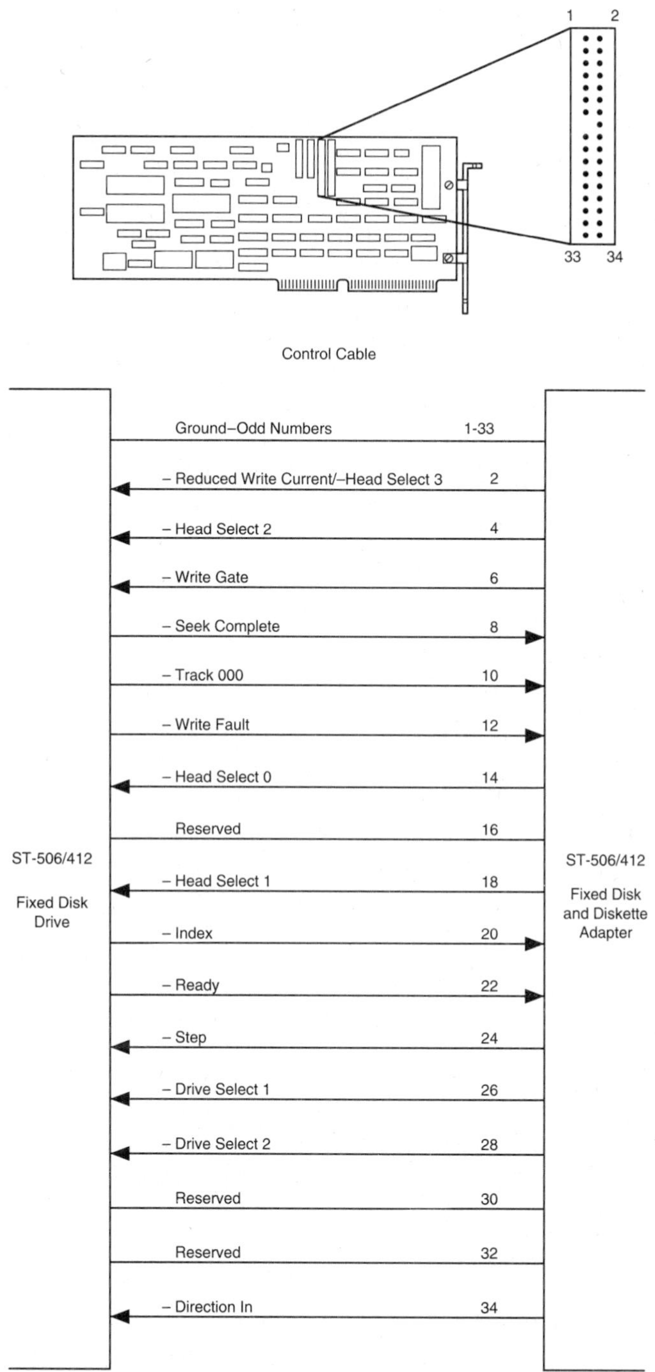

Figure 15.1

ST-506/412 control cable connector.

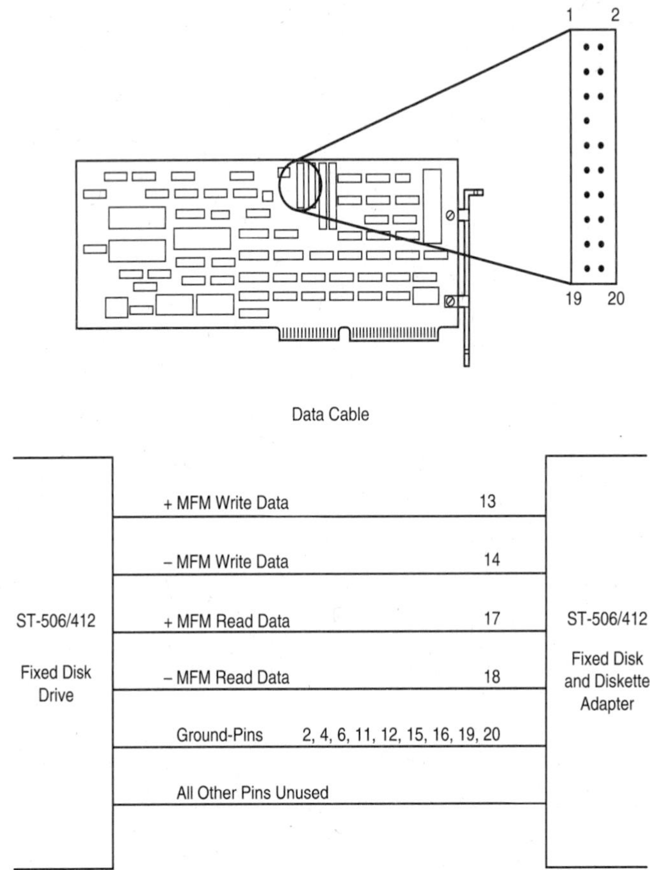

Figure 15.2

ST-506/412 data cable connectors.

do so only with excessive problems). Improper termination also may damage the controller because of improper electrical loads.

Control and Data Cables. The control cable connects to the controller and daisy chains to the secondary and primary drives, and separate data cables (20-pin) run from the controller to each drive. The data cable connector closest to the control-cable connector on the controller is used for the primary (C) drive.

When connecting cables, you should observe the proper pin-1 orientation from end to end. On ribbon cables, the pin-1 line usually is a different color from the other lines. (In most ribbon cables, for example, the pin-1 line is red or blue, and the rest of the cable is gray). You need to ensure that this pin-1 line is plugged into pin-1 of the controller and drive connectors. Both the controller and drive should have the pin-1 position on each connector marked. Sometimes the mark is the number 1; other times, it is a dot or some other symbol that is silkscreened on the circuit board. The cable connectors at the controller end may be keyed, in which case pin-15 will be missing from the control-cable connector on the controller connector, and the corresponding hole will be plugged in the control cable. The data cable connectors will be missing pin-8, and the corresponding hole also will be plugged in the data cables. The edge connectors used at the drive end are normally keyed to a notch in the drive connectors. The side of the connector with the notch cut out indicates the pin-1 orientation at the drive end.

Notice that the 34-pin control cable is very similar to the 34-pin control/data cable used for floppy drives; these cables, however, usually are not interchangeable. The ST-506/412 control cable has lines 25 through 29 twisted between the secondary and primary drive connectors, whereas the 34-pin floppy cable has lines 10 through 17 twisted. As a result, the cables are incompatible and therefore noninterchangeable.

ST-506/412 Interface Connectors. The ST-506/412 Interface uses two connections, a 34-pin control connector and a 20-pin data connector. Table 15.1 and 15.2 show the pinouts for these connectors.

Power Cables. To complete the required cable connections to the hard drive, you need a spare power connector (Table 15.3 shows the pinouts for the connector). Some older power supplies have only two-drive power connectors. Several companies sell a power splitter cable, or Y cable, that can adapt one cable from the power supply so that it powers two drives. If you add a power splitter to a system, make sure that the power supply can handle the load of the additional drive or drives.

Table 15.1 ST-506/412 34-Pin Control Connector

Signal Name	Pin	Pin	Signal Name
GROUND	1	2	-HD SLCT 3
GROUND	3	4	-HD SLCT 2
GROUND	5	6	-WRITE GATE
GROUND	7	8	-SEEK CMPLT
GROUND	9	10	-TRACK 0
GROUND	11	12	-WRITE FAULT
GROUND	13	14	-HD SLCT 0
KEY (no pin)	15	16	Not Connected
GROUND	17	18	-HD SLCT 1
GROUND	19	20	-INDEX
GROUND	21	22	-READY
GROUND	23	24	-STEP
GROUND	25	26	-DRV SLCT 0
GROUND	27	28	-DRV SLCT 1
GROUND	29	30	Not Connected
GROUND	31	32	Not Connected
GROUND	33	34	-DIRECTION IN

Table 15.2 ST-506/412 20-Pin Data Connector

Signal Name	Pin	Pin	Signal Name
-DRV SLCTD	1	2	GROUND
Not Connected	3	4	GROUND
Not Connected	5	6	GROUND
Not Connected	7	8	KEY (no pin)
Not Connected	9	10	Not Connected
GROUND	11	12	GROUND
+MFM WRITE	13	14	-MFM WRITE
GROUND	15	16	GROUND
+MFM READ	17	18	-MFM READ
GROUND	19	20	GROUND

Table 15.3 Disk Drive Power Connector

Pin	Wire Color	Signal
1	Yellow	+12v
2	Black	Gnd
3	Black	Gnd
4	Red	+5v

If the original power supply is not adequate, purchase an aftermarket unit that can supply adequate power. Most better aftermarket supplies have four-drive power connectors, eliminating the need for the splitter cables. Power splitter cables are available from several of the cable and accessory vendors listed in Appendix B, as well as from electronic supply stores such as Radio Shack.

Historical Notes. The following sections list some information on the original ST-506/412 controllers used in the PC environment. These were the controllers that IBM supplied in the XT and AT systems. At the time of introduction, these controllers set standards that, especially in the case of the AT controller, we still live with today. In fact, the entire IDE interface standard is based on the controller that IBM designed and used in the AT. All the conventions and standards for the hard disk interfaces that we use today started with these controllers.

Original IBM 8-Bit Controllers. The first ST-506/412 controller standard sold for PC systems was the hard disk controller used in the original 10MB IBM XT. This controller actually was made for IBM by Xebec Corporation and also was sold under the Xebec name as the Xebec 1210 controller. The Xebec 1210 is an ST-506/412 controller that uses Modified Frequency Modulation (MFM) encoding to record data on a drive. This controller's ROM, produced by IBM, contained an 8K hard disk BIOS with an internal table that had entries for four different drives. Each drive was selected by jumpers on the controller, which actually were soldered in the early IBM units. If you purchased the controller from Xebec, you got a slightly different but completely compatible ROM, and the jumpers were not soldered, so you easily could select one of the four BIOS table entries. Xebec also allowed system integrators to copy its ROM to modify the built-in drive tables for a specific drive.

Later IBM XT systems with a 20M hard disk still used the Xebec 1210, but it had a new 4K ROM that contained different drive tables, as well as jumpers like those found on the versions also sold separately by Xebec. Xebec never sold an autoconfigure version of this controller, which would have made integrating different drives easier.

The Xebec 1210 is one of the slowest ST-506/412 controllers ever made, supporting at best a 5:1 interleave on a stock IBM PC or IBM XT system. If you use the IBM Advanced Diagnostics program for the IBM PC or IBM XT, the low-level formatter produces a standard 6:1 interleave, which results in a paltry 85K-per-second data-transfer rate. By changing the interleave to 5:1, you can wring 102K per second from this controller—still unbelievably slow by today's standards.

Xebec also made a Model 1220 that combined a hard disk and floppy disk controller, was hardware-compatible with the 1210, and worked with the IBM or standard Xebec ROM. The separate floppy controller then could be removed from the system, and you could save a slot.

I recommend replacing this controller with an autoconfigure controller whenever you get the chance. Most other controllers also are significantly faster than the Xebec.

Original IBM 16-Bit Controllers. For the AT, IBM used two controllers made by Western Digital: the WD1002-WA2 and the WD1003A-WA2. The WD1003 is an upgraded WD1002 with a much lower chip count. The WD1003 also was shorter than the WD1002 to fit into the IBM XT 286.

The WD1002 is used in the IBM AT as a combination hard disk and floppy disk controller. The WD1002 and the WD1003 are standard ST-506/412 controllers that supply MFM encoding to the drive. Neither controller contains a ROM BIOS; instead, BIOS support is built into the motherboard ROM. Both controllers support a 2:1 interleave, even on a standard 6-MHz IBM AT system. The IBM Advanced Diagnostics low-level formatter can put down a 2:1 interleave, but the default is 3:1. Most users of these controllers can realize a performance gain if they simply reformat to the lower interleave.

The ESDI Interface

ESDI, or Enhanced Small Device Interface, is a specialized hard disk interface established as a standard in 1983, primarily by Maxtor Corporation. Maxtor led a consortium of drive manufacturers to adopt its proposed interface as a high-performance standard to succeed ST-506/412. ESDI later was adopted by the ANSI (American National Standards Institute) organization and published under the ANSI X3T9.2 Committee. The latest version of the ANSI ESDI document is known as X3.170a-1991. You can obtain this document, and other ANSI-standard documents, from ANSI itself or from Global Engineering Documents. These companies are listed in Appendix B.

Compared with ST-506/412, ESDI has provisions for increased reliability, such as building the Endec (encoder/decoder) into the drive. ESDI is a very-high-speed interface, capable of a maximum 24-megabits-per-second transfer rate. Most drives running ESDI, however, are limited to a maximum 10 or 15 megabits per second. Unfortunately, compatibility problems between different ESDI implementations combined with pressure from low-cost, high-performance IDE interface drives have served to make the ESDI interface obsolete. Few, if any, new systems today include ESDI drives, although ESDI became somewhat popular in high-end systems during the late '80s.

Enhanced commands enabled some ESDI controllers to read a drive's capacity parameters directly from the drive, as well as to control defect mapping, but several manufacturers had different methods for writing this information on the drive. When you install an ESDI drive, in some cases the controller automatically reads the parameter and defect information directly from the drive. In other cases, however, you still have to enter this information manually, as with ST-506/412.

The ESDI's enhanced defect-mapping commands provide a standard way for the PC system to read a defect map from a drive, which means that the manufacturer's defect list can be written to the drive as a file. The defect-list file then can be read by the controller and low-level format software, eliminating the need for the installer to type these entries from the keyboard and enabling the format program to update the defect list with new entries if it finds new defects during the low-level format or the surface analysis.

Most ESDI implementations have drives formatted to 32 sectors per track or more (80 or more sectors per track are possible)—many more sectors per track than the standard ST-506/412 implementation of 17 to 26 sectors per track. The greater density results in two or more times the data-transfer rate, with a 1:1 interleave. Almost without exception, ESDI controllers support a 1:1 interleave, which allows for a transfer rate of 1MB per second or greater.

Because ESDI is much like the ST-506/412 interface, it can replace that interface without affecting software in the system. Most ESDI controllers are register-compatible with the older ST-506/412 controllers, which enables OS/2 and other non-DOS operating systems to run with few or no problems. The ROM BIOS interface to ESDI is similar to the ST-506/412 standard, and many low-level disk utilities that run on one interface will run on the other. To take advantage of ESDI defect mapping and other special features, however, use a low-level format and surface-analysis utility designed for ESDI (such as the ones usually built into the controller ROM BIOS and called by DEBUG).

During the late 1980s, most high-end systems from major manufacturers were equipped with ESDI controllers and drives. More recently, manufacturers have been equipping high end systems with SCSI. The SCSI interface allows for much greater expandability, supports more types of devices than ESDI, and offers equal or greater performance. I no longer recommend installing ESDI drives unless you are upgrading a system that already has an ESDI controller.

ESDI Interface Connectors. ESDI (Enhanced Small Device Interface) uses two connections, a 34-pin control connector and a 20-pin data connector. Tables 15.4 and 15.5 show the pinouts for these connectors.

Table 15.4 ESDI (Enhanced Small Device Interface) 34-Pin Control Connector

Signal Name	Pin	Pin	Signal Name
GROUND	1	2	-HD SLCT 3
GROUND	3	4	-HD SLCT 2
GROUND	5	6	-WRITE GATE
GROUND	7	8	-CNFG/STATUS
GROUND	9	10	-XFER ACK
GROUND	11	12	-ATTENTION
GROUND	13	14	-HD SLCT 0
KEY (no pin)	15	16	-SECTOR
GROUND	17	18	-HD SLCT 1
GROUND	19	20	-INDEX
GROUND	21	22	-READY
GROUND	23	24	-XFER REQ
GROUND	25	26	-DRV SLCT 0
GROUND	27	28	-DRV SLCT 1
GROUND	29	30	Reserved
GROUND	31	32	-READ GATE
GROUND	33	34	-CMD DATA

Table 15.5 ESDI (Enhanced Small Device Interface) 20-Pin Data Connector

Signal Name	Pin	Pin	Signal Name
-DRV SLCTD	1	2	-SECTOR
-CMD COMPL	3	4	-ADDR MK EN
GROUND	5	6	GROUND
+WRITE CLK	7	8	-WRITE CLK
GROUND	9	10	+RD/REF CLK
-RD/REF CLK	11	12	GROUND
+NRZ WRITE	13	14	-NRZ WRITE
GROUND	15	16	GROUND
+NRZ READ	17	18	-NRZ READ
GROUND	19	20	-INDEX

ESDI Drive Configuration. The ESDI interface was modeled after the ST-506/412 interface and shares virtually all the same types of configuration items and procedures. The 34-pin control and 20-pin data cables are identical to those used in an ST-506/412 installation, and all the configuration procedures with regard to Drive Select jumpers, twisted cables, and terminating resistors are the same as with ST-506/412.

Follow the configuration procedures for ST-506/412 drives when configuring ESDI drives. Because ESDI was developed from the ST-506/412 interface, it shares many characteristics including the type of cabling used as well as how it is configured.

The IDE Interface

Integrated Drive Electronics (IDE) is a generic term applied to any drive with an integrated (built-in) disk controller. The IDE interface as we know it is officially called ATA (AT Attachment) and is an ANSI standard, however IDE can roughly apply to any disk drive with a built-in controller. The first drives with integrated controllers were Hardcards; today, a variety of drives with integrated controllers are available. In a drive with IDE, the disk controller is integrated into the drive, and this combination drive/controller assembly usually plugs into a bus connector on the motherboard or on a bus adapter card. Combining the drive and controller greatly simplifies installation because there are no separate power or signal cables from the controller to the drive. Also, when the controller and the drive are assembled as a unit, the number of total components is reduced, signal paths are shorter, and the electrical connections are more noise-resistant, resulting in a more reliable design than is possible when a separate controller, connected to the drive by cables, is used.

Placing the controller (including Endec) on the drive gives IDE drives an inherent reliability advantage over interfaces with separate controllers. Reliability is increased because the data encoding, from digital to analog, is performed directly on the drive in a tight noise-free environment; the timing-sensitive analog information does not have to travel along crude ribbon cables that are likely to pick up noise and to insert propagation delays into the signals. The integrated configuration allows for increases in the clock rate of the encoder, as well as the storage density of the drive.

Integrating the controller and drive also frees the controller and drive engineers from having to adhere to the strict standards imposed by the earlier interface standards. Engineers can design what essentially are custom drive and controller implementations because no other controller would ever have to be connected to the drive. The resulting drive and controller combinations can offer higher performance than earlier stand-alone controller and drive setups. IDE drives sometimes are called drives with embedded controllers.

The IDE connector on motherboards in many systems is nothing more than a stripped-down bus slot. In ATA IDE installations, these connectors normally contain a 40-pin subset of the 98 pins that would be available in a standard 16-bit ISA bus slot. The pins used are only the signal pins required by a standard-type XT or AT hard disk controller. For example, because an AT-style disk controller uses only interrupt line 14, the motherboard AT IDE connector supplies only that interrupt line; no other interrupt lines are needed. The XT IDE motherboard connector supplies interrupt line 5 because that is what an XT controller would use.

Many people who use systems with IDE connectors on the motherboard believe that a hard disk controller is built into their motherboard, but the controller really is in the drive. I do not know of any PC systems that have hard disk controllers built into the motherboard.

When IDE drives are discussed, the ATA IDE variety usually is the only kind mentioned because it is so popular. But other forms of IDE drives exist, based on other buses. For example, several PS/2 systems came with Micro Channel (MCA) IDE drives, which plug directly into a Micro Channel Bus slot (through an angle adapter or Interposer card). An 8-bit ISA form of IDE also existed but was never very popular. Most IBM-compatible systems with the ISA or EISA Bus use AT-Bus (16-bit) IDE drives. The ATA IDE interface is by far the most popular type of drive interface available.

The primary advantage of IDE drives is cost. Because the separate controller or host adapter is eliminated and the cable connections are simplified, IDE drives cost much less than a standard controller-and-drive combination. These drives also are more reliable because the controller is built into the drive. Therefore, the Endec or data separator (the converter between the digital and analog signals on the drive) stays close to the media. Because the drive has a short analog-signal path, it is less susceptible to external noise and interference.

Another advantage is performance. IDE drives are some of the highest-performance drives available—but they are also among the lowest-performance drives. This apparent contradiction is a result of the fact that all IDE drives are different. You cannot make a blanket statement about the performance of IDE drives because each drive is unique. The high-end models, however, offer performance that is equal or superior to that of any other type of drive on the market for a single-user, single-tasking operating system.

IDE Origins. Technically, the first IDE drives were Hardcards. Companies such as the Plus Development division of Quantum took small 3.5-inch drives (either ST-506/412 or ESDI) and attached them directly to a standard controller. The assembly then was plugged into a bus slot as though it were a normal disk controller. Unfortunately, the mounting of a heavy, vibrating hard disk in an expansion slot with nothing but a single screw to hold it in place left a lot to be desired—not to mention the possible interference with adjacent cards due to the fact that many of these units were much thicker than a controller card alone.

Several companies got the idea that you could redesign the controller to replace the logic-board assembly on a standard hard disk and then mount it in a standard drive bay just like any other drive. Because the built-in controller in these drives still needed to plug directly into the expansion bus just like any other controller, a cable was run between the drive and one of the slots.

These connection problems were solved in different ways. Compaq was the first to incorporate a special bus adapter in its system to adapt the 98-pin AT bus edge connector on the motherboard to a smaller 40-pin header style connector that the drive would plug into. The 40-pin connectors were all that were needed because it was known that a disk controller would never need more than 40 of the bus lines.

In 1987, IBM developed its own MCA IDE drives and connected them to the bus through a bus adapter device called an interposer card. These bus adapters (sometimes called paddle boards) needed only a few buffer chips and did not require any real circuitry because the drive-based controller was designed to plug directly into the bus. The paddle board nickname came from the fact that they resembled game paddle or joystick adapters, which do not have much circuitry on them. Another 8-bit variation of IDE appeared in 8-bit ISA systems such as the PS/2 Model 30. The XT IDE interface uses a 40-pin connector and cable that is similar to, but not compatible with, the 16-bit version.

IDE Bus Versions. Three main types of IDE interfaces are available, with the differences based on three different bus standards:

- AT Attachment (ATA) IDE (16-bit ISA)
- XT IDE (8-bit ISA)
- MCA IDE (16-bit Micro Channel)

The XT and ATA versions have standardized on 40-pin connectors and cables, but the connectors have slightly different pinouts, rendering them incompatible with one another. MCA IDE uses a completely different 72-pin connector and is designed for MCA bus systems only.

In most cases, you must use the type of IDE drive that matches your system bus. This situation means that XT IDE drives work only in XT-class 8-bit ISA slot systems, AT IDE drives work only in AT-class 16-bit ISA or EISA slot systems, and MCA IDE drives work only in Micro Channel systems (such as the IBM PS/2 Model 50 or higher). A company called Silicon Valley offers adapter cards for XT systems that will run ATA IDE drives. Other companies, such as Arco Electronics and Sigma Data, have IDE adapters for Micro Channel systems that allow ATA IDE drives to be used on these systems. (You can find these vendors in Appendix B.) These adapters are very useful for XT or PS/2 systems, because there is a very limited selection of XT or MCA IDE drives, whereas the selection of ATA drives is virtually unlimited.

In most modern ISA and EISA systems, you will find an ATA connector on the motherboard. If your motherboard does not have one of these connectors and you want to attach an AT IDE drive to your system, you can purchase an adapter card that changes your 98-pin slot connector to the 40-pin IDE connector. These adapter cards are nothing more than buffered cables; they are not really controllers. The controller is built into the drive. Some of the cards offer additional features, such as an on-board ROM BIOS or cache memory.

ATA IDE. CDC, Western Digital, and Compaq actually created what could be called the first ATA type IDE interface drive and were the first to establish the 40-pin IDE connector pinout. The first ATA IDE drives were 5-1/4-inch half-height CDC 40M units (I believe that they had a green activity LED) with integrated WD controllers sold in the first Compaq 386 systems way back in '86. After that, Compaq helped found a company called Conner Peripherals to supply Compaq with IDE drives. Conner originally made drives only for Compaq, but later, Compaq sold much of its ownership of Conner.

Eventually, the 40-pin IDE connector and drive interface method was placed before one of the ANSI standards committees, which, in conjunction with drive manufacturers, ironed out some deficiencies, tied up some loose ends, and published what is known as the CAM ATA (Common Access Method AT Attachment) interface. The CAM Committee was formed in October 1988, and the first working document of the AT Attachment interface was introduced in March 1989. Before the CAM ATA standard, many companies that followed CDC, such as Conner Peripherals, made proprietary changes to what had been done by CDC. As a result, many older ATA drives are very difficult to integrate into a dual-drive setup that has newer drives.

Some areas of the ATA standard have been left open for vendor-specific commands and functions. These vendor-specific commands and functions are the main reason why it is so difficult to low-level format IDE drives. To work properly, the formatter that you are using usually must know the specific vendor-unique commands for rewriting sector headers and remapping defects. Unfortunately, these and other specific drive commands differ from OEM to OEM, clouding the "standard" somewhat.

It is important to note that only the ATA IDE interface has been standardized by the industry. The XT IDE and MCA IDE were never adopted as industry-wide standards and never became very popular. These interfaces are no longer in production, and no new systems of which I am aware come with these nonstandard IDE interfaces.

The ATA Specification. The ATA specification was introduced in March 1989 as an ANSI standard. ATA-1 was finally approved in 1994, and ATA-2 (also called Enhanced IDE) was approved in 1995. ATA-3 is currently in the works. You can obtain the current version of these standards from Global Engineering Documents, which is listed in Appendix B. The ATA standards have gone a long way toward eliminating incompatibilities and problems with interfacing IDE drives to ISA and EISA systems. The ATA specifications define the signals on the 40-pin connector, the functions and timings of these signals, cable specifications, and so on. The following section lists some of the elements and functions defined by the ATA specification.

Dual-Drive Configurations. Dual-drive ATA installations can be problematic because each drive has its own controller and both controllers must function while being connected to the same bus. There has to be a way to ensure that only one of the two controllers will respond to a command at a time.

The ATA standard provides the option of operating on the AT Bus with two drives in a daisy-chained configuration. The primary drive (drive 0) is called the master, and the secondary drive (drive 1) is the slave. You designate a drive as being master or slave by setting a jumper or switch on the drive or by using a special line in the interface called the Cable Select (CSEL) pin.

When only one drive is installed, the controller responds to all commands from the system. When two drives (and, therefore, two controllers) are installed, all commands from the system are received by both controllers. Each controller then must be set up to respond only to commands for itself. In this situation, one controller then must be designated as the master and the other as the slave. When the system sends a command for a specific drive, the controller on the other drive must remain silent while the selected controller and drive are functioning. You handle discrimination between the two controllers by setting a special bit (the DRV bit) in the Drive/Head Register of a command block.

ATA I/O Connector. The ATA interface connector is a 40-pin header-type connector that should be keyed to prevent the possibility of installing it upside down. A key is provided by the removal of pin 20, and the corresponding pin on the cable connector should be plugged to prevent a backward installation. The use of keyed connectors and cables is highly recommended because plugging an IDE cable in backward can damage both the drive and the bus adapter circuits (although I have done it myself many times with no smoked parts yet!).

Table 15.6 shows the ATA-IDE interface connector pinout.

Table 15.6 ATA (AT Attachment) IDE (Integrated Drive Electronics) Connector

Signal Name	Pin	Pin	Signal Name
-RESET	1	2	GROUND
Data Bit 7	3	4	Data Bit 8
Data Bit 6	5	6	Data Bit 9
Data Bit 5	7	8	Data Bit 10
Data Bit 4	9	10	Data Bit 11
Data Bit 3	11	12	Data Bit 12
Data Bit 2	13	14	Data Bit 13
Data Bit 1	15	16	Data Bit 14
Data Bit 0	17	18	Data Bit 15
GROUND	19	20	KEY (pin missing)
DRQ 3	21	22	GROUND
-IOW	23	24	GROUND
-IOR	25	26	GROUND
I/O CH RDY	27	28	SPSYNC:CSEL
-DACK 3	29	30	GROUND
IRQ 14	31	32	-IOCS16
Address Bit 1	33	34	-PDIAG
Address Bit 0	35	36	Address Bit 2
-CS1FX	37	38	-CS3FX
-DA/SP	39	40	GROUND
+5 Vdc (Logic)	41	42	+5 Vdc (Motor)
GROUND	43	44	-TYPE (0=ATA)

ATA I/O Cable. A 40-conductor ribbon cable is specified to carry signals between the bus adapter circuits and the drive (controller). To maximize signal integrity and to eliminate potential timing and noise problems, the cable should not be longer than 0.46 meters (18 inches).

ATA Signals. The ATA interface signals and connector pinout are listed in Appendix A. This section describes some of the most important signals in more detail.

Pin 20 is used as a key pin for cable orientation and is not connected through in the interface. This pin should be missing from any ATA connectors, and the cable should have the pin-20 hole in the connector plugged off to prevent the cable from being plugged in backward.

Pin 39 carries the Drive Active/Slave Present (DASP) signal, which is a dual-purpose, time-multiplexed signal. During power-on initialization, this signal indicates whether a slave drive is present on the interface. After that, each drive asserts the signal to indicate that it is active. Early drives could not multiplex these functions and required special jumper settings to work with other drives. Standardizing this function to allow for compatible dual-drive installations is one of the features of the ATA standard.

Pin 28 carries the Cable Select or Spindle Synchronization signal (CSEL or SPSYNC), which is a dual-purpose conductor; a given installation, however, may use only one of the two functions. The CSEL (Cable Select) function is the most widely used and is designed to control the designation of a drive as master (drive 0) or slave (drive 1) without requiring jumper settings on the drives. If a drive sees the CSEL as being grounded, the drive is a master; if CSEL is open, the drive is a slave.

You can install special cabling to ground CSEL selectively. This installation is normally accomplished through a Y-cable arrangement, with the IDE bus connector in the middle and each drive at opposite ends of the cable. One leg of the Y has the CSEL line connected through, indicating a master drive; the other leg has the CSEL line open (conductor interrupted or removed), making the drive at that end the slave.

ATA Commands. One of the best features of the ATA IDE interface is the enhanced command set. The ATA IDE interface was modeled after the WD1003 controller that IBM used in the original AT system. All ATA IDE drives must support the original WD command set (eight commands), with no exceptions, which is why IDE drives are so easy to install in systems today. All IBM-compatible systems have built-in ROM BIOS support for the WD1003, which means that essentially, they support ATA IDE as well.

In addition to supporting all the WD1003 commands, the ATA specification added numerous other commands to enhance performance and capabilities. These commands are an optional part of the ATA interface, but several of them are used in most drives available today and are very important to the performance and use of ATA drives in general.

Perhaps the most important is the Identify Drive command. This command causes the drive to transmit a 512-byte block of data that provides all details about the drive. Through this command, any program (including the system BIOS) can find out exactly what type of drive is connected, including the drive manufacturer, model number, operating parameters, and even the serial number of the drive. Many modern BIOSes use this information to automatically receive and enter the drive's parameters into CMOS memory, eliminating the need for the user to enter these parameters manually during system configuration. This arrangement helps prevent mistakes that later can lead to data loss when the user no longer remembers what parameters he or she used during setup.

The Identify Drive data can tell you many things about your drive, including the following:

- Number of cylinders in the recommended (default) translation mode
- Number of heads in the recommended (default) translation mode

- Number of sectors per track in the recommended (default) translation mode
- Number of cylinders in the current translation mode
- Number of heads in the current translation mode
- Number of sectors per track in the current translation mode
- Manufacturer and model number
- Firmware revision
- Serial number
- Buffer type, indicating sector buffering or caching capabilities

Several public-domain programs can execute this command to the drive and report the information on-screen. I use the IDEINFO program (which can be downloaded from the IBM Hardware Forum on CompuServe) or the IDEDIAG utility (which can be downloaded from the Western Digital BBS). Phone numbers for these information services appear in Appendix B. I find these programs especially useful when I am trying to install IDE drives and need to know the correct parameters for a user-definable BIOS type. These programs get the information directly from the drive itself.

Two other very important commands are the Read Multiple and Write Multiple commands. These commands permit multiple-sector data transfers and, when combined with block-mode Programmed I/O (PIO) capabilities in the system, can result in incredible data-transfer rates many times faster than single-sector PIO transfers.

Tip

If you want the ultimate in IDE performance and installation ease, make sure that your motherboard BIOS and IDE adapter supports ATA-2 or Enhanced IDE (EIDE). This support allows your BIOS to execute data transfers to and from the IDE drive several times faster than normal, and also makes installation and configuration easier because the BIOS will be able to detect the drive-parameter information automatically. High speed PIO (Programmed Input Output) and automatic detection of the drive type are included in the latest versions of most PC BIOSes.

There are many other enhanced commands, including room for a given drive manufacturer to implement what are called vendor-unique commands. These commands often are used by a particular vendor for features unique to that vendor. Often, features such as low-level formatting and defect management are controlled by vendor-unique commands. This is why low-level format programs can be so specific to a particular manufacturer's IDE drives and why many manufacturers make their own LLF programs available.

ATA IDE Drive Categories. ATA-IDE drives can be divided into three main categories. These categories separate the drives by function (such as translation capabilities) and design (which can affect features such as low-level formatting). The three drive categories are:

- Non-Intelligent ATA-IDE drives
- Intelligent ATA-IDE drives
- Intelligent Zoned Recording ATA-IDE drives

The following sections describe these categories.

Non-Intelligent IDE. As I stated earlier, the ATA standard requires that the built-in controller respond exactly as though it were a Western Digital WD1003 controller. This controller responds to a command set of eight commands. Early IDE drives supported these commands and had few, if any, other options. These early drives actually were more like regular ST-506/412 or ESDI controllers bolted directly to the drive than the more intelligent drives that we consider today to be IDE.

These drives were not considered to be intelligent IDE drives; an intelligent drive is supposed to have several capabilities that these early IDE drives lacked. The drives could not respond to any of the enhanced commands that were specified as (an optional) part of the ATA IDE specification, including the Identify Drive command. These drives also did not support sector translation, in which the physical parameters could be altered to appear as any set of logical cylinders, heads, and sectors. Enhanced commands and sector-translation support are what make an IDE drive an intelligent IDE drive, and these features were not available in the early IDE drives.

These drives could be low-level formatted in the same manner as any normal ST-506/412 or ESDI drive. They were universally low-level formatted at the factory, with factory-calculated optimum interleave (usually, 1:1) and head- and cylinder-skew factors. Also, factory defects were recorded in a special area on the drive; they no longer were written on a sticker pasted to the exterior. Unfortunately, this arrangement means that if you low-level format these drives in the field, you most likely will alter these settings (especially the skew factors) from what the factory set as optimum, as well as wipe out the factory-written defect table.

Some manufacturers released special low-level format routines that would reformat the drives while preserving these settings, but others did not make such programs available. Because they did not want you to overwrite the defect list or potentially slow the drive, most manufacturers stated that you should never low-level format their IDE drives.

This statement started a myth that the drives could somehow be damaged or rendered inoperable by such a format, which truly is not the case. One rumor was that the servo information could be overwritten, which would mean that you would have to send the drive back to the manufacturer for re-servoing. This also is not true; the servo information is protected and cannot be overwritten. The only consequence of an improper low-level format of these drives is the possible alteration of the skew factors and the potential loss of the factory defect maps.

The Disk Manager program by Ontrack is the best special-purpose format utility to use on these drives for formatting because it is aware of these types of drives and often can restore the skew factors and preserve the defect information. If you are working with a drive that already has had the defect map overwritten, Disk Manager can perform a very good surface analysis that will mark off any of these areas that it finds. Disk Manager allows you to specify the skew factors and to mark defects at the sector level so that they will not cause problems later. Other general-purpose diagnostics that work especially well with IDE drives such as this include the Microscope program by Micro 2000.

Intelligent IDE. Later IDE drives became known as intelligent IDE drives. These drives support enhanced ATA commands, such as the Identify Drive command, and sector-translation capabilities.

These drives can be configured in two ways: in raw physical mode or in translation mode. To configure the drive in raw physical mode, you simply enter the CMOS drive parameters during setup so that they match the true physical parameters of the drive. For example, if the drive physically has 800 cylinders, 6 heads, and 50 sectors per track, you enter these figures during setup. To configure the drive in translation mode, you simply enter any combination of cylinders, heads, and sectors that adds up to equal or less than the true number of sectors on the drive.

In the example I just used, the drive has a total of 240,000 sectors (800×6×50). All I have to do is figure out another set of parameters that adds up to equal or less than 240,000 sectors. The simplest way to do this is to cut the number of cylinders in half and double the number of heads. Thus, the new drive parameters become 400 cylinders, 12 heads, and 50 sectors per track. This method adds up to 240,000 sectors and enables the drive to work in translation mode.

When these drives are in translation mode, a low-level format cannot alter the interleave and skew factors; neither can it overwrite the factory defect-mapping information. A low-level format program can, however, perform additional defect mapping or sector sparing while in this mode.

If the drive is in true physical mode, a low-level format rewrites the sector headers and modifies the head and cylinder skewing. If done incorrectly, the format can be repaired by a proper low-level format program that allows you to set the correct head and cylinder skew. This task can be accomplished automatically by the drive manufacturer's recommended low-level format program (if available) or by other programs, such as Disk Manager by Ontrack. When you use Disk Manager, you have to enter the skew values manually; otherwise, the program uses predetermined defaults. To get the correct skew values, it is best to contact the drive manufacturer's technical-support department. You can calculate the skew values if the manufacturer cannot provide them.

To protect the skew factors and defect information on intelligent IDE drives, all you have to do is run them in translation mode. In translation mode, this information cannot be overwritten.

Intelligent Zoned Recording IDE. The last and most sophisticated IDE drives combine intelligence with Zoned Recording. With Zoned Recording, the drive has a variable number sectors per track in several zones across the surface of the drive. Because the PC BIOS can handle only a fixed number of sectors on all tracks, these drives must always run in translation mode. Because these drives are always in translation mode, you cannot alter the factory-set interleave and skew factors or wipe out the factory defect information.

You still can low-level format these drives, however, and use such a format to map or spare additional defective sectors that crop up during the life of the drive. To low-level format intelligent Zoned Recording drives, you need either a specific utility from the drive manufacturer or an IDE-aware program, such Disk Manager by Ontrack or Micro-scope by Micro 2000.

ATA-2 (Enhanced IDE). ATA-2 is an extension of the original ATA (IDE) specification. The most important additions are performance enhancing features such as fast PIO and DMA modes. ATA-2 also features improvements in the Identify Drive command allowing a drive to tell the software exactly what its characteristics are; this is essential for both Plug-n-Play and compatibility with future revisions of the standard.

ATA-2 is often called Enhanced IDE (EIDE). EIDE is technically a marketing program from Western Digital. Fast-ATA and Fast-ATA-2 are similar Seagate-inspired marketing programs, which are also endorsed by Quantum. As far as the hard disk and BIOS are concerned, these are all different terms for basically the same thing.

There are four main areas where ATA-2 and EIDE have improved the original ATA/IDE interface:

- Increased Maximum Drive Capacity
- Faster Data Transfer
- Secondary Two-Device Channel
- ATAPI (ATA Program Interface)

The following section describes these improvements.

Increased Drive Capacity. ATA-2/EIDE allows for increased drive capacity over the original ATA/IDE specification. This is done through an Enhanced BIOS, which makes it possible to use hard disks exceeding the 504M (528 million bytes) barrier. The origin of this limit is the disk geometry (cylinders, heads, sectors) supported by the combination of an IDE drive and the BIOS' software interface. Both IDE and the BIOS are capable of supporting huge disks, but their combined limitations conspire to restrict the useful capacity to 504MB.

An Enhanced BIOS circumvents this by using a different geometry when talking to the drive than when talking to the software. What happens in between is called *translation*. For example, if your drive has 2,000 cylinders and 16 heads, a translating BIOS will make programs think that the drive has 1,000 cylinders and 32 heads.

You can usually tell if your BIOS is enhanced by the ability to specify more than 1,024 cylinders in the BIOS setup, although this is not conclusive. If you see drive-related settings like "LBA," "ECHS," or even "Large," these are tell-tale signs of a BIOS with translation support. Most BIOSes with a date of 1994 or later are enhanced. If your system currently does not have an Enhanced BIOS you may be able to get an upgrade.

BIOS Translation. There are roughly three ways today's BIOSes can handle translation: standard CHS addressing, Extended CHS addressing, and LBA addressing. They are summarized in the following table:

BIOS Mode	Operating System to BIOS	BIOS to Drive Ports
Standard CHS	Logical CHS Parameters	Logical CHS Parameters
Extended CHS	Translated CHS Parameters	Logical CHS Parameters
LBA	Translated CHS Parameters	LBA Parameters

Standard CHS (Cylinder Head Sector). In Standard CHS, there is only one possible translation step internal to the drive. The drive's actual, physical geometry is completely invisible from the outside with all zoned recorded ATA drives today. The Cylinders, Heads, and Sectors printed on the label for use in the BIOS setup are purely logical geometry, and do not represent the actual physical parameters. Standard CHS addressing is limited to 16 heads and 1,024 cylinders, which gives the us a limit of 504 Megabytes (528 Million Bytes).

This is often called "Normal" in the BIOS setup, and causes the BIOS to behave like an old fashioned one without translation. Use this setting if your drive has fewer than 1,024 cylinders or if you want to use the drive with a non-DOS operating system that doesn't understand translation.

Extended CHS (Cylinder Head Sector). In Extended CHS, a translated logical geometry is used to communicate between the drive and the BIOS, while a different, translated geometry is used to communicate between the BIOS and everything else. In other words, there are normally two translation steps. The drive still translates internally, but has logical parameters that exceed the 1,024 cylinder limitation of the standard BIOS. In this case, the drive's cylinder count is usually divided by two, and the head count is multiplied by two to get the translated values from those actually stored in the CMOS SETUP. This type of setting breaks the 504/528M barrier.

This is often called "Large" or "ECHS" in the BIOS setup, and tells the BIOS to use Extended CHS translation. It uses a different geometry (cylinders/heads/sectors) when talking to the drive than when talking to the BIOS. This type of translation should be used with drives that have more than 1,024 cylinders but that do not support LBA (Logical Block Addressing). Note that the geometry entered in your BIOS setup is the logical geometry, not the translated one.

LBA (Logical Block Addressing). LBA is a means of linearly addressing sector's addresses, beginning at Cylinder 0, Head 0, Sector 1 as LBA 0, and proceeding on to the last physical sector on the drive. This is new in ATA-2, but has always been the one and only addressing mode in SCSI.

With LBA, each sector on the drive is numbered starting from 0. The number is a 28-bit binary number internally, which translates to a sector number of from 0 to 268,435,456. Since each sector represents 512 bytes, this results in a maximum drive capacity of exactly 128G, or 137 billion bytes. Unfortunately, the operating system still needs to see a translated CHS, so the BIOS determines how many sectors there are, and comes up with Translated CHS to match. The BIOS CHS limits are 1,024 cylinders, 256 Heads, and 63 Sectors per track which limits total drive capacity to just under 8GB.

In other words, this breaks the 528MB barrier in essentially the same way as Extended CHS does. Because it is somewhat simpler to use a single linear number to address a sector on the hard disk compared to a CHS type address, this is the preferred method if the drive supports LBA.

A word of warning with these BIOS translation settings. If you switch between standard CHS, Extended CHS, or LBA, the BIOS may change the (translated) geometry. The same thing may happen if you transfer a disk that has been formatted on an old, non-LBA computer to a new one that uses LBA. This will cause the logical CHS geometry seen by the operating system to change, and will cause the date to appear in the wrong locations! This can cause you to lose access to your data if you are not careful. I always recommend recording the CMOS setup screens associated with the hard disk configuration so that you can properly match the setup of a drive to the settings it was originally at.

Faster Data Transfer. ATA-2/EIDE defines several high performance modes for transferring data to and from the drive. These faster modes are the main part of the new specifications and were the main reason they were initially developed. Most of the faster drives on the market today will support either Programmed I/O transfer Mode 3 or Mode 4, which results in a very fast transfer. The following section discusses these modes.

PIO (Programmed I/O Modes). The PIO mode determines how fast data is transferred to and from the drive. In the slowest possible mode, PIO mode 0, the data cycle time cannot exceed 600 nanoseconds. In a single cycle, 16 bits are transferred in or out of the drive making the theoretical transfer rate of PIO Mode 0 (600ns cycle time) 3.3 megabytes per second. Most of the high performance ATA-2 (EIDE) drives today support PIO Mode 4, which offers a 16.6MB per second transfer rate.

The following table shows the PIO modes, with their respective transfer rates:

PIO Mode	Cycle time (ns)	Transfer rate (MB/s)	Specification
0	600	3.3	ATA
1	383	5.2	ATA
2	240	8.3	ATA
3	180	11.1	ATA-2
4	120	16.6	ATA-2

To run in Mode 3 or 4 requires that the IDE port on the system be a local bus port. This means that it must operate through either a VL-Bus or PCI bus connection. Most modern motherboards with ATA-2/EIDE support have dual IDE connectors on the motherboard, with only the primary connector running through the system's PCI local bus. The secondary connector usually runs through the ISA bus, and therefore supports up to Mode 2 operation only.

When interrogated with an Identify Drive command, a hard disk returns, among other things, information about the PIO and DMA modes it is capable of using. Most enhanced BIOSes will automatically set the correct mode to match the capabilities of the drive. If you set a mode faster than the drive can handle, data corruption will result.

ATA-2 drives also perform Block Mode PIO, which means that they use the Read/Write Multiple commands that greatly reduce the number of interrupts sent to host processor. This lowers the overhead, and the resulting transfers are even faster.

DMA Transfer Modes. Although it is not used by most operating system or BIOS software, ATA-2 drives also support DMA transfers. DMA (Direct Memory Access) means that the data is transferred directly between drive and memory without using the CPU as an intermediary, as opposed to PIO.

There are two distinct types of direct memory access: DMA and busmastering DMA. Ordinary DMA relies on the DMA controller on the system's mainboard to perform the complex task of arbitration, grabbing the system bus and transferring the data. In the case of busmastering DMA, all this is done by logic on the interface card itself. Of course, this adds considerably to the complexity and the price of a busmastering interface.

Unfortunately, the DMA controller on ISA systems is ancient and slow, and out of the question for use with a modern hard disk. Today, proper software support for DMA is still rare.

ATAPI (ATA Packet Interface). ATAPI is a standard designed for devices such as CD-ROMs and tape drives that plug into an ordinary ATA (IDE) connector. The principal advantage of ATAPI hardware is that it's cheap and works on your current adapter. For CD-ROMs, it has a somewhat lower CPU usage compared to proprietary adapters but there's no performance gain otherwise. For tape drives, ATAPI has potential for superior performance and reliability compared to the popular "floppy" tape devices.

While ATAPI CD-ROMs use the hard disk interface, this does not mean that they look like an ordinary hard disk; to the contrary, from a software point of view they are a completely different kind of animal. They actually most closely resemble a SCSI device.

This means that intelligent (e.g. caching) controllers that are not ATAPI aware will NOT work with these devices. This also means that, at present, you cannot boot from an ATAPI CD-ROM and you still must load a driver to use it under DOS or Windows. Windows 95 has native ATAPI support, and the first ATAPI-aware BIOS that will even allow booting from an ATAPI CD-ROM has already been introduced.

IDE Drive Configuration. IDE (Integrated Drive Electronics) drives can be both simple and troublesome to configure. Single-drive installations usually are very simple, with few, if any, special jumper settings to worry about. Multiple-drive configurations, however, can be a problem. Jumpers have to be set on both drives; and the names, locations, and even functions of these jumpers can vary from drive to drive.

Because the CAM ATA (Common Access Method AT Attachment) IDE specification was ironed out only after many companies were already making and selling drives, many older IDE drives have problems in dual-drive installations, especially when the drives are from different manufacturers. In some cases, two particular drives may not function together at all. Fortunately, most of the newer drives follow the CAM ATA specification, which clears up this problem. Drives that follow the specification have no problems in dual-drive installations.

Cable Configuration. The cable connection to IDE drives is usually very simple. There is a single 40-pin cable that normally has three pin-header style connectors on it. One of the connectors plugs into the IDE interface connector; the other two plug into the primary and secondary drives. The cable normally runs from the IDE connector to both drives in a daisy-chain arrangement. On one end, this cable plugs into the IDE interface connector, which is located on the motherboard in many systems but also may be located on an IDE interface adapter card. The cable then connects to the secondary (D) and primary (C) drives in succession, with the primary drive usually (but not always) being at the end of the cable opposite the IDE interface connector.

There are no terminating resistors to set with IDE drives; instead, a distributed termination circuit is built into all IDE drives. The last drive on the cable need not be the primary drive, so you actually may find the primary or secondary drive at either connector. Jumpers on the drives themselves normally control whether a drive responds as primary or secondary.

You may see a different arrangement of cable connections in some IDE installations. In some installations, the middle connector is plugged into the motherboard, and the primary and secondary drives are at opposite ends of the cable in a Y arrangement. If you see this arrangement, be careful; in some of these Y-cable installations, the cable, rather than jumpers on the drives, actually controls which drive is primary and which is secondary.

Controlling master/slave selection via the cable rather than jumpers on the drive is performed via a special signal on the IDE interface called CSEL (Cable SELect), which is on pin 28 of the interface. If the CSEL line is connected through from the drive to the IDE interface connector, the drive automatically is designated as primary. If the CSEL line is open between a drive and the IDE interface connector, that drive automatically is designated as secondary.

In the Y-cable approach, the IDE interface connector is in the middle of the cable, and a separate length of cable goes to each drive. Study this type of cable closely. If one of the ends of the Y has line 28 open (usually, a hole in the cable through that wire), only the secondary drive can be plugged into that connector. HP Vectra PC systems use exactly this type of IDE cable arrangement. This type of setup eliminates the need to set jumpers on the IDE drives to configure them for primary or secondary operation, but the setup can be troublesome if you do not know about it.

IDE Drive Jumper Settings. Configuring IDE drives can be simple, as is the case with most single-drive installations, or troublesome, especially where it comes to mixing two drives from different manufacturers on a single cable.

Most IDE drives come in three configurations:

- Single-drive (master)
- Master (dual-drive)
- Slave (dual-drive)

Because each IDE drive has its own controller, you must specifically tell one drive to be the master and the other to be the slave. There's no functional difference between the two, except that the drive that's specified as the slave will assert the DASP signal after a system reset that informs the master that a slave drive is present in the system. The master drive then pays attention to the Drive Select line, which it otherwise ignores. Telling a drive that it's the slave also usually causes it to delay its spinup for several seconds to allow the master to get going and thus to lessen the load on the system's power supply.

Until the ATA IDE specification, no common implementation for drive configuration was in use. Some drive companies even used different master/slave methods for different models of drives. Because of these incompatibilities, some drives work together only in a specific master/slave or slave/master order. This situation affects mostly older IDE drives that were introduced before the ATA specification.

Most drives that fully follow the ATA specification now need only one jumper (Master/Slave) for configuration. A few also need a Slave Present jumper as well. Table 15.7 shows the jumper settings required by most ATA IDE drives.

Table 15.7 Jumper Settings for Most ATA IDE-Compatible Drives

Jumper Name	Single-Drive	Dual-Drive Master	Dual-Drive Slave
Master (M/S)	On	On	Off
Slave Present (SP)	Off	On	Off

The Master jumper indicates that the drive is a master or a slave. Some drives also require a Slave Present jumper, which is used only in a dual-drive setup and then installed only on the master drive, which is somewhat confusing. This jumper tells the master that a slave drive is attached. With many ATA IDE drives, the Master jumper is optional and may be left off. Installing this jumper doesn't hurt in these cases and may eliminate confusion, so I recommend that you install the jumpers listed here.

Conner Peripherals Drives. Because they were introduced before the ATA IDE specification was formalized, Conner Peripherals drives often are different in configuration from many other-brand drives. When you mix and match IDE hard drives from different manufacturers, the drives are not always fully compatible. Table 15.8 shows the jumper settings that are correct for most Conner IDE drive installations.

The C/D jumper is used to determine whether the drive is a master (drive C) or a slave (drive D). The drive is configured as master when this jumper is on. The DSP jumper indicates that a slave drive is present. The HSP jumper causes the drive to send the Slave Present signal to the master drive. The ACT jumper enables the master drive to signal when it is active.

Table 15.8 Jumper Settings for Conner Peripherals IDE Drives

Jumper Name	Single-Drive	Dual-Drive Master	Dual-Drive Slave
Master or Slave (C/D)	On	On	Off
Drive Slave Present (DSP)	Off	On	Off
Host Slave Present (HSP)	Off	Off	On
Drive Active (ACT)	On	On	Off

Some Conner drives are not set up to support the industry-standard CAM ATA (Common Access Method AT Attachment) interface by default. The problems show up when you attempt to connect another manufacturer's drive to some Conner drives in either a master or slave role. Fortunately, you can correct many of these situations by changing the configuration of the drive.

You can make this change in two ways. One way is to use a special program to semipermanently change the mode of the drive. A special file available on the Conner BBS, called FEATURE.COM, contains a program that displays the current ISA/ATACAM setting and allows the setting to be changed. The change is actually stored in a feature byte in the firmware of the drive, and after this byte is changed, most other manufacturers' drives will work with the Conner drives. The program also can be used to reset the feature byte back to its original configuration, which is best when you are connecting to other Conner drives.

The second method for changing this configuration is available on some Conner drives. These drives also have a special jumper called ATA/ISA. This jumper almost always should be installed in the ATA position to provide compatibility with the ATA standard. If you are using only Conner drives, you can leave this jumper in ISA mode if you want. Some Conner drives have a separate jumper (E1) that can delay startup of the drive to minimize the load on the power supply. This jumper should be enabled on any drive that is configured as a slave. Most other drives automatically delay startup of the slave drive for a few seconds.

Most Conner drives also have a special 12-pin connector that is used to drive an optional LED (pin 1, LED +5v; and pin 2, ground), as well as to connect to special factory equipment for low-level formatting and configuration. A company called TCE (see Appendix B) sells a device called The Conner, which connects to this port and permits full factory-level initialization, formatting, and testing of Conner drives. I consider this piece of gear to be essential to anybody who services or supports a large number of Conner Peripherals drives. Notice that Compaq uses Conner drives in most of its systems.

For more information on any specific Conner drive, you can use the company's FaxBack system (see the vendor list in Appendix B) at (800) 4CONNER. Through this system, you can get drive information and jumper settings that are specific to Conner drives.

XT-Bus (8-bit) IDE. Many systems with XT ISA bus architecture used XT IDE hard drives. The IDE interface in these systems is usually built into the motherboard. The IBM PS/2 Model 25, 25-286, 30, and 30-286 systems used an 8-bit XT IDE interface. These 8-bit XT IDE drives are difficult to find; few manufacturers other than IBM, Western

Digital, and Seagate made them; and none of these drives were available in capacities beyond 40M.

Since the ATA IDE interface is a 16-bit design, it could not be used in 8-bit (XT type) systems, so some of the drive manufacturers standardized on an XT-Bus (8-bit) IDE interface for XT class systems. These drives were never very popular, and were usually only available in capacities from 20M to 40M. Table 15.9 shows the industry standard 8-bit IDE connector pinout.

Table 15.9 XT-Bus IDE (Integrated Drive Electronics) Connector

Signal Name	Pin	Pin	Signal Name
-RESET	1	2	GROUND
Data Bit 7	3	4	GROUND
Data Bit 6	5	6	GROUND
Data Bit 5	7	8	GROUND
Data Bit 4	9	10	GROUND
Data Bit 3	11	12	GROUND
Data Bit 2	13	14	GROUND
Data Bit 1	15	16	GROUND
Data Bit 0	17	18	GROUND
GROUND	19	20	KEY (pin missing)
AEN	21	22	GROUND
-IOW	23	24	GROUND
-IOR	25	26	GROUND
-DACK 3	27	28	GROUND
DRQ 3	29	30	GROUND
IRQ 5	31	32	GROUND
Address Bit 1	33	34	GROUND
Address Bit 0	35	36	GROUND
-CS1FX	37	38	GROUND
-Drive Active	39	40	GROUND

Notice that IBM used a custom version of the XT-Bus IDE interface in the PS/2 Model 25 and Model 30 systems. The pinout for the custom IBM XT-Bus IDE connector is shown in table 15.10.

Table 15.10 IBM Unique XT-Bus (PS/2 Model 25 and 30) IDE Connector

Signal Name	Pin	Pin	Signal Name
-RESET	1	2	-Disk Installed
Data Bit 0	3	4	GROUND
Data Bit 1	5	6	GROUND
Data Bit 2	7	8	GROUND

Signal Name	Pin	Pin	Signal Name
Data Bit 3	9	10	GROUND
Data Bit 4	11	12	GROUND
Data Bit 5	13	14	GROUND
Data Bit 6	15	16	GROUND
Data Bit 7	17	18	GROUND
-IOR	19	20	GROUND
-IOW	21	22	GROUND
-CS1FX	23	24	GROUND
Address Bit 0	25	26	GROUND
Address Bit 1	27	28	GROUND
Address Bit 2	29	30	+5 Vdc
RESERVED	31	32	+5 Vdc
-DACK 3	33	34	GROUND
DRQ 3	35	36	GROUND
IRQ 5	37	38	GROUND
I/O CH RDY	39	40	+12 Vdc
Spare	41	42	+12 Vdc
Spare	39	44	+12 Vdc

The newer PS/1, PS/Valuepoint, and PS/2 systems with 16-bit ISA architecture use ATA IDE drives. Because nearly all hard disk manufacturers make a multitude of drives with the ATA IDE interface, these systems are easy to upgrade or repair. ATA IDE drives are available in capacities up to and beyond 1G.

MCA IDE. The IBM PS/2 Models 50 and higher come with Micro Channel Architecture (MCA) bus slots. Although most of these systems now use SCSI drives, for some time IBM used a type of MCA IDE drive in these systems. MCA IDE is a form of IDE interface, but it is designed for the MCA bus and is not compatible with the more industry-standard ATA IDE interface. Few companies other than IBM and Western Digital make replacement MCA IDE drives for these systems. I recommend replacing these drives with ATA IDE drives, using adapters from Arco Electronics or Sigma Data, or switching to SCSI drives instead. The IBM MCA IDE drives are expensive for the limited capacity that they offer.

The pinout of the MCA IDE connector is shown in table 15.11.

Table 15.11 MCA (Micro Channel Architecture) IDE Connector

Signal Name	Pin	Pin	Signal Name
-CD SETUP	A1	B1	Address Bit 15
Address Bit 13	A2	B2	Address Bit 14
GROUND	A3	B3	GROUND
Address Bit 11	A4	B4	OSC (14.3 MHz)

(continues)

Table 15.11 Continued

Signal Name	Pin	Pin	Signal Name
Address Bit 10	A5	B5	GROUND
Address Bit 9	A6	B6	Address Bit 12
+5 Vdc	A7	B7	-CMD
Address Bit 8	A8	B8	-CD SFDBK
Address Bit 7	A9	B9	GROUND
Address Bit 6	A10	B10	Data Bit 1
+5 Vdc	A11	B11	Data Bit 3
Address Bit 5	A12	B12	Data Bit 4
Address Bit 4	A13	B13	GROUND
Address Bit 3	A14	B14	CHRESET
+5 Vdc	A15	B15	Data Bit 8
Address Bit 2	A16	B16	Data Bit 9
Address Bit 1	A17	B17	GROUND
Address Bit 0	A18	B18	Data Bit 12
+12 Vdc	A19	B19	Data Bit 14
-ADL	A20	B20	Data Bit 15
-PREEMPT	A21	B21	GROUND
-BURST	A22	B22	Data Bit 0
+5 Vdc	A23	B23	Data Bit 2
ARB 0	A24	B24	Data Bit 5
ARB 1	A25	B25	GROUND
ARB 2	A26	B26	Data Bit 6
+12 Vdc	A27	B27	Data Bit 7
ARB 3	A28	B28	Data Bit 10
+ARB/-GRANT	A29	B29	GROUND
-TC	A30	B30	Data Bit 11
+5 Vdc	A31	B31	Data Bit 13
-S0	A32	B32	-SBHE
-S1	A33	B33	GROUND
+M/-IO	A34	B34	-CD DS 16
GROUND	A35	B35	-IRQ 14
CD CHRDY	A36	B36	GROUND

Introduction to SCSI

SCSI (pronounced "scuzzy") stands for Small Computer System Interface. This interface has its roots in SASI, the Shugart Associates System Interface. SCSI is not a disk interface, but a systems-level interface. SCSI is not a type of controller, but a bus that supports as many as eight devices. One of these devices, the host adapter, functions as the gateway between the SCSI bus and the PC system bus. The SCSI bus itself does not talk directly with devices such as hard disks; instead, it talks to the controller that is built into the drive.

A single SCSI bus can support as many as eight physical units, usually called SCSI IDs. One of these units is the adapter card in your PC; the other seven can be other peripherals. You could have hard disks, tape drives, CD-ROM drives, a graphics scanner, or other devices (up to seven total) attached to a single SCSI host adapter. Most systems support up to 4 host adapters, each with 7 devices, for a total 28 devices! Some of the newer SCSI implementations allow for 15 devices on each bus.

When you purchase a SCSI hard disk, you are usually purchasing the drive, controller, and SCSI adapter in one circuit. This type of drive is usually called an embedded SCSI drive; the SCSI interface is built into the drive. Most SCSI hard drives actually are IDE drives with SCSI bus adapter circuits added. You do not need to know what type of controller is inside the SCSI drive because your system cannot talk directly to the controller as though it were plugged into the system bus, like a standard controller. Instead, communications go through the SCSI host adapter installed in the system bus. You can access the drive only with the SCSI protocols.

Apple originally rallied around SCSI as being an inexpensive way out of the bind in which it put itself with the Macintosh. When the engineers at Apple realized the problem in making the Macintosh a closed system (with no slots), they decided that the easiest way to gain expandability was to build a SCSI port into the system, which is how external peripherals can be added to the slotless Macs. Because PC systems always have been expandable, the push toward SCSI has not been as urgent. With eight bus slots supporting different devices and controllers in IBM and IBM-compatible systems, it seemed as though SCSI was not needed.

SCSI now is becoming popular in the IBM-based computer world because of the great expandability that it offers and the number of devices that are available with built-in SCSI. One thing that stalled acceptance of SCSI in the PC marketplace was the lack of a real standard; the SCSI standard was designed primarily by a committee. No single manufacturer has led the way, at least in the IBM arena; each company has its own interpretation of how SCSI should be implemented, particularly at the host-adapter level.

SCSI is a standard, in much the same way that RS-232 is a standard. The SCSI standard (like the RS-232 standard), however, defines only the hardware connections, not the driver specifications required to communicate with the devices. Software ties the SCSI subsystem into your PC, but unfortunately, most of the driver programs work only for a specific device and a specific host adapter. For example, a graphics scanner comes with its own SCSI host adapter to connect to the system; a CD-ROM drive comes with another (different) SCSI host adapter and driver software that works only with that SCSI adapter. On a system with those two SCSI adapters, you would need a third SCSI host adapter to run SCSI hard disk drives because the host adapters supplied by the scanner and CD-ROM companies do not include a built-in, self-booting BIOS that supports hard disk drives.

SCSI has become something of a mess in the IBM world because of the lack of a host-adapter standard, a software interface standard, and standard ROM BIOS support for hard disk drives attached to the SCSI bus. Fortunately, some simple recommendations can keep you from living this compatibility nightmare!

The lack of capability to run hard disks off the SCSI bus, to boot from these drives and use a variety of operating systems, is a problem that results from the lack of an interface standard. The standard IBM XT and AT ROM BIOS software was designed to talk to ST-506/412 hard disk controllers. The software easily was modified to work with ESDI because ESDI controllers are similar to ST-506/412 controllers at the register level. (This similarity at the register level enabled manufacturers to easily design self-booting, ROM-BIOS-supported ESDI drives.) The same can be said of IDE, which completely emulates the WD1003 ST-506/412 controller interface and works perfectly with the existing BIOS as well. SCSI is so different from these other standard disk interfaces that a new set of ROM BIOS routines are necessary to support the system so that it can self-boot. The newer IBM PS/2 systems that come with SCSI drives have this support built into the motherboard BIOS or as an extension BIOS on the SCSI host adapter.

Companies such as Adaptec and Future Domain have produced SCSI cards with built-in ROM BIOS support for several years, but these BIOS routines were limited to running the drives only under DOS. The BIOS would not run in the AT-protected mode, and other operating systems included drivers for only the standard ST-506/412 and ESDI controllers. Thus, running SCSI was impossible under many non-DOS operating systems. This situation has changed significantly, however; IBM now supports many third-party SCSI host adapters in OS/2, especially those from Adaptec and Future Domain. For compatibility reasons, I usually recommend using SCSI adapters from these two companies, or any other adapters that are fully hardware-compatible with the Adapted and Future Domain adapters.

Because of the lead taken by Apple in developing systems software (operating systems and ROM) support for SCSI, peripherals connect to Apple systems in fairly standard ways. Until recently, this kind of standard-setting leadership was lacking for SCSI in the IBM world. This situation changed on March 20, 1990, when IBM introduced several "standard" SCSI adapters and peripherals for the IBM PS/2 systems, with complete ROM BIOS and full operating-system support.

IBM has standardized on SCSI for nearly all its high-end systems. In these systems, a SCSI host adapter card is in one of the slots, or the system has a SCSI host adapter built into the motherboard. This arrangement is similar in appearance to the IDE interface because a single cable runs from the motherboard to the SCSI drive, but SCSI supports as many as seven devices (some of which may not be hard disks), whereas IDE supports only two devices, which must be either a hard disk or a tape drive. PS/2 systems with SCSI drives are easy to upgrade because virtually any third-party SCSI drive will plug in and function.

The example set by IBM is causing other manufacturers to supply systems with either SCSI host adapters or SCSI interfaces integrated into the motherboards. As SCSI becomes more and more popular in the PC world, SCSI peripheral integration will be easier, due to better operating-system and device-driver support.

ANSI SCSI standards. The SCSI standard defines the physical and electrical parameters of a parallel I/O bus used to connect computers and peripheral devices in daisy-chain fashion. The standard supports devices such as disk drives, tape drives, and CD-ROM drives. The original SCSI standard (ANSI X3.131-1986) was approved in 1986; SCSI-2 was approved in January of 1994, and a new revision called SCSI-3, is being developed.

The SCSI interface is defined as a standard by ANSI (American National Standards Institute), an organization that approves and publishes standards. The X3 Task Group operates as an ASC (Accredited Standards Committee) under ANSI to develop Information Processing System standards. X3T9 is the I/O Interfaces group, and X3T9.2 specifically is in charge of low-level interfaces such as SCSI and ATA-IDE (among others). The original SCSI-1 standard was published by the X3T9 ANSI group in 1986 and is officially published by ANSI as X3.131-1986.

One problem with the original SCSI-1 document was that many of the commands and features were optional, and there was little or no guarantee that a particular peripheral would support the expected commands. This problem caused the industry as a whole to define a set of 18 basic SCSI commands called the Common Command Set (CCS), which would become the minimum set of commands supported by all peripherals. This Common Command Set became the basis for what is now the SCSI-2 specification.

In addition to formal support for the CCS, SCSI-2 provided additional definitions for commands to access CD-ROM drives (and their sound capabilities), tape drives, removable drives, optical drives, and several other peripherals. In addition, an optional higher speed called FAST SCSI-2 and a 16-bit version called WIDE SCSI-2 were defined. Another feature of SCSI-2 is command queuing, which enables a device to accept multiple commands and execute them in the order that the device deems to be most efficient. This feature is most beneficial when you are using a multitasking operating system that could be sending several requests on the SCSI bus at the same time.

The X3T9 group approved the SCSI-2 standard as X3.131-1990 in August 1990, but the document was recalled in December 1990 for changes before final ANSI publication. Final approval for the SCSI-2 document was finally made in January of 1994(!), although it has changed little from the original 1990 release. The SCSI-2 document is now called ANSI X3.131-1994. The official document is available from Global Engineering Documents or the ANSI committee, which are listed in Appendix B. You can also download working drafts of these documents from the NCR SCSI BBS, listed in the vendor list under NCR Microelectronics.

Most companies indicate that their host adapters follow both the ANSI X3.131-1986 (SCSI-1) as well as the x3.131-1994 (SCSI-2) standards. Note that since virtually all parts of SCSI-1 are supported in SCSI-2, virtually any SCSI-1 device is also considered SCSI-2 by default. Many manufacturers advertise that their devices are SCSI-2, but this does not mean that they support any of the additional optional features that were incorporated in the SCSI-2 revision.

For example, an optional part of the SCSI-2 specification includes a fast synchronous mode that doubles the standard synchronous transfer rate from 5MB per second to 10MB per second. This Fast SCSI transfer mode can be combined with 16-bit Wide SCSI for transfer rates of up to 20MB per second. There was an optional 32-bit version defined in SCSI-2, but component manufacturers have shunned this as too expensive. In essence,

32-bit SCSI was a stillborn specification. Most SCSI implementations are 8-bit standard SCSI or Fast/Wide SCSI. Even devices which support none of the fast or wide modes can still be considered SCSI-2.

The SCSI-3 standard is still being defined and is still a long way from being approved. However, portions of this specification, although not final, are being sold in products today. One of these developments is the new Fast-20 mode, which is also called Ultra-SCSI. This essentially is quad-speed SCSI, and will run 20MB per second on an 8-bit standard SCSI bus, and 40MB per second on Wide (16-bit) SCSI.

Table 15.12 shows the maximum transfer rates for the SCSI bus at various speeds and widths, as well as the cable type required for the specific transfer widths.

Table 15.12 SCSI Data-Transfer Rates

Bus Width	Std. SCSI	Fast SCSI	Fast-20 (Ultra) SCSI	Cable Type
8-bit	5MB/s	10MB/s	20MB/s	A (50-pin)
16-bit (Wide)	10MB/s	20MB/s	40MB/s	P (68-pin)

MB/s = MegaBytes per second.
Fast-20 SCSI is also called Ultra-SCSI.

Note

The A cable is the standard 50-pin SCSI cable, whereas the P cable is a 68-pin cable designed for 16-bit. Maximum cable length is 6 meters (about 20 feet) for standard speed SCSI, and only 3 meters (about 10 feet) for Fast or Fast-20 (Ultra) SCSI. Pinouts for these cable connections are listed in this chapter.

So-called SCSI-1 adapters have no problems with SCSI-2 peripherals. In fact, as was stated earlier, virtually any SCSI-1 device can also legitimately be called SCSI-2 (or even SCSI-3). You can't take advantage of Fast, Fast-20, or Wide transfer capabilities, but the extra commands defined in SCSI-2 can be sent by means of a SCSI-1 controller. In other words, nothing is different between SCSI-1 and SCSI-2 compliant hardware. For example, I am running a Seagate Barracuda 4G Fast SCSI-2 drive with my standard IBM SCSI-1 host adapter, and it runs fine. Most adapters are similar, in that they actually are SCSI-2 compatible, even if they advertise only SCSI-1 support. Because the SCSI-2 standard was not actually approved before January 1994, any devices that claimed to be SCSI-2 before that time were not officially in compliance with the standard. This is really not a problem, however, since the SCSI-2 document had not changed appreciably since it was nearly approved in 1990. The same thing is currently happening with advertisers listing devices as "SCSI-3." The SCSI-3 specification is not yet approved, although certain areas are being worked out.

SCSI Hard Disk Evolution and Construction. SCSI is not a disk interface, but a bus that supports SCSI bus interface adapters connected to disk and other device controllers. The first SCSI drives for PCs simply were standard ST-506/412 or ESDI drives with a separate SCSI bus interface adapter (sometimes called a bridge controller) that converted the ST-506/412 or ESDI interfaces to SCSI. This interface originally was in the form of a secondary logic board, and the entire assembly often was mounted in an external case.

The next step was to build the SCSI bus interface "converter" board directly into the drive's own logic board. Today, we call these drives embedded SCSI drives because the SCSI interface is built in.

At that point, there was no need to conform to the absolute specifications of ST-506/412 or ESDI on the internal disk interface because the only other device that the interface would ever have to talk to was built in as well. Thus, the disk-interface and controller-chipset manufacturers began to develop more customized chipsets that were based on the ST-506/412 or ESDI chipsets already available but offered more features and higher performance. Today, if you look at a typical SCSI drive, you often can identify the chip or chipset that serves as the disk controller on the drive as being exactly the same kind that would be used on an ST-506/412 or ESDI controller or as being some evolutionary customized variation thereof.

Consider some examples. An ATA (AT Attachment interface) IDE drive must fully emulate the system-level disk-controller interface introduced with the Western Digital WD1003 controller series that IBM used in the AT. These drives must act as though they have a built-in ST-506/412 or ESDI controller; in fact, they actually do. Most of these built-in controllers have more capabilities than the original WD1003 series (usually in the form of additional commands), but they must at least respond to all the original commands that were used with the WD1003.

If you follow the hard drive market, you usually will see that drive manufacturers offer most of their newer drives in both ATA IDE and SCSI versions. In other words, if a manufacturer makes a particular 500MB IDE drive, you invariably will see that the company also make a SCSI model with the same capacity and specifications, which uses the same HDA (Head Disk Assembly) and even looks the same as the IDE version. If you study these virtually identical drives, the only major difference you will find is the additional chip on the logic board of the SCSI version, called a SCSI Bus Adapter Chip (SBIC).

Figures 15.3 and 15.4 show the logic-block diagrams of the WD-AP4200 (a 200MB ATA-IDE drive) and WD-SP4200 (a 200MB SCSI drive), respectively. These drives use the same HDA; they differ only in their logic boards, and even the logic boards are the same except for the addition of an SBIC (SCSI Bus Adapter Chip) on the SCSI drive's logic board.

Notice that even the circuit designs of these two drives are almost identical. Both drives use an LSI (Large Scale Integrated circuit) chip called the WD42C22 Disk Controller and Buffer manager chip. In the ATA drive, this chip is connected through a DMA control chip directly to the AT bus. In the SCSI version, a WD33C93 SCSI bus interface controller chip is added to interface the disk-controller logic to the SCSI bus. In fact, the logic diagrams of these two drives differ only in the fact that the SCSI version has a complete subset of the ATA drive with the SCSI bus interface controller logic added. This essentially is a very condensed version of the separate drive and bridge controller setups that were used in the early days of PC SCSI!

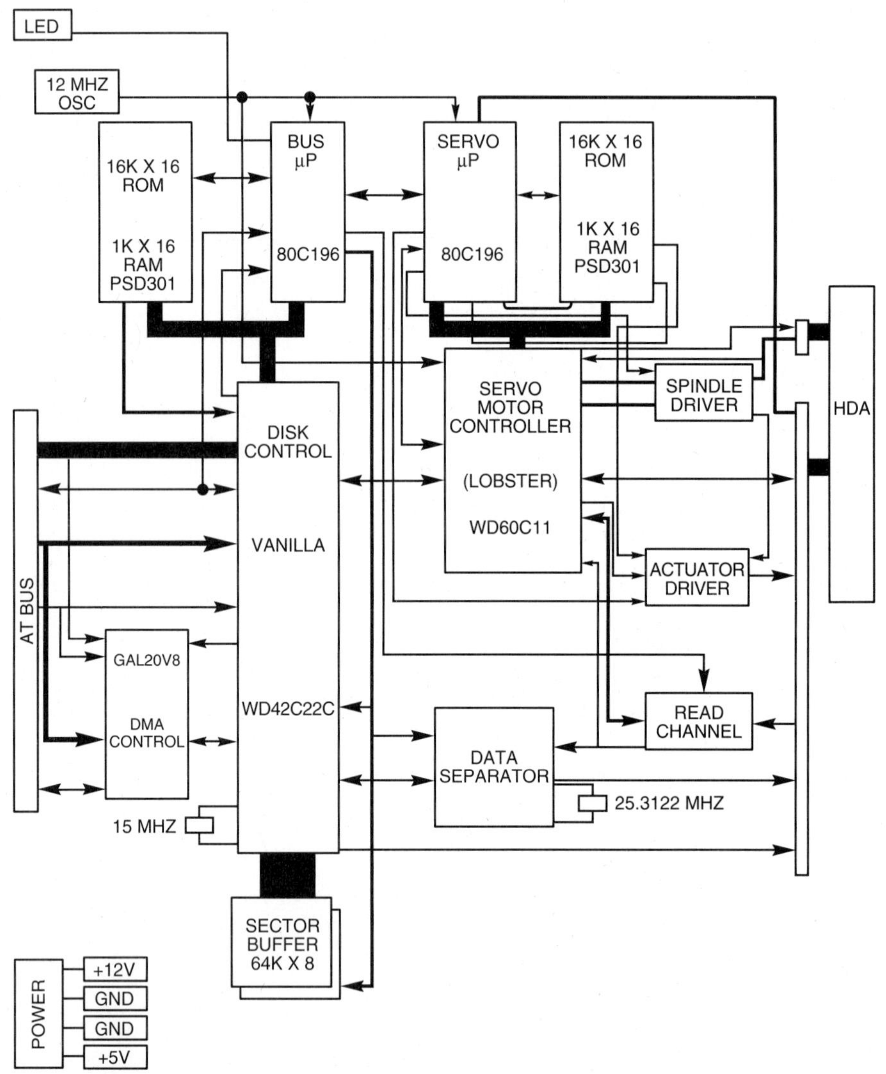

Figure 15.3

Western Digital WD-AP4200 200MB ATA-IDE drive logic-board block diagram.

To top off this example, study the following logic diagram for the WD 1006V-MM1, which is an ST-506/412 controller (see fig. 15.5).

You can clearly see that the main LSI chip on board is the same WD42C22 disk controller chip used in the IDE and SCSI drives. Here is what the technical reference literature says about that chip:

> The WD42C22 integrates a high performance, low cost Winchester controller's architecture. The WD42C22 integrates the central elements of a Winchester

controller subsystem such as the host interface, buffer manager, disk formatter/controller, encoder/decoder, CRC/ECC (Cyclic Redundancy Check/Error Correction Code) generator/checker, and drive interface into a single 84-pin PQFP (Plastic Quad Flat Pack) device.

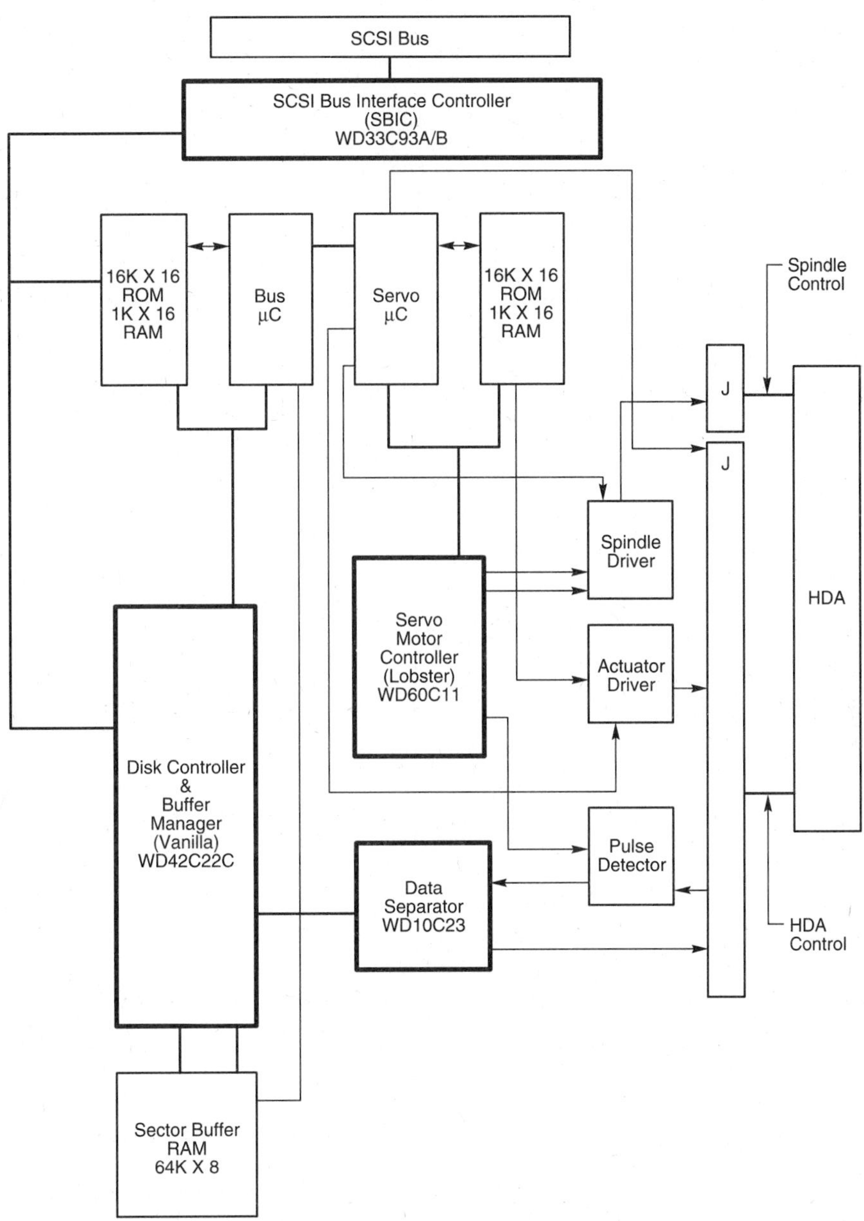

Figure 15.4

Western Digital WD-SP4200 200MB SCSI drive logic-board block diagram.

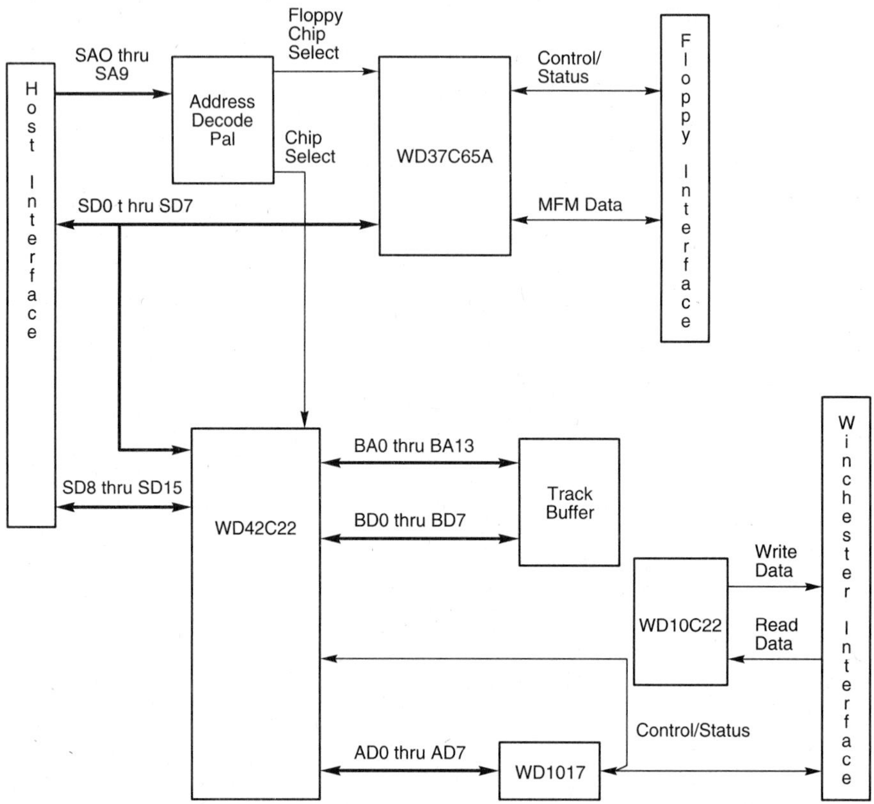

Figure 15.5

Western Digital WD1006V-MM1 ST-506/412 Disk Controller block diagram.

The virtually identical design of ATA-IDE and SCSI drives is not unique to Western Digital. Most drive manufacturers design their ATA-IDE and SCSI drives the same way, often using these very same Western Digital chips as well as disk controller and SCSI bus interface chips from other manufacturers. You now should be able to understand that most SCSI drives simply are "regular" ATA-IDE drives with SCSI bus logic added. This fact will come up again later in this chapter, in the section "SCSI versus IDE," which discusses performance and other issues differentiating these interfaces.

For another example, I have several IBM 320MB and 400MB embedded SCSI-2 hard disks; each of these drives has on-board a WD-10C00 Programmable Disk Controller in the form of a 68-pin PLCC (Plastic Leaded Chip Carrier) chip. The technical literature states, "This chip supports ST412, ESDI, SMD and Optical interfaces. It has 27-Mbit/sec maximum transfer rate and an internal, fully programmable 48- or 32-bit ECC, 16-bit CRC-CCITT or external user defined ECC polynomial, fully programmable sector sizes and 1.25 micron low power CMOS design."

In addition, these particular embedded SCSI drives include the 33C93 SCSI Bus Interface Controller chip, which is also used in the other SCSI drive that I mentioned. Again, there is a distinctly separate disk controller, and the SCSI interface is added on.

So again, most embedded SCSI drives have a built-in disk controller (usually based on previous ST-506/412 or ESDI designs) and additional logic to interface that controller to the SCSI bus (a built-in bridge controller, if you like). Now think about this from a performance standpoint. If virtually all SCSI drives really are ATA IDE drives with a SCSI Bus Interface Controller chip added, what conclusions can you draw?

First, no drive can perform sustained data transfers faster than the data can actually be read from the disk platters. In other words, the HDA (Head Disk Assembly) limits performance to whatever it is capable of achieving. Drives can transmit data in short bursts at very high speeds because they often have built-in cache or read-ahead buffers that store data. Many of the newer high-performance SCSI and ATA-IDE drives have 1M or more of cache memory on-board! No matter how big or intelligent the cache is, however, sustained data transfer still will be limited by the HDA.

Data from the HDA must pass through the disk controller circuits which, as you have seen, are virtually identical between similar SCSI and ATA-IDE drives. In the ATA IDE drive, this data then is presented directly to the system bus. In the SCSI drive, however, the data must pass through a SCSI Bus Interface adapter on the drive, travel through the SCSI bus itself, and then pass through another SCSI Bus Interface controller in the SCSI host adapter card in your system. The longer route that a SCSI transfer must take makes this type of transfer slower than the much more direct ATA IDE transfer.

The conventional wisdom has been that SCSI is always much faster than IDE; unfortunately, this wisdom usually is wrong! This incorrect conclusion was derived by looking at the raw SCSI and ISA bus performance capabilities. An 8-bit Fast SCSI-2 bus can transfer data at 10MB (million bytes) per second, whereas the 16-bit ISA bus used directly by IDE drives can transfer data at rates ranging from 2MB to 8MB per second. Based on these raw transfer rates, SCSI seems to be faster, but the raw transfer rate of the bus is not the limiting factor. Instead, the actual HDA and disk-controller circuitry place the limits on performance. Another point to remember is that unless you are using a PCI, VL-Bus, EISA, or 32-bit MCA SCSI adapter, the SCSI data-transfer speeds will be limited by the host bus performance as well as by the drive performance.

Single-Ended or Differential SCSI. "Normal" SCSI also is called single-ended SCSI. For each signal that needs to be sent across the bus, a wire exists to carry it. With differential SCSI, for each signal that needs to be sent across the bus, a pair of wires exists to carry it. The first in this pair carries the same type of signal that the single-ended SCSI carries. The second in this pair, however, carries the logical inversion of the signal. The receiving device takes the difference of the pair (hence the name differential), which makes it less susceptible to noise and allows for greater cable length. Because of this, differential SCSI can be used with cable lengths up to 25 meters, whereas single-ended SCSI is good only for 6 meters with standard asynchronous or synchronous transfers or for only 3 meters for Fast SCSI.

You cannot mix single-ended and differential devices on a single SCSI bus; the result would be catastrophic. (That is to say that you probably will see smoke!) Notice that the cables and connectors are the same, so it's entirely possible to make this mistake. This usually is not a problem, however, because very few differential SCSI implementations exist. Especially with SCSI in the PC environment, single-ended is about all you will ever see. If, however, you to come upon a peripheral that you believe might be differential, there are a few ways to tell. One way is to look for a special symbol on the unit; the industry has adopted different universal symbols for single-ended and differential SCSI. Figure 15.6 shows these symbols.

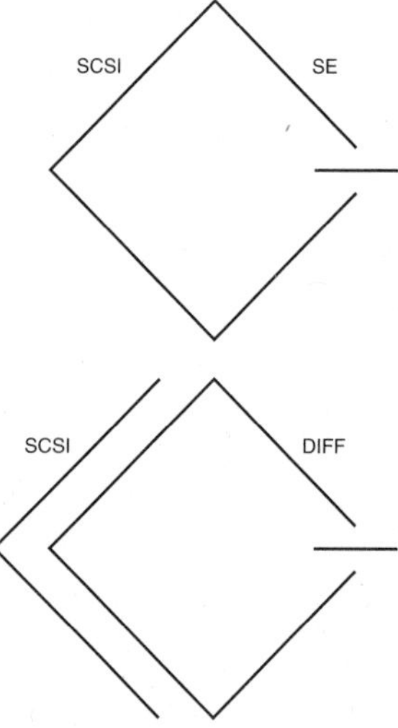

Figure 15.6

Single-ended and differential SCSI universal symbols.

If you do not see such symbols, you can tell whether you have a differential device by using an ohm meter to check the resistance between pins 21 and 22 on the device connector. On a single-ended system, the pins should be tied together and also tied to Ground. On a differential device, the pins should be open or have significant resistance between them. Again, this generally should not be a problem because virtually all devices used in the PC environment are single-ended.

SCSI-1 and SCSI-2. The SCSI-2 specification essentially is an improved version of SCSI-1 with some parts of the specification tightened and with several new features and options added. Normally, SCSI-1 and SCSI-2 devices are compatible, but SCSI-1 devices ignore the additional features in SCSI-2.

Some of the changes in SCSI-2 are very minor. For example, SCSI-1 allowed SCSI Bus parity to be optional, whereas parity must be implemented in SCSI-2. Another requirement is that initiator devices, such as host adapters, provide terminator power to the interface; most devices already did so.

SCSI-2 also has several optional features:

- Fast SCSI
- Wide SCSI
- Command queuing
- High-density cable connectors
- Improved Active (Alternative 2) termination

These features are not required; they are optional under the SCSI-2 specification. If you connect a standard SCSI host adapter to a Fast SCSI drive, for example, the interface will work, but only at standard SCSI speeds.

Fast SCSI. Fast SCSI refers to high-speed synchronous transfer capability. Fast SCSI achieves a 10MB per second transfer rate on the standard 8-bit SCSI cabling. When combined with a 16-bit Wide SCSI interface, this configuration results in data-transfer rates of 20MB per second (called Fast/Wide).

Fast-20 (Ultra) SCSI. Fast-20 or Ultra SCSI refers to high-speed synchronous transfer capability that is twice as fast as Fast-SCSI. This has been introduced in the Draft (unfinished) SCSI-3 specification and has already been adopted by the marketplace, especially for high speed hard disks. Ultra SCSI achieves a 20MB per second transfer rate on the standard 8-bit SCSI cabling. When combined with a 16-bit Wide SCSI interface, this configuration results in data-transfer rates of 40MB per second (called Ultra/Wide).

Wide SCSI. Wide SCSI allows for parallel data transfer at a bus width of 16 bits. The wider connection requires a new cable design. The standard 50-conductor 8-bit cable is called the A-cable. SCSI-2 originally defined a special 68-conductor B-cable that was supposed to be used in conjunction with the A cable for wide transfers, but the industry ignored this specification in favor of a newer 68-conductor P-cable that was introduced as part of the SCSI-3 specification. The P-cable superseded the A- and B-cable combination because the P-Cable can be used alone (without the A cable) for 16-bit Wide SCSI.

A 32-bit Wide SCSI version was originally defined on paper as a part of the SCSI-2 specification, but has not found popularity and probably never will in the PC environment. Theoretically, 32-bit SCSI implementations would require two cables: a 68-conductor P-cable and a 68-conductor Q-cable.

Termination. The single-ended SCSI bus depends on very tight termination tolerances to function reliably. Unfortunately, the original 132-ohm passive termination defined in the SCSI-1 document was not designed for use at the higher synchronous speeds now possible. These passive terminators can cause signal reflections to cause errors when transfer rates increase or when more devices are added to the bus. SCSI-2 defines an active (voltage-regulated) terminator that lowers termination impedance to 110 ohms and improves system integrity.

Command Queuing. In SCSI-1, an initiator device, such as a host adapter, was limited to sending one command per device. In SCSI-2, the host adapter can send as many as 256 commands to a single device, which will store and process those commands internally before responding on the SCSI bus. The target device even can resequence the commands to allow for the most efficient execution or performance possible. This feature is especially useful in multitasking environments, such as OS/2 and Windows NT, that can take advantage of this feature.

New Commands. SCSI-2 took the Common Command Set that was being used throughout the industry and made it an official part of the standard. The CCS was designed mainly for disk drives and did not include specific commands designed for other types of devices. In SCSI-2, many of the old commands are reworked and several new commands have been added. New command sets have been added for CD-ROMs, optical drives, scanners, communications devices, and media changers (jukeboxes).

SCSI-3. Even though the SCSI-2 specification has only recently been approved (although it has remained stable for some time), the SCSI-3 specification is already being developed. SCSI-3 will have everything that SCSI-2 has and definitely will add new commands, features, and implementations. For example, SCSI-3 will provide support for up to 32 devices on the bus instead of only 8.

One of the most exciting things about SCSI-3 is the proposed Serial SCSI, a scheme that may use only a six-conductor cable and that will be able to transfer data at up to 100MB per second! The switch to serial instead of parallel is designed to control the delay, noise, and termination problems that have plagued SCSI-2, as well as to simplify the cable connection. Serial SCSI will be capable of transferring more data over 6 wires than 32-bit Fast Wide SCSI-2 can over 128 wires! The intention is that Serial SCSI be implemented on the motherboard of future systems, giving them incredible expansion and performance capabilities.

Although Serial SCSI may not make the older host adapters and cables obsolete overnight, it does make future cabling possibilities even more of a puzzle. Serial SCSI offers the possibility of longer cable lengths; less electromagnetic interference; and easier connections on laptops, notebooks, and docking stations. Expect SCSI-3 to offer almost pain-free installations with automatic plug-and-play SCSI ID setup and termination schemes.

In any practical sense, SCSI-3 is still some ways away from being approved. Because the standard exists in draft documents before being officially approved, if the portions of the standard become stable, we may very well see products claiming SCSI-3 compatibility well before the standard truly exists. Since SCSI-3 actually incorporates all of what is in SCSI-2, technically anybody can call any SCSI-1 or SCSI-2 device a SCSI-3 device as well. Beware of product hype along these lines. Some of the new SCSI-3 features will likely be incompatible with previous SCSI implementations, and may take a while to appear on the market.

SCSI Cables and Connectors. The SCSI standards are very specific when it comes to cables and connectors. The most common connectors specified in this standard are the

50-position unshielded pin header connector for internal SCSI connections and the 50-position shielded Centronics latch-style connectors for external connections. The shielded Centronics style connector is also called Alternative 2 in the official specification. Passive or Active termination (Active is preferred) is specified for both single-ended and differential buses. The 50-conductor bus configuration is defined in the SCSI-2 standard as the A-cabled.

The SCSI-2 revision added a high-density, 50-position, D-shell connector option for the A-cable connectors. This connector is now called Alternative 1. The Alternative 2 Centronics latch-style connector remains unchanged from SCSI-1. A 68-conductor B-cable specification was added to the SCSI-2 standard to provide for 16- and 32-bit data transfers; the connector, however, had to be used in parallel with an A-cable. The industry did not widely accept the B-cable option, which has been dropped from the SCSI-3 standard.

To replace the ill-fated B-cable, a new 68-conductor P-cable was developed as part of the SCSI-3 specification. Shielded and unshielded high-density D-shell connectors are specified for both the A-cable and P-cable. The shielded high-density connectors use a squeeze-to-release latch rather than the wire latch used on the Centronics-style connectors. Active termination for single-ended buses is specified, providing a high level of signal integrity.

SCSI Cable and Connector Pinouts. The following section details the pinouts of the various SCSI cables and connectors. There are two electrically different version of SCSI, Single Ended and Differential. These two versions are electrically incompatible, and must not be interconnected or damage will result. Fortunately, there are very few Differential SCSI applications available in the PC industry, so you will rarely (if ever) encounter it. Within each electrical type (Single Ended or Differential), there are basically three SCSI cable types:

- A-Cable (Standard SCSI)
- P-Cable (16- and 32-bit Wide SCSI)
- Q-Cable (32-bit Wide SCSI)

The A-Cable is used in most SCSI-1 and SCSI-2 installations, and is the most common cable you will encounter. SCSI-2 Wide (16-bit) applications use a P-Cable instead, which completely replaces the A-Cable. You can intermix standard and wide SCSI devices on a single SCSI bus by interconnecting A- and P-Cables with special adapters. 32-bit wide SCSI-3 applications use both the P- and Q-Cables in parallel to each 32-bit device. Today there are virtually no PC applications for 32-bit Wide SCSI-3, and because of the two cable requirement, it is not likely to catch on.

The A-Cables can have Pin Header (Internal) type connectors or External Shielded connectors, each with a different pinout. The P- and Q-Cables feature the same connector pinout on either Internal or External cable connections.

The following tables show all the possible interface, cable, and connector pinout specifications. A hyphen preceding a signal name indicates the signal is Active Low. The RESERVED lines have continuity from one end of the SCSI bus to the other. In an A-Cable bus, the RESERVED lines should be left open in SCSI devices (but may be connected to ground), and are connected to ground in the bus terminator assemblies. In the P- and Q-Cables, the RESERVED lines are left open in SCSI devices as well as in the bus terminator assemblies.

Single-Ended SCSI Cables and Connectors. The single-ended electrical interface is the most popular type for PC systems. The following tables show all the possible single-ended cable and connector pinouts. The A-Cable is available in both internal unshielded as well as external shielded configurations. Both are shown in tables 15.13 and 15.14.

Table 15.13 A-Cable (Single-Ended) Internal Unshielded Header Connector

Signal Name	Pin	Pin	Signal Name
GROUND	1	2	-DB(0)
GROUND	3	4	-DB(1)
GROUND	5	6	-DB(2)
GROUND	7	8	-DB(3)
GROUND	9	10	-DB(4)
GROUND	11	12	-DB(5)
GROUND	13	14	-DB(6)
GROUND	15	16	-DB(7)
GROUND	17	18	-DB(Parity)
GROUND	19	20	GROUND
GROUND	21	22	GROUND
RESERVED	23	24	RESERVED
Open	25	26	TERMPWR
RESERVED	27	28	RESERVED
GROUND	29	30	GROUND
GROUND	31	32	-ATN
GROUND	33	34	GROUND
GROUND	35	36	-BSY
GROUND	37	38	-ACK
GROUND	39	40	-RST
GROUND	41	42	-MSG
GROUND	43	44	-SEL
GROUND	45	46	-C/D
GROUND	47	48	-REQ
GROUND	49	50	-I/O

Table 15.14 A-Cable (Single-Ended) External Shielded Connector

Signal Name	Pin	Pin	Signal Name
GROUND	1	26	-DB(0)
GROUND	2	27	-DB(1)
GROUND	3	28	-DB(2)
GROUND	4	29	-DB(3)
GROUND	5	30	-DB(4)
GROUND	6	31	-DB(5)
GROUND	7	32	-DB(6)
GROUND	8	33	-DB(7)
GROUND	9	34	-DB(Parity)
GROUND	10	35	GROUND
GROUND	11	36	GROUND
RESERVED	12	37	RESERVED
Open	13	38	TERMPWR
RESERVED	14	39	RESERVED
GROUND	15	40	GROUND
GROUND	16	41	-ATN
GROUND	17	42	GROUND
GROUND	18	43	-BSY
GROUND	19	44	-ACK
GROUND	20	45	-RST
GROUND	21	46	-MSG
GROUND	22	47	-SEL
GROUND	23	48	-C/D
GROUND	24	49	-REQ
GROUND	25	50	-I/O

IBM has standardized on the SCSI interface for virtually all PS/2 systems introduced since 1990. These systems use a Micro Channel SCSI adapter or have the SCSI Host Adapter built into the motherboard. In either case, IBM's SCSI interface uses a special 60-pin mini-Centronics type external shielded connector that is unique in the industry. A special IBM cable is required to adapt this connector to the standard 50-pin Centronics style connector used on most external SCSI devices. The pinout of the IBM 60-pin mini-Centronics style External Shielded connector is shown in the following table. In the following table, notice that although the pin arrangement is unique, the pin number to signal designations correspond with the standard unshielded internal pin header type of SCSI connector.

The P-Cable (Single-Ended) and connectors are used in 16-bit wide SCSI-2 applications (see table 15.15 for the pinout).

Table 15.15 IBM PS/2 SCSI External Shielded 60-Pin Connector

Signal Name	Pin	Pin	Signal Name
GROUND	1	60	Not Connected
-DB(0)	2	59	Not Connected
GROUND	3	58	Not Connected
-DB(1)	4	57	Not Connected
GROUND	5	56	Not Connected
-DB(2)	6	55	Not Connected
GROUND	7	54	Not Connected
-DB(3)	8	53	Not Connected
GROUND	9	52	Not Connected
-DB(4)	10	51	GROUND
GROUND	11	50	-I/O
-DB(5)	12	49	GROUND
GROUND	13	48	-REQ
-DB(6)	14	47	GROUND
GROUND	15	46	-C/D
-DB(7)	16	45	GROUND
GROUND	17	44	-SEL
-DB(Parity)	18	43	GROUND
GROUND	19	42	-MSG
GROUND	20	41	GROUND
GROUND	21	40	-RST
GROUND	22	39	GROUND
RESERVED	23	38	-ACK
RESERVED	24	37	GROUND
Open	25	36	-BSY
TERMPWR	26	35	GROUND
RESERVED	27	34	GROUND
RESERVED	28	33	GROUND
GROUND	29	32	-ATN
GROUND	30	31	GROUND

Table 15.16 P-Cable (Single-Ended) Internal or External Shielded Connector

Signal Name	Pin	Pin	Signal Name
GROUND	1	35	-DB(12)
GROUND	2	36	-DB(13)
GROUND	3	37	-DB(14)
GROUND	4	38	-DB(15)
GROUND	5	39	-DB(Parity 1)
GROUND	6	40	-DB(0)

Signal Name	Pin	Pin	Signal Name
GROUND	7	41	-DB(1)
GROUND	8	42	-DB(2)
GROUND	9	43	-DB(3)
GROUND	10	44	-DB(4)
GROUND	11	45	-DB(5)
GROUND	12	46	-DB(6)
GROUND	13	47	-DB(7)
GROUND	14	48	-DB(Parity 0)
GROUND	15	49	GROUND
GROUND	16	50	GROUND
TERMPWR	17	51	TERMPWR
TERMPWR	18	52	TERMPWR
RESERVED	19	53	RESERVED
GROUND	20	54	GROUND
GROUND	21	55	-ATN
GROUND	22	56	GROUND
GROUND	23	57	-BSY
GROUND	24	58	-ACK
GROUND	25	59	-RST
GROUND	26	60	-MSG
GROUND	27	61	-SEL
GROUND	28	62	-C/D
GROUND	29	63	-REQ
GROUND	30	64	-I/O
GROUND	31	65	-DB(8)
GROUND	32	66	-DB(9)
GROUND	33	67	-DB(10)
GROUND	34	68	-DB(11)

The Q-Cable (Single-Ended) and connector is defined only for 32-bit SCSI implementations, which also require a P-Cable (see table 15.16 for the pinout). 32-bit SCSI applications are rare to virtually nonexistent.

Table 15.17 Q-Cable (Single-Ended) Internal or External Shielded Connector

Signal Name	Pin	Pin	Signal Name
GROUND	1	35	-DB(28)
GROUND	2	36	-DB(29)
GROUND	3	37	-DB(30)
GROUND	4	38	-DB(31)
GROUND	5	39	-DB(Parity 3)

(continues)

Table 15.17 Continued

Signal Name	Pin	Pin	Signal Name
GROUND	6	40	-DB(16)
GROUND	7	41	-DB(17)
GROUND	8	42	-DB(18)
GROUND	9	43	-DB(19)
GROUND	10	44	-DB(20)
GROUND	11	45	-DB(21)
GROUND	12	46	-DB(22)
GROUND	13	47	-DB(23)
GROUND	14	48	-DB(Parity 2)
GROUND	15	49	GROUND
GROUND	16	50	GROUND
TERMPWRQ	17	51	TERMPWRQ
TERMPWRQ	18	52	TERMPWRQ
RESERVED	19	53	RESERVED
GROUND	20	54	GROUND
GROUND	21	55	TERMINATED
GROUND	22	56	GROUND
GROUND	23	57	TERMINATED
GROUND	24	58	-ACKQ
GROUND	25	59	TERMINATED
GROUND	26	60	TERMINATED
GROUND	27	61	TERMINATED
GROUND	28	62	TERMINATED
GROUND	29	63	-REQQ
GROUND	30	64	TERMINATED
GROUND	31	65	-DB(24)
GROUND	32	66	-DB(25)
GROUND	33	67	-DB(26)
GROUND	34	68	-DB(27)

Differential SCSI Signals. Differential SCSI is not normally used in a PC environment but is very popular with minicomputer installations due to the very long bus lengths that are allowed. Although not popular in PC systems, the interface connector specifications are shown here for reference.

The A-Cable (Differential) Connector is available in both internal unshielded form as well as an external shielded form. Table 15.18 shows the pinout for the Internal cable, while table 15.19 shows the pinout for the External cable.

Table 15.18 A-Cable (Differential) Internal Unshielded Header Connector

Signal Name	Pin	Pin	Signal Name
GROUND	1	2	GROUND
+DB(0)	3	4	-DB(0)
+DB(1)	5	6	-DB(1)
+DB(2)	7	8	-DB(2)
+DB(3)	9	10	-DB(3)
+DB(4)	11	12	-DB(4)
+DB(5)	13	14	-DB(5)
+DB(6)	15	16	-DB(6)
+DB(7)	17	18	-DB(7)
+DB(Parity)	19	20	-DP(Parity)
DIFFSENS	21	22	GROUND
RESERVED	23	24	RESERVED
TERMPWR	25	26	TERMPWR
RESERVED	27	28	RESERVED
+ATN	29	30	-ATN
GROUND	31	32	GROUND
+BSY	33	34	-BSY
+ACK	35	36	-ACK
+RST	37	38	-RST
+MSG	39	40	-MSG
+SEL	41	42	-SEL
+C/D	43	44	-C/D
+REQ	45	46	-REQ
+I/O	47	48	-I/O
GROUND	49	50	GROUND

Table 15.19 A-Cable (Differential) External Shielded Connector

Signal Name	Pin	Pin	Signal Name
GROUND	1	26	GROUND
+DB(0)	2	27	-DB(0)
+DB(1)	3	28	-DB(1)
+DB(2)	4	29	-DB(2)
+DB(3)	5	30	-DB(3)
+DB(4)	6	31	-DB(4)
+DB(5)	7	32	-DB(5)
+DB(6)	8	33	-DB(6)
+DB(7)	9	34	-DB(7)

(continues)

Table 15.19 Continued

Signal Name	Pin	Pin	Signal Name
+DB(Parity)	10	35	-DP(Parity)
DIFFSENS	11	36	GROUND
RESERVED	12	37	RESERVED
TERMPWR	13	38	TERMPWR
RESERVED	14	39	RESERVED
+ATN	15	40	-ATN
GROUND	16	41	GROUND
+BSY	17	42	-BSY
+ACK	18	43	-ACK
+RST	18	44	-RST
+MSG	20	45	-MSG
+SEL	21	46	-SEL
+C/D	22	47	-C/D
+REQ	23	48	-REQ
+I/O	24	49	-I/O
GROUND	25	50	GROUND

The P-Cable (Differential) and Connector is used for 16-bit wide SCSI connections. Table 15.20 has the pinouts for the P-Cable (Differential).

Table 15.20 P-Cable (Differential) Internal or External Shielded Connector

Signal Name	Pin	Pin	Signal Name
+DB(12)	1	35	-DB(12)
+DB(13)	2	36	-DB(13)
+DB(14)	3	37	-DB(14)
+DB(15)	4	38	-DB(15)
+DB(Parity 1)	5	39	-DB(Parity 1)
GROUND	6	40	GROUND
+DB(0)	7	41	-DB(0)
+DB(1)	8	42	-DB(1)
+DB(2)	9	43	-DB(2)
+DB(3)	10	44	-DP(3)
+DB(4)	11	45	-DB(4)
+DB(5)	12	46	-DB(5)
+DB(6)	13	47	-DB(6)
+DB(7)	14	48	-DB(7)
+DB(Parity 0)	15	49	-DB(Parity 0)
DIFFSENS	16	50	GROUND
TERMPWR	17	51	TERMPWR

Signal Name	Pin	Pin	Signal Name
TERMPWR	18	52	TERMPWR
RESERVED	19	53	RESERVED
+ATN	20	54	-ATN
GROUND	21	55	GROUND
+BSY	22	56	-BSY
+ACK	23	57	-ACK
+RST	24	58	-RST
+MSG	25	59	-MSG
+SEL	26	60	-SEL
+C/D	27	61	-C/D
+REQ	28	62	-REQ
+I/O	29	63	-I/O
GROUND	30	64	GROUND
+DB(8)	31	65	-DB(8)
+DB(9)	32	66	-DB(9)
+DB(10)	33	67	-DB(10)
+DB(11)	34	68	-DB(11)

The Q Cable (Differential) and connector is used only with the proposed 32-bit wide SCSI implementations (which have not been implemented by the marketplace as of yet), and in that case would also require a 16-bit wide P-cable. Table 15.21 shows the Q-Cable (Differential) pinout.

Table 15.21 Q-Cable (Differential) Internal or External Shielded Connector

Signal Name	Pin	Pin	Signal Name
+DB(28)	1	35	-DB(28)
+DB(29)	2	36	-DB(29)
+DB(30)	3	37	-DB(30)
+DB(31)	4	38	-DB(31)
+DB(Parity 3)	5	39	-DB(Parity 3)
GROUND	6	40	GROUND
+DB(16)	7	41	-DB(16)
+DB(17)	8	42	-DB(17)
+DB(18)	9	43	-DB(18)
+DB(19)	10	44	-DP(19)
+DB(20)	11	45	-DB(20)
+DB(21)	12	46	-DB(21)
+DB(22)	13	47	-DB(22)
+DB(23)	14	48	-DB(23)
+DB(Parity 2)	15	49	-DB(Parity 2)

(continues)

Table 15.21 Continued

Signal Name	Pin	Pin	Signal Name
DIFFSENS	16	50	GROUND
TERMPWRQ	17	51	TERMPWRQ
TERMPWRQ	18	52	TERMPWRQ
RESERVED	19	53	RESERVED
TERMINATED	20	54	TERMINATED
GROUND	21	55	GROUND
TERMINATED	22	56	TERMINATED
+ACKQ	23	57	-ACKQ
TERMINATED	24	58	TERMINATED
TERMINATED	25	59	TERMINATED
TERMINATED	26	60	TERMINATED
TERMINATED	27	61	TERMINATED
+REQQ	28	62	-REQQ
TERMINATED	29	63	TERMINATED
GROUND	30	64	GROUND
+DB(24)	31	65	-DB(24)
+DB(25)	32	66	-DB(25)
+DB(26)	33	67	-DB(26)
+DB(27)	34	68	-DB(27)

Termination. All busses need to be electrically terminated at each end, and the SCSI bus is no exception. Improper termination is still one of the most common problems in SCSI installations. Three types of terminators typically are available for the SCSI bus:

- Passive
- Active (also called Alternative 2)
- Forced Perfect Termination (FPT)

  FPT-3

  FPT-18

  FPT-27

Typical passive terminators (a network of resistors) allow signal fluctuations in relation to the terminator power signal on the bus. Usually, passive terminating resistors suffice over short distances, such as 2 or 3 feet, but for longer distances, active termination is a real advantage. Active termination is required with Fast SCSI.

An active terminator actually has one or more voltage regulators to produce the termination voltage, rather than resistor voltage dividers. This arrangement helps ensure that the SCSI signals are always terminated to the correct voltage level. The SCSI-2 specification recommends active termination on both ends of the bus and requires active termination whenever Fast or Wide SCSI devices are used.

A variation on active termination is available: Forced Perfect Termination. Forced Perfect Termination is an even better form of active termination, in which diode clamps are added to eliminate signal overshoot and undershoot. The trick is that instead of clamping to +5 and Ground, these terminators clamp to the output of two regulated voltages. This arrangement enables the clamping diodes to eliminate signal overshoot and undershoot, especially at higher signaling speeds and over longer distances.

FPT terminators are available in several versions. FPT-3 and FPT-18 versions are available for 8-bit standard SCSI, while the FPT-27 is available for 16-bit (Wide) SCSI. The FPT-3 version forces perfect the three most highly active SCSI signals on the 8-bit SCSI bus, while the FPT-18 forces perfect all the SCSI signals on the 8-bit bus except grounds. FPT-27 also forces perfect all of the 16-bit Wide SCSI signals except grounds.

Several companies make high-quality terminators for the SCSI bus, including Aeronics and the Data Mate division of Methode. Both of these companies make a variety of terminators, but Aeronics is well noted for some unique FPT versions that are especially suited to problem configurations that require longer cable runs or higher signal integrity. One of the best investments that you can make in any SCSI installation is in high-quality cables and terminators.

SCSI Drive Configuration. SCSI drives are not too difficult to configure, especially compared with IDE drives. The SCSI standard controls the way that the drives must be set up. You need to set two or three items when you configure an SCSI drive:

- SCSI ID setting (0 through 7)
- Terminating resistors

SCSI ID Setting. The SCSI ID setting is very simple. Up to eight SCSI devices can be used on a single SCSI bus, and each device must have a unique SCSI ID address. The host adapter takes one address, and up to seven SCSI peripherals take the others. Most SCSI host adapters are factory-set to ID 7, which is the highest-priority ID. All other devices must have unique IDs that do not conflict with one another. Some host adapters boot only from a hard disk set to a specific ID. In my system, for example, the IBM SCSI host adapter requires the boot drive to be set to ID 6. Newer IBM host adapters and systems enable you to boot from a hard disk at any SCSI ID. Older Adaptec host adapters required the boot hard disk to be ID 0; newer ones can boot from any ID.

Setting the ID usually involves changing jumpers on the drive itself. If the drive is installed in an external chassis, the chassis may have an ID selector switch that is accessible at the rear. This selector makes ID selection a simple matter of pressing a button or rotating a wheel until the desired ID number appears. If no external selector is present, you must open the external device chassis and set the ID via the jumpers on the drive.

Three jumpers are required to set the SCSI ID; the particular ID selected actually is derived from the binary representation of the jumpers themselves. For example, setting all three ID jumpers off results in a binary number of 000b, which translates to an ID of 0. A binary setting of 001b equals ID 1, 010b equals 2, 011b equals 3, and so on. Notice that as I list these values, I append a lowercase b to indicate binary numbers.

Unfortunately, the jumpers can appear either forward or backward on the drive, depending on how the manufacturer set them up. To keep things simple, I have recorded all the different ID jumper settings in the following tables. Table 15.22 shows the settings for drives that order the jumpers with the Most Significant Bit (MSB) to the left; Table 15.23 shows the settings for drives that have the jumpers ordered so that the MSB is to the right.

Table 15.22 SCSI ID Jumper Settings with the Most Significant Bit to the Left

SCSI	ID	Jumper	Settings
0	0	0	0
1	0	0	1
2	0	1	0
3	0	1	1
4	1	0	0
5	1	0	1
6	1	1	0
7	1	1	1

1 = Jumper On, 0 = Jumper Off

Table 15.23 SCSI ID Jumper Settings with the Most Significant Bit to the Right

SCSI	ID	Jumper	Settings
0	0	0	0
1	1	0	0
2	0	1	0
3	1	1	0
4	0	0	1
5	1	0	1
6	0	1	1
7	1	1	1

1 = Jumper On, 0 = Jumper Off

Termination. SCSI termination is very simple. Termination is required at both ends of the bus; there are no exceptions. If the host adapter is at one end of the bus, it must have termination enabled. If the host adapter is in the middle of the bus, and if both internal and external bus links are present, the host adapter must have its termination disabled, and the devices at each end of the bus must have terminators installed. Several types of terminators are available, differing both in quality and in appearance. Active terminators are the minimum recommended, and Forced Perfect Terminators (FPT) are considered the best available. For more information on the different types, see the previous section on terminators in this chapter.

The rules are simple: use the best terminators possible, and make sure that only the ends of the SCSI bus are terminated. The majority of problems that I see with SCSI installations are the result of improper termination. Some devices have built-in termination resistors that are enabled or disabled through a jumper or by being physically removed. Other devices do not have built-in terminating resistors; these devices instead rely on external terminator modules for termination.

When installing an external SCSI device, you usually will find the device in a storage enclosure with both input and output SCSI connectors so that you can use the device in a daisy chain. If the enclosure is at the end of the SCSI bus, an external terminator module most likely will have to be plugged into the second (outgoing) SCSI port to provide proper termination at that end of the bus (see fig. 15.7).

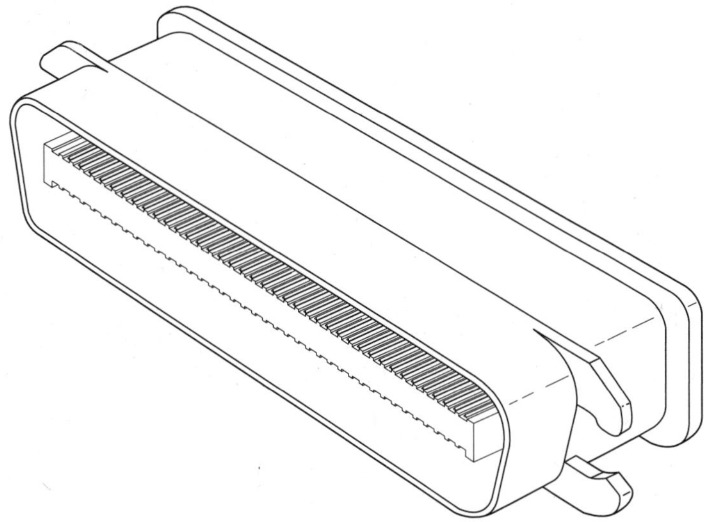

Figure 15.7

External SCSI device terminator.

External terminator modules are available in a variety of connector configurations, including pass-through designs, which are needed if only one port is available. Pass-through terminators also are commonly used in internal installations in which the device does not have built-in terminating resistors. Many hard drives use pass-through terminators for internal installations to save space on the logic-board assembly (see fig. 15.8).

The pass-through models are required when a device is at the end of the bus and only one SCSI connector is available.

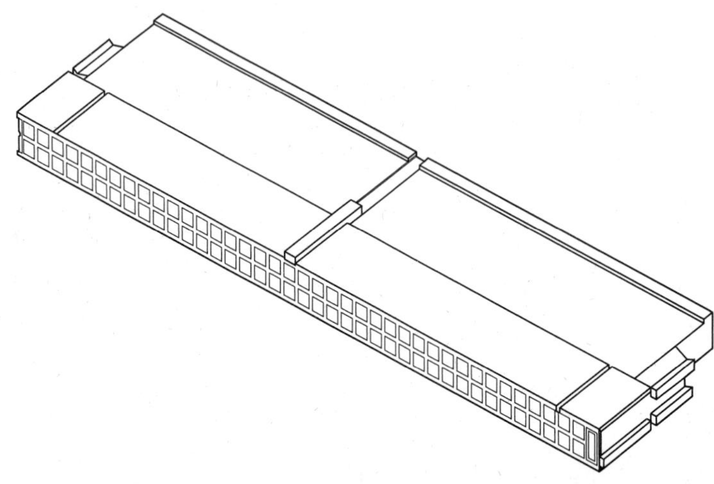

Figure 15.8

Internal pin-header connector pass-through SCSI terminator.

Remember to stick with high-quality active or Forced Perfect terminators at each end of the bus, and you will eliminate most common termination problems.

Other Settings. Other configuration items on a SCSI drive can be set via jumpers. Following are several of the most common additional settings that you will find:

- Start on command (delayed start)
- SCSI parity
- Terminator power
- Synchronous negotiation

These configuration items are described in the following sections.

Start On Command (Delayed Start). If you have multiple drives installed in a system, it is wise to set them up so that all the drives do not start to spin immediately when the system is powered on. A hard disk drive can consume three or four times more power during the first few seconds after power-on than during normal operation. The motor requires this additional power to get the platters spinning quickly. If several drives are drawing all this power at the same time, the power supply may be overloaded, which can cause the system to hang or to have intermittent startup problems.

Nearly all SCSI drives provide a way to delay drive spinning so that this problem does not occur. When most SCSI host adapters initialize the SCSI bus, they send out a command called Start Unit to each of the ID addresses in succession. By setting a jumper on the hard disk, you can prevent the disk from spinning until it receives the Start Unit command from the host adapter. Because the host adapter sends this command to all the ID addresses in succession, from the highest-priority address (ID 7) to the lowest (ID 0), the higher-priority drives can be made to start first, with each lower-priority drive spinning up sequentially. Because some host adapters do not send the Start Unit command, some drives may simply delay spinup for a fixed number of seconds rather than wait for a command that never will arrive.

If drives are installed in external chassis with separate power supplies, you need not implement the delayed-start function. This function is best applied to internal drives that must be run from the same power supply that runs the system. For internal installations, I recommend setting Start on Command (delayed start) even if you have only one SCSI drive; this setting will ease the load on the power supply by spinning the drive up after the rest of the system has full power. This method is especially good for portable systems and other systems in which the power supply is limited.

SCSI Parity. SCSI parity is a limited form of error checking that helps ensure that all data transfers are reliable. Virtually all host adapters support SCSI parity checking, so this option should be enabled on every device. The only reason why it exists as an option is that some older host adapters do not work with SCSI parity, so the parity must be turned off.

Terminator Power. The terminators at each end of the SCSI bus require power from at least one device on the bus. In most cases, the host adapter supplies this terminator power; in some cases, however, it does not. For example, parallel port SCSI host adapters typically do not supply terminator power. It is not a problem if more than one device supplies terminator power because each source is diode protected. For simplicity's sake, many will configure all devices to supply terminator power. If no device supplies terminator power, the bus will not be terminated correctly and will not function properly.

SCSI Synchronous Negotiation. The SCSI bus can run in two modes: asynchronous (the default) and synchronous. The bus actually switches modes during transfers through a protocol called synchronous negotiation. Before data is transferred across the SCSI bus, the sending device (called the initiator) and the receiving device (called the target) negotiate how the transfer will take place. If both devices support synchronous transfers, they will discover this fact through the negotiation, and the transfer will take place at the faster synchronous rate.

Unfortunately, some older devices do not respond to a request for synchronous transfer and actually can be disabled when such a request is made. For this reason, both host adapters and devices that support synchronous negotiation often have a jumper that can be used to disable this negotiation so that it can work with older devices. By default, all devices today should support synchronous negotiation, and this function should be enabled.

Plug and Play (PnP) SCSI. Plug and Play SCSI was originally released in April 1994. This specification allows SCSI device manufacturers to build Plug and Play peripherals that will automatically configure when used with a Plug and Play operating system. This will allow you to easily connect or reconfigure external peripherals, such as hard disk drives, backup tapes, and CD-ROMs.

To connect SCSI peripherals to the host PC, the specification requires a Plug and Play SCSI host adapter such as Plug and Play ISA or PCI. Plug and Play add-in cards enable a Plug and Play operating system automatically to configure software device drivers and system resources for the host bus interface.

The Plug and Play SCSI specification version 1.0 includes these technical highlights:

- A single cable-connector configuration
- Automatic termination of the SCSI bus
- SCAM (SCSI Configured Automagically) automatic ID assignment
- Full backward compatibility of Plug and Play SCSI devices with the installed base of SCSI systems

This should go a long way in making SCSI easier to use for the normal user.

SCSI Drivers. Each SCSI peripheral that you add to your SCSI bus (other than hard disk drives) requires an external driver to make the device work. Hard disks are the exception; driver support for them normally is provided as part of the SCSI host adapter BIOS. These external drivers are specific not only to a particular device, but also to the host adapter.

Recently, two types of standard host adapter interface drivers have become popular, greatly reducing this problem. By having a standard host adapter driver to write to, peripheral makers can more quickly create new drivers that support their devices and then talk to the universal host adapter driver. This arrangement eliminates dependence on one particular type of host adapter. These primary or universal drivers link the host adapter and the operating system.

The Advanced SCSI Programming Interface (ASPI) currently is the most popular universal driver, with most peripheral makers writing their drivers to talk to ASPI. The A in ASPI used to stand for Adaptec, the company that introduced it, but other SCSI device vendors have licensed the right to use ASPI with their products. DOS does not support ASPI directly, but it does when the ASPI driver is loaded. Windows 95, NT, OS/2 2.1, and later versions provide automatic ASPI support for several SCSI host adapters.

Future Domain and NCR have created another interface driver called the Common Access Method (CAM). CAM is an ANSI-approved protocol that enables a single driver to control several host adapters. In addition to ASPI, OS/2 2.1 and later versions currently offer support for CAM. Future Domain also provides a CAM-to-ASPI converter in the utilities that go with its host adapters.

SCSI Configuration Tips. When you are installing a chain of devices on a single SCSI bus, the installation can get complicated very quickly. Here are some tips for getting your setup to function quickly and efficiently:

- *Start by adding one device at a time.* Rather than plug numerous peripherals into a single SCSI card and then try to configure them at the same time, start by installing the host adapter and a single hard disk. Then you can continue installing devices one at a time, checking to make sure that everything works before moving on.

- *Keep good documentation.* When you add a SCSI peripheral, write down the SCSI ID address as well as any other switch and jumper settings, such as SCSI Parity, Terminator Power, and Remote Start. For the host adapter, record the BIOS addresses, Interrupt, DMA channel, and I/O Port addresses used by the adapter, as well as any other jumper or configuration settings (such as termination) that might be important to know later.
- *Use proper termination.* Each end of the bus must be terminated, preferably with active or Forced Perfect Terminators (FPT). If you are using any Fast SCSI-2 device, you must use active terminators rather than the cheaper passive types. Even with standard (slow) SCSI devices, active termination is highly recommended. If you have only internal or external devices on the bus, the host adapter and last device on the chain should be terminated. If you have external and internal devices on the chain, you generally will terminate the first and last of these devices but not the SCSI host adapter itself (which is in the middle of the bus).
- *Use high-quality shielded SCSI cables.* Make sure that your cable connectors match your devices. Use high-quality shielded cables, and observe the SCSI bus-length limitations. Use cables designed for SCSI use, and if possible, stick to the same brand of cable throughout a single SCSI bus. Different brands of cables have different impedance values; this situation sometimes causes problems, especially in long or high-speed SCSI implementations.

Following these simple tips will help minimize problems and leave you with a trouble-free SCSI installation.

IDE versus SCSI

When you compare the performance and capabilities of IDE (Integrated Drive Electronics) and SCSI (Small Computer System Interface) interfaced drives, you need to consider several factors. These two types of drives are the most popular drives used in PC systems today, and a single manufacturer may make identical drives in both interfaces. Deciding which drive type is best for your system is a difficult decision that depends on many factors.

In most cases, you will find that an IDE drive outperforms an equivalent SCSI drive at a given task or benchmark and that IDE drives usually cost less than SCSI drives, thus offering better value. In some cases, however, SCSI drives have significant performance and value advantages over IDE drives.

Performance. ATA (AT Attachment) IDE drives currently are used in most PC configurations on the market today, because the cost of an IDE-drive implementation is low and the performance capabilities are high. In comparing any given IDE and SCSI drive for performance, you have to look at the capabilities of the HDAs (Head Disk Assemblies) that are involved.

To minimize the variables in this type of comparison, it is easiest to compare IDE and SCSI drives from the same manufacturer that also use the identical HDA. You will find that in most cases, a drive manufacturer makes a given drive available in both IDE and

SCSI forms. For example, Seagate makes the ST-3600A (ATA-IDE) and ST-3600N (Fast SCSI-2) drives, both of which use identical HDAs and which differ only in the logic board. The IDE version has a logic board with a built-in disk controller and a direct AT bus interface. The SCSI version has the same built-in disk controller and bus interface circuits, and also a SCSI Bus Interface Controller (SBIC) chip. The SBIC chip is a SCSI adapter that places the drive on the SCSI bus. What you will find, in essence, is that virtually all SCSI drives actually are IDE drives with the SBIC chip added.

The HDAs in these example drives are capable of transferring data at a sustained rate of 2.38M to 4M per second. Because the SCSI version always has the additional overhead of the SCSI bus to go through, in almost all cases the directly attached IDE version performs faster.

SCSI versus IDE: Advantages and Limitations. IDE drives have much less command overhead for a given sector transfer than SCSI drives do. In addition to the drive-to-controller command overhead that both IDE and SCSI must perform, a SCSI transfer involves negotiating for the SCSI bus; selecting the target drive; requesting data; terminating the transfer over the bus; and finally converting the logical data addresses to the required cylinder, head, and sector addresses.

This arrangement gives IDE an advantage in sequential transfers handled by a single-tasking operating system. In a multitasking system that can take advantage of the extra intelligence of the SCSI bus, SCSI can have the performance advantage.

SCSI drives offer significant architectural advantages over IDE and other drives. Because each SCSI drive has its own embedded disk controller that can function independently of the system CPU, the computer can issue simultaneous commands to every drive in the system. Each drive can store these commands in a queue and then perform the commands simultaneously with other drives in the system. The data could be fully buffered on the drive and transferred at high speed over the shared SCSI bus when a time slot was available.

Although IDE drives also have their own controllers, they do not operate simultaneously, and command queuing is not supported. In effect, the dual controllers in a dual-drive IDE installation work one at a time so as not to step on each other.

Although SCSI drives require an additional-cost host adapter card, more and more PCs require tape-backup, CD-ROM, or optical-drive support and thus must still be configured with a SCSI host bus adapter. This means that the incremental cost of supporting SCSI drives is virtually nil, because the SCSI host bus adapter is shared with other devices, such as tape and optical drives. In addition, all major operating systems today include software support for a wide range of SCSI devices.

What are the limitations of IDE?

- IDE does not support overlapped, multitasked I/O.
- IDE does not support command queuing.
- IDE does not support bus mastering.

As you can see, SCSI has some advantages over IDE, especially where expansion is concerned, and also with regard to support for multitasking operating systems. Unfortunately it also costs much more to implement.

Recommended Aftermarket Controllers and Host Adapters

Many companies manufacture disk controllers for IBM and IBM-compatible systems. Many newer systems include IDE drives, which have built-in controllers and offer a high level of performance at a low cost. Other systems are using SCSI drives because of the inherent flexibility of the SCSI bus in supporting many drives and other peripherals.

I recommend IDE drives for most standard installations because the connections are simple and the drives are inexpensive for the power. For higher-end systems, or for systems in which upgradability and flexibility are most important, I recommend SCSI drives.

Silicon Valley makes a line of IDE adapters that are excellent for systems that do not have the special IDE connector on the motherboard. The company also makes a special adapter that enables you to put AT IDE drives in 8-bit XT systems, which few other cards do. Arco Electronics and Sigma Data make IDE adapters that enable you to install ATA IDE drives in PS/2 MCA bus systems. These companies even have unique versions for the Model 50z and 70 that replace the interposer card, therefore using no MCA slots in the system. All these companies are listed in Appendix B.

Recommended SCSI Host Adapters. For SCSI host adapters, I normally recommend Adaptec. Their adapters work well and come with the necessary formatting and operating software. Windows 95, Windows NT, and OS/2 have built-in support for Adaptec SCSI adapters. This support is a consideration in many cases because it frees you from having to deal with additional drivers.

Standard or Fast SCSI is adequately supported by the ISA bus, but if you are going to install a Fast-Wide SCSI bus, or especially an Ultra-Wide bus, then you should consider some form of local bus SCSI adapter, normally PCI. This is because the ISA bus supports a maximum transfer speed of about 8MB/sec, while a Fast-Wide SCSI bus runs up to 20MB/sec, and an Ultra-Wide SCSI bus runs up to a blazing 40MB/sec! In most cases a local bus SCSI adapter would be a PCI bus version, which is supported in most current PC systems.

One example of a popular SCSI adapter for the ISA bus is the Adaptec AHA-1540C and 1542C. The 1542 has a built-in floppy controller; the 1540 does not. These adapters are most notable for their ease of installation and use. Virtually all functions on the card can be configured and set through software. No more digging through manuals, looking for Interrupt, DMA, I/O Port, and other jumper settings—everything is controlled by software and saved in a flash memory module on the card. Following are some of the features of this card:

- Complete configuration utility built into the adapter's ROM
- Software-configurable IRQ, ROM Addresses, DMA, I/O Port Addresses, SCSI Parity, SCSI ID, and other settings
- Software-selectable termination (no resistors to pull out!)

- Enhanced BIOS support for up to eight 7.88G drives
- No drivers required for more than two hard disks
- Drive spinup on a per-drive basis available
- Boots from any SCSI ID

The 1542C model includes an Intel 82077 floppy controller chip (which supports 2.88M drives); 2.88M BIOS support also must be provided by your motherboard BIOS (see fig. 15.9).

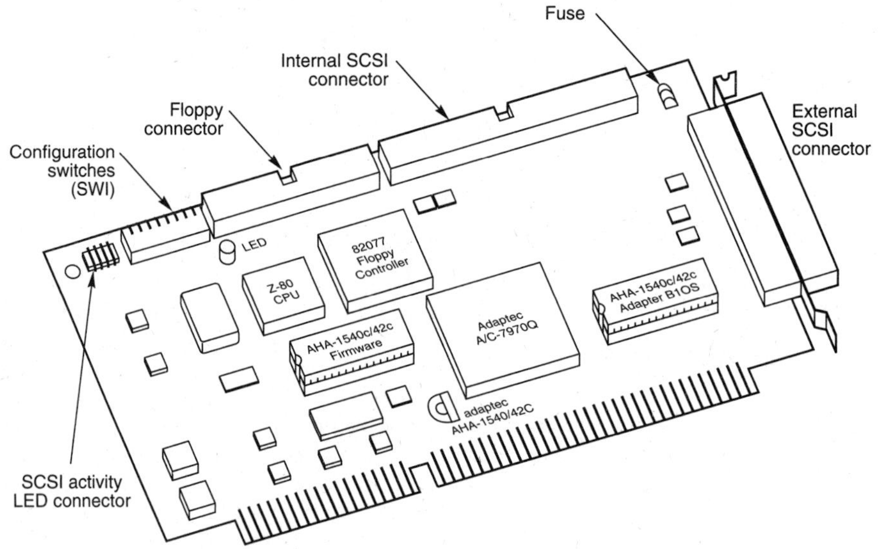

Figure 15.9

An Adaptec AHA-1542C SCSI host adapter.

More recently, Adaptec has released full Plug and Play versions of their SCSI adapters. These adapters will be automatically configured in any PC that supports the Plug and Play (PnP) specification, or they can be configured manually through supplied software in non-PnP systems. The PnP SCSI adapters are highly recommended because they can be configured without opening up the PC! All functions are set by software, and there are no jumpers or switches to attend to. Most peripheral manufacturers write drivers for Adaptec's cards first, so you will not have many compatibility or driver-support problems with any Adaptec card.

If you are using the older AHA-1542B SCSI host adapter, the current ROM revision available is version 3.20, which adds Enhanced BIOS support for multiple drives up to 7.88G with no drivers.

IBM SCSI Adapters. IBM has shipped several types of SCSI adapters since it introduced PC SCSI in 1990. Three basic types of adapters are available:

- 16-bit SCSI MCA adapter
- 32-bit SCSI MCA adapter with cache
- 16-bit Fast SCSI ISA adapter

The IBM host adapters (especially the MCA versions) are among the easiest to install and configure in the industry. Much of this ease comes from the Micro Channel architecture, which eliminates the need to worry about interrupts, DMA channels, I/O Port addresses, and even BIOS addresses. By virtue of MCA, these adapters are virtually self-configuring.

The only real problem is drivers. All these adapters have built-in support for hard disk drives, but no drivers are included for any other devices. This is important to know if you decide to attach external peripherals to these cards because you will need drivers to make the peripherals work.

IBM makes DOS drivers available only for the peripherals that it sells. Amazingly, however, IBM OS/2 includes SCSI drivers not only for numerous IBM and non-IBM peripherals, but also for non-IBM SCSI host adapters. If you cannot use OS/2, one way around the driver-support problem is to use the same peripherals that IBM sells, in which case you can get the drivers from IBM. For example, IBM sells a CD-ROM drive that actually incorporates a Toshiba mechanism. If I purchase a Toshiba CD-ROM drive, I can make it work simply by using the drivers that IBM supplies with its (Toshiba) CD-ROM drive.

IBM makes its drivers available free for the downloading on the IBM NSC BBS (the phone number is in Appendix B). I am also using a Hewlett Packard DAT (digital audiotape) drive for backup because that is the same mechanism that IBM sells in its own DAT drive. Again, I get the drivers from IBM. This system does not always work, however. For example, I want to attach a Hewlett Packard scanner to my IBM host adapter, but neither HP nor IBM (or anybody else so far) makes drivers to run the scanner with the IBM card. My only choice would be to use a different SCSI card to run the scanner—not a very good alternative, in my estimation.

The 16- and 32-bit MCA adapters have been available in two versions. The original version of the 16-bit (noncached) MCA adapter was known as FRU (Field Replacement Unit) # 15F6561 and was recalled for a defect. The replacement was labeled FRU # 85f0002. Some of the earlier cards were reworked and returned to the field without having the new FRU # applied over the old one. These repaired adapters can be identified by two yellow wires running from the upper to the lower side of the module (the module is labeled ZM10). If you have the original version of this card, getting the replacement is important (IBM should replace it free) because the original card could cause random lockups and data corruption.

The original 32-bit cached MCA adapter did not have a serious problem that required replacement, but it was updated over the years with improved functionality. The original SCSI adapter with cache does not support drive capacities greater than 1G. If you install a drive larger than 1G, the drive will work, but only the first 1G will be recognized. A new version of this card has an improved BIOS that supports drives up to 8G.

You can tell which SCSI adapter with cache you have by inspecting the adapter. The new adapter comes with an orange terminating resistor on the end of the card, similar to the noncached adapter. If you do not have both internal and external devices installed, this orange resistor should be located on the adapter. If you do have both internal and external devices, the resistor should be removed; there will be an empty socket on the adapter where the resistor originally was located. The new SCSI adapter with cache is sold under the part number 6451133 and known as FRU # 85F0063. If you have the original SCSI adapter with cache, you will not have either an orange resistor or an empty socket where the resistor is supposed to go. The original adapter does not implement termination on the card itself.

It is not widely known that you can upgrade the cache on the IBM SCSI adapter with cache from the standard 512K to 2MB simply by replacing the 256K (9-bit) SIMMs with 1MB SIMMs. The only caveat is that you must use the IBM-style 9-bit SIMMs, which have a slightly different pinout from so-called industry-standard 9-bit SIMMs. I have done this to my IBM SCSI card and have achieved perhaps a 10 percent improvement in throughput.

IBM also sells a new Fast/Wide MCA SCSI-2 adapter under part number G451280. IBM also has a Fast SCSI-2 adapter for ISA bus systems, which actually is made by Future Domain. This adapter is sold for use in ISA bus systems such as PS/1 and PS/Valuepoints. Because of Future Domain support, many more drivers are available for this adapter than for the MCA adapters, making it very easy to add a variety of peripherals under DOS as well as OS/2. This adapter also supports Fast SCSI transfers, whereas the original MCA IBM adapters do not.

Disk Hardware and Software Limitations

By studying the capabilities of the different disk interfaces as well as the ROM BIOS and operating systems, it is possible to determine the limits on disk storage. The following section details the limits under the different interfaces and operating systems.

Disk Interface Capacity Limitations

Different disk interfaces have different limitations on the theoretical maximum drive capacities that they may support. These limitations are due to variations in the way that each interface operates at the hardware level. It is important to note that even though a particular interface may permit access to a given amount of disk real estate, the BIOS and DOS usually are much more limiting and end up being the true limits for system disk capacity.

ST-506/412, ESDI, and IDE. To determine the capacity limits for the ST-506/412, ESDI, or IDE interface, you first need to determine the limits on the maximum number of cylinders, heads, and sectors per track. To do so, look at the size of the registers that hold this data in the controller. All these interfaces have the same controller register specifications, so the capacity limits calculated here apply to all of them. As you will see, the interface capacity limits are quite high. The drive parameter limits are as follows:

Cylinders (16 bits) = 65,536

Heads (4 bits) = 16

Sectors (8 bits) = 256

This calculates to a maximum theoretical drive size of:

65,536 Cyls × 16 Hds × 256 Secs × 512 Bytes = 137,438,953,472 Bytes (128G)

Unfortunately, the maximum capacity—128G—is limited by the BIOS. There are two different BIOS types with regards to disk size limitations. The standard BIOS built into most systems is limited to 1,024 cylinders, 16 heads, and 63 sectors per track. If the BIOS is an enhanced version, it will be limited to 1,024 cylinders, 256 heads, and 63 sectors per track. Combining the BIOS and interface limits results in the following maximum capacities (assuming 512-byte sectors):

Limit w/ Std. BIOS: 1,024 Cyls × 16 Hds × 63 Secs = 528,482,304 Bytes (504M)

Limit w/ Enh. BIOS: 1,024 Cyls × 256 Hds × 63 Secs = 8,455,716,864 Bytes (7.88G)

If you do not have enhanced BIOS support on your motherboard, you could add an IDE bus adapter that has an on-board enhanced BIOS. To get around such BIOS problems, some IDE drive implementations over 528 million bytes split the drive to act as two physical units. In this case, the drive would appear on the IDE bus connector as being both master and slave, and could be used only as two 504M-maximum-size drives.

ATA-2 has defined LBA support for EIDE. This is a logical block address mode where each sector on the drive is numbered from 0 to x. The limitations are that x is a 28-bit number that has a maximum value of 268,435,456. Using 512 byte sectors, this brings the maximum drive capacity to 137,438,953,472. That is coincidentally the same as the IDE internal limit has always been. The LBA is translated by the ATA-2/EIDE enhanced BIOS to the extended Cylinder, Head, and Sector (CHS) parameters which allow a maximum of 1,024 cylinders, 256 heads, and 63 sectors respectively.

SCSI. According to the SCSI specification, drives are not addressed by cylinders, heads, and sectors but instead by what is called a Logical Block Address (LBA). This is a sector number in which all the sectors on the drive are numbered sequentially from start to finish. The LBA is specified by a 32-bit number with 512-byte sectors, results in the following limitation:

4,294,967,296 LBAs (sectors) × 512 Bytes = 2,199,023,255,552 Bytes (2,048G or 2 terabytes)

As you can see, SCSI drive capacity limits are extremely high. However, because the SCSI drive must appear to the BIOS as being a given number of cylinders, heads, and sectors per track, the BIOS limits SCSI capacity. Virtually all SCSI adapters have an enhanced BIOS that supports a maximum drive capacity as follows (assuming 512-byte sectors):

SCSI w/ Enh. BIOS: 1,024 Cyls × 256 Hds × 63 Secs = 8,455,716,864 Bytes (7.88G)

If you do not have enhanced BIOS support in your SCSI adapter or motherboard, in some cases, you can load an external driver for your adapter to provide this support.

Most systems support up to 4 SCSI host adapters, each with up to 7 hard disk drives for a total of 28 physically installed drives.

ROM BIOS Capacity Limitations

In addition to the capacity limit of 504M, the standard ROM BIOS is limited to supporting only two hard disk drives. The enhanced BIOS is limited to 128 drives maximum. Most SCSI and IDE adapters get around the two-drive standard BIOS limits by incorporating an enhanced BIOS on board that takes over the disk interface. Some of the newer adapter on-board BIOS versions support booting from CD-ROM drives as well.

Operating-System Capacity Limitations

IBM and Microsoft officially say that DOS 5 and later versions will support up to eight physical hard disks. IBM says that OS/2 1.30.1 and later versions (including 2.x) support up to 24 physical hard disks, and because OS/2 includes DOS, that implies that DOS under OS/2 would support 24 physical drives as well. OS/2 HPFS (High Performance File System) also supports a maximum partition size of 8G and a maximum single-file size of 2G, whereas DOS and OS/2 FAT partitions have a maximum size of 2G and a maximum single-file size of 2G also. As you have seen, BIOS limitations currently limit the maximum physical hard disk size to about 7.88G (or about 8.46 million bytes).

Summary

This chapter examined hard disk interfaces and controllers. You learned about the different types of interfaces, their benefits and limitations. You also learned how to select and configure these interfaces. You can use this information to upgrade an existing system with a new type of hard disk or to troubleshoot and repair an existing system.

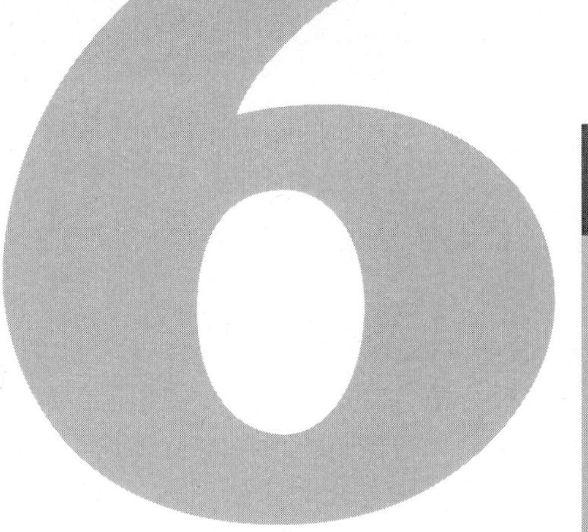

Chapter 16

Hard Disk Drive Installation

This chapter thoroughly describes hard disk installation. In particular, the chapter examines the configuration, physical installation, and formatting of a hard disk drive. This chapter also covers the basic procedures necessary to install a hard disk drive into a PC system.

Hard Disk Installation Procedures

This section describes the installation of a typical hard disk and its integration into a particular PC system. To install a hard drive in an IBM-compatible system, you must perform several procedures:

- Configure the drive
- Configure the controller or interface
- Physically install the drive
- Configure the system
- Low-level format the drive (not required with IDE and SCSI)
- Partition the drive
- High-level format the drive

Drive configuration was discussed in Chapter 15, "Hard Disk Interfaces." For complete configuration information, consult the section that covers the type of drive that you are installing.

The following sections describe the other steps, which are simple to execute and, if done properly, result in the successful installation of a bootable hard disk. Special attention is given to issues of reliability and data integrity to ensure that the installation is long-lasting and trouble-free.

To begin the setup procedure, you need to know several details about the hard disk drive, controller or host adapter, and system ROM BIOS, as well as most of the other devices in the system. This information usually appears in the various OEM manuals that come with these devices. Make sure when you purchase these items that the vendor includes these manuals. (Many vendors do not include the manuals unless you ask for them.) For most equipment sold today, you will get enough documentation from the vendor or reseller of the equipment to enable you to proceed.

If you are like me, however, and want all the technical documentation on the device, you will want to contact the original manufacturer of the device and order the technical specification manual. For example, if you purchase an IBM-compatible system that comes with a Western Digital IDE hard disk, the seller probably will give you some limited information on the drive, but not nearly the amount that the actual Western Digital technical specification manual provides. To get this documentation, you have to call Western Digital and order it. The same goes for any of the other components in most clones that are assembled rather than manufactured. I find the OEM technical manuals to be essential in providing the highest level of technical support possible.

Controller Configuration

Configuring a disk controller involves setting the different system resources that the controller requires. Some controllers have these resources fixed, which means that they cannot be altered. Other controllers provide jumpers, switches, or even software that enable you to reconfigure or change the resources used. Controllers with adjustable resource settings can often be used in conjunction with other controllers in a system, but controllers with fixed resources usually cannot coexist with others.

All hard disk controllers and SCSI host adapters require one or more of the following system resources:

- ROM addresses
- Interrupt Request Channel (IRQ)
- DMA channel (DRQ)
- I/O port addresses

Not all adapters use every one of these resources, but some will use them all. In most cases, these resources must be configured so that they are unique and cannot be shared among several adapters. For example, if a disk controller is using I/O port addresses from 1F0-1F7h, no other device in the system can use those addresses.

When a conflict in resource use occurs, not all of the adapters involved may function. In the case of disk controllers, the controller will not function, and disk access will be impossible or corrupted. You need to identify which boards in the system have overlapping resources and then change the configuration of one or more of those boards to eliminate the conflict. Before installing a board, you should know which resources the board will require, and you should make sure that these resources are not being used by other boards.

In most systems, this is a manual procedure that requires you to know exactly what every adapter in the system is using. If your system supports Plug and Play (PnP), this will be much easier. On older MCA and EISA systems, the procedure is also under software control. PnP ISA, PCI, MCA, and EISA systems can automatically determine whether two adapters use the same resource and then change the configuration to eliminate the conflict.

For most systems, you need the documentation for every adapter in the system to ensure that no conflicts exist and to find out how to reconfigure a card to eliminate a conflict. Software included with your system, such as MSD (Microsoft Diagnostics, which comes with Windows 3.x and DOS 6.x) or the Device Manager in Windows 95, can help when documentation is not available or is limited. Aftermarket diagnostics and utility programs can also be helpful. Unless your system conforms to the Plug and Play (PnP) specification, software will normally not be able to identify direct conflicts, but if you install one board at a time, they can identify the addresses or resources that a given board is using.

Many system resources simply cannot be identified by software alone. Several companies, including AllMicro, Quarterdeck, Data Depot, and others, manufacture cards that can be used to monitor interrupt and DMA channels. These boards are very helpful in identifying which of these resources are used in your system. These companies and others are listed in Appendix B.

ROM Addresses. Many disk controllers and SCSI host adapters require an on-board BIOS to function. An on-board BIOS can provide many functions, including:

- Low-level formatting
- Drive-type (parameter) control
- Adapter configuration
- Support for nonstandard I/O port addresses and interrupts

If the motherboard BIOS supports a hard disk controller, an on-board BIOS is not needed—and, in fact, is undesirable because it uses memory in the Upper Memory Area (UMA). Fortunately, the on-board BIOS usually can be disabled if it is not required.

Only controllers that meet certain standards can run off the motherboard BIOS, including ST-506/412 controllers, ESDI controllers, and IDE bus adapters. These standards include the use of I/O port addresses 170-17Fh and interrupt 14. If you are installing a controller that uses other I/O port addresses or interrupt settings (such as when adding a second controller to a system), the motherboard BIOS will not be able to support it, and an on-board BIOS will be required. XT controllers universally need an on-board BIOS because the motherboard BIOS has no hard disk support whatsoever.

SCSI adapters normally do not emulate the WD1003-type disk interface and almost always require an on-board BIOS to provide disk driver functions. This on-board BIOS supports any of the adapter's settings; and in most cases, multiple SCSI host adapters can use the BIOS of the first adapter, in which case the BIOSes on all but the first adapter can be disabled.

If an on-board BIOS is required and enabled, it will use specific memory address space in the UMA (Upper Memory Area). The UMA is the top 384K in the first megabyte of system memory. The UMA is divided into three areas of two 64K segments each, with the first and last areas being used by the video-adapter circuits and the motherboard BIOS, respectively. Segments C000h and D000h are reserved for use by adapter ROMs such as those found on disk controllers or SCSI host adapters.

You need to ensure that any adapters using space in these segments do not overlap with another adapter that uses this space. No two adapters can share this memory space. Most adapters have jumpers, switches, or even software that can adjust the configuration of the board and change the addresses that are used to prevent conflict.

Interrupt Request Channel (IRQ). All disk controllers and SCSI host adapters require an interrupt line to gain the system's attention. These devices invoke a hardware interrupt to gain timely access to the system for data transfers and control. The original 8-bit ISA systems have only 8 interrupt levels, with interrupts 2 through 7 available to any adapter. AT bus (16-bit ISA), EISA, and MCA systems have 16 interrupt levels, with interrupts 3 through 7, 9 through 12, and 14 through 15 available to any adapter cards. IRQs 10 through 12 and 14 through 15 are 16-bit interrupts available only to 16- or 32-bit adapters.

Tables 16.1 and 16.2 show the normally used and normally available interrupts in ISA, EISA, and MCA systems and in 8-bit ISA systems. The tables list the default use for each interrupt and indicate whether the interrupt is available in a bus slot.

Table 16.1 ISA, EISA, and MCA Default Interrupt Assignments

IRQ	Function	Bus Slot
0	System Timer	No
1	Keyboard Controller	No
2	Second IRQ Controller	No
8	Real-Time Clock	No
9	Network/Available (Redirected IRQ 2)	Yes (8-bit)
10	Available	Yes (16-bit)
11	SCSI/Available	Yes (16-bit)
12	Motherboard Mouse Port	Yes (16-bit)
13	Math Coprocessor	No
14	Hard Disk Controller	Yes (16-bit)
15	Secondary IDE	Yes (16-bit)
3	Serial Port 2 (COM2:)	Yes (8-bit)
4	Serial Port 1 (COM1:)	Yes (8-bit)
5	Sound/Parallel Port 2 (LPT2:)	Yes (8-bit)

IRQ	Function	Bus Slot
6	Floppy Disk Controller	Yes (8-bit)
7	Parallel Port 1 (LPT1:)	Yes (8-bit)

Table 16.2 XT-Bus (8-Bit ISA) Default Interrupt Assignments

IRQ	Function	Bus Slot
0	System Timer	No
1	Keyboard Controller	No
2	Network/Available	Yes (8-bit)
3	Serial Port 2 (COM2:)	Yes (8-bit)
4	Serial Port 1 (COM1:)	Yes (8-bit)
5	Hard Disk Controller	Yes (8-bit)
6	Floppy Disk Controller	Yes (8-bit)
7	Parallel Port 1 (LPT1:)	Yes (8-bit)

Notice that some of the interrupts simply are not available in slots; they are reserved for use only by the indicated system function. Any interrupt that is listed as being in use by an item that is not installed in your system would be available. For example, if your system does not have a motherboard mouse port, IRQ 12 would be available; if your system does not have a second serial port, IRQ 3 would be available.

You must discover which interrupts currently are in use and which currently are available in a system, and then configure any new cards to use only the available interrupts. In a standard configuration, the hard disk controller uses interrupt (IRQ) 14. Any secondary controllers would have to use other interrupts. The standard interrupt for a secondary controller is IRQ 15. If the system does not support EIDE (Enhanced IDE) in the motherboard BIOS, then any controllers that do not use IRQ 14 must have an on-board BIOS to function. The older motherboard BIOS supports disk controllers only at IRQ 14, whereas a BIOS with EIDE support will run IDE ports at both IRQ 14 and 15. Most newer systems have integral EIDE support and automatically include a secondary IDE port, which is at IRQ 15.

Standard IDE adapters come preconfigured for IRQ 14, which is fine if the adapter is the only disk adapter in the system. Many SCSI host adapters, such as the Adaptec 1540/1542C, come configured to one of the other available 16-bit interrupts, such as IRQ 11. Old XT (8-bit) hard disk controllers normally use IRQ 5.

DMA Channel. Direct Memory Access (DMA) is a technique for transferring blocks of data directly into system memory without the complete attention of the main processor. The motherboard has DMA control circuits that orchestrate and govern DMA transfers. In the original 8-bit XT bus, DMA was the highest-performance transfer method, and XT hard disk controllers universally used DMA channel 3 for high-speed transfers.

In AT-bus (16-bit ISA) systems, most 16-bit disk controllers and SCSI host adapters do not use a DMA channel, partly because the performance of the AT bus DMA circuitry turned out to be very poor. Therefore, most adapters use a technique called Programmed I/O (PIO), which simply sends bytes of data through the I/O ports. PIO transfers are faster than DMA transfers in most cases, especially if the motherboard BIOS and device support block-mode PIO, such as with the new IDE drives. If an adapter does not use DMA, you can assume that PIO is used as the data-transfer method and that no DMA channel is required.

Some adapters have found a way around the poor performance of the ISA bus by becoming what is known as a bus master. A bus master actually takes control of the bus and can override the DMA controller circuitry of the motherboard to perform fast DMA transfers. These transfers can exceed the performance of a PIO transfer (even block-mode PIO), so you will find that many of the highest-performing controllers have bus-master capabilities.

You have to select a DMA channel for bus-master adapters to use. In an 8-bit ISA bus, normally only DMA channel 1 is available; in a 16-bit ISA bus, however, DMA channels 0 through 1, 3, and 5 through 7 are available. DMA channels 5 through 7 are 16-bit channels that most high-performance bus-master adapters would want to use. XT disk controllers always use DMA channel 3, whereas most 16-bit AT or IDE controllers do not use DMA at all.

Tables 16.3 and 16.4 show the normally used and normally available DMA channels. The tables list the default use for each DMA channel and indicate whether the DMA channel is available in a bus slot.

Table 16.3 16-bit ISA Default DMA Channel Assignments

DMA	Function	Transfer	Bus Slot
0	Available	8-bit	Yes(16-bit)
1	Sound/Available	8-bit	Yes (8-bit)
2	Floppy Disk Controller	8-bit	Yes (8-bit)
3	ECP Parallel/Available	8-bit	Yes (8-bit)
4	First DMA Controller	N/A	No
5	Sound/Available	16-bit	Yes(16-bit)
6	SCSI/Available	16-bit	Yes(16-bit)
7	Available	16-bit	Yes(16-bit)

Table 16.4 8-Bit ISA Default DMA Channel Assignments

DMA	Function	Transfer	Bus Slot
0	Dynamic RAM Refresh	N/A	No
1	Sound/Available	8-bit	Yes (8-bit)
2	Floppy Disk Controller	8-bit	Yes (8-bit)
3	Hard Disk Controller	8-bit	Yes (8-bit)

Notice that some of the DMA channels simply are not available in slots; they are reserved for use only by the indicated system function. Any DMA channel that is listed as being in use by an item that is not installed in your system would be available. For example, if your 8-bit ISA bus system does not have a hard disk controller, DMA channel 3 would be available.

MCA and EISA bus systems have additional DMA capabilities that support even faster transfers without the performance problems associated with non-bus-master cards. The MCA and EISA buses also provide even better support for bus-master devices that offer even higher performance.

To configure an adapter that requires a DMA channel, you first must find out which DMA channels currently are in use and which channels are available in your system. Unless you have an MCA or EISA system, software techniques for determining this are very limited. Most programs that claim to be capable of discovering which DMA channels are being used are only reporting what any standard configuration would be. In standard ISA systems, the only way to know for sure is to check the documentation for each adapter or to use a special hardware device that monitors DMA transfers. Allied Electronics makes a card called the Trapcard II that monitors IRQ and DMA lines and can tell you for certain which are used and which are not. This inexpensive card plugs into a slot and monitors the bus, with LEDs indicating which resources are being used. Allied is listed in Appendix B.

After determining what DMA channels are free, you can set your adapter to any of those free channels. DMA conflicts usually result in improper operation or corrupted data transfers, so if you made a mistake, you will usually know quickly.

MCA and EISA systems automatically set up the boards so that no DMA conflicts exist. This method works fully only in EISA systems with all EISA 32-bit adapters installed.

I/O Port Addresses. I/O port addresses are like mailboxes through which data and commands are sent to and from an adapter. These addresses are different from memory addresses. I/O ports must be used exclusively and cannot be shared among different adapters. Each adapter usually uses a group of sequential port addresses for communication with the bus.

The standard I/O port addresses used by disk controllers are 1F0-1F7h. These are the only addresses that the motherboard BIOS supports, so if you have a disk controller at any other port address, it must have an on-board BIOS. Obviously, if you are adding a secondary controller to a system, that controller must use different I/O addresses and also must have an on-board BIOS. Most controllers use 170-177h as secondary I/O addresses, which would be used if another disk controller were in the system; however, you can use any I/O addresses that are free.

I/O port conflicts are rare unless you are installing multiple disk controllers in a system. In that case, each controller needs different I/O port address settings so as not to conflict with the others. To determine what I/O ports are currently in use, you normally have to refer to the documentation that comes with each device in your system. Software normally cannot identify all used I/O port addresses unless you have a Micro Channel or

EISA system. When port conflicts exist, the devices in conflict do not function, or they function improperly.

Physical Installation

The procedure for physical installation of a hard disk is much the same as the procedure for installing a floppy drive. You must have the correct screws, brackets, and faceplates for the specific drive and system before you can install the drive.

IBM AT systems require plastic rails that are secured to the sides of the drives so that they can slide into the proper place in the system (see fig. 16.1). Compaq uses a different type of rail. When you purchase a drive, the vendor usually includes the IBM-type rails, so be sure to specify whether you need the special Compaq type. IBM PC-type and XT-type systems do not need rails, but they may need a bracket to enable double-stacking of half-height drives. Several companies listed in Appendix B specialize in drive-mounting brackets, cables, and other hardware accessories.

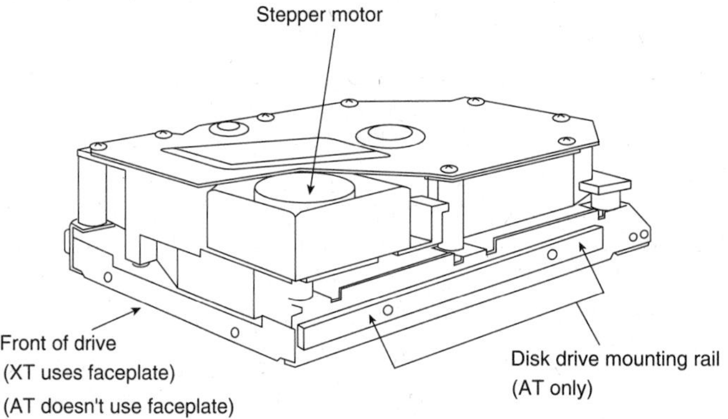

Figure 16.1

A full-height hard disk with AT mounting rails.

Different faceplate, or bezel, options are available; make sure that you have the correct bezel for your application. Some systems, for example, do not need a bezel; if a bezel is on the drive, it must be removed. If you are installing a half-height drive in a full-height bay, you may need a blank half-height bezel to fill the hole, or you may want to order a half-height drive with a full-height bezel so that no hole is created. Several vendors listed in Appendix B sell a variety of drive mounting kits, hardware, rails, adapters, and cables.

System Configuration

When the drive is physically installed, you can begin configuring the system to the drive. You have to tell the system about the drive so that the system can boot from it when it is powered on. How you set and store this information depends on the type of drive and system you have. Standard setup procedures are used for most hard disks except SCSI drives. SCSI drives normally follow a custom setup procedure that varies depending on the host adapter that you are using. If you have SCSI drives, follow the instructions included with the host adapter to configure the drives.

AT-Class System Setup Program and Drive Types. If the system is an AT type and you are using the motherboard BIOS to support the hard disks, you need to know some information about the BIOS, such as what drives are supported in the hard drive table. Many BIOS versions now have user-definable drive types that enable you to enter any set of parameters required to match your drive. For IDE drives, many new BIOS versions have automatic typing, which interrogates the drive and automatically enters the parameter information returned by the drive. This procedure eliminates errors or confusion in parameter selection.

Normally, the information about the drive table appears in the technical manuals provided with the motherboard or the BIOS. Appendix A includes a list of drive types for many different BIOS versions. For systems that are not listed, you can find this information in the system's technical reference manual. Often, the BIOS setup program shows you all the available selections on-screen, enabling you to select the best choice interactively and eliminating the need to research this information.

After you collect the necessary information, the next step is to tell the system what kind of drive is attached so that the system can boot from the drive (eventually). This chapter discusses the installation of an example drive in both an XT-type and an AT-type of system. The same drive is installed in both systems. With knowledge of drive interfacing, you can install just about any drive in any system.

The example drive is a Maxtor XT-1140, which is an ST-506/412 drive designed for MFM encoding. This drive is a full-height 5 1/4-inch platter drive that fits into any 5 1/4-inch full-height drive bay. The drive capacity is 140MB unformatted and 119.85MB formatted, with MFM encoding or 183.31MB formatted, with RLL 2,7 encoding. You can use the drive in a system with an ST-506/412 interface controller. In its day, this drive was a fairly high-performance drive (as far as ST-506/412 drives go, anyway), with an advertised 27-ms seek time. This drive is a voice coil drive with thin-film media; it has 8 platters with 15 read/write heads and 1 dedicated servo head.

First, you need to read the drive manual and locate the required information. The manual for the example drive contains the following drive-parameter information:

- 918 cylinders
- 15 heads
- 17 or 26 sectors per track (MFM or RLL encoding)
- No write precompensation required
- 2 to 3,100[230] head step pulse timing acceptable
- 2 to 13[230] head step pulse timing optimum
- 7 defective tracks:

  Cyl 188, Head 7
  Cyl 217, Head 5

Cyl 218, Head 5

Cyl 219, Head 5

Cyl 601, Head 13

Cyl 798, Head 10

Cyl 835, Head 5

To install this Maxtor XT-1140 in an IBM AT, I could simply use the original IBM AT controller (Western Digital WD1003A-WA2); however, I would have to live with the slow 2:1 interleave that this controller provides. A better choice is to upgrade the controller with a Data Technology Corporation DTC7287 controller. This controller not only supports a 1:1 interleave, but also has an RLL Endec, which will increase the storage capacity of the drive by 50 percent compared with the original MFM encoding controller. Because this drive is a high-quality voice coil actuated drive with thin-film media, it should work well with RLL encoding.

This controller also has an optional on-board ROM that can be used to set the drive type if the motherboard does not have a matching or user-definable type. The on-board ROM (if enabled) also has a low-level format program. For most systems, you set the drive type by looking up the drive information in the table of types located in the system ROM. You match the drive parameters to one of the table entries in the system ROM or set the parameters by using the user-definable drive type.

The following information is required for installing the DTC7287 controller:

- Interrupt Request Channel (IRQ) = 14
- I/O ports = 1F0 to 1F7
- Step pulse rate = 35µs (selected by BIOS)
- Best interleave = 1:1

This controller uses Programmed I/O (PIO) transfers and does not require a DMA channel for the hard disk controller portion. Because this controller also contains a floppy controller, some additional information specific to the floppy controller portion of the card is required:

- Interrupt Request Channel (IRQ) = 6
- DMA channel (DRQ) = 2
- I/O ports = 3F0 to 3F7

You need some of this information to ensure that the card is uniquely configured compared with other cards in the system. The system cannot have other cards using the same IRQ, DMA, ROM, or I/O ports as this card. Keep this information for future reference, and cross-check for conflicts when you add other cards to the system. The step pulse rates and interleave information are all that you need to complete the setup.

As mentioned earlier, the Maxtor XT-1140 manual states that the drive's seek performance degrades if step pulses are sent at intervals greater than 13µs. Unfortunately, the IBM AT ROM BIOS hard-codes this specification to 35µs, which slows the drive's performance. In my experience, the drive runs 25-ms seeks with the proper step pulse rate but an average 29-ms seeks with the slower step pulse rate selected in the IBM AT. If you want to bother with patching the AT ROM BIOS, you can change the controller's step pulse rate to 16µs; this change would probably make up a few milliseconds of average seek time. The instructions for making this patch appear in Chapter 7, "Memory," in the section "Upgrading the ROM BIOS." I made this modification to my own system to see whether it could be done, and I learned a lot in the process, but the results really are not worth the trouble.

After you find the information about the drive and controller, you need to match the drive's parameters to one of the drive-table entries in the motherboard ROM. ROM drive tables for IBM and many other compatible systems are listed in Appendix A, which also includes a detailed list of a large number of hard disk drives with parameter specifications. The information in Appendix A saved me several times when the original manuals were nowhere to be found.

With the drive tables and drive information in hand, try to find a table entry that matches on heads, cylinders, and write-precompensation starting cylinder. If you do not find an exact match for any of these values, use a type that has fewer cylinders and heads than your drive; you cannot use a type that has more. Remember that many compatible ROMs (such as those from Phoenix, Award, and AMI) have a user-definable drive type that enables you to support any drive parameters you want simply by typing them during setup.

Because the Maxtor XT-1140 drive has 918 cylinders and 15 heads, type 9, with 900 cylinders and 15 heads, is the best match in an IBM AT—if you are running an MFM controller, that is. Notice that all the types in an original AT BIOS have 17 sectors per track, whereas the drive actually has 26 sectors per track with RLL encoding. If the BIOS has a user-definable type entry (the original AT does not), you are home free; simply select the user-definable type and enter the exact parameters, including the correct number of sectors per track. If you select or define a type that indicates more cylinders, heads, or sectors than your drive has, you probably will see 1790 or 1791 Power-On Self Test (POST) error codes. These error codes indicate a fixed-disk 0 (or disk 1) read error, which most likely means that your selection is improper. If you are installing an intelligent IDE drive, it translates the parameters that you enter, which means that those parameters will work as long as they do not add up to more total sectors than the drive actually has.

The Maxtor XT-1140 drive requires no write precompensation. Type 9 in the original AT BIOS indicates a precompensation start cylinder of 65535—the largest number that can be stored with 16 bits. Essentially, this means that write precompensation never will be done, because you will never reach an actual cylinder number that high. For entries that have a value of 0 for the write-precompensation figure, write precompensation is performed on all cylinders, starting with 0.

The landing-cylinder designation is superfluous because this drive automatically parks and locks its heads at power-down, although it would be used if you ever ran a correctly written head-parking program.

Because there is no acceptable type in the original AT BIOS, and because there is no user-definable type either, this controller has an on-board BIOS that can override the motherboard BIOS and provide the drive-type information to the system. In this case, the motherboard BIOS is set to type 1, and the on-board controller BIOS takes over. To run the format program in the on-board BIOS, you use the DOS DEBUG program to point to the starting address of the BIOS format routine.

IBM AT Drive Type Tables. Rather than use a ROM on the controller card to support the card and drive tables, IBM incorporated the hard disk ROM BIOS into the main system ROM that resides on the motherboard. This ROM contains a hard disk table with at least 15 entries; later AT ROMs have tables with 23 entries. The XT 286 (really a late-model AT) has a table with 24 entries, and some PS/1 and PS/2 systems have as many as 44 entries. In each of these tables, entry 15 is reserved and not usable.

The tables are downward-compatible in the newer systems. For example, the PS/2 Model 80-111 has 32 table entries in its ROM, and the entries in the earlier systems match the specifications. Drive type 9, for example, is the same in all these systems, from the earliest AT to the newest PS/2 systems.

Notice that compatible systems are not consistent in regard to drive tables. Appendix A lists several hard disk drive tables for different compatible systems.

Table 16.5 lists the entries in the IBM motherboard ROM BIOS hard disk parameter table for AT or PS/2 systems using ST-506/412 (standard or IDE) controllers.

Table 16.5 IBM AT and PS/2 Hard Disk Drive Types

Type	Cyls	Heads	WPC	Ctrl	LZ	S/T	Meg	MB
1	306	4	128	00h	305	17	10.16	10.65
2	615	4	300	00h	615	17	20.42	21.41
3	615	6	300	00h	615	17	30.63	32.12
4	940	8	512	00h	940	17	62.42	65.45
5	940	6	512	00h	940	17	46.82	49.09
6	615	4	65,535	00h	615	17	20.42	21.41
7	462	8	256	00h	511	17	30.68	32.17
8	733	5	65,535	00h	733	17	30.42	31.90
9	900	15	65,535	08h	901	17	12.06	117.50
10	820	3	65,535	00h	820	17	20.42	21.41
11	855	5	65,535	00h	855	17	35.49	37.21
12	855	7	65,535	00h	855	17	49.68	52.09
13	306	8	128	00h	319	17	20.32	21.31
14	733	7	65,535	00h	733	17	42.59	44.66

Type	Cyls	Heads	WPC	Ctrl	LZ	S/T	Meg	MB
15	0	0	0	00h	0	0	0	0
16	612	4	0	00h	663	17	20.32	21.31
17	977	5	300	00h	977	17	40.55	42.52
18	977	7	65,535	00h	977	17	56.77	59.53
19	1024	7	512	00h	1023	17	59.50	62.39
20	733	5	300	00h	732	17	30.42	31.90
21	733	7	300	00h	732	17	42.59	44.66
22	733	5	300	00h	733	17	30.42	31.90
23	306	4	0	00h	336	17	10.16	10.65
24	612	4	305	00h	663	17	20.32	21.31
25	306	4	65,535	00h	340	17	10.16	10.65
26	612	4	65,535	00h	670	17	20.32	21.31
27	698	7	300	20h	732	17	40.56	42.53
28	976	5	488	20h	977	17	40.51	42.48
29	306	4	0	00h	340	17	10.16	10.65
30	611	4	306	20h	663	17	20.29	21.27
31	732	7	300	20h	732	17	42.53	44.60
32	1023	5	65,535	20h	1023	17	42.46	44.52
33	614	4	65,535	20h	663	25	29.98	31.44
34	775	2	65,535	20h	900	27	20.43	21.43
35	921	2	65,535	20h	1000	33	29.68	31.12
36	402	4	65,535	20h	460	26	20.41	21.41
37	580	6	65,535	20h	640	26	44.18	46.33
38	845	2	65,535	20h	1023	36	29.71	31.15
39	769	3	65,535	20h	1023	36	40.55	42.52
40	531	4	65,535	20h	532	39	40.45	42.41
41	577	2	65,535	20h	1023	36	20.29	21.27
42	654	2	65,535	20h	674	32	20.44	21.43
43	923	5	65,535	20h	1023	36	81.12	85.06
44	531	8	65,535	20h	532	39	80.89	84.82
45	0	0	0	00h	0	0	0.00	0.00
46	0	0	0	00h	0	0	0.00	0.00
47	0	0	0	00h	0	0	0.00	0.00

Type = drive type number
Cyls = total cylinders
Heads = total heads
WPC = write-precompensation starting cylinder
Ctrl = control byte; values as follows:
Bit 0 01h, not used (XT = drive step rate)
Bit 1 02h, not used (XT = drive step rate)
Bit 2 04h, not used (XT = drive step rate)
Bit 3 08h, more than 8 heads
Bit 4 10h, not used (XT = embedded servo)
Bit 5 20h, OEM defect map at (Cyls + 1)
Bit 6 40h, disable disk retries
Bit 7 80h, disable disk retries
LZ = landing-zone cylinder for head parking
S/T = number of sectors per track
Meg = drive capacity, in megabytes
MB = drive capacity, in millions of bytes

Table entry 15 is reserved as a CMOS pointer to indicate that the actual type is greater than 15.

Type tables for compatible BIOS versions are listed in Appendix A. Notice that most IBM systems do not have every entry in this table. The maximum usable type number varies for each specific ROM version. The maximum usable type for each IBM ROM is indicated in table 16.6.

Table 16.6 Number of Drive Types in Various IBM BIOS Versions

System Description	ROM BIOS Date	ID Byte	Submodel Byte	Revision	No. of ST-506/412 Drive types
PS/2 25	06/26/87	FA	01	00	26
PS/2 30	09/02/86	FA	00	00	26
PS/2 30	12/12/86	FA	00	01	26
PS/2 30	02/05/87	FA	00	02	26
PC-AT	01/10/84	FC	N/A	N/A	15
PC-AT	06/10/85	FC	00	01	23
PC-AT	11/15/85	FC	01	00	23
PC-XT 286	04/21/86	FC	02	00	24
PS/1	12/01/89	FC	0B	00	44
PS/2 25-286	06/28/89	FC	09	02	37
PS/2 30-286	08/25/88	FC	09	00	37
PS/2 30-286	06/28/89	FC	09	02	37
PS/2 35 SX	03/15/91	F8	19	05	37
PS/2 35 SX	04/04/91	F8	19	06	37
PS/2 40 SX	03/15/91	F8	19	05	37
PS/2 40 SX	04/04/91	F8	19	06	37
PS/2 L40 SX	02/27/91	F8	23	02	37
PS/2 50	02/13/87	FC	04	00	32
PS/2 50	05/09/87	FC	04	01	32
PS/2 50 Z	01/28/88	FC	04	02	33
PS/2 50 Z	04/18/88	FC	04	03	33
PS/2 55 SX	11/02/88	F8	0C	00	33
PS/2 60	02/13/87	FC	05	00	32
PS/2 65 SX	02/08/90	F8	1C	00	33
PS/2 70 386	01/29/88	F8	09	00	33
PS/2 70 386	04/11/88	F8	09	02	33
PS/2 70 386	12/15/89	F8	09	04	33
PS/2 70 386	01/29/88	F8	04	00	33
PS/2 70 386	04/11/88	F8	04	02	33
PS/2 70 386	12/15/89	F8	04	04	33

System Description	ROM BIOS Date	ID Byte	Submodel Byte	Revision	No. of ST-506/412 Drive types
PS/2 70 386	06/08/88	F8	0D	00	33
PS/2 70 386	02/20/89	F8	0D	01	33
PS/2 P70 386	01/18/89	F8	0B	00	33
PS/2 80 386	03/30/87	F8	00	00	32
PS/2 80 386	10/07/87	F8	01	00	32

Numbers in the ID Byte, Submodel Byte, and Revision columns are in hexadecimal.

If you have an IBM-compatible, this table probably will be inaccurate for any of the entries past type 15. (Most compatibles follow the IBM table for at least the first 15 entries.) Several compatible-system drive tables appear in Appendix A of this book, including tables for compatible systems ranging from Compaq to Zenith.

Most IBM PS/2 systems' hard disk drives have the defect map written as data on the cylinder that is one cylinder beyond the highest reported cylinder. This special data is read by the IBM PS/2 Advanced Diagnostics low-level format program, which automates the entry of the defect list and eliminates the chance of human error (as long as you use only the IBM PS/2 Advanced Diagnostics program for hard disk low-level formatting).

This drive-table information does not apply to IBM ESDI or SCSI hard disk controllers, host adapters, and drives. Because ESDI and SCSI controllers and host adapters query the drive directly for the required parameters, no table-entry selection is necessary. The table for ST-506/412 drives, however, still appears in the ROM BIOS of most PS/2 systems, even if the model came standard with the ESDI or SCSI disk subsystem.

The manufacturers of most compatibles have enhanced the motherboard ROM BIOS tables in three ways:

- *Additional types.* The first thing that the manufacturers did was add more drive types to the table. Because the table had room for 47 or more entries, many compatible BIOS versions simply filled out all the entries with values that matched the most popular drives on the market, generally making drive installations easier. IBM tables often were short of the maximum number of possible entries.

- *User-definable drive types.* Most makers of compatibles then added a user-definable type, which used unused areas of the CMOS memory to store all the drive-parameter information. This was an excellent solution, because during setup, you can type a parameter that matches any drive on the market. The only drawback is that if the CMOS battery dies or the saved values are corrupted in some way, you would have to re-enter the information exactly as it was before to regain access to the drive. Many people did not write down the parameters that they used, or they used improper parameters that caused problems.

- *Automatic detection.* Most of the newer BIOS versions include a feature that is specific to IDE drives. Because most IDE drives are intelligent and will respond to a command called Identify Drive, the BIOS sends this command to the drive, which then responds with the correct parameters. This feature eliminates the need to type the parameters because the BIOS will accept what the drive tells it.

Most of the newer compatible BIOS versions have both the user-definable type feature and automatic determination for IDE drives.

Drive-Table Alteration. Some drives do not match the table entries well. One way around the table-match problem is to purchase drives that match your tables. This solution can be limiting, however, especially if you have one of the earlier ROM-equipped systems. Most IBM-compatible systems have table entries all the way to type 47, but IBM AT systems stop much earlier than that.

ROM Patching. A second way around the drive-table limitation is to patch the correct entries for the desired drive and then reburn your own ROMs. This solution is illegal commercially and therefore is limited to "hacker" status, which means that you can do it to your own system but cannot legally sell patched IBM ROMs. For those who are so inclined, instructions for patching the BIOS are included in Chapter 7, "Memory".

ROM Replacement. A third way around the drive-table limits is to purchase and install a new ROM BIOS. A Phoenix ROM BIOS set, for example, costs about $50. These ROMs include a user-definable drive-type setting, which is the most elegant solution to this problem. A new set of ROMs probably will give you additional features, such as a built-in setup program, support for HD or ED 3 1/2-inch floppy drives, and Enhanced Keyboard support.

RLL/ESDI System Configuration. RLL and ESDI drives are usually not represented in the internal drive tables of older BIOS versions. Consequently, the controllers for these drives often have an on-board ROM BIOS that either contains an internal list of choices for the interface or enables you to dynamically configure (define) the controller to the specific geometry of the drive.

If you have a motherboard BIOS with a user-defined drive type (recommended), you can simply enter the correct parameters and the drive will be supported. (Remember to write down the parameters that you use; if you lose them, you can lose access to the drive if you don't re-enter the parameters properly.) When using a user-definable type, you can disable the controller BIOS.

IDE System Configuration. Intelligent IDE drives can use the geometry that represents their true physical parameters, or they can translate to other drive geometries that have the same number of sectors or fewer. Simply select a type, or enter a user-definable type that is less than or equal to the total capacity of the drive.

SCSI System Configuration. Almost all SCSI drives use DRIVE TYPE 0 or NONE, because the host adapter BIOS and the drive communicate to establish the drive geometry. The low-level formatting routines are usually accessed on the host adapter through DEBUG or are on disk in the form of a configuration, setup, and format program. All SCSI drives are low-level formatted at the factory.

XT-Type System Drive Configuration. XT-type systems typically store the drive setup or type information in ROM. The IBM XT uses a controller with a ROM that contains the hard disk controller BIOS and a table of four drive types indicating the supported drives. You set jumpers or switches on that controller to indicate which of the four drives you are installing. XT systems lack the CMOS memory and setup methods used by AT-class systems.

Because the on-board BIOS in IBM's original XT controllers supported only four drives, most aftermarket controllers rapidly evolved into having an autoconfigure capability. This capability is essentially equivalent to the user-definable type in most later compatible AT BIOS versions, enabling you to dynamically configure the controller and drive by entering parameters through the controller BIOS configuration routine. These parameters often were stored in a hidden sector on the drive and were loaded each time the system was powered on. This technique was used because XT-class systems do not have CMOS memory in which to store information such as this.

XT-Class System Drive Selection. IBM XT hard disk controllers have used two different ROMs over the years, but each has only four entry tables, which means that a single ROM can support only four drives. Therefore, virtually every time you want to add a different type of hard disk to an IBM XT, you must reburn the ROM with the correct values for the new drive. You can try to anticipate future upgrades and burn in the values for those drives as well.

A new generation of controllers for the IBM PC and IBM XT alleviates the problem with the IBM XT disk controller. These new controllers request the type of drive being connected and store that information in a specially reserved track on the drive. Every time the system is booted, the information is read from that location, and the system has the correct drive type. Therefore, a drive table with an infinite number of entries is possible.

Regardless of the parameters of your drive, the system can support it because this "autoconfigure ROM" is built into the controller. No matter what type of disk drive you select, make sure that your controller is an autoconfigure type; it eliminates problems with table entries that do not match your drives.

Tables 16.7 and 16.8 list the ROM BIOS drive parameters in IBM XT (Xebec 1210) hard disk controllers.

Table 16.7 IBM 10MB Hard Disk Controller (Xebec 1210) Drive Parameter Tables

Entry	Type	Cyls	Heads	WPC	Ctrl	LZ	S/T	Meg	MB
0	_	306	2	0	00h	00h	00h	5.08	5.33
1	_	375	8	0	05h	00h	00h	24.90	26.11
2	_	306	6	256	05h	00h	00h	15.24	15.98
3	_	306	4	0	05h	00h	00h	10.16	10.65

Table 16.8 IBM 20MB Hard Disk Controller (Xebec 1210) Drive Parameter Tables

Entry	Type	Cyls	Heads	WPC	Ctrl	LZ	S/T	Meg	MB
0	1	306	4	0	05h	305	17	10.16	10.65
1	16	612	4	0	05h	663	17	20.32	21.31
2	2	615	4	300	05h	615	17	20.42	21.41
3	13	306	8	128	05h	319	17	20.32	21.31

Entry = controller table position
Type = drive-type number
Cyls = total cylinders
Heads = total heads
WPC = write-precompensation starting cylinder
Ctrl = control byte; values as follows:
Bit 0 01h, drive step rate
Bit 1 02h, drive step rate
Bit 2 04h, drive step rate
Bit 3 08h, more than eight heads
Bit 4 10h, embedded servo drive
Bit 5 20h, OEM defect map at (Cyls + 1)
Bit 6 40h, disable ECC retries
Bit 7 80h, disable disk access retries
Xebec 1210 Drive Step Rate Coding (control byte, bits 0–3)
00h, 3-ms step rate
04h, 200-microsecond buffered step
05h, 70-microsecond buffered step
06h, 30-microsecond buffered step
07h, 15-microsecond buffered step
LZ = landing-zone cylinder for head parking
S/T = number of sectors per track
Meg = drive capacity, in megabytes
MB = drive capacity, in millions of bytes

The Landing Zone field and Sectors per Track fields are not used in the 10M (original) controller and contain 00h values for each entry.

Note

MB and Meg sometimes are used interchangeably, but this is not exactly correct. MB is 1 million bytes, or 1,000,000 bytes. Meg (or M) is one megabyte, which is equal to 1,048,576 bytes. (1 megabyte = 1 kilobyte times 1 kilobyte, and 1 kilobyte = 1,024 bytes. Thus, 1 megabyte = 1,024 × 1,024 = 1,048,576.)

To select one of the drive-table entries in the IBM XT controllers (Xebec 1210), you would set the drive-table selection jumper (Jumper W5). Table 16.9 shows how these jumpers should be set to select a particular table entry. To select table entry 2 for drive 0 (C), for example, you would set the jumper off at position 1 and on at position 2.

Table 16.9 IBM XT Controller (Xebec 1210) Drive-Table Jumper (W5) Settings

Drive 0 Table Entry	1	2	3	4
Jumper 1	On	On	Off	Off
Jumper 2	On	Off	On	Off

Drive 1 Table Entry	1	2	3	4
Jumper 3	On	On	Off	Off
Jumper 4	On	Off	On	Off

Autoconfigure Controllers. To install the example drive in an IBM XT, I could use the original IBM XT controller (Xebec 1210), but the built-in tables in that controller do not match my drive. I would have to download the ROM to disk and patch it to contain the correct drive-table values. If you can wield the DOS DEBUG program and have access to an EPROM burner, you can patch the correct table into one of the existing four table positions on the controller, and the controller will operate correctly with the drive. (I used this procedure on my vintage 1983 XT controller. The system works fine, but its best interleave is 5:1.)

Faster autoconfigure ROM controllers are available at such low prices that a better alternative is to purchase one. This example describes the installation of a Scientific Micro Systems Omti 5520A-10 controller, which has complete autoconfigure capability and supports a 2:1 interleave in the IBM PC and XT. Although this controller no longer is available, Data Technology Corporation (DTC) makes a DTC5150XL controller that offers even more features. The installation and configuration of all autoconfigure controllers are very similar.

DTC also makes a DTC5160XL controller that is an RLL version of the preceding controller. These controllers support co-residency, which means that they can be added to a system that already has an existing controller. These controllers can be installed with no hassle, run three times faster than the old Xebec controller, and cost less than $100. (Times have changed; an original Xebec 1210 cost me $795 in 1983.)

Following is the required information for the example installation:

- Interrupt Request Channel (IRQ) = 5
- DMA channel (DRQ) = 3
- ROM locations used = C8000 to C9FFF
- I/O ports = 320 to 32F
- Autoconfigure start location = C8006
- Step pulse rates = 10, 25, 50, 70, 200, and 3000μs
- Best interleave = 2:1 (4.77-MHz XT)

You need some of this information to ensure that the card is uniquely configured compared with other cards in the system. The system cannot have another card using the same IRQ, DMA, ROM, or I/O ports as this card. Keep this information for future reference, and cross-check for conflicts when you add other cards to the system. The autoconfigure start location, step pulse rates, and interleave information are necessary for completing the drive setup.

The next step is to activate the controller's built-in autoconfigure routine. When you do so, an autoconfigure controller prompts you for information about the drive (otherwise found in ROM tables) and then records the information directly on the drive in an area reserved by the controller on the first track. The advantage of the autoconfigure controller is that when you change drives, the controller can adapt. You never have to patch ROM-based tables with an EPROM burner because this drive stores them on the drive dynamically. After the routine is completed, the controller reads this information every time the system is powered up and "knows" how to boot from the drive.

One potential problem with storing the parameters on the drive is that if they are accidentally overwritten, the drive is inaccessible. For this reason, you must be careful with any program that performs a low-level format on the drive. Most nondestructive formatters, such as the Norton Utilities Calibrate program, refuse to reformat the first track of any drive so as to avoid overwriting any of this special autoconfigure data.

To run the autoconfigure routine, follow these steps:

1. Boot DOS 3.3 or later.
2. Run the DOS DEBUG program.
3. At the DEBUG prompt, enter the information to tell DEBUG to move the system instruction pointer to the autoconfigure ROM start location. For this specific controller, you enter G=C800:6.

Because autoconfigure controllers from different manufacturers have different starting locations for the ROM BIOS format routine built into the controller, look in the manual to find the starting location for the specific controller that you are installing. Table 16.10 provides the controller BIOS low-level format addresses used with DEBUG for several popular controller brands.

Table 16.10 Controller BIOS Low-Level Format Addresses

Controller Manufacturer	Low-Level Format Address
Western Digital	g = XXXX:5
DTC	g = XXXX:5
Adaptec	g = XXXX:CCC
Seagate	g = XXXX:5
SMS-OMTI	g = XXXX:6

Replace the XXXX value with the starting segment address of the ROM as configured in the controller. Most controller ROMs can be configured for a variety of starting addresses in segments C000h and D000h. Most controllers have C800h or D800h as starting segment addresses, but you will have to consult the controller documentation and controller jumper settings to be sure. Note that when you enter this number, you do not type the "h", which is used here simply to indicate that these are hexadecimal numbers.

After you enter the last DEBUG instruction, the autoconfigure routine asks several questions about the drive and controller: how many heads and cylinders the drive has, what the starting write-precompensation cylinder is, and how quickly the step pulses should be sent. Use the information that you gathered about the drive and controller to answer these questions.

In the example, you would indicate that the controller should pulse the drive with step pulses spaced 10µs apart. To establish this figure, look at the range of spacing that the drive will accept, compare it with what the controller can send, and select the fastest rate that both can agree on. This procedure is similar to configuring a serial printer and serial port for 9,600 bps transmission. Why not go as fast as the hardware will allow? The Maxtor XT-1140 manual states that seek performance on this particular drive degrades if step pulses are sent at intervals greater than 13µs. Setting this specification to a setting that is optimum for your drive can tweak a drive's seek performance.

The autoconfigure program also asks you to specify the desired interleave. An interleave of 2:1 is the best value for the example controller in a 4.77-MHz IBM PC or IBM XT system. This interleave value was determined by a simple trial-and-error testing session in which the disk was formatted at various interleaves, from 6:1 (the IBM XT default) down to 1:1. The transfer rate improved with each lower interleave until 1:1, at which point the transfer rate slowed by more than 800 percent. At 1:1, this controller cannot keep up with the rate at which the next sector passes below the heads; it requires 17 full revolutions of the disk to read a track, compared with 2 revolutions to read a track at a 2:1 interleave.

Finally, the autoconfigure program asks whether the drive has defects and gives you the opportunity to enter them. The example drive has seven defects (printed on a sticker on top of the drive, as well as included on a printed sheet). Entering this information causes the low-level format program to specially mark these tracks with invalid checksum figures, ensuring that these locations never are read or written to. Later, when DOS is used to high-level format the disk, the DOS format program will be unable to read these locations and will mark the file allocation table with information so that the locations never will be used. If you do not enter these locations properly, data or program files could use these defective tracks and become corrupted. Always mark these locations.

For the controller used in this example, the low-level format is part of the autoconfigure routine. After you answer the questions, the drive is low-level formatted, the defects are marked, and a scan is made for defects that were marked improperly or that became bad after the manufacturer's original tests. Finally, the autoconfigure information is written to a specially reserved track on the disk. When this process is complete, the drive is ready for DOS installation.

Formatting and Software Installation

Proper setup and formatting are critical to a drive's performance and reliability. This section describes the procedures used to format a hard disk drive correctly. Use these procedures when you install a new drive in a system or immediately after you recover data from a hard disk that has been exhibiting problems.

Three major steps complete the formatting process for a hard disk drive subsystem:

- Low-level formatting
- Partitioning
- High-level formatting

Considerations Before Low-Level Formatting. In a low-level format (LLF), which is a "real" format, the tracks and sectors of the disk are outlined and written. During the LLF, data is written across the entire disk. An improper low-level format results in lost data and in many read and write failures. You need to consider several things before initiating a low-level format.

Data Backup. Low-level formatting is the primary standard repair procedure for hard disk drives that are having problems. Because data values are copied to the drive at every possible location during an LLF, necessary data-recovery operations must be performed before an LLF operation.

Caution

After an LLF has been performed, you cannot recover any information previously written to the drive.

Because an LLF overwrites all the data on a drive, it is a good way to erase an entire drive if you are trying to ensure that nobody will be able to get data from it. Government standards for this type of procedure actually require the data to be overwritten several times with different patterns, but for most intents and purposes, if the drive is overwritten one time, nobody will be able to read any data that was on it.

System Temperature. Sector header and trailer information is written or updated only during the LLF operation. During normal read and write activity, only the 512 bytes plus the CRC (Cyclic Redundancy Check) bytes in the trailer are written in a sector. Temperature-induced dimensional changes in the drive platters during read and write operations can become a problem.

When a 5 1/4-inch platter drive is low-level formatted five minutes after power-up at a relatively cold platter temperature of 70 degrees F, the sector headers and trailers and the 512-byte dummy data values are written to each track on each platter at specific locations.

Suppose that you save a file on a drive that has been running for several hours at a platter temperature of 140 degrees F. The data areas of only several sectors are updated. But with the drive platters as much as 70 degrees warmer than when the drive was formatted, each aluminum drive platter will have expanded in size by 2.5 thousandths of an inch (taking into account the coefficient of linear thermal expansion of aluminum). Each track, therefore, would have moved outward a distance of approximately 1.25 thousandths of an inch. Most 5 1/4-inch hard disks have track densities between 500 and 1,000 tracks per inch, with distances of only 1 to 2 thousandths of an inch between adjacent tracks. As a result, the thermal expansion of a typical 5 1/4-inch hard disk platter could cause the tracks to migrate from one-half to more than one full track of distance below the heads. If the drive head-movement mechanism does not compensate for these thermally induced dimensional changes in the platters, severe mistracking results.

When mistracking occurs, the data areas in each sector that have been updated at the higher temperature fail to line up with the sector header and trailer information. If the sector header and trailer information cannot be read properly, DOS usually issues an error message like this one:

```
Sector not found reading drive C
Abort, Retry, Ignore, Fail?
```

The data is misaligned with the sector boundaries on those tracks. This thermal effect also can work in reverse: if the drive is formatted and written to while it is extremely hot, it may not read properly while cold because of dimensional changes in the platters. This problem occurs with drives that have the "Monday-morning blues," in which they spin but cannot read data properly when they are first powered on, especially after being off for an extended period (over a weekend, for example). If you leave the power to the system on for some time so that the drive can warm up, the system then may boot and run normally.

If this happens, the next step is to back up the drive completely and initiate a new low-level format at the proper operating temperature (described next). This procedure enables the drive to work normally again until temperature-induced mistracking becomes great enough to cause the problem again.

Knowing that temperature fluctuations can cause mistracking, you should understand the reasons for the following basic rules of disk use:

- Leave the system's power on for at least 30 minutes before performing a low-level format on its hard disk. This step ensures that the platters are at a normal operating temperature and have stabilized dimensionally.

- If possible, allow a system some time to warm up before storing any data on the hard disk. This procedure is not required for voice coil drives.

If you have a cheap stepper motor drive that consistently exhibits temperature-related mistracking problems, you may want to consider running the drive constantly. Doing so would extend its trouble-free life span significantly because the temperature and dimensions of the platters would stay relatively constant.

These kinds of temperature-fluctuation problems are more of a problem with drives that have open-loop stepper motor actuators (which offer no thermal compensation) than with the closed-loop voice coil actuators (which follow temperature-induced track migration and compensate completely, resulting in no tracking errors even with large changes in platter dimensions).

Modern voice coil actuator drives do not exhibit these dimensional instabilities due to thermal expansion and contraction of the platters because they have a track-following servo mechanism. As the tracks move, the positioner automatically compensates. Many of these drives undergo a noticeable thermal compensation sequence every 5 minutes or so for the first 30 minutes after being powered on, and usually every 30 minutes after that. During these thermal-compensation routines, you hear the heads move back and forth as they measure and compensate for platter-dimension changes.

Drive Operating Position. Another consideration before formatting a drive is ensuring that the drive is formatted in the operating position it will have when it is installed in the system. Gravity can place on the head actuator different loads that can cause mistracking if the drive changes between a vertical and a horizontal position. This effect is minimized or even eliminated in most voice coil drives, but this procedure cannot hurt.

Additionally, drives that are not properly shock-mounted (such as the Seagate ST 2xx series) should be formatted only when they are installed in the system because the installation screws exert twisting forces on the drive's Head Disk Assembly (HDA), which can cause mistracking. If you format the drive with the mounting screws installed tightly, it may not read with the screws out, and vice versa. Be careful not to overtighten the mounting screws, because doing so can stress the HDA. This usually is not a problem if the drive's HDA is isolated from the frame by rubber bushings.

In summary, for a proper low-level format, the drive should be:

- at a normal operating temperature
- in a normal operating position
- mounted in the host system (if the drive HDA is not shock-mounted or isolated from the drive frame by rubber bushings)

Because many different makes and models of controllers differ in the way that they write data to a drive, especially with respect to the encoding scheme, it is best to format the drive using the same make and model of controller as the controller that will be used in the host system. Some brands of controllers work exactly alike, however, so this is not an absolute requirement even if the interface is the same. This problem does not occur with IDE or SCSI drives, of course, because the controller is built into the drive. Usually, if the controller establishes the drive type by using its own on-board ROM rather than the system setup program, it will be incompatible with other controllers.

Low-Level Format. Of these procedures, the low-level format is most important to ensure trouble-free operation of the drive. This format is the most critical of the operations and must be done correctly for the drive to work properly. The low-level format includes several subprocedures:

- Scanning for existing defect mapping
- Selecting the interleave

- Formatting and marking (or remarking) manufacturer defects
- Running a surface analysis

On some systems, such as the IBM PS/2, these subprocedures are performed automatically by the system's low-level format program and require no user intervention. On other systems, you must take the initiative.

To perform the drive defect mapping, to select an interleave, and to complete a surface analysis of the drive, you need information about the drive, the controller, and possibly the system. This information usually is provided in separate manuals or documents for each item; therefore, be sure that you get the complete documentation for your drive and controller products when you purchase them. The specific information required depends on the type of system, controller, and low-level format program that you are using.

Defect Mapping. Before formatting the disk, you need to know whether the drive has defects that have to be mapped out. Most drives come with a list of defects discovered by the manufacturer during the drive's final quality-control testing. These defects must be marked so that they are not used later to store programs or data.

Defect mapping is one of the most critical aspects of low-level formatting. To understand the defect-mapping procedures, you first must understand what happens when a defect is mapped on a drive.

The manufacturer's defect list usually indicates defects by cylinder and track. When this information is entered, the low-level format program marks these tracks with invalid checksum figures in the header of each of the sectors, ensuring that nothing can read or write to these locations. When DOS performs a high-level format of the disk, the DOS FORMAT program cannot read these locations, and it marks the involved clusters in the file allocation table (FAT) so that they never will be used.

The list of defects that the manufacturer gives you probably is more extensive than what a program could determine from your system, because the manufacturer's test equipment is far more sensitive than a regular disk controller. Do not expect a format program to find the defects automatically; you probably will have to enter them manually. An exception is the new IBM PS/2 systems, in which the defect list is encoded in a special area of the drive that normal software cannot access. The IBM PS/2 low-level format program (included on the Reference disk that comes with IBM PS/2 systems) reads this special map, thereby eliminating the need to enter these locations manually.

Most new drives are not low-level formatted by the manufacturer. Even if you bought a drive that had been low-level formatted, you would not know the temperature and the operating position of the drive when it was formatted. For best results, perform your own low-level format on a drive after you receive it. If you bought a system with a drive already installed by the manufacturer or dealer, a low-level format probably was done for you. To be safe, however, you might want to do a new low-level format in the system's new environment.

Although an actual defect is technically different from a marked defect, these defects should correspond to one another if the drive is formatted properly. For example, I can enter the location of a good track into the low-level format program as a defective track. The low-level format program then corrupts the checksum values for the sectors on that track, rendering them unreadable and unwriteable. When the DOS FORMAT program encounters that track, it finds the track unreadable and marks the clusters occupying that track as bad. After that, as the drive is used, DOS ensures that no data ever is written to that track. The drive stays in that condition until you redo the low-level format of that track, indicate that the track is not to be marked defective, and redo the high-level format that no longer will find the track unreadable and therefore permit those clusters to be used. In general, unless an area is marked as defective in the low-level format, it will not be found as defective by the high-level format, and DOS will subsequently use it for data storage.

Defect mapping becomes a problem when someone formats a hard disk and fails to enter the manufacturer's defect list, which contains actual defect locations, so that the low-level format can establish these tracks or sectors as marked defects. Letting a defect go unmarked will cost you data when the area is used to store a file that you subsequently cannot retrieve. Unfortunately, the low-level format program does not automatically find and mark any areas on a disk that are defective. The manufacturer's defect list is produced by very sensitive test equipment that tests the drive at an analog level. Most manufacturers indicate areas as being defective even if they are just marginal. The problem is that a marginal area today may be totally unreadable in the future. You should avoid any area suspected as being defective by entering the location during the low-level format so that the area is marked; then DOS is forced to avoid the area.

Currently Marked Defects Scan. Most low-level format programs have the capability to perform a scan for previously marked defects on a drive. Some programs call this operation a defect scan; IBM calls it Read Verify in the IBM Advanced Diagnostics. This type of operation is nondestructive and reports by cylinder and head position all track locations marked bad. Do not mistake this for a true scan for defective tracks on a disk, which is a destructive operation normally called a surface analysis (discussed in the section "Surface Analysis" later in this chapter).

If a drive was low-level formatted previously, you should scan the disk for previously marked defects before running a fresh low-level format for several reasons:

- To ensure that the previous low-level format correctly marked all manufacturer-listed defects. Compare the report of the defect scan with the manufacturer's list and note any discrepancies. Any defects on the manufacturer's list that were not found by the defect scan were not marked properly.

- To look for tracks that are marked as defective but are not on the manufacturer's list. These tracks may have been added by a previously run surface-analysis program (in which case they should be retained), or they may result from the previous formatter's typographical errors in marking the manufacturer's defect. One of my drive manufacturer's lists showed Cylinder 514 Head 14 as defective. A defect scan, however, showed that track as good but Cylinder 814, Head 14 as bad. Because the latter location was not on the manufacturer's list, and because typing 5 instead of 8 would be an easy mistake to make, I concluded that a typographical error was the cause and then reformatted the drive, marking Cylinder 514, Head 14 as bad and enabling Cylinder, 814 Head 14 to be formatted as a good track, thus "unmarking" it.

If you run a surface analysis and encounter defects in addition to those on the manufacturer's list, you can do one of two things. If the drive is under warranty, consider returning it. If the drive is out of warranty, grab a pen and write on the defect-list sticker, adding the bad tracks discovered by the surface-analysis program. (The IBM PS/2 low-level formatter built into the Reference disk automatically performs a surface analysis immediately after the low-level format; if it discovers additional defects, it automatically adds them to the defect list recorded on the drive.) Adding new defects to the sticker in this manner means that these areas are not forgotten when the drive is subsequently reformatted.

Manufacturer's Defect List. The manufacturer tests a new hard disk by using sophisticated analog test instruments that perform an extensive analysis of the surface of the platters. This kind of testing can indicate the functionality of an area of the disk with great accuracy, precisely measuring information such as the signal-to-noise ratio and recording accuracy.

Some manufacturers have more demanding standards than others about what they consider to be defects. Many people are bothered by the fact that when they purchase a new drive, it comes with a list of defective locations; some even demand that the seller install a defect-free drive. The seller can satisfy this request by substituting a drive made by a company with less-stringent quality control, but the drive will be of poorer quality. The manufacturer that produces drives with more listed defects usually has a higher-quality product because the number of listed defects depends on the level of quality control. What constitutes a defect depends on who is interpreting the test results.

To mark the manufacturer defects listed for the drive, consult the documentation for your low-level format program. For most drives, the manufacturer's defect list shows the defects by cylinder and head; other lists locate the defect down to the bit on the track that is bad, starting with the index location.

Caution

Make sure that all manufacturer's defects have been entered before proceeding with the low-level format.

Some systems automatically mark the manufacturer's defects, using a special defect file recorded on the drive by the manufacturer. For such a system, you need a special low-level format program that knows how to find and read this file. Automatic defect-map entry is standard for IBM PS/2 systems and for most ESDI and all SCSI systems. Consult the drive or controller vendor for the proper low-level format program and defect-handling procedures for your drive.

Note

Data recovery utilities such as Scandisk (DOS/Windows) or the Norton Utilities cannot mark the sectors or tracks at the physical format level. The bad cluster marks that they make are stored only in the FAT and are easily erased during the next high-level format operation. You should also use a Low Level Format utility designed for your drive (contact the manufacturer), which will properly mark bad sectors and assign spares at the physical disk level.

Surface Analysis. A defect scan is a scan for marked defects; a surface analysis is a scan for actual defects. A surface analysis ignores tracks already marked defective by a low-level format and tests the unmarked tracks. The surface-analysis program writes 512 bytes to each sector on the good tracks, reads the sectors back, and compares the data read to what was written. If the data does not verify, the program (like a low-level format) marks the track bad by corrupting the checksum values for each sector on that track. A proper surface analysis is like a low-level format program in that it should bypass the DOS and the BIOS so that it can turn off controller retry operations and also see when ECC (Error Correction Code) is invoked to correct soft errors.

Surface-analysis programs are destructive: they write over every sector except those that already are marked as bad. You should run a surface analysis program immediately after running a low-level format to determine whether defects have appeared in addition to the manufacturer's defects entered during the low-level format. A defect scan after the low-level format and the surface analysis shows the cumulative tracks that were marked bad by both programs.

If you have lost the manufacturer's defect list, you can use the surface analysis program to indicate which tracks are bad, but this program can never duplicate the accuracy or sensitivity of the original manufacturer testing.

For example, if a spot in the sector were performing at 51 percent of capacity, it would be good enough to pass a PC surface analysis. The next day, due to variances in the drive and electronics, that same spot might perform at only 49 percent of capacity, failing a surface analysis. If you must use a surface analysis as your only source of defect information for a drive, be sure to use the option of increasing the number of times that each track will be tested, and run the program over an evening or weekend for a higher probability of catching an elusive or intermittent bad track.

Some low-level format and surface analysis programs have hype-filled advertisements that make misleading and even false claims of performance and capability. Some programs even "unmark" defects that have been purposely marked by the initial, properly done low-level format according to the manufacturer's supplied list of defects, because the program determines that the area in question is not defective. (This is unbelievable!) If the drive is a good one, no surface analysis program can possibly find all the defects on the manufacturer's list. Only factory testing at the analog level could indicate these defects because most manufacturers include even slightly marginal areas on their list.

For example, I have a 40MB drive that has 27 manufacturer defects on the bad-track list; this drive probably is the highest-quality 40MB sold. Most cheaper 40MB drives would have five or fewer defects on the bad-track list. I have run virtually every surface-analysis program on this drive, and none could find more than 5 of the 27 defects.

Although it is recommended if you have been experiencing any problems with a drive, on new drives I normally do not run a surface analysis after low-level formatting, for several reasons:

- Compared with formatting, surface analysis takes a long time. Most surface analysis programs take two to five times longer than a low-level format. A low-level format of a 120MB drive takes about 15 minutes; a surface analysis of the same drive takes an hour or more. Moreover, if you increase the accuracy of the surface analysis by allowing multiple passes or multiple patterns, the surface analysis takes even longer.

- With high-quality drives, I never find defects beyond those that the manufacturer specified. In fact, the surface-analysis programs do not find all the manufacturer's defects if I do not enter them manually. Because the high-quality (voice coil) drives that I use have been tested by the manufacturer to a greater degree than a program can perform on my system, I simply mark all the defects from the manufacturer's list in the low-level format. If I were using a low-quality (stepper motor) drive or installing a used and out-of-warranty drive, I would consider performing a surface analysis after the low-level format.

Defect-Free Drives. Although some manufacturers claim that the drives that they sell or install are defect-free, this really is not true. The defects are mapped out and replaced by spare sectors and tracks. This type of defect mapping, usually called sector sparing, insulates the operating system from having to handle the defects. IDE and SCSI drives universally use sector sparing to hide defects, so all these drives seem to be defect-free.

When you finish the low-level format and surface analysis of a hard disk in non-IDE or non-SCSI installations, several areas on the disk have been marked defective by corrupting the checksum values in the sector headers on the indicated tracks. When the high-level format scans the disk, it locates the defective sectors by failing to read them during the defect-scan portion of the high-level format operation. The clusters or allocation units that contain these unreadable sectors then are marked as bad in the FAT. When the CHKDSK command is executed, you get a report of how many of these bad clusters are on the disk. The CHKDSK report looks like this (although yours will have different numbers):

```
Volume DRIVE C   created 06-02-1990 9:14p
Volume Serial Number is 3311-1CD3

 117116928 bytes total disk space
    73728 bytes in 3 hidden files
```

```
  593920 bytes in 268 directories
106430464 bytes in 4068 user files
  143360 bytes in bad sectors
  9875456 bytes available on disk

    2048 bytes in each allocation unit
   57186 total allocation units on disk
    4822 available allocation units on disk

  655360 total bytes memory

  561216 bytes free
```

The 143360 bytes in bad sectors really are only 70 clusters, or allocation units, because each allocation unit contains 2048 bytes.

When I performed the low-level format of this disk, I entered 14 defects, which caused 14 tracks to be corrupted. This disk has 17 sectors per track; therefore, 238 total sectors (17 sectors times 14 tracks) have been corrupted by the low-level format program. Therefore, 121,856 total bytes have been marked bad (238 sectors times 512 bytes per sector).

This number does not agree with the total reported by CHKDSK, because DOS must mark entire allocation units, not individual sectors. Each allocation unit is made up of four sectors (2,048 bytes) on this disk. Therefore:

1 track = 17 sectors = 4 allocation units plus 1 extra sector

DOS must mark an entire allocation unit as being bad, even if only one sector in the unit is bad; therefore, DOS marks five allocation units for each marked track as being bad. In bytes, this becomes:

5 allocation units = 20 sectors = 10,240 bytes (20 sectors times 512 bytes)

Therefore, 10,240 bytes are marked as bad in the FAT for each track marked in the low-level format. And 10,240 bytes per track marked bad times 14 total marked tracks equals 143,360 total bytes marked bad.

From these calculations, you can see that all the correct defect mapping is in place. The bytes in bad sectors never will be used by files, so they won't bother you. This number should not change over the life of the drive unless new defects are entered during a subsequent low-level format or surface analysis.

The relationship between CHKDSK results and disk defects is not as clear with all drives and controllers. For example, I have an IBM PS/2 Model 70-121 that has a 120MB IBM drive and an MCA IDE drive with an embedded ESDI controller. (The controller is built into the drive.) I formatted this drive by using IBM Advanced Diagnostics for the IBM PS/2 (included free with the system). After finishing the high-level format, I ran CHKDSK, and it reported no bad sectors. Could this be true? Not really. In fact, this drive has more than 140 defects, and all have been correctly marked. How could that be? If the defects were marked, the high-level format should have been unable to read those locations, and CHKDSK would have reported the xxxxxx bytes in bad sectors message. The answer lies in how the drive and controller operate together.

IBM advertises this drive as having 32 sectors per track and 920 cylinders with 8 heads, but it actually has 33 sectors per track—or a spare sector on every track. When a defect location is given to the low-level format program, the program removes the defective sector from use by not numbering it as one of the 32 sectors on that track. Then the program gives the spare sector the number that the defective one would have been given; the defective sector becomes the spare. Through this technique, the disk can have up to one defect for every track on the drive (7,360 total) without losing capacity. Moreover, entire spare tracks are available on several spare cylinders past 920; if more than one sector on a track is defective, those extra tracks can be used. The disk has enough spare sectors and tracks to accommodate all possible defects.

Sector sparing is standard on all intelligent IDE and all SCSI drives; it also is an option on many ESDI controllers. This is why IDE and SCSI drives never seem to have any bytes in bad sectors. Of course they do, but they are replaced with good sectors from the spare-sector pool.

Why Low-Level Format?. Even though it generally is not necessary (or even recommended) to low-level format IDE or SCSI drives, there are a few good reasons to consider a low-level format. One reason is that a low-level format will wipe out all the data on a drive, ensuring that other people will not be able to read or recover that data. This procedure is useful if you are selling a system and do not want your data to be readable by the purchaser. Another reason for wiping all the data from a drive is to remove corrupted or non-DOS operating-system partitions and even virus infections. The best reason is for defect management. As you may have noticed, most ATA-IDE drives appear to have no "bytes in bad sectors" under CHKDSK or any other software.

Any defects that were present on the drive after manufacturing were reallocated by the factory low-level format. Essentially, any known bad sectors are replaced by spare sectors stored in different parts of the drive. If any new defects occur, such as from a minor head/platter contact or drive mishandling, a proper IDE-aware low-level format program can map the new bad sectors to other spares, hiding them and restoring the drive to what appears to be defect-free status.

Because the IDE (ATA) specification is an extension of the IBM/WD ST-506/412 controller interface, the specification includes several new CCB commands that were not part of the original INT 13h/CCB support. Some of these new CCB commands are vendor-specific and are unique to each IDE drive manufacturer. Some manufacturers use these special CCB commands for tasks such as rewriting the sector headers to flag bad sectors, which in essence means LLF. When using these commands, the drive controller can rewrite the sector headers and data areas and then carefully step over any servo information (if the drive uses an embedded servo).

IDE drives can be low-level formatted, although some drives require special vendor-specific commands to activate certain low-level formatting features and defect-management options. Seagate, Western Digital, Maxtor, IBM, and others make specific low-level format and spare-sector defect-management software specific to their respective IDE drives. Conner drives are unique in that to actually low-level format them, you need a special hardware device that attaches to a diagnostic port connector on the Conner IDE drive.

A company called TCE (they are in the vendor list in Appendix B) sells such a device for $99. Coincidentally, this device is called The Conner. It includes software and the special adapter device that permits true low-level formatting (including rewriting all sectors and sector headers, as well as completely managing spare sector defects) at the factory level.

Other companies have developed low-level format software that recognizes the particular IDE drive and uses the correct vendor-specific commands for the low-level format and defect mapping. The best of these programs is Ontrack's Disk Manager. A general-purpose diagnostic program that also supports IDE-drive formatting is the MicroScope package by Micro 2000.

Intelligent IDE drives must be in nontranslating, or native, mode to low-level format them. Zoned recording drives can perform only a partial low-level format, in which the defect map is updated and new defective sectors can be marked or spared, but the sector headers usually are rewritten only partially, and only for the purpose of defect mapping. In any case, you are writing to some of the sector headers in one form, and physical (sector-level) defect mapping and sector sparing can be performed. This procedure is, by any standard definition, an LLF.

On an embedded servo drive, all the servo data for a track is recorded at the same time by a specialized (usually, laser-guided) servowriter. This servo information is used to update the head position continuously during drive function, so that the drive automatically compensates for thermal effects. As a result, all the individual servo bursts are in line on the track. Because the servo controls head position, there is no appreciable head-to-sector drift, as there could be on a nonservo drive.

This is why even though it is possible to low-level format embedded servo drives, it rarely is necessary. The only purpose for performing an LLF on an embedded servo drive is to perform additional physical- (sector-) level defect mapping or sector sparing for the purpose of managing defects that occur after manufacture. Because no drift occurs, when a sector is found to contain a flaw, it should remain permanently marked bad; a physical flaw cannot be repaired by reformatting.

Most IDE drives have three to four spare sectors for each physical cylinder of the drive. These hundreds of spare sectors are more than enough to accommodate the original defects and any subsequent defects. If more sectors are required, the drive likely has serious physical problems that cannot be fixed by software.

Software for Low-Level Formatting. You often can choose among several types of low-level format programs, but no single low-level format program works on all drives or all systems. Because low-level format programs must operate very closely with the controller, they often are specific to a controller or controller type. Therefore, ask the controller manufacturer for the formatting software it recommends.

If the controller manufacturer supplies a low-level format program (usually in the controller's ROM), use that program because it is the one most specifically designed for your system and controller. The manufacturer's program can take advantage of special defect-mapping features, for example. A different format program not only might fail to use a manufacturer-written defect map, but also might overwrite and destroy it.

IBM supplies a low-level format program for its PS/2 systems. For Models 50 and higher, the program is included in the Advanced Diagnostics portion of the Reference disk that comes with the system. For system models before 50, users can purchase the Advanced Diagnostics program separately.

For a general-purpose ST-506/412, ESDI, or IDE low-level format program, I recommend the Disk Manager program by Ontrack. For the ST-506/412 interface only, I recommend the IBM Advanced Diagnostics or the HDtest program by Jim Bracking, a user-supported product found on many electronic bulletin boards, including CompuServe. (These companies are listed in the vendor list at the back of this book.) For SCSI systems and systems on which the other recommended programs do not work, you will normally use the format program supplied with the SCSI host adapter.

Low-Level Format Software. There are several ways that a program can LLF (low-level format) a drive. The simplest way is to call the BIOS by using INT 13h functions such as the INT 13h, function 05h (Format Track) command. The BIOS then converts this command to what is called a CCB (Command Control Block) command: a block of bytes sent from the proper I/O ports directly to the disk controller. In this example, the BIOS would take INT 13h, 05h and convert it to a CCB 50h (Format Track) command that would be sent through the Command Register Port (I/O address 1F7h for ST-506/412 or IDE). When the controller receives the CCB Format Track command, it may actually format the track or may simply fill the data areas of each sector on the track with a predetermined pattern.

The best way to LLF a drive is to bypass the ROM BIOS and send the CCB commands directly to the controller. Probably the greatest benefit in sending commands directly to the drive controller is being able to correctly flag defective sectors via the CCB Format Track command, including the capability to perform sector sparing. This is why IDE drives that are properly low-level formatted never show any bad sectors.

By using the CCB commands, you also gain the ability to read the Command Status and Error registers (which enable you to detect things such as ECC corrected data, which is masked by DOS INT 13h). You also can detect whether a sector was marked bad by the manufacturer or during a previous LLF and can maintain those marks in any subsequent Format Track commands, thereby preserving the defect list. I do not recommend unmarking a sector (returning it to "good" status), especially if the manufacturer previously marked it as bad.

When you use CCB commands, you can read and write sector(s) with automatic retries as well as ECC turned off. This capability is essential for any good surface analysis or LLF program, and this is why I recommend programs that use the CCB hardware interface rather than the DOS INT 13h interface.

Advanced Diagnostics Formatters. The standard low-level format program for IBM systems is the Advanced Diagnostics program. For IBM PS/2 Models 50 and higher, this formatting software is provided on the Reference disk included with the system. To get this software for other IBM PS/2 systems (lower than 50), you must purchase the hardware-maintenance service manuals, which cost several hundred dollars.

To access the Advanced Diagnostics portion of the Reference disk, press Ctrl-A (for Advanced) at the Reference disk main menu. The "secret" advanced diagnostics appear. IBM does not document this feature in the regular system documentation, because it does not want the average user wandering around in the software. The Ctrl-A procedure is documented in the service manuals.

The IBM PS/2 low-level format programs are excellent and are the only low-level format programs that you should use on these systems. Only the IBM-format tools know to find, use, and update the IBM-written defect map.

For standard IBM AT or IBM XT systems, the Advanced Diagnostics low-level format program is fine for formatting and testing hard disks; it has the standard features associated with this type of program. The AT version, however, does not allow an interleave setting of 1:1; this may not be a problem, but it renders the program useless if you upgrade to a controller that can handle a 1:1 interleave.

The IBM PC/XT version permits only a 6:1 interleave selection, which renders it useless on most IBM PC and IBM XT systems because most controllers can handle between 2:1 and 5:1 interleaves. Using the IBM XT formatting program results in a very slow system. An additional problem with the IBM PC/XT version is that it does not permit the entry of the manufacturer's defect list—an unforgivable oversight that makes the IBM PC/XT low-level format program definitely not recommended. Fortunately, most PC- or XT-type system users use aftermarket autoconfigure-type controllers that come with a proper built-in ROM-based formatter.

Ontrack Disk Manager. For AT-type systems and other systems with controllers that do not have an autoconfigure routine, the Disk Manager program from Ontrack is excellent. It probably is the most sophisticated hard disk format tool available and has many capabilities that make it a desirable addition to your toolbox.

Disk Manager is a true register-level format program that goes around the BIOS and manipulates the disk controller directly. This direct controller access gives it powerful capabilities that simply are not possible in programs that work through the BIOS.

Some of these advanced features include the capability to set head- and cylinder-skew factors. Disk Manager also can detect intermittent (soft) errors much better than most other programs can because it can turn off the automatic retries that most controllers perform. The program also can tell when ECC (Error Correction Code) has been used to correct data, indicating that an error occurred, as well as directly manipulate the bytes that are used for ECC. Disk Manager has been written to handle most IDE drives and uses vendor-specific commands to unlock the capability to perform a true low-level format on IDE drives.

All these capabilities make Disk Manager one of the most powerful and capable LLF programs available. Ontrack also offers an excellent package of hard disk diagnostic and data-recovery utilities called DOS Utils. Anybody who has to support, maintain, troubleshoot, repair, or upgrade PCs needs a powerful disk formatter such as Disk Manager.

HDtest. HDtest is an excellent BIOS-level format program that will function on virtually any drive that has an INT 13h ROM BIOS interface, which includes most drives. HDtest does not have some of the capabilities of true register-level format programs, but it can be used when the additional capabilities of a register-level program are not required. For example, you can use this program to do a quick wipe of all the data on a drive, no matter what the interface or controller type is. HDtest also is good for BIOS-level read and write testing, and has proved to be especially useful in verifying the functions of disk interface BIOS code.

HDtest, by Jim Bracking, is a user-supported software program. This program is distributed through electronic bulletin boards and public-domain software libraries. You also can obtain the program from the Public Software Library, listed in Appendix B. It costs $35, but you can try it for free.

HDtest has an easy-to-use interface and pull-down menu system. The program offers all functions that normally are associated with a standard low-level format program, as well as some extras:

- Normal formatting
- Defect mapping
- Surface analysis
- Interleave test
- Nondestructive low-level reformat
- Hard disk tests (duplicate of the IBM Advanced Diagnostics hard disk tests), including tests for drive seek, head selection, and error detection and correction, and well as a read/write/verify of the diagnostics cylinder. This program also can run low-level ROM BIOS commands to the controller.

HDtest includes most of what you would want in a generic low-level format program and hard disk diagnostics utility. Its real limitation is that it works only through the BIOS and cannot perform functions that a true register-level format program can. In some cases, the program cannot format a drive that a register-level program could format. Only register-level programs can perform defect mapping in most IDE and SCSI environments.

SCSI Low-Level Format Software. If you are using a SCSI drive, you must use the low-level format program provided by the manufacturer of the SCSI host adapter. The design of these devices varies enough that a register-level program can work only if it is tailored to the individual controller. Fortunately, all SCSI host adapters include such format software, either in the host adapter's BIOS or in a separate disk-based program.

The interface to the SCSI drive is through the host adapter. SCSI is a standard, but there are no true standards for what a host adapter is supposed to look like. This means that any formatting or configuration software will be specific to a particular host adapter. For example, IBM supplies formatting and defect-management software that works with the IBM PS/2 SCSI host adapters directly on the PS/2 Reference disk. That software performs everything that needs to be done to a SCSI hard disk connected to an IBM host adapter. IBM has defined a standard interface to its adapter through an INT 13h and INT 4Bh

BIOS interface in a ROM installed on the card. The IBM adapters also include a special ABIOS (Advanced BIOS) interface that runs in the processor's protected mode of operation (for use under protected-mode operating systems such as OS/2).

Other SCSI host adapters often include the complete setup, configuration, and formatting software in the host adapter's on-board ROM BIOS. Most of these adapters also include an INT 13h interface in the BIOS. The best example is the Adaptec 1540/1542C adapters, which include software in ROM that completely configures the card and all attached SCSI devices.

Notice that SCSI format and configuration software is keyed to the host adapter and is not specific in any way to the particular SCSI hard disk drive that you are using.

IDE Low-Level Format Software. IDE drive manufacturers have defined extensions to the standard Western Digital 1002/1003 AT interface, which was further standardized for IDE drives as the ATA (AT Attachment) interface. The ATA specification provides for vendor-unique commands, which are manufacturer proprietary extensions to the standard. To prevent improper low-level formatting, many of these IDE drives have special codes that must be sent to the drive to unlock the format routines. These codes vary among manufacturers. If possible, you should obtain low-level format and defect-management software from the drive manufacturer; this software usually is specific to that manufacturer's products.

The custom nature of the ATA interface drives is the source of some myths about IDE. Many people say, for example, that you cannot perform a low-level format on an IDE drive, and that if you do, you will wreck the drive. This statement is untrue! What can happen is that in some drives, you may be able to set new head and sector skew factors that are not as optimal for the drive as the ones that the manufacturer set, and you also may be able to overwrite the defect-map information. This situation is not good, but you still can use the drive with no problems provided that you perform a proper surface analysis.

Most ATA IDE drives are protected from any alteration to the skew factors or defect map erasure because they are in a translated mode. Zoned Recording drives always are in translation mode and are fully protected. Most ATA drives have a custom command set that must be used in the format process; the standard format commands defined by the ATA specification usually do not work, especially with intelligent or Zoned Recording IDE drives. Without the proper manufacturer-specific format commands, you will not be able to perform the defect management by the manufacturer-specified method, in which bad sectors often can be spared.

Currently, the following manufacturers offer specific LLF and defect-management software for their own IDE drives:

- Seagate
- Western Digital
- Maxtor
- IBM

These utilities are available for downloading on the various BBSes run by these companies. The numbers appear in Appendix B.

Conner Peripherals drives are unique in that they cannot be low-level formatted through the standard interface; they must be formatted by a device that attaches to a special diagnostics and setup port on the drive. You see this device as a 12-pin connector on Conner drives. A company called TCE sells an inexpensive device that attaches your PC to this port through a serial port in your system, and includes special software that can perform sophisticated test, formatting, and surface analysis operations. The product is called The Conner. (TCE is listed in Appendix B.)

For other drives, I recommend Disk Manager by Ontrack, as well as the MicroScope program by Micro 2000. These programs can format most IDE drives because they know the manufacturer-specific IDE format commands and routines. They also can perform defect-mapping and surface analysis procedures.

Nondestructive Formatters. General-purpose, BIOS-level, nondestructive formatters such as Calibrate and SpinRite are not recommended in most situations for which a real low-level format (LLF) is required. These programs have several limitations and problems that limit their effectiveness; in some cases, they can even cause problems with the way defects are handled on a drive. These programs attempt to perform a track-by-track LLF by using BIOS functions, while backing up and restoring the track data as they go. These programs do not actually perform a complete LLF, because they do not even try to LLF the first track (Cylinder 0, Head 0) due to problems with some controller types that store hidden information on the first track.

These programs also do not perform defect mapping in the way that standard LLF programs do, and they can even remove the carefully applied sector header defect marks applied during a proper LLF. This situation potentially allows data to be stored in sectors that originally were marked defective and may actually void the manufacturer's warranty on some drives. Another problem is that these programs work only on drives that are already formatted and can format only drives that are formattable through BIOS functions.

A true LLF program bypasses the system BIOS and send commands directly to the disk controller hardware. For this reason, many LLF programs are specific to the disk controller hardware for which they are designed. It is virtually impossible to have a single format program that will run on all different types of controllers. Many hard drives have been incorrectly diagnosed as being defective because the wrong format program was used and the program did not operate properly.

For example, I was helping somebody with an IBM PS/2 Model 30, which uses an 8-bit IDE interface 20MB drive. This drive was having serious problems reading and writing files. To start, CHKDSK showed about 40K bytes in bad sectors, and several programs would not load because they were corrupted. I could not copy files to the drive without getting Data error writing drive C: messages. Also, the system was having problems with booting; sometimes it would boot, and at other times it wouldn't, returning a Non-System disk or disk error message.

The owner first ran SpinRite II Version 2.0, using the deepest (level-4) pattern testing and formatting. This operation took an incredible 72 hours to complete, and it ended up marking more than 4MB of the drive as being bytes in bad sectors. SpinRite also indicated bad sectors in cylinders 00 and 01 in the FAT and root-directory areas. After SpinRite finished running, the drive owner tried running FDISK to repartition the drive from scratch, but FDISK crashed, displaying the error message No space to create a DOS partition. At this point, FDISK also had trashed the existing partition table. Fortunately, however, the owner was wise enough to have previously made a partition-table backup and stored it on a floppy disk with the DOS MIRROR /PARTN command. The owner then recovered this partition table backup with the UNFORMAT /PARTN command, which reads the backup file from the floppy and uses it to restore the partition data.

At this point, even though SpinRite had marked out more than 4MB of the disk as being bad during a 72 hour test, the owner still could not load any additional software on the drive without getting write-error messages from DOS. At this point, many people would have considered the drive to be defective and replaced it with a new one. Fortunately, the owner did not do this, and called me instead!

I decided that we needed to low-level format the drive, and that this time, we would use a real LLF program that bypassed the BIOS routines and worked directly with the disk controller hardware registers.

IBM publishes a Hardware Maintenance Service package for the PS/2 Model 30 (about $60), which includes a troubleshooting pamphlet and a special Advanced Diagnostics disk. Notice that all Micro Channel-based PS/2 systems come with a free Advanced Diagnostics disk; for most of the ISA-bus systems, you have to purchase the disk separately. The IBM NSC BBS also makes many of these disks available free for the downloading (see Appendix B for the phone number), but the Model 30 disk was not available through the BBS.

Using the IBM Advanced Diagnostics, we ran an unconditional format and then a surface analysis; these operations together took less than an hour. During the surface analysis, only one sector was marked bad on the entire drive. After the format and surface analysis were complete, we ran FDISK (which worked perfectly this time) and, by accepting the defaults, partitioned the entire drive as a primary DOS partition and marked it as active. Then we formatted the drive with DOS 5, which picked up the sector flagged bad during the surface analysis and marked the cluster containing the flagged sector as bad in the FAT. When the DOS format was complete, we ran CHKDSK, and it showed only 2,048 bytes in bad sectors (equal to the single cluster marked bad in the FAT). The owner of the system then was able to reinstall all the software that had been on the drive with no problems or glitches, and the drive has been working flawlessly ever since!

The moral of this story (well, perhaps the most important part) is that you should not replace a hard disk unless you have tried to format it with a real register-level LLF program. I have little use for "partial" LLF programs and recommend that when a real format is needed, you use a program that works directly with the controller hardware registers. When in doubt, contact the manufacturer of the controller or drive; find out whether the manufacturer has something specific that you should use or can recommend something. If the manufacturer doesn't have its own special program, most controller and drive manufacturers recommend the Disk Manager program from Ontrack for real low-level formatting. I also highly recommend the Ontrack software (listed in Appendix B).

Drive Partitioning. Partitioning a hard disk is the act of defining areas of the disk for an operating system to use as a volume. To DOS, a volume is an area of a disk denoted as a drive letter; for example, drive C is volume C, drive D is volume D, and so on. Some people think that you have to partition a disk only if you are going to divide it into more than one volume. This is a misunderstanding; a disk must be partitioned even if it will be the single volume C.

When a disk is partitioned, a master partition boot sector is written at cylinder 0, head 0, sector 1—the first sector on the hard disk. This sector contains data that describes the partitions by their starting and ending cylinder, head, and sector locations. The partition table also indicates to the ROM BIOS which of the partitions is bootable and, therefore, where to look for an operating system to load. A single hard disk can have 1 to 24 partitions. This number includes all the hard drives installed in the system, which means that you can have as many as 24 separate hard disks with one partition each, a single hard disk with 24 partitions, or a combination of disks and partitions such that the total number of partitions is no more than 24. If you have more than 24 drives or partitions, DOS does not recognize them, although other operating systems may. What limits DOS is that a letter is used to name a volume, and the Roman alphabet ends with Z—the 24th volume, when you begin with C.

FDISK. The DOS FDISK program is the accepted standard for partitioning hard disks. Partitioning prepares the boot sector of the disk in such a way that the DOS FORMAT program can operate correctly; it also enables different operating systems to coexist on a single hard disk.

If a disk is set up with two or more partitions, FDISK shows only two total DOS partitions: the primary partition and the extended partition. The extended partition then is divided into logical DOS volumes, which are partitions themselves. FDISK gives a false impression of how the partitioning is done. FDISK reports that a disk divided as C, D, E, and F is set up as two partitions, with a primary partition having a volume designator of C and a single extended partition containing logical DOS volumes D, E, and F. But in the real structure of the disk, each logical DOS volume is a separate partition with an extended partition boot sector describing it. Each drive volume constitutes a separate partition on the disk, and the partitions point to one another in a daisy-chain arrangement.

Different versions of DOS have had different partitioning capabilities, as follows:

- DOS 1.x had no support whatsoever for hard disk drives.
- DOS 2.x was the first version to include hard disk support, including the capability to partition a drive as a single volume with a maximum partition size of 16MB. DOS versions 2.x support only 16MB-maximum partitions due to the limitations of the 12-bit FAT system. A 12-bit FAT can manage a maximum of only 4,096 total clusters on a disk.

- The limit of 16MB did not come from the FAT, but from the high-level DOS FORMAT command, which aborts with an Invalid media or Track 0 bad - disk unusable error message if the partition is larger than 16MB. On a disk that has no bad sectors beyond the first 16MB, you could ignore the error message and continue the setup of the disk with the SYS command. If the disk has defects beyond 16MB, those defects will not be properly marked in the FAT. Most vendors supplied modified high-level format programs that permitted partitions of up to 32MB to be formatted properly. Unfortunately, each cluster or minimum allocation unit on the disk then is 8,192 bytes (8K) because of the 12-bit FAT.

- DOS 3.x increased the maximum partition and, therefore, volume size to 32MB but still could support only a single partition for DOS (assigned the C volume designator). The size limit is 32MB, due to the limit of 65,536 total sectors in a partition.

- DOS 3.3 introduced the concept of extended partitions, which enables DOS to see the drive as multiple volumes (drive letters). The extended partition's logical DOS volumes actually are partitions themselves. In the organization of the disk, the primary partition is assigned drive letter C, and the extended partitions are assigned letters sequentially from D through Z. Each drive letter (which is a volume or partition) can be assigned only as much as 32MB of disk space.

- DOS 4.x increased the size of a single DOS partition or volume to 2GB. FDISK was modified to allocate disk space in megabytes rather than in individual cylinders, as with previous versions of DOS. IBM DOS FDISK handled up to eight physical hard disk drives.

- DOS 5.x had no changes in partitioning capabilities, but MS-DOS now could universally handle up to eight physical hard drives. (IBM had this capability in IBM DOS 4.x.)

- DOS 6.x had no changes in partitioning capabilities, although both Microsoft and IBM added disk-compression software to DOS that created additional compressed volumes.

The minimum size for a partition in any version of DOS is one cylinder; however, FDISK in DOS 4 and later versions allocate partitions in megabytes, meaning that the minimum-size partition is 1MB. DOS 4.x and later versions permit individual partitions or volumes to be as large as 2GB, whereas versions of DOS earlier than 4.0 have a maximum partition size of 32MB.

The current DOS limits—8 physical hard disks with a maximum 24 total volumes between them, and up to 2GB per volume—do not seem to be too restrictive for most people.

FDISK Undocumented Functions. FDISK is a very powerful program, and in DOS 5 and later versions, it gained some additional capabilities. Unfortunately, these capabilities were never documented in the DOS manual and remain undocumented even in DOS 6.x. The most important undocumented parameter in FDISK is the /MBR (Master Boot Record) parameter, which causes FDISK to rewrite the Master Boot Sector code area, leaving the partition tables intact. Beware: It will overwrite the partition tables if the two signature bytes at the end of the sector (55AAh) are damaged. This situation is highly unlikely, however. In fact, if these signature bytes were damaged, you would know; the system would not boot and would act as though there were no partitions at all.

The /MBR parameter seems to be tailor-made for eliminating boot-sector virus programs that infect the Master Partition Boot Sector (Cylinder 0, Head 0, Sector 1) of a hard disk. To use this feature, you simply enter

```
FDISK /MBR
```

FDISK then rewrites the boot sector code, leaving the partition tables intact. This should not cause any problems on a normally functioning system, but just in case, I recommend backing up the partition table information to floppy disk before trying it. You can do this with the following command:

```
MIRROR /PARTN
```

This procedure uses the MIRROR command to store partition-table information in a file called PARTNSAV.FIL, which should be stored on a floppy disk for safekeeping. To restore the complete partition-table information, including all the master and extended partition boot sectors, you would use the UNFORMAT command as follows:

```
UNFORMAT /PARTN
```

This procedure causes the UNFORMAT command to ask for the floppy disk containing the PARTNSAV.FIL file and then to restore that file to the hard disk.

Note that if you are using Windows 95, the MIRROR and UNFORMAT programs have been eliminated, and you will have to purchase the Norton Utilities instead.

FDISK also has three other undocumented parameters: /PRI:, /EXT:, and /LOG:. These parameters can be used to have FDISK create master and extended partitions, as well as logical DOS volumes in the extended partition, directly from the command line rather than through the FDISK menus. This feature was designed so that you can run FDISK in a batch file to partition drives automatically. Some system vendors probably use these parameters (if they know about them, that is!) when setting up systems on the production line. Other than that, these parameters have little use for a normal user, and in fact may be dangerous!

Other Partitioning Software. Since DOS 4 became available, there has been little need for aftermarket disk partitioning utilities, except in special cases. If a system is having problems that cause you to consider using a partitioning utility, I recommend that you upgrade to a newer version of DOS instead. Using nonstandard partitioning programs to partition your disk jeopardizes the data in the partitions and makes recovery of data lost in these partitions extremely difficult.

The reason why disk partitioning utilities other than FDISK even existed is that the maximum partition size in older DOS versions was restricted: 16MB for DOS 2.x and 32MB for DOS 3.x. These limits are bothersome for people whose hard disks are much larger than 32M because they must divide the hard disk into many partitions to use all of the disk.

Versions of DOS before 3.3 cannot even create more than a single DOS-accessible partition on a hard disk. If you have a 120MB hard disk and are using DOS 3.2 or an earlier version, you can access only 32MB of that disk as a C partition.

To overcome this limitation, several software companies created enhanced partitioning programs, which you can use rather than FDISK. These programs create multiple partitions and partitions larger than 32MB on a disk that DOS can recognize. These partitioning programs include a high-level format program because the FORMAT program in DOS 3.3 and earlier versions can format partitions only up to 32MB.

Disk Manager by Ontrack is probably the best-known of the partitioning utilities. These programs include low-level format capabilities, so you can use one of them as a single tool to set up a hard disk. The programs even include disk driver software that provides the capability to override the physical type selections in the system ROM BIOS, enabling a system to use all of a disk, even though the drive-type table in the system ROM BIOS does not have an entry that matches the hard disk.

Many drive vendors and integrators gave away these nonstandard partitioning and formatting programs, which makes some purchasers of such products feel that they must use those drivers to operate the drive. In most cases, however, better alternatives are available; nonstandard disk partitioning and formatting can cause more problems than it solves.

For example, Seagate shipped Ontrack Disk Manager with its drives larger than 32MB. One purpose of the program is to perform low-level formatting of the drive, which Disk Manager does well, and I recommend it highly for this function. If possible, however, you should avoid the partitioning and high-level formatting functions and stick with FDISK and FORMAT.

When you use a program other than standard FDISK and FORMAT to partition and high-level (DOS) format a drive, the drive is set up in a nonstandard way, different from pure DOS. This difference can cause trouble with utilities—including disk cache programs, disk test and interleave check programs, and data recovery or retrieval programs—written to function with a standard DOS disk structure. In many situations that a standard format would avoid, a nonstandard disk format can cause data loss and also can make data recovery impossible.

Caution

You should use only standard DOS FDISK and FORMAT to partition or high-level format your hard disks. If you use aftermarket partitioning software to create a nonstandard disk system, some programs that bypass DOS for disk access will not understand the disk properly and may write in the wrong place. Windows is an example of a program that bypasses DOS when you turn on the Use 32-bit Disk Access option in the Control Panel.

It is especially dangerous to use these partitioning programs to override your ROM BIOS disk-table settings. Consider the following disaster scenario.

Suppose that you have a Seagate ST-4096 hard disk, which has 1,024 cylinders and 9 heads, and requires that your controller never perform a data-write modification called write precompensation to cylinders of the disk. Some drives require this precompensation on the inner cylinders to compensate for the peak shifting that takes place because of the higher density of data on the (smaller) inner cylinders. The ST-4096 internally compensates for this effect and therefore needs no precompensation from the controller.

Now suppose that you install this drive in an IBM AT that does not have a ROM BIOS drive table that matches the drive. The best matching type you can select is type 18, which enables you to use only 977 cylinders and 7 heads—56.77MB of what should be a 76.5MB hard disk. If your IBM AT is one of the older ones with a ROM BIOS dated 01/10/84, the situation is worse, because its drive-table ends with type 14. In that case, you would have to select type 12 as the best match, giving you access to 855 cylinders and 7 heads, or only 49.68MB of a 76.5MB drive.

ROM BIOS drive tables are listed in Appendix A. Most IBM-compatibles have a more complete drive-type table and would have an exact table match for this drive, allowing you to use the full 76.5MB with no problems. In most compatibles with a Phoenix ROM BIOS, for example, you would select type 35, which would support the drive entirely.

Now suppose that you are not content with using only 50MB or 57MB of this 76.5MB drive. You invoke the SuperPartition aftermarket partitioning program that came with the drive and use it to low-level format the drive. Then you use the aftermarket program to override the type 18 or type 12 settings in the drive table. The program instructs you to set up a very small C partition (of only 1M) and then partitions the remaining 75.5MB of the disk as D. This partitioning overrides the DOS 3.3 32MB partition limitation. (If you had an IBM-compatible system that did not require the drive-type override, you still would need to use the aftermarket partitioner to create partitions larger than the DOS 3.3 standard 32MB.) Following that, you use the partitioner to high-level format the C and D partitions, because the DOS high-level format in DOS 3.3 works only on volumes of 32MB or less.

Most aftermarket partitioners create a special driver file that they install in the CONFIG.SYS file through the DEVICE command. After the system boots from the C partition and loads the device driver, the 75.5MB D partition is completely accessible.

Along comes an innocent user of the system who always boots from her own DOS floppy disk. After booting from the floppy, she tries to log into the D partition. No matter what version of DOS this user boots from on the floppy disk, the D partition seems to have vanished. An attempt to log into that partition results in an Invalid drive specification error message. No standard version of DOS can recognize that specially created D partition if the device driver is not loaded.

An attempt by this user to recover data on this drive with a utility program such as Norton or PC Tools results in failure because these programs interpret the drive as having 977 cylinders and 7 heads (type 18) or 855 cylinders and 7 heads (type 12). In fact, when these programs attempt to correct what seems to be partition-table damage, data will be corrupted in the vanished D partition.

Thinking that there may be a physical problem with the disk, the innocent user boots and runs the Advanced Diagnostics software to test the hard disk. Because Advanced Diagnostics incorporates its own special boot code and does not use standard DOS, it does not examine partitioning, but goes to the ROM BIOS drive-type table to determine the capacity of the hard disk. It sees the unit as having only 977 or 855 cylinders (indicated by the type 18 or 12 settings), as well as only 7 heads. The user then runs the Advanced Diagnostics hard disk tests that use the last cylinder of the disk as a test cylinder for diagnostic read and write tests. This cylinder subsequently is overwritten by the diagnostics tests, which the drive passes because there is no physical problem with the drive.

This innocent user has just wiped out the D-drive data that happened to be on cylinder 976 in the type-18 setup or on cylinder 854 in the type-12 setup. Had the drive been partitioned by FDISK, the last cylinder indicated by the ROM BIOS drive table would have been left out of any partitions, being reserved so that diagnostics tests could be performed on the drive without damaging data.

Beyond the kind of disaster scenario just described, other potential problems can be caused by nonstandard disk partitioning and formatting, such as the following:

- Problems in using the 32-bit Disk Access feature provided by Windows, which bypasses the BIOS for faster disk access in 386 Enhanced Mode.
- Data loss by using OS/2, UNIX, XENIX, Novell Advanced NetWare, or other non-DOS operating systems that do not recognize the disk or the nonstandard partitions.
- Difficulty in upgrading a system from one DOS version to another.
- Difficulty in installing a different operating system, such as OS/2, on the hard disk.
- Data loss by using a low-level format utility to run an interleave test; the test area for the interleave test is the diagnostics cylinder, which contains data on disks formatted with Disk Manager.
- Data loss by accidentally deleting or overwriting the driver file and causing the D partition to disappear after the next boot.
- Data-recovery difficulty or failure because nonstandard partitions do not follow the rules and guidelines set by Microsoft and IBM, and no documentation on their structure exists. The sizes and locations of the FATs and root directory are not standard, and the detailed reference charts in this book (which are valid for an FDISK-created partition) are inaccurate for nonstandard partitions.

I could continue, but I think you get the idea. If these utility programs are used only for low-level formatting, they do not cause problems; it is the drive-type override, partitioning, and high-level format operations that cause difficulty. If you consider data integrity to be important, and you want to be able to perform data recovery, follow these disk support and partitioning rules:

- Every hard disk must be properly supported by system ROM BIOS, with no software overrides. If the system does not have a drive table that supports the full capacity of the drive, accept the table's limit, upgrade to a new ROM BIOS (preferably with a user-definable drive-type setting), or use a disk controller with an on-board ROM BIOS for drive support.
- Use only FDISK to partition a hard disk. If you want partitions larger than 32MB, use DOS 4 or a later version.

High-Level (Operating-System) Format. The final step in the software preparation of a hard disk is the DOS high-level format. The primary function of the high-level format is to create a FAT and a directory system on the disk so that DOS can manage files.

Usually, you perform the high-level format with the standard DOS FORMAT program, using the following syntax:

```
FORMAT C: /S /V
```

This step high-level formats drive C (or volume C, in a multivolume drive), places the hidden operating-system files in the first part of this partition, and prompts for the entry of a volume label to be stored on the disk at completion.

The high-level format program performs the following functions and procedures:

1. Scans the disk (read only) for tracks and sectors marked as bad during the low-level format, and notes these tracks as being unreadable.
2. Returns the drive heads to the first cylinder of the partition, and at that cylinder, head 1, sector 1, writes a DOS volume boot sector.
3. Writes a file allocation table (FAT) at head 1, sector 2. Immediately after this FAT, it writes a second copy of the FAT. These FATs essentially are blank except for bad-cluster marks noting areas of the disk that were found to be unreadable during the marked-defect scan.
4. Writes a blank root directory.
5. If the /S parameter is specified, copies the system files (IBMBIO.COM and IBMDOS.COM or IO.SYS and MSDOS.SYS, depending on which DOS you run) and COMMAND.COM files to the disk (in that order).
6. If the /V parameter is specified, prompts the user for a volume label, which is written as the fourth file entry in the root directory.

Now DOS can use the disk for storing and retrieving files, and the disk is a bootable disk.

Note that the Format command can be run through the Windows Explorer within Windows 95 even on hard disks, as long as no files are open. You cannot format the drive where Windows 95 resides.

During the first phase of the high-level format, a marked defect scan is performed. Defects marked by the low-level format operation show up during this scan as being unreadable tracks or sectors. When the high-level format encounters one of these areas, it automatically performs up to five retries to read these tracks or sectors. If the unreadable area was marked by the low-level format, the read fails on all attempts.

After five retries, the DOS FORMAT program gives up on this track or sector and moves to the next. Areas that remain unreadable after the initial read and the five retries are noted in the FAT as being bad clusters. DOS 3.3 and earlier versions can mark only entire tracks bad in the FAT, even if only one sector was marked in the low-level format. DOS 4 and later versions individually check each cluster on the track and recover clusters that do not involve the low-level format marked-bad sectors. Because most low-level format programs mark all the sectors on a track as bad, rather than the individual sector that contains the defect, the result of using DOS 3.3 or 4 is the same: all clusters involving sectors on that track are marked in the FAT as bad.

Note

Some low-level format programs mark only the individual sector that is bad on a track, rather than the entire track. This is true of the IBM PS/2 low-level formatters on the IBM PS/2 Advanced Diagnostics or Reference disk. In this case, high-level formatting with DOS 4 or later versions results in fewer lost bytes in bad sectors because only the clusters that contain the marked bad sectors are marked bad in the FAT. DOS 4 and later versions display the Attempting to recover allocation unit x message (in which x is the number of the cluster) in an attempt to determine whether a single cluster or all of the clusters on the track should be marked bad in the FAT.

If the controller and low-level format program together support sector and track sparing, the high-level format finds the entire disk defect-free, because all the defective sectors have been exchanged for spare good ones.

If a disk has been low-level formatted correctly, the number of bytes in bad sectors is the same before and after the high-level format. If the number does change after you repeat a high-level format (reporting fewer bytes or none), the low-level format was not done correctly. The manufacturer's defects were not marked correctly; or Norton, Mace, PC Tools, or a similar utility was used to mark defective clusters on the disk. The utilities cannot mark the sectors or tracks at the low-level format level; the bad-cluster marks that they make are stored only in the FAT and erased during the next high-level format operation. Defect marks made in the low-level format consistently show up as bad bytes in the high-level format, no matter how many times you run the format.

Only a low-level format or a surface analysis tool can correctly mark defects on a disk; anything else makes only temporary bad-cluster marks in the FAT. This kind of marking may be acceptable temporarily, but when additional bad areas are found on a disk, you should run a new low-level format of the disk and either mark the area manually or run a surface analysis to place a more permanent mark on the disk.

Hard Disk Drive Troubleshooting and Repair

If a hard disk drive has a problem inside its sealed HDA (Head Disk Assembly), repairing the drive usually is not feasible. If the failure is in the logic board, you can replace that assembly with a new or rebuilt assembly easily and at a much lower cost than replacing the entire drive.

Most hard disk problems really are not hardware problems; instead, they are soft problems that can be solved by a new low-level format and defect-mapping session. Soft problems are characterized by a drive that sounds normal but produces various read and write errors.

Hard problems are mechanical, such as when the drive sounds as though it contains loose marbles. Constant scraping and grinding noises from the drive, with no reading or writing capability, also qualify as hard errors. In these cases, it is unlikely that a low-level format will put the drive back into service. If a hardware problem is indicated, first replace the logic-board assembly. You can make this repair yourself, and if successful, you can recover the data from the drive.

If replacing the logic assembly does not solve the problem, contact the manufacturer or a specialized repair shop that has clean-room facilities for hard disk repair. (See Appendix B for a list of drive manufacturers and companies that specialize in hard disk drive repair.)

The cost of HDA repair may be more than half the cost of a new drive, so you may want to consider replacing rather than repairing the drive. If the failed drive is an inexpensive 20MB or 30MB stepper motor drive, the better option is to purchase something better. If the drive is a larger, voice coil drive, however, it usually is more economical to repair the drive rather than replace it, because the replacement cost is much higher.

17xx, 104xx, and 210xxxx Hardware Error Codes

When a failure occurs in the hard disk subsystem at power-on, the Power-On Self Test (POST) finds the problem and reports it with an error message. The 17xx, 104xx, and 210xxxx errors during the POST or while running the Advanced Diagnostics indicate problems with hard disks, controllers, or cables. The 17xx codes apply to ST-506/412 interface drives and controllers; 104xx errors apply to ESDI drives and controllers; and 210xxxx errors apply to SCSI drives and host adapters.

Table 16.11 shows a breakdown of these error messages and their meanings.

Table 16.11 Hard Disk and Controller Diagnostic Error Codes

ST-506/412 Drive and Controller Error Codes	
1701	Fixed disk general POST error
1702	Drive/controller time-out error
1703	Drive seek error
1704	Controller failed

(continues)

Table 16.11 Contined

ST-506/412 Drive and Controller Error Codes

1705	Drive sector not found error
1706	Write fault error
1707	Drive track 0 error
1708	Head select error
1709	Error Correction Code (ECC) error
1710	Sector buffer overrun
1711	Bad address mark
1712	Internal controller diagnostics failure
1713	Data compare error
1714	Drive not ready
1715	Track 0 indicator failure
1716	Diagnostics cylinder errors
1717	Surface read errors
1718	Hard drive type error
1720	Bad diagnostics cylinder
1726	Data compare error
1730	Controller error
1731	Controller error
1732	Controller error
1733	BIOS undefined error return
1735	Bad command error
1736	Data corrected error
1737	Bad track error
1738	Bad sector error
1739	Bad initialization error
1740	Bad sense error
1750	Drive verify failure
1751	Drive read failure
1752	Drive write failure
1753	Drive random read test failure
1754	Drive seek test failure
1755	Controller failure
1756	Controller Error Correction Code (ECC) test failure
1757	Controller head select failure
1780	Seek failure; drive 0
1781	Seek failure; drive 1
1782	Controller test failure
1790	Diagnostic cylinder read error; drive 0
1791	Diagnostic cylinder read error; drive 1

ESDI Drive and Controller Error Codes

10450	Read/write test failed
10451	Read verify test failed
10452	Seek test failed
10453	Wrong device type indicated
10454	Controller test failed sector buffer test
10455	Controller failure
10456	Controller diagnostic command failure
10461	Drive format error
10462	Controller head select error
10463	Drive read/write sector error
10464	Drive primary defect map unreadable
10465	Controller; Error Correction Code (ECC) 8-bit error
10466	Controller; Error Correction Code (ECC) 9-bit error
10467	Drive soft seek error
10468	Drive hard seek error
10469	Drive soft seek error count exceeded
10470	Controller attachment diagnostic error
10471	Controller wrap mode interface error
10472	Controller wrap mode drive select error
10473	Read verify test errors
10480	Seek failure; drive 0
10481	Seek failure; drive 1
10482	Controller transfer acknowledge error
10483	Controller reset failure
10484	Controller; head select 3 error
10485	Controller; head select 2 error
10486	Controller; head select 1 error
10487	Controller; head select 0 error
10488	Controller; read gate - command complete 2 error
10489	Controller; write gate - command complete 1 error
10490	Diagnostic area read error; drive 0
10491	Diagnostic area read error; drive 1
10499	Controller failure

SCSI Drive and Host Adapter Error Codes

096xxxx	SCSI adapter with cache (32-bit) errors
112xxxx	SCSI adapter (16-bit without cache) errors
113xxxx	System board SCSI adapter (16-bit) errors
210xxxx	SCSI fixed disk errors

The first x in xxxx is the SCSI ID number.
The second x in xxxx is the logical unit number (usually, 0).
The third x in xxxx is the host adapter slot number.
The fourth x in xxxx is a letter code indicating drive capacity.
A list of all IBM SCSI error codes appears in Appendix A.

Most of the time, a seek failure indicates that the drive is not responding to the controller. This failure is usually caused by one of the following problems:

- Incorrect drive-select jumper setting
- Loose, damaged, or backward control cable
- Loose or bad power cable
- Stiction between drive heads and platters
- Bad power supply

If a diagnostics cylinder read error occurs, the most likely problems are these:

- Incorrect drive-type setting
- Loose, damaged, or backward data cable
- Temperature-induced mistracking

The methods for correcting most of these problems are obvious. If the drive-select jumper setting is incorrect, for example, correct it. If a cable is loose, tighten it. If the power supply is bad, replace it. You get the idea.

If the problem is temperature-related, the drive usually will read data acceptably at the same temperature at which it was written. Let the drive warm up for a while and then attempt to reboot it, or let the drive cool and reread the disk if the drive has overheated.

The stiction problem may not have an obvious solution; the next section addresses this problem.

Drive Spin Failure (Stiction)

Other than a faulty power-supply cable connection or a faulty power supply, stiction is the primary cause of a hard disk drive's failure to spin. *Stiction* (static friction) is a condition in which the drive heads are stuck to the platters in such a way that the platter motor cannot overcome the sticking force and spin the drive up for operation. This situation happens more frequently than you might imagine.

The heads stick to the platters in the same way that two very smooth pieces of glass might stick together. The problem is especially noticeable if the drive has been off for a week or more. It also seems to be more noticeable if the drive is operated under very hot conditions and then shut down. In the latter case, the excessive heat buildup in the drive softens the lubricant coating on the platter surface; after the drive is powered off, the platters cool rapidly and contract around the heads, which have settled in this lubricant coating. Drives that have more platters and heads are more susceptible to this problem than are drives that have fewer platters and heads.

To solve this problem, you must spin the platters with enough force to rip the heads loose from the platters. Usually, you accomplish this by twisting the drive violently in the same plane as the platters, using the platter's inertia to overcome the sticking force.

The heavy platters tend to remain stationary while you twist the drive and essentially make the heads move around the platters.

Another technique is to spin the spindle motor manually, which rotates the platters inside the drive. To do this, you may have to remove the circuit board from the bottom of the drive to get to the spindle motor. In other cases, you can insert a thin wooden stick into the gap between the bottom of the drive and the circuit board, and push on the spindle motor drum with the stick. You probably will feel heavy resistance to rotation; then the platters will suddenly move free as the heads are unstuck.

Many drives today have spindle motors located inside the platter hub area, which is totally enclosed within the HDA. You will not be able to spin these platters by hand unless you open the HDA, which is recommended only in situations in which nothing else has worked. In most cases, simply twisting the entire drive in the same plane as the platters uses the inertia of the platters to jerk the heads free from their stuck position.

Another problem that can cause the appearance of stiction is a stuck spindle motor (platter) brake. Many drives use a solenoid actuated spindle motor brake to rapidly stop the platters when the drive is powered off (see fig. 16.2). This brake is designed to minimize the distance that the heads skid on the platter surface when the drive is powered down. When the brake solenoid fails, it does not release the spindle motor and can produce the same symptoms as stiction.

Because this device almost always is outside the HDA, you can easily remove if it fails, allowing the drive to spin freely. Because every drive is designed differently, consult the drive manual to see whether your drive has such a spindle braking system and where it is located. Of course, long-term reliability may be affected, because the heads will skid for a much longer distance every time the drive is powered off, accelerating wear of the heads and media.

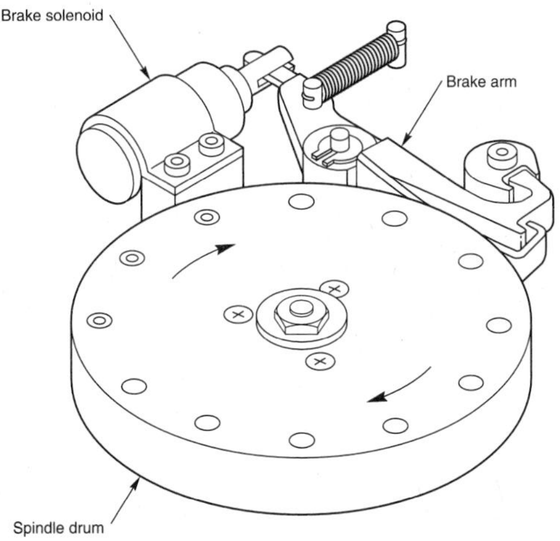

Figure 16.2

A typical spindle motor solenoid and brake assembly.

After you free the platters, reapply the power; the drive should spin up normally. I have used these methods to solve stiction problems many times and have never lost data as long as I could get the drive to spin. If you cannot make the drive spin, you certainly will not be able to recover any data from it. Notice that most drive failures occur in the logic board, which also contains motor control circuits in most drives. This means that a no-spin situation can be caused by a defective logic board. Unless you have a spare drive with the same type of logic board to swap with, it is difficult to know whether the logic board is truly at fault.

Some drive manufacturers and repair depots sell logic boards individually, but I usually find it easier simply to purchase another (duplicate) entire drive. It is often cheaper to purchase a used drive exactly like the one that failed than to buy a single part, such as a logic board. You then can cannibalize the used drive for parts that can restore the failed drive to operation. This is not designed to be a cost-effective way to repair a drive, but it will allow you to possibly recover the data from the failed drive, which usually is worth much more than the drive itself. Most good data-recovery operations have a variety of functioning used drives available to be cannibalized for parts in recovering data from failed drives.

In some cases, I have had to open the HDA to forcibly spin the platters by hand so as to recover data. In many cases, this worked to free the platters and start the drive operation, after which I was able to close the HDA and back up all the data on the drive. If you are nervous about handling your drive in this manner, consult a professional drive repair facility.

I know that the impression that everybody normally has is that opening a drive will destroy or damage it in some way (head crash?), especially considering the extremely close proximity between the heads and the disk platters. I can say from experience, however, that most hard drives are much sturdier than people think. I have not only opened many functioning hard drives, but also operated them for extended periods while they were exposed in this manner, all the while reliably reading and writing data. In fact, I have several drives that I regularly use in my PC Hardware/Troubleshooting and Data Recovery seminars; I have been operating these drives with the lids off practically every week for several years now, with no lost data. Even more amazing is the fact that I often use the drives to perform torture demonstrations, in which I literally bend the HDA with my bare hands while the drive is reading files. This procedure instantly causes the file-read operation to fail (Abort, Retry, Ignore) due to the heads being forced away from their proper track positions. When I release the bending force, the heads return to normal track position, and the files can be read with no problem!

Although I use these seminar demonstrations to get people's attention, these lid-off techniques have helped me at times in extreme data-recovery situations. Of course, I am obligated to give you the standard "Don't try this at home" warning!

Logic Board Failures

A disk drive, including a hard disk drive, has one or more logic boards mounted on it. These boards contain the electronics that control the drive's spindle and head actuator systems and that present data to the controller. Some drives have built-in controllers.

Logic boards on hard disks fail more often than the mechanical components do. Most professional data-recovery companies stock a number of functional logic boards for popular drives. When a drive comes in for recovery, data-recovery professionals check the drive for problems such as installation or configuration errors, temperature mistracking, and stiction. If these situations are not the problem, the technicians replace the logic board on the drive with a known good unit. Often, the drive then works normally, and data can be read from it.

The logic boards on most hard disks can be removed and replaced easily; they simply plug into the drive and usually are mounted with standard screw hardware. If a drive is failing, and you have a spare of the same type, you may be able to verify a logic-board failure by removing the board from a known good drive and mounting it on the bad one. Then, if your suspicions are confirmed, in some cases you can order a new logic board from the drive's manufacturer. Be prepared for sticker shock; parts like this may cost more than replacing the entire drive with a new or refurbished unit.

A less-expensive option is buying a refurbished unit or trading in the old board (the drive manufacturer will have details on these options). Purchasing a new logic board may not always be cost-effective, but borrowing one from a drive that works is one of the only ways to verify that the logic board has failed, and it may be the only way to recover all the data from the problem drive.

Summary

This chapter examined the installation of hard disks and controllers. You learned about configuring, installing, and troubleshooting hard disk installations. Now you can use this information to upgrade an existing system with a new hard disk or to troubleshoot and repair an existing configuration. A properly installed hard disk system will give you fewer problems than a haphazardly installed system will. Most problems are related to software, installation, or formatting, so you can use the information in this chapter to restore many failing drives to normal operation.

Chapter 17

CD-ROM Drives

This chapter explains the technology behind CD-ROM drives, delineates the various recording formats used on PC CD-ROMs, and examines the performance characteristics of the typical CD-ROM drive. After showing you the process of selecting a good drive for a system upgrade, the chapter guides you through the installation of the CD-ROM interface card, the drive itself, and the software that must be added to your PC for the drive to communicate with the system. This chapter also focuses on the latest CD technology, including CD-R (CD-Recordable), CD-E (CD-Erasable), and the new DVD (Digital Video Disc) drives.

What is CD-ROM?

Within minutes of inserting a compact disc into your computer, you have access to information that might have taken you days, or even weeks, to find a few short years ago. Science, medicine, law, business profiles, and educational materials—every conceivable form of human endeavor or pursuit of knowledge—are making their way to aluminum-coated, five-inch plastic data discs called *CD-ROMs*, or *compact disc read-only memory*.

Note

The CD-ROM (compact disc read-only memory) is a read-only optical storage medium capable of holding up to 682MB (650 megabytes) of data (approximately 333,000 pages of text), 74 minutes of high-fidelity audio, or some combination of the two. The CD-ROM is very similar to the familiar audio compact disc, and can, in fact, play in a normal audio player. The result would be noise unless audio accompanies the data on the CD-ROM. Accessing data from a CD-ROM is somewhat faster than floppy disk, but considerably slower than a modern hard drive. The term CD-ROM refers to both the discs themselves and the drive that reads them.

Although only dozens of CD-ROM discs, or titles, were published for personal computer users in all of 1988, there are currently thousands of individual titles, containing data and programs ranging from world-wide agricultural statistics to preschool learning games. Individual businesses, local and federal government offices, and small businesses also publish thousands of their own, limited-use titles.

CD-ROM, a Brief History

In 1978, Philips and Sony Corporations joined forces to produce the current audio CD. Philips had already developed commercial laser-disc players, whereas Sony had a decade of digital recording research under its belt. The two companies were poised for a battle—the introduction of potentially incompatible audio laser disc formats—when they came to terms on an agreement to formulate a single audio technology.

Sony pushed for a 12-inch platter. Philips wanted to investigate smaller sizes, especially when it became clear that they could pack an astonishing 12 hours of music on the 12-inch discs.

By 1982, the companies announced the standard, which included the specifications for recording, sampling, and—above all—the 4.72-inch format we live with today. To be specific, the discs are precisely 120mm in diameter, have a 15mm hole in the center, and are 1.2mm thick. This size was chosen, legend has it, because it could contain Beethoven's Ninth Symphony.

With the continued cooperation of Sony and Philips through the 1980s, additional specifications were announced concerning the use of CD technology for computer data. These recommendations evolved into the computer CD-ROM drives in use today. Where once engineers struggled to find the perfect fit between disc form-factor and the greatest symphony ever recorded, software developers and publishers are cramming these little discs with the world's information.

CD Technology

Although identical in appearance to audio CDs, computer CDs store data in addition to audio. The CD drives that read the data discs when attached to PCs also bear a strong resemblance to an audio CD. How you must handle the CDs—insert them into the CD drive and eject them when finished—are all familiar to anyone who has used an audio CD. Both forms of CD operate on the same general mechanical principles.

The disc itself, 120mm (nearly 4.75 inches in diameter), is made of a polycarbonate wafer. This wafer base is coated with a metallic film, usually an aluminum alloy. The aluminum film is the portion of the disc that the CD-ROM drive reads for information. The aluminum film or strata is then covered by plastic polycarbonate coating that protects the underlying data. A label is usually placed on the top of the disc, and all reading occurs from the bottom. CD-ROMs are single-sided.

Note

CD-ROM media should be handled with the same care afforded a photographic negative. The CD-ROM is an optical device and degrades as its optical surface becomes dirty or scratched. If your drive uses a "caddy"—a container for the disc that does not require handling the disc itself—you should purchase a sufficient supply of these to reduce disc handling.

Mass-Producing CD-ROMs

Although a laser is used to etch data onto a master disc, this technique would be impractical for the reproduction of hundreds or thousands of copies. Each production of a master disc can take over one-half hour to encode. In addition, these master discs are made of materials that aren't as durable as a mass-produced disc for continued or prolonged use.

For limited run productions of CDs, an original master is coated with metal in a process similar to electroplating. After the metal is formed and separated from the master, the metal imprint of the original can be used to stamp copies, not unlike the reproduction of vinyl records. This process works effectively for small quantities—eventually the stamp wears out.

To produce a large volume of discs, the following three-step process is employed:

1. The master is, once again, plated and a stamp is produced.
2. This stamp is used to create a duplicate master, made of a more resilient metal.
3. The duplicate master can then be used to produce numerous stamps.

This technique allows a great many production stamps to be made from the duplicate master, preserving the original integrity of the first encoding. It also allows for the mass production to be made from inexpensive materials. The CDs you buy are coated with aluminum after they are stamped into polycarbonate, and then protected with a thin layer of plastic. The thin, aluminum layer that coats the etched pits, as well as smooth surfaces, enables the reading laser to determine the presence or absence of strongly relented light, as described earlier.

This mass manufacturing process is identical for both data and audio CDs.

Reading the information back is a matter of reflecting a lower-powered laser off the aluminum strata. A receiver or light receptor notes where light is strongly reflected or where it is absent or diffused. Diffused or absent light is caused by the pits etched in the CD. Strong reflection of the light indicates no pit—this is called a *land*. The light receptors within the player collect the reflected and diffused light as it is refracted from the surface. As the light sources are collected from the refraction, they are passed along to microprocessors that translate the light patterns back into data or sound.

Individual pits are 0.12 microns deep and about 0.6 microns wide. They are etched into a spiral track with a spacing of 1.6 microns between turns, corresponding to a track density of nearly 16,000 tracks per inch! The pits and lands run from 0.9 to 3.3 microns long. The track starts at the inside of the disc and ends as close as 5mm from the edge of the disc. This single spiral track is nearly three miles long!

When a CD—audio or data—seeks out a bit of data on the disc, it looks up the address of the data from a table of contents and positions itself near the beginning of this data across the spiral, waiting for the right string of bits to flow past the laser beam.

CD-ROM data is recorded using a technique called *Constant Linear Velocity (CLV)*. This means that the track data is always moving past the read laser at the same linear speed. In other words, the disk must spin faster when reading the inner track area and slower when reading the outer track area. Because CDs were originally designed to record audio, the speed at which the data was read had to be a constant. Thus each disc is broken up into blocks, or sectors, which are stored at the rate of 75 blocks per second on a disc that can hold a total of 74 minutes of information, resulting in a maximum of 333,000 blocks (sectors).

In a CD-DA (Digital Audio) disc, each block stores 2,352 bytes. In a CD-ROM disc, 304 of these bytes are used for Sync (Synchronizing bits), ID (Identification bits), and ECC (Error Correcting Code) information, leaving 2,048 bytes for user data. Because these blocks are read at a constant speed of 75 per second, this results in a standard CD-ROM transfer rate of 153,600 bytes per second, which is exactly 150K bytes per second (150 KB/s).

Because a disc can hold a maximum of 74 minutes of data, and each second contains 75 blocks of 2,048 bytes each, one can calculate the absolute maximum storage capacity of a CD-ROM at 681,984,000 bytes (rounded as 682MB or 650 megabytes).

Recordable CDs come in 74-minute and 63-minute versions.

Inside Data CDs

The microprocessor that decodes the electrical impulses is the key difference between music and data compact players. Audio CDs convert the digital information stored on the disc into analog signals for a stereo amplifier to process. In this scheme, some imprecision is acceptable, since it would be virtually impossible to hear in the music. CD-ROMs, however cannot tolerate any imprecision. Each bit of data must be accurately read. For this reason, CD-ROM discs have a great deal of additional *ECC (Error Correcting Code)* information written to the disc. The ECC can be used to detect and correct most minor errors, improving the reliability and precision to levels which are acceptable for data storage.

CD-ROM drives operate in the following manner:

1. The *laser diode* (see fig. 17.1) emits a low-energy infra-red beam toward a reflecting mirror.
2. The *servo motor*, on command from the microprocessor, positions the beam onto the correct track on the CD-ROM by moving the reflecting mirror.
3. When the beam hits the disc, its refracted light is gathered and focused through the first lens beneath the platter, bounced off the mirror, and sent toward the beam splitter.
4. The *beam splitter* directs the returning laser light toward another focusing lens.
5. The last lens directs the light beam to a photo detector that converts the light into electric impulses.
6. These incoming impulses are decoded by the microprocessor and sent along to the host computer as data.

The pits that are etched into the CD-ROM vary in length. The reflected light beam changes in intensity as it crosses over from a land to a pit area. The corresponding electrical signal from the photodetector varies with the reflected light intensity. Data bits are read as the transitions between high and low signals, which is physically recorded as the start and end of each pit area.

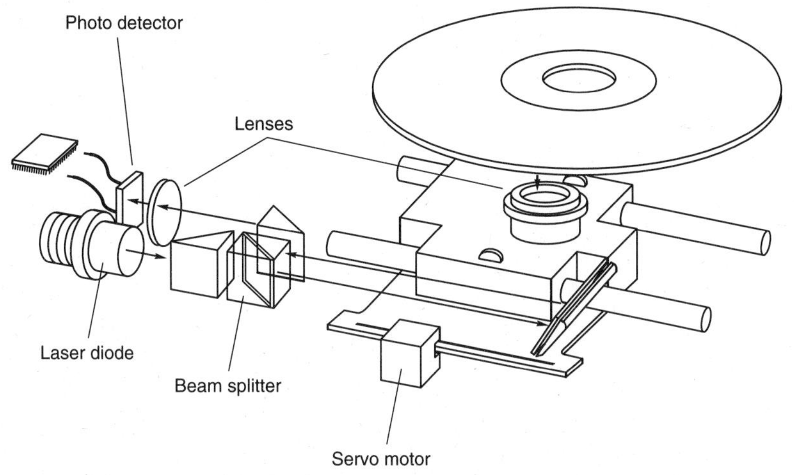

Figure 17.1
Inside a CD-ROM drive.

Because a single bit error can be disastrous in a program or data file, extensive error detection and correction algorithms are utilized. These routines allow for the probability of a non-detected error to be less than 1 in 10 to the 25th power. In more physical terms, this means that there would be only one undetected error in two quadrillion discs (this would form a stack one billion miles high!).

Error correction alone requires 288 bytes for every 2,048 bytes of disc data. This allows for the correction of numerous bad bits, including bursts of bad data over 1,000 bits long. This powerful error correction capability is required since physical defects can cause errors, and because the CD media was originally designed for audio reproduction in which minor errors or even missing data can be tolerated.

In the case of an audio CD, missing data can be *interpolated*—that is, the information follows a predictable pattern that allows the missing value to be guessed at. For example, if three values are stored on an audio disc, say 10, 13, and 20 appearing in a series, and the middle value is missing—due to damage or dirt on the CD's surface—you can interpolate a middle value of 15, which is midway between the 10 and 20 values. Although this is not exactly correct, in the case of audio recording it will not be noticeable to the listener. If those same three values appear on a CD-ROM in an executable program, there is no way to guess at the correct value for the middle sample. Interpolation cannot work because executable program data follows no natural law, for the data is a series of values. To guess 15 is not just slightly off, it is completely wrong.

Because of the need for such precision, CD-ROM drives for use on PCs were later to market than their audio counterparts. When first introduced, CD-ROM drives were too expensive for widespread adoption. In addition, drive manufacturers were slow in adopting standards, causing a lag time for the production of CD-ROM titles. Without a wide base of software to drive the industry, acceptance was slow.

What Types of Drives are Available?

When purchasing a CD-ROM drive for your PC, consider three distinct sets of attributes of CD-ROM drives, as follows:

1. The drive's performance specifications.
2. The interface it requires for connection to your PC.
3. The physical disc handling system used.

The variance in any of these categories is enormous; in fact, single vendors offer entire lines of drives that vary in performance specifications, disc handling mechanisms, and type of adapters they can use to interface with your PC. For these reasons, drive prices vary widely. CD-DA (Compact Disc-Digital Audio) drives, for example, are very inexpensive since they don't require the precision in reproducing music that is required by a drive used for storing data. So before you buy, know the drive's characteristics.

All three drive characteristics are discussed in this section, giving you a better understanding of what type of drive you need to buy.

CD-ROM Drive Specifications

Drive specifications tell you the drive's performance capabilities. If you're shopping for a sports car, for instance, and the dealer tells you the car can accelerate from a standing stop to 60 miles per hour in five seconds, you know you've got a hot car. The car's horsepower, weight, suspension design, and other specifications can be used to understand the vehicle's performance.

CD-ROM drive specifications tell the shopper much the same thing. Typical performance figures published by manufacturers are the data transfer rate, access time, internal cache or buffers (if any), and the interface used.

Data Transfer Rate. The data transfer rate tells you how much data the drive can read from a data CD and transfer to the host computer when reading one large, sequential chunk of data. The standard measurement in the industry is kilobytes per second, usually abbreviated as KB/s. If a manufacturer claims a drive can transfer data at 150 KB/s, it means that a drive reading a sequential stream of data from the CD will achieve 150 kilobytes a second after it has come up to speed. Note that this is a sustained and sequential read, not access across the data disc from different portions of the platter. Obviously, the data transfer specification is meant to convey the drive's peak data reading capabilities. A higher rate of transfer might be better, but a number of other factors come into play.

The standard CD format dictates that there are 75 blocks (or sectors) of data per second, with each block containing 2,048 bytes of data. This gives a transfer rate of exactly 150 KB/s. This is the standard for CD-DA (Digital Audio) drives, and is also called *Single-speed* in CD-ROM drives. The term *Single-speed* is used since CD discs are recorded in a *Constant Linear Velocity (CLV) format,* which means that the rotational speed of the disc will vary to keep the track speed a constant.

Because CD-ROM drives can read data which is not time based like audio, it is possible to speed up the reading of these discs by spinning them at a higher linear velocity. There are currently several different speed drives available, all of which are multiples of the original Single-speed drives. Table 17.1 shows the speeds at which CD-ROM drives can operate.

Table 17.1 CD-ROM Drive Speeds and Data Transfer Rates

Drive Speed	Transfer Rate (Bps)	Transfer Rate (KB/s)
Single-speed (1x)	153,600	150
Double-speed (2x)	307,200	300
Triple-speed (3x)	460,800	450
Quad-speed (4x)	614,400	600
Six-speed (6x)	921,600	900
Eight-speed (8x)	1,228,800	1,200
Ten-speed (10x)	1,536,000	1,500

Note: Bps = Bytes per second
KB/s = K Bytes per second

The 4x and 8x drives are currently the most popular, and at least 4x drives are the minimum recommended today that meet the new MPC-3 (Multimedia Personal Computer) standard. There are some 6x (six-speed) drives on the market now, but they have already being overshadowed by 8x (eight-speed) drives in popularity. Unless you are using a laptop system, I don't recommend the 6x drives because they cost significantly more than 4x drives, yet do not offer a significant jump in performance to be worthwhile. For laptop multimedia computers with integrated CD-ROM drives, 6x drives are becoming popular; however for desktop systems the 6x drives were quickly passed over by cheaper 8x drives, just as the 3x drives were passed over by cheaper 4x units. For an increase to be worthwhile, it should be double the previous standard. It remains to be seen how the 10x drives fare in the marketplace.

Even the fastest CD-ROM drives pale in comparison to hard disk drive transfer rates, which are usually 6MB or more per second. This means that the SCSI or ATA-IDE interfaces used by CD-ROM drives are more than up to the task. If you expect to run a variety of CD-based software on your system, you need a drive with a high data transfer rate. Applications that employ full-motion video, animation, and sound require high transfer rates, and you'll be disappointed in the results of a slower drive. The minimum recommended drive should be a Quad-speed drive which means it can transfer data at a rate of 600 KB/s.

Access Time. A CD-ROM drive's access time is measured the same way as for PC hard drives. In other words, the *access time* is the delay between the drive receiving the command to read and its actual first reading of a bit of data. The time is recorded in milliseconds; a typical manufacturer's rating for a Quad-speed drive would be listed as 200ms. This is an average access rate; the true access rate depends entirely on where the data is located on the disc. Positioning the read mechanism to a portion of the disc near the narrower center of the disc gives you a faster access rate than positioning at the wider outer perimeter. Access rates quoted by many manufacturers are an average taken by calculating a series of random reads from a disc.

Obviously, a faster average access rate is desirable, especially when you are relying on the drive to locate and pull up data quickly. Access times for CD-ROM drives are steadily improving, and the advancements are discussed later in this chapter. Note that these average times are significantly slower than PC hard drives, ranging from 500 to 100 milliseconds when compared to 10 milliseconds found on your typical hard disk. Most of the speed difference lies in the construction of the drive itself; hard drives have multiple read heads and range over a smaller surface area of media. CD-ROM drives have but one laser read beam, and it must be positioned over the entire range of the disc. In addition, the data on a CD is organized in a long spiral from outer edge inward. When the drive positions its head to read a "track" it must estimate the distance into the disc and skip forward or backward to the appropriate point in the spiral. Reading off the outer edge requires a longer access time than the inner segments.

Access times have been falling since the original Single-speed drives came out. With each subsequent boost in data transfer speed, usually we have also seen an increase in access time as well. Table 17.2 lists typical access times for good quality drives of several different speed drives:

Table 17.2 Typical CD-ROM Drive Access Times

Drive Speed	Access Time (ms)
Single-speed (1x)	400
Double-speed (2x)	300
Triple-speed (3x)	200
Quad-speed (4x)	150
Six-speed (6x)	150
Eight-speed (8x)	100
Ten-speed (8x)	100

The times listed here are typical examples for good drives—within each speed category there will be drives that are faster and slower. Because I recommend Quad-speed drives as a minimum, this means you can also expect a 150ms access time rating to go along with that.

Buffer/Cache. Most drives are shipped with internal buffers or caches of memory installed on-board. These *buffers* are actual memory chips installed on the drive's board and allow data to be staged or stored in larger segments before they are sent to the PC. A typical buffer for a CD-ROM drive is 256 kilobytes or KB, although drives are available that have either more or less (more is generally better!). Generally the faster speed drives will come with more buffer to handle the higher transfer rates.

Having buffer or cache memory on the CD-ROM drive offers a number of advantages. Buffers can ensure that the PC receives data at a constant rate; when an application requests data from the CD-ROM disc, the data is probably scattered across different segments of the disc. Because the drive has a relatively slow access time, the pauses between data reads can cause a drive to send data to the PC sporadically. You might not notice this in typical text applications, but a slower access rate drive coupled with no data buffering is very noticeable, even irritating, in the display of video or some audio segments. In addition, a drive's buffer, when under control of sophisticated software, can read and have ready the disc's table of contents, making the first request for data faster to find on the disc platter. I recommend a minimum size for a built-in buffer or cache of 256K, which is standard on most Quad-speed drives.

Interface

A CD-ROM's *interface* is the physical connection of the drive to the PC's expansion bus. The interface is the pipeline of data from the drive to the computer, and its importance shouldn't be minimized. There are three different types of interfaces available for attaching a CD-ROM drive to your system. They are:

- SCSI/ASPI (Small Computer System Interface, Advanced SCSI Programming Interface)
- IDE/ATAPI (Integrated Drive Electronics/AT Attachment Packet Interface)
- Proprietary

This next section will examine these different interface choices.

SCSI/ASPI. *SCSI* (pronounced SKUH-zee), or the *Small Computer System Interface,* is a name given to a special interface bus that allows many different types of peripherals to communicate. The current version of the standard is called *SCSI-2*. A standard software interface called *ASPI (Advanced SCSI Programming Interface)* is most commonly used to communicate between the CD-ROM drive (or other SCSI peripherals) and the host adapter. SCSI offers the greatest flexibility and performance of the interfaces available for CD-ROM drives, and can be used to connect many other types of peripherals to your system as well.

The SCSI bus enables computer users to string a group of devices along a chain from one SCSI host adapter, avoiding the complication of inserting a different adapter card into the PC bus slots every time a new hardware device, such as a tape unit or additional CD-ROM drive, is added to the system. These traits make SCSI interfaces preferable for connecting peripherals such as your CD-ROM to your PC.

All SCSI adapters are not created equal, however. Although they may share a common command set, they can implement these commands differently, depending on how the adapter's manufacturer designed the hardware. To eliminate these incompatibilities, ASPI was created. ASPI stands for Advanced SCSI Programming Interface and was originally developed by Adaptec, Inc., a leader in the development of SCSI controller cards and adapters. ASPI consists of two main parts. The primary part is an ASPI-Manager program, which is a driver that is written to work between the particular operating system used and the specific SCSI host adapter. The ASPI-Manager sets up the ASPI interface to the SCSI bus.

The second part of an ASPI system are the individual ASPI device drivers. For example, you would get an ASPI driver for your SCSI CD-ROM drive. You can also get ASPI drivers for your other SCSI peripherals such as tape drives, scanners, and so on. The ASPI driver for the peripheral talks to the ASPI-Manager for the host adapter. This is what allows the devices to communicate together on the SCSI bus.

The bottom line is that if you are getting a SCSI interface CD-ROM, make sure that it includes an ASPI driver which runs under your particular operating system. Also be sure that your SCSI host adapter has the corresponding ASPI-Manager driver, as well.

The SCSI interface offers the most powerful and flexible connection for CD-ROM and other devices. It allows for higher performance, and up to seven or more drives can be connected to a single host adapter. The drawback is cost. If you do not need SCSI for other peripherals, and intend on connecting only one CD-ROM drive to the SCSI bus, then you will be spending a lot of money on unused potential. In that case, an IDE/ATAPI interface CD-ROM drive would be a more cost-effective choice.

IDE/ATAPI. The *IDE/ATAPI (Integrated Drive Electronics/AT Attachment Packet Interface)* is an extension of the same ATA (AT Attachment) interface most people connect their hard disk drives to. Specifically, ATAPI is an industry standard Enhanced IDE interface for CD-ROM drives. ATAPI is a software interface that adapts the SCSI/ASPI commands to the IDE/ATA interface. This has allowed drive manufacturers to take their high-end CD-ROM drive products and quickly adapt them to the IDE interface. This also allows the IDE CD-ROM drives to remain compatible with the MSCDEX (Microsoft CD-ROM Extensions) that are used to interface with DOS. With Windows 95, the CD-ROM extensions are contained in the CDFS (CD File System) VxD (virtual device) driver.

ATAPI drives are sometimes also called Enhanced IDE drives, since this is an extension of the original IDE (technically the ATA) interface. In most cases, an IDE/ATA CD-ROM drive will connect to the system via a second IDE interface connector and channel, leaving the primary one for hard disk drives only. This is done because IDE does not share the single channel well, and would cause the hard disk to wait for CD-ROM commands to complete and vice versa. SCSI does not have this problem because you can send commands to different devices without having to wait for each previous command to complete.

The IDE/ATAPI interface represents the most cost effective, yet high performance interface for CD-ROM drives. Most new systems that include a CD-ROM drive will have it connected through IDE/ATAPI. To prevent performance problems, be sure that your CD-ROM drive is connected on a secondary IDE channel that is separate from the primary channel used by your hard disk drive. Many sound cards now include an ATAPI interface driver and the requisite secondary IDE interface connector specifically for a CD-ROM drive. Up to two drives can be connected to the secondary IDE connector, but for more than that, SCSI would be a better choice.

Proprietary Interfaces. The last type of interface you will see for CD-ROM drives are the *proprietary* ones. These are often included in the very low cost CD-ROM drive kits that come with their own adapter card. These interfaces are nonstandard and although inexpensive, are not flexible and do not offer high performance. I recommend you stay away from any of the proprietary CD-ROM interfaces and only use drives that interface via SCSI or IDE/ATAPI.

Loading Mechanism

There are two distinctly different mechanisms for loading a CD into a CD-ROM drive. They are the Caddy or the Tray. Each one offers some benefits and features. Which type you select will have a major impact on your use of the drive because you will interact with this every time you load a disc!

There are some multiple disc drives on the market now that allow you to insert more than one disc at a time. Most of these use a special cartridge that you fill with discs, much like a multi-disc player for automotive use.

Caddy. The *caddy system* is used on most high-end CD-ROM drives. This system requires that you place the CD itself into a special caddy, which is a sealed container with a metal shutter. The caddy has a hinged lid that allows you to open it for inserting the CD, but after that the lid remains shut. When you insert the caddy containing the CD into the drive, the drive will open a metal shutter on the caddy, allowing access to the CD by the laser.

The caddy is definitely the most convenient loading mechanism. If all of your CDs are in their own caddies, then all you have to do is grab the caddy containing the disc you want and shove it into the drive! This makes the CD operate much like a 3.5-inch diskette. You can handle the caddy without worrying about touching or contaminating the disc or the drive, making this the most accurate and durable mechanism as well. Young children can easily handle the caddies and don't have to touch the delicate CD discs themselves.

Because the caddy is sealed, the discs are protected from damage caused by handling. The only time the disc is actually handled is when it is first put into the caddy. The caddy loading system also ensures that the disc is properly located when inside the drive. This allows for more accurate laser head positioning mechanisms, and caddy drives generally have faster access times as well.

The only drawback to the caddy is the expense. You only get one caddy with the drive, and I see many users who fail to understand that they need many more! I watch them in agony as each time they insert a new disc into their drive, they first have to eject the caddy/disc, remove the disc from the caddy, put the disc back into the original jewel case, open the jewel case for the new disc, put the new disc into the caddy, and finally insert the caddy/disc back into the drive. What a nightmare! Don't even think about using a caddy drive without purchasing separate caddies for all of your most commonly used CDs! Caddies cost about $3 each in quantity, and I recommend you have at least 20 or so on hand, or at least as many as you have discs that you regularly use. Of course this will add $60 or more to the cost of your CD-ROM drive, but that is the price you pay for convenience, durability, reliability, and higher performance.

After you have caddies for all of your discs, the disc swap procedure is much easier; simply eject the one in the drive, grab the new caddy/disc and shove it back in! The caddy essentially takes the place of the jewel case, and the disc should be left in the caddy permanently.

A final advantage of caddy loaded drives is that they can be mounted in either a horizontal or vertical plane, meaning that the drive can be installed sideways. This cannot be done with the cheaper tray loaded drives.

Tray. Most of the lower end drives use a *tray loading* mechanism. This is exactly the same as you would find in a CD-DA (Digital Audio) drive used with your stereo system. Because you don't need to put each disc into a separate caddy, this mechanism is much less expensive overall. However, it also means that you have to handle each disc every time you insert or remove it, which gets the disc dirty and can damage it as well.

Tray loading is also much less convenient than a caddy system. Every time you want to use a disc, you have to eject the disc that is in the drive, replace it in the jewel case, remove the new disk from the jewel case, and place it in the tray. This makes it much more difficult for young children to use the discs without smudging or damaging them due to the excess handling.

The tray loader itself is also subject to damage. I have seen several drives with the trays broken as they were bumped or something was dropped on them while the tray was extended. Also, any contamination you place on the tray or disc is brought right into the drive when the tray is retracted. Tray loaded drives should never be used in a harsh environment such as a commercial or industrial application.

The tray mechanism also does not hold the disc as securely as the caddy. If you don't have the disc placed in the tray properly when it is retracted, then the disc or tray can be damaged. Tray drives obviously cannot be run in a vertical (sideways) position, as gravity would prevent proper loading and operation.

The only advantage to the tray mechanism over the caddy system is in cost, but that is a big factor. If you do not have young children, the drive will be run in a clean environment where careful handling and cleanliness can be assured, and convenience is not important, then I would recommend the tray mechanism due to its significantly lower cost. On the other hand, if these things are important to you, then the additional cost of the caddies brings with it a host of other benefits.

Other Drive Features

Although drive specifications are of the utmost importance, other factors and features should be taken into consideration as well. Besides quality of construction, the following criteria bear scrutiny when making a purchase decision:

- Drive sealing
- Self-cleaning lenses
- Internal versus external drive

Drive Sealing. Dirt is your CD-ROM's biggest enemy. Dust or dirt, when it collects on the lens portion of the mechanism, can cause read errors or severe performance loss. Many manufacturers "seal" the lens and internal components in airtight enclosures from the drive bay. Other drives, although not sealed, have double dust doors—one external and one internal—to keep dust from the inside of the drive. All these features help prolong the life of your drive.

Caddy loaded drives are inherently sealed better and are much more resistant to the external environment than tray loaded drives. Always use a caddy loaded drive in harsh industrial or commercial environments.

Self-Cleaning Lenses. If the laser lens gets dirty, so does your data. The drive will spend a great deal of time seeking and reseeking—or finally giving up. Lens cleaning discs are available, but built-in cleaning mechanisms are now included on virtually all good quality drives. This might be a feature you'll want to consider, particularly if you work in a less than pristine work environment, or you have trouble keeping your desk clean, let alone your CD-ROM drive lens.

Internal versus External Drives. When deciding whether you want an internal or external drive, think about where and how you're going to use your CD-ROM drive. What about the future expansion of your system? Both types of drives have pluses and minuses. The following lists some of the issues:

- *External Enclosure.* These tend to be rugged, portable, and large—in comparison to their internal versions. Buy an external only if you lack the space inside the system. You might also consider an external if you want to move the drive from one PC to another easily. If each PC has its own SCSI adapter, all you need to do is unplug the drive from one adapter and plug it in to the other.

- *Internal Enclosure.* Internal drives will clear off a portion of your desk. Buy an internal drive if you have a free drive bay, or plan on keeping the CD-ROM drive exclusively on one machine. All modern PCs should have a CD-ROM drive; it is no longer looked upon as a peripheral. The internal drives are nice because you can connect the audio connector to your sound card and leave the external audio connectors free for other inputs.

CD-ROM Disc and Drive Formats

Compact discs are pitted to encode the binary bits of 0 and 1. Without this logical organization to this disc full of digits, the CD-ROM drive and PC would be at a loss to find any discernible data amid all those numbers. To this end, the data is encoded to conform to particular standards. When a drive encounters particular patterns, it—and the PC—can "recognize" the organization of the disc and find its way around the platter. Without standard data formats, the CD-ROM industry would be dead in the water; vendors of particular discs and disc drives would be producing incompatible software discs and drives and thereby limiting the number of units that could be sold.

Formats are also needed to advance the technology. For instance, hard rubber wheels and no suspension were just fine for the first automobiles as they cruised along at the breakneck speed of 30 miles an hour. But hitting a pothole at 60 mph could cause serious damage to the vehicle—and the riders. Inflatable tires and shock absorbers became necessary components of the modern car.

Similarly, the standards for disc formats evolved as well. The first compact data discs stored only text information, which was relatively easy to encode onto a disc. Graphics produced a greater challenge, and the standards evolved to incorporate them. The use of animation with synchronized sound, and then live-motion video, called for other expansions to the standards in which CDs store data.

It is extremely important to note that advanced CD-ROM standards are in the process of evolution right now. Multiple vendors are deploying a number of different techniques for expanding the capabilities of CD-ROM technology. They may be incompatible with each other or are immature in their development, and acceptance of these newer standards by software vendors is essential to the widespread use of these standards. It is important that you are familiar with these issues before you purchase a drive: consider the formats it is capable of reading now—and in the future.

The majority of drives available today, however, do comply with earlier CD-ROM formats, ensuring that the vast library of CD-ROM applications available today can be used on these drives.

Data Standard: ISO 9660

Manufacturers of the first CD-ROM data discs produced their discs for one particular drive. In other words, a data disc produced for company A's drive could not be read by anyone who had purchased company B's CD-ROM drive—the disc needed to be formatted for each manufacturer's drive. Obviously, this stalled the development of the industry. Philips and Sony—the original collaborators for the standards incorporated in audio CDs—developed the "Yellow Book" specifications for data CD-ROMs.

When Philips and Sony first published the audio CD specifications, the material was released in a red binder and became known as "Red Book." Subsequent CD-ROM specifications have been dubbed by color as well, such as "Orange Book" and "Green Book."

An extension of the way in which audio data was stored on disc, the Yellow Book specification details how data—rather than audio—can be organized on a disc for its later retrieval. The International Standards Organization (ISO) refined this specification (called ISO 9660) in such a way that every vendor's drive and disc would expect to find a table of contents for a data disc. This is known as a *Volume Table of Contents*, and really is quite similar to a standard book's table of contents in theory. ISO 9660 did not completely solve compatibility problems, however. The incorporation of additional data to aid and refine the search for data on a disc and even how to format the data blocks were still left to each separate vendor's design.

High Sierra Format

It was in all manufacturer's interests to resolve this issue. In a meeting in 1985 at the High Sierra Hotel and Casino in Lake Tahoe, California, leading manufacturers of CD-ROM drives and CD-ROM discs came together to resolve the differences in their implementation of the ISO 9660 format. The agreement has become known as the *High Sierra format* and is now a part of the ISO 9660 specification document. This expansion enabled all drives to read all ISO 9660-compliant discs, opening the way for the mass production of CD-ROM software publishing. Adoption of this standard also enabled disc publishers to provide cross-platform support for their software, easily manufacturing discs for DOS, UNIX, and other operating system formats. Without this agreement, the maturation of the CD-ROM marketplace would have taken years longer and stifled the production of available CD ROM-based information.

The exact and entire specifications for how to format the CD media are complex, strewn with jargon you may never need, and superfluous to your understanding of drive capabilities. You should know the basics, however, because it gives you a glimpse of the inner workings of retrieving data so quickly from such an enormous well.

To put basic High Sierra format in perspective, the disc layout is roughly analogous to a floppy disk. A floppy has a system track that not only identifies itself as a floppy and its density and operating system, but also tells the computer how it's organized—into directories, and within the directories, files.

Basic CD-ROM formats are much the same. The initial track of a data CD identifies itself as a CD and begins synchronization between the drive and the disc. Beyond the synchronization lies a system level that details how the entire disc is structured; as a part of the system area, the disc identifies the location of the volume area—where the actual data is held. The system also contains the directories of this volume, with pointers or addresses to various named areas, as illustrated in figure 17.2. A significant difference between CD directory structures and that of DOS is that the system area also contains direct addresses of files within their subdirectories, allowing the CD to seek to a specific location on the spiral data track.

Because the CD data is all really on one, long spiral track, when speaking of tracks in the context of a CD, we're talking about sectors or segments of data along the spiral.

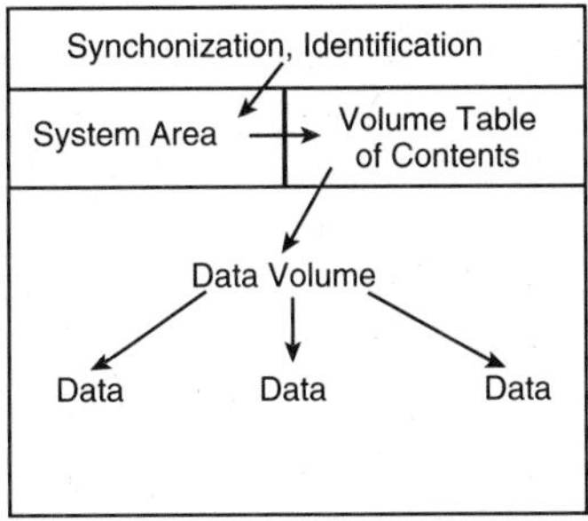

Figure 17.2

CD-ROM basic organizational format.

CD-DA (Digital Audio)

Data drives that can read data and audio are called *CD-DA*. Virtually any data drive now being sold reads both types of discs. When you insert a disc, the drive reads the first track of the disc to determine what type you loaded. Most drives ship with audio CD software, which enables you to play music CDs from your PC. You can use headphones or, with an installed sound card, connect speakers to the system. Some external drives ship with standard Left/Right audio plugs; just plug them into any external amplifier.

CD+

Philips and Sony have recently introduced a new CD format called CD+. This is a new format that enables audio CD players and multimedia PCs to easily play the same compact discs. This new format allows both audio and data to be integrated on the same CD.

CD+ uses a new technology called *stamped multisession*, which solves the problem of trying to use a computer CD-ROM title in an audio player. Because the first track of a computer CD-ROM contains data and not music, the audio player attempts to play it and static results. If the volume is turned up, the speakers can be damaged.

The new CD+ format will allow a new type of CD to appear that contains not only music, but data such as song lyrics, biographies, and any other text that is desired.

PhotoCD

First announced back in 1990, but not available until 1992, CD drives or players that display your own CD-ROM recorded photographs over your television are now being sold by Kodak. You merely drop off a roll of film at a participating Kodak developer; later you take home a PhotoCD and drop it into your Kodak PhotoCD compatible disc player. But what's a PhotoCD compatible player?

This is a home A/V (Audio Visual) entertainment system component that is designed to play your PhotoCDs and your audio CDs as well. Because virtually all data-ready CD drives also can interpret audio, it's no mean feat for the Kodak CD players to play audio discs. The player merely reads off the first track and determines what type of disc you've fed it. The real breakthrough is in the drive's capability to determine whether one, two, or dozens of individual photo "sessions" are on the data disc.

CD Sessions. Remember from the High Sierra format discussion that each data disc holds a VTOC, or Volume Table of Contents, which tells the CD reader where—and how—the data is laid out on disc. CD data has, until this point, been single-session in its encoding. In other words, when a CD is mastered, all the data that will ever reside on the disc must be recorded in one session. The format, or the media, has no provision for returning later to append more information. The PhotoCD format—along with the XA and CD-I formats discussed later—not only allow for multiple sessions, but allow multiple sessions to be read back on a fully PhotoCD-capable CD-ROM drive. The drive must be capable of finding the multiple VTOCs associated with the appended sessions, however.

And this is where some confusion now reigns. When Kodak first released the PhotoCD, the company maintained that a drive must be CD-ROM XA compliant to use PhotoCD.

An explanation of the XA spec follows. As of January 1992, however, Kodak has tested non-XA drives with new software drivers and approved them as single-session PhotoCD compatible. In other words, many of the drives shipping right now—in fact a majority—may be perfectly suited to reading PhotoCD discs that contain a single session of photos. The drive can only recognize the first session, and ignores any data or subsequent volume entries made after the initial session.

PC-based CD-ROM drives, if supplied with the proper device driver and Kodak-based software, can read single-session PhotoCD images. Kodak is licensing the "viewer" portion of its software so that it can be incorporated into existing software packages. Special filters—or decoders—will be added to desktop publishing, word processing, and PC paint software that will allow them to import PhotoCD images into their documents.

Kodak has future plans to incorporate synchronized audio and text to the existing photo format. For these capabilities, the drive that reads these advanced discs must be XA-compatible. In addition, drives must be XA-compatible to read any disc that has multiple recordings.

PhotoCD Production

When you drop off your roll of film, the Kodak developers produce prints, just as they normally do. After prints are made, however, the process goes high-tech. Using high-speed UNIX operating system-based SUN SparcStations, the prints are scanned into the SparcStation at very high resolution using ultra-high resolution scanners. To give you an idea of the amount of information each scan carries, one color photograph can take 15–20 megabytes of storage. When the image is stored on disc, it is compressed using Kodak's own custom software. The compressed, stored images are then encoded onto special writable CD discs. The finished product is packaged in a familiar CD case and shipped back to your local developer for pickup.

Even though these scanned images occupy an enormous amount of media space, the capacity of CD technology can easily carry 100 photos, at the highest possible resolution. Because existing television, and even most home computers, cannot use these ultra-high resolutions, the typical home or PC-based PhotoCD can hold hundreds of images. See table 17.3 for more details. Because most of us rarely have that many photos developed at the same time, Kodak developed the system in conjunction with Philips so that multiple sessions can be recorded on one disc. You can have your Thanksgiving photos developed and recorded to disc in November, for example, and then bring the same disc back in late December to have your other holiday photos added to the remaining portion of the disc. Keep bringing the disc in until it fills up.

Table 17.3 PhotoCD Resolutions

Resolution	Description
256 lines × 384	Fine for most conventional TVs
512 × 768	Good for S-VHS TVs and VGA PCs
1024 × 1536	Beyond current TV technology, even Super VGA can't use all
2048 × 3072	Beyond TV or current PC capacities

As of this writing, Kodak PhotoCD discs run fine in single session mode in many current CD-ROM drives—in Philips CD-I home entertainment systems as well as the Kodak systems.

For multisession capabilities and the capability to use audio and text on a PhotoCD for the PC, you must have an XA-compatible CD-ROM drive.

CD-ROM-XA, or Extended Architecture

CD-ROM XA, or *Extended Architecture*, is backwards compatible with the earlier High Sierra or ISO 9660 CD-ROMs. It adds another dimension to the world of CD-ROM technology.

Interleaving. CD-ROM XA drives employ a technique known as *interleaving*. The specification calls for the capability to encode on disc whether the data directly following an identification mark is graphics, sound, or text. Graphics can include standard graphics pictures, animation, or full-motion video. In addition, these blocks can be *interleaved*, or interspersed, with each other. For example, a frame of video may start a track followed by a segment of audio, which would accompany the video, followed by yet another frame of video. The drive picks up the audio and video sequentially, buffering the information in memory, and then sending it along to the PC for synchronization.

In short, the data is read off the disc in alternating pieces, and then synchronized at playback so that the result is a simultaneous presentation of the data.

Mode 1 and Mode 2, Form 1 and Form 2. To achieve this level of sophistication, the CD format is broken up so that the data types are layered. *Mode 1* is CD data with error correction. *Mode 2* is CD data without error correction. The Mode 2 track, however, allows what are called Form 1 and Form 2 tracks to exist one after the other on the Mode 2 track, thereby allowing the interleaving. These interleaved tracks may include their own error correction and can be any type of data. Figure 17.3 shows a visual representation of the breakdowns of Mode and Form structure.

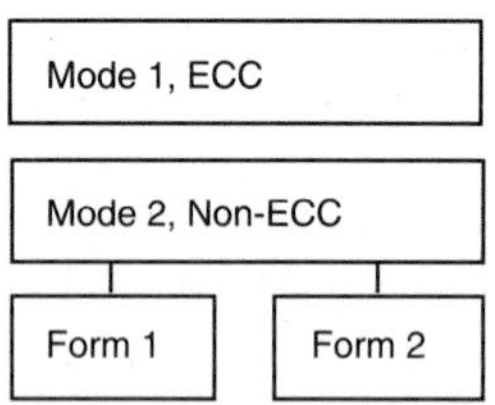

Figure 17.3

Mode and Form format for CD-ROM XA.

For a drive to be truly XA-compatible, the Form 2 data encoded on the disc as audio must be *ADPCM (Adaptive Differential Pulse Code Modulation) audio*—specially compressed and encoded audio. This requires that the drive or the SCSI controller have a signal processor chip that can decompress the audio during the synchronization process.

What all this translates into is that drives currently available may be partially XA-compliant. They might be capable of the interleaving of data and reading of multisession discs, but may not have the ADPCM audio component on the disc or its controller.

Presently, the only drives with full XA compliance are produced by Sony and IBM. The Sony drive incorporates the ADPCM chip on its drive. The IBM XA drive is for IBM's proprietary Micro Channel bus and is designed for its high-end PS/2 Model computers.

Manufacturers may claim that their drives are "XA-ready," which means that they are capable of multisession and Mode 1 and Mode 2, Form 1 and Form 2 reading, but they do not incorporate the ADPCM chip. Software developers, including Kodak, have yet to produce many XA software titles. IBM has a few under its Multimedia program, but others have not yet hit the market.

If you get a drive that is fully mode and form compatible, and is capable of reading multiple sessions, you may have the best available at this time. XA is a specification waiting for acceptance right now. Audio and video interleaving is possible without full XA compliance, as MPC applications under Microsoft Windows demonstrate.

CD-R

Sometimes known as *CD-WORM* and *CD-WO, CD-R (CD-Recordable)* enables you to write your own CDs.

As with mastering any CD, your data must be laid out or formatted before recording it to the CD-R unit. Often this layout is performed on a PC with large hard disks or other magnetic and removable media.

The CD-R is not quite the CD you might expect, however. Instead of the recording beam burning pits into a metallic or glass strata, the CD-R media is coated with a dye that has the same reflective properties as a "virgin" CD disc—in other words, a CD reader would see an unrecorded CD-R disc as one long land. When the recording laser begins to burn data into the CD-R media, it heats the gold layer and the dye layer beneath. The result of heating these areas causes the dye and gold areas to diffuse light in exactly the same way that a pit would on a glass master disc or a mass-produced CD. The reader is fooled into thinking a pit exists; there is no actual pit, however—just a spot of less-reflective disc caused by the chemical reaction of heating the dye and gold.

Many of the newer recordable CD-ROM drives support all the formats discussed—ISO 9660 all the way through CD-ROM XA. In addition, these drives read the formats as well, serving as a ROM reader. Prices have been falling steadily, and are now in the $1,000 area for a drive, and under $7 for the blank media. These drives are now affordable for small businesses, who can distribute databases easily on CD-ROM discs. After you make a master, it can cost less than $1 per disc to have duplicates made, bringing the price of distributing your data to a very reasonable figure.

CD-E

Although CD-R is a write-once standard, soon it will be possible to purchase fully rerecordable CD drives. Philips Electronics and Ricoh have already introduced and demonstrated erasable CD-ROMs (called CD-E). The CD-E standard is currently being developed and supported by more than ten manufacturers, including IBM, Hewlett-Packard, Mitsubishi, Mitsumi, Matsushita, Sony, 3M, Olympus, Philips, and Ricoh.

The new medium has an archival life of more than 10 years, or roughly 10,000 access cycles, and will allow at least 1,000 overwrites to occur. As such it is not intended to replace magnetic media for primary online storage, but can supplement it for archival purposes. The media has a lower optical reflectability than standard CDs, requiring a five-times increase in read/write gain for the drive units.

This new technology is backward compatible with standard CD-ROM and CD-R technology, meaning that CD-E drives would read existing CD and CD-R discs. These new drives will initially be expensive, but if the price falls, it may catch on as a viable backup and online storage solution.

DVD (Digital Video Disc)

The future of CD-ROM is called DVD (Digital Video Disc). This is a new standard that dramatically increases the storage capacity of, and therefore the useful applications for CD-ROMs. The problem with current CD-ROM technology is that it is severely limited in storage capacity. A CD-ROM can only hold a maximum of about 680 MB of data, which may sound like a lot, but is simply not enough for many up and coming applications, especially where the use of video is concerned.

One of the primary applications envisioned for the new DVD standard is a replacement for video tapes. In the future instead of renting a tape at your local video store, you will be able to rent or purchase a movie on a CD-ROM disc! As such, DVD will have applications not only in computers, but in the consumer entertainment market as well.

DVD had a somewhat confusing beginning. During 1995, two competing standards for high capacity CD-ROM drives emerged to compete with each other for future market share. A standard called Multimedia CD was introduced and backed by Sony and Philips Electronics, while a competing standard called the Super Density (SD) disk was introduced and backed by Toshiba, Time Warner, and several other companies. If both of these standards had hit the market as is, consumers as well as entertainment and software producers would have been in a quandary over which one to choose!

Fearing a repeat of the Beta/VHS situation, several organizations including the Hollywood Video Disc Advisory Group and the Computer Industry Technical Working Group banded together and insisted on a single format and refused to endorse either competing proposal. With this incentive, both groups worked out an agreement on a single new high capacity CD-ROM in September of 1995. The new standard, called DVD (Digital Video Disc), combines elements of both previously proposed standards. The single DVD standard has avoided a confusing replay of the VHS/Betamax fiasco and has given the software, hardware, and movie industries a single unified standard to support.

DVD offers an initial storage capacity of 4.7 GB of digital information on a single-sided, single-layer disc the same diameter and half the thickness (0.6mm) of a current CD-ROM. With MPEG-2 (Motion Picture Experts Group) compression, that's enough to contain 135 minutes of video, enough for a full-length, full-screen, full-motion feature film—including three channels of CD-quality audio and four channels of subtitles. The initial capacity is no coincidence: the creation of DVD was driven by the film industry, which has long sought a storage medium cheaper and more durable than videotape.

Future plans for DVD include 9.4-GB double-layer discs as well as double-sided, double-layer discs that will store 18.8 GB—which is nearly 30 times the capacity of today's CD-ROMs! With advancements coming in blue light lasers, this capacity may be increased several fold in the future. DVD drives are also very fast compared to current CD-ROM technology. The standard transfer rate is 1.3MB per second, which is approximately equivalent to a 9X CD-ROM drive.

DVD drives will be fully backwards compatible, and, as such, will be able to play today's CD-ROMs as well as audio CDs. When playing existing CDs, the performance will be equivalent to a standard 4x CD-ROM drive. As such, users who currently own 4x CD-ROM drives should probably consider waiting for DVD drives instead of upgrading to a 6x or faster drives. Any products that require faster than 4x speeds will likely come out in DVD form and not use current CD-ROM technology anyway.

If you want to take advantage of DVD's multimedia capabilities you will need to have a sound-and-video card that can handle MPEG-2 and the three DVD audio formats. This type of hardware is expected to be available along with the drives.

In the future it is expected that DVD drives, multimedia players for TV (Set Top Box) connection, and over 300 DVD movies and software titles will be available by the end of 1996. Movies will be the initial application for DVD, and large numbers of DVD-ROM titles will be available during 1997 and 1998.

Multimedia CD-ROM

Multimedia is not a specific standard but a descriptive term. Any CD that incorporates text with graphics, sound, or video is by definition multimedia. Multimedia CDs exist for DOS, Macintosh System 7, Windows, OS/2, and UNIX operating systems and can be in many different formats.

MPC CD-ROMs

A consortium of hardware and software manufacturers led by Microsoft Corporation announced the formation of the Multimedia PC Marketing Council at Fall COMDEX in 1991. This council described the recommended platform for implementing multimedia on PC systems, and as more manufacturers joined the council, applications and hardware conformed to the prescribed specifications.

The MPC Council recommends minimum performance requirements for MPC-compatible CD-ROM drives, however. They are as follows:

Specification Transfer Rate	**MPC Level 1 Single-speed (1x)**	**MPC Level 2 Double-speed (2x)**	**MPC Level 3 Quad-speed (4x)**
Average Access	1000 ms	400 ms	200 ms

The minimum recommended specifications today are the MPC Level 3 standard. In other words, your drive should meet or exceed those performance standards.

Far from being an exact specification or format for data, MPC CD-ROM is a convention for storing audio, animation, video, and text for synchronization under the Microsoft Windows operating system from data received from an MPC-compliant CD-ROM. Microsoft has developed Windows Application Programmer's Interface software, which allows CD-ROM software manufacturers to organize the data on their CDs in such a way that information can be passed to Windows for processing.

Note that discs labeled as MPC only run under Microsoft Windows 3.0 or higher with the Microsoft Multimedia Extensions, or under OS/2 with MMPM. If a drive meets the minimum MPC Council recommendation for performance, it will run MPC CD-ROMs under Windows.

Audio drives deliver sound at a preset transfer rate to the amplifiers. Today's CD-ROM drives can spin at faster rates when retrieving data. The minimum recommended speed today would be the Quad-speed drive. Particular applications, such as live-motion video, especially benefit from this technology. Data is delivered in a constant stream, allowing the PC to process the video frames at a smoother rate. Some drives without high-speed technology, especially those that have no buffering capabilities, deliver video in a jerky and uneven manner.

Installing Your Drive

You decided on the drive you want. You ordered it. Now it's arrived at your doorstep. What next?

Installation of a CD-ROM drive is as difficult—or easy—as you make it. If you know a little about SCSI interface devices, such as your CD drive, and plan ahead, the installation should go smoothly.

This section walks you through the installation of typical internal and external CD-ROM drives with tips that often aren't included in your manufacturer's installation manuals. Even after you install the hardware, it isn't enough to just turn on the drive and toss in a CD. Special software must be loaded onto your PC first.

Avoiding Conflict: Get Your Cards in Order

Regardless of your type of installation—internal or external drive—you need to check your CD-ROM drive's SCSI host adapter before installation.

Carefully remove the adapter card from its protective, anti-static bag.

Note

Never handle the card by its gold, edge connector contacts—a simple spark of static electricity sent to the card is enough to do potential damage. The oils and contaminants from your skin can also cause corrosion and poor connections over time.

Lay the card out on the static bag with the IC chips, transistors, and processors face up, and the external connector to your right. Virtually all documentation for adapter cards assumes that cards are oriented this way when you configure them.

The single most important step in installing any SCSI device, including this new CD-ROM, is the proper configuration, or settings, for the adapter card in front of you. If you pay special attention to this part of the installation, you avoid 90 percent of the problems with installing SCSI devices.

Check the adapter's documentation or pamphlet for the default settings for the card. These should be indicated by a list near the front, or by notation throughout the manual. DO NOT worry about pin settings, jumpers, or anything else other than copying the default settings to a piece of paper. Look for the following default settings:

- IRQ
- DMA channel
- I/O Port address
- Adapter and Drive SCSI ID

The following is a typical list of recommended settings for a SCSI adapter:

Resource	Recommended Setting
IRQ	11
DMA channel	6
I/O address	334h-337h
SCSI ID	7

The IRQ and DMA settings indicated here should be followed or you may have conflicts with other adapters such as sound cards or network cards. The I/O port address setting can vary from what I have indicated here depending on what SCSI host adapter card you are installing, but make sure that whatever settings you use do not conflict with other adapters. Each setting is discussed later in the chapter.

Note

Some proprietary SCSI host adapters may have some, all, or just a few of these settings available to you. In any case, jot down the defaults they list in the manual.

If you want to avoid hair-pulling, teeth-gnashing, and general frustration, check these default settings for your SCSI card for possible conflicts with other cards already installed in your PC. You *cannot* have two cards set for the same IRQ, DMA, or I/O address, or the drive—and possibly your PC—will lock up or operate erratically.

The following are some typical cards you should check for IRQ, DMA, and I/O port address settings:

- Network interface cards (Ethernet, ARCNet, and so on)
- Sound cards
- Scanner interfaces
- Internal modems and fax-modems
- Other SCSI cards for hard drives, tape drives, scanners, or other added peripherals

If you value your time and your sanity, it's a good idea to keep handy a record of these important settings for all your adapter cards. Write down the current settings on a piece of paper and tape it into your PC's owner manual, for example. Any time you add a new adapter card or must reconfigure one already installed, you'll have a reference. Otherwise, you might find yourself pulling out every peripheral adapter in your machine to check its settings. Obviously, any time you add a new card or change the settings of one installed, change your note card.

Make a note of any conflicts. It probably is easier to reset the defaults on your CD-ROM SCSI card—it's already out of the PC and sitting in front of you. Don't make changes yet. Just take notes.

The next step is to make sure that the defaults listed in the manual are, in fact, the defaults actually set on the board. Everyone makes mistakes, and your manufacturer is included. Although this is relatively uncommon, it's best to double-check things now, before you go too far into the installation.

Jumpers. Adapter card configurations are set with *jumpers*—tiny plastic-covered shunts that fit over pin-pairs on the adapter card (see fig. 17.4). These rows of jumper pins may run left to right or up and down across the card. Configuration is a matter of having the jumpers on or off a pair of pins.

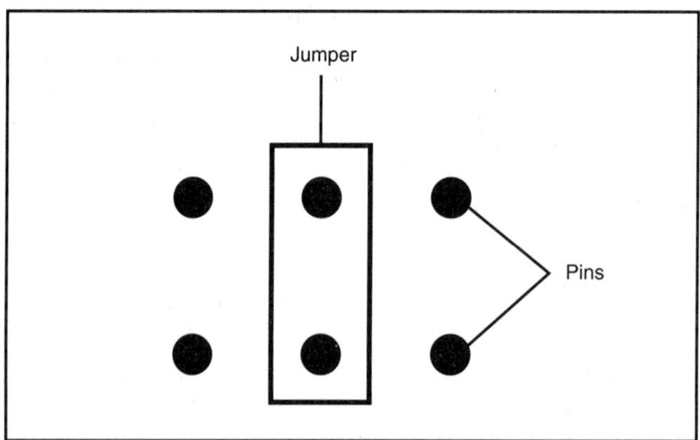

Figure 17.4
A SCSI card with jumper banks.

These rows of jumper pins are labeled on the card as J5 or W1, for example. Your adapter card manual or pamphlet has a diagram of these jumper rows, or *blocks*, as they're called. Carefully check the pin settings against your manual. Make sure that pins are jumpered where they should be, and just as important, that no extra jumpers are on any of the pins.

Note

Some SCSI adapters use rocker switches rather than jumpers to configure the cards.

If you believe you've found an error, double check. You might have multiple jumper blocks on your card—make sure that you're checking the right ones.

After you make sure that you have the pins set to the correct defaults, you're ready to resolve any possible conflicts.

IRQ Conflicts. The most common cause of a system lock-up after an installation is an IRQ conflict. Avoid problems up front by making sure that you have no conflicts now. Table 17.4 lists common IRQ numbers and which ones are typically open. Remember, you may already have an installed card occupying one of the interrupt request lines.

Table 17.4 Recommended IRQ Assignments

IRQ	Standard Function	Bus Slot	Card Type
0	System Timer	No	-
1	Keyboard Controller	No	-
2	2nd IRQ Controller Cascade	No	-
8	Real-Time Clock	No	-
9	Network/Available (Appears as IRQ 2)	Yes	8/16-bit
10	Available	Yes	16-bit
11	SCSI/Available	Yes	16-bit
12	Motherboard Mouse Port	Yes	16-bit
13	Math Coprocessor	No	-
14	Primary IDE (Hard Disk)	Yes	16-bit
15	Secondary IDE (IDE CDROM)	Yes	16-bit
3	Serial Port 2 (COM2:)	Yes	8/16-bit
4	Serial Port 1 (COM1:)	Yes	8/16-bit
5	Sound Card/LPT2:	Yes	8/16-bit
6	Floppy Disk Controller	Yes	8/16-bit
7	Parallel Port 1 (LPT1:)	Yes	8/16-bit

If you find a conflict, consult your adapter card manual for selecting a different IRQ. At this point, remove or move a jumper from one pin pair to another. Although jumper blocks can be removed with your fingers, you risk handling chips that may be near the jumpers. It's better to use a pair of claw grabbers, especially those sold in a computer tool kit, to carefully remove the jumper. Reset the jumper blocks according to the manual's diagrams for the new IRQ. For more information on these settings, see Chapter 5, "Bus Slots and I/O Cards."

DMA Conflicts. *DMA*, or *Direct Memory Address*, settings can also have serious consequences when in conflict. Typical symptoms of a DMA conflict are no response from one of the cards in conflict, or corruption of the data manipulated by one of the cards. For example, if you have a sound card and your CD-ROM SCSI card set for the same DMA channels, one—or both—of the cards might not function. If you also have a hard disk drive attached to the SCSI card in conflict, then data written to the drive could be corrupted, and could corrupt all of the other data on the drive! Check DMA settings on the card, but be aware that the card may require that the DMA request and acknowledge channel be set using different jumpers, even though the settings must be the same. Most cards use a single jumper or software setting for DMA which covers both the request and acknowledge signals.

Note

Direct Memory Access (DMA) is a technique that speeds up access to memory for expansion cards. Because it avoids the intervention of the CPU, this technique is "direct." Seven DMA channels are available in an IBM-AT compatible machine.

Many SCSI cards come with a default of DMA channel 5 set. This should be changed for most PCs because most of the newer, 16-bit sound cards also have DMA channel 5 set as default, so they are likely culprits in any conflict. For more information about these settings, see Chapter 5, "Bus Slots and I/O Cards."

I/O Port Addresses. No two cards can live at the same I/O port address. More important, these I/O addresses are really base addresses—they describe the address start that the card occupies. The full range of the memory address must be taken into consideration when resolving conflict with other cards. For example, if a sound card occupies address 220, you might assume that the SCSI card could exist at 230. This is not necessarily so. If the sound card's port address range is really 220–235, you've just introduced a conflict.

I've noticed some typical conflicts of late in the way types of adapter cards are shipped in their default state. Most SCSI cards ship with base memory I/O addresses of 300, 330, or 220. Many sound boards and internal fax modem cards may also occupy these addresses in their default configurations. Network interface cards are often set in the 280–360 range also. This means that if you are installing a sound card, SCSI card, and network card, then you will likely have conflicts to work out. I recommend that you always let the sound card have its default settings, and change the settings on the other cards if there are any conflicts. This is because some commercial software is improperly written to work with the sound cards alternate addresses.

If you need to change an adapter's I/O port address settings due to a conflict, make sure that you know the range of the possible conflict. Typical symptoms of I/O conflict are lockups or a failure of one or both of the conflicting devices to operate. Another symptom of conflict is disconcerting but harmless. Your machine may go through the boot process of checking memory, loading drivers, and so on, get to the end of the boot, and then reboot all over again. If this happens, remove the adapters one at a time until the conflict goes away, then you know at least one of the cards involved!

Plug and Play. If you have a system that includes a Plug and Play (PnP) BIOS, and you use all Plug and Play (PnP) adapter cards, setting the resources will be simple. If you have a PnP BIOS but use legacy (non-PnP) adapters, you will still have to set jumpers and switches as has been described.

Plug and Play systems include a BIOS that manages systems resource conflicts, which works extremely well with the newer PnP adapters. If you have a PnP system you can use the Configuration Manager program that came with it, which resides in your operating system to configure the PnP cards. Windows 95 calls this the Device Manager. For non-PnP cards, you will still need to set the jumpers and switches in order to change resource usage. The Device Manager in Windows 95 will find most of the popular legacy adapters, but in many cases, you may have to work out a configuration conflict manually. Use the resource listings in this section as a guide, and configure your adapters according to these listings. This will help minimize the chance for conflicts.

Selecting a Slot. After you configure your card correctly, resolve all potential conflicts, and are thoroughly tired of looking at the manual's hazy diagrams for jumper blocks, you're ready to insert the SCSI card into the PC.

Turn off the power. Unscrew the case cover and remove it. Look at the available or unoccupied slots in your PC bus. These card slots may come in 8, 16, or 32-bit lengths—with 8 being the shortest and the 32-bit slots the longest—and usually the last slots in the case. If your CD SCSI adapter is an 8-bit adapter, it will have one set of gold edge-connectors; the 16-bit cards have two sets—one short and one long. Make the most of the real estate inside your PC case. Don't put an 8-bit card in a 16-bit slot unless you have no other choice—you may want that 16-bit slot later on for a true 16-bit card. The main point is simple, though—you can put the SCSI card in any of the available slots in the case. Unscrew the slot cover for the bus slot you've selected from the back of the PC. Hang onto this screw.

Holding the card by its top edges slide it firmly into the expansion bus, connector edge facing through the open slot in the back of the PC chassis. Press down firmly. You'll feel the card seat itself—pop into the connector. Be careful not to press down too hard—you might damage the motherboard below. Make sure that the card is evenly seated, front to back. Most SCSI cards have cable hooks on either side of the outside connector. These can get in the way when you put the card into the bus.

If one of these hooks gets caught between the chassis and the card, you'll have a difficult time seating the card properly (see fig. 17.5). Move the hooks straight up, parallel with the connector so that they'll slide easily through the slot in the back of the PC.

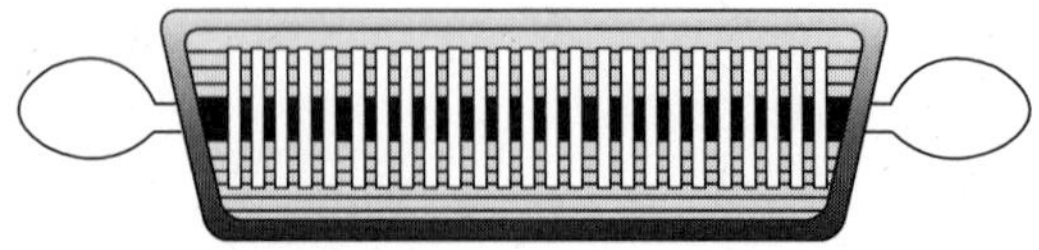

Figure 17.5
A SCSI-1 connector, showing the latching hooks.

Gently move the adapter flange with its slotted top away from the screw hole of the PC chassis. Put the screw from the slot plate into the hole and give it a few turns, enough to start it solidly. Slide the card flange under the screw head and secure it firmly. By starting the screw into the chassis first, and then sliding the card into place beneath it, you can avoid the problems of trying—often without luck—to align the adapter bracket flange and PC chassis hole with the screw. A common hassle here is dropping the screw into your PC case while attempting to secure the card. It's a good idea to have a flashlight around to peer between the cards to find dropped screws; those tweezers you used for changing jumpers might come in handy here to carefully remove the misplaced screws. If you've grounded yourself, you won't do any damage if you're careful in removing a dropped screw.

Never, under any circumstances, leave a loose or dropped screw in the case. It will inevitably short something out, doing severe damage to your main PC board and any cards in the expansion bus.

DO NOT replace the cover of the PC yet. If some lingering conflicts exist or the card is not fully seated in the slot, you might need to do more inside work. You can replace the PC case after you install the drive, reboot your system, install the driver software, and (whew!) tested the drive—not before.

External CD-ROM Hook-Up

Unpack the CD-ROM carefully. With the purchase of an external drive, you should receive the following items:

- CD-ROM drive
- SCSI adapter cable
- SCSI adapter card

This is the bare minimum to get the drive up and running. You'll probably also find a CD caddy, a manual or pamphlet for the adapter card, and possibly a sampling of CDs to get you started.

Take a look at your work area and the SCSI cable that came with the drive. Where will the drive find a new home? You're limited by the length of the cable. Find a spot for the drive, and insert the power cable into the back of the unit; make sure that you have an outlet, or preferably, a free socket in a surge-suppressing power strip to plug in the new drive.

Plug one end of the supplied cable into the connector socket of the drive, and one into the SCSI connector on the adapter card. Most external drives have two connectors on the back—either connector can be hooked to the PC (see fig. 17.6). The following sections discuss the extra connector. Secure the cable with the guide hooks on both the drive and adapter connector, if provided. Some SCSI cables supplied with Future Domain 16-bit controllers have a micro-connector for the adapter end, and simply clip into place.

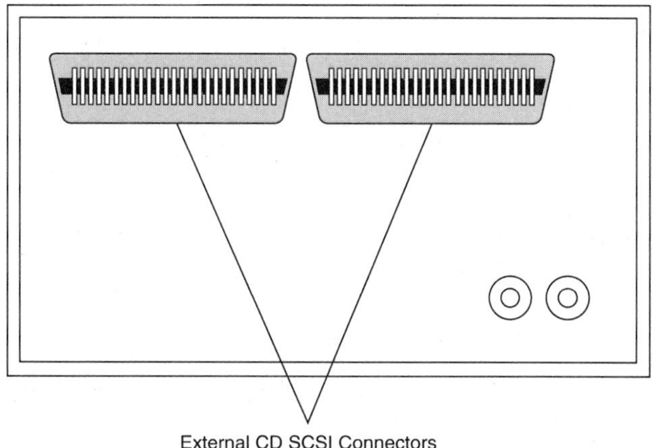

Figure 17.6

External CD-ROM drive SCSI connectors.

Finally, your external CD-ROM drive should have a SCSI ID select switch on the back. This switch sets the identification number for the drive when hooked to the host adapter. The adapter, by most manufacturer's defaults, should be set for SCSI ID 7. Make sure that you set the SCSI ID for the CD-ROM drive to any other number—6, 5, or 4, for example. The only rule to follow is to make sure that you do not set the drive for an ID that is already occupied—by either the card or any other SCSI peripheral on the chain.

Internal Drive Installation

Unpack your internal drive kit. You should have the following pieces:

- The drive
- Power cord
- SCSI interface board
- Internal SCSI ribbon cable
- Internal CD-Audio cable
- Floppy disks with device driver software and manual
- Drive rails and/or mounting screws

Your manufacturer also may have provided a *power cable splitter*—a bundle of wires with plastic connectors on each of three ends. A disc caddy and owner's manual may also be included.

Make sure that the PC is off and leave the cover off the PC for now. Before installing the card into the PC bus, however, connect the SCSI ribbon cable onto the adapter card (see fig. 17.7).

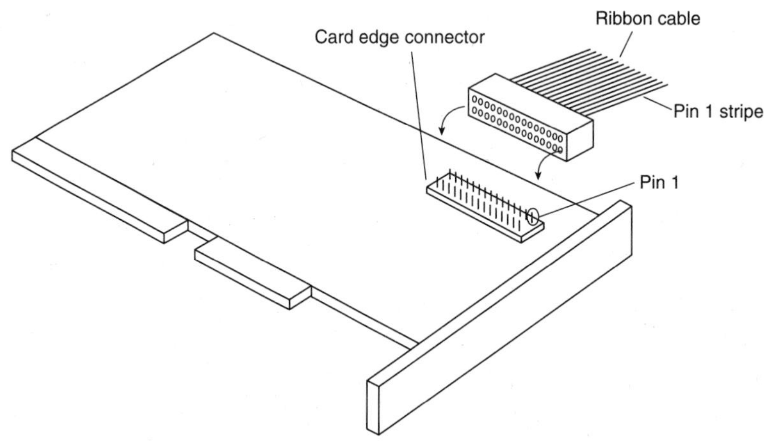

Figure 17.7

Ribbon cable connection to SCSI adapter.

Ribbon Cable and Card Edge Connector. The ribbon cable should be identical on both ends. You'll find a red stripe of dotted line down one side of the outermost edge of the cable. This stripe indicates a pin-1 designation and ensures that the SCSI cable is connected properly into the card and into the drive. If you're lucky, the manufacturer supplied a cable with notches or keys along one edge of the connector. With such a key, you can insert the cable into the card and drive in only one way. Unkeyed cables must be hooked up according to the pin-1 designation.

Along one edge of your SCSI adapter, you'll find a double row of 50 brass-colored pins. This is the card edge connector. In small print along the base of this row of pins you should find at least two numbers next to the pins—1 and 50. Aligning the ribbon cable's marked edge over pin 1, carefully and evenly insert the ribbon cable connector.

Now insert the adapter card, leaving the drive end of the cable loose for the time being.

Choose a slot in the front bay for your internal drive. Make sure that it's easily accessible and not blocked by other items on your desk. You'll be inserting the CDs here, and you'll need the elbow room.

Remove the drive bay cover. Inside the drive bay you should find a metal enclosure with screw holes for mounting the drive. If the drive has mounting holes along its side and fits snugly into the enclosure, you won't need mounting rails. If it's a loose fit, however, mount the rails along the sides of the drive with the rail screws and then slide the drive into the bay. Secure the drive into the bay with four screws—two on each side. If the rails or drive don't line up evenly with four mounting holes, make sure that you use at least two—one mounting screw on each side. Because you'll be inserting and ejecting many CDs over the years, mounting the drive securely is a must.

Once again, find the striped side of the ribbon cable and align it with pin 1 on the drive's edge connector. Either a diagram in your owner's manual or designation on the connector itself tells you which is pin 1.

The back of the CD drive has a power connector outlet. Inside the case of your PC, at the back of your floppy or hard disk, are power cords—bundled red and yellow wires with plastic connectors on them. You may already have an open power connector laying open in the case. Take the open connector and plug it into the back of the power socket on the CD-ROM drive. These connectors only go in one way. If you do not have an open connector, use the splitter (see fig. 17.8). Disconnect a floppy drive power cord. Attach the splitter to the detached power cord. Plug one of the free ends into the floppy drive, the other into the CD-ROM drive.

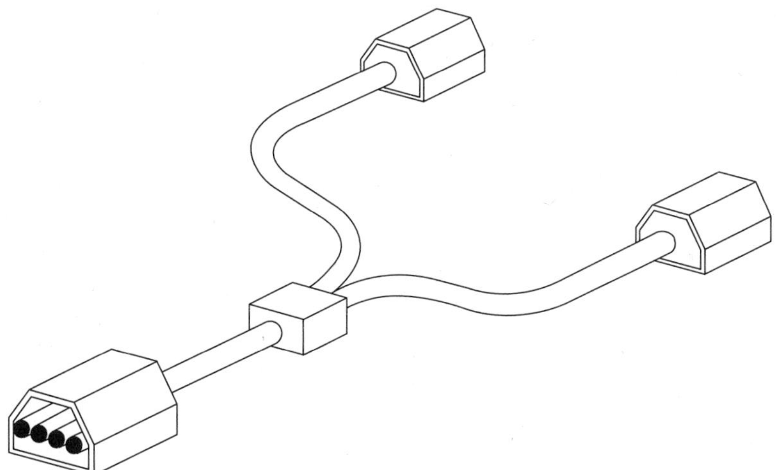

Figure 17.8

Power cord splitter and connector.

Note

It's best to "borrow" juice from the floppy drive connector in this way. Your hard drive may require more power or be more sensitive to sharing this line than the floppy is. If you have no choice—the splitter and ribbon cable won't reach, for example—you can split off any power cord that hasn't already been split. Check the power cable to ensure that you have a line not already overloaded with a split.

DO NOT replace the PC cover yet—you need to make sure that everything is running perfectly before you seal the case. You're now ready to turn on the computer. For the drive to work, however, you need to install the software drivers.

SCSI Chains: Internal, External, a Little of Both

Remember, one of the primary reasons for using a SCSI controller for your CD-ROM drive is the capability to chain a string of peripherals from one adapter card—saving card slots inside the PC, and limiting the nightmare of tracking IRQs, DMAs, and I/O memory addresses.

You can add scanners, tape backup units, and other SCSI peripherals to this chain (see fig. 17.9). You must keep a few things in mind; chief among them is SCSI termination.

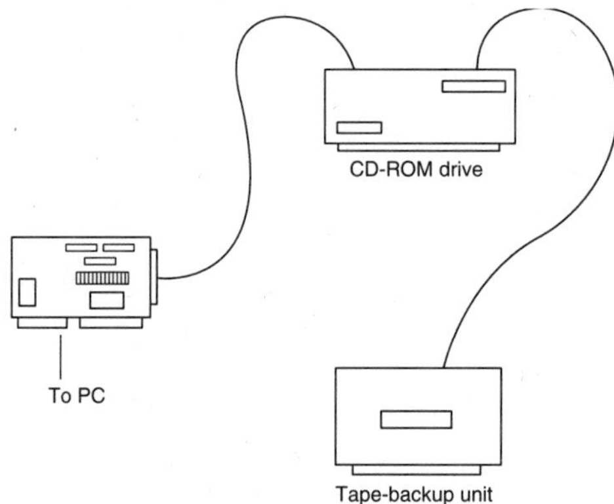

Figure 17.9

A SCSI chain of devices on one adapter card.

Identify and Terminate with Care. The first rule of SCSI device chaining is simple: each end of the SCSI chain must be terminated. The first device must contain a termination resistor and the last must also have a terminator attached. All devices between the first and last should be free of any terminator.

The second SCSI rule you must follow is that all SCSI devices must be set to a unique ID number. In the external drive installed earlier, the SCSI adapter is set for ID 7, and the CD-ROM drive is set for ID 6. Any additional SCSI devices added must then take IDs 1,2,3,4, or 5. *Remember: the SCSI adapter takes an ID, and its default is usually ID 7.*

Example One: All External SCSI Devices. Say that you installed your CD-ROM drive and added a tape device to the chain with the extra connector on the back of the CD-ROM drive. The first device in this SCSI chain is the adapter card itself. On all SCSI cards you find a series of long, reddish, ceramic tipped components plugged into the board in a group of three. These are the terminating resistors for the card (see fig. 17.10). From the card, you ran an external cable to the CD-ROM drive, and from the CD-ROM drive you added another cable to the back of the tape unit. The tape unit must then be terminated as well. Most external units are terminated with a SCSI cap—a small connector that plugs into the unused external SCSI connector. These external drive connectors come in two varieties: a SCSI cap and a pass-through terminator. The cap is just that; it plugs over the open connector and covers it. The pass-through terminator, however, plugs into the connector and has an open end that you can use to plug the SCSI cable into. This type of connector is essential if your external drive has only one SCSI connector; you can plug the drive in and make sure that it's terminated all with one connector.

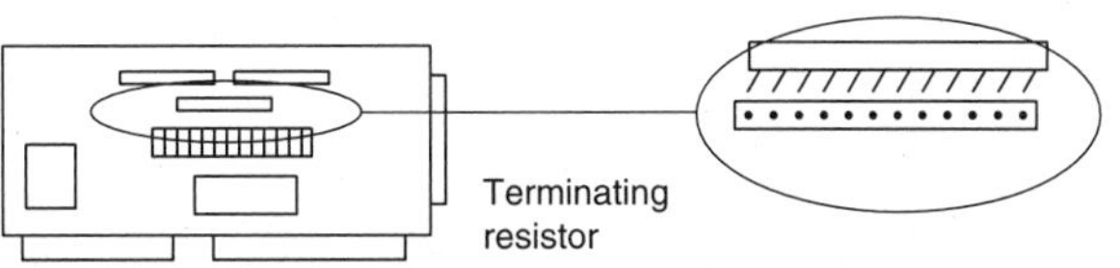

Figure 17.10

SCSI adapter card built-in terminating resistors.

> **Note**
>
> Some external drives have internal termination. In other words, the manufacturer installed terminating resistors, much like the ones installed on the adapter card, onto the drive's IC board inside the drive case. If your drive has internal termination, you must not put a terminator cap on the external connector.

Example Two: Internal Chain and Termination. The same rules apply—all the internal devices must have unique SCSI ID numbers, and the first and last devices must be terminated. In the case of internal devices, however, you must check for termination. Internal devices have terminator packs or resistors similar to the ones installed on your adapter card. If you install a tape unit as the last device on the chain, it must have resistors on its circuit board. If you place your CD-ROM drive in the middle of this chain, its resistors must be removed. The adapter card, at the end of the chain, keeps its resistors intact.

> **Note**
>
> Most internal SCSI devices ship with terminating resistors on board. Check your user's manuals for their locations. Any given device may have one, two, or even three such resistors.

Example Three: Internal and External SCSI Devices. If you mix and match external as well as internal devices, follow the rules. The example shown in figure 17.11 has an internal CD-ROM drive, terminated and set for SCSI ID 6; the external tape unit also is terminated, and we assign it SCSI ID 5. The SCSI adapter itself is set for ID 7, and—most important—its terminating resistor packs have been removed.

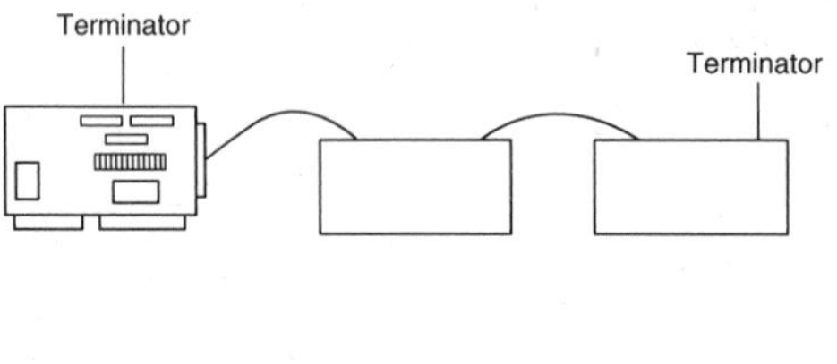

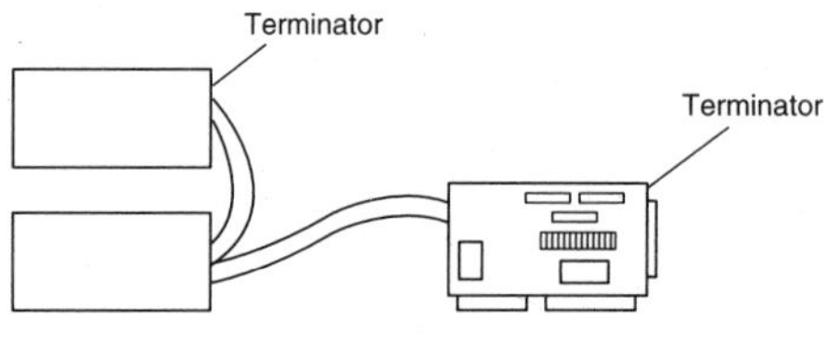

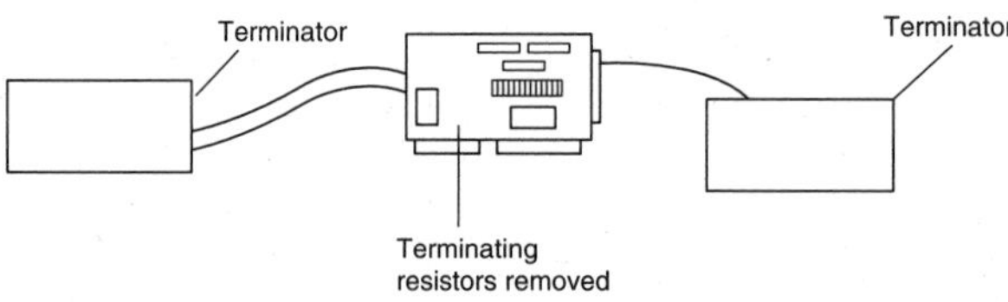

Figure 17.11

Examples of SCSI termination.

> **Note**
>
> As with any adapter card, be careful when handling the card itself. Make sure that you ground yourself first. Chip pullers—specially made tweezers found in most computer tool kits—are especially useful in removing resistor packs from adapter cards and internal peripherals such as CD-ROM drives. The resistor packs have very thin teeth that are easily bent. Once bent, they're tough to straighten out and reinsert, so be careful when removing the packs.

CD-ROM Software on Your PC

After you configure the adapter card correctly, insert it into the PC, and make sure that the drives are connected and terminated properly, you're ready for the last step—installation of the CD-ROM software. The CD-ROM needs the following three software components for it to operate on a PC:

- A SCSI adapter driver (not needed for ATAPI IDE CD-ROM drives). Most popular SCSI adapter drivers are built-in to Windows 95.
- A SCSI driver for the specific CD-ROM drive you've installed. An ASPI driver is built in to Windows 95, as is an ATAPI IDE CD-ROM driver.

- MSCDEX—Microsoft CD Extensions for DOS, which is built in to Windows 95 as the CDFS VxD.

You can have the first two drivers—the SCSI adapter driver and CD-ROM driver—load into your system at startup by placing command lines in your CONFIG.SYS file. The MSCDEX, or DOS extension, is an executable file added into your system through your AUTOEXEC.BAT file.

If you are using Windows 95 along with a CD-ROM drive that conforms to the ATAPI (AT Attachment Packet Interface) IDE specification, there is literally nothing to do. All the driver support for these drives is built in to Windows 95, including the ATAPI driver and the CDFS VxD driver.

If you are running a SCSI CD-ROM drive under Windows 95, you will still need the ASPI (Advanced SCSI Programming Interface) driver that goes with your drive. The ASPI driver for your drive will normally come from the drive manufacturer and is included with the drive in most cases. Windows 95 includes the corresponding ASPI driver for most SCSI host adapters, and also automatically runs the CDFS VxD virtual device driver.

SCSI Adapter Driver. Each SCSI adapter model has a specific driver that allows communications between the PC and the SCSI interface. Normally these drivers conform to the ASPI (Advanced SCSI Programming Interface). The ASPI driver that goes with the drive will connect with the ASPI driver that goes with the SCSI host adapter and allow the adapter and drive to communicate. An ASPI driver should have been provided with your SCSI drive and adapter kit. Documentation should also have been included that walks you through the installation of the software. You can manually add the SCSI device driver to your CONFIG.SYS file as follows:

At the front of the CONFIG.SYS file, add the name and path of the driver with the DEVICE= command:

```
DEVICE=C:\DRIVERS\MYSCSI.SYS
```

C:\DRIVERS is the subdirectory in which you copied the SCSI ASPI device drivers. Some drivers have option switches or added commands that, for example, enable you to view the progress of the driver being loaded.

CD-ROM Device Driver. This driver, as well, should be a part of your basic installation kit. If not, contact the drive's manufacturer for the proper device driver for your SCSI card.

The device driver should come with an installation program that prompts you for the memory I/O address for the SCSI adapter on which you installed your CD-ROM drive. This device driver allows communication with the drive through the SCSI bus to your PC. Installation programs add a line similar to the following to your CONFIG.SYS file:

```
DEVICE=C:\DRIVERS\MYCDROM.SYS /D:mscd001
```

C:\DRIVERS is the subdirectory that contains the driver MYCDROM.SYS, the CD-ROM driver for your specific CD-ROM drive.

Note the /D:mscd001 option after the preceding statement. This designates this CD-ROM driver as controlling the first (001), and only, CD-ROM drive on the system. This portion of the device driver statement is for the Microsoft DOS Extension driver, which designates CD-ROM drives in this fashion.

MSCDEX: Adding CDs to DOS. The Microsoft CD Extensions for DOS allow the DOS operating system to identify and use data from CD-ROMs attached to the system. The original DOS operating system had no provisions for this technology, so "hooks" or handling of this unique media are not a part of the basic operating environment. Using these extensions is convenient for all involved, however. As CD-ROM technology changes, the MSCDEX can be changed, independent of the DOS system. For example, most PhotoCD, multiple session CD-ROM drives require MSCDEX.EXE version 2.21, which has been modified from earlier versions to accommodate the newer CD format.

MSCDEX.EXE should be in your software kit with your drive. If not, you can obtain the latest copy from Microsoft directly. The latest version of the DOS extension also is available on CompuServe in the Microsoft forum. If you are a registered user of the DOS operating system, the MSCDEX is free. Read the licensing agreement that appears on the disk or in your manual concerning the proper licensing of your MSCDEX files.

Your installation software should add a line similar to the following to your AUTOEXEC.BAT file:

```
C:\WINDOWS\MSCDEX.EXE /d:mscd001
```

C:\WINDOWS is the directory in which you copied the MSCDEX.EXE file. The /d:mscd001 portion of the command line tells the MSCDEX extension the DOS name of the device defined in the CD-ROM device driver of your CONFIG.SYS file.

Note

The MSCDEX and CD-ROM device driver names must match. The defaults that most installations provide are used in this example. As long as the two names are the same, the drivers can "find" one another.

Sounds complicated? Don't worry. As long as you have these three drivers—the SCSI adapter driver, the CD-ROM driver, and the DOS CD extensions—loaded properly in your system, the CD-ROM drive will operate as transparently as any other drive in your system.

Table 17.5 lists the options MSCDEX.EXE has that you can add to its command line.

Note that Windows 95 uses a built-in CDFS (CD File System) driver that takes the place of MSCDEX. It is configured through the SYSTEM.DAT registry in Windows 95.

Table 17.5 MSCDEX Command Line Options

Switch	Function
/V	This option is called *Verbose*; lists information about memory allocation, buffers, drive letter assignments, and device driver names on your screen at boot up when this option is added to the command line.
/L: <letter>	Designates which DOS drive letter you will assign the drive. For instance, /L:G assigns the drive letter G: to your CD-ROM drive. Two conditions apply: first, you must not have another drive assigned to that letter; and second, your lastdrive= statement in your CONFIG.SYS file must be equal to or greater than the drive letter you're assigning. LASTDRIVE=G would be fine. LASTDRIVE=F would cause an error if you attempt to assign the CD-ROM drive to the G: drive through the /L: switch.
/M: <buffers>	Enables you to buffer the data from the CD-ROM drive. This is useful if you want faster initial access to the drive's directory. Buffers of 10 to 15 are more than enough for most uses. Any more is overkill. Each buffer, however, is equal to 2K of memory. So a /M:10 buffer argument, for instance, would take 20K of memory. Note that this does not significantly increase the overall performance of the drive, just DOS's initial access to the drive and the access of large data blocks when the drive is gulping down live-motion video, for example. You can't turn a 400 millisecond drive into a speed demon by adding a 200K buffer. With no /M: argument added, MSCDEX will add, as a default, 6 buffers anyway. That may be fine for most PCs and CD-ROM drives.
/E	Loads the aforementioned buffers into DOS high memory, freeing up space in the conventional 640K. Early versions of MSCDEX—anything below version 2.1—does not load into extended memory. You must have DOS 5.0 for this option to load.
/K	Kanji (Japanese) support
/S	Enables you to share your CD-ROM drive on a peer-to-peer network, like Windows for Workgroups

Software Loading

As mentioned earlier, your drive should come with installation software that copies the device driver files to your hard drive and adds the necessary command lines to your CONFIG.SYS and AUTOEXEC.BAT files, or to the SYSTEM.DAT registry file for Windows 95.

When this is accomplished, you can reboot your machine and look for signs that all went smoothly in the software installation.

Following is a series of sample portions of your boot up screens to give you an idea of what messages you'll receive when a given driver is properly loaded into the system.

When you're sure that the software is loaded correctly, try out the drive by inserting a CD into the disc caddy and loading it into the CD-ROM drive. Then get a directory of the disc from the DOS prompt by issuing the following command:

```
DIR/w G:
```

This command gives you a directory of the CD you've inserted, if your CD has been assigned the drive letter G.

You can log in to the CD-ROM drive, just as you would any DOS drive. The only DOS commands not possible on a CD-ROM drive are those that write to the drive. CDs, remember, are media that cannot be overwritten, erased, or formatted.

If you logged into the CD-ROM and received a directory of a sample CD, you're all set.

Now you can power down the PC and replace the cover.

CD-ROM in Microsoft Windows 3.x

When your drive is added to your system, Windows already knows about it through the device drivers and DOS. The CD-ROM drive is accessible through File Manager by double-clicking its file cabinet icon. You see your CD-ROM drive among the drive icons across the top. Windows knows that the drive is a CD-ROM drive is through the DOS extensions discussed earlier.

Media Player. You can set your CD-ROM player to play audio CDs while you are working in Windows. You need to hook up your drive to a sound card and speakers or connect the CD's audio ports to a stereo first. Go to Window's Control Panel and select Drivers. If you do not see [MCI] CD Audio among the files in the driver's list, choose Add. Insert the Windows installation disk that contains the CDAUDIO driver. When the driver appears on the list, exit the Drivers and Control Panel windows.

Double-click on the Media Player icon. Under Devices, select CD. A listing of the track numbers on your audio CD appears along the bottom edge of the media player. The controls on Media Player are similar to those of an audio CD player, including track select, continuous play, and pause (see fig. 17.12).

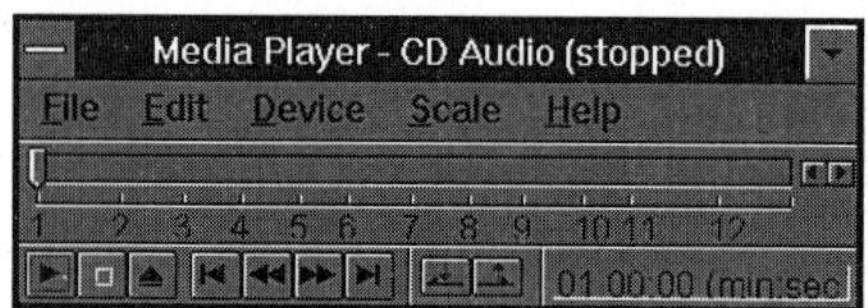

Figure 17.12

The Media Player with an audio CD loaded.

Many drive manufacturer's supply DOS-based CD audio players with their systems. Check your installation manual and software disks for these utilities.

CD-ROM in Windows 95

As stated earlier, Windows 95 includes virtually all the drivers you will need to run your CD-ROM drive, making the software installation automatic. Windows automatically recognizes most IDE CD-ROM drives, and with the addition of the appropriate drive specific ASPI driver, most SCSI CD-ROM drives as well.

There are several new capabilities with CDs in Windows 95. The most dramatic is the Autoplay feature. Autoplay is a feature integrated into Windows 95 that allows you to simply insert a CD into the drive, and Windows will automatically run it without any user intervention. It will also detect whether that particular CD has already been installed on your system, and if not, it will automatically start the install program. If the disc has already been installed, it will start the application program on the disc.

The autoplay feature is simple. When you insert a disc, Windows 95 automatically spins it and looks for a file called AUTORUN.INF. If this file exists, Windows 95 opens it and follows the instructions contained within. As you can see, this autoplay feature will only work on new CDs that have this file. Most software companies are now shipping CD-ROM titles that incorporate the autoplay feature.

CD-Player. Windows 95 includes a new version of the Media Player found in Windows 3.x called the CD-Player. This application allows you to play audio CDs in your drive while you work at the computer. The CD-Player features graphical controls that look like a standard audio CD-ROM drive and even has advanced features found in audio drives like random play, programmable playback order, and the ability to save play list programs.

Troubleshooting CD-ROMs

Some people believe that CD-ROM discs and drives are indestructible compared to their magnetic counterparts. Actually, the modern CD-ROM drive is far less reliable than the modern hard disk! Reliability is the bane of any removable media, and CD-ROMs are no exception.

By far the most common cause of problems with CDs or CD-ROM drives is scratches, dirt or other contamination. Small scratches or fingerprints on the bottom of the disc should not affect performance because the laser focuses on a point inside the actual disk, but dirt or deep scratches can interfere with reading a disc.

To remedy this type of problem, you can clean the bottom surface of the CD with a soft cloth, but be careful not to scratch the surface in the process. The best technique is to wipe the disc in a radial fashion, using strokes that start from the center of the disc and emanate towards the outer edge. This way any scratches will be perpendicular to the tracks rather than parallel to them, minimizing the interference they might cause. You can use any type of solution on the cloth to clean the disc, so long as it will not damage plastic. Most window cleaners are excellent at removing fingerprints and other dirt from the disc, and will not damage the plastic surface.

If there are deep scratches, then often they can be buffed or polished out. I recommend using commercial plastic cleaner like that sold in auto parts stores for cleaning plastic instrument cluster and tail lamp lenses. This type of plastic polish or cleaner has a very mild abrasive that serves to polish scratches out of a plastic surface. Products labeled as cleaners are usually designed for more serious scratches, while those labeled as a polish are usually milder and work well as a final buff after using the cleaner, or can be used alone if the surface is not scratched very deeply.

Read errors can also occur when dust accumulates on the read lens of your CD-ROM drive. You can try to clean out the drive and lens with a blast of "canned air" or by using a CD drive cleaner (which can be purchased at most music stores that sell audio CDs).

If your discs and your drive are clean, and yet you still can't read a particular CD-ROM, then your trouble might be due to disc capacity. Early CD-ROM discs had a capacity of about 550MB (equivalent to about 60 minutes of CD audio). More recently, the capacity of a standard CD has been pushed to 680MB (74 minutes of CD audio). Many older CD-ROM drives are unreliable when they try to read the outermost tracks of newer discs where the last bits of data are stored. You're more likely to run into this problem with a CD that has lots of data—including some Microsoft multimedia titles such as Ancient Lands, Art Gallery, and Complete Baseball. If you have this problem, you may be able to solve it with a firmware or driver upgrade for your CD-ROM drive, but it's possible that the only solution will be to replace the drive.

Sometimes too little data on the disc can be problematic as well. Some older CD-ROM drives use an arbitrary point on the disc's surface to calibrate their read mechanism and if there happens to be no data at that point on the disc, the drive will have problems calibrating successfully. For example, some CD-ROM drives are not able to calibrate successfully with the Microsoft Flight Simulator 5.1 CD-ROM because that disc does not have very much data on it. Fortunately, this problem can usually be corrected by a firmware or driver upgrade for your CD-ROM drive.

Many older drives have had problems in working under Windows 95. If you are having problems, contact your drive manufacturer to see if there is a firmware or software driver upgrade that may take care of your problem. With new quad-speed drives approaching $50 in cost, it may not make sense to spend any time messing with an older drive that is having problems, it would be more cost effective to simply upgrade to a new 4x drive instead!

If you are having problems with only one particular disc, and not the drive in general, then you may find that your difficulties are in fact caused by a defective disc. See if you can exchange the disc for another to determine if that was indeed the cause.

Summary

This chapter should aid you in selecting, installing, and configuring a typical CD-ROM drive in a DOS- or Windows-based PC. When selecting a drive, remember to pay careful attention to drive specifications, drive quality, and other drive features, such as self-cleaning lenses and tray versus caddy operations.

When installing your drive, make sure you follow the manufacturer's recommendations and instructions. What we offer in this chapter is a generic or basic guide for installation and tips on avoiding trouble spots and misconfiguration.

Finally, whenever possible update your SCSI, CD-ROM, and MSCDEX drivers to the latest revisions; these latest versions may increase performance and compatibility with other PC components and software.

Chapter 18

Tape and Other Mass-Storage Drives

The data backup needs on a personal computer can be overwhelming. People with large hard drives with numerous application programs installed, and those who generate a large amount of data, should find it necessary to back up their computers on a weekly or even a daily basis.

In addition, a critical need on today's PCs is data storage space. Sometimes it seems the storage requirements of a PC can never be satisfied. On nearly any PC used for business, study, or even for fun, the amount of software you need to install and the amount of data you need to store can overwhelm what just a short time before was considered a power user's jumbo hard drive.

This chapter focuses on tape backup drives and removable media disk drives, which increasingly are used to solve the problems of the growing need for data storage space and the need for a fast and efficient way to back up many megabytes of data.

Tape Backup Drives

Any computer book worth reading warns repeatedly that you should back up your system regularly. Backups are necessary because at any time a major problem, or even some minor ones, can corrupt the important information and the programs stored on your computer's hard drive, rendering this information useless. A wide range of problems can damage the data on your hard drive. Here is a list of some of these data-damaging problems:

1. Sudden fluctuations in the electricity that powers your computer (power spikes) resulting in data damage or corruption.
2. Overwriting a file by mistake.
3. Mistakenly formatting your hard disk when you meant to format a floppy.

4. Hard drive failure resulting in loss of data that has not been backed up. Not only do you have to install a new drive but, because you have no backup, you also must reinstall your software programs, disk by disk.

5. Catastrophic damage to your computer (storm, flood, lightning strike, fire, theft). A single lightning strike near your office or home can destroy the circuitry of your computer, including your hard drive. Theft of your computer, of course, is equally devastating. A recent, complete, backup greatly simplifies the process of setting up a replacement computer.

Backups are also the cure for such common headaches as a full hard drive and the need to transfer data between computers. By backing up data you rarely use, then deleting the original data from your hard drive, you free up the space once occupied by that data. If you later need a particular data file, you can retrieve that file from your backup. Sharing large amounts of data between computers—as when you send data from one city to another, for example—is more easily accomplished by backing up the data to a tape and sending the tape.

Regardless of how important regular backups are, many people avoid making them. A major reason for this lapse is that for many people, backing up their system is tedious work when they have to use their floppy disk drive. When you use your floppy drive, you may have to insert and remove hundreds of diskettes to back up all of the important programs and data, depending on whether your backup software includes *data compression*, the capability to specially encode backed up data in less space than it takes to store the same data on your hard drive.

Tape backup drives are the most simple and efficient device for backing up your system. With a tape backup drive installed in your system, you simply insert a tape into the drive, start your backup software, and select the drive and files you want to back up. The backup software copies your selected files onto the tape while you attend to other business. Later, when you need to retrieve some or all of the files on the backup tape, you insert the tape in the drive, start your backup program, and select the files you want to restore. The tape backup drive takes care of the rest of the job.

This section examines the various types of tape backup drives on the market, describing the capacities of different drives as well as the system requirements for installation and use of a tape drive. The following topics are covered in this section:

- Common standards for tape backup drives, including QIC-40 and QIC-80 drives
- Common backup tape capacities
- Newer higher-capacity tape drives
- Common tape drive interfaces
- The QIC standards for tape backup drives
- Portable tape drives
- Tape backup software

The Origins of Tape Backup Standards

The evolution of tape backup standards is similar to that of standards for many computer components. Using tape to back up computer data became a common practice long before accepted tape backup standards existed. At first, reel-to-reel systems (somewhat similar to old reel-to-reel audio tape recorders) were used to store data. The most commonly used tape—quarter-inch—eventually developed into a de facto standard. But each tape system manufacturer used its own data-encoding specifications for backup tapes. Variations included not only the number of tracks and data density on the tape, but also the interface used to connect the drive to the computer.

In 1972, more than a decade before the introduction of the first IBM-PC, the 3M company introduced the first quarter-inch tape cartridge designed for data storage. The cartridge measured 6 inches by 4 inches by 5/8 inch. Inside this cartridge, the tape was threaded onto two reels. The tape was moved from one reel to another during the recording or read-back process by a drive belt. Because of the reliability of this tape cartridge, the demand for tape backup systems began to grow, despite the lack of established standards for storing data on these cartridges.

The result of this lack of standardization was that quarter-inch tapes written on one manufacturer's tape backup drive generally could not be read on another manufacturer's quarter-inch tape drive. One problem created by this situation was that the way particular manufacturers encoded data on a tape continued to change. If a particular model of tape drive became disabled and the manufacturer had discontinued that particular drive and no longer used its encoding format, the data stored on tapes written on the disabled drive could be unavailable until the drive had been sent for repairs. In the event the manufacturer could not repair the drive, the data was lost forever.

As with other computer components, such as hard drive interface cards, consumers were the force behind standardization. Consumers clamored for standardized tape drives that could read tapes created on different tape drives manufactured by different companies.

The QIC Standards

In response to this demand for standardization, the tape drive industry formed the Quarter-Inch Cartridge Drive Standards Inc., sometimes simply referred to as the Quarter-Inch Committee (QIC). In 1983–84, the first tape drive based on a QIC standard was shipped—the QIC-02, which stored 60M of data encoded in 9 data tracks on roughly 300 feet of tape.

As the technology improved, and because the 4-by-6-by-5/8-inch size of the first tape cartridges was difficult to adapt to the 5 1/2-inch drive bays in most IBM-compatible personal computers, QIC adopted a second standard for tape cartridges roughly the size of an audio cassette. These minicartridges measure roughly 3 1/4-by-2 1/2-by-3/5 inches.

These two cartridge sizes are currently used in various QIC-standard tape drives. A two-letter code at the end of the QIC standard number designates whether the tape standard is based on the full-sized cartridge or the minicartridge. These two-letter codes are shown in the following:

- DC in a QIC standard number stands for data cartridge, the 4-by-6-by-5/8-inch cassette.
- MC in a QIC standard number stands for minicartridge, the 3 1/4-by-2 1/2-by-3/5-inch cassette.

The new QIC-5B-DC, for example, is a 5G-capacity tape based on the QIC standard for the full-sized cartridge. The new QIC-5010-MC, which has 13G capacity, is based on the minicartridge standard.

Table 18.1 shows the common QIC-standard tape formats and their technical specifications.

Table 18.1 Specifications of QIC-Standard Quarter-inch Tape Cassettes and Minicartridges

QIC Minicartridge Tape Standards

DC-2000 QIC Tape Standards (Approximate Dimensions 3 1/4-by-2 1/2-by-3/5)

QIC Standard Number	Capacity (w/o Compression) (1)	Tracks	Data Transfer Rate (Approximate)
QIC-40	40MB/60MB	20	2MB-to-8MB minute
QIC-80	80MB/120MB	28	3MB-to-9MB minute
QIC-100 (obsolete)	20MB/40MB	12 or 24	—
QIC-128	86MB/128MB	32	—
QIC-3010	255MB	40	9MB minute
QIC-3020	500MB	40	9MB minute
QIC-3030	555MB	40	
QIC-3040	840MB (3)	42 or 52	
QIC-3050	750MB	40	
QIC-3060 (inactive)	875MB	38	
QIC-3070	4GB	144	
QIC-3080	1.6GB	50	
QIC-3110	2GB	48	
QIC-5010	13GB	144	
QIC-11 (DC-300)	45MB	9	—
QIC-24	45MB/60MB	9	—

(1) Tape capacity may vary according to tape length.
(2) Tape lengths may vary by manufacturer.
(3) 1GB with drives based on 0.315-inch tape cartridge.
(4) SCSI: Small Computer Systems Interface.

Unlike software whose version numbers (1.0, 1.1, 2.0, 2.1) tell you which version of the software is the most recent, the QIC number designation does not serve as an accurate guide to understanding which QIC-standard tape drives are the latest technology. The designations QIC-100 and QIC-128, for example, were used for tape drives marketed long before today's QIC-40 and QIC-80 drives. Furthermore, the QIC-standard version numbers frequently have no correlation with the capacity of the tape cassettes or mini-cartridges used with a drive bearing a QIC designation. For example, the QIC-40 tapes have a capacity of 60M; the QIC-80 tapes have a capacity of 120M.

QIC-standard backup tapes are magnetic media, primarily ferric oxide, and are recorded in a manner similar to the way data is encoded on your hard drive, using either modified frequency modulation (MFM) or run-length limited (RLL) technologies.

Data Density	Tape Length (2)	Encoding Method	Interface Type
10,000bpi	205 ft. /307.5 ft.	MFM adapter card	Floppy or optional
14,700bpi	205 ft./ 307.5 ft.	MFM	Floppy or optional adapter card
10,000bpi	—	MFM	SCSI (4) or QIC
16,000bpi	—	MFM	SCSI or QIC
22,000bpi	300 ft.	MFM	Floppy or IDE
42,000bpi	400 ft.	MFM	Floppy or IDE
51,000bpi	275 ft.	MFM	SCSI-2 or QIC
41,000bpi	400 ft.	RLL	SCSI-2 or QIC
—	295 ft.	RLL	SCSI-2 or QIC
—	295 ft.	RLL	—
68,000	295 ft.	RLL	SCSI-2 or QIC
60,000	—	RLL	SCSI-2 or QIC
—	—	RLL	SCSI-2 or QIC
—	—	RLL	SCSI-2 or QIC
—	450 ft.	MFM	QIC-02
8,000	450 ft. 600 ft.	MFM	SCSI or QIC-02

(continues)

Table 18.1 Continued
QIC Minicartridge Tape Standards
DC-2000 QIC Tape Standards (Approximate Dimensions 3 1/4-by-2 1/2-by-3/5)

QIC Standard Number	Capacity (w/o Compression)	Tracks	Data Transfer Rate (Approximate)
QIC-120	125MB	15	—
QIC-150	150MB/250MB	18	—
QIC-525	320MB/525MB	26	12MB minute
QIC-1000	1GB	30	18MB minute
QIC-1350	1.35GB	30	18MB minute
QIC-2100	2.1GB	30	18MB minute
QIC-2GB	2.0GB	42	18MB minute
QIC-5GB	5GB	44	18MB minute
QIC-5010	13GB	144	18MB minute

(1) Tape capacity may vary according to tape length.
(2) Tape lengths may vary by manufacturer.

Common QIC Tape Backup Types

The most common QIC-standard drives, QIC-40 and QIC-80, are based on minicartridges. Millions of drives based on the QIC-40 and QIC-80 standards are currently installed in computer systems. There are several reasons for the success of QIC-40 and QIC-80, not the least of which is that these two standards resulted in the first generation of economically attractive tape drives which stored data in a manner compatible from one manufacturer to another. In other words, QIC-40 and QIC-80 tape drives and tapes are quite affordable, and backups made on one QIC-40 or QIC-80 tape drive can be read in a tape drive built by another manufacturer.

In addition, the compact size of the minicartridge used for QIC-40 and QIC-80 tapes has resulted in drives made by numerous manufacturers that fit easily into both 5 1/2-inch half-height drive bays and 3 1/2-by-1-inch drive bays. Portable tape drives that read and write QIC-40 and QIC-80 format tapes are quite common. Unlike a drive that is installed in a computer's drive bay, portable drives can be used to back up any number of computers.

Another reason for the success of QIC-40 and QIC-80 tape drives is that the cost of tapes themselves is considerably lower per megabyte than the cost of a stack of floppy disks that can store the same amount of backup data. For example, a name brand QIC-80 tape that can hold 250M of data (with data compression) costs between $14 and $25. The street price of 13 boxes (of 10) name brand 1.44M 3 1/2-inch floppy disks, which hold roughly the same amount of compressed data, is about $90. The same number of generic,

Data Density	Tape Length (2)	Encoding Method	Interface Type
10,000	600 ft.	MFM	SCSI or QIC-02
10,000bpi	600 ft. 1,000 ft.	MFM	SCSI or QIC-02
16,000bpi	1,000 ft.	MFM	SCSI or SCSI-2
36,000bpi	760 ft.	MFM	SCSI or SCSI-2
51,000bpi	760 ft.	RLL	SCSI-2
68,000bpi	875 ft.	RLL	SCSI-2
40,640bpi	900 ft.	MFM	SCSI-2
96,000bpi	1,200 ft.	RLL	SCSI-2
68,000bpi	—	RLL	SCSI-2

bulk floppy disks, which many people are hesitant to rely upon for backing up important data, costs nearly $50.

One major shortcoming of QIC-40 or QIC-80 tape drives is that the use of the floppy drive interface, especially on an older PC, makes the tape drive performance extremely slow. Data transfers occur at roughly the same slow rate as when data is written to a floppy disk. Controllers that support only the Double Density (DD) floppy drives can only write data at 250 Kbps (K bits per second), which is less than 2M (Millions of bytes) per minute. A floppy controller that supports HD (High Density) drives can operate at 300 or 500 Kbps, which is up to 3.75M per minute. The latest ED (Extra-high Density) controllers can operate at rates of up to 7.5M per minute, which is quite good (see table 18.2). Notice that these rates are the maximum raw throughput of the controller, and due to overhead, you will never achieve these actual figures in practice.

Table 18.2 Floppy Controller Raw Data Transfer Rates

Controller Type	DD	HD	HD	ED
Transfer rate in K bits per second (Kbps)	250	300	500	1,000
Transfer rate in K Bytes per second (KBps)	31.25	37.50	62.50	125.00
Transfer rate in M Bytes per second (M/s)	1.88	2.25	3.75	7.50

Backup tapes, like floppy disks and hard drives, must be formatted before use. And one aspect of using a QIC-40 or QIC-80 tape drive that has not been improved is the time it takes to format a tape. Formatting a 60M-length QIC-40 tape can take quite a long time—90 minutes or more. Formatting a 125M length QIC-80 tape can take more than three hours. You can buy preformatted tapes but, as is true with many timesaving products, formatted tapes do cost slightly more than unformatted ones.

Data is stored on QIC-40 and QIC-80 tapes in Modified Frequency Modulation (MFM) format, the format used on floppy disks (and older hard drives). Another similarity between formatting a backup tape, floppy disks, or a hard drive is that the formatting process creates a record-keeping system. The record-keeping system used on QIC-40 and QIC-80 tapes is similar to that on a hard drive or floppy disk.

The QIC standard calls for a file allocation table (FAT) that keeps track of where data is stored on the tape and keeps bad sectors from being used for data storage. A QIC-40 tape is divided into 20 tracks, with each track divided into 68 segments of 29 sectors each. Each sector stores one kilobyte (1,024 bytes). This record-keeping system and the error-correcting system that ensures reliably stored backup data use a total of 30 percent or more of each QIC-40 tape.

Despite the slow backup speeds of tape backup drives on some computers and the time it takes to format tapes, the ease of using a backup tape drive makes it easy to understand the popularity of QIC-40 and QIC-80 tape drives. And that popularity has its benefits. Prices of QIC-80 tape drives—the smallest-capacity tape drives anyone should consider—have plunged in recent years. Brand name QIC-80 tape backup drives often cost less than $150; sometimes you can buy them for as little as $100 by shopping mail order.

QIC-40 Drives. The first tape backup drives to gain wide acceptance were based on the QIC-40 standard, adopted in 1986. Most early QIC-40 tape drives were built to fit a 5 1/2-inch drive bay, although models designed for 3 1/2-by-1-inch bays became available. The QIC-40-standard drives use an internal power connector and send and receive data through a cable linked to the floppy controller. The first QIC-40 tapes, which had a *native capacity* of 40M (they could hold 40M of data without data compression), were soon followed by QIC-40 tapes capable of holding 60M without data compression.

One disadvantage of the first QIC-40 tape drives was that, because a spare connector had to be used on the floppy drive cable, only one floppy drive could be used on a system in which a tape drive was installed. But with the use of a special cable, more recent QIC-40 drives are easily installed on systems with two floppy drives.

Although a major goal of the QIC organization was to achieve compatibility between tape backup systems, a tape created on one brand of tape drive could not necessarily be read in another brand. Manufacturers still clung to their individual arrangements for the physical placement of data on the tape. The goal of compatibility between tape backup systems became more of a reality with the introduction of QIC-80 drives.

QIC-80 Drives. The QIC-80 tape backup drive is the most popular tape backup drive on the market and the minimum any buyer should consider. QIC-80 tape drives generally are built to fit 3 1/2-by-1-inch bays, although they usually include a frame and faceplate that enable them to be used in a larger 5 1/2-inch bay. Like the QIC-40 drives, QIC-80 tape systems use an internal power connector. The data connection for a QIC-80 tape backup can be the same type of floppy disk controller connection used for QIC-40 drives or a special high-speed interface installed in an available expansion slot on the motherboard. The use of a high-speed interface card can greatly increase the data transfer rate and decrease the amount of time needed for a backup.

Generally, a tape created on one brand of QIC-80 tape drive can be read and written to by another manufacturer's drive. This improved compatibility is due in large measure to the QIC-80 standard itself, which specifies not only the type of record-keeping system for each tape, but also the logical data structure of the tape. QIC-80-standard drives can read, but not write, QIC-40 tapes.

Portable Tape Drives. The portable tape drive is one of the most popular tape drive configurations because portables can be moved easily from system to system—desktops, laptops, a single system, or multisystem installations. Portable tape drives are particularly useful to people who use laptops (in which an internal tape backup drive will not fit) and those who want to back up a number of systems on a single tape backup drive. Portable tape drives are good also for people who want to use a tape backup drive for their desktop system but whose system has no available drive bay, as is often the case with small profile, or slim-line, desktop systems.

Portable tape drives can meet so many needs because these drives are self-contained. The drive itself is contained in a rectangular box. The unit connects to the computer's parallel port and is powered by a transformer that plugs into a common AC socket.

To set up a portable tape drive, you simply plug the transformer cord into the system unit and an AC socket, connect the data cable to the computer's parallel port, and run the backup software. One limitation of portable units is availability of compatible backup software. Although portable tape drive manufacturers include software that operates the drive, some popular third-party backup software cannot be used with portable drives.

The most popular portable tape drives are available in QIC-40 and QIC-80 standards. The QIC-40 models ordinarily can achieve a data transfer rate of 1M to 3M per minute; the QIC-80 models, a rate of 3M to 6M per minute.

Newer High-Capacity QIC-Standard Drives

Using a QIC-40 or QIC-80 tape drive to back up a network server's 4B drive or other large hard drive packed with data can be as frustrating as swapping floppies during a backup on a system with a more common 200M–500M drive. To back up a 4G network server hard drive with a QIC-40 tape drive without using data compression, for example, you need about 64 tapes. With data compression, the number of tapes drops to 32—but making the backup takes longer.

The solution to this tape-swapping problem is to use a larger-capacity tape drive system. QIC has established a number of standards for higher-capacity tape drive systems ranging from 86M to 13G. Generally, these larger-capacity systems pack data more densely on the tape, using as many as 144 tracks to pack 60,000 bits per inch (bpi) or more onto the tape (compared to the QIC-40's 20 tracks and 10,000 bpi). To achieve these higher capacities, QIC-standards call for tape media with a higher coercivity level of 1,300 oersted or more (compared to QIC-40 and QIC-80 tape media, which has a coercivity level of 550 oersted). High-capacity tapes are also longer. QIC-5010 tapes, for example, are 1,200 feet long (compared to QIC-40 and QIC-80 tapes, both of which are roughly 300 feet long).

Note

Just as the higher coercivity level of 1.44M floppy disks enables a high-density drive to write more densely packed tracks than is possible with 720K floppy disks, higher-coercivity tape media enables higher densities as well.

Although tape systems based on the minicartridge dominate the market for lower capacity tape drives (the QIC-40 60M and QIC-80 120M systems), high-capacity tape backup systems are based on both minicartridge-sized tapes and full-sized data cartridge tapes. For example, the QIC-525 standard, which has a capacity of 525M (without data compression), is based on the full-sized (4-by-6-by-5/8) cartridge. The QIC-5010 standard is based on a minicartridge (3 1/4-by-2 1/2-by-3/5).

QIC-Tape Compatibility

Although QIC-standard drives are based on the standard minicartridge and the full-sized data cartridge, it would be a mistake to assume that tapes based on the same cartridge standard are always compatible. For example, QIC-5010-standard tapes are incompatible with QIC-40 and QIC-80 tape backup systems, although both standards are based on the minicartridge. Similarly, QIC-525-standard tapes are incompatible with earlier standards based on the full-sized data cartridge. The lack of compatibility between tapes based on the same sized cartridge is due to differences in tape drive mechanisms, as well as the coercivity differences between tape standards. Table 18.3 shows the compatibility of common QIC-standard backup tapes.

Table 18.3. QIC-Tape-Standard Compatibility

QIC Minicartridge Standard	Compatibility
QIC-40	—
QIC-80	QIC-40 (read-only)
QIC-100	—
QIC-128	QIC-100 (read-only)
QIC-3010	QIC-40 and QIC-80 (read only)
QIC-3030	QIC-3010 (read-only)
QIC-3070	QIC-3030 (read-only)

QIC Full-Sized Cartridge Standard	Compatibility
QIC-24	—
QIC-120	QIC-24 (read-only)
QIC-150	QIC-24 and QIC-120 (read-only)
QIC-525	QIC-24, QIC-120, and QIC-150 (read-only)
QIC-1000	QIC-120, QIC-150, and QIC-525 (read-only)
QIC-1350	QIC-525 and QIC-1000 (read-only)
QIC-2G	QIC-120, QIC-150, QIC-525, and QIC-1000 (read-only)
QIC-2100	QIC-525 and QIC-1000 (read-only)
QIC-5G	QIC-24, QIC-120, QIC-150, QIC-525, and QIC-1000 (read-only)
QIC-5010	QIC-150, QIC-525, and QIC-1000 (read-only)

Tape compatibility is an important issue to consider when you choose a tape backup system. For example, as you can see from table 18.3, the 4G QIC-3070-standard drive can read only its own tapes and those that conform to the QIC-3030 standard. If you have many QIC-80 tapes containing data you must be able to continue to access, a better choice might be a drive based on the 2G QIC-3010 standard. The QIC-3010 can read QIC-40 and QIC-80 tapes. This chapter's "Choosing a Tape Backup Type" section covers similar issues to be considered when you purchase a new tape backup drive.

Other High-Capacity Tape Drive Standards

Although ferric oxide QIC-standard tapes continue to be popular, two other types of tape backup systems are becoming increasingly popular for backing up networks and other systems with large amounts of data: 4mm digital audio tape (DAT) and 8mm videotape.

Sony, which introduced both DAT tape and 8mm videotape, licenses DAT tape technologies to other manufacturers, in effect setting the standard for drives and tapes manufactured by those companies. Because the 8mm tape backup drive technologies have been developed by a variety of manufacturers, there is no recognized 8mm standard. For that reason, a QIC-standard or DAT tape drive might be a better choice for most potential buyers of backup tape systems. Table 18.4 shows the basic specifications of the DAT and 8mm technology tapes.

Helical scan recording is similar in many ways to the way video images are recorded to videotape. As with QIC-standard tape drives, DAT and 8mm tapes move past the recording heads, which are mounted on a drum. These read/write heads rotate at a slight angle to the tape, writing a section of a *helix*, or spiral. The tape drive mechanism wraps the tape about half way around the read/write heads, causing the heads to touch the tape at an angle. With helical scan technology, the entire surface of the tape is used to record data, unlike other technologies in which data tracks are separated by areas of unrecorded tape. This use of the entire tape surface enables helical scan backup drives to pack a much greater amount of data on a particular length of tape.

Table 18.4 DAT and 8mm Tape Specifications

Tape Standard	Capacity (w/o Compression)	Data Density	Tracks (Approximate)
DAT tape (4mm metal particle)	2G/4G	114 megabits	1,869
8mm video tape (Sony-standard)	10G	NA	NA

(1)DDS: digital data storage

The DAT Tape Drive Standard. DAT (Digital Audio Tape) is a tape standard that has primarily been developed and marketed by Hewlett Packard. HP chairs the DDS (Digital Data Storage) Manufacturers Group, and has led the development of the DDS standards.

The technology behind digital audio tape is similar in many ways to the techniques used to record music and encode it on musical compact discs (CDs). Data is not recorded on the tape in the MFM or RLL formats used by QIC-standard drives; rather, bits of data received by the tape drive are assigned numerical values, or digits. Then these digits are translated into a stream of electronic pulses that are placed in the tape. Later, when information is being restored to a computer system from the tape, the DAT tape drive translates these digits back into binary bits that can be stored on the computer.

DAT is a helical scan technology, which means that the heads rotate and record strips of information on the tape at an angle as the tape passes across the heads. This allows for a very high capacity with accuracy and reliability.

DAT tapes can store up to 12G of uncompressed data, or about 24G compressed. Two types of data formats—digital data storage (DDS) and DataDAT—are used for DAT tapes; however, DDS type drives are by far the most common. DDS drives are available in three types, DDS-1, DDS-2, and DDS-3. DDS-1 drives store 2G of uncompressed data (4G compressed) should be; DDS-2 drives can store 4G of data uncompressed (up to 8G with compression), while DDS-3 drives have a native 12M capacity, or 24M compressed. Both the DDS-2 and DDS-3 drives are what I usually recommend for tape backup as they are proven technology and offer a great deal of performance for the dollar.

The new DDS-3 drives offer full read and write compatibility with all DDS-2 and DDS-1 drives. DDS-3 offers three times the capacity and double the data-transfer rates of current DDS-2 drives. DDS-3 drives are designed to provide reliable high-performance backup for medium to large networks at a substantially lower price than 8mm or DLT (digital linear tape) products with similar capacities.

The new HP DDS-3 drive (Model C1537A) has a native capacity of 12G with a transfer rate of 1M/second. The DDS-3 drive typically can store 24G on a single 125m tape at a rate of 2M/second using built-in hardware data compression. The new HP DDS-3 drive incorporates several innovations, including the use of a partial response maximum likelihood (PRML) data-channel detection scheme that allows the tape's read head to differentiate between bits of data picked up simultaneously.

Tape Length	Recording Technology	Encoding Format	Interface
195 ft./300 ft.	Helical Scan DataDAT	DDS, (1)	SCSI
2-hour video	Helical Scan /proprietary	NTSC	Proprietary

A typical DDS-2 drive costs about $750 while DDS-3 drives are right around $1,000. DDS technology has an excellent track record and a reputation for reliability that has made it the technology of choice for workstation, end user, and network backup.

The 8mm Tape Drive. A single manufacturer, Exabyte, offers tape backup drives that take advantage of 8mm videotape cartridges. These drives are offered in two capacities—1.5G (3G with hardware data compression), for the least expensive drives, and 5G (10G with hardware compression) for the more expensive models. Although these drives use 8mm videotapes, video technology is not used in the process of recording computer data to these drives. Rather, Exabyte developed its own technology for encoding data on the tapes. The helical scan method is used to record data to the tape.

The highest capacity 8mm tape backup drives are somewhat expensive. For example, one hardware vendor specializing in network hardware recently offered the 5G to 10G capacity Exabyte 8505i half-height internal drive for $2,265. That might seem expensive when the Exabyte drive is compared, gigabyte for gigabyte, with the 2G (4G with software data compression) Colorado Memory Systems PowerDAT 6000 tape drive, offered by the same vendor for $1,295.

But the 30M per minute data throughput rate of the Exabyte 8mm tape backup drive, compared with the 10M per minute throughput of the DAT drive, makes the 8mm tape drive a more attractive choice. The extraordinary speed and huge capacity of these 8mm tape drives makes them extremely attractive for backing up network servers and for backing up workstations from the server.

DLT (Digital Linear Tape). Over the last year, a new tape technology has taken off because of its capability to provide high-capacity, high-speed, and highly reliable backup. Digital linear tape (DLT) is now considered one of the hottest products in the high-end tape-backup market. DLT started as a proprietary technology belonging to Digital Equipment Corp. The technology has been on the market since 1991; but in December 1994, Quantum purchased Digital's DLT and magneto-resistive drive technology.

DLT has a capacity of up to 20G to 40G compressed, and a data-transfer rate of 1.5M to 3M per second or more. This is as much as four times the capacity and speed of traditional 8mm or DAT tape products.

DLT segments the tape into parallel horizontal tracks and records data by streaming the tape across a single stationary head at 100 inches to 150 inches per second during read/write operations. This is a dramatic contrast to traditional helical-scan technology, in which the data is recorded in diagonal stripes with a rotating drum head while a much slower tape motor draws the media past the recording head.

The result is a very durable drive and a robust medium. DLT drive heads have a minimum life expectancy of 15,000 hours under worst-case temperature and humidity conditions, and the tapes have a life expectancy of 500,000 passes. DLT drives are designed primarily for network server backup and cost $6,000 to $8,000 or more, depending on capacity. With automatic tape changers, DLT drives can be left unattended for many network backup tasks. I expect to see DLT drives and tapes become more popular mainly as a replacement for 8mm drives used in network server applications.

Travan Cartridge Tape. 3M has created an entirely new tape cartridge standard based on the QIC format called Travan. Tape drives based on Travan technology will have a significant impact on the tape market for PCs and workstations and drives based on this technology will dominate this market over the next several years.

The Travan platform features a unique drive/minicartridge interface that is patented by 3M. The Travan platform fits in a 3.5-inch form factor, making it easy to install in a variety of systems and enclosures. Travan drives can accept current QIC and Travan minicartridges—a critical need for users, given the installed base of more than 200 million QIC-compatible minicartridges worldwide.

Travan cartridges contain 750 feet of .315-inch wide tape. There are currently several different levels of Travan cartridges and drives available called TR-1 through TR-4, each based on a particular QIC standard. The TR-1 minicartridge provides users with 400M of uncompressed storage, more than doubling the capacity of the industry's top-selling QIC-80 minicartridge (125M). The TR-2 minicartridge, a new modified QIC-3010 drive/cartridge, stores 800M of uncompressed data, which is significantly more than the 340M available in QIC-3010 form. The capacity of the TR-3 minicartridge, a new modified 3020 drive/cartridge, is 1.6G of uncompressed data (up from 670M in QIC-3020 form). The newest Travan cartridge, TR-4, stores 4G of uncompressed data! The Travan migration path for the new drive and minicartridge products should exceed 15 gigabytes (G) of uncompressed storage capacity by 1997, according to 3M.

Notice that virtually all Travan drives offer 2:1 data compression, which doubles the uncompressed native capacity. This means that a Travan TR-4 drive can store up to 8G on a single cartridge! A typical TR-4 based drive, like those from HP/Colorado sell for under $400. Because Travan tapes sell in the $40 price range and are available through any of 3M's worldwide network of distributors and resellers, the low cost and high availability of these drives and cartridges make Travan one of the best backup solutions possible for most individuals.

The TR-1 through TR-3 drives usually interface to the system via the floppy controller or parallel port. I recommend using an EPP or ECP parallel port for ease of use and performance. The higher end TR-4 drives often use a SCSI-2 interface, which offers greater performance than either floppy or parallel port interfaces. A typical TR-4 system such as the HP T4000 drive operates at 514K/second, which is approximately four times faster than floppy-interface systems, providing backup speeds up to 31M/minute native and up to 62M/minute with 2:1 data compression. Using a typical Pentium system, users can back up a 1G hard drive in about 30 minutes. If you are using the floppy controller or parallel port, you can expect backup times about four times longer or about two hours for a 1G drive.

Storage industry leaders like 3M, Hewlett Packard's Colorado Memory Systems Division, Conner Peripherals, Exabyte, Iomega, Tandberg Data, AIWA, Pertec Memories, TEAC, Rexon, and Sony offer Travan drives and support future development of Travan drive and recording formats.

Choosing a Tape Backup Drive

Choosing a tape backup drive can be a simple job if you need to back up a single stand-alone system with a 500M (or smaller) hard drive. The decision becomes more complex if the system has a larger hard drive or if you must back up not only a desktop system, but also a laptop. Choosing a backup tape drive type can be an even more complex program if you must back up a network server's 4G hard drive and perhaps even back up the workstations from the server. As you ponder which backup tape drive type you should choose, consider the following factors:

- The amount of data you must back up
- The data throughput you need
- The tape standard that is best for your needs
- The cost of the drive and tapes

By balancing the considerations of price, capacity, throughput, and tape standard, you can find a tape drive that best meets your needs.

> **Note**
>
> When purchasing a tape backup drive, take the time to look through magazines where dealers or distributors advertise. Several publications specialize in PCs and carry advertising from many hardware and software distributors. I recommend publications like the *Computer Reseller News, Computer Hotline*, the *Processor*, and the *Computer Shopper*. These publications cater to people or companies willing to go around the middlemen and buy more direct. By reading such publications, you can get an excellent idea of the drives available and the price you can expect to pay.

Capacity. The first rule for choosing a tape backup drive is to buy a drive whose capacity is large enough for your needs, now and for the foreseeable future. The ideal is to buy a drive with enough capacity that you can start your backup software, insert a blank tape in the drive, walk away from the system (or go about other work), and find the backup completed when you return. You can safely store the tape and resume working.

Given that ideal, an internal QIC-80 drive might be just the ticket if you need to back up a single system with a hard drive of 250M or less. If you need to back up several systems, including laptops, with hard drives of 250M or less, a portable QIC-80 drive might be the solution.

But if you must back up a large network server hard drive, relying on a QIC-80 tape drive with its 125M capacity (250M with software data compression) is a bad idea. A better choice would be one of the larger-capacity tape backup drive systems detailed earlier in this chapter.

Lately, no matter what the capacity, I have been recommending either DAT drives or the newer Travan drives. These are simply the most cost effective, highest performing drives on the market today. The tapes are pre-formatted, which saves a lot of time, and can store up to 8G on a single Travan TR-4 tape or 24G on a single DDS-3 DAT tape. You should always make sure that your tape backup media supports a capacity larger than your largest single drive or partition. This will make automated backups possible since you won't have to change a tape in the middle of a backup. Since the DAT drives normally interface via SCSI, you can use a parallel port SCSI adapter to connect the drive to a system's parallel port as well as an internal SCSI adapter. Of course the internal adapter will perform better, but a portable DAT drive connected via the parallel port can be used to back up many different systems. The DAT media is also cheaper than any other media, and is more reliable as well. All in all, I would say that because of its reliability, low cost, and excellent track record, DAT is the tape backup solution I normally recommend for most situations.

Tape Standards. The next most important consideration, after adequate capacity, is choosing a drive whose tapes meet a standard that is useful to you. For example, if you must be able to restore backup data using any of a number of different tape backup drives, you should ensure that all these drives can at least read the tapes. For this reason, if you have several systems to work with, you should choose a tape standard that will work in them all.

There is no quick, simple answer as to which standard is the best. Many people stick with QIC-standard drives because QIC created the first standards and continues to develop new standards for large-capacity tape backups. But if you need a large-capacity backup tape system, DAT or 8mm may be the correct choice.

If you need backward compatibility with tapes or tape drives you already have, you will need to buy drives that are the same standard or a higher compatible standard. For example, if you need a large-capacity tape drive that is backwardly compatible with your QIC-80 tapes, you should consider the 2G-capacity QIC-3010, which reads QIC-40 and QIC-80 tapes. If, on the other hand, you don't have to worry about data already stored on old tapes, the important considerations may be capacity and performance. Therefore, DAT or 8mm drives may be the best choice.

It is important that you make a choice you can live with. If you manage a large installation of computers, mixing QIC, Travan, DAT, and 8mm drives among systems is seldom a good idea.

Data Throughput. You should consider the 8mm drives if performance is more important to you than price or compatibility. These drives offer huge capacity and tremendous data throughput—as high as 30M per minute. Large-capacity drives based on newer QIC-standards are capable of 18M per minute throughput. DAT tape drives offer throughput of 10M per minute.

The low end of the tape backup drive performance spectrum is older QIC-80 standard drives. When linked to a floppy controller, these drives achieve 3M to 4M per minute throughput. Even with a dedicated interface card purchased at added cost, QIC-80 drives are lucky to achieve their advertised throughput of 9M per minute. Portable QIC-80 drives are advertised at 3M to 8M per minute, but 2M or 3M a minute is a more realistic figure.

The Cost of the Drive and Tapes. The price of tape drives varies considerably based upon where you buy, so it pays to shop enthusiastically for price after you have settled on the type of drive you want to buy.

The cost of backup tapes also varies widely, depending on where you buy. The same name brand 12G DAT tape that costs as much as $14 from one vendor can cost $12 from another. The cost of a formatted name brand QIC-80 (120M) tape can range from $15 to $26, depending on where you buy it. Because many computer retailers and direct channel vendors offer lower prices when you buy three or more tapes at a time, it pays to shop for price and buy the largest quantity of tapes you expect to need.

One point worth remembering when you evaluate whether to buy a tape drive is that the cost of the tapes and drive, taken as a whole, is nowhere near as high as the costs (in terms of frustration and lost productivity) of a single data-damaging hard drive problem. Considering that most people are more likely to back up their system if they have a tape drive installed than if they must use floppy disks for the backup, the cost of a drive and tapes is quite small, even on a stand-alone PC used mostly for fun.

Tape Drive Installation Issues

Each of the tape drive standards covered in this chapter provides a range of options for installation. These options include both internal and external installation. Whether to choose an internal or external drive, and which external drive to choose if that appears to be the best choice for you, is not always a cut-and-dried issue. If you must back up a single computer with a relatively small hard drive (500M or less), an internal QIC-80 drive might be your best choice. If you have to back up several computers with 500M hard drives, or if you must be able to share data between several computers, you might be able to make do with a QIC-80 portable. If your backup needs are not that simple, however, here are some additional considerations:

- If your computer has a large hard drive and you back up often, or if you administer a large number of systems and want to minimize the amount of work you must do and the number of tapes you have to store for each computer, installing large-capacity QIC, DAT, or 8mm tape drives in each computer might be what you need to do.

- If your best choice is a large capacity QIC, DAT, or 8mm tape drive and almost all the computers you administer have an available drive bay, you might choose a portable DAT or 8mm tape system, which can be moved from system to system.

Caution

Steer away from nonstandard tape backup drives. For example, some drives may not conform to QIC, DAT, or Exabyte standards. Since Exabyte is the only manufacturer of 8mm tape backup drives, you can be confident that tapes made on this manufacturer's drives can be read on their drives. I would avoid drives based on VHS videotape, for example, since these types of drives are not a true standard and are not very well supported.

The following sections cover some important installation issues for internally- and externally-mounted drives.

Internal Installation. Virtually all internal tape backup drives available today are designed to be installed in a half-height drive bay. Many are designed to be installed in either half-height drive bays or the smaller drive bays generally used for 3 1/2-inch floppy drives. Drives that can be installed in 3 1/2-inch floppy drive bays generally are shipped in a cage, or frame, that enables them to be installed in a 5 1/4-inch bay. To install the drive in a 3 1/2-inch bay, you remove the cage and the 5 1/4-inch bay faceplate. Most tape drives are between about 5 and 9 inches deep; they require approximately 5–9 inches of clearance inside the system case. To mount tape drives inside the system, use the same rails or cage apparatus used for floppy drives, hard drives, and devices such as CD-ROM drives.

Note

Half-height drive bays measure roughly 1.7 inches high by 5.9 inches wide. The smaller drive bays measure 1 by 4 inches.

Internal tape drives require a spare power connector, usually the larger connector used for hard drives, although some may require the smaller power connector common to 3 1/2-inch floppy drives. If a power connector is not available inside your system, you can buy a power splitter from a computer store or cable supply vendor. A *power splitter* looks like the letter Y and acts like an extension cord. You unplug the power connector from a device (such as a floppy drive) that's already installed. Then plug the bottom point of the Y into that power connector. The two arms of the Y then provide you with two power connectors.

Internal tape drives also require an interface to the system. QIC-40 and QIC-80 drives most often connect to the system through the floppy controller. On a system with only one floppy drive you connect the tape drive to an unused connector on the floppy disk data cable. On systems with two floppy disk drives you use a special cable linked to the floppy disk data cable, in effect, a splitter cable.

Internal drives other than QIC-40s and QIC-80s usually require a special adapter card, or they may link to a card already installed in your system. This card is usually one of the following: a QIC-standard adapter card, a Small Computer Systems Interface (SCSI) adapter, a SCSI-2 adapter card, or an Integrated Drive Electronics (IDE) card. When purchasing a drive, you must determine which interface you need; make sure that the drive kit includes the adapter card you need or that you purchase the correct card.

External Installation. If you want to move an external tape drive from computer to computer, you must install an adapter card in each system on which you want to use the tape drive. Portable tape backup drives like the DAT portables have a SCSI to parallel port converter that uses the computer's parallel port connector. Adapter cards designed for use with external tape drives have a different connector, depending on the interface used, that is accessible from the back panel of the system unit. These cards generally are QIC-standard, SCSI, SCSI-2, or IDE.

When you buy an external tape backup drive that requires an adapter, you must ensure either that the drive includes the necessary adapter card or that you purchase the card at the same time you purchase the drive. In addition, if you plan to use the external tape drive to back up a number of systems, you must buy a card for each system on which you plan to use the drive.

Power is supplied to external units by a transformer that plugs into an ordinary 120v AC wall socket. Generally, the transformer connects to the external tape drive with a small connector. When you choose an external tape drive, be sure you have enough AC power sockets available for your computer, its peripherals, and the tape drive.

Tape Drive Backup Software

The most important decision you can make after you choose the tape standard and capacity of your backup tape drive is the backup software you will use with it. Most tape drives are shipped with backup software that generally is adequate for your basic backup needs.

Often, however, third-party software compatible with the drive you have chosen gives you greater flexibility and functionality. For example, some tape drives may be shipped with only DOS-based software. If you want to use one of these drives from within Windows, or on a system running OS/2 or UNIX, you may need to purchase third-party backup software. And if you will be backing up network workstations from a server, you must make sure that the drive is shipped with software capable of performing this function; otherwise, you will need to acquire third-party software.

One important issue with backup software is data compression. Most backup software offers *data compression*, special programming that stores data on the backup tape in less space than is needed on the original source disk. Some companies produce backup software that is well known for especially efficient data compression. In other words, backup software produced by these companies does a better job of compressing large data files into a small amount of space.

Note

Microsoft Backup (MSBACKUP.EXE) and Windows Backup (MWBACKUP.EXE), which are included with DOS 6.0 and later versions, do not work with tape drives, however, the software included with IBM's PC-DOS does. IBM includes a version of Central Point Backup with its copy of DOS. This does an excellent job and will work on virtually any drive or interface. In any case, your best bet is to get software that is included with your tape drive, so you have something to fall back on.

The backup software built into Windows 95 supports a variety of QIC 40, 80, and 3010 tape drives that are connected via the floppy controller card, as well as the Colorado Memory Systems QIC 40, 80, and 3010 drives attached via the parallel port. Unfortunately, the Windows 95 backup does NOT support the majority of tape drives currently on the market! For example, SCSI tape drives of any kind are not supported, and neither are the newer QIC type drives such as 3020 or Travan. Fortunately, many superior backup programs are available from aftermarket sources. Most of the time you will get this software with the drive itself. Check with your tape drive manufacturer to verify Windows 95 support.

You may want to take the time to read reviews on backup software in one of the many monthly computer magazines. The reviews can help you determine which backup software does the best job of compressing data; they also provide information on how quickly backup software programs perform a typical backup. The speed of the backup software and its data-compression capabilities are important considerations. Also of great importance is whether the software is easy to use. If your backup software makes backing up more difficult than it has to be, chances are you won't back up as often as you should.

Bundled Software. Before you buy a backup tape drive you should always check whether the drive includes software that will meet your needs and, if it doesn't, be sure to buy third-party software that does the job. Generally, the software bundled with most tape backup drives will do the job for you—provided that you don't plan to place great demands on the tape drive.

The software included with a QIC-80 drive, for example, generally cannot be used to back up network workstations from the server. If you want to use a QIC-80 drive for this task, you may need to buy special software compatible with your network and the tape backup drive. If you use Windows, Windows NT, OS/2, or UNIX, your backup software must be compatible with your operating system as well as the drive, and you must determine whether the software shipped with the drive will do the job for you.

Third-Party Software. A large number of companies manufacture backup software designed for different types of tape drives and different uses. For example, many manufacturers design their backup software to be compatible with most networks. Others specialize in DOS and Windows backup software. Some specialize in OS/2 software. Others are well known among those whose computers run in UNIX. You may need to ask a trusted retailer or call the software company itself to determine whether a particular type of software is compatible not only with the tape drive you have chosen, but also with your network and operating environment.

Often, third-party software is easier to use than the software designed by a tape manufacturer. The tape manufacturer's software may have an unfamiliar interface or its commands may seem cryptic to you, even if you have used backup software for years. It is not uncommon for tape manufacturers to include inadequate or even incomplete documentation for the backup software included with the drive, although this generally is the case only with lower cost models. In such a case, you may be able to solve the problem by purchasing third-party software.

Third-party software often does a better job of data compression than the software designed by a tape manufacturer. In addition, third-party software often includes capabilities not included with the software bundled with many drives. Some of the capabilities you might want to look for include the following:

- *Unattended backup scheduling*. Enabling you to schedule a backup for a time when you won't need to use your computer.
- *Macro capability*. For selecting options and the files to back up.
- *A quick tape-erase capability*. For erasing the entire contents of a tape.
- *Partial tape-erase capability*. For erasing only part of a tape.
- *Tape unerase capability*. For recovering erased data.
- *Password protect capability*. To protect backup data from access by unauthorized persons.

You can find backup software manufacturers by reading some of the many monthly computer magazines, paying particular attention to their usability reviews. Generally, if a backup software product gets good reviews, works on a system configuration like yours, and has the features you need, it is worth the price you pay.

Removable Storage Drives

The reason for the shortage of storage space on today's PCs is easy enough to understand. Just take a look at the sheer number and size of the files stored in the two main directories used by Windows (usually C:\WINDOWS and C:\WINDOWS\SYSTEM). The amount of disk space used by the files in those two directories alone can quickly balloon to 40M or more after you also install a few Windows applications. The reason is simple: Nearly all Windows applications place files in one of the Windows directories that the application will use later. These files include those with extensions like DLL, 386, VBX, DRV, TTF, and many others. Similarly, Windows NT, OS/2, and UNIX, as well as the software applications that run in these operating systems, can require enormous amounts of storage space.

The remainder of this chapter focuses on some of the more advanced data storage options on the market: removable media large-capacity storage drives. Some removable media drives use media as small as a 3 1/2-inch floppy disk, others use media about the size of a 5 1/4-inch floppy.

These drives, whose capacities range from 35M to 1GB or more, offer fairly speedy performance, the ability to store data or less frequently used programs on a removable disk, and the ability to easily transport huge data files—Computer Aided Drawing (CAD) files and graphics files, for example—from one computer to another. Or you can use a removable media disk to remove sensitive data from your office so that you can lock it safely away from prying eyes.

There are two commonly used types of removable media drives: magnetic media and optical media, also called *magneto-optical media*. Magnetic media drives use much the same technology used on a floppy disk or hard drive to encode data for storage. Magneto-optical media drives encode information on disk by using newer technology, a combination of traditional magnetic and laser technologies.

Magnetic media drives are considerably faster than magneto-optical drives and offer similar capacities. The SyQuest magnetic media drives, for example, offer 14ms average access times, compared to the 30ms (or slower) access times of magneto-optical drives. Magneto-optical drives can be more than twice as expensive as magnetic media drives. If you have a great deal of data to store, however, the comparative cost of using a magneto-optical drive drops because magneto-optical media cartridges are considerably less expensive than magnetic media. For example, 10, 270M SyQuest cartridges can cost roughly $80 each and 150M Bernoulli cartridges can cost about $90 apiece. The 128M magneto-optical cartridges can cost as little as $25 apiece when you buy 10.

The following section provides information on magnetic media and magneto-optical drive types.

Magnetic Media Drives

A small group of companies dominate the market for magnetic removable media drives. One company, Iomega, always tops the list because it developed the first popular large-capacity removable magnetic media drives, and because its disk cartridges are known as the most rugged in the industry. Two other leading names in removable magnetic media drives are SyQuest and 3M.

Removable magnetic media drives are usually floppy or hard disk based. For example, the popular Zip drive is merely a 3.5" version of the original Bernoulli drive made by Iomega. The new 3M LS-120 drive stores 120MB on a disk that looks exactly like a 1.44M floppy!

Both the Bernoulli and SyQuest designs are their own de facto standard. Other manufacturers market drives based on the Bernoulli and SyQuest designs (and some actually manufactured by Bernoulli or SyQuest). For example, the Jaz drive from Iomega uses a hard disk cartridge similar to the Syquest. Generally these manufacturers' drives are somewhat less expensive than the Bernoulli and SyQuest models. If you are considering one of these compatible drives, however, make sure that the drive you are buying has the same performance characteristics (average access speed, and so on) as the original and that the drive manufacturer offers the same warranty as the original (Bernoulli, three years; SyQuest/SyDOS, two years).

Bernoulli Removable Media Drives. The disk used in the Bernoulli drive is roughly the same size as a 5 1/4-inch floppy disk, although a large shutter, similar to the shutter on a 3 1/2-inch floppy disk, easily differentiates Bernoulli disks from floppy disks. Modern Bernoulli cartridges are available in 35M, 65M, 105M, and 150M capacities. The Iomega Bernoulli MultiDisk 150 drive, the company's newest model, reads and writes all of these drive capacities. In addition, the MultiDisk reads and writes to older Bernoulli 90M disks and reads older 40M disks. The MultiDisk is available in both internal and external models.

Bernoulli disks are widely known as the most durable of the removable media drive types. It is probably safer to mail a Bernoulli cartridge than another type of removable disk because the media is well protected inside the cartridge. Bernoulli encases a magnetic-media-covered flexible disk (in effect, a floppy disk) in a rigid cartridge in the same way the thin disk of a 1.44M floppy is encased in a rigid plastic shell.

When it rotates in the drive, the disk is pulled by air pressure towards the drive heads. Many people do not think that there is head-to-disk contact in a Bernoulli drive, but indeed there is. As the disk spins, the airflow generated by the disk movement encounters what is called a *Bernoulli plate,* a stationary plate designed to control the air flow so that the disk is pulled toward the read/write head. At full speed the head does touch the disk, which causes wear. Bernoulli drives have built-in random seek functions that prevent any single track on the disk from wearing excessively during periods of inactivity. Bernoulli disk cartridges should be replaced periodically since they can wear out. The disk itself spins at speeds approaching the 3,600 rpm of relatively slow hard drives. The drive has an average seek time of 18ms, not a great deal slower than today's medium-priced hard drives.

The Bernoulli MultiDisk 150 drive is available in an internal model, which requires a half-height drive bay and an external model. The internal model connects to the IDE hard drive adapter already installed in your system. The external model requires a SCSI adapter card with an external connector. The external model is powered by a transformer that connects to a grounded AC wall plug.

Another form of Bernoulli drive from Iomega is the popular Zip Drive. This device is available as a external or internal SCSI unit and is also available as an external parallel port device. The drive is capable of storing up to 100 MB of data on a small removable magnetic cartridge that resembles a 3.5 inch floppy disk, and has approximately a 29ms access time and a 1M/sec transfer rate when used with a SCSI connection. If the parallel connection is used, the drive's speed is often limited by the speed of the parallel port.

The Zip drives use a proprietary 3.5-inch disk made by Iomega. It is about twice as thick as a standard 3.5-inch floppy disk. The Zip drives do not accept standard 1.44MB or 720KB floppy disks, making this an unlikely candidate for a floppy drive replacement. Zip drives have become popular in use as an external drive for exchanging data between systems, but the major PC manufacturers have not recognized the proprietary format directly in the system BIOS or in the operating system. The popularity and functionality of the Zip drive has now been greatly exceeded by the new LS-120 "floptical" drive introduced by 3M and Matsushita and supported by Compaq and other major PC manufacturers. More information about the revolutionary LS-120 drive follows in the next few sections.

Removable Media Hard Disk Drives. SyQuest manufactures some drives that use 5 1/4-inch cartridges and others that use 3 1/2-inch cartridges. But the SyQuest disks, like the Bernoulli cartridges, are easily differentiated from floppy disks. The 5 1/4-inch 44M and 88M cartridges used in some SyDOS drives are encased in clear plastic, as are the SyDOS 3 1/2-inch 105M and SyQuest 270M cartridges. The disk spins inside the cartridge at several thousand rpm. SyQuest claims a 14ms average access time for the drives it manufactures.

The disks for the SyQuest and SyDOS drives are composed of a rigid platter inside a plastic cartridge but are not as well protected as the disk in a Bernoulli cartridge. Some people consider these disks fragile. If the SyQuest and SyDOS cartridges are not severely jostled or dropped, however, they can be transported safely. These cartridges must be carefully protected when they are mailed or shipped.

The SyQuest/SyDOS drives are available in internal and external models. The internal models require a connection to the existing IDE hard drive interface card. The external models require a SCSI interface card with an external connector and are powered by a transformer that connects to a grounded AC wall plug.

Another type of removable hard disk drive is the Jaz drive from Iomega. This is physically and functionally identical to the Syquest drives in that it is a true removable cartridge hard disk, except the capacity of the cartridge has been increased to 1GB. Unfortunately, the cartridges themselves cost about $100, which is about seven times the cost of a DAT (Digital Audio Tape) cartridge, which stores 4 to 8 times more data! The high cost of the media makes the Jaz drive unsuitable for backup compared to traditional tape media but possibly useful as an add-on external SCSI hard disk.

Floptical Drives

Floptical drives are another popular form of increased-capacity removable magnetic media drives. A 21MB as well as a 120MB version have been available over the years, and the 21MB version has become obsolete. The older 21MB version was created by Insite Peripherals and packed 21M of data on the same size disk as a 3 1/2-inch floppy. More recently, 3M and Matsushita have introduced a drive called the LS-120 that can store 120MB on a single 3 1/2-inch floppy disk! In addition, all floptical drives can read and write 1.44M and 720KB floppy disks (although they cannot handle 2.88M disks). Because of their greatly increased storage capacity and ability to use common floppy disks, the newer 120MB flopticals are considered by many as the perfect replacement floppy disk drive.

The name "floptical" might suggest the use of laser beams to burn or etch data onto the disk or to excite the media in preparation for magnetic recording—as is the case with the CD-ROM, Write Once, Read Many (WORM), and magneto-optical disks discussed later in this chapter. But this suggestion is erroneous. The read/write heads of a floptical drive use magnetic recording technology, much like that of floppy drives. The floptical disk itself is composed of the same ferrite materials common to floppy and hard disks. Floptical drives are capable of such increased capacity because many more tracks are packed on each disk, compared with a standard 1.44M floppy. Obviously, in order to fit so many tracks on the floptical disk, the tracks must be much more narrow than those on a floppy disk.

That's where optical technology comes into play. Flopticals use a special optical mechanism to properly position the drive read/write heads over the data tracks on the disk. The way this works, *servo information*, which specifically defines the location of each track, is embedded in the disk during the manufacturing process. Each track of servo information is actually etched or stamped on the disk and is never disturbed during the recording process. Each time the floptical drive writes to the disk, the recording mechanism (including the read/write heads) is guided by a laser beam precisely into place by this servo information. When the floptical drive reads the encoded data, this servo information again is used by the laser to guide the read/write heads precisely into place.

21MB Floptical Drives. The original Insite 21MB floptical disks used tracks formatted to 27 sectors of 512 bytes. The disks themselves revolved at 720 rpm. Flopticals are capable of nearly 10M per minute data throughput. These drives used a SCSI interface to the system.

Unfortunately, the 21MB drives by Insite never really caught on due to several reasons. One is that no leading manufacturer has included these drives in a standard configuration with built-in BIOS drivers and support. Also, Microsoft, IBM, and Apple have not built support for these drives directly into their operating systems.

LS-120 (120MB) Floptical Drives. The LS-120 drive is designed to become the new standard floppy disk drive in the PC industry. This new drive was developed by 3M and Matsushita-Kotobuki Electronics Industries, Ltd., and stores 120MB of data, or about 80 times more data than current 1.44MB floppy disks. In addition to storing more, these drives read and write up to five times the speed of standard floppy disk drives.

Unlike the Iomega Zip drive, the LS-120 floppy drive can act as the PC's bootable A: drive, and is fully compatible with Windows NT and Windows 95. In addition to the new 120MB floppy disks, the LS-120 drive accepts standard 720 KB and 1.44MB floppy disks and actually reads and writes those disks up to three times faster than standard floppy drives. Zip drives are not backwards compatible and cannot use existing floppy disks, and the proprietary Zip media stores less and is more expensive than the 3M LS-120 media. The LS-120 also uses a standard IDE interface, which is already built-in to most existing systems. Zip drives, on the other hand, use either the slower external parallel port as an interface, or require the addition of a SCSI adapter, which adds to the expense.

The LS-120 drives are perfect for portable systems, providing a solution that not only replaces the existing floppy, but which can even be used in place of the floppy drive internally. Having one of these high-capacity drives in a portable will allow the use of the relatively inexpensive 120MB removable disks while on the road. They are perfect for storing entire applications or datasets, which can be removed and secured when the portable system is not in use.

Compaq was the first PC maker to offer computers equipped with LS-120 drives. Other leading PC manufacturers are now incorporating LS-120 drives in their products, making this the new standard for PC floppy drives. Besides coming in new systems, these drives are also available separately at a cost of about $200 in internal or external versions for upgrading older systems. The 120MB floppy disks are available for about $15 per disk or less.

The 3M LS-120 disk has the same shape and size as a standard 1.44MB 3.5-inch floppy disk; however, it uses a combination of magnetic and optical technology to enable greater capacity and performance. Named after the Laser Servo (LS) mechanism it employs, LS-120 technology places optical reference tracks on the diskette that are both written and read by a laser system. The optical sensor in the drive allows the read-write head to be precisely positioned over the magnetic data tracks, enabling track densities of 2,490 tracks per inch (tpi) versus the 135 tpi for a 1.44MB floppy disk.

On the Web

3M has recently moved it's disk and tape drive division into an independent, publicly owned data storage and imaging company called Imation. If you want more information on the LS-120 drives or any of the 3M tape products, Imation can be reached on the Web at the following address:

http://www.imation.com

Unlike the previous Insite Floptical or Zip drives, the LS-120 is being endorsed by major PC manufacturers, starting with Compaq, and will be supported by the system BIOS. Microsoft and IBM are also building support for the LS-120 drives into Windows and OS/2, meaning that the LS-120 will probably be the next true standard for PC floppy drives.

Magneto-Optical Drives

Magneto-optical drives, which are manufactured by a large number of companies, use an ingenious combination of magnetic and laser technology to pack data on 5 1/4-inch and 3 1/2-inch disks contained in cartridges. The media itself and the construction of the platter are similar in ways to the media of a CD-ROM disc. An aluminum base is covered with clear plastic, then a layer of magnetic, optically active media particles—an alloy of cobalt, iron, and terbium. A clear plastic coating seals the disk, rendering it nearly impervious to shock, contamination, and damage.

Although the magneto-optical disks are similar to CD-ROM discs, there is a world of difference in the way data is stored. When manufacturers write CD-ROM discs, the laser actually burns pits into the media to represent the data. These pits are read by the laser and translated into the form of computer data. In the case of magneto-optical disks, the magnetically/optically active media is not burned or pitted. Instead, during the writing process a magneto-optical drive focuses a laser beam onto a very tight track—a much thinner track than could be used to store data on a purely magnetic media platter. The laser beam heats the track and a weak magnetic signal is applied. The result is that only the thin track of heated media receives the magnetic signal and stores the data it contains.

Unlike a CD-ROM disc, a magneto-optical disk theoretically can be rewritten an infinite number of times because the media is never burned, or pitted. When the time comes to erase data from or rewrite the disk, the disk is simply reheated with the laser and the old data removed magnetically so that new data can be recorded. When the magneto-optical drive reads the disk, the drive functions optically—that is, the laser reads the data from the disk (without heating the media).

Because of the thin tracks on which data is written to magneto-optical disks, the data is packed extremely densely: large amounts of data can be packed on a platter about the same size as common 3 1/2-inch and 5 1/4-inch floppy disks. The current maximum capacity of the 3 1/2-inch cartridges is 230M; the 5 1/2-inch cartridges can hold as much as a gigabyte of data. It is important to note, however, that capacity ratings of magneto-optical disks can be misleading. Magneto-optical disks are double sided, like floppy disks, but magneto-optical drives have only one read/write head. Therefore, to read or write to the second side you must manually flip over the cartridge. So only half the disk capacity is available at any one time.

For many applications, magneto-optical drives are tediously slow, although some drives—using refinements of the basic magneto-optical technology—offer data-access speeds that are inching more closely to those of removable magnetic media drives. One reason that magneto-optical drives are slow is that they typically spin the disk at roughly 2,000 rpm—much slower than the 3,600 rpm of a relatively slow hard drive. Another reason for the slow speeds is that the read/write head mechanism, although optically and magnetically advanced, is mechanically a kludge. The massive mechanism of a magneto-optical drive's read/write heads takes much longer to move and settle than the read/write heads of a hard drive or even a removable magnetic media drive.

Magneto-optical drives typically are rated with average access speeds of about 30ms. However, these average access speed figures do not tell the entire story. The process of rewriting a disk can take nearly twice the time it takes to read the disk. Because of the way magneto-optical technology works, all the bias magnetic field of the area of the disk to be written must be oriented in a single direction during the write process. Because of this limitation, during the write process most magneto-optical drives must make a first pass over the disk to align the tracks of the disk that are to be rewritten. Then, the drive makes a second pass over the disk to realign, or change the alignment of, the necessary areas. This alignment/realignment process is known as *two pass recording.*

New magneto-optical technologies are emerging which use single pass recording of disks. If speed is an important factor in choosing a magneto-optical drive, you should be prepared to pay extra for a drive whose performance is not penalized by two pass recording technology. In addition, several manufacturers are offering drives that spin the platter at speeds approaching the 3,600 rpm speeds of a hard drive. The performance boost offered by these drives is considerable, but this technology also boosts considerably the prices of these drives.

Most manufacturers adhere to the International Standards Organization specifications for magneto-optical disks and drives. The ISO standard calls for all drives to use a SCSI host adapter to interface with the computer. Under the ISO standard, 5 1/4-inch drives must be able to read two different disk formats: disks with 512-byte sectors and disks with 1,024-byte sectors. The disks with 512-byte sectors have a capacity of roughly 600M; those 1,024-byte sectors hold 650M of data. Under the ISO standard, the 3 1/2-inch drives, which are quite popular among first-time purchasers, are required to read only the 128M disks. Some manufacturers, in addition to designing their drives to meet ISO standards, also design their drives to use a proprietary data format that can increase the capacity of 5 1/4-inch disks to about 1.3G. Both 5 1/4-inch and 3 1/2-inch drives are available as internal and external units.

Write-Once, Read Many (WORM) Drives

The removable media drive known as *write-once, read many (WORM)* is designed to serve as a nearly bulletproof data archival system. If you have extremely important data files that absolutely must remain in an unaltered state, perhaps accounting or database data, a WORM drive can provide the kind of security you are looking for. Data written to a WORM disk cannot be changed.

The WORM disk is encased in a high-impact cartridge with a sliding shutter similar to the shutter on a 3 1/2-inch floppy disk. The cartridge and the extremely durable nature of the disk inside make WORM disks worry free for data exchange. A WORM drive cartridge is very difficult to damage. The disk itself, with the media sandwiched in plastic, is not unlike a CD-ROM disc or a magneto-optical disk. The technology used to write a WORM disk, however, is more like the technology used for CD-ROM recording than that used for writing to magneto-optical disks. The WORM drive uses a laser to burn microscopic patches of darkness into the light-colored media.

A number of companies manufacture WORM drives but follow no single standard. Therefore, a WORM disk written on one manufacturer's drive is quite unlikely to be readable on another manufacturer's drive. Each manufacturer (sometimes small groups of manufacturers) uses its own proprietary data format and disk capacity and many use a cartridge size only their drives can handle. For example, most WORM drives are designed for 5 1/4-inch cartridges, but some WORM drives handle only 12-inch disks. In addition, although most WORM drives interface the computer via SCSI host adapter, others use different interfaces, some of them proprietary.

Certainly, at least in part because of these incompatibility problems, WORM drives are not big sellers. No more than several thousand are sold each year at prices soaring to the heights—some 5 1/4-inch drives cost several thousand dollars. The 5 1/4-inch-drive cartridges, which range in capacity from 650M to 1.3G, can cost more than $180.

The term *niche market* is used occasionally to describe a computer product or peripheral that lacks broad appeal or usefulness. Because of its cost and incompatibility problems, WORM drive technology is a niche market product. Unless you must be able to store massive amounts of data and ensure it can never be altered, you are better off buying a magneto-optical drive, or perhaps even a tape backup drive.

Note that a variation on WORM technology is also found in CD-R (CD-Recordable) drives. CD-R drives are indeed WORM, however, they use a special recordable CD-ROM disc that, once recorded, can be played back or read in any standard CD-ROM drive. CD-R drives are very useful for creating master CDs, which can be duplicated for distribution within a company. For example, using such a drive, a company can generate a new master CD each month that contains their inventory or customer database and then have the master CD copied for distribution to their sales force. For more information on CD-R drives, see Chapter 17, "CD-ROM Drives."

Summary

This chapter examined a wide range of data storage options, including backup tape drives and large-capacity removable media drives. The QIC standards for tape backup drives as well as DAT and 8mm tape drives also were covered. In addition, you were given some useful guidelines for choosing the tape backup drive that is right for your computer or the computer installation you administer.

In addition, this chapter covered magnetic media drives, such as the popular Zip and Jaz drives by Iomega and the revolutionary new LS-120 floppy drive from 3M and Matsushita. In each case, the similarities and the differences between these removable magnetic media drives was discussed.

This chapter also discussed magneto-optical drives, detailing their strengths and weaknesses, explaining the technology of writing data to and reading it from magneto-optical disks, and offering some guidelines that may help you decide whether magneto-optical drive technology will meet your needs.

Finally, this chapter discussed WORM drives and their uses. It also discussed the incompatibilities between WORM drives and different media, and it explained why WORM drives are appropriate only for a small segment of computer users.

Part V

System Assembly and Maintenance

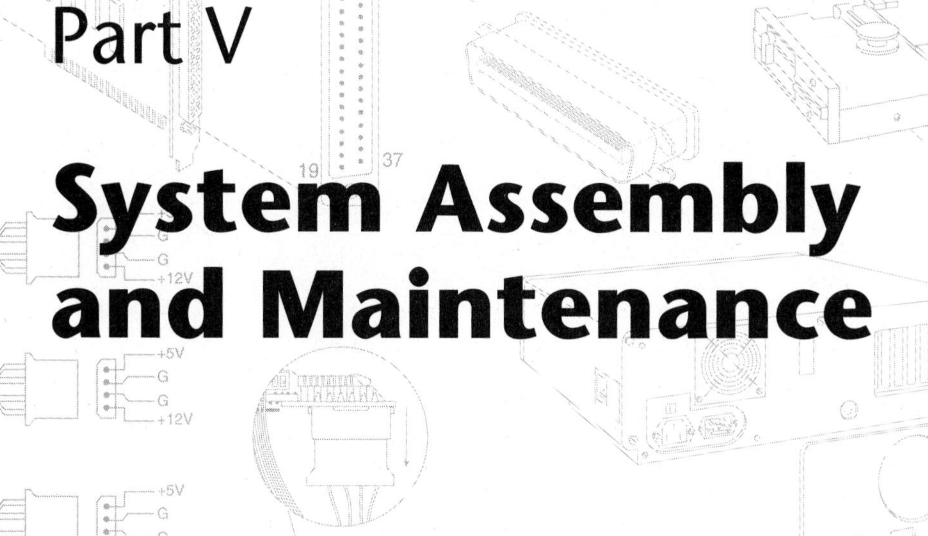

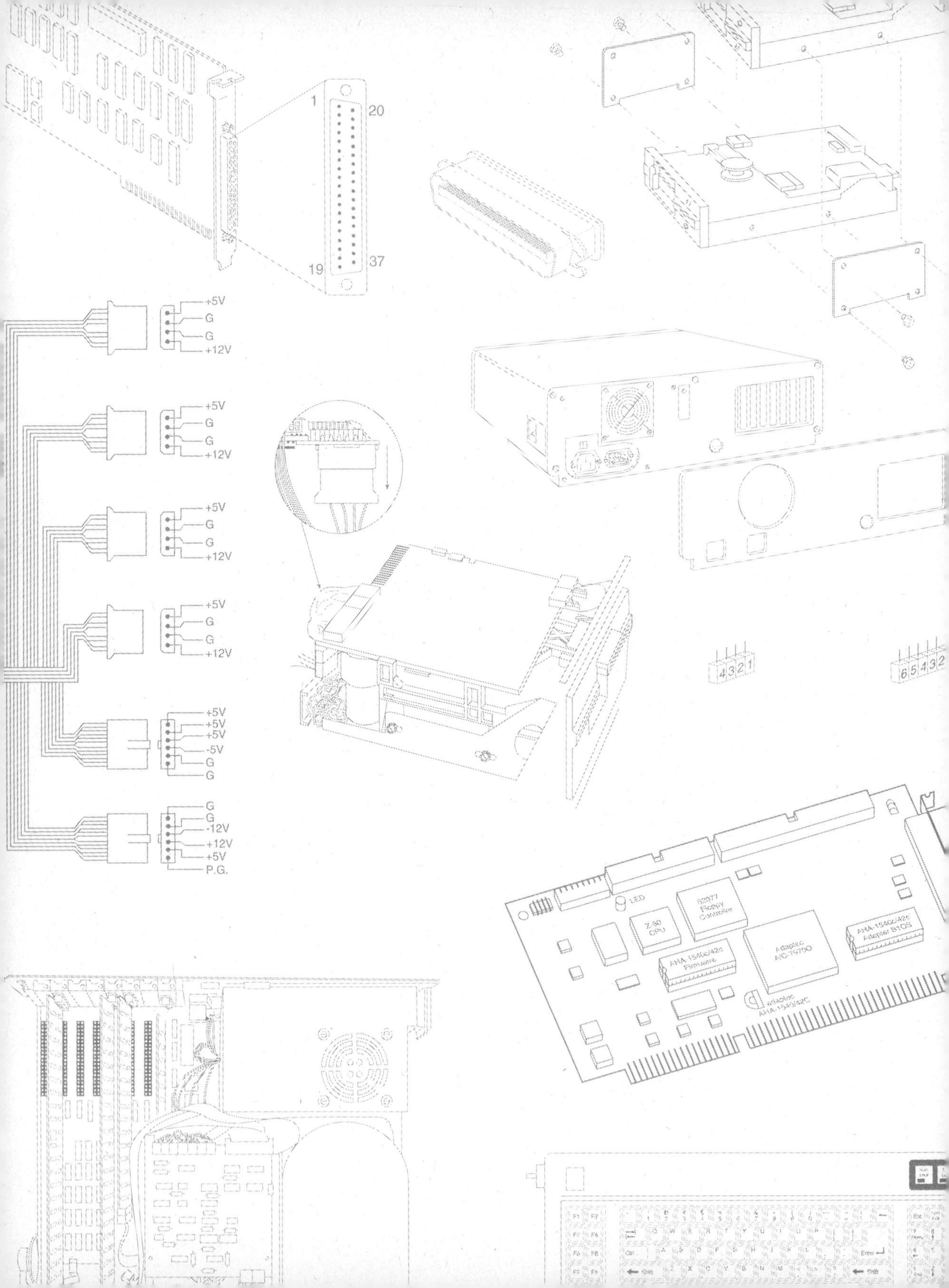

1
20
19
37
+5V
G
G
+12V
+5V
G
G
+12V
+5V
G
G
+12V
+5V
G
G
+12V
+5V
+5V
+5V
-5V
G
G
G
G
-12V
+12V
+5V
P.G.
4 3 2 1
6 5 4 3 2
LED
Z-80 CPU
82077 Floppy Controller
AHA-1540c/42c Firmware
Adaptec AIC-7970C
AHA-1540c/42c Adapter BIOS
adaptec AHA-1540/42C

Chapter 19

Building a System

In these days of commodity parts and component pricing, building your own system from scratch is no longer the daunting process it once was. Every component necessary to build a PC compatible system is available off the shelf, and at very competitive pricing. In many cases, the system you build can use the same components as the top name brand systems.

There are, however, some cautions. The main thing to note is that rarely will you save money when building your own system compared to purchasing a complete system from a mail order vendor or mass merchandiser. The reasoning for this is simple. Most system vendors today who build systems to order use many if not all the same components you can when building your own. The difference is that they buy these components in quantity and receive a much larger discount than you can purchasing only one of a particular item. There will also be only one shipping or handling charge when purchasing a complete system as opposed to the individual shipping charges when purchasing separate components. In fact, the shipping, handling, and even phone charges from ordering all of the separate parts needed to build a PC will often add up to $100 or more. This cost will rise if you encounter problems with any of the components and have to make additional calls or send improper or malfunctioning parts back for replacement.

It is clear that the reasons for building a system from scratch will often have less to do with saving money than with the experience and end result. In the end, you will have a custom system that contains the exact components and features you have selected. The experience itself will also be very rewarding. You will know exactly how your system is constructed and configured, since you will have done it yourself. This will make future support and the installation of additional accessories much easier.

So if you are interested in a rewarding experience, wish to have a custom system that is not exactly offered by any vendor, and you are not in a hurry, then building your own PC compatible may be the way to go. On the other hand, if you are interested in getting a PC compatible for the best price, want one stop support that is a single place to go for warranty claims, and need an operational system quickly, then building your own system should definitely be avoided!

This chapter will detail the components needed to assemble your own system, the assembly procedures, and list some recommendations for components and their sources.

System Components

The components used in building a typical PC compatible are:

- Case and power supply
- Motherboard

    Processor
    Memory

- I/O ports

    Serial
    Parallel
    IDE
    Floppy

- Floppy disk drive(s)
- Hard disk drive(s)
- CD-ROM drive
- Keyboard and pointing device (mouse)
- Video card and display
- Sound card and speakers
- Accessories

    Heat sinks/cooling fans
    Cables
    Hardware
    Operating system software

Each of these components is discussed in the following sections.

Case and Power Supply

The case and power supply is usually sold as a unit. There are several designs to choose from, most of which will take a standard baby-AT or the new ATX form factor motherboards. The size of the case, power supply, and even the motherboard are called the *form factor*. The most popular case form factors are as follows:

- Full Tower
- Mid-Tower
- Mini-Tower
- Desktop
- Low Profile (also called Slimline)

Out of these choices, it is recommended that you avoid the Low Profile systems. These cases require a special type of motherboard called a *Low Profile* or *LPX board.* LPX motherboards have virtually everything built-in, even video, and do not have any normal adapter slots. Instead, all of the expansion slots are mounted on a "tree" board called a *riser card,* which plugs into a special slot on the motherboard. Adapter cards then plug sideways into the riser card, making expansion somewhat limited and difficult.

Most of the case designs other than the Low Profile (or Slimline) take a standard sized motherboard called a *baby-AT* type. This designation refers to the form factor or shape of the motherboard, which is to say that it mimics the original IBM AT, but is slightly smaller. Actually, the baby-AT form factor is a kind of a cross between the IBM XT and AT motherboard sizes. There is more information on these form factors in Chapter 4, "Motherboards."

Many of the newer cases accept the standard baby-AT form factor motherboards as well as the ATX style boards, but an older case designed for baby-AT motherboards does *not* accept an ATX motherboard. The ATX form factor will eventually replace the baby-AT style for most newer motherboards. So if you are interested in the most flexible type of case and power supply that will support future upgrades, look for a unit that conforms to the ATX and baby-AT motherboard form factors.

Whether you choose a Desktop or one of the Tower cases is really a personal preference. Most feel that the Tower systems are easier to work on, and the full sized Tower cases have lots of bays for different storage devices. Tower cases have enough bays to hold floppy drives, multiple hard disks, CD-ROM drives, tape drives, and anything else you might want to install. Some of the Desktop cases also can have as much room as the Towers, particularly the Mini- or Mid-Tower models. In fact a Tower case can really be considered a Desktop case turned sideways or vice versa. Some cases are convertible; that is they can be used in either a desktop or tower orientation.

Motherboard

There are several compatible form factors used for motherboards. The form factor refers to the physical dimensions and size of the board, and dictates what type of case the board will fit into. The types of motherboard form factors generally available are the following:

- Full-size AT
- Baby-AT
- ATX
- LPX

The full-size AT motherboard is so named because it matches the original IBM AT motherboard design. This allows for a very large board of up to 12 inches wide by 13.8 inches deep. The keyboard connector and slot connectors must conform to specific placement requirements to fit the holes in the case. This type of board will fit into the Tower or full-sized Desktop cases only. Because the cases that will fit these boards are more limited in availability, and due to component miniaturization, the full-size AT boards are no longer being produced by most motherboard manufacturers.

The baby-AT form factor is essentially the same as the original IBM XT motherboard, with modifications in screw hole positions to fit into an AT-style case (see fig. 19.1). These motherboards also have specific placement of the keyboard connector and slot connectors to match the holes in the case. Note that virtually all full size AT and baby-AT motherboards use the standard 5-pin DIN type connector for the keyboard. Baby-AT motherboards will fit into every type of case except the low profile or Slimline cases. Because of their flexibility, this is now the most popular motherboard form factor. Figure 19.1 shows the dimensions and layout of a baby-AT motherboard.

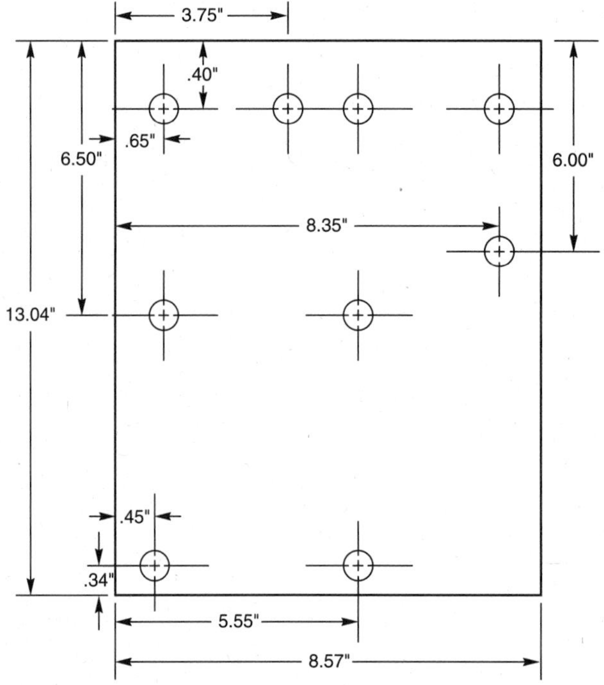

Figure 19.1

Baby-AT motherboard form factor.

The newest form factor on the market today is the ATX form factor, which was released by Intel in July 1995 (see fig. 19.2). This motherboard design will be featured on many new Pentium and Pentium Pro-based motherboards over the next few years, and it is destined to replace the baby-AT form factor. ATX-shaped boards are the same basic dimensions as baby-AT; however, they are rotated 90 degrees from the standard baby-AT orientation. This places the slots parallel to the short side of the board, allowing more space for other components without interfering with expansion boards. High heat producing components like the CPU and memory are located next to the power supply, which is redesigned to feature an internal fan blowing directly across the board. The ATX-style power supply also features a redesigned single keyed (foolproof!) connector that cannot be plugged in backwards, and it also supplies the motherboard with 3.3 volts for many of the newer CPUs and other components.

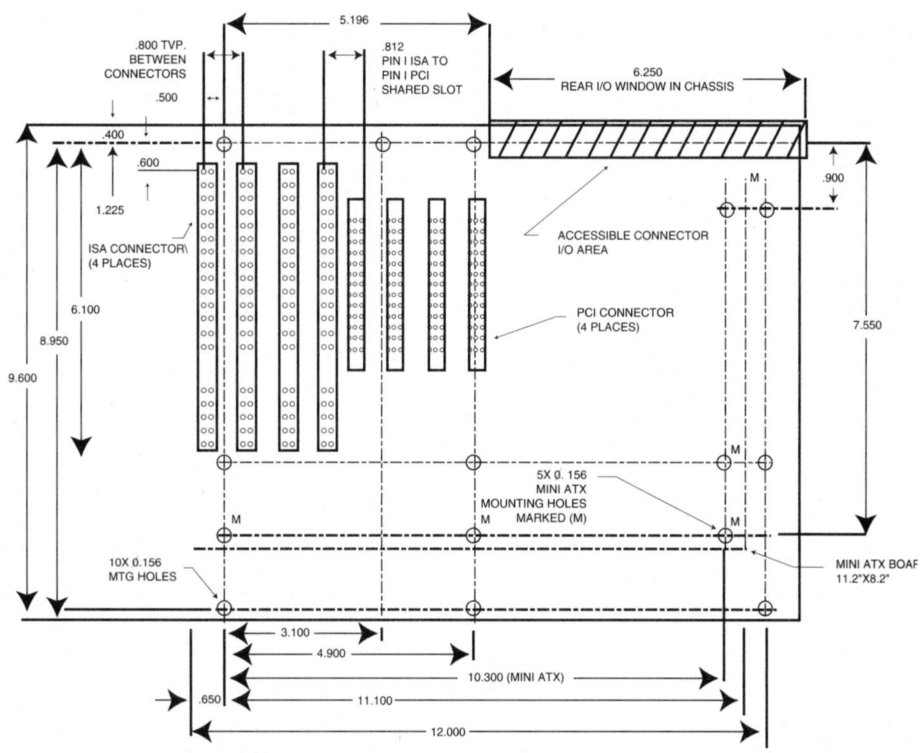

Figure 19.2

ATX motherboard form factor.

Consider that if you don't purchase an ATX form factor motherboard this time, the next time you probably will. Virtually all motherboard manufacturers have committed to the new ATX design in the long run, as the ATX motherboard designs will be cheaper, easier to access for user serviceability, and more reliable in the long run.

Another form factor used in motherboards today are the LPX and Mini-LPX form factors. This form factor requires the use of a Low Profile case, also known as SlimLine case, and is normally not recommended when building your own system. This is due to the number of different variations on case and riser card designs. This type of form factor is popular with many of the PC systems sold through retail outlets and appliance stores.

There can be some differences between systems with LPX motherboards, so it is possible to find interchangability problems between different motherboards and cases. I usually do not recommend LPX style systems if future upgradability is a factor; it is not only difficult to locate a new motherboard that will fit, but LPX systems are also limited in expansion slots and drive bays as well. Generally, the baby AT configuration is the most popular and the most flexible type of system to consider.

Besides the form factor, there are several other features you should consider in a motherboard. The primary considerations would be the processor type and chipset. Motherboards you should consider would have a socket for one of three different processor families:

- 486
- Pentium
- Pentium Pro

The 486 class motherboards today will typically include a Zero Insertion Force (ZIF) Socket 3 (237-pin) and will accept any 486 processor from the 486 SX through the 486 DX4. A special class of low-cost 486 boards may come with an integrated (soldered in) 16-bit 486 SLC2 (IBM manufactured) and be upgradable to the 32-bit 486 processors via the ZIF Socket 3. Pentium motherboards will normally have a Zero Insertion Force (ZIF) Socket 5 (320-pin) or Socket 7 (321-pin) for the second generation Pentium processor, which is available in speeds from 75 MHz to 166 MHz and up. The Pentium Pro processor is Intel's newest processor family and is becoming a popular alternative among the highest end systems.

Depending on the exact processor version you install, and the speed at which it is to be run, there may be jumpers on the motherboard to set. There may also be jumpers to control the voltage supplied to the processor, and these should be carefully checked or the board and processor will not operate properly.

There are a few other items to consider when purchasing a motherboard. Besides the processor, the main component on the board would be the chipset. This is normally a set of one to five chips that contain the main motherboard circuits. These chipsets replace the 100 or more discrete components that were used in the original IBM AT systems, and allow a motherboard designer to easily create a functional system. The chipset will contain the local bus controller (usually PCI), the cache controller, main memory controller, DMA and Interrupt controllers, and several other circuits as well. The chipset used in a given motherboard will have a profound effect on the performance of the board, and will dictate performance parameters and limitations such as cache size and speed, main memory size and speed, processor types and speeds, etc.

Because chipsets are constantly being introduced and improved over time, I cannot possibly list all of them and their functions, but as an example, I will discuss some of the popular ones for Pentium based systems. There are several very popular high performance chipsets designed for Pentium motherboards on the market today. The best of these offer support for EDO (Extended Data Out) RAM, pipeline burst cache SRAM (Static RAM), PCI local bus, Advanced Power Management (APM), as well as other functions such as IDE interfaces.

Here are several of the high performance chipsets available for Pentium based motherboards:

- Intel Triton/Triton II. The 82430FX PCIset (called Triton) and HX (called Triton II) are both 4 chipsets. The Triton chipset consists of the 82437FX Triton System Controller (TSC), two 82438FX Triton Data Paths (TDP), and the 82371FB PCI ISA IDE Xcelerator (PIIX). The TSC integrates the cache and main memory control functions and provides bus control for transfers between the CPU, cache, main memory, and the PCI Bus. The L2 cache controller in the TSC supports write-back cache for cache sizes of 256 and 512K, as well as lower cost cacheless designs. Cache memory can be implemented with either standard, burst, or pipeline burst SRAMs (Static RAMs). The TSC and TDPs together support up to 128M of EDO (Extended Data Out) or standard main memory. The PIIX acts as a PCI to ISA bridge, and includes the DMA controllers, interrupt controllers, timer/counter, power management support, and an enhanced IDE interface with up to two IDE connectors for four IDE devices.

- The original (FX suffix) version Triton chipset unfortunately does NOT support parity checked RAM. This means that any motherboard built with this chipset will not be able to detect memory errors during system operation. Even if you purchase parity SIMMs, the parity will not be used. Many system integrators will not use non-parity RAM in mission critical systems such as file servers. Because of market pressures demanding such support, Intel has released a second generation (HX suffix) Triton II chipset that includes both parity and ECC (Error Correcting Code) memory support.

- Opti Viper. The 82C550 Viper-DP from Opti supports not only the Pentium, but the AMD K5 and Cyrix M1 processors as well, in both single and dual processor configurations. The Viper-DP chipset consists of three chips, the 82C556 Data Buffer Controller (DBC), the 82C557 System Controller (SC), and the 82C558 Integrated Peripherals Controller (IPC). The SC is the main chip and contains the main memory controller, L2 cache controller, and the PCI and VL-Bus interfaces. The IPC contains the ISA bus controller, DMA and Interrupt controllers, and PCI to ISA bridge. The DBC buffers the CPU and main memory and contains the parity generation and checking circuits. Viper supports up to 512 MB of EDO (Extended Data Out) or standard main memory with or without parity checking, and up to 2 MB of L2 write back cache using either asynchronous, burst, or pipeline burst SRAMs.

- ALI Aladdin. The Aladdin M1510 chipset from Acer Laboratories Inc. also supports the Pentium, AMD K5, and Cyrix M1 series processors in both single and dual processor configurations. Aladdin M1510 is a four-chip set. It includes the M1511 Memory/Cache Controller that supports EDO RAM as well as standard RAM up to 768 MB with or without parity checking. This chip also supports up to 1 MB of L2 write-back cache, including support for standard, burst, and pipeline burst SRAMs. The M1513 System I/O Controller contains the PCI bus interface, DMA and Interrupt controllers, timer circuits, PCI enhanced IDE interface, as well as an integrated keyboard controller. Finally, two M1512 Data Buffers are used which serve as an intermediate between the CPU and main memory.

The choices for Pentium Pro motherboard chipsets are a little more restricted. So far only a couple of chipsets are available, including the Intel Orion and Natoma chipsets. Intel's original Pentium Pro chipset was codenamed Orion and is technically known as the 82450GX or KX. This chipset is generally made up of 7 individual chips and supports up to 4 Pentium Pro processors and 2 separate PCI busses in the GX server version. A desktop version of Orion, the 82450KX, supports 2 processors and a single PCI bus.

More recently Intel released a less expensive and more efficient Natoma chipset for Pentium Pro machines. Natoma is technically called the 82440FX chipset and consists of only three chips rather than seven as with Orion. Natoma will support only two Pentium Pro processors and a single PCI bus, making it less suited to servers than the GX version of the Orion chipset. However, the greater internal efficiency of Natoma will make it a better performer overall than Orion.

No matter what Pentium class chipset you look for, I would recommend looking for the following supported features:

- EDO (Extended Data Out) RAM (main memory)
- Pipeline Burst (also called Synchronous) SRAM cache
- Parity generation and checking
- ECC (Error Correcting Code) memory support
- APM (Advanced Power Management) energy saving functions
- PCI Local Bus

Most of the better Pentium chipsets on the market today should have these features. If you are buying a motherboard, I highly recommend you contact the chipset manufacturer and obtain the documentation (usually called the *Data Book*) for your particular chipset. This will explain how the memory and cache controllers, as well as many other devices in your system, operate. This documentation will also describe the Advanced Chipset Setup functions in your system's SETUP program. With this information you may be able to fine tune the motherboard configuration by altering the chipset features. Because chipsets are discontinued and new ones are introduced all the time, don't wait too long to get the chipset documentation as most manufacturers only make it available for chips currently in production.

One interesting tidbit about the chipset is that in the volume that the motherboard manufacturers purchase them, the chipsets usually cost about $40 each. If you have an older motherboard and need repair, you normally cannot purchase the chipset because they are normally not stocked by the manufacturer after they are discontinued. The low cost chipset is one of the reasons that motherboards have become disposable items and are rarely if ever repaired.

Another feature on your motherboard will be the BIOS (Basic Input Output System). This is also called the ROM BIOS, since the code is stored in a Read Only Memory (ROM) chip. There are several things to look for here. One is that the BIOS be supplied by one of the major BIOS manufacturers such as AMI (American Megatrends International), Phoenix, Award, or Microid Research. Also make sure that the BIOS is contained in a special type of reprogrammable chip called a Flash ROM or EEPROM (Electrically Erasable Programmable Read Only Memory). This will allow you to download BIOS updates from the manufacturer and using a program they supply, easily update the code in your BIOS. If you do not have the Flash ROM or EEPROM type, you will have to physically replace the chip if an update is required.

Make sure that the Motherboard and BIOS support the new Plug and Play (PnP) specification. This will make installing new cards, especially PnP cards, much easier. PnP automates the installation and uses special software that is both built in to the BIOS as well as the operating system (such as Windows 95) to automatically configure adapter cards and resolve adapter resource conflicts.

Processor. In most cases your motherboard will come with the processor already installed. Most of the name brand motherboard manufacturers like to install the processor, and warranty both the board and processor as a unit. This is not always the case, and it is definitely possible to purchase the motherboard and processor separately.

The processor will be installed normally in a special *ZIF (Zero Insertion Force) socket* on the motherboard. Make sure the jumpers on the board are set to match the correct processor type, speed, and voltage.

Memory. Your system will require memory for the Level 2 (secondary) cache as well as the main memory. The cache memory will be in the form of individual SRAM (Static RAM) chips, or possibly in what is called COAST (Cache On A Stick) or CELP (Card Edge Low Profile). COAST and CELP are different names for the same thing. This is a new standard for cache SIMMs. COAST/CELP SIMMs have a different number of pins and pinout from standard main memory SIMMs, and are not interchangeable with them.

Most 486 and Pentium motherboards will support at least 256K to 512K of cache memory. The chips themselves are available in three basic types; standard asynchronous cache, burst cache, and pipeline burst cache. The latter offers the highest performance, and should be the choice providing your motherboard supports it. Most of the newer Pentium boards support the pipeline burst cache chips, while most of the 486 boards do not. This is because these faster cache chips are not really needed at the slower 33 to 40 MHz memory bus speeds on the 486 compared to the 60 and 66 MHz memory bus speeds in a Pentium system.

Main memory will normally be installed in the form of *SIMMs (Single Inline Memory Modules)* or in some cases the newer *DIMMs (Dual Inline Memory Modules)*. There are three different physical types of main memory modules used in PC systems today, with several variations of each. The three main types are as follows:

- 30-pin SIMMs
- 72-pin SIMMs
- 168-pin DIMMs

The 72-pin SIMMs are by far the most common type of memory module used today; however, just a few years ago most systems came with 30-pin modules. Many of the high-end systems use the DIMMs, because they are 64-bits wide and can be used as a single bank on a Pentium or Pentium Pro system. Depending on the type of processor, a different number of SIMMs must be installed to make a complete memory bank, and the 72-pin SIMMs are four times as dense as the 30-pin types.

For example, in a 486-based system, you would need four 30-pin SIMMs to make a single bank of memory, while only one 72-pin SIMM would be required for a single bank. This is because the 72-pin SIMMs hold data 32-bits wide, while the 30-pin SIMMs only hold data 8-bits wide. A 64-bit Pentium system, then, would require two 72-pin SIMMs or a single 168-pin DIMM to make a single bank.

Memory modules can include an extra bit for each eight to be used for parity checking. These are called *parity SIMMs* or *parity DIMMs* and are required by most older boards. Many newer motherboards do not employ parity checking, which means that you will not be able to use the slightly more expensive parity SIMMs. You can install them, but the extra parity bits will not function. I do not necessarily agree with this philosophy, but nevertheless, many newer motherboards (such as those based on the Intel Triton chipset) simply cannot utilize parity checking at all! Most other chipsets, including the newer Triton II, do support memory parity checking.

Another thing to watch out for is the type of metal on the memory module contacts. They are available with either tin- or gold-plated contacts. While it may seem that gold-plated contacts are better (they are) you should not use them in all systems. You should instead always match the type of plating on the module contacts to what is also used on the socket contacts. In other words, if the motherboard SIMM or DIMM sockets have tin-plated contacts, then you MUST use SIMMs or DIMMs with tin-plated contacts also.

If you mix dissimilar metals (tin with gold), there will be a rapidly accelerated corrosion occurring on the tin side, and also tiny electrical currents will be generated. The combination of the corrosion and tiny currents causes havoc and all types of memory problems and errors occur. In some systems I have observed that everything will seem fine for about a year, during which the corrosion develops. After that, random memory errors result. Removing and cleaning the memory module and socket contacts postpones the problem for another year, upon which the problems return again. How would you like this problem if you had 100 or more systems to support? Of course you can avoid these problems if you insist on using SIMMs with contacts whose metal matches the metal found in the sockets in which they will be installed.

Finally, some systems now use a special type of memory called *EDO (Extended Data Out)*. These memory chips are slightly redesigned and do not cost much more than standard non-EDO memory, but they can operate at increased efficiency in a motherboard designed for them. The actual speed increase varies but is usually not more than a couple of percentage points. Motherboards that use EDO memory also can use standard non-EDO memory, but they will not enjoy the increased performance. You also can install EDO memory in older systems that do not support it, because EDO is backwards compatible with standard (called fast page mode) memory. Of course installing the more expensive EDO modules in an older system will not improve performance.

I/O Ports

Most motherboards today have built-in I/O ports. If these ports are not built-in, then they will have to be supplied via a plug-in expansion board that unfortunately wastes a slot. The following ports should be included in any new system you assemble:

- Mouse port (so-called PS/2 type)
- Two local bus enhanced IDE ports (primary and secondary)
- Floppy controller (2.88M capable)
- Two serial ports (16550A buffered type)
- Parallel port (EPP/ECP type)

The standard thing today is to include these ports directly on the motherboard. This is possible because there are several chip companies that have implemented all of these features except the mouse port (which uses the keyboard controller) on a single "Super I/O" chip! These chips often cost less than $5 in quantities of 1,000 or more, so adding these items directly to the motherboard saves a more expensive board taking up an expansion slot.

If these devices are not present on the motherboard, then various "Super-" or "Multi-I/O" boards are available that implement all of these ports. Again, most of the newer versions of these boards will use a single chip implementation since it is cheaper and more reliable.

Floppy Disk Drive

Obviously, your system will need some type of floppy drive to load software. Most commonly this would be a 1.44M 3-1/2 inch drive, but I usually recommend a 2.88M drive these days. The 2.88M drives are superior to the 1.44M drives, and they are fully backwards compatible. Virtually all controllers and ROM BIOS these days will fully support the 2.88M drives.

If you are interested in saving a drive bay, most of the floppy drive manufacturers make combo drives that include both a 3-1/2 inch 1.44M and 5-1/4 inch 1.2M drive in a single unit, which installs in a half-height 5-1/4 inch bay. At least one company (Teac) offers a combo drive that combines a 1.44M floppy and a quad-speed CD-ROM drive in a single unit as well. One drawback of these combo units is that if one of the components fails, the entire combo drive will have to be replaced. Also nobody seems to make these with the more desirable 2.88M floppy drives.

Hard Disk Drive

Your system will also need a hard disk. In most cases, a drive with a minimum capacity of 1G is recommended, although in some cases you can get away with only 500M for a low-end configuration. High-end systems should have drives of 2-4G or higher. The most popular interface is IDE, although SCSI can also be used. IDE generally offers greater performance for single or dual drive installations, but SCSI is better for more drives or with multi-tasking operating systems. This is due to the greater intelligence in the SCSI interface, which relieves some of the I/O processing from the CPU in the system.

There are several brands of drives to choose from, but most of them offer similar performance within their price and capacity category.

CD-ROM Drive

A CD-ROM drive should be considered a mandatory item in any PC you construct these days. This is because most software is now being distributed on CD-ROM, especially multimedia programs. In the future, systems will be able to boot from CD-ROM drives. There are several types of CD-ROM drives to consider these days, but mostly I recommend a minimum of a Quad-speed drive interfaced via an IDE connection. This results in the best possible performance with the minimum amount of hassle.

Keyboard and Pointing Device (Mouse)

Obviously your system will need a keyboard and some type of pointing device such as a mouse. There is a lot of subjectivity here as to what is appropriate. Different people prefer different types of keyboards, and the "feel" of one type can vary considerably from other types. I suggest that you try a variety of keyboards until you find what suits you best. I prefer a stiff action with tactile feedback myself, but others prefer a lighter, quieter touch.

Because there are two types of keyboard connectors found in systems today, make sure that the keyboard you purchase matches the connector on your motherboard. Most baby-AT boards use the larger 5-pin DIN connector, and most LPX boards use the 6-pin mini-DIN connector, however the trend now seems to be changing to the mini-DIN connector for all boards. On some motherboards you have an option of choosing either connector when you purchase the board. If you end up with a keyboard and motherboard that do not match, there are several companies that sell adapters that will mate either type of keyboard to either type of motherboard connector.

The same thing applies to mice or other pointing devices, that is there are a number of different choices that suit different individuals. Try several before deciding on the type you want. If your motherboard includes a built-in mouse port, make sure that you get a mouse that is designed for that interface. These are often called PS/2 type mice, since the IBM PS/2 systems were the first with this type of mouse port. Many systems use a serial mouse connected to a serial port, but if you have the choice of using a motherboard integrated mouse port, that would be better. Having an integrated motherboard mouse port will allow you to have both serial ports free for other devices.

Video Card and Display

You will need a video adapter or interface as well as a monitor or display to complete your system. There are numerous choices in this area, but the biggest piece of advice I have is to choose a good monitor. The display is your main interface to the system, and can be the cause of many hours of either pain or pleasure depending on what you choose. I normally recommend a minimum of a 17" display these days, as anything smaller will not acceptably display 1,024x768 pixel resolution. If you opt for a smaller

15" display, you will find that the maximum tolerable resolution will be 800x600. This may sound confusing since practically all 15" monitors claim to be able to display 1,024x768 resolution or even higher, but the problem is that the characters and features will be so small on the screen at that resolution that excessive eyestrain and headaches will result. If you spend a lot of time in front of your system, and want to display the higher resolution, a 17" display should be considered mandatory.

Sound Card and Speakers

A sound card will be required for any system that is to be multimedia capable, as will a set of external speakers. The sound card should be compatible with the Creative Labs Sound Blaster cards, which have set the standards in this area. Speakers are really a personal choice, you can go with very inexpensive and tiny speakers or spend much more money on larger ones.

Accessories

Often you will need various accessories to complete your system. These are the small parts that can make or break the assembly process.

Heat Sinks/Cooling Fans. Most of today's faster processors produce a lot of heat, and this heat has to be dissipated or your system will operate intermittently or even fail completely. Heat sinks are available in two main types, passive or active.

Passive heat sinks are simply finned chunks of metal (usually aluminum) that are clipped or glued on to the top of the processor. They act as a radiator, and in effect give the processor more surface area to dissipate the heat. I normally recommend this passive design type of heat sink, because there are no mechanical parts to fail. In some cases, you should use a thermal transfer grease or sticky tape to fill any air gaps between the heat sink and the processor. This allows for maximum heat transfer and the best efficiency.

An *active heat sink* includes a fan. These can offer greater cooling capacity than the passive types, but require power and are not known for reliability. They often use a cheap fan mechanism that fails after a year or so, thus allowing the processor to overheat and the system to fail. If you do use an active heat sink with a fan, stay away from cheaper units that may be more failure prone.

Notice that the newer ATX form factor motherboards are designed to eliminate the troublesome and unreliable active heat sink (CPU fan). These systems feature a power supply with reverse flow cooling that blows air directly over the CPU, which is relocated in these systems to take advantage of this. Due to a superior design, the ATX motherboard form factor eliminates the need for any sort of cooling fan mounted directly to the CPU.

Cables. Any PC system will need a number of different cables to hook everything up. These can include power cables or adapters, disk drive cables, CD-ROM cables, and many others. Most of the time the devices you purchase will come with included cables, but in some cases they will not be supplied. The vendor list in Appendix B of this book has several cable and small parts suppliers listed that can get you the cables or other parts you need to complete your system.

Another advantage of the ATX motherboard form factor is that these boards feature externally accessible I/O connectors directly mounted to the rear of the board. This eliminates the "rats nest" of cables found in the common baby-AT form factor systems. This feature also makes the ATX system a little cheaper and more reliable as well.

Hardware. You will need screws, standoffs, and other miscellaneous hardware to assemble your system. Most of this will come with the case, but in some situations you may need more. Again, you can consult the vendor list in Appendix B for suppliers of small parts and hardware needed to get your system operational.

Operating System Software. You will need operating system software to run your PC, such as DOS, Windows, or OS/2. Most software houses will carry a selection of appropriate operating system software, and any applications you need as well.

System Assembly

Actually assembling the system is easy after you have lined up all of the components! In fact, you will find the procurement phase the most lengthy and trying of the entire experience. Completing the system is simply a matter of screwing everything together, plugging in all of the cable and connectors, and configuring everything to operate properly together.

More explicit instructions for installing any of the system components can be found in the section of this book that covers that particular component. For example, to find out about configuring and installing the floppy drive, consult Chapter 13, "Floppy Disk Drives."

In short order, you will find out whether your system operates as you had planned, or whether there are some incompatibilities between some of the components. Be careful and pay attention to how you install all of your components. It is rare that a newly assembled system operates perfectly the first time, even for those who are somewhat experienced. It is easy to forget a jumper, switch, cable connection, and so on, which would cause problems in system operation. The first reaction if there are problems is to blame the problem on defective hardware, but that is usually not the case. Usually the problem can be traced to some missed step or error made in the assembly process.

Sources and Suppliers

One of the most valuable (to me anyway) parts of this book is the vendor list in Appendix B. Here you will find a number of vendors of different PC components including addresses, phone numbers, and other information as it is available. These vendors are in this list usually because I recommend their products, or because they are an important company whose products are very popular. There are companies listed in the vendor list covering all of the components needed to build your system. In some cases, the manufacturers of the components listed will not sell direct to end users, and you may find yourself purchasing through a distributor instead. That is OK, I normally include the actual manufacturer in my list because they can best recommend a distributor for their own products, and of course they should support their own products as well.

Summary

Building your own system is an excellent learning experience, and I highly recommend it. Not only will you learn more about PCs and how they operate, but you will know your own system inside and out. In addition, you will end up with a system that uses precisely the components you want, and is, in effect, custom tailored to your own specifications. That is something that is hard to get in an off-the-shelf PC.

On the other hand, building your own system will generally cost more money than a store bought (especially mail ordered) system. Not only will you spend more on the hardware, but you will spend more on phone calls and shipping charges as well. Also, you will not have a central source for support or warranty claims, which may be problematic for a new PC user. In short, if you are inexperienced, or simply wish to save money, then building your own system is generally not recommended.

For those who are willing to go through the experience, the rewards can be well worth the additional expense and trouble!

Chapter 20

Maintaining Your System: Preventive Maintenance, Backups, and Warranties

Preventive maintenance is the key to obtaining years of trouble-free service from your computer system. A properly administered preventive maintenance program pays for itself by reducing problem behavior, data loss, component failure, and by ensuring a long life for your system. In several cases, I have "repaired" an ailing system with nothing more than a preventive maintenance session. Preventive maintenance also increases your system's resale value because it will look and run better. This chapter describes preventive maintenance procedures and how often you should perform them.

You also will learn the importance of creating backup files of data and the various backup procedures available. A sad reality in the computer repair and servicing world is that hardware can always be repaired or replaced, but data cannot. Most hard disk troubleshooting and service procedures, for example, require that a low-level format be done. This low-level format overwrites any data on the disk.

In Chapter 22, "Operating Systems Software and Troubleshooting," simple techniques for recovering data from a damaged disk or disk drive are explained. These procedures, however, are not perfect.

Because data recovery depends a great deal on the type and severity of damage and the expertise of the recovery specialist, data-recovery services are very expensive. Most recovery services charge a premium and offer no guarantees that the data will be completely recovered. Backing up your system as discussed in this chapter is the only guarantee you have of seeing your data again.

Most of the discussion of backing up systems in this chapter is limited to professional solutions that require special hardware and software. Backup solutions that employ floppy disk drives, such as the DOS backup software, are insufficient and too costly in most cases for hard disk backups. It would take 2,867 1.44M floppy disks, for example, to backup the 4 gigabyte hard disk in my portable system! That would cost more than $1,000 in disks, not to mention the time involved. A DAT (Digital Audio Tape) system, on the other hand, can put 4G to 8G or more on a single $15 tape.

Although the DAT drive itself will cost $500 or more, the media costs are really far more significant than the cost of the drive. If you are doing responsible backups, you will have at least three sets of media for each system you are backing up. The media sets would be used on a rotating basis, and one of them should be moved off-site. The media sets should be changed out at an interval of a year or less to prevent excessive wear. If you are backing up more than one system, these media costs will add up quickly.

You should also factor in the cost of time. If a backup requires manual intervention to change the media during the backup, I don't recommend it. A backup system should be able to fit a complete backup on a single tape so that the backup can be done unattended. If somebody has to hang around to switch tapes every so often, the backup becomes a real chore and is less likely to be performed. Also, every time a media change occurs, there is a substantial increase in the likelihood of errors and problems that may not be realized until a restore is performed. Backup is far more important than most people realize, and spending a little more on a quality piece of hardware like a DAT drive will pay off in the long run with greater reliability, lower media costs, higher performance, and unattended backups that contain the entire system file structure.

Finally, the last section in this chapter discusses the standard warranties and optional service contracts available for many systems. Although most of this book is written for people who want to perform their own maintenance and repair service, taking advantage of a good factory warranty that provides service for free definitely is prudent. Some larger computer companies, such as IBM, offer attractive service contracts that, in some cases, are cost-justified over self service. These types of options are examined in the final section.

Developing a Preventive Maintenance Program

Developing a preventive maintenance program is important to everyone who uses or manages personal computer systems. Two types of preventive maintenance procedures exist—active and passive.

Active preventive maintenance includes steps you apply to a system that promote a longer, trouble-free life. This type of preventive maintenance primarily involves periodic cleaning of the system and its components. This section describes several active preventive maintenance procedures, including cleaning and lubricating all major components, reseating chips and connectors, and reformatting hard disks.

Passive preventive maintenance includes steps you can take to protect a system from the environment, such as using power-protection devices; ensuring a clean, temperature-controlled environment; and preventing excessive vibration. In other words, passive preventive maintenance means treating your system well. This section also describes passive preventive maintenance procedures.

Active Preventive Maintenance Procedures

How often you should implement active preventive maintenance procedures depends on the system's environment and the quality of the system's components. If your system is in a dirty environment, such as a machine shop floor or a gas station service area, you might need to clean your system every three months or less. For normal office environments, cleaning a system every one to two years is usually fine. However, if you open your system after one year and find dust bunnies inside, you should probably shorten the cleaning interval.

Another active preventive maintenance technique discussed in this section is reformatting hard disks. Low-level reformatting restores the track and sector marks to their proper locations and forces you to back up and restore all data on the drive. Not all drives require this procedure, but if you are using drives with a stepper-motor head actuator, periodic reformatting is highly recommended. Most drives with voice-coil head actuators run indefinitely without reformatting due to their track following servo mechanisms that prevent temperature induced mistracking.

Other hard disk preventive maintenance procedures include making periodic backups of critical areas such as Boot Sectors, File Allocation Tables, and Directory structures on the disk.

Cleaning a System. One of the most important operations in a good preventive maintenance program is regular and thorough cleaning of the system. Dust buildup on the internal components can lead to several problems. One is that the dust acts as a thermal insulator, which prevents proper system cooling. Excessive heat shortens the life of system components and adds to the thermal stress problem caused by wider temperature changes between power-on and power-off states. Additionally, the dust may contain conductive elements that can cause partial short circuits in a system. Other elements in dust and dirt can accelerate corrosion of electrical contacts and cause improper connections. In all, the removal of any layer of dust and debris from within a computer system benefits that system in the long run.

All PC-compatible systems use a forced-air cooling system that allows for even cooling inside the system. A fan is mounted in, on, or near the power supply and pushes air outside. This setup depressurizes the interior of the system relative to the outside air. The lower pressure inside the system causes outside air to be drawn into openings in the system chassis and cover. This draw-through, or depressurization, is the most efficient cooling system that can be designed without an air filter. Air filters typically are not used with depressurization systems because there is no easy way to limit air intake to a single port that can be covered by a filter.

Some industrial computers use a forced-air system that uses the fan to pressurize, rather than to depressurize, the case. This system forces air to exhaust from any holes in the chassis and case or cover. The key to the pressurization system is that all air intake for the system is at a single location—the fan. The air flowing into the system, therefore, can be filtered by simply integrating a filter assembly into the fan housing. The filter must be cleaned or changed periodically. Because the interior of the case is pressurized relative to the outside air, airborne contaminants are not drawn into the system even though it may not be sealed. Any air entering the system must pass through the fan and filter housing, which removes the contaminants. Pressurization cooling systems are used primarily in industrial computer models designed for extremely harsh environments.

Most systems you have contact with are depressurization systems. Mounting any sort of air filter on these types of systems is impossible because air enters the system from too many sources. With any cooling system in which incoming air is not filtered, dust and other chemical matter in the environment is drawn in and builds up inside the computer. This buildup can cause severe problems if left unchecked.

One problem that can develop is overheating. The buildup of dust acts as a heat insulator, which prevents the system from cooling properly. Some of the components in a modern PC can generate an enormous amount of heat that must be dissipated for the component to function. The dust also might contain chemicals that conduct electricity. These chemicals can cause minor current shorts and create electrical signal paths where none should exist. The chemicals also cause rapid corrosion of cable connectors, socket-installed components, and areas where boards plug into slots. All can cause intermittent system problems and erratic operation.

Tip

Cigarette smoke contains chemicals that can conduct electricity and cause corrosion of computer parts. The smoke residue can infiltrate the entire system, causing corrosion and contamination of electrical contacts and sensitive components such as floppy drive read/write heads and optical drive lens assemblies. You should avoid smoking near computer equipment and encourage your company to develop and enforce a similar policy.

Floppy disk drives are particularly vulnerable to the effects of dirt and dust. Floppy drives are a large "hole" within the system through which air continuously flows. Therefore, they accumulate a large amount of dust and chemical buildup within a short time. Hard disk drives do not present quite the same problem. Because the head disk assembly (HDA) in a hard disk is a sealed unit with a single barometric vent, no dust or dirt can enter without passing through the barometric vent filter. This filter ensures that contaminating dust or particles cannot enter the interior of the HDA. Thus, cleaning a hard disk requires simply blowing the dust and dirt off from outside the drive. No internal cleaning is required.

Disassembly and Cleaning Tools. To properly clean the system and all the boards inside requires certain supplies and tools. In addition to the tools required to disassemble the unit, you should have these items:

- Contact cleaning solution
- Canned air

- A small brush
- Lint-free foam cleaning swabs
- Antistatic wrist-grounding strap

You also might want to acquire these optional items:

- Foam tape
- Low-volatile room-temperature vulcanizing (RTV) sealer
- Silicone type lubricant
- Computer vacuum cleaner

These simple cleaning tools and chemical solutions will allow you to perform most common preventive maintenance tasks.

Chemicals. You can use several different types of cleaning solutions with computers and electronic assemblies. Most fall into the following categories:

- Standard cleaners
- Contact cleaner/Lubricants
- Dusters

Tip

The makeup of many of the chemicals used for cleaning electronic components has been changing because many of the chemicals originally used are now considered environmentally unsafe. They have been attributed to damaging the earth's ozone layer, a natural protective barrier in the stratosphere which prevents harmful ultraviolet (UV-B) radiation from reaching earth. Chlorine atoms from chlorofluorocarbons (CFCs) and chlorinated solvents attach themselves to ozone molecules and destroy them. Many of these chemicals are now strictly regulated by federal and international agencies in an effort to preserve the ozone layer. Most of the companies that produce chemicals used for system cleaning and maintenance have had to introduce environmentally safe replacements. The only drawback is that many of these safer chemicals cost more and usually do not work as well as those they replace.

Many specific chemicals are used in cleaning and dusting solutions, but five types are of particular interest. The EPA has classified ozone-damaging chemicals into two classes—Class I and Class II. Chemicals that fall into these two classes have their usage regulated. Other chemicals are nonregulated. Class I chemicals include:

- Chlorofluorocarbons (CFCs)
- Chlorinated solvents

Class I chemicals can only be sold for use in professional service and not to consumers. A law that went into effect on May 15, 1993, requires that the containers for Class I chemicals be labeled with a warning that the product "Contains substances that harm public health and the environment by destroying ozone in the atmosphere." Additionally, electronics manufacturers and other industries must also apply a similar warning label to any products that use Class I chemicals in the production process. This means that any circuit board or computer that is manufactured with CFCs will have this label!

The most popular Class I chemicals are the various forms of Freon, which are CFCs. A very popular cleaning solution called 1,1,1 Trichloroethane is a chlorinated solvent and also is strictly regulated. Up until the last year or so, virtually all computer or electronic cleaning solutions contained one or both of these chemicals. While you can still purchase them, regulations and limited production have made them more expensive and more difficult to find.

Class II chemicals include hydrochlorofluorocarbons (HCFCs). These are not as strictly regulated as Class I chemicals because they have a lower ozone depletion potential. Many cleaning solutions have switched to HCFCs because they do not require the restrictive labeling required by Class I chemicals and are not as harmful. Most HCFCs have only one tenth the ozone damaging potential of CFCs.

Other nonregulated chemicals include Volatile Organic Compounds (VOCs) and Hydrofluorocarbons (HFCs). These chemicals do not damage the ozone layer but actually contribute to ozone production, which, unfortunately, appears in the form of smog or ground level pollution. Pure isopropyl alcohol is an example of a VOC that is commonly used in electronic part and contact cleaning. HFCs are used as a replacement for CFCs because the HFCs do not damage the ozone layer.

The EPA has developed a method to measure the ozone damaging capability of a chemical. The Ozone Depletion Potential (ODP) of a chemical solution is the sum of the depletion potentials of each of the chemicals used in the solution by weight. The ODP of Freon R12 (Automotive Air Conditioning Freon), is 1.0 on this scale. Most modern CFC replacement chemicals have an ODP rating of 0.0 to 0.1, as opposed to those using CFCs and chlorinated solvents that usually have ODP ratings of 0.75 or higher.

Standard Cleaners. Standard cleaning solutions are available in a variety of types and configurations. You can use pure isopropyl alcohol, acetone, Freon, trichloroethane, or a variety of other chemicals. Most board manufacturers and service shops are now leaning to the alcohol, acetone, or other chemicals that do not cause ozone depletion and that comply with government regulations and environmental safety. You should be sure that your cleaning solution is designed to clean computers or electronic assemblies. In most cases this means that the solution should be chemically pure and free from contaminants or other unwanted substances. You should not, for example, use drugstore rubbing alcohol for cleaning electronic parts or contacts because it is not pure and could contain water or perfumes. The material must be moisture-free and residue-free. The solutions should be in liquid form, not a spray. Sprays can be wasteful and you almost never spray the solution directly on components. Instead, wet a foam or chamois swab used for wiping the component. These electronic-component cleaning solutions are available at any good electronics parts stores.

Contact Cleaner/Lubricants. These are very similar to the standard cleaners but include a lubricating component. The lubricant eases the force required when plugging and unplugging cables and connectors, which reduces strain on the devices. The lubricant coating also acts as a conductive protectant that insulates the contacts from corrosion. These chemicals can greatly prolong the life of a system by preventing intermittent contacts in the future.

Contact cleaner/lubricants are especially effective on I/O slot connectors, adapter card edge and pin connectors, disk drive connectors, power supply connectors, and virtually any connectors in the PC.

An excellent contact enhancer and lubricant is Stabilant 22. It is more effective than conventional contact cleaners or lubricants. This chemical is available in several forms. Stabilant 22 is the full strength concentrated version, while Stabilant 22a is a version diluted with isopropyl alcohol in a 4 to 1 ratio. An even more diluted 8 to 1 ratio version is sold in many high end stereo and audio shops under the name "Tweek." Just 15ml of Stabilant 22a sells for about $40, while a liter of the concentrate costs about $4,000. While Stabilant 22 is expensive, very little is required and an application can provide protection for a long time. Stabilant is manufactured by D. W. Electrochemicals, which is listed in the Vendor List in Appendix B.

Dusters. Compressed gas often is used as an aid in system cleaning. The compressed gas is used as a blower to remove dust and debris from a system or component. Originally, these dusters used CFCs such as Freon, while modern dusters now use HFCs or carbon dioxide, neither of which is damaging to the ozone layer. Be careful when you use these devices because some of them can generate a static charge when the compressed gas leaves the nozzle of the can. Be sure that you are using the kind approved for cleaning or dusting off computer equipment, and consider wearing a static grounding strap as a precaution. The type of compressed-air cans used for cleaning camera equipment can sometimes differ from the type used for cleaning static sensitive computer components.

Most older computer-grade canned gas dusters consisted of dichlorodifluoromethane (Freon R12), the same chemical used in many automotive air-conditioning systems built until 1996, when a ban of the manufacture and use of R12 takes place. In 1992 many automobile manufacturers began switching to an ozone-safe chemical called R134a, and most had switched to the new refrigerant by 1994. Manufacturing of R12 has ceased, and the regulations placed on its use have forced companies to use other products such as carbon dioxide for compressed gas dusters. In addition to the environmental concerns about depleting the ozone layer, Freon can be dangerous if exposed to an open flame.

Caution

If you use any chemical with the propellant Freon R12 (dichlorodifluoromethane), do not expose the gas to an open flame or other heat source. If you burn this substance, a highly toxic gas called phosgene is generated. Phosgene, used as a choking agent in World War I, can be deadly.

Related to compressed-air products are chemical-freeze sprays. These sprays are used to quickly cool down a suspected failing component, which often temporarily restores it to operation. These substances are not used to repair a device, but to confirm that you have found a failed device. Often, a component's failure is heat-related and cooling it temporarily restores it to function. If the circuit begins operating normally, the device you are cooling is the suspect device.

Vacuum Cleaners. Some people prefer to use a vacuum cleaner instead of canned gas dusters for cleaning a system. Canned gas is usually better for cleaning in small areas. A vacuum cleaner is more useful when you are cleaning a system loaded with dust and dirt. You can use the vacuum cleaner to suck out dust and debris instead of blowing them on other components, which sometimes happens with canned air. For outbound servicing (when you are going to the location of the equipment instead of the equipment coming to you), canned air is easier to carry in a toolkit than a small vacuum cleaner. There are also tiny vacuum cleaners available for system cleaning. These small units are easy to carry and may serve as an alternative to compressed air cans.

Note that there are special vacuum cleaners specifically designed for using on and around electronic components. They are designed to minimize ESD (Electro Static Discharge) while in use. If you are using a regular vacuum cleaner and not one specifically designed with ESD protection, then you should take precautions such as wearing a grounding wrist strap. Also be careful if the cleaner has a metal nozzle not to touch it to the circuit boards or components you are cleaning.

Brushes and Swabs. A small brush (makeup, photographic, or paint) can be used to carefully loosen accumulated dirt and dust before spraying with canned air or using the vacuum cleaner. Be careful about generating static electricity. In most cases the brushes should not be used directly on circuit boards but should be used instead on the case interior and other parts such as fan blades, air vents, and keyboards. Wear a grounded wrist strap if you are brushing on or near any circuit boards, and brush slowly and lightly to prevent static discharges from occurring.

Use cleaning swabs to wipe off electrical contacts and connectors, disk drive heads, and other sensitive areas. The swabs should be made of foam or synthetic chamois material that does not leave lint or dust residue. Unfortunately, proper foam or chamois cleaning swabs are more expensive than the typical cotton swabs. Do not use cotton swabs because they leave cotton fibers on everything they touch. Cotton fibers are conductive in some situations and can remain on drive heads, which can scratch disks. Foam or chamois swabs can be purchased at most electronics-supply stores.

One item to avoid is an eraser for cleaning contacts. Many people (including myself) have recommended using a soft pencil type eraser for cleaning circuit board contacts. Testing has proven this to be bad advice for several reasons. One is that any such abrasive wiping on electrical contacts generates friction and an Electro-Static Discharge (ESD). This ESD can be damaging to boards and components, especially with newer low voltage devices made using CMOS (Complimentary Metal Oxide Semiconductor) technology. These devices are especially static sensitive, and cleaning the contacts without a proper liquid solution is not recommended. Also, the eraser will wear off the gold coating on many contacts, exposing the tin contact underneath, which will rapidly corrode when exposed to air. Some companies sell premoistened contact cleaning pads that are soaked in a proper contact cleaner and lubricant. These pads are safe to wipe on conductor and contacts with no likelihood of ESD damage or abrasion of the gold plating.

Foam Tape or RTV Sealer. Hard disks usually use a small copper strap to ground the spindle of the disk assembly to the logic board, thus bleeding off any static charge carried by the spinning disk platters. Unfortunately, with most older drives, this strap often can begin to harmonize, or vibrate, and result in an annoying squealing or whining noise. (Sometimes the noise is similar to fingernails dragged across a chalkboard.) This spindle motor ground strap has been redesigned and can be hidden on newer drives, making it difficult to see. Fortunately, it rarely makes noise on the 3.5 inch or smaller drives.

To eliminate the source of irritation, you can stop the strap from vibrating by weighting it. One method is to use a piece of foam tape cut to match the size of the strap and stuck to the strap's back side. Another way to dampen the vibration is to apply a low-volatile RTV sealer. You apply this silicone-type rubber to the back of the grounding strap. After it hardens to a rubber-like material, the sealer stops the vibrations that produce the annoying squeal. You can buy the RTV sealer from an automotive-supply house.

I prefer using the foam tape rather than the RTV because it is easier and neater to apply. If you use the RTV, be sure that it is the low-volatile type, which does not generate acid when it cures. This acid produces the vinegar smell common to the standard RTV sealer, and can be highly corrosive to the strap and anything else it contacts. The low-volatile RTV also eliminates the bad vinegar smell. You can purchase the foam tape at most electronics-supply stores, where it often is sold for attaching alarm switches to doors or windows. The low-volatile RTV is available from most auto-supply stores. To be sure that you buy low-volatile RTV, look for the packaging to state specifically that the product is either a low-volatile type or is compatible with automobile oxygen sensors.

Silicone Lubricants. Silicone lubricants are used to lubricate the door mechanisms on floppy disk drives and any other part of the system that may require clean, non-oily lubrication. Other items you can lubricate are the disk drive head slider rails or even printer-head slider rails, which allow for smooth operation.

Using silicone instead of conventional oils is important because silicone does not gum up and collect dust and other debris. Always use the silicone sparingly. Do not spray it anywhere near the equipment as it tends to migrate and will end up where it doesn't belong (such as on drive heads). Instead, apply a small amount to a toothpick or foam swab and dab the silicone on the components where needed. You can use a lint-free cleaning stick soaked in silicone lubricant to lubricate the metal print-head rails in a printer.

Remember that some of the cleaning operations described in this section might generate a static charge. You may want to use a static grounding strap in cases in which static levels are high to ensure that you do not damage any boards as you work with them.

Obtaining Required Tools and Accessories. Most cleaning chemicals and tools can be obtained from a number of electronics supply houses, or even the local Radio Shack. A company called Chemtronics specializes in chemicals for the computer and electronics industry. These and other companies that supply tools, chemicals, and other computer and electronic cleaning supplies are listed in the Vendor List in the Appendix. With all these items on hand, you should be equipped for most preventive maintenance operations.

Disassembling and Cleaning Procedures. To properly clean your system, it must be at least partially disassembled. Some people go as far as to remove the motherboard. Removing the motherboard results in the best possible access to other areas of the system but in the interest of saving time, you probably need to disassemble the system only to where the motherboard is completely visible.

All plug-in adapter cards must be removed, along with the disk drives. Although you can clean the heads of a floppy drive with a cleaning disk without opening the system unit's cover, you probably will want to do more thorough cleaning. In addition to the heads, you also should clean and lubricate the door mechanism and clean any logic boards and connectors on the drive. This procedure usually requires removing the drive.

Next, do the same procedure with a hard disk: clean the logic boards and connectors, as well as lubricate the grounding strap. To do so, you must remove the hard disk assembly. As a precaution, be sure it is backed up before removal.

Reseating Socketed Chips. A primary preventive maintenance function is to undo the effects of chip creep. As your system heats and cools, it expands and contracts, and the physical expansion and contraction causes components plugged into sockets to gradually work their way out of those sockets. This process is called chip creep. To correct its effects, you must find all socketed components in the system and make sure that they are properly reseated.

In most systems, all the memory chips are socketed or are installed in socketed SIMMs (Single Inline Memory Modules). SIMM devices are retained securely in their sockets by a positive latching mechanism and cannot creep out. Memory SIPP (Single Inline Pin Package) devices (SIMMs with pins rather than contacts) are not retained by a latching mechanism and therefore can creep out of their sockets. Standard socketed memory chips are prime candidates for chip creep. Most other logic components are soldered in. You can also expect to find the ROM chips, the main processor or CPU, and the math coprocessor in sockets. In most systems, these items are the only components that are socketed; all others are soldered in.

Exceptions, however, might exist. A socketed component in one system might not be socketed in another—even if both are from the same manufacturer. Sometimes this difference results from a parts-availability problem when the boards are manufactured. Rather than halt the assembly line when a part is not available, the manufacturer adds a socket instead of the component. When the component becomes available, it is plugged in and the board is finished. Many newer systems place the CPU in a Zero Insertion Force (ZIF) socket, which has a lever that can release the grip of the socket on the chip. In most cases there is very little creep with a ZIF socket.

To make sure that all components are fully seated in their sockets, place your hand on the underside of the board and then apply downward pressure with your thumb (from the top) on the chip to be seated. For larger chips, seat the chip carefully in two movements, and press separately on each end of the chip with your thumb to be sure that the chip is fully seated. (The processor and math coprocessor chips can usually be seated in this manner.) In most cases, you hear a crunching sound as the chip makes its way back into the socket. Because of the great force sometimes required to reseat the chips, this operation is difficult if you do not remove the board.

For motherboards, forcibly seating chips can be dangerous if you do not directly support the board from the underside with your hand. Too much pressure on the board can cause it to bow or bend in the chassis, and the pressure can crack it before seating takes place. The plastic standoffs that separate and hold the board up from the metal chassis are spaced too far apart to properly support the board under this kind of stress. Try this operation only if you can remove and support the board adequately from underneath.

You may be surprised to know that, even if you fully seat each chip, they might need reseating again within a year. The creep usually is noticeable within a year or less.

Cleaning Boards. After reseating any socketed devices that may have crept out of their sockets, the next step is to clean the boards and all connectors in the system. For this step, the cleaning solutions and the lint-free swabs described earlier are needed.

First, clean the dust and debris off the board and then clean any connectors on the board. To clean the boards, it is usually best to use a vacuum cleaner designed for electronic assemblies and circuit boards or a duster can of compressed gas. The dusters are especially effective at blasting any dust and dirt off the boards.

Also blow any dust out of the power supply, especially around the fan intake and exhaust areas. You do not need to disassemble the power supply to do this, just use a duster can and blast the compressed air into the supply through the fan exhaust port. This will blow the dust out of the supply and clean off the fan blades and grille, which will help with system airflow.

Caution

Be careful with electrostatic discharge (ESD), which can damage components, when cleaning electronic components. Take extra precautions in the dead of winter in an extremely dry, high-static environment. You can apply antistatic sprays and treatments to the work area to reduce the likelihood of ESD damage.

An antistatic wrist-grounding strap is recommended. This should be connected to a ground on the card or board you are wiping. This strap ensures that no electrical discharge occurs between you and the board. An alternative method is to keep a finger or thumb on the ground of the motherboard or card as you wipe it off. It is easier to ensure proper grounding while the motherboard is still installed in the chassis, so it is a good idea not to remove it.

Cleaning Connectors and Contacts. Cleaning the connectors and contacts in a system promotes reliable connections between devices. On a motherboard, you will want to clean the slot connectors, power-supply connectors, keyboard connector, and speaker connector. For most plug-in cards, you will want to clean the edge connectors that plug into slots on the motherboard as well as any other connectors, such as external ones mounted on the card bracket.

Submerge the lint-free swabs in the liquid cleaning solution. If you are using the spray, hold the swab away from the system and spray a small amount on the foam end until the solution starts to drip. Then, use the soaked foam swab to wipe the connectors on the boards. Pre-soaked wipes are the easiest to use. Simply wipe them along the contacts to remove any accumulated dirt and leave a protective coating behind.

On the motherboard, pay special attention to the slot connectors. Be liberal with the liquid; resoak the foam swab repeatedly, and vigorously clean the connectors. Don't worry if some of the liquid drips on the surface of the motherboard. These solutions are entirely safe for the whole board and will not damage the components.

Use the solution to wash the dirt off the gold contacts in the slot connectors, and then douse any other connectors on the board. Clean the keyboard connector, the grounding positions where screws ground the board to the system chassis, power-supply connectors, speaker connectors, battery connectors, and so on.

If you are cleaning a plug-in board, pay special attention to the edge connector that mates with the slot connector on the motherboard. When people handle plug-in cards, they often touch the gold contacts on these connectors. Touching the gold contacts coats them with oils and debris, which prevents proper contact with the slot connector when the board is installed. Make sure that these gold contacts are free of all finger oils and residue. It is a good idea to use one of the contact cleaners that has a conductive lubricant, which both allows connections to be made with less force, and also protects the contacts from corrosion.

Caution

Many people use a common pink eraser to rub the edge connectors clean. I do not recommend this procedure for two reasons. One, the eraser eventually removes some of the gold and leaves the tin solder or copper underneath exposed. Without the gold, the contact corrodes rapidly and requires frequent cleaning. The second reason to avoid cleaning with the eraser is that the rubbing action can generate a static charge. This charge can harm any component on the board. Rather than use an eraser, use the liquid solution and swab method described earlier.

You also will want to use the swab and solution to clean the ends of ribbon cables or other types of cables or connectors in a system. Clean the floppy drive cables and connectors, the hard disk cables and connectors, and any others you find. Don't forget to clean off the edge connectors that are on the disk drive logic boards as well as the power connectors to the drives.

Cleaning Floppy Drives. Because Chapter 13 explains the procedure for cleaning floppy drives, the information is not repeated here. The basic idea is to use a canned gas duster to dust off the interior of the drive, use the silicone lubricant on whatever items need lubrication, and follow up with a head cleaning, either manually with a foam swab or most likely with a chemical soaked cleaning disk.

For hard disks, take this opportunity to dampen or lubricate the grounding strap if you have a noise problem as described earlier. Dampening is the recommended solution because if you lubricate this point, the lubricant eventually dries up and the squeal can come back. Because the dampening is usually a more permanent fix for this sort of problem, I recommend it whenever possible. Most newer hard disks have this dampening material applied at the factory and are not likely to generate noise like older drives.

Cleaning the Keyboard and Mouse. Keyboards and mice are notorious for picking up dirt and garbage. If you have ever opened up an older keyboard, you often will be amazed at the junk you will find in there.

To prevent problems, it is a good idea to periodically clean out the keyboard with a vacuum cleaner. An alternative method is to turn the keyboard upside down and shoot it with a can of compressed gas. This will blow out the dirt and debris that has accumulated inside the keyboard and possibly prevent future problems with sticking keys or dirty keyswitches.

If a particular key is stuck or making intermittent contact, you can soak or spray that switch with contact cleaner. The best way to do this is to first remove the keycap and then spray the cleaner into the switch. This usually does not require complete disassembly of the keyboard. Periodic vacuuming or compressed gas cleaning will prevent more serious problems with sticking keys and keyswitches.

Most mice are easily cleaned. In most cases there is a twist off locking retainer that keeps the mouse ball retained in the body of the mouse. By removing the retainer, the ball will drop out. After removing the ball, you should clean it with one of the electronic cleaners. I would recommend a pure cleaner instead of a contact cleaner with lubricant because you do not want any lubricant on the mouse ball. Then you should clean off the rollers in the body of the mouse with the cleaner and some swabs.

Periodic cleaning of a mouse in this manner will eliminate or prevent skipping or erratic movement that can be frustrating. I also recommend a mouse pad for most ball type mice because the pad will prevent the mouse ball from picking up debris from your desk.

Mice often need frequent cleaning before they start sticking and jumping, which can be frustrating. If you never want to clean a mouse again, I suggest you look into the Honeywell mouse. These mice have a revolutionary new design that uses two external wheels rather than the conventional ball and roller system. The wheels work directly on the desk surface and are unaffected by dirt and dust. Because the body of the mouse is sealed, dirt and dust cannot enter it and gum up the positional sensors. I find this mouse excellent to use with my portable system because it works well on any surface. This mouse is virtually immune to the sticking and jumping that plagues ball and roller designs and never needs to be cleaned, so it is less frustrating than conventional mice.

Other pointing devices requiring little or no maintenance are the IBM designed Trackpoint and similar systems introduced by other manufacturers, such as the Glidepoint by Alps. These devices are totally sealed, and use pressure transducers to control pointer movement. Because they are sealed, cleaning need only be performed externally, and is as simple as wiping the device off with a mild cleaning solution to remove oils and other deposits that have accumulated from handling them.

Hard Disk Maintenance

Certain preventive maintenance procedures protect your data and ensure that your hard disk works efficiently. Some of these procedures actually minimize wear and tear on your drive, which will prolong its life. Additionally, a high level of data protection can be implemented by performing some simple commands periodically. These commands provide methods for backing up (and possibly later restoring) critical areas of the hard disk that, if damaged, would disable access to all your files.

Defragmenting Files. Over time, as you delete and save files to a hard disk, the files become fragmented. This means that they are split into many noncontiguous areas on the disk. One of the best ways to protect both your hard disk and the data on it is to periodically defragment the files on the disk. This serves two purposes. One is that by ensuring that all of the files are stored in contiguous sectors on the disk, head movement and drive wear and tear will be minimized. This has the added benefit of improving the speed at which files will be retrieved from the drive by reducing the head thrashing that occurs every time a fragmented file is accessed.

The second major benefit, and in my estimation the more important of the two, is that in the case of a disaster where the File Allocation Tables (FATs) and Root Directory are severely damaged, the data on the drive can usually be recovered very easily if the files are contiguous. On the other hand, if the files are split up in many pieces across the drive, it is virtually impossible to figure out which pieces belong to which files without an intact File Allocation Table (FAT) and directory system. For the purposes of data integrity and protection, I recommend defragmenting your hard disk drives on a weekly basis, or immediately after you perform any major backup.

Three main functions are found in most defragmenting programs:

- File Defragmentation
- File Packing (Free Space Consolidation)
- File Sorting

Defragmentation is the basic function but most other programs also add file packing. Packing the files is optional on some programs because it usually takes additional time to perform. This function packs the files at the beginning of the disk so that all free space is consolidated at the end of the disk. This feature minimizes future file fragmentation by eliminating any empty holes on the disk. Because all free space is consolidated into one large area, any new files written to the disk will be able to be written in a contiguous manner with no fragmentation necessary.

The last function, file sorting, is not usually necessary and is performed as an option by many defragmenting programs. This function adds a tremendous amount of time to the operation, and has little or no effect on the speed at which information is accessed. It can be somewhat beneficial for disaster recovery purposes because you will have an idea of which files came before or after other files if a disaster occurs. These benefits would be minimal compared to having the files be contiguous no matter what their order. Not all defragmenting programs offer file sorting and the extra time it takes is probably not worth any benefits you will receive. Other programs can sort the order that files are listed in directories, which is a quick and easy operation compared to sorting the file ordering the disk.

Several programs are available that can defragment the files on a hard disk. Both the Windows 95 and DOS contain built-in degragmenters. The Windows 95 version is a graphical application that runs within the Win 95 environment. It has the ability to defragment disks in the background while other applications are running, making it more convenient than conventional defragmenters. While it is running, you can see details of the defragmenting process or display a minimal status view of the process.

DOS 6 and newer versions also include a defragmenting program called DEFRAG. This is a reduced function version of the SPEEDISK program that is normally sold as a part of the Symantec Norton Utilities. If you have the Norton Utilities, by all means use the higher function (and faster) SPEEDISK program instead of DEFRAG. The DOS DEFRAG program offers all three functions including defragmenting, packing, and sorting. The SPEEDISK program performs these operations faster and with more efficient use of memory. Many of these programs will have problems on very large disks, and SPEEDISK will work on drives as large as 2G (the maximum DOS volume size), while DEFRAG is limited to disks of about 512M or less due to memory constraints.

Several aftermarket defragmenting programs are more powerful or faster than the DOS DEFRAG program. They include:

- SPEEDISK by Symantec (Norton Utilities)
- Power Disk by PC-KWIK
- Optune by Gazelle
- VOPT by Golden Bow

All of these are highly recommended and usually perform much better than the DEFRAG program in DOS. The Power Disk, Optune, and VOPT programs are also much faster than DEFRAG. The VOPT program is the simplest and quickest of these, and is the one I use myself. It is a simple command-line program—not a menu driven program—like the others. Although VOPT does not offer a sort capability, the speed at which it operates is second to none, and the visual display is very entertaining as well! VOPT offers the ultimate in speed and efficiency in defragmenting and packing files.

Currently, some of these programs may have problems with large partitions and lots of files, however VOPT will handle partitions of up to 2G (the maximum allowable under

DOS). These types of programs are updated constantly; contact the manufacturer for more detailed specifications if you are interested. Each of these manufacturers is listed in Appendix B.

No matter which program you end up using, defragmenting and packing your disk helps to reduce drive wear and tear by minimizing the amount of work required to load files. It also greatly increases the chances for data recovery in the case of serious corruption in the File Allocation Tables (FATs) and directories on the disk.

Backing Up the FAT and Directory System. The operating system uses several areas on a formatted disk to manage the files stored on the disk. These areas are extremely critical. If they are damaged, all access to the drive volume may be compromised or completely disabled. In some cases, these critical areas can be rebuilt using known data recovery procedures and tools, but the easiest and best way to recover from damage to these areas is to simply have a backup of them to restore.

The critical areas of a hard disk file system are the following:

- Master (Partition) Boot Record (MBR)
- Extended (Partition) Boot Record (EBR)
- DOS Boot Record (DBR)
- File Allocation Tables (FATs)
- Root Directory

These areas are stored on the disk in the order listed, except that each volume will start with an MBR or EBR but not both. Unlike complete file backups of the entire hard disk, a backup of these system areas is relatively quick and easy. This is because these areas are very small in comparison to the remainder of the drive and normally occupy a fixed amount of space on the disk. For example, the MBR, EBRs, and DBRs are only one sector long each, while the two FATs used on each volume cannot exceed 256 sectors each (512 sectors or up to 256K total for both), and the Root Directory is limited to 32 sectors (16K). This means that even for the largest hard disk drive, these areas will not consume more than about 300K of space.

The boot record (sector) areas do not change during day to day usage of the disk. These areas will change only if you reformat, repartition, or change operating system versions. Because they are relatively constant, it makes good sense to back up these areas to a file on a floppy disk for later restoring if necessary.

Each normal disk volume will have two File Allocation Tables and a single Root Directory. These areas change constantly as files are written and deleted from the disk. A backup of these areas is only good for temporary purposes and can be useful when trying to undelete files. Because of this, these backups are often written on the hard disk in a special hidden file near the end of the disk. Other recovery or restoration programs can then look for this special file and use the information within it to rebuild the FATs or directory system. Often this type of backup is very useful in a situation where files need to be undeleted.

DOS 5.0 provided the MIRROR command for backups of all of these areas. MIRROR has two functions: it can back up the boot sector areas on the hard disk to a file on a floppy disk as well as back up the FAT and directory areas to the end of the hard disk as a special hidden file that recovery programs can find. To use MIRROR to back up the boot sectors to a floppy disk, execute the command as follows:

```
MIRROR /PARTN
```

This will create a special file called PARTNSAV.FIL on a floppy disk you designate. This file contains an image of all of the boot sectors across all of the DOS accessible partitions on your hard disk. This information can later be restored by the UNFORMAT command as follows:

```
UNFORMAT /PARTN
```

The UNFORMAT program will ask for the disk containing the PARTNSAV.FIL file and restore the boot sector information to the hard disk.

MIRROR can also be used to backup the FATs and Directory structure to a special hidden file on the disk by simply executing the command with no parameters at all:

```
MIRROR
```

By executing the command in this manner, a special file called MIRROR.FIL, as well as a hidden file called MIRRORSAV.FIL, will be created in the root directory, and a copy of the FAT and Directory structures will be copied into some free space at the end of the drive. The actual FAT and Directory data is not stored in a normal file with a filename but is instead written to empty sectors at the end of the drive. These sectors will eventually be overwritten, which is why it is a good idea to run the MIRROR command frequently. The second time you run it, it will actually create a second backup and retain the first. Every subsequent run will retain the previous one as a secondary backup. It is a good idea to put the MIRROR command in your AUTOEXEC.BAT file so that these critical areas of the disk are backed up every time your system boots. Usually, MIRROR only takes a few seconds to perform its backup functions so there will be little delay in booting.

To restore the FAT and Directory area backups, you would use the UNFORMAT program, also with no parameters. This program will then search the disk for the MIRROR backups and prompt you for a possible restore. Be careful in restoring these areas as they may be out of sync somewhat with the actual files on your disk. You should always run MIRROR after defragmenting your drive because the defragmenting process moves many files on the disk, making the MIRROR backup obsolete.

There is one unfortunate problem with the MIRROR program; both Microsoft and IBM removed it from DOS 6 and higher versions. Fortunately, you can retain your copy of MIRROR from DOS 5, or you can download the DOS 6 supplemental disk from the Microsoft BBS or the MSDOS forum on CompuServe. This package will provide you with a number of utilities left out of DOS 6 but the MIRROR command is the most useful. You can also order this disk directly from Microsoft for $5 using an order form in the back of the DOS 6 manual from Microsoft.

Many other data recovery programs offer the ability to back up these areas on the disk. The Norton Utilities by Symantec is one of the best and most well known data recovery packages on the market. It offers this capability and does a much better job than DOS alone. Norton uses an IMAGE command instead of MIRROR, and also has a special program called RESCUE that creates a rescue disk with not only the boot sector areas on it, but copies of your AUTOEXEC.BAT and CONFIG.SYS files, the DOS system files, and the CMOS RAM data from your system. Also included on the rescue disk are copies of the appropriate Norton Utilities programs that can be used to restore these areas.

Checking for Virus Programs. Both Microsoft and IBM now provide standard anti-virus software in DOS. The Microsoft Anti-Virus program is actually a reduced function version of the Central Point Anti-Virus software. IBM has written a package called the IBM Anti-Virus program. Many aftermarket utility packages are available that will scan for and remove virus programs. One of the best known is the McAfee Associates SCANV program, which is also one of the easiest to run because it is a command-line utility. The McAfee program is also distributed through BBS systems and is often site-licensed to large companies.

Because Windows 95 does not include an anti-virus program, you may want to invest in one of the aftermarket utilities such as the McAfee program.

No matter which of these programs you use, it is a good idea to perform a scan for virus programs periodically, especially before making hard disk backups. This will help to ensure that you catch any potential virus problem before it spreads and becomes a major hassle.

Reformatting a Hard Disk. Periodically reformatting a hard disk is an operation that applies mostly to older drives as part of a preventive maintenance plan. Modern IDE and SCSI drives are preformatted from the factory, and already have all the known defects mapped out.

Reformatting serves two purposes. On non-servo controlled drives (stepper motor head actuators) the low level format rewrites the sector header information in alignment with current head positions, which can drift in stepper motor head-actuator drives because of temperature- and stress-induced dimensional changes between the platters and heads. If these alignment variations continue unchecked, they eventually will cause read and write errors. Note that this reformatting operation applies to stepper motor head-actuator drives only and not to voice-coil drives, which maintain their positional accuracy due to the closed loop servo control mechanism that guides the heads.

The second function of a Low Level Format is to locate and mark or spare out any new defective sectors. This can be accomplished during the Low Level Format and also by a subsequent surface analysis.

Reformatting a hard disk lays down new track and sector ID marks and boundaries, remarks the manufacturer's defects, and performs a surface scan for new defects that might have developed since the last format. With Zone Recorded drives, only the defect mapping and surface analysis are performed. The sector headers are usually not completely rewritten. Temperature variations, case flexing, and physical positioning can add up to eventual read and write errors in a stepper-motor-actuated hard disk. This type of failure sometimes appears as a gradually increasing number of disk retries and other read and write problems. You also might notice difficulties when you boot the disk for the first time each day or if the system has been turned off for some time. The cause of these problems is a mistracking between where the data has actually written on the drive and where the track and sector ID marks are located. If the drive is used in a variety of temperatures and environmental conditions, dimensional changes between the heads and platters can cause the data to be written at various improper offsets from the desired track locations.

The reformatting procedure for hard disks is the equivalent of aligning a floppy drive. For hard disks, however, the concern is not for the actual locations of each track, but that the drive heads are positioned accurately to the same track location each time. Because of the inherent problems in tracking with stepper motor drives and the lack of a track-following system, mistracking errors accumulate and eventually cause a failure to read or write a particular location. To correct this problem, you must lay down a new set of track and sector ID marks that correspond as closely as possible to the position from which the heads actually read and write data. To do this (with stepper motor drives), you must perform a low-level format.

To make the new format effective, you must do it at the drive's full operating temperature and with the drive in its final mounted position. If the drive runs on its side when it is installed, the format must be done in that position.

For inexpensive drives that lack a proper shock-mounting system (such as the older Seagate ST-225, -238, -251, or any ST-2XX drive), make sure that the drive is completely installed before beginning low-level formatting. When you attach the mounting screws to these drives, you are placing screws almost directly into the Head Disk Assembly (HDA), which can cause the HDA to bend or warp slightly depending on how much you tighten the screws. Turn the screws just until they are snug. Do not over tighten them, or your drive might fail if the screws ever loosen and the HDA stress is relaxed. Screws that are too tight can cause continuous read and write problems from stress in the HDA. Having this type of drive completely installed when you are formatting places the HDA under the same physical stress and distortion that it will be under when data is read and written, which makes the format much more accurate.

The frequency with which you should reformat a hard disk depends primarily on the types of drives you have. If the drives are inexpensive stepper motor types (the Seagate ST-2XX series, for example) you probably should reformat the drives once a year. People who must support large numbers of these cheaper drives become known as "hard disk reformatting specialists." A joke in the industry is that some of these drives require winter and summer formats because of temperature sensitivity. This joke, unfortunately, can be somewhat truthful in some cases. Fortunately the modern IDE and SCSI drives today use high quality voice coil head actuators and are virtually immune to these problems.

High-quality voice coil drives usually are formatted only once, either at the factory, as in the case of most IDE or SCSI drives, or by the installer, as is the case with most other types of hard disks. With these drives, a reformat is only performed when the drive begins to exhibit problems reading or writing any sectors on the disk. This might appear in the form of DOS "Abort, Retry, Fail, Ignore" error messages, or other read or write errors. Upon encountering difficulty with any sectors on the disk, it should be fully backed up and then a reformat should be performed. In this case, the reformat and subsequent surface analysis will locate and mark off or spare out the marginal sectors, thus restoring the drive to proper operation.

As mentioned earlier, voice coil drives do not require reformatting the hard disk as do stepper motor drives. Voice coil drives do not usually develop difficulties with hysteresis, a measurement of how accurately a drive can repeatedly locate to a specified position. Hysteresis is measured by commanding a drive to position itself at a particular cylinder and later (at a different temperature), commanding the drive to position itself at the same cylinder. The voice coil drive always positions itself at the same position relative to the disk platter because of the track-following servo guide head. The stepper motor drive, however, is fooled by temperature and other environmental or physical stress changes because it is essentially a blind positioning system.

Refer to Chapter 16, "Hard Disk Drive Installation," for more information about the proper tools and procedures for reformatting the different types of hard disk drives.

Passive Preventive Maintenance Procedures

Passive preventive maintenance involves taking care of the system in an external manner: basically, providing the best possible environment—both physical as well as electrical—for the system to operate in. Physical concerns are conditions such as ambient temperature, thermal stress from power cycling, dust and smoke contamination, and disturbances such as shock and vibration. Electrical concerns are items such as electrostatic discharge (ESD), power-line noise and radio-frequency interference. Each of these environmental concerns is discussed in this section.

Examining the Operating Environment. Oddly enough, one of the most overlooked aspects of microcomputer preventive maintenance is protecting the hardware—and the sizable financial investment it represents—from environmental abuse. Computers are relatively forgiving, and they generally are safe in an environment that is comfortable for people. Computers, however, often are treated with no more respect than desktop calculators. The result of this type of abuse is many system failures.

Before you acquire a system, prepare a proper location for your new system, free of airborne contaminants such as smoke or other pollution. Do not place your system in front of a window: The system should not be exposed to direct sunlight or temperature variations. The environmental temperature should be as constant as possible. Power should be provided through properly grounded outlets, and should be stable and free from electrical noise and interference. Keep your system away from radio transmitters or other sources of radio frequency energy. This section examines these issues in more detail.

Heating and Cooling. Thermal expansion and contraction from temperature changes place stress on a computer system. Therefore, keeping the temperature in your office or room relatively constant is important to the successful operation of your computer system.

Temperature variations can lead to serious problems. You might encounter excessive chip creep, for example. If extreme variations occur over a short period, signal traces on circuit boards can crack and separate, solder joints can break, and contacts in the system undergo accelerated corrosion. Solid-state components such as chips can be damaged also, and a host of other problems can develop.

Temperature variations can play havoc with hard disk drives also. Writing to a disk at different ambient temperatures can, on some drives, cause data to be written at different locations relative to the track centers. Read and write problems then might accelerate later.

To ensure that your system operates in the correct ambient temperature, you first must determine your system's specified functional range. Most manufacturers provide data about the correct operating temperature range for their systems. Two temperature specifications might be available, one indicating allowable temperatures during operation and another indicating allowable temperatures under non-operating conditions. IBM, for example, indicates the following temperature ranges as acceptable for most of its systems:

System on: 60 to 90 degrees Fahrenheit

System off: 50 to 110 degrees Fahrenheit

For the safety of the disk and the data it contains, avoid rapid changes in ambient temperatures. If rapid temperature changes occur—for example, when a new drive is shipped to a location during the winter and then brought indoors—let the drive acclimate to room temperature before turning it on. In extreme cases, condensation forms on the platters inside the drive Head Disk Assembly—disastrous for the drive if you turn it on before the condensation can evaporate. Most drive manufacturers specify a timetable to use as a guide in acclimating a drive to room temperature before operating it. You usually must wait several hours to a day before a drive is ready to use after it has been shipped or stored in a cold environment.

Most office environments provide a stable temperature in which to operate a computer system, but some do not. Be sure to give some consideration to the placement of your equipment.

Power Cycling (On/Off). As you have just learned, the temperature variations a system encounters greatly stress the system's physical components. The largest temperature variations a system encounters, however, are those that occur during system warm-up when you initially turn it on. Turning on (also called powering on) a cold system subjects it to the greatest possible internal temperature variations. For these reasons, limiting the number of power-on cycles a system is exposed to greatly improves its life and reliability.

If you want a system to have the longest, most trouble-free life possible, you should limit the temperature variations in its environment. You can limit the extreme temperature cycling in two simple ways during a cold start-up: leave the system off all the time or leave it on all the time. Of these two possibilities, of course, you want to choose the latter option. Leaving the power on is the best way I know to promote system reliability. If your only concern is system longevity, the simple recommendation would be to keep the system unit powered on (or off!) continuously. In the real world, however there are more variables to consider, such as the cost of electricity, the potential fire hazard of unattended running equipment, and other concerns as well.

If you think about the way light bulbs typically fail, you can begin to understand that thermal cycling can be dangerous. Light bulbs burn out most often when you first turn them on, because the filament must endure incredible thermal stresses as it changes temperature—in less than one second—from ambient to several thousands of degrees. A bulb that remains on continuously lasts longer than one that is turned on and off repeatedly.

Some people argue that the reason you should leave a computer system on continuously is to prevent the electrical "shock" from the inrush of power when you start up a system. The cause of failure in a low-voltage solid-state circuit repeatedly powered on and off, however, is not in-rushing electrons, but rather physical stresses caused by thermal expansion and contraction of the components. Component engineers agree, and tests prove, that a device left on continuously outlasts one that is powered on and off repeatedly.

Where problems can occur immediately at power-on is in the power supply. The start-up current draw for the system and for any motor during the first few seconds of operation is very high compared to the normal operating-current draw. Because the current must come from the power supply, the supply has an extremely demanding load to carry for the first few seconds of operation, especially if several disk drives will be started. Motors have an extremely high power-on current draw. This demand often overloads a marginal circuit or component in the supply and causes it to burn or break with a "snap." I have seen several power supplies die the instant a system was powered up. To enable your equipment to have the longest possible life, try to keep the temperature of solid-state components relatively constant, and limit the number of start-ups on the power supply. The only way I know to do so is to leave the system on.

Although it sounds as though I am recommending that you leave all of your computer equipment on 24 hours a day, seven days a week, I no longer recommend this type of operation. A couple of concerns have tempered my urge to leave everything running continuously. One is that an unattended system that is powered on represents a fire hazard. I have seen monitors start themselves on fire after internally shorting, and systems whose cooling fans have frozen, enabling the power supply and entire system to overheat. I do not leave any system running in an unattended building. Another problem is wasted electrical power. Many companies have adopted austerity programs that involve turning lights and other items off when not in use. The power consumption of some of today's high-powered systems and accessories is not trivial. Also, an unattended operating system is more of a security risk than one that is powered off and locked.

Realities—such as the fire hazard of unattended systems running during night or weekend hours, security problems, and power-consumption issues—might prevent you from leaving your system on all the time. Therefore, you must compromise. Power on the system only one time daily. Don't power the system on and off several times every day. This good advice is often ignored, especially when several users share systems. Each user powers on the system to perform work on the PC and then powers off the system. These systems tend to have many more problems with component failures.

If you are concerned about running your hard disk continuously, let me dispel your fears. Running your hard disk continuously might be the best thing you can do for your drive. Leaving the drive powered on is the best method for reducing read and write failures caused by temperature changes. If you are using extremely inexpensive or older drives with stepper motor actuators, leaving the drive on greatly improves reliability and increases the time between low-level formats caused by mistracking. A drive's bearings and motors also function longer if you reduce the power-on temperature cycling. You might have had a disk that didn't boot after you turned the drive off for a prolonged period (over the weekend, for example) and you fixed the problem with a subsequent low-level format, but you most likely wouldn't have had the problem if you had left your drive on.

If you are in a building with a programmable thermostat, you have another reason to be concerned about temperatures and disk drives. Some buildings have thermostats programmed to turn off the heat overnight or over the weekend. These thermostats are programmed also to quickly raise the temperature just before business hours every day. In Chicago, for example, outside temperatures in the winter can dip to 20 degrees below 0 (not including a wind-chill factor). An office building's interior temperature can drop as low as 50 degrees during the weekend. When you arrive Monday morning, the heat has been on for only an hour or so, but the hard disk platters might have not yet reached even 60 degrees when you turn on the system unit. During the first 20 minutes of operation, the disk platters rapidly rise in temperature to 120 degrees or more. If you have an inexpensive stepper motor hard disk and begin writing to the disk at these low temperatures, you are setting yourself up for trouble. Again, many systems with these "cheap" drives don't even boot properly under these circumstances and must be warmed up before they even boot DOS.

Tip

If you do not leave a system on continuously, at least give it 15 minutes or more to warm up after a cold start before writing to the hard disk. Power up the system and go get a cup of coffee, read the paper, or do some other task. This practice does wonders for the reliability of the data on your disk, especially cheaper units.

If you do leave your system on for long periods of time, make sure that the screen is blank or displays a random image if the system is not in use. The phosphor on the picture tube can burn if a stationary image is left on-screen continuously. Higher-persistence phosphor monochrome screens are most susceptible, and the color displays with low-persistence phosphors are the least susceptible. If you ever have seen a monochrome display with the image of some program permanently burned in—even with the display off—you know what I mean. Look at the monitors that display flight information at the airport—they usually show some of the effects of phosphor burn.

Most modern displays that have power saving features can automatically enter a standby mode on command by the system. If your system has these power saving functions, enable them as they will help to reduce energy costs as well as preserve the monitor.

Screen savers or blankers will either blank the screen completely or display some sort of moving random image to prevent burn in. This can be accomplished by either a manual or automatic procedure as follows:

- Manual. Turn the brightness and contrast levels all the way down, or even power the display off completely. This technique is effective but it is a manual method; you must remember to do it.

- Automatic. Many types of programs can cause the screen to blank or display random images automatically at a predetermined interval. Screen savers are built in to most Graphical User Interfaces (GUIs) such as Windows and OS/2. These can easily be enabled and you can also specify the time delay before they activate. If you run under plain DOS, you can use a number of public domain as well as commercial screen saver programs. These programs usually run as terminate-and-stay-resident (TSR) programs. The program watches the clock as well as the keyboard and mouse ports. If several minutes pass with nothing typed at the keyboard or no mouse movement, the program activates and either shuts off all signals to the display or creates an image that moves around on the screen to prevent burn in.

Screen savers are obsolete in a modern green PC that features power management capabilities. In fact in these systems, using a screen saver can defeat the power management functions by keeping the hard disk drive and the screen fully powered up at all times.

Static Electricity. Static electricity can cause numerous problems within a system. The problems usually appear during the winter months when humidity is low or in extremely dry climates where the humidity is low year-round. In these cases, you might need to take special precautions to ensure that the system functions properly.

Static discharges outside a system-unit chassis are rarely a source of permanent problems within the system. The usual effect of a static discharge to the case, keyboard, or even in close proximity to a system, is a parity check (memory) error or a locked-up system. In some cases, I have been able to cause parity checks or system lockups by simply walking past a system. Most static-sensitivity problems such as this one are caused by improper grounding of the system power. Be sure that you always use a three-prong, grounded power cord plugged into a properly grounded outlet. If you are unsure about the outlet, you can buy an outlet tester at most electronics-supply or hardware stores for only a few dollars.

Whenever you open a system unit or handle circuits removed from the system, you must be much more careful with static. You can permanently damage a component with a static discharge if the charge is not routed to a ground. I usually recommend handling boards and adapters first by a grounding point such as the bracket to minimize the potential for static damage.

An easy way to prevent static problems is with good power-line grounding, which is extremely important for computer equipment. A poorly designed power-line grounding system is one of the primary causes of poor computer design. The best way to prevent static damage is to prevent the static charge from getting into the computer in the first place. The chassis ground in a properly designed system serves as a static guard for the computer, which redirects the static charge safely to ground. For this ground to be complete, therefore, the system must be plugged into a properly grounded three-wire outlet.

If the static problem is extreme, you can resort to other measures. One is to use a grounded static mat underneath the computer. Touch the mat first before you touch the computer, to ensure that any static charges are routed to ground and away from the system unit's internal parts. If problems still persist, you might want to check out the electrical building ground. I have seen installations in which three-wire outlets exist but are not grounded properly. You can use an outlet tester to be sure that the outlet is wired properly.

Power-Line Noise. To run properly, a computer system requires a steady supply of clean noise-free power. In some installations, however, the power line serving the computer serves heavy equipment also, and the voltage variations resulting from the on-off cycling of this equipment can cause problems for the computer. Certain types of equipment on the same power line also can cause voltage spikes—short transient signals of sometimes 1,000 volts or more—that can physically damage a computer. Although these spikes are rare, they can be crippling. Even a dedicated electrical circuit used only by a single computer can experience spikes and transients, depending on the quality of the power supplied to the building or circuit.

During the site-preparation phase of a system installation, you should be aware of these factors to ensure a steady supply of clean power:

- If possible, the computer system should be on its own circuit with its own circuit breaker. This setup does not guarantee freedom from interference but it helps.
- The circuit should be checked for a good, low-resistance ground, proper line voltage, freedom from interference, and freedom from brownouts (voltage dips).
- A three-wire circuit is a must but some people substitute grounding-plug adapters to adapt a grounded plug to a two-wire socket. This setup is not recommended; the ground is there for a reason.
- Power-line noise problems increase with the resistance of the circuit, which is a function of wire size and length. To decrease resistance, therefore, avoid extension cords unless absolutely necessary, and then use only heavy-duty extension cords.
- Inevitably, you will want to plug in other equipment later. Plan ahead to avoid temptations to use too many items on a single outlet. If possible, provide a separate power circuit for noncomputer-related accessories.

Air conditioners, coffee makers, copy machines, laser printers, space heaters, vacuum cleaners, and power tools are some of the worst corrupters of a PC system's power. Any of these items can draw an excessive amount of current and play havoc with a PC system on the same electrical circuit. I've seen offices in which all the computers begin to crash at about 9:05 a.m. daily, which is when all the coffee makers are turned on!

Also, try to ensure that copy machines and laser printers do not share a circuit with other computer equipment. These devices draw a large amount of power.

Another major problem in some companies is partitioned offices. Many of these partitions are prewired with their own electrical outlets and are plugged into one another in a sort of power-line daisy chain, similar to chaining power strips together. I pity the person in the cubicle at the end of the electrical daisy chain, who will have very flaky power!

As a real-world example of too many devices sharing a single circuit, I can describe several instances in which a personal computer had a repeating parity check problem. All efforts to repair the system had been unsuccessful. The reported error locations from the parity check message also were inconsistent, which normally indicates a problem with power. The problem could have been the power supply in the system unit or the external power supplied from the wall outlet. This problem was solved one day as I stood watching the system. The parity check message was displayed at the same instant someone two cubicles away turned on a copy machine. Placing the computers on a separate line solved the problem.

By following the guidelines in this section, you can create the proper power environment for your systems and help to ensure trouble-free operation.

Radio-Frequency Interference. Radio-frequency interference (RFI) is easily overlooked as a problem factor. The interference is caused by any source of radio transmissions near a computer system. Living next door to a 50,000-watt commercial radio station is one sure way to get RFI problems, but less powerful transmitters cause problems too. I know of many instances in which portable radio-telephones have caused sporadic random keystrokes to appear, as though an invisible entity were typing on the keyboard. I also have seen RFI cause a system to lock up. Solutions to RFI problems are more difficult to state because every case must be handled differently. Sometimes, reorienting a system unit eliminates the problem because radio signals can be directional in nature. At other times, you must invest in specially shielded cables for cables outside the system unit, such as the keyboard cable.

One type of solution to an RFI noise problem with cables is to pass the cable through a toroidal iron core, a doughnut-shaped piece of iron placed around a cable to suppress both the reception and transmission of electromagnetic interference (EMI). If you can isolate an RFI noise problem in a particular cable, you often can solve the problem by passing the cable through a toroidal core. Because the cable must pass through the center hole of the core, it often is difficult, if not impossible, to add a toroid to a cable that already has end connectors installed.

Radio Shack sells a special snap-together toroid designed specifically to be added to cables already in use. This toroid looks like a thick-walled tube that has been sliced in half. You just lay the cable in the center of one of the halves, and snap the other half over the first. This type of construction makes it easy to add the noise-suppression features of a toroid to virtually any existing cable.

IBM also makes a special 6-foot long PS/2 keyboard cable with a built-in toroid core (part number 27F4984) that can greatly reduce interference problems. This cable has the smaller 6-pin DIN (PS/2 style) connector at the system end and the standard SDL (Shielded Data Link) connector at the keyboard end; it costs about $40.

The best, if not the easiest, way to eliminate the problem probably is to correct it at the source. You likely won't convince the commercial radio station near your office to shut down but if you are dealing with a small radio transmitter that is generating RFI, sometimes you can add to the transmitter a filter that suppresses spurious emissions. Unfortunately, problems sometimes persist until the transmitter is either switched off or moved some distance away from the affected computer.

Note that your own computer systems can be a source of RFI. Computer equipment must meet one of these two classifications to be certified and salable, according to the FCC (Federal Communications Commission): Class A or Class B. The Class A specification applies to computing devices sold for use in commercial, business, and industrial environments. Class B indicates that the equipment has passed more stringent tests and can be used in residential environments, in addition to any environments allowed under Class A.

The FCC does not really police users or purchasers of computer equipment so much as it polices the equipment manufacturers or vendors. Therefore, if you are using a Class A-rated system in your home, you don't need to worry about radio police showing up at your door. If, however, you are making or selling PCs that meet one of these conditions:

- Marketed through retail or direct-mail outlets
- Sold to the general public rather than commercial users only
- Operates on battery or 120-volt AC electrical power

You must obtain a Class B certification for these systems. Notice that a system has to fit each of these three categories to be considered a personal computer and be subject to the stricter Class B rules. Notice also that the FCC considers all portable computer systems as meeting Class B standards because their portability makes them likely to be used in a residential setting.

The FCC standards for Class A and Class B certification govern two kinds of emissions: conductive emissions, radiated from the computer system into the power cord, and radio-frequency emissions, radiated from the computer system into space. Table 20.1 shows the conductive and radio-frequency emissions limitations to be eligible for both Class A and Class B ratings.

Table 20.1 FCC Class A and Class B Emission Limitations

Frequency	Class A (10M)	Class B (3M)
Conductive Emissions:	**Maximum Signal Level (mv)**	
0.45 to 1.705 MHz	1000	250
1.705 to 30.0 MHz	3000	250
Radiated Emissions:	**Maximum Field Strength (uv/M)**	
30 to 88 MHz	90	100
88 to 216 MHz	150	150
217 to 960 MHz	210	200
960 MHz and up	300	500

MHz = Megahertz
10M = Measured at 10 meters
3M = Measured at 3 meters
mv = Millivolts
uv/M = Microvolts per meter

Notice that although some of the specific numbers listed for Class A seem lower than those required for Class B, you must consider that field-strength measurements normally decline under the inverse square law: The strength of the signal decreases as the square of the distance from the source. A rating of 100 microvolts per meter at 3 meters, therefore, would be approximately equal to a rating of about 9 microvolts per meter at 10 meters. This calculation just means that the limits to pass Class B certification are much tougher than they look, and certainly are much tougher than Class A limits. Additionally, Class A certification is tested and verified entirely by the manufacturer; Class B certification requires a sample of the equipment to be sent to the FCC for testing.

IBM and most other responsible manufacturers ensure that all systems they sell meet the stricter Class B designations. One of the benefits of the Micro Channel Architecture and PCI bus designs are that they meet, and greatly exceed, these FCC classifications. As bus clock speeds go up, so do the radio emissions. Today the PCI bus runs at 33 MHz, but a 66 MHz version is already on the drawing board. Even at these higher bus speeds, PCI systems will continue to be able to meet the FCC class B requirements.

Dust and Pollutants. Dirt, smoke, dust, and other pollutants are bad for your system. The power-supply fan carries airborne particles through your system, and they collect inside. If your system is used in an extremely harsh environment, you might want to investigate some of the industrial systems on the market designed for harsh conditions. IBM used to sell industrial-model XT and AT systems but discontinued them after introducing the PS/2. IBM has licensed several third-party companies to produce industrial versions of PS/2 systems.

Compatible vendors also have industrial systems; many companies make special hardened versions of their systems for harsh environments. Industrial systems usually use a different cooling system from the one used in a regular PC. A large cooling fan is used to pressurize the case rather than depressurize it, as most systems do. The air pumped into the case passes through a filter unit that must be cleaned and changed periodically. The system is pressurized so that no contaminated air can flow into it; air flows only outward. The only way air can enter is through the fan and filter system.

These systems also might have special keyboards impervious to liquids and dirt. Some flat-membrane keyboards are difficult to type on, but are extremely rugged; others resemble the standard types of keyboards, but have a thin, plastic membrane that covers all the keys. You can add this membrane to normal types of keyboards to seal them from the environment.

A new breed of humidifier can cause problems with computer equipment. This type of humidifier uses ultrasonics to generate a mist of water sprayed into the air. The extra humidity helps cure problems with static electricity resulting from a dry climate, but the airborne water contaminants can cause many problems. If you use one of these systems, you might notice a white ash-like deposit forming on components. The deposit is the result of abrasive and corrosive minerals suspended in the vaporized water. If these deposits collect on the disk drive heads, they will ruin the heads and scratch disks. The only safe way to run one of these ultrasonic humidifiers is with pure distilled water. If you use a humidifier, be sure it does not generate these deposits.

If you do your best to keep the environment for your computer equipment clean, your system will run better and last longer. Also, you will not have to open your unit as often for complete preventive maintenance cleaning.

Using Power-Protection Systems

Power-protection systems do just what the name implies: They protect your equipment from the effects of power surges and power failures. In particular, power surges and spikes can damage computer equipment, and a loss of power can result in lost data. In this section, you learn about the four primary types of power-protection devices available and under what circumstances you should use them.

Before considering any further levels of power protection, you should know that the power supply in your system (if your system is well-made) already affords you a substantial amount of protection. The power supplies in IBM equipment are designed to provide protection from higher-than-normal voltages and currents, and provide a limited amount of power-line noise filtering. Some of the inexpensive aftermarket power supplies probably do not have this sort of protection; be careful if you have an inexpensive clone system. In those cases, further protecting your system might be wise.

IBM's PS/2 power supplies will stay within operating specifications and continue to run a system if any of these power line disturbances occur:

- Voltage drop to 80 volts for up to 2 seconds
- Voltage drop to 70 volts for up to .5 seconds
- Voltage surge of up to 143 volts for up to 1 second

IBM also states that neither their power supplies nor systems will be damaged by the following occurrences:

- Full power outage
- Any voltage drop (brownout)
- A spike of up to 2,500 volts

Because of the high quality power supply design that IBM uses, they state in their documentation that external surge suppressors are not needed for PS/2 systems. Most other high quality name brand manufacturers also use high quality power supply designs. Companies like Astec, PC Power and Cooling, and others make very high quality units.

To verify the levels of protection built in to the existing power supply in a computer system, an independent laboratory subjected several unprotected PC systems to various spikes and surges up to 6,000 volts—considered the maximum level of surge that can be transmitted to a system by an electrical outlet. Any higher voltage would cause the power to arc to ground within the outlet itself. Note that none of the systems sustained permanent damage in these tests; the worst thing that happened was that some of the systems rebooted or shut down if the surge was more than 2,000 volts. Each system restarted when the power switch was toggled after a shutdown.

I do not use any real form of power protection on my systems, and they have survived near-direct lightning strikes and powerful surges. The most recent incident, only 50 feet from my office, was a direct lightning strike to a brick chimney that blew the top of the chimney apart. None of my systems (which were running at the time) was damaged in any way from this incident; they just shut themselves down. I was able to restart each system by toggling the power switches. An alarm system located in the same office, however, was destroyed by this strike. I am not saying that lightning strikes or even much milder spikes and surges cannot damage computer systems—another nearby lightning strike did destroy a modem and serial adapter installed in one of my systems. I was just lucky that the destruction did not include the motherboard.

This discussion points out an important oversight in some power-protection strategies: you may elect to protect your systems from electrical power disturbances, but do not forget to provide similar protection also from spikes and surges on the phone line.

The automatic shutdown of a computer during power disturbances is a built-in function of most high-quality power supplies. You can reset the power supply by flipping the power switch from on to off and back on again. Some power supplies, such as those in most of the PS/2 systems, have an auto-restart function. This type of power supply acts the same as others in a massive surge or spike situation: it shuts down the system. The difference is that after normal power resumes, the power supply waits for a specified delay of three to six seconds and then resets itself and powers the system back up. Because no manual switch resetting is required, this feature is desirable in systems functioning as a network file server or in a system in a remote location.

The first time I witnessed a large surge cause an immediate shutdown of all my systems, I was extremely surprised. All the systems were silent, but the monitor and modem lights were still on. My first thought was that everything was blown, but a simple toggle of each system-unit power switch caused the power supplies to reset, and the units powered up with no problem. Since that first time, this type of shutdown has happened to me several times, always without further problems.

The following types of power-protection devices are explained in the sections that follow:

- Surge suppressors
- Line conditioners
- Standby power supplies (SPS)
- Uninterruptible power supplies (UPS)

Surge Suppressors (Protectors)

The simplest form of power protection is any of the commercially available surge protectors; that is, devices inserted between the system and the power line. These devices, which cost between $20 and $200, can absorb the high-voltage transients produced by nearby lightning strikes and power equipment. Some surge protectors can be effective for certain types of power problems, but they offer only very limited protection.

Surge protectors use several devices, usually metal-oxide varistors (MOVs), that can clamp and shunt away all voltages above a certain level. MOVs are designed to accept voltages as high as 6,000 volts and divert any power above 200 volts to ground. MOVs can handle normal surges, but powerful surges such as a direct lightning strike can blow right through them. MOVs are not designed to handle a very high level of power, and self-destruct while shunting a large surge. These devices therefore cease to function after either a single large surge or a series of smaller ones. The real problem is that you cannot easily tell when they no longer are functional; the only way to test them is to subject the MOVs to a surge, which destroys them. Therefore, you never really know if your so-called surge protector is protecting your system.

Some surge protectors have status lights that let you know when a surge large enough to blow the MOVs has occurred. A surge suppressor without this status indicator light is useless because you never know when it has stopped protecting.

Underwriters Laboratories has produced an excellent standard that governs surge suppressors, called UL 1449. Any surge suppressor that meets this standard is a very good one, and definitely offers an additional line of protection beyond what the power supply in your PC already does. The only types of surge suppressors worth buying, therefore, should have two features: conformance to the UL 1449 standard and a status light indicating when the MOVs are blown. Units that meet the UL 1449 specification say so on the packaging or directly on the unit. If this standard is not mentioned, it does not conform, and you should avoid it.

Another good feature to have in a surge suppressor is a built-in circuit breaker that can be reset rather than a fuse. The breaker protects your system if the system or a peripheral develops a short. These better surge suppressors usually cost about $40.

Phone Line Surge Protectors

In addition to protecting the power lines, it is critical to provide protection to your systems from any phone lines that are connected. If you are using a modem or fax board that is plugged into the phone system, any surges or spikes that travel the phone line can potentially damage your system. In many areas, the phone lines are especially susceptible to lightning strikes, which is the largest cause of fried modems and any computer equipment attached to them.

Several companies manufacture or sell simple surge protectors that plug between your modem and the phone line. These inexpensive devices can be purchased from most electronics supply houses. Most of the cable and communication products vendors listed in Appendix B sell these phone line surge protectors.

Line Conditioners

In addition to high-voltage and current conditions, other problems can occur with incoming power. The voltage might dip below the level needed to run the system and result in a brownout. Other forms of electrical noise other than simple voltage surges or spikes might be on the power line, such as radio-frequency interference or electrical noise caused by motors or other inductive loads.

Remember two things when you wire together digital devices (such as computers and their peripherals). A wire is an antenna and has a voltage induced in it by nearby electromagnetic fields, which can come from other wires, telephones, CRTs, motors, fluorescent fixtures, static discharge, and, of course, radio transmitters. Digital circuitry also responds with surprising efficiency to noise of even a volt or two, making those induced voltages particularly troublesome. The wiring in your building can act as an antenna and pick up all kinds of noise and disturbances. A line conditioner can handle many of these types of problems.

A line conditioner is designed to remedy a variety of problems. It filters the power, bridges brownouts, suppresses high-voltage and current conditions, and generally acts as a buffer between the power line and the system. A line conditioner does the job of a surge suppressor, and much more. It is more of an active device functioning continuously rather than a passive device that activates only when a surge is present. A line conditioner provides true power conditioning and can handle myriad problems. It contains transformers, capacitors, and other circuitry that temporarily can bridge a brownout or low-voltage situation. These units usually cost several hundreds of dollars, depending on the power-handling capacity of the unit.

Backup Power

The next level of power protection includes backup power-protection devices. These units can provide power in case of a complete blackout, which provides the time needed for an orderly system shutdown. Two types are available: the standby power supply (SPS) and the uninterruptible power supply (UPS). The UPS is a special device because it does much more than just provide backup power: it is also the best kind of line conditioner you can buy.

Standby Power Supplies (SPS). A standby power supply is known as an offline device: It functions only when normal power is disrupted. An SPS system uses a special circuit that can sense the AC line current. If the sensor detects a loss of power on the line, the system quickly switches over to a standby battery and power inverter. The power inverter converts the battery power to 110-volt AC power, which then is supplied to the system.

SPS systems do work, but sometimes a problem occurs with the switch to battery power. If the switch is not fast enough, the computer system unit shuts down or reboots anyway, which defeats the purpose of having the backup power supply. A truly outstanding SPS adds to the circuit a ferroresonant transformer, a large transformer with the capability to store a small amount of power and deliver it during the switch time. Having this device is similar to having on the power line a buffer that you add to an SPS to give it almost truly uninterruptible capability.

SPS units also may or may not have internal line conditioning of their own; most cheaper units place your system directly on the regular power line under normal circumstances and offer no conditioning. The addition of a ferroresonant transformer to an SPS gives it additional regulation and protection capabilities due to the buffer effect of the transformer. SPS devices without the ferroresonant transformer still require the use of a line conditioner for full protection. SPS systems usually cost from $200 to several thousands of dollars, depending on the quality and power-output capacity.

Uninterruptible Power Supplies (UPS). Perhaps the best overall solution to any power problem is to provide a power source that is both conditioned and that also cannot be interrupted—which describes an uninterruptible power supply. UPSs are known as online systems because they continuously function and supply power to your computer systems. Because some companies advertise ferroresonant SPS devices as though they were UPS devices, many now use the term true UPS to describe a truly online system. A true UPS system is constructed much the same as an SPS system; however, because you always are operating from the battery, there is no switching circuit.

In a true UPS, your system always operates from the battery, with a voltage inverter to convert from 12 volts DC to 110 volts AC. You essentially have your own private power system that generates power independently of the AC line. A battery charger connected to the line or wall current keeps the battery charged at a rate equal to or greater than the rate at which power is consumed.

When power is disconnected, the true UPS continues functioning undisturbed because the battery-charging function is all that is lost. Because you already were running off the battery, no switch takes place and no power disruption is possible. The battery then begins discharging at a rate dictated by the amount of load your system places on the unit, which (based on the size of the battery) gives you plenty of time to execute an orderly system shutdown. Based on an appropriately scaled storage battery, the UPS functions continuously, generating power and preventing unpleasant surprises. When the line power returns, the battery charger begins recharging the battery, again with no interruption.

UPS cost is a direct function of both the length of time it can continue to provide power after a line current failure, and how much power it can provide; therefore, purchasing a

UPS that gives you enough power to run your system and peripherals as well as enough time to close files and provide an orderly shutdown would be sufficient. In most PC applications, this solution is the most cost-effective because the batteries and charger portion of the system must be much larger than the SPS type of device, and will be more costly.

Many SPS systems are advertised as though they were true UPS systems. The giveaway is the unit's "switch time." If a specification for switch time exists, the unit cannot be a true UPS because UPS units never switch. Understand, however, that a good SPS with a ferroresonant transformer can virtually equal the performance of a true UPS at a lower cost.

Because of a UPS's almost total isolation from the line current, it is unmatched as a line conditioner and surge suppressor. The best UPS systems add a ferroresonant transformer for even greater power conditioning and protection capability. This type of UPS is the best form of power protection available. The price, however, can be very high. A true UPS costs from $1 to $2 per watt of power supplied. To find out just how much power your system requires, look at the UL sticker on the back of the unit. This sticker lists the maximum power draw in watts, or sometimes in just volts and amperes. If only voltage and amperage are listed, multiply the two figures to calculate a wattage figure.

As an example, the back of an IBM PC AT Model 339 indicates that the system can require as much as 110 volts at a maximum current draw of 5 amps. The maximum power this AT can draw is about 550 watts. This wattage is for a system with every slot full, two hard disks and one floppy—in other words, the maximum possible level of expansion. The system should never draw any more power than that; if it does, a 5-ampere fuse in the power supply blows. This type of system normally draws an average 300 watts; to be safe when you make calculations for UPS capacity, however, be conservative and use the 550-watt figure. Adding a monitor that draws 100 watts brings the total to 650 watts or more. To run two fully loaded AT systems, you need an 1100-watt UPS. Don't forget two monitors, each drawing 100 watts; the total, therefore, is 1300 watts. Using the $1 to $2 per watt figure, a UPS of at least that capacity or greater will cost from $1300 to $2600—expensive, but unfortunately what the best level of protection costs. Most companies can justify this type of expense for only a critical-use PC, such as a network file server.

In addition to the total available output power (wattage), several other factors can differentiate one UPS from another. The addition of a ferroresonant transformer improves a unit's power conditioning and buffering capabilities. Good units have also an inverter that produces a true sine wave output; the cheaper ones may generate a square wave. A square wave is an approximation of a sine wave with abrupt up-and-down voltage transitions. The abrupt transitions of a square wave signal are not compatible with some computer equipment power supplies. Be sure that the UPS you purchase produces a signal compatible with your computer equipment. Every unit has a specification for how long it can sustain output at the rated level. If your systems draw less than the rated level, you have some additional time. Be careful, though: Most UPS systems are not designed for you to sit and compute for hours through an electrical blackout. They are designed to provide power to whatever is needed, to remain operating long enough to allow for an orderly shutdown. You pay a large amount for units that provide power for more than 15 minutes or so.

There are many sources of power protection equipment, but two of the best are Best Power and Tripp Lite. These companies sell a variety of UPS, SPS, line, and surge protectors. They are listed in Appendix B.

Using Data-Backup Systems

Making a backup of important data on a computer system is one thing that many users fail to do. A backup is similar to insurance: You need it only when you are in big trouble! Because of the cost in not only dollars, but also in time and effort, many users do not have adequate backup—which is not a problem until the day you have a catastrophe and suddenly find yourself without your important data or files. This section discusses several forms of backup hardware and software that can make the job both easier and faster, and, hopefully, cause more users to do it.

Backup is something a service technician should be aware of. After I repair a system that has suffered some kind of disk crash, I can guarantee that the disk subsystem will be completely functional. I cannot guarantee, however, that the original files are on the disks; in fact, the drive may have to be replaced. Without a backup, the system can be physically repaired, but the original data may be lost forever.

Nothing destroys someone's faith in computer technology faster than telling them that the last year or more of work (in the form of disk files) no longer exists. When I visit a customer site to do some troubleshooting or repair, I always tell my clients to back up the system before I arrive. They may be reluctant to do so at first, but it is better than paying a technician by the hour to do it. A backup must be done before I operate on a system, because I do not want to be liable if something goes wrong and data is damaged or lost. If the system is so dysfunctional that a backup cannot be performed, I make sure that the client knows that the service technician is not responsible for the data.

A good general rule is never to let a backup interval be longer than what you are willing to lose some day. You always can reload or even repurchase copies of software programs that might have been lost, but you cannot buy back your own data. Because of the extremely high value of data compared to the system itself, I have recommended for some time that service technicians become familiar with data-recovery principles and procedures. Being able to perform this valuable service gives you a fantastic edge over technicians who can only fix or replace the hardware.

Backup Policies

All users and managers of computer systems should develop a plan for regular disk backups. I recommend that one person in an office have the responsibility of performing these backups so that the job is not left undone.

A backup interval should be selected based on the amount of activity on the system. Some users find that daily backups are required, and others find that a weekly arrangement is more suitable. Backups rarely must be scheduled at more than weekly intervals.

Some users settle on a mixed plan: perform weekly disk backups and daily backups of only the changed files.

The procedures for backing up and for dealing with copy protection are explained in the following sections.

Backup Procedures. You should back up to removable media such as cartridge or tape, which you remove from a system and store in a safe place. Backups performed on non-removable media, such as another hard disk, are much more vulnerable to damage, theft, or fire; also, having multiple backups is much more expensive.

Because of the relatively low cost of hard disks, some users unfortunately install two hard disks and back up one to the other. Worse, some users split a single disk into two partitions and back up one partition to the other. These backups are false backups. If the system were subjected to a massive electrical surge or failure, the contents of both drives could be lost. If the system were stolen, again, both backups would be lost. Finally, if the system were physically damaged, such as in a fire or other mishap, both the data and the backup would be lost. These are good reasons that it is important to back up to removable media.

Perform your backups on a rotating schedule. I recommend using a tape-backup system with at least three tapes per drive, in which you back up data to the first tape the first week. The second week, you use a second tape. That way, if the second tape has been damaged, you can use the preceding week's backup tape to restore data. The third week, you should use still another, third, tape and place the first tape in a different physical location as protection against damage from fire, flood, theft, or another disaster.

The fourth week, you begin to rotate each tape so that the first (off-site) tape is used again for backup, and the second tape is moved off-site. This system always has two progressively older backups on-site, with the third backup off-site to provide for disaster insurance. Only removable media can provide this type of flexibility, and tape is one of the best forms of removable media for backup.

Dealing with Copy Protection. One thing standing in the way of proper backups of some of your software is copy protection, a system in which the original disk the software is on is modified so that it cannot be copied exactly by your system. When the programs on the disk are run, they look for this unique feature to determine whether the original disk is in the system. Some software makers force you to use master copies of their programs by using this technique to require that the original disks be placed in the floppy drive for validation even though the system might have the software loaded on the hard disk.

Some forms of copy protection load the software on a hard disk only from an original disk, and modify the hard disk loaded version so that it runs only if it remains on the system in a specified set of sectors. If the program ever is moved on the disk, it fails to operate. Because these requirements make the software highly prone to failure, copy protection has no place on software used in a business environment.

My personal response to copy protection is to refuse to use, buy, or recommend any software from a company engaged in this practice. With rare exceptions, I simply do not buy copy-protected software. Unprotected alternatives are normally available for whatever type of program you want. You might even discover that the unprotected alternative is a better program. If you don't make the software-purchasing decisions in your organization, however, you may have little choice in this matter.

Experienced computer users know that you never should use original disks when you install or configure software. After I purchase a new program, I first make a copy and store the original disks. In fact, I use the original disks solely for making additional backup copies. Following this procedure protects me if I make a mistake in installing or using the software. Because of the need for backup and the fact that copy protection essentially prevents proper backup, a solution has been devised.

When you must use a piece of protected software, you can purchase special programs that enable you to back up and even to remove the protection from most copy-protected programs on the market. Two such programs are CopyWrite, by Quaid Software Ltd., and Copy II PC, by Central Point Software. These programs cost about $50 and are absolutely necessary when you are forced to deal with copy-protected software.

Note that no matter what a software license agreement says, you have a legal right to back up your software; this right is guaranteed under U.S. copyright law. Do not let a software license agreement bamboozle you into believing otherwise. Only a few remaining programs have this unfortunate defect; I hope that the protection will be eradicated from them as well.

Backup Software. In considering how to back up your system, you should be aware of both the hardware and software options available. This section first explores the software-only options; that is, using either what you get with DOS, or some more-powerful aftermarket software to back up using a floppy drive. You will learn that the aftermarket software usually offers many features and capabilities that the standard DOS BACKUP program does not have. After discussing software alternatives, this section looks at complete, dedicated hardware and software backup systems. Using specialized hardware is the best way to have an easy, effective, and safe way of backing up your system.

The DOS BACKUP Command. The most basic backup software you can use are the DOS commands BACKUP and RESTORE. Since their introduction in version 2.0 of DOS, and up to version 3.3, these commands have frustrated users with their bugs and other problems. The versions supplied with DOS 4.0 and higher have been greatly improved, but they still do not offer what many aftermarket products offer. Because of the way BACKUP and RESTORE use the floppy drive as the hardware device, you can use this software only for backing up systems with low-capacity hard drives.

New Backup Software with DOS 6.x. Both Microsoft and IBM have included new backup software with their respective versions of DOS 6 or higher. These programs far outstrip the capabilities of the original BACKUP command and are much easier and safer to use.

In MS-DOS, Microsoft supplies a limited version of the Norton Backup software called MSBACKUP in both a standard DOS and a Windows version. This program is a full featured menu driven program that is designed to back up to floppy drives only. It is very easy to use, and represents a great leap from the older BACKUP and RESTORE commands. Because it is really a restricted version of the Norton Backup program by Symantec, you can easily upgrade to the more full featured Norton Backup program and still retain compatibility with all of your existing backups.

IBM went a different route in PC DOS and supplies an only slightly limited version of the Central Point Backup program called CPBACKUP. This offers a great deal more functionality than the MSBACKUP program supplied by Microsoft. CPBACKUP can back up to a variety of different devices, including tape drives. It is also an easy-to-use menu driven program, but can also be completely automated with an extensive number of command line options.

Windows 95 includes a new backup program that takes full advantage of the Windows 95 user interface. The Win 95 Backup includes the ability to drag and drop file sets and backup sets onto a link to the Backup application. This can be placed on the desktop to make starting a backup operation much easier. Essentially all you have to do is click and drag to start a backup procedure. Access to the Backup application can be invoked by explicitly running the Backup application, or by choosing the Backup option from the Tools tab on the Disk Property sheet. The Win 95 Backup application supports a variety of drives including those that connect to the floppy controller or parallel port.

Aftermarket Software for Floppy Backups. Most aftermarket software offers convenience and performance features not found in the DOS BACKUP and RESTORE commands. If you are relegated to using the floppy disk drive as your backup hardware, you should do yourself a favor and investigate some of the aftermarket software designed for backup. I recommend FASTBACK, by Fifth Generation Systems, as well as the Norton (Symantec) and Central Point backup programs. The latter two are included in utility packages from these companies, including Norton Desktop for Windows and PC Tools.

Even with these programs, however, backing up a hard disk larger than 20 to 40 megabytes is not recommended because it requires using a large number of floppy disks. To explain, consider the system I use. My main portable system has a 4-gigabyte disk drive, which requires 2,867 1.44M floppy disks for backup! Some backup programs perform data compression that can reduce that number by a third to a half; even optimistically, therefore, I would need 1,000 or more high-density disks. Because I always perform backups to a rotating set of media, with three backups in the rotation, I would need somewhere between 3,000 to 8,602 HD diskettes for my backup. That number handles only one of my systems; what about the other systems I have with 1G or larger drives? When you imagine trying to manage more than three thousand floppy disks, not to mention feeding 1,000 or more of them into a system to perform each backup, you can see the problem associated with backing up large drives to floppy disks!

One solution is to back up the drive using either an 8mm (video-type) tape drive or a 4mm Digital Audio Tape (DAT) drive. Either type of tape system easily backs up several gigabytes worth of data to a single tape and can perform a complete backup of a full drive in just a few hours. Partial backups take only seconds or minutes.

Another feature of a tape drive is that, because it is an external unit, I can carry it around and use it to back up all my systems. Also, the media costs for tape are much less than for floppy disks: the 4mm 4 gigabyte tapes cost only $15 or less. Therefore, I can have three backups that cost less than $45—using floppy media would cost from $1,000 to $2,000 or more. You may not have a gigabyte of online storage to back up, but any amount over 40 megabytes starts to become unwieldy when you are using a floppy drive.

For a total of about $500 or so for some of the less-expensive DAT or 8mm units, I have a reliable, complete, high-speed, and simple backup of every system I own. If you have more than 40M to back up—or more than one system—a tape-backup device is the best way. Various tape-backup products are discussed in the following section.

Dedicated Backup Hardware

As explained earlier, you can choose from software and hardware options when you consider backup equipment. In this section, you learn about dedicated backup hardware, usually a tape or cartridge device designed for high-speed, high-capacity backup purposes.

Backup Systems. A good, reliable backup is important when you're using a large hard disk. With a disk of 40M or more, you should consider some form of hardware backup device other than only the floppy drive. Tape backup is available in configurations easily supporting hundreds of megabytes and more. Tape backup is fast and accurate.

Because your data is probably worth much more to you than the physical hardware on which it is stored, it is important to develop a backup system you will use. A tape system makes the backup convenient and, therefore, helps to ensure that you will complete it. If backing up your system is a difficult, time-consuming operation, you or the person responsible for doing it probably will not do it regularly (if ever). Tape units also can be set to perform unattended automatic backups during times when you are not using your computer, such as during the middle of the night.

These parameters describe the basic parameters of different tape-backup devices:

- Type of media used
- Hardware interface
- Backup software

These parameters and more are discussed in Chapter 18, "Tape and other Mass-Storage Drives."

Purchasing Warranty and Service Contracts

Extended warranties are a recent trend in the computer industry. With the current fierce competition among hardware vendors, a good warranty is one way for a specific manufacturer to stand out from the crowd. Although most companies offer a one-year warranty on their systems, others offer longer warranty periods, such as two years or more.

In addition to extended-length warranties, some manufacturers offer free or nearly free on-site service during the warranty period. Many highly competitive mail-order outfits offer service such as this for little or no extra cost.

Tip

Most companies offer extended-length warranties and free or low-cost on-site service. If your system is "mission critical," meaning it absolutely must be functioning all the time, such as with a network file or print server application, you might want to consider an on-site service contract. Such contracts are often overkill for a standard PC.

In most normal cases, service contracts are not worth the price. In the retail computer environment, a service contract is often a way for a dealer or vendor to add income to a sale. Most annual service contracts add 5 to 10 percent of the cost of the system. A service contract for a $5,000 system, for example, costs $250 to $500 per year. Salespeople in most organizations are trained to vigorously sell service contracts. Much like in the automobile sales business, these contracts are largely unnecessary except in special situations.

The high prices of service contracts also might affect the quality of service you receive. Technicians could try to make their work seem more complex than it actually is to make you believe that the contract's price is justified. For example, a service technician might replace your hard disk or entire motherboard with a spare when all you need is low-level formatting for the hard disk or a simple fix for the motherboard such as a single memory chip. A "defective" drive, for example, probably is just returned to the shop for low-level formatting. Eventually, it ends up in somebody else's system. Replacing a part is faster and leaves the impression that your expensive service contract is worth the price because you get a "new" part. You might be much less impressed with your expensive service contract if the service people visit, do a simple troubleshooting procedure, and then replace a single $2 cable or spend 15 minutes reformatting the hard disk.

With some basic troubleshooting skills, some simple tools, and a few spare parts, you can eliminate the need for most of these expensive service contracts. Unfortunately, some companies practice deceptive servicing procedures to justify the expensive service contracts they offer. Users are made to believe that these types of component failures are the norm, and they have a mistaken impression about the overall reliability of today's systems.

Tip

If you have many systems, you can justify carrying a spare-parts inventory, which can also eliminate the need for a service contract. For less than what a service contract costs for five to ten systems, you often can buy a complete spare system each year. Protecting yourself with extra equipment rather than service contracts is practical if you have more than ten computers of the same make or model. For extremely time-sensitive applications, you might be wise to buy a second system along with the primary unit—such as in a network file-server application. Only you can make the appropriate cost-justification analysis to decide whether you need a service contract or a spare system.

In some instances, buying a service contract can be justified and beneficial. If you have a system that must function at all times and is so expensive that you cannot buy a complete spare system, or for a system in a remote location far away from a centralized service operation, you might be wise to invest in a good service contract that provides timely repairs. Before contracting for service, you should consider your options carefully. These sources either supply or authorize service contracts:

- Manufacturers
- Dealers or vendors
- Third parties

Although most users take the manufacturer or dealer service, sometimes a third-party tries harder to close the deal; for example, it sometimes includes all the equipment installed, even aftermarket items the dealers or manufacturers don't offer. In other cases, a manufacturer might not have its own service organization; instead, it makes a deal with a major third-party nationwide service company to provide authorized service.

After you select an organization, several levels of service often are available. Starting with the most expensive, these levels of service typically include:

- Four-hour on-site response
- Next-day on-site response
- Courier service (a service company picks up and returns a unit)
- Carry-in, or "depot," service

The actual menu varies from manufacturer to manufacturer. For example, IBM offers only a full 24-hours-a-day, 7-days-a-week, on-site service contract. IBM claims that a technician is dispatched usually within four hours of your call. For older systems, but not the PS/2, IBM also offers a courier or carry-in service contract. Warranty work, normally a customer carry-in depot arrangement, can be upgraded to a full on-site contract for only $40. After the first-year $40 contract upgrade expires, you can continue the full on-site service contract for standard rates.

If you have ever bought a service contract, you may be surprised by the pricing. In most cases the price of a service contract will be so high that you will only be able to justify it for mission critical systems such as file servers.

Tip

In summary, for most standard systems, a service contract beyond what is included with the original warranty is probably a waste of money. For special or proprietary systems where parts might be difficult to locate, or for systems that must be up and running at all times, you might want to investigate a service-contract option, even though you might be fully qualified and capable of servicing the system. Only after carefully weighing every option and cost involved can you decide how your systems should be serviced.

Summary

This chapter has presented the steps you can take to ensure proper operation of your system. It has examined active and passive preventive maintenance—the key to a system that gives many years of trouble-free service. You have learned about the procedures involved in preventive maintenance and the frequency with which these procedures should be performed.

Backup was discussed as a way to be prepared when things go wrong. The only guarantee for being able to retrieve data is to back it up. In this chapter, you also have learned about backup options.

Finally, you have learned about the commonly available warranty and service contracts provided by computer manufacturers. Sometimes the contracts can save you from worrying about tough-to-service systems or systems whose parts are largely unavailable on short notice.

Part VI

Troubleshooting and Diagnostics

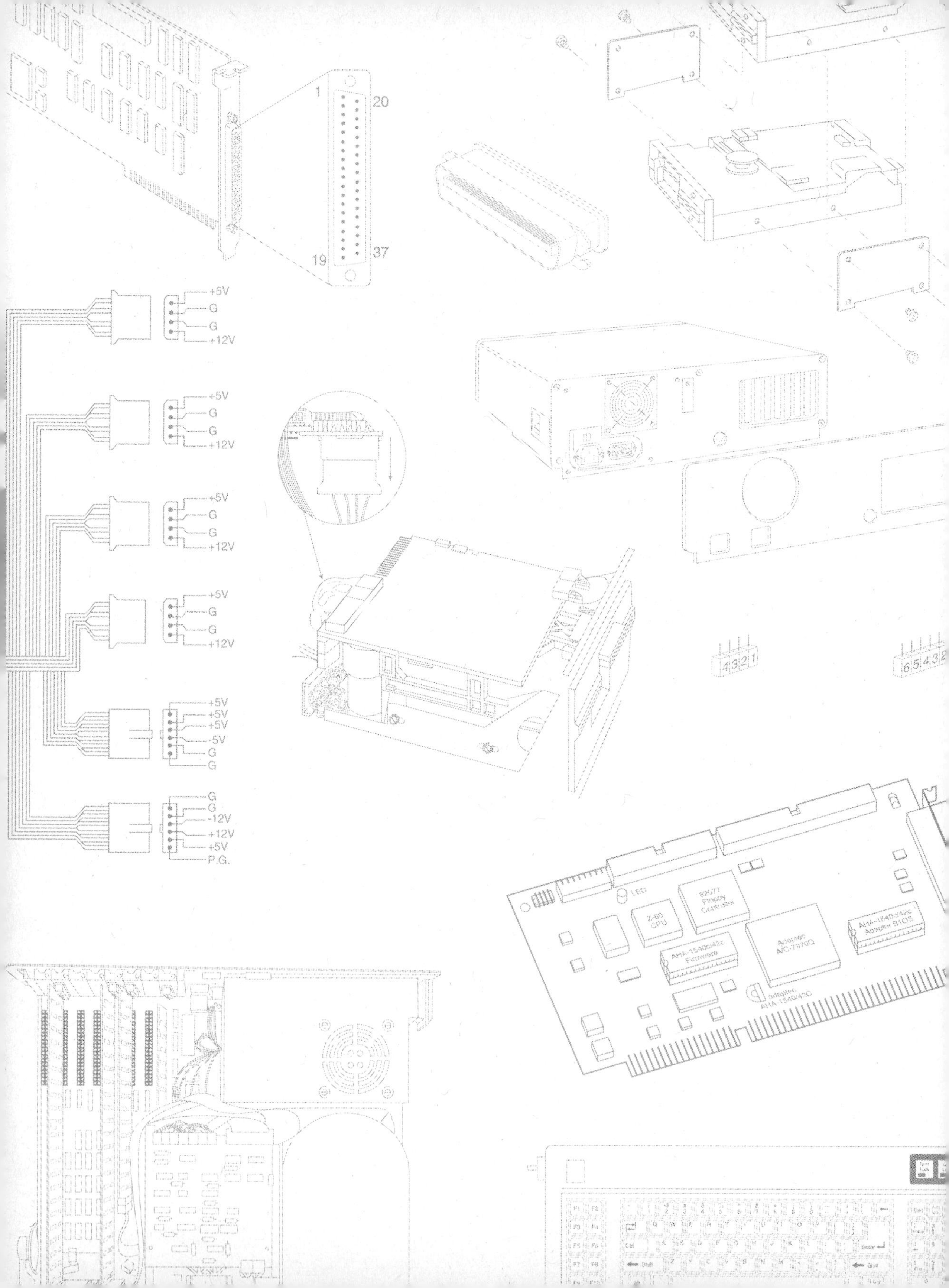

1
20
19
37
+5V
G
G
+12V
+5V
G
G
+12V
+5V
G
G
+12V
+5V
G
G
+12V
+5V
+5V
+5V
-5V
G
G
G
G
-12V
+12V
+5V
P.G.
4 3 2 1
LED
Z-80 CPU
AHA-1540B/42C Adapter BIOS

Chapter 21

Software and Hardware Diagnostic Tools

Diagnostic software, the kind that comes with your computer as well as the types of available third-party software, is vitally important to you any time your computer malfunctions or you begin the process of upgrading a system component or adding a new device. Even when you attempt a simple procedure, such as adding a new adapter card, or begin the sometimes tedious process of troubleshooting a hardware problem that causes a system crash or lockup when you are working, you need to know more about your system than you can learn from the packing list sent with the system. Diagnostic software provides the portal through which you can examine your system hardware and the way your components are working.

This chapter describes three levels of diagnostic software (POST, system, and advanced) included with many computers, or that is available from your computer manufacturer. The chapter describes how you can get the most from this software. It also details IBM's audio codes and error codes, which are similar to the error codes used by most computer manufacturers, and examines aftermarket diagnostics and public-domain diagnostic software.

Diagnostics Software

Several types of diagnostic software are available for PC-compatible systems. This software, some of which is included with the system when purchased, assists users in identifying many problems that can occur with a computer's components. In many cases, these programs can do most of the work in determining which PC component is defective. Three programs that can help you locate a problem are available; each program is more complex and powerful than the preceding one. The diagnostic programs include the following three items:

- *POST*. The Power-On Self Test operates whenever any PC is powered up (switched on).

- *Manufacturer supplied diagnostics software.* Many of the larger, especially high-end name-brand manufacturers such as IBM, Compaq, Hewlett-Packard, and others, make special diagnostics software that is expressly designed for their systems. This manufacturer specific software normally consists of a suite of tests that thoroughly examines the system. IBM's diagnostics software is on the reference disk for the PS/2 systems, and on an advanced diagnostics disk for their other systems. Both Compaq and Hewlett-Packard also produce diagnostics that are designed for a technician to use in troubleshooting their respective systems. In some cases these diagnostics can be downloaded from their electronic bulletin boards, or it may have to be purchased from the manufacturer. Some of the PC compatible vendors like Gateway and Dell include a limited version of one of the aftermarket packages that has been customized for their systems.

- *Aftermarket diagnostics software.* There are a number of manufacturers making general purpose diagnostics software for PC compatible systems. This includes utilities such as Symantec's Norton Utilities, MicroScope by Micro 2000, Qa-Plus by Diagsoft, PC-Technician by Windsor Technologies, and others which provide detailed diagnostics of any PC compatible systems. This chapter also mentions software from numerous other companies.

Many computer operators use the first and last of these software systems to test and troubleshoot most systems—the POST tests and a third-party diagnostic package.

Manufacturer diagnostics can sometimes be expensive, but they are usually complete and work well with the systems they are designed for.

The Power-On Self Test (POST)

When IBM first began shipping the IBM PC in 1981, it included safety features that had never been seen in a personal computer. These features were the POST and parity-checked memory. The parity-checking feature is explained in Chapter 7, "Memory." The following provides much more detail on the POST, a series of program routines buried in the motherboard ROM-BIOS chip that tests all the main system components at power-on time. This program series causes the delay when you turn on an IBM-compatible system; the POST is executed before the computer loads the operating system.

What is Tested?

Whenever you start up your computer, the computer automatically performs a series of tests that check various components—the primary components—in your system. Items such as the CPU, ROM, motherboard support circuitry, memory, and major peripherals (such as an expansion chassis) are tested. These tests are brief and not very thorough compared with available disk-based diagnostics. The POST process provides error or warning messages whenever a faulty component is encountered.

Although the diagnostics performed by the system POST are not always very thorough, they are the first line of defense, especially in handling severe motherboard problems.

If the POST encounters a problem severe enough to keep the system from operating properly, it halts bootup of the system and produces an error message that often leads you directly to the cause of the problem. Such POST-detected problems are sometimes called fatal errors. The POST tests normally provide three types of output messages: audio codes, display-screen messages, and hexadecimal numeric codes to an I/O port address.

POST Audio Error Codes

POST audio error codes usually are audio codes consisting of a number of beeps that identify the faulty component. If your computer is functioning normally, you hear one short beep when the system starts up. If a problem is detected, a different number of beeps sounds—sometimes in a combination of short and long beeps. These BIOS-dependent codes can vary among different BIOS manufacturers. Table 21.1 lists the beep codes for IBM systems and the problem indicated by each series of beeps.

Table 21.1 IBM POST Audio Error Codes and Indicated Problem

Audio code	Sound	Problem (Fault domain)
1 short beep	.	Normal POST-system OK
2 short beeps	..	POST error-error code
No beep		Power supply, system board
Continuous beep	————————	Power supply, system board
Repeating short beeps	......	Power supply, system board
One long, one short beep	-.	System board
One long, two short beeps	-..	Display adapter (MDA, CGA)
One long, three short beeps	-...	Enhanced Graphics Adapter (EGA)
Three long beeps	- - -	3270 keyboard card

. = short beep
- = long beep

Appendix A lists the audio POST codes for the AMI BIOS and Phoenix BIOS, both of which have a much more detailed set of audio error codes than IBMs, which are much more helpful in diagnosing problems with a system motherboard. In particular, the Phoenix BIOS POST is so well done that many times I do not need to use any other diagnostics to isolate a problem—the BIOS does it for me. The sophisticated POST procedure is one of the reasons I like the Phoenix BIOS.

POST Visual Error Codes

On the XT, AT, PS/2, and most compatibles, the POST also displays on the system monitor the test of system memory. The last number displayed is the amount of memory that tested properly. For example, a modern system might display the following:

```
32768 KB OK
```

In most cases, the number displayed by the memory test should agree with the total amount of memory installed on your system motherboard, including conventional and extended memory. Some systems will display a slightly lower total since they will deduct all or part of the 384K of UMA (Upper Memory Area) from the count. The RAM on an expanded memory card is not tested by the POST and does not count in the numbers reported. However, if you are using an expanded memory driver such as EMM386.EXE or Quarterdeck's QEMM to configure extended memory installed on the motherboard as expanded, the POST executes before this driver is loaded so that all installed memory is counted. If the POST memory test stops short of the expected total, the number displayed often indicates how far into system memory a memory error lies. This number alone is a valuable troubleshooting aid.

If an error is detected during the POST procedures, an error message is displayed onscreen. These messages usually are in the form of a numeric code several digits long; for example, 1790-Disk 0 Error. The information in the hardware-maintenance service manual identifies the malfunctioning component. I have researched all available IBM documentation and have included an abbreviated list of the on-screen error codes in this chapter, as well as a complete list in Appendix A. By looking in the error-code chart in Appendix A, you can see that a 1790 error code indicates a read error on the diagnostics cylinder for hard disk drive 0.

I/O Port POST Codes

A less-well-known feature of the POST is that at the beginning of each POST, the BIOS sends test codes to a special I/O port address. These POST codes can be read only by a special adapter card plugged into one of the system slots. These cards originally were designed to be used by the system manufacturers for burn-in testing of the motherboard during system manufacturing without the need for a video display adapter or display. Several companies now make these cards available to technicians. Micro 2000, JDR Microdevices, Data Depot, Ultra-X, Quarterdeck, and Trinitech are just a few manufacturers of these POST cards.

On the Web

Here are some Web sites to visit for information on some of the POST cards:

http://sacb.co.za/dion/micro2.htm

http://www.jdr.com/cgi-bin/wander?PATH:jdr/catalog/Interface_Cards@HTML:Diagnostic_Cards.html@BACK_PATH:jdr/catalog/Interface_Cards@BACK_HTML:subcat_list.html@WID:70796@SETUP:JDR

http://www.datadepo.com/catalog1.htm

http://www.merriweb.com.au/cblock/phd16.html

When one of these adapter cards is plugged into a slot, during the POST you see two-digit hexadecimal numbers flash on a display on the card. If the system stops unexpectedly or hangs, you can just look at the two-digit display on the card for the code indicating the test in progress during the hang. This step usually identifies the failed part. A complete list of these POST codes is in Appendix A; the list covers several different manufacturer's BIOS, including IBM, AMI, Award, and Phoenix.

Most BIOS on the market in systems with an ISA or EISA bus output the POST codes to I/O port address 80h. Compaq is different: its systems send codes to port 84h. IBM PS/2 models with ISA bus slots, such as the Model 25 and 30, send codes to port 90h. Some EISA systems send codes to port 300h (most EISA systems also send the same codes to 80h). IBM MCA bus systems universally send codes to port 680h.

Several cards read only port address 80h. This port address is certainly the most commonly used and works in most situations, but those cards would not work in Compaq systems, some EISA systems, and IBM PS/2 systems. A POST card designed specifically for the PS/2 MCA bus needs to read only port address 680h because the card cannot be used in ISA or EISA bus systems anyway. With all these different addresses, make sure that the card you purchase reads the port addresses you need.

The two most common types of POST cards are those that plug into the 8-bit connector that is a part of the ISA or EISA bus, and those that plug into the MCA bus. Some companies offer both types of POST cards—one for MCA bus systems and one for ISA/EISA bus systems. Micro 2000 and Data Depot do not offer a separate MCA bus card; rather, they have slot adapters that enable their existing ISA bus cards to work in MCA bus systems as well as in ISA and EISA systems. Most other companies offer only ISA/EISA POST cards and ignore the MCA bus.

To read a port address, a POST card needs to have only an 8-bit design; it does not have to be a 16-bit or 32-bit card. At least one manufacturer sold a separate EISA card that it claimed was designed specifically for the EISA bus. However, because the EISA bus was designed to enable the use of 8-bit and 16-bit ISA adapter cards as well as 32-bit EISA cards, and only the 8-bit portion of the ISA bus is needed to read the required port addresses, it is unnecessary to have a separate card specific to EISA bus systems. As long as an ISA card is properly designed to latch the correct port addresses, there is no reason for it not to function perfectly in both ISA and EISA bus systems. There is absolutely no need for a separate (and expensive) EISA card.

Most systems today include PCI slots, and there are a large number of older systems with VL-Bus slots as well. These systems also have ISA slots, and that is where the POST codes can be read from. In other words, there is no need for a PCI or VL-Bus specific POST card.

POST-code cards are invaluable in diagnosing systems where the motherboard seems dead even though the power supply comes on (you can hear the fan). Just pop the card into a slot and observe the code on the card's display. Then look up the code in a list corresponding to the specific BIOS on the motherboard. These cards also can be very helpful with tough problems such as a memory-bit failure in Bank 0, which does not allow error codes to be displayed on a CRT in most EGA or VGA systems.

An important feature that separates the many POST cards on the market is that some provide extensive documentation of different BIOS, and others do not. Each computer manufacturer's BIOS runs different tests in a different sequence and even outputs different code numbers for the same tests. Therefore, without the proper documentation specific to the BIOS on the motherboard you are testing, the numbers shown on the POST card are meaningless.

The documentation supplied with the Micro 2000, Landmark, Data Depot, and Ultra-X cards offers excellent information covering a wide variety of different BIOS manufacturers' codes. Some companies supply their documentation both in printed form and on a disk with a built-in POST Code lookup program. This method is unique and desirable especially if you carry a laptop or portable system with you when you troubleshoot. The JDR Microdevices card offers less than most of the others in the way of documentation, but is also the least expensive card by a wide margin. Another thing that distinguishes the JDR card is that it is designed so that it can be left in a system permanently. The two-digit display can be moved to the back bracket of the card so that it can be read outside the system. There is also a connector for an external two-digit display. The other cards have the display on the card only, which is impossible to read unless you open the system case.

Some cards have additional features worth mentioning. Several of the cards, including the Micro 2000 card (called the POST Probe) as well as the Pocket POST by Data Depot, include a built-in logic probe for testing signals on the major motherboard components. The POST Probe includes a series of separate LED readouts for several important bus signals as well as power-supply voltage levels. The separate LEDs enable these bus signals to be monitored simultaneously. Sometimes you can help to determine the cause of a failure by noting which bus LED is lit at a certain time. The power-supply LEDs verify the output of the +5, -5, +12, and -12 volt signals from the supply. Another feature is meter-probe attachment points on which you can easily connect a voltmeter to the card for more accurate measurements.

The Data Depot Pocket POST is a unique card that includes an LED for monitoring bus signals. It can monitor a single signal at a time, which is selected by a jumper. The card includes LEDs for testing power-supply voltage levels and includes attachment points for a voltmeter as well. The Pocket POST is designed for ISA and EISA bus systems and can connect to any port addresses used in these systems for POST codes. As its name suggests, the card is small compared to most others, and therefore is easy to carry around. The entire package, including the comprehensive manual, fits in a standard (included) floppy disk case.

Trinitech has a Post card and IRQ/DMA diagnostic card combined in one called the OmniPOST. They also have a Power Supply diagnostic card called the PC Power Patroller and a diagnostics program called ExperTrace. The OmniPOST card is unique in that it combines the functions of a standard POST card, an IRQ/DMA trap card, a simple power supply test card, and even has software built into a flash ROM on the card. This makes it one of the most powerful test boards on the market.

Data Depot also has a unique card called the Mini-POST, which is the smallest POST code card on the market. Not much larger than a SIMM module, it works in most any system and is very inexpensive.

Ultra-X has two cards: the Quick-POST PC for ISA/EISA bus systems and the Quick-POST PS/2 for MCA bus systems. Because the Quick-POST cards monitor only one port address each—80h for the PC card and 680h for the PS/2 card—the ISA/EISA version is less flexible than some others. The included documentation is excellent and covers a variety of BIOS versions. Both cards also include LEDs used to monitor power-supply voltages.

A second type of diagnostics card goes beyond the function of a basic POST-code card. In addition to monitoring POST codes, these cards include an on-board ROM chip that contains a more sophisticated diagnostics program than the suite of tests in the motherboard ROM BIOS. Among the cards that offer this function are the Kickstart Irq card, by Quarterdeck, the RACER II card, by Ultra-X, and the Omni-POST by Trinitech. These cards monitor POST codes as well as use their own on-board ROM-based diagnostics program. Because of the extra expense of having these programs and other options on-board, the cards are more expensive than the standard POST-code cards.

Although a higher-level diagnostics card can be handy, I normally do not recommend them because the standard POST-code cards provide 95 percent of the capabilities of these cards with no BIOS conflicts or other problems. In many cases, before you can use a higher-level diagnostics card, other adapters must be removed from the system to eliminate conflicts with ROMs on other cards. Although these cards are quite capable and function as a basic POST-code card if necessary, I find it more valuable to spend the extra money on a disk-based diagnostics program and stick to the basic POST-code cards. This way, I get the most functionality for my money.

IBM Diagnostics

IBM systems usually have two levels of diagnostics software. One is a general purpose diagnostics that is more user-oriented, and the second is a technician level program that can be somewhat cryptic at times. In many cases, both of these programs are provided free with the system when it is purchased, and in some cases, the diagnostics and documentation has to be purchased separately. Since the troubleshooting procedures for most systems these days are fairly simple, most people have no problems running the diagnostics software without any official documentation. IBM runs a BBS system that has virtually all of its general and advanced diagnostics available free for downloading. You can find the number for this BBS listed in the vendor list in Appendix B.

IBM Advanced Diagnostics

For technician-level diagnostics, IBM sells hardware-maintenance and service manuals for each system, which include the Advanced Diagnostics disks for that system. These disks contain the real diagnostics programs and, combined with the hardware-maintenance service manuals, represent the de facto standard diagnostics information and software for IBM and compatible systems. For PS/2 machines, IBM includes the Advanced Diagnostics on the Reference Disk that comes with the system; however, the instructions for using the diagnostics are still found in the separately available service manuals.

If you need a copy of the Advanced Diagnostics for any IBM system, check the IBM National Support Center (NSC) Bulletin Board System (BBS). The IBM BBS has virtually all of the IBM Advanced Diagnostics and Reference Disks available for download at no charge! They are stored on the BBS in a compressed disk image format, and you will need one of two utilities to uncompress the file depending on how it was originally compressed. Follow the instructions presented online for more information on which uncompress program you need. The phone number for the IBM NSC BBS is listed in the Vendor list under the IBM PC Company.

These programs produce error messages in the form of numbers you can use to identify the cause of a wide range of problems. The number codes used are the same as those used in the POST and general-diagnostics software. The meaning of the numbers is consistent across all IBM diagnostic programs. This section explores the advanced diagnostics and lists most of the known error-code meanings. IBM constantly adds to this error-code list as it introduces new equipment.

Using IBM Advanced Diagnostics. If you have a PS/2 system with the MCA (Micro Channel Architecture) bus slots (models produced later than the Models 25 to 40), you may already have IBM's Advanced Diagnostics, even if you don't know it. These diagnostics are usually hidden on the PS/2 Reference Disk. To access these diagnostics, boot the PS/2 Reference Disk. When the main menu is displayed, press Ctrl-A (for Advanced). The program changes to the advanced diagnostics menu. In some of the PS/2 systems, the Advanced Diagnostics were large enough to require a separate disk or disks. All the PS/2 Reference and Diagnostics disks are available for downloading on the IBM NSC BBS (see Appendix B).

Hiding advanced diagnostics from average users is probably a good idea. For example, inexperienced users can easily wipe out all their data by using this disk's option of low-level formatting the hard disk.

The PS/2 service manuals are fairly skimpy because the average PS/2 system doesn't have that many parts, and they are easy to repair. One drawback of the PS/2 Service manuals is that they often end a troubleshooting session with this advice: Replace the system board. Although I recommend the hardware-maintenance and service manuals, if all you are looking for is the advanced-diagnostics software (and you have a PS/2 system with the MCA bus), you already have it and do not need to purchase any additional items.

Non-MCA systems, such as the PS/2 25 to 40 systems, come with a Starter Disk, equivalent to the Setup and Diagnostics Disk that came with the original AT system. This Starter Disk includes the Setup program and limited diagnostics that lack many functions found in the advanced diagnostics. You get the advanced diagnostics for these systems included with the PS/2 Hardware Maintenance and Service (HMS) Manual, which includes the advanced diagnostics disks for Models 25, 30, and 30-286. If you want the diagnostics for later systems, such as Models 35 or 40, you must purchase the respective update package for the PS/2 HMS manual. These updates usually cost about $30. If all you need are the Advanced Diagnostics disks, they can be downloaded at no charge from the IBM NSC BBS (see the vendor list).

If you really want in-depth information about troubleshooting your system, you can purchase the *IBM Hardware Maintenance Service Manual*. This single book covers the earlier IBM systems, including the PC, XT, and AT. Updates cover the XT-286 and PS/2 Models 25 and 30. Later PS/2 systems have their own separate version of this book, called

PS/2 Hardware Maintenance and Service. This book includes spare copies of the standard reference disks. The newer versions of the PS/2 book now cover also all PS/2 systems, those with ISA (Industry Standard Architecture), as well as MCA (Micro Channel Architecture) slots.

Although the guide-to-operations manual is good only for identifying a problem component, the HMS manual provides information for you to more accurately isolate and repair the failure of any field-replaceable unit (FRU).

The HMS manual includes an Advanced Diagnostics disk as well as provides maintenance-analysis procedures (MAPs), which are instructions to help you to isolate and identify problem components.

Examining Error Codes. Nearly all the personal computer error codes for the POST, general diagnostics, and advanced diagnostics are represented by the display of the device number followed by two digits other than 00. When the tests display the device number plus the number 00, it indicates a test was completed without an error being found.

The following list is a compilation from various sources including technical reference manuals, hardware-maintenance service manuals, and hardware-maintenance reference manuals. In each three-digit number, the first number indicates a device. The other two digits indicate the exact problem. For example, 7xx indicates the math coprocessor. A display of 700 means all is well. Any other number (701 to 799) indicates that the math coprocessor is bad or having problems. The last two digits (01 to 99) indicate what is wrong. Table 21.2 lists the basic error codes and their descriptions.

Table 21.2 Personal Computer Error Codes

Code	Description
1xx	System Board errors
2xx	Memory (RAM) errors
3xx	Keyboard errors
4xx	Monochrome Display Adapter (MDA) errors
4xx	PS/2 System Board Parallel Port errors
5xx	Color Graphics Adapter (CGA) errors
6xx	Floppy Drive/Controller errors
7xx	Math Coprocessor errors
9xx	Parallel Printer adapter errors
10xx	Alternate Parallel Printer Adapter errors
11xx	Primary Async Communications (serial port COM1:) errors
12xx	Alternate Async Communications (serial COM2:, COM3: and COM4:)
13xx	Game Control Adapter errors
14xx	Matrix Printer errors
15xx	Synchronous Data Link Control (SDLC) Communications Adapter errors

(continues)

Table 21.2 Continued

Code	Description
16xx	Display Station Emulation Adapter (DSEA) errors (5520, 525x)
17xx	ST-506/412 Fixed Disk and Controller errors
18xx	I/O Expansion Unit errors
19xx	3270 PC Attachment Card errors
20xx	Binary Synchronous Communications (BSC) Adapter errors
21xx	Alternate Binary Synchronous Communications (BSC) Adapter errors
22xx	Cluster Adapter errors
23xx	Plasma Monitor Adapter errors
24xx	Enhanced Graphics Adapter (EGA) errors
24xx	PS/2 System Board Video Graphics Array (VGA) errors
25xx	Alternate Enhanced Graphics Adapter (EGA) errors
26xx	XT or AT/370 370-M (Memory) and 370-P (Processor) Adapter errors
27xx	XT or AT/370 3277-EM (Emulation) Adapter errors
28xx	3278/79 Emulation Adapter or 3270 Connection Adapter errors
29xx	Color/Graphics Printer errors
30xx	Primary PC Network Adapter errors
31xx	Secondary PC Network Adapter errors
32xx	3270 PC or AT Display and Programmed Symbols Adapter errors
33xx	Compact Printer errors
35xx	Enhanced Display Station Emulation Adapter (EDSEA) errors
36xx	General Purpose Interface Bus (GPIB) Adapter errors
38xx	Data Acquisition Adapter errors
39xx	Professional Graphics Adapter (PGA) errors
44xx	5278 Display Attachment Unit and 5279 Display errors
45xx	IEEE Interface Adapter (IEEE-488) errors
46xx	A Real-Time Interface Coprocessor (ARTIC) Multiport/2 Adapter errors
48xx	Internal Modem errors
49xx	Alternate Internal Modem errors
50xx	PC Convertible LCD errors
51xx	PC Convertible Portable Printer errors
56xx	Financial Communication System errors
70xx	Phoenix BIOS/Chip Set Unique Error Codes
71xx	Voice Communications Adapter (VCA) errors
73xx	3 1/2-inch External Diskette Drive errors
74xx	IBM PS/2 Display Adapter (VGA card) errors
74xx	8514/A Display Adapter errors
76xx	4216 PagePrinter Adapter errors
84xx	PS/2 Speech Adapter errors
85xx	2M XMA Memory Adapter or Expanded Memory Adapter/A errors
86xx	PS/2 Pointing Device (Mouse) errors

Code	Description
89xx	Musical Instrument Digital Interface (MIDI) Adapter errors
91xx	IBM 3363 Write-Once Read Multiple (WORM) Optical Drive/Adapter errors
096xxxx	SCSI Adapter with Cache (32-bit) errors
100xx	Multiprotocol Adapter/A errors
101xx	300/1200bps Internal Modem/A
104xx	ESDI Fixed Disk or Adapter errors
107xx	5 1/4-inch External Diskette Drive or Adapter errors
112xxxx	SCSI Adapter (16-bit w/o Cache) errors
113xxxx	System Board SCSI Adapter (16-bit) errors
129xx	Model 70 Processor Board errors; Type 3 (25MHz) System Board
149xx	P70/P75 Plasma Display and Adapter errors
165xx	6157 Streaming Tape Drive or Tape Attachment Adapter errors
166xx	Primary Token Ring Network Adapter errors
167xx	Alternate Token Ring Network Adapter errors
180xx	PS/2 Wizard Adapter errors
194xx	80286 Memory Expansion Option Memory Module errors
208xxxx	Unknown SCSI Device errors
209xxxx	SCSI Removable Disk errors
210xxxx	SCSI Fixed Disk errors
211xxxx	SCSI Tape Drive errors
212xxxx	SCSI Printer errors
213xxxx	SCSI Processor errors
214xxxx	SCSI Write-Once Read Multiple (WORM) Drive errors
215xxxx	SCSI CD-ROM Drive errors
216xxxx	SCSI Scanner errors
217xxxx	SCSI Optical Memory errors
218xxxx	SCSI Jukebox Changer errors
219xxxx	SCSI Communications errors

Appendix A contains a detailed list of every IBM error code I have encountered. Also listed are charts I developed concerning IBM SCSI errors. The SCSI interface has introduced a whole new set of error codes because of the large number and variety of devices that can be attached.

General Purpose Diagnostics Programs

A large number of third-party diagnostics programs are available for PC-compatible systems. Specific programs are available also to test memory, floppy drives, hard disks, video boards, and most other areas of the system. Although some of these utility packages should be considered essential in any tool kit, many fall short of the level needed by professional-level troubleshooters. Many products, geared more toward end users, lack the accuracy, features, and capabilities needed by technically proficient people who are serious about troubleshooting. In this section I present information about some of the diagnostics programs I recommend.

Most of the better diagnostics on the market offer several advantages over the IBM diagnostics. They usually are better at determining where a problem lies within a system, especially in IBM-compatible systems. Serial- and parallel-port loopback connectors, or wrap plugs, are often included in these packages, or are available for a separate charge. The plugs are required to properly diagnose and test serial and parallel ports. (IBM always charges extra for these plugs.)

Many of these programs can be run in a batch mode, which enables a series of tests to be run from the command line without operator intervention. You then can set up automated test suites, which can be especially useful in burning in a system or executing the same tests on many systems.

These programs test all types of memory including conventional (base) memory, extended memory, and expanded memory. Failures can usually be identified down to the individual chip or SIMM (bank and bit) level.

One question I commonly receive is about which diagnostic program I would recommend above all others. This is impossible to answer! There are so many programs available, and each seems to have strengths in some areas and weaknesses in others. I almost never rely on the "opinion" of one program, and usually try several to see if they corroborate the diagnosis. Having a second or third opinion in some cases is a good idea before replacing an expensive piece of equipment or getting involved in a lengthy repair procedure. Although many of these programs can be somewhat expensive for casual troubleshooters, if you work in a service or support role, these professional-level programs can save you money in the long run with increased accuracy and capabilities in troubleshooting and servicing your systems.

The remainder of this section describes some of the different diagnostics programs I recommend.

AMIDiag

AMI (American Megatrends, Inc.) makes the most popular PC ROM BIOS software in use today. The AMI BIOS can be found on the majority of newer IBM compatible systems that are currently being sold. If you have seen the AMI BIOS, you know that most versions have a diagnostic program built in. Few people know that AMI now markets an enhanced disk-based version of the same diagnostics that is built into the AMI ROM.

AMIDiag, as the program is called, has numerous features and enhancements not found in the simpler ROM version. AMIDiag is a comprehensive, general purpose diagnostic that is designed for any IBM compatible system, not just those with an AMI ROM BIOS.

On the Web

This ftp site contains a demo version of AMIDiag:

http://www.cyf-kr.edu.pl/ftp/ami/

Checkit Pro

Touchstone Software Corp.'s Checkit products offer an excellent suite of testing capabilities, including tests of the system CPU; conventional, extended, and expanded memory; hard and floppy drives; and video card and monitor (including VESA-Standard cards and monitors, mouse, and keyboard). Several versions of the Checkit product are available—Checkit Pro Deluxe is the company's most complete hardware diagnostic program. Checkit Pro Analyst for Windows performs Windows-based diagnostics. Checkit Plus, which is included by some system manufacturers with their systems, is less complete.

Checkit Pro Deluxe provides limited benchmarking capabilities but gives detailed information about your system hardware such as the following: total installed memory, hard drive type and size, current memory allocation (including upper memory usage), IRQ availability and usage, modem/fax modem speed, and a variety of other tests important to someone troubleshooting a PC. Checkit Pro Deluxe includes a text editing module that opens automatically to CONFIG.SYS and AUTOEXEC.BAT. If you use Windows, Checkit Pro's Windows option makes it easy to edit your Windows SYSTEM.INI and WIN.INI files.

Some of the testing performed by Checkit Pro is uncommon for diagnostic utility packages (for example, its capability to test modem/fax modem settings). Still, Checkit Pro lacks important features such as an easy-to-use listing of available DMA channels, which is crucial if you are trying to install a sound card and other hardware devices.

For additional information on Checkit, be sure to check its Web site at:

On the Web

http://www.checkit.com/products/index.htm

Micro-Scope

Micro-Scope by Micro 2000 is a full featured general purpose diagnostic program for IBM compatible systems. It has many features and capabilities that can be very helpful in troubleshooting or diagnosing hardware problems.

The Micro-Scope package is one of only a few diagnostics packages that are truly PS/2 aware. Micro-Scope not only helps you troubleshoot PS/2 systems, but also does some things that even IBM advanced diagnostics cannot do. For example, it can format industry-standard ESDI hard disk drives attached to the IBM PS/2 ESDI controller. When you attach an ESDI drive to the IBM ESDI controller, the BIOS on the controller queries the drive for its capacity and defect map information. IBM apparently chose a proprietary format for this information on its drives; if the controller cannot read the information, you cannot set up the drive nor format it by using the PS/2 Reference Disk.

Although IBM used an ESDI controller in its PS/2 system, you could not get just any ESDI drive to work on that system. Some drive manufacturers produced special PS/2 versions of their drives that had this information on them. Another way around the problem was to use an aftermarket ESDI controller in place of the IBM controller so that you could use the IBM ESDI drive as well as any other industry-standard ESDI drive. With this method, however, you could not use the Reference Disk format program anymore because it works only with IBM's controller. Micro-Scope solves many of these problems because it can format an industry-standard ESDI drive attached to the IBM ESDI controller and save you from having to purchase an aftermarket controller or a special drive when you add drives to these systems.

Micro-Scope also has a hardware interrupt and I/O port address check feature that is more accurate than the same feature in most other software. It enables you to accurately identify the interrupt or I/O port address a certain adapter or hardware device in your system is using—a valuable capability in solving conflicts between adapters. Some user-level diagnostics programs have this feature, but the information they report can be grossly inaccurate, and they often miss items installed in the system. Micro-Scope goes around DOS and the BIOS; because the program has its own operating system and its tests bypass the ROM BIOS when necessary, it can eliminate the masking that occurs with these elements in the way. For this reason, the program also is useful for technicians who support PCs that run under non-DOS environments such as UNIX or on Novell file servers. For convenience, you can install Micro-Scope on a hard disk and run it under regular DOS.

Finally, Micro 2000 offers excellent telephone technical support. Its operators do much more than explain how to operate the software—they help you with real troubleshooting problems. This information is augmented by good documentation and online help built in to the software so that, in many cases, you don't have to refer to the manual.

On the Web

http://sacb.co.za/dion/micro2.htm

Norton Utilities Diagnostics

When you consider that Norton Diagnostics (NDIAGS) comes with the Norton Utilities, and that Norton Utilities is already an essential collection of system data safeguarding, troubleshooting, testing, and repairing utilities, NDIAGS probably is one of the best values in diagnostic programs.

If you already have a version of Norton Utilities earlier than 8.0, get an upgrade. They also have a new version that is designed for Windows 95. If you don't already have Norton Utilities, you'll want to strongly consider this package, not only for NDIAGS, but also for enhancements to other utilities such as Speedisk, Disk Doctor, and Calibrate. These three hard drive utilities basically represent the state of the art in hard drive diagnostics and software-level repair. SYSINFO still handles benchmarking for the Norton Utilities, and it does as good a job as any other diagnostic package on the market.

NDIAGS adds diagnostic capabilities that previously were not provided by the Norton Utilities, including comprehensive information about the overall hardware configuration of your system—the CPU, system BIOS, math coprocessor, video adapter, keyboard and mouse type, hard and floppy drive types, amount of installed memory (including extended and expanded), bus type (ISA, EISA, or MCA), and the number of serial and parallel ports. Unlike some other programs, loopback plugs do not come in the box for NDIAGS, but a coupon is included that enables you to get loopback plugs free. Note that this program uses wrap plugs that are wired a bit differently than what has been commonly used by others. The different wiring allows you to run some additional tests.

Fortunately, the documentation includes a diagram for these plugs, allowing you to make your own if you desire.

NDIAGS thoroughly tests the major system components and enables you to check minor details such as the NumLock, CapsLock, and ScrollLock LEDs on your keyboard. NDIAGS also provides an on-screen grid you can use to center the image on your monitor and test for various kinds of distortion that may indicate a faulty monitor. The Norton Utilities 8.0, as mentioned previously, is available for registered users of an earlier version and can be purchased for $100 or less.

The following Web site contains information about all the Symantec utilities:

On the Web

http://www.symantec.com/lit/util/doswinut/doswinut.html

PC Technician

PC Technician by Windsor Technologies is one of the longest running PC diagnostics products on the market. As such, it has been highly refined and continuously updated to reflect the changing PC market.

PC Technician is a full-featured comprehensive hardware diagnostic and troubleshooting tool, and tests all major areas of a system. Like several of the other more capable programs, PC Technician has its own operating system that isolates it from problems caused by software conflicts. The program is written in assembly language and has direct access to the hardware in the system for testing. This program also includes all the wrap plugs needed for testing serial and parallel ports.

PC Technician has long been a favorite with field service companies, who equip their technicians with the product for troubleshooting. This program was designed for the professional service technician; however, it is easy to use for the amateur as well. As a bonus, PC Technician costs much less than many of the other programs in its class.

On the Web

http://www.windsortech.com/

QAPlus/FE

QAPlus/FE by Diagsoft is one of the most advanced and comprehensive sets of diagnostics you can buy for 386, 486, or Pentium-based computers, including PS/2s. Its testing is extremely thorough, and its menu-based interface makes it downright easy to use, even for someone who is not particularly well-versed in diagnosing problems with personal computers. QAPlus/FE also includes some of the most accurate system benchmarks you can get, which can be used to find out if that new system you are thinking of buying is really all that much faster than the one you already have. More importantly, QAPlus/FE comes on bootable 3 1/2- and 5 1/4-inch disks that (regardless of whether your operating system is DOS, OS/2, or UNIX) can be used to start your system when problems are so severe that your system hardware cannot even find the hard drive. You also can install QAPlus/FE on your hard drive if you are using DOS 3.2 or later.

Many of you may already have a less comprehensive version of this program oriented toward end users called QAPlus. The basic QAPlus version is often included with systems sold by a number of different PC system vendors. Although the simple QAPlus program is okay, I much prefer the full-blown QAPlus/FE version for serious troubleshooting.

QAPlus/FE can be used to test your motherboard, system RAM (conventional, extended, and expanded), video adapter, hard drive, floppy drives, CD-ROM drive, mouse, keyboard, printer, and parallel and serial ports (the QAPlus/FE package includes loopback plugs for full testing of these ports). It also provides exhaustive information on your system configuration, including the hardware installed on your system, its CPU, and the total amount of RAM installed on your system. It provides full interrupt mapping—crucial when installing new adapter boards and other hardware devices—and gives you a full picture of the device drivers and memory resident programs loaded in CONFIG.SYS and AUTOEXEC.BAT, as well as other information about DOS and system memory use.

QAPlus/FE also includes various other utilities that are more likely to appeal to the serious PC troubleshooter than to the average PC user. These special capabilities include a CMOS editor that can be used to change system date and time, as well as the hard drive type; installed memory size and other CMOS information; a COM port debugger; a hard drive test and low-level formatting utility; a floppy drive test utility; and a configuration file editor that can be used to edit AUTOEXEC.BAT, CONFIG.SYS, a remote system communication host program that enables service people with the full remote package to operate your computer via modem, as well as other text files.

Unlike some diagnostics programs, QAPlus/FE has a system burn-in capability, meaning it can be used to run your system non-stop under a full load of computations and hardware activity for the purpose of determining whether any system component is likely to fail in real life use. Many people use a burn-in utility when they receive a new system, and then again just before the warranty runs out. A true system burn-in usually lasts 48 to 72 hours, or even longer. The amount of time QAPlus/FE can burn-in a system is user-configurable by setting the number of times the selected tests are to be run.

On the Web

http://www.diagsoft.com/

Disk Diagnostics

All the general purpose diagnostics programs will test both floppy and hard disk drives. However, because these programs are general-purpose in nature, the drive tests are not always as complete as one would like. For this reason there are a number of specific programs designed expressly for performing diagnostics and servicing on disk drives. The following section discusses some of the best disk diagnostic and testing programs on the market and what they can do for you.

Drive Probe

Many programs on the market evaluate the condition of floppy disk drives by using a disk created or formatted on the same drive. A program that uses this technique cannot make a proper evaluation of a disk drive's alignment. A specially-created disk produced by a tested and calibrated machine is required. This type of disk can be used as a reference standard by which to judge a drive. Accurite, the primary manufacturer of such reference standard floppy disks, helps specify floppy disk industry standards. Accurite produces the following three main types of reference standard disks used for testing drive function and alignment:

- Digital Diagnostic Diskette (DDD)
- High-Resolution Diagnostic Diskette (HRD)
- Analog Alignment Diskette (AAD)

The DDD disk, introduced in 1982, enables you to test drive alignment by using only software; no oscilloscope or special tools are needed. This disk is accurate to only 500μ-inches (millionths of an inch)—good enough for a rough test of drive alignment, but not nearly enough to use for aligning a drive.

The HRD disk, introduced in 1989, represents a breakthrough in floppy disk drive testing and alignment. The disk is accurate to within 50μ-inches (millionths of an inch)—accurate enough to use not only for precise testing of floppy drives, but also for aligning drives. With software that uses this HRD disk, you can align a floppy drive without having to use special tools or an oscilloscope. Other than the program and the HRD disk, you need only an IBM-compatible system to which to connect the drive. This product has lowered significantly the cost of aligning a drive and has eliminated much hassling with special test equipment.

The AAD disk has been the standard for drive alignment for many years. The disks, accurate to within 50μ inches (millionths of an inch), require that you use special test gear, such as an oscilloscope, to read the disk. These disks have no computer-readable data, only precisely placed analog tracks. Until HRD disks became available, using an AAD was the only way to align drives properly.

The Accurite program Drive Probe is designed to work with the HRD disks (also from Accurite). Drive Probe is the most accurate and capable floppy disk testing program on the market, thanks to the use of HRD disks. Until other programs utilize the HRD disks for testing, Drive Probe is my software of choice for floppy disk testing. Because the Drive Probe software also acts as a disk exerciser, for use with AAD disks and an oscilloscope, you can move the heads to specific tracks for controlled testing.

Disk Manager

Disk Manager by Ontrack stands today as the most comprehensive and capable hard disk test and format utility available. This program works with practically every hard disk and controller on the market, including the newer SCSI and IDE types.

The Disk Manager program allows testing of the controller as well as the drive. Read-only testing may be performed as well as read/write tests. One of the best features is the comprehensive low-level formatting capability, which allows a user to set not only interleave but skew factors as well. The low-level format portion is also capable of truly formatting most IDE drives, a feature that few other programs have.

If you do any testing and formatting of hard disks, this program should be in your utility library. I included more information about Disk Manager in Chapter 14, "Hard Disk Drives."

http://www.ontrack.com/ontrack/products.html

Data Recovery Utilities

There are several programs designed for data recovery rather than just hardware troubleshooting and repair. These data recovery programs can troubleshoot and repair disk formatting structures (boot sectors, file allocation tables, directories) as well as files and file structures (database files, spreadsheet files, and so on).

Norton Utilities

The Norton Utilities by Symantec stands as perhaps the premier data recovery package on the market today. This package is very comprehensive and will automatically repair most types of disk problems.

What really makes this package stand out for me is the fantastic Disk Editor program. Currently there simply is no other program that is as comprehensive or as capable of editing disks at the sector level. For the professional PC troubleshooter or repair person, the Disk Editor included with the Norton Utilities can give you the ability to work directly with any sector on the disk. Unfortunately, this does require extensive knowledge of sector formats and disk structures. The documentation with the package is excellent and can be very helpful if you are learning data recovery on your own.

I find that data recovery is a lucrative service that the more advanced technician can provide. People are willing to pay much more to get their data back than to simply replace a hard drive.

For more automatic recovery that anybody can perform, Norton Utilities has several other useful modules. Disk Doctor and Calibrate are two of the modules included with the Norton Utilities version 8.0 and later, including the Windows 95 version. Together, these two utilities provide exhaustive testing of the data structures and sectors of a hard drive. Disk Doctor works with both hard disks and floppies and tests the capability of the drive to work with the system in which it is installed, including the drive's boot sector, file allocation tables (FAT), file structure, and data areas. Calibrate, which is used for the most intensive testing of the data area of a drive, also tests the hard drive controller electronics.

Calibrate also can be used to perform deep-pattern testing of IDE, SCSI, and ST-506/412-interface drives, writing literally millions of bytes of data to every sector of the drive to see whether it can properly retain data; moving data if the sector where it is stored is flawed; and marking the sector as bad in the FAT.

Calibrate can perform a nondestructive low-level format of ST-506/412 drives, which means that the data stored on the drive is not destroyed as it is when you use the controller BIOS to perform a low-level format on these drives. Often, in performing deep-pattern testing and low-level formatting of ST-506/412 drives, Calibrate can refresh, or remagnetize, bad sectors and return them to service so that they can be safely used again for data storage. Calibrate also can be used to test for the optimal interleave on ST-506/412 drives and nondestructively change the format if system performance would benefit.

Due to the excellent Disk Editor, anybody serious about data recovery needs a copy of Norton Utilities. The many other modules that are included are excellent as well, and the latest versions now include NDIAGS, which is a comprehensive PC hardware diagnostic.

http://www.symantec.com/lit/util/doswinut/doswinut.html

On the Web

Configuration Utilities

Many utilities that are on the market today specialize not only in hardware diagnostics, but instead in hardware configuration. These programs are designed to tell you what type of hardware you have and how it is configured. I find this type of program to be one of the most useful, since most PC problems result from improper system configuration.

MSD (Microsoft Diagnostics)

Since the introduction of Windows 3.1 and now with DOS 6.0 and higher, Microsoft has included a little-known program called MSD (Microsoft Diagnostics). MSD is not really a full-blown diagnostics program but is more of a system configuration utility. MSD provides quick answers to system configuration problems such as interrupt request line (IRQ) conflicts and memory address problems.

In addition, MSD provides basic information about the system it is running on, including the BIOS, processor type, video adapter, network (if any), the mouse, disk drives (including CD-ROM drives), parallel and serial ports, and the DOS version. Also provided is extensive information on any device drivers and memory resident programs loaded into memory. This information can be very useful in locating conflicts between two programs or especially when trying to fit different programs into different areas of memory. MSD can present in a visual manner the locations in memory where each module occupies; this can be much more helpful than the text listings provided by the DOS MEM command.

MSD is provided free with Windows 3.1 and higher and MS-DOS 6.0 or higher. This means that if you are not using Windows and are using other OEM versions of DOS such as IBM's PC-DOS, you may not have MSD installed on your system. In that case, you can still get the program for free by downloading it from the Microsoft BBS (see the vendor list for the number). Microsoft has decided to treat MSD as a public domain program and it can be downloaded for free by anyone with access to a modem. Although it may not be the greatest system configuration utility available, it certainly does a very good job, especially on memory, and the price is right!

Windows Diagnostic Software

With the startling success of Windows 3.0, 3.1, and of course the new Windows 95, software utility manufacturers have raced to fill what was perceived as a shortage of diagnostic programs that run under Windows. The results have been mixed. But some good utility packages have emerged.

For example, the Norton Desktop for Windows, which many users think of first as a replacement for Program Manager, includes SYSINFO, an excellent system hardware information program that offers details on your drives, available IRQs, memory, video adapter, printer, and other system information. SYSINFO also offers a benchmark that measures your CPU performance.

Another excellent Windows diagnostic program is WinSleuth, which benchmarks your system and performs extremely thorough testing of your system hardware. It also details your drives, memory, video adapter, printer, and other system components.

But a real treasure is WinSleuth's capability to tell you the IRQs available when Windows is running, and also available direct memory access (DMA) channels. Although numerous DOS-based utility packages provide this information, few do so in Windows. And WinSleuth Gold can save you literally hours of scratching your head while trying to configure a sound board or other adapter to run in Windows.

First Aid 95 Deluxe by Cybermedia is another excellent Windows diagnostic program. Unlike others that focus mainly on hardware, First Aid focuses on software conflicts and Windows-specific problems. This program works on all Windows versions, including Windows 95.

Notice that all of these companies have newer versions of these programs that have been especially updated for Windows 95.

On the Web

http://arachnid.qdeck.com/qdeck/products/WinProbe/

Shareware and Public-Domain Diagnostics

Many excellent public-domain diagnostic programs are available, including programs for diagnosing problems with memory, hard disks, floppy disks, monitors and video adapters, as well as virtually any other part of the system. These programs can be excellent for users who do not perform frequent troubleshooting or who are on a budget.

Many programs assumed to be "public domain" are really not. These are often called shareware or user-distributed software. These programs are not free like true public domain programs, but are in fact commercial software that is merely distributed for free. In most cases you are allowed to try the program for a period of time before registering and paying for the software. Be sure to register; this will allow the author to stay in business, providing excellent software through the shareware concept, and you will then be notified of any updates or improvements. In some cases registration entitles you to the next version of the program for free, and may include other incentives such as an enhanced version of the program with additional features.

Shareware is a set of commercial-quality programs distributed under a try now, pay later concept. The authors of shareware programs depend on honest users to pay for the shareware they use (generally only a few dollars). Public domain software has been released by the author to be used by anyone without the payment of a fee of any kind to the author.

Most often, you obtain shareware programs by downloading them from a BBS using a modem. However, some companies distribute shareware on disk. One of these companies stands out: the Public Software Library. This organization, which began as an outgrowth of a Houston computer users' group, has acquired the single best collection of public-domain and user-supported software. What makes this company extraordinary is that all the software is tested before entering the library, which eliminates virus or Trojan-horse programs that can damage a system. Buggy programs also usually don't make it into the Public Software Library. All the programs are the latest available versions, and earlier versions are purged from the library. Many other shareware disk distribution companies don't think twice about sending you a disk full of old programs.

The programs in this library are not sold but distributed. The authors are aware of how these programs are distributed, and no excessive fees are charged for the disk and copying services. This truly legitimate company has the program authors' approval to distribute software in this manner. All disks are guaranteed, unlike many comparable organizations that seem bent on making as much money as they can.

Besides the Public Software Library, you can find many shareware and public domain programs on local Bulletin Board Systems (BBSs), CompuServe, or the Internet. If you have access to CompuServe, one of the best places to look for this type of software is in the PCHW forum.

Summary

This chapter examined the diagnostic hardware and software utilities you can use as a valuable aid in diagnosing and troubleshooting a system. First, the chapter described the three levels of diagnostic software (POST, system, and advanced) and explained how you can get the most from the POST each time your system boots. This chapter also included detailed information about IBM error codes and a reference chart showing the meanings of some of these codes.

In addition, this chapter covered diagnostic and benchmarking utility packages, such as IBM's system diagnostics and advanced diagnostics, as well as many other aftermarket general and special purpose diagnostics. Each of these packages, although taking different approaches to troubleshooting a PC, provides specialized diagnostics for particular areas of the system, such as system memory, hard drives, floppy drives, COM ports, parallel ports, video adapters, keyboards, the mouse, and other components.

Finally, this chapter included a discussion of diagnostic utilities distributed as shareware or released into the public domain. Shareware and public domain software are a rich source of utilities that are relatively inexpensive, or free for the downloading.

Chapter 22

Operating Systems Software and Troubleshooting

This chapter focuses on the problems that occur in PC systems because of faulty or incompatible software. First, it describes the structure of DOS and how DOS works with hardware in a functioning system. Topics of particular interest are as follows:

- DOS file structure
- DOS disk organization
- DOS programs for data and disk recovery (their capabilities and dangers)

Additionally, the chapter examines two other important software-related issues: using memory-resident software (and dealing with the problems it can cause) and distinguishing a software problem from a hardware problem.

Disk Operating System (DOS)

Information about DOS may seem out of place in a book about hardware upgrade and repair, but if you ignore DOS and other software when you troubleshoot a system, you can miss a number of problems. The best system troubleshooters and diagnosticians know the entire system—hardware and software.

This book cannot discuss DOS in depth, but if you need to read more about it, Que Corporation publishes some good books on the subject (*Using MS DOS 6.2, Special Edition*, for example).

Note that Windows 95 still uses the same structures on the disk as DOS does, such as the Master Boot Record (MBR), DOS Boot Record (DBR), File Allocation Tables (FATs), and Directories. There are a few enhancements to the directory structure in order to support long filenames, but that's about it. Microsoft has indicated that future versions of Windows 95 will incorporate a 32-bit FAT that will break the current partition size barrier of 2GB for DOS and Windows 95 partitions. Note that the HPFS (High Performance File

System) and NTFS (Windows NT File System) already support single partitions of up to 8GB, which is currently the maximum drive capacity allowed.

This section describes the basics of DOS: where it fits into the PC system architecture, what its components are, and what happens when a system boots (starts up). Understanding the booting process can be helpful when diagnosing startup problems. This section also explains DOS configuration—an area in which many people experience problems—and the file formats DOS uses, as well as how DOS manages information on a disk.

Operating System Basics

DOS is just one component in the total system architecture. A PC system has a distinct hierarchy of software that controls the system at all times. Even when you are operating within an application program such as a word processor, several other layers of programs are always executing underneath. Usually the layers can be defined distinctly, but sometimes the boundaries are vague.

Communications generally occur only between adjoining layers in the architecture, but this rule is not absolute. Many programs ignore the services provided by the layer directly beneath them and eliminate the middleman by skipping one or more layers. An example is a program that ignores the DOS and ROM BIOS video routines and communicates directly with the hardware in the interest of the highest possible screen performance. Although the high performance goal is admirable, many operating systems (such as OS/2 and Windows 95) no longer allow direct access to the hardware. Programs that do not play by the rules must be rewritten to run in these new environments.

The hardware is at the lowest level of the system hierarchy. By placing various bytes of information at certain ports or locations within a system's memory structure, you can control virtually anything connected to the CPU. Maintaining control at the hardware level is difficult; doing so requires a complete and accurate knowledge of the system architecture. The level of detail required in writing the software operating at this level is the most intense. Commands to the system at this level are in *machine language* (binary groups of information applied directly to the microprocessor). Machine language instructions are limited in their function: You must use many of them to perform even the smallest amount of useful work. The large number of instructions required is not really a problem because these instructions are executed extremely rapidly, wasting few system resources.

Programmers can write programs consisting of machine language instructions, but generally they use a tool—an *assembler*—to ease the process. They write programs using an *editor*, and then use the assembler to convert the editor's output to pure machine language. Assembler commands are still very low level, and using them effectively requires that programmers be extremely knowledgeable. No one (in his or her right mind) writes directly in machine code anymore; assembly language is the lowest level of programming environment typically used today. Even assembly language, however, is losing favor among programmers because of the amount of knowledge and work required to complete even simple tasks and because of its lack of portability between different kinds of systems.

When you start a PC system, a series of machine code programs, the ROM BIOS, assumes control. This set of programs, always present in a system, talks (in machine code) to the hardware. The BIOS accepts or interprets commands supplied by programs above it in the system hierarchy and translates them to machine code commands that then are passed on to the microprocessor. Commands at this level typically are called *interrupts* or *services*. A programmer generally can use nearly any language to supply these instructions to the BIOS. A complete list of these services is supplied in the IBM *BIOS Interface Technical Reference Manual*.

DOS itself is made up of several components. It attaches to the BIOS, and part of DOS actually becomes an extension of the BIOS, providing more interrupts and services for other programs to use. DOS provides for communication with the ROM BIOS in PCs and with higher level software (such as applications). Because DOS gives the programmer interrupts and services to use in addition to those provided by the ROM BIOS, a lot of reinventing the wheel in programming routines is eliminated. For example, DOS provides an extremely rich set of functions that can open, close, find, delete, create, rename, and perform other file handling tasks. When programmers want to include some of these functions in their programs, they can rely on DOS to do most of the work.

This standard set of functions that applications use to read from and write data to disks makes data recovery operations possible. Imagine how tough writing programs and using computers would be if every application program had to implement its own custom disk interface, with a proprietary directory and file retrieval system. Every application would require its own special disks. Fortunately, DOS provides a standard set of documented file storage and retrieval provisions that all software can use; as a result, you can make some sense out of what you find on a typical disk.

Another primary function of DOS is to load and run other programs. As it performs that function, DOS is the *shell* within which another program can be executed. DOS provides the functions and environment required by other software—including operating environments such as Windows 3.x to run on PC systems in a standard way. Windows 95 finally marries DOS and the Windows environment into a more seamless operating system. You can still drop to a DOS prompt within Win 95, however the graphical interface is now the standard one.

The System ROM BIOS

Think of the system ROM BIOS as a form of compatibility glue that sits between the hardware and an operating system. Why is it that IBM can sell the same DOS to run on the original IBM PC and on the latest Pentium systems—two very different hardware platforms? If DOS were written to talk directly to the hardware on all systems, it would be a very hardware-specific program. Instead, IBM developed a set of standard services and functions each system should be capable of performing and coded them as programs in the ROM BIOS. Each system then gets a completely custom ROM BIOS that talks directly to the hardware in the system and knows exactly how to perform each specific function on that hardware only.

This convention enables operating systems to be written to what amounts to a standard interface that can be made available on many different types of hardware. Any applications written to the operating system standard interface can run on that system. Figure 22.1 shows that two very different hardware platforms can each have a custom ROM BIOS that talks directly to the hardware and still provides a standard interface to an operating system.

The two different hardware platforms described in figure 22.1 can run not only the exact same version of DOS, but also the same application programs because of the standard interfaces provided by the ROM BIOS and DOS. Keep in mind, however, that the actual ROM BIOS code differs among the specific machines and that it is not usually possible therefore to run a ROM BIOS designed for one system in a different system. ROM BIOS upgrades must come from a source that has an intimate understanding of the specific motherboard on which the chip will be placed because the ROM must be custom written for that particular hardware.

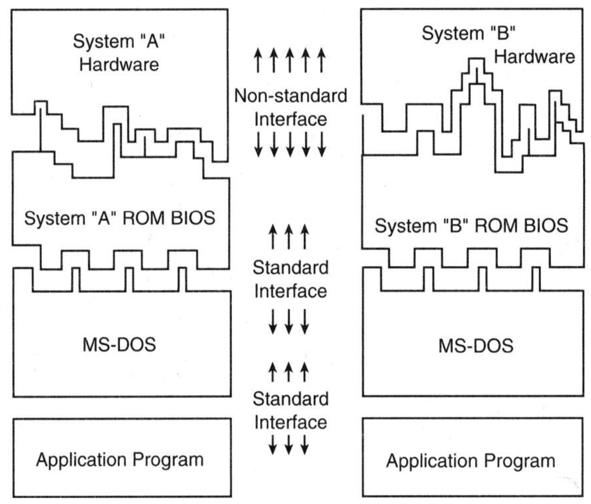

Figure 22.1

A representation of the software layers in an IBM-compatible system.

The portion of DOS shown in figure 22.1 is the system portion, or core, of DOS. This core is found physically as the two system files on any bootable DOS disk. These hidden system files usually have one of two sets of names, IBMBIO.COM and IBMDOS.COM (used in IBM and Compaq DOS), or IO.SYS and MSDOS.SYS (used in MS-DOS and versions of DOS licensed from Microsoft by original equipment manufacturers (OEMs). In Windows 95, both IO.SYS and MSDOS.SYS still exist. The IO.SYS actually contains all of the code previously in both of the system files, while MSDOS.SYS is a text file containing some configuration information. In some installations a single file WINBOOT.SYS replaces the I0.SYS file. These files are normally the first files listed in the directory on a bootable disk.

Figure 22.1 represents a simplified view of the system; some subtle but important differences exist. Ideally, application programs are insulated from the hardware by the ROM BIOS and DOS, but in reality many programmers write portions of their programs to talk directly to the hardware, circumventing DOS and the ROM BIOS. A program therefore might work only on specific hardware, even if the proper DOS and ROM BIOS interfaces are present in other hardware.

Programs designed to go directly to the hardware are written that way mainly to increase performance. For example, many programs directly access the video hardware to improve screen update performance. These applications often have install programs that require you to specify exactly what hardware is present in your system so that the program can load the correct hardware-dependent routines into the application.

Additionally, some utility programs absolutely must talk directly to the hardware to perform their function. For example, a low-level format program must talk directly to the hard disk controller hardware to perform the low-level format of the disk. Such programs are very specific to a certain controller or controller type. Another type of system-specific utility, the driver programs, enables extended memory to function as expanded memory on an 80386-based system. These drivers work by accessing the 80386 directly and utilizing specific features of the chip.

Another way that reality might differ from the simple view is that DOS itself communicates directly with the hardware. In fact, much of the IBMBIO.COM file consists of low-level drivers designed to supplant and supersede ROM BIOS code in the system. People who own both IBM systems and compatibles might wonder why IBM never seems to have ROM BIOS upgrades to correct bugs and problems with its systems, although for vendors of most compatible systems, a ROM upgrade is at least a semiannual occurrence. The reason is simple: IBM distributes its ROM patches and upgrades in DOS. When IBM DOS loads, it determines the system type and ID information from the ROM and loads different routines depending on which version of ROM it finds. For example, at least four different hard disk code sections are in IBM DOS, but only one is loaded for a specific system.

I have taken a single DOS boot disk with only the system files (COMMAND.COM and CHKDSK.COM) on it, and booted the disk on both an XT and an AT system, each one with an identical 640K of memory. After loading DOS, CHKDSK reported different amounts of free memory, which showed that DOS had taken up different amounts of memory in the two systems. This is because of the different code routines loaded, based on the ROM ID information. In essence, DOS, the ROM BIOS, and the hardware are much more closely related than most people realize.

DOS Components

DOS consists of two primary components: the input/output (I/O) system and the shell. The I/O system consists of the underlying programs that reside in memory while the system is running; these programs are loaded first when DOS boots. The I/O system is stored in the form of two files hidden on a bootable DOS disk. The files are called IBMBIO.COM and IBMDOS.COM on an IBM DOS disk, but might go by other names for other manufacturers' versions of DOS. For example, IO.SYS and MSDOS.SYS are the MS-DOS file names. No matter what the exact names are, the function of these two files is basically the same for all versions of DOS. However, each individual system's ROM BIOS looks for the system files by name, and often does not recognize them by another name.

This is one reason that the OEM version of DOS that you use must be the correct one for your system. In Windows 95, both of these components are replaced by a single file called WINBOOT.SYS.

The user interface program, or shell, is stored in the COMMAND.COM file, which also is loaded during a normal DOS boot-up. The shell is the portion of DOS that provides the DOS prompt and that normally communicates with the user of the system.

The following sections examine the DOS I/O system and shell in more detail to help you properly identify and solve problems related to DOS rather than to hardware. Also included is a discussion on how DOS allocates disk file space.

The I/O System and System Files

This section briefly describes the two files that make up the I/O system: IBMBIO.COM (IO.SYS) and IBMDOS.COM (MSDOS.SYS) as well as WINBOOT.SYS from Windows 95.

IO.SYS (or IBMBIO.COM). IO.SYS is one of the hidden files that the CHKDSK command reports on any system (bootable) disk. This file contains the low-level programs that interact directly with devices on the system and the ROM BIOS. IO.SYS usually is customized by the particular original equipment manufacturer (OEM) of the system to match perfectly with that OEM's ROM BIOS. The file contains low-level drivers loaded in accord with a particular ROM BIOS, based on the ROM ID information, as well as on a system initialization routine. During boot-up, the DOS volume boot sector loads the file into low memory and gives it control of the system (see the section, "DOS Volume Boot Sectors," later in this chapter). The entire file, except the system initializer portion, remains in memory during normal system operation.

The name used for the file that performs the functions just described varies among versions of DOS from different OEMs. Most versions of DOS, including Microsoft's MS-DOS, use IO.SYS as the name of this file. IBM, Compaq, and Hewlett-Packard call the file IBMBIO.COM, whereas some other manufacturers call the file MIO.SYS, and Toshiba calls it TBIOS.SYS. Using different names for this file is not normally a problem, until you try to upgrade from one OEM version of DOS to a different OEM version. If the different OEMs use different names for this file, the SYS command might fail with the error message `No room for system on destination`. Today most OEMs use either the standard IO.SYS or IBMBIO.COM name for this file to eliminate problems in upgrading and otherwise remain standard.

For a disk to be bootable, IO.SYS or its equivalent must be listed as the first file in the directory of the disk and must occupy at least the first cluster on the disk (cluster number 2). The remainder of the file might be placed in clusters anywhere across the rest of the disk (versions 3 and higher). The file normally is marked with hidden, system, and read-only attributes, and placed on a disk by the FORMAT command or the SYS command.

MSDOS.SYS (or IBMDOS.COM). MSDOS.SYS, the core of DOS, contains the DOS disk handling programs. The routines present in this file make up the DOS disk and device handling programs. MSDOS.SYS is loaded into low memory at system boot-up by the DOS volume boot sector and remains resident in memory during normal system operation.

The MSDOS.SYS program collection is less likely to be customized by an OEM, but still might be present on a system by a name different from MSDOS.SYS. The most common alternative name, IBMDOS.COM, is used by IBM, Compaq, and some other OEM versions of DOS. Another name is TDOS.SYS (used by Toshiba). Many OEMs like Compaq and HP use the IBM naming convention.

MSDOS.SYS or its equivalent must be listed as the second entry in the root directory of any bootable disk. This file usually is marked with hidden, system, and read-only attributes, and is normally placed on a disk by the FORMAT command or the SYS command. There are no special requirements for the physical positioning of this file on a disk.

WINBOOT.SYS. When running Windows 95, a replacement for the previous two system files is used. Called WINBOOT.SYS, this file is loaded into base memory at system bootup by the DOS Boot Record and remains resident in memory during normal system operation. WINBOOT contains virtually all the code found in the older system files, and shows the DOS roots built in to Windows 95.

The Shell or Command Processor (COMMAND.COM). The DOS command processor COMMAND.COM is the portion of DOS with which users normally interact. The commands can be categorized by function, but IBM DOS divides them into two types by how they are made available: *resident* or *transient.*

Resident commands are built into COMMAND.COM and are available whenever the DOS prompt is present. They are generally the simpler, frequently used commands such as CLS and DIR. Resident commands execute rapidly because the instructions for them are already loaded into memory. They are *memory-resident.*

When you look up the definition of a command in the DOS manual, you find an indication of whether the command is resident or transient. You then can determine what is required to execute that command. A simple rule is that, at a DOS prompt, all resident commands are instantly available for execution, with no loading of the program from disk required. Resident commands are also sometimes termed *internal.* Commands run from a program on disk are termed *external,* or *transient,* and also are often called *utilities.*

Transient commands are not resident in the computer's memory, and the instructions to execute the command must be located on a disk. Because the instructions are loaded into memory only for execution and then are overwritten in memory after they are used, they are called *transient commands.* Most DOS commands are transient; otherwise, the memory requirements for DOS would be astronomical. Transient commands are used less frequently than resident commands and take longer to execute because they must be found and loaded before they can be run.

Most executable files operate like transient DOS commands. The instructions to execute the command must be located on a disk. The instructions are loaded into memory only for execution and are overwritten in memory after the program is no longer being used.

DOS Commands. Tables 22.1 through 22.3 show all the resident, batch, and transient DOS commands and in which DOS version they are supported. If you are responsible for providing technical support, you should know what DOS commands are available to the users at the other end of the phone. These tables identify which commands are supported in any version of DOS released to date.

Table 22.1 Resident DOS Commands

Command Name	DOS Version Number 1.0	1.1	2.0	2.1	3.0	3.1	3.2	3.3	4.x	5.x	6.x
CD/CHDIR			X	X	X	X	X	X	X	X	X
CHCP									X	X	X
CLS			X	X	X	X	X	X	X	X	X
COPY	X	X	X	X	X	X	X	X	X	X	X
CTTY			X	X	X	X	X	X	X	X	X
DATE	X	X	X	X	X	X	X	X	X	X	X
DEL/ERASE	X	X	X	X	X	X	X	X	X	X	X
DIR	X	X	X	X	X	X	X	X	X	X	X
EXIT					X	X	X	X	X	X	X
EXPAND										X	X
LOADHIGH/LH										X	X
MD/MKDIR			X	X	X	X	X	X	X	X	X
PATH			X	X	X	X	X	X	X	X	X
PROMPT			X	X	X	X	X	X	X	X	X
RD/RMDIR			X	X	X	X	X	X	X	X	X
REN/RENAME	X	X	X	X	X	X	X	X	X	X	X
SET			X	X	X	X	X	X	X	X	X
TIME	X	X	X	X	X	X	X	X	X	X	X
TYPE	X	X	X	X	X	X	X	X	X	X	X
VER					X	X	X	X	X	X	X
VERIFY			X	X	X	X	X	X	X	X	X
VOL			X	X	X	X	X	X	X	X	X

Table 22.2 DOS Batch File Commands

Command Name	DOS Version Number 1.0	1.1	2.0	2.1	3.0	3.1	3.2	3.3	4.x	5.x	6.x
CALL								X	X	X	X
ECHO	X	X	X	X	X	X	X	X	X	X	X
FOR	X	X	X	X	X	X	X	X	X	X	X
GOTO	X	X	X	X	X	X	X	X	X	X	X
IF	X	X	X	X	X	X	X	X	X	X	X
PAUSE	X	X	X	X	X	X	X	X	X	X	X
REM	X	X	X	X	X	X	X	X	X	X	X
SHIFT	X	X	X	X	X	X	X	X	X	X	X

Table 22.3 Transient DOS Commands											
Command	**DOS Version Number**										
Name	**1.0**	**1.1**	**2.0**	**2.1**	**3.0**	**3.1**	**3.2**	**3.3**	**4.x**	**5.x**	**6.x**
APPEND								X	X	X	X
ASSIGN			X	X	X	X	X	X	X	X	X
ATTRIB					X	X	X	X	X	X	X
BACKUP			X	X	X	X	X	X	X	X	X
BASIC	X	X	X	X	X	X	X	X	X	X	X
BASICA	X	X	X	X	X	X	X	X	X	X	X
CHCP								X	X	X	X
CHKDSK	X	X	X	X	X	X	X	X	X	X	X
CHOICE											X
COMMAND			X	X	X	X	X	X	X	X	X
COMP	X	X	X	X	X	X	X	X	X	X	X
DEBUG	X	X	X	X	X	X	X	X	X	X	X
DEFRAG										X	X
DELTREE											X
DISKCOMP	X	X	X	X	X	X	X	X	X	X	X
DISKCOPY	X	X	X	X	X	X	X	X	X	X	X
DOSKEY										X	X
DOSKEY										X	X
DOSSHELL									X	X	X
EDIT										X	X
EDIT										X	X
EDLIN	X	X	X	X	X	X	X	X	X	X	X
EMM386										X	X
EXE2BIN			X	X	X	X	X			X	X
EXPAND										X	X
FASTOPEN								X	X	X	X
FC										X	X
FDISK			X	X	X	X	X	X	X	X	X
FIND			X	X	X	X	X	X	X	X	X
FORMAT	X	X	X	X	X	X	X	X	X	X	X
GRAFTABL			X	X	X	X	X	X	X	X	X
GRAPHICS			X	X	X	X	X	X	X	X	X
HELP										X	X
HELP										X	
INTERLNK											X
INTERSVR											X
JOIN					X	X	X	X	X	X	X
KEYB								X	X	X	X

(continues)

Table 22.3 Continued

Command Name	DOS Version Number 1.0	1.1	2.0	2.1	3.0	3.1	3.2	3.3	4.x	5.x	6.x
KEYBFR					X	X	X				
KEYBGR					X	X	X				
KEYBIT					X	X	X				
KEYBSP					X	X	X				
KEYBUK					X	X	X				
LABEL					X	X	X	X	X	X	X
LIB	X	X	X	X	X	X	X				
LINK	X	X	X	X	X	X	X				
MEM									X	X	X
MEMMAKER											X
MIRROR										X	X
MODE	X	X	X	X	X	X	X	X	X	X	X
MORE			X	X	X	X	X	X	X	X	X
MSCDEX											X
MSD											X
NLSFUNC								X	X	X	X
POWER											X
PRINT			X	X	X	X	X	X	X	X	X
QBASIC										X	X
QBASIC										X	
RECOVER			X	X	X	X	X	X	X	X	X
REPLACE					X	X	X	X	X	X	X
RESTORE			X	X	X	X	X	X	X	X	X
SCANDISK											X
SETVER										X	X
SHARE						X	X	X	X	X	X
SORT			X	X	X	X	X	X	X	X	X
SUBST					X	X	X	X	X	X	X
SYS	X	X	X	X	X	X	X	X	X	X	X
TREE			X	X	X	X	X	X	X	X	X
UNDELETE										X	X
UNDELETE										X	X
UNFORMAT										X	X
UNFORMAT										X	X
XCOPY							X	X	X	X	X

LIB, LINK, and EXE2BIN are included with the DOS technical-reference manual for DOS versions 3.3 and higher. EXE2BIN is included with DOS 5.0.

DOS Command File Search Procedure. DOS looks only in specific places for the instructions for a transient command, or a software application's executable file. The instructions that represent the command or program are in files on one or more disk drives. Files that contain execution instructions have one of three specific extensions to indicate to DOS that they are program files: .COM (command files), .EXE (executable files), or .BAT (batch files). .COM and .EXE files are machine code programs; .BAT files contain a series of commands and instructions using the DOS batch facilities. The places in which DOS looks for these files is controlled by the current directory and the PATH command.

In other words, if you type several characters, like **WIN**, at the DOS prompt and press the Enter key, DOS attempts to find and run a program named WIN. DOS performs a two- or three-level search for program instructions (the file). The first step in looking for command instructions is to see whether the command is a resident one and, if so, run it from the program code already loaded. If the command is not resident, DOS looks in the current directory for .COM, .EXE, and .BAT files, in that order, and loads and executes the first file it finds with the specified name. If the command is not resident and not in the current directory, DOS looks in all the directories specified in the DOS PATH setting (which the user can control); DOS searches for the file within each directory in the extension order just indicated. Finally, if DOS fails to locate the required instructions, it displays the error message `Bad command or filename`. This error message can be misleading because the command instructions usually are missing from the search areas rather than actually being bad.

Suppose that, at the DOS prompt, I type the command **XYZ** and press Enter. This command sends DOS on a search for the XYZ program's instructions. If DOS is successful, the program starts running within seconds. If DOS cannot find the proper instructions, an error message is displayed. Here is what happens:

1. DOS checks internally to see whether it can find the XYZ command as one of the resident commands whose instructions are already loaded. It finds no XYZ command as resident.

2. DOS looks next in the current directory on the current drive for files named XYZ.COM, then for files named XYZ.EXE, and finally for files named XYZ.BAT. Suppose that I had logged in to drive C:, and the current directory is \ (the root directory); therefore, DOS did not find the files in the current directory.

3. DOS looks to see whether a PATH is specified. If not, the search ends here. In this scenario, I do have a PATH specified when my system was started, so DOS checks every directory listed in that PATH for the first file it can find named XYZ.COM, XYZ.EXE, or XYZ.BAT (in that order). My PATH lists several directories, but DOS does not find an appropriate file in any of them.

4. The search ends, and DOS gives me the message `Bad command or filename`.

For this search-and-load procedure to be successful, I must ensure that the desired program or command file exists in the current directory on the current drive, or I must set my DOS PATH to point to the drive and directory in which the program does exist. This is why the PATH is so powerful in DOS.

A common practice is to place all simple command files or utility programs in one directory and set the PATH to point to that directory. Then each of those programs (commands) is instantly available by simply typing its name, just as though it were resident.

This practice works well only for single-load programs such as commands and other utilities. Major applications software often consists of many individual files and might have problems if they are called up from a remote directory or drive using the DOS PATH. The reason is that when the application looks for its overlay and accessory files, the DOS PATH setting has no effect.

On a hard disk system, users typically install all transient commands and utilities in subdirectories and ensure that the PATH points to those directories. The path literally is a list of directories and subdirectories in the AUTOEXEC.BAT file that tells DOS where to search for files when these files are not in the same directory you are in when you enter a command. The system then functions as though all the commands were resident because DOS finds the necessary files without further thought or effort on the part of the user. A path on such a hard drive may look like this:

```
PATH=C:\DOS;C:\BAT;C:\UTILS;
```

It is important to know that when DOS loads each time you power up your system, it looks for two such text files. The first text file DOS looks for is CONFIG.SYS, which also can be edited by the system user. This file loads device drivers like ANSI.SYS. The following is an example of a common CONFIG.SYS file:

```
FILES=30
BUFFERS=17
SHELL=C:\DOS\COMMAND.COM C:\DOS /E:512 /P
LASTDRIVE=G
DEVICE=C:\DOS\ANSI.SYS
```

The second text file DOS looks for each time you power up your system is AUTOEXEC.BAT, which sets the PATH, loads memory-resident programs, and performs other system configuration tasks like creating a C:\> prompt. A typical AUTOEXEC.BAT file might look like the following:

```
@ECHO OFF
PROMPT $P$G
PATH=C:\DOS;C:\BAT;C:\UTILS;
\DOS\MODE CON: RATE=32 DELAY=1
\DOS\DOSKEY
```

The PATH normally cannot exceed 128 characters in length (including colons, semicolons, and backslashes). As a result of that limitation, you cannot have a PATH that contains all your directories if the directory names exceed 128 characters. For more information on the AUTOEXEC.BAT and CONFIG.SYS files, consult Que's *Using DOS 6.2, Special Edition*, or *Using IBM PC DOS 6.1*.

You can completely short-circuit the DOS command search procedure by simply entering at the command prompt the complete path to the file. For example, rather than include C:\DOS in the PATH and enter this command

```
C:\>CHKDSK
```

you can enter the full name of the program

```
C:\>C:\DOS\CHKDSK.COM
```

The latter command immediately locates and loads the CHKDSK program with no search through the current directory or PATH setting. This method of calling up a program speeds the location and execution of the program and works especially well to increase the speed of DOS batch file execution.

A few major software applications have problems if they are called up from a remote directory or drive using the DOS PATH. Such an application often is made up of many individual files, including overlay and accessory files. Problems can occur when an application expects you to run it from its own directory by making that directory current and then running the program's .COM or .EXE file. Such applications look for their own files in the current directory. If you did not change to the application's directory, because the program does not look for its files by checking the path, the program does not find its own files. The path entry in AUTOEXEC.BAT has no effect.

Such applications can be called up through batch files or aided by programs that "force feed" a path type setting to the programs; the software then works as though files are "here" even when they are in some other directory. The best utility for this purpose is the APPEND command in DOS 3.0 and later versions. For information on the use of the APPEND command see Que's *Using MS-DOS 6*.

DOS History

The following section details some of the differences between the DOS versions that have appeared over the years.

IBM and MS DOS 1.x to 3.x Versions. There have been many specific DOS versions in the 1.x to 3.x range from both IBM and Microsoft, as well as a few other OEMs. Table 22.4 lists the file dates and sizes for the major IBM and Microsoft DOS versions. You can see how DOS has grown over the years!

Table 22.4 System File Sizes

DOS Version	File Dates	COMMAND.COM	IO.SYS IBMBIO.COM	MSDOS.SYS IBMDOS.COM
IBM PC 1.0	08-04-81	3,231	1,920	6400
IBM PC 1.1	05-07-82	4,959	1,920	6400
IBM PC 2.0	03-08-83	17,792	4,608	17,152
IBM PC 2.1	10-20-83	17,792	4,736	17,024
IBM PC 3.0	08-14-84	22,042	8,964	27,920

(continues)

Table 22.4 Continued

DOS Version	File Dates	COMMAND.COM	IO.SYS IBMBIO.COM	MSDOS.SYS IBMDOS.COM
IBM PC 3.1	03-07-85	23,210	9,564	27,760
IBM PC 3.2	12-30-85	23,791	16,369	28,477
MS 3.2	07-07-86	23,612	16.138	28,480
IBM PC 3.3	03-17-87	25,307	22,100	30,159
MS 3.3	07-24-87	25,276	22,357	30,128

IBM DOS 4.xx Versions. DOS 4.xx has had many revisions since being introduced in mid-1988. Since the first release, IBM has released different Corrective Service Diskettes (CSDs), which fix a variety of problems with DOS 4. Each CSD is cumulative, which means that the later ones include all previous fixes. Note that these fixes are for IBM DOS and not for any other manufacturer's version.

Table 22.5 shows a summary of the different IBM DOS 4.xx releases and specific information about the system files and shell so that you can identify the release you are using. To obtain the latest Corrective Service Diskettes (CSD) that update you to the latest release, contact your dealer—the fixes are free.

Table 22.5 IBM DOS 4.xx Releases

File Name	Size	Date	Version	SYSLEVEL	Comments
IBMBIO.COM	32810	06/17/88	4.00	—	Original release.
IBMDOS.COM	35984	06/17/88			
COMMAND.COM	37637	06/17/88			
IBMBIO.COM	32816	08/03/88	4.01	CSD UR22624	EMS fixes.
IBMDOS.COM	36000	08/03/88			
COMMAND.COM	37637	06/17/88			
IBMBIO.COM	32816	08/03/88	4.01	CSD UR24270	Date change fixed.
IBMDOS.COM	36000	11/11/88			
COMMAND.COM	37652	11/11/88			
IBMBIO.COM	33910	04/06/89	4.01	CSD UR25066	"Death disk" fixed.
IBMDOS.COM	37136	04/06/89			
COMMAND.COM	37652	11/11/88			
IBMBIO.COM	34660	03/20/90	4.01	CSD UR29015	SCSI support added.
IBMDOS.COM	37248	02/20/90			
COMMAND.COM	37765	03/20/90			
IBMBIO.COM	34660	04/27/90	4.01	CSD UR31300	HPFS compatibility.
IBMDOS.COM	37264	05/21/90			
COMMAND.COM	37765	06/29/90			
IBMBIO.COM	34692	04/08/91	4.01	CSD UR35280	HPFS and CHKDSK.
IBMDOS.COM	37280	11/30/90			
COMMAND.COM	37762	09/27/91			

IBM DOS 5.xx Versions. DOS 5.xx has had several different revisions since being introduced in mid-1991. Since the first release, IBM has released various Corrective Service Diskettes (CSDs), which fix a variety of problems with DOS 5. Each CSD is cumulative, which means that the later ones include all previous fixes. Note that these fixes are for IBM DOS and not any other manufacturer's version. IBM typically provides more support in the way of fixes and updates than any other manufacturer. Note that IBM now supports the installation of IBM DOS on clone systems.

Table 22.6 shows a summary of the different IBM DOS 5.xx releases and specific information about the system files and shell so that you can identify the release you are using. To obtain the latest Corrective Service Diskettes (CSD) that update you to the latest release, contact your dealer—the fixes are free.

Table 22.6 IBM DOS 5.xx Releases

File Name	Size	Date	Version	SYSLEVEL	Comments
IBMBIO.COM	33430	05/09/91	5.00	—	Original release.
IBMDOS.COM	37378	05/09/91			
COMMAND.COM	47987	05/09/91			
IBMBIO.COM	33430	05/09/91	5.00	CSD UR35423	XCOPY and
IBMDOS.COM	37378	05/09/91			QEDIT fixed.
COMMAND.COM	48005	08/16/91			
IBMBIO.COM	33430	05/09/91	5.00	CSD UR35748	SYS fixed.
IBMDOS.COM	37378	05/09/91			
COMMAND.COM	48006	10/25/91			
IBMBIO.COM	33446	11/29/91	5.00	CSD UR35834	EMM386, FORMAT,
IBMDOS.COM	37378	11/29/91			and BACKUP
COMMAND.COM	48006	11/29/91			fixed.
IBMBIO.COM	33446	02/28/92	5.00.1	CSD UR36603	Many fixes;
IBMDOS.COM	37378	11/29/91	Rev. A		clone support;
COMMAND.COM	48006	02/28/92			new retail version.
IBMBIO.COM	33446	05/29/92	5.00.1	CSD UR37387	RESTORE and
IBMDOS.COM	37362	05/29/92	Rev. 1		UNDELETE fixed;
COMMAND.COM	48042	09/11/92			>1GB HD fix.
IBMBIO.COM	33718	09/01/92	5.02	—	New retail version;
IBMDOS.COM	37362	09/01/92	Rev. 0		several new
COMMAND.COM	47990	09/01/92			commands added.

IBM and MS DOS 6.xx Versions. There are several different versions of DOS 6.xx from both Microsoft and IBM. The original release of MS DOS 6.0 came from Microsoft. One of the features included in 6.0 was the new DoubleSpace disk compression. Unfortunately, DoubleSpace had some problems with certain system configurations and hardware types. In the meantime, IBM took DOS 6.0 from Microsoft, updated it to fix several small problems, removed the disk compression, and sold it as IBM DOS 6.1. Microsoft had many problems with the DoubleSpace disk compression used in 6.0 and released 6.2 as a free bug fix upgrade. Microsoft then ran into legal problems in a lawsuit brought by Stacker Corporation. Microsoft was found to have infringed on the Stacker software and was forced to remove the DoubleSpace compression from DOS 6.2, which was released as 6.21. Microsoft then quickly developed a non-infringing disk compression utility called DriveSpace, which was released in 6.22, along with several minor bug fixes. IBM skipped over the 6.2 version number and released DOS 6.3 (now called PC DOS), which also included a different type of compression program than that used by Microsoft. By avoiding the DoubleSpace software, IBM also avoided the bugs and legal problems that Microsoft had encountered. Also included in the updated IBM releases are enhanced PCMCIA and power management commands.

Table 22.7 shows a summary of the different IBM DOS 6.xx releases.

Table 22.7 IBM and Microsoft DOS 6.xx Releases

File Name	Size	Date	Version	SYSLEVEL	Comments
IO.SYS	40470	03/10/93	MS	—	Original Microsoft
MSDOS.SYS	38138	03/10/93	6.00		release.
COMMAND.COM	52925	03/10/93	Rev. A		
IBMBIO.COM	40694	06/29/93	IBM	—	Original IBM
IBMDOS.COM	38138	06/29/93	6.10		release. Has fixes
COMMAND.COM	52589	06/29/93	Rev. 0		over MS version.
IBMBIO.COM	40964	09/30/93	PC	—	SuperStor/DS
IBMDOS.COM	38138	09/30/93	6.10		compression;
COMMAND.COM	52797	09/30/93	Rev. 0		enhanced PCMCIA.
IO.SYS	40566	09/30/93	MS	—	DoubleSpace fixes.
MSDOS.SYS	38138	09/30/93	6.20		Enhanced cleanboot
COMMAND.COM	54619	09/30/93	Rev. A		and data recovery.
IO.SYS	40774	05/31/94	MS	—	New DriveSpace disk
MSDOS.SYS	38138	05/31/94	6.22		compression software
COMMAND.COM	54645	05/31/94	Rev. A		and minor fixes.
IBMBIO.COM	40758	12/31/93	IBM	—	Numerous bug fixes;
IBMDOS.COM	38138	12/31/93	6.30		new disk compression
COMMAND.COM	54804	08/12/94	Rev. 0		software.

The Boot Process

The term *boot* comes from the term bootstrap and describes the method by which the PC becomes operational. Just as you pull on a large boot by the small strap attached to the back, a PC can load a large operating system program by first loading a small program that then can pull in the operating system. A chain of events begins with the application of power and finally results in an operating computer system with software loaded and running. Each event is called by the event before it and initiates the event after it.

Tracing the system boot process might help you find the location of a problem if you examine the error messages the system displays when the problem occurs. If you can see an error message displayed only by a particular program, you can be sure that the program in question was at least loaded and partially running. Combine this information with the knowledge of the boot sequence, and you can at least tell how far along the system's startup procedure is. You usually want to look at whatever files or disk areas were being accessed during the failure in the boot process. Error messages displayed during the boot process as well as those displayed during normal system operation can be hard to decipher, but the first step in decoding an error message is to know where the message came from—what program actually sent or displayed the message. The following programs are capable of displaying error messages during the boot process:

- Motherboard ROM BIOS
- Adapter card ROM BIOS extensions
- Master partition boot sector
- DOS volume boot sector
- System files (IBMBIO.COM/IO.SYS and IBMDOS.COM/MSDOS.SYS or WINBOOT.SYS)
- Device drivers (loaded through CONFIG.SYS or the Win 95 Registry SYSTEM.DAT)
- Shell program (COMMAND.COM, can be skipped in Win 95)
- Programs run by AUTOEXEC.BAT (can be skipped in Win 95)
- Windows (WIN.COM)

This section examines the system startup sequence and provides a detailed account of many of the error messages that might occur during this process.

How DOS Loads and Starts

If you have a problem with your system during startup and you can determine where in this sequence of events your system has stalled, you know what events have occurred and you probably can eliminate each of them as a cause of the problem. The following steps occur in a typical system startup:

1. You switch on electrical power to the system.
2. The power supply performs a self-test. When all voltages and current levels are acceptable, the supply indicates that the power is stable and sends the Power Good signal to the motherboard. The time from switch-on to Power Good is normally between .1 and .5 seconds.
3. The microprocessor timer chip receives the Power Good signal, which causes it to stop generating a reset signal to the microprocessor.
4. The microprocessor begins executing the ROM BIOS code, starting at memory address FFFF:0000. Because this location is only 16 bytes from the very end of the available ROM space, it contains a JMP (jump) instruction to the actual ROM BIOS starting address.
5. The ROM BIOS performs a test of the central hardware to verify basic system functionality. Any errors that occur are indicated by audio codes because the video system has not yet been initialized.
6. The BIOS performs a video ROM scan of memory locations C000:0000 through C780:0000, looking for video adapter ROM BIOS programs contained on a video adapter card plugged into a slot. If a video ROM BIOS is found, it is tested by a checksum procedure. If it passes the checksum test, the ROM is executed; the video

ROM code initializes the video adapter; and a cursor appears on-screen. If the checksum test fails, the following message appears:

```
C000 ROM Error
```

7. If the BIOS finds no video adapter ROM, it uses the motherboard ROM video drivers to initialize the video display hardware, and a cursor appears on-screen.

8. The motherboard ROM BIOS scans memory locations C800:0000 through DF80:0000 in 2K increments for any other ROMs located on any other adapter cards. If any ROMs are found, they are checksum-tested and executed. These adapter ROMs can alter existing BIOS routines as well as establish new ones.

9. Failure of a checksum test for any of these ROM modules causes this message to appear:

```
XXXX ROM Error
```

10. The address `XXXX` indicates the segment address of the failed ROM module.

11. The ROM BIOS checks the word value at memory location 0000:0472 to see whether this start is a cold start or a warm start. A word value of 1234h in this location is a flag that indicates a warm start, which causes the memory test portion of the POST (Power On Self Test) to be skipped. Any other word value in this location indicates a cold start and full POST.

12. If this is a cold start, the POST executes. Any errors found during the POST are reported by a combination of audio and displayed error messages. Successful completion of the POST is indicated by a single beep.

13. The ROM BIOS searches for a DOS volume boot sector at cylinder 0, head 0, sector 1 (the very first sector) on the A: drive. This sector is loaded into memory at 0000:7C00 and tested. If a disk is in the drive but the sector cannot be read, or if no disk is present, the BIOS continues with the next step.

14. If the first byte of the DOS volume boot sector loaded from the floppy disk in A: is less than 06h, or if the first byte is greater than or equal to 06h, and the first nine words contain the same data pattern, this error message appears and the system stops:

```
602-Diskette Boot Record Error
```

15. If the disk was prepared with FORMAT or SYS using DOS 3.3 or an earlier version and the specified system files are not the first two files in the directory, or if a problem was encountered loading them, the following message appears:

```
Non-System disk or disk error
Replace and strike any key when ready
```

16. If the disk was prepared with FORMAT or SYS using DOS 3.3 or an earlier version and the boot sector is corrupt, you might see this message:

```
Disk Boot failure
```

17. If the disk was prepared with FORMAT or SYS using DOS 4.0 and later versions, and the specified system files are not the first two files in the directory, or if a problem was encountered loading them, or the boot sector is corrupt, this message appears:

```
Non-System disk or disk error
Replace and press any key when ready
```

18. If no DOS volume boot sector can be read from drive A:, the BIOS looks for a master partition boot sector at cylinder 0, head 0, sector 1 (the very first sector) of the first fixed disk. If this sector is found, it is loaded into memory address 0000:7C00 and tested for a signature.

19. If the last two (signature) bytes of the master partition boot sector are not equal to 55AAh, software interrupt 18h (Int 18h) is invoked on most systems. On an IBM PS/2 system, a special character graphics message is displayed that depicts inserting a floppy disk in drive A: and pressing the F1 key. For non-PS/2 systems made by IBM, an Int 18h executes the ROM BIOS-based Cassette BASIC Interpreter. When this occurs, the message looks like this:

```
The IBM Personal Computer Basic
Version C1.10 Copyright IBM Corp 1981
62940 Bytes free
Ok
```

Because no BIOS versions other than IBM's systems ever had the Cassette BASIC interpreter in ROM, other BIOS manufacturers had to come up with different messages to display for the same situations in which an IBM system would invoke this BASIC. PCs that have an AMI BIOS, in fact, display a confusing message as follows:

```
NO ROM BASIC - SYSTEM HALTED
```

This message is a BIOS error message that is displayed by the AMI BIOS when the same situations occur that would cause an IBM system to dump into Cassette BASIC, which of course is not present in an AMI BIOS (or any other compatible BIOS for that matter). Other BIOS versions display different messages. For example, under the same circumstances, a Compaq BIOS displays the following:

```
Non-System disk or disk error
replace and strike any key when ready
```

This is somewhat confusing on Compaq's part because this very same (or similar) error message is contained in the DOS Boot Sector, and would normally be displayed if the DOS system files were missing or corrupted.

In the same situations that you would see Cassette BASIC on an IBM system, a system with an Award BIOS would display the following:

```
DISK BOOT FAILURE, INSERT SYSTEM DISK AND PRESS ENTER
```

Phoenix BIOS systems will display either:

```
No boot device available -
strike F1 to retry boot, F2 for setup utility
```

or

```
No boot sector on fixed disk -
strike F1 to retry boot, F2 for setup utility
```

The first or second Phoenix message displays depending on exactly which error actually occurred.

Although the message displayed varies from BIOS to BIOS, the cause is the same for all of them. Two things can generally cause any of these messages to be displayed, and they both relate to specific bytes in the Master Boot Record, which is the first sector of a hard disk at the physical location Cylinder 0, Head 0, Sector 1.

The first problem relates to a disk that has either never been partitioned or has had the Master Boot Sector corrupted. During the boot process, the BIOS checks the last two bytes in the Master Boot Record (first sector of the drive) for a "signature" value of 55AAh. If the last two bytes are not 55AAh, an Interrupt 18h is invoked, which calls the subroutine that displays the message you received as well as the others indicated, or on an IBM system invokes Cassette (ROM) BASIC itself.

The Master Boot Sector (including the signature bytes) is written to the hard disk by the DOS FDISK program. Immediately after you low level format a hard disk, all the sectors are initialized with a pattern of bytes, and the first sector does NOT contain the 55AAh signature. In other words, these ROM error messages are exactly what you see if you attempt to boot from a hard disk that has been low level formatted, but has not yet been partitioned.

20. The master partition boot sector program searches its partition table for an entry with a system indicator byte indicating an extended partition. If the program finds such an entry, it loads the extended partition boot sector at the location indicated. The extended partition boot sector also has a table that is searched for another extended partition. If another extended partition entry is found, that extended partition boot sector is loaded from the location indicated, and the search continues until either no more extended partitions are indicated or the maximum number of 24 total partitions has been reached.

21. The master partition boot sector searches its partition table for a boot indicator byte marking an active partition.

22. On an IBM system, if none of the partitions is marked active (bootable), ROM BIOS-based Cassette BASIC is invoked. On most IBM-compatible systems, some type of disk error message is displayed.

23. If any boot indicator in the master partition boot record table is invalid, or if more than one indicates an active partition, the following message is displayed, and the system stops:

```
Invalid partition table
```

24. If an active partition is found in the master partition boot sector, the volume boot sector from the active partition is loaded and tested.

25. If the DOS volume boot sector cannot be read successfully from the active partition within five retries because of read errors, this message appears and the system stops:

```
Error loading operating system
```

26. The hard disk DOS volume boot sector is tested for a signature. If the DOS volume boot sector does not contain a valid signature of 55AAh as the last two bytes in the sector, this message appears and the system stops:

```
Missing operating system
```

27. The volume boot sector is executed as a program. This program checks the root directory to ensure that the first two files are IBMBIO.COM and IBMDOS.COM. If these files are present, they are loaded.

28. If the disk was prepared with FORMAT or SYS using DOS 3.3 or an earlier version and the specified system files are not the first two files in the directory, or if a problem is encountered loading them, the following message appears:

```
Non-System disk or disk error
Replace and strike any key when ready
```

29. If the disk was prepared with FORMAT or SYS using DOS 3.3 or an earlier version and the boot sector is corrupt, you might see this message:

```
Disk Boot failure
```

30. If the disk was prepared with FORMAT or SYS using DOS 4.0 or a later version and the specified system files are not the first two files in the directory, or if a problem is encountered loading them, or the boot sector is corrupt, the following message appears:

```
Non-System disk or disk error
Replace and press any key when ready
```

31. If no problems occur, the DOS volume boot sector executes IBMBIO.COM/IO.SYS or WINBOOT.SYS.

32. The initialization code in IBMBIO.COM/IO.SYS copies itself into the highest region of contiguous DOS memory and transfers control to the copy. The initialization code copy then relocates IBMDOS over the portion of IBMBIO in low memory that contains the initialization code, because the initialization code no longer needs to be in that location. WINBOOT.SYS combines the functions of both IBMBIO.COM/IO.SYS and IBMDOS.COM/MSDOS.SYS.

33. The initialization code executes IBMDOS, which initializes the base device drivers, determines equipment status, resets the disk system, resets and initializes attached devices, and sets the system default parameters.

34. The full DOS filing system is active, and the IBMBIO initialization code is given back control.

35. The IBMBIO or WINBOOT.SYS initialization code reads CONFIG.SYS multiple times. WINBOOT.SYS then also looks for the SYSTEM.DAT registry file.

36. If loading CONFIG.SYS, DEVICE statements are first processed in the order in which they appear, and any device driver files named are loaded and executed. Then any INSTALL statements are processed in the order in which they appear, and the programs named are loaded and executed. The SHELL statement is processed and loads the specified command processor with the specified parameters. If the CONFIG.SYS file contains no SHELL statement, the default \COMMAND.COM processor is loaded with default parameters. Loading the command processor overwrites the initialization code in memory (because the job of the initialization code is finished).

    In Windows 95, the COMMAND.COM program is loaded only if an AUTOEXEC.BAT exists, so it can process the commands contained within.

    During the final reads of CONFIG.SYS, all the remaining statements are read and processed in a predetermined order. Thus, the order of appearance for statements other than DEVICE, INSTALL, and SHELL in CONFIG.SYS is of no significance.

37. If AUTOEXEC.BAT is present, COMMAND.COM loads and runs AUTOEXEC.BAT. After the commands in AUTOEXEC.BAT have been executed, the DOS prompt appears (unless the AUTOEXEC.BAT calls an application program or shell of some kind, in which case the user might operate the system without ever seeing a DOS prompt).

38. If no AUTOEXEC.BAT is present, COMMAND.COM executes the internal DATE and TIME commands, displays a copyright message, and displays the DOS prompt.

    In Windows 95, WINBOOT.SYS automatically loads HIMEM.SYS, IFSHLP.SYS, and SETVER.EXE. Finally, it loads WIN.COM and Windows 95 is officially started.

Some minor variations from this scenario are possible, such as those introduced by other ROM programs in the various adapters that might be plugged into a slot. Also, depending on the exact ROM BIOS programs involved, some of the error messages and sequences might vary. Generally, however, a computer follows this chain of events in "coming to life."

You can modify the system startup procedures by altering the CONFIG.SYS, AUTOEXEC.BAT, or SYSTEM.DAT files. These files control the configuration of DOS or Windows 95 and allow special startup programs to be executed every time the system starts.

File Management

DOS uses several elements and structures to store and retrieve information on a disk. These elements and structures enable DOS to communicate properly with the ROM BIOS as well as application programs to process file storage and retrieval requests. Understanding these structures and how they interact help you to troubleshoot and even repair these structures.

DOS File Space Allocation

DOS allocates disk space for a file on demand (space is not preallocated). The space is allocated one *cluster* (or allocation unit) at a time. A cluster is always one or more sectors. (For more information about sectors, refer to Chapter 14, "Hard Disk Drives.")

The clusters are arranged on a disk to minimize head movement for multisided media. DOS allocates all the space on a disk cylinder before moving to the next cylinder. It does this by using the sectors under the first head, and then all the sectors under the next head, and so on until all sectors of all heads of the cylinder are used. The next sector used is sector 1 of head 0 on the next cylinder. (You find more information on floppy disks and drives in Chapter 13, "Floppy Disk Drives," and on hard disks in Chapter 14, "Hard Disk Drives.")

DOS version 2.x uses a simple algorithm when it allocates file space on a disk. Every time a program requests disk space, DOS scans from the beginning of the FAT until it finds a free cluster in which to deposit a portion of the file; then the search continues for the next cluster of free space, until all the file is written. This algorithm, called the *First Available Cluster algorithm,* causes any erased file near the beginning of the disk to be overwritten during the next write operation because those clusters would be the first available to the next write operation. This system prevents recovery of that file and promotes file fragmentation because the first available cluster found is used regardless of whether the entire file can be written there. DOS simply continues searching for free clusters in which to deposit the remainder of the file.

The algorithm used for file allocation in DOS 3.0 and later versions is called the *Next Available Cluster algorithm*. In this algorithm, the search for available clusters in which to write a file starts not at the beginning of the disk, but rather from where the last write occurred. Therefore, the disk space freed by erasing a file is not necessarily reused immediately. Rather, DOS maintains a *Last Written Cluster pointer* indicating the last written cluster and begins its search from that point. This pointer is maintained in system RAM and is lost when the system is reset or rebooted, or when a disk is changed in a floppy drive.

In working with 360K drives, all versions of DOS always use the First Available Cluster algorithm because the Last Written Cluster pointer cannot be maintained for floppy disk drives that do not report a disk change (DC) signal to the controller, and because 360K drives do not supply the DC signal. With 360K floppy drives, therefore, DOS always assumes that the disk could have been changed, which flushes any buffers and resets the Last Written Cluster pointer.

The Next Available Cluster algorithm in DOS 3.0 and later versions is faster than the First Available Cluster algorithm and helps minimize fragmentation. Sometimes this type of algorithm is called *elevator seeking* because write operations occur at higher and higher clusters until the end of the disk area is reached. At that time, the pointer is reset, and writes work their way from the beginning of the disk again.

Files still end up becoming fragmented using the new algorithm, because the pointer is reset after a reboot, a disk change operation, or when the end of the disk is reached. Nevertheless, a great benefit of the newer method is that it makes unerasing files more likely to succeed even if the disk has been written to since the erasure, because the file just erased is not likely to be the target of the next write operation. In fact, it might be some time before the clusters occupied by the erased file are reused.

Even when a file is overwritten under DOS 3.0 and later versions, the clusters occupied by the file are not actually reused in the overwrite. For example, if you accidentally save on a disk a file using the same name as an important file that already exists, the existing file clusters are marked as available, and the new file (with the same name) is written to the disk in other clusters. It is possible, therefore, that the original copy of the file can still be retrieved. You can continue this procedure by saving another copy of the file with the same name, and each file copy is saved to higher numbered clusters, and each earlier version overwritten might still be recoverable on the disk. This process can continue until the system is rebooted or reset, or until the end of the available space is reached. Then the pointer is set to the first cluster, and previous file data is overwritten.

Because DOS always uses the first available directory entry when it saves or creates a file, the overwritten or deleted files whose data is still recoverable on the disk no longer appear in a directory listing. No commercial quick unerase or other unerase utilities therefore can find any record of the erased or overwritten file on the disk—true, of course, because these programs look only in the directory for a record of an erased file. Some newer undelete programs have a memory-resident delete tracking function that, in essence, maintains a separate directory listing from DOS. Unless an unerase program has a memory-resident delete tracking function, and that function has been activated before the deletion, no program can recall the files overwritten in the directory entry.

Table 22.8 Floppy Disk Format Specifications

	Current Formats			
Disk Size (in.)	**3 1/2"**	**3 1/2"**	**3 1/2"**	**5 1/4"**
Disk Capacity (KB)	**2,880**	**1,440**	**720**	**1,200**
Media Descriptor Byte	F0h	F0h	F9h	F9h
Sides (Heads)	2	2	2	2
Tracks per Side	80	80	80	80
Sectors per Track	36	18	9	15
Bytes per Sector	512	512	512	512
Sectors per Cluster	2	1	2	1
FAT Length (Sectors)	9	9	3	7
Number of FATs	2	2	2	2
Root Dir. Length (Sectors)	15	14	7	14
Maximum Root Entries	240	224	112	224
Total Sectors per Disk	5,760	2,880	1,440	2,400
Total Available Sectors	5,726	2,847	1,426	2,371
Total Available Clusters	2,863	2,847	713	2,371

Because unerase programs do not look at the FAT, or at the data clusters themselves (unless they use delete tracking), they see no record of the files' existence. By scanning the free clusters on the disk one by one using a disk editor tool, you can locate the data from the overwritten or erased file and manually rebuild the FAT and directory entries. This procedure enables you to recover erased files even though files have been written to the disk since the erasure took place.

Interfacing to Disk Drives

DOS uses a combination of disk management components to make files accessible. These components differ slightly between floppies and hard disks and between disks of different sizes. They determine how a disk appears to DOS and to applications software. Each component used to describe the disk system fits as a layer into the complete system. Each layer communicates with the layer above and below it. When all the components work together, an application can access the disk to find and store data. Table 22.8 lists the DOS format specifications for floppy disks.

The four primary layers of interface between an application program running on a system and any disks attached to the system consist of software routines that can perform various functions, usually to communicate with the adjacent layers. These layers are shown in the following list:

- DOS Interrupt 21h (Int 21h) routines
- DOS Interrupt 25/26h (Int 25/26h) routines
- ROM BIOS disk Interrupt 13h (Int 13h) routines
- Disk controller I/O port commands

	Obsolete Formats		
5 1/4" 360	**5 1/4" 320**	**5 1/4" 180**	**5 1/4" 160**
FDh	FFh	FCh	FEh
2	2	1	1
40	40	40	40
9	8	9	8
512	512	512	512
2	2	1	1
2	1	2	1
2	2	2	2
7	7	4	4
112	112	64	64
720	640	360	320
708	630	351	313
354	315	351	313

Each layer accepts various commands, performs different functions, and generates results. These interfaces are available for both floppy disk drives and hard disks, although the floppy disk and hard disk Int 13h routines differ widely. The floppy disk controllers and hard disk controllers are very different as well, but all the layers perform the same functions for both floppy disks and hard disks.

Interrupt 21h. The DOS Int 21h routines exist at the highest level and provide the most functionality with the least amount of work. For example, if an application program needs to create a subdirectory on a disk, it can call Int 21h, Function 39h. This function performs all operations necessary to create a subdirectory on the disk, including updating the appropriate directory and FAT sectors. The only information this function needs is the name of the subdirectory to create. DOS Int 21h would do much more work by using one of the lower-level access methods to create a subdirectory on the disk. Most applications programs you run access the disk through this level of interface.

Interrupt 25h and 26h. The DOS Int 25h and Int 26h routines provide much lower-level access to the disk than the Int 21h routines. Int 25h reads only specified sectors from a disk, and Int 26h only writes specified sectors to a disk. If you were to write a program that used these functions to create a subdirectory on a disk, the work required would be much greater than that required by the Int 21h method. For example, your program would have to perform all of these tasks:

- Calculate exactly which directory and FAT sectors need to be updated
- Use Int 25h to read these sectors
- Modify the sectors appropriately to contain the new subdirectory information
- Use Int 26h to write the sectors back out

The number of steps would be even greater considering the difficulty in determining exactly what sectors have to be modified. According to Int 25/26h, the entire DOS-addressable area of the disk consists of sectors numbered sequentially from 0. A program designed to access the disk using Int 25h and Int 26h must know the location of everything by this sector number. A program designed this way might have to be modified to handle disks with different numbers of sectors or different directory and FAT sizes and locations. Because of all the overhead required to get the job done, most programmers would not choose to access the disk in this manner, and instead would use the higher-level Int 21h—which does all the work automatically.

Only disk- and sector-editing programs typically access a disk drive at the Int 25h and Int 26h level. Programs that work at this level of access can edit only areas of a disk that have been defined to DOS as a logical volume (drive letter). For example, DEBUG can read sectors from and write sectors to disks with this level of access.

Interrupt 13h. The next lower level of communications with drives, the ROM BIOS Int 13h routines, usually are found in ROM chips on the motherboard or on an adapter card in a slot; however, an Int 13h handler also can be implemented by using a device driver loaded at boot time. Because DOS requires Int 13h access to boot from a drive (and a device driver cannot be loaded until after boot-up), only drives with ROM BIOS based Int 13h support can become bootable. Int 13h routines need to talk directly to the controller using the I/O ports on the controller. Therefore, the Int 13h code is very controller specific.

Table 22.9 lists the different functions available at the Interrupt 13h BIOS interface. Some functions are available to floppy drives or hard drives only, whereas others are available to both types of drives.

Table 22.9 Int 13h BIOS Disk Functions

Function	Floppy Disk	Hard Disk	Description
00h	X	X	Reset disk system.
01h	X	X	Get status of last operation.
02h	X	X	Read sectors.
03h	X	X	Write sectors.
04h	X	X	Verify sectors.
05h	X	X	Format track.
06h		X	Format bad track.
07h		X	Format drive.
08h	X	X	Read drive parameters.
09h		X	Initialize drive characteristics.
0Ah		X	Read long.
0Bh		X	Write long.
0Ch		X	Seek.
0Dh		X	Alternate hard disk reset.
0Eh		X	Read sector buffer.
0Fh		X	Write sector buffer.
10h		X	Test for drive ready.
11h		X	Recalibrate drive.
12h		X	Controller RAM diagnostic.
13h		X	Controller drive diagnostic.
14h		X	Controller internal diagnostic.
15h	X	X	Get disk type.
16h	X		Get floppy disk change status.
17h	X		Set floppy disk type for format.
18h	X		Set media type for format.
19h		X	Park hard disk heads.
1Ah		X	ESDI—Low-level format.
1Bh		X	ESDI—Get manufacturing header.
1Ch		X	ESDI—Get configuration.

Table 22.10 shows the error codes that may be returned by the BIOS INT 13h routines. In some cases, you may see these codes referred to when running a low-level format program, disk editor, or other program that can directly access a disk drive through the BIOS.

Table 22.10 INT 13h BIOS Error Codes

Code	Description
00h	No error.
01h	Bad command.
02h	Address mark not found.
03h	Write protect.
04h	Request sector not found.
05h	Reset failed.
06h	Media change error.
07h	Initialization failed.
09h	Cross 64K DMA boundary.
0Ah	Bad sector flag detected.
0Bh	Bad track flag detected.
10h	Bad ECC on disk read.
11h	ECC corrected data error.
20h	Controller has failed.
40h	Seek operation failed.
80h	Drive failed to respond.
AAh	Drive not ready.
BBh	Undefined error.
CCh	Write fault.
0Eh	Register error.
FFh	Sense operation failed.

If you design your own custom disk controller device, you need to write an IBM-compatible Int 13h handler package and install it on the card using a ROM BIOS that will be linked into the system at boot time. To use Int 13h routines, a program must use exact cylinder, head, and sector coordinates to specify sectors to read and write. Accordingly, any program designed to work at this level must be intimately familiar with the parameters of the specific disk on the system on which it is designed to run. Int 13h functions exist to read the disk parameters, format tracks, read and write sectors, park heads, and reset the drive.

A low-level format program for ST-506/412 drives needs to work with disks at the Int 13h level or lower. Most ST-506/412 controller format programs work with access at the Int 13h level because virtually any operation a format program needs is available through the Int 13h interface. This is not true, however, for other types of controllers (such as IDE, SCSI, or ESDI), for which defect mapping and other operations differ considerably from the ST-506/412 types. Controllers that must perform special operations during a low-level format, such as defining disk parameters to override the motherboard ROM BIOS drive tables, would not work with any formatter that used only the standard Int 13h interface. For these reasons, most controllers require a custom formatter designed to bypass the Int 13h interface. Most general purpose, low-level reformat programs that perform a nondestructive format (such as Norton Calibrate and SpinRite II) access the controller through the Int 13h interface (rather than going direct) and therefore cannot be used for an initial low-level format; the initial low-level format must be done by a controller-specific utility.

Few high-powered disk utility programs, other than some basic formatting software, can talk to the disk at the Int 13h level. The DOS FDISK program communicates at the Int 13h level. The Norton DISKEDIT and older NU programs can communicate with a disk at the Int 13h level when these programs are in their absolute sector mode; they are some of the few disk repair utilities that can do so. These programs are important because they can be used for the worst data recovery situations, in which the partition tables have been corrupted. Because the partition tables, as well as any non-DOS partitions, exist outside the area of a disk that is defined by DOS, only programs that work at the Int 13h level can access them. Most utility programs for data recovery work only at the DOS Int 25/26h level, which makes them useless for accessing areas of a disk outside of DOS' domain.

Disk Controller I/O Port Commands. In the lowest level of interface, programs talk directly to the disk controller in the controller's own specific native language. To do this, a program must send controller commands through the I/O ports to which the controller responds. These commands are specific to the particular controller and sometimes differ even among controllers of the same type, such as different ESDI controllers. The ROM BIOS in the system must be designed specifically for the controller because the ROM BIOS talks to the controller at this I/O port level. Most manufacturer type low-level format programs also need to talk to the controller directly because the higher-level Int 13h interface does not provide enough specific features for many of the custom ST-506/412 or ESDI and SCSI controllers on the market.

Figure 22.2 shows that most application programs work through the Int 21h interface, which passes commands to the ROM BIOS as Int 13h commands; these commands then are converted into direct controller commands by the ROM BIOS. The controller executes the commands and returns the results through the layers until the desired information reaches the application. This process enables applications to be written without worrying about such low-level system details, leaving such details up to DOS and the ROM BIOS. It also enables applications to run on widely different types of hardware, as long as the correct ROM BIOS and DOS support is in place.

Any software can bypass any level of interface and communicate with the level below it, but doing so requires much more work. The lowest level of interface available is direct communication with the controller using I/O port commands. As figure 22.2 shows, each different type of controller has different I/O port locations as well as differences among the commands presented at the various ports, and only the controller can talk directly to the disk drive.

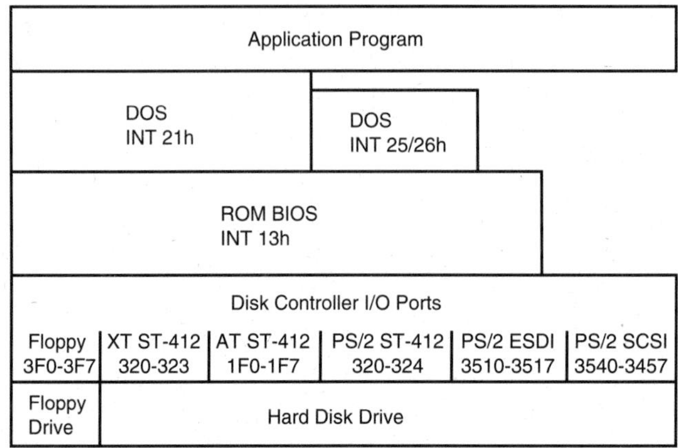

Figure 22.2

Relationships between various interface levels.

If not for the ROM BIOS Int 13h interface, a unique DOS would have to be written for each available type of hard and floppy disk drive and disk. Instead, DOS communicates with the ROM BIOS using standard Int 13h function calls translated by the Int 13h interface into commands for the specific hardware. Because of the standard ROM BIOS interface, DOS can be written relatively independently of specific disk hardware and can support many different types of drives and controllers.

DOS Structures

To manage files on a disk and enable all application programs to see a consistent disk interface no matter what type of disk is used, DOS uses several structures. The following list shows all the structures and areas that DOS defines and uses to manage a disk, in roughly the order in which they are encountered on a disk:

- Master and extended partition boot sectors
- DOS volume boot sector
- Root directory
- File allocation tables (FAT)
- Clusters (allocation units)
- Data area
- Diagnostic read-and-write cylinder

A hard disk has all these DOS disk management structures allocated, and a floppy disk has all but the master and extended partition boot sectors and the diagnostic cylinder. These structures are created by the DOS FDISK program, which has no application on a floppy disk because floppy disks cannot be partitioned. Figure 22.3 is a simple diagram showing the relative locations of these DOS disk management structures on the 32M hard disk in an IBM AT Model 339.

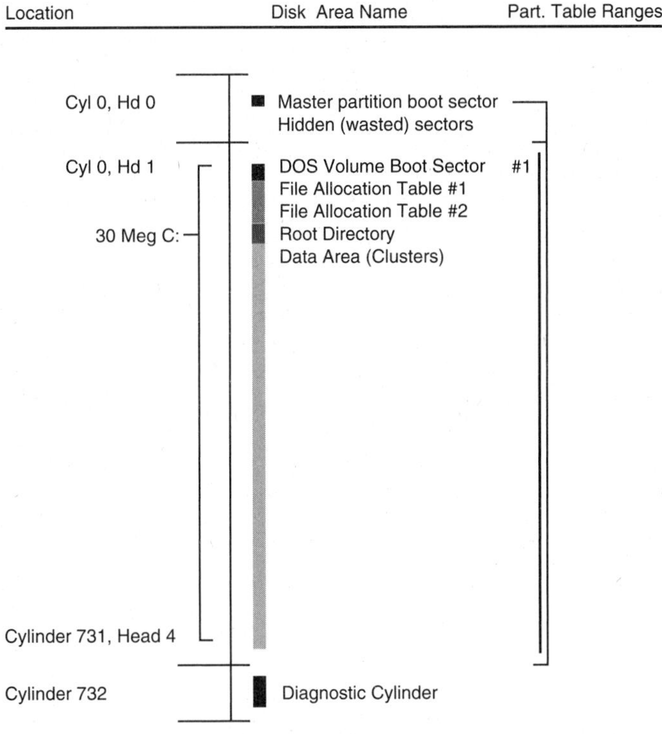

Figure 22.3

DOS disk management structures on an IBM AT Model 339 32M hard disk.

Each disk area has a purpose and function. If one of these special areas is damaged, serious consequences can result. Damage to one of these sensitive structures usually causes a domino effect and limits access to other areas of the disk or causes further problems in using the disk. For example, DOS cannot read and write files if the FAT is damaged or corrupted. You therefore should understand these data structures well enough to be able to repair them when necessary. Rebuilding these special tables and areas of the disk is essential to the art of data recovery.

Master Partition Boot Sectors. To share a hard disk among different operating systems, the disk might be logically divided into one to four master partitions. Each operating system, including DOS (through versions 3.2), might own only one partition. DOS 3.3 and later versions introduced the extended DOS partition, which allows multiple DOS partitions on the same hard disk. With the DOS FDISK program, you can select the size of each partition. The partition information is kept in several partition boot sectors on the disk, with the main table embedded in the master partition boot sector. The master partition boot sector is always located in the first sector of the entire disk (cylinder 0, head 0, sector 1). The extended partition boot sectors are located at the beginning of each extended partition volume.

Each DOS partition contains a DOS volume boot sector as its first sector. With the DOS FDISK utility, you might designate a single partition as active (or bootable). The master partition boot sector causes the active partitions volume boot sector to receive control when the system is started or reset. Additional master disk partitions can be set up for Novell NetWare, and for OS/2 HPFS, PCIX (UNIX), XENIX, CP/M-86, or other operating systems. Any of these foreign operating system partitions cannot be accessible under DOS, nor can any DOS partitions normally be accessible under other operating systems. (OS/2 and DOS share FAT partitions, the high-performance file system (HPFS) is exclusive to OS/2, and the NTFS is exclusive to Windows NT.)

A hard disk must be partitioned to be accessible by an operating system. You must partition a disk even if you want to create only a single partition. Table 22.11 shows the format of the Master Boot Record (MBR) with partition tables.

Table 22.11 Master Boot Record (Partition Table)

Offset	Length	Description
Partition Table Entry #1		
1BEh 446	1 byte	Boot Indicator Byte (80h = Active, else 00h)
1BFh 447	1 byte	Starting Head (or Side) of Partition
1C0h 448	16 bits	Starting Cylinder (10 bits) and Sector (6 bits)
1C2h 450	1 byte	System Indicator Byte (see table)
1C3h 451	1 byte	Ending Head (or Side) of Partition
1C4h 452	16 bits	Ending Cylinder (10 bits) and Sector (6 bits)
1C6h 454	1 dword	Relative Sector Offset of Partition
1CAh 458	1 dword	Total Number of Sectors in Partition
Partition Table Entry #2		
1CEh 462	1 byte	Boot Indicator Byte (80h = Active, else 00h)
1CFh 463	1 byte	Starting Head (or Side) of Partition
1D0h 464	16 bits	Starting Cylinder (10 bits) and Sector (6 bits)
1D2h 466	1 byte	System Indicator Byte (see table)
1D3h 467	1 byte	Ending Head (or Side) of Partition
1D4h 468	16 bits	Ending Cylinder (10 bits) and Sector (6 bits)
1D6h 470	1 dword	Relative Sector Offset of Partition
1DAh 474	1 dword	Total Number of Sectors in Partition
Partition Table Entry #3		
1DEh 478	1 byte	Boot Indicator Byte (80h = Active, else 00h)
1DFh 479	1 byte	Starting Head (or Side) of Partition
1E0h 480	16 bits	Starting Cylinder (10 bits) and Sector (6 bits)

Offset	Length	Description
Partition Table Entry #3		
1E2h 482	1 byte	System Indicator Byte (see table)
1E3h 483	1 byte	Ending Head (or Side) of Partition
1E4h 484	16 bits	Ending Cylinder (10 bits) and Sector (6 bits)
1E6h 486	1 dword	Relative Sector Offset of Partition
1EAh 490	1 dword	Total Number of Sectors in Partition
Partition Table Entry #4		
1EEh 494	1 byte	Boot Indicator Byte (80h = Active, else 00h)
1EFh 495	1 byte	Starting Head (or Side) of Partition
1F0h 496	16 bits	Starting Cylinder (10 bits) and Sector (6 bits)
1F2h 498	1 byte	System Indicator Byte (see table)
1F3h 499	1 byte	Ending Head (or Side) of Partition
1F4h 500	16 bits	Ending Cylinder (10 bits) and Sector (6 bits)
1F6h 502	1 dword	Relative Sector Offset of Partition
1FAh 506	1 dword	Total Number of Sectors in Partition
Signature Bytes		
1FEh 510	2 bytes	Boot Sector Signature (55AAh)

A WORD equals two bytes read in reverse order, and a DWORD equals two WORDs read in reverse order.

Table 22.12 shows the standard values and meanings of the System Indicator Byte.

Table 22.12 Partition Table System Indicator Byte Values

Value	Description
00h	No allocated partition in this entry
01h	Primary DOS, 12-bit FAT (Partition < 16M)
04h	Primary DOS, 16-bit FAT (16M <= Partition <= 32M)
05h	Extended DOS (Points to next Primary Partition)
06h	Primary DOS, 16-bit FAT (Partition > 32M)
07h	OS/2 HPFS Partition
02h	MS-XENIX Root Partition
03h	MS-XENIX usr Partition
08h	AIX File System Partition
09h	AIX boot Partition
50h	Ontrack Disk Manager READ-ONLY Partition
51h	Ontrack Disk Manager READ/WRITE Partition

(continues)

Table 22.12 Continued

Value	Description
56h	Golden Bow Vfeature Partition
61h	Storage Dimensions Speedstor Partition
63h	IBM 386/ix or UNIX System V/386 Partition
64h	Novell NetWare Partition
75h	IBM PCIX Partition
DBh	Digital Research Concurrent DOS/CPM-86 Partition
F2h	Some OEM's DOS 3.2+ second partition
FFh	UNIX Bad Block Table Partition

DOS Volume Boot Sectors. The *volume boot sector* is the first sector on any area of a drive addressed as a volume (or logical DOS disk). On a floppy disk, for example, this sector is the first one on the floppy disk because DOS recognizes the floppy disk as a volume with no partitioning required. On a hard disk, the volume boot sector or sectors are located as the first sector within any disk area allocated as a nonextended partition, or any area recognizable as a DOS volume.

This special sector resembles the master partition boot sector in that it contains a program as well as some special data tables. The first volume boot sector on a disk is loaded by the system ROM BIOS for floppies or by the master partition boot sector on a hard disk. This program is given control; it performs some tests and then attempts to load the first DOS system file (IBMBIO.COM). The volume boot sector is transparent to a running DOS system; it is outside the data area of the disk on which files are stored.

You create a volume boot sector with the DOS FORMAT command (high-level format). Hard disks have a volume boot sector at the beginning of every DOS logical drive area allocated on the disk, in both the primary and extended partitions. Although all the logical drives contain the program area as well as a data table area, only the program code from the volume boot sector in the active partition on a hard disk is executed. The others are simply read by the DOS system files during boot-up to obtain their data table and determine the volume parameters.

The volume boot sector contains program code and data. The single data table in this sector is called the *media parameter block* or *disk parameter block*. DOS needs the information it contains to verify the capacity of a disk volume as well as the location of important features such as the FAT. The format of this data is very specific. Errors can cause problems with booting from a disk or with accessing a disk. Some non-IBM OEM versions of DOS have not adhered to the standards set by IBM for the format of this data, which can cause interchange problems with disks formatted by different versions of DOS. The later versions can be more particular, so if you suspect that boot sector differences are causing inability to access a disk, you can use a utility program such as DOS DEBUG or Norton Utilities to copy a boot sector from the newer version of DOS to a disk formatted by the older version. This step should enable the new version of DOS to read the older disk and should not interfere with the less particular older version. This has never been a problem in using different DOS versions from the same OEM, but might occur in mixing different OEM versions.

Table 22.13 shows the format and layout of the DOS Boot Record (DBR).

Table 22.13 DOS Boot Record (DBR) Format

Offset Hex	Dec	Field Length	Description
00h	0	3 bytes	Jump Instruction to Boot Program Code
03h	3	8 bytes	OEM Name and DOS Version ("IBM 5.0")
0Bh	11	1 word	Bytes / Sector (usually 512)
0Dh	13	1 byte	Sectors / Cluster (Must be a power of 2)
0Eh	14	1 word	Reserved Sectors (Boot Sectors, usually 1)
10h	16	1 byte	FAT Copies (usually 2)
11h	17	1 word	Maximum Root Directory Entries (usually 512)
13h	19	1 word	Total Sectors (If Partition <= 32M, else 0)
15h	21	1 byte	Media Descriptor Byte (F8h for Hard Disks)
16h	22	1 word	Sectors / FAT
18h	24	1 word	Sectors / Track
1Ah	26	1 word	Number of Heads
1Ch	28	1 dword	Hidden Sectors (If Partition <= 32M, 1 word only)
For DOS 4.0 or Higher Only, Else 00h			
20h	32	1 dword	Total Sectors (If Partition > 32M, else 0)
24h	36	1 byte	Physical Drive No. (00h=floppy, 80h=hard disk)
25h	37	1 byte	Reserved (00h)
26h	38	1 byte	Extended Boot Record Signature (29h)
27h	39	1 dword	Volume Serial Number (32-bit random number)
2Bh	43	11 bytes	Volume Label ("NO NAME " stored if no label)
36h	54	8 bytes	File System ID ("FAT12 " or "FAT16 ")
For All Versions of DOS			
3Eh	62	448 bytes	Boot Program Code
1FEh	510	2 bytes	Signature Bytes (55AAh)

A WORD is two bytes read in reverse order, and a DWORD is two WORDs read in reverse order.

Root Directory. A *directory* is a simple database containing information about the files stored on a disk. Each record in this database is 32 bytes long, and no delimiters or separating characters are between the fields or records. A directory stores almost all the information that DOS knows about a file: name, attribute, time and date of creation, size, and where the beginning of the file is located on the disk. (The information a directory does not contain about a file is where the file continues on the disk and whether the file is contiguous or fragmented. The FAT contains that information.)

Two basic types of directories exist: the *root directory* and *subdirectories*. They differ primarily in how many there can be and in where they can be located. Any given volume can have only one root directory, and the root directory is always stored on a disk in a fixed location immediately following the two FAT copies. Root directories vary in size because of the varying types and capacities of disks, but the root directory of a given disk is fixed. After a root directory is created, it has a fixed length and cannot be extended to hold more entries. Normally, a hard disk volume has a root directory with room for 512 total entries. Subdirectories are stored as files in the data area of the disk and therefore have no fixed length limits.

Every directory, whether it is the root directory or a subdirectory, is organized in the same way. A directory is a small database with a fixed record length of 32 bytes. Entries in the database store important information about individual files and how files are named on a disk. The directory information is linked to the FAT by the starting cluster entry. In fact, if no file on a disk were longer than one single cluster, the FAT would be unnecessary. The directory stores all the information needed by DOS to manage the file, with the exception of all the clusters that the file occupies other than the first one. The FAT stores the remaining information about other clusters the file uses.

To trace a file on a disk, you start with the directory entry to get the information about the starting cluster of the file and its size. Then you go to the file allocation table. From there, you can follow the chain of clusters the file occupies until you reach the end of the file.

DOS directory entries are 32 bytes long and are in the format shown in table 22.14.

Table 22.14 DOS Directory Format

Offset Hex	Dec	Field Length	Description
00h	0	8 bytes	File name
08h	8	3 bytes	File extension
0Bh	11	1 byte	File attributes
0Ch	12	10 bytes	Reserved (00h)
16h	22	1 word	Time of creation
18h	24	1 word	Date of creation
1Ah	26	1 word	Starting cluster
1Ch	28	1 dword	Size in bytes

Note

File names and extensions are left-justified and padded with spaces (32h). The first byte of the file name indicates the file status as follows:

Hex	File Status
00h	Entry never used; entries past this point not searched.
05h	Indicates first character of filename is actually E5h.
E5h	"σ" (lowercase sigma) indicates file has been erased.
2Eh	"." (period) indicates this entry is a directory. If the second byte is also 2Eh, the cluster field contains the cluster number of parent directory (0000h if the parent is the root).

Table 22.15 describes the DOS Directory file attribute byte.

Table 22.15 DOS Directory File Attribute Byte

Bit Positions Hex 7 6 5 4 3 2 1 0	Value	Description
0 0 0 0 0 0 0 1	01h	Read-only file
0 0 0 0 0 0 1 0	02h	Hidden file
0 0 0 0 0 1 0 0	04h	System file
0 0 0 0 1 0 0 0	08h	Volume label
0 0 0 1 0 0 0 0	10h	Subdirectory
0 0 1 0 0 0 0 0	20h	Archive (updated since backup)
0 1 0 0 0 0 0 0	40h	Reserved
1 0 0 0 0 0 0 0	80h	Reserved
Examples		
0 0 1 0 0 0 0 1	21h	Read-only, archive
0 0 1 1 0 0 1 0	32h	Hidden, subdirectory, archive
0 0 1 0 0 1 1 1	27h	Read-only, hidden, system, archive

File Allocation Tables (FATs). The *file allocation table (FAT)* is a table of number entries describing how each cluster is allocated on the disk. The data area of the disk has a single entry for each cluster. Sectors in the nondata area on the disk are outside the range of the disk controlled by the FAT. The sectors involved in any of the boot sectors, file allocation table, and root directory are outside the range of sectors controlled by the FAT.

The FAT does not manage every data sector specifically, but rather allocates space in groups of sectors called *clusters* or *allocation units*. A cluster is one or more sectors designated by DOS as allocation units of storage. The smallest space a file can use on a disk is one cluster; all files use space on the disk in integer cluster units. If a file is one byte larger than one cluster, two clusters are used. DOS determines the size of a cluster when the disk is high-level formatted by the DOS FORMAT command.

You can think of the FAT as a sort of spreadsheet that controls the cluster use of the disk. Each cell in the spreadsheet corresponds to a single cluster on the disk; the number stored in that cell is a sort of code telling whether the cluster is used by a file, and if so where the next cluster of the file is located.

The numbers stored in the FAT are hexadecimal numbers that are either 12 or 16 bits long. The 16-bit FAT numbers are easy to follow because they take an even two bytes of space and can be edited fairly easily. The 12-bit numbers are 1 1/2 bytes long, which presents a problem when most disk sector editors show data in byte units. To edit the FAT, you must do some hex/binary math to convert the displayed byte units to FAT numbers. Fortunately, (unless you are using the DOS DEBUG program), most of the available tools and utility programs have a FAT editing mode that automatically converts the numbers for you. Most of them also show the FAT numbers in decimal form, which most people find easier to handle.

The DOS FDISK program determines whether a 12-bit or 16-bit FAT is placed on a disk, even though the FAT is written during the high-level format (FORMAT). All floppy disks use a 12-bit FAT, but hard disks can use either. On hard disk volumes with more than 16 megabytes (32,768 sectors), DOS creates a 16-bit FAT; otherwise, DOS creates a 12-bit FAT.

DOS keeps two copies of the FAT. Each one occupies contiguous sectors on the disk, and the second FAT copy immediately follows the first. Unfortunately, DOS uses the second FAT copy only if sectors in the first FAT copy become unreadable. If the first FAT copy is corrupted, which is a much more common problem, DOS does not use the second FAT copy. Even the DOS CHKDSK command does not check or verify the second FAT copy. Moreover, whenever DOS updates the first FAT, large portions of the first FAT automatically are copied to the second FAT. If, therefore, the first copy was corrupted and then subsequently updated by DOS, a large portion of the first FAT would be copied over the second FAT copy, damaging it in the process. After the update, the second copy is usually a mirror image of the first one, complete with any corruption. Two FATs rarely stay out of sync for very long. When they are out of sync and DOS writes to the disk and causes the first FAT to be updated, it also causes the second FAT to be overwritten by the first FAT. Because of all this, the usefulness of the second copy of the FAT is limited to manual repair operations, and even then it is useful only if the problem is caught immediately, before DOS has a chance to update the disk.

Clusters (Allocation Units). The term *cluster* was changed to *allocation unit* in DOS 4.0. The newer term is appropriate because a single cluster is the smallest unit of the disk that DOS can handle when it writes or reads a file. A cluster is equal to one or more sectors, and although a cluster can be a single sector, it is usually more than one. Having more than one sector per cluster reduces the size and processing overhead of the FAT and enables DOS to run faster because it has fewer individual units of the disk to manage. The trade-off is in wasted disk space. Because DOS can manage space only in full cluster units, every file consumes space on the disk in increments of one cluster.

Table 22.16 shows default cluster (or allocation unit) sizes used by DOS for the various floppy disk formats.

Table 22.16 Default Floppy Disk Cluster (Allocation Unit) Sizes

Drive Type	Cluster (Allocation Unit) Size
5 1/4-inch 360K	2 sectors (1,024 bytes)
5 1/4-inch 1.2M	1 sector (512 bytes)
3 1/2-inch 720K	2 sectors (1,024 bytes)
3 1/2-inch 1.44M	1 sector (512 bytes)
3 1/2-inch 2.88M	2 sectors (1,024 bytes)

It seems strange that the high-density disks, which have many more individual sectors than low-density disks, sometimes have smaller cluster sizes. The larger the FAT, the more entries DOS must manage, and the slower DOS seems to function. This sluggishness is due to the excessive overhead required to manage all the individual clusters; the more clusters to be managed, the slower things become. The trade-off is in the minimum cluster size.

Smaller clusters generate less slack (space wasted between the actual end of each file and the end of the cluster). With larger clusters, the wasted space grows larger. High-density floppy drives are faster than their low-density counterparts, so perhaps IBM and Microsoft determined that the decrease in cluster size balances the drive's faster operation and offsets the use of a larger FAT.

For hard disks, the cluster size can vary greatly among different versions of DOS and different disk sizes. Table 22.17 shows the cluster sizes DOS selects for a particular volume size.

Table 22.17 Default Hard Disk Cluster (Allocation Unit) Sizes

Hard Disk Volume Size	Cluster (Allocation Unit) Size	FAT type
0 MB to less than 16 MB	8 sectors or 4,096 bytes	12-bit
16 MB through 128 MB	4 sectors or 2,048 bytes	16-bit
Over 128 MB through 256 MB	8 sectors or 4,096 bytes	16-bit
Over 256 MB through 512 MB	16 sectors or 8,192 bytes	16-bit
Over 512 MB through 1,024 MB	32 sectors or 16,384 bytes	16-bit
Over 1,024 MB through 2,048MB	64 sectors or 32,768 bytes	16-bit

In most cases, these cluster sizes, selected by the DOS FORMAT command, are the minimum possible for a given partition size. Therefore, 8K clusters are the smallest possible for a partition size of greater than 256M. Although most versions of DOS work like this, some versions might use cluster sizes different from what this table indicates. For example, Compaq DOS 3.31 shifts to larger cluster sizes much earlier than IBM or MS-DOS does. Compaq DOS shifts to 4K clusters at 64M partitions, 8K clusters at 128M partitions, and 16K clusters at 256M partitions. A 305M partition that uses 8K clusters under IBM DOS has clusters of 16K under Compaq DOS 3.31. Later versions of Compaq DOS changed to the standard partitioning scheme.

The effect of these larger cluster sizes on disk use can be substantial. A drive containing about 5,000 files, with average slack of one-half of the last cluster used for each file, wastes about 20M [5000*(.5*8)K] of file space on a disk set up with IBM DOS or MS-DOS. Using Compaq DOS 3.31, this wasted space doubles to 40M for the same 5,000 files. Someone using a system with Compaq DOS 3.31 could back up, repartition, and reformat with IBM DOS, and after restoring all 5,000 files, gain 20M of free disk space.

The reason that Compaq DOS 3.31 does not use the most efficient (or smallest) cluster size possible for a given partition size is because its makers were interested in improving the performance of the system at the expense of great amounts of disk space. Larger cluster sizes get you a smaller FAT, with fewer numbers to manage; DOS overhead is reduced when files are stored and retrieved, which makes the system seem faster. For example, the CHKDSK command runs much faster on a disk with a smaller FAT. Unfortunately, the trade-off for speed here is a tremendous loss of space on the disk. (Compaq DOS 4.0 and 5.0 use IBM DOS and MS-DOS conventions.)

Windows 95 will soon be available with a new 32-bit FAT system that allows for more than 64K clusters. Since there can be more clusters, the individual clusters can be smaller. This will alleviate the large cluster size problem for larger drives, and will extend the size of a FAT partition on a hard disk to beyond the current 2GB limit. Note that Windows NT and OS/2 already have more sophisticated file systems that do away with the FAT structure and that are not limited in the way that FAT partitions are.

The Data Area. The data area of a disk is the area that follows the boot sector, file allocation tables, and root directory on any volume. This area is managed by the FAT and the root directory. DOS divides it into allocation units sometimes called clusters. These clusters are where normal files are stored on a volume.

Diagnostic Read-and-Write Cylinder. The FDISK partitioning program always reserves the last cylinder of a hard disk for use as a special diagnostic read-and-write test cylinder. That this cylinder is reserved is one reason FDISK always reports fewer total cylinders than the drive manufacturer states are available. DOS (or any other operating system) does not use this cylinder for any normal purpose, because it lies outside the partitioned area of the disk.

On systems with IDE, SCSI, or ESDI disk interfaces, the drive and controller might allocate an additional area past the logical end of the drive for a bad-track table and spare sectors. This situation may account for additional discrepancies between FDISK and the drive manufacturer.

The diagnostics area enables diagnostics software such as the manufacturer-supplied Advanced Diagnostics disk to perform read-and-write tests on a hard disk without corrupting any user data. Low-level format programs for hard disks often use this cylinder as a scratch-pad area for running interleave tests or preserving data during nondestructive formats. This cylinder is also sometimes used as a head landing or parking cylinder on hard disks that do not have an automatic parking facility.

Potential DOS Upgrade Problems

You already know that the DOS system files have special placement requirements on a hard disk. Sometimes these special requirements cause problems when you are upgrading from one version of DOS to another.

If you have attempted to upgrade a PC system from one version of DOS to another, you know that you use the DOS SYS command to replace old system files with new ones. The SYS command copies the existing system files (stored on a bootable disk with hidden, system, and read-only attributes) to the disk in the correct position and with the correct names and attributes. The COPY command does not copy hidden or system files (nor would it place the system files in the required positions on the destination disk if their other attributes had been altered so that they could be copied using COPY).

In addition to transferring the two hidden system files from one disk to another, SYS also updates the DOS volume boot sector on the destination disk so that it is correct for the new version of DOS. Common usage of the SYS command is as follows:

SYS C: (for drive C)

or

SYS A: (to make a floppy in drive A bootable)

The syntax of the command is as follows:

SYS*[d:][path]***d:**

In this command line, *d:/path* specifies an optional source drive and path for the system files. If the source drive specification is omitted, the boot drive is used as the source drive. This parameter is supported in DOS 4.0 and later versions only. Versions of DOS older than 4.0 automatically look for system files on the default drive (not on the boot drive). The *d* in the syntax specifies the drive to which you want to transfer the system files.

When the SYS command is executed, you usually are greeted by one of two messages:

```
System transferred
```

or

```
No room for system on destination disk
```

If a disk has data on it before you try to write the system files to it, the SYS command from DOS versions 3.3 and earlier probably will fail because they are not capable of moving other files out of the way. The SYS command in DOS 4.0 and higher versions rarely fail because they can and do move files out of the way.

Some users think that the cause of the `No room` message on a system that has an older version of DOS is that the system files in any newer version of DOS are always larger than the previous version, and that the new version files cannot fit into the space allocated for older versions. Such users believe that the command fails because this space cannot be provided at the beginning without moving other data away. This belief is wrong. The SYS command fails in these cases because you are trying to install a version of DOS that has file names different from the names already on the disk. There is no normal reason for the SYS command to fail when you update the system files on a disk that already has them.

Although the belief that larger system files cannot replace smaller ones might be popular, it is wrong for DOS 3.0 and later versions. The system files can be placed virtually anywhere on the disk, except that the first clusters of the disk must contain the file IBMBIO.COM (or its equivalent). After that requirement is met, the IBMDOS.COM file might be fragmented and placed just about anywhere on the disk, and the SYS command implements it with no problems whatsoever. In version 3.3 or later, even the IBMBIO.COM file can be fragmented and spread all over the disk, as long as the first cluster of the file occupies the first cluster of the disk (cluster 2). The only other requirement is that the names IBMBIO.COM and IBMDOS.COM (or their equivalents) must use the first and second directory entries.

DOS 4.0 and Later Versions. Under DOS 4.0 and later versions, the SYS command is much more powerful than under previous versions. Because the system files must use the first two entries in the root directory of the disk as well as the first cluster (cluster 2) of the disk, the DOS 4.0 and later versions' SYS command moves any files that occupy the first two entries but that do not match the new system file names to other available entries in the root directory; the SYS command also moves the portion of any foreign file occupying the first cluster to other clusters on the disk. Whereas the SYS command in older versions of DOS would fail and require a user to make adjustments to the disk, the DOS 4.0 and later versions' SYS command automatically makes the required adjustments. For example, even if you are updating a Phoenix DOS 3.3 disk to IBM DOS 4.0, the IBM DOS SYS command relocates the Phoenix IO.SYS and MSDOS.SYS files so that the new IBMBIO.COM and IBMDOS.COM files can occupy the correct locations in the root directory as well as on the disk.

The SYS command in DOS versions 5.0 and 6.0 go one step farther: They replace old system files with the new ones. Even if the old system files had other names, DOS 5.0 and higher ensure that they are overwritten by the new system files. If you are updating a disk on which the old system file names match the new ones, the SYS command of any version of DOS overwrites the old system files with the new ones with no moving of files necessary. With the enhanced SYS command in DOS 4.0 and later versions, it is difficult to make a DOS upgrade fail.

DOS 3.3. The DOS 3.3 SYS command does not move other files out of the way (as SYS does in DOS 4.0 and later versions); therefore, you must ensure that the first two root directory entries are either free or contain names that match the new system file names. As in DOS 4.0 and later versions, the first cluster on the disk must contain the first portion of IBMBIO.COM; unlike DOS 4.0 and later versions, however, the SYS command under DOS 3.3 does not move any files for you. Necessary manual adjustments, such as clearing the first two directory entries or relocating a file that occupies the first cluster on the disk, must be done with whatever utility programs you have available. The DOS 3.3 system files can be fragmented and occupy various areas of the disk.

SYS under DOS 3.3 does not automatically handle updating from one version of DOS to a version that has different system file names. In that case, because the system file names are not the same, the new system files do not overwrite the old ones. If you are making this kind of system change, use a directory editing tool to change the names of the current system files to match the new names so that the system file overwrite can occur.

DOS 3.2. DOS 3.2 or earlier requires that the entire IBMBIO.COM file be contiguous starting with cluster 2 (the first cluster) on the disk. The other system file (IBMDOS.COM) can be fragmented or placed anywhere on the disk; it does not have to follow the first system file physically on the disk.

DOS 2.x. DOS 2.x requires that both system files (IBMBIO.COM and IBMDOS.COM) occupy contiguous clusters on the disk starting with the first cluster (cluster 2). The DOS 2.1 system files are slightly larger than the DOS 2.0 files in actual bytes, but the size change is not enough to require additional clusters on the disk. A SYS change from DOS 2.0 to DOS 2.1 therefore is successful in most cases.

Windows 95. Windows 95 includes its own automatic install program that will rename the existing system files with a .DOS extension. The file WINBOOT.SYS will then be installed on the disk in its place.

Upgrading DOS from the Same OEM. Updating from one version of DOS to a later version from the same OEM by simply using the SYS command has never been a problem. I verified this with IBM DOS by installing IBM DOS 2.0 on a system with a hard disk through the normal FORMAT /S command. I copied all the subsequent DOS transient programs into a \DOS subdirectory on the disk and then updated the hard disk, in succession, to IBM DOS 2.1, 3.0, 3.1, 3.2, 3.3, 4.0, 5.0, and even 6.3 using nothing more than the SYS and COPY (or XCOPY or REPLACE) commands. Between each version change, I verified that the hard disk would boot the new version of DOS with no problems. Based on this experiment, I have concluded that you never have to use the FORMAT command to update one DOS version to a later version, as long as both versions are from the same OEM. I also verified the same operations on a floppy disk. Starting with a bootable floppy disk created by IBM DOS 2.0, I used SYS and COPY to update that disk to all subsequent versions of DOS through 6.3 without ever reformatting it. After each version change, the floppy disk was bootable with no problems.

You should be able to update a bootable hard disk or floppy disk easily from one DOS version to another without reformatting the disk. If you are having problems, you probably are attempting to upgrade to a version of DOS that uses names for the system files different from those used by the existing DOS, which means that you are moving from a DOS made by one OEM to a DOS made by a different company. If you are having trouble and this is not the case, carefully examine the boot sequence at the beginning of this section. That will help you determine where things are going wrong.

Downgrading DOS. One important and often overlooked function of the SYS command is its capability to update the DOS volume boot sector of a disk on which it is writing system files. Later versions of SYS are more complete than earlier versions in the way they perform this update; therefore, using SYS to go from a later version of DOS to an earlier version is sometimes difficult. For example, you cannot use SYS to install DOS 2.1 on a disk that currently boots DOS 3.0 and later versions. Changing from DOS 4.0 or higher versions back to DOS 3.3 usually works, if the partition is less than or equal to 32 megabytes in capacity. You probably will never see a problem with a later version of SYS updating a DOS volume boot sector created by an earlier version, but earlier versions might leave something out when they attempt to change back from a later version. Fortunately, few people ever attempt to install a lower version of DOS over a higher version.

Known Bugs in DOS

Few things are more frustrating than finding out that software you depend on every day has bugs. It's even worse when DOS does. Every version of DOS ever produced has had bugs, and users must learn to anticipate them. Some problems are never resolved; you must live with them.

Sometimes the problems are severe enough, however, that Microsoft, IBM, and other OEM distributors of DOS issue a patch disk that corrects the problems. If you use IBM DOS, you can get them from an IBM dealer or download them from the IBM National Support Center (NSC) BBS (the number is in the vendor list in Appendix B). With MS-DOS, you can request a patch by calling the technical support number in the front of your DOS manual. Or, if you have a modem, you can download patches from the Microsoft Download Service BBS (see Appendix B).

If you have IBM PC DOS, check with your system vendor periodically to find out whether patches are available. You do not have to go to the dealer from which you purchased PC DOS; any dealer must provide the patches for free when you show you have a legal license for PC DOS. The proof-of-license page from the PC DOS 4.0 manual satisfies as a license check. If you ask a dealer who does not know about these patches, or who does not provide them for some reason, try another dealer. PC DOS is a warranted product, and the patches are part of the warranty service.

On the Web

Here are some of the common Web sites for DOS patches:

http://www.microsoft.com/kb/softlib/

http://ps.software.ibm.com/pbin-usa-ps/getobj.pl?/pdocs-usa/alldos.html

http://www.compaq.com/support/

The following sections detail IBM patches for PC DOS 3.3, 4.0, 5.0, and 6.0. These versions have official IBM-produced patch disks available at no cost from your nearest IBM dealer, or available from the IBM BBS.

PC DOS 3.3 Bugs and Patches. The PC DOS 3.3 official patches and fixes from IBM originally were issued by IBM's National Support Center on September 9, 1987. A second update, issued October 24, 1987, superseded the first update. These disks fix the following two general problems with DOS 3.3:

- BACKUP did not work properly in backing up a large number of subdirectories in a given directory. A new version of BACKUP was created to resolve this problem.
- Systems that had slow serial printers with small input buffers sometimes displayed a false `Out Of Paper` error message when attempting to print. A new program, I17.COM, resolves this problem.

In addition to the two general problems resolved by this patch, IBM PS/2 systems had a particular problem between their ROM BIOS and DOS 3.3; a special DASDDRVR.SYS driver was provided on the patch disk to fix these BIOS problems. The versions of DASDDRVR.SYS supplied on the DOS 3.3 patch disks have been superseded by later versions supplied elsewhere; DASDDRVR.SYS was placed on the IBM PS/2 Reference disks for more widespread distribution, and you can obtain it directly from IBM on a special system update floppy disk. This driver and the problems it can correct are discussed later in this chapter, in the section "PS/2 BIOS Update (DASDDRVR.SYS)."

PC DOS 4.0 and 4.01 Bugs and Patches. Six different versions of IBM DOS 4.0 have been issued, counting the first version and the five patch disks subsequently released. The disks are not called patch disks anymore; they are called *Corrective Service Disks (CSDs)*. Each level of CSD contains all the previous level CSDs. The first CSD issued for PC DOS 4.0 (UR22624) contained a series of problem fixes that later were incorporated into the standard release version of DOS 4.01. Several newer CSDs have been released since version 4.01 appeared. Unfortunately, these more recent updates were never integrated into the commercially packaged DOS. The only way to obtain these fixes is to obtain the CSDs from your dealer or from the IBM BBS.

The VER command in any level of IBM DOS 4.x always shows 4.00, which causes much confusion about which level of CSD fixes are installed on a specific system. To eliminate this confusion and allow for the correct identification of installed patches, the CSD UR29015 and later levels introduce to DOS 4.x a new command: SYSLEVEL. This command is resident in COMMAND.COM and is designed to identify conclusively to the user the level of corrections installed. On a system running PC DOS 4.x with CSD UR35284 installed, the SYSLEVEL command reports the following:

DOS Version: 4.00 U.S. Date: 06/17/88

CSD Version: UR35284 U.S. Date: 09/20/91

The following list notes each of the IBM DOS 4.0 Corrective Service Diskettes (CSDs) and when they first became available:

CSD	Date available
UR22624	08/15/88 (this equals 4.01)
UR24270	03/27/89
UR25066	05/10/89
UR29015	03/20/90
UR31300	06/29/90
UR35284	09/20/91

These CSDs are valid only for the IBM version of DOS—PC DOS 4.0. Microsoft and OEM versions of DOS may not have corresponding patches. Some OEMs provide patches or corrections in different ways, and some may not even offer them. Because most OEMs release their versions of DOS after IBM, other manufacturers have had a chance to incorporate fixes in their standard version and may not need to provide patches. If you have a version of DOS by a manufacturer other than Microsoft or IBM, contact its source to find out which patch corrections have been applied to your version of DOS. With a system that can run standard MS-DOS, you can get patches from Microsoft. If you have an IBM, you must rely on a reputable dealer to get the latest version of DOS.

MS-DOS 4. Microsoft released its version of DOS 4 after IBM had fixed most of the bugs in PC DOS 4.0. Yet MS-DOS 4.01 introduced some bugs of its own. A patch for MS-DOS 4.x is available for download from the Microsoft Download Service or by calling Microsoft technical service. The patch disk for MS-DOS 4.0x is available on the Microsoft Download service as PD0255.EXE.

IBM DOS 5.0 Bugs and Patches. With the release of its DOS version 5.0, IBM changed the product name from PC DOS to IBM DOS. (Version 6.0 of IBM's DOS has been changed back to PC DOS.) IBM DOS version 5.0 has several CSDs that fix a couple of problems. The most significant is a defect in the XCOPY command that causes it to fail sometimes when it uses the /E or /S switches. The following list notes the IBM DOS 5.0 CSDs and indicates when they first became available:

CSD	Date available
UR35423	08/91
UR35748	10/91
UR35834	11/91
UR36603	02/92
UR37387	09/92

Table 22.18 lists the problems fixed by these patch disks.

Table 22.18 IBM DOS 5 Corrective Service Disks (CSDs)

CSD	Item	Problem
UR35423	XCOPY	Wrong output when using /E and /S switches.
UR35423	QBASIC	Enables QBASIC and QEDIT compatibility.
UR35748	SYS	Corrupted hard file after installing UR35423.
UR35834	DOSSHELL	DOSSHELL takes 27 seconds to load.
UR35834	MEUTOINI	4.0 .MEU to 5.0 .INI conversion incomplete.
UR35834	MEM	MEM switch hangs system with PC3270.
UR35834	IBMBIO	L40SX will not SUSPEND or RESUME.
UR35834	DOSSHELL	Can't edit Dialog Box if length is maximum.
UR35834	EMM386	Int 19H fails with EMM386 and DOS=HIGH.
UR35834	FORMAT	FORMAT on unpartitioned drive; rc = 0.

CSD	Item	Problem
UR35834	REPLACE	REPLACE /a returns error.
UR35834	XCOPY	XCOPY /s incorrectly sets error level.
UR35834	GRAPHICS	PrtScr of graphics display produces garbage.
UR35834	DOSSHELL	DOSSHELL.INI corrupted from CTRL+ALT+DEL.
UR35834	BACKUP	BACKUP calls wrong FORMAT.COM from OS/2.
UR35834	MIRROR	MIRROR doesn't enable Interrupts correctly.
UR35834	BACKUP	BACKUP /a backs up too large a file.
UR36603	EDIT	Alt ### key combo doesn't work in EDIT.
UR36603	MIRROR	MIRROR fails with /T switch and DOS=UMB.
UR36603	IBMBIO	L40SX will not SUSPEND or RESUME if DOS=LOW.
UR36603	BACKUP	BACKUP fails to back up all files.
UR36603	QBASIC	QBASIC help msgs missing in nls versions.
UR36603	CHKDSK	CHKDSK Data loss when sectors per FAT>256.
UR36603	EMM386	DMA transfer may not function on EISA systems.
UR36603	RECOVER	RECOVER can corrupt disks with 12-bit FAT.
UR36603	RECOVER	RECOVER may not adjust file size correctly.
UR36603	DOSSHELL	DOSSHELL incorrectly copies certain file sizes.
UR36603	DOSSWAP	Task Swapper destroys CX register.
UR36603	DOSSWAP	Task Swapper does not swap EMS memory.
UR36603	DOSSWAP	Task Swapper incorrectly swaps large XMS memory.
UR36603	DOSSWAP	DOSSHELL overwrites an interrupt vector.
UR36603	DOSSWAP	DOSSHELL random skip of swapping application memory.
UR36603	DOSSHELL	DOSSHELL uses environment var to set 2nd swap path.
UR37387	RESTORE	RESTORE fails to display backup files.
UR37387	IBMDOS	FASTOPEN causes bad FAT message.
UR37387	KEYB	Pause key doesn't work on PS/2 25 and 30.
UR37387	IBMDOS	Unmapped network drive returns error.
UR37387	MODE	MODE and off-line printer across net hangs.
UR37387	IBMDOS	RAMDRIVE errors with certain combinations.
UR37387	DOSSHELL	Unattended start mode—lose keyboard with DOSSHELL.
UR37387	COMMAND	Error with greater than 1GB free space.
UR37387	IBMDOS	INT 27 returns no data after file create.
UR37387	IBMBIO	L40SX loses time during suspend.
UR37387	DOSSHELL	CTRL+ESC hangs when returning to DOSSHELL.
UR37387	IBMDOS	Extended File Open returns incorrect code.
UR37387	HIMEM	Device driver fails to load.
UR37387	HIMEM	HIMEM incorrectly identifies memory on EISA.
UR37387	UNDELETE	Doesn't work if partition is a multiple of 128 MB.
UR37387	UNDELETE	Doesn't handle foreign characters correctly.
UR37387	BACKUP	Restore does not ask for second diskette.

(continues)

Table 22.18 Continued

CSD	Item	Problem
UR37387	KEYBOARD	Keyboard changes for Latin II countries.
UR37387	MEM	Finland MEM/C displays invalid characters.
UR37387	DOSSHELL	INT 33 DOSSHELL reentry problem with BASIC.
UR37387	MODE	MODE LPT1:,,P reports Bad mode.
UR37387	BACKUP	Occasionally gets Cannot Restore File error.

MS-DOS 5.0 Bugs and Patches. As mentioned earlier, the Microsoft Download Service DOS files listing includes fixes for MS-DOS versions 4.0 and 5.0. When you call the Microsoft Download Service, you are asked to enter your name and city and to choose a password. Choose a password you will not forget because when you realize how simple it is to always have the most current bug fixes for MS-DOS, you will want to call back.

MS-DOS 6.0 and IBM PC DOS 6.1. As of this writing, there had been one bug fix for MS-DOS version 6.0—a new version of SmartDrive, which fixes a problem on some systems when SmartDrive is used at the same time as DoubleSpace. The fix can be used if you have experienced cross-linked files you think are related to upgrading to DOS 6.0. You can download the file, named PD0805.EXE, from the Microsoft Download Service. The Microsoft Download Services also enables you (free of charge) to download the MS-DOS 6.0 Supplemental Disk. This supplemental disk contains utilities helpful to the disabled. The disk also contains new versions of various utilities that were part of DOS 5.0, but not included on the DOS 6.0 upgrade disks, including MIRROR, EDLIN, ASSIGN, JOIN, BACKUP (MSBACKUP is a new menu-based backup program included with DOS 6), COMP, PRINTER.SYS, the DVORAK keyboard. Also available is a utility to fix a problem using the Shift key in Quick Basic 1.1, named PD0415.EXE.

In addition, numerous technical papers on setting up and running MS-DOS 6.0 are available on the download service. Some of them are listed in table 22.19.

Table 22.19 MS-DOS Technical Papers

File Name	Subject
PD0456.TXT	Running MS-DOS in the High Memory Area
PD0457.TXT	HIMEM.SYS "ERROR: Unable to Control A20 Line"
PD0459.TXT	EMM386.EXE: No Expanded Memory Available
PD0460.TXT	Running Both Extended and Expanded Memory
PD0462.TXT	Mouse Doesn't Work with MS-DOS Shell
PD0463.TXT	Using the Setver Command
PD0465.TXT	Problems Formatting or Reading a Floppy Disk
PD0470.TXT	System Fails When You Are Using EMM.386
PD0471.TXT	Explanation of the WINA20.386 File
PD0473.TXT	Installing MS-DOS from Drive B
PD0474.TXT	Windows 3.0 Doesn't Run in 386 Enhanced Mode

File Name	Subject
PD0476.TXT	IBM PS/1 Fails After MS-DOS Is Installed
PD0477.TXT	Setup Stops Before Completing Upgrade to MS
PD0743.TXT	MS-DOS 6.0 Installation and Partition Q&A
PD0744.TXT	MS-DOS 6.0 General Installation Q&A
PD0745.TXT	DoubleSpace Questions and Answers
PD0746.TXT	MemMaker Questions and Answers
PD0747.TXT	MS-DOS 6.0 Configuration Q&A
PD0748.TXT	Backup and Miscellaneous Q&A
PD0771.TXT	Repartitioning Your Hard Disk To Upgrade to MS-DOS 6.0
PD0785.TXT	Upgrading DR DOS to MS-DOS 6

IBM has since released PC DOS 7.0, which has many fixes and updates.

PS/2 BIOS Update (DASDDRVR.SYS)

The DASDDRVR.SYS (direct access storage device driver) file is a set of software patches that fixes various ROM BIOS bugs in several models of the older IBM PS/2s. DASDDRVR.SYS is required for specific PS/2 systems using IBM's PC DOS versions 3.30 or later, to correct several bugs in the IBM PS/2 ROM BIOS. Before IBM's PC DOS 4.00 was released, conflicting information indicated that PC DOS 4.00 would include the updates to correct the PS/2 ROM BIOS problems fixed by DASDDRVR.SYS under PC DOS 3.30. This information was not accurate, however. In fact, an IBM PS/2 system needs DASDDRVR.SYS with IBM DOS 7.00 (or any higher version of DOS) even with the most current corrective service disk (CSD) update.

The older PS/2 systems need the DASDDRVR.SYS fixes only in the DOS environment. Some users assume, therefore, that the PS/2 problems with DOS are DOS bugs; they are not. The DASDDRVR.SYS program is provided on the PS/2 Reference disk (included with every PS/2 system) and is available separately on a special PS/2 system update disk. The disks contain the device driver program (DASDDRVR.SYS) and an installation program.

The PS/2 ROM BIOS bugs in the following list are fixed by DASDDRVR.SYS (the problem numbers are shown in table 22.19, and more detailed information is provided later in this section):

1. Failures occur in reading some 720K program floppy disks (Models 8530, 8550, 8560, and 8580).
2. Intermittent `Not ready` or `General failure` error messages appear (Models 8550, 8560, and 8580).
3. 3 1/2-inch floppy disk format fails when user tries to format more than one floppy disk (Models 8550, 8560, and 8580).
4. Combined 301 and 8602 error messages appear at power-on or after power interruption (Models 8550 and 8560).
5. System clock loses time, or combined 162 and 163 errors appear during system initialization (Models 8550 and 8560).

6. User is unable to install Power-On Password program with DASDDRVR.SYS installed (Models 8550, 8560, and 8580).
7. Devices attached to COM2:, COM3:, or COM4: are not detected (Model 8530).
8. Devices that use Interrupt Request level 2 (IRQ2) fail (Model 8530).
9. 3 1/2-inch floppy disk format fails when user tries to format more than one floppy disk (Model 8570).
10. System performance degradation occurs from processor intensive devices (Models 8550, 8555, and 8560).
11. Error occurs in a microcode routine that enhances long-term reliability of 60/120M disk drives (Models 8550, 8555, 8570, and 8573).
12. Time and date errors occur when user resets the time or date. Intermittent date changes occur when the system is restarted by pressing Ctrl+Alt+Del (Model 8530).

If you are an IBM PS/2-system user running PC DOS 3.3 or higher and experiencing any of these problems, load the DASDDRVR.SYS file. The problems are system specific, and DASDDRVR.SYS fixes the problems for only the systems listed. IBM requires its dealers to distribute the System Update disk containing DASDDRVR.SYS to anyone who requests it. Neither the dealer nor the customer pays a fee for the System Update disk. You also can obtain copies directly from IBM by calling (800) IBM-PCTB (800-426-7282) and ordering the PS/2 System Update disk.

Check table 22.20 for detailed descriptions of each of these problems and for the specific systems affected. Models not listed for a particular problem do not need DASDDRVR.SYS, and no benefit results from installing it.

Table 22.20 DASDDRVR.SYS Version Summary

Version	File Size	Problems Fixed	Source
1.10	648 bytes	1-3	DOS 3.3 Fix Disk (08/24/87)
1.20	698 bytes	1-5	Reference Disk, DOS 3.3 Fix Disk (09/09/87)
1.30	734 bytes	1-6	Reference Disk
1.56	1170 bytes	1-10	Reference Disk (03/90), System Update Disk 1.01 (part number 64F1500)
1.56	3068 bytes	1-12	Reference Disk (xx/xx), System Update Disk 1.02 (part number 04G3288)

The first three problem fixes originally were provided by the DASDDRVR.SYS version 1.10 file supplied on the first PC DOS 3.3 fix disk. Fixes for problems 4 and 5 were added in DASDDRVR.SYS version 1.20, included on all IBM PS/2 Reference disks (30-286, 50/60, and 70/80), version 1.02 or later, as well as on an updated version of the PC DOS 3.3 fix disk. The fix for problem 6 was added in DASDDRVR.SYS Version 1.30, included on all 50/60 and 70/80 Reference Disks, version 1.03 or later. Fixes for problems 7 through 10 were added to DASDDRVR.SYS Version 1.56, included on all IBM PS/2 Reference Disks dated March 1990 or later. This version of DASDDRVR.SYS also was available separately, on the IBM PS/2 System Update disk version 1.01. The latest DASDDRVR.SYS (also called version 1.56, but dated January 1991) can be found on newer reference disks or on the IBM PS/2 System Update disk version 1.02.

By using the DASDDRVR.SYS driver file, IBM can correct specific ROM BIOS problems and bugs without having to issue a new set of ROM chips for a specific system. Using this file eliminates service time or expense in fixing simple problems, but causes the inconvenience of having to load the driver. The driver does not consume memory, nor does it remain in memory (as does a typical driver or memory-resident program); it either performs functions on boot only and then terminates, or overlays existing code or tables in memory, thereby consuming no additional space. Because DASDDRVR.SYS checks the exact ROM BIOS by model, submodel, and revision, it performs functions only on those for which it is designed. If it detects a BIOS that does not need fixing, the program terminates without doing anything. You can load DASDDRVR.SYS on any system; it functions only on systems for which it is designed.

Because a system BIOS occasionally needs revising or updating, IBM used disk-based BIOS programs for most newer PS/2 systems. The Models 57, P75, 90, and 95, in fact, load the system BIOS from the hard disk every time the system is powered up, during a procedure called *initial microcode load (IML)*. You can get a ROM upgrade for these systems by obtaining a new Reference disk and loading the new IML file on the hard disk. This system makes DASDDRVR.SYS or other such patches obsolete.

Note that most modern PCs use an EEPROM (Electrically Erasable Programmable ROM) otherwise called a Flash ROM to store their BIOS code. This means they can be updated by running a special program from the motherboard manufacturer that erases the BIOS chip and rewrites it with the new code. This eliminates the need for a special partition on the hard disk for the BIOS code, and allows easy field updates.

Installing DASDDRVR.SYS. To install DASDDRVR.SYS, you must update the CONFIG.SYS file with the following entry and restart the system:

DEVICE=*[d:\path\]*DASDDRVR.SYS

The drive and path values must match the location and name of the DASDDRVR.SYS file on your system.

Detailed Problem Descriptions. This section gives a detailed description of the problems corrected by the most current release of DASDDRVR.SYS and indicates for which systems the corrections are necessary.

1. Failures occur in reading some 720K program disks.

    IBM PS/2 systems affected:
    Model 30 286 8530-E01, -E21
    Model 50 8550-021
    Model 60 8560-041, -071
    Model 80 8580-041, -071

VI

Troubleshooting

Intermittent read failures on some 720K original application software disks. Example: `Not ready reading drive A:` appears when a user attempts to install an application program. Attempting to perform DIR or COPY commands from the floppy disk also produces the error message.

2. Intermittent `Not ready` or `General failure` error messages are displayed.

IBM PS/2 systems affected:
Model 50 8550-021
Model 60 8560-041, -071
Model 80 8580-041, -071

A very intermittent problem with a floppy disk drive `Not ready` or a fixed disk `General failure` message. This problem can be aggravated by certain programming practices that mask off (or disable) interrupts for long periods. The update ensures that interrupts are unmasked on each disk or floppy disk request.

3. A 3 1/2-inch floppy disk format fails when the user tries to format more than one floppy disk.

IBM PS/2 systems affected:
Model 50 8550-021
Model 60 8560-041, -071
Model 80 8580-041, -071

The DOS FORMAT command fails when a user tries to format multiple 3 1/2-inch floppy disks. The failure appears as an `Invalid media` or `Track 0 bad—disk unusable` message when the user replies Yes to the prompt `Format another (Y/N)?` after the format of the first floppy disk is complete. The error message appears when the user tries to format the second disk. If a system is booted from a floppy disk, the problem does not occur. This problem occurs only with DOS 3.3, not with later versions.

4. Combined 301 and 8602 error messages at power-on or after power interruption.

IBM PS/2 systems affected:
Model 50 8550-021
Model 60 8560-041, -071

When power is interrupted momentarily or a system is otherwise switched on and off quickly, a 301 (keyboard) and 8602 (pointing device) error message may appear during the Power On Self Test (POST). This error occurs because the system powers on before the keyboard is ready. The problem is more likely to occur if the system was reset previously by pressing Ctrl+Alt+Del.

5. System clock loses time or combined 162 and 163 errors during system initialization.

IBM PS/2 systems affected:
Model 50 8550-021
Model 60 8560-041, -071

Intermittent 162 (CMOS checksum or configuration) and 163 (Clock not updating) Power On Self Test (POST) errors occur. Various time-of-day problems on specified IBM PS/2 Model 50 systems; for example, the user turns on the machine in the morning and finds the time set to the same time the machine was turned off the day before.

6. User is unable to install Power-On Password program with DASDDRVR.SYS installed.

   IBM PS/2 systems affected:
   Model 50 8550-021
   Model 60 8560-041, -071
   Model 80 8580-041, -071

   When a user tries to install the Power-On Password feature with DASDDRVR.SYS Version 1.3 or earlier installed, a message appears that states (incorrectly) that a password already exists. The user also may be prompted for a password (on warm boot), even though password security has not been implemented.

7. Devices attached to COM2:, COM3:, or COM4: are not detected.

   IBM PS/2 systems affected:
   Model 30 286 8530-E01, -E21

8. Devices that use Interrupt Request level 2 (IRQ2) fail.

   IBM PS/2 systems affected:
   Model 30 286 8530-E01, -E21

9. A 3 1/2-inch disk format fails when user tries to format more than one disk.

   IBM PS/2 systems affected:
   Model 70 8570-Axx (all)
   Model 80 8580-Axx (all)

   The DOS FORMAT command fails when the user tries to format multiple 3 1/2-inch disks. The failure appears as an `Invalid media` or `Track 0 bad — disk unusable` message when the user replies Yes to the prompt `Format another (Y/N)?` after the format of the first disk is complete. The error message appears when the user tries to format the second disk. If the system is booted from a floppy disk, the problem does not occur.

10. System performance degradation occurs from processor intensive devices.

    IBM PS/2 systems affected:
    Model 50 8550-021, -031, -061
    Model 55 SX 8555-031, -061
    Model 60 8560-041, -071

11. Error occurs in a microcode routine that enhances long-term reliability of 60/120M disk drives.

    IBM PS/2 systems affected:
    Model 50 8550-061

Model 55 SX 8555-061
Model 70 8570-061, -121, -A61, -A21, -B61, -B21
Model P70 8573-061, -121

12. Time and date errors occur when the user resets the time or date. Intermittent date changes occur when the system is restarted by pressing Ctrl+Alt+Del.

    IBM PS/2 systems affected:
    Model 30 8530 (all)

OS/2 versions 1.2 and earlier contained these BIOS fixes in the form of a .BIO file for each specific BIOS needing corrections. These files were automatically loaded by OS/2 at boot time, depending on the specific system on which it was being loaded.

OS/2 Versions 1.3 and later contain the fixes directly in-line in the system files, not as separate files. When a system running one of these OS/2 versions is booted, OS/2 determines the model, submodel, and revision bytes for the particular BIOS under which it is running. Based on this information, OS/2 determines the correct .BIO file to load or the correct in-line code to run. For example, the IBM PS/2 55SX BIOS is Model F8, Submodel 0C, Revision 00, which causes IBM OS/2 Version 1.2 to load the file F80C00.BIO automatically during boot-up. OS/2 Versions 1.3 or later use this information to run the proper fix code contained in the system files. This procedure enables execution of only those BIOS fixes necessary for this particular system.

Any symptom described as being resolved by the DASDDRVR.SYS update may have other causes. If you install the DASDDRVR.SYS update and continue to have problems, consider the errors valid and follow normal troubleshooting procedures to find the causes.

DOS Disk and Data Recovery

The CHKDSK, RECOVER, SCANDISK, and DEBUG commands are the DOS damaged disk recovery team. These commands are crude, and their actions sometimes are drastic, but at times they are all that is available or needed. RECOVER is best known for its function as a data recovery program, and CHKDSK usually is used for inspection of the file structure. Many users are unaware that CHKDSK can implement repairs to a damaged file structure. DEBUG, a crude, manually controlled program, can help in the case of a disk disaster, if you know exactly what you are doing.

SCANDISK is basically a more powerful replacement for CHKDSK and RECOVER and should be used in their place if you have DOS 6 or higher.

The CHKDSK Command. The useful and powerful DOS CHKDSK command also is generally misunderstood. To casual users, the primary function of CHKDSK seems to be providing a disk space allocation report for a given volume and a memory allocation report. CHKDSK does those things, but its primary value is in discovering, defining, and repairing problems with the DOS directory and FAT system on a disk volume. In handling data recovery problems, CHKDSK is a valuable tool, although it is crude and simplistic compared to some of the after-market utilities that perform similar functions.

The output of the CHKDSK command that runs on a typical (well maybe not typical, but from my own personal) hard disk is as follows:

```
Volume 4GB_SCSI    created 08-31-1994 5:05p
Volume Serial Number is 1882-18CF

2,146,631,680 bytes total disk space
      163,840 bytes in 3 hidden files
   16,220,160 bytes in 495 directories
  861,634,560 bytes in 10,355 user files
1,268,613,120 bytes available on disk

       32,768 bytes in each allocation unit
       65,510 total allocation units on disk
       38,715 available allocation units on disk

      655,360 total bytes memory
      632,736 bytes free
```

A little known CHKDSK function is reporting a specified file's (or files') level of fragmentation. CHKDSK also can produce a list of all files (including hidden and system files) on a particular volume, similar to a super DIR command. By far, the most important CHKDSK capabilities are its detection and correction of problems with the DOS file management system.

The name of the CHKDSK program is misleading: It seems to be a contraction of CHECK DISK. The program does not actually check a disk, or even the files on a disk, for integrity. CHKDSK cannot even truly show how many bad sectors are on a disk, much less locate and mark them. The real function of CHKDSK is to inspect the directories and FATs to see whether they correspond with each other or contain discrepancies. CHKDSK does not detect (and does not report on) damage in a file; it checks only the FAT and directory areas (the table of contents) of a disk. Rather than CHKDSK, the command should have been called CKDIRFAT (for CHECK DIRECTORY FAT) because its most important job is to verify that the FATs and directories correspond with one another. The name of the program gives no indication of the program's capability to repair problems with the directory and FAT structures.

CHKDSK also can test files for contiguity. Files loaded into contiguous tracks and sectors of a disk or floppy disk naturally are more efficient. Files spread over wide areas of the disk make access operations take longer. DOS always knows the location of all of a file's fragments by using the pointer numbers in the file allocation table (FAT). These pointers are data that direct DOS to the next segment of the file. Sometimes, for various reasons, these pointers might be lost or corrupted and leave DOS incapable of locating some portion of a file. Using CHKDSK can alert you to this condition and even enable you to reclaim the unused file space for use by another file.

CHKDSK Command Syntax. The syntax of the CHKDSK command is as follows:

CHKDSK *[d:\path\] [filename] [/F] [/V]*

The *d:* specifies the disk volume to analyze. The *\path* and *filename* options specify files to check for fragmentation in addition to the volume analysis. Wild cards are allowed in the filename specification, to include as many as all the files in a specified directory for fragmentation analysis. One flaw with the fragmentation analysis is that it does not check for fragmentation across directory boundaries, only within a specified directory.

The switch */F* (Fix) enables CHKDSK to perform repairs if it finds problems with the directories and FATs. If /F is not specified, the program is prevented from writing to the disk, and all repairs are not really performed.

The switch */V* (Verbose) causes the program to list all the entries in all the directories on a disk and give detailed information, in some cases, when errors are encountered.

The drive, path, and file specifiers are optional. If no parameters are given for the command, CHKDSK processes the default volume or drive and does not check files for contiguity. If you specify *[path]* and *[filename]* parameters, CHKDSK checks all specified files to see whether they are stored contiguously on the disk. One of two messages is displayed as a result:

```
All specified file(s) are contiguous
```

or

```
[filename] Contains xxx non-contiguous blocks
```

The second message is displayed for each file fragmented on the disk and displays the number of fragments the file is in. A *fragmented file* is one that is scattered around the disk in pieces rather than existing in one contiguous area of the disk. Fragmented files are slower to load than contiguous files, which reduces disk performance. Fragmented files are also much more difficult to recover if a problem with the FAT or directory on the disk occurs.

Utility programs that can defragment files are discussed in Chapter 20, "Maintaining Your System: Preventive Maintenance, Backups, and Warranties." But if you have only DOS, you have several possible ways to accomplish a full defragmentation. To defragment files on a floppy disk, you can format a new floppy disk and use COPY or XCOPY to copy all the files from the fragmented disk to the replacement. For a hard disk, you must completely back up, format, and then restore the disk. This procedure on a hard disk is time-consuming and dangerous, which is why so many defragmenting utilities have been developed.

CHKDSK Limitations. In several instances, CHKDSK operates only partially or not at all. CHKDSK does not process volumes or portions of volumes that have been created as follows:

- SUBST command volumes
- ASSIGN command volumes
- JOIN command subdirectories
- Network volumes

SUBST Problems. The SUBST command creates a virtual volume, which is actually an existing volume's subdirectory using another volume specifier (drive letter) as an alias. To analyze the files in a subdirectory created with SUBST, you must give the TRUENAME or actual path name to the files. TRUENAME is an undocumented command in DOS 4.0 and later versions that shows the actual path name for a volume that has been created by the SUBST command.

You also can use the SUBST command to find out the TRUENAME of a particular volume. Suppose that you use SUBST to create volume E: from the C:\AUTO\SPECS directory, as follows:

```
C:\>SUBST E: C:\AUTO\SPECS
```

After entering the following two commands to change to the E: volume and execute a CHKDSK of the volume and files there, you see the resulting error message:

```
C:\>E:

E:\>CHKDSK *.*

Cannot CHKDSK a SUBSTed or ASSIGNed drive
```

To run CHKDSK on the files on this virtual volume E:, you must find the actual path the volume represents. You can do so by entering the SUBST command (with no parameters):

```
E:\>SUBST

E: => C:\AUTO\SPECS
```

You can also find the actual path with the undocumented TRUENAME command (in DOS 4.0 and later versions only), as follows:

```
E:\>TRUENAME E:

C:\AUTO\SPECS
```

After finding the path to the files, you can issue the appropriate CHKDSK command to check the volume and files:

```
E:\>CHKDSK C:\AUTO\SPECS\*.*

Volume 4GB_SCSI    created 08-31-1994 5:05p
Volume Serial Number is 1882-18CF

2,146,631,680 bytes total disk space
      163,840 bytes in 3 hidden files
   16,220,160 bytes in 495 directories
  861,634,560 bytes in 10,355 user files
1,268,613,120 bytes available on disk

       32,768 bytes in each allocation unit
       65,510 total allocation units on disk
       38,715 available allocation units on disk

      655,360 total bytes memory
      632,736 bytes free

All specified file(s) are contiguous
```

ASSIGN Problems. Similarly, CHKDSK does not process a disk drive that has been altered by the ASSIGN command. For example, if you have given the command ASSIGN A=B, you cannot analyze drive A: unless you first unassign the disk drive with the ASSIGN command, that is, ASSIGN A=A.

JOIN Problems. CHKDSK does not process a directory tree section created by the JOIN command (which joins a physical disk volume to another disk volume as a subdirectory), nor does it process the actual joined physical drive because such a drive is an invalid drive specification, according to DOS. On volumes on which you have used the JOIN command, CHKDSK processes the actual portion of the volume and then displays this warning error message:

```
Directory is joined
tree past this point not processed
```

This message indicates that the command cannot process the directory on which you have used JOIN. CHKDSK then continues processing the rest of the volume and outputs the requested volume information.

Network Problems. CHKDSK does not process a networked (shared) disk on either the server or workstation side. In other words, at the file server, you cannot use CHKDSK on any volume that has any portion of itself accessible to remote network stations. At any network station, you can run CHKDSK only on volumes physically attached to that specific station and not on any volume accessed through the network software. If you attempt to run CHKDSK from a server or a workstation on a volume shared on a network, you see this error message:

```
Cannot CHKDSK a network drive
```

If you want to run CHKDSK on the volume, you must go to the specific PC on which the volume physically exists and suspend or disable any sharing of the volume during the CHKDSK.

CHKDSK Command Output. CHKDSK normally displays the following information about a disk volume:

- Volume name and creation date
- Volume serial number
- Number of bytes in total disk space
- Number of files and bytes in hidden files
- Number of files and bytes in directories
- Number of files and bytes in user files
- Number of bytes in bad sectors (unallocated clusters)
- Number of bytes available on disk
- Number of bytes in total memory (RAM)

- Number of bytes in free memory
- Error messages if disk errors are encountered

By using optional parameters, CHKDSK also can show the following:

- Names and number of fragments in noncontiguous files
- Names of all directories and files on disk

If a volume name or volume serial number does not exist on a particular volume, that information is not displayed. If no clusters are marked as bad in the volume's FAT, CHKDSK returns no display of bytes in bad sectors.

For example, suppose that a disk was formatted under DOS 6.2 with the following command:

C:\>FORMAT A: /F:720 /U /S /V:floppy_disk

The output of the FORMAT command looks like this:

```
Insert new diskette for drive A:
and press ENTER when ready...

Formatting 720K
Format complete.
System transferred


      730,112 bytes total disk space
      135,168 bytes used by system
      594,944 bytes available on disk

        1,024 bytes in each allocation unit.
          581 allocation units available on disk.

Volume Serial Number is 266D-1DDC

Format another (Y/N)?
```

The status report at the end of the FORMAT operation is similar to the output of the CHKDSK command. The output of the CHKDSK command when run on this disk would appear as follows:

```
C:\>CHKDSK A:

Volume FLOPPY_DISK created 01-16-1994 10:18p
Volume Serial Number is 266D-1DDC

      730,112 bytes total disk space
       79,872 bytes in 2 hidden files
       55,296 bytes in 1 user files
      594,944 bytes available on disk

        1,024 bytes in each allocation unit
```

```
         713 total allocation units on disk
         581 available allocation units on disk

     655,360 total bytes memory
     632,736 bytes free
```

In this case, CHKDSK shows the volume name and serial number information because the FORMAT command placed a volume label on the disk with the /V: parameter, and FORMAT under DOS 4.0 and later versions automatically places the volume serial number on a disk. Note that three total files are on the disk, two of which have the HIDDEN attribute. DOS versions earlier than 5.0 report the Volume Label "FLOPPY_DISK" as a third hidden file. To see the names of the hidden files, you can execute the CHKDSK command with the /V parameter, as follows:

```
C:\>CHKDSK A: /V

Volume FLOPPY_DISK created 01-16-1994 10:18p
Volume Serial Number is 266D-1DDC
Directory A:\
A:\IO.SYS
A:\MSDOS.SYS
A:\COMMAND.COM

     730,112 bytes total disk space
      79,872 bytes in 2 hidden files
      55,296 bytes in 1 user files
     594,944 bytes available on disk

       1,024 bytes in each allocation unit
         713 total allocation units on disk
         581 available allocation units on disk

     655,360 total bytes memory
     632,736 bytes free
```

With the /V parameter, CHKDSK lists the names of all directories and files across the entire disk, which in this example is only three total files. CHKDSK does not identify which of the files are hidden, it simply lists them all. Note that the DIR command in DOS versions 5.0 and higher can specifically show hidden files with the /AH parameter. The DOS System files are the first two files on a bootable disk and normally have HIDDEN, SYSTEM, and READ-ONLY attributes. After listing how many bytes are used by the hidden and normal files, CHKDSK lists how much total space is available on the disk.

If you are using DOS 4.0 or a later version, CHKDSK also tells you the size of each allocation unit (or cluster), the total number of allocation units present, and the number not currently being used.

Finally, CHKDSK counts the total amount of conventional memory or DOS-usable RAM (in this case, 640K or 655,360 bytes) and displays the number of bytes of memory currently unused or free. This information tells you the size of the largest executable program you can run.

CHKDSK under DOS versions 3.3 and earlier does not recognize the IBM PS/2 Extended BIOS Data Area (which uses the highest 1K of addresses in contiguous conventional memory) and therefore reports only 639K, or 654,336 bytes, of total memory. For most IBM PS/2 systems with 640K of contiguous memory addressed before the video wall, the Extended BIOS Data Area occupies the 640th K. DOS 4.0 and later versions provide the correct 640K report.

During the FORMAT of the disk in the example, the FORMAT program did not find any unreadable sectors. Therefore, no clusters were marked in the FAT as bad or unusable, and CHKDSK did not display the `xxxxxxxxx Bytes in bad sectors` message. Even if the disk had developed bad sectors since the FORMAT operation, CHKDSK still would not display any bytes in bad sectors because it does not test for and count bad sectors: CHKDSK reads the FAT and reports on whether the FAT says that there are any bad sectors. CHKDSK does not really count sectors; it counts clusters (allocation units) because that is how the FAT system operates.

Although bytes in bad sectors sounds like a problem or error message, it is not. The report is simply stating that a certain number of clusters are marked as bad in the FAT and that DOS therefore will never use those clusters. Because nearly all hard disks are manufactured and sold with defective areas, this message is not uncommon. In fact, the higher quality hard disks on the market tend to have more bad sectors than the lower quality drives, based on the manufacturer defect list shipped with the drive (indicating all the known defective spots). Many of the newest controllers allow for sector and track sparing, in which the defects are mapped out of the DOS readable area so that DOS never has to handle them. This procedure is almost standard in drives that have embedded controllers, such as IDE (Integrated Drive Electronics) or SCSI (Small Computer Systems Interface) drives.

Suppose that you use a utility program to mark two clusters (150 and 151, for example) as bad in the FAT of the 720K floppy disk formatted earlier. CHKDSK then reports this information:

```
Volume FLOPPY_DISK created 01-16-1994 10:18p
Volume Serial Number is 266D-1DDC

      730,112 bytes total disk space
       79,872 bytes in 2 hidden files
       55,296 bytes in 1 user files
        2,048 bytes in bad sectors
      592,896 bytes available on disk

        1,024 bytes in each allocation unit
          713 total allocation units on disk
          579 available allocation units on disk

      655,360 total bytes memory
      632,736 bytes free
```

CHKDSK reports 2,048 bytes in bad sectors, which corresponds exactly to the two clusters just marked as bad. These clusters, of course, are perfectly good—you simply marked them as bad in the FAT. Using disk editor utility programs such as those supplied with the Norton or Mace Utilities, you can alter the FAT in almost any way you want.

CHKDSK Operation. Although bytes in bad sectors do not constitute an error or problem, CHKDSK reports problems on a disk volume with a variety of error messages. When CHKDSK discovers an error in the FAT or directory system, it reports the error with one of several descriptive messages that vary to fit the specific error. Sometimes the messages are cryptic or misleading. CHKDSK does not specify how an error should be handled; it does not tell you whether CHKDSK can repair the problem or whether you must use some other utility, or what the consequences of the error and the repair will be. Neither does CHKDSK tell you what caused the problem or how to avoid repeating the problem.

The primary function of CHKDSK is to compare the directory and FAT to determine whether they agree with one another—whether all the data in the directory for files (such as the starting cluster and size information) corresponds to what is in the FAT (such as chains of clusters with end-of-chain indicators). CHKDSK also checks subdirectory file entries, as well as the special . and .. entries that tie the subdirectory system together.

The second function of CHKDSK is to implement repairs to the disk structure. CHKDSK patches the disk so that the directory and FAT are in alignment and agreement. From a repair standpoint, understanding CHKDSK is relatively easy. CHKDSK almost always modifies the directories on a disk to correspond to what is found in the FAT. In only a couple of special cases does CHKDSK modify the FAT; when it does, the FAT modifications are always the same type of simple change.

Think of CHKDSK's repair capability as a directory patcher. Because CHKDSK cannot repair most types of FAT damage effectively, it simply modifies the disk directories to match whatever problems are found in the FAT.

CHKDSK is not a very smart repair program and often can do more damage repairing the disk than if it had left the disk alone. In many cases, the information in the directories is correct and can be used (by some other utility) to help repair the FAT tables. If you have run CHKDSK with the /F parameter, however, the original directory information no longer exists, and a good FAT repair is impossible. You therefore should never run CHKDSK with the /F parameter without first running it in read-only mode (without the /F parameter) to determine whether and to what extent damage exists.

Only after carefully examining the disk damage and determining how CHKDSK would fix the problems do you run CHKDSK with the /F parameter. If you do not specify the /F parameter when you run CHKDSK, the program is prevented from making corrections to the disk. Rather, it performs repairs in a mock fashion. This limitation is a safety feature because you do not want CHKDSK to take action until you have examined the problem. After deciding whether CHKDSK will make the correct assumptions about the damage, you might want to run it with the /F parameter.

Sometimes people place a CHKDSK /F command in their AUTOEXEC.BAT file—*a very dangerous practice*. If a system's disk directories and FAT system become damaged, attempting to load a program whose directory and FAT entries are damaged might lock the system. If, after you reboot, CHKDSK is fixing the problem because it is in the AUTOEXEC.BAT, it can irreparably damage the file structure of the disk. In many cases, CHKDSK ends up causing more damage than originally existed, and no easy way exists to undo the CHKDSK repair. Because CHKDSK is a simple utility that makes often faulty assumptions in repairing a disk, you must run it with great care when you specify the /F parameter.

Problems reported by CHKDSK are usually problems with the software and not the hardware. You rarely see a case in which lost clusters, allocation errors, or cross-linked files reported by CHKDSK were caused directly by a hardware fault, although it is certainly possible. The cause is usually a defective program or a program that was stopped before it could close files or purge buffers. A hardware fault certainly can stop a program before it can close files, but many people think that these error messages signify fault with the disk hardware—almost never the case.

I recommend running CHKDSK at least once a day on a hard disk system because it is important to find out about file structure errors as soon as possible. Accordingly, placing a CHKDSK command in your AUTOEXEC.BAT file is a good idea, but do not use the /F parameter. Also run CHKDSK whenever you suspect that directory or FAT damage might have occurred. For example, whenever a program terminates abnormally or a system crashes for some reason, run CHKDSK to see whether any file system damage has occurred.

Common Errors. All CHKDSK can do is compare the directory and FAT structures to see whether they support or comply with one another; as a result, CHKDSK can detect only certain kinds of problems. When CHKDSK discovers discrepancies between the directory and the FAT structures, they almost always fall into one of the following categories (these errors are the most common ones you will see with CHKDSK):

- Lost allocation units
- Allocation errors
- Cross-linked files
- Invalid allocation units

The RECOVER Command

The DOS RECOVER command is designed to mark clusters as bad in the FAT when the clusters cannot be read properly. When a file cannot be read because of a problem with a sector on the disk going bad, the RECOVER command can mark the FAT so that those clusters are not used by another file. Used improperly, this program is highly dangerous.

Many users think that RECOVER is used to recover a file or the data within the file in question. What really happens is that only the portion of the file before the defect is recovered and remains after the RECOVER command operates on it. RECOVER marks the defective portion as bad in the FAT and returns to available status all the data after the defect. Always make a copy of the file to be recovered before using RECOVER because the COPY command can get all the information, including the portion of the file after the location of the defect.

Suppose that you are using a word processing program. You start the program and tell it to load a file called DOCUMENT.TXT. The hard disk has developed a defect in a sector used by this file, and in the middle of loading it, you see this message appear on-screen:

```
Sector not found error reading drive C
Abort, Retry, Ignore, Fail?
```

You might be able to read the file on a retry, so try several times. If you can load the file by retrying, save the loaded version as a file with a different name to preserve the data in the file. You still have to repair the structure of the disk to prevent the space from being used again.

After 10 retries or so, if you still cannot read the file, the data will be more difficult to recover. This operation has two phases, as follows:

- Preserve as much of the data in the file as possible.
- Mark the FAT so that the bad sectors or clusters of the disk are not used again.

Preserving Data. To recover the data from a file, use the DOS COPY command to make a copy of the file with a different name; for example, if the file you are recovering has the name DOCUMENT.TXT and you want the copy to be named DOCUMENT.NEW, enter the following at the DOS prompt:

COPY document.txt document.new

In the middle of the copy, you see the `Sector not found` error message again. The key to this operation is to answer with the (I)gnore option. Then the bad sectors are ignored, and the copy operation can continue to the end of the file. This procedure produces a copy of the file with all the file intact, up to the error location and after the error location. The bad sectors appear as gibberish or garbage in the new copied file, but the entire copy is readable. Use your word processor to load the new copy and remove or retype the garbled sectors. If this file were a binary file (such as a part of a program), you probably would have to consider the whole thing a total loss because you generally do not have the option of retyping the bytes that make up a program file. Your only hope then is to replace the file from a backup. This step completes phase one, which recovers as much of the data as possible. Now you go to phase two, in which you mark the disk so that these areas will not be used again.

Marking Bad Sectors. You mark bad sectors on a disk by using the RECOVER command. After making the attempted recovery of the data, you can use the following RECOVER command at the DOS prompt to mark the sectors as bad in the FAT:

RECOVER document.txt

In this case, the output of the RECOVER command looks like this:

```
Press any key to begin recovery of the file(s) on drive C:
XXXXX of YYYYY bytes recovered
```

The DOCUMENT.TXT file still is on the disk after this operation, but it has been truncated at the location of the error. Any sectors the RECOVER command cannot read are marked as bad sectors in the FAT and will show up the next time you run CHKDSK. You might want to run CHKDSK before and after running RECOVER to see the effect of the additional bad sectors.

After using RECOVER, delete the DOCUMENT.TXT file because you have already created a copy of it that contains as much good data as possible.

This step completes phase two—and the entire operation. You now have a new file that contains as much of the original file as possible, and the disk FAT is marked so that the defective location will not be a bother.

Caution

Be very careful when you use RECOVER. Used improperly, it can do much damage to your files and the FAT. If you enter the RECOVER command without a filename for it to work on, the program assumes that you want every file on the disk recovered, and operates on every file and subdirectory on the disk; it converts all subdirectories to files, places all filenames in the root directory, and gives them new names (FILE0000.REC, FILE0001.REC, and so on). This process essentially wipes out the file system on the entire disk. *Do not use RECOVER without providing a filename for it to work on.* This program should be considered as dangerous as the FORMAT command.

When you get the `Sector not found` error reading drive C:, rather than using the DOS RECOVER command, use the Norton Disk Doctor, or a similar utility, to repair the problem. If the error is on a floppy disk, use Norton's DiskTool before you use Disk Doctor. DiskTool is designed to help you recover data from a defective floppy disk. Disk Doctor and DiskTool preserve as much of the data in the file as possible, and afterward mark the FAT so that the bad sectors or clusters of the disk are not used again. These Norton Utilities also save UNDO information, making it possible for you to reverse any data recovery operation.

http://www.symantec.com/lit/util/doswinut/doswinut.html

On the Web

SCANDISK

SCANDISK is included with DOS 6 and higher versions as well as Windows 95. This program is more thorough and comprehensive than CHKDSK or RECOVER, and can perform the functions of both of them. It is more like a scaled down version of the Norton Disk Doctor program, and it can verify both file structure as well as disk sector integrity. If problems are found, the directory and File Allocation Tables (FATs) can be repaired. If bad sectors are found in the middle of a file, the clusters (allocation units) containing the bad sectors will be marked bad in the FAT, and an attempt to read the file data and reroute around the defect will be made. Although SCANDISK is good, I would normally recommend using one of the commercial packages like the Norton Utilities for any major problems. These utilities go far beyond what is included in DOS or Windows.

The DEBUG Program

The DOS DEBUG program is a powerful debugging tool for programmers who develop programs in assembly language. The following list shows some of the things you can do with DEBUG:

- Display data from any memory location.

- Display or alter the contents of the CPU registers.
- Display the assembly source code of programs.
- Enter data directly into any memory location.
- Input from a port.
- Move blocks of data between memory locations.
- Output to a port.
- Perform hexadecimal addition and subtraction.
- Read disk sectors into memory.
- Trace the execution of a program.
- Write disk sectors from memory.
- Write short assembly language programs.

To use the DEBUG program, make sure that DEBUG.COM is in the current directory or in the current DOS PATH. The following is the DEBUG command syntax:

DEBUG *[d:][path][filename][arglist]*

Entering DEBUG alone at the DOS prompt launches DEBUG. The *d\path* option represents the drive and directory where the file you want to debug is located. The *filename* entry represents the file you want to debug, and when you want to use DEBUG to work on a file, the filename is mandatory. The *arglist* entry represents parameters and switches that are passed to a program being debugged and can be used only if the file name is present.

After DEBUG is executed, its prompt is displayed (the DEBUG prompt is a hyphen). At the DEBUG hyphen prompt, you can enter a DEBUG command.

Because more powerful programs are available for debugging and assembling code, the most common use for DEBUG is patching assembly language programs to correct problems, changing an existing program feature, or patching disk sectors.

DEBUG Commands and Parameters

The documentation for DEBUG no longer is provided in the standard DOS manual. If you are serious about using DEBUG, you should purchase the *DOS Technical Reference Manual*, which contains the information you need to use this program. Many third-party books also provide documentation of the DEBUG commands and parameters.

As a quick reference to the DEBUG program, the following is a brief description of each command:

A address assembles macro assembler statements directly into memory.

C range address compares the contents of two blocks of memory.

D address or *D range* displays the contents of a portion of memory.

E address displays bytes sequentially and enables them to be modified.

E address list replaces the contents of one or more bytes, starting at the specified address, with values contained in the list.

F range list fills the memory locations in the range with the values specified.

G processes the program you are debugging without breakpoints.

G =address processes instructions beginning at the address specified.

G =address address processes instructions beginning at the address specified. This command stops the processing of the program when the instruction at the specified address is reached (breakpoint), and displays the registers, flags, and the next instruction to be processed. As many as 10 breakpoints can be listed.

H value value adds the two hexadecimal values and then subtracts the second from the first. It displays the sum and the difference on one line.

I portaddress inputs and displays (in hexadecimal) one byte from the specified port.

L address loads a file.

L address drive sector sector loads data from the disk specified by drive and places the data in memory beginning at the specified address.

M range address moves the contents of the memory locations specified by range to the locations beginning at the address specified.

N filename defines file specifications or other parameters required by the program being debugged.

O portaddress byte sends the byte to the specified output port.

P =address value causes the processing of a subroutine call, a loop instruction, an interrupt, or a repeat-string instruction to stop at the next instruction.

Q ends the DEBUG program.

R displays the contents of all registers and flags and the next instruction to be processed.

R F displays all flags.

R registername displays the contents of a register.

S range list searches the range for the characters in the list.

T =address value processes one or more instructions starting with the instructions at CS:IP, or at =address if it is specified. This command also displays the contents of all registers and flags after each instruction is processed.

U address unassembles instructions (translates the contents of memory into assembler-like statements) and displays their addresses and hexadecimal values, together with assembler-like statements.

W address enables you to use the WRITE command without specifying parameters or by specifying only the address parameter.

W address drive sector sector writes data to disk beginning at a specified address.

XA count allocates a specified number of expanded memory pages to a handle.

XD handle deallocates a handle.

XM lpage ppage handle maps an EMS logical page to an EMS physical page from an EMS handle.

XS displays the status of expanded memory.

Changing Disks and Files. DEBUG can be used to modify sectors on a disk. Suppose that you use the following DEBUG command:

```
-L 100 1 0 1
```

This command loads into the current segment at an offset of 100h, sectors from drive B:\ (1), starting with sector 0 (the DOS volume boot sector), for a total of 1 or more sectors.

You then could write this sector to a file on drive C:\ by using these commands:

```
-N C:\B-BOOT.SEC

-R CX

CX 0000

:200

-W

Writing 00200 bytes

-Q
```

The Name command sets up the name of the file to read or write.

The Register command enables you to inspect and change the contents of registers. The CX register contains the low-order bytes indicating the size of the file to load or save, and the BX register contains the high-order bytes. You would not need to set the BX register to anything but 0 unless the file was to be more than 65535 (64K) bytes in size. Setting the CX register to 200 indicates a file size of 200h, or 512 bytes.

The Write command saves 512 bytes of memory, starting at the default address of offset 100, to the file indicated in the Name command.

After quitting the program, your C:\ drive will have a file called B-BOOT.SEC that contains an image of the DOS volume boot sector on drive B:\.

Memory-Resident Software Conflicts

One area that gives many users trouble is a type of memory-resident software called Terminate and Stay Resident (TSR) or *pop-up utilities*. This software loads itself into memory and stays there, waiting for an activation key (usually a keystroke combination).

The problem with pop-up utilities is that they often conflict with each other, as well as with application programs and even DOS. Pop-up utilities can cause many types of problems. Sometimes the problems appear consistently, and at other times they are intermittent. Some computer users do not like to use pop-up utilities unless absolutely necessary because of their potential for problems.

Other memory-resident programs, such as MOUSE.COM, are usually loaded in AUTOEXEC.BAT. These memory-resident programs usually do not cause the kind of conflicts that pop-up utilities do, mainly because pop-up utilities are constantly monitoring the keyboard for the hotkey that activates them (and pop-up utilities are known to barge into memory addresses being used by other programs in order to monitor the keyboard, or to activate). Memory-resident programs like MOUSE.COM are merely installed in memory, do not poll the keyboard for a hotkey, and generally do not clash with the memory addresses used by other programs.

Device drivers loaded in CONFIG.SYS are another form of memory-resident software and can cause many problems.

If you are experiencing problems that you have traced to any of the three types of memory-resident programs, a common way to correct the problem is to eliminate the conflicting program. Another possibility is to change the order in which device drivers and memory-resident programs are loaded into system memory. Some programs must be loaded first, and others must be loaded last. Sometimes this order preference is indicated in the documentation for the programs, but often it is discovered through trial and error.

Unfortunately, conflicts between memory-resident programs are likely to be around as long as DOS is used. The light at the end of the tunnel is operating systems like Windows 95, Windows NT, and OS/2. The problem with DOS is that it establishes no real rules for how resident programs must interact with each other and the rest of the system. Windows 95, Windows NT, and OS/2 are built on the concept of many programs being resident in memory at one time, and all multitasking. These operating systems should put an end to the problem of resident programs conflicting with each other.

Hardware Problems versus Software Problems

One of the most aggravating situations in computer repair is opening up a system and troubleshooting all the hardware just to find that the cause of the problem is a software program, not the hardware. Many people have spent large sums of money on replacement hardware such as motherboards, disk drives, adapter boards, cables, and so on, all on the premise that the hardware was causing problems, when software was actually the culprit. To eliminate these aggravating, sometimes embarrassing, and often expensive situations, you must be able to distinguish a hardware problem from a software problem.

Fortunately, making this distinction can be relatively simple. Software problems often are caused by device drivers and memory-resident programs loaded in CONFIG.SYS and

AUTOEXEC.BAT on many systems. One of the first things to do when you begin having problems with your system is to boot the system from a DOS disk that has no CONFIG.SYS or AUTOEXEC.BAT configuration files on it. Then test for the problem. If it has disappeared, the cause was probably something in one or both of those files. To find the problem, begin restoring device drivers and memory-resident programs to CONFIG.SYS and AUTOEXEC.BAT one at a time (starting with CONFIG.SYS). For example, add one program back to CONFIG.SYS, reboot your system, and then determine if the problem has reappeared. When you discover the device driver or memory-resident program causing the problem, you might be able to solve the problem by editing CONFIG.SYS and AUTOEXEC.BAT to change the order in which device drivers and memory-resident programs are loaded, or you might have to eliminate the problem device driver or memory-resident program.

If you are using these files in Windows 95, the same procedures apply. Windows 95 also adds the SYSTEM.DAT registry file, which contains the equivalent functions of CONFIG.SYS and AUTOEXEC.BAT. By changing or removing entries from the registry, you can perform the same troubleshooting procedures with Windows 95 as with plain DOS.

DOS can cause other problems, such as bugs or incompatibilities with certain hardware items. For example, DOS 3.2 does not support the 1.44M floppy drive format; therefore, using DOS 3.2 on a system equipped with a 1.44M floppy drive might lead you to believe (incorrectly) that the drive is bad. Make sure that you are using the correct version of DOS and that support is provided for your hardware. Find out whether your version of DOS has any official patches available; sometimes a problem you are experiencing might be one that many others have had, and IBM or Microsoft might have released a fix disk that takes care of the problem. For example, many PS/2 users have a floppy formatting problem under DOS 3.3. They get a `track 0 bad` message after answering Yes to the `Format another diskette` message. This problem is solved by a special driver file on the DOS 3.3 patch disk.

If you are having a problem related to a piece of application software, a word processor or spreadsheet, for example, contact the company that produces the software and explain the problem. If the software has a bug, the company might have a patched or fixed version available, or it might be able to help you operate the software in a different way to solve the problem.

Summary

This chapter examined the software side of your system. Often a system problem is in the software and is not hardware-related. The chapter also examined DOS and Windows, showing how information is organized on a disk. You learned about the CHKDSK, RECOVER, SCANDISK, and DEBUG commands to see how these utilities can help you with data and disk recovery. Finally, the chapter described memory-resident software and some of the problems it can cause, and informed you how to distinguish a software problem from a hardware problem.

Chapter 23

IBM Personal Computer Family Hardware

This chapter serves as a technical reference to IBM's original family of personal computer system units and accessories. It separates and identifies each personal computer system originally offered by IBM, including the complete line of PC systems that have been discontinued. Because the entire original line was discontinued long ago, much of this chapter can be considered a history lesson. The information still is valuable, however, because many people still own and manage these older systems, which are more likely to break down than newer ones. Also nearly every PC-compatible or clone system on the market today is based on one or more of these IBM products. The original line of systems are often called Industry Standard Architecture (ISA) systems, or Classic PCs. IBM calls them Family/1 systems.

This chapter is a reference specific to the original line of true IBM PC, XT, and AT systems. Issues affecting PC-compatible systems are examined in more detail separately in Chapter 19, "Building a System," but even people that do not own IBM systems will find this chapter filled with interesting and useful information. After all, the entire PC-compatible market was started by companies who cloned, copied, or emulated the features of a particular IBM system or combination of systems. For upgrade and repair purposes, most PC-compatible systems are treated in the same manner as the original IBM systems. Most compatible systems can exchange parts easily with these original IBM systems and vice versa. These original IBM systems defined the form factors or shapes that are still in use in the PC compatibles today.

In Chapter 2, "Overview of System Features and Components," you learned that all systems can be broken down into two basic types: 8-bit (PC/XT type) or 16/32/64-bit (AT type). The AT types of systems can be broken down into several subtypes. These subtypes can be classified according to their main bus design, including systems with Industry Standard Architecture (ISA), Extended Industry Standard Architecture (EISA), VL (VESA Local) Bus, PCI (Peripheral Component Interconnect), or Micro Channel Architecture (MCA) slots. Use this chapter to compare a compatible system with a specific IBM system in a feature-by-feature comparison. This kind of comparison is often interesting because compatibles usually offer many more features and options at a lower price. I find this information is also useful from a historical perspective. Because the PC compatibles are mostly based on the IBM XT and especially AT systems, you can see where things like the motherboard, case, and power supply shapes came from, the positions of slots, connectors and other components on the boards, and the levels of performance these systems originally offered.

System-Unit Features by Model

In the following sections, you learn the makeup of all the various versions or models of the specific systems and also technical details and specifications of each system. Every system unit has a few standard parts. The primary component is the motherboard, which has the CPU (central processing unit, or microprocessor) and other primary computer circuitry. Each unit also includes a case with an internal power supply, a keyboard, certain standard adapters or plug-in cards, and usually some form of disk drive.

You receive an explanation of each system's various submodels and details about the differences between and features of each model. You learn about the changes from model to model and version to version of each system.

Included for your reference is part-number information for each system and option. This information is for comparison and reference purposes only; all these systems have been discontinued and generally are no longer available. IBM still stocks and sells component parts and assemblies, however, for even these discontinued units. You can (and usually should) replace failed components in these older systems with non-IBM replacement parts because you invariably can obtain upgraded or improved components compared to what IBM offers, and at a greatly reduced price.

An Introduction to the PC

IBM introduced the IBM Personal Computer on August 12, 1981, and officially withdrew the machine from marketing on April 2, 1987. During the nearly six-year life of the PC, IBM made only a few basic changes to the system. The basic motherboard circuit design was changed in April 1983 to accommodate 64K RAM chips. Three different ROM BIOS versions were used during the life of the system; most other specifications, however, remained unchanged. Because IBM no longer markets the PC system, and because of the PC's relatively limited expansion capability and power, the standard PC is obsolete by most standards.

The system unit supports only floppy disk drives unless the power supply is upgraded or an expansion chassis is used to house the hard disk externally. IBM never offered an internal hard disk for the PC but many third-party companies stepped in to fill this void with upgrades. The system unit included many configurations with single or dual floppy disk drives. Early on, one version even was available with no disk drives, and others used single-sided floppy drives. The PC motherboard was based on the 16-bit Intel 8088 microprocessor and included the Microsoft Cassette BASIC language built into ROM. For standard memory, the PC offered configurations with as little as 16K of RAM (when the system was first announced) and as much as 256K on the motherboard. Two motherboard designs were used. Systems sold before March 1983 had a motherboard that supported a maximum of only 64K of RAM, and later systems supported a maximum of 256K on the motherboard. In either case, you added more memory (as much as 640K) by installing memory cards in the expansion slots.

The first bank of memory chips in every PC is soldered to the motherboard. Soldered memory is reliable but not conducive to easy servicing because the solder prevents you from easily exchanging failing memory chips located in the first bank. The chips must be unsoldered and the defective chip replaced with a socket so that a replacement can be plugged in. When IBM services the defective memory, IBM advises you to exchange the entire motherboard. Considering today's value of these systems, replacing the motherboard with one of the many compatible motherboards on the market may be a better idea. Repairing the same defective memory chip in the XT system is much easier because all memory in an XT is socketed.

The only disk drive available from IBM for the PC is a double-sided (320 or 360K) floppy disk drive. You can install a maximum of two drives in the system unit by using IBM-supplied drives, or four using half-height third-party drives and mounting brackets.

The system unit has five slots that support expansion cards for additional devices, features, or memory. All these slots support full-length adapter cards. In most configurations, the PC included at least a floppy disk controller card. You need a second slot for a monitor adapter, which leaves three slots for adapter cards.

All models of the PC have a fan-cooled, 63.5-watt power supply. This low-output power supply doesn't support much in the way of system expansion, especially power-hungry items such as hard disks. Usually, this low-output supply must be replaced by a higher-output unit, such as the one used in the XT. Figure 23.1 shows an interior view of a PC system unit.

An 83-key keyboard with an adjustable typing angle is standard equipment on the PC. The keyboard is attached to the rear of the system unit by a six-foot coiled cable. Figure 23.2 shows the back panel of the PC.

Most model configurations of the PC system unit included these major functional components:

- Intel 8088 microprocessor
- ROM-based diagnostics (POST)
- BASIC language interpreter in ROM
- 256 kilobytes of dynamic RAM
- Floppy disk controller
- One or two 360K floppy drives

- A 63.5-watt power supply
- Five I/O expansion slots
- Socket for the 8087 math coprocessor

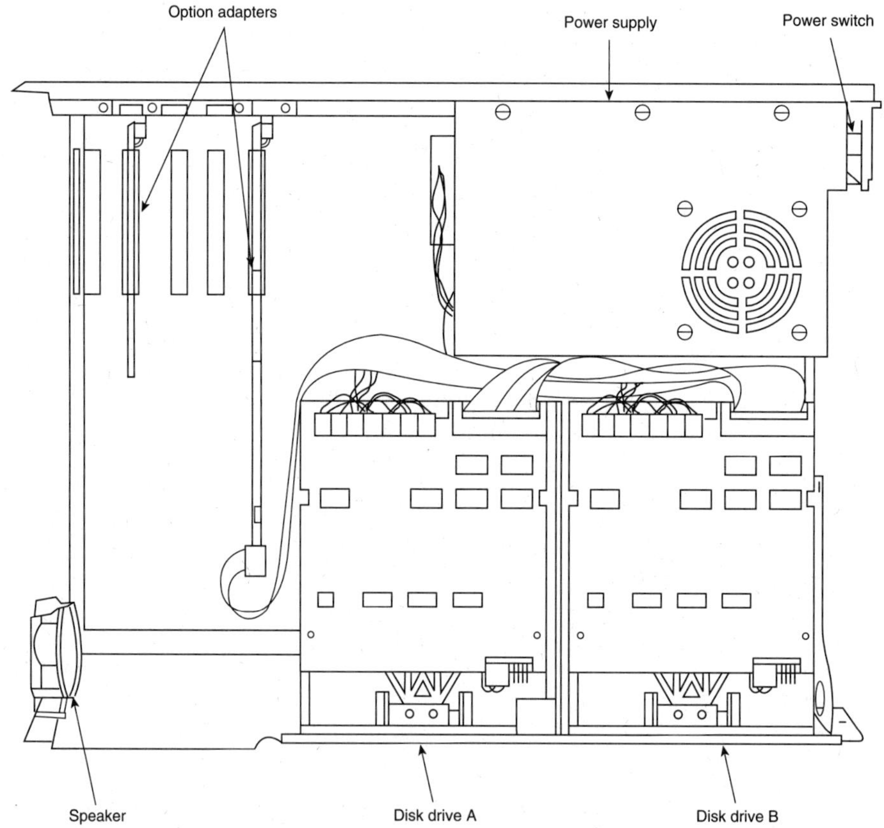

Figure 23.1
The IBM PC interior view.

PC Models and Features

Although several early-model configurations of the IBM PC were available before March 1983, only two models were available after that time. The later models differ only in the number of floppy drives—one or two. IBM designated these models as follows:

IBM PC 5150 Model 166: 256K RAM, one 360K drive

IBM PC 5150 Model 176: 256K RAM, two 360K drives

The PC never was available with a factory-installed hard disk, primarily because the system unit has a limited base for expansion and offered few resources with which to work. After IBM started selling XTs with only floppy disk drives (on April 2, 1985), the PC became obsolete. The XT offered much more for virtually the same price. Investing in a PC after the XT introduction was questionable.

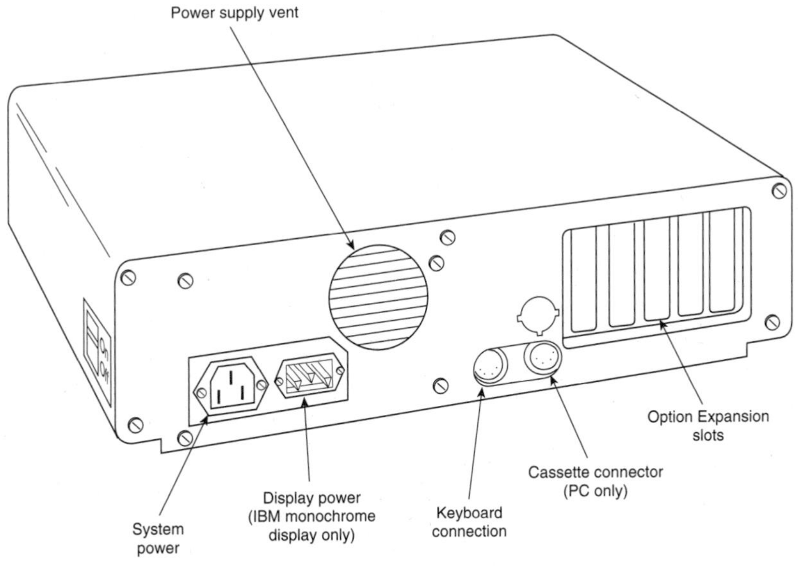

Figure 23.2

The IBM PC rear view.

IBM finally withdrew the PC from the market April 2, 1987. IBM's plans for the system became obvious when the company didn't announce a new model with the Enhanced Keyboard, as it did with other IBM systems.

With some creative purchasing, you can make a usable system of a base PC by adding the requisite components, such as a full 640K of memory and hard and floppy drives. You still may have a slot or two to spare. Unfortunately, expanding this system requires replacing many of the boards in the system unit with boards that combine the same functions in less space. Only you can decide when your money is better invested in a new system.

Before you can think of expanding a PC beyond even a simple configuration, and to allow for compatibility and reliability, you must address the following two major areas:

- ROM BIOS level (version)
- Power supply

In most cases, the power supply is the most critical issue because all PCs sold after March 1983 already have the latest ROM BIOS. If you have an earlier PC system, you also must upgrade the ROM because the early versions lack some required capabilities. Table 23.1 shows the part numbers for the IBM PC system unit.

Table 23.1 IBM PC Part Numbers

Description	Number
PC system unit, 256K, one double-sided drive	5150166
PC system unit, 256K, two double-sided drives	5150176
Options	
PC expansion-unit Model 001 with 10M fixed disk	5161001
Double-sided disk drive	1503810
8087 math coprocessor option	1501002
BIOS update kit	1501005

PC Technical Specifications

Technical information for the personal computer system and keyboard is described in this section. Here, you find information about the system architecture, memory configurations and capacities, standard system features, disk storage, expansion slots, keyboard specifications, and physical and environmental specifications. This kind of information may be useful in determining what parts you need when you are upgrading or repairing these systems. Figure 23.3 shows the layout and components on the PC motherboard.

System Architecture

Microprocessor	8088
Clock speed	4.77 MHz
Bus type	ISA (Industry Standard Architecture)
Bus width	8-bit
Interrupt levels	8
Type	Edge-triggered
Shareable	No
DMA channels	3
DMA burst mode supported	No
Bus masters supported	No
Upgradable processor complex	No

Memory

Standard on system board	16K, 64K, or 256K
Maximum on system board	256K
Maximum total memory	640K
Memory speed (ns) and type	200ns dynamic RAM
System board memory-socket type	16-pin DIP
Number of memory-module sockets	27 (3 banks of 9)
Memory used on system board	27 16K×1-bit or 64K×1-bit DRAM chips in 3 banks of 9, one soldered bank of 9 16K×1-bit or 64K×1-bit chips

Memory

Memory cache controller	No
Wait states:	
System board	1
Adapter	1

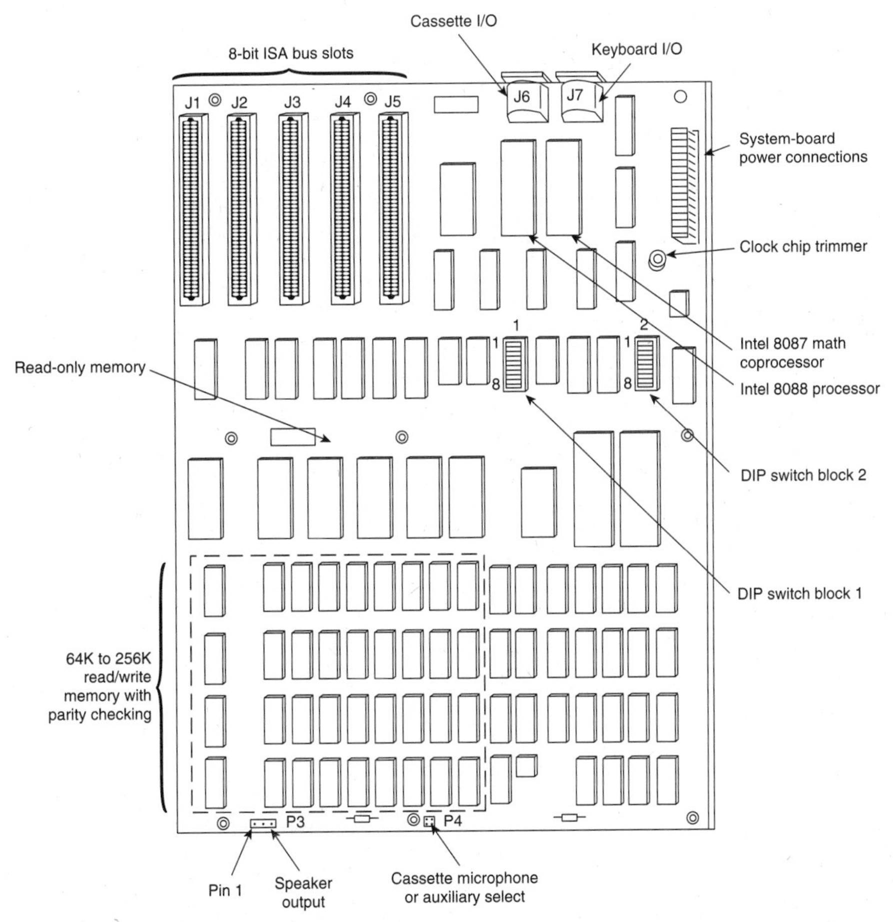

Figure 23.3

The IBM PC motherboard.

Standard Features

ROM size	40K
ROM shadowing	No
Optional math coprocessor	8087
Coprocessor speed	4.77 MHz

(continues)

(continued)

Standard Features	
Standard graphics	None standard
RS232C serial ports	None standard
UART chip used	NS8250B
Maximum speed (bits per second)	9,600 bps
Maximum number of ports supported	2
Pointing device (mouse) ports	None standard
Parallel printer ports	None standard
Bi-directional	No
Maximum number of ports supported	3
CMOS real-time clock (RTC)	No
CMOS RAM	None

Disk Storage	
Internal disk and tape drive bays	2 full-height
Number of 3 1/2-/5 1/4-inch bays	0/2
Standard floppy drives	1×360K
Optional floppy drives:	
5 1/4-inch 360K	Optional
5 1/4-inch 1.2M	No
3 1/2-inch 720K	Optional
3 1/2-inch 1.44M	No
3 1/2-inch 2.88M	No
Hard disk controller included	None

Expansion Slots	
Total adapter slots	5
Number of long and short slots	5/0
Number of 8-/16-/32-bit slots	5/0/0
Available slots (with video)	3

Keyboard Specifications	
101-key Enhanced Keyboard	No, 83-key
Fast keyboard speed setting	No
Keyboard cable length	6 feet

Physical Specifications

Footprint type	Desktop
Dimensions:	
Height	5.5 inches
Width	19.5 inches
Depth	16.0 inches
Weight	25 pounds

Environmental Specifications

Power-supply output	63.5 watts
Worldwide (110/60,220/50)	No
Auto-sensing/switching	No
Maximum current:	
104-127 VAC	2.5 amps
Operating range:	
Temperature	60–90 degrees F
Relative humidity	8–80 percent
Maximum operating altitude	7,000 feet
Heat (BTUs/hour)	505
Noise (Average dB, operating, 1m)	43
FCC classification	Class B

Tables 23.2 and 23.3 show the Switch Settings for the PC (and XT) motherboard. The PC has two eight-position switch blocks (Switch Block 1 and Switch Block 2), whereas the XT has only a single Switch Block 1. The PC used the additional switch block to control the amount of memory the system would recognize, and the XT automatically counted up the memory amount.

Table 23.2 IBM PC/XT Motherboard Switch Settings

SWITCH BLOCK 1 (PC and XT)

Switch 1	**IBM PC Function (PC Only):**
Off	Boot From Floppy Drives
On	Do Not Boot From Floppy Drives
Switch 1	**IBM XT Function (XT Only):**
Off	Normal POST (Power-On Self Test)
On	Continuous Looping POST
Switch 2	**Math Coprocessor (PC/XT):**
Off	Installed
On	Not Installed

(continues)

Table 23.2 Continued

SWITCH BLOCK 1 (PC and XT)		
Switch 3	**Switch 4**	**Installed Motherboard Memory (PC/XT):**
On	On	Bank 0 only
Off	On	Banks 0 and 1
On	Off	Banks 0, 1, and 2
Off	Off	All 4 Banks
Switch 5	**Switch 6**	**Video Adapter Type (PC/XT):**
Off	Off	Monochrome (MDA)
Off	On	Color (CGA) - 40x25 mode
On	Off	Color (CGA) - 80x25 mode
On	On	Any Video Card w/onboard BIOS (EGA/VGA)
Switch 7	**Switch 8**	**Number of Floppy Drives (PC/XT):**
On	On	1 floppy drive
Off	On	2 floppy drives
On	Off	3 floppy drives
Off	Off	4 floppy drives

Table 23.3 SWITCH BLOCK 2 (PC only) Memory Settings

	Switch Number (Switch Block 2, PC Only)							
Memory	**1**	**2**	**3**	**4**	**5**	**6**	**7**	**8**
16K	On	On	On	On	On	Off	Off	Off
32K	On	On	On	On	On	Off	Off	Off
48K	On	On	On	On	On	Off	Off	Off
64K	On	On	On	On	On	Off	Off	Off
96K	Off	On	On	On	On	Off	Off	Off
128K	On	Off	On	On	On	Off	Off	Off
160K	Off	Off	On	On	On	Off	Off	Off
192K	On	On	Off	On	On	Off	Off	Off
224K	Off	On	Off	On	On	Off	Off	Off
256K	On	Off	Off	On	On	Off	Off	Off
288K	Off	Off	Off	On	On	Off	Off	Off
320K	On	On	On	Off	On	Off	Off	Off
352K	Off	On	On	Off	On	Off	Off	Off
384K	On	Off	On	Off	On	Off	Off	Off
416K	Off	Off	On	Off	On	Off	Off	Off
448K	On	On	Off	Off	On	Off	Off	Off
480K	Off	On	Off	Off	On	Off	Off	Off
512K	On	Off	Off	Off	On	Off	Off	Off
544K	Off	Off	Off	Off	On	Off	Off	Off

Memory	Switch Number (Switch Block 2, PC Only) 1	2	3	4	5	6	7	8
576K	On	On	On	On	Off	Off	Off	Off
608K	Off	On	On	On	Off	Off	Off	Off
640K	On	Off	On	On	Off	Off	Off	Off

An Introduction to the PC Convertible

IBM marked its entry into the laptop computer market on April 2, 1986 by introducing the IBM 5140 PC Convertible. The system superseded the 5155 Portable PC (IBM's transportable system), which no longer was available. The IBM 5140 system wasn't a very successful laptop system. Other laptops offered more disk storage, higher processor speeds, more readable screens, lower cost, and more compact cases, which pressured IBM to improve the Convertible. Because the improvements were limited to the display, however, this system never gained respect in the marketplace.

The PC Convertible was available in two models. The Model 2 had a CMOS 80C88 4.77 MHz microprocessor, 64K of ROM, 256K of Static RAM, an 80-column-by-25-line detachable liquid crystal display, two 3 1/2-inch floppy disk drives, a 78-key keyboard, an AC adapter, and a battery pack. Also included were software programs called Application Selector, SystemApps, Tools, Exploring the IBM PC Convertible, and Diagnostics. The Model 22 is the same basic computer as the Model 2 but with the diagnostics software only. You can expand either system to 512K of RAM by using 128K RAM memory-cards, and you can include an internal 1,200 bps modem in the system unit. With aftermarket memory expansion, the computers can reach 640K.

Although the unit was painfully slow at 4.77 MHz, one notable feature is the use of Static memory chips for the system's RAM. Static RAM does not require the refresh signal that normal Dynamic RAM requires, which would normally require about seven percent of the processor's time in a standard PC or XT system. This means that the Convertible is about seven percent faster than an IBM PC or XT even though they all operate at the same clock speed of 4.77 MHz. Because of the increased reliability of the Static RAM (compared to Dynamic RAM) used in the Convertible, as well as the desire to minimize power consumption, none of the RAM in the Convertible is parity checked.

At the back of each system unit is an extendable bus interface. This 72-pin connector enables you to attach the following options to the base unit: a printer, a serial or parallel adapter, and a CRT display adapter. Each feature is powered from the system unit. The CRT display adapter operates only when the system is powered from a standard AC adapter. A separate CRT display or a television set attached through the CRT display adapter requires a separate AC power source.

Each system unit includes a detachable liquid crystal display (LCD). When the computer is not mobile, the LCD screen can be replaced by an external monitor. When the LCD is latched in the closed position, it forms the cover for the keyboard and floppy disk drives. Because the LCD is attached with a quick-disconnect connector, you can remove it easily to place the 5140 system unit below an optional IBM 5144 PC Convertible monochrome or IBM 5145 PC Convertible color display. During the life of the Convertible, IBM offered three different LCD displays. The first display was a standard LCD, which suffered from problems with contrast and readability. Due to complaints, IBM then changed the LCD to a Super Twisted type LCD display, which had much greater contrast. Finally, in the third LCD they added a fluorescent backlight to the Super Twisted LCD display, which not only offered greater contrast, but made the unit usable in low light situations.

The PC Convertible system unit has these standard features:

- Complementary Metal-Oxide Semiconductor (CMOS) 80C88 4.77 MHz microprocessor
- Two 32K CMOS ROMs containing these items:

  POST (Power On Self Test) of system components
  BIOS (basic input-output system) support
  BASIC language interpreter
- 256K CMOS Static RAM (expandable to 512K)
- Two 3 1/2-inch 720K (formatted) floppy drives
- An 80-column-by-25-line detachable LCD panel (graphics modes: 640-by-200 resolution and 320-by-200 resolution)
- LCD controller
- 16K RAM display buffer
- 8K LCD font RAM
- Adapter for optional printer (#4010)
- Professional keyboard (78 keys)
- AC adapter
- Battery pack

The system-unit options for the 5140 are shown in this list:

- 128K Static RAM memory card (#4005)
- Printer (#4010)
- Serial/parallel adapter (#4015)
- CRT display adapter (#4020)
- Internal modem (#4025)
- Printer cable (#4055)
- Battery charger (#4060)
- Automobile power adapter (#4065)

The following two optional displays were available for the PC Convertible:

- IBM 5144 PC Convertible Monochrome Display Model 1
- IBM 5145 PC Convertible Color Display Model 1

PC Convertible Specifications and Highlights

This section lists some technical specifications for the IBM 5140 PC Convertible system. The weights of the unit and options are listed because weight is an important consideration when you carry a laptop system. Figure 23.4 shows the PC Convertible motherboard components and layout.

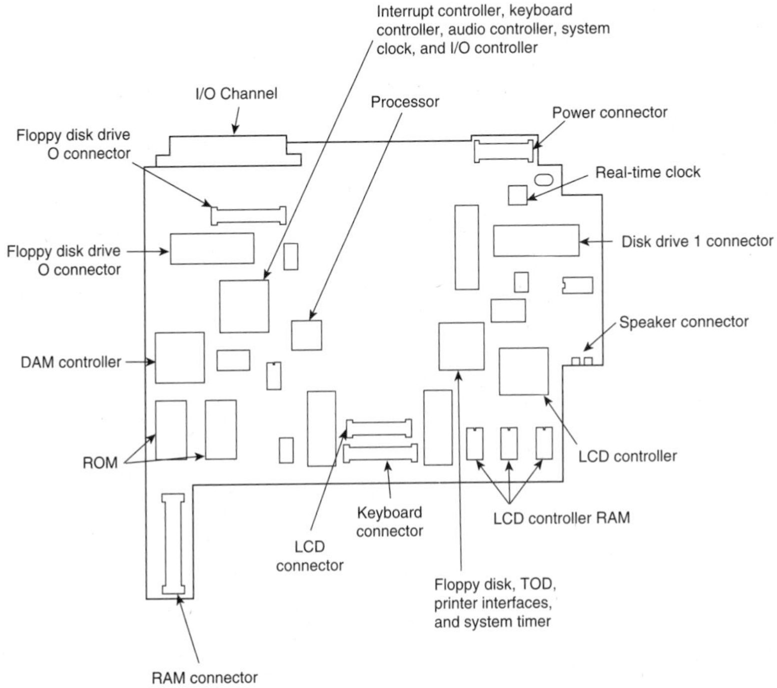

Figure 23.4
The PC Convertible motherboard.

Dimensions

Depth:	360 mm (14.17 inches)
	374 mm (14.72 inches) including handle
Width:	309.6 mm (12.19 inches)
	312 mm (12.28 inches) including handle
Height:	67 mm (2.64 inches)
	68 mm (2.68 inches) including footpads

Weight	
Models 2 and 22 (including battery)	5.5 kg (12.17 pounds)
128K/256K memory card	40 g (1.41 ounces)
Printer	1.6 kg (3.50 pounds)
Serial/parallel adapter	470 g (1.04 pounds)
CRT display adapter	630 g (1.40 pounds)
Internal modem	170 g (6 ounces)
Printer cable	227 g (8 ounces)
Battery charger	340 g (12 ounces)
Automobile power adapter	113 g (4 ounces)
5144 PC Convertible monochrome display	7.3 kg (16 pounds)
5145 PC Convertible color display	16.9 kg (37.04 pounds)

To operate the IBM 5140 PC Convertible properly, you must have PC DOS version 3.2 or later. Previous DOS versions aren't supported because they don't support the 720K floppy drive. Using the CRT display adapter and an external monitor requires that the system unit be operated by power from the AC adapter rather than from the battery.

PC Convertible Models and Features

This section covers the options and special features available for the PC Convertible. Several kinds of options were available, from additional memory to external display adapters, serial/parallel ports, modems, and even printers.

Memory Cards. A 128K or 256K memory card expands the base memory in the system unit. You can add two of these cards, for a system-unit total of 640K with one 256K card and one 128K card.

Optional Printers. An optional printer attaches to the back of the system unit or to an optional printer-attachment cable for adjacent printer operation. The printer's intelligent, microprocessor-based, 40 cps, non-impact dot-matrix design makes it capable of low-power operation. The optional printer draws power from and is controlled by the system unit. Standard ASCII 96-character, upper- and lowercase character sets were printed with a high-resolution, 24-element print head. A mode for graphics capability is provided also. You can achieve near-letter-quality printing by using either a thermal transfer ribbon on smooth paper or no ribbon on heat-sensitive thermal paper.

Serial/Parallel Adapters. A serial/parallel adapter attaches to the back of the system unit, a printer, or other feature module attached to the back of the system unit. The adapter provides an RS-232C asynchronous communications interface and a parallel printer interface, both compatible with the IBM personal computer asynchronous communications adapter and the IBM personal computer parallel printer adapter.

CRT Display Adapters. A CRT display adapter attaches to the back of the system unit, printer, or other feature module attached to the back of the system unit. This adapter enables you to connect to the system a separate CRT display, such as the PC Convertible monochrome display or PC Convertible color display. By using optional connectors or cables, you can use the CRT display adapter also to attach a standard CGA monitor. Because composite video output is available, you also can use a standard television set.

Internal Modems. With an internal modem, you can communicate with compatible computers over telephone lines. It runs Bell 212A (1,200 bps) or Bell 103A (300 bps) protocols. The modem comes as a complete assembly, consisting of two cards connected by a cable. The entire assembly is installed inside the system unit. Over the life of the system, IBM made two different internal modems for the Convertible. The original modem was made for IBM by Novation, and did not follow the Hayes standard for commands and protocols. This rendered the modem largely incompatible with popular software designed to use the Hayes command set. Later, IBM changed the modem to one that was fully Hayes compatible, and this resolved the problems with software. IBM never introduced a modem faster than 1,200 bps for the Convertible. Fortunately, you still can operate a standard external modem through the serial port, although you lose the convenience of having it built in.

Printer Cables. The printer cable is 22 inches (0.6 meter) long with a custom 72-pin connector attached to each end. With this cable, you can operate the Convertible printer when it is detached from the system unit and place the unit for ease of use and visibility.

Battery Chargers. The battery charger is a 110-volt input device that charges the system's internal batteries. It does not provide sufficient power output for the system to operate while the batteries are being charged.

Automobile Power Adapters. An automobile power adapter plugs into the cigarette-lighter outlet in a vehicle with a 12-volt, negative-ground electrical system. You can use the unit while the adapter charges the Convertible's battery.

The IBM 5144 PC Convertible Monochrome Display. The 5144 PC Convertible monochrome display is a nine-inch (measured diagonally) composite video display attached to the system unit through the CRT display adapter. It comes with a display stand, an AC power cord, and a signal cable that connects the 5144 to the CRT display adapter. This display does not resemble—and is not compatible with—the IBM monochrome display for larger PC systems. The CRT adapter emits the same signal as the one supplied by the Color Graphics Adapter for a regular PC. This display is functionally equivalent to the display on the IBM Portable PC.

The IBM 5145 PC Convertible Color Display. The 5145 PC Convertible color display is a 13-inch color display attached to the system unit through the CRT display adapter. It comes with a display stand, an AC power cord, a signal cable that connects the 5145 to the CRT display adapter, and a speaker for external audio output. The monitor is a low-cost unit compatible with the standard IBM CGA display.

Special software available for the Convertible includes these programs:

- The Application Selector program, installed as an extension to DOS, provides a menu-driven interface to select and run applications software, the SystemApps, and Tools.

- The SystemApps program provides basic functions similar to many memory-resident programs on the market. This application, which includes Notewriter, Schedule, Phone List, and Calculator, is equivalent in function to the popular SideKick program.
- You can use the menu-driven Tools program as a front end for DOS to control and maintain the system (copying and erasing files, copying disks, and so on). With DOS, additional functions are available, including printing, formatting, and configuring the Application Selector function keys. This program presents many DOS functions in an easy-to-use menu format.

This additional software, except system diagnostics, is not included with the Model 23. Table 23.4 shows the part numbers of the IBM Convertible system units.

Table 23.4 IBM Convertible Part Numbers

5140 PC Convertible System Units	Number
Two drives, 256K with system applications	5140002
Two drives, 256K without system applications	5140022

An Introduction to the XT

Introduced March 8, 1983, the PC XT with a built-in 10M hard disk (originally standard, later optional) caused a revolution in personal computer configurations. At the time, having even a 10M hard disk was something very special. XT stands for eXTended. IBM chose this name because the IBM PC XT system includes many features not available in the standard PC. The XT has eight slots, allowing increased expansion capabilities; greater power-supply capacity; completely socketed memory; motherboards that support memory expansion to 640K without using an expansion slot; and optional hard disk drives. To obtain these advantages, the XT uses a different motherboard circuit design than the PC.

The system unit was available in several models, with a variety of disk drive configurations: one 360K floppy disk drive; two 360K floppy disk drives; one floppy disk and one hard disk drive; or two floppy disk drives and one hard disk drive. The floppy disk drives were full-height drives in the earlier models, and half-height drives in more recent models. With the four available drive bays, IBM had standard configurations with two floppy drives and a single hard disk, with room for a second hard disk provided all half-height units were used.

IBM offered 10M and 20M, full-height hard disks. In some cases they also installed half-height hard disks, but they were always installed in a bracket and cradle assembly that took up the equivalent space of a full-height drive. If you wanted half-height hard disks (to install two of them stacked, for example), you had to use non-IBM supplied drives or modify the mounting of the IBM supplied half-height unit so that two could fit. Most aftermarket sources for hard disks had mounting kits that would work.

IBM also used double-sided (320/360K) floppy disk drives in full- or half-height configurations. A 3 1/2-inch 720K floppy disk drive was available in more recent models. The 3 1/2-inch drives were available in a normal internal configuration or as an external device. You could install a maximum of two floppy disk drives and one hard disk drive in the system unit, using IBM-supplied drives. With half-height hard disks, you could install two hard drives in the system unit.

The XT is based on the same 8- and 16-bit Intel 8088 microprocessor (the CPU has 16-bit registers but only an 8-bit data bus) as the PC and runs at the same clock speed. Operationally, the XT systems are identical to the PC systems except for the hard disk. All models have at least one 360K floppy disk drive and a keyboard. For standard memory, the XT offers 256K or 640K on the main board. The hard disk models also include a serial adapter.

The system unit has eight slots that support cards for additional devices, features, or memory. Two of the slots support only short option cards because of physical interference from the disk drives. The XT has at least a disk drive adapter card in the floppy-disk-only models, and a hard disk controller card and serial adapter in the hard disk models. Either five or seven expansion slots (depending on the model) therefore are available. Figure 23.5 shows the interior of an XT.

All XT models include a heavy-duty, fan-cooled, 130-watt power supply to support the greater expansion capabilities and disk drive options. The power supply has more than double the capacity of the PC's supply, and can easily support hard disk drives as well as the full complement of expansion cards.

An 83-key keyboard was standard equipment with the early XT models, but was changed to an enhanced 101-key unit in the more recent models. The keyboard is attached to the system unit by a six-foot coiled cable.

All models of the PC XT system unit contain these major functional components:

- Intel 8088 microprocessor
- ROM-based diagnostics (POST)
- BASIC language interpreter in ROM
- 256K or 640K of dynamic RAM
- Floppy disk controller
- One 360K floppy drive (full- or half-height)
- 10M or 20M hard disk drive with interface (enhanced models)
- Serial interface (enhanced models)
- Heavy-duty, 135-watt power supply
- Eight I/O expansion slots
- Socket for 8087 math coprocessor

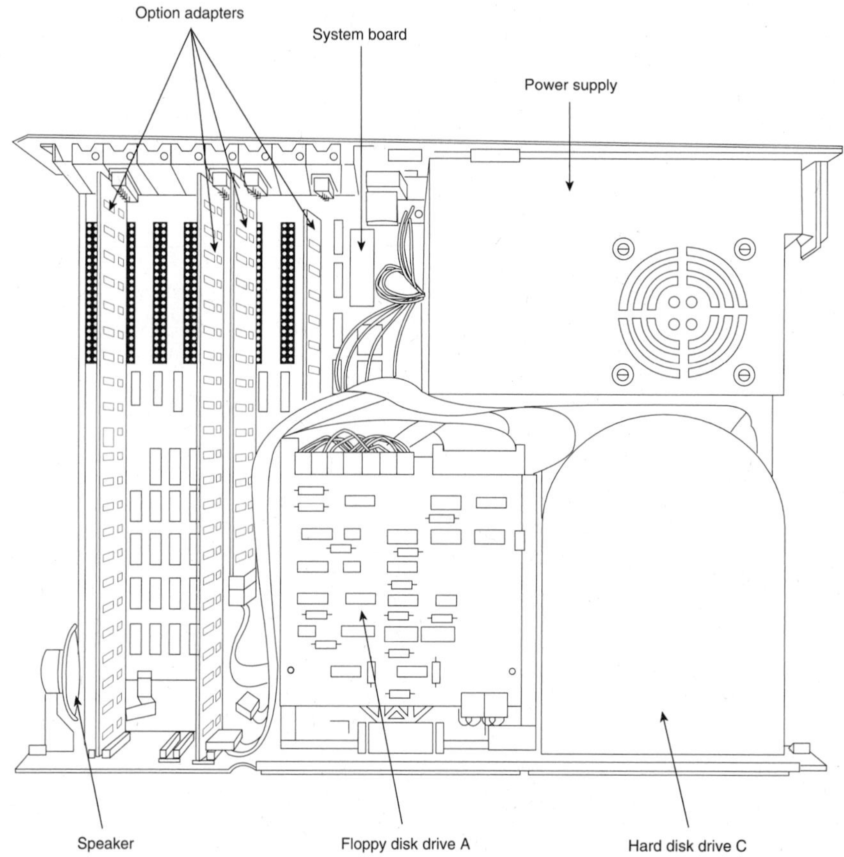

Figure 23.5

The IBM PC XT interior.

XT Models and Features

The XT was available in many different model configurations, but originally only one model was available. This model included a 10M hard disk, marking the first time that a hard disk was standard equipment in a personal computer and was properly supported by the operating system and peripherals. This computer helped change the industry standard for personal computers from normally having one or two floppy disk drives only to now including one or more hard disks.

Today, most people wouldn't consider a PC to be even remotely usable without a hard disk. The original XT was expensive, however, and buyers couldn't unbundle, or delete, the hard disk from the system at purchase time for credit and add it later. This fact distinguished the XT from the PC and misled many people to believe that the only difference between the two computers was the hard disk. People who recognized and wanted the greater capabilities of the XT without the standard IBM hard disk unfortunately had to wait for IBM to sell versions of the XT without the hard disk drive.

The original Model 087 of the XT included a 10M hard disk, 128K of RAM, and a standard serial interface. IBM later increased the standard memory in all PC systems to 256K. The XT reflected the change in Model 086, which was the same as the preceding 087 except for a standard 256K of RAM.

On April 2, 1985, IBM introduced new models of the XT without the standard hard disk. Designed for expansion and configuration flexibility, the new models enabled you to buy the system initially at a lower cost and add your own hard disk later. The XT therefore could be considered in configurations that previously only the original PC could fill. The primary difference between the PC and the XT is the XT's expansion capability, provided by the larger power supply, eight slots, and better memory layout. These models cost only $300 more than equivalent PCs, rendering the original PC no longer a viable option.

The extra expense of the XT can be justified with the first power-supply replacement you make with an overworked PC. The IBM PC XT is available in two floppy disk models:

5160068 XT with one full-height 360K disk drive

5160078 XT with two full-height 360K disk drives

Both these models have 256K of memory and use the IBM PC XT motherboard, power supply, frame, and cover. The serial (asynchronous communications) adapter isn't included as a standard feature with these models.

IBM introduced several more models of the PC XT on April 2, 1986. These models were significantly different from previous models. The most obvious difference, the enhanced keyboard, was standard with these newer computers. A 20M (rather than 10M) hard disk and high-quality, half-height floppy disk drives were included. The new half-height floppy disk drives allow for two drives in the space that previously held only one floppy drive. With two drives, backing up floppy disks became easy. A new 3 1/2-inch floppy disk drive, storing 720K for compatibility with the PC Convertible laptop computer, was released also. These more recent XT system units were configured with a new memory layout allowing for 640K of RAM on the motherboard without an expansion slot. This feature conserves power, improves reliability, and lowers the cost of the system.

One 5 1/4-inch, half-height, 360K floppy disk drive and 256K of system-board memory was standard with the XT Models 267 and 268. Models 277 and 278 have a second 5 1/4-inch floppy disk drive. Models 088 and 089 were expanded PC XTs with all the standard features of the Models 267 and 268, a 20M hard disk, a 20M fixed disk drive adapter, a serial port adapter, and an additional 256K of system-board memory—a total of 512K.

The following list shows the highlights of these new models:

- Enhanced keyboard standard on Models 268, 278, and 089
- 101 keys

  Recappable

Selectric typing section

Dedicated numeric pad

Dedicated cursor and screen controls

Two additional function keys

Nine-foot cable

- Standard PC XT keyboard on Models 267, 277, and 088
- More disk capacity (20M)
- Standard 5 1/4-inch, half-height, 360K floppy drive
- Available 3 1/2-inch, half-height, 720K floppy drive
- Capacity for four half-height storage devices within the system unit
- Capacity to expand to 640K bytes memory on system board without using expansion slots

These newest XT models have an extensively changed ROM BIOS. The new BIOS is 64K and is internally similar to the BIOS found in ATs. The ROM includes support for the new keyboard and 3 1/2-inch floppy disk drives. The POST also was enhanced.

The new XTs were originally incompatible in some respects with some software programs. These problems centered on the new 101-key enhanced keyboard and the way the new ROM addressed the keys. These problems weren't major and were solved quickly by the software companies.

Seeing how much IBM changed the computer without changing the basic motherboard design is interesting. The ROM is different, and the board now could hold 640K of memory without a card in a slot. The memory trick is a simple one. IBM designed this feature into the board originally and chose to unleash it with these models of the XT.

During the past several years, I have modified many XTs to have 640K on the motherboard, using a simple technique designed into the system by IBM. A jumper and chip added to the motherboard can alter the memory addressing in the board to enable the system to recognize 640K. The new addressing is set up for 256K chips, installed in two of the four banks. The other two banks of memory contain 64K chips—a total of 640K. Chapter 7, "Memory," has a set of detailed instructions for modifying an IBM XT in this way.

XT Technical Specifications

Technical information for the XT system, described in this section, provides information about the system architecture, memory configurations and capacities, standard system features, disk storage, expansion slots, keyboard specifications, and also physical and environmental specifications. This information can be useful in determining what parts you need when you are upgrading or repairing these systems. Figure 23.6 shows the layout and components on the XT motherboard.

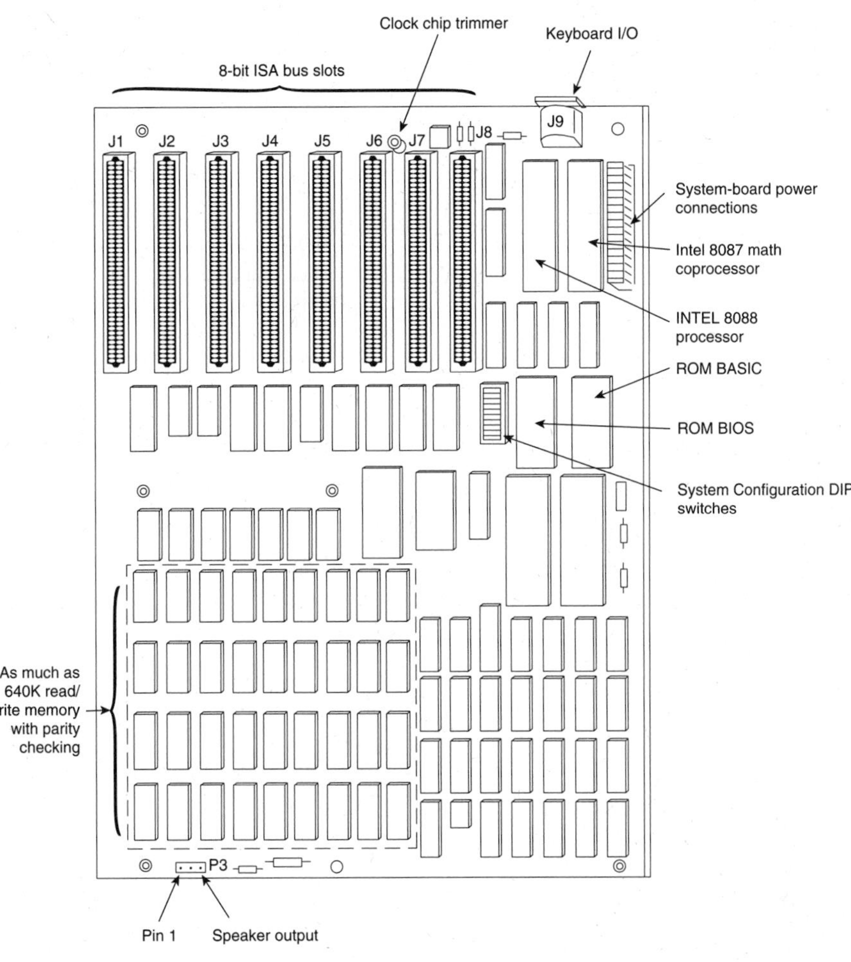

Figure 23.6

The XT motherboard.

System Architecture

Microprocessor	8088
Clock speed	4.77 MHz
Bus type	ISA (Industry Standard Architecture)
Bus width	8-bit
Interrupt levels	8
Type	Edge-triggered
Shareable	No
DMA channels	3
DMA burst mode supported	No
Bus masters supported	No
Upgradable processor complex	No

Memory	
Standard on system board	256K or 640K
Maximum on system board	256K or 640K
Maximum total memory	640K
Memory speed (ns) and type	200ns dynamic RAM
System board memory-socket type	16-pin DIP
Number of memory-module sockets	36 (4 banks of 9)
Memory used on system board	36 64K×1-bit DRAM chips in 4 banks of 9, or 2 banks of 9 256K×1-bit and 2 banks of 9 64K×1-bit chips
Memory cache controller	No
Wait states:	
System board	1
Adapter	1

Standard Features	
ROM size	40K or 64K
ROM shadowing	No
Optional math coprocessor	8087
Coprocessor speed	4.77 MHz
Standard graphics	None standard
RS232C serial ports	1 (some models)
UART chip used	NS8250B
Maximum speed (bits per second)	9,600 bps
Maximum number of ports supported	2
Pointing device (mouse) ports	None standard
Parallel printer ports	1 (some models)
Bi-directional	No
Maximum number of ports supported	3
CMOS real-time clock (RTC)	No
CMOS RAM	None

Disk Storage	
Internal disk and tape drive bays	2 full-height or 4 half-height
Number of 3 1/2 or 5 1/4-inch bays	0/2 or 0/4
Standard floppy drives	1×360K
Optional floppy drives:	
5 1/4-inch 360K	Optional
5 1/4-inch 1.2M	No
3 1/2-inch 720K	Optional
3 1/2-inch 1.44M	No
3 1/2-inch 2.88M	No

Disk Storage

Hard disk controller included:	ST-506/412 (Xebec Model 1210)	
ST-506/412 hard disks available	10/20M	
Drive form factor	5 1/4-inch	
Drive interface	ST-506/412	
Drive capacity	10M	20M
Average access rate (ms)	85	65
Encoding scheme	MFM	MFM
BIOS drive type number	1	2
Cylinders	306	615
Disk storage		
Heads	4	4
Sectors per track	17	17
Rotational speed (RPMs)	3600	3600
Interleave factor	6:1	6:1
Data transfer rate (kilobytes/second)	85	85
Automatic head parking	No	No

Expansion Slots

Total adapter slots	8
Number of long/short slots	6/2
Number of 8-/16-/32-bit slots	8/0/0
Available slots (with video)	4

Keyboard Specifications

101-key Enhanced Keyboard	Yes
Fast keyboard speed setting	No
Keyboard cable length	6 feet

Physical Specifications

Footprint type	Desktop
Dimensions:	
Height	5.5 inches
Width	19.5 inches
Depth	16.0 inches
Weight	32 pounds

Environmental Specifications

Power-supply output	130 watts
Worldwide (110v/60Hz,220v/50Hz)	No

(continues)

(continued)

Environmental Specifications	
Auto-sensing/switching	No
Maximum current:	
90-137 VAC	4.2 amps
Operating range:	
Temperature	60–90 degrees F
Relative humidity	8–80 percent
Maximum operating altitude	7,000 feet
Heat (BTUs/hour)	717
Noise (Average dB, operating, 1m)	56
FCC classification	Class B

Table 23.5 shows the XT motherboard switch settings. The XT motherboard uses a single eight-position switch block to control various functions as detailed in the table.

Table 23.5 IBM PC/XT Motherboard Switch Settings

SWITCH BLOCK 1 (PC and XT)		
	Switch 1	**IBM PC Function (PC Only):**
	Off	Boot From Floppy Drives
	On	Do Not Boot From Floppy Drives
	Switch 1	**IBM XT Function (XT Only):**
	Off	Normal POST (Power-On Self Test)
	On	Continuous Looping POST
	Switch 2	**Math Coprocessor (PC/XT):**
	Off	Installed
	On	Not Installed
Switch 3	**Switch 4**	**Installed Motherboard Memory (PC/XT):**
On	On	Bank 0 only
Off	On	Banks 0 and 1
On	Off	Banks 0, 1, and 2
Off	Off	All 4 Banks
Switch 5	**Switch 6**	**Video Adapter Type (PC/XT):**
Off	Off	Monochrome (MDA)
Off	On	Color (CGA) - 40x25 mode
On	Off	Color (CGA) - 80x25 mode
On	On	Any Video Card w/onboard BIOS (EGA/VGA)
Switch 7	**Switch 8**	**Number of Floppy Drives (PC/XT):**
On	On	1 floppy drive
Off	On	2 floppy drives

SWITCH BLOCK 1 (PC and XT)

On	Off	3 floppy drives
Off	Off	4 floppy drives

Table 23.6 shows the part numbers of the XT system units.

Table 23.6 IBM XT Model Part Numbers

Description	Number
XT system unit/83-key keyboard, 256K:	
one full-height 360K drive	5160068
one half-height 360K drive	5160267
two full-height 360K drives	5160078
two half-height 360K drives	5160277
XT system unit/101-key keyboard, 256K:	
one half-height 360K drive	5160268
two half-height 360K drives	5160278
XT system unit/83-key keyboard, 256K, one serial, one full-height 360K drive, 10M hard disk	5160086
Description Number	
XT system unit/83-key keyboard, 640K, one serial, one half-height 360K drive, 20M fixed disk	5160088
XT system unit/101-key keyboard, 640K, one serial, one half-height 360K drive, 20M fixed disk	5160089
Option Numbers	
PC expansion-unit Model 002, 20M fixed disk	5161002
20M fixed disk drive	6450326
20M fixed disk adapter	6450327
10M fixed disk drive	1602500
10M fixed disk adapter	1602501
5 1/4-inch, half-height, 360K drive	6450325
5 1/4-inch, full-height, 360K drive	1503810
3 1/2-inch, half-height, 720K internal drive	6450258
3 1/2-inch, half-height, 720K external drive	2683190
8087 math coprocessor option	1501002
Asynchronous serial adapter	1502074
Enhanced Keyboard Accessories	
Clear keycaps (60) with paper inserts	6341707
Blank light keycaps	1351710
Blank dark keycaps	1351728
Paper inserts (300)	6341704
Keycap-removal tools (6)	1351717

An Introduction to the 3270 PC

On October 18, 1983, IBM announced a special version of the XT, the 3270 PC. The 3270 PC combines the functions of IBM's 3270 display system with those of the XT. This system was basically a standard XT system unit with three to six custom adapter cards added to the slots. The keyboard and display for this system also were special and attach to some of the special adapter cards. The 3270 PC Control Program runs all this hardware. This combination can support as many as seven concurrent activities: one local PC DOS session, four remote mainframe sessions, and two local electronic notepads. With the help of the 3270 PC Control Program, information can be copied between windows, but a PC DOS window cannot receive information.

The 3270 PC included a new keyboard that addressed some complaints about the Personal Computer keyboard. The keyboard has more keys and an improved layout. The Enter and Shift keys are enlarged. The cursor keys are separate from the numeric keypad and form a small group between the main alphanumeric keys and the numeric keypad. At the top of the keyboard, 20 function keys are arranged in two rows of ten. To help clarify keystroke operations, the new keyboard is annotated. Blue legends designate PC-specific functions; black legends indicate 3270 functions. The keyboard is greatly improved, but most new keys and features don't work in PC mode. Often, you must obtain special versions of programs or disregard most of the new keys.

3270 PC Models and Features

The 3270 PC includes several specialized expansion boards that can be added to an XT. This section examines those expansion boards.

The 3270 System Adapter. The 3270 system adapter supports communication between the 3270 PC and the remote 3274 controller through a coaxial cable. One physical 3274 connection can support four logical connections.

The Display Adapter. A display adapter is used in place of the PC's monochrome or Color/Graphics Display Adapter and provides text-only displays in eight colors. The PC's extended-character graphics are available, but bitmapped graphics capabilities are not supported unless you add the accessory extended graphics card.

The Extended Graphics Adapter. The Extended Graphics Adapter provides storage and controls necessary for displaying local graphics in high- or medium-resolution mode. High-resolution mode is available in two colors at 720-by-350 or 640-by-200 pixels. Note that this isn't the same as the newer XGA (eXtended Graphics Array), which is either available for, or included with, certain PS/2 systems.

Medium-resolution mode is available with a choice of two sets of four colors at 360-by-350 or 320-by-200 pixels. To run in medium-resolution mode, your system must have an available system-expansion slot adjacent to the display adapter card. If you install a Programmed Symbols feature (discussed in the following section) next to the display adapter, you must use the slot adjacent to the PS feature. Because the aspect ratio differs for each display monitor, applications programs must control the aspect ratio parameter; a circle on the 5150/5160 PC with the Color Graphics Adapter looks slightly elliptical on the 3270 PC with the XGA unless you change this parameter.

Programmed Symbols. The Programmed Symbols (PS) adapter provides graphics capabilities available on IBM 3278/3279 display stations. This card provides storage for as many as six 190-symbol sets whose shapes and codes are definable. Symbol sets are loaded (and accessed for display) under program control. To accept this board, your system must have an available system-expansion slot adjacent to the display adapter card. If an XGA feature is installed, you must use the slot adjacent to the XGA. The PS card is available in distributed-function terminal (DFT) mode only and can be used in only one of the four host sessions.

The Keyboard Adapter. You use the keyboard adapter to adapt the 3270-style keyboard to the system unit. The keyboard connects to this board rather than to the motherboard, as it does for the PC. The board is short and must be installed in the special eighth slot in the XT system unit.

The standard XT system unit provides eight expansion slots; at least five of the slots normally were filled upon delivery with the 3270 system adapter, the display adapter, the keyboard adapter, the disk drive adapter, and the hard disk controller. If you add options such as the graphics adapter and a memory multifunction card, you can see that even with the XT as a base, slots are at a premium in this system.

Software. The 3270 PC runs under control of the 3270 PC Control Program in conjunction with PC DOS and supports concurrent operation of as many as four remote-host interactive sessions, two local notepad sessions, and one PC DOS session. The Control Program enables users to associate sessions with display screen windows and to manage the windows by a set of functions that IBM named advanced screen management.

Windows. You can define windows that permit viewing of all (as many as 2,000 characters) or part of a presentation space. In IBM's vocabulary, a presentation space is a logical display area presented by a single host. PC DOS presentation spaces are 2,000 characters (25 lines by 80 characters); remote host spaces are as many as 3,440 characters; and notepad presentation spaces are 1,920 characters.

As many as seven windows can appear on-screen at one time. Every window is associated with a distinct presentation space. Windows can be as large as the screen or as small as one character and can be positioned at any point within their presentation space. A window 20 characters wide and four lines long, for example, shows the first 20 characters of the last four lines of a host session display. You can change window size and position in the presentation space at any time without affecting the content of the presentation space.

At any time, only one window on the 3270 PC screen can be the active window. When you enter information from the keyboard, the information is directed to the session associated with the active window. You can switch between active windows by using keystroke commands.

You can define the foreground and background colors of host session windows not using extended data-stream attributes. You can define the background color for the 5272 screen also (the color to be displayed in areas not occupied by windows).

Special Facilities. In addition to advanced screen-management functions, the Control Program offers a number of related special facilities that help you take further advantage of the 3270 environment.

Data can be copied within or between any presentation spaces except into the PC DOS screen. You copy by marking a block of data in one window and a destination in some other window, much the same as a block copy in a word processor.

Think of the notepads as local electronic scratch pads that you can use at your convenience. You can save and restore the contents of a notepad at any time by using PC DOS files as the storage medium.

You can define as many as 10 screen configurations, each of which describes a set of windows configured in any way, and they can display on command any one configuration. Use PC DOS files to store the configuration information.

You can print a full copy of the display screen on a local printer. Similarly, you can print a full copy of a PC DOS presentation space on a local printer. You also can print a full copy of any host presentation space on a local printer, a 3274 attached printer, or a 43xx display/printer.

The Control Program maintains at the bottom of the screen a status line that displays current configuration information, including the name of the active window. The program includes a help function and displays active workstation functions and sessions and an online tutorial that explains and simulates system functions. The tutorial is a standard PC DOS program that can be run on any IBM PC.

The Control Program, assisted by a host-based IBM 3270 PC file-transfer program, can initiate transfers of ASCII, binary, and EBCDIC files to and from remote hosts.

A drawback to this software is that it is memory resident and consumes an enormous amount of space. The result is that in the PC DOS session, not many applications can run in the leftover workspace. Your only option—reboot the computer without loading the Control Program—is a clumsy and time-consuming procedure. Even with this tactic, the drastic differences in the display hardware and the keyboard still render this computer much less than "PC compatible." The AT version of this system offers a solution to the memory problem by enabling much of the Control Program to reside in the AT's extended memory, above the 1M memory limit of the PC and XT.

The Significance of the 3270

The 3270 PC is a great system to use if you are a corporate worker who deals every day with many information sources (most of which are available through an IBM mainframe SNA network). Corporate information managers greatly appreciate the concurrent access to several SNA-based databases. The 3270 PC provides essential tools for viewing, extracting, combining, and manipulating information: multiple concurrent-terminal sessions, cut-and-paste capability between sessions, PC productivity tools, and up- and downloading host files from PC DOS files.

For simple 3270 terminal-emulation capability, however, this system is more than you need. In addition, the display and keyboard make this system partially incompatible with the rest of the PC world. Many PC applications do not run properly on this system. If you depend more on PC DOS applications than on the mainframe, or if you consider the multiple mainframe sessions unimportant, using one of the simpler 3270 emulation adapters is more cost-effective.

An Introduction to the XT 370

On October 18, 1983, IBM introduced another special version of the XT, the XT 370, consisting of a standard PC XT chassis with three special cards added. These adapters were special S/370-emulation cards that enable the computer to execute the mainframe system 370 instruction set. The boards enable you to run VM/CMS and emulate 4M of virtual memory. You can download programs and compilers from the mainframe and execute them directly on the XT. You switch between 370 mode and the standard XT by using a hot key, or special keystroke sequence.

XT 370 Models and Features

The three cards that make up the XT 370—the PC 370-P card, the PC 370-M card, and the PC 3277-EM card—are examined in this section.

The P card implements an emulation of the 370 instruction set. The card has three microprocessors. One processor is a heavily modified Motorola 68000 produced under license to IBM. This chip implements the general-purpose registers, the PSW, instruction fetch and decode logic, and 72 commonly used S/370 instructions. Because Motorola manufactures the chip under license to IBM, the chip probably will not appear as a Motorola product.

A second processor is a slightly modified Motorola 68000, which is listed in Motorola's catalog. The chip emulates the remaining nonfloating-point instructions, manipulates the page table, handles exception conditions, and performs hardware housekeeping.

The third microprocessor, a modified Intel 8087 that executes S/370 floating-point instructions, is interfaced as a peripheral rather than the normal 8087 coprocessor linkage.

The M card has 512K of parity-checked RAM. You can access this memory from the P card or from the XT's native 8088 processor. Concurrent requests are arbitrated in favor of the 8088. The M card resides in an XT expansion slot but is connected to the P card by a special edge connector. Sixteen-bit-wide transfers between M card memory and the P card are carried out through this connector (normal XT memory transfers operate in 8-bit-wide chunks).

Operating in native PC mode, the M card's memory is addressed as contiguous memory beginning at the end of the 256K memory of the system's motherboard. In native PC mode, the XT 370 has 640K of usable RAM; some of the M card's memory is not used.

Operating in 370 mode, only the 512K RAM of the M card is usable. (The memory on the motherboard is not available.) The first 480K of this memory implements 480K of real S/370 space. The remaining 32K on the M card functions as a microcode control-storage area for the second P card microprocessor.

The first 64K (of 480K) of S/370 memory are consumed by VM/PC; 416K of real memory remains for user programs. User programs larger than 416K are handled through paging.

The PC 3277-EM card attaches the XT 370 to an S/370 mainframe by a local or remote 3274 control unit (connection through coaxial cable). When VM/PC is running, the EM card uses the IBM monochrome or color display. Under VM/PC, the EM card is used also to up- and download data between a host VM system and the XT 370.

The XT 370 can run in native PC XT mode or in S/370 mode under the VM/PC Control Program. Under VM/PC, the user can use a "hot key" to alternate between a local CMS session and a remote 3277 session (or, optionally, a 3101-emulation session). VM/PC does not offer a true VM-like environment. Rather, VM/PC provides an environment in which CMS applications can run. Non-CMS VM applications do not run on the XT 370.

The VM/PC system, which must be licensed, is provided on six floppy disks and includes the VM/PC Control Program, CMS, XEDIT, EXEC2, local and remote file-transfer utilities, and the 370 Processor Control package.

Estimations of the XT 370 CPU's performance indicate that it is about half of a 4331 when the XT 370 is running a commercial instruction mix. When the XT 370 is running scientific codes, you can expect twice the performance as from the 4331. The CPU generally is categorized as a 0.1 MIPS (million instructions per second) processor. This size does not sound impressive when you're used to multi-MIPS, single-chip microprocessors, but remember that 0.1-million S/370 instructions likely will produce substantially more computing than 0.1-million instructions of your standard microprocessor chip.

The XT 370 running in S/370 mode can access the 512K on the M card. Of this 512K, 32K is reserved for microcode control storage, and 65K is used by the VM/PC Control Program; 416K remains for user programs. If a user program requires more memory than 416K, VM/PC uses a paging area on the XT 370's hard disk and swaps pieces of the program in and out of memory according to use.

Swapping on the small 10M or 20M hard disks is considerably slower than on the large disks used with mainframes. Programs larger than 416K, therefore, probably will run very slowly. Field test users report long delays in loading large programs into memory, even when the programs are well under the maximum for nonpaging operation. Delays are due to the relatively slow operation of the XT 370 hard disks. Because of size and speed problems, many users of these systems should consider larger and faster hard disks.

An Introduction to the Portable PC

IBM introduced the Portable PC on February 16, 1984. The IBM Portable PC, a "transportable" personal computer, has a built-in nine-inch, amber composite video monitor;

one 5 1/4-inch, half-height floppy disk drive (with space for an optional second drive); an 83-key keyboard; two adapter cards; a floppy disk controller; and a Color Graphics Adapter (CGA). The unit has also a universal-voltage power supply capable of overseas operation on 220-volt power. Figure 23.7 shows the Portable PC exterior.

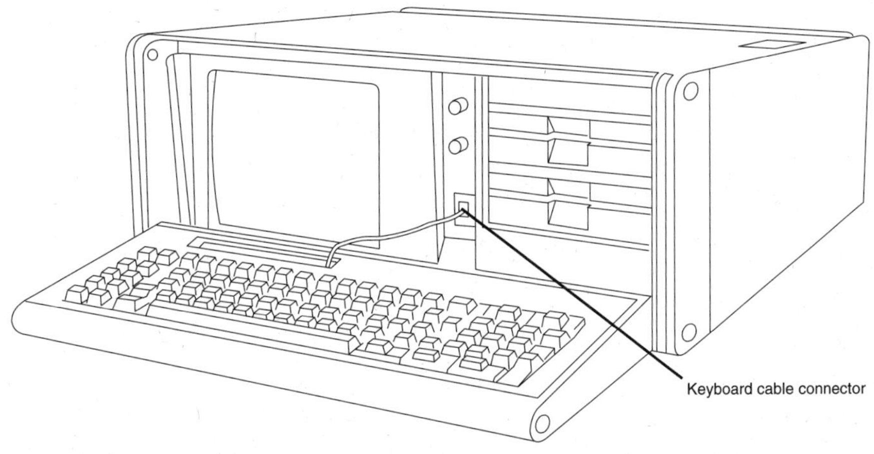

Figure 23.7
The IBM Portable PC.

The system board used in the IBM Portable PC is the same board used in the original IBM XTs, with 256K of memory. Because the XT motherboard was used, eight expansion slots are available for the connection of adapter boards, although only two slots can accept a full-length adapter card due to internal space restrictions. The power supply is basically the same as an XT's, with physical changes for portability and a small amount of power drawn to run the built-in monitor. In function and performance, the Portable PC system unit has identical characteristics to an equivalently configured IBM PC XT system unit. Figure 23.8 shows the Portable PC interior view.

IBM withdrew the Portable PC from the market on April 2, 1986, a date that coincides with the introduction of the IBM Convertible laptop PC. The Portable PC is rare because not many were sold. The system was largely misunderstood by the trade press and user community. Most did not understand that the system was really a portable XT and had more to offer than the standard IBM PC. Maybe if IBM had called the system the Portable XT, it would have sold better.

The Portable PC system unit has these major functional components:

- Intel 8088 4.77 MHz microprocessor
- ROM-based diagnostics (POST)
- BASIC language interpreter in ROM
- 256K of dynamic RAM

- Eight expansion slots (two long slots, one 3/4-length slot, and five short slots)
- Socket for 8087 math coprocessor
- Color/Graphics Monitor Adapter
- 9-inch, amber, composite video monitor
- Floppy disk interface
- One or two half-height 360K floppy drives
- 114-watt universal power supply (115 V to 230 V, 50 Hz to 60 Hz)
- Lightweight 83-key keyboard
- Enclosure with carrying handle
- Carrying bag for the system unit

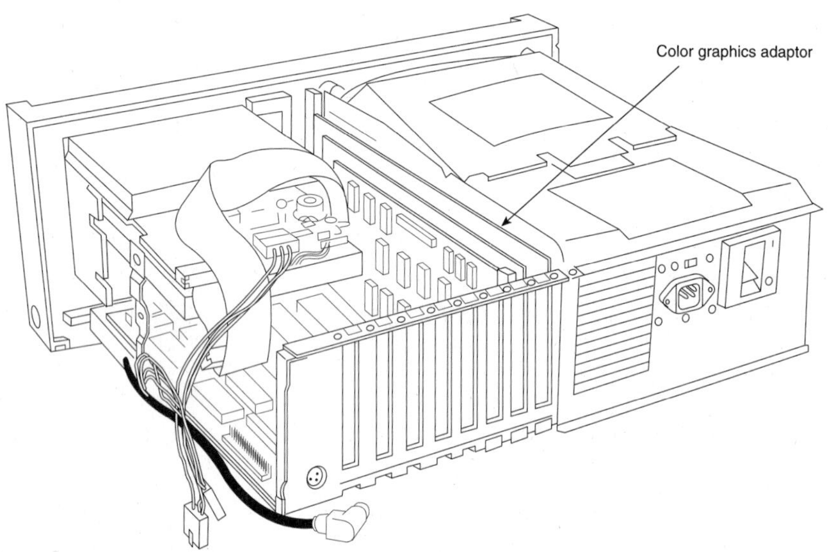

Figure 23.8

The IBM Portable PC interior.

Portable PC Technical Specifications

The technical data for the Portable PC system is described in this section, which includes information about the system architecture, memory configurations and capacities, standard system features, disk storage, expansion slots, keyboard specifications, and also physical and environmental specifications. This information can be useful in determining what kinds of parts you need when you are upgrading or repairing these systems. Figure 23.6 previously showed the XT motherboard, also used in the Portable PC.

System Architecture

Microprocessor	8088
Clock speed	4.77 MHz
Bus type	ISA (Industry Standard Architecture)
Bus width	8-bit
Interrupt levels	8
Type	Edge-triggered
Shareable	No
DMA channels	3
DMA burst mode supported	No
Bus masters supported	No
Upgradeable processor complex	No

Memory

Standard on system board	256K
Maximum on system board	256K
Maximum total memory	640K
Memory speed (ns) and type	200ns dynamic RAM
System board memory-socket type	16-pin DIP
Number of memory-module sockets	36 (4 banks of 9)
Memory used on system board	36 64K×1-bit DRAM chips in 4 banks of 9 chips
Memory cache controller	No
Wait states:	
System board	1
Adapter	1

Standard Features

ROM size	40K
ROM shadowing	No
Optional math coprocessor	8087
Coprocessor speed	4.77 MHz
Standard graphics	CGA adapter with built-in 9" amber CRT
RS232C serial ports	None standard
UART chip used	NS8250B
Maximum speed (bits per second)	9,600 bps
Maximum number of ports supported	2
Pointing device (mouse) ports	None standard
Parallel printer ports	None standard
Bi-directional	No
Maximum number of ports supported	3
CMOS real-time clock (RTC)	No
CMOS RAM	None

Disk Storage

Internal disk and tape drive bays	2 half-height
Number of 3 1/2-/5 1/4-inch bays	0/2
Standard floppy drives	1 or 2×360K
Optional floppy drives:	
5 1/4-inch 360K	Optional
5 1/4-inch 1.2M	No
3 1/2-inch 720K	Optional
3 1/2-inch 1.44M	No
3 1/2-inch 2.88M	No
Hard disk controller included	None

Expansion Slots

Total adapter slots	8
Number of long/short slots	2/6
Number of 8-/16-/32-bit slots	8/0/0
Available slots (with video)	6

Keyboard Specifications

101-key Enhanced Keyboard	No
Fast keyboard speed setting	No
Keyboard cable length	6 feet

Physical Specifications

Footprint type	Desktop
Dimensions:	
Height	8.0 inches
Width	20.0 inches
Depth	17.0 inches
Weight	31 pounds

Environmental Specifications

Power-supply output	114 watts
Worldwide (110/60,220/50)	Yes
Auto-sensing/switching	No
Maximum current:	
90-137 VAC	4.0 amps
Operating range:	
Temperature	60–90 degrees F
Relative humidity	8–80 percent
Maximum operating altitude	7,000 feet

Environmental Specifications	
Heat (BTUs/hour)	650
Noise (Average dB, operating, 1m)	42
FCC classification	Class B

Table 23.7 shows the part numbers for the Portable PC.

Table 23.7 IBM Portable PC Model Part Numbers

Description	Number
256K, one 360K half-height drive	5155068
256K, two 360K half-height drives	5155076
Half-height 360K floppy disk drive	6450300

Description Number	
256K, one 360K half-height drive	5155068
256K, two 360K half-height drives	5155076
Half-height 360K floppy disk drive	6450300

The disk drive used in the Portable PC was a half-height drive, the same unit specified for use in the PCjr. When the Portable PC was introduced, PCjr was the only one IBM sold with the half-height drive.

An Introduction to the AT

IBM introduced the Personal Computer AT (Advanced Technology) on August 14, 1984. The IBM AT system included many features previously unavailable in IBM's PC systems such as increased performance, an advanced 16-bit microprocessor, high-density floppy disk and hard disk drives, larger memory space, and an advanced coprocessor. Despite its new design, the IBM AT incredibly retained compatibility with most existing hardware and software products for the earlier systems.

In most cases, IBM AT system performance was from three to five times faster than the IBM XT for single applications running DOS on both computers. The performance increase is due to the combination of a reduced cycle count for most instructions by the 80286 processor, an increased system clock rate, 16-bit memory, and faster hard disk and controller.

The AT system unit has been available in several models: a floppy-disk-equipped base model (068) and several hard-disk-enhanced models. Based on a high-performance, 16-bit, Intel 80286 microprocessor, each computer includes Cassette BASIC language in ROM and a CMOS (Complementary Metal Oxide Semiconductor) clock and calendar with battery backup. All models are equipped with a high-density (1.2M) floppy disk drive, a keyboard, and a lock. For standard memory, the base model offers 256K, and the enhanced models offer 512K. In addition, the enhanced models have a 20M or a 30M hard disk drive and a serial/parallel adapter. Each system can be expanded through customer-installable options. You can add memory (to 512K) for the base model by adding chips to the system board. You can expand all models to 16M by installing memory cards.

Besides the standard drives included with the system, IBM only offered two different hard disks as upgrades for the AT: a 30M hard disk drive and a 20M hard disk drive. IBM also offered only three different types of floppy drives for the AT; a second, high-density (1.2M) floppy disk drive; a double-density (320/360K) floppy disk drive; and a new 3 1/2-inch 720K drive. The original 068 and 099 models of the AT did not support the 720K drive in the BIOS; you had to add a special driver (DRIVER.SYS—supplied with DOS) for the drive to work. The later model ATs also supported a 1.44M high-density 3 1/2-inch floppy drive; however, IBM never sold or supported such a drive.

You can install as many as two floppy disk drives and one hard disk drive or one floppy disk drive and two hard disk drives in the system unit. To use the high-density 5 1/4-inch floppy disk drives properly, you must have special floppy disks—5 1/4-inch, high-coercivity, double-sided, soft-sectored disks. Due to track width problems between the high-density (1.2M) drives and the double-density (360K) drives, a double-density floppy disk drive (320/360K) was available for compatibility with the standard PC or XT systems. You can exchange disks reliably between the 1.2M and the standard 360K drives if you use the proper method and understand the recording process. For transferring data between a system with a 1.2M drive to a system with a 360K drive you must start with a blank (never previously formatted) 360K disk, which must be formatted and written only by the 1.2M drive. No special precautions to transfer the data the other way. This information is covered in Chapter 13. For complete interchange reliability, however, IBM recommended you purchase the 360K drive.

The system unit has eight slots that support cards for additional devices, features, or memory. Six slots support the advanced 16-bit or 8-bit option cards. Two slots support only 8-bit option cards. All system-unit models, however, use one 16-bit slot for the fixed disk and floppy disk drive adapter. The enhanced models use an additional 8-bit slot for the serial/parallel adapter. The result is seven available expansion slots for the base model and six available expansion slots for enhanced models. Figure 23.9 shows the interior of an AT system unit.

All models include a universal power supply; a temperature-controlled, variable-speed cooling fan; and a security lock with key. The user selects the power supply for a country's voltage range. The cooling fan significantly reduces the noise in most environments; the fan runs slower when the system unit is cool and faster when the system unit is hot. When the system is locked, no one can remove the system-unit cover, boot the system, or enter commands or data from the keyboard, thereby enhancing the system's security.

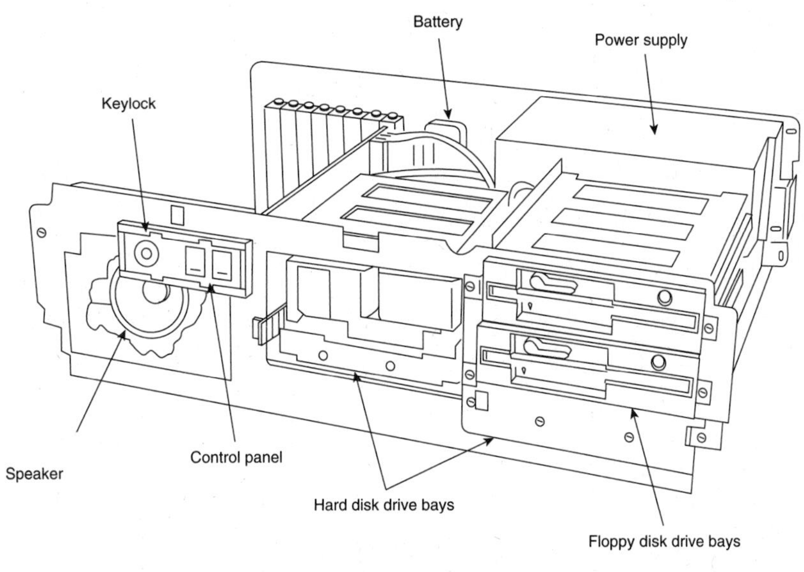

Figure 23.9
The IBM AT unit interior.

The keyboard is attached to the system unit by a nine-foot, coiled cable that enables the AT to adapt to a variety of workspace configurations. The keyboard includes key-location enhancements and mode indicators for improved keyboard usability. Figure 23.10 shows the rear panel of an AT.

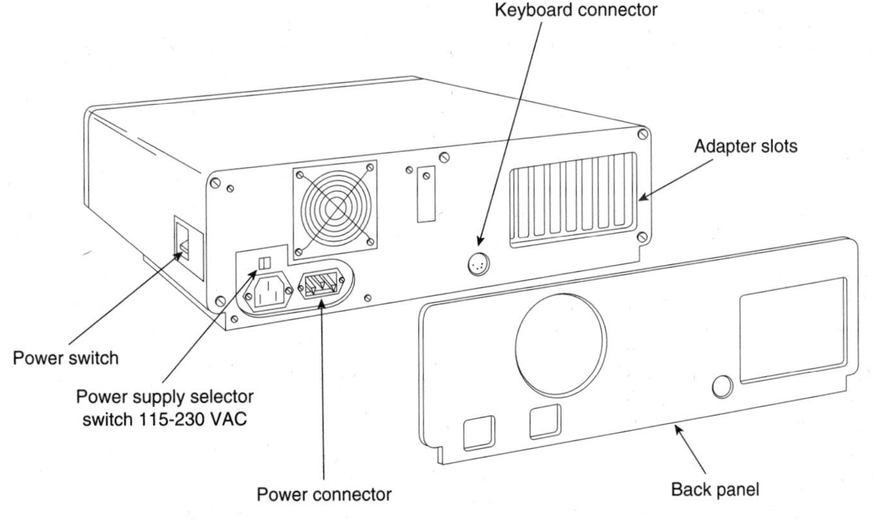

Figure 23.10
The IBM AT rear panel.

Every system unit for the AT models has these major functional components:

- Intel 80286 (6 MHz or 8 MHz) microprocessor
- Socket for 80287 math coprocessor
- 8086-compatible real address mode
- Protected virtual address mode
- Eight I/O expansion slots (six 16-bit, two 8-bit)
- 256K of dynamic RAM (base model)
- 512K of dynamic RAM (enhanced models)
- ROM-based diagnostics (POST)
- BASIC language interpreter in ROM
- Hard/floppy disk controller
- 1.2M HD floppy drive
- 20M or 30M hard disk drive (enhanced models)
- Serial/parallel interface (enhanced models)
- CMOS Clock-calendar and configuration with battery backup
- Keylock
- 84-key keyboard
- Enhanced, 101-key keyboard (standard on newer models)
- Switchable worldwide power supply

AT Models and Features

Since the introduction of the AT, several models have become available. First, IBM announced two systems: a base model (068) and an enhanced model (099). The primary difference between the two systems is the standard hard disk that came with the enhanced model. IBM has introduced two other AT systems since the first systems, each offering new features.

The first generation of AT systems have a 6 MHz system clock that dictates the processor cycle time. The cycle time, the system's smallest interval of time, represents the speed at which operations occur. Every operation in a computer takes at least one or (usually) several cycles to complete. Therefore, if two computers are the same in every way except for the clock speed, the system with the faster clock rate executes the same operations in a shorter time proportional to the difference in clock speed. Cycle time and clock speed are two different ways of describing the same thing. Discussions of clock speed are significant when you consider buying the AT because not all models have the same clock speed.

All models of the AT included a combination hard/floppy disk controller that was really two separate controllers on the same circuit board. The board was designed by IBM and Western Digital, and manufactured for IBM by Western Digital. This controller had no on-board ROM BIOS like the Xebec hard disk controller used in the XT. In the AT, IBM built full support for the hard disk controller directly into the motherboard ROM BIOS. To support different types of hard disks, IBM encoded a table into the motherboard ROM that listed the parameters of various drives that could be installed. In the first version of the AT, with a ROM BIOS dated 01/10/84, only the first 14 types in the table were filled in. Type 15 itself was reserved for internal reasons, and was not usable. Other table entries from 16 through 47 were left unused at all and were actually filled with zeros. Later versions of the AT added new drive types to the tables, starting from type 16 and up.

The first two AT models were the 068 (base) model, which had 256K on the motherboard and a single 1.2M floppy disk drive; and the model 099 (enhanced), which had a 20M hard disk drive, a serial/parallel adapter, and 512K on the motherboard. IBM designated the motherboard on these computers as Type 1, which is larger than the later Type 2 board and used an unusual memory layout. The memory is configured as four banks of 128K chips—a total of 512K on the board. This configuration sounds reasonable until you realize that a 128K chip does not really exist in the physical form factor that IBM used. IBM actually created this type of memory device by stacking a 64K chip on top of another one and soldering the two together. My guess is that IBM had many 64K chips to use, and the AT was available to take them.

On October 2, 1985, IBM announced a new model of the AT—the Personal Computer AT Model 239. The system has all the standard features of the AT Model 099, but also has a 30M hard disk rather than a 20M hard disk. A second, optional 30M hard disk drive expands the Model 239's hard disk storage to 60M. This unit's motherboard, a second-generation design IBM calls Type 2, is about 25 percent smaller than the Type 1 but uses the same mounting locations, for physical compatibility. All important items, such as the slots and connectors, remain in the same locations. Other major improvements in this board are in the memory. The 128K memory chips have been replaced by 256K devices. Now only two banks of chips were needed to get the same 512K on the board.

The AT Model 239 includes these items:

- 512K of RAM (standard)
- 6 MHz Type 2 motherboard with 256K memory chips
- Serial/parallel adapter (standard)
- 30M hard disk (standard)
- New ROM BIOS (dated 06/10/85)

  ROM supports 3 1/2-inch 720K floppy drives without using external driver programs

  ROM supports 22 hard disk types (up to type 23), including the supplied 3

  POST fixes clock rate to 6 MHz

The Type 2 motherboard's design is much improved over Type 1's; the Type 2 motherboard improved internal-circuit timing and layout. Improvements in the motherboard indicated that the system would be pushed to higher speeds—exactly what happened with the next round of introductions.

In addition to obvious physical differences, the Model 239 includes significantly different ROM software from the previous models. The new ROM supports more types of hard and floppy disks, and its new POST prevents alteration of the clock rate from the standard 6 MHz models. Because support for the 30M hard disk is built into the new ROM, IBM sold a 30M hard disk upgrade kit that included the new ROM for the original AT systems. This $1,795 kit represented the only legal way to obtain the newer ROM.

The 30M hard disk drive upgrade kit for the Personal Computer AT Models 068 and 099 included all the features in the 30M hard disk drive announced for the AT Model 239. The upgrade kit also had a new basic input-output subsystem (BIOS), essential to AT operation. The new ROM BIOS supports 22 drive types (compared to the original 14 in earlier ATs), including the new 30M drive. To support the 30M hard disk drive, a new diagnostics floppy disk and an updated guide-to-operations manual were shipped with this kit.

The 30M update kit included these items:

- 30M hard disk drive
- Two new ROM BIOS modules
- Channel keeper bar (a bracket for the fixed disk)
- Data cable for the hard disk
- Diagnostics and Setup disk
- An insert to the AT guide-to-operations manual

Some people were upset initially that IBM had "fixed the microprocessor clock" to 6 MHz n the new model, thereby disallowing any possible "hot rod" modifications. Many ople realized that the clock crystal on all the AT models was socketed so that the crys- could be replaced easily by a faster one. More important, because the AT circuit de- is modular, changing the clock crystal does not have repercussions throughout the f the system, as is the case in the PC and PC XT. For the price of a new crystal (from 30) and the time needed to plug it in, someone easily could increase an AT's speed ercent, and sometimes more. Because IBM now retrofits the ROM into earlier r the 30M hard disk upgrade, you no longer can implement a simple speedup without also changing the ROM BIOS as well.

e believed that this change was made to prevent the AT from being "too fast" competing with IBM's minicomputers. In reality, the earlier motherboard ionally at 6 MHz because IBM did not believe that the ROM BIOS software em timing was fully operational at a higher speed. Also, IBM used some were rated only for 6 MHz operation, starting of course with the CPU.

Users who increased the speed of their early computers often received DOS error messages from timing problems, and in some cases, total system lockups due to components not functioning properly at the higher speeds. Many companies selling speedup kits sold software to help smooth over some of these problems, but IBM's official solution was to improve the ROM BIOS software and motherboard circuitry and to introduce a complete new system running at the faster speed. If you want increased speed no matter what model you have, several companies used to sell clock-crystal replacements that were frequency synthesizers rather than a fixed type of crystal. The units can wait until the POST is finished and change midstream to an increased operating speed. Unfortunately, I don't know of anyone who is still making or selling these upgrades. If you are really interested in speeding up your AT in this manner, Chapter 18, "System Upgrades and Improvements," discusses a technique for patching the existing ROM to ignore the speed test so that a faster crystal will still pass the POST procedure.

On April 2, 1986, IBM introduced the Personal Computer AT Models 319 and 339. These two similar systems were an enhancement of the earlier Model 239. The primary difference from the Model 239 is a faster clock crystal that provides 8 MHz operation. The Model 339 has a new keyboard, the Enhanced Keyboard, with 101 keys rather than the usual 84. Model 319 is the same as Model 339, but includes the original keyboard.

Highlights of the Models 319 and 339 are shown in this list:

- Faster processor speed (8 MHz)
- Type 2 motherboard, with 256K chips
- 512K of RAM (standard)
- Serial/parallel adapter (standard)
- 30M hard disk (standard)
- New ROM BIOS (dated 11/15/85)

  ROM Support for 22 types (up to type 23) of hard disks

  ROM Support for 3 1/2-inch drives, at both 720K and 1.44M capacities

  POST fixes clock rate to 8 MHz
- 101-key Enhanced Keyboard (standard on Model 339)

  Recappable keys

  Selectric typing section

  Dedicated numeric pad

  Dedicated cursor and screen controls

  12 function keys

  Indicator lights

  Nine-foot cable

The most significant physical difference in these new systems is the Enhanced Keyboard on the Model 339. The keyboard, similar to a 3270 keyboard, has 101 keys. It could be called the IBM "corporate" keyboard because it is standard on all new desktop systems. The 84-key PC keyboard still was available, with a new 8 MHz model, as the Model 319.

These new 8 MHz systems were available only in an enhanced configuration with a standard 30M hard drive. If you wanted a hard disk larger than IBM's 30M, you could either add a second drive or simply replace the 30M unit with something larger.

ROM support for 3 1/2-inch disk drives at both 720K and 1.44M exists only in Models 339 and 319. In particular the 1.44M drive, although definitely supported by the ROM BIOS and controller, was not ever offered as an option by IBM. This means that the IBM Setup program found on the Diagnostics and Setup disk did not offer the 1.44M floppy drive as a choice when configuring the system. Anybody adding such a drive had to use one of the many Setup replacement programs available in the public domain, or "borrow" one from an IBM-compatible system that used a floppy disk-based setup program. Adding the 1.44M drive became one of the most popular upgrades for the AT systems because many newer systems came with that type of drive as standard equipment. Earlier AT systems still can use the 720K and 1.44M drives, but they need to either upgrade the ROM to support it (recommended) or possibly use software drivers to make them work.

AT Technical Specifications

Technical information for the AT system is described in this section. You will find information about the system architecture, memory configurations and capacities, standard system features, disk storage, expansion slots, keyboard specifications, as well as physical and environmental specifications. This type of information can be useful in determining what types of parts are needed when you are upgrading or repairing these systems. Figures 23.11 and 23.12 show the layout and components on the two different AT motherboards.

System Architecture

Microprocessor	80286
Clock speed	6 or 8 MHz
Bus type	ISA (Industry Standard Architecture)
Bus width	16-bit
Interrupt levels	16
Type	Edge-triggered
Shareable	No
DMA channels	7
DMA burst mode supported	No
Bus masters supported	No
Upgradeable processor complex	No

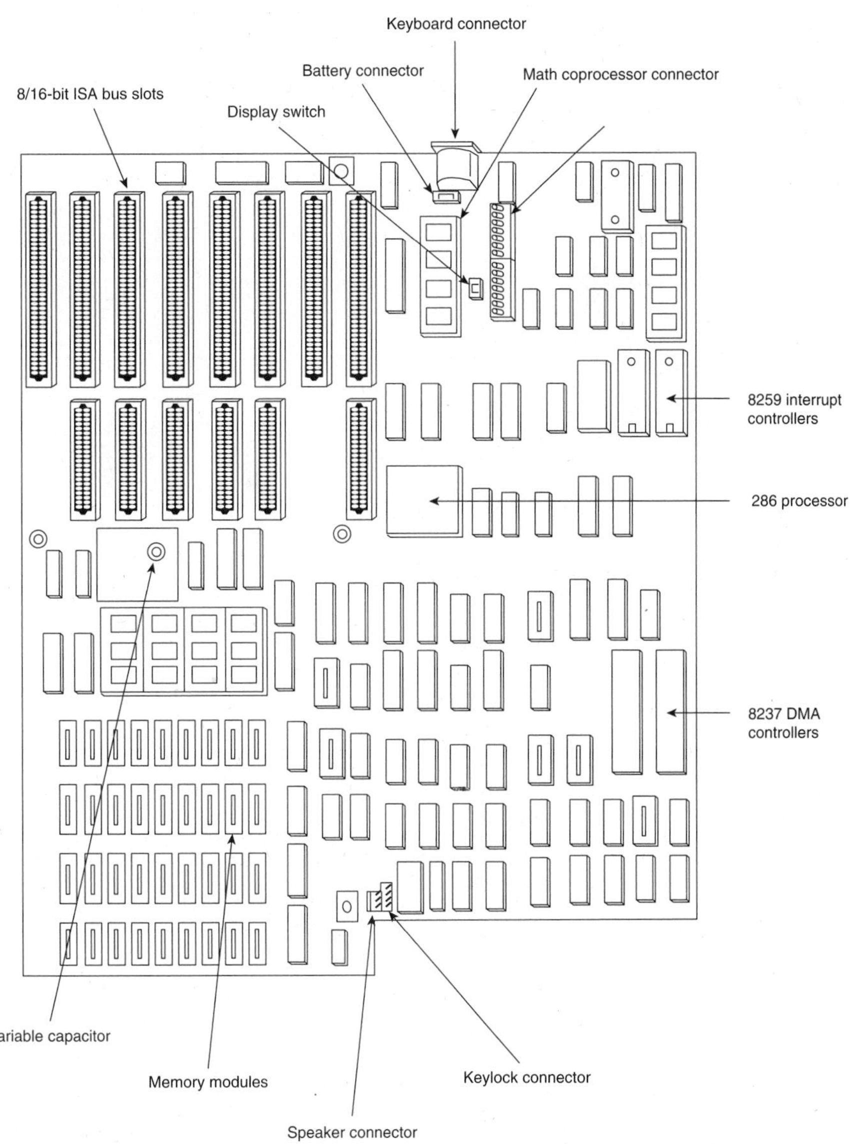

Figure 23.11

The IBM AT Type 1 motherboard.

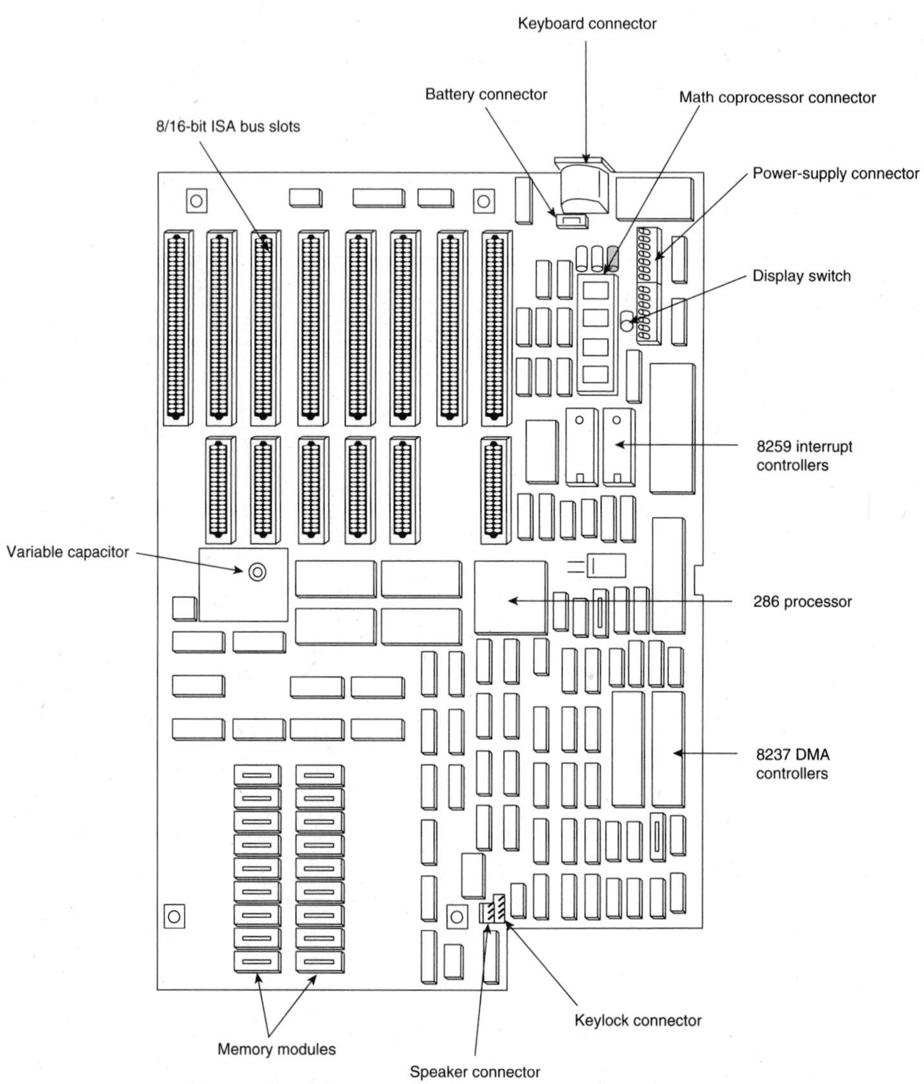

Figure 23.12

The IBM AT Type 2 motherboard.

Memory

Standard on system board	512K
Maximum on system board	512K
Maximum total memory	16M
Memory speed (ns) and type	150ns dynamic RAM
System board memory-socket type	16-pin DIP
Number of memory-module sockets	18 or 36 (2 or 4 banks of 18)

Memory

Memory used on system board	36 128K×1-bit DRAM chips in 2 banks of 18, or 18 256K×1-bit chips in one bank
Memory cache controller	No
Wait states:	
System board	1
Adapter	1

Standard Features

ROM size	64K
ROM shadowing	No
Optional math coprocessor	80287
Coprocessor speed	4 or 5.33 MHz
Standard graphics	None standard
RS232C serial ports	1 (some models)
UART chip used	NS16450
Maximum speed (bits per second)	9,600 bps
Maximum number of ports supported	2
Pointing device (mouse) ports	None standard
Parallel printer ports	1 (some models)
Bi-directional	Yes
Maximum number of ports supported	3
CMOS real-time clock (RTC)	Yes
CMOS RAM	64 bytes
Battery life	5 years

Disk Storage

Internal disk and tape drive bays	1 full-height and 2 half-height
Number of 3 1/2-, 5 1/4-inch bays	0/3
Standard floppy drives	1×1.2M
Optional floppy drives:	
5 1/4-inch 360K	Optional
5 1/4-inch 1.2M	Standard
3 1/2-inch 720K	Optional
3 1/2-inch 1.44M	Optional (8 MHz models)
3 1/2-inch 2.88M	No
Hard disk controller included:	ST-506/412 (Western Digital WD1002-WA2 or WD1003-WA2)
ST-506/412 hard disks available	20/30M
Drive form factor	5 1/4-inch
Drive interface	ST-506/412

(continues)

(continued)

Disk Storage

Drive capacity	20M	30M
Average access rate (ms)	40	40
Encoding scheme	MFM	MFM
BIOS drive type number	2	20
Cylinders	615	733
Heads	4	5
Sectors per track	17	17
Rotational speed (RPMs)	3600	3600
Disk storage		
Interleave factor	3:1	3:1
Data transfer rate (kilobytes/second)	170	170
Automatic head parking	Yes	Yes

Expansion Slots

Total adapter slots	8
Number of long and short slots	8/0
Number of 8-/16-/32-bit slots	2/6/0
Available slots (with video)	5

Keyboard Specifications

101-key Enhanced Keyboard	Yes (8 MHz models)
Fast keyboard speed setting	Yes
Keyboard cable length	6 feet

Physical Specifications

Footprint type	Desktop
Dimensions:	
Height	6.4 inches
Width	21.3 inches
Depth	17.3 inches
Weight	43 pounds

Environmental Specifications

Power-supply output	192 watts
Worldwide (110/60,220/50)	Yes
Auto-sensing/switching	No
Maximum current:	
90-137 VAC	5.0 amps

Environmental Specifications

Operating range:	
Temperature	60–90 degrees F
Relative humidity	8–80 percent
Maximum operating altitude	7,000 feet
Heat (BTUs/hour)	1229
Noise (Average dB, operating, 1m)	42
FCC classification	Class B

Table 23.8 shows the AT system-unit part-number information.

Table 23.8 IBM AT Model Part Numbers

Description	Number
AT 6 MHz/84-key keyboard, 256K:	
one 1.2M floppy drive	5170068
AT 6 MHz/84-key keyboard, 512K, serial/parallel:	
one 1.2M floppy drive, 20M hard disk	5170099
one 1.2M floppy drive, 30M hard disk	5170239
AT 8 MHz/84-key keyboard, 512K, serial/parallel:	
one 1.2M floppy drive, 30M hard disk	5170319
AT 8 MHz/101-key, 512K, serial/parallel:	
one 1.2M floppy drive, 30M hard disk	5170339
System Options	
20M fixed disk drive	6450205
30M fixed disk	6450210
30M fixed disk drive upgrade kit	6450468
360K half-height floppy disk drive (AT)	6450207
1.2M high-density drive	6450206
3 1/2-inch, half-height, 720K external drive (AT)	2683191
Serial/parallel adapter	6450215
80287 math coprocessor option	6450211
Floor-standing enclosure	6450218
Enhanced Keyboard Accessories	
Clear keycaps (60) with paper inserts	6341707
Blank light keycaps	1351710
Blank dark keycaps	1351728
Paper inserts (300)	6341704
Keycap-removal tools (6)	1351717

AT 3270

IBM announced the AT 3270 on June 18, 1985. This computer, basically the same as the original 3270 PC, is configured with an AT, rather than an XT, as the base. New software enhancements and adapter cards use the DOS memory space better and can place much of the Control Program in the extended-memory area, beyond the 1M boundary. Much of this capability comes from the XMA card, from IBM. Because much of the Control Program can reside in the area above 1M, DOS can find more room for applications software. Although this configuration doesn't eliminate the incompatibilities in the display hardware or keyboard, it at least makes available the memory needed to run an application.

The AT 3270 system has the same basic adapters as the standard 3270 PC. This system differs, however, in the capability of enabling the Control Program to reside in the memory space above 1M (extended memory), which doesn't exist on a standard PC or XT. IBM made several changes in the Control Program for this system and in special memory adapters, such as the XMA card. These changes enhanced the compatibility of the AT 3270 system over the original 3270 PC.

For more information about the AT 3270 system, refer to the section on the 3270 PC in this chapter.

The AT 370

The AT 370 is basically the same system as the XT 370 except for its use of an AT as the base unit. The same three custom processor boards that convert an XT into an XT 370 also plug into an AT. This system is at least two to three times faster than the XT version. The custom processor boards also were available as an upgrade for existing ATs. For a more complete description of this system, refer to the section "3270 PC Models and Features" earlier in this chapter.

An Introduction to the XT Model 286

On September 9, 1986, IBM introduced a new AT-type system disguised inside the chassis and case of an XT. This XT Model 286 system featured increased memory, an Intel 80286 microprocessor, and as many as three internal drives standard. The computer combined an XT's cost-effectiveness, flexibility, and appearance with the high-speed, high-performance technology of the Intel 80286 microprocessor. This model looked like an XT, but underneath the cover, it was all AT.

The IBM XT Model 286 can operate as much as three times faster than earlier models of the XT in most applications. It has a standard 640K of memory. Various memory-expansion options enable users to increase its memory to 16M.

Standard features in this system include a half-height, 1.2M, 5 1/4-inch, high-density floppy disk drive; a 20M hard disk drive; a serial/parallel adapter card; and the IBM Enhanced Keyboard. You can select an optional, internal, second floppy disk drive from the following list:

- Half-height, 3 1/2-inch, 720K floppy drive
- Half-height, 3 1/2-inch, 1.44M floppy drive
- Half-height, 5 1/4-inch, 1.2M floppy drive
- Half-height, 5 1/4-inch, 360K floppy drive

The IBM XT Model 286's performance stems primarily from the AT motherboard design, with 16-bit I/O slots and an Intel 80286 processor running at 6 MHz. In addition to the type of processor used, clock speed and memory architecture are the primary factors in determining system performance. Depending on the model, the IBM AT's clock speed is 6 or 8 MHz, with one wait state; and the XT Model 286 processes data at 6 MHz, with zero wait states. The elimination of a wait state improves performance by increasing processing speed for system memory access. The zero-wait-state design makes the XT Model 286 definitely faster than the original AT models that ran at 6 MHz and about equal in speed to the 8 MHz AT systems. Based on tests, the XT Model 286 also is about three times faster than an actual XT.

Because the XT Model 286 is an AT-class system, the processor supports both real and protected modes. Operating in real address mode, the 80286 is 8088 compatible; therefore, you can use most software that runs on the standard PC systems. In real address mode, the system can address as much as 1M of RAM. Protected mode provides a number of advanced features to facilitate multitasking operations. Protected mode provides separation and protection of programs and data in multitasking environments. In protected mode, the 80286 can address as much as 16M of real memory and 1 gigabyte of virtual memory. In this mode, the XT Model 286 can run advanced operating systems such as OS/2 and UNIX. When the XT Model 286 was introduced, it was the least-expensive IBM system capable of running a true multitasking operating system.

The IBM XT Model 286 has a standard 640K of RAM. Memory options enable the system to grow to 15 1/2M, much higher than the 640K limit in other PC XTs. If you add an operating system such as OS/2 or Windows, you can take advantage of the larger memory capacities that the XT Model 286 provides.

A 20M hard disk drive is a standard feature in the XT Model 286, as is a 5 1/4-inch, 1.2M, high-density floppy disk drive. A similar floppy disk drive is standard on all models of the AT. Floppy disks formatted on a 1.2M floppy disk drive therefore can be read by an AT or an XT Model 286. The 1.2M floppy disk drive also can read floppy disks formatted with PC-family members that use a 360K floppy disk drive. Figure 23.13 shows the interior of an XT 286 system unit.

The XT Model 286 features the IBM Enhanced Keyboard with indicator lights. Many IBM personal computers use the Enhanced Keyboard, but the XT Model 286 was the first PC XT to feature keyboard indicator lights. The Caps Lock, Num Lock, and Scroll Lock lights remind users of keyboard status, which helps to prevent keyboard-entry errors.

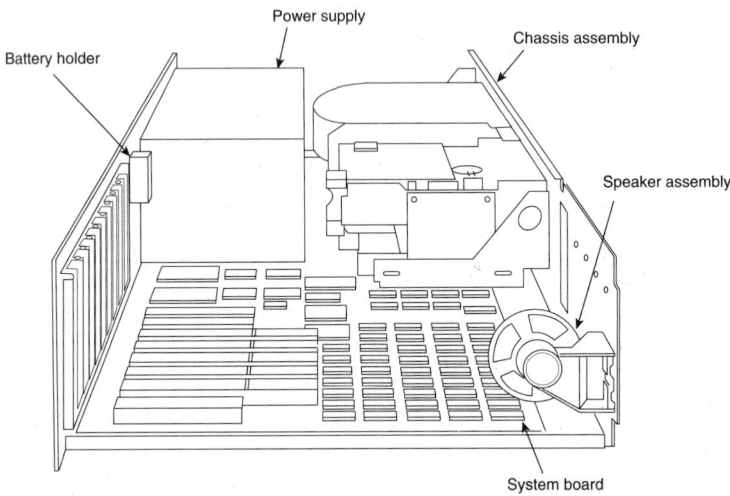

Figure 23.13
The IBM XT 286 interior.

The IBM XT Model 286 has eight I/O slots to accommodate peripheral-device adapter cards and memory-expansion options. Five slots support the advanced 16-bit cards or 8-bit cards; three support only 8-bit cards. Two of the three 8-bit slots support only short cards.

A hard disk and floppy drive adapter card are standard features in the XT Model 286. This multifunction card takes only one 16-bit slot and supports as many as four disk drives (two floppy disk drives and two hard disk drives).

The serial/parallel adapter, another standard feature, is a combination card that requires only one slot (either type) and provides a serial and a parallel port. The parallel portion of the adapter has the capacity to attach devices, such as a parallel printer, that accept eight bits of parallel data. The fully programmable serial portion supports asynchronous communications from 50 bps to 9,600 bps, although even higher speeds are possible with the right software. The serial portion requires an optional serial-adapter cable or a serial-adapter connector. When one of these options is connected to the adapter, all the signals in a standard EIA RS-232C interface are available. You can use the serial port for interfacing a modem, a remote display terminal, a mouse, or other serial device. The XT Model 286 supports as many as two serial/parallel adapters.

A standard IBM XT Model 286 offers these features:

- 80286 processor at 6 MHz with 0 wait states
- 640K of motherboard memory
- 1.2M floppy drive

- 20M hard disk
- Five 16-bit and three 8-bit expansion slots
- Fixed disk/floppy disk drive adapter (occupies one 16-bit expansion slot)
- Serial/parallel adapter (occupies one 16-bit expansion slot)
- Enhanced Keyboard with indicator lights
- CMOS time-and-date clock with battery backup

XT Model 286 Models and Features

The XT Model 286 processor is as much as three times faster internally than the preceding XT family and as much as 25 percent faster than the AT Model 239, depending on specific applications. A 20M fixed disk and a 1.2M, 5 1/4-inch floppy disk drive were standard on the XT Model 286. One additional floppy disk drive can be installed internally as drive B. You can add as a second half-height floppy drive any type of floppy drive, including both the double and high-density versions of the 5 1/4- and 3 1/2-inch drives.

If you want to be able to read standard 5 1/4-inch data or program floppy disks created by the XT Model 286 on other PC systems, you might want to add a 5 1/4-inch 360K floppy disk drive, which provides full read/write compatibility with those systems. This is due to the fact that the 1.2M drives write a narrower track than the 360K drives, and are unable to properly overwrite a floppy disk written on first by a 360K drive. If full read/write compatibility with 360K drives is not important, you can add a second 1.2M high-density floppy disk drive.

You can add any 3 1/2-inch drive, including the 720K and 1.44M versions. Because the 1.44M does not have any read/write compatibility problems with the 720K drives, however, and the 1.44M drives always can operate in 720K mode, I suggest adding only the 1.44M 3 1/2-inch drives rather than the 720K versions. The higher-density drive is only a small extra expense compared to the double-density version. Most people do not know that full ROM BIOS support for these 1.44M drives is provided in the XT Model 286. Unfortunately, because IBM never offered the 1.44M drive as an option, the supplied Setup program does not offer the 1.44M drive as a choice in the Setup routine. Instead you have to use one of the many available public domain AT type setup programs, or "borrow" such a program from an AT-compatible system.

XT Model 286 Technical Specifications

The technical information for the XT 286 system described in this section covers the system architecture, memory configurations and capacities, standard system features, disk storage, expansion slots, keyboard specifications, and also physical and environmental specifications. You can use this information to determine the parts you need when you are upgrading or repairing these systems. Figure 23.14 shows the layout and components on the XT 286 motherboard.

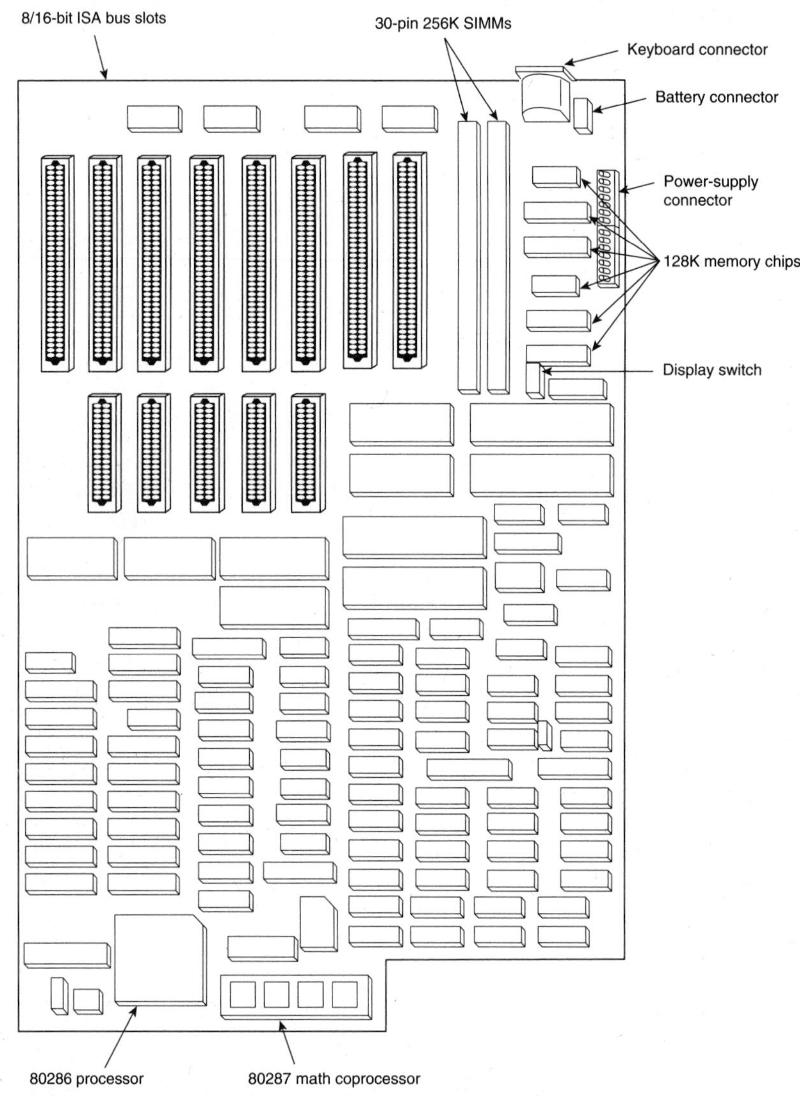

Figure 23.14

The IBM XT 286 motherboard.

System Architecture

Microprocessor	80286
Clock speed	6 MHz
Bus type	ISA (Industry Standard Architecture)
Bus width	16-bit

System Architecture

Interrupt levels	16
Type	Edge-triggered
Shareable	No
DMA channels	7
DMA burst mode supported	No
Bus masters supported	No
Upgradeable processor complex	No

Memory

Standard on system board	640K
Maximum on system board	640K
Maximum total memory	16M
Memory speed (ns) and type	150ns dynamic RAM
System board memory-socket type	9-bit SIMM
Number of memory-module sockets	2
Memory used on system board	One bank of 4 64K×4-bit and 2 64K×1-bit DRAM parity chips, and one bank of 2 9-bit SIMMs
Memory cache controller	No
Wait states:	
System board	0
Adapter	1

Standard Features

ROM size	64K
ROM shadowing	No
Optional math coprocessor	80287
Coprocessor speed	4.77 MHz
Standard graphics	None standard
RS232C serial ports	1
UART chip used	NS16450
Maximum speed (bits per second)	9,600 bps
Maximum number of ports supported	2
Pointing device (mouse) ports	None standard
Parallel printer ports	1
Bi-directional	Yes
Maximum number of ports supported	3
CMOS real-time clock (RTC)	Yes
CMOS RAM	64 bytes
Battery life	5 years

Disk Storage	
Internal disk and tape drive bays	1 full-height and 2 half-height
Number of 3 1/2-/5 1/4-inch bays	0/3
Standard floppy drives	1×1.2M
Optional floppy drives:	
5 1/4-inch 360K	Optional
5 1/4-inch 1.2M	Standard
3 1/2-inch 720K	Optional
3 1/2-inch 1.44M	Optional
3 1/2-inch 2.88M	No
Hard disk controller included:	ST-506/412 (Western Digital WD1003-WA2)
ST-506/412 hard disks available	20M
Drive form factor	5 1/4-inch
Drive interface	ST-506/412
Drive capacity	20M
Average access rate (ms)	65
Encoding scheme	MFM
BIOS drive type number	2
Cylinders	615
Heads	4
Sectors per track	17
Rotational speed (RPMs)	3600
Interleave factor	3:1
Data transfer rate (kilobytes/ second)	170
Automatic head parking	No

Expansion Slots	
Total adapter slots	8
Number of long and short slots	6/2
Number of 8-/16-/32-bit slots	3/5/0
Available slots (with video)	5

Keyboard Specifications	
101-key Enhanced Keyboard	Yes
Fast keyboard speed setting	Yes
Keyboard cable length	6 feet

Physical Specifications	
Footprint type	Desktop
Dimensions:	
Height	5.5 inches
Width	19.5 inches
Depth	16.0 inches
Weight	28 pounds

Environmental Specifications	
Power-supply output	157 watts
Worldwide (110v/60Hz,220v/50Hz)	Yes
Auto-sensing/switching	Yes
Maximum current:	
90-137 VAC	4.5 amps
Operating range:	
Temperature	60–90 degrees F
Relative humidity	8–80 percent
Maximum operating altitude	7,000 feet
Heat (BTUs/hour)	824
Noise (Average dB, operating, 1m)	42
FCC classification	Class B

Table 23.9 lists the XT Model 286 system-unit part numbers.

Table 23.9 IBM XT-286 Model Part Numbers

Description	Number
XT Model 286 system unit, 6 MHz 0 wait state,640K, serial/parallel, 1.2M floppy drive, one 20M hard disk	5162286
Optional Accessories	
5 1/4-inch, half-height 360K drive	6450325
3 1/4-inch, half-height 720K internal drive	6450258
3 1/2-inch, half-height 720K external drive	2683190
80287 math coprocessor option	6450211
Enhanced Keyboard Accessories	
Clear keycaps (60) with paper inserts	6341707
Blank light keycaps	1351710
Blank dark keycaps	1351728
Paper inserts (300)	6341704
Keycap removal tools (6)	1351717

Summary

This chapter examined all the systems that make up the original line of IBM personal computers. Although these systems have long since been discontinued, I am amazed to find many of these systems still in everyday use. From individuals to large corporations to the United States government, I regularly encounter many of these old systems in my training and consulting practice. Because these systems still are used, and probably will be for years, the information in this chapter is useful as a reference tool. Much of this information also is a sort of history lesson; it is easy to see how far IBM-compatible computing has come when you look over the specifications of these older systems!

The chapter described the makeup of all the versions or models of each system, as well as their technical details and specifications. Each system unit's main components also were listed. Each system's submodels were discussed, which should help you better understand the differences among systems that might look the same on the outside but differ internally.

Chapter 24

A Final Word

The contents of this book cover most of the components of a PC-compatible system. In this book, you discover how all the components operate and interact and how these components should be set up and installed. You see the ways that components fail and learn the symptoms of these failures. You review the steps in diagnosing and troubleshooting the major components in a system so that you can locate and replace a failing component. You also learn about upgrades for components, including what upgrades are available, the benefits of an upgrade, and how to obtain and perform the actual upgrade. Because failing components so often are technically obsolete, it is often desirable to combine repair and upgrade procedures to replace a failing part with an upgraded or higher performance part.

The information I present in this book represents many years of practical experience with PC-compatible systems. A great deal of research and investigation have gone into each section. This information has saved companies many thousands of dollars. By reading this book, you also take advantage of this wealth of information, and may save you and your company time, energy, and most importantly, money!

Bringing PC service and support in-house is one of the best ways to save money. Eliminating service contracts for most systems and reducing downtime are just two of the benefits of applying the information presented in this book. As I indicate many times in this book, you can also save a lot of money on component purchases by eliminating the middleman and purchasing the components directly from distributors or manufacturers. The vendor list in Appendix B provides the best of these sources for you to contact. If you intend to build your own systems, the vendor list will be extremely useful as I list sources for all of the components needed to assemble a complete system—from the screws and brackets all the way to the cases, power supplies, and motherboards. I've found that this list is one of the most frequently used parts of this book. Many people have been unable to make direct purchases because doing so requires a new level of understanding of the components involved. Also, many of the vendors are unable to provide support for beginning users. I hope that this book gives you the deeper level of knowledge and understanding you need so that you can purchase the components you want directly from the vendors who manufacture and distribute them, saving a great deal of money in the long run.

I used many sources to gather the information in this book, starting with my own real world experiences. I also taught this information to thousands of people in seminars presented over the last 15 years by my company, Mueller Technical Research. During these seminars, I am often asked where more of this type of information can be obtained and whether I have any "secrets" for acquiring this knowledge. Well, I won't keep any secrets! I can freely share the following four key sources of information that can help you become a verifiable expert in PC upgrading and repairing:

- Manuals
- Machines
- Modems
- Magazines

Manuals

Manuals are the single most important source of computer information. Unfortunately, manuals also are one of the most frequently overlooked sources of information. Much of my knowledge has come from poring over technical-reference manuals and other original equipment manufacturer's (OEM) manuals. I would not even consider purchasing a system that does not have a detailed technical-reference manual available. This statement applies also to system components—whether it's a floppy drive, hard disk, power supply, motherboard, or memory card. I have to have a detailed reference manual to help me understand what future upgrades are possible and to provide valuable insight into the proper installation, use, and support of a product. Oftentimes these manuals must be obtained from the OEM of the equipment you purchase, meaning the vendor or reseller will not supply them. Where possible, you should make an effort to discover who the real OEM of each component in your system is, and try to obtain documentation from them on the product or component.

Large manufacturers such as Intel, IBM, Compaq, Hewlett-Packard, and others both manufacture their own components as well as purchase components from other sources. Many of these manufacturers also make available complete libraries of technical documentation for their systems. I have included a list of some of IBM's technical documents in Appendix A, which are quite detailed and, unfortunately, often fairly expensive. These are excellent at detailing the operations of CPU, memory, bus, and other architectures in the system, and are even appropriate when discussing compatible systems because most systems must be compatible with IBMs in most elements. In other words, the IBM documentation would be interesting to those who do not even own a single piece of true IBM hardware.

Other companies, such as Compaq and HP, also have extensive documentation libraries. IBM, HP, and Compaq make their technical libraries available in a CD-ROM version, which is very convenient and easy to search. These CD-ROMs contain detailed information about PC systems from these companies. In addition to IBM, both Compaq and HP also have BBS services available for technical support. Check the vendor list for phone number information on these and other BBS systems.

A simple analogy explains the importance of manuals, as well as other issues concerning repair and maintenance of a system. Compare your business use of computers to a taxicab company. The company has to purchase automobiles to use as cabs. The owners purchase not one car but an entire fleet of cars. Do you think that they would purchase a fleet of automobiles based solely on reliability, performance, or even gas-mileage statistics? Would they neglect to consider ongoing maintenance and service of these automobiles? Would they purchase a fleet of cars that could be serviced only by the original manufacturer and for which parts could not be obtained easily? Do you think that they would buy a car that did not have available a detailed service and repair manual? Would they buy an automobile for which parts were scarce and that was supported by a sparse dealer network with few service and parts outlets, making long waits for parts and service inevitable? The answer (of course) to all these questions is no, no, no!

You can see why most taxi companies as well as police departments use "standard" automobiles such as the Chevrolet Caprice or Ford Crown Victoria. If ever there were "generic" cars, these models would qualify! Dealers, parts, and documentation for these particular models are everywhere. They share parts with many other automobiles as well, which makes them easy to service and maintain.

Doesn't your business (especially if it is large) use what amounts to a "fleet" of computers? If so, why don't you think of this fleet as being similar to the cars of a cab company, which would go out of business quickly if these cars could not be kept running smoothly and inexpensively. Now you know why the Checker Marathon automobile used to be so popular with cab companies: its design barely changed from the time it was introduced in 1956 until it was discontinued in July 1982. (At last report, there were only eight still in service in New York City!) In many ways, the standard XT- and AT-compatible systems are like the venerable Checker Marathon. You can get technical information by the shelf-full for these systems. You can get parts and upgrade material from so many sources that anything you need is always immediately available and at a discounted price. I'm not saying that you should standardize on using older XT or AT systems. However, there are good reasons for standardizing on systems that follow the "generic" physical design of the XT or AT, but use newer internal components. This results in systems that are completely modern in performance and capabilities, and which are easily supported, repaired, and upgraded.

It's amazing that people purchase computers that have no technical documentation and no spare-parts program, or parts available only through dealers, or that use nonstandard form-factor components, and so on. The upgrade, repair, and maintenance of a company's computer systems always seem to take a back seat to performance and style.

In addition to the system OEM manuals, I like to collect documentation from the different Original Equipment Manufacturers that make the components used in various systems. For example, I recently worked with Gateway 2000 and Hewlett-Packard systems, both of which use Epson floppy drives. The OEM documentation for these systems did not include detailed information on the Epson floppy drives, so I called Epson and ordered the specification manual for these drives. I also ordered the specification manuals for several other drives used in these systems, including Western Digital and Quantum hard disks. I now have detailed information on these drives, which covers jumper settings, service and repair information, and other technical specifications not provided otherwise. I recommend that you inventory each major component of your system by manufacturer and model number. If you don't have the specification or technical reference manuals for these components, call the manufacturers (the vendor list in Appendix B will help), and ask for them. You'll be amazed at the wealth of information you can get.

If you want information about the electronics and chip level components in the system, you can contact the manufacturers of these devices and get their data books. Intel, for example, has volumes of information available on their processors, motherboard chipsets, cache controller chips, and other components they make. Other chipset manufacturers have data books on their chips that tell you about all the esoteric settings you see in your CMOS setup. Most of the BIOS manufacturers also produce documentation specific to their BIOS software. Check the vendor list in Appendix B for the manufacturers of the components in your system and call them to see what documentation they have available.

If you're looking for more general purpose documentation, especially on operating systems or applications software, try Que Corporation, which specializes in this type of computer book. These books combine basic hardware information with more extensive software and operating system coverage. Microsoft and IBM also publish books of interest to computer enthusiasts and technicians. For example, Microsoft sells both Windows 95 and Windows NT Resource Kits, which should be considered mandatory additions to any technical library.

Machines

The term "machines" refers to the systems themselves. Machines are one of my best sources of information. For example, suppose that I need to answer the question, "Will the XYZ SCSI host adapter work with the ABC tape drive?" The answer is as simple as plugging everything in and pressing the switch. (Simple to talk about, that is.) Seriously, experimenting with and observing running systems are some of the best learning tools at your disposal. I recommend that you try everything; rarely will anything you try harm the equipment. Harming valuable data is definitely possible, if not likely, however, so make regular backups as insurance. You should not use a system you depend on for day-to-day operations as an experimental system, if possible use a secondary machine. People sometimes are reluctant to experiment with systems that cost a lot of money, but much can be learned through direct tests and studies of the system. I often find that vendor claims about a product are somewhat misleading when I actually install it and run some tests. If you are unsure that something will really work, make sure that the company has a return policy that allows you to return the item for a refund if it does not meet your expectations.

Support people in larger companies have access to quantities of hardware and software I can only dream about. Some larger companies have "toy stores," where they regularly purchase equipment solely for evaluation and testing. Dealers and manufacturers also have access to an enormous variety of equipment. If you are in this position, take advantage of this access to equipment, and learn from this resource. When new systems are purchased, take notes on their construction and components.

Every time I encounter a system I have not previously worked with, I immediately open it up and start taking notes. I want to know the make and model of all the internal components, such as disk drives, power supplies, and motherboards. As far as motherboards, I like to record the numbers of the primary IC chips on the board, such as the processor (of course), integrated chip sets, floppy controller chips, keyboard controller chips, video chipsets, and any other major chips on the board. By knowing which chip set your system uses, you can often infer other capabilities of the system, such as enhanced setup or configuration capabilities. I like to know which BIOS version is in the system, and I even make a copy of the BIOS on disk for backup and further study purposes. I want to know the hard drive tables from the BIOS, and any other particulars involved in setting up and installing a system. Write down the type of battery a system uses so that you can obtain spares. Note any unique brackets or construction techniques such as specialized hardware (Torx screws, for example) so that you can be prepared for servicing the system later. Some programs have been designed to help you maintain an inventory of systems and components, but I find that these fall far short of the detail I am talking about here.

This discussion brings up a pet peeve of mine. Nothing burns me up as much as reading a review of computer systems in a major magazine, in which reviewers test systems and produce benchmark and performance results for, let's say, the hard disks or video displays in a system. Then, they do not open up the machines and tell me (and the world) exactly which components the manufacturer of the system is using! I want to know exactly which disk controller, hard drive, BIOS, motherboard, video adapter, and so on are found in each system. Without this information, their review and benchmark tests are useless to me. Then they run a test of disk performance between two systems with the same disk controller and drives and say (with a straight face) that the one that came out a few milliseconds ahead of the other wins the test. With the statistical variation that normally occurs in any manufactured components, these results are meaningless. The point is perhaps to be very careful of what you trust in a normal magazine review. If it tells me exactly which components were tested, I can draw my own conclusions and even make comparisons to other systems not included in that review.

Modems

Modems refers to the use of public- and private-information utilities and online services, which are a modem and a phone call away. With a modem, you can tie into everything from local electronic bulletin board systems (BBSs) to major information networks such as CompuServe and of course the Internet featuring the World Wide Web. Many hardware and software companies offer technical support and even software upgrades over their own public bulletin boards or the Internet. The public-access information networks such as the Internet, CompuServe, and other BBS systems include computer enthusiasts and technical-support people from various organizations, as well as experts in virtually all areas of computer hardware and software. Bulletin boards are a great way to have questions answered and to collect useful utility and help programs that can make your job much easier. The world of public-domain and user-supported software awaits, as well as more technical information and related experiences than you can imagine.

Appendix B includes not only the name, address, and voice phone number for the company, but also the Internet addresses (Websites) and or BBS numbers where available. If you need more information on a vendor's products, or need technical support, try using the vendor's online connection. Many companies today provide on-line services to facilitate obtaining updated software or driver files which you can download quickly and easily. When a vendor provides an online connection, I consider that service a major advantage in comparison to other vendors who do not provide such a service. Using vendor provided online connections either through the Internet or via a private BBS or even CompuServe has saved me money and countless hours of time.

Many companies that provide online services do so through a public access utility, such as CompuServe, or through their own Website on the Internet, rather than running their own BBS. The CompuServe Information Service (CIS) is a public information access utility with an extensive network of dial-in nodes that allows you to log on to its cluster of mainframe systems (based in Ohio) from virtually anywhere in the world through a local telephone call. Among CompuServe's resources are the forums sponsored or attended by most of the major software and hardware companies, as well as enthusiasts of all types. CompuServe also provides access to the Internet, including the World Wide Web. CompuServe or other Internet providers, combined with a local electronic bulletin board or two, can greatly supplement the information you gather from other sources. In fact, CompuServe electronic mail is probably the most efficient method of reaching me. My CompuServe ID is **73145,1566** (on the Internet it is **73145.1566@compuserve.com**), and if you have questions or just a comment or useful information you think I might be interested in, please send me a message. Because of the extra steps in processing, my standard mail can get backed up and it can take me quite a while to answer a regular postal letter; electronic mail, however, involves fewer steps for me to send, and always seems to have a higher priority. If you do send a regular letter, be sure to include a SASE (Self-Addressed Stamped Envelope) so that I will be able to reply.

Magazines

The last source of information, magazines, is one of the best sources of up-to-date reviews and technical data. Featured are "bug fixes," problem alerts, and general industry news. Keeping a printed book up-to-date with the latest events in the computer industry is extremely difficult or even impossible. Things move so fast that the magazines themselves barely keep pace. I subscribe to most of the major computer magazines and am hard-pressed to pick one as the best. They all are important to me, and each one provides different information or the same information with a different angle or twist. Although the reviews usually leave me wanting, the magazines still are a valuable way to at least hear about products, most of which I never would have known about without the magazines' reports and advertisements. Most computer magazines are also available on CD-ROM, which can ease the frantic search for a specific piece of information you remember reading about. If CD-ROM versions are too much for your needs, be aware that you can access and search most major magazines on the Internet. This capability is valuable when you want to research everything you can about a specific subject.

One of the best kept secrets in the computer industry is the excellent trade magazines that offer free subscriptions. Although many of these magazines are directed toward the wholesale or technical end of the industry, I like to subscribe to them. Some of my favorites magazines include:

- *Computer Design*
- *Computer Hotline*
- *Computer Reseller News*
- *Electronic Design News*
- *Electronic Buyer's News*
- *Electronic Engineering Times*
- *Electronic News*
- *Electronic Products*
- *Processor*
- *Service News*
- *Test and Measurement World*

These magazines offer free subscriptions to anyone who qualifies. Aimed at people in the computer and electronics industries, these magazines offer a much greater depth and breadth of technical and industry information compared to the more "public" magazines that most people are familiar with. You'll find these and other recommended magazines in the vendor list in Appendix B.

The Appendixes

The appendixes provide a collection of technical information, tables, charts, and lists especially useful to people in a computer support, troubleshooting, service, or upgrading role. Whether you're looking for the meaning of a word in the glossary, seeking the address and phone number of a company or vendor in the vendor list, or searching for something as technical as determining the pinout of the ISA bus connector, you'll most likely find the information in the appendixes.

The appendixes started out as a brief collection of essential information, but have grown into a complete reference resource of its own. No other book currently on the market contains such a complete and informative technical reference, which is one reason why so many large companies and educational institutions have standardized on this book for their technicians and students. This book is currently being used as an official textbook for many corporate and college-level computer training courses, as well as my own PC training seminars, for which the book was originally designed.

In Conclusion

I hope that *Upgrading and Repairing PCs, Sixth Edition,* is beneficial to you and I hope that you have enjoyed reading it as much as I have enjoyed writing it. If you have questions about this book, or if you have ideas for future versions, I can be reached at the following address:

Scott Mueller
Mueller Technical Research
21718 Mayfield Lane
Barrington, IL 60010-9733
(847)726-0709
(847)726-0710 Fax
73145,1566 = CompuServe ID
73145.1566@compuserve.com = Internet Address

I am especially interested in any ideas you have for new topics and information to be included in future releases of this book. Remember that the best way to contact me is through e-mail, often time constraints prevent me from responding to regular mail. If you do need a response through the mail, please include a self-addressed stamped envelope so that I can reply to you. If you are interested in one of my many intensive PC training seminars or videotapes, please call my office.

Thank you again for reading this book, and a special thanks to those people who have been loyal readers since the first edition came out in January 1989.

Sincerely,

Scott Mueller

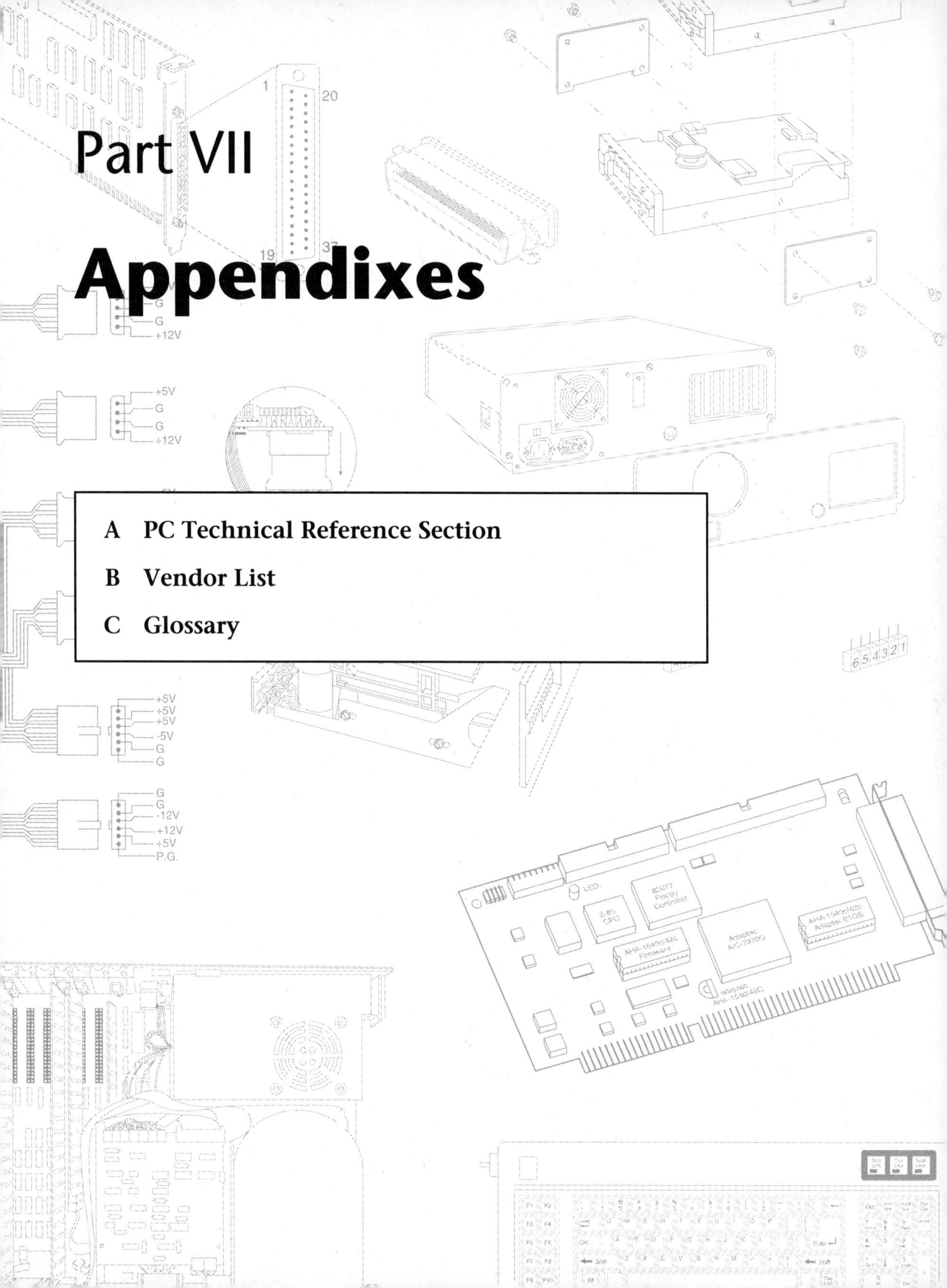

Part VII

Appendixes

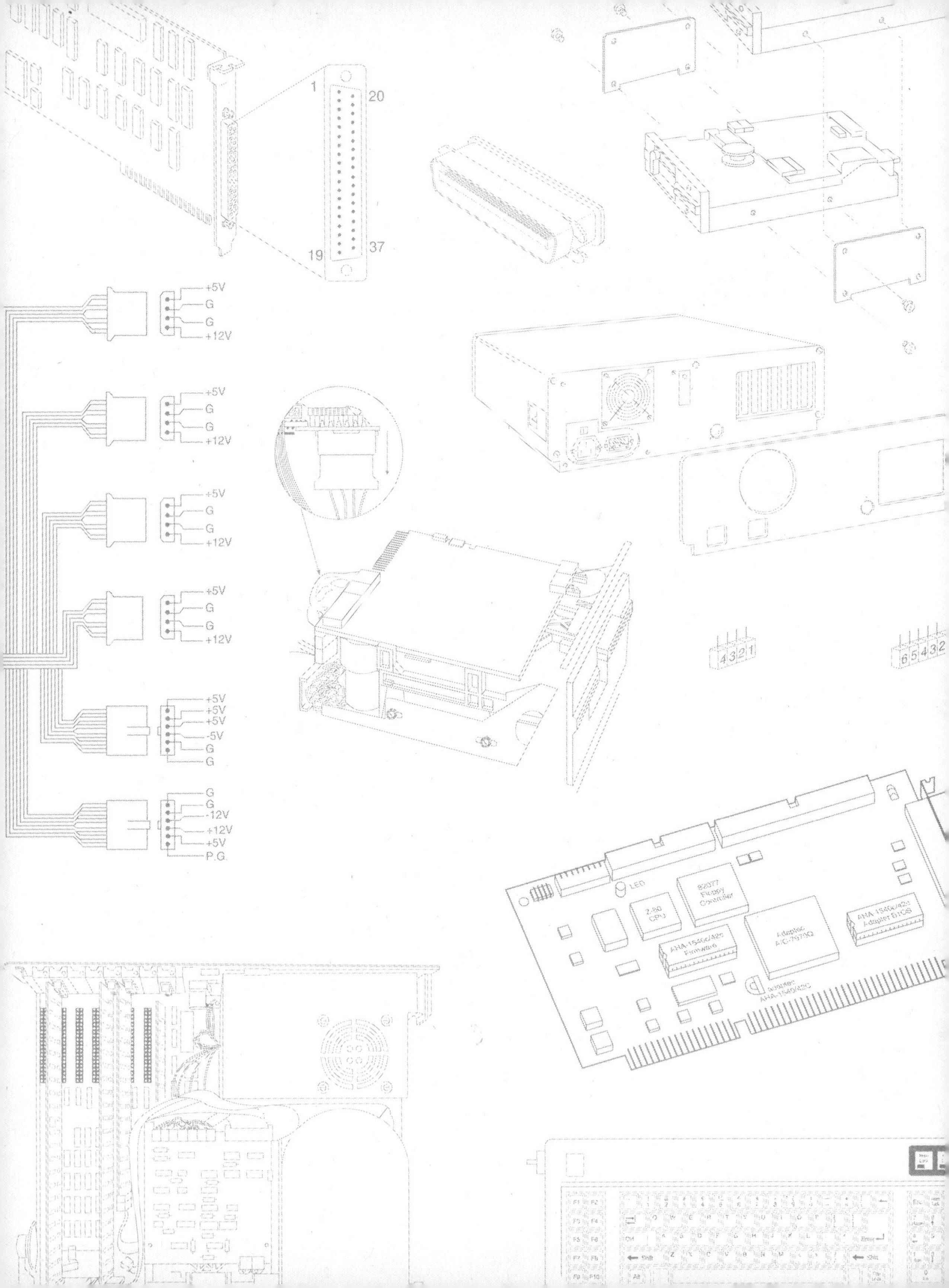
1
20
19
37
+5V
G
G
+12V
+5V
G
G
+12V
+5V
G
G
+12V
+5V
G
G
+12V
+5V
+5V
+5V
-5V
G
G
G
G
-12V
+12V
+5V
P.G.
4 3 2 1
6 5 4 3 2
LED
Z-80 CPU
82077 Floppy Controller
Adaptec AIC-7970Q
AHA-1540c/42c Adapter BIOS
AHA-1540C/42C Firmware
Adaptec AHA-1540/42C

Appendix A

PC Technical Reference Section

This book has a great deal of useful information, primarily reference information, that is not designed to be read but to be looked up. Important technical information not provided in specific chapters is listed in this appendix. This type of information can be very useful in troubleshooting or upgrading sessions, but usually is spread out among many sources. In this edition of *Upgrading and Repairing PCs*, virtually all types of reference information you will need for troubleshooting and upgrading systems can be found quickly and easily.

This information is organized into charts and tables—in particular, information about the default interrupt, and DMA channel use of the primary system and most standard options. This information is invaluable if you install new boards or upgrade a system in any way, and can be important when you troubleshoot a conflict between two devices.

This book has information about various system connectors—from serial and parallel ports to power supply connections. Diagrams for making serial and parallel wrap (test) plugs are shown also.

Tables indicate the hard disk drive parameters found in XT, AT, PS/2, and other IBM-compatible systems. Many compatible BIOS drive tables are included. This information is often necessary when adding a hard disk to a system.

One of the most useful tables is a concise listing of the IBM, AMI, Phoenix, Award, and Hewlett Packard diagnostics error codes. These codes can be generated by the POST and by the disk-based diagnostic programs. This information can be very useful in deciphering the codes quickly and efficiently, without having to look through a stack of books.

This book also has a listing of all the available IBM technical manuals and a description of all the documentation available. The included listing has part numbers and pricing information, as well as information useful in ordering this documentation.

Although all of this information comes from a wide range of sources, most of it comes from the technical-reference manuals and hardware-maintenance service manuals available for various systems from IBM and other manufacturers. These documents are invaluable if you want to pursue this topic more extensively.

General Information

ASCII Character Code Charts

Figure A.1 lists ASCII control character values. Figure A.2 shows the IBM extended ASCII line-drawing characters in an easy-to-use format. I frequently use these extended ASCII line-drawing characters for visual enhancement in documents I create.

DEC	HEX	CHAR	NAME		CONTROL CODE
0	00		Ctrl-@	NUL	Null
1	01	☺	Ctrl-A	SOH	Start of Heading
2	02	●	Ctrl-B	STX	Start of Text
3	03	♥	Ctrl-C	ETX	End of Text
4	04	♦	Ctrl-D	EOT	End of Transit
5	05	♣	Ctrl-E	ENQ	Enquiry
6	06	♠	Ctrl-F	ACK	Acknowledge
7	07	•	Ctrl-G	BEL	Bell
8	08	◘	Ctrl-H	BS	Back Space
9	09	○	Ctrl-I	HT	Horizontal Tab
10	0A	◙	Ctrl-J	LF	Line Feed
11	0B	♂	Ctrl-K	VT	Vertical Tab
12	0C	♀	Ctrl-L	FF	Form Feed
13	0D	♪	Ctrl-M	CR	Carriage Return
14	0E	♫	Ctrl-N	SO	Shift Out
15	0F	☼	Ctrl-O	SI	Shift In
16	10	►	Ctrl-P	DLE	Data Line Escape
17	11	◄	Ctrl-Q	DC1	Device Control 1
18	12	↕	Ctrl-R	DC2	Device Control 2
19	13	‼	Ctrl-S	DC3	Device Control 3
20	14	¶	Ctrl-T	DC4	Device Control 4
21	15	§	Ctrl-U	NAK	Negative Acknowledge
22	16	■	Ctrl-V	SYN	Synchronous Idle
23	17	↨	Ctrl-W	ETB	End of Transmit Block
24	18	↑	Ctrl-X	CAN	Cancel
25	19	↓	Ctrl-Y	EM	End of Medium
26	1A	←	Ctrl-Z	SUB	Substitute
27	1B	→	Ctrl-[	ESC	Escape
28	1C	∟	Ctrl-\	FS	File Separator
29	1D	↔	Ctrl-]	GS	Group Separator
30	1E	▲	Ctrl-^	RS	Record Separator
31	1FA	▼	Ctrl-_	US	Unit Separator

Figure A.1

ASCII control codes.

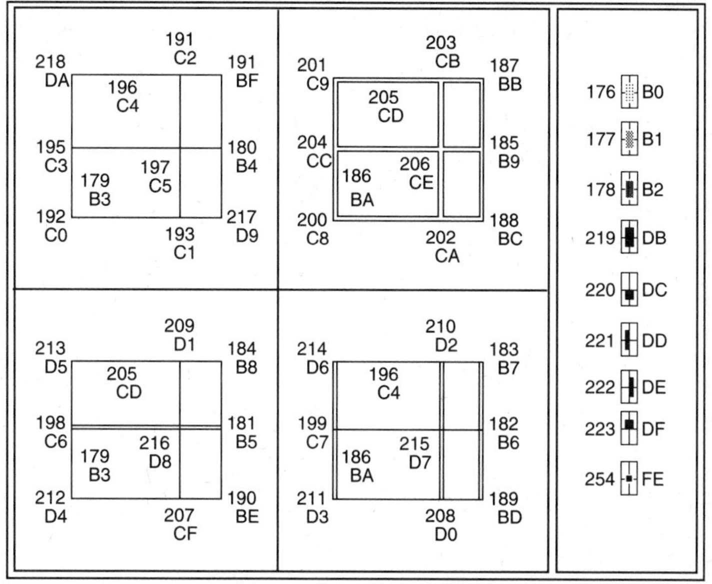

Figure A.2

Extended ASCII line-drawing characters.

Hexadecimal/ASCII Conversions

Table A.1 Hexadecimal/ASCII Conversions

Dec	Hex	Octal	Binary	Name	Character
0	00	000	0000 0000	blank	
1	01	001	0000 0001	happy face	☺
2	02	002	0000 0010	inverse happy face	☻
3	03	003	0000 0011	heart	♥
4	04	004	0000 0100	diamond	♦
5	05	005	0000 0101	club	♣
6	06	006	0000 0110	spade	♠
7	07	007	0000 0111	bullet	•
8	08	010	0000 1000	inverse bullet	◘
9	09	011	0000 1001	circle	o
10	0A	012	0000 1010	inverse circle	○
11	0B	013	0000 1011	male sign	♂
12	0C	014	0000 1100	female sign	♀
13	0D	015	0000 1101	single note	♪
14	0E	016	0000 1110	double note	♫
15	0F	017	0000 1111	sun	☼
16	10	020	0001 0000	right triangle	►
17	11	021	0001 0001	left triangle	◄
18	12	022	0001 0010	up/down arrow	↕

(continues)

Table A.1 Continued

Dec	Hex	Octal	Binary	Name	Character
19	13	023	0001 0011	double exclamation	‼
20	14	024	0001 0100	paragraph sign	¶
21	15	025	0001 0101	section sign	§
22	16	026	0001 0110	rectangular bullet	■
23	17	027	0001 0111	up/down to line	↨
24	18	030	0001 1000	up arrow	↑
25	19	031	0001 1001	down arrow	↓
26	1A	032	0001 1010	right arrow	→
27	1B	033	0001 1011	left arrow	←
28	1C	034	0001 1100	lower left box	∟
29	1D	035	0001 1101	left/right arrow	↔
30	1E	036	0001 1110	up triangle	▲
31	1F	037	0001 1111	down triangle	▼
32	20	040	0010 0000	space	Space
33	21	041	0010 0001	exclamation point	!
34	22	042	0010 0010	quotation mark	"
35	23	043	0010 0011	number sign	#
36	24	044	0010 0100	dollar sign	$
37	25	045	0010 0101	percent sign	%
38	26	046	0010 0110	ampersand	&
39	27	047	0010 0111	apostrophe	'
40	28	050	0010 1000	opening parenthesis	(
41	29	051	0010 1001	closing parenthesis	)
42	2A	052	0010 1010	asterisk	*
43	2B	053	0010 1011	plus sign	+
44	2C	054	0010 1100	comma	,
45	2D	055	0010 1101	hyphen or minus sign	-
46	2E	056	0010 1110	period	.
47	2F	057	0010 1111	slash	/
48	30	060	0011 0000	zero	0
49	31	061	0011 0001	one	1
50	32	062	0011 0010	two	2
51	33	063	0011 0011	three	3
52	34	064	0011 0100	four	4
53	35	065	0011 0101	five	5
54	36	066	0011 0110	six	6
55	37	067	0011 0111	seven	7
56	38	070	0011 1000	eight	8
57	39	071	0011 1001	nine	9
58	3A	072	0011 1010	colon	:
59	3B	073	0011 1011	semicolon	;
60	3C	074	0011 1100	less-than sign	<
61	3D	075	0011 1101	equal sign	=

Dec	Hex	Octal	Binary	Name	Character
62	3E	076	0011 1110	greater-than sign	>
63	3F	077	0011 1111	question mark	?
64	40	100	0100 0000	at sign	@
65	41	101	0100 0001	capital A	A
66	42	102	0100 0010	capital B	B
67	43	103	0100 0011	capital C	C
68	44	104	0100 0100	capital D	D
69	45	105	0100 0101	capital E	E
70	46	106	0100 0110	capital F	F
71	47	107	0100 0111	capital G	G
72	48	110	0100 1000	capital H	H
73	49	111	0100 1001	capital I	I
74	4A	112	0100 1010	capital J	J
75	4B	113	0100 1011	capital K	K
76	4C	114	0100 1100	capital L	L
77	4D	115	0100 1101	capital M	M
78	4E	116	0100 1110	capital N	N
79	4F	117	0100 1111	capital O	O
80	50	120	0101 0000	capital P	P
81	51	121	0101 0001	capital Q	Q
82	52	122	0101 0010	capital R	R
83	53	123	0101 0011	capital S	S
84	54	124	0101 0100	capital T	T
85	55	125	0101 0101	capital U	U
86	56	126	0101 0110	capital V	V
87	57	127	0101 0111	capital W	W
88	58	130	0101 1000	capital X	X
89	59	131	0101 1001	capital Y	Y
90	5A	132	0101 1010	capital Z	Z
91	5B	133	0101 1011	opening bracket	[
92	5C	134	0101 1100	backward slash	\
93	5D	135	0101 1101	closing bracket	]
94	5E	136	0101 1110	caret	^
95	5F	137	0101 1111	underscore	_
96	60	140	0110 0000	grave	`
97	61	141	0110 0001	lowercase A	a
98	62	142	0110 0010	lowercase B	b
99	63	143	0110 0011	lowercase C	c
100	64	144	0110 0100	lowercase D	d
101	65	145	0110 0101	lowercase E	e
102	66	146	0110 0110	lowercase F	f
103	67	147	0110 0111	lowercase G	g
104	68	150	0110 1000	lowercase H	h
105	69	151	0110 1001	lowercase I	i

(continues)

Table A.1 Continued

Dec	Hex	Octal	Binary	Name	Character
106	6A	152	0110 1010	lowercase J	j
107	6B	153	0110 1011	lowercase K	k
108	6C	154	0110 1100	lowercase L	l
109	6D	155	0110 1101	lowercase M	m
110	6E	156	0110 1110	lowercase N	n
111	6F	157	0110 1111	lowercase O	o
112	70	160	0111 0000	lowercase P	p
113	71	161	0111 0001	lowercase Q	q
114	72	162	0111 0010	lowercase R	r
115	73	163	0111 0011	lowercase S	s
116	74	164	0111 0100	lowercase T	t
117	75	165	0111 0101	lowercase U	u
118	76	166	0111 0110	lowercase V	v
119	77	167	0111 0111	lowercase W	w
120	78	170	0111 1000	lowercase X	x
121	79	171	0111 1001	lowercase Y	y
122	7A	172	0111 1010	lowercase Z	z
123	7B	173	0111 1011	opening brace	{
124	7C	174	0111 1100	vertical line	|
125	7D	175	0111 1101	closing brace	}
126	7E	176	0111 1110	tilde	~
127	7F	177	0111 1111	small house	Δ
128	80	200	1000 0000	C cedilla	Ç
129	81	201	1000 0001	u umlaut	ü
130	82	202	1000 0010	e acute	é
131	83	203	1000 0011	a circumflex	â
132	84	204	1000 0100	a umlaut	ä
133	85	205	1000 0101	a grave	à
134	86	206	1000 0110	a ring	å
135	87	207	1000 0111	c cedilla	ç
136	88	210	1000 1000	e circumflex	ê
137	89	211	1000 1001	e umlaut	ë
138	8A	212	1000 1010	e grave	è
139	8B	213	1000 1011	I umlaut	ï
140	8C	214	1000 1100	I circumflex	î
141	8D	215	1000 1101	I grave	ì
142	8E	216	1000 1110	A umlaut	Ä
143	8F	217	1000 1111	A ring	Å
144	90	220	1001 0000	E acute	É
145	91	221	1001 0001	ae ligature	æ
146	92	222	1001 0010	AE ligature	Æ
147	93	223	1001 0011	o circumflex	ô
148	94	224	1001 0100	o umlaut	ö

Dec	Hex	Octal	Binary	Name	Character
149	95	225	1001 0101	o grave	ò
150	96	226	1001 0110	u circumflex	û
151	97	227	1001 0111	u grave	ù
152	98	230	1001 1000	y umlaut	ÿ
153	99	231	1001 1001	O umlaut	Ö
154	9A	232	1001 1010	U umlaut	Ü
155	9B	233	1001 1011	cent sign	¢
156	9C	234	1001 1100	pound sign	£
157	9D	235	1001 1101	yen sign	¥
158	9E	236	1001 1110	Pt	₧
159	9F	237	1001 1111	function	ƒ
160	A0	240	1010 0000	a acute	á
161	A1	241	1010 0001	I acute	í
162	A2	242	1010 0010	o acute	ó
163	A3	243	1010 0011	u acute	ú
164	A4	244	1010 0100	n tilde	ñ
165	A5	245	1010 0101	N tilde	Ñ
166	A6	246	1010 0110	a macron	ª
167	A7	247	1010 0111	o macron	º
168	A8	250	1010 1000	opening question mark	¿
169	A9	251	1010 1001	upper-left box	⌐
170	AA	252	1010 1010	upper-right box	¬
171	AB	253	1010 1011	1/2	½
172	AC	254	1010 1100	1/4	¼
173	AD	255	1010 1101	opening exclamation	¡
174	AE	256	1010 1110	opening guillemets	«
175	AF	257	1010 1111	closing guillemets	»
176	B0	260	1011 0000	light block	░
177	B1	261	1011 0001	medium block	▒
178	B2	262	1011 0010	dark block	▓
179	B3	263	1011 0011	single vertical	│
180	B4	264	1011 0100	single right junction	┤
181	B5	265	1011 0101	2 to 1 right junction	╡
182	B6	266	1011 0110	1 to 2 right junction	╢
183	B7	267	1011 0111	1 to 2 upper-right	╖
184	B8	270	1011 1000	2 to 1 upper-right	╕
185	B9	271	1011 1001	double right junction	╣
186	BA	272	1011 1010	double vertical	║
187	BB	273	1011 1011	double upper-right	╗
188	BC	274	1011 1100	double lower-right	╝
189	BD	275	1011 1101	1 to 2 lower-right	╜
190	BE	276	1011 1110	2 to 1 lower-right	╛
191	BF	277	1011 1111	single upper-right	┐
192	C0	300	1100 0000	single lower-left	└

(continues)

Table A.1 Continued

Dec	Hex	Octal	Binary	Name	Character
193	C1	301	1100 0001	single lower junction	┴
194	C2	302	1100 0010	single upper junction	┬
195	C3	303	1100 0011	single left junction	├
196	C4	304	1100 0100	single horizontal	─
197	C5	305	1100 0101	single intersection	┼
198	C6	306	1100 0110	2 to 1 left junction	╞
199	C7	307	1100 0111	1 to 2 left junction	╟
200	C8	310	1100 1000	double lower-left	╚
201	C9	311	1100 1001	double upper-left	╔
202	CA	312	1100 1010	double lower junction	╩
203	CB	313	1100 1011	double upper junction	╦
204	CC	314	1100 1100	double left junction	╠
205	CD	315	1100 1101	double horizontal	═
206	CE	316	1100 1110	double intersection	╬
207	CF	317	1100 1111	1 to 2 lower junction	╧
208	D0	320	1101 0000	2 to 1 lower junction	╨
209	D1	321	1101 0001	1 to 2 upper junction	╤
210	D2	322	1101 0010	2 to 1 upper junction	╥
211	D3	323	1101 0011	1 to 2 lower-left	╙
212	D4	324	1101 0100	2 to 1 lower-left	╘
213	D5	325	1101 0101	2 to 1 upper-left	╒
214	D6	326	1101 0110	1 to 2 upper-left	╓
215	D7	327	1101 0111	2 to 1 intersection	╫
216	D8	330	1101 1000	1 to 2 intersection	╪
217	D9	331	1101 1001	single lower-right	┘
218	DA	332	1101 1010	single upper-right	┌
219	DB	333	1101 1011	inverse space	█
220	DC	334	1101 1100	lower inverse	▄
221	DD	335	1101 1101	left inverse	▌
222	DE	336	1101 1110	right inverse	▐
223	DF	337	1101 1111	upper inverse	▀
224	E0	340	1110 0000	alpha	α
225	E1	341	1110 0001	beta	β
226	E2	342	1110 0010	Gamma	Γ
227	E3	343	1110 0011	pi	π
228	E4	344	1110 0100	Sigma	Σ
229	E5	345	1110 0101	sigma	σ
230	E6	346	1110 0110	mu	µ
231	E7	347	1110 0111	tau	τ
232	E8	350	1110 1000	Phi	Φ
233	E9	351	1110 1001	theta	θ
234	EA	352	1110 1010	Omega	Ω
235	EB	353	1110 1011	delta	δ

Dec	Hex	Octal	Binary	Name	Character
236	EC	354	1110 1100	infinity	∞
237	ED	355	1110 1101	phi	σ
238	EE	356	1110 1110	epsilon	ε
239	EF	357	1110 1111	intersection of sets	∩
240	F0	360	1111 0000	is identical to	≡
241	F1	361	1111 0001	plus/minus sign	±
242	F2	362	1111 0010	greater/equal sign	≥
243	F3	363	1111 0011	less/equal sign	≤
244	F4	364	1111 0100	top half integral	⌠
245	F5	365	1111 0101	lower half integral	⌡
246	F6	366	1111 0110	divide-by sign	÷
247	F7	367	1111 0111	approximately	≈
248	F8	370	1111 1000	degree	°
249	F9	371	1111 1001	filled-in degree	•
250	FA	372	1111 1010	small bullet	·
251	FB	373	1111 1011	square root	√
252	FC	374	1111 1100	superscript n	^{n}
253	FD	375	1111 1101	superscript 2	^{2}
254	FE	376	1111 1110	box	■
255	FF	377	1111 1111	phantom space	

Extended ASCII Keycodes for ANSI.SYS

Table A.2 Extended ASCII Keycodes for ANSI.SYS

Code	Keystroke	Code	Keystroke	Code	Keystroke
0;1	<Alt> Esc	0;36	<Alt> J	0;64	F6
0;3	Null Character	0;37	<Alt> K	0;65	F7
0;14	<Alt> Backspace	0;38	<Alt> L	0;66	F8
0;15	<Shift> Tab	0;39	<Alt> ;	0;67	F9
0;16	<Alt> Q	0;40	<Alt> '	0;68	F10
0;17	<Alt> W	0;41	<Alt> '	0;71	Home
0;18	<Alt> E	0;43	<Alt> \	0;72	Up Arrow
0;19	<Alt> R	0;44	<Alt> Z	0;73	Page Up
0;20	<Alt> T	0;45	<Alt> X	0;74	<Alt> Keypad -
0;21	<Alt> Y	0;46	<Alt> C	0;75	Left Arrow
0;22	<Alt> U	0;47	<Alt> V	0;76	Keypad 5
0;23	<Alt> I	0;48	<Alt> B	0;77	Right Arrow
0;24	<Alt> O	0;49	<Alt> N	0;78	<Alt> Keypad +
0;25	<Alt> P	0;50	<Alt> M	0;79	End
0;26	<Alt> [	0;51	<Alt> ,	0;80	Down Arrow
0;27	<Alt>]	0;52	<Alt> .	0;81	Page Down
0;28	<Alt> Enter	0;53	<Alt> /	0;82	Insert
0;30	<Alt> A	0;55	<Alt> Keypad *	0;83	Delete
0;31	<Alt> S	0;59	F1	0;84	<Shift> F1
0;32	<Alt> D	0;60	F2	0;85	<Shift> F2
0;33	<Alt> F	0;61	F3	0;86	<Shift> F3
0;34	<Alt> G	0;62	F4	0;87	<Shift> F4
0;35	<Alt> H	0;63	F5	0;88	<Shift> F5

(continues)

Table A.2 Continued

Code	Keystroke	Code	Keystroke	Code	Keystroke
0;89	<Shift> F6	0;114	<Ctrl> Print Screen	0;139	<Alt> F11
0;90	<Shift> F7	0;115	<Ctrl> Left Arrow	0;140	<Alt> F12
0;91	<Shift> F8	0;116	<Ctrl> Right Arrow	0;141	<Ctrl> Up Arrow
0;92	<Shift> F9	0;117	<Ctrl> End	0;142	<Ctrl> Keypad -
0;93	<Shift> F10	0;118	<Ctrl> Page Down	0;143	<Ctrl> Keypad 5
0;94	<Ctrl> F1	0;119	<Ctrl> Home	0;144	<Ctrl> Keypad +
0;95	<Ctrl> F2	0;120	<Alt> 1	0;145	<Ctrl> Down Arrow
0;96	<Ctrl> F3	0;121	<Alt> 2	0;146	<Ctrl> Insert
0;97	<Ctrl> F4	0;122	<Alt> 3	0;147	<Ctrl> Delete
0;98	<Ctrl> F5	0;123	<Alt> 4	0;148	<Ctrl> Tab
0;99	<Ctrl> F6	0;124	<Alt> 5	0;149	<Ctrl> Keypad /
0;100	<Ctrl> F7	0;125	<Alt> 6	0;150	<Ctrl> Keypad *
0;101	<Ctrl> F8	0;126	<Alt> 7	0;151	<Alt> Home
0;102	<Ctrl> F9	0;127	<Alt> 8	0;152	<Alt> Up Arrow
0;103	<Ctrl> F10	0;128	<Alt> 9	0;153	<Alt> Page Up
0;104	<Alt> F1	0;129	<Alt> 0	0;155	<Alt> Left Arrow
0;105	<Alt> F2	0;130	<Alt> -	0;157	<Alt> Right Arrow
0;106	<Alt> F3	0;131	<Alt> =	0;159	<Alt> End
0;107	<Alt> F4	0;132	<Ctrl> Page Up	0;160	<Alt> Down Arrow
0;108	<Alt> F5	0;133	F11	0;161	<Alt> Page Down
0;109	<Alt> F6	0;134	F12	0;162	<Alt> Insert
0;110	<Alt> F7	0;135	<Shift> F11	0;163	<Alt> Delete
0;111	<Alt> F8	0;136	<Shift> F12	0;164	<Alt> Keypad /
0;112	<Alt> F9	0;137	<Ctrl> F11	0;165	<Alt> Tab
0;113	<Alt> F10	0;138	<Ctrl> F12	0;166	<Alt> Keypad Enter

EBCDIC Character Codes

Table A.3 EBCDIC Character Codes

Dec	Hex	Octal	Binary	Name	Character
0	00	000	0000 0000	NUL	
1	01	001	0000 0001	SOH	
2	02	002	0000 0010	STX	
3	03	003	0000 0011	ETX	
4	04	004	0000 0100	SEL	
5	05	005	0000 0101	HT	
6	06	006	0000 0110	RNL	
7	07	007	0000 0111	DEL	
8	08	010	0000 1000	GE	
9	09	011	0000 1001	SPS	
10	0A	012	0000 1010	RPT	
11	0B	013	0000 1011	VT	
12	0C	014	0000 1100	FF	
13	0D	015	0000 1101	CR	
14	0E	016	0000 1110	SO	
15	0F	017	0000 1111	SI	
16	10	020	0001 0000	DLE	
17	11	021	0001 0001	DC1	
18	12	022	0001 0010	DC2	

Dec	Hex	Octal	Binary	Name	Character
19	13	023	0001 0011	DC3	
20	14	024	0001 0100	RES/ENP	
21	15	025	0001 0101	NL	
22	16	026	0001 0110	BS	
23	17	027	0001 0111	POC	
24	18	030	0001 1000	CAN	
25	19	031	0001 1001	EM	
26	1A	032	0001 1010	UBS	
27	1B	033	0001 1011	CU1	
28	1C	034	0001 1100	IFS	
29	1D	035	0001 1101	IGS	
30	1E	036	0001 1110	IRS	
31	1F	037	0001 1111	IUS/ITB	
32	20	040	0010 0000	DS	
33	21	041	0010 0001	SOS	
34	22	042	0010 0010	FS	
35	23	043	0010 0011	WUS	
36	24	044	0010 0100	BYP/INP	
37	25	045	0010 0101	LF	
38	26	046	0010 0110	ETB	
39	27	047	0010 0111	ESC	
40	28	050	0010 1000	SA	
41	29	051	0010 1001	SFE	
42	2A	052	0010 1010	SM/SW	
43	2B	053	0010 1011	CSP	
44	2C	054	0010 1100	MFA	
45	2D	055	0010 1101	ENQ	
46	2E	056	0010 1110	ACK	
47	2F	057	0010 1111	BEL	
48	30	060	0011 0000		
49	31	061	0011 0001		
50	32	062	0011 0010	SYN	
51	33	063	0011 0011	IR	
52	34	064	0011 0100	PP	
53	35	065	0011 0101	TRN	
54	36	066	0011 0110	NBS	
55	37	067	0011 0111	EOT	
56	38	070	0011 1000	SBS	
57	39	071	0011 1001	IT	
58	3A	072	0011 1010	RFF	
59	3B	073	0011 1011	CU3	
60	3C	074	0011 1100	DC4	
61	3D	075	0011 1101	NAK	
62	3E	076	0011 1110		
63	3F	077	0011 1111	SUB	
64	40	100	0100 0000	SP	
65	41	101	0100 0001	RSP	
66	42	102	0100 0010		
67	43	103	0100 0011		
68	44	104	0100 0100		
69	45	105	0100 0101		
70	46	106	0100 0110		
71	47	107	0100 0111		

(continues)

Table A.3 Continued

Dec	Hex	Octal	Binary	Name	Character
72	48	110	0100 1000		
73	49	111	0100 1001		
74	4A	112	0100 1010		¢
75	4B	113	0100 1011		.
76	4C	114	0100 1100		<
77	4D	115	0100 1101		(
78	4E	116	0100 1110		+
79	4F	117	0100 1111		|
80	50	120	0101 0000		&
81	51	121	0101 0001		
82	52	122	0101 0010		
83	53	123	0101 0011		
84	54	124	0101 0100		
85	55	125	0101 0101		
86	56	126	0101 0110		
87	57	127	0101 0111		
88	58	130	0101 1000		
89	59	131	0101 1001		
90	5A	132	0101 1010		!
91	5B	133	0101 1011		$
92	5C	134	0101 1100		*
93	5D	135	0101 1101		)
94	5E	136	0101 1110		;
95	5F	137	0101 1111		¬
96	60	140	0110 0000		–
97	61	141	0110 0001		/
98	62	142	0110 0010		
99	63	143	0110 0011		
100	64	144	0110 0100		
101	65	145	0110 0101		
102	66	146	0110 0110		
103	67	147	0110 0111		
104	68	150	0110 1000		
105	69	151	0110 1001		
106	6A	152	0110 1010		|
107	6B	153	0110 1011		,
108	6C	154	0110 1100		%
109	6D	155	0110 1101		-
110	6E	156	0110 1110		>
111	6F	157	0110 1111		?
112	70	160	0111 0000		
113	71	161	0111 0001		
114	72	162	0111 0010		
115	73	163	0111 0011		
116	74	164	0111 0100		
117	75	165	0111 0101		
118	76	166	0111 0110		
119	77	167	0111 0111		
120	78	170	0111 1000		
121	79	171	0111 1001		`
122	7A	172	0111 1010		:
123	7B	173	0111 1011		#

Dec	Hex	Octal	Binary	Name	Character
124	7C	174	0111 1100		@
125	7D	175	0111 1101		'
126	7E	176	0111 1110		=
127	7F	177	0111 1111		"
128	80	200	1000 0000		
129	81	201	1000 0001		a
130	82	202	1000 0010		b
131	83	203	1000 0011		c
132	84	204	1000 0100		d
133	85	205	1000 0101		e
134	86	206	1000 0110		f
135	87	207	1000 0111		g
136	88	210	1000 1000		h
137	89	211	1000 1001		i
138	8A	212	1000 1010		
139	8B	213	1000 1011		
140	8C	214	1000 1100		
141	8D	215	1000 1101		
142	8E	216	1000 1110		
143	8F	217	1000 1111		
144	90	220	1001 0000		
145	91	221	1001 0001		j
146	92	222	1001 0010		k
147	93	223	1001 0011		l
148	94	224	1001 0100		m
149	95	225	1001 0101		n
150	96	226	1001 0110		o
151	97	227	1001 0111		p
152	98	230	1001 1000		q
153	99	231	1001 1001		r
154	9A	232	1001 1010		
155	9B	233	1001 1011		
156	9C	234	1001 1100		
157	9D	235	1001 1101		
158	9E	236	1001 1110		
159	9F	237	1001 1111		
160	A0	240	1010 0000		
161	A1	241	1010 0001		~
162	A2	242	1010 0010		s
163	A3	243	1010 0011		t
164	A4	244	1010 0100		u
165	A5	245	1010 0101		v
166	A6	246	1010 0110		w
167	A7	247	1010 0111		x
168	A8	250	1010 1000		y
169	A9	251	1010 1001		z
170	AA	252	1010 1010		
171	AB	253	1010 1011		
172	AC	254	1010 1100		
173	AD	255	1010 1101		
174	AE	256	1010 1110		
175	AF	257	1010 1111		
176	B0	260	1011 0000		

(continues)

Table A.3 Continued

Dec	Hex	Octal	Binary	Name	Character
177	B1	261	1011 0001		
178	B2	262	1011 0010		
179	B3	263	1011 0011		
180	B4	264	1011 0100		
181	B5	265	1011 0101		
182	B6	266	1011 0110		
183	B7	267	1011 0111		
184	B8	270	1011 1000		
185	B9	271	1011 1001		
186	BA	272	1011 1010		
187	BB	273	1011 1011		
188	BC	274	1011 1100		
189	BD	275	1011 1101		
190	BE	276	1011 1110		
191	BF	277	1011 1111		
192	C0	300	1100 0000		{
193	C1	301	1100 0001		A
194	C2	302	1100 0010		B
195	C3	303	1100 0011		C
196	C4	304	1100 0100		D
197	C5	305	1100 0101		E
198	C6	306	1100 0110		F
199	C7	307	1100 0111		G
200	C8	310	1100 1000		H
201	C9	311	1100 1001		I
202	CA	312	1100 1010	SHY	
203	CB	313	1100 1011		
204	CC	314	1100 1100		
205	CD	315	1100 1101		
206	CE	316	1100 1110		
207	CF	317	1100 1111		
208	D0	320	1101 0000		}
209	D1	321	1101 0001		J
210	D2	322	1101 0010		K
211	D3	323	1101 0011		L
212	D4	324	1101 0100		M
213	D5	325	1101 0101		N
214	D6	326	1101 0110		O
215	D7	327	1101 0111		P
216	D8	330	1101 1000		Q
217	D9	331	1101 1001		R
218	DA	332	1101 1010		
219	DB	333	1101 1011		
220	DC	334	1101 1100		
221	DD	335	1101 1101		
222	DE	336	1101 1110		
223	DF	337	1101 1111		
224	E0	340	1110 0000		\
225	E1	341	1110 0001	NSP	
226	E2	342	1110 0010		S
227	E3	343	1110 0011		T

Dec	Hex	Octal	Binary	Name	Character
228	E4	344	1110 0100		U
229	E5	345	1110 0101		V
230	E6	346	1110 0110		W
231	E7	347	1110 0111		X
232	E8	350	1110 1000		Y
233	E9	351	1110 1001		Z
234	EA	352	1110 1010		
235	EB	353	1110 1011		
236	EC	354	1110 1100		
237	ED	355	1110 1101		
238	EE	356	1110 1110		
239	EF	357	1110 1111		
240	F0	360	1111 0000		0
241	F1	361	1111 0001		1
242	F2	362	1111 0010		2
243	F3	363	1111 0011		3
244	F4	364	1111 0100		4
245	F5	365	1111 0101		5
246	F6	366	1111 0110		6
247	F7	367	1111 0111		7
248	F8	370	1111 1000		8
249	F9	371	1111 1001		9
250	FA	372	1111 1010		
251	FB	373	1111 1011		
252	FC	374	1111 1100		
253	FD	375	1111 1101		
254	FE	376	1111 1110		
255	FF	377	1111 1111	EO	

Metric System (SI) Prefixes

Table A.4 Metric System Prefixes

Multiplier	Exponent Form	Prefix	SI Symbol
1 000 000 000 000 000 000 000 000	10^{24}	yotta	Y
1 000 000 000 000 000 000 000	10^{21}	zetta	Z
1 000 000 000 000 000 000	10^{18}	exa	E
1 000 000 000 000 000	10^{15}	peta	P
1 000 000 000 000	10^{12}	tera	T
1 000 000 000	10^{9}	giga	G
1 000 000	10^{6}	mega	M
1 000	10^{3}	Kilo	k
100	10^{2}	hecto	h
10	10^{1}	deca	da
0.1	10^{-1}	deci	d
0.01	10^{-2}	centi	c
0.001	10^{-3}	milli	m
0.000 001	10^{-6}	micro	µ
0.000 000 001	10^{-9}	nano	n
0.000 000 000 001	10^{-12}	pico	p
0.000 000 000 000 001	10^{-15}	femto	f
0.000 000 000 000 000 001	10^{-18}	atto	a
0.000 000 000 000 000 000 001	10^{-21}	zepto	z
0.000 000 000 000 000 000 000 001	10^{-24}	yocyo	y

Powers of 2

Table A.5 Powers of 2

n	2n	Hexadecimal
0	1	1
1	2	2
2	4	4
3	8	8
4	16	10
5	32	20
6	64	40
7	128	80
8	256	100
9	512	200
10	1,024	400
11	2,048	800
12	4,096	1000
13	8,192	2000
14	16,384	4000
15	32,768	8000
16	65,536	10000
17	131,072	20000
18	262,144	40000
19	524,288	80000
20	1,048,576	100000
21	2,097,152	200000
22	4,194,304	400000
23	8,388,608	800000
24	16,777,216	1000000
25	33,554,432	2000000
26	67,108,864	4000000
27	134,217,728	8000000
28	268,435,456	10000000
29	536,870,912	20000000
30	1,073,741,824	40000000
31	2,147,483,648	80000000
32	4,294,967,296	100000000
33	8,589,934,592	200000000
34	17,179,869,184	400000000
35	34,359,738,368	800000000
36	68,719,476,736	1000000000
37	137,438,953,472	2000000000
38	274,877,906,944	4000000000
39	549,755,813,888	8000000000
40	1,099,511,627,776	10000000000
41	2,199,023,255,552	20000000000
42	4,398,046,511,104	40000000000
43	8,796,093,022,208	80000000000
44	17,592,186,044,416	100000000000
45	35,184,372,088,832	200000000000
46	70,368,744,177,664	400000000000
47	140,737,488,355,328	800000000000
48	281,474,976,710,656	1000000000000

n	2n	Hexadecimal
49	562,949,953,421,312	2000000000000
50	1,125,899,906,842,624	4000000000000
51	2,251,799,813,685,248	8000000000000
52	4,503,599,627,370,496	10000000000000
53	9,007,199,254,740,992	20000000000000
54	18,014,398,509,481,984	40000000000000
55	36,028,797,018,963,968	80000000000000
56	72,057,594,037,927,936	100000000000000
57	144,115,188,075,855,872	200000000000000
58	288,230,376,151,711,744	400000000000000
59	576,460,752,303,423,488	800000000000000
60	1,152,921,504,606,846,976	1000000000000000
61	2,305,843,009,213,693,952	2000000000000000
62	4,611,686,018,427,387,904	4000000000000000
63	9,223,372,036,854,775,808	8000000000000000
64	18,446,744,073,709,551,616	10000000000000000

Hardware and ROM BIOS Data

This section has an enormous amount of detailed reference information covering a variety of hardware and ROM BIOS topics. These figures and tables cover very useful information, such as Interrupt and DMA channel default usage, IBM PC and XT motherboard switch settings (see fig. A.3), AT CMOS RAM addresses, and diagnostic status-byte information. This section also has a variety of other hardware information. Finally, this section has a number of cable and connector pinouts for serial, parallel, keyboard, video, and other connectors.

Interrupts (IRQs)

Interrupt request channels (IRQs), or *hardware interrupts,* are used by various hardware devices to signal the motherboard that a request must be fulfilled.

8-Bit ISA Bus Interrupts. The PC and XT (the systems based on the 8-bit 8086 CPU) provide for eight different external hardware interrupts. Table A.6 shows the typical uses for these interrupts, which are numbered 0 through 7.

Table A.6 8-Bit ISA Bus Default Interrupt Assignments

IRQ	Function	Bus Slot
0	System Timer	No
1	Keyboard Controller	No
2	Network/Available	Yes (8-bit)
3	Serial Port 2 (COM2:)	Yes (8-bit)
4	Serial Port 1 (COM1:)	Yes (8-bit)
5	Hard Disk Controller	Yes (8-bit)
6	Floppy Disk Controller	Yes (8-bit)
7	Parallel Port 1 (LPT1:)	Yes (8-bit)

16-Bit ISA, EISA, and MCA Bus Interrupts. The introduction of the AT, based on the 286 processor, was accompanied by an increase in the number of external hardware interrupts that the bus would support. The number of interrupts was doubled (to 16) by using two Intel 8259 interrupt controllers, piping the interrupts generated by the second one through the unused IRQ 2 in the first controller. This arrangement effectively means that only 15 IRQ assignments are available, and IRQ 2 effectively became inaccessible.

IBM PC and XT Motherboard Switch Settings

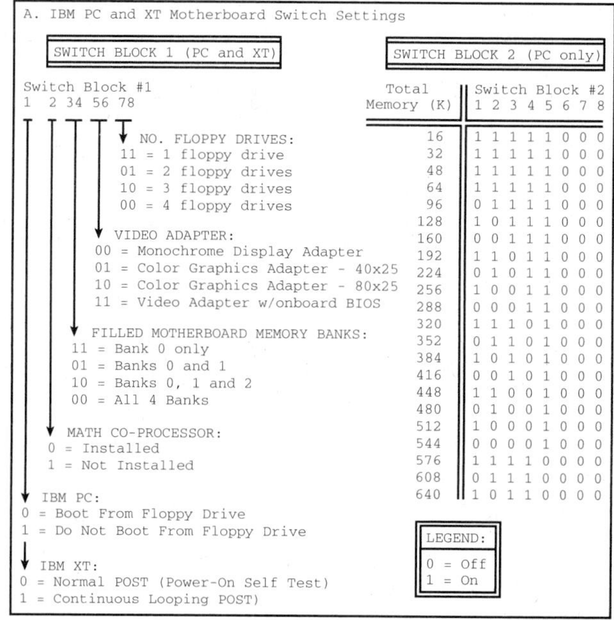

A. IBM PC and XT Motherboard Switch Settings
SWITCH BLOCK 1 (PC and XT)
SWITCH BLOCK 2 (PC only)
Switch Block #1
1 2 34 56 78
NO. FLOPPY DRIVES:
11 = 1 floppy drive
01 = 2 floppy drives
10 = 3 floppy drives
00 = 4 floppy drives
VIDEO ADAPTER:
00 = Monochrome Display Adapter
01 = Color Graphics Adapter - 40x25
10 = Color Graphics Adapter - 80x25
11 = Video Adapter w/onboard BIOS
FILLED MOTHERBOARD MEMORY BANKS:
11 = Bank 0 only
01 = Banks 0 and 1
10 = Banks 0, 1 and 2
00 = All 4 Banks
MATH CO-PROCESSOR:
0 = Installed
1 = Not Installed
IBM PC:
0 = Boot From Floppy Drive
1 = Do Not Boot From Floppy Drive
IBM XT:
0 = Normal POST (Power-On Self Test)
1 = Continuous Looping POST)
Total Memory (K)
Switch Block #2
1 2 3 4 5 6 7 8
16 1 1 1 1 1 0 0 0
32 1 1 1 1 1 0 0 0
48 1 1 1 1 1 0 0 0
64 1 1 1 1 1 0 0 0
96 0 1 1 1 1 0 0 0
128 1 0 1 1 1 0 0 0
160 0 0 1 1 1 0 0 0
192 1 1 0 1 1 0 0 0
224 0 1 0 1 1 0 0 0
256 1 0 0 1 1 0 0 0
288 0 0 0 1 1 0 0 0
320 1 1 1 0 1 0 0 0
352 0 1 1 0 1 0 0 0
384 1 0 1 0 1 0 0 0
416 0 0 1 0 1 0 0 0
448 1 1 0 0 1 0 0 0
480 0 1 0 0 1 0 0 0
512 1 0 0 0 1 0 0 0
544 0 0 0 0 1 0 0 0
576 1 1 1 1 0 0 0 0
608 0 1 1 1 0 0 0 0
640 1 0 1 1 0 0 0 0
LEGEND:
0 = Off
1 = On

Figure A.3

IBM PC and XT motherboard switch settings.

To prevent problems with boards set to use IRQ 2, the AT system designers routed one of the new interrupts (IRQ 9) to fill the slot position left open after removing IRQ 2. This means that any card you install in a modern system that claims to use IRQ 2 is really using IRQ 9 instead. Some cards now label this selection as IRQ 2/9, while others may only call it IRQ 2 or IRQ 9. No matter what the labeling says, you must never set two cards to use that interrupt!

Table A.7 shows the typical uses for interrupts in the 16-bit ISA, EISA, and MCA buses, and lists them in priority order from highest to lowest.

Table A.7 16-Bit ISA, EISA, and MCA Default Interrupt Assignments

IRQ	Standard Function	Bus Slot	Card Type
0	System Timer	No	—
1	Keyboard Controller	No	—
2	2nd IRQ Controller Cascade	No	—
8	Real-Time Clock	No	—
9	Network/Available (Appears as IRQ 2)	Yes	8/16-bit
10	Available	Yes	16-bit
11	SCSI/Available	Yes	16-bit
12	Motherboard Mouse Port/Available	Yes	16-bit

IRQ	Standard Function	Bus Slot	Card Type
13	Math Coprocessor	No	—
14	Primary IDE	Yes	16-bit
15	Secondary IDE/Available	Yes	16-bit
3	Serial Port 2 (COM2:)	Yes	8/16-bit
4	Serial Port 1 (COM1:)	Yes	8/16-bit
5	Sound Card/Parallel Port 2 (LPT2:)	Yes	8/16-bit
6	Floppy Disk Controller	Yes	8/16-bit
7	Parallel Port 1 (LPT1:)	Yes	8/16-bit

DMA Channels

DMA (*direct memory access*) channels are used by high-speed communications devices that must send and receive information at high speed.

8-Bit ISA Bus DMA Channels. In the 8-bit ISA bus, four DMA channels support high-speed data transfers between I/O devices and memory. Three of the channels are available to the expansion slots. Table A.8 shows the typical uses of these DMA channels.

Table A.8 8-Bit ISA Default DMA-Channel Assignments

DMA	Standard Function	Bus Slot
0	Dynamic RAM Refresh	No
1	Available	Yes (8-bit)
2	Floppy disk controller	Yes (8-bit)
3	Hard disk controller	Yes (8-bit)

16-Bit ISA DMA Channels. Since the introduction of the 286 CPU, the ISA bus has supported eight DMA channels, with seven channels available to the expansion slots. Like the expanded IRQ lines described earlier in this chapter, the added DMA channels were created by cascading a second DMA controller to the first one. DMA channel 4 is used to cascade channels 0 through 3 to the microprocessor. Channels 0 through 3 are available for 8-bit transfers, and channels 5 through 7 are for 16-bit transfers only. Table A.9 shows the typical uses for the DMA channels.

Table A.9 16-Bit ISA, EISA, and MCA Default DMA-Channel Assignments

DMA	Standard Function	Bus Slot	Card Type	Transfer
0	Available	Yes	16-bit	8-bit
1	Sound/Available	Yes	8/16-bit	8-bit
2	Floppy Disk Controller	Yes	8/16-bit	8-bit
3	ECP Parallel/Available	Yes	8/16-bit	8-bit
4	1st DMA Controller Cascade	No	16-bit	—
5	Sound/Available	Yes	16-bit	16-bit
6	SCSI/Available	Yes	16-bit	16-bit
7	Available	Yes	16-bit	16-bit

AT CMOS RAM Addresses

Table A.10 shows the information maintained in the 64-byte AT CMOS RAM module. This information controls the configuration of the system much like the switches control the PC and XT configurations. This memory is read and written by the system SETUP program.

Table A.10 AT CMOS RAM Addresses

Offset Hex	Offset Dec	Field Size	Function
00h	0	1 byte	Current second in binary coded decimal (BCD)
01h	1	1 byte	Alarm second in BCD
02h	2	1 byte	Current minute in BCD
03h	3	1 byte	Alarm minute in BCD
04h	4	1 byte	Current hour in BCD
05h	5	1 byte	Alarm hour in BCD
06h	6	1 byte	Current day of week in BCD
07h	7	1 byte	Current day in BCD
08h	8	1 byte	Current month in BCD
09h	9	1 byte	Current year in BCD
0Ah	10	1 byte	Status register A Bit 7 = Update in progress 0 = Date and time can be read 1 = Time update in progress Bits 6–4 = Time frequency divider 010 = 32.768 kHz Bits 3–0 = Rate selection frequency 0110 = 1.024 kHz square wave frequency
0Bh	11	1 byte	Status register B Bit 7 = Clock update cycle 0 = Update normally 1 = Abort update in progress Bit 6 = Periodic interrupt 0 = Disable interrupt (default) 1 = Enable interrupt Bit 5 = Alarm interrupt 0 = Disable interrupt (default) 0 = Disable interrupt (default) 1 = Enable interrupt Bit 4 = Update-ended interrupt 0 = Disable interrupt (default) 1 = Enable interrupt Bit 3 = Status register A square wave frequency 0 = Disable square wave (default) 1 = Enable square wave Bit 2 = Date format 0 = Calendar in BCD format (default) 1 = Calendar in binary format Bit 1 = 24-hour clock 0 = 24-hour mode (default) 1 = 12-hour mode Bit 0 = Daylight Savings Time 0 = Disable Daylight Savings (default) 1 = Enable Daylight Savings
0Ch	12	1 byte	Status register C Bit 7 = IRQF flag Bit 6 = PF flag Bit 5 = AF flag Bit 4 = UF flag Bits 3-0 = Reserved
0Dh	13	1 byte	Status register D Bit 7 = Valid CMOS RAM bit 0 = CMOS battery dead 1 = CMOS battery power good Bits 6–0 = Reserved

Offset Hex	Offset Dec	Field Size	Function
0Eh	14	1 byte	Diagnostic status Bit 7 = Real-time clock power status 0 = CMOS has not lost power 1 = CMOS has lost power Bit 6 = CMOS checksum status 0 = Checksum is good 1 = Checksum is bad Bit 5 = POST configuration information status 0 = Configuration information is valid 1 = Configuration information is invalid Bit 4 = Memory size compare during POST 0 = POST memory equals configuration 1 = POST memory not equal to configuration Bit 3 = Fixed disk/adapter initialization 0 = Initialization good 1 = Initialization failed Bit 2 = CMOS time status indicator 0 = Time is valid 1 = Time is Invalid Bits 1-0 = Reserved
0Fh	15	1 byte	Shutdown code 00h = Power on or soft reset 01h = Memory size pass 02h = Memory test pass 03h = Memory test fail 04h = POST end; boot system 05h = JMP double word pointer with EOI 06h = Protected mode tests pass 07h = Protected mode tests fail 07h = Protected mode tests fail 08h = Memory size fail 09h = Int 15h block move 0Ah = JMP double word pointer without EOI 0Bh = used by 80386
10h	16	1 byte	Floppy disk drive types Bits 7-4 = Drive 0 type Bits 3-0 = Drive 1 type 0000 = None 0001 = 360K 0010 = 1.2M 0011 = 720K 0100 = 1.44M
11h	17	1 byte	Reserved
12h	18	1 byte	Hard disk types Bits 7–4 = Hard disk 0 type (0–15) Bits 3–0 = Hard disk 1 type (0–15)
13h	19	1 byte	Reserved
14h	20	1 byte	Installed equipment Bits 7–6 = Number of floppy disk drives 00= 1 floppy disk drive 01= 2 floppy disk drives Bits 5–4 = Primary display 00= Use display adapter BIOS 01= CGA 40-column 10= CGA 80-column 11= Monochrome Display Adapter Bits 3–2 = Reserved Bit 1 = Math coprocessor present Bit 0 = Floppy disk drive present
15h	21	1 byte	Base memory low-order byte
16h	22	1 byte	Base memory high-order byte

(continues)

Table A.10 Continued

Offset Hex	Offset Dec	Field Size	Function
17h	23	1 byte	Extended memory low-order byte
18h	24	1 byte	Extended memory high-order byte
19h	25	1 byte	Hard Disk 0 Extended Type (0–255)
1Ah	26	1 byte	Hard Disk 1 Extended Type (0–255)
1Bh	27	9 bytes	Reserved
2Eh	46	1 byte	CMOS checksum high-order byte
2Fh	47	1 byte	CMOS checksum low-order byte
30h	48	1 byte	Actual extended memory low-order byte
31h	49	1 byte	Actual extended memory high-order byte
32h	50	1 byte	Date century in BCD
33h	51	1 byte	POST information flag Bit 7 = Top 128K base memory status 0 = Top 128K base memory not installed 1 = Top 128K base memory installed Bit 6 = Setup program flag 0 = Normal (default) 1 = Put out first user message Bits 5–0 = Reserved
34h	52	2 bytes	Reserved

Table A.11 shows the values that may be stored by your system BIOS in a special CMOS byte called the diagnostics status byte. By examining this location with a diagnostics program, you can determine whether your system has set "trouble codes," which indicates that a problem previously has occurred.

Table A.11 CMOS RAM (AT and PS/2) Diagnostic Status Byte Codes

Bit Number 7 6 5 4 3 2 1 0	Hex	Function
1	80	Real-time clock (RTC) chip lost power
. 1	40	CMOS RAM checksum is bad
. . 1	20	Invalid configuration information found at POST
. . . 1	10	Memory size compare error at POST
. . . . 1 . . .	08	Fixed disk or adapter failed initialization
. . . . . 1 . .	04	Real-time clock (RTC) time found invalid
. . . . . . 1 .	02	Adapters do not match configuration
. . . . 1	01	Time-out reading an adapter ID
. . . .	00	No errors found (Normal)

IBM BIOS Model, Submodel, and Revision Codes

Table A.12 shows information about the different ROM BIOS versions that have appeared in various IBM systems.

Table A.12 IBM BIOS Model, Submodel, and Revision Codes

System Description	CPU	Clock Speed	Bus Type /Width	ROM BIOS Date	ID Byte	Sub-model Byte	Rev.	ST506 Drive Types
PC	8088	4.77 MHz	ISA/8	04/24/81	FF	—	—	—
PC	8088	4.77 MHz	ISA/8	10/19/81	FF	—	—	—
PC	8088	4.77 MHz	ISA/8	10/27/82	FF	—	—	—

System Description	CPU	Clock Speed	Bus Type /Width	ROM BIOS Date	ID Byte	Sub-model Byte	Rev.	ST506 Drive Types
PC-XT	8088	4.77 MHz	ISA/8	11/08/82	FE	—	—	—
PC-XT	8088	4.77 MHz	ISA/8	01/10/86	FB	00	01	—
PC-XT	8088	4.77 MHz	ISA/8	05/09/86	FB	00	02	—
PCjr	8088	4.77 MHz	ISA/8	06/01/83	FD	—	—	—
PC Convertible	80C8	4.77 MHz	ISA/8	09/13/85	F9	00	00	—
PS/2 25	8086	8 MHz	ISA/8	06/26/87	FA	01	00	26
PS/2 30	8086	8 MHz	ISA/8	09/02/86	FA	00	00	26
PS/2 30	8086	8 MHz	ISA/8	12/12/86	FA	00	01	26
PS/2 30	8086	8 MHz	ISA/8	02/05/87	FA	00	02	26
PC-AT	286	6 MHz	ISA/16	01/10/84	FC	—	—	15
PC-AT	286	6 MHz	ISA/16	06/10/85	FC	00	01	23
PC-AT	286	8 MHz	ISA/16	11/15/85	FC	01	00	23
PC-XT 286	286	6 MHz	ISA/16	04/21/86	FC	02	00	24
PS/1	286	10 MHz	ISA/16	12/01/89	FC	0B	00	44
PS/2 25 286	286	10 MHz	ISA/16	06/28/89	FC	09	02	37
PS/2 30 286	286	10 MHz	ISA/16	08/25/88	FC	09	00	37
PS/2 30 286	286	10 MHz	ISA/16	06/28/89	FC	09	02	37
PS/2 35 SX	386SX	20 MHz	ISA/16	03/15/91	F8	19	05	37
PS/2 35 SX	386SX	20 MHz	ISA/16	04/04/91	F8	19	06	37
PS/2 40 SX	386SX	20 MHz	ISA/16	03/15/91	F8	19	05	37
PS/2 40 SX	386SX	20 MHz	ISA/16	04/04/91	F8	19	06	37
PS/2 L40 SX	386SX	20 MHz	ISA/16	02/27/91	F8	23	02	37
PS/2 50	286	10 MHz	MCA/16	02/13/87	FC	04	00	32
PS/2 50	286	10 MHz	MCA/16	05/09/87	FC	04	01	32
PS/2 50Z	286	10 MHz	MCA/16	01/28/88	FC	04	02	33
PS/2 50Z	286	10 MHz	MCA/16	04/18/88	FC	04	03	33
PS/2 55 SX	386SX	16 MHz	MCA/16	11/02/88	F8	0C	00	33
PS/2 55 LS	386SX	16 MHz	MCA/16	?	F8	1E	00	33
PS/2 57 SX	386SX	20 MHz	MCA/16	07/03/91	F8	26	02	None
PS/2 60	286	10 MHz	MCA/16	02/13/87	FC	05	00	32
PS/2 65 SX	386SX	16 MHz	MCA/16	02/08/90	F8	1C	00	33
PS/2 70 386	386DX	16 MHz	MCA/32	01/29/88	F8	09	00	33
PS/2 70 386	386DX	16 MHz	MCA/32	04/11/88	F8	09	02	33
PS/2 70 386	386DX	16 MHz	MCA/32	12/15/89	F8	09	04	33
PS/2 70 386	386DX	20 MHz	MCA/32	01/29/88	F8	04	00	33
PS/2 70 386	386DX	20 MHz	MCA/32	04/11/88	F8	04	02	33
PS/2 70 386	386DX	20 MHz	MCA/32	12/15/89	F8	04	04	33
PS/2 70 386	386DX	25 MHz	MCA/32	06/08/88	F8	0D	00	33
PS/2 70 386	386DX	25 MHz	MCA/32	02/20/89	F8	0D	01	33
PS/2 70 486	486DX	25 MHz	MCA/32	12/01/89	F8	0D	?	?
PS/2 70 486	486DX	25 MHz	MCA/32	09/29/89	F8	1B	00	?
PS/2 P70 386	386DX	16 MHz	MCA/32	?	F8	50	00	?
PS/2 P70 386	386DX	20 MHz	MCA/32	01/18/89	F8	0B	00	33
PS/2 P75 486	486DX	33 MHz	MCA/32	10/05/90	F8	52	00	33
PS/2 80 386	386DX	16 MHz	MCA/32	03/30/87	F8	00	00	32
PS/2 80 386	386DX	20 MHz	MCA/32	10/07/87	F8	01	00	32
PS/2 80 386	386DX	25 MHz	MCA/32	11/21/89	F8	80	01	?
PS/2 90 XP 486	486SX	20 MHz	MCA/32	?	F8	2D	00	?
PS/2 90 XP 486	487SX	20 MHz	MCA/32	?	F8	2F	00	?
PS/2 90 XP 486	486DX	25 MHz	MCA/32	?	F8	11	00	?
PS/2 90 XP 486	486DX	33 MHz	MCA/32	?	F8	13	00	?

(continues)

Table A.12 Continued

System Description	CPU	Clock Speed	Bus Type /Width	ROM BIOS Date	ID Byte	Sub-model Byte	Rev.	ST506 Drive Types
PS/2 90 XP 486	486DX	50 MHz	MCA/32	?	F8	2B	00	?
PS/2 95 XP 486	486SX	20 MHz	MCA/32	?	F8	2C	00	?
PS/2 95 XP 486	487SX	20 MHz	MCA/32	?	F8	2E	00	?
PS/2 95 XP 486	486DX	25 MHz	MCA/32	?	F8	14	00	?
PS/2 95 XP 486	486DX	33 MHz	MCA/32	?	F8	16	00	?
PS/2 95 XP 486	486DX	50 MHz	MCA/32	?	F8	2A	00	?

The ID byte, Submodel byte, and Revision numbers are in hexadecimal.
— = This feature is not supported.
None = Only SCSI drives are supported.
? = Information unavailable.

Disk Software Interfaces

Figure A.4 shows a representation of the relationship between the different disk software interfaces at work in an IBM-compatible system. This figure shows the chain of command from the hardware, which is the drive controller, to the ROM BIOS, DOS, and, finally, an application program.

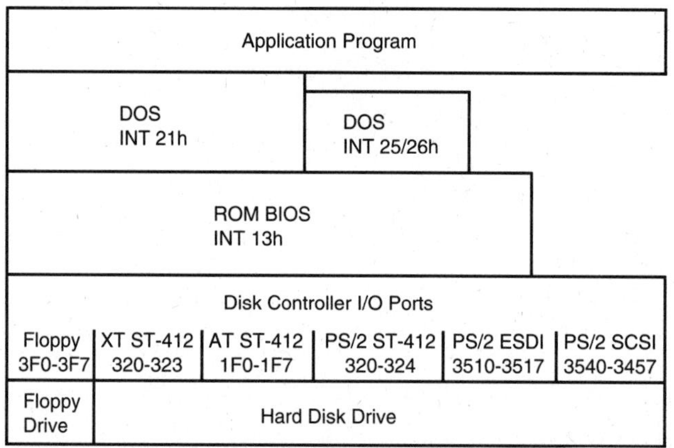

Figure A.4

Disk Software Interface levels and relationships.

The following table shows the different functions available at the Interrupt 13h BIOS interface. Some functions are available to floppy drives or hard drives only, and others are available to both types of drives.

Table A.13 Int 13h BIOS Disk Functions

Function	Floppy Disk	Hard Disk	Description
00h	×	×	Reset disk system
01h	×	×	Get status of last operation
02h	×	×	Read sectors
03h	×	×	Write sectors
04h	×	×	Verify sectors

Function	Floppy Disk	Hard Disk	Description
05h	×	×	Format track
06h		×	Format bad track
07h		×	Format drive
08h	×	×	Read drive parameters
09h		×	Initialize drive characteristics
0Ah		×	Read long
0Bh		×	Write long
0Ch		×	Seek
0Dh		×	Alternate hard disk reset
0Eh		×	Read sector buffer
0Fh		×	Write sector buffer
10h		×	Test for drive ready
11h		×	Recalibrate drive
12h		×	Controller RAM diagnostic
13h		×	Controller drive diagnostic
14h		×	Controller internal diagnostic
15h	×	×	Get disk type
16h	×		Get floppy disk change status
17h	×		Set floppy disk type for format
18h	×		Set media type for format
19h		×	Park hard disk heads
1Ah		×	ESDI—Low-level format
1Bh		×	ESDI—Get manufacturing header
1Ch		×	ESDI—Get configuration

Table A.14 shows the error codes that may be returned by the BIOS INT 13h routines. In some cases you may see these codes be referred to when running a Low Level Format program, disk editor or other program that can directly access a disk drive through the BIOS.

Table A.14 IINT13h BIOS Error Codes

Code	Description
00h	No error
01h	Bad command
02h	Address mark not found
03h	Write protect
04h	Request sector not found
05h	Reset failed
06h	Media change error
07h	Initialization failed
09h	Cross 64K DMA boundary
0Ah	Bad sector flag detected
0Bh	Bad track flag detected
10h	Bad ECC on disk read
11h	ECC corrected data error
20h	Controller has failed
40h	Seek operation failed
80h	Drive failed to respond
AAh	Drive not ready
BBh	Undefined error
CCh	Write fault
0Eh	Register error
FFh	Sense operation failed

Motherboard Connectors

Table A.15 Battery Connector

Pin	Signal
1	Gnd
2	Unused
3	KEY
4	+6v

Table A.16 LED and Keylock Connector

Pin	Signal
1	LED Power (+5v)
2	KEY
3	Gnd
4	Keyboard Inhibit
5	Gnd

Table A.17 Speaker Connector

Pin	Signal
1	Audio
2	KEY
3	Gnd
4	+5v

Wrap Plug Diagrams

Many of the third party diagnostics packages do not have correctly wired loopback connectors (also called wrap plugs). These plugs may pass their own tests, but will fail tests by other diagnostics, especially IBM's Advanced Diagnostics. The following diagrams show the wiring of IBM's Tri-Connector Wrap Plug P/N 72X8546. These plugs will pass IBM Advanced Diagnostics as well as virtually all compatible diagnostics software tests which check serial and parallel ports.

IBM 25-Pin Serial (Female DB25S) Loopback Connector (Wrap Plug):

Connect these pins:

1 to 7

2 to 3

4 to 5 to 8

6 to 11 to 20 to 22

15 to 17 to 23

18 to 25

IBM 9-Pin Serial (Female DB9S) Loopback Connector (Wrap Plug):

Connect these pins:

1 to 7 to 8

2 to 3

4 to 6 to 9

IBM 25-Pin Parallel (Male DB25P) Loopback Connector (Wrap Plug):

Connect these pins:

1 to 13

2 to 15

10 to 16

11 to 17

The Norton Diagnostics program (NDIAGS.EXE) from the Norton Utilities 7.x and up (by Symantec) uses somewhat non-standard loopback connectors that are wired differently from most everybody else. If you use standard loopback connectors that follow the original IBM wiring specification, the serial and parallel port tests will fail. Of course Symantec sells a set of wrap plugs wired to their specifications for about $30, but you can make your own by using the following wiring diagrams:

SYMANTEC 25-Pin Serial (Female DB25S) Loopback Connector (Wrap Plug):

Connect these pins:

2 to 3

4 to 5

6 to 8 to 20 to 22

SYMANTEC 9-Pin Serial (Female DB9S) Loopback Connector (Wrap Plug):

Connect these pins:

2 to 3

7 to 8

1 to 4 to 6 to 9

SYMANTEC 25-Pin Parallel (Male DB25P) Loopback Connector (Wrap Plug):

Connect these pins:

2 to 15

3 to 13

4 to 12

5 to 10

6 to 11

Interlink Cables

The DOS Interlink program connects two computers via parallel or serial ports and enables the computers to share disks and printers. For example, you could connect a laptop computer to a desktop computer and share files.

The entire Interlink set consists of two programs, called INTERLNK and INTERSVR. The INTERLNK program functions both as a device driver as well as an executable program, while the INTERSVR program is an executable program only.

To link two computers together, the INTERLNK program must be loaded as a device driver (INTERLNK.EXE) on the client system, while the INTERSVR command must be executed on the server. A cable must also be run between the two systems to act as the transfer medium. Either a serial or parallel cable may be used, but the parallel option offers much higher data transfer rates and is preferred.

The Interlink program will allow the server's drives to appear as new drive letters on the client system. In other words, if you have both client and server systems with a single floppy A: and a single hard disk partition C:, the server drives will appear on the client as follows:

```
Client   Server
---------------
   A:
   C:
   D: ---> A:
   E: ---> C:
```

If the client or server system has more than two drive letters, INTERLNK will try to assign letters higher than E: on the client. This will not be possible unless LASTDRIVE command in your CONFIG.SYS file is set high enough to accomodate that number of redirected drives.

In addition, the position of the DEVICE command that loads INTERLNK.EXE can affect pre-existing drive assignments. If you place the INTERLINK.EXE driver before other drivers that create drive volumes (such as for a CD-ROM drive), the drive letters allocated by the other drivers will be changed. To prevent this from happening, load INTERLNK.EXE after other disk volume drivers in your CONFIG.SYS file.

There can be special problems using Interlink with Windows. If you are using a serial mouse with Microsoft Windows, specify either the /LPT switch or a /COM switch that designates a COM port other than the one the mouse is using. For example, if the serial mouse uses COM1, and you are using a parallel connection, specify the /LPT switch to prevent Interlink from scanning all COM ports. Also if you redirect LPT1 or LPT2 and print from Microsoft Windows, use Control Panel to assign the printer to either LPT1.DOS or LPT2.DOS.

Although Interlink is very powerful, commands that work directly with disk drive hardware or file systems will usually not work on a redirected (remote) drive. This includes several DOS commands such as:

CHKDSK	FORMAT
DEFRAG	MIRROR
DISKCOMP	SYS
DISKCOPY	UNDELETE
FDISK	UNFORMAT

Interlink Serial Cables

You can make an Interlink serial cable with either a 9-pin or a 25-pin female connector on both ends. Three wires are required for data transmission: Ground-Ground, Transmit-Receive, and Receive-Transmit. Seven wires are required if you want to use the remote copy feature. Wire the cable as shown in the following table:

9-pin	25-pin	Signal Descriptions			25-pin	9-pin
pin 3	pin 2	Transmit	<-->	Receive	pin 3	pin 2
pin 2	pin 3	Receive	<-->	Transmit	pin 2	pin 3
pin 7	pin 4	RTS	<-->	CTS	pin 5	pin 8
pin 8	pin 5	CTS	<-->	RTS	pin 4	pin 7
pin 6	pin 6	DSR	<-->	DTR	pin 20	pin 4
pin 4	pin 20	DTR	<-->	DSR	pin 6	pin 6
pin 5	pin 7	Ground	<-->	Ground	pin 7	pin 5

Interlink Parallel Cables

You can make a parallel Interlink cable with male DB-25 connectors at both ends. Eleven wires are required for data transmission. Wire the cable as shown in the following table:

25-pin	Signal Descriptions			25-pin
pin 2	Data Bit 0	<-->	Error	pin 15
pin 3	Data Bit 1	<-->	Select	pin 13
pin 4	Data Bit 2	<-->	Paper End	pin 12
pin 5	Data Bit 3	<-->	-Acknowledge	pin 10
pin 6	Data Bit 4	<-->	Busy	pin 11
pin 15	-Error	<-->	Data Bit 0	pin 2
pin 13	Select	<-->	Data Bit 1	pin 3
pin 12	Paper End	<-->	Data Bit 2	pin 4
pin 10	-Acknowledge	<-->	Data Bit 3	pin 5
pin 11	Busy	<-->	Data Bit 4	pin 6
pin 25	Ground	<-->	Ground	pin 25

There are additional pins you can connect if you want to create a "Turbo" cable as developed by Rupp Corp. for their Fastlynx program. Most other high speed commercial programs will use a parallel cable with these additional pins connected, which offers the highest possible throughput. This type of cable adds 7 wires to the standard Interlink parallel cable, making for an 18-wire cable. The following table shows the additional wires required for a "Turbo" cable:

25-pin	Signal Descriptions			25-pin
pin 1	-Strobe	<-->	Data Bit 5	pin 7
pin 7	Data Bit 5	<-->	-Strobe	pin 1
pin 8	Data Bit 6	<-->	-Auto Feed	pin 14
pin 9	Data Bit 7	<-->	-Initialize	pin 16
pin 14	-Auto Feed	<-->	Data Bit 6	pin 8
pin 16	-Initialize	<-->	Data Bit 7	pin 9
pin 17	-Select Input	<-->	-Select Input	pin 17

System Video Information

Table A.18 Video Adapter and Display Modes and Standards

Video Std.	Intro-duced	Reso-lution	No. of Colors	Mode Type	BIOS Modes	Char. For-mat	Char. Box	Vert. (Hz)	Horiz. (kHz)	Scan Mode
MDA	08/12/81	720×350	4	Text	07h	80×25	9×14	50	8.432	Std
CGA	08/12/81	320×200	16	Text	00/01h	40×25	8×8	60	15.75	Std
		640×200	16	Text	02/03h	80×25	8×8	60	15.75	Std
		160×200	16	APA	—	—	—	60	15.75	Std
		320×200	4	APA	04/05h	40×25	8×8	60	15.75	Std
		640×200	2	APA	06h	80×25	8×8	60	15.75	Std
EGA	09/10/84	320×350	16	Text	00/01h	40×25	8×14	60	21.85	Std
		640×350	16	Text	02/03h	80×25	8×14	60	21.85	Std
		720×350	4	Text	07h	80×25	9×14	50	18.432	Std
		320×200	16	APA	0Dh	40×25	8×8	60	15.75	Std
		640×200	16	APA	0Eh	80×25	8×8	60	15.75	Std
		640×350	4	APA	0Fh	80×25	8×14	50	18.432	Std
		640×350	16	APA	10h	80×25	8×14	60	21.85	Std
PGA	09/10/84	320×200	16	Text	00/01h	40×25	8×8	60	15.75	Std
		640×200	16	Text	02/03h	80×25	8×8	60	15.75	Std
		320×200	4	APA	04/05h	40×25	8×8	60	15.75	Std
		640×200	2	APA	06h	80×25	8×8	60	15.75	Std
		640×480	256	APA	—	—	—	60	30.48	Std
MCGA	04/02/87	320×400	16	Text	00/01h	40×25	8×16	70	31.5	Std
		640×400	16	Text	02/03h	80×25	8×16	70	31.5	Std
		320×200	4	APA	04/05h	40×25	8×8	70	31.5	DBL
		640×200	2	APA	06h	80×25	8×8	70	31.5	DBL
		640×480	2	APA	11h	80×30	8×16	60	31.5	Std
		320×200	256	APA	13h	40×25	8×8	70	31.5	DBL
VGA	04/02/87	360×400	16	Text	00/01h	40×25	9×16	70	31.5	Std
		720×400	16	Text	02/03h	80×25	9×16	70	31.5	Std
		320×200	4	APA	04/05h	40×25	8×8	70	31.5	DBL
		640×200	2	APA	06h	80×25	8×8	70	31.5	DBL
		720×400	16	Text	07h	80×25	9×16	70	31.5	Std
		320×200	16	APA	0Dh	40×25	8×8	70	31.5	DBL
		640×200	16	APA	0Eh	80×25	8×8	70	31.5	DBL
		640×350	4	APA	0Fh	80×25	8×14	70	31.5	Std
		640×350	16	APA	10h	80×25	8×14	70	31.5	Std
		640×480	2	APA	11h	80×30	8×16	60	31.5	Std
		640×480	16	APA	12h	80×30	8×16	60	31.5	Std
		320×200	256	APA	13h	40×25	8×8	70	31.5	DBL
8514	04/02/87	1024×768	256	APA	H-0h	85×38	12×20	43.48	35.52	IL
		640×480	256	APA	H-1h	80×34	8×14	60	31.5	Std
		1024×768	256	APA	H-3h	146×51	7×15	43.48	35.52	IL
XGA	10/30/90	360×400	16	Text	00/01h	40×25	9×16	70	31.5	Std
		720×400	16	Text	02/03h	80×25	9×16	70	31.5	Std
		320×200	4	APA	04/05h	40×25	8×8	70	31.5	DBL
		640×200	2	APA	06h	80×25	8×8	70	31.5	DBL
		720×400	16	Text	07h	80×25	9×16	70	31.5	Std
		320×200	16	APA	0Dh	40×25	8×8	70	31.5	DBL
		640×200	16	APA	0Eh	80×25	8×8	70	31.5	DBL
		640×350	4	APA	0Fh	80×25	8×14	70	31.5	Std
		640×350	16	APA	10h	80×25	8×14	70	31.5	Std

Video Std.	Intro-duced	Reso-lution	No. of Colors	Mode Type	BIOS Modes	Char. For-mat	Char. Box	Vert. (Hz)	Horiz. (kHz)	Scan Mode
		640×480	2	APA	11h	80×30	8×16	60	31.5	Std
		640×480	16	APA	12h	80×30	8×16	60	31.5	Std
		320×200	256	APA	13h	40×25	8×8	70	31.5	DBL
		1056×400	16	Text	14h	132×25	8×16	70	31.5	Std
		1056×400	16	Text	14h	132×43	8×9	70	31.5	Std
		1056×400	16	Text	14h	132×56	8×8	70	31.5	Std
		1056×400	16	Text	14h	132×60	8×6	70	31.5	Std
		1024×768	256	APA	H-0h	85×38	12×20	43.48	35.52	IL
		640×480	65536	APA	H-1h	80×34	8×14	60	31.5	Std
		1024×768	256	APA	H-2h	128×54	8×14	43.48	35.52	IL
		1024×768	256	APA	H-3h	146×51	7×15	43.48	35.52	IL

MDA = Monochrome Display Adapter
CGA = Color Graphics Adapter
EGA = Enhanced Graphics Adapter
PGA = Professional Graphics Adapter
MCGA = Multi-Color Graphics Array
VGA = Video Graphics Array
8514 = 8514/A Adapter
XGA = eXtended Graphics Array
APA = All Points Addressable (Graphics)
DBL = Double Scan
IL = Interlaced
— = Not supported

Note

The 8514/A adapter allows the System Board VGA signals to pass through via the Auxiliary Video Connector (slot); therefore, all VGA modes will function normally. The XGA Adapter shuts down the System Board VGA and contains a full 16-bit VGA adapter circuit onboard.

Monitor ID Pins

The following table shows the settings used for the Monitor ID bits for several different IBM displays. By sensing which of these four pins are grounded, the video adapter can determine what type of display is attached. This is especially used with regards to monochrome or color display detection. In this manner, the VGA or XGA circuitry can properly select the color mapping and image size to suit the display.

Table A.19 IBM Display Monitor ID Settings

Display	Size	Type	ID0	ID1	ID2	ID3
8503	12-inch	Mono	No Pin	Ground	No Pin	No Pin
8512	13-inch	Color	Ground	No Pin	No Pin	No Pin
8513	12-inch	Color	Ground	No Pin	No Pin	No Pin
8514	15-inch	Color	Ground	No Pin	Ground	No Pin
8515	14-inch	Color	No Pin	No Pin	Ground	No Pin
9515	14-inch	Color	No Pin	No Pin	Ground	No Pin
9517	17-inch	Color	Ground	No Pin	Ground	Ground
9518	14-inch	Color	Ground	No Pin	Ground	No Pin

Modem Control Codes

This section lists the command and control codes for popular modems. If you have ever had to work with these devices without the original documentation, you will appreciate these tables. The following table shows the commands recognized by the popular Hayes and U.S. Robotics modems. These modems have a standard command set that can get quite complicated in the higher end models. Table A.20 comes in handy when you need to reconfigure a modem without the original manual. Even if your modem is not Hayes or U.S. Robotics, it probably follows most of these commands because this command set has become somewhat of a standard.

Table A.20 U.S. Robotics and Hayes Modem Commands and Supported Features

Command	Modem Functions and Options		USR	2400	Hayes 2400	1200
&	See Extended Command Set		×			
%	See Extended Command Set		×			
A	Force Answer mode when modem has not received an incoming call		×	×	×	×
A/	Reexecute last command once		×	×	×	×
A>	Repeat last command continuously		×			
Any key	Terminate current connection attempt; exit Repeat mode		×	×		
AT	Attention: must precede all other commands, except A/, A>, and +++		×	×	×	×
Bn	Handshake options		×		×	
	B0	CCITT answer sequence	×		×	
	B1	Bell answer tone	×		×	
Cn	Transmitter On/Off		×	×	×	×
	C0	Transmitter Off	×	×	×	×
	C1	Transmitter On—Default	×	×	×	×
Dn	Dial number n and go into originate mode					
	Use any of these options:		×	×	×	×
	P	Pulse dial—Default	×	×	×	×
	T	Touch-Tone dial	×	×	×	×
	,	(Comma) Pause for 2 seconds	×	×	×	×
	;	Return to command state after dialing	×	×	×	×
	"...	Dial the letters that follow	×	×		
	!	Flash switch-hook to transfer call	×	×	×	
	W	Wait for 2nd dial tone (if X3 or higher is set)	×	×	×	
	@	Wait for an answer (if X3 or higher is set)	×	×	×	
	R	Reverse frequencies	×	×	×	×
	S	Dial stored number			×	
DL	Dial the last-dialed number		×			
DSn	Dial number stored in NVRAM at position n		×			
En	Command mode local echo; not applicable after a connection has been made		×	×	×	×
	E0	Echo Off	×	×	×	×
	E1	Echo On	×	×	×	×

Command	Modem Functions and Options	USR	2400	Hayes 2400	1200
Fn	Local echo On/Off when a connection has been made	×	×	×	×
	F0 Echo On (Half duplex)	×	×	×	×
	F1 Echo Off (Full duplex)—Default	×	×	×	×
Hn	On/Off hook control	×	×	×	×
	H0 Hang up (go on hook)—Default	×	×	×	×
	H1 Go off hook	×	×	×	×
In	Inquiry	×	×	×	×
	I0 Return product code	×	×	×	×
	I1 Return memory (ROM) checksum	×	×	×	×
	I2 Run memory (RAM) test	×	×	×	
	I3 Return call duration/real time	×	×		
	I4 Return current modem settings	×	×		
	I5 Return NVRAM settings	×			
	I6 Return link diagnostics	×			
	I7 Return product configuration	×			
Kn	Modem clock operation	×			
	K0 ATI3 displays call duration—Default	×			
	K1 ATI3 displays real time; set with ATI3=HH:MM:SSK1	×			
Ln	Loudness of speaker volume;			×	
	L0 Low			×	
	L1 Low			×	
	L2 Medium			×	
	L3 High			×	
Mn	Monitor (speaker) control	×	×	×	×
	M0 Speaker always Off	×	×	×	×
	M1 Speaker On until carrier is established—Default	×	×	×	×
	M2 Speaker always On	×	×	×	×
	M3 Speaker On after last digit dialed, Off at carrier detect	×	×	×	×
O	Return on-line after command execution	×	×	×	×
	O0 Return on-line, normal	×	×	×	×
	O1 Return on-line, retrain	×	×	×	×
P	Pulse dial	×	×	×	×
Qn	Result codes display	×	×	×	×
	Q0 Result codes displayed	×	×	×	×
	Q1 Result codes suppressed (quiet mode)	×	×	×	×
	Q2 Quiet in answer mode only	×			
Sr=n	Set Register commands: r is any S-register; n must be a decimal number between 0 and 255.	×	×	×	×
Sr.b=n	Set bit .b of register r to n (0/Off or 1/On)	×			
Sr?	Query register r	×	×	×	×
T	Tone dial	×	×	×	×
Vn	Verbal/Numeric result codes	×	×	×	×
	V0 Numeric mode	×	×	×	×
	V1 Verbal mode	×	×	×	×
Xn	Result code options	×	×	×	×

(continued)

Table A.20 Continued

Command	Modem Functions and Options	USR	2400	Hayes 2400	1200
Yn	Long space disconnect			×	
	Y0 Disabled			×	
	Y1 Enabled; disconnects after 1.5-second break			×	
Z	Software reset	×	×	×	×
+++	Escape code sequence, preceded and followed by at least one second of no data transmission	×	×		
/(Slash)	Pause for 125 msec	×			
>	Repeat command continuously or up to 10 dial attempts Cancel by pressing any key	×	×		
$	Online Help—Basic command summary	×	×		
&$	Online Help—Ampersand command summary	×			
%$	Online Help—Percent command summary	×			
D$	Online Help—Dial command summary	×	×		
S$	Online Help—S-register summary	×	×		
<Ctrl>-S	Stop/restart display of HELP screens		×		
<Ctrl>-C	Cancel display HELP screens		×		
<Ctrl>-K	Cancel display HELP screens		×		
Extended Command Set					
&An	ARQ result codes 14–17, 19	×			
	&A0 Suppress ARQ result codes	×			
	&A1 Display ARQ result codes —Default	×			
	&A2 Display HST and V.32 result codes	×			
	&A3 Display protocol result codes	×			
&Bn	Data Rate, terminal-to-modem (DTE/DCE)	×			
	&B0 DTE rate follows connection rate—Default	×			
	&B1 Fixed DTE rate	×			
	&B2 Fixed DTE rate in ARQ mode; variable DTE rate in non-ARQ mode	×			
&Cn	Carrier Detect (CD) operations	×		×	
	&C0 CD override	×		×	
	&C1 Normal CD operations	×		×	
&Dn	Data Terminal Ready (DTR) operations	×		×	
	&D0 DTR override	×		×	
	&D1 DTR Off; goes to command state			×	
	&D2 DTR Off; goes to command state and on hook	×		×	
	&D3 DTR Off; resets modem			×	
&F	Load factory settings into RAM	×		×	
&Gn	Guard tone	×		×	
	&G0 No guard tone; U.S., Canada—Default	×		×	
	&G1 Guard tone; some European countries	×		×	
	&G2 Guard tone; U.K., requires B0	×		×	
&Hn	Transmit Data flow control	×			
	&H0 Flow control disabled—Default	×			
	&H1 Hardware (CTS) flow control	×			

Command	Modem Functions and Options	USR	2400	Hayes 2400	1200
	&H2 Software (XON/XOFF) flow control	×			
	&H3 Hardware and software control	×			
&In	Received Data software flow control	×			
	&I0 Flow control disabled—Default	×			
	&I1 XON/XOFF to local modem and remote computer	×			
	&I2 XON/XOFF to local modem only	×			
	&I3 Host mode, Hewlett Packard protocol	×			
	&I4 Terminal mode, Hewlett Packard protocol	×			
	&I5 ARQ mode-same as &I2; non-ARQ mode; look for incoming XON/XOFF	×			
&Jn	Telephone jack selection			×	
	&J0 RJ-11/ RJ-41S/ RJ-45S			×	
	&J1 RJ-12/ RJ-13			×	
&Kn	Data compression	×			
	&K0 Disabled	×			
	&K1 Auto enable/disable—Default	×			
	&K2 Enabled	×			
	&K3 V.42bis only	×			
&Ln	Normal/Leased line operation	×		×	
	&L0 Normal phone line—Default	×		×	
	&L1 Leased line	×		×	
&Mn	Error Control/Synchronous Options	×		×	
	&M0 Normal mode, no error control	×		×	
	&M1 Synch mode	×		×	
	&M2 Synch mode 2—stored number dialing			×	
	&M3 Synch mode 3—manual dialing	×			
	&M4 Normal/ARQ mode-Normal if ARQ connection cannot be made-Default	×			
	&M5 ARQ mode-hang up if ARQ connection cannot be made	×			
&Nn	Data Rate, data link (DCE/DCE)	×			
	&N0 Normal link operations—Default	×			
	&N1 300 bps	×			
	&N2 1200 bps	×			
	&N3 2400 bps	×			
	&N4 4800 bps	×			
	&N5 7200 bps	×			
	&N6 9600 bps	×			
	&N7 12K bps	×			
	&N8 14.4K bps	×			
&Pn	Pulse dial make/break ratio	×		×	
&P0	North America—Default	×		×	
&P1	British Commonwealth	×		×	
&Rn	Received Data hardware (RTS) flow control	×		×	
	&R0 CTS tracks RTS	×		×	
	&R1 Ignore RTS—Default	×		×	
	&R2 Pass received data on RTS high; used Pass received data on RTS high	×			

(continues)

Table A.20 Continued

Command	Modem Functions and Options	USR	2400	Hayes 2400	1200
Extended Command Set					
&Sn	Data Set Ready (DSR) override	×		×	
	&S0 DSR override (always On—Default)	×		×	
	&S1 Modem controls DSR	×		×	
	&S2 Pulsed DSR; CTS follows CD	×			
	&S3 Pulsed DSR	×			
&Tn	Modem Testing	×		×	
	&T0 End testing	×		×	
	&T1 Analog loopback	×		×	
	&T2 Reserved	×			
	&T3 Digital loopback	×		×	
	&T4 Grant remote digital loopback	×		×	
	&T5 Deny remote digital loopback	×		×	
	&T6 Initiate remote digital loopback	×		×	
	&T7 Remote digital loopback with self-test	×		×	
	&T8 Analog loopback with self-test	×		×	
&W	Write current settings to NVRAM	×		×	
&Xn	Synchronous timing source	×		×	
	&X0 Modem's transmit clock—Default	×		×	
	&X1 Terminal equipment	×		×	
	&X2 Modem's receiver clock	×		×	
&Yn	Break handling. Destructive breaks clear the buffer; expedited Breaks are sent immediately to remote system.	×			
	&Y0 Destructive, but don't send break	×			
	&Y1 Destructive, expedited—Default	×			
	&Y2 Nondestructive, expedited	×			
	&Y3 Nondestructive, unexpedited	×			
&Zn=L	Store last-dialed phone number in NVRAM at position n	×			
&Zn=s	Write phone number(s) to NVRAM at position n (0–3); 36 characters maximum	×			
&Zn?	Display phone number in NVRAM at position n (n=0–3)	×		×	
%Rn	Remote access to Rack Controller Unit (RCU)	×			
	%R0 Disabled	×			
	%R1 Enabled	×			
%T	Enable Touch-Tone recognition	×			
Modem S-Register Functions and Defaults					
S0	Number of rings before automatic answering when DIP switch 5 is UP. Default = 1. S0 = 0 disables Auto Answer, equivalent to DIP switch 5 Down	SW5	SW5	0	SW5
S1	Counts and stores number of rings from incoming call	0	0	0	0
S2	Define escape code character. Default = +	43	43	43	43
S3	Define ASCII carriage return	13	13	13	13

Command	Modem Functions and Options	USR	2400	Hayes 2400	1200
S4	Define ASCII line feed	10	10	10	10
S5	Define ASCII Backspace	8	8	8	8
S6	Number of seconds modem waits before dialing	2	2	2	2
S7	Number of seconds modem waits for a carrier	60	30	30	30
S8	Duration (sec) for pause (,) option in Dial command and pause between command reexecutions for Repeat (>) command	2	2	2	2
S9	Duration (.1 sec units) of remote carrier signal before recognition	6	6	6	6
S10	Duration (.1 sec units) modem waits after loss of carrier before hanging up	7	7	7	7
S11	Duration and spacing (ms) of dialed Touch-Tones	70	70	70	70
S12	Guard time (in .02 sec units) for escape code sequence (+++)	50	50	50	50
S13	Bit-mapped register:	0			
	1 Reset when DTR drops				
	2 Auto answer in originate mode				
	4 Disable result code pause				
	8 DS0 on DTR low-to-high				
	16 DS0 on power up, ATZ				
	32 Disable HST modulation				
	64 Disable MNP Level 3				
	128 Watchdog hardware reset				
S15	Bit-mapped register:	0			
	1 Disable high-frequency equalization				
	2 Disable on-line fallback				
	4 Force 300-bps back channel				
	8 Set non-ARQ transmit buffer to 128 bytes				
	16 Disable MNP Level 4				
	32 Set Del as Backspace key				
	64 Unusual MNP incompatibility				
	128 Custom applications only				
S16	Bit-mapped register:	0	0	0	
	1 Analog loopback				
	2 Dial test				
	4 Test pattern				
	8 Initiate remote digital loopback				
	16 Reserved				
	32 Reserved				
	64 Reserved				
	128 Reserved				
S18	&Tn Test timer, disabled when set to 0	0		0	
S19	Set inactivity timer in minutes	0			
S21	Length of Break, DCE to DTE, in 10ms units	10		0	
S22	Define ASCII XON	17		17	
S23	Define ASCII XOFF	19		19	

(continues)

Table A.20 Continued

Command	Modem Functions and Options		USR	2400	Hayes 2400	1200
Modem S-Register Functions and Defaults						
S24	Duration (20ms units) of pulsed DSR when modem is set to &S2 or &S3		150			
S25	Delay to DTR in 10ms units		5			
S26	Duration (10ms units) of delay between RTS and CTS, synchronous mode		1		1	
S27	Bit-mapped register:		0			
	1	Enable V.21 modulation, 300 bps				
	2	Enable unencoded V.32 modulation				
	4	Disable V.32 modulation				
	8	Disable 2100 Hz answer tone				
	16	Disable MNP handshake				
	32	Disable V.42 Detect phase				
	64	Reserved				
	128	Unusual software incompatibility				
S28	Duration (.1 sec units) of V.21/V.23 handshake delay		8			
S32	Voice/Data switch options:		1			
	0	Disabled				
	1	Go off hook in originate mode				
	2	Go off hook in answer mode				
	3	Redial last-dialed number				
	4	Dial number stored at position 0				
	5	Auto answer toggle On/Off				
	6	Reset modem				
	7	Initiate remote digital loopback				
S34	Bit-mapped register:		0			
	1	Disable V.32bis				
	2	Disable enhanced V.32 mode				
	4	Disable quick V.32 retrain				
	8	Enable V.23 modulation				
	16	Change MR LED to DSR				
	32	Enable MI/MIC				
	64	Reserved				
	128	Reserved				
S38	Duration (sec) before disconnect when DTR drops during an ARQ call		0			

ARQ = Automatic repeat request
ASCII = American Standard Code for Information Interchange
BPS = Bits per second
CCITT = Consultative Committee for International Telephone and Telegraph
CD = Carrier cetect
CRC = Cyclic redundancy check
DCE = Data communications equipment
DTE = Data terminal equipment
EIA = Electronic Industries Association
HDLC = High-level data link control
HST = High-speed technology
Hz = Hertz

LAPM = Link access procedure for modems
MI/MIC = Mode indicate/Mode indicate common
MNP = Microcom networking protocol
NVRAM = Non-volatile memory
RAM = Random-access memory
ROM = Read-only memory
SDLC = Synchronous Data Link Control
MR = Modem ready
LED = Light-emitting diode
DTR = Data terminal ready
CTS = Clear to send
RTS = Ready to send
DSR = Data set ready

Printer Control Codes

Table A.21 IBM Printer-Control Codes

Function	Codes in ASCII	Codes in Hex	Pro-Printer	Graphics Printer	Color Printer
Job-Control Commands					
Escape (command start)	<ESC>	1B	×	×	×
Null (command end)	<NUL>	00	×	×	×
Ring bell	<BELL>	07	×	×	×
Cancel (clear printer buffer)	<CAN>	18	×	×	×
Select printer	<DC1>	11	×		×
Deselect printer n	<ESC>Q#	1B 51#	×		×
Deselect printer	<DC3>	13	×		×
Automatic ribbon band shift	<ESC>a	1B 61			×
Select ribbon band 1	<ESC>y	1B 79			×
Select ribbon band 2	<ESC>m	1B 6D			×
Select ribbon band 3	<ESC>c	1B 63			×
Select ribbon band 4 (black)	<ESC>b	1B 62			×
Home print head	<ESC><	1B 3C		×	×
Form feed	<FF>	0C	×	×	×
Horizontal tab	<HT>	09	×	×	×
Backspace	<BS>	08	×		×
Initialize function On	<ESC>?<SOH>	1B 3F 01			×
Initialize function Off	<ESC>?<NUL>	1B 3F 00			×
Unidirectional printing On	<ESC>U<SOH>	1B 55 01	×	×	×
Unidirectional printing Off	<ESC>U<NUL>	1B 55 00	×	×	×
Space #/120 fwd to next character	<ESC>d#	1B 64 #			×
Space #/120 bwd to next character	<ESC>e#	1B 65 #			×
Set aspect ratio to 1:1	<ESC>n<SOH>	1B 6E 01			×
Set aspect ratio to 5:6	<ESC>n<NUL>	1B 6E 00			×
Select control values = binary	<ESC>@#<NUL>	1B 40 # 00			×
Select control values = ASCII	<ESC>@<SOH>	1B 40 01			×

(continues)

Table A.21 Continued

Function	Codes in ASCII	Codes in Hex	Pro-Printer	Graphics Printer	Color Printer
Job-Control Commands					
Ignore paper end On	<ESC>8	1B 38		×	
Ignore paper end Off	<ESC>9	1B 39		×	
Set length of page in lines (1–127)	<ESC>C#	1B 43 #	×	×	×
Set length of page in inches (1–22)	<ESC>C<SOH>#	1B 43 01 #	×	×	×
Automatic line justification On	<ESC>M<SOH>	1B 4D 01			×
Automatic line justification Off	<ESC>M<NUL>	1B 4D 00			×
Perforation skip On (1–127)	<ESC>N #	1B 4E #	×	×	×
Perforation skip Off	<ESC>O	1B 4F	×	×	×
Set top of page (form)	<ESC>4	1B 34	×		×
Set left and right margins	<ESC>X #	1B 58 #			×
Clear tabs (set to power-on defaults)	<ESC>R	1B 52	×		×
Set horizontal tab stops	<ESC>D # <NUL>	1B 44 # 00	×	×	×
Set vertical tab stops	<ESC>B # <NUL>	1B 42 # 00	×	×	×
Carriage return	<CR>	0D	×	×	×
Line feed	<LF>	0A		×	×
Set n/72 lines per inch	<ESC>A #	1B 41 #	×	×	×
Set n/216 lines per inch	<ESC>3 #	1B 33 #	×	×	#/144"
Set 8 lines per inch	<ESC>0	1B 30	×	×	×
Set 7/72nd line per inch	<ESC>1	1B 31	×	×	6/72"
Start new line spacing	<ESC>2	1B 32	×	×	×
Vertical tab	<VT>	0B	×	×	×
Reverse line feed	<ESC>]	1B 5D			×
Automatic line feed On	<ESC>5<SOH>	1B 35 01	×		×
Automatic line feed Off	<ESC>5<NUL>	1B 35 00	×		×
Font Selection					
Select character set 1	<ESC>7	1B 37	×	×	×
Select character set 2	<ESC>6	1B 36	×	×	×
10 cpi (compressed Off)	<DC2>	12	×	×	×
17.1 cpi (compressed On)	<SI>	0F	×	×	×
Doublestrike On	<ESC>G	1B 47	×	×	×
Doublestrike Off	<ESC>H	1B 48	×	×	×
Doublewidth On (lines)	<ESC>W<SOH>	1B 57 01	×	×	×
Doublewidth Off (lines)	<ESC>W<NUL>	1B 57 00	×	×	×
Doublewidth by line On	<SO>	0E	×	×	×
Doublewidth by line Off	<DC4>	14	×	×	×
Emphasized printing On	<ESC>E	1B 45	×	×	×
Emphasized printing Off	<ESC>F	1B 46	×	×	×
Subscript On	<ESC>S<SOH>	1B 53 01	×	×	×
Superscript On	<ESC>S<NUL>	1B 53 00	×	×	×
Subscript/superscript Off	<ESC>T	1B 54	×	×	×
Set draft quality	<ESC>I<SOH>	1B 49 01			×
Set text quality (near-letter quality)	<ESC>I<STX>	1B 49 02	×		×
Set letter quality	<ESC>I<ETX>	1B 49 03			×

Function	Codes in ASCII	Codes in Hex	Pro-Printer	Graphics Printer	Color Printer
Proportional spacing On	<ESC>P<SOH>	1B 50 01			×
Proportional spacing Off	<ESC>P<NUL>	1B 50 00			×
12-characters-per-inch spacing	<ESC>:	1B 3A	×		×
Print all characters	<ESC>\ #	1B 5C #	×		×
Print next character	<ESC>^	1B 5E	×		×
Underline On	<ESC>-<SOH>	1B 2D 01	×	×	×
Underline Off	<ESC>-<NUL>	1B 2D 00	×	×	×
Graphics					
Graphics, 60 dots per inch (dpi)	<ESC>K #	1B 4B #	×	×	
Graphics, 70/84 dpi	<ESC>K #	1B 4B #			×
Graphics, 120 DPI half-speed	<ESC>L #	1B 4C #	×	×	
Graphics, 140/168 dpi half-speed	<ESC>L #	1B 4C #			×
Graphics, 120 dpi normal speed	<ESC>Y #	1B 59 #	×	×	
Graphics, 140/168 dpi normal speed	<ESC>Y #	1B 59 #			×
Graphics, 240 dpi half-speed	<ESC>Z #	1B 5A #	×	×	
Graphics, 280/336 dpi half-speed	<ESC>Z #	1B 5A #			×

 # indicates a variable number in the code.

Table A.22 Epson Printer-Control Codes

Function	Codes in ASCII	Codes in Hex
Job-Control Commands		
Ring bell	<BELL>	07
Clear line	<CAN>	18
Select printer	<DC1>	11
Deselect printer	<DC3>	13
Set justification	<ESC>a	1B 61
Cut sheet-feeder control	<ESC>	EM1B 19
Select character space	<ESC>	SP1B 20
Select mode combinations	<ESC>!	1B 21
Select active character set	<ESC>%	1B 25
Copies ROM to user RAM	<ESC>:	1B 3A
Defines user characters	<ESC>&	1B 26
Set MSB = 0	<ESC>>	1B 3E
Set MSB = 1	<ESC>=	1B 3D
Select international character set	<ESC>R#	1B 72#
Select 15 width	<ESC>g	1B 67
Select immediate print (typewriter mode)	<ESC>i	1B 69
Half-speed printing Off	<ESC>s<NUL>	1B 73 00
Half-speed printing On	<ESC>s<SOH>	1B 73 01
Set horizontal tab unit	<ESC>e<NUL>	1B 65 00
Set vertical tab unit	<ESC>e<SOH>	1B 6D 01
Special character-generator selection (control codes accepted)	<ESC>m<NUL>	1B 6D 00
Special character-generator selection (graphic characters accepted)	<ESC>m<SOH>	1B 6D 01

(continues)

Table A.22 Continued

Function	Codes in ASCII	Codes in Hex
Job-Control Commands		
Unidirectional printing On	<ESC>U<SOH>	1B 55 01
Unidirectional printing Off	<ESC>U<NUL>	1B 55 00
Turn unidirectional (left to right) On	<ESC><	1B 3C
Form feed	<FF>	0C
Horizontal tab	<HT>	09
Initialize printer	<ESC>@	1B 40
Backspace	<BS>	08
Printer-Control Commands		
Ignore paper end On	<ESC>8	1B 38
Ignore paper end Off	<ESC>9	1B 39
Set length of page in lines (1–127)	<ESC>C#	1B 43#
Set length of page in inches (1–22)	<ESC>C<NUL>#	1B 43 00#
Set absolute tab	<ESC>$	1B 24
Set vertical tab	<ESC>/	1B 2F
Set vertical tab	<ESC>b	1B 62
Set horizontal tab unit	<ESC>e<NUL>	1B 65 00
Set vertical tab unit	<ESC>e<SOH>	1B 65 01
Set horizontal skip position	<ESC>f<NUL>	1B 66 00
Set vertical skip position	<ESC>f<SOH>	1B 66 01
Perforation skip On (1–127)	<ESC>N#	1B 4E#
Perforation skip Off	<ESC>O	1B 4F
Set horizontal tab stop	<ESC>D	1B 44
Set vertical tab stop	<ESC>B	1B 42
Carriage return	<CR>	0D
Line feed	<LF>	0A
Set variable line feed to #/72 inch (1–85)	<ESC>A#	1B 41#
Set variable line feed to #/216 inch	<ESC>J#	1B 4A#
Set spacing at 1/8 inch	<ESC>0	1B 30
Set spacing at 7/72 inch	<ESC>1	1B 31
Set line spacing at 1/6 inch	<ESC>2	1B 32
Set #/216 inch line feed (0–225)	<ESC>3#	1B 33#
Vertical tab	<VT>	0B
Font Selection		
Deactivate high-order control codes	<ESC>6	1B 36
Turn alternate character (italics) On	<ESC>4	1B 34
10 CPI (compressed Off) spacing	<DC2>	12
17.1 CPI (compressed On) spacing	<SI>	0F
Doublestrike On	<ESC>G	1B 47
Doublestrike Off	<ESC>H	1B 48
Doublewidth On (lines)	<ESC>W<SOH>	1B 57 01
Doublewidth Off (lines)	<ESC>W<NUL>	1B 57 00
Enlarged print mode On	<SO>	0E
Enlarged print mode Off	<DC4>	14
Emphasized printing On	<ESC>E	1B 45
Emphasized printing Off	<ESC>F	1B 46
Turn alternate character (italics) On	<ESC>4	1B 34
Turn alternate character (italics) Off	<ESC>5	1B 35

Function	Codes in ASCII	Codes in Hex
Elite mode On (Pica mode off)	<ESC>M	1B 4D
Select family of type styles	<ESC>k	1B 6B
Proportional printing Off	<ESC>p<NUL>	1B 70 00
Proportional printing On	<ESC>p<SOH>	1B 70 01
Select letter- or draft-quality printing	<ESC>z	1B 7A
Subscript On	<ESC>S<SOH>	1B 53 01
Superscript On	<ESC>S<NUL>	1B 53 00
Subscript/superscript Off	<ESC>T	1B 54
Control code select	<ESC>I	1B 49
Elite mode Off (Pica mode On)	<ESC>P	1B 50
Nine-pin graphics mode	<ESC>^	1B 5E
Underline On	<ESC>-<SOH>	1B 2D 01
Underline Off	<ESC>-<NUL>	1B 2D 00
Graphics		
Normal-density bit image	<ESC>K	1B 4B##
Dual-density bit image	<ESC>L	1B 4C##
Double-speed, dual-density bit image	<ESC>Y	1B 59##
Quadruple-density bit image	<ESC>Z	1B 5A##

International character sets:
0 = U.S.
1 = France
2 = Germany
3 = England
4 = Denmark
5 = Sweden
6 = Italy
7 = Spain
8 = Japan
9 = Norway
10 = Denmark II
Characters in brackets are ASCII code names.
 # indicates a variable numeric value.

Table A.23 HP LaserJet Printer-Control Codes

Function Type	Function	Codes in ASCII	Codes in Hex
Job-Control Commands			
Printer control	Reset printer	<ESC>E	1B 45
	Self-test mode	<ESC>z	1B 7A
	Number of copies	<ESC>&l#X	1B 26 6C # 58
	Long-edge (left) offset registration	<ESC>&l#U	1B 26 6C # 55
	Short-edge (top) offset registration	<ESC>&l#Z	1B 26 6C # 5A
Printer-Control Commands			
Paper source	Eject page	<ESC>&l0H	1B 26 6C 30 48
	Paper-tray auto feed	<ESC>&l1H	1B 26 6C 31 48
	Manual feed	<ESC>&l2H	1B 26 6C 32 48
	Manual envelope feed	<ESC>&l3H	1B 26 6C 33 48
	Feed from lower cassette	<ESC>&l4H	1B 26 6C 34 48

(continues)

Table A.23 Continued

Function Type	Function	Codes in ASCII	Codes in Hex
Job-Control Commands			
Page size	Executive	<ESC>&l1A	1B 26 6C 31 41
	Letter	<ESC>&l2A	1B 26 6C 32 41
	Legal	<ESC>&l3A	1B 26 6C 33 41
	A4	<ESC>&l26A	1B 26 6C 32 36 41
	Monarch (envelope)	<ESC>&l80A	1B 26 6C 38 30 41
	COM 10 (envelope)	<ESC>&l81A	1B 26 6C 38 31 41
	DL (envelope)	<ESC>&l90A	1B 26 6C 39 30 41
	C5 (envelope)	<ESC>&l91A	1B 26 6C 39 31 41
Orientation	Portrait mode	<ESC>&l0O	1B 26 6C 30 4F
	Landscape mode	<ESC>&l1O	1B 26 6C 31 4F
	Reverse portrait	<ESC>&l2O	1B 26 6C 32 4F
	Reverse landscape	<ESC>&l3O	1B 26 6C 33 4F
	Print direction	<ESC>&a#P	1B 26 61 # 50
Page settings	Page length	<ESC>&l#P	1B 26 6C # 50
	Top margin	<ESC>&l#E	1B 26 6C # 45
	Text length	<ESC>&l#F	1B 26 6C # 46
	Clear horizontal margins	<ESC>9	1B 39
	Set left margin	<ESC>&a#L	1B 26 61 # 4C
	Set right margin	<ESC>&a#M	1B 26 61 # 4D
	Perforation skip enable	<ESC>&l1L	1B 26 6C 31 4C
	Perforation skip disable	<ESC>&l0L	1B 26 6C 30 4C
Line spacing	Vertical motion index	<ESC>&l#C	1B 26 6C # 43
	Horizontal motion index	<ESC>&k#H	1B 26 6B # 4B
	1 line/inch	<ESC>&l1D	1B 26 6C 31 44
	2 lines/inch	<ESC>&l2D	1B 26 6C 32 44
	3 lines/inch	<ESC>&l3D	1B 26 6C 33 44
	4 lines/inch	<ESC>&l4D	1B 26 6C 34 44
	6 lines/inch	<ESC>&l6D	1B 26 6C 36 44
	8 lines/inch	<ESC>&l8D	1B 26 6C 38 44
	12 lines/inch	<ESC>&l12D	1B 26 6C 31 32 44
	16 lines/inch	<ESC>&l16D	1B 26 6C 31 36 44
	24 lines/inch	<ESC>&l24D	1B 26 6C 32 34 44
	48 lines/inch	<ESC>&l48D	1B 26 6C 34 38 44
	Half line feed	<ESC>=	1B 3D
Stacking position	Default	<ESC>&l0T	1B 26 6C 30 54
	Toggle	<ESC>&l1T	1B 26 6C 31 54
Cursor Positioning			
Vertical position	Number of rows	<ESC>&a#R	1B 26 61 # 52
	Number of dots	<ESC>*p#Y	1B 2A 70 # 59
	Number of decipoints	<ESC>&a#V	1B 26 61 # 56
Horizontal position	Number of rows	<ESC>&a#C	1B 26 61 # 43
	Number of dots	<ESC>*p#X	1B 2A 70 # 58
	Number of decipoints	<ESC>&a#H	1B 26 61 # 48
End-of-line	CR=CR; LF=LF; FF=FF	<ESC>&k0G	1B 26 6B 30 47
	CR=CR+LF; LF=LF; FF=FF	<ESC>&k1G	1B 26 6B 31 47
	CR=CR; LF=CR+LF; FF=CR+FF	<ESC>&k2G	1B 26 6B 32 47
	CR=CR+LF; LF=CR+LF; FF=CR+FF	<ESC>&k3G	1B 26 6B 33 47
Push/Pop position	Push position	<ESC>&f0S	1B 26 66 30 53
	Pop position	<ESC>&f1S	1B 26 66 31 53

Function Type	Function	Codes in ASCII	Codes in Hex
Font Selection			
Font symbol set	Roman-8	<ESC>(8U	1B 28 38 55
	USASCII	<ESC>(0U	1B 28 30 55
	Danish/Norwegian	<ESC>(0D	1B 28 30 44
	British (U.K.)	<ESC>(1E	1B 28 31 45
	French	<ESC>(1F	1B 28 31 46
	German	<ESC>(1G	1B 28 31 47
	Italian	<ESC>(0I	1B 28 30 49
	Swedish/Finnish	<ESC>(0S	1B 28 30 53
	Spanish	<ESC>(2S	1B 28 32 53
	Legal	<ESC>(1U	1B 28 31 55
	Linedraw	<ESC>(0B	1B 28 30 42
	Math8	<ESC>(8M	1B 28 38 4D
	Math7	<ESC>(0A	1B 28 30 41
	PiFont	<ESC>(15U	1B 28 31 35 55
	ECMA-94 Latin	<ESC>(0N	1B 28 30 4E
	PC-8	<ESC>(10U	1B 28 31 30 55
	PC-8 D/N	<ESC>(11U	1B 28 31 31 55
	PC 850	<ESC>(12U	1B 28 31 32 55
Primary spacing	Proportional	<ESC>(s1P	1B 28 73 31 50
	Fixed	<ESC>(s0P	1B 28 73 30 50
Character pitch	10 characters per inch	<ESC>(s10H	1B 28 73 31 30 48
	12 characters per inch	<ESC>(s12H	1B 28 73 31 32 48
	16.6 characters per inch	<ESC>(s16.6H	1B 28 73 31 36 2E 36 48
	Standard pitch (10 cpi)	<ESC>&k0S	1B 26 6B 30 53
	Compressed pitch (16.6 cpi)	<ESC>&k2S	1B 26 6B 32 53
	Elite (12.0)	<ESC>&k4s	1B 26 6B 34 53
Character point size	7 point	<ESC>(s7V	1B 28 73 37 56
	8 point	<ESC>(s8V	1B 28 73 38 56
	8.5 point	<ESC>(s8.5V	1B 28 73 38 2E 35 56
	10 point	<ESC>(s10V	1B 28 73 31 30 56
	12 point	<ESC>(s12V	1B 28 73 31 32 56
	14.4 point	<ESC>(s14.4V	1B 28 73 31 34 2E 34 56
Character style	Upright	<ESC>(s0S	1B 28 73 30 53
	Italic	<ESC>(s1S	1B 28 73 31 53
Character weight	Ultra thin	<ESC>(s-7B	1B 28 73 -37 42
	Extra thin	<ESC>(s-6B	1B 28 73 -36 42
	Thin	<ESC>(s-5B	1B 28 73 -35 42
	Extra light	<ESC>(s-4B	1B 28 73 -34 42
	Light	<ESC>(s-3B	1B 28 73 -33 42
	Demi light	<ESC>(s-2B	1B 28 73 -32 42
	Semi light	<ESC>(s-1B	1B 28 73 -31 42
	Medium (normal)	<ESC>(s0B	1B 28 73 30 42
	Semi bold	<ESC>(s1B	1B 28 73 31 42
	Demi bold	<ESC>(s2B	1B 28 73 32 42
	Bold	<ESC>(s3B	1B 28 73 33 42
	Extra bold	<ESC>(s4B	1B 28 73 34 42
	Black	<ESC>(s5B	1B 28 73 35 42
	Extra black	<ESC>(s6B	1B 28 73 36 42
	Ultra black	<ESC>(s7B	1B 28 73 37 42

(continues)

Table A.23 Continued

Function Type	Function	Codes in ASCII	Codes in Hex
Font Selection			
Character typeface	Courier	<ESC>(s3T	1B 28 73 33 54
	Univers	<ESC>(s52T	1B 28 73 35 32 54
	Line printer	<ESC>(s0T	1B 28 73 30 54
	CG Times	<ESC>(s4101T	1B 28 73 34 31 30 31 54
	Helvetica	<ESC>(s4T	1B 28 73 34 54
	TMS RMN	<ESC>(s5T	1B 28 73 33 54
Font default	Primary font	<ESC>(3@	1B 28 33 40
	Secondary font	<ESC>)3@	1B 29 33 40
Underlining	Underline On	<ESC>&d#D	1B 26 64 30 44
	Underline floating	<ESC>&d3D	1B 26 64 33 44
	Underline Off	<ESC>&d@	1B 26 64 40
Transparent print	Number of bytes	<ESC>&p#X[Data]	1B 26 70 # 58
Font Management			
Assign font ID	Font ID number	<ESC>*c#D	1B 2A 63 # 44
Font and character	Delete all font controls	<ESC>*c0F	1B 2A 63 30 46
	Delete all temporary fonts	<ESC>*c1F	1B 2A 63 31 46
	Delete last font ID specified	<ESC>*c2F	1B 2A 63 32 46
	Delete last font ID and char code	<ESC>*c3F	1B 2A 63 33 46
	Make temporary font	<ESC>*c4F	1B 2A 63 34 46
	Make permanent font	<ESC>*c5F	1B 2A 63 35 46
	Copy/assign font	<ESC>*c6F	1B 2A 63 36 46
Select font (ID)	Primary font ID number	<ESC>(#X	1B 28 # 58
	Secondary font ID number	<ESC>)#X	1B 29 # 58
Soft Font Creation			
Font descriptor	Create font	<ESC>)s#W[Data]	1B 29 73 # 57
	Download character	<ESC>(s#W[Data]	1B 28 73 # 57
	ASCII character code number	<ESC>*c#E	1B 2A 63 # 45
Graphics			
Vector graphics	Enter HP-GL/2 mode	<ESC>%0B	1B 25 30 42
	HP-GL/2 plot horizontal size	<ESC>%1B	1B 25 31 42
	HP-GL/2 plot vertical size	<ESC>*c#K	1B 2A 63 # 4B
	Set picture frame	<ESC>*0T	1B 2A 63 30 54
	Picture frame horizontal size	<ESC>*c#X	1B 2A 63 # 58
	Picture frame vertical size	<ESC>*c#Y	1B 2A 63 # 59
Raster resolution	75 dpi resolution	<ESC>*t75R	1B 2A 74 37 35 52
	100 dpi resolution	<ESC>*t100R	1B 2A 74 31 30 30 52
	150 dpi resolution	<ESC>*t150R	1B 2A 74 31 35 30 52
	300 dpi resolution	<ESC>*t300R	1B 2A 74 33 30 30 52
	Start at leftmost position	<ESC>*r0A	1B 2A 72 30 41
	Start at current cursor	<ESC>*r1A	1B 2A 72 31 41
Raster graphics presentation	Rotate image	<ESC>*r0F	1B 2A 72 30 46
	LaserJet landscape compatible	<ESC>*r3F	1B 2A 72 33 46
	Left raster graphics margin	<ESC>*r0A	1B 2A 72 30 41
	Current cursor	<ESC>*r1A	1B 2A 72 31 41
	Raster Y offset	<ESC>*b0M	1B 2A 62 # 59
Set raster compression	Uncoded	<ESC>*b0M	1B 2A 62 30 41
	Mode run-length encoded	<ESC>*b1M	1B 2A 62 31 41

Function type	Function	Codes in ASCII	Codes in Hex
	Tagged image file format	<ESC>*b2M	1B 2A 62 32 41
	Delta row	<ESC>*b3M	1B 2A 62 33 41
	Transfer graphic rows	<ESC>*b#W[Data]	1B 2A 62 # 57
	End graphics	<ESC>*rB	1B 2A 72 42
	Raster height	<ESC>*r#T	1B 2A 72 # 54
	Raster width	<ESC>*r#S	1B 2A 72 # 53
The Print Model			
Select pattern	Solid black (default)	<ESC>*v0T	1B 2A 76 30 54
	Solid white	<ESC>*v1T	1B 2A 76 31 54
	HP-defined shading pattern	<ESC>*v2T	1B 2A 76 32 54
	HP-defined cross-hatched pattern	<ESC>*v3T	1B 2A 76 33 54
Select source	Transparent	<ESC>*v0N	1B 2A 76 30 42
Transparency	Opaque	<ESC>*v1N	1B 2A 76 31 42
Select pattern	Transparent	<ESC>*v0O	1B 2A 76 30 43
Transparency	Opaque	<ESC>*v1O	1B 2A 76 31 43
Rectangle width	Horizontal # dots in pattern	<ESC>*c#A	1B 2A 63 # 41
	Horizontal # decipoints in pattern	<ESC>*c#H	1B 2A 63 # 48
Rectangle height	Vertical # dots in pattern	<ESC>*c#B	1B 2A 63 # 42
	Vertical # decipoints in pattern	<ESC>*c#V	1B 2A 63 # 56
Fill rectangular	Solid black	<ESC>*c0P	1B 2A 63 30 50
Area	Erase (solid white area fill)	<ESC>*c1P	1B 2A 63 31 50
	Shade fill	<ESC>*c2P	1B 2A 63 32 50
	Cross-hatched fill	<ESC>*c3P	1B 2A 63 33 50
	User defined	<ESC>*c4P	1B 2A 63 34 50
	Current pattern	<ESC>*c5P	1B 2A 63 35 50
Pattern ID	Percent of shading or type of pattern	<ESC>*c#G	1B 2A 63 # 47
Shading	Print 2% grayscale	<ESC>*c2G	1B 2A 63 32 47
	Print 10% grayscale	<ESC>*c10G	1B 2A 63 31 30 47
	Print 15% grayscale	<ESC>*c15G	1B 2A 63 31 35 47
	Print 30% grayscale	<ESC>*c30G	1B 2A 63 33 30 47
	Print 45% grayscale	<ESC>*c45G	1B 2A 63 34 35 47
	Print 70% grayscale	<ESC>*c70G	1B 2A 63 37 30 47
	Print 90% grayscale	<ESC>*c90G	1B 2A 63 39 30 47
	Print 100% grayscale	<ESC>*c100G	1B 2A 63 31 30 30 47
Pattern	1 horizontal line	<ESC>*c1G	1B 2A 63 31 47
	2 vertical lines	<ESC>*c2G	1B 2A 63 32 47
	3 diagonal lines	<ESC>*c3G	1B 2A 63 33 47
	4 diagonal lines	<ESC>*c4G	1B 2A 63 34 47
	5 square grid	<ESC>*c5G	1B 2A 63 35 47
	6 diagonal grid	<ESC>*c6G	1B 2A 63 36 47
Macros			
Macro ID	Macro ID number	<ESC>&f#Y	1B 26 66 # 59
Macro control	Start macro	<ESC>&f0X	1B 26 66 30 58
	Stop macro definition	<ESC>&f1X	1B 26 66 31 58
	Execute macro	<ESC>&f2X	1B 26 66 32 58
	Call macro	<ESC>&f3X	1B 26 66 33 58
	Enable overlay	<ESC>&f4X	1B 26 66 34 58
	Disable overlay	<ESC>&f5X	1B 26 66 35 58
	Delete macros	<ESC>&f6X	1B 26 66 36 58
	Delete all temporary macros	<ESC>&f7X	1B 26 66 37 58

(continues)

Table A.23 Continued

Function Type	Function	Codes in ASCII	Codes in Hex
Macros			
	Delete macro ID	<ESC>&f8X	1B 26 66 38 58
	Make temporary	<ESC>&f9X	1B 26 66 39 58
	Make permanent	<ESC>&f10X	1B 26 66 31 30 58
Programming Hints			
Display functions	Display functions On	<ESC>Y	1B 59
	Display functions Off	<ESC>Z	1B 5A
End-of-line wrap	Enable	<ESC>&s0C	1B 26 73 30 43
	Disable	<ESC>&s1C	1B 26 73 31 43

 # indicates a variable numeric value
[Data] indicates a bitstream of appropriate data

DOS Disk Structures and Layout

Table A.24 Master Boot Record (Partition Table)

Offset	Length	Description
Partition Table Entry #1		
1BEh 446	1 byte	Boot Indicator Byte (80h = Active, else 00h)
1BFh 447	1 byte	Starting Head (or Side) of Partition
1C0h 448	16 bits	Starting Cylinder (10 bits) and Sector (6 bits)
1C2h 450	1 byte	System Indicator Byte (see table)
1C3h 451	1 byte	Ending Head (or Side) of Partition
1C4h 452	16 bits	Ending Cylinder (10 bits) and Sector (6 bits)
1C6h 454	1 dword	Relative Sector Offset of Partition
1CAh 458	1 dword	Total Number of Sectors in Partition
Partition Table Entry #2		
1CEh 462	1 byte	Boot Indicator Byte (80h = Active, else 00h)
1CFh 463	1 byte	Starting Head (or Side) of Partition
1D0h 464	16 bits	Starting Cylinder (10 bits) and Sector (6 bits)
1D2h 466	1 byte	System Indicator Byte (see table)
1D3h 467	1 byte	Ending Head (or Side) of Partition
1D4h 468	16 bits	Ending Cylinder (10 bits) and Sector (6 bits)
1D6h 470	1 dword	Relative Sector Offset of Partition
1DAh 474	1 dword	Total Number of Sectors in Partition
Partition Table Entry #3		
1DEh 478	1 byte	Boot Indicator Byte (80h = Active, else 00h)
1DFh 479	1 byte	Starting Head (or Side) of Partition
1E0h 480	16 bits	Starting Cylinder (10 bits) and Sector (6 bits)
1E2h 482	1 byte	System Indicator Byte (see table)
1E3h 483	1 byte	Ending Head (or Side) of Partition
1E4h 484	16 bits	Ending Cylinder (10 bits) and Sector (6 bits)
1E6h 486	1 dword	Relative Sector Offset of Partition
1EAh 490	1 dword	Total Number of Sectors in Partition

Offset	Length	Description
Partition Table Entry #4		
1EEh 494	1 byte	Boot Indicator Byte (80h = Active, else 00h)
1EFh 495	1 byte	Starting Head (or Side) of Partition
1F0h 496	16 bits	Starting Cylinder (10 bits) and Sector (6 bits)
1F2h 498	1 byte	System Indicator Byte (see table)
1F3h 499	1 byte	Ending Head (or Side) of Partition
1F4h 500	16 bits	Ending Cylinder (10 bits) and Sector (6 bits)
1F6h 502	1 dword	Relative Sector Offset of Partition
1FAh 506	1 dword	Total Number of Sectors in Partition
Signature Bytes		
1FEh 510	2 bytes	Boot Sector Signature (55AAh)

A WORD equals two bytes which are read in reverse order, and a DWORD equals two WORDS that are read in reverse order.

Table A.25 Partition Table System Indicator Byte Values

Value	Description
00h	No Partition allocated in this entry
01h	Primary DOS, 12-bit FAT (Partition < 16M)
04h	Primary DOS, 16-bit FAT (16M <= Partition <= 32M)
05h	Extended DOS (Points to next Primary Partition)
06h	Primary DOS, 16-bit FAT (Partition > 32M)
07h	OS/2 HPFS Partition
02h	MS-XENIX root Partition
03h	MS-XENIX user Partition
08h	AIX File System Partition
09h	AIX Boot Partition
50h	Ontrack Disk Manager READ-ONLY Partition
51h	Ontrack Disk Manager READ/WRITE Partition
56h	Golden Bow Vfeature Partition
61h	Storage Dimensions Speedstor Partition
63h	IBM 386/ix or UNIX System V/386 Partition
64h	Novell Netware Partition
75h	IBM PCIX Partition
DBh	Digital Research Concurrent DOS/CPM-86 Partition
F2h	Some OEM's DOS 3.2+ second partition
FFh	UNIX Bad Block Table Partition

DOS Boot Record

Table A.26 DOS Volume Boot Sector (DVB) Format

Offset Hex	Dec	Field Length	Description
00h	0	3 bytes	Jump Instruction to Boot Program Code
03h	3	8 bytes	OEM Name and DOS Version ("IBM 5.0")
0Bh	11	1 word	Bytes/Sector (usually 512)
0Dh	13	1 byte	Sectors/Cluster (Must be a power of 2)
0Eh	14	1 word	Reserved Sectors (Boot Sectors, usually 1)

(continues)

Table A.26 Continued

Offset Hex	Dec	Field Length	Description
10h	16	1 byte	FAT Copies (usually 2)
11h	17	1 word	Maximum Root Directory Entries (usually 512)
13h	19	1 word	Total Sectors (If Partition <= 32M, else 0)
15h	21	1 byte	Media Descriptor Byte (F8h for hard disks)
16h	22	1 word	Sectors/FAT
18h	24	1 word	Sectors/Track
1Ah	26	1 word	Number of Heads
1Ch	28	1 dword	Hidden Sectors (If Partition <= 32M, 1 word only)
DOS 4.0 or Higher Only (Others 00h)			
20h	32	1 dword	Total Sectors (If Partition > 32M, else 0)
24h	36	1 byte	Physical Drive No. (00h=floppy, 80h=hard disk)
25h	37	1 byte	Reserved (00h)
26h	38	1 byte	Extended Boot Record Signature (29h)
27h	39	1 dword	Volume Serial Number (32-bit random number)
2Bh	43	11 bytes	Volume Label ("NO NAME" stored if no label)
36h	54	8 bytes	File System ID ("FAT12" or " FAT16")
All Versions of DOS			
3Eh	62	450 bytes	Boot Program Code
1FEh	510	2 bytes	Signature Bytes (55AAh)

A WORD is two bytes which are read in reverse order, and a DWORD is two WORDS that are read in reverse order.

Directory Structure

Table A.27 DOS Directory Entries

Offset Hex	Dec	Field Length	Description
00h	0	8 bytes	Filename
08h	8	3 bytes	File Extension
0Bh	11	1 byte	File Attributes (see table)
0Ch	12	10 bytes	Reserved (00h)
16h	22	1 word	Time of Creation (see table)
18h	24	1 word	Date of Creation (see table)
1Ah	26	1 word	Starting Cluster
1Ch	28	1 dword	Size in Bytes

Note

File names and extensions are left-justified and padded with spaces (32h). The first byte of the file name indicates the file status as follows:

Hex	File Status
00h	Entry never used; entries past this point not searched.
05h	Indicates first character of filename is actually E5h.
E5h	"[lcs]" (lowercase Sigma) indicates file has been erased.
2Eh	"." (period) indicates this entry is a direcotry. If the second byte is also 2Eh, the cluster field contains the cluster number of parent directory (0000h if the parent is the Root).

DOS Directory File Attribute Byte

Bit Positions 7 6 5 4 3 2 1 0	Hex Value	Description
0 0 0 0 0 0 0 1	01h	Read Only file
0 0 0 0 0 0 1 0	02h	Hidden file
0 0 0 0 0 1 0 0	04h	System file
0 0 0 0 1 0 0 0	08h	Volume Label
0 0 0 1 0 0 0 0	10h	Subdirectory
0 0 1 0 0 0 0 0	20h	Archive (updated since backup)
0 1 0 0 0 0 0 0	40h	Reserved
1 0 0 0 0 0 0 0	80h	Reserved
Examples		
0 0 1 0 0 0 0 1	21h	Read Only, Archive
0 0 1 1 0 0 1 0	32h	Hidden, Subdirectory, Archive
0 0 1 0 0 1 1 1	27h	Read Only, Hidden, System, Archive

Hard Disk Drives

This section has a great deal of information concerning all aspects of hard disk drives, including a table that lists a large number of different drive parameters, organized by manufacturer. Because Seagate is the largest supplier of hard disks in the world, and its product line is so extensive, a separate table references Seagate's hard disk product line and shows the parameters of all of its drives. This section also shows BIOS hard drive parameter tables for a number of different ROM BIOS versions, including those from IBM, Compaq, AMI, Award, Phoenix, and Zenith. Finally, this section includes the pinouts of popular hard disk interfaces such as ST-506/412, ESDI, IDE, and SCSI.

Table A. 28 shows parameters and specifications for a large number of different hard disk drives. This table can be very helpful when you are trying to install one of these drives in a system with no documentation for the drive.

Table A.28 Hard Disk Drive Specifications

Make/ Model	Capacity (MB)	Cyls	Hds	Sectors per Track	Write Pre-comp	Park Cyl
Atasi						
502	46.0	755	7	17	—	—
504	46.0	755	7	17	—	—
514	117.2	1,224	11	17	—	—
519MFM	159.8	1,224	15	17	—	—
519RLL	244.4	1,224	15	26	—	—
617	149.0	1,223	7	34	—	—

(continues)

Table A.28 Continued

Make/ Model	Capacity (MB)	Cyl	Hds	Sectors per Track	Write Pre-comp	Park Cyl
Atasi						
628	234.2	1,223	11	34	—	—
638	319.3	1,223	15	34	—	—
3046	39.3	645	7	17	323	644
3051	42.9	704	7	17	352	703
3051+	44.7	733	7	17	368	732
3085	71.3	1,024	8	17	0	—
V130	25.8	987	3	17	128	—
V150	43.0	987	5	17	128	—
V170	60.1	987	7	17	128	—
V185	71.0	1,166	7	17	128	—
Brand Technology						
BT8085	71.3	1,024	8	17	512	—
BT8128	109.1	1,024	8	26	—	—
BT8170E	142.5	1,023	8	34	—	—
Conner Peripherals						
CP-342	42.7	981	5	17	—	—
CP-344	42.9	805	4	26	—	—
CP-3024	21.4	634	2	33	—	—
CP-3044	43.1	526	4	40	—	—
CP-3102-A	104.9	776	8	33	—	—
CP-3102-B	104.3	772	8	33	—	—
CP-3104	104.9	776	8	33	—	—
CP-3184	84.3	832	6	33	—	—
CP-3204	209.8	1,348	8	38	—	—
CP-3204F	212.9	684	16	38	—	—
CP-30104	121.6	1,522	4	39	—	—
CMI						
CM-6626	22.3	640	4	17	256	615
CM-6640	33.4	640	6	17	256	615
Data-Tech Memories						
DTM-553	44.6	1,024	5	17	850	—
DTM-853	44.6	640	8	17	256	—
DTM-885	71.3	1,024	8	17	850	—
Fujitsu						
M2225D	21.4	615	4	17	—	615
M2227D	42.8	615	8	17	—	615
M2241AS	26.3	754	4	17	128	—
M2242AS	45.9	754	7	17	128	—
M2243AS	72.2	754	11	17	128	—
M2244E	71.5	822	5	34	—	—
M2245E	100.2	822	7	34	—	—
M2246E	143.1	822	10	34	—	—
M2247E	151.3	1,242	7	34	—	—
M2248E	237.8	1,242	11	34	—	—

Make/ Model	Capacity (MB)	Cyls	Hds	Sectors per Track	Write Pre-comp	Park Cyl
M2249E	324.3	1,242	15	34	—	—
M2261E	359.7	1,657	8	53	—	—
M2263E	674.5	1,657	15	53	—	—
M2611T	45.1	1,334	2	33	—	—
M2612T	90.2	1,334	4	33	—	—
M2613T	135.2	1,334	6	33	—	—
M2614T	180.3	1,334	8	33	—	—
Hewlett Packard						
97544EF	339.9	1,456	8	57	128	—
97548EF	679.9	1,456	16	57	128	—
Hitachi						
DK511-3	30.4	699	5	17	300	699
DK511-5	42.6	699	7	17	300	699
DK511-8	71.6	823	10	17	256	—
DK512-8	71.5	822	5	34	—	—
DK512-10	85.9	822	6	34	—	—
DK512-12	100.2	822	7	34	—	—
DK512-17	143.1	822	10	34	—	—
DK514-38	329.7	902	14	51	—	—
DK522-10	85.9	822	6	34	—	—
Imprimis (CDC)						
9415-519	18.2	697	3	17	128	—
9415-536	30.3	697	5	17	128	—
9415-538	31.9	733	5	17	128	—
94155-48	40.3	925	5	17	128	—
94155-57	48.3	925	6	17	128	—
94155-67	56.4	925	7	17	128	—
94155-77	64.4	925	8	17	128	—
94155-85	71.3	1,024	8	17	—	—
94155-85P	71.3	1,024	8	17	128	—
94155-86	72.5	925	9	17	128	—
94155-96	80.2	1,024	9	17	—	—
94155-96P	80.2	1,024	9	17	128	—
94155-120	102.2	960	8	26	—	—
94155-120P	102.2	960	8	26	128	—
94155-135	115.0	960	9	26	—	—
94155-135P	115.0	960	9	26	128	—
94156-48	40.3	925	5	17	128	—
94156-67	56.4	925	7	17	128	—
94156-86	72.5	925	9	17	128	—
94166-101	84.3	968	5	34	—	—
94166-141	118.0	968	7	34	—	—
94166-182	151.7	968	9	34	—	—
94186-383	319.3	1,411	13	34	—	—
94186-383H	319.3	1,223	15	34	—	—
94186-442H	368.4	1,411	15	34	—	—
94196-766	663.9	1,631	15	53	—	—
94204-65	65.5	941	8	17	128	—
94204-71	71.3	1,024	8	17	128	—

(continues)

Table A.28 Continued

Make/ Model	Capacity (MB)	Cyls	Hds	Sectors per Track	Write Pre-comp	Park Cyl
Imprimis (CDC)						
94205-51	43.0	989	5	17	128	—
94205-77	65.8	989	5	26	128	—
94211-106	89.0	1,023	5	34	—	—
94244-383	338.1	1,747	7	54	—	—
94246-383	331.7	1,746	7	53	—	—
94354-160	143.3	1,072	9	29	128	—
94354-200	177.8	1,072	9	36	—	—
94354-230	211.0	1,272	9	36	—	—
94355-100	84.0	1,072	9	17	128	—
94355-150	128.4	1,072	9	26	128	—
94356-111	93.2	1,071	5	34	—	—
94356-155	130.5	1,071	7	34	—	—
94356-200	167.8	1,071	9	34	—	—
Kalok						
KL320	21.4	615	4	17	—	660
KL330	32.7	615	4	26	—	660
KL343	42.5	670	4	31	—	669
Kyocera						
KC20A	21.4	616	4	17	0	—
KC20B	21.4	615	4	17	0	664
KC30A	32.8	616	4	26	0	—
KC30B	32.7	615	4	26	0	664
KC40GA	42.5	977	5	17	0	980
Lapine						
TITAN20	21.4	615	4	17	0	615
Maxtor						
LXT50S	48.0	733	4	32	—	—
LXT100S	96.1	733	8	32	—	—
LXT200A	200.5	816	15	32	—	—
LXT200S	212.9	1,320	7	45	—	—
LXT213A	212.6	683	16	38	—	—
LXT340S	352.2	1,560	7	63	—	—
LXT340AT	352.2	1,560	7	63	—	—
XT1050	39.3	902	5	17	—	—
XT1065	55.9	918	7	17	—	—
XT1085	71.3	1,024	8	17	—	—
XT1105	87.9	918	11	17	—	—
XT1120R	109.1	1,024	8	26	—	—
XT1140	119.9	918	15	17	—	—
XT1160	133.7	1,024	15	17	—	—
XT1240R	204.5	1,024	15	26	—	—
XT2085	74.6	1,224	7	17	—	—
XT2140	117.2	1,224	11	17	—	—
XT2190	159.8	1,224	15	17	—	—
XT4170E	149.2	1,224	7	34	—	—
XT4170S	149.2	1,224	7	34	—	—

Make/ Model	Capacity (MB)	Cyls	Hds	Sectors per Track	Write Pre-comp	Park Cyl
XT4175	149.2	1,224	7	34	—	—
XT4230E	203.0	1,224	9	36	—	—
XT4280	234.4	1,224	11	34	—	—
XT4380E	338.4	1,224	15	36	—	—
XT4380S	338.4	1,224	15	36	—	—
XT8380E	361.0	1,632	8	54	—	—
XT8380S	361.0	1,632	8	54	—	—
XT8610E	541.5	1,632	12	54	—	—
XT8760E	676.8	1,632	15	54	—	—
XT8760S	676.8	1,632	15	54	—	—
XT8702S	617.9	1,490	15	54	—	—
XT8800E	694.7	1,274	15	71	—	—
Micropolis						
1323	35.7	1,024	4	17	—	—
1323A	44.6	1,024	5	17	—	—
1324	53.5	1,024	6	17	—	—
1324A	62.4	1,024	7	17	—	—
1325	71.3	1,024	8	17	—	—
1333	35.7	1,024	4	17	—	—
1333A	44.6	1,024	5	17	—	—
1334	53.5	1,024	6	17	—	—
1334A	62.4	1,024	7	17	—	—
1335	71.3	1,024	8	17	—	—
1353	71.2	1,023	4	34	—	—
1353A	89.0	1,023	5	34	—	—
1354	106.9	1,023	6	34	—	—
1354A	124.7	1,023	7	34	—	—
1355	142.5	1,023	8	34	—	—
1551	149.0	1,223	7	34	—	—
1554	234.2	1,223	11	34	—	—
1555	255.5	1,223	12	34	—	—
1556	276.8	1,223	13	34	—	—
1557	298.1	1,223	14	34	—	—
1558	319.3	1,223	15	34	—	—
1568-15	663.9	1,631	15	53	—	—
1653-4	86.9	1,248	4	34	—	—
1653-5	108.6	1,248	5	34	—	—
1654-6	130.4	1,248	6	34	—	—
1654-7	152.1	1,248	7	34	—	—
1664-7	337.9	1,779	7	53	—	—
1743-5	110.9	1,140	5	38	—	—
Microscience						
HH-325	21.4	615	4	17	—	615
HH-725	21.4	615	4	17	—	615
HH-1050	44.6	1,024	5	17	—	—
HH-1060	68.2	1,024	5	26	—	—
HH-1075	62.4	1,024	7	17	—	—
HH-1090	80.1	1,314	7	17	—	—
HH-1095	95.4	1,024	7	26	—	—

(continues)

Table A.28 Continued

Make/ Model	Capacity (MB)	Cyls	Hds	Sectors per Track	Write Pre-comp	Park Cyl
Microscience						
HH-1120	122.4	1,314	7	26	—	—
HH-2120	124.7	1,023	7	34	—	—
HH-2160	155.4	1,275	7	34	—	—
4050	44.6	1,024	5	17	768	—
4060	68.2	1,024	5	26	768	—
4070	62.4	1,024	7	17	768	—
4090	95.4	1,024	7	26	768	—
5040-00	45.9	854	3	35	—	—
5070-00	76.5	854	5	35	—	—
5070-20	85.9	959	5	35	—	—
5100-00	107.1	854	7	35	—	—
5100-20	120.3	959	7	35	—	—
5160-00	159.3	1,270	7	35	—	—
7040-00	46.0	855	3	35	—	—
7070-00	76.6	855	5	35	—	—
7070-20	86.0	960	5	35	—	—
7100-00	107.3	855	7	35	—	—
7100-20	120.4	960	7	35	—	—
Miniscribe						
1006	5.3	306	2	17	128	336
1012	10.7	306	4	17	128	336
2006	5.3	306	2	17	128	336
2012	10.7	306	4	17	128	336
3012	10.7	612	2	17	128	656
3053	44.6	1,024	5	17	512	—
3085	71.3	1,170	7	17	512	—
3130E	112.0	1,250	5	35	—	—
3180E	156.8	1,250	7	35	—	—
3180S	161.9	1,255	7	36	—	—
3212	10.7	612	2	17	128	656
3412	10.7	306	4	17	128	336
3425	21.4	615	4	17	128	656
3425P	21.4	615	4	17	128	656
3438	32.7	615	4	26	128	656
3438P	32.7	615	4	26	128	656
3650	42.2	809	6	17	128	852
3650R	64.6	809	6	26	128	852
3675	64.6	809	6	26	128	852
4010	8.4	480	2	17	128	522
4020	16.7	480	4	17	128	522
6032	26.7	1,024	3	17	512	—
6053	44.6	1,024	5	17	512	—
6079	68.2	1,024	5	26	512	—
6085	71.3	1,024	8	17	512	—
6128	109.1	1,024	8	26	512	—
7040A	42.7	981	5	17	—	—
7080A	85.4	981	10	17	—	—
8051A	42.7	745	4	28	—	—

Make/ Model	Capacity (MB)	Cyls	Hds	Sectors per Track	Write Pre-comp	Park Cyl
8051S	42.7	745	4	28	—	—
8212	10.7	615	2	17	128	656
8225	20.5	771	2	26	128	810
8225A	21.4	615	4	17	—	810
8225XT	21.4	805	2	26	—	820
8412	10.7	306	4	17	128	336
8425	21.4	615	4	17	128	664
8425F	21.4	615	4	17	128	664
8425S	21.4	615	4	17	—	664
8425XT	21.4	615	4	17	—	664
8438	32.7	615	4	26	128	664
8438F	32.7	615	4	26	128	664
8450	41.1	771	4	26	128	810
8450A	42.7	745	4	28	—	810
8450XT	42.9	805	4	26	—	820
9380E	329.0	1,224	15	35	—	—
9380S	336.8	1,218	15	36	—	—
9780E	676.1	1,661	15	53	—	—
Mitsubishi						
MR522	21.3	612	4	17	300	612
MR535	42.5	977	5	17	0	—
MR535RLL	65.0	977	5	26	0	—
MR5310E	85.0	976	5	34	—	—
NEC						
D3126	21.4	615	4	17	256	664
D3142	44.7	642	8	17	128	664
D3146H	42.8	615	8	17	256	664
D3661	111.4	914	7	34	—	—
D3741	45.0	423	8	26	—	423
D5126	21.4	615	4	17	128	664
D5126H	21.4	615	4	17	128	664
D5127H	32.7	615	4	26	128	664
D5128	21.4	615	4	17	128	664
D5146H	42.8	615	8	17	128	664
D5147H	65.5	615	8	26	128	664
D5452	71.6	823	10	17	512	—
D5652	143.1	822	10	34	—	—
D5655	149.0	1,223	7	34	—	—
D5662	319.3	1,223	15	34	—	—
D5682	664.3	1,632	15	53	—	—
Newbury						
NDR320	21.4	615	4	17	—	615
NDR340	42.8	615	8	17	—	615
NDR360	65.5	615	8	26	—	615
NDR1065	55.9	918	7	17	—	—
NDR1085	71.3	1,024	8	17	—	—
NDR1105	87.9	918	11	17	—	—
NDR1140	119.9	918	15	17	—	—
NDR2190	159.8	1,224	15	17	—	—
NDR4170	149.0	1,223	7	34	—	—
NDR4380	319.3	1,223	15	34	—	—

(continues)

Table A.28 Continued

Make/ Model	Capacity (MB)	Cyls	Hds	Sectors per Track	Write Pre-comp	Park Cyl
Pacific Magtron						
4115E	114.6	1,599	4	35	—	—
4140E	143.3	1,599	5	35	—	—
4170E	171.9	1,599	6	35	—	—
Plus Development						
40AT	42.0	965	5	17	—	—
80AT	84.0	965	10	17	—	—
120AT	120.0	814	9	32	—	—
170AT	168.5	968	10	34	—	—
210AT	209.2	873	13	36	—	—
52AT/LP	52.3	751	8	17	—	—
80AT/LP	85.8	616	16	17	—	—
105AT/LP	105.1	755	16	17	—	—
Priam						
502	46.0	755	7	17	—	—
504	46.0	755	7	17	—	—
514	117.2	1,224	11	17	—	—
519	159.8	1,224	15	17	—	—
617	143.8	751	11	34	—	—
623	196.1	751	15	34	—	—
638	319.3	1,223	15	34	—	—
V130	25.8	987	3	17	128	—
V150	43.0	987	5	17	128	—
V170	60.1	987	7	17	128	—
V185	71.0	1,166	7	17	128	—
PTI						
PT225	21.4	615	4	17	410	—
PT234	28.5	820	4	17	547	—
PT338	32.1	615	6	17	410	—
PT351	42.8	820	6	17	547	—
PT238R	32.7	615	4	26	410	—
PT251R	43.7	820	4	26	547	—
PT357R	49.1	615	6	26	410	—
PT376R	65.5	820	6	26	547	—
Quantum						
40AT	42.0	965	5	17	—	—
80AT	84.0	965	10	17	—	—
120AT	120.0	814	9	32	—	—
170AT	168.5	968	10	34	—	—
210AT	209.2	873	13	36	—	—
LPS52	52.3	751	8	17	—	—
LPS80	85.8	616	16	17	—	—
LPS105	105.1	755	16	17	—	—
Q520	17.8	512	4	17	256	512
Q530	26.7	512	6	17	256	512
Q540	35.7	512	8	17	256	512

Make/ Model	Capacity (MB)	Cyls	Hds	Sectors per Track	Write Pre-comp	Park Cyl
Rodime						
203	16.8	321	6	17	132	321
204	22.4	321	8	17	132	321
202E	22.3	640	4	17	0	640
203E	33.4	640	6	17	0	640
204E	44.6	640	8	17	0	640
3099A	80.2	373	15	28	—	—
3139A	112.5	523	15	28	—	—
3259A	212.9	990	15	28	—	—
3000A-NAT	43.2	625	5	27	0	—
3000A-XLAT	43.2	992	5	17	0	—
3060R	49.9	750	5	26	0	—
3075R	59.9	750	6	26	0	—
3085R	69.9	750	7	26	0	—
5040	32.0	1,224	3	17	0	—
5065	53.3	1,224	5	17	0	—
5090	74.6	1,224	7	17	0	—
Samsung						
SHD2020	21.8	820	2	26	—	—
SHD2021	23.5	820	2	28	—	—
SHD2030	28.5	820	4	17	—	—
SHD2040	43.7	820	4	26	—	—
SHD2041	47.0	820	4	28	—	—
Siemens						
MF-1200	169.2	1,215	8	34	—	—
MF-1300	253.8	1,215	12	34	—	—
MF-4410	321.9	1,099	11	52	—	—
Syquest						
SQ312RD	10.7	612	2	17	0	615
SQ315F	21.3	612	4	17	0	615
SQ338F	32.0	612	6	17	0	615
Tandon						
TN262	21.4	615	4	17	0	615
TN362	21.4	615	4	17	0	615
TN703	25.2	578	5	17	0	615
TN703AT	31.9	733	5	17	0	733
TN705	41.9	962	5	17	0	962
TN755	42.7	981	5	17	128	981
Toshiba						
MK-53F	36.1	830	5	17	—	—
MK-53FRLL	55.2	830	5	26	—	—
MK-54F	50.6	830	7	17	—	—
MK-54FRLL	77.3	830	7	26	—	—
MK-56F	72.2	830	10	17	—	—
MK-56FRLL	110.5	830	10	26	—	—

(continues)

Table A.28 Continued

Make/ Model	Capacity (MB)	Cyls	Hds	Sectors per Track	Write Pre-comp	Park Cyl
Toshiba						
MK-72PCMFM	72.2	830	10	17	—	—
MK-72PCRLL	110.5	830	10	26	512	—
MK-134FAMFM	44.7	733	7	17	—	—
MK-134FARLL	68.3	733	7	26	512	—
MK-153FA	72.2	829	5	34	—	—
MK-154FA	101.0	829	7	34	—	—
MK-156FA	144.3	829	10	34	—	—
MK-232FC	45.4	845	3	35	—	—
MK-234FC-I	106.0	845	7	35	—	—
MK-355FA	398.3	1,631	9	53	—	—
MK-358FA	663.9	1,631	15	53	—	—
MK-538FB	1229.0	1,980	15	80	—	—
Tulin						
TL226	22.3	640	4	17	—	640
TL240	33.4	640	6	17	—	640
Vertex						
V130	25.8	987	3	17	128	—
V150	43.0	987	5	17	128	—
V170	60.1	987	7	17	128	—
V185	71.0	1,166	7	17	128	—
Western Digital						
WD-93024A	21.6	782	2	27	—	—
WD-93028A	21.6	782	2	27	—	—
WD-93044A	43.2	782	4	27	—	—
WD-93048A	43.2	782	4	27	—	—
WD-95028A	21.6	782	2	27	—	—
WD-95044A	43.2	782	4	27	—	—
WD-95048A	43.2	782	4	27	—	—
WD-AC140	42.6	980	5	17	—	—
WD-AC280	85.3	980	10	17	—	—
WD-AP4200	212.2	987	12	35	—	—
WD-SP4200	209.7	1,280	8	40	—	—
WD-SC8320	326.5	949	14	48	—	—
WD-SC8400	413.2	1,201	14	48	—	—

— = No write precompensation required, or no parking cylinder required (autopark)

Table A.29 Seagate Hard Disk Drive Specifications

Seagate Model #	Imprimis Model #	Cyls	Hds	WPC	Park Cyl	Sectors per Track	Capacity (MB)	Total Sectors
ST1057a		1024	6	-1	1024	17*	53.5	104448
ST1090a	94354-90	1072	5	-1	1072	29	79.6	155440
Opt. CMOS Values:		335	16	335	335	29	79.6	155440

Seagate Model #	Imprimis Model #	Cyls	Hds	WPC	Park Cyl	Sectors per Track	Capacity (MB)	Total Sectors
ST1090n	94351-90	1068	5	-1	1068	29	79.3	154860
ST1096n		906	7	-1	906	26	84.4	164892
ST1100	94355-100	1072	9	-1	1072	17	84.0	164016
ST1102a		1024	10	-1	1024	17*	89.1	174080
ST1106r		977	7	-1	977	26	91.0	177814
ST1111a	94354-111	1072	5	-1	1072	36	98.8	192960
Opt. CMOS Values:		402	10	402	402	48	98.8	192960
ST1111e	94356-111	1072	5	-1	1072	36	98.8	192960
ST1111n	94351-111	1068	5	-1	1068	36	98.4	192240
ST11200n		1872	15	-1	1872	73*	1049.5	2049840
ST1126a	94354-126	1072	7	-1	1072	29	111.4	217616
Opt. CMOS Values:		469	16	469	469	29	111.4	217616
ST1126n	94351-125	1068	7	-1	1068	29	111.0	216804
ST1133a	94354-133	1272	5	-1	1272	36	117.2	228960
Opt. CMOS Values:		477	8	477	477	60	117.2	228960
ST1133n	94351-133s	1268	5	-1	1268	36	116.9	228240
ST1144a		1001	15	-1	1001	17*	130.7	255255
ST1150r	94355-150	1072	9	300	1072	26	128.4	250848
ST1156a	94354-156	1072	7	-1	1072	36	138.3	270144
Opt. CMOS Values:		536	9	536	536	56	138.3	270144
ST1156e	94356-156	1072	7	-1	1072	36	138.3	270144
ST1156n	94351-155	1068	7	-1	1068	36	137.8	269136
ST1156r	94355-156	1072	7	300	1072	36	138.3	270144
ST1162a	94354-162	1072	9	-1	1072	29	143.3	279792
Opt. CMOS Values:		603	16	603	603	29	143.3	279792
ST1162n	94351-160	1068	9	-1	1068	29	142.7	278748
ST1182e		972	9	-1	972	36	161.2	314928
ST1186a	94354-186	1272	7	-1	1272	36	164.1	320544
Opt. CMOS Values:		636	9	636	636	56	164.1	320544
ST1186n	94351-186	1268	7	-1	1268	36	163.6	319536
ST11950n		2706	15	-1	2706	99*	2057.4	4018410
ST1201a	94354-201	1072	9	-1	1072	36	177.8	347328
Opt. CMOS Values:		804	9	804	804	48	177.8	347328
ST1201e	94356-201	1072	9	-1	1072	36	177.8	347328
ST1201n	94351-200	1068	9	-1	1068	36	177.2	346032
ST1239a	94354-239	1272	9	-1	1272	36	211.0	412128
Opt. CMOS Values:		848	9	848	848	54	211.0	412128
ST1239n	94351-230	1268	9	-1	1268	36	210.3	410832
ST124		615	4	-1	670	17	21.4	41820
ST12400n		2626	19	-1	2626	82*	2094.7	4091308
ST125		615	4	-1	615	17	21.4	41820
ST125-1		615	4	-1	615	17	21.4	41820
ST12550N		2707	19	—	2707	81*	2133.0	4166073
ST12551N		2707	19	—	2707	81*	2133.0	4166073
ST12550ND		2707	19	—	2707	81*	2133.0	4166073
ST12551ND		2707	19	—	2707	81*	2133.0	4166073
ST125a		404	4	-1	404	26	21.5	42016
Opt. CMOS Values:		615	4	615	615	17	21.4	41820
ST125n		407	4	-1	408	26	21.7	42328
ST137r		615	6	-1	670	26	49.1	95940

(continues)

Table A.29 Continued

Seagate Model #	Imprimis Model #	Cyls	Hds	WPC	Park Cyl	Sectors per Track	Capacity (MB)	Total Sectors
ST138		615	6	-1	615	17	32.1	62730
ST138a		604	4	-1	604	26	32.2	62816
Opt. CMOS Values:		615	6	615	615	17	32.1	62730
ST138n		615	4	-1	615	26	32.7	63960
ST138r		615	4	-1	615	26	32.7	63960
ST1400a		1018	12	-1	1018	53*	331.5	647448
ST1400n		1476	7	-1	1476	62*	328.0	640584
ST1400ns		1476	7	-1	1476	62*	328.0	640584
ST1401a		726	15	-1	726	61*	340.1	664290
ST1401n		1100	9	-1	1100	66*	334.5	653400
ST1401ns		1100	9	-1	1100	66*	334.5	653400
ST1480a		1474	9	-1	1474	62*	421.1	822492
Opt. CMOS Values:		1015	15	1015	1015	54*	420.9	822150
ST1480n		1476	9	-1	1476	62*	421.7	823608
ST1480ns		1476	9	-1	1476	62*	421.7	823608
ST1481n		1476	9	-1	1476	62*	421.7	823608
ST151		977	5	-1	977	17	42.5	83045
ST157a		560	6	-1	560	26	44.7	87360
Opt. CMOS Values:		733	7	733	733	17	44.7	87227
ST157n		615	6	-1	615	26	49.1	95940
ST157r		615	6	-1	615	26	49.1	95940
ST1581n		1476	9	-1	1476	77*	523.7	1022868
ST177n		921	5	-1	921	26	61.3	119730
ST1980n		1730	13	-1	1730	74*	852.1	1664260
ST2106e	94216-106	1024	5	-1	1024	36	94.4	184320
ST2106n	94211-091	1024	5	-1	1024	36	94.4	184320
ST2106n	94211-106	1024	5	-1	1024	36	94.4	184320
ST2106nm	94211-106	1024	5	-1	1024	36	94.4	184320
ST212		306	4	128	319	17	10.7	20808
ST2125n	94221-125	1544	3	-1	1544	45*	106.7	208440
ST2125nm	94221-125	1544	3	-1	1544	45*	106.7	208440
ST2125nv	94221-125	1544	3	-1	1544	45*	106.7	208440
ST213		615	2	300	670	17	10.7	20910
ST2182e	94246-182	1453	4	-1	1453	54	160.7	313848
ST2209n	94221-209	1544	5	-1	1544	45*	177.9	347400
ST2209nm	94221-209m	1544	5	-1	1544	45*	177.9	347400
ST2209nv	94221-209	1544	5	-1	1544	45*	177.9	347400
ST224n		615	2	-1	615	17	10.7	20910
ST225		615	4	300	670	17	21.4	41820
ST225n		615	4	-1	615	17	21.4	41820
ST225r		667	2	-1	670	31	21.2	41354
ST2274a	94244-274	1747	5	-1	1747	54	241.5	471690
Opt. CMOS Values:		536	16	536	536	55	241.5	471680
ST238		615	4	-1	670	26	32.7	63960
ST2383a	94244-383	1747	7	-1	1747	54	338.1	660366
Opt. CMOS Values:		737	16	737	737	56	338.1	660352
ST2383e	94246-383	1747	7	-1	1747	54	338.1	660366
ST2383n	94241-383	1260	7	-1	1260	74*	334.2	652680
ST2383nm	94241-383	1260	7	-1	1260	74*	334.2	652680

Seagate Model #	Imprimis Model #	Cyls	Hds	WPC	Park Cyl	Sectors per Track	Capacity (MB)	Total Sectors
ST238r		615	4	-1	670	26	32.7	63960
ST2502n	94241-502	1756	7	-1	1755	69*	434.3	848148
ST2502nm	94241-502	1756	7	-1	1755	69*	434.3	848148
ST2502nv	94241-502	1756	7	-1	1755	69*	434.3	848148
ST250n		667	4	-1	670	31	42.3	82708
ST250r		667	4	-1	670	31	42.3	82708
ST251		820	6	-1	820	17	42.8	83640
ST251n-0		820	4	-1	820	26	43.7	85280
ST251n-1		630	4	-1	630	34	43.9	85680
ST252		820	6	-1	820	17	42.8	83640
ST253	94205-51	989	5	128	989	17	43.0	84065
ST274a	94204-74	948	5	-1	948	27	65.5	127980
ST277n-0		820	6	-1	820	26	65.5	127920
ST277n-1		628	6	-1	628	34	65.6	128112
ST277r		820	6	-1	820	26	65.5	127920
ST278r		820	6	-1	820	26	65.5	127920
ST279r	94205-77	989	5	-1	989	26	65.8	128570
ST280a	94204-71	1032	5	-1	1032	27	71.3	139320
Opt. CMOS Values:		1024	8	1024	1024	17	71.3	139264
ST280a	94204-81	1032	5	-1	1032	27	71.3	139320
Opt. CMOS Values:		1024	8	1024	1024	17	71.3	139264
ST296n		820	6	-1	820	34	85.6	167280
ST3051a		820	6	-1	820	17	42.8	83640
ST3096a		1024	10	-1	1024	17	89.1	174080
ST31200n		2626	9	-1	2626	79*	955.9	1867086
ST3120a		1024	12	-1	1024	17*	107.0	208896
ST3123a		1024	12	-1	1024	17*	107.0	208896
ST3144a		1001	15	-1	1001	17*	130.7	255255
ST3145a		1001	15	-1	1001	17*	130.7	255255
ST3195a		981	10	-1	981	34*	170.8	333540
ST3243a		1024	12	-1	1024	34*	213.9	417792
ST325a		615	4	-1	615	17	21.4	41820
ST325a/x		615	4	-1	615	17	21.4	41820
ST325n		654	2	-1	654	32	21.4	41856
ST325x		615	4	-1	615	17	21.4	41820
ST3283a		978	14	-1	978	35*	245.4	479220
ST3283n		1689	5	-1	1689	57*	246.5	481365
ST3290a		1001	15	-1	1001	34*	261.4	510510
ST3385a		767	14	-1	767	62*	340.9	665756
ST3390a		768	14	-1	768	62*	341.3	666624
ST3390n		2676	3	-1	2676	83*	341.2	666324
ST3500a		895	15	-1	895	62*	426.2	832350
ST351a		820	6	-1	820	17	42.8	83640
ST351a/x		820	6	-1	820	17	42.8	83640
ST351x		820	6	-1	820	17	42.8	83640
ST3550a		1018	14	-1	1018	62*	452.4	883624
ST3550n		2126	5	-1	2126	83*	451.7	882290
ST3600a		1872	7	-1	1872	79*	530.0	1035216
Opt. CMOS Values:		1024	16	1024	1024	63*	528.5	1032192
ST3600n		1872	7	-1	1872	79*	530.0	1035216

(continues)

Table A.29 Continued

Seagate Model #	Imprimis Model #	Cyls	Hds	WPC	Park Cyl	Sectors per Track	Capacity (MB)	Total Sectors
ST3610n		1872	7	-1	1872	52*	348.9	681408
ST3655a		1024	16	-1	1024	63*	528.5	1032192
ST3655n		2676	5	-1	2676	79*	541.2	1057020
ST4026		615	4	-1	670	17	21.4	41820
ST4038		733	5	-1	733	17	31.9	62305
ST4038m		733	5	-1	733	17	31.9	62305
ST4051		977	5	-1	977	17	42.5	83045
ST4053		1024	5	-1	1024	17	44.6	87040
ST406		306	2	128	319	17	5.3	10404
ST4085		1024	8	-1	1024	17	71.3	39264
ST4086	94155-86	925	9	-1	925	17	72.5	141525
ST4086p	94155-86p	925	9	128	925	17	72.5	141525
ST4096		1024	9	-1	1024	17	80.2	156672
ST4097	94155-96	1024	9	-1	1024	17	80.2	156672
ST4097p	94155-96p	1024	9	128	1024	17	80.2	156672
ST412		306	4	128	319	17	10.7	20808
ST41200n	94601-12g	1931	15	-1	1931	71*	1052.9	2056515
ST41200nm	94601-12g	1931	15	-1	1931	71*	1052.9	2056515
ST41200nv	94601-12g	1931	15	-1	1931	71*	1052.9	2056515
ST4135r	94155-135	960	9	-1	960	26	115.0	224640
ST4144r		1024	9	-1	1024	26	122.7	239616
ST41520n		2101	17	-1	2101	77*	1408.1	2750209
ST41600n		2098	17	-1	2098	74*	1351.3	2639284
ST41650n		2110	15	-1	2110	88*	1426.0	2785200
ST41651n		2107	15	-1	2107	87*	1407.8	2749635
ST4182e	94166-155	969	9	-1	969	36	160.7	313956
ST4182e	94166-182	969	9	-1	969	36	160.7	313956
ST4182n	94161-182	967	9	-1	967	36	160.4	313308
ST4182nm	94161-182	967	9	-1	967	36	160.4	313308
ST419		306	6	128	319	17	16.0	31212
ST42000n		2624	16	-1	2624	83*	1784.2	3484672
ST42100n		2573	15	-1	2573	96*	1897.0	3705120
ST42400n		2624	19	-1	2624	83*	2118.7	4138048
ST425		306	8	128	319	17	21.3	41616
ST43400n		2735	21	-1	2735	99*	2911.3	5686065
ST4350n	94171-300	1412	9	-1	1412	46*	299.3	584568
ST4350n	94171-307	1412	9	-1	1412	46*	299.3	584568
ST4350n	94171-327	1412	9	-1	1412	46*	299.3	584568
ST4350n	94171-350	1412	9	-1	1412	46*	299.3	584568
ST4350nm	94171-327	1412	9	-1	1412	46*	299.3	584568
ST4376n	94171-344	1549	9	-1	1549	45*	321.2	627345
ST4376n	94171-376	1549	9	-1	1549	45*	321.2	627345
ST4376nm	94171-344	1549	9	-1	1549	45*	321.2	627345
ST4376nv	94171-344	1549	9	-1	1549	45*	321.2	627345
ST4383e	94186-383	1412	13	-1	1412	36	338.3	660816
ST4384e	94186-383h	1224	15	-1	1224	36	338.4	660960
ST4385n	94181-385h	791	15	-1	791	55*	334.1	652575
ST4385nm	94181-385h	791	15	-1	791	55*	334.1	652575
ST4385nv	94181-385h	791	15	-1	791	55*	334.1	652575
ST4442e	94186-442	1412	15	-1	1412	36	390.4	762480

Seagate Model #	Imprimis Model #	Cyls	Hds	WPC	Park Cyl	Sectors per Track	Capacity (MB)	Total Sectors
ST4702n	94181-702	1546	15	-1	1546	50*	593.7	1159500
ST4702nm	94181-702	1546	15	-1	1546	50*	593.7	1159500
ST4766e	94196-766	1632	15	-1	1632	54	676.8	1321920
ST4766n	94191-766	1632	15	-1	1632	54	676.8	1321920
ST4766nm	94191-766	1632	15	-1	1632	54	676.8	1321920
ST4766nv	94191-766	1632	15	-1	1632	54	676.8	1321920
ST4767e		1399	15	-1	1399	63	676.9	1322055
ST4767n	94601-767h	1356	15	-1	1356	64*	666.5	1301760
ST4767nm	94601-767h	1356	15	-1	1356	64*	666.5	1301760
ST4767nv	94601-767h	1356	15	-1	1356	64*	666.5	1301760
ST4769e		1552	15	-1	1552	58	691.3	1350240
ST506		153	4	128	157	17	5.3	10404
ST9025a		1024	4	-1	1024	17	35.7	69632
ST9051a		1024	6	-1	1024	17	53.5	104448
ST9052a		980	5	-1	980	17*	42.6	83300
ST9077a		669	11	-1	669	17	64.1	125103
ST9080a		823	4	-1	823	38*	64.0	125096
ST9096a		980	10	-1	980	17*	85.3	166600
ST9100a		748	14	-1	748	16*	85.8	167552
ST9140a		980	15	-1	980	17*	127.9	249900
ST9144a		980	15	-1	980	17*	127.9	249900
ST9145a		980	15	-1	980	17*	127.9	249900
ST9190a		873	16	-1	873	24*	171.6	335232
ST9235a		985	13	-1	985	32*	209.8	409760
ST9235n		985	13	-1	985	32*	209.8	409760
ST----	9415-521	697	3	0	697	17	18.2	35547
ST----	9415-525	697	4	0	697	17	24.3	47396
ST----	9415-536	697	5	0	697	17	30.3	59245
ST----	9415-538	733	5	0	733	17	31.9	62305
ST----	94151-42	921	5	-1	921	17	40.1	78285
ST----	94151-62	921	7	-1	921	17	56.1	109599
ST----	94151-80	921	9	-1	921	17	72.1	140913
ST----	94155-48	925	5	-1	925	17	40.3	78625
ST----	94155-48p	925	5	128	925	17	40.3	78625
ST----	94155-57	925	6	-1	925	17	48.3	94350
ST----	94155-57p	925	6	128	925	17	48.3	94350
ST----	94155-67	925	7	-1	925	17	56.4	110075
ST----	94155-67p	925	7	128	925	17	56.4	110075
ST----	94155-92	989	9	-1	989	17	77.5	151317
ST----	94155-92p	989	9	128	989	17	77.5	151317
ST----	94155-130	024	9	128	1024	26	122.7	239616
ST----	94156-48	925	9	-1	925	17	72.5	141525
ST----	94156-67	925	7	-1	925	17	56.4	110075
ST----	94156-86	925	7	-1	925	17	56.4	110075
ST----	94161-86	969	5	-1	969	35	86.8	169575
ST----	94161-103	969	6	-1	969	35	104.2	203490
ST----	94161-121	969	7	-1	969	35	121.6	237405
ST----	94161-138	969	8	-1	969	35	138.9	271320
ST----	94166-86	969	5	-1	969	35	86.8	169575
ST----	94166-103	969	6	-1	969	35	104.2	203490
ST----	94166-121	969	7	-1	969	35	121.6	237405

(continues)

Table A.29 Continued

Seagate Model #	Imprimis Model #	Cyls	Hds	WPC	Park Cyl	Sectors per Track	Capacity (MB)	Total Sectors
ST----	94166-138	969	8	-1	969	35	138.9	271320
ST----	94244-219	1747	4	-1	1747	54	193.2	377352
Opt. CMOS Values:		536	16	536	536	44	193.2	377344

* *Because these drives use zoned recording, the sectors-per-track value is an average, rounded down to the next-lower integer.*

"Opt. CMOS Values" indicates optional translated values for the preceeding drive in the table that can be entered if the CMOS Setup program will not accept the actual values for the drive.

Seagate Model designations follow a specific format shown as follows:

ST-FXXXI PR-A

The various parts of each model number designation have meanings according to the following tables.

Table A.30 Hard Drive Model Number Code Legend

Code	Description
ST	Seagate Technologies
F	Form factor (see following table)
XXX	Unformatted capacity in MB
I	Interface type (see following table)
PR	Paired Solution (shipped with controller and installation software)
A	Access time; 0 = Standard, 1= Fast

Table A.31 F-Code Descriptions

F-Code	Description
1	3.5-inch, half-height (41mm)
2	5.25-inch, half-height (41mm)
3	3.5-inch, 1-inch high (25mm)
4	5.25-inch, full-height (82mm)
6	9-inch
8	8-inch
9	2.5-inch, .75-inch high (19mm)

Table A.32 I-Code Descriptions

I Code	Description
None	ST-412 MFM interface
R	ST-412 (RLL certified) interface
E	ESDI interface
A	ATA (AT Attachment) IDE interface
X	XT-Bus (8-bit) IDE interface
A/X	Switchable ATA IDE or XT-Bus interface
M or P	Modified Precompensation

I Code	Description
N	SCSI Single Ended (SE) interface
NM	SCSI SE interface (Macintosh Plus)
NV	SCSI SE interface (Novell NetWare)
NS	SCSI SE interface (Synchronized Spindle)
ND	SCSI Differential interface

For example, the model designation ST112550N equates to a 3.5-inch half-height drive with an unformatted capacity of approximately 2550MB, and a SCSI Single Ended interface.

AT Motherboard BIOS Hard Drive Tables

This section consists of motherboard ROM BIOS hard disk parameters for AT systems. The following explains the column headings used in Tables A.29–A.39:

Type = Drive type number

Cylinders = Total number of cylinders

Heads = Total number of heads

WPC = Write precompensation starting cylinder

65535 = No write precompensation

0 = Write precompensation on all cylinders

Ctrl = Control byte, with values according to the following table.

Bit Number	Hex	Meaning
Bit 0	01h	Not used (XT = drive step rate)
Bit 1	02h	Not used (XT = drive step rate)
Bit 2	04h	Not used (XT = drive step rate)
Bit 3	08h	More than eight heads
Bit 4	10h	Not used (XT = imbedded servo drive)
Bit 5	20h	OEM defect map at (cylinders + 1)
Bit 6	40h	Disable ECC retries
Bit 7	80h	Disable disk access retries

LZ = Landing-zone cylinder for head parking

S/T = Number of sectors per track

Meg = Drive capacity in megabytes

MB = Drive capacity in millions of bytes

Table A.33 shows the IBM motherboard ROM BIOS hard disk parameters for AT or PS/2 systems using ST-506/412 (standard or IDE) controllers.

Table A.33 IBM AT and PS/2 BIOS Hard Disk Table

Type	Cylinders	Heads	WPC	Ctrl	LZ	S/T	Meg	MB
1	306	4	128	00h	305	17	10.16	10.65
2	615	4	300	00h	615	17	20.42	21.41
3	615	6	300	00h	615	17	30.63	32.12
4	940	8	512	00h	940	17	62.42	65.45
5	940	6	512	00h	940	17	46.82	49.09
6	615	4	65535	00h	615	17	20.42	21.41
7	462	8	256	00h	511	17	30.68	32.17
8	733	5	65535	00h	733	17	30.42	31.90
9	900	15	65535	08h	901	17	112.06	117.50
10	820	3	65535	00h	820	17	20.42	21.41
11	855	5	65535	00h	855	17	35.49	37.21
12	855	7	65535	00h	855	17	49.68	52.09
13	306	8	128	00h	319	17	20.32	21.31
14	733	7	65535	00h	733	17	42.59	44.66
15	0	0	0	00h	0	0	0	0
16	612	4	0	00h	663	17	20.32	21.31
17	977	5	300	00h	977	17	40.55	42.52
18	977	7	65535	00h	977	17	56.77	59.53
19	1024	7	512	00h	1023	17	59.50	62.39
20	733	5	300	00h	732	17	30.42	31.90
21	733	7	300	00h	732	17	42.59	44.66
22	733	5	300	00h	733	17	30.42	31.90
23	306	4	0	00h	336	17	10.16	10.65
24	612	4	305	00h	663	17	20.32	21.31
25	306	4	65535	00h	340	17	10.16	10.65
26	612	4	65535	00h	670	17	20.32	21.31
27	698	7	300	20h	732	17	40.56	42.53
28	976	5	488	20h	977	17	40.51	42.48
29	306	4	0	00h	340	17	10.16	10.65
30	611	4	306	20h	663	17	20.29	21.27
31	732	7	300	20h	732	17	42.53	44.60
32	1023	5	65535	20h	1023	17	42.46	44.52
33	614	4	65535	20h	663	25	29.98	31.44
34	775	2	65535	20h	900	27	20.43	21.43
35	921	2	65535	20h	1000	33	29.68	31.12
36	402	4	65535	20h	460	26	20.41	21.41
37	580	6	65535	20h	640	26	44.18	46.33
38	845	2	65535	20h	1023	36	29.71	31.15
39	769	3	65535	20h	1023	36	40.55	42.52
40	531	4	65535	20h	532	39	40.45	42.41
41	577	2	65535	20h	1023	36	20.29	21.27
42	654	2	65535	20h	674	32	20.44	21.43
43	923	5	65535	20h	1023	36	81.12	85.06
44	531	8	65535	20h	532	39	80.89	84.82
45	0	0	0	00h	0	0	0.00	0.00
46	0	0	0	00h	0	0	0.00	0.00
47	0	0	0	00h	0	0	0.00	0.00

The landing zone and sectors per track fields are not used in the 10MB (original) controller and contain 00h values for each entry.

Table entry 15 is reserved to act as a pointer to indicate that the type is greater than 15. Most IBM systems do not have every entry in this table. The maximum usable type number varies for each particular ROM version. The maximum usable type for each IBM ROM is indicated in the table on IBM ROM versions, earlier in this appendix. If you have a compatible, this table may be inaccurate for many of the entries past type 15. Instead, you should see whether one of the other tables listed here applies to your specific compatible ROM. Most compatibles follow the IBM table for at least the first 15 entries.

Most IBM PS/2 systems now are supplied with hard disk drives that have the defect map written as data on the cylinder—one cylinder beyond the highest reported cylinder. This special data is read by the IBM PS/2 Advanced Diagnostics low-level format program. This process automates the entry of the defect list and eliminates the chance of human error, as long as you use only the IBM PS/2 Advanced Diagnostics for hard disk low-level formatting.

This type of table does not apply to IBM ESDI or SCSI hard disk controllers, host adapters, and drives. Because the ESDI and SCSI controllers or host adapters query the drive directly for the required parameters, no table-entry selection is necessary. Note, however, that the table for the ST-506/412 drives can still be found currently in the ROM BIOS of most of the PS/2 systems, even if the model came standard with an ESDI or SCSI disk subsystem.

Table A.34 shows the Compaq motherboard ROM BIOS hard disk parameters for the Compaq Deskpro 386.

Table A.34 Compaq Deskpro 386 Hard Disk Table

Type	Cylinders	Heads	WPC	Ctrl	LZ	S/T	Meg	MB
1	306	4	128	00h	305	17	10.16	10.65
2	615	4	128	00h	638	17	20.42	21.41
3	615	6	128	00h	615	17	30.63	32.12
4	1024	8	512	00h	1023	17	68.00	71.30
5	940	6	512	00h	939	17	46.82	49.09
6	697	5	128	00h	696	17	28.93	30.33
7	462	8	256	00h	511	17	30.68	32.17
8	925	5	128	00h	924	17	38.39	40.26
9	900	15	65535	08h	899	17	112.06	117.50
10	980	5	65535	00h	980	17	40.67	42.65
11	925	7	128	00h	924	17	53.75	56.36
12	925	9	128	08h	924	17	69.10	72.46
13	612	8	256	00h	611	17	40.64	42.61
14	980	4	128	00h	980	17	32.54	34.12
15	0	0	0	00h	0	0	0	0
16	612	4	0	00h	612	17	20.32	21.31
17	980	5	128	00h	980	17	40.67	42.65
18	966	6	128	00h	966	17	48.11	50.45
19	1023	8	65535	00h	1023	17	67.93	71.23
20	733	5	256	00h	732	17	30.42	31.90
21	733	7	256	00h	732	17	42.59	44.66
22	805	6	65535	00h	805	17	40.09	42.04
23	924	8	65535	00h	924	17	61.36	64.34
24	966	14	65535	08h	966	17	112.26	117.71
25	966	16	65535	08h	966	17	128.30	134.53
26	1023	14	65535	08h	1023	17	118.88	124.66

(continues)

Table A.34 Continued

Type	Cylinders	Heads	WPC	Ctrl	LZ	S/T	Meg	MB
27	966	10	65535	08h	966	17	80.19	84.08
28	748	16	65535	08h	748	17	99.34	104.17
29	805	6	65535	00h	805	26	61.32	64.30
30	615	4	128	00h	615	25	30.03	31.49
31	615	8	128	00h	615	25	60.06	62.98
32	905	9	128	08h	905	25	99.43	104.26
33	748	8	65535	00h	748	34	99.34	104.17
34	966	7	65535	00h	966	34	112.26	117.71
35	966	8	65535	00h	966	34	128.30	134.53
36	966	9	65535	08h	966	34	144.33	151.35
37	966	5	65535	00h	966	34	80.19	84.08
38	611	16	65535	08h	611	63	300.73	315.33
39	1023	11	65535	08h	1023	33	181.32	190.13
40	1023	15	65535	08h	1023	34	254.75	267.13
41	1023	15	65535	08h	1023	33	247.26	259.27
42	1023	16	65535	08h	1023	63	503.51	527.97
43	805	4	65535	00h	805	26	40.88	42.86
44	805	2	65535	00h	805	26	20.44	21.43
45	748	8	65535	00h	748	33	96.42	101.11
46	748	6	65535	00h	748	33	72.32	75.83
47	966	5	128	00h	966	25	58.96	61.82

Table entry 15 is reserved to act as a pointer to indicate that the type is greater than 15.

Table A.35 shows the Compaq motherboard ROM BIOS hard disk parameters for the Compaq Deskpro 286 Revision F.

Table A.35 Compaq Deskpro 286 Revision F Hard Disk Table

Type	Cylinders	Heads	WPC	Ctrl	LZ	S/T	Meg	MB
1	306	4	128	00h	305	17	10.16	10.65
2	615	4	128	00h	638	17	20.42	21.41
3	615	6	128	00h	615	17	30.63	32.12
4	1024	8	512	00h	1023	17	68.00	71.30
5	940	6	512	00h	939	17	46.82	49.09
6	697	5	128	00h	696	17	28.93	30.33
7	462	8	256	00h	511	17	30.68	32.17
8	925	5	128	00h	924	17	38.39	40.26
9	900	15	65535	08h	899	17	112.06	117.50
10	980	5	65535	00h	980	17	40.67	42.65
11	925	7	128	00h	924	17	53.75	56.36
12	925	9	128	08h	924	17	69.10	72.46
13	612	8	256	00h	611	17	40.64	42.61
14	980	4	128	00h	980	17	32.54	34.12
15	0	0	0	00h	0	0	0	0
16	612	4	0	00h	612	17	20.32	21.31
17	980	5	128	00h	980	17	40.67	42.65
18	966	6	128	00h	966	17	48.11	50.45
19	1023	8	65535	00h	1023	17	67.93	71.23
20	733	5	256	00h	732	17	30.42	31.90
21	733	7	256	00h	732	17	42.59	44.66

Type	Cylinders	Heads	WPC	Ctrl	LZ	S/T	Meg	MB
22	768	6	65535	00h	768	17	38.25	40.11
23	771	6	65535	00h	771	17	38.40	40.26
24	966	14	65535	08h	966	17	112.26	117.71
Type	Cylinders	Heads	WPC	Ctrl	LZ	S/T	Meg	MB
25	966	16	65535	08h	966	17	128.30	134.53
26	1023	14	65535	08h	1023	17	118.88	124.66
27	966	10	65535	08h	966	17	80.19	84.08
28	771	3	65535	00h	771	17	19.20	20.13
29	578	4	65535	00h	578	17	19.19	20.12
30	615	4	128	00h	615	25	30.03	31.49
31	615	8	128	00h	615	25	60.06	62.98
32	966	3	65535	00h	966	34	48.11	50.45
33	966	5	65535	00h	966	34	80.19	84.08
34	966	7	65535	00h	966	34	112.26	117.71
35	966	8	65535	00h	966	34	128.30	134.53
36	966	9	65535	08h	966	34	144.33	151.35
37	966	5	65535	00h	966	34	80.19	84.08
38	1023	9	65535	08h	1023	33	148.35	155.56
39	1023	11	65535	08h	1023	33	181.32	190.13
40	1023	13	65535	08h	1023	33	214.29	224.70
41	1023	15	65535	08h	1023	33	247.26	259.27
42	1023	16	65535	08h	1023	34	271.73	284.93
43	756	4	65535	00h	756	26	38.39	40.26
44	756	2	65535	00h	756	26	19.20	20.13
45	768	4	65535	00h	768	26	39.00	40.89
46	768	2	65535	00h	768	26	19.50	20.45
47	966	5	128	00h	966	25	58.96	61.82

Table entry 15 is reserved to act as a pointer to indicate that the type is greater than 15.

Table A.36 shows the Compaq motherboard ROM BIOS hard disk parameters for the Compaq Deskpro 286e Revision B (03/22/89).

Table A.36 Compaq Deskpro 286e Revision B Hard Disk Table

Type	Cylinders	Heads	WPC	Ctrl	LZ	S/T	Meg	MB
1	306	4	128	00h	305	17	10.16	10.65
2	615	4	128	00h	638	17	20.42	21.41
3	615	6	128	00h	615	17	30.63	32.12
4	1024	8	512	00h	1023	17	68.00	71.30
5	805	6	65535	00h	805	17	40.09	42.04
6	697	5	128	00h	696	17	28.93	30.33
7	462	8	256	00h	511	17	30.68	32.17
8	925	5	128	00h	924	17	38.39	40.26
9	900	15	65535	08h	899	17	112.06	117.50
10	980	5	65535	00h	980	17	40.67	42.65
11	925	7	128	00h	924	17	53.75	56.36
12	925	9	128	08h	924	17	69.10	72.46
13	612	8	256	00h	611	17	40.64	42.61
14	980	4	128	00h	980	17	32.54	34.12
15	0	0	0	00h	0	0	0	0

(continues)

Table A.36 Continued

Type	Cylinders	Heads	WPC	Ctrl	LZ	S/T	Meg	MB
16	612	4	0	00h	612	17	20.32	21.31
17	980	5	128	00h	980	17	40.67	42.65
18	966	5	128	00h	966	17	40.09	42.04
19	754	11	65535	08h	753	17	68.85	72.19
20	733	5	256	00h	732	17	30.42	31.90
21	733	7	256	00h	732	17	42.59	44.66
22	524	4	65535	00h	524	40	40.94	42.93
23	924	8	65535	00h	924	17	61.36	64.34
24	966	14	65535	08h	966	17	112.26	117.71
25	966	16	65535	08h	966	17	128.30	134.53
26	1023	14	65535	08h	1023	17	118.88	124.66
27	832	6	65535	00h	832	33	80.44	84.34
28	1222	15	65535	08h	1222	34	304.31	319.09
29	1240	7	65535	00h	1240	34	144.10	151.10
30	615	4	128	00h	615	25	30.03	31.49
31	615	8	128	00h	615	25	60.06	62.98
32	905	9	128	08h	905	25	99.43	104.26
33	832	8	65535	00h	832	33	107.25	112.46
34	966	7	65535	00h	966	34	112.26	117.71
35	966	8	65535	00h	966	34	128.30	134.53
36	966	9	65535	08h	966	34	144.33	151.35
37	966	5	65535	00h	966	34	80.19	84.08
38	611	16	65535	08h	611	63	300.73	315.33
39	1023	11	65535	08h	1023	33	181.32	190.13
40	1023	15	65535	08h	1023	34	254.75	267.13
41	1630	15	65535	08h	1630	52	620.80	650.96
42	1023	16	65535	08h	1023	63	503.51	527.97
43	805	4	65535	00h	805	26	40.88	42.86
44	805	2	65535	00h	805	26	20.44	21.43
45	748	8	65535	00h	748	33	96.42	101.11
46	748	6	65535	00h	748	33	72.32	75.83
47	966	5	128	00h	966	25	58.96	61.82

Table entry 15 is reserved to act as a pointer to indicate that the type is greater than 15.

Table A.37 shows the AMI ROM BIOS (286 BIOS version 04/30/89) hard disk parameters.

Table A.37 AMI ROM BIOS (286 BIOS Version 04/30/89) Hard Disk Table

Type	Cylinders	Heads	WPC	Ctrl	LZ	S/T	Meg	MB
1	306	4	128	00h	305	17	10.16	10.65
2	615	4	300	00h	615	17	20.42	21.41
3	615	6	300	00h	615	17	30.63	32.12
4	940	8	512	00h	940	17	62.42	65.45
5	940	6	512	00h	940	17	46.82	49.09
6	615	4	65535	00h	615	17	20.42	21.41
7	462	8	256	00h	511	17	30.68	32.17
8	733	5	65535	00h	733	17	30.42	31.90
9	900	15	65535	08h	901	17	112.06	117.50
10	820	3	65535	00h	820	17	20.42	21.41
11	855	5	65535	00h	855	17	35.49	37.21
12	855	7	65535	00h	855	17	49.68	52.09

Type	Cylinders	Heads	WPC	Ctrl	LZ	S/T	Meg	MB
13	306	8	128	00h	319	17	20.32	21.31
14	733	7	65535	00h	733	17	42.59	44.66
15	0	0	0	00h	0	0	0	0
16	612	4	0	00h	663	17	20.32	21.31
17	977	5	300	00h	977	17	40.55	42.52
18	977	7	65535	00h	977	17	56.77	59.53
19	1024	7	512	00h	1023	17	59.50	62.39
20	733	5	300	00h	732	17	30.42	31.90
21	733	7	300	00h	732	17	42.59	44.66
22	733	5	300	00h	733	17	30.42	31.90
23	306	4	0	00h	336	17	10.16	10.65
24	925	7	0	00h	925	17	53.75	56.36
25	925	9	65535	08h	925	17	69.10	72.46
26	754	7	526	00h	754	17	43.81	45.94
27	754	11	65535	08h	754	17	68.85	72.19
28	699	7	256	00h	699	17	40.62	42.59
29	823	10	65535	08h	823	17	68.32	71.63
30	918	7	874	00h	918	17	53.34	55.93
31	1024	11	65535	08h	1024	17	93.50	98.04
32	1024	15	65535	08h	1024	17	127.50	133.69
33	1024	5	1024	00h	1024	17	42.50	44.56
34	612	2	128	00h	612	17	10.16	10.65
35	1024	9	65535	08h	1024	17	76.50	80.22
36	1024	8	512	00h	1024	17	68.00	71.30
37	615	8	128	00h	615	17	40.84	42.82
38	987	3	805	00h	987	17	24.58	25.77
39	987	7	805	00h	987	17	57.35	60.14
40	820	6	820	00h	820	17	40.84	42.82
41	977	5	815	00h	977	17	40.55	42.52
42	981	5	811	00h	981	17	40.72	42.69
43	830	7	512	00h	830	17	48.23	50.57
44	830	10	65535	08h	830	17	68.90	72.24
45	917	15	65535	08h	918	17	114.18	119.72
47	0	0	0	00h	0	0	0.00	0.00

Table entry 15 is reserved to act as a pointer to indicate that the type is greater than 15.
This BIOS uses type 47 as a user-definable entry.

Table A.38 shows the Award ROM BIOS (286 BIOS version 04/30/89) (Modular 286, 386SX, and 386 BIOS version 3.05) hard disk parameters.

Table A.38 Award ROM BIOS Version 3.05 Hard Disk Table

Type	Cylinders	Heads	WPC	Ctrl	LZ	S/T	Meg	MB
1	306	4	128	00h	305	17	10.16	10.65
2	615	4	300	00h	615	17	20.42	21.41
3	615	6	300	00h	615	17	30.63	32.12
4	940	8	512	00h	940	17	62.42	65.45
5	940	6	512	00h	940	17	46.82	49.09
6	615	4	65535	00h	615	17	20.42	21.41
7	462	8	256	00h	511	17	30.68	32.17

(continues)

Table A.38 Continued

Type	Cylinders	Heads	WPC	Ctrl	LZ	S/T	Meg	MB
8	733	5	65535	00h	733	17	30.42	31.90
9	900	15	65535	08h	901	17	112.06	117.50
10	820	3	65535	00h	820	17	20.42	21.41
11	855	5	65535	00h	855	17	35.49	37.21
12	855	7	65535	00h	855	17	49.68	52.09
13	306	8	128	00h	319	17	20.32	21.31
14	733	7	65535	00h	733	17	42.59	44.66
15	0	0	0	00h	0	0	0	0
16	612	4	0	00h	663	17	20.32	21.31
17	977	5	300	00h	977	17	40.55	42.52
18	977	7	65535	00h	977	17	56.77	59.53
19	1024	7	512	00h	1023	17	59.50	62.39
20	733	5	300	00h	732	17	30.42	31.90
21	733	7	300	00h	732	17	42.59	44.66
22	733	5	300	00h	733	17	30.42	31.90
23	306	4	0	00h	336	17	10.16	10.65
24	977	5	65535	00h	976	17	40.55	42.52
25	1024	9	65535	08h	1023	17	76.50	80.22
26	1224	7	65535	00h	1223	17	71.12	74.58
27	1224	11	65535	08h	1223	17	111.76	117.19
28	1224	15	65535	08h	1223	17	152.40	159.81
29	1024	8	65535	00h	1023	17	68.00	71.30
30	1024	11	65535	08h	1023	17	93.50	98.04
31	918	11	65535	08h	1023	17	83.82	87.89
32	925	9	65535	08h	926	17	69.10	72.46
33	1024	10	65535	08h	1023	17	85.00	89.13
34	1024	12	65535	08h	1023	17	102.00	106.95
35	1024	13	65535	08h	1023	17	110.50	115.87
36	1024	14	65535	08h	1023	17	119.00	124.78
37	1024	2	65535	00h	1023	17	17.00	17.83
38	1024	16	65535	08h	1023	17	136.00	142.61
39	918	15	65535	08h	1023	17	114.30	119.85
40	820	6	65535	00h	820	17	40.84	42.82
41	1024	5	65535	00h	1023	17	42.50	44.56
42	1024	5	65535	00h	1023	26	65.00	68.16
43	809	6	65535	00h	808	17	40.29	42.25
44	820	6	65535	00h	819	26	62.46	65.50
45	776	8	65535	00h	775	33	100.03	104.89
46	0	0	0	00h	0	0	0.00	0.00
47	0	0	0	00h	0	0	0.00	0.00

Table entry 15 is reserved to act as a pointer to indicate that the type is greater than 15.
This BIOS uses types 46 and 47 as user-definable entries.

Table A.39 shows the Award ROM BIOS hard disk parameters (modular 286, 386SX, and 386 BIOS version 3.1).

Table A.39 Award ROM BIOS Version 3.1 Hard Disk Table

Type	Cylinders	Heads	WPC	Ctrl	LZ	S/T	Meg	MB
1	306	4	128	00h	305	17	10.16	10.65
2	615	4	300	00h	615	17	20.42	21.41
3	615	6	300	00h	615	17	30.63	32.12
4	940	8	512	00h	940	17	62.42	65.45
5	940	6	512	00h	940	17	46.82	49.09
6	615	4	65535	00h	615	17	20.42	21.41
7	462	8	256	00h	511	17	30.68	32.17
8	733	5	65535	00h	733	17	30.42	31.90
9	900	15	65535	08h	901	17	112.06	117.50
10	820	3	65535	00h	820	17	20.42	21.41
11	855	5	65535	00h	855	17	35.49	37.21
12	855	7	65535	00h	855	17	49.68	52.09
13	306	8	128	00h	319	17	20.32	21.31
14	733	7	65535	00h	733	17	42.59	44.66
15	0	0	0	00h	0	0	0	0
16	612	4	0	00h	663	17	20.32	21.31
17	977	5	300	00h	977	17	40.55	42.52
18	977	7	65535	00h	977	17	56.77	59.53
19	1024	7	512	00h	1023	17	59.50	62.39
20	733	5	300	00h	732	17	30.42	31.90
21	733	7	300	00h	732	17	42.59	44.66
22	733	5	300	00h	733	17	30.42	31.90
23	306	4	0	00h	336	17	10.16	10.65
24	977	5	65535	00h	976	17	40.55	42.52
25	1024	9	65535	08h	1023	17	76.50	80.22
26	1224	7	65535	00h	1223	17	71.12	74.58
27	1224	11	65535	08h	1223	17	111.76	117.19
28	1224	15	65535	08h	1223	17	152.40	159.81
29	1024	8	65535	00h	1023	17	68.00	71.30
30	1024	11	65535	08h	1023	17	93.50	98.04
31	918	11	65535	08h	1023	17	83.82	87.89
32	925	9	65535	08h	926	17	69.10	72.46
33	1024	10	65535	08h	1023	17	85.00	89.13
34	1024	12	65535	08h	1023	17	102.00	106.95
35	1024	13	65535	08h	1023	17	110.50	115.87
36	1024	14	65535	08h	1023	17	119.00	124.78
37	1024	2	65535	00h	1023	17	17.00	17.83
38	1024	16	65535	08h	1023	17	136.00	142.61
39	918	15	65535	08h	1023	17	114.30	119.85
40	820	6	65535	00h	820	17	40.84	42.82
41	1024	5	65535	00h	1023	17	42.50	44.56
42	1024	5	65535	00h	1023	26	65.00	68.16
43	809	6	65535	00h	852	17	40.29	42.25
44	809	6	65535	00h	852	26	61.62	64.62
45	776	8	65535	00h	775	33	100.03	104.89
46	684	16	65535	08h	685	38	203.06	212.93
47	615	6	65535	00h	615	17	30.63	32.12

Table entry 15 is reserved to act as a pointer to indicate that the type is greater than 15.
This BIOS uses types 48 and 49 as user-definable entries.

Table A.40 shows the Phoenix 286 ROM BIOS (80286 ROM BIOS version 3.01, dated 11/01/86) hard disk parameters.

Table A.40 Phoenix 286 (80286 ROM BIOS Version 3.01) Hard Disk Table

Type	Cylinders	Heads	WPC	Ctrl	LZ	S/T	Meg	MB
1	306	4	128	00h	305	17	10.16	10.65
2	615	4	300	00h	638	17	20.42	21.41
3	615	6	300	00h	615	17	30.63	32.12
4	940	8	512	00h	940	17	62.42	65.45
5	940	6	512	00h	940	17	46.82	49.09
6	615	4	65535	00h	615	17	20.42	21.41
7	462	8	256	00h	511	17	30.68	32.17
8	733	5	65535	00h	733	17	30.42	31.90
9	900	15	65535	08h	901	17	112.06	117.50
10	820	3	65535	00h	820	17	20.42	21.41
11	855	5	65535	00h	855	17	35.49	37.21
12	855	7	65535	00h	855	17	49.68	52.09
13	306	8	128	00h	319	17	20.32	21.31
14	733	7	65535	00h	733	17	42.59	44.66
15	0	0	0	00h	0	0	0.00	0.00
16	612	4	0	00h	633	17	20.32	21.31
17	977	5	300	00h	977	17	40.55	42.52
18	977	7	65535	00h	977	17	56.77	59.53
19	1024	7	512	00h	1023	17	59.50	62.39
20	733	5	300	00h	732	17	30.42	31.90
21	733	7	300	00h	733	17	42.59	44.66
22	733	5	300	00h	733	17	30.42	31.90
23	0	0	0	00h	0	0	0.00	0.00
24	0	0	0	00h	0	0	0.00	0.00
25	0	0	0	00h	0	0	0.00	0.00
26	0	0	0	00h	0	0	0.00	0.00
27	0	0	0	00h	0	0	0.00	0.00
28	0	0	0	00h	0	0	0.00	0.00
29	0	0	0	00h	0	0	0.00	0.00
30	0	0	0	00h	0	0	0.00	0.00
31	0	0	0	00h	0	0	0.00	0.00
32	0	0	0	00h	0	0	0.00	0.00
33	0	0	0	00h	0	0	0.00	0.00
34	0	0	0	00h	0	0	0.00	0.00
35	0	0	0	00h	0	0	0.00	0.00
36	1024	5	512	00h	1024	17	42.50	44.56
37	830	10	65535	08h	830	17	68.90	72.24
38	823	10	256	08h	824	17	68.32	71.63
39	615	4	128	00h	664	17	20.42	21.41
40	615	8	128	00h	664	17	40.84	42.82
41	917	15	65535	08h	918	17	114.18	119.72
42	1023	15	65535	08h	1024	17	127.38	133.56
43	823	10	512	08h	823	17	68.32	71.63
44	820	6	65535	00h	820	17	40.84	42.82
45	1024	8	65535	00h	1024	17	68.00	71.30
46	925	9	65535	08h	925	17	69.10	72.46
47	1024	5	65535	00h	1024	17	42.50	44.56

Table entry 15 is reserved to act as a pointer to indicate that the type is greater than 15.

Table A.41 shows the Phoenix 286 ROM BIOS (286 BIOS Plus version 3.10) hard disk parameters.

Table A.41 Phoenix 286 ROM BIOS (286 BIOS Plus Version 3.10) Hard Disk Table

Type	Cylinders	Heads	WPC	Ctrl	LZ	S/T	Meg	MB
1	306	4	128	00h	305	17	10.16	10.65
2	615	4	300	00h	615	17	20.42	21.41
3	615	6	300	00h	615	17	30.63	32.12
4	940	8	512	00h	940	17	62.42	65.45
5	940	6	512	00h	940	17	46.82	49.09
6	615	4	65535	00h	615	17	20.42	21.41
7	462	8	256	00h	511	17	30.68	32.17
8	733	5	65535	00h	733	17	30.42	31.90
9	900	15	65535	08h	901	17	112.06	117.50
10	820	3	65535	00h	820	17	20.42	21.41
11	855	5	65535	00h	855	17	35.49	37.21
12	855	7	65535	00h	855	17	49.68	52.09
13	306	8	128	00h	319	17	20.32	21.31
14	733	7	65535	00h	733	17	42.59	44.66
15	0	0	0	00h	0	0	0	0
16	612	4	0	00h	663	17	20.32	21.31
17	977	5	300	00h	977	17	40.55	42.52
18	977	7	65535	00h	977	17	56.77	59.53
19	1024	7	512	00h	1023	17	59.50	62.39
20	733	5	300	00h	732	17	30.42	31.90
21	733	7	300	00h	732	17	42.59	44.66
22	733	5	300	00h	733	17	30.42	31.90
23	306	4	0	00h	336	17	10.16	10.65
24	0	0	0	00h	0	0	0.00	0.00
25	615	4	0	00h	615	17	20.42	21.41
26	1024	4	65535	00h	1023	17	34.00	35.65
27	1024	5	65535	00h	1023	17	42.50	44.56
28	1024	8	65535	00h	1023	17	68.00	71.30
29	512	8	256	00h	512	17	34.00	35.65
30	615	2	615	00h	615	17	10.21	10.71
31	989	5	0	00h	989	17	41.05	43.04
32	1020	15	65535	08h	1024	17	127.00	133.17
33	0	0	0	00h	0	0	0.00	0.00
34	0	0	0	00h	0	0	0.00	0.00
35	1024	9	1024	08h	1024	17	76.50	80.22
36	1024	5	512	00h	1024	17	42.50	44.56
37	830	10	65535	08h	830	17	68.90	72.24
38	823	10	256	08h	824	17	68.32	71.63
39	615	4	128	00h	664	17	20.42	21.41
40	615	8	128	00h	664	17	40.84	42.82
41	917	15	65535	08h	918	17	114.18	119.72
42	1023	15	65535	08h	1024	17	127.38	133.56
43	823	10	512	08h	823	17	68.32	71.63
44	820	6	65535	00h	820	17	40.84	42.82
45	1024	8	65535	00h	1024	17	68.00	71.30
46	925	9	65535	08h	925	17	69.10	72.46
47	699	7	256	00h	700	17	40.62	42.59

Table entry 15 is reserved to act as a pointer to indicate that the type is greater than 15. This BIOS uses types 48 and 49 as user-definable entries.

Table A.42 shows the Pheonix 386 ROM BIOS (A386 BIOS 1.01 Reference ID 08, dated 04/19/90) hard disk parameters.

Table A.42 Phoenix 386 ROM BIOS (A386 BIOS 1.01) Hard Disk Table

Type	Cylinders	Heads	WPC	Ctrl	LZ	S/T	Meg	MB
1	306	4	128	00h	305	17	10.16	10.65
2	615	4	300	00h	615	17	20.42	21.41
3	615	6	300	00h	615	17	30.63	32.12
4	940	8	512	00h	940	17	62.42	65.45
5	940	6	512	00h	940	17	46.82	49.09
6	615	4	65535	00h	615	17	20.42	21.41
7	462	8	256	00h	511	17	30.68	32.17
8	733	5	65535	00h	733	17	30.42	31.90
9	900	15	65535	08h	901	17	112.06	117.50
10	820	3	65535	00h	820	17	20.42	21.41
11	855	5	65535	00h	855	17	35.49	37.21
12	855	7	65535	00h	855	17	49.68	52.09
13	306	8	128	00h	319	17	20.32	21.31
14	733	7	65535	00h	733	17	42.59	44.66
15	0	0	0	00h	0	0	0	0
16	987	12	65535	08h	988	35	202.41	212.24
17	977	5	300	00h	977	17	40.55	42.52
18	977	7	65535	00h	977	17	56.77	59.53
19	1024	7	512	00h	1023	17	59.50	62.39
20	733	5	300	00h	732	17	30.42	31.90
21	733	7	300	00h	732	17	42.59	44.66
22	1024	16	0	08h	0	17	136.00	142.61
23	914	14	0	08h	0	17	106.22	111.38
24	1001	15	0	08h	0	17	124.64	130.69
25	977	7	815	00h	977	26	86.82	91.04
26	1024	4	65535	00h	1023	17	34.00	35.65
27	1024	5	65535	00h	1023	17	42.50	44.56
28	1024	8	65535	00h	1023	17	68.00	71.30
29	980	10	812	08h	990	17	81.35	85.30
30	1024	10	0	08h	0	17	85.00	89.13
31	832	6	832	00h	832	33	80.44	84.34
32	1020	15	65535	08h	1024	17	127.00	133.17
33	776	8	0	00h	0	33	100.03	104.89
34	782	4	0	00h	862	27	41.24	43.24
35	1024	9	1024	08h	1024	17	76.50	80.22
36	1024	5	512	00h	1024	17	42.50	44.56
37	830	10	65535	08h	830	17	68.90	72.24
38	823	10	256	08h	824	17	68.32	71.63
39	980	14	65535	08h	990	30	200.98	210.74
40	615	8	128	00h	664	17	40.84	42.82
41	917	15	65535	08h	918	17	114.18	119.72
42	1023	15	65535	08h	1024	17	127.38	133.56
43	823	10	512	08h	823	17	68.32	71.63
44	820	6	65535	00h	820	17	40.84	42.82
45	1024	8	65535	00h	1024	17	68.00	71.30
46	0	0	0	00h	0	0	0.00	0.00
47	0	0	0	00h	0	0	0.00	0.00

Table entry 15 is reserved to act as a pointer to indicate that the type is greater than 15. This BIOS uses types 46 and 47 as user-definable entries.

Table A.43 shows the Zenith motherboard BIOS (80286 Technical Reference 1988) hard disk parameters.

Table A.43 Zenith BIOS Hard Disk Table

Type	Cylinders	Heads	WPC	Ctrl	LZ	S/T	Meg	MB
1	306	4	128	00h	305	17	10.16	10.65
2	615	4	300	00h	615	17	20.42	21.41
3	699	5	256	00h	710	17	29.01	30.42
4	940	8	512	00h	940	17	62.42	65.45
5	940	6	512	00h	940	17	46.82	49.09
6	615	4	65535	00h	615	17	20.42	21.41
7	699	7	256	00h	710	17	40.62	42.59
8	733	5	65535	00h	733	17	30.42	31.90
9	900	15	65535	08h	901	17	112.06	117.50
10	925	5	0	00h	926	17	38.39	40.26
11	855	5	65535	00h	855	17	35.49	37.21
12	855	7	65535	00h	855	17	49.68	52.09
13	306	8	128	00h	319	17	20.32	21.31
14	733	7	65535	00h	733	17	42.59	44.66
15	0	0	0	00h	0	0	0	0
16	612	4	0	00h	663	17	20.32	21.31
17	977	5	300	00h	977	17	40.55	42.52
18	977	7	65535	00h	977	17	56.77	59.53
19	1024	7	512	00h	1023	17	59.50	62.39
20	733	5	300	00h	732	17	30.42	31.90
21	733	7	300	00h	732	17	42.59	44.66
22	733	5	300	00h	733	17	30.42	31.90
23	306	4	0	00h	336	17	10.16	10.65
24	612	2	65535	00h	611	17	10.16	10.65
25	615	6	300	00h	615	17	30.63	32.12
26	462	8	256	00h	511	17	30.68	32.17
27	820	3	65535	00h	820	17	20.42	21.41
28	981	7	65535	00h	986	17	57.00	59.77
29	754	11	65535	08h	754	17	68.85	72.19
30	918	15	65535	08h	918	17	114.30	119.85
31	987	5	65535	00h	987	17	40.96	42.95
32	830	6	400	00h	830	17	41.34	43.35
33	697	4	0	00h	696	17	23.14	24.27
34	615	4	65535	00h	615	17	20.42	21.41
35	615	4	128	00h	663	17	20.42	21.41
36	1024	9	65535	08h	1024	17	76.50	80.22
37	1024	5	512	00h	1024	17	42.50	44.56
38	820	6	65535	00h	910	17	40.84	42.82
39	615	4	306	00h	684	17	20.42	21.41
40	925	9	0	08h	924	17	69.10	72.46
41	1024	8	512	00h	1023	17	68.00	71.30
42	1024	5	1024	00h	1023	17	42.50	44.56
43	615	8	300	00h	615	17	40.84	42.82
44	989	5	0	00h	988	17	41.05	43.04
45	0	0	0	00h	0	0	0.00	0.00
46	0	0	0	00h	0	0	0.00	0.00
47	0	0	0	00h	0	0	0.00	0.00

Table entry 15 is reserved to act as a pointer to indicate that the type is greater than 15.

Troubleshooting Error Codes

The following sections list a variety of system error codes. Included are manufacturer test POST codes, display POST error codes, and advanced diagnostics error codes. This section includes also a detailed list of SCSI interface error codes, which can be very helpful in troubleshooting SCSI devices.

ROM BIOS Port 80h Power-On Self Test (POST) Codes

When the ROM BIOS is performing the Power-On Self Test, in most systems the results of these tests are sent to I/O Port 80h so they can be monitored by a special diagnostics card. These tests sometimes are called manufacturing tests because they were designed into the system for testing systems on the assembly line without a video display attached. The POST-code cards have a two-digit hexadecimal display used to report the number of the currently executing test routine. Before executing each test, a hexadecimal numeric code is sent to the port, and then the test is run. If the test fails and locks up the machine, the hexadecimal code of the last test being executed remains on the card's display.

Many tests are executed in a system before the video display card is enabled, especially if the display is EGA or VGA. Therefore, many errors can occur that would lock up the system before the system could possibly display an error code through the video system. To most normal troubleshooting procedures, a system with this type of problem (such as a memory failure in Bank 0) would appear completely "dead." By using one of the commercially available POST-code cards, however, you can correctly diagnose the problem.

These codes are completely BIOS dependent because the card does nothing but display the codes sent to it. Some BIOSes have better Power-On Self Test procedures and therefore send more informative codes. Some BIOS versions also send audio codes that can be used to help diagnose such problems. The Phoenix BIOS, for example, sends the most informative set of audio codes, which eliminates the need for a Port 80h POST card. Tables A.50, A.51, and A.52 list the Port 80h codes and audio codes sent by a number of different BIOS manufacturers and versions.

AMI BIOS Audio and Port 80h Error Codes.

Table A.44 AMI BIOS Audio POST Codes

Beep Code	Fatal Errors
1 short	DRAM refresh failure
2 short	Parity circuit failure
3 short	Base 64K RAM failure
4 short	System timer failure
5 short	Processor failure
6 short	Keyboard controller Gate A20 error
7 short	Virtual mode exception error
8 short	Display memory Read/Write test failure
9 short	ROM BIOS checksum failure
10 short	CMOS Shutdown Read/Write error
11 short	Cache Memory error
Beep Code	**Nonfatal Errors**
1 long, 3 short	Conventional/extended memory failure
1 long, 8 short	Display/retrace test failed

Table A.45 AMI 286 BIOS Plus Port 80h POST Codes

Checkpoint	Meaning
01h	NMI disabled and 286 register test about to start
02h	286 register test over
03h	ROM checksum OK
04h	8259 initialization OK
05h	CMOS pending interrupt disabled
06h	Video disabled and system timer counting OK
07h	CH-2 of 8253 test OK
08h	CH-2 of delta count test OK
09h	CH-1 delta count test OK
0Ah	CH-0 delta count test OK
0Bh	Parity status cleared
0Ch	Refresh and system timer OK
0Dh	Refresh link toggling OK
0Eh	Refresh period On/Off 50% OK
10h	Confirmed refresh On and about to start 64K memory
11h	Address line test OK
12h	64K base memory test OK
13h	Interrupt vectors initialized
14h	8042 keyboard controller test OK
15h	CMOS read/write test OK
16h	CMOS checksum/battery check OK
17h	Monochrome mode set OK
18h	Color mode set OK
19h	About to look for optional video ROM
1Ah	Optional video ROM control OK
1Bh	Display memory R/W test OK
1Ch	Display memory R/W test for alternate display OK
1Dh	Video retrace check OK
1Eh	Global equipment byte set for video OK
1Fh	Mode set call for Mono/Color OK
20h	Video test OK
21h	Video display OK
22h	Power-on message display OK
30h	Virtual mode memory test about to begin
31h	Virtual mode memory test started
32h	Processor in virtual mode
33h	Memory address line test in progress
34h	Memory address line test in progress
35h	Memory below IMB calculated
36h	Memory size computation OK
37h	Memory test in progress
38h	Memory initialization over below IMB
39h	Memory initialization over above IMB
3Ah	Display memory size
3Bh	About to start below 1M memory test
3Ch	Memory test below 1M OK
3Dh	Memory test above 1M OK
3Eh	About to go to real mode (shutdown)
3Fh	Shutdown successful and entered in real mode
40h	About to disable gate A-20 address line
41h	Gate A-20 line disabled successfully
42h	About to start DMA controller test

(continues)

Table A.45 Continued

Checkpoint	Meaning
4Eh	Address line test OK
4Fh	Processor in real mode after shutdown
50h	DMA page register test OK
51h	DMA unit-1 base register test about to start
52h	DMA unit-1 channel OK, about to begin CH-2
53h	DMA CH-2 base register test OK
54h	About to test f/f latch for unit-1
55h	f/f latch test both unit OK
56h	DMA unit 1 and 2 programmed OK
57h	8259 initialization over
58h	8259 mask register check OK
59h	Master 8259 mask register OK, about to start slave
5Ah	About to check timer and keyboard interrupt level
5Bh	Timer interrupt OK
5Ch	About to test keyboard interrupt
5Dh	ERROR! timer/keyboard interrupt not in proper level
5Eh	8259 interrupt controller error
5Fh	8259 interrupt controller test OK
70h	Start of keyboard test
71h	Keyboard BAT test OK
72h	Keyboard test OK
73h	Keyboard global data initialization OK
74h	Floppy setup about to start
75h	Floppy setup OK
76h	Hard disk setup about to start
77h	Hard disk setup OK
79h	About to initialize timer data area
7Ah	Verify CMOS battery power
7Bh	CMOS battery verification done
7Dh	About to analyze diagnostics test result for memory
7Eh	CMOS memory size update OK
7Fh	About to check optional ROM C000:0.
80h	Keyboard sensed to enable SETUP
81h	Optional ROM control OK
82h	Printer global data initialization OK
83h	RS-232 global data initialization OK
84h	80287 check/test OK
85h	About to display soft error message
86h	About to give control to system ROM E000.0
87h	System ROM E000.0 check over
00h	Control given to Int 19, boot loader

Table A.46 AMI Color BIOS Port 80h POST Codes

Port 80h Code	Test Description
01h	Processor register test about to start, and NMI to be disabled
02h	NMI is disabled; power-on delay starting
03h	Power-on delay complete; any initialization before keyboard BAT is in progress
04h	Any initialization before keyboard BAT is complete; reading keyboard SYS bit to check soft reset/power-on

Port 80h Code	Test Description
05h	Soft reset/power-on determined; going to enable ROM (that is, disable shadow RAM/cache if any)
06h	ROM enabled; calculating ROM BIOS checksum and waiting for KB controller input buffer to be free
07h	ROM BIOS checksum passed, KB controller I/B free; going to issue BAT command to keyboard controller
08h	BAT command to keyboard controller issued; going to verify BAT command
09h	Keyboard controller BAT result verified; keyboard command byte to be written next
0Ah	Keyboard-command byte code issued; going to write command byte data
0Bh	Keyboard controller command byte written; going to issue Pin-23,24 blocking/ unblocking command
0Ch	Pin-23,24 of keyboard controller blocked/unblocked; NOP command of keyboard controller to be issued next
0Dh	NOP command processing done; CMOS shutdown register test to be done next
0Eh	CMOS shutdown register R/W test passed; going to calculate CMOS checksum and update DIAG byte
0Fh	CMOS checksum calculation done and DIAG byte written; CMOS initialization to begin (If INIT CMOS IN EVERY BOOT is set.)
10h	CMOS initialization done (if any); CMOS status register about to initialize for date and time
11h	CMOS status register initialized; going to disable DMA and interrupt controllers
12h	DMA controller #1,#2, interrupt controller #1,#2 disabled; about to disable video display and init port-B
13h	Video display is disabled and port-B initialized; chipset init/auto memory detection to begin
14h	Chipset initialization/auto memory detection over; 8254 timer test about to start
15h	CH-2 timer test halfway; 8254 CH-2 timer test to be complete
16h	Ch-2 timer test over; 8254 CH-1 timer test to be complete
17h	CH-1 timer test over; 8254 CH-0 timer test to be complete
18h	CH-0 timer test over; about to start memory refresh
19h	Memory refresh started; memory refresh test to be done next
1Ah	Memory refresh line is toggling; going to check 15 micro-second On/Off time
1Bh	Memory refresh period 30 micro-second test complete; base 64K memory test about to start
20h	Base 64K memory test started; address line test to be done next
21h	Address line test passed; going to do toggle parity
22h	Toggle parity over; going for sequential data R/W test
23h	Base 64K sequential data R/W test passed; any setup before interrupt vector initialization about to start
24h	Setup required before vector initialization complete; interrupt vector initialization about to begin
25h	Interrupt vector initialization done; going to read I/O port of 8042 for turbo switch (if any)
26h	I/O port of 8042 is read; going to initialize global data for turbo switch
27h	Global data initialization is over; any initialization after interrupt vector to be done next
28h	Initialization after interrupt vector is complete; going for monochrome mode setting
29h	Monochrome mode setting is done; going for color mode setting
2Ah	Color mode setting is done; about to go for toggle parity before optional ROM test
2Bh	Toggle parity over; about to give control for any setup required before optional video ROM check
2Ch	Processing before video ROM control is done; about to look for optional video ROM and give control
2Dh	Optional video ROM control is done; about to give control to do any processing after video ROM returns control

(continues)

Table A.46 Continued

Port 80h Code	Test Description
2Eh	Return from processing after the video ROM control; if EGA/VGA not found, then do display memory R/W test
2Fh	EGA/VGA not found; display memory R/W test about to begin
30h	Display memory R/W test passed; about to look for the retrace checking
31h	Display memory R/W test or retrace checking failed; about to do alternate display memory R/W test
32h	Alternate display memory R/W test passed; about to look for the alternate display retrace checking
33h	Video display checking over; verification of display type with switch setting and actual card to begin
34h	Verification of display adapter done; display mode to be set next
35h	Display mode set complete; BIOS ROM data area about to be checked
36h	BIOS ROM data area check over; going to set cursor for power-on message
37h	Cursor setting for power-on message ID complete; going to display the power-on message
38h	Power-on message display complete; going to read new cursor position
39h	New cursor position read and saved; going to display the reference string
3Ah	Reference string display is over; going to display the Hit <Esc> message
3Bh	Hit <Esc> message displayed; virtual mode memory test about to start
40h	Preparation for virtual mode test started; going to verify from video memory
41h	Returned after verifying from display memory; going to prepare the descriptor tables
42h	Descriptor tables prepared; going to enter virtual mode for memory test
43h	Entered in virtual mode; going to enable interrupts for diagnostics mode
44h	Interrupts enabled (if diagnostics switch is on); going to initialize data to check memory wrap-around at 0:0
45h	Data initialized; going to check for memory wrap-around at 0:0 and find total system memory size
46h	Memory wrap-around test done; memory-size calculation over; about to go for writing patterns to test memory
47h	Pattern to be test-written in extended memory; going to write patterns in base 640K memory
48h	Patterns written in base memory; going to determine amount of memory below 1M memory
49h	Amount of memory below 1M found and verified; going to determine amount of memory above 1M memory
4Ah	Amount of memory above 1M found and verified; going for BIOS ROM data area check
4Bh	BIOS ROM data area check over; going to check <Esc> and clear memory below 1M for soft reset
4Ch	Memory below 1M cleared (Soft Reset); going to clear memory above 1M
4Dh	Memory above 1M cleared (Soft Reset); going to save the memory size
4Eh	Memory test started (No Soft Reset); about to display the first 64K memory test
4Fh	Memory size display started; will be updated during memory test; going for sequential and random memory test
50h	Memory test below 1M complete; going to adjust memory size for relocation and shadow
51h	Memory size adjusted due to relocation/shadow; memory test above 1M to follow
52h	Memory test above 1M complete; going to prepare to go back to real mode
53h	CPU registers are saved including memory size; going to enter in real mode
54h	Shutdown successful, CPU in real mode; going to restore registers saved during preparation for shutdown
55h	Registers restored; going to disable Gate A20 address line
56h	A20 address line disable successful; BIOS ROM data area about to be checked
57h	BIOS ROM data area check halfway; BIOS ROM data area check to be complete

Port 80h Code	Test Description
58h	BIOS ROM data area check over; going to clear Hit <ESC> message
59h	Hit <ESC> message cleared; <WAIT...> message displayed; about to start DMA and interrupt controller test
60h	DMA page-register test passed; about to verify from display memory
61h	Display memory verification over; about to go for DMA #1 base register test
62h	DMA #1 base register test passed; about to go for DMA #2 base register test
63h	DMA #2 base register test passed; about to go for BIOS ROM data area check
64h	BIOS ROM data area check halfway; BIOS ROM data area check to be complete
65h	BIOS ROM data area check over; about to program DMA unit 1 and 2
66h	DMA unit 1 and 2 programming over; about to initialize 8259 interrupt controller
67h	8259 initialization over; about to start keyboard test
80h	Keyboard test started, clearing output buffer, checking for stuck key; about to issue keyboard reset command
81h	Keyboard reset error/stuck key found; about to issue keyboard controller interface test command
82h	Keyboard controller interface test over; about to write command byte and initialize circular buffer
83h	Command byte written, global data initialization done; about to check for lock-key
84h	Lock-key checking over; about to check for memory-size mismatch with CMOS
85h	Memory size check done; about to display soft error and check for password or bypass setup
86h	Password checked; about to do programming before setup
87h	Programming before setup complete; going to CMOS setup program
88h	Returned from CMOS setup program and screen is cleared; about to do programming after setup
89h	Programming after setup complete; going to display power-on screen message
8Ah	First screen message displayed; about to display <WAIT...> message
8Bh	<WAIT...> message displayed; about to do main and video BIOS shadow
8Ch	Main and video BIOS shadow successful; Setup options programming after CMOS setup about to start
8Dh	Setup options are programmed, mouse check and initialization to be done next
8Eh	Mouse check and initialization complete; going for hard disk, floppy reset
8Fh	Floppy check returns that floppy is to be initialized; floppy setup to follow
90h	Floppy setup is over; test for hard disk presence to be done
91h	Hard disk presence test over; hard disk setup to follow
92h	Hard disk setup complete; about to go for BIOS ROM data area check
93h	BIOS ROM data area check halfway; BIOS ROM data area check to be complete
94h	BIOS ROM data area check over; going to set base and extended memory size
95h	Memory size adjusted due to mouse and hard disk type 47 support; going to verify display memory
96h	Returned after verifying display memory; going to do initialization before C800 optional ROM control
97h	Any initialization before C800 optional ROM control is over; optional ROM check and control to be done next
98h	Optional ROM control is done; about to give control to do any required processing after optional ROM returns control
99h	Any initialization required after optional ROM test over; going to set up timer data area and printer base address
9Ah	Return after setting timer and printer base address; going to set the RS-232 base address
9Bh	Returned after RS-232 base address; going to do any initialization before coprocessor test
9Ch	Required initialization before coprocessor is over; going to initialize the coprocessor next

(continues)

Table A.46 Continued

Port 80h Code	Test Description
9Dh	Coprocessor initialized; going to do any initialization after coprocessor test
9Eh	Initialization after coprocessor test is complete; going to check extended keyboard, keyboard ID, and Num Lock
9Fh	Extended keyboard check is done, ID flag set, Num Lock on/off; keyboard ID command to be issued
A0h	Keyboard ID command issued; keyboard ID flag to be reset
A1h	Keyboard ID flag reset; cache memory test to follow
A2h	Cache memory test over; going to display any soft errors
A3h	Soft error display complete; going to set the keyboard typematic rate
A4h	Keyboard typematic rate set; going to program memory wait states
A5h	Memory wait states programming over; screen to be cleared next
A6h	Screen cleared; going to enable parity and NMI
A7h	NMI and parity enabled; going to do any initialization required before giving control to optional ROM at E000
A8h	Initialization before E000 ROM control over; E000 ROM to get control next
A9h	Returned from E000 ROM control; going to do any initialization required after E000 optional ROM control
AAh	Initialization after E000 optional ROM control is over; going to display the system configuration
00h	System configuration is displayed; going to give control to Int 19h boot loader

Award BIOS Port 80h POST Codes. Table A.47 provides information on the majority of Award POST codes displayed during the POST sequence. These POST codes are output to I/O port address 80h. Although this chart specifically lists all the POST codes output by the Award Modular BIOS, version 3.1, the codes are valid also for these Award Modular BIOS types:

PC/XT Version 3.0 and greater
AT Version 3.02 and greater

Not all these POST codes apply to all the BIOS types. Note that the POST tests do not necessarily execute in the numeric order shown. The POST sequence may vary depending on the BIOS.

Table A.47 Award BIOS Port 80h POST Codes

Port 80h Code	Code Meaning
01h	Processor Test 1. Processor status verification. Tests the following processor-status flags; carry, zero, sign, and overflow. The BIOS sets each flag, verifies that they are set, and turns each flag off and verifies that it is off. Failure of a flag causes a fatal error.
02h	Determine POST Type. This test determines whether the status of the system is manufacturing or normal. The status can be set by a physical jumper on some motherboards. If the status is normal, the POST continues through and, assuming no errors, boot is attempted. If manufacturing POST is installed, POST is run in continuous loop, and boot is not attempted.
03h	8042 Keyboard Controller. Tests controller by sending TEST_KBRD command (AAh) and verifying that controller reads command.
04h	8042 Keyboard Controller. Verifies that keyboard controller returned AAh, sent in test 3.
05h	Get Manufacturing Status. The last test in the manufacturing cycle. If test 2 found the status to be manufacturing, this POST triggers a reset and POSTs 1 through 5 are repeated continuously.
06h	Initialize Chips. POST 06h performs these functions: disables color and mono video, disables parity circuits, disables DMA (8237) chips, resets math co-processor, initializes timer 1 (8255), clears DMA chip, clears all page registers, and clears CMOS shutdown byte.

Port 80h Code	Code Meaning
07h	Processor Test 2. Reads, writes, and verifies all CPU registers except SS, SP, and BP with data pattern FF and 00.
08h	Initialize CMOS Timer. Updates timer cycle normally.
09h	EPROM Checksum. Checksums EPROM; test failed if sum not equal to 0. Also checksums sign-on message.
0Ah	Initialize Video Interface. Initializes video controller register 6845 to the following: 80 characters per row 25 rows per screen 8/14 scan lines per row for mono/color First scan line of cursor 6/11 Last scan line of cursor 7/12 Reset display offset to 0
0Bh	Test Timer (8254) Channel 0. These three timer tests verify that the 8254 timer chip is functioning properly.
0Ch	Test Timer (8254) Channel 1.
0Dh	Test Timer (8254) Channel 2.
0Eh	Test CMOS Shutdown Byte. Uses a walking bit algorithm to check interface to CMOS circuit.
0Fh	Test Extended CMOS. On motherboards with chipsets that support extended CMOS configurations, such as Chips & Technologies, the BIOS tables of CMOS information are used to configure the chip set. These chip sets have an extended storage mechanism that enables the user to save a desired system configuration after the power is turned off. A checksum is used to verify the validity of the extended storage and, if valid, permit the information to be loaded into extended CMOS RAM.
10h	Test DMA Channel 0. These three functions initialize the DMA (direct memory access) chip and then test the chip using an AA, 55, FF, 00 pattern. Port addresses are used to check the address circuit to DMA page registers.
11h	DMA Channel 1.
12h	DMA Page Registers.
13h	Keyboard Controller. Tests keyboard controller interface.
14h	Test Memory Refresh. RAM must be refreshed periodically to keep the memory from decaying. This function ensures that the memory-refresh function is working properly.
15h	First 64K of System Memory. An extensive parity test is performed on the first 64K of system memory. This memory is used by the BIOS.
16h	Interrupt Vector Table. Sets up and loads interrupt vector tables in memory for use by the 8259 PIC chip.
17h	Video I/O Operations. This function initializes the video, either CGA, MDA, EGA, or VGA. If a CGA or MDA adapter is installed, the video is initialized by the system BIOS. If the system BIOS detects an EGA or VGA adapter, the option ROM BIOS installed on the video adapter is used to initialize and set up the video.
18h	Video Memory. Tests memory for CGA and MDA video boards. This test is not performed by the system BIOS on EGA or VGA video adapters—the board's own EGA or VGA BIOS ensures that it is functioning properly.
19h	Test 8259 Mask Bits—Channel 1. These two tests verify 8259 masked interrupts by alternately turning the interrupt lines off and on. Unsuccessful completion generates a fatal error.
1Ah	8259 Mask Bits—Channel 2.
1Bh	CMOS Battery Level. Verifies that the battery status bit is set to 1. A 0 value can indicate a bad battery or some other problem, such as bad CMOS.
1Ch	CMOS Checksum. This function tests the CMOS checksum data (located at 2Eh, and 2Fh) and extended CMOS checksum, if present, to be sure that they are valid.
1Dh	Configuration from CMOS. If the CMOS checksum is good, the values are used to configure the system.

(continues)

Table A.47 Continued

Port 80h Code	Code Meaning
1Eh	System Memory. The system memory size is determined by writing to addresses from 0K to 640K, starting at 0 and continuing until an address does not respond. Memory size value then is compared to the CMOS value to ensure that they are the same. If they are different, a flag is set, and, at the end of POST an error message is displayed.
1Fh	Found System Memory. Tests memory from 64K to the top of the memory found by writing the pattern FFAA and 5500, and then reading the pattern back, byte by byte, and verifying that it is correct.
20h	Stuck 8259 Interrupt Bits. These three tests verify the functionality of the 8259 interrupt controller.
21h	Stuck NMI Bits (Parity or I/O Channel Check).
22h	8259 Function.
23h	Protected Mode. Verifies protected mode: 8086 virtual mode as well as 8086 page mode. Protected mode ensures that any data about to be written to extended memory (above 1M) is checked to ensure that it is suitable for storage there.
24h	Extended Memory. This function sizes memory above 1M by writing to addresses starting at 1M and continuing to 16M on 286 and 386SX systems, and to 64M on 386 systems until there is no response. This process determines the total extended memory, which is compared with CMOS to ensure that the values are the same. If the values are different, a flag is set and at the end of POST an error message is displayed.
25h	Found Extended Memory. This function tests extended memory using virtual 8086 paging mode and writing an FFFF, AA55, 0000 pattern.
26h	Protected Mode Exceptions. This function tests other aspects of protected mode operations.
27h	Cache Control or Shadow RAM. Tests for shadow RAM and cache controller (386 and 486 only) functionality. Systems with CGA and MDA adapters indicate that video shadow RAM is enabled, even though there is no BIOS ROM to shadow (this is normal).
28h	8242. Optional Intel 8242/8248 keyboard controller detection and support.
29h	Reserved.
2Ah	Initialize Keyboard. Initialize keyboard controller.
2Bh	Floppy Drive and Controller. Initializes floppy disk drive controller and any drives present.
2Ch	Detect and Initialize Serial Ports. Initializes any serial ports present.
2Dh	Detect and Initialize Parallel Ports. Initializes any parallel ports present.
2Eh	Initialize Hard Drive and Controller. Initializes hard drive controller and any drives present.
2Fh	Detect and Initialize Math Coprocessor. Initializes math coprocessor.
30h	Reserved.
31h	Detect and Initialize Option ROMs. Initializes any option ROMs present from C800h to EFFFh.
3Bh	Initialize Secondary Cache with OPTi chipset. Initializes secondary cache controller for systems based on the OPTi chipset (486 only).
CAh	Micronics Cache Initialization. Detects and initializes Micronics cache controller if present.
CCh	NMI Handler Shutdown. Detects untrapped Non-Maskable Interrupts during boot.
EEh	Unexpected Processor Exception.
FFh	Boot Attempt. When the POST is complete, if all the system components and peripherals are initialized, and if no error flags were set (such as memory size error), then the system attempts to boot.

Phoenix BIOS Audio and Port 80h POST Codes. Table A.48 is a list of POST fatal errors that may be reported by the Phoenix BIOS. Table A.49 is a list of nonfatal errors. Fatal errors halt the system and prevent any further processing from occurring; nonfatal errors are less severe.

Table A.48 Phoenix BIOS Fatal System Board Errors

Beep Code	Code at Port 80h	Description
None	01h	CPU register test in progress
1-1-3	02h	CMOS write/read failure
1-1-4	03h	ROM BIOS checksum failure
1-2-1	04h	Programmable interval timer failure
1-2-2	05h	DMA initialization failure
1-2-3	06h	DMA page register write/read failure
1-3-1	08h	RAM refresh verification failure
None	09h	First 64K RAM test in progress
1-3-3	0Ah	First 64K RAM chip or data line failure, multibit
1-3-4	0Bh	First 64K RAM odd/even logic failure
1-4-1	0Ch	Address line failure first 64K RAM
1-4-2	0Dh	Parity failure first 64K RAM
2-1-1	10h	Bit 0 first 64K RAM failure
2-1-2	11h	Bit 1 first 64K RAM failure
2-1-3	12h	Bit 2 first 64K RAM failure
2-1-4	13h	Bit 3 first 64K RAM failure
2-2-1	14h	Bit 4 first 64K RAM failure
2-2-2	15h	Bit 5 first 64K RAM failure
2-2-3	16h	Bit 6 first 64K RAM failure
2-2-4	17h	Bit 7 first 64K RAM failure
2-3-1	18h	Bit 8 first 64K RAM failure
2-3-2	19h	Bit 9 first 64K RAM failure
2-3-3	1Ah	Bit 10 first 64K RAM failure
2-3-4	1Bh	Bit 11 first 64K RAM failure
2-4-1	1Ch	Bit 12 first 64K RAM failure
2-4-2	1Dh	Bit 13 first 64K RAM failure
2-4-3	1Eh	Bit 14 first 64K RAM failure
2-4-4	1Fh	Bit 15 first 64K RAM failure
3-1-1	20h	Slave DMA register failure
3-1-2	21h	Master DMA register failure
3-1-3	22h	Master interrupt mask register failure
3-1-4	23h	Slave interrupt mask register failure
None	25h	Interrupt vector loading in progress
3-2-4	27h	Keyboard controller test failure
None	28h	CMOS power failure/checksum calculation in progress
None	29h	Screen configuration validation in progress
3-3-4	2Bh	Screen initialization failure
3-4-1	2Ch	Screen retrace failure
3-4-2	2Dh	Search for video ROM in progress
None	2Eh	Screen running with video ROM
None	30h	Screen operable
None	31h	Monochrome monitor operable
None	32h	Color monitor (40 column) operable
None	33h	Color monitor (80 column) operable

Table A.49 Nonfatal System Board Errors

Beep Code	Code at Port 80h	Description
4-2-1	34h	Timer tick interrupt test in progress or failure
4-2-2	35h	Shutdown test in progress or failure
4-2-3	36h	Gate A20 failure
4-2-4	37h	Unexpected interrupt in protected mode
4-3-1	38h	RAM test in progress or address failure > FFFFh
4-3-3	3Ah	Interval timer Channel 2 test or failure
4-3-4	3Bh	Time-of-day clock test or failure
4-4-1	3Ch	Serial port test or failure
4-4-2	3Dh	Parallel port test or failure
4-4-3	3Eh	Math coprocessor test or failure
Low 1-1-2	41h	System board select failure
Low 1-1-3	42h	Extended CMOS RAM failure

Low means that a lower pitched beep precedes the other tones.

Hewlett-Packard POST and Diagnostics Error Codes

Table A.50 Hewlett-Packard 386/N and 486/N POST Error Codes

Code	Description
000F	Microprocessor test error. Check CPU and system board.
001x	ROM BIOS memory error. Check ROM BIOS and system board.
008x	Memory error in address range C000–C7FF. Check system board video ROM and/or video adapter.
009x, 00Ax, 00Bx	Memory error in address range C800–DFFF. Check adapter ROMs.
00C0	Memory error in address range E000–EFFF. Check adapters or system board LAN boot ROM.
011x	CMOS register test error; real-time clock (RTC) is not working correctly.
0120, 0130	CMOS real-time clock (RTC) failed or corrupted. Check battery.
0240	CMOS system configuration information corrupted by power failure. Check battery.
0250	CMOS system configuration information does not match system. Run Setup; check battery.
0241, 0280	CMOS power failure; check battery.
02C0, 02C1	EEPROM master configuration information corrupted or not set correctly. Check system board configuration switches. If the fifth switch (Clear EEPROM) is ON, set it to the OFF position, reset the system, and run Setup to reenter the system configuration.
030x, 0311, 0312, 03E0, 03E1, 03E2, 03E3, 03E4, 03EC	Keyboard/mouse controller failed to respond to a command. Check board.
034x, 035x	Keyboard failed to respond during keyboard test. Check keyboard cable, keyboard, and system board.
03E5, 03E6, 03E7, 03E8, 03E9, 03EA, 03EB	Mouse test failure. Check mouse and cable.
0401	Protected mode switch failure. Check system board.
0503, 0505	Serial port failure or configuration error. Check setup and system board.
0543, 0545	Parallel port failure or configuration error. Check setup and system board.
0506, 0546	Serial or parallel port conflict. Check configuration.
06xx	Stuck key failure; xx = the scan code of the stuck key.
0800	System board LAN boot ROM conflict. Check memory address configurations.
0801	Cannot find LAN boot ROM declared in setup. Check configuration and boot ROM.

Code	Description
110x, 1200, 1201	System timer failure. Check the system board.
20xA	SIMM size mismatch; interleaved memory disabled. Check SIMM installation in the affected bank or banks as identified below: 201A = A 205A = A,C 209A = A,D 20DA = A,C,D 202A = B 206A = B,C 20AA = B,D 20EA = B,C,D 203A = A,B 207A = A,B,C 20BA = A,B,D 20FA = A,B,C,D 204A = C 208A = D 20CA = C,D
21xx, 22xx	DMA channel failure. Check system board.
4F01, 4F02, 4F03, 4F04, 4F05, 4F06, 4F07, 4F08	SIMM memory error. Check the defective SIMM as identified below: 4F01 = Bank A, slot 1 4F05 = Bank C, slot 1 4F02 = Bank A, slot 2 4F06 = Bank C, slot 2 4F03 = Bank B, slot 1 4F07 = Bank D, slot 1 4F04 = Bank B, slot 2 4F08 = Bank D, slot 2
61xx	Memory address line failure. Check SIMMs and system board.
63xx	Memory parity error. Check memory and system board.
6500	ROM BIOS shadowing error. Check system memory and ROM BIOS
6510	Video ROM shadowing error. Check system memory and Video ROM BIOS.
6520	LAN option ROM shadowing error. Check system memory and LAN option ROM.
65A0, 65B0, 65C0, 65D0, 65E0, 65F0	ROM BIOS shadowing error; memory segment failure. Check system memory in the segment indicated by the third digit as identified below: A = A000, B = B000, C = C000, D = D000, E = E000, F = F000
66xx	ROM BIOS shadowing error. Check configuration or ROM checksum.
7xxx	Interrupt failure. Check system board.
8003, 8006	Hard drive configuration error; parameters do not match drive. Check configuration and cables.
8004, 8007	CMOS hard disk configuration error. Check drive and battery.
800D, 8010, 8012, 8020, 8021, 8038, 803C, 8040,	Hard disk controller time-out (12 seconds without responding). Check drive and controller.
8045	
800E	Hard disk boot failure. Check cables and disk drive failure.
800F	Hard disk CMOS configuration does not match drive.
8011, 8013, 8030, 8039, 803A, 803B, 8041, 8042, 8043, 8044, 8049, 804B, 8310, 8311, 8313	Hard drive does not respond to commands. Check drive, controller, and cables.
8048, 804A	System failed to identify installed hard disk drive. Check setup and cables.
8050	System failed to identify installed hard disk controller. Check configuration.
8400	Hard disk drive boot sector was corrupted or could not be loaded. Check drive partitions.
9x00, 9x01, 9x02, 9x03, 9x04, 9x05, 9x06, 9x07, 9x08, 9x09	Floppy drive error, check drives and cables. Drive x not responding, where: x = 0 for drive 0 x = 1 for drive 1 x = 2 for drive 2 x = 3 for drive 3
Check cables and drives.	
9x10, 9x0A	CMOS floppy configuration error, where: x = 0 for drive 0 x = 1 for drive 1 x = 2 for drive 2 x = 3 for drive 3
A00x	Math coprocessor error. Check coprocessor and system board.
B300	Memory cache controller error.
Exxx	Memory adapter error. Check adapters or SIMMs.

Table A.51 Hewlett-Packard 486/U POST Error Codes

Code	Description
00Ax, 00Bx, 00Cx, 00Dx	Adapter ROM (read-only memory) checksum error. Check configuration.
008x	Video ROM (read-only memory) checksum error. Check video ROM or adapter.
009x	Adapter ROM (read-only memory) checksum error in addresses between C8000h and CFFFFh. Check configuration and adapter.
0111x, 0120	CMOS real-time clock is not updating. Check battery and system board.
0130	CMOS real-time clock has invalid time and or date. Reset date and time.
0240, 0241	CMOS memory information is incorrect. Check the clear configuration switch on the system board; it should be OFF.
0250	CMOS configuration does not match installed devices.
0280, 0282	CMOS configuration information has been corrupted.
02C0	EEPROM memory has not been set or was corrupted.
0301, 0302, 0303, 0305, 0306, 0307, 0311, 0312, 03E0, 03E1, 03E2, 03E3, 03E4, 03E5, 03EE, 03EC	System board keyboard/mouse controller did not respond.
0342, 0343, 0344, 0345, 0346, 0350, 0351	System board keyboard/mouse controller self-test failure. Check keyboard controller.
0352, 0353	Keyboard not responding to POST tests. Check cable and keyboard controller.
0354	Keyboard self-test failure. Check keyboard.
03E6, 03E7, 03E8, 03E9	Mouse interface test failure. Check mouse, cable, or keyboard/mouse controller.
03EA, 03EB	Keyboard/mouse reset failure. Check mouse and cable.
0401	Gate A20 failure. Check keyboard/mouse controller (8042) on system board or the system board itself.
0503, 0505	Serial port error or conflict. Check system board or adapters.
0543, 0545	Parallel port or configuration failure. Check configuration, system board, or adapters.
06xx	Keyboard stuck key failure; xx = Scan code (hex) of the key.
1100, 1101	System timer failure. Check system board.
1300	Floppy controller conflict. Check configuration.
13x1	Adapter communications error; x = slot containing adapter (e.g., 1351 = slot 5).
13x2	CMOS indicates a slot is empty, but a board is installed; x = slot.
13x3	CMOS indicates a slot contains a board with no readable identification, but a board with a readable identification is present; x = slot.
13x4	CMOS configuration information does not match the board in slot x, where x = slot.
13x5	CMOS configuration information is incomplete.
2002	SIMM not detected. Check SIMMs and system board.
2003, 2005, 2007	Incorrect SIMM configuration; for example, when you have 2MB and 8MB memory modules installed at the same time, the 8MB modules must be in the first sockets.
21xx, 22xx	DMA (Direct Memory Access) controller is not functioning correctly. Check system board.
4F0x	SIMM error; x = SIMM socket (e.g. 4F02 = socket 2)
61xx	Memory addressing error. Check installed SIMMs.
62F0	Memory parity error. Check SIMMs or system board.
62F1	Memory controller error. Check system board.
6300	Adapter RAM error. Check installed adapters and memory.
6500	System board ROM BIOS shadowing error. Check system board and setup for conflicts.

Code	Description
6510	Video ROM shadowing error. Check system board or video adapter.
6520	Adapter ROM shadowing error. Check system board adapters and memory.
65C0, 65D0, 65E0	Reserved memory for shadowing failed tests. Segment indicated by third digit (e.g., 65D0 = segment D000h).
70xx, 71xx, 7400, 7500	Interrupt controller failure. Check system board and adapters.
8003, 8103	Hard disk configuration (number of sectors) is not correct.
8004, 8104	CMOS hard disk parameters are not correct, where 8004 = drive C, and 8104 = drive D.
8005, 8105	CMOS hard disk parameters not supported, where 8005 = drive C, and 8105 = drive D.
8x06	BIOS shadow RAM on your system board must be functioning if you have either a hard disk drive type 33 or type 34 installed.
8007, 8107	The number of hard disk drive cylinders specified for your type 33 or type 34 hard disk drive is not correct, where 8007 = drive C, and 8107 = drive D.
800D, 8010, 800E, 800F	Hard drive controller not responding. Check controller or cables.
8011	Hard disk test failure.
8012, 8013	Hard disk controller test failure.
8020, 8120	Hard drive not ready, where 8020 = drive C, and 8120 = drive D.
8021, 8121	Unable to communicate with hard disk controller, where 8021 = drive C and 8121 = drive D is at fault.
8028	Hard disk controller is configured for drive splitting, but splitting is not supported or is not functioning. Check configuration.
8030, 8130	Identify drive failure, where 8030 = drive C, and 8130 = drive D is at fault. Check the EISA Configuration Manager Utility.
8038, 8138, 803A, 813A, 803B, 813B 803C, 813C	Hard disk (Recalibrate) error, where 8039, 803A, or 803C = hard disk or controller for drive C, and 8139, 8013A, or 813C = drive D or its controller is at fault.
8040, 8140, 8041, 8141, 8042, 8142, 8043, 8143, 8044, 8144, 8045, 8145	Hard disk (Read Verify) command failure, where 804x = hard disk drive or controller for C, and 814x = hard drive or controller for D.
8048, 8148, 804A, 814A	Hard disk (Drive Identify) command failure, where 804x = drive C, and 814x = drive D.
8049, 8149, 804B, 814B	Hard disk (Set Multiple Mode) command failure, where 804x = drive C, and 814x = drive D.
8400	No boot sector (or corrupted boot sector) on hard disk.
900A, 910A, 920A	CMOS floppy configuration does not match actual drives installed, where 900A = drive A, 910A = drive B, and 920A = a third floppy drive.
9000, 9100, 9200, 9001, 9101, 9201	Floppy controller communication error, where 90xx = drive A, 91xx = drive B, and 92xx = a third floppy drive.
9002, 9102, 9202	Floppy drive (Seek) error, where 90xx = drive A, 91xx = drive B, and 9202 = a third floppy drive.
9003, 9103, 9203	Floppy drive (Recalibrate) error, where 90xx = drive A, 9103 = drive B, and 9203 = a third floppy drive.
9005, 9105, 9205	Floppy drive (Reset) error, where 9005 = drive A, 9105 = drive as B, and 9205 = a third floppy drive.
9008, 9108, 9208	Floppy drive command error, where 9008 = drive A, 9108 = drive B, and 9208 = a third floppy drive.
9009, 9109, 9209	Floppy drive track zero error, where 9009 = drive A, 9109 = drive B, and 9209 = a third floppy drive.
A001, A002, A003, A004, A005, A006, A007, A008, A009, A00A, A00B, A00C, A00D, A00E	Math coprocessor failure.
B300	CPU Level 2 cache failure.
Exxx	Memory board failure (non-HP).

IBM POST and Diagnostics Display Error Codes

When an IBM or compatible system is first powered on, the system runs a Power-On Self Test (POST). If errors are encountered during the POST, they are displayed in the form of a code number and possibly some additional text. When you are running the IBM Advanced Diagnostics, which you can purchase from IBM or which is included on many of the PS/2 Reference Diskettes, similar codes are displayed if errors are encountered during the tests. IBM has developed a system in which the first part of the error code indicates the device the error involves, and the last part indicates the exact error meaning. One of the biggest problems with these error codes is that IBM does not publish a complete list of the errors in any single publication; instead, it details specific error codes in many different publications. I have researched these codes for many years; Tables A.48 and A.49 represent all the codes I have found meanings for. These codes have been selected from a number of sources, including all of IBM's technical-reference and hardware-maintenance service manuals.

When diagnostics are run, any code ending in 00 indicates that the particular test has passed. For example, an error code of 1700 indicates that the hard disk diagnostics tests have passed.

After completing the Power-On Self Test (POST), an audio code indicates either a normal condition or that one of several errors has occurred. Table A.52 lists the audio codes for IBM systems, and table A.53 lists the IBM POST and diagnostics error codes.

Table A.52 IBM POST Audio Error Codes

Audio Code	Sound Graph	Fault Domain
1 short beep	•	Normal POST—system OK
2 short beeps	••	POST error—error code on CRT
No beep		Power supply, system board
Continuous beep	———	Power supply, system board
Repeating short beeps	••••••	Power supply, system board
1 long, 1 short beep	–•	System board
1 long, 2 short beeps	–••	Display adapter (MDA, CGA)
1 long, 3 short beeps	–•••	Enhanced Graphics Adapter (EGA)
3 long beeps	– – –	3270 keyboard card

Table A.53 IBM POST and Diagnostics Error-Code List

Code	Description
1xx	**System Board Errors**
101	System board interrupt failure (unexpected interrupt).
102	System board timer failure.
102	PS/2; real-time clock (RTC)/64 byte CMOS RAM test failure.
103	System board timer interrupt failure.
103	PS/2; 2K CMOS RAM extension test failure.
104	System board protected mode failure.
105	System board 8042 keyboard controller command failure.
106	System board converting logic test failure.
107	System board Non-Maskable Interrupt (NMI) test failure; hot NMI.
108	System board timer bus test failure.
109	System board memory select error; low MB chip select test failed.
110	PS/2 system board parity check error (PARITY CHECK 1).
111	PS/2 I/O channel (bus) parity check error (PARITY CHECK 2).
112	PS/2 Micro Channel Arbitration error; watchdog time-out (NMI error).
113	PS/2 Micro Channel Arbitration error; DMA arbitration time-out (NMI error).
114	PS/2 external ROM checksum error.
115	Cache parity error, ROM checksum error or DMA error.

Code	Description
116	System board port read/write failure.
118	System board parity or L2-cache error during previous power-on.
119	"E" Step level 82077 (floppy controller) and 2.88M drive installed (not supported).
120	Microprocessor self-test error.
121	256K ROM checksum error (second 128KB bank).
121	Unexpected hardware interrupts occurred.
131	PC system board cassette port wrap test failure.
131	Direct memory access (DMA) compatibility registers error.
132	Direct memory access (DMA) extended registers error.
133	Direct memory access (DMA) verify logic error.
134	Direct memory access (DMA) arbitration logic error.
151	Battery or CMOS RAM failure.
152	Real-time clock or CMOS RAM failure.
160	PS/2 system board ID not recognized.
161	CMOS configuration empty (dead battery).
162	CMOS checksum error or adapter ID mismatch.
163	CMOS error; date and time not set (clock not updating).
164	Memory size error; CMOS setting does not match memory.
165	PS/2 Micro Channel adapter ID and CMOS mismatch.
166	PS/2 Micro Channel adapter time-out error (card busy).
167	PS/2 CMOS clock not updating.
168	CMOS configuration error (math coprocessor).
169	System board and processor card configuration mismatch. Run Setup.
170	ASCII setup conflict error.
170	PC Convertible; LCD not in use when suspended.
171	Rolling-bit-test failure on CMOS shutdown address byte.
171	PC Convertible; base 128K checksum failure.
172	Rolling-bit-test failure on NVRAM diagnostic byte.
172	PC Convertible; diskette active when suspended.
173	Bad CMOS/NVRAM checksum.
173	PC Convertible; real-time clock RAM verification error.
174	Bad configuration.
174	PC Convertible; LCD configuration changed.
175	Bad EEPROM CRC #1.
175	PC Convertible; LCD alternate mode failed.
176	Tamper evident.
177	Bad PAP (Privileged-Access Password) CRC.
177	Bad EEPROM.
178	Bad EEPROM.
179	NVRAM error log full.
180x	Sub Address data error, where x = the slot number that caused the error.
181	Unsupported configurations.
182	Privileged-access switch (JMP2) is not in the write-enable position.
183	PAP is needed to boot from the system programs.
183	Privileged-access password required.
184	Bad power-on password checksum—erase it.
184	Bad power-on password.
185	Bad startup sequence.
186	Password-protection hardware error.
187	Serial number error.
188	Bad EEPROM checksum CRC #2.
189	Excessive incorrect password attempts.
191	82385 cache controller test failure.
194	System board memory error.
199	User indicated INSTALLED DEVICES list is not correct.
2xx	**Memory (RAM) Errors**
20x	Memory error.
201	Memory test failure; error location may be displayed.
202	Memory address error; lines 00–15.
203	Memory address error; lines 16–23 (ISA) or 16–31 (MCA).
204	Memory remapped due to error (run diagnostics again).
205	Base 128K memory error; memory remapped.
207	ROM failure.
210	System board memory parity error.

(continues)

Table A.53 Continued

Code	Description
2xx	**Memory (RAM) Errors**
211	PS/2 memory; base 64K on system board failed.
212	Watchdog time-out error (reported by NMI interrupt handler).
213	DMA bus arbitration time-out (reported by NMI interrupt handler).
215	PS/2 memory; base 64K on daughter/SIP 2 failed.
216	PS/2 memory; base 64K on daughter/SIP 1 failed.
221	PS/2 memory; ROM to RAM copy failed (ROM shadowing).
225	PS/2 memory; wrong-speed memory on system board, unsupported SIMM.
230	Overlapping adapter and planar memory (Family 1).
231	Non-contiguous adapter memory installed (Family 1).
231	2/4-16MB Enhanced 386 memory adapter; memory module 1 failed.
235	Stuck data line on memory module, microprocessor, or system board.
241	2/4-16MB Enhanced 386 memory adapter; memory module 2 failed.
251	2/4-16MB Enhanced 386 memory adapter; memory module 3 failed.
3xx	**Keyboard Errors**
301	Keyboard reset or stuck key failure (SS 301, SS = scan code in hex).
302	System unit keylock is locked.
303	Keyboard-to-system board interface error; keyboard controller failure.
304	Keyboard or system board error; keyboard clock high.
305	Keyboard +5v dc error; PS/2 keyboard fuse (on system board) error.
306	Unsupported keyboard attached.
341	Keyboard error.
342	Keyboard cable error.
343	Keyboard LED card or cable failure.
365	Keyboard LED card or cable failure.
366	Keyboard interface cable failure.
367	Keyboard LED card or cable failure.
4xx	**Monochrome Display Adapter (MDA) Errors**
4xx	**PS/2 System Board Parallel Port Errors**
401	Monochrome memory, horizontal sync frequency, or video test failure.
401	PS/2 system board parallel port failure.
408	User indicated display attributes failure.
416	User indicated character set failure.
424	User indicated 80525 mode failure.
432	Parallel port test failure; Monochrome Display Adapter.
5xx	**Color Graphics Adapter (CGA) Errors**
*501	CRT error.
501	CGA memory, horizontal sync frequency, or video test failure.
503	CGA adapter controller failed.
508	User indicated display attribute failure.
516	User indicated character set failure.
524	User indicated 80×25 mode failure.
532	User indicated 40×25 mode failure.
540	User indicated 320×200 graphics mode failure.
548	User indicated 640×200 graphics mode failure.
556	User indicated light-pen test failed.
564	User indicated paging test failure.
6xx	**Floppy Drive/Controller Errors**
601	Floppy drive/controller Power-On Self Test failure; disk drive or controller error.
602	Diskette boot sector is not valid.
603	Diskette size error.
604	Non-media sense.
605	Diskette drive locked.
606	Diskette verify test failure.
607	Write protect error.
608	Drive command error.

Code	Description
610	Diskette initialization failure; track 0 bad.
611	Drive time-out error.
612	Controller chip (NEC) error.
613	Direct memory access (DMA) error.
614	Direct memory access (DMA) boundary overrun error.
615	Drive index timing error.
616	Drive speed error.
621	Drive seek error.
622	Drive cyclic redundancy check (CRC) error.
623	Sector not found error.
624	Address mark error.
625	Controller chip (NEC) seek error.
626	Diskette data compare error.
627	Diskette change error.
628	Diskette removed.
630	Index stuck high; drive A.
631	Index stuck low; drive A.
632	Track 0 stuck off; drive A.
633	Track 0 stuck on; drive A.
640	Index stuck high; drive B.
641	Index stuck low; drive B.
642	Track 0 stuck off; drive B.
643	Track 0 stuck on; drive B.
645	No index pulse.
646	Drive track 0 detection failed.
647	No transitions on read data line.
648	Format test failed.
649	Incorrect media type in drive.
650	Drive speed error.
651	Format failure.
652	Verify failure.
653	Read failure.
654	Write failure.
655	Controller error.
656	Drive failure.
657	Write protect stuck protected.
658	Changeline stuck changed.
659	Write protect stuck unprotected.
660	Changeline stuck unchanged.
7xx	**Math Coprocessor Errors**
701	Math coprocessor presence/initialization error.
702	Exception errors test failure.
703	Rounding test failure.
704	Arithmetic test 1 failure.
705	Arithmetic test 2 failure.
706	Arithmetic test 3 (80387 only) failure.
707	Combination test failure.
708	Integer load/store test failure.
709	Equivalent expressions errors.
710	Exception (interrupt) errors.
711	Save state (FSAVE) errors.
712	Protected mode test failure.
713	Special test (voltage/temperature sensitivity) failure.
9xx	**Parallel Printer Adapter Errors**
901	Printer adapter data register latch error.
902	Printer adapter control register latch error.
903	Printer adapter register address decode error.
904	Printer adapter address decode error.
910	Status line(s) wrap connector error.
911	Status line bit 8 wrap error.
912	Status line bit 7 wrap error.

(continues)

Table A.53 Continued

Code	Description
9xx	**Parallel Printer Adapter Errors**
913	Status line bit 6 wrap error.
914	Status line bit 5 wrap error.
915	Status line bit 4 wrap error.
916	Printer adapter interrupt wrap error.
917	Unexpected printer adapter interrupt.
92x	Feature register error.
10xx	**Alternate Parallel Printer Adapter Errors**
1001	Printer adapter data register latch error.
1002	Printer adapter control register latch error.
1003	Printer adapter register address decode error.
1004	Printer adapter address decode error.
1010	Status line(s) wrap connector error.
1011	Status line bit 8 wrap error.
1012	Status line bit 7 wrap error.
1013	Status line bit 6 wrap error.
1014	Status line bit 5 wrap error.
1015	Status line bit 4 wrap error.
1016	Printer adapter interrupt wrap error.
1017	Unexpected printer adapter interrupt.
102x	Feature register error.
11xx	**Primary Async Communications (Serial COM1:) Errors**
1101	16450/16550 chip error; serial port A error.
1102	Card selected feedback error.
1102	PC Convertible internal modem test failed.
1103	Port 102h register test failure.
1103	PC Convertible internal modem dial tone test 1 failed.
1104	PC Convertible internal modem dial tone test 2 failed.
1106	Serial option cannot be put to sleep.
1107	Cable error.
1108	Interrupt request (IRQ) 3 error.
1109	Interrupt request (IRQ) 4 error.
1110	16450/16550 chip register failure.
1111	Internal wrap test of 16450/16550 chip modem control line failure.
1112	External wrap test of 16450/16550 chip modem control line failure.
1113	16450/16550 chip transmit error.
1114	16450/16550 chip receive error.
1115	16450/16550 chip receive error; data not equal to transmit data.
1116	16450/16550 chip interrupt function error.
1117	16450/16550 chip baud rate test failure.
1118	16450/16550 chip receive external data wrap test failure.
1119	16550 chip first-in first-out (FIFO) buffer failure.
1120	Interrupt enable register error; all bits cannot be set.
1121	Interrupt enable register error; all bits cannot be reset.
1122	Interrupt pending; stuck on.
1123	Interrupt ID register; stuck on.
1124	Modem control register error; all bits cannot be set.
1125	Modem control register error; all bits cannot be reset.
1126	Modem status register error; all bits cannot be set.
1127	Modem status register error; all bits cannot be reset.
1128	Interrupt ID error.
1129	Cannot force overrun error.
1130	No modem status interrupt.
1131	Invalid interrupt pending.
1132	No data ready.
1133	No data available interrupt.
1134	No transmit holding interrupt.
1135	No interrupts.
1136	No received sine status interrupt.
1137	No receive data available.
1138	Transmit holding register not empty.

Code	Description
1139	No modem status interrupt.
1140	Transmit holding register not empty.
1141	No interrupts.
1142	No interrupt 4.
1143	No interrupt 3.
1144	No data transferred.
1145	Maximum baud rate error.
1146	Minimum baud rate error.
1148	Time-out error.
11xx	**Primary Async Communications (Serial COM1:) Errors**
1149	Invalid data returned.
1150	Modem status register error.
1151	No data set ready and delta data set ready.
1152	No data set ready.
1153	No delta data set ready.
1154	Modem status register not clear.
1155	No clear to send and delta clear to send.
1156	No clear to send.
1157	No delta clear to send.
12xx	**Alternate Async Communications (Serial COM2:, COM3:, and COM4:) Errors**
1201	16450/16550 chip error.
1202	Card selected feedback error.
1203	Port 102h register test failure.
1206	Serial option cannot be put to sleep.
1207	Cable error.
1208	Interrupt request (IRQ) 3 error.
1209	Interrupt request (IRQ) 4 error.
1210	16450/16550 chip register failure.
1211	Internal wrap test of 16450/16550 chip modem control line failure.
1212	External wrap test of 16450/16550 chip modem control line failure.
1213	16450/16550 chip transmit error.
1214	16450/16550 chip receive error.
1215	16450/16550 chip receive error; data not equal to transmit data.
1216	16450/16550 chip interrupt function error.
1217	16450/16550 chip baud rate test failure.
1218	16450/16550 chip receive external data wrap test failure.
1219	16550 chip first-in first-out (FIFO) buffer failure.
1220	Interrupt enable register error; all bits cannot be set.
1221	Interrupt enable register error; all bits cannot be reset.
1222	Interrupt pending; stuck on.
1223	Interrupt ID register; stuck on.
1224	Modem control register error; all bits cannot be set.
1225	Modem control register error; all bits cannot be reset.
1226	Modem status register error; all bits cannot be set.
1227	Modem status register error; all bits cannot be reset.
1228	Interrupt ID error.
1229	Cannot force overrun error.
1230	No modem status interrupt.
1231	Invalid interrupt pending.
1232	No data ready.
1233	No data available interrupt.
1234	No transmit holding interrupt.
1235	No interrupts.
1236	No received sine status interrupt.
1237	No receive data available.
1238	Transmit holding register not empty.
1239	No modem status interrupt.
1240	Transmit holding register not empty.
1241	No interrupts.
1242	No interrupt 4.
1243	No interrupt 3.
1244	No data transferred.
1245	Maximum baud rate error.

(continues)

Table A.53 Continued

Code	Description
12xx	**Alternate Async Communications (Serial COM2:, COM3:, and COM4:) Errors**
1246	Minimum baud rate error.
1248	Time-out error.
1249	Invalid data returned.
1250	Modem status register error.
1251	No data set ready and delta data set ready.
1252	No data set ready.
1253	No delta data set ready.
1254	Modem status register not clear.
1255	No clear to send and delta clear to send.
1256	No clear to send.
1257	No delta clear to send.
13xx	**Game Control Adapter Errors**
1301	Game control adapter test failure.
1302	Joystick test failure.
14xx	**Matrix Printer Errors**
1401	Printer test failure.
1402	Printer not ready error.
1403	Printer no-paper error.
1404	System board time-out.
1405	Parallel adapter failure.
1406	Printer presence test failed.
15xx	**Synchronous Data Link Control (SDLC) Communications Adapter Errors**
1501	SDLC adapter test failure.
1510	8255 Port B failure.
1511	8255 Port A failure.
1512	8255 Port C failure.
1513	8253 Timer #1 did not reach terminal count.
1514	8253 Timer #1 stuck on.
1515	8253 Timer #0 did not reach terminal count.
1516	8253 Timer #0 stuck on.
1517	8253 Timer #2 did not reach terminal count.
1518	8253 Timer #2 stuck on.
1519	8273 Port B error.
1520	8273 Port A error.
1521	8273 command/read time-out.
1522	Interrupt Level 4 failure.
1523	Ring Indicate stuck on.
1524	Receive Clock stuck on.
1525	Transmit Clock stuck on.
1526	Test Indicate stuck on.
1527	Ring Indicate not on.
1528	Receive Clock not on.
1529	Transmit Clock not on.
1530	Test Indicate not on.
1531	Data Set Ready not on.
1532	Carrier Detect not on.
1533	Clear to Send not on.
1534	Data Set Ready stuck on.
1535	Carrier Detect stuck on.
1536	Clear to Send stuck on.
1537	Interrupt Level 3 failure.
1538	Receive interrupt results error.
1539	Wrap data compare error.
1540	Direct memory access Channel 1 error.
1541	Direct memory access Channel 1 error.
1542	8273 error-checking or status-reporting error.
1547	Stray interrupt Level 4.
1548	Stray interrupt Level 3.
1549	Interrupt presentation sequence time-out.

Code	Description
16xx	**Display Station Emulation Adapter (DSEA) Errors (5520, 525x)**
1604	DSEA or twinaxial network error.
1608	DSEA or twinaxial network error.
1624	DSEA error.
1634	DSEA error.
1644	DSEA error.
1652	DSEA error.
1654	DSEA error.
1658	DSEA error.
1662	DSEA interrupt level error.
1664	DSEA error.
1668	DSEA interrupt level error.
1669	DSEA diagnostics error; use 3.0 or higher.
1674	DSEA diagnostics error; use 3.0 or higher.
1674	DSEA station address error.
1684	DSEA device address error.
1688	DSEA device address error.
17xx	**ST-506/412 Fixed Disk and Controller Errors**
1701	Fixed disk general POST error.
1702	Drive/controller time-out error.
1703	Drive seek error.
1704	Controller failed.
1705	Drive sector not found error.
1706	Write fault error.
1707	Drive track 0 error.
1708	Head select error.
1709	Error-correction code (ECC) error.
1710	Sector buffer overrun.
1711	Bad address mark.
1712	Internal controller diagnostics failure.
1713	Data compare error.
1714	Drive not ready.
1715	Track 0 indicator failure.
1716	Diagnostics cylinder errors.
1717	Surface read errors.
1718	Hard drive type error.
1720	Bad diagnostics cylinder.
1726	Data compare error.
1730	Controller error.
1731	Controller error.
1732	Controller error.
1733	BIOS undefined error return.
1735	Bad command error.
1736	Data corrected error.
1737	Bad track error.
1738	Bad sector error.
1739	Bad initialization error.
1740	Bad sense error.
1750	Drive verify failure.
1751	Drive read failure.
1752	Drive write failure.
1753	Drive random read test failure.
1754	Drive seek test failure.
1755	Controller failure.
1756	Controller error-correction code (ECC) test failure.
1757	Controller head-select failure.
1780	Seek failure; drive 0.
1781	Seek failure; drive 1.
1782	Controller test failure.
1790	Diagnostic cylinder read error; drive 0.
1791	Diagnostic cylinder read error; drive 1.

(continues)

Table A.53 Continued

Code	Description
18xx	**I/O Expansion Unit Errors**
1801	I/O expansion unit POST failure.
1810	Enable/disable failure.
1811	Extender card wrap test failure; disabled.
1812	High-order address lines failure; disabled.
1813	Wait state failure; disabled.
1814	Enable/disable could not be set on.
1815	Wait state failure; disabled.
1816	Extender card wrap test failure; enabled.
1817	High-order address lines failure; enabled.
1818	Disable not functioning.
1819	Wait request switch not set correctly.
1820	Receiver card wrap test failure.
1821	Receiver high order address lines failure.
19xx	**3270 PC Attachment Card Errors**
20xx	**Binary Synchronous Communications (BSC) Adapter Errors**
2001	BSC adapter test failure.
2010	8255 Port A failure.
2011	8255 Port B failure.
2012	8255 Port C failure.
2013	8253 Timer #1 did not reach terminal count.
2014	8253 Timer #1 stuck on.
2015	8253 Timer 2 did not reach terminal count.
2016	8253 Timer #2 output stuck on.
2017	8251 data set ready failed to come on.
2018	8251 clear to send not sensed.
2019	8251 data SET ready stuck on.
2020	8251 clear to send stuck on.
2021	8251 hardware reset failure.
2022	8251 software reset failure.
2023	8251 software "error reset" failure.
2024	8251 transmit ready did not come on.
2025	8251 receive ready did not come on.
2026	8251 could not force "overrun" error status.
2027	Interrupt failure; no timer interrupt.
2028	Interrupt failure; transmit; replace card or planar.
2029	Interrupt failure; transmit; replace card.
2030	Interrupt failure; receive; replace card or planar.
2031	Interrupt failure; receive; replace card.
2033	Ring indicate stuck on.
2034	Receive clock stuck on.
2035	Transmit clock stuck on.
2036	Test indicate stuck on.
2037	Ring indicate stuck on.
2038	Receive clock not on.
2039	Transmit clock not on.
2040	Test indicate not on.
2041	Data set ready not on.
2042	Carrier detect not on.
2043	Clear to send not on.
2044	Data set ready stuck on.
2045	Carrier detect stuck on.
2046	Clear to send stuck on.
2047	Unexpected transmit interrupt.
2048	Unexpected receive interrupt.
2049	Transmit data did not equal receive data.
2050	8251 detected overrun error.
2051	Lost data set ready during data wrap.
2052	Receive time-out during data wrap.

Code	Description
21xx	**Alternate Binary Synchronous Communications (BSC) Adapter Errors**
2101	BSC adapter test failure.
2110	8255 Port A failure.
2111	8255 Port B failure.
2112	8255 Port C failure.
2113	8253 Timer #1 did not reach terminal count.
2114	8253 Timer #1 stuck on.
2115	8253 Timer 2 did not reach terminal count.
2116	8253 Timer #2 output stuck on.
2117	8251 Data set ready failed to come on.
2118	8251 Clear to send not sensed.
2119	8251 Data set ready stuck on.
2120	8251 Clear to send stuck on.
2121	8251 Hardware reset failure.
2122	8251 Software reset failure.
2123	8251 Software "error reset" failure.
2124	8251 Transmit ready did not come on.
2125	8251 Receive ready did not come on.
2126	8251 could not force "overrun" error status.
2127	Interrupt failure; no timer interrupt.
2128	Interrupt failure; transmit; replace card or planar.
2129	Interrupt failure; transmit; replace card.
2130	Interrupt failure; receive; replace card or planar.
2131	Interrupt failure; receive; replace card.
2133	Ring indicate stuck on.
2134	Receive clock stuck on.
2135	Transmit clock stuck on.
2136	Test indicate stuck on.
2137	Ring indicate stuck on.
2138	Receive clock not on.
2139	Transmit clock not on.
2140	Test indicate not on.
2141	Data set ready not on.
2142	Carrier detect not on.
2143	Clear to send not on.
2144	Data set ready stuck on.
2145	Carrier detect stuck on.
2146	Clear to send stuck on.
2147	Unexpected transmit interrupt.
2148	Unexpected receive interrupt.
2149	Transmit data did not equal receive data.
2150	8251 detected overrun error.
2151	Lost data set ready during data wrap.
2152	Receive time-out during data wrap.
22xx	**Cluster Adapter Errors**
23xx	**Plasma Monitor Adapter Errors**
24xx	**Enhanced Graphics Adapter (EGA) or Video Graphics Array (VGA) Errors**
2401	Video adapter test failure.
2402	Video display error.
2408	User indicated display attribute test failed.
2409	Video display error.
2410	Video adapter error; video port error.
2416	User indicated character set test failed.
2424	User indicated 80×25 mode failure.
2432	User indicated 40×25 mode failure.
2440	User indicated 320×200 graphics mode failure.
2448	User indicated 640×200 graphics mode failure.
2456	User indicated light-pen test failure.
2464	User indicated paging test failure.

(continues)

Table A.53 Continued

Code	Description
25xx	**Alternate Enhanced Graphics Adapter (EGA) Errors**
2501	Video adapter test failure.
2502	Video display error.
2508	User indicated display attribute test failed.
2509	Video display error.
2510	Video adapter error.
2516	User indicated character set test failed.
2524	User indicated 80×25 mode failure.
2532	User indicated 40×25 mode failure.
2540	User indicated 320×200 graphics mode failure.
2548	User indicated 640×200 graphics mode failure.
2556	User indicated light-pen test failure.
2564	User indicated paging test failure.
26xx	**XT or AT/370 370-M (Memory) and 370-P (Processor) Adapter Errors**
2601	370-M (memory) adapter error.
2655	370-M (memory) adapter error.
2657	370-M (memory) adapter error.
2668	370-M (memory) adapter error.
2672	370-M (memory) adapter error.
2673	370-P (processor) adapter error.
2674	370-P (processor) adapter error.
2677	370-P (processor) adapter error.
2680	370-P (processor) adapter error.
2681	370-M (memory) adapter error.
2682	370-P (processor) adapter error.
2694	370-P (processor) adapter error.
2697	370-P (processor) adapter error.
2698	XT or AT/370 diagnostic diskette error.
27xx	**XT or AT/370 3277-EM (Emulation) Adapter Errors**
2701	3277-EM adapter error.
2702	3277-EM adapter error.
2703	3277-EM adapter error.
28xx	**3278/79 Emulation Adapter or 3270 Connection Adapter Errors**
29xx	**Color/Graphics Printer Errors**
30xx	**Primary PC Network Adapter Errors**
3001	Processor test failure.
3002	ROM checksum test failure.
3003	Unit ID PROM test failure.
3004	RAM test failure.
3005	Host interface controller test failure.
3006	±12v test failure.
3007	Digital loopback test failure.
3008	Host detected host interface controller failure.
3009	Sync failure and no Go bit.
3010	Host interface controller test OK and no Go bit.
3011	Go bit and no command 41.
3012	Card not present.
3013	Digital failure; fall through.
3015	Analog failure.
3041	Hot carrier; not this card.
3042	Hot carrier; this card!
31xx	**Secondary PC Network Adapter Errors**
3101	Processor test failure.
3102	ROM checksum test failure.
3103	Unit ID PROM test failure.
3104	RAM test failure.
3105	Host interface controller test failure.

Code	Description
3106	±12v test failure.
3107	Digital loopback test failure.
3108	Host detected host interface controller failure.
3109	Sync failure and no Go bit.
3110	Host interface controller test OK and no Go bit.
3111	Go bit and no command 41.
3112	Card not present.
3113	Digital failure; fall through.
3115	Analog failure.
3141	Hot carrier; not this card.
3142	Hot carrier; this card!
32xx	**3270 PC or AT Display and Programmed Symbols Adapter Errors**
33xx	**Compact Printer Errors**
35xx	**Enhanced Display Station Emulation Adapter (EDSEA) Errors**
3504	Adapter connected to Twinaxial cable during off-line test.
3508	Workstation address error.
3509	Diagnostic program failure.
3540	Workstation address invalid.
3588	Adapter address switch error.
3599	Diagnostic program failure.
36xx	**General-Purpose Interface Bus (GPIB) Adapter Errors**
3601	Adapter test failure.
3602	Serial poll mode register write error.
3603	Adapter address error.
3610	Adapter listen error.
3611	Adapter talk error.
3612	Adapter control error.
3613	Adapter standby error.
3614	Adapter Asynchronous control error.
3615	Adapter Asynchronous control error.
3616	Adapter error; cannot pass control.
3617	Adapter error; cannot address to listen.
3618	Adapter error; cannot un-address to listen.
3619	Adapter error; cannot address to talk.
3620	Adapter error; cannot un-address to talk.
3621	Adapter error; cannot address to listen with extended addressing.
3622	Adapter error; cannot unaddress to listen with extended addressing.
3623	Adapter error; cannot address to talk with extended addressing.
3624	Adapter error; cannot unaddress to talk with extended addressing.
3625	Write to self error.
3626	Generate handshake error.
3627	Cannot detect "Device Clear" message error.
3628	Cannot detect "Selected Device Clear" message error.
3629	Cannot detect end with end of identify.
3630	Cannot detect end of transmission with end of identify.
3631	Cannot detect end with 0-bit end of string.
3632	Cannot detect end with 7-bit end of string.
3633	Cannot detect group execute trigger.
3634	Mode 3 addressing error.
3635	Cannot recognize undefined command.
3636	Cannot detect remote, remote changed, lockout, or lockout changed.
3637	Cannot clear remote or lockout.
3638	Cannot detect service request.
3639	Cannot conduct serial poll.
3640	Cannot conduct parallel poll.
3650	Adapter error; direct memory access (DMA) to 7210.
3651	Data error; error on direct memory access (DMA) to 7210.
3652	Adapter error; direct memory access (DMA) from 7210.
3653	Data error on direct memory access (DMA) from 7210.
3658	Uninvoked interrupt received.
3659	Cannot interrupt on address status changed.

(continues)

Table A.53 Continued

Code	Description
36xx	**General-Purpose Interface Bus (GPIB) Adapter Errors**
3660	Cannot interrupt on address status changed.
3661	Cannot interrupt on command output.
3662	Cannot interrupt on data out.
3663	Cannot interrupt on data in.
3664	Cannot interrupt on error.
3665	Cannot interrupt on device clear.
3666	Cannot interrupt on end.
3667	Cannot interrupt on device execute trigger.
3668	Cannot interrupt on address pass through.
3669	Cannot interrupt on command pass through.
3670	Cannot interrupt on remote changed.
3671	Cannot interrupt on lockout changed.
3672	Cannot interrupt on service request In.
3673	Cannot interrupt on terminal count on direct memory access to 7210.
3674	Cannot interrupt on terminal count on direct memory access from 7210.
3675	Spurious direct memory access terminal-count interrupt.
3697	Illegal direct memory access configuration setting detected.
3698	Illegal interrupt level setting detected.
37xx	**System Board SCSI Controller Error**
38xx	**Data Acquisition Adapter Errors**
3801	Adapter test failure.
3810	Timer read test failure.
3811	Timer interrupt test failure.
3812	Delay; binary input 13 test failure.
3813	Rate; binary input 13 test failure.
3814	Binary output 14; interrupt status—interrupt request test failure.
3815	Binary output 0; count-in test failure.
3816	Binary input strobe; count-out test failure.
3817	Binary output 0; binary output clear to send test failure.
3818	Binary output 1; binary input 0 test failure.
3819	Binary output 2; binary input 1 test failure.
3820	Binary output 3; binary input 2 test failure.
3821	Binary output 4; binary input 3 test failure.
3822	Binary output 5; binary input 4 test failure.
3823	Binary output 6; binary input 5 test failure.
3824	Binary output 7; binary input 6 test failure.
3825	Binary output 8; binary input 7 test failure.
3826	Binary output 9; binary input 8 test failure.
3827	Binary output 10; binary input 9 test failure.
3828	Binary output 11; binary input 10 test failure.
3829	Binary output 12; binary input 11 test failure.
3830	Binary output 13; binary input 12 test failure.
3831	Binary output 15; analog input CE test failure.
3832	Binary output strobe; binary output GATE test failure.
3833	Binary input clear to send; binary input HOLD test failure.
3834	Analog input command output; binary input 15 test failure.
3835	Counter interrupt test failure.
3836	Counter read test failure.
3837	Analog output 0 ranges test failure.
3838	Analog output 1 ranges test failure.
3839	Analog input 0 values test failure.
3840	Analog input 1 values test failure.
3841	Analog input 2 values test failure.
3842	Analog input 3 values test failure.
3843	Analog input interrupt test failure.
3844	Analog input 23 address or value test failure.
39xx	**Professional Graphics Adapter (PGA) Errors**
3901	PGA test failure.
3902	ROM1 self-test failure.

Code	Description
3903	ROM2 self-test failure.
3904	RAM self-test failure.
3905	Cold start cycle power error.
3906	Data error in communications RAM.
3907	Address error in communications RAM.
3908	Bad data reading/writing 6845-like register.
3909	Bad data in lower E0h bytes reading/writing 6845-like registers.
3910	Graphics controller display bank output latches error.
3911	Basic clock error.
3912	Command control error.
3913	Vertical sync scanner error.
3914	Horizontal sync scanner error.
3915	Intech error.
3916	Look-up table address error.
3917	Look-up table red RAM chip error.
3918	Look-up table green RAM chip error.
3919	Look-up table blue RAM chip error.
3920	Look-up table data latch error.
3921	Horizontal display error.
3922	Vertical display error.
3923	Light-pen error.
3924	Unexpected error.
3925	Emulator addressing error.
3926	Emulator data latch error.
3927	Base for error codes 3928–3930 (Emulator RAM).
3928	Emulator RAM error.
3929	Emulator RAM error.
3930	Emulator RAM error.
3931	Emulator horizontal/vertical display problem.
3932	Emulator cursor position error.
3933	Emulator attribute display problem.
3934	Emulator cursor display error.
3935	Fundamental emulation RAM problem.
3936	Emulation character set problem.
3937	Emulation graphics display error.
3938	Emulation character display problem.
3939	Emulation bank select error.
3940	Adapter RAM U2 error.
3941	Adapter RAM U4 error.
3942	Adapter RAM U6 error.
3943	Adapter RAM U8 error.
3944	Adapter RAM U10 error.
3945	Adapter RAM U1 error.
3946	Adapter RAM U3 error.
3947	Adapter RAM U5 error.
3948	Adapter RAM U7 error.
3949	Adapter RAM U9 error.
3950	Adapter RAM U12 error.
3951	Adapter RAM U14 error.
3952	Adapter RAM U16 error.
3953	Adapter RAM U18 error.
3954	Adapter RAM U20 error.
3955	Adapter RAM U11 error.
3956	Adapter RAM U13 error.
3957	Adapter RAM U15 error.
3958	Adapter RAM U17 error.
3959	Adapter RAM U19 error.
3960	Adapter RAM U22 error.
3961	Adapter RAM U24 error.
3962	Adapter RAM U26 error.
3963	Adapter RAM U28 error.
3964	Adapter RAM U30 error.
3965	Adapter RAM U21 error.

(continues)

Table A.53 Continued

Code	Description
39xx	**Professional Graphics Adapter (PGA) Errors**
3966	Adapter RAM U23 error.
3967	Adapter RAM U25 error.
3968	Adapter RAM U27 error.
3969	Adapter RAM U29 error.
3970	Adapter RAM U32 error.
3971	Adapter RAM U34 error.
3972	Adapter RAM U36 error.
3973	Adapter RAM U38 error.
3974	Adapter RAM U40 error.
3975	Adapter RAM U31 error.
3976	Adapter RAM U33 error.
3977	Adapter RAM U35 error.
3978	Adapter RAM U37 error.
3979	Adapter RAM U39 error.
3980	Graphics controller RAM timing error.
3981	Graphics controller read/write latch error.
3982	Shift register bus output latches error.
3983	Addressing error (vertical column of memory; U2 at top).
3984	Addressing error (vertical column of memory; U4 at top).
3985	Addressing error (vertical column of memory; U6 at top).
3986	Addressing error (vertical column of memory; U8 at top).
3987	Addressing error (vertical column of memory; U10 at top).
3988	Base for error codes 3989–3991 (horizontal bank latch errors).
3989	Horizontal bank latch errors.
3990	Horizontal bank latch errors.
3991	Horizontal bank latch errors.
3992	RAG/CAG graphics controller error.
3993	Multiple write modes, nibble mask errors.
3994	Row nibble (display RAM) error.
3995	Graphics controller addressing error.
44xx	**5278 Display Attachment Unit and 5279 Display Errors**
45xx	**IEEE Interface Adapter (IEEE-488) Errors**
46xx	**A Real-Time Interface Coprocessor (ARTIC) Multiport/2 Adapter Errors**
4611	ARTIC adapter error.
4612	Memory module error.
4613	Memory module error.
4630	ARTIC adapter error.
4640	Memory module error.
4641	Memory module error.
4650	ARTIC interface cable error
48xx	**Internal Modem Errors**
49xx	**Alternate Internal Modem Errors**
50xx	**PC Convertible LCD Errors**
5001	LCD display buffer failure.
5002	LCD font buffer failure.
5003	LCD controller failure.
5004	User indicated PEL/drive test failed.
5008	User indicated display attribute test failed.
5016	User indicated character set test failed.
5020	User indicated alternate character set test failure.
5024	User indicated 80×25 mode test failure.
5032	User indicated 40×25 mode test failure.
5040	User indicated 320×200 graphics test failure.
5048	User indicated 640×200 graphics test failure.
5064	User indicated paging test failure.

Code	Description
51xx	**PC Convertible Portable Printer Errors**
5101	Portable printer interface failure.
5102	Portable printer busy error.
5103	Portable printer paper or ribbon error.
5104	Portable printer time-out.
5105	User indicated print-pattern test error.
56xx	**Financial Communication System Errors**
70xx	**Phoenix BIOS/Chipset Unique Error Codes**
7000	Chipset CMOS failure.
7001	Chipset shadow RAM failure.
7002	Chipset CMOS configuration error.
71xx	**Voice Communications Adapter (VCA) Errors**
7101	Adapter test failure.
7102	Instruction or external data memory error.
7103	PC to VCA interrupt error.
7104	Internal data memory error.
7105	Direct memory access (DMA) error.
7106	Internal registers error.
7107	Interactive shared memory error.
7108	VCA to PC interrupt error.
7109	DC wrap error.
7111	External analog wrap and tone-output error.
7112	Microphone to speaker wrap error.
7114	Telephone attachment test failure.
73xx	**3 1/2-Inch External Diskette Drive Errors**
7301	Diskette drive/adapter test failure.
7306	Disk changeline failure.
7307	Diskette is write protected.
7308	Drive command error.
7310	Diskette initialization failure; track 0 bad.
7311	Drive time-out error.
7312	Controller chip (NEC) error.
7313	Direct memory access (DMA) error.
7314	Direct memory access (DMA) boundary overrun.
7315	Drive index timing error.
7316	Drive speed error.
7321	Drive seek error.
7322	Drive cyclic redundancy check (CRC) error.
7323	Sector not found error.
7324	Address mark error.
7325	Controller chip (NEC) seek error.
74xx	**IBM PS/2 Display Adapter (VGA Card) Errors**
74xx	**8514/A Display Adapter Errors**
7426	8514 display error.
7440	8514/A memory module 31 error.
7441	8514/A memory module 30 error.
7442	8514/A memory module 29 error.
7443	8514/A memory module 28 error.
7444	8514/A memory module 22 error.
7445	8514/A memory module 21 error.
7446	8514/A memory module 18 error.
7447	8514/A memory module 17 error.
7448	8514/A memory module 32 error.
7449	8514/A memory module 14 error.
7450	8514/A memory module 13 error.
7451	8514/A memory module 12 error.
7452	8514/A memory module 06 error.
7453	8514/A memory module 05 error.

(continues)

Table A.53 Continued

Code	Description
74xx	**8514/1 Display Adapter Errors**
7454	8514/A memory module 02 error.
7455	8514/A memory module 01 error.
7460	8514/A memory module 16 error.
7461	8514/A memory module 27 error.
7462	8514/A memory module 26 error.
7463	8514/A memory module 25 error.
7464	8514/A memory module 24 error.
7465	8514/A memory module 23 error.
7466	8514/A memory module 20 error.
7467	8514/A memory module 19 error.
7468	8514/A memory module 15 error.
7469	8514/A memory module 11 error.
7470	8514/A memory module 10 error.
7471	8514/A memory module 09 error.
7472	8514/A memory module 08 error.
7473	8514/A memory module 07 error.
7474	8514/A memory module 04 error.
7475	8514/A memory module 03 error.
76xx	**4216 PagePrinter Adapter Errors**
7601	Adapter test failure.
7602	Adapter error.
7603	Printer error.
7604	Printer cable error.
84xx	**PS/2 Speech Adapter Errors**
85xx	**2MB XMA Memory Adapter or XMA Adapter/A Errors**
850x	Adapter error.
851x	Adapter error.
852x	Memory module error.
8599	Unusable memory segment found.
86xx	**PS/2 Pointing Device (Mouse) Errors**
8601	Pointing device error; mouse time-out.
8602	Pointing device error; mouse interface.
8603	Pointing device or system-bus failure; mouse interrupt.
8604	Pointing device or system board error.
8611	System bus error—I/F between 8042 and TrackPoint II.
8612	TrackPoint II error.
8613	System bus error or TrackPoint II error.
89xx	**Musical Instrument Digital Interface (MIDI) Adapter Errors**
91xx	**IBM 3363 Write-Once Read Multiple (WORM) Optical Drive/Adapter Errors**
96xx	**SCSI Adapter with Cache (32-Bit) Errors**
100xx	**Multiprotocol Adapter/A Errors**
10001	Presence test failure.
10002	Card selected feedback error.
10003	Port 102h register rest failure.
10004	Port 103h register rest failure.
10006	Serial option cannot be put to sleep.
10007	Cable error.
10008	Interrupt request (IRQ) 3 error.
10009	Interrupt request (IRQ) 4 error.
10010	16550 chip register failure.
10011	Internal wrap test of 16550 chip modem control line failure.
10012	External wrap test of 16550 chip modem control line failure.
10013	16550 chip transmit error.

Code	Description
10014	16550 chip receive error.
10015	16550 chip receive error; data not equal to transmit data.
10016	16550 chip interrupt function error.
10017	16550 chip baud rate test failure.
10018	16550 chip receive external data wrap test failure.
10019	16550 chip first-in first-out (FIFO) buffer failure.
10026	8255 Port A error.
10027	8255 Port B error.
10028	8255 Port C error.
10029	8254 timer 0 error.
10030	8254 timer 1 error.
10031	8254 timer 2 error.
10032	Binary sync data set ready response to data terminal ready error.
10033	Binary sync clear to send response to ready to send error.
10034	8251 hardware reset test failed.
10035	8251 function error.
10036	8251 status error.
10037	Binary sync timer interrupt error.
10038	Binary sync transmit interrupt error.
10039	Binary sync receive interrupt error.
10040	Stray interrupt request (IRQ) 3 error.
10041	Stray interrupt request (IRQ) 4 error.
10042	Binary sync external wrap error.
10044	Binary sync data wrap error.
10045	Binary sync line status/condition error.
10046	Binary sync time-out error during data wrap test.
10050	8273 command acceptance or results ready time-out error.
10051	8273 Port A error.
10052	8273 Port B error.
10053	SDLC modem status change logic error.
10054	SDLC timer interrupt request (IRQ) 4 error.
10055	SDLC modem status change interrupt request (IRQ) 4 error.
10056	SDLC external wrap error.
10057	SDLC interrupt results error.
10058	SDLC data wrap error.
10059	SDLC transmit interrupt error.
10060	SDLC receive interrupt error.
10061	Direct memory access (DMA) channel 1 transmit error.
10062	Direct memory access (DMA) channel 1 receive error.
10063	8273 status detect failure.
10064	8273 error detect failure.
101xx	**300/1200bps Internal Modem/A Errors**
10101	Presence test failure.
10102	Card selected feedback error.
10103	Port 102h register test failure.
10106	Serial option cannot be put to sleep.
10108	Interrupt request (IRQ) 3 error.
10109	Interrupt request (IRQ) 4 error.
10110	16450 chip register failure.
10111	Internal wrap test of 16450 modem control line failure.
10113	16450 transmit error.
10114	16450 receive error.
10115	16450 receive error data not equal transmit data.
10116	16450 interrupt function error.
10117	16450 baud rate test failure.
10118	16450 receive external data wrap test failure.
10125	Modem reset result code error.
10126	Modem general result code error.
10127	Modem S registers write/read error.
10128	Modem turn echo on/off error.
10129	Modem enable/disable result codes error.
10130	Modem enable number/word result codes error.
10133	Connect results for 300 baud not received.
10134	Connect results for 1200 baud not received.

(continues)

Table A.53 Continued

Code	Description
101xx	**300/1200bps Internal Modem/A Errors**
10135	Modem fails local analog loopback test at 300 baud.
10136	Modem fails local analog loopback test at 1200 baud.
10137	Modem does not respond to escape/reset sequence.
10138	S-Register 13 does not show correct parity or number of data bits.
10139	S-Register 15 does not reflect correct bit rate.
104xx	**ESDI or MCA IDE Fixed Disk or Adapter Errors**
10450	Read/write test failed.
10451	Read verify test failed.
10452	Seek test failed.
10453	Wrong drive type indicated.
10454	Controller sector buffer test failure.
10455	Controller invalid failure.
10456	Controller diagnostic command failure.
10461	Drive format error.
10462	Controller head select error.
10463	Drive read/write sector error.
10464	Drive primary defect map unreadable.
10465	Controller; error-correction code (ECC) 8-bit error.
10466	Controller; error-correction code (ECC) 9-bit error.
10467	Drive soft seek error.
10468	Drive hard seek error.
10469	Drive soft error count exceeded.
10470	Controller attachment diagnostic error.
10471	Controller wrap mode interface error.
10472	Controller wrap mode drive select error.
10473	Read verify test errors.
10480	Seek failure; drive 0.
10481	Seek failure; drive 1.
10482	Controller transfer acknowledge error.
10483	Controller reset failure.
10484	Controller; head select 3 error.
10485	Controller; head select 2 error.
10486	Controller; head select 1 error.
10487	Controller; head select 0 error.
10488	Controller; read gate—command complete 2 error.
10489	Controller; write gate—command complete 1 error.
10490	Diagnostic area read error; drive 0.
10491	Diagnostic area read error; drive 1.
10492	Controller error, drive 1.
10493	Reset error, drive 1.
10499	Controller failure.
107xx	**5 1/4-Inch External Diskette Drive or Adapter Errors**
112xx	**SCSI Adapter (16-bit without Cache) Errors**
113xx	**System Board SCSI Adapter (16-Bit) Errors**
129xx	**Processor Complex (CPU Board) Errors**
129005	DMA error.
12901	Processor board; processor test failed.
12902	Processor board; cache test failed.
12904	Second level cache failure.
12905	Cache enable/disable errors.
12907	Cache fatal error.
12908	Cache POST program error.
12912x	Hardware failure.
12913x	Micro channel bus time-out.
12914x	Software failure.
12915x	Processor complex error.

Code	Description
12916x	Processor complex error.
12917x	Processor complex error.
12918x	Processor complex error.
12919x	Processor complex error.
12940x	Processor complex failure.
12950x	Processor complex failure.
129900	Processor complex serial-number mismatch.
149xx	**P70/P75 Plasma Display and Adapter Errors**
14901	Plasma Display Adapter failure.
14902	Plasma Display Adapter failure.
14922	Plasma display failure.
14932	External display failure.
152xx	**XGA Display Adapter/A Errors**
164xx	**120MB Internal Tape Drive Errors**
165xx	**6157 Streaming Tape Drive or Tape Attachment Adapter Errors**
16520	Streaming tape drive failure.
16540	Tape attachment adapter failure.
166xx	**Primary Token Ring Network Adapter Errors**
167xx	**Alternate Token Ring Network Adapter Errors**
180xx	**PS/2 Wizard Adapter Errors**
18001	Interrupt controller failure.
18002	Incorrect timer count.
18003	Timer interrupt failure.
18004	Sync check interrupt failure.
18005	Parity check interrupt failure.
18006	Access error interrupt failure.
18012	Bad checksum error.
18013	Micro Channel interface error.
18021	Wizard memory compare or parity error.
18022	Wizard memory address line error.
18023	Dynamic RAM controller failure.
18029	Wizard memory byte enable error.
18031	Wizard memory-expansion module memory compare or parity error.
18032	Wizard memory-expansion module address line error.
18039	Wizard memory-expansion module byte enable error.
185xx	**DBCS Japanese Display Adapter/A Errors**
194xx	**80286 Memory-Expansion Option Memory-Module Errors**
200xx	**Image Adapter/A Errors**
208xx	**Unknown SCSI Device Errors**
209xx	**SCSI Removable Disk Errors**
210xx	**SCSI Fixed Disk Errors**
210PLSC	"PLSC" codes indicate errors P = SCSI ID number (Physical Unit Number or PUN) L = Logical unit number (LUN, usually 0) S = Host Adapter slot number C = SCSI Drive capacity: A = 60M B = 80M C = 120M D = 160M E = 320M

(continues)

Table A.53 Continued

Code	Description
210xx	**SCSI Fixed Disk Errors**
	F = 400M H = 1,024M (1GB) I = 104M J = 212M U = Undetermined or Non IBM OEM Drive
211xx	**SCSI Tape Drive Errors**
212xx	**SCSI Printer Errors**
213xx	**SCSI Processor Errors**
214xx	**SCSI Write-Once Read Multiple (WORM) Drive Errors**
215xx	**SCSI CD-ROM Drive Errors**
216xx	**SCSI Scanner Errors**
217xx	**SCSI Magneto Optical Drive Errors**
218xx	**SCSI Jukebox Changer Errors**
219xx	**SCSI Communications Errors**
243xxxx	**XGA-2 Adapter/A Errors**
I998xxxx	**Dynamic Configuration Select (DCS) Information Codes**
I998001x	Bad integrity of DCS master boot record.
I988002x	Read failure of DCS master boot record.
I988003x	DCS master boot record is not compatible with the planar ID.
I988004x	DCS master boot record is not compatible with the model/submodel byte.
I988005x	Bad integrity of CMOS/NVRAM (or internal process error).
I988006x	Read failure of header/mask/configuration record.
I988007x	Bad integrity of header/mask/configuration record.
I988008x	Hard disk does not support the command to set the maximum RBA.
I988009x	DCS master boot record is older than system ROM.
I9880402	Copyright notice in E000 segment does not match the one in DCS MBR.
I9880403	DCS MBR is not compatible with the system board ID or model/submodel byte.
I99900xx	**Initial Microcode Load (IML) Error**
I999001x	Invalid disk IML record.
I999002x	Disk IML record load error.
I999003x	Disk IML record incompatible with system board.
I999004x	Disk IML record incompatible with processor/processor card.
I99900xx	**Initial Microcode Load (IML) Error**
I999005x	Disk IML not attempted.
I999006x	Disk stage II System Image load error.
I999007x	Disk stage II image checksum error.
I999008x	IML not supported on priamry disk drive.
I999009x	Disk IML record is older than ROM.
I99900x1	Invalid diskette IML record.
I99900x2	Diskette IML record load error.
I99900x3	Diskette IML record incompatible with system board.
I99900x4	Diskette IML record incompatible with processor card.
I99900x5	Diskette IML recovery prevented (valid password and CE override not set).
I99900x6	Diskette stage II image loade error.
I99900x7	Diskette stage II image checksum error.
I99900x9	Diskette IML record older than ROM.
I99903xx	**No Bootable Device, Initial Program Load (IPL) Errors**
I9990302	Invalid disk boot record, unable to read IPL boot record from disk.

Code	Description
19990303	IML System Partition boot failure.
19990304	No bootable device with ASCII console.
19990305	No bootable media found.
19990306	Invalid SCSI Device boot record.
199904xx	**IML-to-System Mismatch**
19990401	Unauthorized access (manufacturing boot request with valid password).
19990402	Missing ROM IBM Copyright notice.
19990403	IML Boot Record incompatible with system board/processor card.
199906xx	IML Errors

IBM SCSI Error Codes

With the new IBM SCSI adapter and SCSI devices comes a new set of error codes. This section contains tables describing all the known IBM SCSI Power-On Self Test (POST) and advanced diagnostics error codes. These codes can be used to determine the meaning of errors that occur on the IBM SCSI adapters and any attached SCSI devices. The error codes that occur during POST and diagnostics tests have the format shown in figure A.5.

This section shows what each part of the error code indicates.

The DDD field in figure A.5 indicates the SCSI device causing the error. Table A.54 shows the device codes.

The P field indicates the SCSI device physical unit number (PUN) or SCSI ID. This value is between 0 and 7, with the host adapter normally set to 7 and the first (bootable) SCSI hard disk set to 6.

The L field indicates the SCSI device logical unit number (LUN). For most SCSI devices, it is 0 because normally there is only a single LUN per physical unit or SCSI ID.

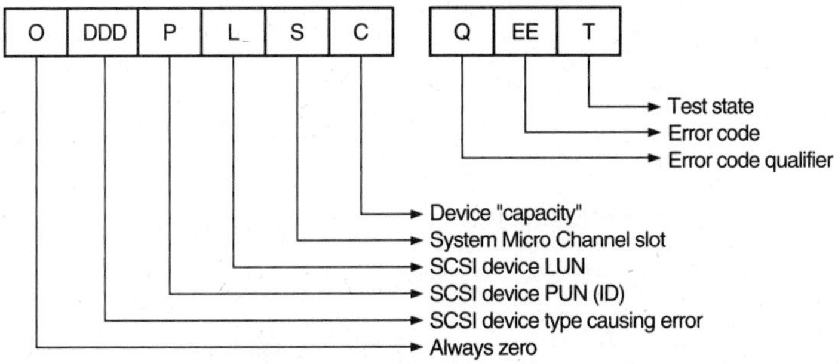

Figure A.5

IBM SCSI POST and diagnostics error code format.

The S field indicates the system Micro Channel Architecture (MCA) slot number containing the SCSI host adapter to which the device in error is connected. If S equals 0, the error is an adapter initialization error (there is no MCA slot 0). In this case, the DDD number is 096, 112, or 113, and you must use the following adapter initialization error chart to determine the error. The specific errors in this chart are indicated by the value in the L field, which immediately precedes the S field. In this case, the L does not represent the logical unit number (as it normally does), but instead shows a specific initialization error for the adapter. If S is not equal to 0, no error is on the adapter (or device attached to the adapter) in slot S. You can determine these standard errors by using the rest of the tables in this section.

Table A.54 SCSI Device Error Codes

DDDxxxx xxxx	Error
096xxxx xxxx	32-bit cached SCSI host adapter.
112xxxx xxxx	16-bit non-cached SCSI host adapter.
113xxxx xxxx	System board SCSI host adapter.
208xxxx xxxx	Unknown SCSI device type.
209xxxx xxxx	Direct access (disk) device with removable media and/or other than 512 byte blocks.
210xxxx xxxx	Direct access (disk) device with nonremovable media and 512 byte blocks (hard disk).
211xxxx xxxx	Sequential access device (magnetic tape).
212xxxx xxxx	Printer device.
213xxxx xxxx	Processor device (host to host).
214xxxx xxxx	Write-Once, Read Multiple device (optical WORM drive).
215xxxx xxxx	Read-only device (CD-ROM drive).
216xxxx xxxx	Scanner device.
217xxxx xxxx	Optical memory device (optical drive).
218xxxx xxxx	Media changer device (multiple tray CD-ROM or jukebox).
219xxxx xxxx	Communications device (LAN bridge).
DDD0LS0 0000	**SCSI Adapter Initialization Errors, Where S = 0**
DDD0100 0000	No extended CMOS setup data available. On systems with Non-Volatile RAM (NVRAM), this means that SCSI setup data was not located or the checksum did not verify. On systems without NVRAM (Model 50, for example), the setup data must be on the first non-SCSI fixed disk.
DDD0200 0000	No hard disk at PUN 6, LUN 0. (Also expect to see 161, 162, or 165 errors.)
DDD0300 0000	No space available in extended BIOS data area for SCSI data table.
DDD0400 0000	ROM modules not found on SCSI adapter.
DDD0500 0000	ROM checksum error in the second 16K portion of 32K SCSI adapter ROM space.

A value of x indicates any number or character.

The C field indicates the capacity of the device originating the error code. The capacity codes for each of the available IBM SCSI hard disk drives are listed in Table A.55. In the case of error codes from a device with no capacity (such as a SCSI adapter or printer), this field is 0.

Table A.55 SCSI Device Capacity Codes

DDDxxxC xxxx	SCSI Device Capacity
DDDxxx0 xxxx	Not a storage device
DDDxxxA xxxx	60M
DDDxxxB xxxx	80M
DDDxxxC xxxx	120M
DDDxxxD xxxx	160M
DDDxxxE xxxx	320M
DDDxxxF xxxx	400M
DDDxxxH xxxx	1,024M (1GB)
DDDxxxI xxxx	104M
DDDxxxJ xxxx	212M
DDDxxxU xxxx	Undetermined device capacity, or non-IBM OEM drive

The Q field is the error code (EE field) qualifier. Q can have a value from 0 through 7. Depending on the value of Q, the error codes take on different meanings, because Q indicates what class of error occurred or what part of the SCSI system the error is coming from. To determine the error code meaning, use one of the following tables that correspond to the value of Q you have.

The Q value defines the origin of the EE code reported. Error codes with Q = 0 or 1 are generated by the SCSI host adapter, and all error codes with Q greater than 1 are developed using information returned by the adapter or a SCSI device. If Q = 2, the EE code indicates the value returned in the Command Error field (word 8, bits 15-8) of the SCSI Command Complete Status Block (CCSB) for values indicating hardware problems (codes of 20h or greater). If Q = 3, then EE also indicates the value returned in the Command Error field (word 8, bits 15-8) of the Command Complete Status Block (CCSB), but for values indicating software problems (codes less than 20h). If Q = 4, then EE indicates the value returned in the Sense Key field (byte 2, bits 3-0) of a Sense Data Block returned to the SCSI host adapter by a device following a SCSI Request Sense command. If Q = 5, then EE indicates the value returned in the Additional Sense Code field (byte 12) of a Sense Data Block returned by a Direct Access (Disk) device following a SCSI Request Sense command. If Q = 6, then EE indicates the value returned in the Device Error Code field (word 8, bits 7-0) of the Command Complete Status Block (CCSB). If Q = 7, a device error has occurred that normally would not be considered an error, but is now considered an error based on when the code was returned—for example, a Medium Corrupted error from a device with nonremovable media.

Although IBM has a unique format for displaying SCSI error codes, almost all except the adapter-specific errors are part of the SCSI specification. Because many of these codes come from the devices attached to the SCSI bus and not the host adapter, a new code not listed here possibly could appear because some errors can be dependent on the particular device, and some devices send manufacturer-specific errors. You then can look up the error code in the manufacturer's documentation for the device to determine the meaning. The tables in this section are standard as defined in the SCSI Common Command Set (CCS) of the ANSI SCSI-1 specification. Further information is in the IBM hardware-maintenance and service manual for the IBM SCSI adapter and the various SCSI devices.

Table A.56 SCSI Host Adapter Error Codes with Q = 0

DDDxxxx QEEx	Error Code
96xxxx 001x	80188 ROM test failure.
96xxxx 002x	Local RAM test failure.
96xxxx 003x	Power protection error (terminator or fuse).
96xxxx 004x	80188 internal peripheral test failure.
96xxxx 005x	Buffer control chip test failure.
96xxxx 006x	Buffer RAM test failure.
96xxxx 007x	System interface control chip test failure.
96xxxx 008x	SCSI interface test failure.
112xxxx 001x	8032 ROM test failure.
112xxxx 002x	Local RAM test failure.
112xxxx 003x	Power protection device error (terminator or fuse).
112xxxx 004x	8032 internal peripheral test failure.
112xxxx 005x	Buffer control chip test failure.
112xxxx 006x	Undefined error condition.
112xxxx 007x	System interface control chip test failure.
112xxxx 008x	SCSI interface test failure.
113xxxx 001x	Microprocessor ROM test failure.
113xxxx 002x	Local RAM test failure.
113xxxx 003x	Power protection device error (terminator or fuse).
113xxxx 004x	Microprocessor internal peripheral test failure.
113xxxx 005x	Buffer control chip test failure.
113xxxx 006x	Undefined error condition.
113xxxx 007x	System interface control chip test failure.
113xxxx 008x	SCSI interface test failure.

Table A.57 SCSI Adapter Error Codes with Q = 1

DDDxxxx QEEx	Error Code
DDDxxxx 107x	Adapter hardware failure.
DDDxxxx 10Cx	Command completed with failure.
DDDxxxx 10Ex	Command error (invalid command or parameter).
DDDxxxx 10Fx	Software sequencing error.
DDDxxxx 180x	Time out.
DDDxxxx 181x	Adapter busy error.
DDDxxxx 182x	Unexpected interrupt presented by adapter.
DDDxxxx 183x	Adapter register test failure.
DDDxxxx 184x	Adapter reset (via basic control register) failure.
DDDxxxx 185x	Adapter buffer test failure (cached adapter only).
DDDxxxx 186x	Adapter reset count expired.
DDDxxxx 187x	Adapter registers not cleared on reset (power-on or channel reset).
DDDxxxx 188x	Card ID in adapter microcode did not match ID in POS registers.
DDDxxxx 190x	Expected device did not respond (target device not powered on).
DDDxxxx 190x	DMA arbitration level conflict (if device number is 096, 112, or 113).

Table A.58 SCSI Hardware Error Codes with Q = 2

DDDxxxx QEEx	Error Code
DDDxxxx 220x	Adapter hardware error.
DDDxxxx 221x	Global command time-out on adapter (device did not respond).
DDDxxxx 222x	Adapter DMA error.
DDDxxxx 223x	Adapter buffer defective.
DDDxxxx 224x	Command aborted by adapter.
DDDxxxx 280x	Adapter microprocessor detected error.

Table A.59 SCSI Software Error Codes with Q = 3

DDDxxxx QEEx	Error Code
DDDxxxx 301x	Invalid parameter in subsystem control block.
DDDxxxx 302x	Reserved.
DDDxxxx 303x	Command not supported.
DDDxxxx 304x	Command aborted by system.
DDDxxxx 305x	Command rejected (buffer not disabled).
DDDxxxx 306x	Command rejected (adapter diagnostic failure).
DDDxxxx 307x	Format rejected (sequence error).
DDDxxxx 308x	Assign rejected (command in progress on device).
DDDxxxx 309x	Assign rejected (device already assigned).
DDDxxxx 30Ax	Command rejected (device not assigned).
DDDxxxx 30Bx	Maximum logical block address exceeded.
DDDxxxx 30Cx	16-bit card slot address range exceeded.
DDDxxxx 313x	Invalid device for command.
DDDxxxx 3FFx	Status not returned by adapter.

Table A.60 SCSI Device Sense Key Error Codes with Q = 4

DDDxxxx QEEx	Error Code
DDDxxxx 401x	Recovered error (not considered an error condition).
DDDxxxx 402x	Device not ready.
DDDxxxx 403x	Device media error.
DDDxxxx 404x	Device hardware error.
DDDxxxx 405x	Illegal request for device.
DDDxxxx 406x	Device unit attention would not clear.
DDDxxxx 407x	Device data protect error.
DDDxxxx 408x	Device blank check error.
DDDxxxx 409x	Device vendor unique error.

DDDxxxx QEEx	Error Code
DDDxxxx 40Ax	Device copy aborted.
DDDxxxx 40Bx	Command aborted by device.
DDDxxxx 40Cx	Device search data command satisfied.
DDDxxxx 40Dx	Device volume overflow (residual data still in buffer).
DDDxxxx 40Ex	Device miscompare (source and medium data don't match).
DDDxxxx 40Fx	Reserved.

Table A.61 SCSI Device Extended Sense Error Codes with Q = 5

DDDxxxx QEEx	Error Code
DDDxxxx 501x	No index or sector signal.
DDDxxxx 502x	Seek incomplete.
DDDxxxx 503x	Write fault.
DDDxxxx 504x	Drive not ready.
DDDxxxx 505x	Drive not selected.
DDDxxxx 506x	No track 0 found.
DDDxxxx 507x	Multiple drives selected.
DDDxxxx 508x	Logical unit communication failure.
DDDxxxx 509x	Head positioning error (track following error).
DDDxxxx 50Ax	Error log overflow.
DDDxxxx 50Cx	Write error.
DDDxxxx 510x	CRC or ECC error on ID field.
DDDxxxx 511x	Unrecoverable read error.
DDDxxxx 512x	Address mark not found for ID field.
DDDxxxx 513x	Address mark not found for data field.
DDDxxxx 514x	Record not found.
DDDxxxx 515x	Seek error.
DDDxxxx 516x	Data synchronization mark error.
DDDxxxx 517x	Recovered read data with retries (without ECC).
DDDxxxx 518x	Recovered read data with ECC correction.
DDDxxxx 519x	Defect list error.
DDDxxxx 51Ax	Parameter list length overrun.
DDDxxxx 51Bx	Synchronous data transfer error.
DDDxxxx 51Cx	Primary defect list not found.
DDDxxxx 51Dx	Data miscompare during verify.
DDDxxxx 51Ex	Recovered ID read with ECC correction.
DDDxxxx 520x	Invalid command operation code.
DDDxxxx 521x	Illegal logical block address (out of range).
DDDxxxx 522x	Illegal function for device type.
DDDxxxx 524x	Invalid field in command descriptor block.
DDDxxxx 525x	Invalid logical unit number (LUN not supported).
DDDxxxx 526x	Invalid field in parameter list.
DDDxxxx 527x	Media write protected.
DDDxxxx 528x	Media changed error (ready went true).
DDDxxxx 529x	Power-on or bus device reset occurred (not an error).
DDDxxxx 52Ax	Mode select parameters changed (not an error).
DDDxxxx 52Bx	Copy command can't execute because host can't disconnect.
DDDxxxx 52Cx	Command sequence error.
DDDxxxx 52Fx	Tagged commands cleared by another initiator.
DDDxxxx 530x	Incompatible media (unknown or incompatible format).
DDDxxxx 531x	Medium format corrupted.
DDDxxxx 532x	Defect spare location unavailable.
DDDxxxx 537x	Rounded parameter error.
DDDxxxx 539x	Saving parameters not supported.
DDDxxxx 53Ax	Media not present.
DDDxxxx 53Cx	Link flag bit not supported.
DDDxxxx 53Dx	Invalid bits in identify message.
DDDxxxx 53Ex	Logical unit has not self-configured.
DDDxxxx 53Fx	Target operating conditions have changed.
DDDxxxx 540x	Device RAM failure.
DDDxxxx 541x	Data path diagnostic failure.
DDDxxxx 542x	Device power-on diagnostic failure.
DDDxxxx 543x	Device message rejected.
DDDxxxx 544x	Target device internal controller error.

(continues)

Table A.61 Continued

DDDxxxx QEEx	Error Code
DDDxxxx 545x	Select/reselect failure (device unable to reconnect).
DDDxxxx 546x	Device soft reset unsuccessful.
DDDxxxx 547x	SCSI interface parity error.
DDDxxxx 548x	Initiator detected error.
DDDxxxx 549x	Illegal command or command out of sequence error.
DDDxxxx 54Ax	SCSI command phase error.
DDDxxxx 54Bx	SCSI data phase error.
DDDxxxx 54Cx	Logical unit failed self-configuration.
DDDxxxx 54Ex	Overlapped commands attempted.
DDDxxxx 560x	Status error from second-party copy command.
DDDxxxx 588x	Not digital audio track.
DDDxxxx 589x	Not CD-ROM data track.
DDDxxxx 58Ax	Drive not in play audio state.
DDDxxxx 5F0x	Format in progress (not an error).
DDDxxxx 5F1x	Spinup in progress.

Table A.62 SCSI Command Complete Status Block Errors with Q = 6

DDDxxxx QEEx	Error Code
DDDxxxx 601x	SCSI bus reset occurred.
DDDxxxx 602x	SCSI interface fault.
DDDxxxx 610x	SCSI selection time-out (device not available).
DDDxxxx 611x	Unexpected SCSI bus free.
DDDxxxx 612x	Mandatory SCSI message rejected.
DDDxxxx 613x	Invalid SCSI phase sequence.
DDDxxxx 620x	Short length record error.

Table A.63 SCSI Device Condition Error Codes with Q = 7

DDDxxxx QEEx	Error Code
DDDxxxx 702x	Device not ready (removable media devices).
DDDxxxx 704x	Device not ready (nonremovable media devices).
DDDxxxx 728x	Media changed error would not clear.
DDDxxxx 731x	Medium format corrupted (format unit interrupted—reissue format).
DDDxxxx 7F0x	Format in progress (prior format unit command being completed).
DDDxxxx 7F1x	Spinup in progress.

Table A.64 shows the diagnostics test state codes used when a failure occurs. Position T indicates the POST or diagnostics test state in which the failure occurred.

Table A.64 SCSI Diagnostics Test State Codes

DDDxxxx xxxT	Test State Code
DDDxxxx xxx0	Not applicable for error code.
DDDxxxx xxxA	Adapter initialization.
DDDxxxx xxxB	Adapter reset.
DDDxxxx xxxC	Adapter register test.
DDDxxxx xxxD	Adapter buffer test Phase 1 (cached adapter only).
DDDxxxx xxxE	Adapter buffer test Phase 2 (cached adapter only).
DDDxxxx xxxF	Adapter buffer test Phase 3 (cached adapter only).
DDDxxxx xxxG	Adapter buffer test Phase 4 (cached adapter only).
DDDxxxx xxxH	Adapter information test state (buffer enable/size, retry enable, etc.).
DDDxxxx xxxI	Device assignment sequence.
DDDxxxx xxxJ	Device not ready (also initial unit attention clearing).
DDDxxxx xxxK	Device reset.
DDDxxxx xxxL	Device starting phase (appropriate devices only).
DDDxxxx xxxM	Device in process of starting (wait for device to become ready).
DDDxxxx xxxN	Device block size determination.

DDDxxxx xxxT	Test State Code
DDDxxxx xxxO	Device self-test.
DDDxxxx xxxP	Device single block (logical block address) read.
DDDxxxx xxxQ	Device double block (logical block address) read.
DDDxxxx xxxS	Error occurred after device testing had completed.

DOS Error Messages

Table A.65 DOS Extended Error Codes

Hex Code	Dec Code	Description
01h	1	Invalid function number
02h	2	File not found
03h	3	Path not found
04h	4	Too many open files (no handles left)
05h	5	Access denied
06h	6	Invalid handle
07h	7	Memory control blocks destroyed
08h	8	Insufficient memory
09h	9	Invalid memory block address
0Ah	10	Invalid environment
0Bh	11	Invalid format
0Ch	12	Invalid access code
0Dh	13	Invalid data
0Eh	14	Reserved
0Fh	15	Invalid drive was specified
10h	16	Attempt to write on write-protected diskette
11h	17	Not same devise
12h	18	No more files
13h	19	Attempt to write-protect diskette
14h	20	Unknown unit
15h	21	Drive not ready
16h	22	Unkown command
17h	23	Cyclic Redundancy Check (CRC) error
18h	24	Bad request structure length
19h	25	Seek error
1Ah	26	Unknown media type
1Bh	27	Sector not found
1Ch	28	Printer out of paper
1Dh	29	Write fault
1Eh	30	Read fault
1Fh	31	General failure
20h	32	Sharing violation
21h	33	Lock violation
22h	34	Invalid disk change
23h	35	FCB unavailable
24h	36	Sharing buffer overflow
25h	37	Reserved by DOS 5.0
26h	38	Unable to complete file operation
27h–31h	39–49	Reserved by DOS 5.0
32h	50	Network request not supported
33h	51	Remote computer not listening
34h	52	Duplicate name on network
35h	53	Network path not found
36h	54	Network busy
37h	55	Network device no longer exists
38h	56	NETBIOS command limit exceeded
39h	57	System error; NETBIOS error
3Ah	58	Incorrect response from network
3Bh	59	Unexpected network error
3Ch	60	Incompatible remote adapter
3Dh	61	Print queue full
3Eh	62	Note enough space for print file
3Fh	63	Print file was cancelled

(continues)

Table A.65 Continued

Hex Code	Dec Code	Description
40h	64	Network name was deleted
41h	65	Access denied
42h	66	Network device type incorrect
43h	67	Network name not found
44h	68	Network name limit exceeded
45h	69	NETBIOS session limit exceeded
46h	70	Sharing temporarily paused
47h	71	Network request not accepted
48h	72	Print or disk redirection is paused
49h–4Fh	73–79	Reserved
50h	80	File exists
51h	81	Reserved
52h	82	Cannot make directory entry
53h	83	Failure on Interrupt 24
54h	84	Too many redirections
55h	85	Duplicate redirection
56h	86	Invalid password
57h	87	Invalid parameter
58h	88	Network data fault
59h	89	Function not supported by network
5Ah	90	Required system component not installed

Table A.66 DOS Parse Error Codes

Code	Description
1	Too many parameters
2	Required parameter missing
3	Invalid switch
4	Invalid keyword
6	Parameter value not in allowed range
7	Parameter value not allowed
8	Parameter value not allowed
9	Parameter format not correct
10	Invalid parameter
11	Invalid parameter combination

IBM Technical Manuals and Updates

IBM has an extensive array of documentation available to help a system troubleshooter responsible for upgrading and repairing any system. These manuals are primarily in three categories: Guide to Operations or Quick Reference Manuals, Hardware-Maintenance Manuals, and Technical-Reference Manuals. You purchase these manuals in basic form and then buy updates that reflect changes in newer systems as they are introduced. All the manuals together with the updates presents a bewildering—and expensive—array of documentation. If you are interested in obtaining any of this documentation, this section is very useful. It explains each manual type and gives information needed for ordering this documentation, and tables describe all the available manuals and updates, including part numbers and prices.

Guide to Operations and Quick-Reference Manuals

These publications contain instructions for system operation, testing, relocation, and option installation. A diagnostics floppy disk is included, which includes the Advanced Diagnostics for most PS/2 Model 50 and higher systems.

Table A.67 Guide to Operations and Quick Reference Manual Part Numbers and Prices

Description	Part Number	Price
Model 25	75X1051	$29.75
Model 25 286	15F2179	37.75
Model 30	68X2230	56.25
Model 30 286	15F2143	44.00
Model 35 SX	84F9844	35.75
Model 40 SX	84F7765	42.50
Model L40 SX	84F7577	81.50
Model 50	68X2321	56.25
Model N51 SX	04G5107	70.75
Model 55 SX	91F8575	49.50
Model 56 SX and 56 SLC	10G6001	66.25
Model 57 SX and 57 SLC	04G3382	64.75
Model 60	68X2213	56.25
Model 65 SX	91F8622	28.75
Model 70	91F8577	50.50
Model 70 486	91F8619	57.75
Model P70 386	68X2380	17.00
Model P75 486	84F7590	39.25
Model 80	91F8580	50.50
Model 90 48	92F2685	90.25
Model 90 (Models 0H5 and 0H9 only)	41G8561	85.25
Model 90 (Models 0L9 and 0LF only)	41G8330	65.00
Model 95 486	92F2684	103.00
Model 95 (Models 0H9 and 0HF only)	41G8562	111.00
Models 95 (Model 0LF only)	41G8331	68.00
External Storage Enclosure for SCSI Devices	15F2159	15.25
FAX Concentrator Adapter/A	15F2260	31.50
Remote Program Load for Ethernet Networks	15F2292	29.00
PC Systems		
AT	6280066	$49.50
AT Model 339	6280102	80.00
PC	6322510	50.00
PC Convertible	6280629	71.50
PCjr	1502292	23.25
Portable PC	6936571	66.75
XT	6322511	50.00
XT Models 089 268 278	6280085	88.00
XT Model 286	6280147	65.00

Hardware-Maintenance Library

The Hardware-Maintenance Library consists of a two-part set of manuals, including a service manual, a reference manual, as well as possible supplements or updates.

The Hardware-Maintenance Service manuals contain all the information necessary to diagnose a failure. Maintenance-analysis procedures (MAPs), the parts catalog, and Reference Disks containing the advanced diagnostics tests are included with these manuals. The Hardware-Maintenance Reference contains product descriptions, field-replaceable unit (FRU) locations and removal procedures, and information about the diagnostics programs. To maintain an accurate library, you should add all available supplements.

Table A.68 PS/2 Hardware-Maintenance Service Manual Part Numbers and Prices

Description	Part Number	Price
PS/2 Hardware-Maintenance Service Library (includes all of the following pamphlets):	**SBOF-3988**	**N/A**
General Information	15F2189	$3.70

(continues)

Table A.68 Continued

Description	Part Number	Price
PS/2 Hardware-Maintenance Service Library (includes all of the following pamphlets):	**SBOF-3988**	**N/A**
Model 25/30	15F2191	$3.70
Model 25 SX	10G6609	2.95
Model 25 286	15F2181	5.75
Model 30 286	91F9231	2.30
Model 35 SX	10G6621	2.05
Model 40 SX	84F7767	1.80
Model L40 SX	15F2266	1.65
Model 50	15F2193	1.60
Model N51 SX	04G5112	4.55
Model 55 SX	91F8637	2.40
Model 56 SX and 56 SLC	10G6003	3.40
Model 57 SX, 57 SLC, & M57 SLC	04G3383	2.70
Model 60	84F9825	3.55
Model 65 SX	84F8549	1.70
Model 70 (includes Model 70 486)	91F8635	2.40
Model P70 386	15F2198	1.60
Model P75 486	84F7593	5.55
Model 80	84F8547	1.70
Model 90 XP 486	04G3389	2.20
Model 95 XP 486	04G3394	2.20
Option Pamphlets		
Communications Cartridge (for L40 SX)	10G5993	$1.95
External Devices Parts Catalog	64F4022	3.55
External SCSI Devices	92F1656	4.65
300/1200/2400 Internal Modem/A	68X2384	10.75
Adapter/A for Ethernet Networks	84F9863	19.50
8504 Monochrome Display	15F2241	11.00
Host Connected Keyboard Errata Sheet	92F1682	6.55

Table A.69 PS/2 Hardware-Maintenance Reference Manual Part Numbers and Prices

Description	Part Number	Price
PS/2 Hardware Maintenance Reference Library (includes all of the following manuals):	**SBOF-3989**	**N/A**
General Information Manual	64F3983	$5.95
Diagnostics for Micro Channel Systems	15F2245	6.00
Diagnostics for Non-Micro Channel Systems	64F3985	5.95
Model 25	64F3986	2.65
Model 25 SX	10G6610	2.80
Model 25 286	64F3811	2.65
Model 30	64F3987	2.65
Model 30 286	64F3988	2.65
Model 35 SX	10G6620	2.45
Model 40 SX	84F7768	5.10
Model L40 SX	15F2267	2.85
Model 50	64F3989	2.65
Model N51 SX	04G5111	5.25
Model 55 SX	15F2250	2.15
Model 56 SX	04G3295	3.55
Model 56 SX and 56 SLC	10G6002	3.55
Model 57 SX, 57 SLC, & M57 SLC	04G3384	2.95
Model 60	64F3991	2.65
Model 65 SX	64F3992	2.65
Model 70	64F3993	2.65
Model P70 386	64F3994	2.65
Model P75 486	84F8525	8.80
Model 80	84F8548	2.85

Description	Part Number	Price
Model 90 XP 486	04G3388	$2.50
Model 95 XP 486	04G3393	5.25
Options and Adapter Information	64F3996	2.65
Option Manuals		
Communications Cartridge (for L40 SX)	10G5992	$1.95
Adapter/A for Ethernet Networks	15F2290	2.20
5.25-inch Slim High Diskette Drive	15F2274	1.55
1–8MB 286 Memory	85F1672	15.75
2.88MB Diskette Drive	85F1648	6.35
FAX Concentrator Adapter/A	15F2262	3.50
External Storage Enclosure for SCSI Devices	91F9233	2.20

Table A.70 PS/2 Hardware Maintenance Library Update Part Numbers and Prices

Description	Part Number	Price
PS/2 Hardware Maintenance Library Supplements (includes HMS and HMR update and diskette):		
Model 25 SX	10G6616	$36.00
Model 25 286	15F2180	17.00
Model 35 SX	92F2735	28.50
Model 40 SX	85F1645	13.75
Model L40 SX	15F2271	38.00
Model N51 SX and N51 SLC	04G5108	33.25
Model 56 SX and 56 SLC	10G6005	28.75
Model M57 SLC	10G3340	23.00
Model 57 SX and 57 SLC	04G3385	11.25
Model P70 386	15F2149	44.00
Model 90 486	04G3391	14.50
Model 95 486	04G3396	14.50
Communications Cartridge (for L40 SX)	10G5994	27.95
400MB Hard Disk Drive	15F2233	2.00
Image Adapter/A	15F2240	36.25
2.3GB Full Height SCSI Tape Drive	91F9250	20.00
Rewritable Optical Drive	91F9234	13.25
8517 Color Display	92F2676	11.75
8518 Color Display	85F1692	25.50
Cached Processor Option	04G5106	13.00
Manual Binders and Inserts		
Empty HMS (Service) Binder	85F8542	$41.00
HMS Vinyl Insert (pkg. of 6)	84F8543	11.75
Empty HMR (Reference) Binder	01F0200	17.00

Table A.71 PC Family Hardware Maintenance Service Manual Part Numbers and Prices

Description	Part Number	Price
PC Hardware Maintenance Service (PC,XT,AT,PPC)	6280087	$244.00
Supplements to 6280087		
AT Model 339	6280139	$12.00
XT Model 286	68X2211	12.00
XT Models 089, 268, 278	6280109	12.00
PS/2 Display Adapter (VGA Card)	68X2216	37.00
PC Music Feature	75X1049	52.00
2MB Expanded Memory Adapter	74X9923	67.25
3 1/2-inch internal Floppy Disk Drive	6280159	7.05
3 1/2-inch external Floppy Disk Drive	6280111	12.25

(continues)

Table A.71 Continued

Description	Part Number	Price
Supplements to 6280087		
5 1/4-inch external Floppy Disk Drive	68X2273	$12.25
20MB Hard Disk Drive Model 25	01F0246	9.45
Empty supplement binder	1502561	9.45
Color Printer Model 5182	68X2237	63.75
Graphics and Compact Printer	6280079	43.00
PCjr	1502294	96.75
PC Convertible	6280641	101.00
Supplement to 6280641		
Speech Adapter	59X9964	$23.00

Table A.72 PC Family Hardware Maintenance Reference Manual Part Numbers and Prices

Description	Part Number	Price
PC Hardware Maintenance Reference (PC,XT,AT,PPC)	6280088	$187.00
Supplements to 6280088		
AT Model 339	6280138	$7.40
XT Model 286	68X2212	12.00
XT Models 089, 268, and 278	6280108	7.40
PS/2 Display Adapter (VGA Card)	68X2238	7.50
Color Display 8514	68X2218	7.50
3.5-Inch Internal Floppy Disk Drive	6280160	7.40
20MB Hard Disk Drive Model 25	01F0244	4.30
Empty supplement binder	01F0200	21.00

Technical-Reference Library

The publications listed in the following table provide system-specific hardware and software interface information for the IBM PC and PS/2 products. They are intended for developers who provide hardware and software products to operate with these systems. The library is divided into system, options and adapters, and BIOS interface publications.

Table A.73 PC and AT-Bus System Technical Reference Manual Part Numbers and Prices

Description	Part Number	Price
Hardware Interface Technical Reference AT-Bus Systems:	85F1646	$63.00
Updates to 85F1646		
PS/2 Model 25 SX	10G6457	$10.60
PS/2 Models 35 and 40	41G2950	10.60
Keyboard/Auxiliary Device and AT-Bus Architecture	41G5096	10.75
PS/2 Model L40 SX (Laptop)	15F2270	59.00
PS/2 Model 25	75X1055	35.75
Supplement to 75X1055		
20MB Hard Disk Drive	01F0245	$4.20
PS/2 Model 30	68X2201	94.25
PS/2 Model 30 286	01F0237	30.25

Description	Part Number	Price
Supplements to 01F0237		
PS/2 Model 25 286	15F2182	$20.00
PC	6322507	37.50
PC AT	6280070	131.00
Supplements to 6280070		
PC AT Model 339	6280099	$62.00
PC XT Model 286	68X2210	62.75
PC XT and Portable PC	6280089	62.00
PC Convertible	6280648	94.25
Supplements to 6280648		
Speech Adapter	59X9965	$23.00
256KB Memory and Enhanced Modem	75X1035	5.20
PCjr	1502293	51.25

Hardware Interface Technical Reference. These publications provide interface and design information for the system units. Information is included for the system board, math coprocessor, power supply, video subsystem, keyboard, instruction sets, and other features of the system.

Table A.74 MCA-Bus Hardware Interface Technical Reference Manual Part Numbers and Prices

Description	Part Number	Price
PS/2 Hardware Interface Technical Reference Manuals		
System Specific Information Technical Reference	84F9807	$75.00
Updates to 84F9807		
Models 90, 95 and Model 57	04G3280	$20.75
Models 56 SX and 56 SLC	41G2912	10.00
Supplements to 84F9807		
Model N51 SX	04G5120	$16.75
Model P75 486	84F7592	35.50
Architectures Technical Reference	84F9808	55.00
Update to 84F9808		
Micro Channel Architecture and Setup	04G3282	$16.00
Supplements to 84F9808		
Subsystem Control Block Architecture	85F1678	$15.00
Common Interfaces Technical Reference	84F9808	75.00
Update to 84F9809		
Floppy Controller, Keyboard, Keyboard/Auxiliary Device Controller, Serial Port Controller, Video Subsystem, and SCSI	04G3281	$21.75
Supplement to 84F9809		
Model P70 386	68X2377	$15.50

BIOS Interface Technical Reference. This publication provides basic input-output system (BIOS) interface information. It is intended for developers of hardware or software products that operate with the IBM PC and PS/2 products.

Table A.75 BIOS Interface Technical Reference Manual Part Numbers and Prices

Description	Part Number	Price
BIOS Interface Technical Reference (4th edition)	04G3283	$55.00

Options and Adapters Technical Reference. These publications provide interface and design information for the options and adapters available for various systems. This information includes a hardware description, programming considerations, interface specifications, and BIOS information (where applicable).

Table A.76 Options and Adapters Technical Reference Manual Part Numbers and Prices

Description	Part Number	Price
Options and Adapters Technical Reference, includes:	6322509	$156.00
Asynchronous Communications Adapter		
Bisynchronous Communications Adapter		
Cluster Adapter		
Color Display		
Color/Graphics Monitor Adapter		
Color, Compact, and Graphics Printers		
Expansion Unit		
Hard Disk Drive Adapter		
Game Control Adapter		
Monochrome Display		
Monochrome/Printer Adapter		
Printer Adapter		
SDLC Adapter		
Slimline Floppy Disk Drive		
10M Hard Disk Drive		
5.25-Inch Floppy Disk Drive and Adapter		
64/256K Memory Option		
Engineering/Scientific Adapters, includes:	6280133	42.25
Data Acquisition and Control Adapter (DAC)		
DAC Distribution Panel		
General Purpose Interface Bus Adapter		
Professional Graphics Controller		
Professional Graphics Display		
Personal Computer AT, includes:	6280134	16.00
Double-Sided Floppy Disk Drive		
Hard Disk and Floppy Disk Drive Adapter		
High-Capacity Floppy Disk Drive		
Serial/Parallel Adapter		
128K Memory Expansion Option		
20MB Hard Disk Drive		
512K Memory Expansion Option		
Communications		
Dual Async Adapter/A (Second Edition)	68X2315	$7.50
Multiprotocol Adapter/A (Second Edition)	68X2316	14.75
300/1200 Internal Modem/A	68X2275	7.50
300/1200/2400 Internal Modem/A	68X2378	6.40
Displays		
PS/2 Color Display 8514	68X2214	$7.50
PS/2 Display Adapter (VGA Card)	68X2251	12.25
PS/2 Display Adapter 8514/A	68X2248	12.25
PS/2 Displays 8503, 8512, and 8513	68X2206	7.50
EGA, EGA Display, and EGA Memory Expansion Card	6280131	12.00

Description	Part Number	Price
Floppy Disk Drives and Adapters		
3.5-Inch External Drive	59X9945	$6.50
3.5-Inch External Drive Adapter	59X9946	6.50
3.5-Inch 720K/1.44M/2.88M Drive	15F2258	11.50
5.25-Inch External Drive (360K)	68X2272	12.25
5.25-Inch External Drive (1.2MB)	68X2348	11.75
5.25-Inch Internal Drive (1.2MB)	68X2350	11.75
5.25-Inch Drive Adapter (1.2MB)	68X2349	11.75
Floppy Disk Drive Half Height (XT,AT)	6280093	7.40
Hard Disk Drive and Adapters		
Hard Disk Drive Adapter/A	68X2226	$14.75
Hard Disk Drive Adapter/A, ESDI	68X2234	14.75
Hard Disk/Floppy Disk Adapter (for XT Model 286)	68X2215	7.50
20MB Drive (XT-089,-278,-286)	68X2208	8.75
20MB Adapter (XT-089,-268,-278)	6280092	7.40
20MB Drive and Adapter (Model 25)	01F0247	3.45
3.5-Inch 20MB Drive (Model 30)	68X2205	7.50
3.5-Inch 20MB Drive (Model 50)	68X2219	12.25
30MB Drive (AT)	68X2310	23.00
30MB Drive (Model 50-031)	68X2324	12.25
20/30/45MB Drive (Model 25 and 30)	92F1655	13.00
40MB/80MB Drive	91F9230	17.25
44MB Drive (Second Edition)	68X2317	7.50
60MB Adapter (50-021 and 50-031)	68X2343	4.95
60/120MB Drives (Models 50 and 70)	68X2314	11.00
70/115/314MB Drives	68X2236	7.50
Other Storage Devices and Adapters		
CD-ROM Drive	15F2134	$13.00
Rewritable Optical Drive	64F1513	17.50
2.3GB SCSI Tape Drive	84F9801	19.75
Micro Channel SCSI Adapter	68X2397	16.25
Micro Channel SCSI Adapter w/Cache	68X2365	17.25
FAX Concentrator Adapter/A Device Driver Reference	15F2263	18.00
FAX Concentrator Adapter/A Extended Device Driver Ref.	15F2276	30.00
Internal Data/FAX Modem for the L40 SX	15F2268	14.00
Memory		
128/640K Memory Adapter	1502544	$7.40
256K Memory Expansion	6280132	12.00
512KB/2MB Memory Adapter	6183075	7.40
2MB Expanded Memory Adapter	75X1086	10.75
Expanded Memory Adapter/A (0–8MB)	01F0228	7.80
80286 Memory Expansion Option	68X2227	7.50
80286 Memory Expansion Option 2–8MB	68X2356	7.60
80386 Memory Expansion Option 2–6MB	68X2257	12.25
80386 Memory Expansion Option 2–8MB	68X2339	14.75
Other		
PS/2 Speech Adapter	68X2207	$15.75
Voice Communications Adapter	55X8864	7.40
PS/2 Mouse	68X2229	7.50
PC Music Feature	75X1048	21.75
Empty Options and Adapters Binder	6280115	9.30
Software Reference Manuals		
Basic Reference Version 3.30	6280189	$56.00
DOS Technical Reference Version 5.02	53G1686	85.00

Ordering Information

IBM technical and service publications can be ordered by calling toll-free, 1-800-IBM-PCTB (1-800-426-7282), Monday through Friday, 8 a.m. to 8 p.m. Eastern time. In Canada, call toll-free, 1-800-465-1234, Monday through Friday, from 8:30 a.m. to 4:30 p.m. Eastern time. In British Columbia, call toll-free, 112-800-465-1234. In Alaska, call 1-414-633-8108.

When you order by telephone, you can use a credit card. You also may call to request additional copies of the Technical Directory (catalog) or to inquire about the availability of technical information on newly announced products that may not be listed here.

Appendix B

Vendor List

One of the most frustrating things about supporting PCs is finding a specific adapter board, part, driver program, or whatever you need to make a system work. If you are supporting or installing products, you will often need access to technical support or documentation for products you may not have purchased yourself. Over the years I have compiled a list of companies whose products are popular or I have found to work exceptionally well. I use these contacts regularly to provide information and components to enable me to support PC systems effectively.

Many of these companies have been mentioned in this book, but others not specifically mentioned have been added here. These companies carry many computer products you often will have contact with, or that I simply recommend. I have tried to list as many vendors as possible that are important in day-to-day work with PC systems. These vendors can supply documentation for components you have, provide parts and service, and be used as a source for new equipment and even software. This list is as up-to-date as possible, but companies move or go out of business all the time. If you find any information in this list that no longer is accurate, please call me or leave me a message on CompuServe. My address, phone number, and CIS ID are under the listing for Mueller Technical Research.

Many of the companies listed also provide support via electronic Bulletin Board Systems (BBSs). Ward Christensen (creator of the XModem protocol) and Randy Seuss created the first Computerized Bulletin Board System (CBBS) system that went on-line on February 16, 1978, and is still running today using the original software! You can call Ward and Randy's CBBS at (312)545-8086. Since that first BBS came online, BBS systems have proliferated throughout the world. While originally exclusively the domain of computer enthusiasts, today many companies use BBS systems to provide a high level of technical support. Through a company-run BBS you often can receive detailed technical support on that company's products, as well as download product literature and reference materials. I usually find that the level of support I can obtain through a BBS is superior to traditional phone support, especially since I don't have to wait on hold!

With each company listing, I have included both standard phone numbers as well as 800 numbers where possible, so U.S. and international readers can easily contact these companies. Also included are fax and Bulletin Board System (BBS) numbers where available. I have not included any communications parameter settings, but virtually all BBS systems work with at least 2400 bps (V.22bis), 8 data bits, no parity, and 1 stop bit. Many of these systems also support faster communications rates up to 14,400 bps (V.32bis), or even 28,800 bps (V.34).

Some companies run a FAXBack system, an automated system through which you can request product and technical information to be sent directly to your own fax machine. FAXBack systems are an excellent way to get immediate documentation or technical support to solve tough problems.

Many of these companies also provide online support and services through the CompuServe Information System (CIS). You will find many major hardware and software companies on CIS; however, most of these same companies also run standard BBS systems as well. If you want to access CIS, you can contact them via a voice line and request a startup kit.

Some companies are now providing access through the Internet, including the World Wide Web (WWW). I have tried to include Net and WWW addresses for any companies that offer this access. Companies are adding this type of access rapidly now, so many companies may have added Internet access after this book has been printed. If you discover any such information that I have not included, please send me e-mail detailing what you have found!

If you discover that a company on this list is out of business, or they have moved or changed phone numbers, etc., please leave me an e-mail note describing what you have found. This way I can keep the list as up to date as possible.

Finally, each listing includes a short description of the products or services the company provides. I use this vendor list constantly myself; I hope you find this list as useful as I do!

3Com Corp.
5400 Bayfront Plaza
PO Box 58145
Santa Clara, CA 95052-8145
(408)764-5000
(800)638-3266
(408)764-5001 FAX

WWW.3com.com/

Manufactures network adapters, servers, and other networking equipment.

3M Data Storage Products Division
3M Center Building #223-5N-01
St. Paul, MN 55144
(612)733-1110
(800)328-9438 Technical Info
(800)854-0033 Sales/Delivery Info

www.homepagemmm.3m
datastorage@mmm.com

Manufactures magnetic disk and tape media. DC-600 and DC-2000 media are standards for tape backup data cartridges.

Aavid Thermal Technologies, Inc.
One Kool Path
PO Box 400
Laconia, NH 03247-0400
(603)528-3400
(603)528-1478 FAX

www.aavid.com

Manufactures a line of heat sinks and thermal management materials.

ACC Microelectronics Corp.
2500 Augustine Drive
Santa Clara, CA 95054
(408)480-0622
(408)980-0626 FAX

Manufactures PC motherboard chipsets and other logic.

Accurite Technologies, Inc.
231 Charcot Avenue
San Jose, CA 95131
(408)433-1980
(408)433-1716 FAX

sales@accurite.com
www.accurite.com

Manufactures floppy drive diagnostic products as well as PCMCIA diagnostic products and PCMCIA floppy drive subsystems. Floppy drive diagnostic products include the Accurite Drive Probe floppy disk diagnostics program as well as HRD, DDD, and ADD industry standard test disks. PCMCIA products include the PC ExtenderCard, the PC ReportCard (a PCMCIA diagnostic card), the HeadstartCard (a PCMCIA developers kit), and the Travel Floppy 144 (a PCMCIA interfaced floppy drive subsystem).

Acer America Corp.
2641 Orchard Parkway
San Jose, CA 95134-2073
(408)432-6200
(800)733-2237
(800)445-6495 Technical Support
(408)922-2933 FAX
(800)223-7763 Sales
(800)637-7000 Service Parts
(408)428-0140 BBS

TSUP@SMTPLINK.ACER.COM

Manufactures desktop and notebook PC compatible systems, as well as monitors and printers.

Acer Laboratories Inc. (Ali)
Taipei 105, Taiwan ROC
(886)02-5451588

Pacific Technology Group
4701 Patrick Henry Drive
Suite 2101
Santa Clara, CA 95054
(408)764-0644
(408)496-6142 FAX
(408)492-0107 BBS

Manufactures chipsets including PC motherboard, super I/O, disk controller, and others. They make the Aladdin series chips for Pentium systems.

Acme Electric/Safe Power
9962 Route 446
Cuba, NY 14727
(716)968-2400
(800)325-5848 Sales
(716)968-3948 FAX

Manufactures uninterruptible power supplies (UPS) systems and power conditioners.

Adaptec
691 S. Milpitas Boulevard
Milpitas, CA 95035
(408)945-8600
(408)945-2550 Technical Support
(800)959-7274 Technical Support
(800)934-2766 Literature
(408)262-2533 FAX
(408)957-7150 FAXBack
(408)945-7727 BBS

WWW.Adaptec.COM

Manufactures a variety of excellent hard disk controllers and SCSI host adapters. Their SCSI host adapters have become a de facto standard and have an enormous amount of third-party support. Adaptec bought Trantor Systems, Ltd. company, and now manufactures the MiniSCSI Parallel Port SCSI adapters, including hard disk and CD-ROM drivers for a variety of devices. They recently acquired Future Domain, as well.

Addison-Wesley Publishing Co., Inc.
One Jacob Way
Reading, MA 01867
(617)944-3700
(617)944-2911 Technical Support
(617)944-9338 FAX

www.aw.com

Publishes technical publications and books.

Adobe Systems, Inc.
411 First Avenue South
Seattle, WA 98104
(206)470-7000
(800)833-6687 Technical Support
(206)470-7138 FAX
(206)470-7245 Sales

www.adobe.com

Manufactures (and created) the PostScript language and a variety of graphics software.

ADP Hollander Company
14800 28th Avenue North
Suite 190
Plymouth, MN 55447
(800)825-0644
(612)553-0270 FAX

Publishes automotive parts interchange manuals.

Advanced Digital Information Corporation
10201 Willows Road
Redmond, WA 98052
(206)881-8004
(800)336-1233
(206)881-2296 FAX
(206)883-3211 BBS

www.adic.com

Manufactures high-capacity tape-backup subsystems.

Advanced Integration Research (AIR)
2188 Del Franco Street
San Jose, CA 95131
(408)428-0800
(408)428-0950 FAX
(408)428-1735 BBS

www.airwebs.com

Manufactures a line of PC-compatible Pentium class motherboards.

Advanced Logic Research (ALR)
9401 Jeronimo Street
Irvine, CA 92718
(714)581-6770
(800)444-4257
(714)581-9240 FAX
(714)458-0532 Technical Support
(714)458-6834 BBS

www.alr.com

Manufactures PC compatibles featuring ISA, EISA, and MCA buses.

Advanced Micro Devices (AMD)
One AMD Place
Sunnyvale, CA 94088-3453
(408)732-2400
(800)222-9323 Tech Support
(408)749-5703 Tech Support
(408)749-6555 Internet HOTLINE
(408)749-4753 FAX

www.amd.com

Manufactures Intel-compatible chips and math coprocessors. They have high-end 486 processors as well as a Pentium class chip called the K5.

Advanced Personal Systems
105 Sierra Way
Suite 418
Milpitas, CA 95035
(408)298-3703

Manufactures the excellent SYSCHK diagnostics program, which provides valuable information about devices installed in your system.

Aeronics, Inc.
12741 Research Boulevard
Suite #500
Austin, TX 78759
(512)258-2303
(512)258-4392 FAX

Manufactures the highest quality active and forced perfect terminators for use in SCSI-bus systems. They are known for solving problems with longer distances or multiple-SCSI devices.

AIWA America, Inc. Computer Systems Division
800 Corporate Drive
Mahwah, NJ 07430
(800)321-AIWA ext.3606
(201)512-3606
(201)512-3704 FAX
(407)241-2929 BBS

www.aiwa.com

Markets and sells mass storage solutions for network systems and personal workstations, including an impressive line of fault-tolerant RAID subsystems and tape backup devices.

Alaris
47338 Fremont Boulevard
Fremont, CA 94538
(510)770-5700
(510)770-5759 FAX
(510)770-5765 BBS
(510)770-5766 Technical Support
(800)317-2348 Sales

www.alaris.com

Alaris designs and manufactures a line of video cards and computer systems, including QuickVideo (which allows you to fit up to 60 seconds of high impact video on a single 1.44 floppy with QuickVideo capture card) and Matinee Pro (a high performance PCI graphics adapter/full motion video).

Aldus Corporation/ Adobe Systems
411 1st Avenue South
Seattle, WA 98104
(206)470-7000

Manufactures PageMaker desktop publishing software and a variety of other graphical programs.

Alliance Research/ ORA Electronics
9410 Owensmouth Avenue
Chatsworth, CA 91311
(818)772-2700
(800)431-8124 Tech Support
(800)877-7448 ext. 438 Customer Service
(818)718-8667 FAX Sales

www.orausa.com

Manufactures a complete line of computer accessories and peripheral products.

AllMicro, Inc.
18820 US Highway 19 N
Suite 215
Clearwater, FL 34624
(813)539-7283
(800)653-4933 Sales
(813)535-9042 BBS
(813)531-0200 FAX

www.allmicro.com

Manufacturer and distributor of the Rescue data recovery software, the Post Plus, Discovery Card, Alert Card, and other various hardware and software diagnostic utilities and troubleshooting tools.

Alloy Computer Products
25 Polter Road
Littleton, MA 01460
(508)486-0001
(508)486-3755 FAX
(508)486-4044 BBS

Manufactures tape-backup subsystems.

ALPS Electric
3553 N. First Street
San Jose, CA 95134

(408)432-6000
(800)950-ALPS (2577) Sales
(800)449-ALPS (2577) Tech Support
(800)825-ALPS (2577) Customer Service
(408)432-6035 FAX
(800)825-1445 FAX

www.alpsusa.com

Manufactures high-quality keyboards and keyboard switches. They have an excellent mechanical keyswitch design with a quality tactile feedback. Also makes printers, floppy drives, mice, and keypads.

Altex Electronics, Inc.
11342 IH 35 North
San Antonio, TX 78233
(800)531-5369
(210)637-3264 FAX

altex2@dcci.com

Supplies mail order computer/electronics parts.

Amdek Corporation
3471 N. First Street
San Jose, CA 95134
(408)473-1200
(800)722-WYSE (9973)
(408)473-1972 FAX Sales

www.wyse.com

Division of Wyse Technology that manufactures monitors.

America Online
8619 Westwood Center Drive
Vienna, VA 22182
(703)448-8700
(703)918-1509

Provides a very popular online service that allows access to its own network as well as the Internet.

American Megatrends, Inc. (AMI)
6145-F Northbelt Parkway
Norcross, GA 30071
(770)263-8181
(800)828-9264
(770)246-8780 BBS

www.megatrends.com

Manufactures the most popular IBM-compatible BIOS, excellent ISA, EISA, VL-Bus, and PCI local bus motherboards, and diagnostic software such as AMIDIAG, SCSI DIAG, and Remote.

American National Standards Institute (ANSI)
11 West 42nd Street
13th Floor
New York, NY 10036
(212)642-4900
(212)398-0023 FAX
(212)302-1286 FAX Ordering/Pricing

www.ansi.org

ANSI committees set standards throughout the computer industry. Copies of any ANSI-approved standard can be ordered here.

American Power Conversion (APC)
PO Box 278
132 Fairgrounds Road
West Kingston, RI 02892
(800)800-4APC Customer Support
(401)789-5735
(401)789-3710 FAX

www.apcc.com

Manufactures a line of power protection equipment.

Ameriquest Technology
3 Imperial Promenade
Santa Ana, CA 92707
(714)437-0099
(714)445-5370 FAX
(800)555-1771 Tech Support

www.cmsemh.com

Division of Ameriquest that distributes a variety of system and peripheral products, and specializes in hard disk drives.

AMP, Inc.
AMP Building
PO Box 3608
Harrisburg, PA 17105
(717)564-0100
(800)522-6752 Product Info
(717)986-7605 FAX Customer Service

www.amp.com

Manufactures a variety of computer connectors, sockets, and cables used by many OEMs. They also offer 5v to 3.3v adapters for DX4 processors.

Andromeda Research
PO Box 222
Milford, OH 45150
(513)831-9708
(513)831-7562 FAX

Manufactures an excellent EPROM programmer that runs from a PC parallel port. The device can program up to 4M EPROMS and includes software for menu driven operation on IBM-compatible systems.

Annabooks
11838 Bernardo Plaza Court
Suite 102
San Diego, CA 92128-2417
(619)673-0870

(800)462-1042
(619)673-1432 FAX

www.annabooks.com

Publishes and sells an excellent line of technical books and information on PC hardware and software design. Teaches workshops on PCI, Cardbus, and USB design.

Anthem Technology Systems (ATS)
1160 Ridder Park Drive
San Jose, CA 95131
(408)453-1200
(800)359-3580
(800)359-9877 FAX

A large distributor of Hewlett-Packard DAT tape and hard disk drives. They also distribute other hard disk and storage products.

Anvil Cases
15650 Salt Lake Avenue
Industry, CA 91745
(818)968-4100
(800)359-2684
(818)968-1703 FAX

Manufactures heavy-duty equipment cases.

Apple Computer, Inc.
1 Infinite Loop
Cupertino, CA 95014
(408)996-1010
(800)538-9696
(612)919-2976 FAX

@applelink.apple.com

Manufactures a line of Apple-compatible systems, peripherals, and software.

Apricot Computers, Ltd.
3500 Parkside
Birmingham Business Park
Birmingham, B37 7YS
England
(021)717 7171
(021)717 7799 FAX

Manufactures a popular line of PC-compatible systems sold primarily in Europe. Acquired by Mitsubishi Electric in 1990.

Arco Electronics, Inc.
2750 N. 29th Avenue
Suite 316
Hollywood, FL 33020
(305)925-2688
(305)925-2889 FAX
(305)925-2791 BBS

arco@arcoid.com

Manufactures a complete line of Micro Channel ATA IDE adapters used to upgrade IBM PS/2 systems.

Arrow Electronics, Inc.
25 Hub Drive
Melville, NY 11747
(516)391-1300
(800)777-2776
(516)391-1640 FAX

bmcnally@arrow.e-mail.com —Director of customer marketing

Systems and peripheral distributor.

Arrowfield International, Inc.
2822-C Walnut Avenue
Tustin, CA 92780
(800)227-9628
(714)669-0101
(714)669-0526 FAX

arowfld@ix.netcom.com

Manufactures an incredible array of disk drive brackets, rails, slides, cable adapters, bezels, cabinets, and complete drive upgrade and repair assemblies for IBM, Compaq, and IBM-compatible systems.

Association of Shareware Professionals (ASP)
545 Grover Road
Muskegan, MI 49442
(616)788-5131
(616)788-2765 FAX

www.asp-shareware.org

The ASP shareware marketing association sets standards for shareware products and provides an ombudsman for disputes between users and authors as well as marketing information for shareware authors.

AST Research, Inc.
16215 Alton Parkway
Irvine, CA 92718-9658
(714)727-4141
(800)876-4278
(714)727-9355 FAX
(817)230-6850 BBS

www.ast.com

Manufactures an extensive line of adapter boards and peripherals for IBM and compatible computers, as well as a line of IBM-compatible systems.

Astec America Inc.
6339 Paseo Del Largo
Carlsbad, CA 92009
(619)757-1880
(619)930-4739 FAX

www.astec.com

Manufactures high-end power supplies for PC systems as well as many other applications. Astec power supplies are used as OEM equipment in many of the top manufacturers' systems, including IBM and others.

Asus Computer International (ASUStek)
721 Charcot Avenue
San Jose, CA 95013
(408)474-0567
(408)474-0568 FAX

asustek.asus.com.tw

Manufactures a line of 486 and Pentium class PC-compatible motherboards.

AT&T National Parts Sales Center/Lucent Technologies
7424 Scott Hamilton Drive
Little Rock, AR 72209
(800)222-7278
(800)628-2888 Tech Support
(800)543-9935 Computer Software
(800)527-4360 FAX

Supplies parts and components for AT&T computer systems. Call and ask for the free AT&T parts catalog.

ATI Technologies, Inc.
33 Commerce Valley Drive East
Thornhill, ONT L3T7N6
CANADA
(905)882-2600
(905)882-2626 Technical Support
(905)882-2620 FAX
(905)764-9404 BBS

www.atitech.ca

Manufactures a popular line of high-performance PC video adapters and chipsets.

Autodesk, Inc.
111 McInnis Parkway
San Rasael, CA 94903
(800)445-5415 Product Info
(415)507-5000
(415)507-5100 FAX

www.autodesk.com

Manufactures AutoCAD software.

Autotime Corp.
6605 S.W. Macadam
Portland, OR 97201
(503)452-8577
(503)452-8495

info@autotime.com

Manufactures the Hypercable, which transmits high-speed parallel data up to 200 feet. The new bidirectional cable supports parallel-ported CD-ROM and tape backup peripherals. They also convert DIP chips to SIMMs and sell 30-pin to 72-pin SIMM adapters.

Award Software International, Inc.
777 E. Middlefield Road
Mountain View, CA 94043
(415)968-4433
(415)968-0274 FAX
(415)968-0249 BBS

www.award.com

Manufactures a line of IBM-compatible ROM BIOS software.

AZ-COM, Inc.
3343 Vincent Road
Suite D
Pleasant Hills, CA 94523
(510)254-5400
(510)947-1900 FAX

az-com.com

Manufactures a complete line of Bus-Extender cards for ISA, EISA, MCA, VL-Bus, PCI, and others. These extenders allow you to easily insert and remove adapter cards for testing with the power on.

Belden Wire and Cable
PO Box 1980
Richmond, IN 47375
(317)983-5200
(800)235-3362
(800)235-3361 Sales
(317)983-5656 FAX Sales

belden.e-mail.com

Manufactures cable and wire products.

Berkshire Products
PO Box 1015
Suwanee, GA 30174
(770)271-0088
(770)932-0082 FAX

www.berkprod.com

Manufactures the Serial Watchdog and PC Watchdog system monitor including an optional temperature alarm. This board can automatically restart a server or other system that has locked up.

Best Power Technology, Inc.
PO Box 280
Necedah, WI 54646
(608)565-7200
(800)356-5794
(608)565-2221 FAX

bestpower.com

Manufactures an excellent line of computer power protection equipment from high-end ferroresonent UPS systems to line conditioners and standby power protection systems.

Bitstream, Inc.
215 First Street
Cambridge, MA 02142
(617)497-6222
(800)522-3668
(617)868-0784 FAX

sales@bitstream.com—Information
www.bitstream.com

Manufactures fonts and font software.

Black Box Corporation
PO Box 12800
Pittsburgh, PA 15241
(412)746-5530
(412)746-0746 FAX
(800)321-0746 FAX Ordering

info@blackbox.com
www.blackbox.com.—reference materials

Manufactures and distributes a variety of communications products, including network adapters, cables, and connectors for a variety of applications.

Boca Research, Inc.
1377 Clint Moore
Boca Raton, FL 33487
(407)997-6227
(407)241-8088 Technical Support
(407)994-5848 FAX
(407)241-1601 BBS

Manufactures a low-cost line of adapter card products for IBM compatibles. Recently acquired Hayes, and now carries the Hayes modem line.

Borland International
100 Borland Way
Scotts Valley, CA 95066-3249
(408)431-1000
(800)331-0877
(800)523-7070 Technical Support
(800)822-4269 Technical FAX
(408)431-5096 BBS

www.borland.com

Software manufacturer that features Turbo language products, Paradox, as well as dBASE V.

Bose Corp.
The Mountain
Framingham, MA 01701
(508)879-7330
(508)879-1157 FAX
Manufacturing

Manufactures speakers for multimedia applications.

Boston Computer Exchange
55 Temple Place
Boston, MA 02111
(617)542-4414
(617)542-8849 FAX

A broker for used IBM and compatible computers.

Brooktree Corp.
9868 Scanton Road
San Diego, CA 92121-3707
(619)452-7580
(619)452-2104 FAX
(800)228-2777

www.brooktree.com

Manufactures a line of digital to analog converter (DAC) chips, as well as multimedia chipsets.

Buerg, Vernon D.
850 Petaluma Boulevard North
Petaluma, CA 94952
(707)778-1811
(707)769-5479 FAX
(707)778-8944 BBS
(707)778-8936 BBS

www.buerg.com

Manufactures an excellent line of utility programs, including the popular LIST program. Buerg Software is distributed through BBSs and CompuServe.

Byte Information Exchange (BIX)
1030 Massachusetts Avenue
Cambridge, MA 02138
(800)695-4775
(617)491-6642 FAX

www.bix.com
info@bix.com

An on-line computer information and messaging system.

Byte Magazine/ McGraw Hill
One Phoenix Mill Lane
Peterborough, NH 03458
(603)924-9281
(603)924-7507 Customer Service
(617)861-9764 BBS

editors@bix.com

A monthly magazine covering all lines of microcomputers.

Byte Runner Technologies
406 Monitor Lane
Knoxville, TN 37922
(800)274-7897
(615)966-3667
(615)675-3458 FAX

Carries a line of high performance I/O cards featuring FIFO (16550 type) serial port UART chips, EPP/ECP parallel ports, high speed floppy (1Mb/sec). They also carry adapters that allow any IRQ setting (including IRQs 9-15) to prevent conflicts with other existing ports.

Cables To Go
1501 Webster Street
Dayton, OH 45404

(800)826-7904
(513)224-8646
(800)331-2841 FAX

Manufactures a variety of cable, connector, and switch products.

CAIG Laboratories
16744 W. Bernardo Drive
San Diego, CA 92127-1904
(800)CAIG-123 (224-4123)
(619)451-1799
(619)451-2799 FAX

www.caig.com
caig123@aol.com

Manufactures and sells cleaners and lubricants for electronic applications, featuring for PorGold contact enhancer for gold-plated contacts and connectors.

Cal-Abco
6041 Variel Avenue
Woodland Hills, CA 91367
(800)669-2226
(818)704-7733 FAX

Distributes computer systems and peripherals.

Canon USA, Inc.
One Canon Plaza
Lake Success, NY 11042
(516)488-6700
(516)354-5805 FAX
(516)488-6528 BBS

Manufactures a line of printer and video equipment as well as floppy drives. Supplies floppy drives to Compaq and IBM.

Casio, Inc.
570 Mt. Pleasant Avenue
Dover, NJ 07801
(201)361-5400
(201)328-1670 Product Info
(800)962-2746
(201)361-3819 FAX

www.casio-usa.com

Manufactures digital cameras, personal data systems, and digital watches.

Centon Electronics, Inc.
20 Morgan
Irvine, CA 92718
(714)855-9111
(714)855-3132 FAX Sales

www.centon.com

Manufactures memory enhancement kits, SIMM and DIMM modules, expansion boards, credit cards, and PCMCIA cards.

Chemtronics, Inc.
8125 Cobb Center Drive
Kennesaw, GA 30144
(770)424-4888
(770)424-4267 FAX

Manufactures and sells a complete line of computer and electronic grade chemicals, materials, and supplies.

Cherry Electrical Products
3600 Sunset Avenue
Waukegan, IL 60087
(847)662-9200
(847)360-3498 FAX
(847)360-3566 FAX Sales

www.industry.net/cherry.electrical

Manufactures a line of high-quality keyboards for IBM-compatible systems.

Chicago Case Company
4446 S. Ashland Avenue
Chicago, IL 60609
(312)927-1600
(800)333-8172 FAX

Manufactures equipment-shipping and travel cases.

Chilton Book Company
Chilton Way
Radnor, PA 19089-0230
(610)964-4743

Manufactures a number of excellent automotive service manuals and documentation.

Chinon America, Inc.
615 Hawaii
Torrance, CA 90503
(800)441-0222
(310)533-0274
(310)533-1727 FAX
(310)320-4160 BBS

Manufactures a line of floppy disk and CD-ROM drives.

Chips & Technologies, Inc.
2950 Zanker Road
San Jose, CA 95134
(408)434-0600
(408)894-2079 FAX
(408)456-0721 BBS

Designs, markets, and supports a broad line of semiconductor products that provide peripheral solutions in the areas of media, graphics and core logic. The company's cutting-edge product family of HiQVideo™ flat panel video/graphics controllers for portable computers currently leads the market.

Chrysler Motors Service Publications
Service Publications
PO Box 360450
Strongsville, OH 44136
(800)890-4038
(216)572-0725
(216)572-0815 FAX

Publishes Chrysler service manuals and documentation.

Ci Design Company
1695 W. McCarther Boulevard
Costa Mesa, CA 92626
(714)556-0888
(714)556-0890 FAX

Manufactures custom-made 3 1/2-inch drive mounting kits used by Toshiba, Panasonic, and NEC for their drive products. Also makes drive faceplates, enclosures, and custom cable assemblies.

CIE America
2701 Dow Avenue
Tustin, CA 92680
(714)573-2942
(800)877-1421
(714)757-4488 FAX
(714)573-2645 BBS

Manufactures PC printers and other peripherals.

Cirrus Logic, Inc.
3100 W. Warren Avenue
Fremont, CA 94538
(510)623-8300
(510)226-2240
(800)359-6414 FAX On Demand
(510)252-6020 FAX
(510)440-9080 BBS

www.cirrus.com

Manufactures PC motherboard chipsets for mobile and desktop systems and a line of chipsets for disk controller, video, and communications circuits.

Citizen America Corporation
2450 Broadway
Suite 600
Santa Monica, CA 90404
(310)453-0614
(310)453-2814 FAX

www.citizen-america.com

Manufactures a line of printers and floppy disk drives.

CMD Technology, Inc.
1 Vanderbilt
Irvine, CA 92618
(714)454-0800
(800)426-3832
(714)455-1656 FAX
(7140454-0795 BBS

Manufactures EISA adapters, PCI and VL-Bus IDE, and SCSI disk adapters.

Colorado Memory Systems, Inc. (a division of Hewlett-Packard)
800 S. Taft Avenue
Loveland, CO 80537
(970)669-8000
(970)635-1500
(970)667-0997 FAX
(970)635-0650 BBS

Manufactures tape-backup subsystems specializing in QIC-80 and QIC-40 systems that attach through an interface card, floppy controller, or parallel port connection.

Columbia Data Products
1070B Rainer Drive
Altamonte Springs, FL 32714
(407)869-6700
(407)862-4725 FAX
(407)862-4724 BBS

www.cdp.com

Manufactures image backup software for all PC platforms and tools for quick replication of servers and workstations.

Compaq Computer Corporation
20555 State Highway 249
Houston, TX 77070
(713)370-0670
(800)231-0900
(800)652-6672 Technical Support
(713)378-8754 FAX
(713)378-1418 BBS

support@compaq.com

Manufactures high-end IBM-compatible computer systems.

CompTIA (Computing Technology Industry Association)
450 East 22nd Street
Suite 230
Lombard, IL 60148-6158
(847)268-1818
(847)268-1384 FAX

A non-profit trade association that sponsors the A+ Certification program.

Compton's NewMedia, Inc. (a division of Softkey International, Inc.)
1 Anthanaeum Street
Cambridge, MA 02142
(617)494-1200
(617)494-1279 FAX

www.softkey.com

Produces entertainment, multimedia and education software for floppy and CD-ROM users. CD-ROM titles include Compton's Interactive Encyclopedia.

CompUSA, Inc.
15167 Business Avenue
Dallas, TX 75244
(214)888-5700

(800)266-7872
(800)932-2667
(800)329-2212 FAX

Computer retail superstore and mail-order outlet.

CompuServe Information Service (CIS)
5000 Arlington Centre Boulevard
Columbus, OH 43220
(614)457-8600
(800)848-8990
(614)529-1610 FAX Business Accounts
(614)529-1611 FAX Private Accounts

Largest online information and messaging service; offers Internet access and manufacturer- and vendor-sponsored forums for technical support.

Computer Component Source, Inc.
135 Eileen Way
Syosset, NY 11791-9022
(516)496-8727
(800)356-1227
(800)926-2062 FAX

Distributes a large number of computer components for repair. Specializes in display parts such as flyback transformers and other components.

Computer Design Magazine
PennWell Publishing Co.
Advanced Technology Group
10 Tara Boulevard, 5th Floor
Nashua, NH 03062-2801
(603)891-0123
(603)891-0539 FAX
(800)331-4463 Subscriptions
(918)835-3161 Subscriptions
(918)831-9497 FAX Subscription

atd.pennwell.com

An excellent industry magazine for electronic engineers and engineering managers, featuring articles on all types of computer components and hardware.

Computer Discount Warehouse (CDW)
1020 E. Lake Cook Road
Buffalo Grove, IL 60089
(708)465-6000
(800)726-4239
(800)383-4239 Technical Support
(708)465-6800 FAX
(708)465-6899 BBS

Computer retail superstore and mail-order catalog outlet.

Computer Graphics World Magazine
PennWell Publishing Co.
Advanced Technology Group
10 Tara Boulevard, 5th Floor
Nashua, NH 03062-2801
(603)891-0123
(603)891-0539
(800)331-4463 Subscriptions
(918)835-3161 Subscriptions
(918)831-9497 FAX Subscription

An industry magazine covering graphics hardware, software, and applications.

Computer Hotline Magazine
15400 Knoll Trail
Suite #500
Dallas, TX 75248
(214)233-5131
(800)999-5131
(214)233-5514 FAX

A publication that features advertisers offering excellent sources of replacement and repair parts as well as new and used equipment at wholesale prices.

Computer Library
1 Park Avenue
New York, NY 10016
(212)503-4400
(212)503-4414 FAX
(800)419-0313

www.iacnet.com

Manufactures the Computer Select CD-ROM database including full text and abstracts from over 120 computer publications. This is a valuable research tool.

Computer Reseller News Magazine
CMP Media, Inc.
1 Jericho Plaza
Jericho, NY 11753
(516)733-6700
(847)647-6834 Subscriptions
(516)733-6916 FAX

An excellent industry trade weekly news magazine featuring news for computer professionals involved in value-added reselling of computer equipment. Subscriptions are free to those who qualify.

Computer Retail Week Magazine
CMP Publications, Inc.
1 Jericho Plaza
Jericho, NY 11753
(516)733-6700
(847)647-6834 Subscriptions
(516)733-8577 FAX

An excellent industry trade weekly news magazine featuring news for computer superstores, mass merchants, and retailers. Subscriptions are free to those who qualify.

Computer Shopper Magazine
Ziff-Davis Publishing
One Park Avenue
New York, NY 10016
(212)503-5926
(800)825-4237 Reprints

Monthly magazine for experimenters and bargain hunters; features a large number of advertisements.

Computer Technology Review Magazine
West World Productions, Inc.
924 Westwood Boulevard
Suite 650
Los Angeles, CA 90024-2910
(310)208-1335
(310)208-1054 FAX

An excellent monthly technical magazine for systems integrators, value-added resellers, and original equipment manufacturers. Subscriptions are free to those who qualify.

Comtech Publishing Ltd.
P.O. Box 12340
Reno, NV 89510
(702)825-9000
(800)456-7005
(702)825-1818 FAX

www.accutek.com/comtech

Manufactures dSalvage Professional, the best and most comprehensive xBASE data-recovery and file repair software available.

Connector Resources Unlimited (CRU)
1005 Ames Avenue
Milpitas, CA 95035
(408)957-5757
(800)260-9800
(408)942-0862 FAX

www.cruinc.com

Manufactures a large variety of disk enclosures, mounting kits, cables, and connectors for IBM and Mac systems.

Conner Peripherals, Inc.
Seagate Technology
920 Disc Drive
Scotts Valley, CA 95066
(408)438-6550
(408)456-4500
(408)429-6356 FAX
(407)262-4225 FAX
(408)438-2620 FAXBack Info
(800)468-3472 Service
(408)438-8771 BBS
(407)263-3502 BBS

Manufactures a line of hard disk drives, tape-backup products, and CD-ROM drives. They are an OEM supplier to Compaq and other companies.

Conner Tape Products, Inc.
Seagate Technology
1650 Sunflower Avenue
Costa Mesa, CA 92626
(714)641-1230
(800)626-6637 Sales
(714)641-2590 FAX
(408)456-4415 BBS

www.seagate.com

Manufactures a line of tape-backup products and high-capacity tape drives.

Corel Systems, Inc.
1600 Carling Avenue
Ottawa, ONT K1Z8R7
CANADA
(613)728-8200
(613)728-9790 FAX
(613)728-4752 BBS

www.corel.com

Manufactures the CorelDraw graphics program as well as Corel SCSI, a SCSI driver kit featuring drivers for a variety of SCSI host adapters and devices. Also manufactures the WordPerfect suite.

Creative Labs, Inc.
1901 McCarthy Boulevard
Milpitas, CA 95035
(408)428-6600
(800)544-6146
(800)998-1000 Customer Service
(408)742-6600 Technical Support
(408)428-6611 FAX
(405)742-6660 BBS

www.creaf.com

Manufactures the Sound Blaster series of audio cards for multimedia and sound applications.

CS Electronics
1342 Bell Avenue
Tustin, CA 92780
(714)259-9100
(714)259-0911 FAX

www.scsi-cables.com
cablescs@aol.com

Manufactures a very high-quality line of disk and tape drive cables, specializing in SCSI-1, SCSI-2, and SCSI-3 applications. They offer custom lengths, connectors, and impedances for a proper match with an existing installation, and use the highest quality raw cable available.

CST
2336 Lu Field Road
Dallas, TX 75229
(214)241-2662
(214)241-2661 FAX
(214)241-3782 BBS

cst_inc@ix.netcom.com
www.simmtester.com

Manufacturer of memory/ SIMMs testers.

CTX International, Inc.
20470 Walnut Drive
Walnut, CA 91789
(909)595-6146
(800)888-9052
(909)595-6293 FAX

Manufactures a line of high-performance notebook computers.

Curtis Manufacturing Co, Inc.
225 Secaucus
Secaucus, NJ 07094
(201)422-0240
(201)422-0254 FAX

Manufactures a complete line of computer accessories, including copy holders, glare filters, keyboard drawers, media storage, printer stands, data switches, cleaning & tool kits, notebook cases, travel accessories, and surge protectors.

Cypress Semiconductor Corporation
3901 N. First Street
San Jose, CA 95134
(408)943-2600

Manufactures PC chipsets and other semiconductor devices.

Cyrix Corporation
2703 N. Central Expressway
Richardson, TX 75080
(214)968-8388
(800)462-9749
(214)699-9857 FAX
(800)GO-CYRIX (462-9749) FAXBack
(800)340-7501 Cyrix Systems Direct Sales

www.cyrix.com

Manufactures the 6X86 processor and offers a complete line of Computer Systems.

D. W. Electrochemicals, Ltd.
97 Newkirk Road North
Unit 3
Richmond Hill, ONT
L4C3G4
CANADA
(905)508-7500
(905)508-7502 FAX

Manufactures and sells Stabilant 22 contact enhancer and treatment. Stabilant 22 is the gel concentrate, and Stabilant 22a is a 4 to 1 isopropanol diluted form.

DakTech
4900 Ritter Road
Mechanicsburg, PA 17055

(717)795-9544
(800)325-3238
(717)795-9420 FAX

daktech@ix.netcom.com
EMAIL

Distributor of IBM and Compaq parts.

Da-Lite Screen Co.
3100 N. Detroit St.
(shipping address)
PO Box 137
Warsaw, IN 46581-0137
(219)267-8101
(800)622-3737

www.da-lite.com

Manufactures a line of projection screens and computer furniture.

Dallas Semiconductor
4401 S. Beltwood Parkway
Dallas, TX 75244-3292
(214)450-0400
(214)450-0448 Customer Service
(214)450-3715 FAX

www.dalsemi.com

Manufactures real-time clock and non-volatile RAM modules used by a number of OEMs, including IBM, Compaq, and others.

Damark International, Inc.
7101 Winnetka Avenue North
Minneapolis, MN 55429
(612)531-0066
(800)729-9000 Sales
(612)531-0281 FAX

www.internetmci.com/ marketplace

Liquidates and distributes a variety of discontinued products, including PC-compatible systems and peripherals.

Darkhorse Systems
12201 Technology Boulevard
Suite 135
Austin, TX 78727
(512)258-5721
(512)257-0296 FAX

Manufactures the SIGMA.LC memory test system. This is a high-quality memory test device that can accurately test SIMMs, individual chips and other types of memory modules.

Data Based Advisor Magazine
Advisor Publications
4010 Morena Boulevard
Suite 200
San Diego, CA 92117
(619)483-6400
(619)483-9851 FAX
(800)336-6060 Subcriptions

www.advisor.com
70007,1614 CompuServe — Customer service

An excellent magazine featuring articles on database applications software and programming routines. They also publish *Access Visual Basic Advisor, Internet Advisor, FoxPro Advisor, Lotus Notes Advisor*, and *Power Builder Advisor*.

Data Communications Magazine
McGraw-Hill Inc.
1221 Avenue of the Americas
New York, NY 10020
(212)512-2000
(800)525-5003 Subscriptions
(212)512-6833 FAX

www.data.com

An excellent industry publication featuring articles on networking and communications.

Data Depot
1710 Drew Street
Clearwater, FL 34615-6213
(813)446-3402
(800)SOS-DIAG (767-3424) Sales
(813)443-4377 FAX

datadepo@ix.net_com.com

Manufactures the PocketPOST diagnostic card for ISA and EISA systems, as well as several other excellent diagnostics hardware and software products.

Data Exchange Corp.
3600 Via Pescador
Camarillo, CA 93012
(805)388-1711
(800)237-7911
(805)482-4856 FAX Sales

sales@dex.com EMAIL
www.dex.com

Specializes in contract manufacturing, end-of-life support, and depot repair and refurbishment of most major computer components.

Data Retrieval Services, Inc.
1040 Kapp Drive
Clearwater, FL 34625
(813)461-5900
(310)398-2764 LA Office
(813)461-5668 FAX

Specialists in data retrieval from head-crashed disk packs, damaged disk drives, floppies and tapes.

Data Technology Corporation (DTC)
1515 Centre Pointe Drive
Milpitas, CA 95035-8010
(408)942-4000
(408)262-7700 Technical Support
(408)942-4027 FAX
(408)942-4005 FAXBack
(408)942-4197 BBS
(408)942-4010 BBS

www.datatechnology.com

Manufactures a complete line of PC peripherals and multimedia products.

Datamation Magazine
Cahners Publishing Co.
275 Washington Street
Newton, MA 02158-1630
(617)964-3030
(800)446-6551 Subscriptions
(617)558-4506 FAX

www.datamation.com

An excellent industry publication, featuring articles on networking and communications.

Datastorm Technologies, Inc.
2401 Lemone Boulevard
Columbia, MO 65205
(573)443-3282
(573)875-0530 Tech Support
(573)875-0595 FAX Customer Service
(573)875-0503 BBS
(800)474-1573

www.datastorm.com

Manufactures ProCOMM, ProCOMM Plus, and ProCOMM Plus for Windows internet, FAX, and data communications software.

Dell Computer Corporation
2214 W. Braker Lane, Suite D
Austin, TX 78759
(512)338-4400
(800)426-5150
(800)624-9896 Technical Support
(800)727-8320 FAX
(512)728-3653 FAX
(512)338-8528 BBS

Manufactures a line of low-cost, high-performance IBM-compatible computer systems.

DiagSoft, Inc.
5615 Scotts Valley Drive
Suite 140

Scotts Valley, CA 95066
(408)438-8247
(408)438-8997
(800)342-4763
(408)438-7113 FAX

diagsoft.com

Manufactures the QAPlus user-level PC diagnostics software, as well as the high-end QAPlus/FE (Field Engineer) software, which is an excellent program that includes complete high-resolution floppy drive testing and the Power Meter benchmarking utility.

Diamond Flower, Inc. (DFI)
8 Elkins Road
East Brunswick, NJ 08816
(908)390-2815
(908)390-2817 FAX
(800)275-3342 Sales

Manufactures a line of PC-compatible systems, motherboards, adapter cards, and other products.

Diamond Multimedia Systems, Inc.
2880 Junction Avenue
San Jose, CA 95134-1922
(408)325-7000
(408)325-7070 FAX
(800)468-5846 Sales

www.diamondmm.com

Manufactures a line of high-performance video and multimedia adapters.

Digi-Key Corporation
701 Brooks Avenue South
PO Box 677
Thief River Falls, MN 56701-0677
(218)681-6674
(800)344-4539 Sales
(218)681-3380 FAX

www.digikey.com

Sells an enormous variety of electronic and computer components, tools, and test equipment. Publishes a complete catalog listing all items.

Distributed Processing Tech. (DPT)
140 Candace Drive
Maitland, FL 32751
(407)830-5522
(800)322-4378 Sales
(407)260-6690 FAX
(407)831-6432 BBS
(407)830-1070 BBS

sales@dpt. com
techsupp@dpt.com
www.dpt.com

Manufactures high-performance caching SCSI host adapters and disk array (RAID) controllers.

Diversified Technology
PO Box 748
Ridgeland, MS 39158
(601)856-4121 Domestic
(201)891-8718 International
(800)443-2667
(601)856-2888 FAX

Manufactures industrial and rack-mount PC-compatible systems as well as a variety of backplane-design CPU boards and multifunction adapters.

Dolch Computer Systems
3178 Laurelview Court
Fremont, CA 94538
(510)661-2220
(510)490-2360 FAX

Manufactures a series of very powerful portable computers that are also very expandable and rugged. If you need something more powerful than a laptop, they have lunchbox-sized portables with large hard disks and high-end video displays.

DTK Computer, Inc.
770 Epperson Drive
City of Industry, CA 91748
(818)810-0098
(818)810-0090 FAX
(818)854-0797 BBS

Manufactures PC-compatible systems and BIOS software.

Dukane Corporation
2900 Dukane Drive
St. Charles, IL 60174
(630)584-2300
(800)676-2485
(630)584-5156 FAX

www.industry.net/dukane.av

Manufactures a complete line of high-intensity overhead projectors, LCD panels, and LCD data/video projectors. They specialize in portable high-brightness overhead projectors designed for LCD-panel projection applications.

Duracell, Inc.
Berkshire Industrial Park
Bethel, CT 06801
(203)796-4000
(203)791-3257 Sales

www.duracell.com

Manufactures high-performance consumer application batteries including alkaline, lithium, and standard-sized nickel-metal hydride rechargeable batteries.

Edmund Scientific
101 E. Gloucester Pike
Barrington, NJ 08007-1380
(609)573-6280
(609)573-6233 FAX
(609)573-6250 Sales
(609)573-6295 FAX orders only

techsup@edsci.com

They offer a wide range of optical components and scientific equipment for industry and research. Volume discounts offered. Free catalog offered to those who qualify.

Electronic Buyers' News Magazine
CMP Publications, Inc.
600 Community Drive
Manhasset, NY 11030-3875
(516)562-5000
(800)291-5215 Subscriptions
(516)562-5123 FAX

An excellent industry trade weekly magazine featuring news and information for those involved in electronics purchasing, materials, and management. Subscriptions are free to those who qualify.

Electronic Engineering Times Magazine
CMP Publications, Inc.
600 Community Drive
Manhasset, NY 11030-3875
(516)562-5000
(800)291-5215 Subscriptions
(516)562-5325 FAX

An excellent industry trade weekly news magazine featuring news for engineers and technical management. Subscriptions are free to those who qualify.

Electronic Products Magazine
Hearst Business Publications, Inc.
645 Stewart Avenue
Garden City, NY 11530
(516)227-1300
(516)227-1444 FAX

electronicproducts.com

An excellent industry trade magazine featuring engineering type information on electronic and computer components and in-depth technical articles. Subscriptions are free to those who qualify.

Electroservice Laboratories
6085 Sikorsky Street
Ventura, CA 93003
(805)644-2944
(805)644-5006 FAX
(805)644-7810 BBS

www.esl.com—Internet

Provides repair parts for most major computer OEMs, including all major PC components.

Elek-Tek, Inc.
7350 North Linder Avenue
Skokie, IL 60077
(847)677-7660
(800)395-1000
(847)677-1081 FAX

www.elektek.com—Catalog

Computer retail superstore offering a large selection of brand-name equipment at discount pricing.

Elitegroup Computer Systems, Inc.
45225 Northport Court
Fremont, CA 94538
(510)226-7333
(800)829-8890
(510)226-7350 FAX

www.ecsusa.com

One of the largest Taiwan-based PC motherboard manufacturers.

Endl Publications
14426 Black Walnut Court
Saratoga, CA 95070
(408)867-6642
(408)867-6630
(408)867-2115 FAX
(408)741-1600 FAXBack

2501752@mclmail.com

Publishes the SSF Reflector, containing specs for local bus disk drive attachments. Also publishes SCSI technical documentation such as The SCSI Bench Reference and The SCSI Encyclopedia.

Epson America, Inc. OEM Division
20770 Madrona Avenue
Torrance, CA 90509-2842
(310)787-6300
(310)782-5350 FAX
(800)922-8911 FAXBack
(408)782-4531 BBS

www.epson.com

Manufactures printers, floppy disk drives, and complete PC-compatible systems.

Everex Systems, Inc.
5020 Brandin Court
Fremont, CA 94538
(510)498-1111
(800)821-0806 Sales
(510)498-4411 Technical Support
(510)683-2062 FAX
(510)226-9694 BBS

www.everex.com
support@everex.com—EMAIL

Manufactures PC-compatible systems and peripherals.

Exabyte Corporation
1685 38th Street
Boulder, CO 80301
(303)442-4333
(303)417-7170 FAX

sales@exabyte.com
www.exabyte.com

Manufactures high-performance 8mm and minicartridge tape-backup systems and 8mm and 4mm tape libraries.

Extron Electronics
1230 S. Lewis Street
Anaheim, CA 92805
(714)491-1500
(714)491-1517 FAX
(800)633-9876

www.extron.com

Manufactures computer-video interface products used to connect PCs to large-screen video projectors and monitors. The company also manufactures VGA, Mac, and RGB distribution amplifiers and switchers used to connect multimedia classroom and boardroom equipment, and VGA- and Mac-to-NTSC/PAL converters for recording computer information and graphics on videotape.

Fantasy Productions (division of Fortner & Assoc.)
1305 Bert Street
Claremore, OK 74017
(800)358-5887 Sales & Limited Tech Support
(918)341-4577 Publications & Administration
(918)445-1586 Tech Support
(918)341-6545 Shipping

The source for discontinued IBM reference manuals and technical support. Call for a complete listing.

Fedco Electronics, Inc.
184 W. 2nd Street
Fond du Lac, WI 54936
(414)922-6490
(800)542-9761
(414)922-6750 FAX

Manufactures and supplies a large variety of computer batteries.

Fessenden Technologies
116 N. 3rd Street
Ozark, MO 65721
(417)485-2501
(417)485-3133 FAX

fessenden@o2net.com
76660.1035@Compuserve.com
EMAIL

Service company that offers monitor and terminal depot repair. They also repair hard drives for older Seagate and Miniscribe MFM/RLL drives.

First International Computer, Inc, (FIC)
980-A Mission Court
Fremont, CA 94539
(510)252-7777
(800)FICA-OEM (342-2636)
(510)252-8888 FAX

www.fica.com

The largest Taiwan-based manufacturer of PC-compatible motherboards.

Fluke, John Manufacturing Company, Inc.
6920 Seaway Boulevard
P.O. Box 9090
Everett, WA 98206-9090
(206)347-6100
(800)443-5853
(206)356-5019 FAX

www.fluke.com

Manufactures a line of high-end digital troubleshooting tools, including the Scopemeter handheld scope.

Folio Corp.
5072 N. 300 W.
Provo, UT 84604
(801)229-6700
(801)229-6787 FAX
(800)543-6546 Sales

www.folio.com

Manufactures the Folio VIEWS infobase software. Also publishes the annual Comdex exhibitors list on disk.

Framatome Connectors USA
51 Richards Avenue
Norwalk, CT 06856
(203)838-4444
(203)852-8629 FAX

Manufactures electronic connector products for portable and desktop PCs and workstations.

Fujitsu America, Inc.
3055 Orchard Drive
San Jose, CA 95134
(800)626-4686
(408)894-3950 Tech Support
(408)432-1318 FAX
(408)944-9899 BBS

customerserv@fujitsu.com
root@fujitsu.com
www.fujitsu.com

Manufactures a line of high-capacity hard disk drives.

Future Domain Corporation (Adaptec)
9701 Jeronimo Road
Irvine, CA 92718
(800)959-7274 Sales
(408)934-7274 Tech Support
(408)957-6776 FAX
(408)945-7727 BBS

www.adaptec.com

Manufactures a line of high-performance SCSI host adapters and software. Recently acquired by Adaptec.

Gateway 2000
P.O. Box 2000
610 Gateway Drive
North Sioux City, SD 57049
(605)232-2000
(800)523-2000
(800)846-2000 Tech Support
(605)232-2023 FAX Customer Service
(605)232-2224 BBS

gw2k.com

Manufactures a popular line of PC-compatible systems sold by mail order. Their systems use primarily Micronics Motherboards, Phoenix BIOS, and industry standard form factors.

Gazelle/GTM Software
289 E. 950 S.
Orem, UT 84058
(801)235-7000
(801)235-7099 FAX

www.shopsite.com/gtm

Manufactures the Optune disk defragmenter and disk performance utility program.

GigaTrend, Inc.
2234 Rutherford Road
Carlsbad, CA 92008
(619)931-9122
(619)931-9959 FAX
(619)931-9469 BBS
(800)743-4442 Sales

www.gigatrend.com

Manufactures high-capacity tape drives.

Global Engineering Documents
15 Inverness Way East
Englewood, CO 80112-5704
(303)792-2181
(800)854-7179
(303)792-2192 FAX

A source for various ANSI and other industry standard documents, including SCSI-1, 2, and 3, ATA IDE, ESDI, and many others. Unlike ANSI, they sell draft documents of standards that are not yet fully ANSI approved.

Globe Manufacturing, Inc.
1159 Route 22
Mountainside, NJ 07092
(908)232-7301
(800)227-3258
(908)232-4729 FAX

Manufactures assorted PC adapter card brackets.

Golden Bow Systems
PO Box 3039
San Diego, CA 92163-1039
(619)298-9349
(800)284-3269
(619)298-9950 FAX

75471.1007@compuserve.com

Manufactures VOPT, the best and fastest disk optimizer software available. They also offer Vcache, VQ and VLock.

GoldStar Technology, Inc.
1000 Sylvan Avenue
Englewood Cliff, NJ 07632
(201)816-2000
(201)816-0636 FAX

Manufactures a line of color monitors.

GRACE Specialty Polymers/ WR GRACE, Emerson & Cuming, Inc.
869 Washington Street
Canton, MA 02021
(800)832-4929 Technical Support
(800)225-9936 Orders
(617)828-3300
(800)472-2391 Info Center
(617)828-3104 FAX

Manufactures structurally, thermally, and electronically conductive epoxy and silicone adhesives, coatings and encapsulates. Also room temperature, heat cured and UV cured systems as well as circuit board fabrication materials. These include solder mask, solder resist, and polymer thick films.

GSI (Great Software Ideas), Inc.
17951-H Skypark Circle
Irvine, CA 92714-6343
(714)261-7949
(800)486-7800
(714)757-1778 FAX

Manufactures an extremely flexible and powerful line of IDE adapters and floppy controllers, including units with security locks, and support for 2.88M drives. Also offers complete 2.88M drive upgrade kits. Their IDE controllers have a flexible on-board BIOS that allows them to coexist with other drive interfaces.

Harbor Electronics
650 Danbury Road
Ridgefield, CT 06877
(203)438-9625
(203)431-3001 FAX

Manufactures a line of high-quality SCSI-1, -2, and -3 interconnect cables.

Hauppauge Computer Works, Inc.
91 Cabot Court
Hauppauge, NY 11788
(516)434-1600
(800)443-6284
(516)434-3197 Customer Support
(516)434-3198 FAX
(516)434-8454 BBS

www.hauppauge.com/hcw/index.htm

Manufactures video capture cards.

Hayes Microcomputer Products
5835 Peachtree Corners East
Norcross, GA 30092-3405
(770)840-9200
(800)874-3734
(770)441-1213 FAX
(800)429-3739 FAXBack
(770)429-3734 BBS

www.hayes.com

Manufactures a complete line of modems.

Heathkit Education Systems
Heath Company
455 Riverview Drive
Benton Harbor, MI 49023
(616)925-6000
(800)253-0570
(616)925-2982 FAX

Sells courses and training materials for learning electronics and computer design including A+ Certification for Computer Technicians.

Helm, Inc.
Publications Division
PO Box 07130
Detroit, MI 48207
(313)865-5000
(313)865-5927 FAX

Publishes General Motors service manuals and documentation.

Hermann Marketing
1400 North Price Road
St. Louis, MO 63132-2308
(800)523-9009
(314)432-1818 FAX

Distributes a line of "Uniquely Intel" products and accessories. My favorites are the T-shirts, coffee cups, and especially the keychains containing actual Intel 486 and Pentium processors encased in clear plastic.

Hewlett-Packard
16399 W. Bernardo Drive
San Diego, CA 92127-1899
(800)752-0900
(970)635-1000 Customer Support Center
(800)333-1917 HP FIRST (Fax Information Retrieval System)
(208)344-4809 HP FIRST (Fax Information Retrieval System)
(800)333-1917 HP Audio Tips
(408)720-3416 BBS

www.hp.com
www.dmo.hp.com

Manufactures an extensive line of excellent printers and PC-compatible systems.

Hewlett-Packard, Disk Memory Division
11413 Chinden Boulevard
Boise, ID 83714
(800)826-4111
(208)396-6000
(208)396-2896 FAX

www.hp.com
ftp-boi.external.hp.com

Manufactures high-capacity 3 1/2-inch hard disk drives.

Hitachi America, Ltd.
Semiconductor & IC Division
2000 Sierra Point Parkway
Brisbane, CA 94005
(415)589-8300
(415)583-4207 FAX

www.hitatchi.com

Manufactures a variety of memory and other semiconductor devices.

Hitatchi America, Ltd.
50 Prospect Avenue
Tarrytown, NY 10591
(914)332-5800
(914)332-1787 FAX

www.hitatchi.com

Manufactures computer peripherals, including Office automation, digital graphics products and LCD devices.

Hypertech
1910 Thomas Road
Memphis, TN 38134
(901)382-8888
(901)373-5290 FAX

Manufactures and sells a wide variety of well-engineered, high-performance automotive computer EPROM replacements for many different types of vehicles. Also makes the Power Programmer for reprogramming vehicle PCMs with EEPROMs (Flash ROMs).

Hyundai Electronics America
3101 N. 1st Street
San Jose, CA 95134
(408)473-9200

www.hea.com

Manufactures PC-compatible systems.

IBM Fulfillment Center
PO Box 3558
Shiremans Town, PA 17011
(800)426-7282

The source for OS/2 software developer kits, reseller liturature and orders for server guides.

IBM Microelectronics
3605 Hwy. 52
Rochester, MN 55901
(507)253-4011
(507)253-3256 FAX

Manufactures a variety of processors, memory and other semiconductor devices, including the IBM 486SLC2, Blue Lightning, PowerPC, and other processors. Also makes high speed Static RAM for cache, and produces processor chips and motherboards for a variety of PC-compatible manufacturers.

IBM National Publications
4800 Falls of The Neause
Raleigh, NC 27609
(800)879-2755 option 1
(800)445-9269 FAX IBM Publications 5th Flr.

The source for current books, reference manuals, documentation, software toolkits, and language products for IBM systems. For discontinued publications contact Fantasy Productions or Annabooks.

IBM OEM Division
44 Broadway Road
White Plains, NY 10601
(914)288-3000
(914)642-3000
(914)686-4527 FAX

Manufactures and distributes IBM products such as high-capacity 3 1/2-inch hard disk drives, networking and chipset products.

IBM Parts Order Center
PO Box 9022
Boulder, CO 80301
(303)924-4100 Orders
(303)924-4015 Part Number ID and Lookup

IBM's nationwide service parts ordering center.

IBM PC Company
11400 Burnet Road
Austin, TX 78758
(512)823-0000
(800)IBM-3333
(800)426-7015 Factory Outlet (discontinued/used equipment)
(800)426-4329 IBM FAXBack system
(800)426-3395 IBM Tech Support FAXBack system
(919)517-0001 IBM National Support Center BBS
(919)517-0095 IBM NSC BBS Status Line (voice)
(800)547-1283 OS/2 Setup and Register
(800)992-4777 Corporate Customer Software Support
(800)3IBMOS2 (342-6672) OS/2 orders
(800)776-8284 Order other Products

ibm.watson.com

Manufactures and supports IBM Personal Computers.

IBM PC Direct
3039 Cornwallis Road
Building 203
Research Triangle Park, NC 27709-9766
(800)IBM-2YOU (426-2968)
(800)465-7999 Canada
(800)426-4182 FAX
(800)426-3332 Information
(800)426-2968 PC Direct Catalog Orders

www.pc.ibm.com

IBM PC Company's direct mail order catalog sales division. They sell IBM and approved third-party systems and peripherals at a discount from list price, and publish a catalog listing all items.

IBM Personal Systems Technical Solutions Magazine
NCM
PO Box 165447
Irving, TX 75016
(800)678-8014
(214)550-0433
(214)518-2507 FAX

Publishes an excellent bi-monthly magazine covering IBM Personal Computer systems and software.

Illinois Lock
301 West Hintz Road
Wheeling, IL 60090-5754
(847)537-1800
(847)537-1881 FAX

illock@aol.com

Manufactures keylocks used in many different IBM and IBM-compatible computer systems.

InfoWorld Magazine
375 Cochituate Road
Framingham, MA 01701
(508)879-0700
(800)227-8365
(508)879-0446 FAX

Publishes *InfoWorld* magazine, featuring excellent product reviews.

Inline, Inc.
1901 E. Lambert Road
Suite 110
La Habra, CA 90631
(310)690-6767
(800)882-7117
(310)691-5247 FAX

Manufactures a complete line of video-connection accessories, including distribution amplifiers, scan converters, line drivers, projector interfaces, and cables. They also offer interactive training systems for computer-based training facilities.

Innerworks Technology, Inc.
319 Sundance Drive
Bartlett, IL 60103
(630)372-0884
(630)372-0885 FAX

Manufactures an excellent PC diagnostic program called the Third Degree.

Integrated Device Technology, Inc.
2975 Stender Way
Santa Clara, CA 95054-3090
(800)345-7015
(408)727-6116

www.idt.com

Manufactures chipsets and other semiconductor devices.

Integrated Micro Solutions, Inc.
2085 Hamilton Avenue
3rd Floor
San Jose, CA 95125
(408)369-8282
(408)369-0128 FAX

users.aol.com\imsteksup

Manufactures graphic accelerator chips and boards and ATM network products.

Intel Corporation
2200 Mission College Blvd.
Santa Clara, CA 95054-1537
(408)765-8080
(800)548-4725 Intel Literature
(800)468-3548 Customer Support U.S. & Canada
(916)356-7368 Customer Support International
(408)765-9904 FAX

www.intel.com

Manufactures microprocessors used in IBM and compatible systems. Also makes a line of memory and accelerator boards, as well as one of the most popular lines of PC-compatible Pentium motherboards.

Intel PC Enhancement Operations
5200 NE Elam Young Parkway
Hillsboro, OR 97124
(503)629-7354
(503)696-8080 Intel Operator
(800)321-4044 End User Cutomer Support
(800)628-8686 End User Tech Support
(800)538-3373 Networking Sales
(503)264-7000 Networking Tech Support
(503)264-7969 FAX
(503)264-7999 BBS
(503)645-6275 BBS

Manufactures Overdrive CPU upgrades and networking devices.

International Electronic Research Corp. (IERC)
135 W. Magnolia Boulevard
Burbank, CA 91502
(213)849-2481
(818)848-8872 FAX

Manufactures a line of excellent CPU heat sink products, including clip-on, low-profile models especially for 486 and Pentium processors that do not require a special socket.

Iomega Corporation
1821 West Iomega Way
Roy, UT 84067
(801)778-1000
(800)777-6654 Sales
(801)778-3461 FAX Customer Service
(801)778-5888 BBS

info@iomega.com

Manufactures the Jaz, Ditto and Zip drive removable-cartridge drives.

IQ Technologies, Inc.
26425 NE Allen Street
Suite 2
Duvall, WA 98034
(206)788-5811
(800)227-2817
(206)788-5905 FAX
(206)788-2522 BBS

www.iqtech.com

Manufactures a complete line of notebook computer

connectivity products including Ethernet, Token-Ring and FAX/Modem PCMCIA adapter cards. They also manufacture Ethernet-FAX/ Modem 28.8 and Token-Ring-FAX/Modem 28.8 combo cards.

J. Bond Computer Systems
93 W. Montague Expressway
Milpitas, CA 95035
(408)946-9622
(408)946-2898 FAX

www.jbond.com

Manufactures PC motherboard.

Jameco Computer Products
1355 Shoreway Road
Belmont, CA 94002
(415)592-8097
(800)831-4242
(415)592-2503 FAX
(415)637-9025 BBS

www.jameco.com

Supplies computer components, parts, and peripherals by mail order.

JDR Microdevices
1850 S. 10th
San Jose, CA 95112
(408)494-1400
(800)538-5000
(408)494-1430 BBS

www.jdr.com

A vendor for chips, disk drives, and various computer and electronic parts and components.

Jensen Tools
7815 S. 46th Street
Phoenix, AZ 85044
(602)968-6231
(800)426-1194
(800)366-9662 FAX

www.jensentools.com

Supplies and manufactures high-quality tools and test equipment.

JTS Corporation
1289 Anvilwood Avenue
Sunnyvale, CA 94089
(408)468-1800
(408)747-1319 FAX

Manufactures a line of low-cost 3 1/2-inch hard disk drives.

JVC Information Products
17811 Mitchell Avenue
Irvine, CA 92714
(714)261-1292
(714)261-9690 FAX

Manufactures CD-Recordable and CD-ROM drives.

Kensington Microware, Ltd.
2855 Campus Drive
San Mateo, CA 94403
(415)572-2700
(415)572-9675 FAX
(800)535-4242

www.kensington.com

Manufactures and supplies computer accessories.

Key Tronic Corporation
PO Box 14687
Spokane, WA 99214
(509)928-8000
(800)262-6006 Technical Support/Sales
(509)927-5248 FAX
(509)927-5288 BBS

www.keytronic.com

Manufactures a variety of high-quality keyboards and mice for PC-compatible systems. Acquired the Honeywell Keyboard division. The Honeywell mouse uses revolutionary new technology that never needs cleaning and works on any surface, unlike traditional ball and roller mice. Supplies Compaq and Microsoft with keyboards.

Kingston Technology Corporation
17600 Newhope Street
Fountain Valley, CA 92708
(714)435-2600
(800)835-6575 Sales
(714)435-2699 FAX

kingston.com

Manufactures an excellent line of direct processor upgrade modules for 286 and 386 IBM and Compaq systems, as well as the slot-based MCMaster bus master processor upgrade card for Micro Channel systems. They also sell numerous SIMM memory modules and disk upgrades for other systems.

Labconco Corporation
8811 Prospect
Kansas City, MO 64132
(816)333-8811
(800)821-5525
(816)363-0130 FAX

Manufactures a variety of clean room cabinets and clean benches for use in hard disk drive and other sensitive component repair.

Labtec Enterprises, Inc.
3801 N.E. 109 Avenue
Suite J
Vancouver, WA 98682

(360)896-2000
(360)896-2020

www.labtec.com

Manufactures amplified speakers for multimedia applications.

Lantronix
15353 Barranca Parkway
Irvine, CA 92718-2216
(714)453-3990
(800)422-7055 Sales
(714)453-3995 FAX
(714)450-7232 FAX Sales

www.lantronix.com

Manufactures a variety of network hardware including servers, bridges, repeaters, hubs, converters and transceivers.

Laser Magnetic Storage
4425 Arrowswest Drive
Colorado Springs, CO 80907
(719)593-7900
(714)599-8713 FAX
(719)593-4081 BBS

Division of DPMG that manufactures a variety of optical & tape disk products.

LearnKey, Inc.
1845 West Sunset Boulevard
St. George, UT 84770
(800)937-3279
(801)674-9733
(801)674-9734 FAX

Produces and distributes the highest quality computer training videos, including *Your PC—The Inside Story* featuring Scott Mueller.

Lexmark
740 New Circle Road
Lexington, KY 40511
(606)232-2000
(606)232-1206 Helpline
(606)232-3557 Sales FAX
(606)232-5238 BBS
(606)232-5653 BBS

www.Lexmark.com

Manufactures IBM keyboards and printers for retail distribution. Spun off from IBM in 1991, now sells to other OEMs and distributors.

Liebert Assoc.
9650 Jeronimo Road
Irvine, CA 92718
(714)457-3600
(800)222-5877 Sales
(719)457-3677 FAX Sales

Manufactures a line of computer power-protection devices.

Liuski International
10 Hub Drive
Melville, NY 11747
(516)454-8220
(800)854-8754
(800)731-5611 Tech Support

www.liuski.com

Hardware distributor that carries a variety of peripherals and systems. They are the exclusive distributor of Magitronic PC systems and motherboards.

Logicraft Information Systems, Inc.
22 Cotton Road
Nashua, NH 03063
(603)880-0300
(800)880-5644
(603)880-7229

www.logicraft.com

Manufacturer of CD-ROM networking and optical storage solutions for the DOS, Windows, Window 95, Windows NT and Macintosh environments. The company's products provide fast access to CD-ROM databases over a wide range of networks and technologies in the industry, featuring the FastCD Personal Edition.

Longshine Microsystems, Inc.
10400-9 Pioneer Blvd.
Santa Fe Springs, CA 90670
(310)903-0899
(310)944-2201 FAX

Manufactures PC interface boards including disk controllers, super I/O adapters, network cards, and more.

Lotus Development Corporation
55 Cambridge Parkway
Cambridge, MA 02142
(617)577-8500
(800)343-5414 Customer Service
(617)693-3899 FAX
(617)693-7000 BBS

www.lotus.com

Manufactures Lotus 1-2-3, Symphony, and Magellan software. Acquired by IBM.

LSI Logic, Inc.
1551 McCarthy Boulevard
Milpitas, CA 95035
(408)433-8000
(800)433-8778
(408)433-2882 FAX Sales
(408)954-3353 FAX Sales

www.lsilogic.com

Manufactures motherboard logic and chipsets.

Ma Laboratories, Inc.
1972 Concourse Drive
San Jose, CA 95131

(408)954-8188
(408)954-0944 FAX

www.malabs.com

Manufactures and supplies CPUs and SIMMs, PC boards, hard disk drives, floppy drives, motherboards and math coprocessors. They also manufacture a dummy parity chip that allows fake parity SIMMs to be constructed, which they also sell.

Macworld Communications, Inc.
501 Second Street
San Francisco, CA 94107
(415)243-0505
(415)442-1891 FAX

An excellent publication covering news in the Macintosh universe.

MAG InnoVision
2801 S. Yale Street
Santa Ana, CA 92704
(714)751-2008
(800)827-3998 Sales
(714)751-5522 FAX

www.maginnovision.com

Manufactures Flat Square Technology monitors with advanced performance features.

MAGNI Systems, Inc.
9500 S.W. Gemini Drive
Beaverton, OR 97008
(503)626-8400
(800)624-6465 Sales
(503)626-6225 FAX

Manufactures a line of products for converting VGA graphics screens to either NTSC (VHS) or S-video (S-VHS).

MapInfo Corp.
One Global View
Troy, NY 12180
(518)285-6000
(518)285-6070 FAX
(800)552-2511

www.mapinfo.com

Produced desktop mapping software for Windows, Mac, Sun, HP and DOS systems.

Mastersoft, Inc. (acquired by Adobe Systems)
8737 E. Via de Commercio
Scottsdale, AZ 85258
(602)948-4888
(800)624-6107
(602)948-8261 FAX
(602)596-5871 BBS

info@mastersoft.com

Manufactures Word for Word, a word processing file-conversion program.

Matrox Graphics, Inc.
1025 St. Regis Boulevard
Dorval, PQ H9P 2T4
CANADA
(514)969-6300
(514)969-6363 FAX
(514)969-6330 Sales
(514)969-6320 International Sales

Manufactures a line of high-performance PC graphics chipsets and adapters.

Maxell Corporation of America
22-08 Route 208
Fair Lawn, NJ 07410
(800)533-2836
(201)796-8790 FAX

Manufactures magnetic media products, including disks and tape cartridges.

Maxi Switch, Inc.
2901 East Elvira Road
Tuscon, AZ 85706
(602)294-5450
(602)294-6890 FAX
(602)741-9230 BBS

www.maxiswitch.com

Manufactures a line of high-quality PC keyboards, including some designed for harsh or industrial environments and programmable keyboards. Maxi Switch keyboards are used by many compatible system manufacturers, including Gateway 2000.

Maxoptix
3342 Gateway Boulevard
Fremont, CA 94538
(800)848-3092
(510)353-1845 FAX
(510)353-1448 BBS

Manufactures a line of optical WORM and magneto-optical drives. Joint venture with Maxtor Corporation and Kubota Corporation.

Maxtor Corporation
211 River Oaks Parkway
San Jose, CA 95134
(408)432-1700
(800)262-9867
(408)432-4510 FAX
(303)678-2222 BBS

www.maxtor.com

Manufactures a line of large-capacity, high-quality hard disk drives.

Maynard Electronics, Inc. (Seagate Technologies)
36 Skyline Drive
Lake Mary, FL 32746

(407)263-3500
(800)821-8782 Seagate Technologies
(800)626-6637 Sales Support
(800)537-2248 Customer Service
(800)73204283 FAXBack Information
(407)262-4225 FAX
(407)263-3662 BBS
(408)438-5382 TDD

www.seagate.com

Manufactures a line of tape-backup products. Acquired by Conner Peripherals. Acquired by Seagate Technologies.

McAfee Associates
4423 Cheeney Street
Santa Clara, CA 95054
(408)988-3832
(408)970-9727 FAX
(408)988-4044 BBS

www.mcafee.com

Manufactures the SCAN virus-scanning software, which is nonresident and updated frequently to handle new viruses as they are discovered.

McGraw-Hill, Inc.
148 Princeton Road N-1
Hightstown, NJ 08520
(609)426-5000
(800)262-4729
(614)755-5645 FAX

gopher.mcgraw.infor.com

Publishes technical information and books.

McKenzie Technology
910 Page Avenue
Fremont, CA 94538
(510)651-2700
(510)651-1020 FAX

Manufactures sockets for processors and IC chips.

Megahertz Corporation (Division of U.S. Robotics)
605 N 5600 W
Salt Lake City, UT 84116
(801)320-7000
(800)527-8677
(800)856-1045 FAXBack
(801)320-6020 Tech Support FAX
(801)320-6022 Sales FAX
(801)320-6020 RMA FAX
(801)320-6021 Marketing FAX

Manufactures laptop modems and external network adapters. Also makes AT-speedup products.

Mentor Electronics, Inc.
7560 Tyler Boulevard #E
Mentor, OH 44060
(216)951-1884
(216)951-0107 FAX

Supplies ICs.

Merisel
200 N. Continental Boulevard
El Segundo, CA 90245
(310)615-3080
(800)542-9955
(800)462-5241 Customer Service
(800)845-3744 FAX Customer Service
(800)468-0030 Service Support Line

www.merisel.com

World's largest distributor of PC hardware and software products from many manufacturers.

Meritec
1359 West Jackson Street
P.O. Box 8003
Painesville, OH 44077
(216)354-3148
(216)354-0509 FAX
(800)627-7752

Manufactures a line of SCSI 8-bit to 16-bit (Wide SCSI) adapters in a variety of configurations. These adapters allow Wide SCSI devices to be installed in a standard 8-bit SCSI bus and vice versa.

Merritt Computer Products, Inc.
5565 Red Bird Center Drive #150
Dallas, TX 75237
(214)339-0753
(214)339-1313 FAX

Manufactures the SafeSkin keyboard protector.

Methode Electronics, Inc.
DataMate Division
7444 W. Wilson Avenue
Chicago, IL 60656
(708)867-9600
(708)867-3149 FAX

Manufactures and sells a complete line of SCSI terminators.

Micro 2000, Inc.
1100 E. Broadway
Third Floor
Glendale, CA 91205
(818)547-0125
(818)547-0397 FAX

www.micro2000.com

Manufactures the MicroScope PC diagnostics program, as well as the POSTProbe ISA, EISA, and MCA POST diagnostics card.

They are extending 25 percent discount to anyone who mentions this book when purchasing.

Micro Accessories, Inc.
6036 Stewart Avenue
Fremont, CA 94538
(510)226-6310
(800)777-6687
(510)226-6316 FAX

Manufactures a variety of cables and disk drive mounting brackets and accessories, including PS/2 adapter kits.

Micro Channel Developers Association
169 Hartnel Avenue
Redding, CA 96002
(916)222-2262
(800)GET-MCDA (438-6232)
(916)222-2528 FAX

microchannel.inter.net/microchannel

An independent organization established to facilitate the evolution of the Micro Channel Architecture (MCA) as an industry-wide standard. Its primary focus is to assist developers to build compatible MCA products, and to explain to users the benefits of this architecture. The association also provides microchannel products direct to ender users. They publish the "International Catalog of Micro Channel Products and Services."

Micro Computer Cable Company, Inc.
12200 Delta Drive
Taylor, MI 48180
(313)946-9700
(313)946-9645 FAX

Manufactures and sells a complete line of computer cables, connectors, switchboxes and cabling accessories.

Micro Design International (MDI)
6985 University Boulevard
Winter Park, FL 32792
(407)677-8333
(800)228-0891
(407)677-8365 FAX
(407)677-4854 BBS

Manufactures the SCSI Express driver software for integration of SCSI peripherals in a variety of environments. Recently acquired PC-Kwik Corp.

Micro House International
2477 N. 55th Street
Boulder, CO 80301
(303)443-3388
(303)443-3389
(800)926-8299
(303)443-3323 FAX
(303)443-9957 BBS

Publishes the Micro House Technical Library on CD-ROM. The technical library is a Windows- compatible reference tool designed for PC service technicians that covers adapter cards, network cards, motherboards, and disk drives.

Micro Industries Corp.
8399 Green Meadows Drive North
North Westerville, OH 43081-9486
(614)548-7878
(800)369-1086
(614)548-6184 FAX

Manufactures PC-compatible motherboards.

Micro Solutions, Inc.
132 W. Lincoln Hwy.
DeKalb, IL 60115
(815)756-3411
(800)890-7227
(815)756-6417 FAX
(815)756-9100 BBS

www.microsolutions.com

Manufactures a complete line of floppy controllers and subsystems, including 2.88M versions. Also offers floppy drive and tape-backup systems that run from a standard parallel port, using no expansion slots.

Micro Tech Corporation
685 Battle Mountain Road
Amissville, VA 20106
(540)937-3298
(540)937-3299 FAX

A service company specializing in computer repair and data recovery.

Micro Warehouse
535 Conneticut Avenue
Norwalk, CT 06854
(203)899-4000
(203)853-2267 FAX Sales
(800)547-5444 Sales

Distributes a large variety of computers, computer supplies, floppy disks, cables, and so on.

Microcom, Inc.
500 River Ridge Drive
Norwood, MA 02062
(617)551-1000
(800)822-8224
(617)551-1898 FAX
(617)255-1125 BBS

www.microcom.com

Manufactures error-correcting modems, remote

access products; created and develops the MNP communications protocols.

Micrografx, Inc.
1303 E. Arapaho Road
Richardson, TX 75081
(800)733-3729
(800)417-8312 Sales
(214)234-1769 Information
(214)234-2684 Tech Support/
Customer Service
(214)994-6476 FAX
(214)644-4194 BBS

www.micrografx.com
go micrografx—CompuServe
micrografx—America Online

Manufactures the Micrografx Designer, Windows Draw, ABC Toolkit, Photomagic, and Charisma software. Specializes in Windows and OS/2 development.

Microid Research, Inc.
1538 Turnpike Street
North Andover, MA 01845
(508)683-8209
(508)683-1630 FAX

mrbios@mrbio.com

Manufactures the MR BIOS, one of the most flexible and configurable BIOS versions available. They have versions available for a variety of different chip sets and motherboards.

Microlink/Micro Firmware, Inc.
330 West Gray Street
Suite 170
Norman, OK 73069-7111
(800)767-5465
(405)573-5535 FAX
(405)573-5538 BBS

www.firmware.com
go pcvend—CompuServe

The largest distributor of Phoenix ROM BIOS upgrades. Develops custom versions for specific motherboards and supplies many other BIOS vendors with products.

Micron Technologies (Parent Company of Micron Electronics & Micron Custom Manufacturing)
8000 S. Federal Way
Boise, ID 83707
(208)368-3900
(800)388-6334
(208)368-3809 FAX
(208)368-4530 BBS

www.micron.com

Manufactures various memory boards, memory chips, SIMMs, DRAM, SRAM and other semi conductors, as well as a line of IBM-compatible systems.

Micronics Computers/ Orchid Technology, Inc.
232 E. Warren Avenue
Fremont, CA 94539
(510)651-2300
(510)651-5612 FAX Sales
(510)661-3000 FAXBack
(510)651-6837 BBS

Manufactures PC-compatible motherboards and complete laptop and portable systems. Micronics motherboards feature the Phoenix BIOS.

Micropolis Corporation
21211 Nordhoff Street
Chatsworth, CA 91311
(818)709-3300
(800)395-DRIV (3748)
(818)709-3396 FAX
(818)709-3310 BBS

Manufactures a line of high-capacity 5 1/4- and 3 1/2-inch hard disk drives.

Microprocessors Unlimited, Inc.
24000 S. Peoria Avenue
Beggs, OK 74421
(918)267-4961
(918)267-3879 FAX

Distributes memory chips, SIMMs, math coprocessors, UART chips, and other integrated circuits.

Microsoft Corporation
One Microsoft Way
Redmond, WA 98052-6399
(206)882-8080
(800)426-9400 Sales
(206)936-7329 FAX
(206)936-6735 BBS

ftp.microsoft.com

Manufactures MS-DOS, Windows, Windows NT, and a variety of applications software.

MicroWay, Inc.
Research Park
Box 79
Kingston, MA 02364
(508)746-7341
(508)746-4678
(508)746-7946 BBS

tech@microway.com
www.microway.com

Manufactures a line of accelerator products for IBM and compatible systems. Also specializes in math co-processor chips, math chip accelerators, alpha based systems, and language products.

Mini Micro
4900 Patrick Henry Lane
Santa Clara, CA 95054

(408)327-0388
(800)275-4642
(408)327-0389 FAX
(408)434-9319 BBS

postmaster@mm.sco.com

Partly owned by Greenleaf Corp., wholesale distributor of Conner Peripherals, Inc.

Mitsubishi Electronics America, Inc.
Information Technologies Group
5665 Plaza Drive
Cypress, CA 90630
(714)220-2500
(714)236-6380 FAX

Electronic Device Group
1050 E. Arques Avenue
Sunnyvale, CA 94086
(408)730-5900
(800)843-2515
(800)344-6352 Technical Support

Manufactures monitors, printers, and consumables. For hard disks and floppy disk storage products contact the Electronic Device Group.

Mitsumi Electronics Corp.
6210 N. Beltline Road
Suite 170
Irving, TX 75063
(214)550-7300
(214)550-7424 FAX

www.mitsumi.com
www.eclusa.com

Manufactures a line of CD-ROM and floppy drives, as well as keyboards.

Molex, Inc.
2222 Wellington Court
Lisle, IL 60532
(630)969-4550
(800)78MOLEX (786-6539)
(630)969-2321 FAX

www.molex.com

Manufactures a variety of connectors used in PC systems.

Motor Magazine
Hearst Corporation
645 Stewart Avenue
Garden City, NY 11530
(516)227-1300
(800)AUTO-828
(516)227-1444 FAX

The essential trade magazine for the automotive technician, including troubleshooting tips and service product information. Subscriptions are free to those who qualify.

Motorola, Inc.
Microprocessor and Memory Technology Group
3501 Ed Bluestein Boulevard
Austin, TX 78762
(512)891-2000
(800)521-6274
(512)891-2652 FAX

Manufactures PC memory including fast static RAM for cache. Also makes the Power PC and Motorola Processors.

Mountain Network Solutions, Inc.
360 El Pueblo Road
Scotts Valley, CA 95066
(800)458-0300
(408)438-7623 FAX
(408)438-2665 BBS

techsupport@mountain.com

Manufactures tape drives and backup subsystems, including hardware and software.

Mueller Technical Research
21718 Mayfield Lane
Barrington, IL 60010-9733
(847)726-0709
(847)726-0710 FAX

73145.1566@compuserve.com

You found me! I run a service company that offers the best in custom on-site PC hardware and software technical seminars and training, specializing in all aspects of PC hardware, software, and data recovery. We can present a custom seminar for your organization. My new Video Tape "Your PC, The Inside Story" is also available from Learnkey. Scott Mueller.

Mustang Software
PO Box 2264
Bakersfield, CA 93303
(805)873-2500
(800)999-9619
(805)873-2599 FAX
(805)873-2400 BBS

sales@mustang.com
www.mustang.com
bbs.mustang.com
ftp.mustang.com

Manufactures Wildcat! BBS software.

Mylex Corporation
34551 Ardenwood Boulevard
Fremont, CA 94555
(510)796-6100
(800)776-9539
(510)745-8016 FAX

Manufactures high-performance motherboards and SCSI host adapters.

Myoda Computer Centers
1070 N. Roselle Road
Hoffman Estates, IL 60195

(847)885-7600
(847)885-7661 FAX

Assembles PC systems for retail sale.

National Semiconductor Corporation
2900 Semiconductor Drive
Santa Clara, CA 95052-8090
(408)721-5000
(408)721-7582 FAX
(408)721-5151 FAX
(408)245-0671 BBS

www.national.com
www.nsc.com

Manufactures a variety of chips for PC circuit applications. Known especially for its UART and Super I/O chips.

NCL America, Inc.
1031 E. Duane Avenue
Suite H
Sunnyvale, CA 94086
(408)737-2496
(408)730-1621 FAX

Manufactures IDE host adapters.

NCR Microelectronics
1635 Aeroplaza
Colorado Springs, CO 80916
(719)596-5795
(800)334-5454
(719)573-3286 FAX Sales
(719)574-0424 SCSI BBS
(800)262-7782 AT&T GIS Hardware Support
(800)856-3093 Literature Fulfillment

For latest software drivers and installation documentation:
(719)573-3562 BBS Symbios Logics

ftp.hmpd.com

Manufactures a variety of integrated circuits for PC systems, including SCSI protocol chips used by many OEMs. They also sponsor the SCSI BBS, an excellent source for standard documents covering SCSI, IDE, and other interfaces.

NEC Electronics, Inc.
475 Ellis Street
Mountain View, CA
94039-7241
(415)960-6000

Manufactures memory and other semiconductor devices.

NEC Technologies, Inc.
1414 Massachusetts Avenue
Boxborough, MA 01719
(508)264-8000
(800)632-4636
(508)264-8245 FAX
(708)860-2602 BBS

www.nec.com

Manufactures Multisync monitors, CD-ROM drives, video adapters, printers, and other peripherals, as well as complete PC-compatible systems.

Newark Electronics
4801 N. Ravenswood
Chicago, IL 60640-4496
(312)784-5100
(312)907-5217 FAX

An electronic component and product supplier with a huge catalog of products. Their 1500+ page catalog is an excellent source of components and information.

NexGen, Inc.
(A division of AMD)
1623 Buckeye Drive
Milpitas, CA 95035
(408)432-2400
(800)8NEXGEN (863-9436)
(408)435-0262 FAX

Manufactures the Nx586 family of processors, which are being marketed as alternatives to the Intel Pentium family.

Northgate Computer Systems, Inc.
6840 Hayvenhurst
VanNuys, CA 91406
(818)781-0300
(800)947-6211
(888)NORTHGATE
(667-8442) Sales
(818)779-3767 FAX Sales
(612)947-4640 BBS

www.northgate.net

Manufactures PC-compatible systems and keyboards sold through mail order.

Novell, Inc.
122 E. 1700 South
Provo, UT 84601
(801)379-5588
(800)526-7937
(801)228-6160 Public Relations
(801)429-5157 FAX
(801)429-3030 BBS

www.novell.com
ftp.novell.com
go netwire—forum on CompuServe

Manufactures the NetWare LAN operating system.

Number Nine Visual Technology Corp.
18 Hartwell Avenue
Lexington, MA 02173
(617)674-0009
(617)674-2919 FAX
(617)862-7502 BBS

www.numbernine.com (or)
www.9.com

Manufactures a line of high-end PC video graphics accelerator cards.

Oak Technology, Inc.
139 Kifer Court
Sunnyvale, CA 94086
(408)737-0888
(408)737-3838 FAX
(408)774-5308 BBS

www.oaktech.com

Manufactures graphics chipsets.

Ocean Information Systems
688 Arrow Grand Circle
Covina, CA 91722
(818)339-8888
(818)859-7668 FAX

Manufactures high-performance PC motherboards.

OEM Magazine
CMP Publications
600 Community Drive
Manhasset, NY 11030
(516)562-5000

An excellent magazine for the systems integrator or systems assembler. Free subscription for those who qualify.

Okidata
532 Fellowship Road
Mount Laurel, NJ 08054
(609)235-2600
(800)OKIDATA (654-3282)
(609)424-7423 FAX
(800)283-5474 BBS

Manufactures printers and modems.

Olivetti
765 US Hwy. 202
Somerville, NJ 08876
(908)526-8200
(908)526-8405 FAX
(800)243-2324

mscetar@royalnet.com

Manufactures Olivetti and many AT&T PC systems.

Ontrack Data Internationa, Inc. (formerly Ontrack Computer Systems)
6321 Bury Drive
Suites 13-21
Eden Prairie, MN 55346
(612)937-1107
(612)937-5815 FAX
(800)752-1333
(612)937-2121 Technical Support
(612)937-5161 Ontrack Data Recovery
(800)872-2599 Ontrack Data Recovery
(612)937-5750 FAX Data Recovery
(612)937-0860 BBS (2400bps)
(612)937-8567 BBS (9600+bps)

www.ontrack.com
sales@ontrack.com
Technet@ontrack.com

Manufactures the Disk Manager hard disk utilities for PC, PS/2, and Macintosh. Disk Manager is the most comprehensive and flexible low-level format program available, supporting even IDE drives. Also provides extensive data recovery services.

Opti, Inc.
888 Tasman Drive
Milpitas, CA 95035
(408)486-8000
(800)398-6784
(408)486-8001 FAX
(408)486-8051 BBS

www.opti.com

Manufactures PC motherboard chipsets including the Viper series for Pentium systems.

Orchid Technology (Micronics)
45365 Northport Loop West
Fremont, CA 94538

Sales/Customer Support
232 E. Warren Avenue
Fremont, CA 94539
(510)683-0300
(800)767-2443 Customer Service
(510)651-2300 Sales
(510)651-5612 FAX Sales
(510)661-3000 Technical Support
(510)661-3199 FAXBack
(510)651-6837 BBS

www.orchid.com

Manufactures a line of video and memory board products for IBM and compatible systems.

Osborne/McGraw Hill
2600 10th Street
Berkeley, CA 94710
(800)227-0900
(510)549-6600
(510)549-6603 FAX

www.osborne.com

Publishes computer books.

Pacific Data Products
9855 Scranton Road
San Diego, CA 92121
(619)552-0880
(619)552-0889 FAX
(619)452-6329 BBS

Manufactures the Pacific Page XL and PacificPage PE PostScript compatible enhancement products for HP LaserJet printers.

Packard Bell
31717 La Tienda Drive
Westlake Village, CA 91362
(818)865-1555
(800)733-4411
(818)865-0379 FAX
(818)313-8601 BBS

Manufactures a popular line of low-cost PC-compatible computer systems.

Palo Alto Design Group
360 University Avenue
Palo Alto, CA 94301
(415)327-9444

marcom@padg.com

Manufactures enclosures that accept Intel ATX motherboards.

Panasonic Communications & Systems
2 Panasonic Way
Secaucus, NJ 07094
(201)392-6502
(800)233-8182
(201)392-4858 FAX
(201)863-7845 BBS

www.panasonic.com

Manufactures monitors, optical drive products, floppy drives, printers, and PC-compatible laptop systems.

Panasonic Industrial Co.
2 Panasonic Way
Secaucus, NJ 07094
(800)848-3979

Manufactures IC memory cards; batteries (nickel metal hydride); cellular components (planar filters and resonators); optical and floppy disk drives; CD-ROM drives; printer mechanisms; power supplies (custom AC adapters); semiconductors (video digital signal processors, CCD card camera); microphones; speakers; high-resolution color monitors; TV tuners; ceramic receivers; and video camera modules.

Parallel Technologies, Inc.
PO Box 7
Redmond, WA 98073-0007
(206)869-1136
(206)869-9767 FAX

76640.203@compuserve.com

Manufactures the Parallel Port Information Utility.

PARTS NOW!, Inc.
810 Stewart Street
Madison, WI 53713
(608)276-8688
(608)276-9134 FAX

dkrceo—America Online

Sells a large variety of laser printer parts for HP, Canon, Apple, and other laser printers using Canon engines.

PC & MAC Connection
6 Mill Street
Marlow, NH 03456
(603)446-7721
(800)800-5555
(603)446-7791 FAX

Distributes many different hardware and software packages by way of mail order.

PC Magazine
Ziff Communications Co.
One Park Avenue
New York, NY 10016
(212)503-3500
(212)503-5799 FAX
(Editorial)

Magazine featuring product reviews and comparisons.

PC Power & Cooling, Inc.
5995 Avenida Encinas
Carlsbad, CA 92008
(619)931-5700
(800)722-6555
(619)931-6988 FAX

www.pcpowercooling.com

Manufactures a line of high-quality, high-output power supplies and cooling fans for IBM and compatible systems. Known for high-power output and quiet fan operation.

PC Week Magazine
10 Presidents Landing
Medford, MA 02155
(617)393-3700
(617)393-3859 FAX

Weekly magazine featuring industry news and information.

PC World Magazine
375 Chochituate Road
Framingham, MA 01701
(508)879-0700
(800)435-7766
(508)620-7739 FAX

careers.computerworld.com

A monthly magazine featuring product reviews and comparisons.

PC-Kwik Corporation (Micro Design International)
3800 SW Cedar Hills Boulevard
Suite 260
Beaverton, OR 97005

(503)644-5644
(503)646-8267 FAX

Formerly Multisoft, they manufacture the PC-Kwik Power Pak system performance utilities, Super PC-Kwik disk cache, and WinMaster Windows utility programs. Recently acquired by Micro Design International.

PCI Special Interest Group
2727 NE Stanton Street
Portland, OR 97212
(503)693-6232 (outside U.S.)
(800)433-5177
(503)693-8344 FAX

www.teleport.com/~pc2/pcisigindex.html

Formed in June 1992, the PCI SIG (peripheral Component Interconnect Special Interest Group) is the industry organization that owns and manages the PCI Local Bus Specification. More than 500 industry-leading companies are active PCI SIG members. The organization is chartered to support new requirements, while maintaining backward compatibility for all PCI revisions; maintain the specification as an easy-to-implement, stable technology; and contribute to the technical longevity of PCI and its establishment as an industry-wide standard.

PCMCIA—Personal Computer Memory Card International Association
2635 North First Street
Suite 209
San Jose, CA 95314
(408)433-2273
(408)433-9558 FAX
(408)433-2270 BBS

office@pcmcia.org
www.pc-card.com

An independent organization that maintains the PCMCIA bus standard for credit-card-sized expansion adapters.

Philips Consumer Electronics
One Philips Drive
Knoxville, TN 37914
(423)521-4316
(423)521-4586 FAX

www.magnavox.com

Manufactures Magnavox PCs, monitors, and CD-ROM drives.

Phoenix Technologies, Ltd.
2770 De La Cruz Blvd.
Santa Clara, CA 95050
(408)654-9000
(408)452-1985 FAX
(714)440-8026 BBS

www.ptltd.com

Designs IBM-compatible BIOS software for a number of ISA, EISA, and MCA systems.

PicoPower Technology, Inc.
see Cirrus Logic Co. listing

Manufactures PC motherboard chipsets for mobile and desktop systems. Acquired by Cirrus Logic in '94.

Pivar Computing Services, Inc.
165 Arlington Heights Road
Buffalo Grove, IL 60089
(847)459-6010
(800)266-8378
(847)459-6095 FAX

www.pivar.com

Service company that specializes in data and media conversion.

PKWare, Inc.
9025 N. Deerwood Drive
Brown Deer, WI 53223
(414)354-8699
(414)354-8559 FAX
(414)354-8670 BBS

Manufactures the PKZIP, PKUNZIP, and PKLit data compression software. Widely used on BBS systems and by manufacturers for software distribution.

Plextor
4255 Burton Drive
Santa Clara, CA 95054
(408)980-1838
(800)886-3935
(800)4-PLEXTOR (475-3986)
(408)986-1010 FAX
(408)986-1569 BBS

Manufactures a line of high-performance CD-ROM drives.

Practical Enhanced Logic, Corp.
22695 Old Canal Road
Yorba Linda, CA 92687
(714)282-6188
(714)282-6199 FAX

Manufactures the Systo Tek CPU fan failure alarm, as well as the SCSI-Link parallel to SCSI converter and other high performance SCSI adapters.

Processor Magazine
PO Box 85518
Lincoln, NE 68501

(800)247-4880
(402)479-2120 FAX
(402)477-2283 BBS

www.peed.com

Publication that offers excellent sources of replacement and repair parts as well as new equipment at wholesale prices.

Programmer's Shop
33 Riverside Drive
Pembroke, MA 02359
(617)740-2510
(800)421-8006
(617)829-5009 FAX Sales

gopher.std.com

Distributes programming tools and utility software.

Public Software Library
PO Box 35705
Houston, TX 77235
(713)524-6394
(800)242-4775
(713)524-6398 FAX
(713)442-6704 BBS

nelson.ford@pslonline.com

Distributor of high-quality public domain and shareware software. Its library is the most well-researched and tested available. Also offers an excellent newsletter that reviews the software.

Qlogic Corp.
3545 Harbor Boulevard
PO Box 5001
Costa Mesa, CA 92628-5001
(714)438-2200
(714)668-5037 Technical Support
(714)668-5324 FAX Technical Support
(800)TOP-SCSI (867-7274) Product Info
(714)668-5327 FAX Product Info

qlets@qlc.com—Tech Support
qlsales@qlc.com—Sales Inquiries
www.qlc.com

Manufactures a line of high-end PCI SCSI adapters.

Qualitas, Inc.
7101 Wisconsin Avenue #1024
Bethesda, MD 20814
(301)907-6700
(301)907-0905 FAX
(301)718-6060 FAX Tech Service
(301)907-8030 BBS

www.qualitas.com
75300,1107—CompuServe
qualitas—America Online

Manufactures the Qualitas Max 8 memory-manager utility programs.

Quantum Corporation
500 McCarthy Boulevard
Milpitas, CA 95035
(408)894-4000
(800)624-5545
(800)826-8022 Technical Support
(800)434-7532 FAXBack
(800)894-3214 BBS
(408)434-1664 BBS

www.quantum.com

Manufactures a line of 5.24 to 2.5-inch hard disk drives. Supplies drives to Apple Computer, Compaq, IBM, Dell and HP.

Quarter-Inch Cartridge Drive Standards, Inc. (QIC)
311 East Carrillo Street
Santa Barbara, CA 93101
(805)963-3853
(805)962-1541 FAX

www.qic.org
qic@aol.com

An independent industry group that sets and maintains Quarter Inch Cartridge (QIC) tape drive standards for backup and archiving purposes.

Quarterdeck Office Systems
13160 Mindanao
Marina Del Rey, CA 90292
(310)309-3700
(310)314-4218 FAX
(310)3094-3227 BBS

info@qdeck.com
www.qdeck.com

Manufactures the popular DESQview, QEMM, and QRAM memory-manager products.

Que Corporation
201 West 103rd Street
Indianapolis, IN 46290
(317)581-3500
(800)428-5331 Order Line
(800)448-3804 Sales FAX

www.mcp.com

Publishes the highest-quality computer software and hardware books in the industry, including this one!

Qume Corporation (acquired by Wyse Technologies)
500 Yosemite Drive
Milpitas, CA 95035
(408)473-1500
(800)538-3777

Manufactures a variety of peripherals.

Radio Shack
Division of Tandy Corporation
1800 One Tandy Center
Fort Worth, TX 76102
(817)390-3011
(817)390-2774 FAX

Manages the Radio Shack electronics stores, which sell numerous electronics devices, parts, and supplies. Also manufactures a line of PC-compatible computers and computer accessories and supplies.

Ramtron International Corp.
1850 Ramtron Drive
Colorado Springs, CO 80921
(719)481-7000

Manufactures special memory components including EDRAM dynamic RAM products that combine high-speed DRAM with an even faster SRAM cache on a single chip.

Rancho Technology, Inc.
10783 Bell Court
Rancho Cucamonga, CA 91730
(909)-987-3966
(909)989-2365 FAX
(909)980-7699 BBS

scsi@rancho.com
www.rancho.com

Manufactures an extensive line of SCSI products, including host adapters for ISA, EISA, and MCA bus systems, interface and, converters from single-ended to differential and vice versa.

Reply Corporation
4435 Fortran Drive
San Jose, CA 95134
(408)942-4804
(800)955-5295
(408)942-4897 FAX

Designs and sells an exclusive line of complete 386 and 486 motherboard upgrades for IBM PS/2 systems, including the Model 30, 30-286, 50, 55, 60, 65, 70, and 80. These are complete new motherboards with integrated local bus SVGA adapters, Pentium Overdrive support, 2.88M floppy controller, Flash BIOS, built-in ATA IDE adapter, support for up to 32M of motherboard memory, and numerous other features. These upgrade boards are actually manufactured for Reply by IBM, and are fully IBM compatible. They also manufacture a line of Compaq motherboard upgrades as well.

Rinda Technologies Inc.
4563 N. Elston Avenue
Chicago, IL 60630
(312)736-6633
(312)736-2950 FAX

www.mcs.net/~rinda

Manufactures the DIACOM General Motors and Chrysler automotive diagnostics and troubleshooting software. DIACOM includes a hardware adapter that connects your PC directly to the automobile diagnostic connector through a parallel port on your system, and essentially converts you PC into a professional SCAN tool. Vehicle data can then be observed live or stored for analysis and troubleshooting.

Robinson Nugent, Inc.
800 East 8th Street
New Albany, IN 47150
(812)945-0211
(812)945-0804 FAX
(800)457-2412 Sales

Manufactures a variety of computer connectors and sockets. They also manufacture the EPROM carriers used in GM Automotive applications from '81 through '93.

Rockwell Semiconductor Systems
4311 Jamboree Road
Newport Beach, CA 92660-3095
(714)221-4600

Manufactures communications chipsets used in many PC compatible modems and high-speed data, fax, business audio, voice-mail and mobile-communication applications.

Roland Corporation U.S.
7200 Dominion Circle
Los Angeles, CA 90040-3696
(213)685-5141
(213)722-0911 FAX

www.rolandus.com
goroland—CompuServe

Manufactures a variety of musical equipment and MIDI interfaces for computers.

Rupp Technology Corporation
3228 East Indian School Road
Phoenix, AZ 85018
(602)941-4789
(800)852-7877
(800)941-5602 Tech Support
(602)224-0898 FAX

75300,1232—CompuServe
ruptTech—America Online
into@rup.com - Internet

Developer of the DOS Interlink software used in MS- and PC-DOS. Also sells a commercial version called Fastlynx Lite for DOS that offers many enhancements over Interlink. WinLynx is a full windows file transfer and management program. Also makes custom length parallel transfer cables using a high-speed, 18-wire design supported by virtually all parallel transfer programs.

S3 Inc.
PO Box 58058
2770 San Tomas Expressway
Santa Clara, CA 95052-8058
(408)980-5400
(408)980-5444 FAX
(408)654-5676 BBS

www.s3.com

Manufactures a line of very popular high-performance video chipsets.

Safeware Insurance Agency, Inc.
PO Box 656
5760 N. High Street
Worthington, OH 43085
(614)781-1492
(800)848-3469
(614)781-0559 FAX

www.safeware-ins.com

Insurance company that specializes in insurance for computer equipment.

SAMS
201 West 103rd Street
Indianapolis, IN 46290
(317)581-3500

sams.net

Publishes technical books on computers and electronic equipment.

Samsung Semiconductor, Inc.
3655 N. First Street
San Jose, CA 95134
(405)954-7000

Manufactures memory and semiconductor devices.

Seagate Software Storage Management Group (formerly Sytron)
37 Skyline Drive
Lake Mary, FL 32746
(407)333-7500
(407)333-7730 FAX
(800)327-2232 Sales

www.sssmg.seagate.com

Manufactures the SyTOS tape-backup software for DOS and OS/2, the most widely used tape software in the industry.

Seagate Technology
920 Disc Drive
Scotts Valley, CA 95066
(408)438-6550
(408)429-6356 FAX
(800)468-3472 Service
(408)438-2620 FAXBack Information
(408)438-8771 BBS

The largest hard disk manufacturer in the world. Offers the most extensive product line of any disk manufacturer, ranging from low-cost units to the highest-performance, -capacity, and -quality drives available.

Sencore
3200 Sencore Drive
Sioux Falls, SD 57107
(605)339-0100
(800)736-2673 Sales
(605)335-6379 FAX

Manufactures a line of computer monitor signal generators and repair equipment.

Service News Magazine
United Publications Inc.
38 Lafayette Street
PO Box 995
Yarmouth, ME 04096
(207)846-0600
(207)846-0657 FAX

www.servicenews.com

An excellent monthly newspaper for computer service and support personnel featuring articles covering PC service and repair products. Subscriptions are free to those who qualify.

SGS-Thomson Microelectronics, Inc.
55 Old Bedford Road
Lincoln, MA 01773
(617)259-0300
(617)259-4421 FAX

www.st.com

Manufactures a variety of memory and semiconductor devices.

Sharp Electronics Corporation
Sharp Plaza
Mahwah, NJ 07430-2135
(201)529-8200
(201)529-8413 FAX
(800)BE SHARP (237-4277)

www.sharp-usa.com

Manufactures a wide variety of electronic and computer equipment, including the best LCD monochrome and active matrix color displays and panels, as well as scanners, printers, and complete laptop and notebook systems.

Sharp Microelectronics Group
5700 NW Pacific Rim Boulevard
Camas, WA 98607
(800)642-0261 Literature Distribution Center

Manufactures memory and semiconductor devices.

Sigma Data
17 Newport Road
New London, NH 03257-4565
(603)526-6909
(800)446-4525
(603)526-6915 FAX

sigma@sigmadata.com

Manufacturer/distributor of personal computer add-on and peripheral products specializing in easy-to-install hard drives, processors and memory upgrades. They offer a unique line of "Quick Easy" upgrades including the QED (Quick Easy Disk) and QEP (Quick Easy Processor). Their product line also includes high-speed, high-capacity drives for a variety of popular portable, laptop, and notebook computers.

Silicon Integrated Systems Corp. (SiS)
240 North Wolfe Road
Sunnyvale, CA 94086
(408)730-5600
(408)730-5639 FAX

Manufactures PC motherboard chipsets.

Silicon Valley Research
6360 San Ignacio Avenue
San Jose, CA 95119
415-962-3000
415-962-3001 FAX

www.svri.com

Manufactures a complete line of IDE interface adapters, including a unique model that supports 16-bit IDE (ATA) drives on PC and XT systems (8-bit ISA bus) and models, including floppy drive support as well as serial and parallel ports.

Simple Technology
3001 Daimler Street
Santa Ana, CA 92705
(714)476-1180
(800)854-3900
(714)476-1209 FAX

www.simpletech.com

Manufactures the SIMMswitch, which replaces the soldered resistors on a SIMM, allowing it to be easily reconfigured. They also sell SIMMs with the switch already installed.

SL Waber
520 Fellowship Road
Mt. Laurel, NJ 08054
(690)866-888

Manufactures a complete line of power protection equipment for PC computers.

Smart Cable, Inc.
13625 NE 126th Place
Suite 400
Kirkland, WA 98034
(206)823-2273
(800)752-6526
(206)821-3961 FAX

Manufactures the SmartCable universal serial RS-232 cable.

Softbank Comdex, Inc.
300 First Avenue
Needham, MA 02194-2722
(617)449-6600
(617)449-6953 FAX

Producer of the world's leading computer tradeshows.

Softkey International, Inc.
1 Anthenaeum Street
Cambridge, MA 02142
(617)494-1200
(800)227-5609 Sales
(800)323-8088
(617)494-5898 FAX
(423)670-2023 BBS

www.softkey.com

Manufactures the WordStar 7 and distributes over 500 other software programs, including Compton's Encyclopedia and various educational titles.

SofTouch Systems, Inc.
1300 S. Meridian
Suite 600
Oklahoma City, OK 73108-1751
(405)947-8080
(405)947-8169 FAX

www.softouch.com

Manufactures the GammaTech Utilities for OS/2, that can undelete and recover files running under OS/2 even on an OS/2 HPFS partition and UniMaint, a desktop repair and recovery program.

Software Testing Lab (STL)
PO Box 19771
Indianapolis, IN 46219

(317)974-0805
(317)974-0699 FAX

murney@ai2a.net

Sola Heavy Duty Electric
1717 Busse Road
Elk Grove, IL 60007
(708)439-2800
(800)289-7652
(800)377-4384
(800)626-6299 FAX

Manufactures a line of computer power-protection devices.

Sonera Technologies
PO Box 565
Rumson, NJ 07760
(800)932-6323
(908)747-6886
(908)747-4523 FAX

www.displaymate.com

Manufactures the DisplayMate video display utility and diagnostic program. Displaymate exercises, troubleshoots, and diagnoses video display adapter and monitor problems.

Sony Corporation of America
Sony Drive
Park Ridge, NJ 07656
(201)930-1000
(201)930-7669 Product/Service Info
(408)894-0555 Computer products in San Jose, CA
(408)955-5171 FAX
(408)955-5107 BBS

Manufactures all types of high-quality electronic and computer equipment, including displays and magnetic- and optical-storage devices.

Specialized Products Company
3131 Premier Drive
Irving, TX 75063
(214)550-1923
(800)866-5353
(800)234-8286 FAX Sales

Distributes a variety of tools and test equipment.

Sprague Magnetics, Inc.
15720 Stagg Street
Van Nuys, CA 91406
(818)994-6602
(800)553-8712
(818)994-2153 FAX

smicomp@sprague-magnetics.com
www.earthlink.net

Distributes a unique and interesting magnetic developer fluid that can be used to view sectors and tracks on a magnetic disk or tape. Also repairs tape drives.

Stac Incorporated
12636 High Bluff Drive
San Diego, CA 92130
(619)794-4300
(800)522-7822 Sales
(619)794-3715 FAX
(619)794-3711 BBS

Manufactures the Stacker real-time data-compression adapter and software for OS/2 and DOS/Windows. They also have new products which include Reach Out Remote Access/Control software and Replica Server disaster recovery software for netware and CD quick share.

Standard Microsystems Corporation
80 Arkay Drive
Hauppauge, NY 11788
(516)273-3100
(800)SMC-4YOU (768-4768) Sales
(516)273-1803 FAX
(800)762-8329 FAXBack
(516)434-3162 BBS

www.smc.com
techsupport@smc.com

Manufactures Ethernet and ARCnet network adapters, as well as a complete line of Super I/O chipsets, hubs, and switches.

Star Micronics America, Inc.
70-D Ethel Road W.
Piscataway, NJ 08854
(908)572-5550
(908)572-3129 FAX
(908)572-5095 OEM FAX
(908)572-5010 BBS

Manufactures a line of low-cost printers.

STB Systems, Inc.
1651 N. Glenville
Richardson, TX 75085-0957
(214)234-8750
(214)234-1306 FAX
(214)437-9615 BBS

www.stb.com

Manufactures various adapter boards, and specializes in a line of high-resolution VGA video adapters.

Storage Dimensions, Inc.
1656 McCarthy Boulevard
Milpetas, CA 95035
(408)954-0710
(408)944-1200 FAX
(408)944-1221 BBS

www.storagedimensions.com
support@xtor.com
techconnect@xtor.com

Manfactures high-performance disk and tape storage solutions for open system environments. Distributes Maxtor hard disk and optical drives as complete subsystems.

Sun Moon Star
1941 Ringwood Avenue
San Jose, CA 95131
(408)452-7811

Manufactures CD-ROM and multimedia kits and power supplies for PC compatibles.

Super Micro Computer, Inc.
2178 Paragon Drive
San Jose, CA 95131
(408)451-1118
(408)451-1110 FAX

Manufactures a very high quality line of Pentium class PC compatible motherboards.

Superpower Supply, Inc.
990 Norcross Industrial Court
Norcross, GA 30071
(800)736-0007
(310)906-2621 FAX

ourworld.compuserve.com
superpower@delrina.net

Manufactures a line of PC-compatible power supplies and cases. They also distribute PC networking components.

Symantec Corporation
175 W. Broadway
Eugene, OR 97401
(800)441-7234
(541)334-7400 FAX
(541)484-6669 BBS

www.symantec.com
Go Symantec—CompuServe

Manufactures a line of utility and applications software featuring the Norton Utilities for IBM and Apple systems and PC Tools.

SyQuest Technology
47071 Bayside Parkway
Fremont, CA 94538
(510)226-4000
(800)245-2278 Sales
(800)249-2440 Technical Support
(510)226-4102 FAX
(510)656-0473 BBS

sales@syquest.com
support@syquest.com
ftp.netcom.com./pub/sy/syquest

Manufactures removable-cartridge hard disk drives.

Tadiran
2 Seaziew
Port Washington, NY 11050
(516)625-8488
(800)537-1368 Sales
(516)621-4517 FAX

www.echo-on.net\net\mob\tadiran.htm
tadiran@village.ios.com—EMAIL

Manufactures a variety of batteries for computer applications.

Tandy Corporation/ Radio Shack
1800 One Tandy Center
Fort Worth, TX 76102
(817)390-3700
(817)390-2647 FAX

Manufactures a line of IBM-compatible systems, peripherals, and accessories. Also distributes electronic parts and supplies.

Tatung Company of America, Inc.
2850 El Presidio Street
Long Beach, CA 90810
(310)637-2105
(800)827-2850
(310)637-8484 FAX

Manufactures monitors and complete compatible systems.

TDK Electronics Corporation
12 Harbor Park Drive
Port Washington, NY 11050
(516)625-0100
(516)625-0651 FAX

Manufactures a line of magnetic and optical media, including disk and tape cartridges.

Teac America, Inc.
7733 Telegraph Road
Montebello, CA 90640
(213)726-0303
(213)727-7656 FAX
(213)727-7660 BBS
(213)727-7629 FAXBack Info.

Manufactures a line of floppy and tape drives, including a unit that combines both 3 1/2-inch and 5 1/4-inch drives in one half-height package.

Tech Data Corporation
5350 Tech Data Drive
Clearwater, FL 34620
(813)539-7429
(800)237-8931
(813)538-7876 FAX
(813)538-7090 BBS

Distributes computer equipment and supplies.

Tech Spray, Inc.
PO Box 949
Amarillo, TX 79105-0949

(806)372-8523
(806)372-8750 FAX

Manufactures a complete line of computer and electronic cleaning chemicals and products.

Tecmar Technologies, Inc.
1900 Pike Road
Longmont, CO 80501
(303)682-3700
(800)4-BACKUP (422-2587) Sales
(800)344-4463 Tech Support
(800)992-9916 Customer Service
(303)776-7706 FAX

www.tecmar.com

Manufactures Wangtech, WangDAT and Proline tape back up drives.

Tekram Technologies
11500 Metric Boulevard
Suite 190
Austin, TX 78758
(512)833-6550
(512)833-7276 FAX

www.tekram.com

Manufactures a complete line of caching and non-caching disk controllers, PCI motherboards, multimedia products, CD ROM servers, printer servers, and video cards. Specializes in IDE and SCSI adapters, which are fast and flexible.

Test and Measurement World Magazine
275 Washington Street
Newton, MA 02158-1611
(617)558-4671
(617)558-4470 FAX

tmw@cahneis.com

A magazine for quality control and testing in the electronics industry. Free for those who qualify.

Texas Instruments, Inc.
Box 14149
12501 Research Boulevard
Austin, TX 78714-9149
(800)TI-TEXAS (848-3927)
(512)250-7111
(714)274-2000

Manufactures memory and other semiconductor devices.

Thermalloy, Inc.
2021 W. Valley View Lane
PO Box 810839
Dallas, TX 75381-0839
(214)243-4321
(214)241-4656 FAX

www.thermalloy.com

Manufactures a line of excellent CPU heat sink products, including versions with built-in fan modules and DC-DC converters and other thermal management solutions.

THYNX
619 Alexander Road
Princeton,NJ 08540
(609)514-1600
(609)514-1818 FAX

www.Thynx.com

Distributes and publishes software on CD-ROM disks.

Toshiba America Electronic Components, Inc.
9775 Toledo Way
Irvine, CA 92718
(714)455-2000

Manufactures memory and other semiconductor devices.

Toshiba America, Inc.
9740 Irvine Boulevard
Irvine, CA 92718
(714)583-3926
(800)999-4823
(800)950-4373 FAX
(714)837-2116 BBS

Manufactures a complete line of 5 1/4- and 3 1/2-inch floppy and hard disk drives, CD-ROM drives, display products, printers, and a popular line of laptop and notebook IBM-compatible systems.

TouchStone Software Corporation
2124 Main Street
Huntington Beach, CA 92648
(714)969-7746
(800)531-0450
(714)960-1886 FAX

www.checkit.com

Manufactures the CheckIt user level and CheckIt Pro Deluxe high end PC diagnostics and troubleshooting programs. CheckIt Diagnostic Kit also includes CheckIt IV, a self-booting portable diagnostic.

Trace Research and Development Center
University of Wisconsin
S-151 Waisman Center
1500 Highland Avenue
Madison, WI 53705
(608)263-2309
(608)262-8848
(608)263-5408 TDD

trace.wisc.edu
info@trace.wisc.edu

The Trace Center is an interdisciplinary research, development and resource center on technology and disability.

Traveling Software, Inc.
18702 N. Creek Parkway
Bothell, WA 98011
(206)483-8088
(800)662-2652
(206)485-6786 FAX Sales
(206)487-1284 PR FAX
(206)485-1736 BBS

ww.travsoft.com

Manufactures the LapLink file-transfer program for PC and Mac systems as well as several other utility programs.

Trident Microsystems
189 N. Bernado Avenue
Mountain View, CA 94043
(415)691-9211
(415)691-9260 FAX
(415)961-1016 BBS

www.trid.com

Manufactures a line of high-end video chipsets and multimedia video adapters.

TriniTech, Inc.
1430 Court Street
Suite 3
Clearwater, FL 34616
(800)909-3424
(813)442-8882
(813)442-5897 FAX

Manufactures a complete line of PC diagnostics products including the OmniPOST, IRQuest Plus and PC Power Sentry diagnostics cards, and Expertrace diagnostics software.

Tripp Lite Manufacturing
500 N. Orleans
Chicago, IL 60610
(312)329-1777
(312)644-6505 FAX

tripplite.com

Manufactures a complete line of computer power-protection devices.

Tseng Labs, Inc.
6 Terry Drive
Newtown, PA 18940
(215)968-0502
(215)860-7713 FAX
(215)579-7536 BBS

www.tseng.com

Manufactures video controller chipsets, BIOS, and board design for OEMs.

TTI Technologies
5124 Ralston
Ventura, CA 93003
(800)541-1943
(805)650-6515 FAX

www.ttiteck.com
Peter@ttitech.com—EMAIL

Distributes AMI, Award, Phoenix MR BIOS upgrades, and microid research.

Twinhead Corp.
1537 Centre Pointe Drive
Milpitas, CA 95035
(408)945-0808
(800)552-8946

www.twinhead.com
www.slimnote.com

Manufactures notebook, subnotebook and desktop computer systems.

U.S. Robotics, Inc.
8100 N. McCormick Boulevard
Skokie, IL 60076
(847)982-5010
(847)982-5151
(847)933-5300 FAX
(847)982-5092 BBS

www.usr.com
support@usr.com

Manufactures a complete line of modems and communications products. Its modems support more protocols than most others, including V.32bis, HST, and MNP protocols.

Ultra-X, Inc.
1765 Scott Boulevard
Suite 101
Santa Clara, CA 95050
(408)261-7090
(800)722-3789
(408)261-7077 FAX

pcdiag@ultrax.com

Manufactures the excellent QuickPost PC, QuickPost PCI, and QuickPost PRO diagnostic cards, as well as the Quicktech PRO diagnostic software.

Underwriters Laboratories, Inc.
Corporate Headquarters
333 Pfingsten Road
Northbrook, IL 60062-2096
(847)727-8800
(847)272-8129 FAX

The leading third-party product safety certification organization in the United States and the largest in North America. Established in 1894.

Unicomp, Inc.
2501 W. Fifth Street
Santa Ana, CA 92703
(800)359-5092
(714)571-1909 FAX

Distributes new and refurbished printer repair parts for all types of printers.

UNISYS
Township Line and Union Meeting Roads
Blue Bell, PA 19424
(800)448-1424
(716)742-6671 FAX

Manufactures PC-compatible systems that are part of the government Desktop IV contract.

V Communications, Inc.
4320 Stevens Creek Boulevard
Suite 120
San Jose, CA 95129
(408)296-4224
(408)296-4441 FAX

www.v-com.com

Manufactures the Sourcer disassembler and other programming tools.

Varta Batteries, Inc.
300 Executive Boulevard
Elmsford, NY 10523
(914)592-2500
(914)592-2667 FAX

Manufactures a complete line of computer batteries.

Verbatim Corporation
1200 WT Harris Boulevard
Charlotte, NC 28262
(704)547-6500

Manufactures a line of storage media, including optical and magnetic disks and tapes.

VESA—Video Electronic Standards Association
2150 North First Street
Suite 440
San Jose, CA 95131-2029
(408)435-0333
(408)435-8225 FAX

www.vesa.org

An organization of manufacturers dedicated to setting and maintaining video display, adapter, and bus standards. They have created the VESA video standards as well as the VESA Video Local Bus (VL-Bus) standard.

VIA Technologies, Inc.
5020 Brandin Court
Fremont, CA 94538
(510)683-3300
(510)683-3301 FAX

Manufactures PC motherboard chipsets.

ViewSonic
20480 Business Parkway
Walnut, CA 91789
(909)869-7976
(909)869-7958 FAX
(909)444-5219 BBS View Sonic
(909)444-5225 BBS OptiQuest

Manufactures a line of high-quality monitors and displays with plug and play as well as energy star compliance.

Visiflex Seels
16 E. Lafayette Street
Hackensack, NJ 07601
(201)487-8080
(201)487-6637

Manufactures form-fitting clear keyboard covers and other computer accessories.

VLSI Technology, Inc.
1109 McKay Drive
San Jose, CA 95131
(408)434-3000

Manufactures chipsets and circuits for PC-compatible motherboards and adapters.

Volpe, Hank
PO Box 43214
Baltimore, MD 21236
(410)256-5767
(410)256-3631 BBS

modem.doctor@ghawk.com

Manufactures the Modem Doctor Version 6 serial port and modem diagnostics program.

Walling Company
4401 Juniper Street
Tempe, AZ 85282
(602)838-1277 voice/FAX

Manufactures the DataRase EPROM eraser, which can erase as many as four EPROM chips simultaneously using ultraviolet light.

Wang Laboratories, Inc.
600 Technology Park Drive
Billerica, MA 01821-4130
(508)656-1550
(800)225-0654
(508)967-0829

Manufactures a variety of PC-compatible systems, including some with MCA bus slots.

Warshawski/ Whitney & Co.
1104 S. State Street
Chicago, IL 60605
(312)431-6100
(312)431-5625 FAX

70007.1524@compuserve.com

Distributes an enormous collection of bargain-priced tools and equipment. Its products are primarily for automotive applications, but many of the tools have universal uses.

Washburn & Co.
3800 Monroe Avenue
Pittsford, NY 14534
(716)385-5200
(800)836-8026
(716)381-7549 FAX
(770)246-8780 AMI BBS

70305.1211@compuserve.com

The largest distributor of AMI BIOS and AMI motherboard products, known for providing very high-end technical information and support.

Watergate Software
2000 Powell Street
Suite 1200
Emeryville, CA 94608
(510)596-1770
(510)653-4784 FAX

www.ws.com

Manufactures the excellent PC Doctor diagnostic program for PC troubleshooting and repair.

Wave Tech
9145 Balboa Avenue
San Diego, CA 92123
(619)279-2200
(800)854-2708
(619)627-0132 FAX
(619)278-5034 BBS

wavetech.com

Manufactures diagnostics and test equipment.

Weitek Corporation
2801 Orchard Parkway
San Jose, CA 95134
(408)526-0300
(408)577-1066 FAX
(408)522-7512 BBS

www.weitek.com

Manufactures high-performance math coprocessor chips. Moving by January '96.

Western Digital Corporation
8105 Irvine Center Drive
Irvine, CA 92718
(714)932-5000
(800)832-4778
(800)ASK-4WDC (275-4932)
(714)932-6771 Literature
(714)932-4012 FAX
(714)932-4300 FAXBack
(714)753-1234 BBS (2400bps)
(714)753-1068 BBS
(9600+bps)

www.wdc.com

Manufactures many products, including IDE and SCSI hard drives; SCSI and ESDI adapters for ISA, EISA, and MCA bus systems; and Ethernet, Token Ring, and Paradise video adapters. Supplies IBM with IDE and SCSI drives for PS/2 systems.

Winbond (formerly Symphony Laboratories)
2730 Orchard Parkway
San Jose, CA 95134
(408)943-6666
(408)474-1600 FAX

www.winbond.com.tw

Manufactures PC motherboard chipsets.

Windsor Technologies, Inc.
130 Alto Street
San Rafael, CA 94901
(415)456-2200
(415)456-2244 FAX

Manufactures PC Technician, an excellent high-end, technician-level PC diagnostics and troubleshooting program.

WordPerfect (Novell)
1555 N. Technology Way
Orem, UT 84057
(800)453-1267
(801)225-5000
(801)229-1566 FAX
(801)225-4414 BBS

Manufactures the popular WordPerfect word processing program. Acquired by Novell.

Wyse Technology
3471 N. 1st Street
San Jose, CA 95134
(408)473-1200
(800)438-9973
(408)473-1972 FAX
(408)922-4400 BBS

www.wyse.com

Manufactures terminals and monitors.

Xerox Corporation
Xerox Square
Rochester, NY 14644
(716)423-5078
(203)968-3000
(203)968-3368 FAX

Manufactures the Ventura desktop publishing software, as well as an extensive line of computer equipment, copiers, and printers.

Xircom
2300 Corporate Center Drive
Thousand Oaks, CA 91320
(805)376-9300
(800)874-7875
(805)376-9200 Technical Support
(805)376-9311 FAX
(805)376-9130 BBS

cs@xircom.com

Manufactures external Token Ring and Ethernet adapters that attach to a parallel port and PCMCIA cards for laptops.

Y-E Data America, Inc.
5824 Peachtree Corners E
Suite A
Norcross, GA 30092
(404)446-8655
(404)291-4203 FAX

yea_hq@usa.pipeline.com

Manufactures a line of floppy disk drives, tape drives, and printers. Supplied 5 1/4-inch floppy drives to IBM for use in XT, AT, and PS/2 systems.

Young Micro Systems (YMS)
12221 Florence Avenue
Santa Fe Springs, CA 90670
(310)906-1888
(310)906-1889 FAX

Manufactures a variety of PC-compatible motherboards.

Zenith Data Systems
2150 E. Lake Cook Road
Buffalo Grove, IL 60089
(847)808-5000
(800)553-0331
(800)472-7211 FAX

www.zds.com

Manufactures a line of IBM-compatible systems.

Zeos International, Ltd. (purchased by Micron Electronics)
Micron Electronics
900 E. Karcher Road
Napa, ID 83687
(208)893-3434
(800)438-3343
(208)893-3424 FAX Sales
(208)893-8989 FAX
(208)893-8982 BBS
(800)270-1207 BBS

www.mei.micron.com

Manufactures a line of good, low-cost, PC-compatible ISA and EISA bus systems sold by way of mail order.

Ziff-Davis Benchmark Operation
1001 Aviation Parkway
Suite 400
Morrisville, NC 27560
(919)380-2879 FAX

Manufactures Benchmark software; unfortunately at press time all we had was a FAX number. Please write or FAX to company for more information.

Appendix C

Glossary

This glossary contains computer and electronics terms that are applicable to the subject matter in this book. The glossary is meant to be as comprehensive as possible on the subject of upgrading or repairing PCs. Many terms correspond to the latest technology in disk interfaces, modems, video and display equipment, and many standards that govern the PC industry. Although a glossary is a resource not designed to be read from beginning to end, you should find that scanning through this one is interesting, if not enlightening, with respect to some of the newer PC technology.

The computer industry is filled with acronyms used as shorthand for a number of terms. This glossary defines many acronyms, as well as the term on which the acronym is based. The definition of an acronym usually is included under the acronym. For example, Video Graphics Array is defined under the acronym VGA rather than under Video Graphics Array. This organization makes it easier to look up a term—IDE, for example—even if you do not know in advance what it stands for (Integrated Drive Electronics).

For additional reference, Que's *Computer User's Dictionary* is a comprehensive, general-purpose computer dictionary of computer terminology.

10Base2 IEEE standard for baseband Ethernet at 10Mbps over coaxial cable to a maximum distance of 185 meters. Also known as THIN ETHERNET.

10Base5 IEEE standard for baseband Ethernet at 10Mbps over coaxial cable to a maximum distance of 500 meters. Also known as THICK ETHERNET.

10BaseT A 10Mbps CSMA/CD Ethernet local area network that works on Category 3 twisted pair wiring that is very similar to standard telephone cabling. 10BaseT Ethernet local area networks work on a "Star" configuration in which the wire from each workstation routes directly to a central 10BaseT hub.

100BaseT A 100Mbps CSMA/CD Ethernet local area network that works on Category 5 twisted pair wiring. 100BaseT Ethernet local area networks work on a "Star" configuration in which the wire from each workstation routes directly to a central 100Base-T hub. This is the new standard for 100Mbps Ethernet.

100BaseVG The joint Hewlett Packard-AT&T proposal for fast-Ethernet running at 100 million bits per second. It uses four pair of Category 5 cable using the 10BaseT twisted pair wiring scheme to transmit or receive. 100BaseVG splits the signal across the four wire pairs at 25Mhz each.

8086 An Intel microprocessor with 16-bit registers, a 16-bit data bus, and a 20-bit address bus. This processor can operate only in real mode.

8087 An Intel math coprocessor designed to perform floating-point math with much greater speed and precision than the main CPU. The 8087 can be installed in most 8086- and 8088-based systems, and adds more than 50 new instructions to what is available in the primary CPU alone.

8088 An Intel microprocessor with 16-bit registers, an 8-bit data bus, and a 20-bit address bus. This processor can operate only in real mode, and was designed as a low-cost version of the 8086.

8514/A An analog video display adapter from IBM for the PS/2 line of personal computers. Compared to previous display adapters such as EGA and VGA, it provides a high resolution of 1024×768 pixels with as many as 256 colors or 64 shades of gray. It provides a video coprocessor that performs two-dimensional graphics functions internally, thus relieving the CPU of graphics tasks. It is an interlaced monitor; it scans every other line every time the screen is refreshed.

80286 An Intel microprocessor with 16-bit registers, a 16-bit data bus, and a 24-bit address bus. Can operate in real and protected virtual modes.

80287 An Intel math coprocessor designed to perform floating-point math with much greater speed and precision than the main CPU. The 80287 can be installed in most 286- and some 386DX-based systems, and adds more than 50 new instructions to what is available in the primary CPU alone.

80386 *See* 80386DX.

80386DX An Intel microprocessor with 32-bit registers, a 32-bit data bus, and a 32-bit address bus. This processor can operate in real, protected virtual, and virtual real modes.

80386SX An Intel microprocessor with 32-bit registers, a 16-bit data bus, and a 24-bit address bus. This processor, designed as a low-cost version of the 386DX, can operate in real, protected virtual, and virtual real modes.

80387DX An Intel math coprocessor designed to perform floating-point math with much greater speed and precision than the main CPU. The 80387DX can be installed in most 386DX-based systems, and adds more than 50 new instructions to what is available in the primary CPU alone.

80387SX An Intel math coprocessor designed to perform floating-point math with much greater speed and precision than the main CPU. The 80387SX can be installed in most 386SX-based systems, and adds more than 50 new instructions to what is available in the primary CPU alone.

80486 *See* 80486DX.

80486DX An Intel microprocessor with 32-bit registers, a 32-bit data bus, and a 32-bit address bus. The 486DX has a built-in cache controller with 8K of cache memory as well as a built-in math coprocessor equivalent to a 387DX. The 486DX can operate in real, protected virtual, and virtual real modes.

80486DX2 A version of the 486DX with an internal clock doubling circuit that causes the chip to run at twice the motherboard clock speed. If the motherboard clock is 33MHz, the DX2 chip will run at 66MHz. The DX2 designation applies to chips sold through the OEM market, while a retail version of the DX2 is sold as an overdrive processor.

80486DX4 A version of the 486DX with an internal clock tripling circuit that causes the chip to run at three times the motherboard clock speed. If the motherboard clock is 33.33 MHz, the DX4 chip will run at 100MHz.

80486SX An Intel microprocessor with 32-bit registers, a 32-bit data bus, and a 32-bit address bus. The 486SX is the same as the 486DX except that it lacks the built-in math coprocessor function, and was designed as a low-cost version of the 486DX. The 486SX can operate in real, protected virtual, and virtual real modes.

80487SX An Intel microprocessor with 32-bit registers, a 32-bit data bus, and a 32-bit address bus. The 487SX has a built-in cache controller with 8K of cache memory as well as a built-in math coprocessor equivalent to a 387DX. The 487SX can operate in real, protected virtual, and virtual real modes. This processor is a complete processor and math coprocessor unit, not just a math coprocessor. The 487SX is designed to upgrade systems with the 486SX processor, which lacks the math coprocessor function. When a 487SX is installed in a system, it shuts down the 486SX and takes over the system. In effect, the 487SX is a full-blown 486DX modified to be installed as an upgrade for 486SX systems.

abend Short for *abnormal end.* Used when the execution of a program or task is terminated unexpectedly because of a bug or crash.

AC Alternating current. The frequency is measured in cycles per seconds (cps), or hertz. The standard value running through the wall outlet is 120 volts at 60 hertz, through a fuse or circuit breaker that usually can handle about 20 amps.

accelerator board An add-in board replacing the computer's CPU with circuitry that enables the system to run faster.

access time The time that elapses from when the instant information is requested to the point that delivery is completed. Usually described in nanoseconds for memory chips. The IBM PC requires memory chips with an access time of 200 nanoseconds, and the AT requires 150-nanosecond chips. For hard disk drives, access time is described in milliseconds. Most manufacturers rate average access time on a hard disk as the time required for a seek across one-third of the total number of cylinders plus one-half of the time for a single revolution of the disk platters (latency).

accumulator A register (temporary storage) in which the result of an operation is formed.

acronym An acronym is a word or group of letters formed from the first or first few letters of a series of words. For example, CPU is an acronym for Central Processing Unit. This glossary contains definitions for many acronyms popular in the personal computer industry.

active high Designates a digital signal that has to go to a high value to produce an effect. Synonymous with *positive true.*

active low Designates a digital signal that has to go to a low value to produce an effect. Synonymous with *negative true.*

actuator The device that moves a disk drive's read/write heads across the platter surfaces. Also known as an *access mechanism.*

adapter The device that serves as an interface between the system unit and the devices attached to it. A term used by IBM that is synonymous with *circuit board, circuit card,* or *card.*

address Refers to where a particular piece of data or other information is found in the computer. Also can refer to the location of a set of instructions.

address bus One or more electrical conductors used to carry the binary-coded address from the microprocessor throughout the rest of the system.

alphanumeric characters A character set that contains only letters (A-Z) and digits (0-9). Other characters, such as punctuation marks, also may be allowed.

ampere The basic unit for measuring electrical current. Also called *amp.*

analog loopback A modem self-test in which data from the keyboard is sent to the modem's transmitter, modulated into analog form, looped back to the receiver, demodulated into digital form, and returned to the screen for verification.

analog signals Continuously variable signals in which the slightest change may be significant. Analog circuits are more subject to distortion and noise but are capable of handling complex signals with relatively simple circuitry. An alternative to analog is digital, in which signals are in only one of two states.

AND A logic operator having the property that if P is a statement, Q is a statement, R is a statement,..., then the AND of P,Q,R,... is true if all statements are true and is false if any statement is false.

AND gate A logic gate in which the output is 1 only if all inputs are 1.

ANSI American National Standards Institute. A non-governmental organization founded in 1918 to propose, modify, approve, and publish data processing standards for voluntary use in the United States. Also the U.S. representative to the International Standards Organization (ISO) in Paris and the International Electrotechnical Commission (IEC). For more information, see the vendor list.

answer mode A state in which the modem transmits at the predefined high frequency of the communications channel and receives at the low frequency. The transmit/receive frequencies are the reverse of the calling modem, which is in originate mode.

APA All Points Addressable. A mode in which all points of a displayable image can be controlled by the user or a program.

API Application Program Interface. A system call (routine) that gives programmers access to the services provided by the operating system. In IBM-compatible systems, the ROM BIOS and DOS together present an API that a programmer can use to control the system hardware.

APM Advanced Power Management. A specification sponsored by Intel and Microsoft originally proposed to extend the life of batteries in battery-powered computers. APM allows application programs, the system BIOS, and the hardware to work together to reduce power consumption. An APM-compliant BIOS provides built-in power management services to the operating system. The application software communicates power-saving data via predefined APM interfaces.

arbitration A method by which multiple devices attached to a single bus can bid or arbitrate to get control of that bus.

archive bit The bit in a file's attribute byte that sets the archive attribute. Tells whether the file has been changed since it last was backed up.

archive medium A storage medium (floppy disk, tape cartridge, or removable cartridge) to hold files that need not be accessible instantly.

ARCnet Attached Resource Computer Network. A baseband, token-passing local area network technology offering a flexible bus/star topology for connecting personal computers. Operating at 2.5 megabits per second, it is one of the oldest LAN systems, and was popular in low-cost networks. Originally developed by John Murphy, of Datapoint Corporation, although ARCnet interface cards are available from a variety of vendors.

Areal Density A calculation of the bit density (Bits Per Inch, or BPI) multiplied by the track density (Tracks Per Inch, or TPI), which results in a figure indicating how many bits per square inch are present on the disk surface.

ARQ Automatic Repeat Request. A general term for error-control protocols that feature error detection and automatic retransmission of defective blocks of data.

ASCII American Standard Code for Information Interchange. A standard seven-bit code created in 1965 by Robert W. Bemer to achieve compatibility among various types of data processing equipment. The standard ASCII character set consists of 128 decimal numbers, ranging from 0 through 127, assigned to letters, numbers, punctuation marks, and the most common special characters. In 1981 IBM introduced the extended ASCII character set with the IBM PC, extending the code to eight bits and adding characters from 128 through 255 to represent additional special mathematical, graphics, and foreign characters.

ASCII character A 1-byte character from the ASCII character set, including alphabetic and numeric characters, punctuation symbols, and various graphics characters.

ASME American Society of Mechanical Engineers.

assemble To translate a program expressed in an assembler language into a computer machine language.

assembler language A computer-oriented language whose instructions are usually in one-to-one correspondence with machine language instructions.

asymmetrical modulation A duplex transmission technique that splits the communications channel into one high-speed channel and one slower channel. During a call under asymmetrical modulation, the modem with the greatest amount of data to transmit is allocated the high-speed channel. The modem with less data is allocated the slow, or back, channel (450 bps). The modems dynamically reverse the channels during a call if the volume of data transfer changes.

asynchronous communication Data transmission in which the length of time between transmitted characters may vary. Timing is dependent on the actual time for the transfer to take place, as opposed to synchronous communication, which is timed rigidly by an external clock signal. Because the receiving modem must be signaled when the data bits of a character begin and end, start and stop bits are added to each character.

ATA AT Attachment interface. An IDE disk interface standard introduced in March 1989 that defines a compatible register set and a 40-pin connector and its associated signals. *See also* IDE.

ATA-2 The second generation AT Attachment interface specification. This version defines faster transfer modes and Logical Block Addressing schemes to allow high performance large capacity drives. Also called *Fast ATA, Fast ATA-2,* and *Enhanced IDE (EIDE).*

ATAPI AT Attachment Packet Interface. A specification that defines device side characteristics for an IDE connected peripheral, such as CD-ROM or tape drives. ATAPI is essentially an adaptation of the SCSI command set to the IDE interface.

ATM Asynchronous Transfer Mode. ATM is a high bandwidth, low-delay, packet-like switching and multiplexing technique. Usable capacity is segmented into fixed-size cells, consisting of header and information fields, allocated to services on demand. ATM will be the basis for the future broadband network in view of its flexibility and suitability for both transmission and switching.

attribute byte A byte of information, held in the directory entry of any file, that describes various attributes of the file, such as whether it is read-only or has been backed up since it last was changed. Attributes can be set by the DOS ATTRIB command.

audio A signal that can be heard, such as through the speaker of the PC. Many PC diagnostics tests use both visual (on-screen) codes and audio signals.

audio frequencies Frequencies that can be heard by the human ear (approximately 20 to 20,000 hertz).

auto answer A setting in modems enabling them to answer incoming calls over the phone lines automatically.

auto dial A feature in modems enabling them to dial phone numbers without human intervention.

AUTOEXEC.BAT A special batch file that DOS executes at start-up. Contains any number of DOS commands that are executed automatically.

automatic head parking Disk drive head parking performed whenever the drive is powered off. Found in all hard disk drives with a voice-coil actuator.

average access time The average time it takes a disk drive to begin reading any data placed anywhere on the drive. This includes the average seek time, which is when the heads are moved, as well as the latency, which is the average amount of time required for any given data sector to pass underneath the heads. Together these make up the average access time.

average latency The average time required for any byte of data stored on a disk to rotate under the disk drive's read/write head. Equal to one-half the time required for a single rotation of a platter.

average seek time Average seek time for a drive is the average amount of time it takes to move the heads from one random cylinder location to another, usually including any head settling time. In many cases, the average seek is tested across one-third of the total number of cylinders for consistency in measurement.

AVI Audio Video Interleave. A storage technique developed by Microsoft for their "Video for Windows" product that combines audio and video into a single frame or track, saving valuable disk space and keeping audio in synchronization with the corresponding video.

backup The process of duplicating a file or library onto a separate piece of media. Good insurance against loss of an original.

backup disk Contains information copied from another disk. Used to make sure that original information is not destroyed or altered.

bad sector A disk sector that cannot hold data reliably because of a media flaw or damaged format markings.

bad track table A label affixed to the casing of a hard disk drive that tells which tracks are flawed and cannot hold data. The listing is entered into the low-level formatting program.

balanced signal A term referring to signals consisting of equal currents moving in opposite directions. When balanced or nearly balanced signals pass through twisted pair lines, the electromagnetic interference effects such as crosstalk caused by the two opposite currents largely cancel each other out. Differential signaling is a method that uses balanced signals.

balun Short for balanced/unbalanced. A type of transformer that enables balanced cables to be joined with unbalanced cables. Twisted pair (balanced) cables, for example, can be joined with coaxial (unbalanced) cables if the proper balun transformer is used.

bandwidth Generally the measure of the range of frequencies within a radiation band required to transmit a particular signal. Measures in millions of cycles per second the difference between the lowest and highest signal frequencies. The bandwidth of a computer monitor is a measure of the rate that a monitor can handle information from the display adapter. The wider the bandwidth, the more information the monitor can carry, and the greater the resolution. This term is also used to describe the data carrying capacity of a given network circuit. The bandwidth of a network circuit is a measure of the rate that a network can handle information. The higher the bandwidth, the more information the network can carry.

bank The collection of memory chips that make up a block of memory readable by the processor in a single bus cycle. This block therefore must be as large as the data bus of the particular microprocessor. In PC systems, the processor data bus is usually 8, 16, 32, or 64 bits, plus an optional parity bit for each 8 bits, resulting in a total of 9, 18, 36, or 72 bits (respectively) for each bank.

bar code The code used on consumer products and inventory parts for identification purposes. Consists of bars of varying thicknesses that represent characters and numerals that are read with an optical reader. The most common version is called the Universal Product Code (UPC).

baseband The transmission of digital signals over a limited distance. ARCnet and Ethernet local area networks utilize baseband signaling. Contrasts with broadband transmission, which refers to the transmission of analog signals over a greater distance.

BASIC Beginner's All-purpose Symbolic Instruction Code. A popular computer programming language. Originally developed by John Kemeny and Thomas Kurtz in the mid-1960s at Dartmouth College. Normally an interpretive language, meaning that each statement is translated and executed as it is encountered; but can be a compiled language, in which all the program statements are compiled before execution.

batch file A set of commands stored in a disk file for execution by the operating system. A special batch file called AUTOEXEC.BAT is executed by IBM DOS each time the system is started. All DOS batch files have a BAT file extension.

baud A unit of signaling speed denoting the number of discrete signal elements that can be transmitted per second. The word baud is derived from the name of J.M.E. Baudot (1845-1903), a French pioneer in the field of printing telegraphy and the inventor of Baudot code. Although technically inaccurate, baud rate commonly is used to mean bit rate. Because each signal element or baud may translate into many individual bits, bits per second (bps) normally differs from baud rate. A rate of 2400 baud means that 2400 frequency or signal changes per second are being sent, but each frequency change may signal several bits of information. Most people are surprised to learn that 2400 and 1200 bps modems transmit at 600 baud, and that 9600 and 14400 bps modems transmit at 2400 baud.

baud rate *See* baud.

Baudot code A 5-bit code used in many types of data communications including teletype (TTY), radio teletype (RTTY), and telecommunications devices for the deaf (TDD). Baudot code has been revised and extended several times.

bay An opening in a computer cabinet that holds disk drives.

BBS Bulletin Board System. A computer that operates with a program and a modem to enable other computers with modems to communicate with it, often on a round-the-clock basis. Thousands of PC-related bulletin board systems offer a wealth of information and public-domain software that can be downloaded.

bezel A cosmetic panel that covers the face of a drive or some other device.

Bezier Curve A mathematical method for describing a curve, often used in illustration and CAD programs to draw complex shapes.

bidirectional Refers to lines over which data can move in two directions, like a data bus or a telephone line. Also refers to the capability of a printer to print from right to left and from left to right alternately.

binary Refers to the computer numbering system that consists of two numerals, 0 and 1. Also called base-2.

BIOS Basic Input/Output System. The part of an operating system that handles the communications between the computer and its peripherals. Often burned into read-only memory (ROM) chips.

bisynchronous Binary synchronous control. An earlier protocol developed by IBM for software applications and communicating devices operating in synchronous environments. The protocol defines operations at the link level of communications—for example, the format of data frames exchanged between modems over a phone line.

bit Binary digit. Represented logically by 0 or 1 and electrically by 0 volts and (typically) 5 volts. Other methods are used to represent binary digits physically (tones, different voltages, lights, and so on), but the logic is always the same.

bit density Expressed as Bits Per Inch (BPI), bit density defines how many bits can be written onto one linear inch of a track. Sometimes also called *linear density*.

bit map A method of storing graphics information in memory in which a bit devoted to each pixel (picture element) on-screen indicates whether that pixel is on or off. A bit map contains a bit for each point or dot on a video display screen and allows for fine resolution because any point or pixel on-screen can be addressed. A greater number of bits can be used to describe each pixel's color, intensity, and other display characteristics.

block A string of records, words, or characters formed for technical or logic reasons and to be treated as an entity.

block diagram The logical structure or layout of a system in graphics form. Does not necessarily match the physical layout and does not specify all the components and their interconnections.

BMP Bit MaP. A Windows graphics format that may be device-dependent or independent. Device-independent BMP files (DIB) are coded for translation to a wide variety of displays and printers.

BNC British National Connector. A type of connector plug and jack system. Originally designed in England for television set antennas, the BNC is a type of connector designed for use with coaxial cabling. Male and female BNCs are available. Although the term is redundant, BNCs usually are referred to as BNC connectors. Often used in local area network cabling systems that use coaxial cable, such as Ethernet and ARCnet, and also used frequently for video cabling systems.

Boolean operation Any operation in which each of the operands and the result take one of two values.

boot Load a program into the computer. The term comes from the phrase "pulling a boot on by the bootstrap."

boot record A one-sector record that tells the computer's built-in operating system (BIOS) the most fundamental facts about a disk and DOS. Instructs the computer how to load the operating system files into memory, thus booting the machine.

bootstrap A technique or device designed to bring itself into a desired state by means of its own action. The term bootstrap is used to describe the process by which a device such as a PC goes from its initial power-on condition to a running condition without human intervention.

bps Bits per second. The number of binary digits, or bits, transmitted per second. Sometimes confused with baud.

bridge In local area networks, an interconnection between two similar networks. Also the hardware equipment used to establish such an interconnection.

broadband A term used to describe analog transmission. Requires modems for connecting terminals and computers to the network. Using frequency division multiplexing, many different signals or sets of data can be transmitted simultaneously. The alternate transmission scheme is baseband, or digital, transmission.

bubble memory A special type of nonvolatile read/write memory introduced by Intel in which magnetic regions are suspended in crystal film and data is maintained when the power is off. A typical bubble memory chip contains about 512K, or more than 4 million bubbles. Failed to catch on because of slow access times measured in several milliseconds. Has found a niche use as a solid-state "disk" emulator in environments in which conventional drives are unacceptable, such as military or factory use.

buffer A block of memory used as a holding tank to store data temporarily. Often positioned between a slower peripheral device and the faster computer. All data moving between the peripheral and the computer passes through the buffer. A buffer enables the data to be read from or written to the peripheral in larger chunks, which improves performance. A buffer that is x bytes in size usually holds the last x bytes of data that moved between the peripheral and CPU. This method contrasts with that of a cache, which adds intelligence to the buffer so that the most often accessed data rather than the last accessed data remains in the buffer (cache). A cache can improve performance greatly over a plain buffer.

bug An error or defect in a program.

burn-in The operation of a circuit or equipment to establish that components are stable and to screen for failures.

bus A linear electrical signal pathway over which power, data, and other signals travel. It is capable of connecting to three or more attachments. A bus is generally considered to be distinct from radial or point-to-point signal connections. The term bus comes from the Latin "omnibus" meaning "for all." When used to describe a topology, bus always implies a linear structure.

bus master An intelligent device that when attached to the Micro Channel, EISA, VLB, or PCI bus can bid for and gain control of the bus to perform its specific task.

byte A collection of bits that makes up a character or other designation. Generally, a byte is eight data bits. When referring to system RAM, an additional parity (error-checking) bit is also stored, making the total nine bits. *See also* parity.

C A high-level computer programming language. A frequently used programming language on mainframes, minis, and PC computer systems.

cache An intelligent buffer. By using an intelligent algorithm, a cache contains the data that is accessed most often between a slower peripheral device and the faster CPU.

CAM Common Access Method. A committee formed in 1988 that consists of a number of computer peripheral suppliers and is dedicated to developing standards for a common software interface between SCSI peripherals and host adapters. The CAM committee also has set a standard for IDE drives called the ATA interface.

capacitor A device consisting of two plates separated by insulating material and designed to store an electrical charge.

card A printed circuit board containing electronic components that form an entire circuit, usually designed to plug into a connector or slot. Sometimes also called an *adapter*.

carpal tunnel syndrome A painful hand injury that gets its name from the narrow tunnel in the wrist that connects ligament and bone. When undue pressure is put on the tendons, they can swell and compress the median nerve, which carries impulses from the brain to the hand. This causes numbness, weakness, tingling, and burning in the fingers and hands. Computer users get carpal tunnel syndrome primarily from improper keyboard ergonomics that result in undue strain on the wrist and hand.

carrier A continuous frequency signal capable of being either modulated or impressed with another information-carrying signal. The reference signal used for the transmission or reception of data. The most common use of this signal with computers involves modem communications over phone lines. The carrier is used as a signal on which the information is superimposed.

carrier detect signal A modem interface signal that indicates to the attached data terminal equipment (DTE) that it is receiving a signal from the distant modem. Defined in the RS-232 specification. Same as the received line-signal detector.

cathode ray tube (CRT) A device that contains electrodes surrounded by a glass sphere or cylinder and displays information by creating a beam of electrons that strike a phosphor coating inside the display unit. This device is most commonly used in computer monitors and terminals.

CAV Constant Angular Velocity. An optical disk recording format where the data is recorded on the disk in concentric circles. CAV disks are rotated at a constant speed. This is similar to the recording technique used on floppy disk drives. CAV limits the total recorded capacity compared to CLV (Constant Linear Velocity), which is also used in optical recording.

CCITT An acronym for the Comité Consultatif Internationale de Télégraphique et Téléphonique (in English, the International Telegraph and Telephone Consultative Committee or the Consultative Committee for International Telegraph and Telephone). An international committee organized by the United Nations to set international communications recommendations, which frequently are adopted as standards, and to develop interface, modem, and data network recommendations. The Bell 212A standard for 1200 bps communication in North America, for example, is observed internationally as CCITT V.22. For 2400 bps communication, most U.S. manufacturers observe V.22bis, and V.32 and V.32bis are standards for 9600 and 14400 bps, respectively. Work is now under way to define a new standard for 19200 bps called V.32fast.

CCS Common Command Set. A set of SCSI commands specified in the ANSI SCSI-1 Standard X3.131-1986 Addendum 4.B. All SCSI devices must be capable of using the CCS in order to be fully compatible with the ANSI SCSI-1 standard.

CD-DA Compact Disc Digital Audio. CD-DA is also known as "Red Book Audio" and is the digital sound format used by audio CDs. CD-DA uses a sampling rate of 44.1KHz and stores 16 bits of information for each sample. CD audio is not played through the computer, but through a special chip in the CD-ROM drive. Fifteen minutes of CD-DA sound can require about 80M. The highest quality sound that can be utilized by multimedia PCs is the CD-DA format at 44.1KHz sample rate.

CD-R Compact Disc Recordable, sometimes also called CD-Writable. CD-R disks are compact discs that can be recorded several times and read as many times as desired. CD-R is part of the Orange Book Standard defined by ISO. CD-R technology is used for mass production of multimedia applications. CD-R discs can be compatible with CD-ROM, CD-ROM XA, and CD audio. Orange Book specifies multi-session capabilities, which allows data recording on the disk at different times in several recording sessions. Kodak's Photo CD is an example of CD-R technology, and fits up to 100 digital photographs on a single CD. Multi-session capability allows several rolls of 35mm film to be added to a single disc on different occasions.

CD-ROM Compact Disc Read-Only Memory. A computer peripheral device that employs compact disc (CD) technology to store large amounts of data for later retrieval. Phillips and Sony developed CD-ROM in 1983. Current CD-ROM discs hold approximately 600M of information. CD-ROM drives are much slower than conventional hard disks, with normal average-access times of 380 milliseconds or greater and data transfer rates of about 1.2 megabits per second. Most CD-ROM drives use the SCSI (Small Computer Systems Interface) bus for connection to a system.

CD-ROM XA Compact Disc Read Only Memory eXtended Architecture. The XA standard was developed jointly by Sony, Phillips, and Microsoft in 1988 and is now part of the Yellow Book Standard. XA is a built-in feature of newer CD-ROM drives, and supports simultaneous sound playback with data transfer. Non-XA drives support either sound playback or data transfer, but not both simultaneously. XA also provides for data compression right on the disk, which can also increase data transfer rates.

ceramic substrate A thin, flat, fired ceramic part used to hold an IC chip (usually made of beryllium oxide or aluminum oxide).

CERN An acronym for Conseil Europeen pour la Recherche Nucleaire (The European Laboratory for Particle Physics). This is the site in Geneva where the World Wide Web was created in 1989.

CGA Color Graphics Adapter. A type of PC video display adapter introduced by IBM on August 12, 1981, that supports text and graphics. Text is supported at a maximum resolution of 80×25 characters in 16 colors with a character box of 8×8 pixels. Graphics is supported at a maximum resolution of 320×200 pixels in 16 colors or 640×200 pixels in 2 colors. The CGA outputs a TTL (digital) signal with a horizontal scanning frequency of 15.75 KHz, and supports TTL color or NTSC composite displays.

CGI An acronym for Common Gateway Interface. An API (Application Programming Interface) for HTTP that provides the server with the capability to run scripts or compiled applications when requested.

channel A path along which signals can be sent.

character A representation, coded in binary digits, of a letter, number, or other symbol.

checksum Short for summation check, a technique for determining whether a package of data is valid. The package, a string of binary digits, is added up and compared with the expected number.

chip Another name for an IC, or integrated circuit. Housed in a plastic or ceramic carrier device with pins for making electrical connections.

chip carrier A ceramic or plastic package that carries an integrated circuit.

CHS Cylinder Head Sector. The term used to describe the non-translating scheme used by the BIOS to access IDE drives that are less than or equal to 528MB in capacity. *See also* LBA.

circuit A complete electronic path.

circuit board The collection of circuits gathered on a sheet of plastic, usually with all contacts made through a strip of pins. The circuit board usually is made by chemically etching metal-coated plastic.

CISC Complex Instruction-Set Computer. Refers to traditional computers that operate with large sets of processor instructions. Most modern computers, including the Intel 80xxx processors, are in this category. CISC processors have expanded instruction sets that are complex in nature and require several to many execution cycles to complete. This structure contrasts with

RISC (reduced instruction-set computer) processors, which have far fewer instructions that execute quickly.

clean room A dust-free room in which certain electronic components (such as hard disk drives) must be manufactured and serviced to prevent contamination. Rooms are rated by Class numbers. A Class 100 clean room must have fewer than 100 particles larger than .5 microns per cubic foot of space.

clock The source of a computer's timing signals. Synchronizes every operation of the CPU.

clock speed A measurement of the rate at which the clock signal for a device oscillates, usually expressed in millions of cycles per second (MHz).

clone An IBM-compatible computer system that physically as well as electrically emulates the design of one of IBM's personal computer systems, usually the AT or XT. For example, an AT clone has parts (motherboard, power supply, and so on) that are physically interchangeable with the same parts in the IBM AT system.

cluster Also called allocation unit. A group of sectors on a disk that forms a fundamental unit of storage to the operating system. Cluster or allocation unit size is determined by DOS when the disk is formatted.

CLV Constant Linear Velocity. An optical recording format where the spacing of data is consistent throughout the disk, and the rotational speed of the disk varies depending on what track is being read. Additionally, more sectors of data are placed on the outer tracks compared to the inner tracks of the disk, which is similar to Zone Recording on hard drives. CLV drives will adjust the rotational speed to maintain a constant track velocity as the diameter of the track changes. CLV drives rotate faster near the center of the disk and slower toward the edge. Rotational adjustment maximizes the amount of data that can be stored on a disk. CD audio and CD-ROM use CLV recording.

CMOS Complementary Metal-Oxide Semiconductor. A type of chip design that requires little power to operate. In an AT-type system, a battery-powered CMOS memory and clock chip is used to store and maintain the clock setting and system configuration information.

coated media Hard disk platters coated with a reddish iron-oxide medium on which data is recorded.

coaxial cable Also called *coax cable*. A data-transmission medium noted for its wide bandwidth, immunity to interference, and high cost compared to other types of cable. Signals are transmitted inside a fully shielded environment, in which an inner conductor is surrounded by a solid insulating material and then an outer conductor or shield. Used in many local area network systems such as Ethernet and ARCnet.

COBOL COmmon Business-Oriented Language. A high-level computer programming language. The business world's preferred programming language on mainframe computer systems, it has never achieved popularity on smaller computers.

code page switching A DOS feature in versions 3.3 and later that changes the characters displayed on-screen or printed on an output device. Primarily used to support foreign-language characters. Requires an EGA or better video system and an IBM-compatible graphics printer.

CODEC COder-DECoder. A device that converts voice signals from their analog form to digital signals acceptable to more modern digital PBXs and digital transmission systems. It then converts those digital signals back to analog so that you can hear and understand what the other party is saying.

coercivity A measurement in units of oersteads of the amount of magnetic energy to switch or "coerce" the flux change in the magnetic recording media. High-coercivity disk media require a stronger write current.

Color Graphics Adapter *See* CGA.

COM port A serial port on a PC that conforms to the RS-232 standard. *See also* RS-232.

COMDEX The largest international computer trade show and conference in the world. COMDEX/Fall is held in Las Vegas during October, and COMDEX/Spring usually is held in Chicago or Atlanta during April.

command An instruction that tells the computer to start, stop, or continue an operation.

COMMAND.COM An operating system file that is loaded last when the computer is booted. The command interpreter or user interface and program-loader portion of DOS.

common The ground or return path for an electrical signal. If a wire, usually is colored black.

common mode noise Noise or electrical disturbances that can be measured between a current- or signal-carrying line and its associated ground. Common mode noise is frequently introduced to signals between separate computer equipment components through the power distribution circuits. It can be a problem when single-ended signals are used to connect different equipment or components that are powered by different circuits.

compiler A program that translates a program written in a high-level language into its equivalent machine language. The output from a compiler is called an object program.

complete backup A backup of all information on a hard disk, including the directory tree structure.

composite video Television picture information and sync pulses combined. The IBM Color Graphics Adapter (CGA) outputs a composite video signal.

computer Device capable of accepting data, applying prescribed processes to this data, and displaying the results or information produced.

CONFIG.SYS A file that can be created to tell DOS how to configure itself when the machine starts up. Can load device drivers, set the number of DOS buffers, and so on.

configuration file A file kept by application software to record various aspects of the software's configuration, such as the printer it uses.

console The unit, such as a terminal or a keyboard, in your system with which you communicate with the computer.

contiguous Touching or joined at the edge or boundary; in one piece.

continuity In electronics, an unbroken pathway. Testing for continuity normally means testing to determine whether a wire or other conductor is complete and unbroken (by measuring 0 ohms). A broken wire shows infinite resistance (or infinite ohms).

control cable The wider of the two cables that connect an ST-506/412 or ESDI hard disk drive to a controller card. A 34-pin cable that carries commands and acknowledgments between the drive and controller.

controller The electronics that control a device such as a hard disk drive and intermediate the passage of data between the device and the computer.

controller card An adapter holding the control electronics for one or more devices such as hard disks. Ordinarily occupies one of the computer's slots.

convergence Describes the capability of a color monitor to focus the three colored electron beams on a single point. Poor convergence causes the characters on-screen to appear fuzzy and can cause headaches and eyestrain.

coprocessor An additional computer processing unit designed to handle specific tasks in conjunction with the main or central processing unit.

core An "old-fashioned" term for computer memory.

CP/M Control Program/Microcomputer. An operating system created by Gary Kildall, the founder of Digital Research. Created for the old 8-bit microcomputers that used the 8080, 8085, and Z-80 microprocessors. Was the dominant operating system in the late 1970s and early 1980s for small computers used in a business environment.

cps Characters per second. A data transfer rate generally estimated from the bit rate and the character length. At 2400 bps, for example, 8-bit characters with start and stop bits (for a total of 10 bits per character) are transmitted at a rate of approximately 240 characters per second (cps). Some protocols, such as V.42 and MNP, employ advanced techniques such as longer transmission frames and data compression to increase cps.

CPU Central Processing Unit. The computer's microprocessor chip, the brains of the outfit. Typically, an IC using VLSI (very-large-scale integration) technology to pack several different functions into a tiny area. The most common electronic device in the CPU is the transistor, of which several thousand to several million or more are found.

crash A malfunction that brings work to a halt. A system crash usually is caused by a software malfunction, and ordinarily you can restart the system by rebooting the machine. A head crash, however, entails physical damage to a disk and probable data loss.

CRC Cyclic Redundancy Checking. An error-detection technique consisting of a cyclic algorithm performed on each block or frame of data by both sending and receiving modems. The sending modem inserts the results of its computation in each data block in the form of a CRC code. The receiving modem compares its results with the received CRC code and responds with either a positive or negative acknowledgment. In the ARQ protocol implemented in high-speed modems, the receiving modem accepts no more data until a defective block is received correctly.

crosstalk The electromagnetic coupling of a signal on one line with another nearby signal line. Crosstalk is caused by electromagnetic induction, where a signal traveling through a wire creates a magnetic field that induces a current in other nearby wires.

CRT Cathode-Ray Tube. A term used to describe a television or monitor screen tube.

current The flow of electrons, measured in amperes.

cursor The small flashing hyphen that appears on-screen to indicate the point at which any input from the keyboard will be placed.

cyclic redundancy checking *See* CRC.

cylinder The set of tracks on a disk that are on each side of all the disk platters in a stack and are the same distance from the center of the disk. The total number of tracks that can be read without moving the heads. A floppy drive with two heads usually has 160 tracks, which are accessible as 80 cylinders. A typical 4G hard disk has 10 platters with 20 heads (19 for data and one servo head) and 4,000 cylinders, in which each cylinder is composed of 19 tracks.

daisy chain Stringing up components in such a manner that the signals move serially from one to the other. Most microcomputer multiple disk drive systems are daisy-chained. The SCSI bus system is a daisy-chain arrangement, in which the signals move from computer to disk drives to tape units, and so on.

daisywheel printer An impact printer that prints fully formed characters one at a time by rotating a circular print element composed of a series of individual spokes, each containing two characters that radiate from a center hub. Produces letter-quality output.

DAT Digital Audio Tape. A small cassette tape for storing large amounts of digital information, it is sometimes called 4mm tape. DAT technology emerged in Europe and Japan in 1986 as a way to produce high-quality, digital audio recordings. One DAT cassette can hold anywhere from 1GB to 8GB of data.

data Groups of facts processed into information. A graphic or textural representation of facts, concepts, numbers, letters, symbols, or instructions used for communication or processing. Also, an android from the 24th century with a processing speed of 60 trillion operations per second and 800 quadrillion bits of storage who serves on the USS Enterprise NCC-1701-D with the rank of lieutenant commander.

data cable Generically: A cable that carries data. Specific to HD connections: The narrower (20 pin) of two cables that connects an ST-506/412 or ESDI hard disk drive to a controller card.

data communications A type of communication in which computers and terminals can exchange data over an electronic medium.

data compression Data compression is a technique where mathematical algorithms are applied to the data in a file to eliminate redundancies and therefore reduce the size of the file. There are two types of compression: lossy and lossless. Lossy compression deletes some of the original (uncompressed) data needed to reconstruct a file and is normally used only for graphic image or sound files, where the loss of some resolution or information is acceptable. Lossless compression maintains completely the integrity of the original file, allowing it to be reconstructed exactly, and is most commonly used for program or data files.

data separator A device that separates data and clock signals from a single encoded signal pattern. Usually the same device does both data separation and combination and is sometimes called an *endec*, or Encoder/Decoder.

data transfer rate The maximum rate at which data can be transferred from one device to another.

DC Direct current, such as that provided by a power supply or batteries.

DC-600 Data Cartridge 600, a data-storage medium invented by 3M in 1971 that uses a quarter-inch-wide tape 600 feet in length.

DCE Data Communications Equipment. The hardware that does the communication—usually a dial-up modem that establishes and controls the data link through the telephone network. *See also* DTE.

DDE Dynamic Data Exchange. A form of interprocess communications used by Microsoft Windows to support the exchange of commands and data between two applications running simultaneously. This capability has been enhanced further with Object Linking and Embedding (OLE).

DEBUG The name of a utility program included with DOS that is for specialized purposes such as altering memory locations, tracing program execution, patching programs and disk sectors, and performing other low-level tasks.

dedicated line A user-installed telephone line that connects a specified number of computers or terminals within a limited area, such as a single building. The line is a cable rather than a public-access telephone line. The communications channel also may be referred to as nonswitched because calls do not go through telephone company switching equipment.

dedicated servo surface In voice-coil-actuated hard disk drives, one side of one platter given over to servo data that is used to guide and position the read/write heads.

default Any setting assumed at start-up or reset by the computer's software and attached devices and operational until changed by the user. An assumption the computer makes when no other parameters are specified. When you type DIR without specifying the drive to search, for example, the computer assumes that you want it to search the default drive. The term is used in software to describe any action the computer or program takes on its own with embedded values.

defragmentation The process of rearranging disk sectors so that files are stored on consecutive sectors in adjacent tracks.

density The amount of data that can be packed into a certain area on a specific storage media.

desktop A personal computer that sits on a desk.

device driver A memory-resident program loaded by CONFIG.SYS that controls an unusual device, such as an expanded memory board.

Dhrystone A benchmark program used as a standard figure of merit indicating aspects of a computer system's performance in areas other than floating-point math performance. Because the program does not use any floating-point operations, performs no I/O, and makes no operating system calls, it is most useful for measuring the processor performance of a system. The original Dhrystone program was developed in 1984 and was written in Ada, although the C and Pascal versions became more popular by 1989.

diagnostics Programs used to check the operation of a computer system. These programs enable the operator to check the entire system for any problems and to indicate in what area the problems lie.

DifferentialAn electrical signaling method where a pair of lines are used for each signal in "push-pull" fashion. In most cases differential signals are balanced so that the same current flows on each line in opposite directions. This is unlike single-ended signals, which use only one line per signal referenced to a single ground. Differential signals have a large tolerance for common-mode noise and little crosstalk when used with twisted pair wires even in long cables. Differential signaling is expensive because two pins are required for each signal.

digital loopback A test that checks the modem's RS-232 interface and the cable that connects the terminal or computer and the modem. The modem receives data (in the form of digital signals) from the computer or terminal and immediately returns the data to the screen for verification.

digital signals Discrete, uniform signals. In this book, the term refers to the binary digits 0 and 1.

digitize Digitizing refers to transforming an analog wave to a digital signal that a computer can store. Conversion to digital data and back is performed by a Digital to Analog Converter (DAC), often a single chip device. How closely a digitized sample represents an analog wave depends on the number of times the amplitude of a wave is measured and recorded (the rate of digitization), as well as the number of different levels that can be specified at each instance. The number of possible signal levels is dictated by the resolution in bits.

DIP Dual In-line Package. A family of rectangular, integrated-circuit flat packages that have leads on the two longer sides. Package material is plastic or ceramic.

DIP switch A tiny switch (or group of switches) on a circuit board. Named for the form factor of the carrier device in which the switch is housed.

direct memory access A process by which data moves between a disk drive (or other device) and system memory without direct control of the central processing unit, thus freeing it up for other tasks.

directory An area of a disk that stores the titles given to the files saved on the disk and serves as a table of contents for those files. Contains data that identifies the name of a file, the size, the attributes (system, hidden, read-only, and so on), the date and time of creation, and a pointer to the location of the file. Each entry in a directory is 32 bytes long.

disk A floppy disk. Made of a flexible material coated with a magnetic substance, the disk spins inside its protective jacket, and the read/write head comes in contact with the recording surface to read or write data.

dithering Dithering is the process of creating more colors and shades from a given color palette. In monochrome displays or printers, dithering will vary the black and white dot patterns to simulate shades of gray. Grayscale dithering is used to produce different shades of gray when the device can only produce limited levels of black or white outputs. Color screens or printers use dithering to create colors by mixing and varying the dot sizing and spacing.

DLL Dynamic Link Library. An executable driver program module for Microsoft Windows that can be loaded on demand and linked in at runtime, and subsequently unloaded when the driver is no longer needed.

DMA Direct Memory Access. A circuit by which a high-speed transfer of information may be facilitated between a device and system memory. This transfer is managed by a specialized processor that relieves the burden of managing the transfer from the main CPU.

docking station Equipment that allows a laptop or notebook computer to use peripherals and accessories normally associated with desktop systems.

DOS Disk Operating System. A collection of programs stored on the DOS disk that contain routines enabling the system and user to manage information and the hardware resources of the computer. DOS must be loaded into the computer before other programs can be started.

dot pitch A measurement of the width of the dots that make up a pixel. The smaller the dot pitch, the sharper the image.

dot-matrix printer An impact printer that prints characters composed of dots. Characters are printed one at a time by pressing the ends of selected wires against an inked ribbon and paper.

double density (DD) An indication of the storage capacity of a floppy drive or disk in which eight or nine sectors per track are recorded using MFM encoding.

down-time Operating time lost because of a computer malfunction.

DPMI DOS Protected Mode Interface. An industry-standard interface that allows DOS applications to execute program code in the protected mode of the 286 or higher Intel processor. The DPMI specification is available from Intel.

DRAM Dynamic Random Access Memory. The most common type of computer memory, DRAM can be made very inexpensively compared to other types of memory. DRAM chips are small and inexpensive because they normally require only one transistor and a capacitor to represent each bit. The capacitors must be energized every 15ms or so (hundreds of times per second) in order to maintain their charges. DRAM is volatile, meaning it will lose data with no power, or without regular refresh cycles.

drive A mechanical device that manipulates data storage media.

driver A program designed to interface a particular piece of hardware to an operating system or other standard software.

DTE Data Terminal (or terminating) Equipment. The device, usually a computer or terminal, that generates or is the final destination of data. *See also* DCE.

duplex Indicates a communications channel capable of carrying signals in both directions.

DVI Digital Video Interactive. A standard that was originally developed at RCA Laboratories and sold to Intel in 1988. DVI integrates digital motion, still video, sound, graphics, and special effects in a compressed format. DVI is a highly sophisticated hardware compression technique used in interactive multimedia applications.

Dvorak keyboard A keyboard design by August Dvorak that was patented in 1936 and approved by ANSI in 1982. Provides increased speed and comfort and reduces the rate of errors by placing the most frequently used letters in the center for use by the strongest fingers. Finger motions and awkward strokes are reduced by more than 90 percent in comparison with the familiar QWERTY keyboard. The Dvorak keyboard has the five vowel keys, AOEUI, together under the left hand in the center row, and the five most frequently used consonants, DHTNS, under the fingers of the right hand.

EBCDIC Extended Binary Coded Decimal Interchange Code. An IBM-developed 8-bit code for the representation of characters. It allows 256 possible character combinations within a single byte. EBCDIC is the standard code on IBM mini-computers and mainframes, but not on the IBM microcomputers, where ASCII is used instead.

edit The process of rearranging data or information.

EEPROM Electrically Eraseable Programmable Read-Only Memory. A type of non-volatile memory chip used to store semi-permanent information in a computer such as the BIOS. An EEPROM can be erased and reprogrammed directly in the host system without special equipment. Manufacturers can upgrade the ROM code in a system by supplying a special program that erases and reprograms the EEPROM chip with the new code. Also called a *flash ROM.*

EGA Enhanced Graphics Adapter. A type of PC video display adapter, first introduced by IBM on September 10, 1984, that supports text and graphics. Text is supported at a maximum resolution of 80×25 characters in 16 colors with a character box of 8×14 pixels. Graphics is supported at a maximum resolution of 640×350 pixels in 16 (from a palette of 64) colors. The EGA outputs a TTL (digital) signal with a horizontal scanning frequency of 15.75, 18.432, or 21.85KHz, and supports TTL color or TTL monochrome displays.

EIA Electronic Industries Association, which defines electronic standards in the United States.

EIDE Enhanced Integrated Drive Electronics. A specific Western Digital implementation of the ATA-2 specification. *See* ATA-2.

EISA Extended Industry Standard Architecture. An extension of the Industry Standard Architecture (ISA) bus developed by IBM for the AT. The EISA design was led by Compaq Corporation. Later, eight other manufacturers (AST, Epson, Hewlett-Packard, NEC, Olivetti, Tandy, Wyse, and Zenith) joined Compaq in a consortium founded September 13, 1988. This group became known as the "gang of nine." The EISA design was patterned largely after IBM's Micro Channel Architecture (MCA) in the PS/2 systems, but unlike MCA, EISA allows for backward compatibility with older plug-in adapters.

electronic mail A method of transferring messages from one computer to another.

electrostatic discharge (ESD) Static electricity; a sudden flow of electricity between two objects at different electrical potentials. ESD is a primary cause of integrated circuit damage or failure.

embedded servo data Magnetic markings embedded between or inside tracks on disk drives that use voice-coil actuators. These markings enable the actuator to fine-tune the position of the read/write heads.

EMM Expanded Memory Manager. A driver that provides a software interface to expanded memory. EMMs were originally created for expanded memory boards, but can also use the memory management capabilities of the 386 or higher processors to emulate an expanded memory board. EMM386.EXE is an example of an EMM that comes with DOS.

EMS Expanded Memory Specification. Sometimes also called the LIM spec because it was developed by Lotus, Intel, and Microsoft. Provides a way for microcomputers running under DOS to access additional memory. EMS memory management provides access to a maximum of 32M of expanded memory through a small (usually 64K) window in conventional memory.

EMS is a cumbersome access scheme designed primarily for pre-286 systems that could not access extended memory.

emulator A piece of test apparatus that emulates or imitates the function of a particular chip.

encoding The protocol by which data is carried or stored by a medium.

encryption The translation of data into unreadable codes to maintain security.

Endec (Encoder/Decoder) A device that takes data and clock signals and combines or encodes them using a particular encoding scheme into a single signal for transmission or storage. The same device also later separates or decodes the data and clock signals during a receive or read operation. Sometimes called a *data separator*.

Energy Star A certification program started by the EPA. Energy Star certified computers and peripherals are designed to draw less than 30 watts of electrical energy from a standard 110v AC outlet during periods of inactivity. Also called *Green PCs*.

Enhanced Graphics Adapter *See* EGA.

Enhanced Small Device Interface *See* ESDI.

EPROM Erasable Programmable Read-Only Memory. A type of read-only memory (ROM) in which the data pattern can be erased to allow a new pattern. Usually is erased by ultraviolet light and recorded by a higher than normal voltage programming signal.

equalization A compensation circuit designed into modems to counteract certain distortions introduced by the telephone channel. Two types are used: fixed (compromise) equalizers and those that adapt to channel conditions (adaptive). Good-quality modems use adaptive equalization.

error control Various techniques that check the reliability of characters (parity) or blocks of data. V.42, MNP, and HST error-control protocols use error detection (CRC) and retransmission of errored frames (ARQ).

error message A word or combination of words to indicate to the user that an error has occurred somewhere in the program.

ESDI Enhanced Small Device Interface. A hardware standard developed by Maxtor and standardized by a consortium of 22 disk drive manufacturers on January 26, 1983. A group of 27 manufacturers formed the ESDI steering committee on September 15, 1986, to enhance and improve the specification. A high-performance interface used primarily with hard disks, ESDI provides for a maximum data transfer rate to and from a hard disk of between 10 and 24 megabits per second.

Ethernet A type of network protocol developed in the late 1970s by Bob Metcalf at Xerox Corporation and endorsed by the IEEE. One of the oldest LAN communications protocols in the personal computing industry. Ethernet networks use a collision-detection protocol to manage contention.

expanded memory Otherwise known as EMS memory, memory that conforms to the EMS specification. Requires a special device driver and conforms to a standard developed by Lotus, Intel, and Microsoft.

eXtended graphics array *See* XGA.

extended memory Direct processor-addressable memory that is addressed by an Intel (or compatible) 286, 386, or 486 processor in the region beyond the first megabyte. Addressable only in the processor's protected mode of operation.

extended partition A nonbootable DOS partition containing DOS volumes. Starting with DOS V3.3, the DOS FDISK program can create two partitions that serve DOS: an ordinary, bootable partition (called the primary partition) and an extended partition, which may contain as many as 23 volumes from D: through Z:.

extra-high density (ED) An indication of the storage capacity of a floppy drive or disk in which 36 sectors per track are recorded using a vertical recording technique with MFM encoding.

fast ATA Fast AT Attachment interface. Also called *Fast ATA-2,* these are specific Seagate and Quantum implementations of the ATA-2 interface. *See also* ATA-2.

FAT File Allocation Table. A table held near the outer edge of a disk that tells which sectors are allocated to each file and in what order.

FDISK The name of the disk partitioning program under several operating systems used to create the Master Boot Record and allocate partitions for the operating system's use.

FIFO First-In First-Out. A method of storing and retrieving items from a list, table, or stack so that the first element stored is the first one retrieved.

file A collection of information kept somewhere other than in random-access memory.

file attribute Information held in the attribute byte of a file's directory entry.

file name The name given to the disk file. For DOS, must be one to eight characters long and may be followed by a file-name extension, which can be one to three characters long. Windows 95 eases these constraints by allowing file names of up to 255 characters.

firmwareSoftware contained in a read-only memory (ROM) device. A cross between hardware and software.

fixed disk Also called a *hard disk,* a disk that cannot be removed from its controlling hardware or housing. Made of rigid material with a magnetic coating and used for the mass storage and retrieval of data.

flash fROM A type of EEPROM developed by Intel that can be erased and reprogrammed in the host system. *See also* EEPROM.

floppy tape A tape standard that uses drives connecting to an ordinary floppy disk controller.

flow control A mechanism that compensates for differences in the flow of data input to and output from a modem or other device.

FM encoding Frequency modulation encoding. An outdated method of encoding data on the disk surface that uses up half the disk space with timing signals.

folder In a graphical user interface, a simulated file folder that holds documents (text, data, or graphics), applications, and other folders. A folder is like a DOS subdirectory.

form factor The physical dimensions of a device. Two devices with the same form factor are physically interchangeable. The IBM PC, XT, and XT Model 286, for example, all use power supplies that are internally different but have exactly the same form factor.

FORMAT The DOS format program that performs both low- and high-level formatting on floppy disks but only high-level formatting on hard disks.

formatted capacity The total number of bytes of data that can fit on a formatted disk. The unformatted capacity is higher because space is lost defining the boundaries between sectors.

formatting Preparing a disk so that the computer can read or write to it. Checks the disk for defects and constructs an organizational system to manage information on the disk.

FORTRAN An acronym for FORmula TRANslator, a high-level programming language for programs dealing primarily with mathematical formulas and expressions similar to algebra. Used primarily in scientific and technical applications. One of the oldest languages but still widely used because of its compact notation, the many mathematical subroutines available, and the ease with which arrays, matrices, and loops can be handled. FORTRAN was written in 1954 by John Backus at IBM, and the first successful FORTRAN program was executed by Harlan Herrick.

frame A data communications term for a block of data with header and trailer information attached. The added information usually includes a frame number, block size data, error-check codes, and start/end indicators.

FTP File Transfer Protocol. A file-sharing protocol that lets users transfer text and binary files to and from a PC, list directories on the foreign host, delete and rename files on the foreign host, and perform wildcard transfers between hosts. Used on the Internet to transfer files.

full duplex Signal flow in both directions at the same time. In microcomputer communications, also may refer to the suppression of the online local echo.

full-height drive A drive unit that is 3.25 inches high, 5.75 inches wide, and 8 inches deep.

function keys Special-purpose keys that can be programmed to perform various operations. Serve many different functions depending on the program being used.

gas-plasma display Commonly used in portable systems, a type of display that operates by exciting a gas, usually neon or an argon-neon mixture, through the application of a voltage. When sufficient voltage is applied at the intersection of two electrodes, the gas glows an orange-red. Because gas-plasma displays generate light, they require no backlighting.

gateway Officially, a gateway is an application-to-application conversion program or system. For example, an e-mail gateway would convert between SMTP (Internet) e-mail format to MHS (Novell) e-mail format. The term gateway is also used as a slang term for router. *See also* router.

GIF Graphics Interchange Format. A popular raster graphics file format developed by CompuServe that handles 8-bit color (256 colors) and uses the LZW method to achieve compression ratios of approximately 1.5:1 to 2:1.

giga A multiplier indicating 1 billion (1,000,000,000) of some unit. Abbreviated as g or G. When used to indicate a number of bytes of memory storage, the multiplier definition changes to 1,073,741,824. One gigabit, for example, equals 1,000,000,000 bits, and one gigabyte equals 1,073,741,824 bytes.

gigabyte A unit of information storage equal to 1,073,741,824 bytes.

Green Book Green Book is the standard for Compact Disc-Interactive (CD-I). Phillips developed CD-I technology for the consumer market for use with a television instead of a computer monitor. CD-I is not a computer system but a consumer device. CD-I disks require special code and are not compatible with standard CD-ROMs. A CD-ROM cannot be played on the CD-I machine, but Red Book audio can be played on CD-I devices.

GUI Graphical User Interface. A type of program interface that allows users to choose commands and functions by pointing to a graphical icon using either a keyboard or pointing device such as a mouse. Windows and OS/2 are the most popular GUIs available for PC systems.

half duplex Signal flow in both directions but only one way at a time. In microcomputer communications, may refer to activation of the online local echo, which causes the modem to send a copy of the transmitted data to the screen of the sending computer.

half-height drive A drive unit that is 1.625 inches high, and either 5.75 or 4 inches wide and 4 or 8 inches deep.

halftone Halftoning is a process that uses dithering to simulate a continuous tone image such as a photograph or shaded drawing using various sizes of dots. Newspapers, magazines, and many books use halftoning. The human eye will merge the dots to give the impression of gray shades.

hard disk A high-capacity disk storage unit characterized by a normally nonremovable rigid substrate media. The platters in a hard disk normally are constructed of aluminum or glass.

hard error An error in reading or writing data that is caused by damaged hardware.

hardware Physical components that make up a microcomputer, monitor, printer, and so on.

HDLC High-Level Data Link Control. A standard protocol developed by the International Standards Organization for software applications and communicating devices operating in synchronous environments. Defines operations at the link level of communications—for example, the format of data frames exchanged between modems over a phone line.

head A small electromagnetic device inside a drive that reads, records, and erases data on the media.

headh actuator The device that moves read/write heads across a disk drive's platters. Most drives use a stepper-motor or a voice-coil actuator.

head crash A (usually) rare occurrence in which a read/write head strikes a platter surface with sufficient force to damage the magnetic medium.

head parking A procedure in which a disk drive's read/write heads are moved to an unused track so that they will not damage data in the event of a head crash or other failure.

head seek The movement of a drive's read/write heads to a particular track.

heat sink A mass of metal attached to a chip carrier or socket for the purpose of dissipating heat.

helical scan A type of recording technology that has vastly increased the capacity of tape drives. Invented for use in broadcast systems and now used in VCRs. Conventional longitudinal recording records a track of data straight across the width of a single-track tape. Helical scan recording packs more data on the tape by positioning the tape at an angle to the recording heads. The heads spin to record diagonal stripes of information on the tape.

hexadecimal number A number encoded in base-16, such that digits include the letters A through F as well as the numerals 0 through 9 (for example, 8BF3, which equals 35,827 in base-10).

hidden file A file that is not displayed in DOS directory listings because the file's attribute byte holds a special setting.

high density (HD) An indication of the storage capacity of a floppy drive or disk in which 15 or 18 sectors per track are recorded using MFM encoding.

high-level formatting Formatting performed by the DOS FORMAT program. Among other things, it creates the root directory and file allocation tables.

history file A file created by utility software to keep track of earlier use of the software. Many backup programs, for example, keep history files describing earlier backup sessions.

HMA High Memory Area. The first 64K of extended memory, which is controlled typically by the HIMEM.SYS device driver. Real mode programs can be loaded into the HMA to conserve conventional memory. Normally DOS 5.0 and higher use the HMA exclusively to reduce the DOS conventional memory footprint.

home page A top-level Web document that relates to an individual or an organization. Other pages in the document are accessible by links from the home page.

HPT High-Pressure Tin. A PLCC socket that promotes high forces between socket contacts and PLCC contacts for a good connection.

HST High-Speed Technology. The USRobotics proprietary high-speed modem-signaling scheme, developed as an interim protocol until the V.32 protocol could be implemented in a cost-effective manner. Incorporates trellis-coded modulation for greater immunity from variable phone-line conditions, and asymmetrical modulation for more efficient use of the phone channel at speeds of 4800 bps and above. The forward channel transmits at either 9600 bps (older designs) or 14400 bps, and the reverse channel transmits at 450 bps. This technique eliminated the need for the V.32 echo-cancellation hardware that was more costly at the time HST was developed. HST also incorporates MNP-compatible error-control procedures adapted to the asymmetrical modulation.

HTML An acronym for Hypertext Markup Language. A language used to describe and format plain text files on the Web. HTML is based on pairs of tags that allow you to mix graphics with text, change the appearance of text, and create hypertext documents with links to other documents.

HTTP An acronym for Hypertext Transfer Protocol. The protocol that describes the rules that a browser and server use to communicate over the World Wide Web. HTTP allows a Web browser to request HTML documents from a Web server.

hypertext A technology that allows for quick and easy navigation between and within large documents. Hypertext links are pointers to other sections within the same document, other documents, or other resources such as FTP sites, images, or sounds.

Hz An abbreviation for hertz, a frequency measurement unit used internationally to indicate one cycle per second.

I/O Input/Output. A circuit path that enables independent communications between the processor and external devices.

IBMBIO.COM One of the DOS system files required to boot the machine. The first file loaded from disk during the boot. Contains extensions to the ROM BIOS.

IBMDOS.COM One of the DOS system files required to boot the machine. Contains the primary DOS routines. Loaded by IBMBIO.COM, it in turns loads COMMAND.COM.

IC An acronym for integrated circuit, a complete electronic circuit contained on a single chip. May consist of only a few transistors, capacitors, diodes, or resistors, or thousands of them, and generally is classified according to the complexity of the circuitry and the approximate number of circuits on the chip. SSI (small-scale integration) equals 2 to 10 circuits. MSI (medium-scale integration) equals 10 to 100 circuits. LSI (large-scale integration) equals 100 to 1,000 circuits. VLSI (very-large-scale integration) equals 1,000 to 10,000 circuits. ULSI (ultra-large-scale integration) equals more than 10,000 circuits.

IDE Integrated Drive Electronics. Describes a hard disk with the disk controller circuitry integrated within it. The first IDE drives commonly were called hard cards. Also refers to the ATA interface standard, the standard for attaching hard disk drives to ISA bus IBM-compatible computers. IDE drives typically operate as though they were standard ST-506/412 drives. *See also* ATA.

incremental backup A backup of all files that have changed since the last backup.

initiator A device attached to the SCSI bus that sends a command to another device (the target) on the SCSI bus. The SCSI host adapter plugged into the system bus is an example of a SCSI initiator.

inkjet printer A type of printer that sprays one or more colors of ink on the paper. Can produce output with quality approaching that of a laser printer at a lower cost.

input Data sent to the computer from the keyboard, the telephone, the video camera, another computer, paddles, joysticks, and so on.

instruction Program step that tells the computer what to do for a single operation.

integrated circuit *See* IC.

interface A communications device or protocol that enables one device to communicate with another. Matches the output of one device to the input of the other device.

interlacing is a method of scanning alternate lines of pixels on a display screen. The odd lines are scanned first from top to bottom and left to right. The electron gun goes back to the top and makes a second pass scanning the even lines. Interlacing requires two scan passes to construct a single image. Because of this additional scanning, interlaced screens often seem to flicker unless a long persistence phosphor is used in the display.

interleave ratio The number of sectors that pass beneath the read/write heads before the "next" numbered sector arrives. When the interleave ratio is 3:1, for example, a sector is read, two pass by, and then the next is read. A proper interleave ratio, laid down during low-level formatting, enables the disk to transfer information without excessive revolutions due to missed sectors.

internal command In DOS, a command contained in COMMAND.COM so that no other file must be loaded in order to perform the command. DIR and COPY are two examples of internal commands.

internal drive A disk or tape drive mounted inside one of a computer's disk drive bays (or a hard disk card, which is installed in one of the computer's slots).

Internet The Internet is a computer network that joins many government, university, and private computers together over phone lines. The Internet traces its origins to a network set up in 1969 by the Defense Department. You can connect to the Internet through many online services such as CompuServe, BIX, and America Online. Internet computers use the TCP/IP communications protocol. There are several million hosts on the Internet. A host is a mainframe, mini, or workstation that directly supports the Internet Protocol (the IP in TCP/IP).

interpreter A translator program for a high-level language that translates and executes the program at the same time. The program statements that are interpreted remain in their original source language, the way the programmer wrote them—that is, the program does not need to be compiled before execution. Interpreted programs run slower than compiled programs and always must be run with the interpreter loaded in memory.

interrupt A suspension of a process, such as the execution of a computer program, caused by an event external to that process and performed in such a way that the process can be resumed. An interrupt can be caused by internal or external conditions such as a signal indicating that a device or program has completed a transfer of data.

interrupt vector A pointer in a table that gives the location of a set of instructions that the computer should execute when a particular interrupt occurs.

IO.SYS One of the DOS system files required to boot the machine. The first file loaded from disk during the boot. Contains extensions to the ROM BIOS.

IPX Internet Packet eXchange. Novell NetWare's native LAN communications protocol, used to move data between server and/or workstation programs running on different network nodes. IPX packets are encapsulated and carried by the packets used in Ethernet and the similar frames used in Token-Ring networks.

IRQ An acronym for interrupt request. Physical connections between external hardware devices and the interrupt controllers. When a device such as a floppy controller or a printer needs the attention of the CPU, an IRQ line is used to get the attention of the system to perform a task. On PC and XT IBM-compatible systems, 8 IRQ lines, numbered IRQ0 through IRQ7 are included. On the AT and PS/2 systems, 16 IRQ lines are numbered IRQ0 through IRQ15. IRQ lines must be used only by a single adapter in the ISA bus systems, but Micro Channel Architecture (MCA) adapters can share interrupts.

ISDN Integrated Services Digital Network. An international telecommunications standard that enables a communications channel to carry digital data simultaneously with voice and video information.

ISO International Standards Organization. The ISO, based in Paris, develops standards for international and national data communications. The U.S. representative to the ISO is the American National Standards Institute (ANSI).

ISO 9660 ISO 9660 is an international standard that defines file systems for CD-ROM disks, independent of the operating system. ISO (International Standards Organization) 9660 has two levels. Level one provides for DOS file system compatibility, while Level two allows file names of up to 32 characters.

J-lead J-shaped leads on chip carriers, which can be surface-mounted on a PC board or plugged into a socket that then is mounted on a PC board, usually on .050-inch centers.

Java An object-oriented programming language and environment similar to C or C++. Java was developed by Sun Microsystems and is used to create network-based applications.

JEDEC Joint Electron Devices Engineering Council. A group that establishes standards for the electronics industry.

JPEG Joint Photographic Experts Group. A lossy data compression standard that was originally designed for still images, but can also compress real-time video (30 frames per second) and animation. Lossy compression permanently discards unnecessary data, resulting in some loss of precision.

jumper A small, plastic-covered, metal clip that slips over two pins protruding from a circuit board. Sometimes also called a *shunt.* When in place, the jumper connects the pins electrically and closes the circuit. By doing so, it connects the two terminals of a switch, turning it "on."

Kermit A protocol designed for transferring files between microcomputers and mainframes. Developed by Frank DaCruz and Bill Catchings at Columbia University (and named after the talking frog on *The Muppet Show*), Kermit is widely accepted in the academic world. The complete Kermit protocol manual and the source for various versions is available from Kermit Distribution, Columbia University Center for Computing Activities, 612 West 115 Street, New York, NY 10025, (212) 854-3703.

key disk In software copy protection, a distribution floppy disk that must be present in a floppy disk drive for an application program to run.

keyboard macro A series of keystrokes automatically input when a single key is pressed.

kilo A multiplier indicating one thousand (1,000) of some unit. Abbreviated as k or K. When used to indicate a number of bytes of memory storage, the multiplier definition changes to 1,024. One kilobit, for example, equals 1,000 bits, and one kilobyte equals 1,024 bytes.

kilobyte A unit of information storage equal to 1,024 bytes.

landing zone An unused track on a disk surface on which the read/write heads can land when power is shut off. The place that a parking program or a drive with an autopark mechanism parks the heads.

LAPM Link-Access Procedure for Modems. An error-control protocol incorporated in CCITT Recommendation V.42. Like the MNP and HST protocols, uses cyclic redundancy checking (CRC) and retransmission of corrupted data (ARQ) to ensure data reliability.

laptop computer A computer system smaller than a briefcase but larger than a notebook that usually has a clamshell design in which the keyboard and display are on separate halves of the system, which are hinged together. These systems normally run on battery power.

laser printer A type of printer that is a combination of an electrostatic copying machine and a computer printer. The output data from the computer is converted by an interface into a raster feed, similar to the impulses that a TV picture tube receives. The impulses cause the laser beam to scan a small drum that carries a positive electrical charge. Where the laser hits, the drum is discharged. A toner, which also carries a positive charge, is then applied to the drum. This toner, a fine black powder, sticks only to the areas of the drum that have been discharged electrically. As it rotates, the drum deposits the toner on a negatively charged sheet of paper. Another roller then heats and bonds the toner to the page.

latency The amount of time required for a disk drive to rotate half of a revolution. Represents the average amount of time to locate a specific sector after the heads have arrived at a specific track. Latency is part of the average access time for a drive.

LBA Logical Block Addressing. A method used with SCSI and IDE drives to translate the Cylinder, Head, and Sector specifications of the drive to those usable by an enhanced BIOS. LBA is used with drives that are larger than 528MB and causes the BIOS to translate the drive's logical parameters to those usable by the system BIOS.

LCC Leadless Chip Carrier. A type of integrated circuit package that has input and output pads rather than leads on its perimeter.

LCD Liquid Crystal Display. A display that uses liquid crystal sealed between two pieces of polarized glass. The polarity of the liquid crystal is changed by an electric current to vary the amount of light that can pass through. Because LCD displays do not generate light, they depend on either the reflection of ambient light or backlighting the screen. The best type of LCD, the active-matrix or thin-film transistor (TFT) LCD, offers fast screen updates and true color capability.

LED Light-Emitting Diode. A semiconductor diode that emits light when a current is passed through it.

LIF Low Insertion Force. A type of socket that requires only a minimum of force to insert a chip carrier.

light pen A hand-held input device with a light-sensitive probe or stylus connected to the computer's graphics adapter board by a cable. Used for writing or sketching on-screen or as a pointing device for making selections. Unlike mice, not widely supported by software applications.

local bus A generic term used to describe a bus that is directly attached to a processor and that operates at the processor's speed and data transfer width.

local echo A modem feature that enables the modem to send copies of keyboard commands and transmitted data to the screen. When the modem is in command mode (not online to another system), the local echo normally is invoked through an ATE1 command, which causes the modem to display your typed commands. When the modem is online to another system, the local echo is invoked by an ATF0 command, which causes the modem to display the data it transmits to the remote system.

logical drive A drive as named by a DOS drive specifier, such as C: or D:. Under DOS 3.3 or later, a single physical drive can act as several logical drives, each with its own specifier.

logical unit number *See* LUN.

lost clusters Clusters that have been marked accidentally as "unavailable" in the file allocation table even though they don't belong to any file listed in a directory.

low-level formatting Formatting that divides tracks into sectors on the platter surfaces. Places sector-identifying information before and after each sector and fills each sector with null data (usually hex F6). Specifies the sector interleave and marks defective tracks by placing invalid checksum figures in each sector on a defective track.

LUN Logical Unit Number. A number given to a device (a logical unit) attached to a SCSI physical unit and not directly to the SCSI bus. Although as many as eight logical units can be attached to a single physical unit, normally a single logical unit is a built-in part of a single physical unit. A SCSI hard disk, for example, has a built-in SCSI bus adapter that is assigned a physical unit number or SCSI ID, and the controller and drive portions of the hard disk are assigned a logical unit number (usually 0).

magnetic domain A tiny segment of a track just large enough to hold one of the magnetic flux reversals that encode data on a disk surface.

magneto-optical recording An erasable optical-disk recording technique that uses a laser beam to heat pits on the disk surface to the point at which a magnet can make flux changes.

master partition boot sector On hard disks, a one-sector record that gives essential information about the disk and tells the starting locations of the various partitions. Always the first physical sector of the disk.

MCA Micro Channel Architecture. Developed by IBM for the PS/2 line of computers and introduced on April 2, 1987. Features include a 16- or 32-bit bus width and multiple master control. By allowing several processors to arbitrate for resources on a single bus, the MCA is optimized for multitasking, multiprocessor systems. Offers switchless configuration of adapters, which eliminates one of the biggest headaches of installing older adapters.

MCGA MultiColor Graphics Array. A type of PC video display circuit introduced by IBM on April 2, 1987, that supports text and graphics. Text is supported at a maximum resolution of 80×25 characters in 16 colors with a character box of 8×16 pixels. Graphics is supported at a maximum resolution of 320×200 pixels in 256 (from a palette of 262,144) colors or 640×480 pixels in 2 colors. The MCGA outputs an analog signal with a horizontal scanning frequency of 31.5KHz, and supports analog color or analog monochrome displays.

MCI Media Control Interface. A device-independent specification for controlling multimedia devices and files. MCI is a part of the multimedia extensions and offers a standard interface set of device control commands, making it easy to program multimedia applications. MCI commands are used for audio recording and playback and animation playback. Videodisk players and other optional devices are controlled by MCI. Device types include CD audio, digital audio tape players, scanners, MIDI sequencers, videotape players or recorders, and audio devices that play digitized waveform files. MCI classifies compound and simple device drivers. Compound drivers require a device element (usually a file and a path) during operation. Simple devices do not require a device element for playback.

MDA Monochrome Display Adapter. A type of PC video display adapter introduced by IBM on August 12, 1981, that supports text only. Text is supported at a maximum resolution of 80×25 characters in four colors with a character box of 9×14 pixels. Colors, in this case, indicate black, white, bright white, and underlined. Graphics modes are not supported. The MDA outputs a digital signal with a horizontal scanning frequency of 18.432 KHz, and supports TTL monochrome displays. The IBM MDA also included a parallel printer port.

mean time between failure *See* MTBF.

mean time to repair *See* MTTR.

medium The magnetic coating or plating that covers a disk or tape.

mega A multiplier indicating 1 million (1,000,000) of some unit. Abbreviated as m or M. When used to indicate a number of bytes of memory storage, the multiplier definition changes to 1,048,576. One megabit, for example, equals 1,000,000 bits, and one megabyte equals 1,048,576 bytes.

megabyte A unit of information storage equal to 1,048,576 bytes.

memory Any component in a computer system that stores information for future use.

memory caching A service provided by extremely fast memory chips that keeps copies of the most recent memory accesses. When the CPU makes a subsequent access, the value is supplied by the fast memory rather than by relatively slow system memory.

memory-resident program A program that remains in memory after it has been loaded, consuming memory that otherwise might be used by application software.

menu software Utility software that makes a computer easier to use by replacing DOS commands with a series of menu selections.

MFM Modified Frequency Modulation encoding. A method of encoding data on the surface of a disk. The coding of a bit of data varies by the coding of the preceding bit to preserve clocking information.

MHz An abbreviation for megahertz, a unit of measurement indicating the frequency of one million cycles per second. One hertz (Hz) is equal to one cycle per second. Named after Heinrich R. Hertz, a German physicist who first detected electromagnetic waves in 1883.

MI/MIC Mode Indicate/Mode Indicate Common, also called *forced* or *manual originate*. Provided for installations in which equipment other than the modem does the dialing. In such installations, the modem operates in dumb mode (no auto-dial capability), yet must go off-hook in originate mode to connect with answering modems.

micro A prefix indicating one millionth (1/1,000,000 or .000001) of some unit. Abbreviated as u.

microprocessor A solid-state central processing unit much like a computer on a chip. An integrated circuit that accepts coded instructions for execution.

microsecond A unit of time equal to one millionth (1/1,000,000 or .000001) of a second. Abbreviated as us.

MIDI Musical Instrument Digital Interface. An interface and file format standard for connecting a musical instrument to a microcomputer and storing musical instrument data. Multiple musical instruments can be daisy-chained and played simultaneously with the help of the computer and related software. The various operations of the instruments can be captured, saved, edited, and played back. A MIDI file contains note information, timing (how long a note is held), volume, and instrument type for as many as 16 channels. Sequencer programs are used to control MIDI functions such as recording, playback, and editing. MIDI files store only note instructions and not actual sound data.

milli A prefix indicating one thousandth (1/1,000 or .001) of some unit. Abbreviated as m.

millisecond A unit of time equal to one thousandth (1/1,000 or .001) of a second. Abbreviated as ms.

MIPS Million Instructions Per Second. Refers to the average number of machine-language instructions a computer can perform or execute in one second. Because different processors can perform different functions in a single instruction, MIPS should be used only as a general measure of performance among different types of computers.

mnemonic A mnemonic is an abbreviated name for something that is used in a manner similar to an acronym. Computer processor instructions are often abbreviated with a mnemonic such as JMP (Jump), CLR (Clear), STO (Store), INIT (Initialize). A mnemonic name for an instruction or an operation makes it easy to remember and convenient to use.

MNP Microcom Networking Protocol. Asynchronous error-control and data-compression protocols developed by Microcom, Inc. and now in the public domain. Ensure error-free transmission through error detection (CRC) and retransmission of errored frames. MNP Levels 1 through 4 cover error control and have been incorporated into CCITT Recommendation V.42. MNP Level 5 includes data compression but is eclipsed in superiority by V.42bis, an international standard that is more efficient. Most high-speed modems will connect with MNP Level 5 if V.42bis is unavailable.

MO Magneto-Optical. MO drives utilize both magnetic and optical storage properties. MO technology is erasable and recordable, as opposed to CD-ROM (Read-Only) and WORM (Write-Once) drives. MO uses laser and magnetic field technology to record and erase data. The laser is used to heat an area on the disk, which can then be recorded magnetically. MO drives are most commonly used in removable storage applications.

modem MOdulator-DEModulator. A device that converts electrical signals from a computer into an audio form transmittable over telephone lines, or vice versa. Modulates, or transforms, digital signals from a computer into the analog form that can be carried successfully on a phone line; also demodulates signals received from the phone line back to digital signals before passing them to the receiving computer.

module An assembly that contains a complete circuit or subcircuit.

Monochrome Display Adapter *See* MDA.

morphing Morphing is a pseudo-slang term for metamorphosis, the transformation of one object into another. Morphing is performed by software that analyzes any two images and creates several in-between images so that one image appears to become the other. Originally requiring expensive, high powered computer hardware, morphing can now be done on PC systems with sophisticated software now available.

MOS Metal-Oxide Semiconductor. Refers to the three layers used in forming the gate structure of a field-effect transistor (FET). MOS circuits offer low-power dissipation and enable transistors to be jammed close together before a critical heat problem arises. PMOS, the oldest type of MOS circuit, is a silicon-gate P-channel MOS process that uses currents made up of positive charges. NMOS is a silicon-gate N-channel MOS process that uses currents made up of negative charges and is at least twice as fast as PMOS. CMOS, Complementary MOS, is nearly immune to noise, runs off almost any power supply, and is an extremely low-power circuit technique.

motherboard The main circuit board in the computer. Also called *planar, system board,* or *backplane.*

MPEG Moving Pictures Experts Group. A lossy data compression standard for motion video and audio. Lossy compression permanently discards unnecessary data, resulting in some loss of precision. MPEG compression produces about a 50% volume reduction in file size.

MSDOS.SYS One of the DOS system files required to boot the machine. Contains the primary DOS routines. Loaded by IO.SYS, it in turns loads COMMAND.COM.

MTBF Mean Time Between Failure. A statistically derived measure of the probable time a device will continue to operate before a hardware failure occurs, usually given in hours. Because no standard technique exists for measuring MTBF, a device from one manufacturer can be significantly more or significantly less reliable than a device with the same MTBF rating from another manufacturer.

MTTR Mean Time To Repair. A measure of the probable time it will take a technician to service or repair a specific device, usually given in hours.

MultiColor Graphics Array *See* MCGA.

multimedia Multimedia is the integration of sound, graphic images, animation, motion video, and/or text in one environment on a computer. It is a set of hardware and software technologies that are rapidly changing and enhancing the computing environment.

multitask To run several programs simultaneously.

multithread To concurrently process more than one message by an application program. OS/2, Windows 95, and Windows NT are examples of multithreaded operating systems. Each program can start two or more threads, which carry out various interrelated tasks with less overhead than two separate programs would require.

multiuser system A system in which several computer terminals share the same central processing unit (CPU).

nano A prefix indicating one billionth (1/1,000,000,000 or .000000001) of some unit. Abbreviated as n.

nanosecond A unit of time equal to one billionth (1/1,000,000,000 or .000000001) of a second. Abbreviated as ns.

network A system in which a number of independent computers are linked in order to share data and peripherals, such as hard disks and printers.

nonvolatile memory (NVRAM) Random-access memory whose data is retained when power is turned off. Sometimes nonvolatile RAM is retained without any power whatsoever, as in EEPROM or flash memory devices. In other cases the memory is maintained by a small battery. Nonvolatile RAM that is battery maintained is sometimes also called CMOS memory. CMOS NVRAM is used in IBM-compatible systems to store configuration information. True NVRAM often is used in intelligent modems to store a user-defined default configuration loaded into normal modem RAM at power-up.

nonvolatile RAM disk A RAM disk powered by a battery supply so that it continues to hold its data during a power outage.

notebook computer A very small personal computer approximately the size of a notebook.

NTSC The National Television Standards Committee, which governs the standard for television and video playback and recording in the United States. The NTSC was originally organized in 1941 when TV broadcasting first became prevalent. The original standard they created was called RS-170A, which is now simply referred to as NTSC. The NTSC standard provides for 525 scan lines of resolution and is transmitted at 60 half-frames per second. It is an interlaced signal, which means that it scans every other line each time the screen is refreshed. The signal is generated as a composite of red, green, and blue signals for color and includes an FM frequency for audio and a signal for stereo. Twenty years later, higher standards were adopted in Europe with the PAL and SECAM systems, both incompatible with the NTSC standard of North America. NTSC is also called *composite video.*

null modem A serial cable wired so that two data terminal equipment (DTE) devices, such as personal computers, or two data communication equipment (DCE) devices, such as modems or mice, can be connected. Also sometimes called a *modem-eliminator.* To make a null-modem cable with DB-25 connectors, you wire these pins together: 1-1, 2-3, 3-2, 4-5, 5-4, 6-20, 20-6, and 7-7.

object hierarchy Object hierarchy occurs in a graphical program when two or more objects are linked and one object's movement is dependent on the other object. This is known as a parent-child hierarchy. In an example using a human figure, the fingers would be child objects to the hand, which is a child object to the arm, which is a child to the shoulder, and so on. Object hierarchy provides much control for an animator in moving complex figures.

OCR Optical Character Recognition. An information-processing technology that converts human-readable text into computer data. Usually a scanner is used to read the text on a page, and OCR software converts the images to characters.

ODI Open Data-link Interface. A device-driver standard from Novell, ODI allows you to run multiple protocols on the same network adapter card. ODI adds functionality to Novell's NetWare and network computing environments by supporting multiple protocols and drivers.

OEM Original Equipment Manufacturer. Any manufacturer that sells its product to a reseller. Usually refers to the original manufacturer of a particular device or component. Most Compaq hard disks, for example, are made by Conner Peripherals, who is considered the OEM.

OLE Object Linking and Embedding. An enhancement to the original Dynamic Data Exchange (DDE) protocol that allows you to embed or link data created in one application in a document created in another application, and subsequently edit that data directly from the final document.

online fallback A feature that enables high-speed error-control modems to monitor line quality and fall back to the next-lower speed if line quality degrades. The modems fall forward as line quality improves.

operating system A collection of programs for operating the computer. Operating systems perform housekeeping tasks such as input and output between the computer and peripherals and accepting and interpreting information from the keyboard. DOS and OS/2 are examples of popular operating systems.

optical disk A disk that encodes data as a series of reflective pits that are read (and sometimes written) by a laser beam.

Orange Book Orange Book is the standard for recordable compact discs (like CD-ROM, but recordable instead of Read-Only). Recordable compact discs are called CD-R and are becoming popular with the widespread use of multimedia. Publishers use CD-R when transferring paper books to electronic publishing tools. Part of the Orange Book standard defines rewritable Magneto-Optical disks and another section defines optical Write-Once, Read-Many (WORM) disks. Publishers usually record a master onto a CD-R WORM disc prior to mass distribution. Titles recorded on WORM can be played by any standard CD-ROM drive (Yellow Book).

originate mode A state in which the modem transmits at the predefined low frequency of the communications channel and receives at the high frequency. The transmit/receive frequencies are the reverse of the called modem, which is in answer mode.

OS/2 A universal operating system developed jointly by IBM and Microsoft Corporation. The latest operating system from IBM for microcomputers using the Intel 386 or better microprocessors. OS/2 uses the protected-mode operation of the processor to expand memory from 1M to 4G and to support fast, efficient multitasking. The OS/2 Workplace Shell, an integral part of the system, is a graphical interface similar to Microsoft Windows and the Apple Macintosh system. The latest version runs DOS, Windows, and OS/2-specific software.

output Information processed by a computer; or the act of sending that information to a mass storage device such as a video display, a printer, or a modem.

Overdrive An Intel trademark name for its line of upgrade processors.

overlay Part of a program that is loaded into memory only when it is required.

overrun A situation in which data moves from one device faster than a second device can accept it.

overwrite To write data on top of existing data, thus erasing the existing data.

package A device that includes a chip mounted on a carrier and sealed.

PAL Phase Alternating Line system. Invented in 1961, a system of TV broadcasting used in England and other European countries. With its 625-line picture delivered at 25 frames/second, PAL provides a better image and an improved color transmission over the NTSC system used in North America. PAL also can stand for Programmable Array Logic, a type of chip that has logic gates specified by a device programmer.

palmtop computer A computer system smaller than a notebook that is designed so that it can be held in one hand while being operated by the other. Many are now called PDAs or Personal Digital Assistants.

parallel A method of transferring data characters in which the bits travel down parallel electrical paths simultaneously—for example, eight paths for eight-bit characters. Data is stored in computers in parallel form but may be converted to serial form for certain operations.

parity A method of error checking in which an extra bit is sent to the receiving device to indicate whether an even or odd number of binary 1 bits were transmitted. The receiving unit compares the received information with this bit and can obtain a reasonable judgment about the validity of the character. The same type of parity (even or odd) must be used by two communicating computers, or both may omit parity. When parity is used, a parity bit is added to each transmitted character. The bit's value is 0 or 1, to make the total number of 1s in the character even or odd, depending on which type of parity is used.

park program A program that executes a seek to the highest cylinder or just past the highest cylinder of a drive so that the potential of data loss is minimized if the drive is moved.

partition A section of a hard disk devoted to a particular operating system. Most hard disks have only one partition, which is devoted to DOS. A hard disk can have as many as four partitions, each occupied by a different operating system. DOS V3.3 or higher can occupy two of these four partitions.

Pascal A high-level programming language named for the French mathematician Blaise Pascal (1623-1662). Developed in the early 1970s by Niklaus Wirth for teaching programming and designed to support the concepts of structured programming. Easy to learn and often the first language taught in schools.

PCMCIA Personal Computer Memory Card International Association. A nonprofit association founded in 1989 to standardize the PC card, a credit card-sized expansion adapter for notebook and laptop PCs. PC Card is the official PCMCIA trademark; however, both PC Card and PCMCIA card are used to refer to these standards. PCMCIA cards are removable modules that can hold numerous types of devices including memory, modems, fax/modems, radio transceivers, network adapters, solid-state disks, and hard disks.

Pentium An Intel microprocessor with 32-bit registers, a 64-bit data bus, and a 32-bit address bus. The Pentium has a built-in level 1 cache that is segmented into a separate 8K cache for code and another 8K cache for data. The Pentium includes a FPU (Floating Point Unit) or math coprocessor. The Pentium is backwards-compatible with the 486 and can operate in real, protected virtual, and virtual real modes.

Pentium Pro An Intel microprocessor with 32-bit registers, a 64-bit data bus, and a 36-bit address bus. The Pentium Pro has the same segmented level 1 cache as the Pentium, but also includes a 256K or 512K Level 2 cache on a separate die in the same module. The Pentium Pro includes a FPU (Floating Point Unit) or math coprocessor. The Pentium Pro is backwards-compatible with the Pentium and can operate in real, protected virtual, and virtual real modes.

peripheral Any piece of equipment used in computer systems that is an attachment to the computer. Disk drives, terminals, and printers are all examples of peripherals.

PGA Pin-Grid Array. A chip package that has a large number of pins on the bottom designed for socket mounting. Also can mean Professional Graphics Adapter, a limited-production, high-resolution graphics card for XT and AT systems from IBM.

Photo CD Photo CD is a technology developed by Eastman Kodak and Phillips that stores photographic images from 35mm film on a CD-R recordable compact disc. Images stored on the Photo CD may have resolutions as high as 2,048×3,072 pixels. Up to 100 true-color images (24-bit color) can be stored on one disk. Photo CD images are created by scanning 35mm film and digitally recording the images on compact discs (CDs). The digitized images are indexed (given a 4-digit code) and thumbnails of each image on the disc are shown on the front of the case along with its index number. Multi-session capability allows several rolls of 35mm film to be added to a single disk on different occasions.

physical drive A single disk drive. DOS defines logical drives, which are given a specifier, such as C: or D:. A single physical drive may be divided into multiple logical drives. Conversely, special software can span a single logical drive across two physical drives.

physical unit number *See* PUN.

PIF Program Information File. A file that contains information about a non-Windows application specifying optimum settings for running the program under Windows 3.x. These are called Property Sheets in Windows 95.

pixel A mnemonic term meaning picture element. Any of the tiny elements that form a picture on a video display screen. Also called a *pel*.

planar board A term equivalent to *motherboard*, used by IBM in some of its literature.

plated media Hard disk platters plated with a form of thin metal film media on which data is recorded.

platter A disk contained in a hard disk drive. Most drives have two or more platters, each with data recorded on both sides.

PLCC Plastic Leaded-Chip Carrier. A popular chip-carrier package with J-leads around the perimeter of the package.

Plug and Play (PnP) A hardware and software specification developed by Intel that allows a PnP system and PnP adapter cards to automatically configure themselves. PnP cards are free from switches and jumpers and are configured via the PnP BIOS in the host system, or via supplied programs for non PnP systems.

port Plug or socket that enables an external device such as a printer to be attached to the adapter card in the computer. Also a logical address used by a microprocessor for communications between itself and various devices.

port address One of a system of addresses used by the computer to access devices such as disk drives or printer ports. You may need to specify an unused port address when installing any adapter boards in a system unit.

portable computer A computer system smaller than a transportable system, but larger than a laptop system. Most portable systems conform to the lunchbox style popularized by Compaq, or the briefcase style popularized by IBM, each with a fold-down (removable) keyboard and built-in display. These systems characteristically run on AC power and not on batteries, include several expansion slots, and can be as powerful as full-blown desktop systems.

POS Programmable Option Select. The Micro Channel Architecture's POS eliminates switches and jumpers from the system board and adapters by replacing them with programmable registers. Automatic configuration routines store the POS data in a battery-powered

CMOS memory for system configuration and operations. The configuration utilities rely on adapter description (ADF) files that contain the setup data for each card.

POST Power-On Self Test. A series of tests run by the computer at power-on. Most computers scan and test many of their circuits and sound a beep from the internal speaker if this initial test indicates proper system performance.

PostScript A page-description language developed primarily by John Warnock of Adobe Systems for converting and moving data to the laser-printed page. Instead of using the standard method of transmitting graphics or character information to a printer, telling it where to place dots one-by-one on a page, PostScript provides a way for the laser printer to interpret mathematically a full page of shapes and curves.

power supply An electrical/electronic circuit that supplies all operating voltage and current to the computer system.

PPP Point-to-Point Protocol. A protocol that allows a computer to use the Internet with a standard telephone line and a high-speed modem. PPP is a new standard which replaces SLIP. PPP is less common than SLIP; however, it is increasing in popularity.

primary partition An ordinary, single-volume bootable partition. *See also* extended partition.

processor speed The clock rate at which a microprocessor processes data. A standard IBM PC, for example, operates at 4.77 MHz (4.77 million cycles per second).

program A set of instructions or steps telling the computer how to handle a problem or task.

PROM Programmable Read-Only Memory. A type of memory chip that can be programmed to store information permanently—information that cannot be erased.

proprietary Anything invented by a company and not used by any other company. Especially applies to cases in which the inventing company goes to lengths to hide the specifications of the new invention. The opposite of standard.

protected mode A mode available in all Intel 80286- or 80386-compatible processors. In this mode, memory addressing is extended to 16 or 4096 megabytes, and restricted protection levels can be set to trap software crashes and control the system.

protocol A system of rules and procedures governing communications between two or more devices. Protocols vary, but communicating devices must follow the same protocol in order to exchange data. The data format, readiness to receive or send, error detection, and error correction are some of the operations that may be defined in protocols.

PUN Physical Unit Number. A term used to describe a device attached directly to the SCSI bus. Also known as a SCSI ID. As many as eight SCSI devices can be attached to a single SCSI bus, and each must have a unique PUN or ID assigned from 7 to 0. Normally the SCSI host adapter is assigned the highest-priority ID, which is 7. A bootable hard disk is assigned an ID of 6, and other nonbootable drives are assigned lower priorities.

QAM Quadrature Amplitude Modulation. A modulation technique used by high-speed modems that combines both phase and amplitude modulation. This technique enables multiple bits to be encoded in a single time interval. The V.32bis standard-codes six data bits plus an additional trellis coding bit for each signal change. An individual signal is evaluated with respect to phase and amplitude compared to the carrier wave. A plot of all possible QAM signal points is referred to as the signal constellation pattern. The V.32bis constellation pattern has 128 discrete signal points.

QIC Quarter-Inch Committee. An industry association that sets hardware and software standards for tape-backup units that use quarter-inch-wide tapes.

QWERTY keyboard The standard typewriter or computer keyboard, with the characters Q, W, E, R, T, and Y on the top row of alpha keys. Because of the haphazard placement of characters, this keyboard can hinder fast typing.

rails Plastic strips attached to the sides of disk drives mounted in IBM ATs and compatibles so that the drives can slide into place. These rails fit into channels in the side of each disk drive bay position.

RAM Random-Access Memory. All memory accessible at any instant (randomly) by a microprocessor.

RAM disk A "phantom disk drive" in which a section of system memory (RAM) is set aside to hold data, just as though it were a number of disk sectors. To DOS, a RAM disk looks like and functions like any other drive.

random-access file A file in which all data elements (or records) are of equal length and written in the file end to end, without delimiting characters between. Any element (or record) in the file can be found directly by calculating the record's offset in the file.

random-access memory *See* RAM.

raster A pattern of horizontal scanning lines normally on a TV screen. An electromagnetic field causes the beam of the TV tube to illuminate the correct dots to produce the required characters.

raster graphics A technique for representing a picture image as a matrix of dots. It is the digital counterpart of the analog method used in TV. There are several raster graphics standards.

RCA jack Also called a *phono connector.* A plug and socket for a two-wire coaxial cable used to connect audio and video components. The plug is a 1/8" thick prong that sticks out 5/16" from the middle of a cylinder.

read-only file A file whose attribute setting in the file's directory entry tells DOS not to allow software to write into or over the file.

read-only memory *See* ROM.

read/write head A tiny magnet that reads and writes data on a disk track.

real mode A mode available in all Intel 8086-compatible processors that enables compatibility with the original 8086. In this mode, memory addressing is limited to one megabyte.

real time When something is recorded or processed as it is happening in the outside world.

Red Book Red Book is more commonly known as Compact Disc Digital Audio (CD-DA) and is one of four compact disc standards. Red Book got its name from the color of the manual used to describe the CD Audio specifications. The Red Book audio standard requires that digital audio is sampled at a 44.1KHz sample rate using 16 bits for each sample. This is the standard used by audio CDs and many CD-ROMs. Sample rates this high require enormous amounts of disk space.

refresh cycle A cycle in which the computer accesses all memory locations stored by dynamic RAM chips so that the information remains intact. Dynamic RAM chips must be accessed several times a second, or else the information fades.

register Storage area in memory having a specified storage capacity, such as a bit, a byte, or a computer word, and intended for a special purpose.

remote digital loopback A test that checks the phone link and a remote modem's transmitter and receiver. Data entered from the keyboard is transmitted from the initiating modem, received by the remote modem's receiver, looped through its transmitter, and returned to the local screen for verification.

remote echo A copy of the data received by the remote system, returned to the sending system, and displayed on-screen. A function of the remote system.

resolution A reference to the size of the pixels used in graphics. In medium-resolution graphics, pixels are large. In high-resolution graphics, pixels are small.

RFI Radio Frequency Interference. A high frequency signal radiated by improperly shielded conductors, particularly when signal path lengths are comparable to or longer than the signal wavelengths. The FCC now regulates RFI in computer equipment sold in the U.S. under FCC Regulations Part 15, Subpart J.

RISC An acronym for Reduced Instruction Set Computer, as differentiated from CISC, Complex Instruction Set Computer. RISC processors have simple instruction sets requiring only one or a few execution cycles. These simple instructions can be utilized more effectively than CISC systems with appropriately designed software, resulting in faster operations.

RLL Run-Length Limited. A type of encoding that derives its name from the fact that the techniques used limit the distance (run length) between magnetic flux reversals on the disk platter. Several types of RLL encoding techniques exist, although only two are commonly used. (1,7)RLL encoding increases storage capacity by about 30 percent over MFM encoding and is most popular in the very highest capacity drives due to a better window margin, while (2,7)RLL encoding increases storage capacity by 50 percent over MFM encoding and is used in the majority of RLL implementations. Most IDE, ESDI, and SCSI hard disks use one of these forms of RLL encoding.

RMA number Return-Merchandise Authorization number. A number given to you by a vendor when you arrange to return an item for repairs. Used to track the item and the repair.

ROM Read-Only Memory. A type of memory that has values permanently or semi-permanently burned in. These locations are used to hold important programs or data that must be available to the computer when the power initially is turned on.

ROM BIOS Read Only Memory-Basic Input Output System. A BIOS encoded in a form of read-only memory for protection. Often applied to important start-up programs that must be present in a system for it to operate.

root directory The main directory of any hard or floppy disk. Has a fixed size and location for a particular disk volume and cannot be resized dynamically the way subdirectories can.

router A computer system that routes messages from one LAN (local area network) to another. It is used to internetwork similar and dissimilar networks and can select the most expedient route based on traffic load, line speeds, costs, and network failures.

routine Set of frequently used instructions. May be considered as a subdivision of a program with two or more instructions that are related functionally.

RS-232 An interface introduced in August 1969 by the Electronic Industries Association. The RS-232 interface standard provides an electrical description for connecting peripheral devices to computers.

S-Video (Y/C) Y/C video is a video signal in which the luminance and chrominance (Y/C) components are kept separate, providing greater control and quality of each image. The luminance (Y) channel controls light intensity. The greater the luminance, the lighter the color. Chrominance (C) contains hue (color) and saturation (depth) information on an image. Examples of Y/C (S-Video) include S-VHS (Super-VHS) and Hi8 (High band 8mm) video.

scratch disk A disk that contains no useful information and can be used as a test disk. IBM has a routine on the Advanced Diagnostics disks that creates a specially formatted scratch disk to be used for testing floppy drives.

SCSI Small Computer System Interface. A standard originally developed by Shugart Associates (then called SASI for Shugart Associates System Interface) and later approved by ANSI in 1986. SCSI-2 was approved in 1994, and SCSI-3 is currently in the development process. Normally uses a 50-pin connector and permits multiple devices (up to eight including the host) to be connected in daisy-chain fashion.

SDLC Synchronous Data Link Control. A protocol developed by IBM for software applications and communicating devices operation in IBM's Systems Network Architecture (SNA). Defines operations at the link level of communications—for example, the format of data frames exchanged between modems over a phone line.

SECAM A mnemonic term for sequential and memory. Refers to a system of TV broadcasting used in France and in a modified form in the former USSR. Uses an 819-line picture that provides a better resolution than the (British) PAL 625-line and (U.S.) NTSC 525-line formats.

sector A section of one track defined with identification markings and an identification number. Most sectors hold 512 bytes of data.

security software Utility software that uses a system of passwords and other devices to restrict an individual's access to subdirectories and files.

seek time The amount of time required for a disk drive to move the heads across one-third of the total number of cylinders. Represents the average time it takes to move the heads from one cylinder to another randomly selected cylinder. Seek time is a part of the average access time for a drive.

semiconductor A substance, such as germanium or silicon, whose conductivity is poor at low temperatures but is improved by minute additions of certain substances or by the application of heat, light, or voltage. Depending on the temperature and pressure, a semiconductor can control a flow of electricity. Semiconductors are the basis of modern electronic-circuit technology.

sequencer A sequencer is a software program that controls MIDI file messages and keeps track of music timing. Because MIDI files store note instructions instead of actual sounds, a sequencer is needed to play, record, and edit MIDI sounds. Sequencer programs allow for recording and playback of MIDI files by storing the instrument, the note pitch (frequency), the duration in real time that each note is held, and the loudness (amplitude) of each musical or sound effect note.

sequential file A file in which varying-length data elements are recorded end to end, with delimiting characters placed between each element. To find a particular element, you must read the whole file up to that element.

serial The transfer of data characters one bit at a time, sequentially, using a single electrical path.

servo data Magnetic markings written on disk platters to guide the read/write heads in drives that use voice-coil actuators.

Session (Single or Multi-Session) A term used in CD-ROM recording to describe a recording event. In a single session, data is recorded on a CD-ROM disc and an index is created. If additional space is left on the disc, another session can be used to record additional files along with another index. The original index cannot be updated because recordable CD-ROM drives are normally Write-Once, Read-Many (WORM) type drives. Many CD-ROM drives do not expect additional recording sessions and therefore will be unable to read the additional session data on the disk. The advent of Kodak's Photo CD propelled the desire for multisession CD-ROM XA (extended architecture) drives. The first generation of XA drives were capable of single-session reads only. Multi-session CD-ROM XA drives will read all the indices created when images are recorded many times on the same CD-ROM XA drive.

settling time The time required for read/write heads to stop vibrating after they have been moved to a new track.

shadow ROM A copy of a system's slower access ROM BIOS placed in faster access RAM, usually during the start-up or boot procedure. This setup enables the system to access BIOS code without the penalty of additional wait states required by the slower ROM chips. Also called *shadow RAM*.

shell The generic name of any user interface software. COMMAND.COM is the standard shell for DOS. OS/2 comes with three shells: a DOS command shell, an OS/2 command shell, and the OS/2 Presentation Manager, a graphical shell.

shock rating A rating (usually expressed in G force units) of how much shock a disk drive can sustain without damage. Usually two different specifications exist for a drive powered on or off.

SIMM Single in-line memory module. An array of memory chips on a small PC board with a single row of I/O contacts.

single-ended An electrical signaling method where a single line is referenced to a ground path common to other signals. In a single-ended bus intended for moderately long distances, there is commonly one ground line between groups of signal lines to provide some resistance to signal crosstalk. Single-ended signals only require one driver or receiver pin per signal, plus one ground pin per group of signals. Single-ended signals are vulnerable to common mode noise and crosstalk but are much less expensive than differential signaling methods.

SIP Single In-line Package. A DIP-like package with only one row of leads.

skinny dip Twenty-four- and 28-position DIP devices with .300-inch row-to-row centerlines.

SLIP Serial Line Internet Protocol. An Internet protocol that is used to run the Internet Protocol (IP) over serial lines such as telephone circuits. IP allows a packet to traverse multiple networks on the way to its final destination.

SMPTE time code SMPTE is an acronym for the Society of Motion Picture and Television Engineers. The SMPTE time code is a standard used to identify individual video frames in the video editing process. SMPTE time code controls such functions as play, record, rewind, and forward of video tapes. SMPTE time code displays video in terms of hours, minutes, seconds, and frames for accurate video editing.

SO-J Small Outline J-lead. A small DIP package with J-shaped leads for surface mounting or socketing.

soft error An error in reading or writing data that occurs sporadically, usually because of a transient problem such as a power fluctuation.

software A series of instructions loaded in the computer's memory that instructs the computer on how to accomplish a problem or task.

spindle The central post on which a disk drive's platters are mounted.

SQL Structured Query Language. A standard relational database language used especially on midrange and mainframe computers.

SRAM Static Random Access Memory. A form of high-speed memory. SRAM chips do not require a refresh cycle like Dynamic RAM chips and can be made to operate at very high access speeds. SRAM chips are very expensive because they normally require 6 transistors per bit. This also makes the chip larger than conventional dynamic RAM chips. SRAM is volatile, meaning it will lose data with no power.

ST-506/412 A hard disk interface invented by Seagate Technology and introduced in 1980 with the ST-506 5M hard drive. The ST-506 interface requires that the read/write head be stepped or moved across the disk one track at a time by carefully timed pulses. Because these pulses cause the read/write head's stepper motor to advance a notch, they cannot be sent faster than the disk drive can move the heads. The ST-412 interface introduced with the ST-412 10M drive adds buffered seeking, which eliminates this problem. Instead of requiring the controller to slow the pulse rate to whatever the mechanism can handle, ST-412 simply counts the pulses as they come in and then decides how far to step the head to move the required number of tracks. ST-506/412 was formerly the interface of choice for IBM-compatible systems but has since been superseded by the ESDI, IDE, and SCSI interfaces.

standby power supply A backup power supply that quickly switches into operation during a power outage.

start/stop bits The signaling bits attached to a character before the character is transmitted during asynchronous transmission.

starting cluster The number of the first cluster occupied by a file. Listed in the directory entry of every file.

stepper motor actuator An assembly that moves disk drive read/write heads across platters by a sequence of small partial turns of a stepper motor.

storage Device or medium on or in which data can be entered or held and retrieved at a later time. Synonymous with memory.

streaming In tape backup, a condition in which data is transferred from the hard disk as quickly as the tape drive can record the data so that the drive does not start and stop or waste tape.

string A sequence of characters.

subdirectory A directory listed in another directory. Subdirectories themselves exist as files.

subroutine A segment of a program that can be executed by a single call. Also called *program module.*

surface mount Chip carriers and sockets designed to mount to the surface of a PC board.

surge protector A device in the power line that feeds the computer and provides minimal protection against voltage spikes and other transients.

synchronous communication A form of communication in which blocks of data are sent at strictly timed intervals. Because the timing is uniform, no start or stop bits are required. Compare with asynchronous communication. Some mainframes support only synchronous communications unless a synchronous adapter and appropriate software have been installed.

system crash A situation in which the computer freezes up and refuses to proceed without rebooting. Usually caused by faulty software. Unlike a hard disk crash, no permanent physical damage occurs.

system files The two hidden DOS files IBMBIO.COM and IBMDOS.COM; they represent the interface between the BIOS and DOS (IBMBIO) and the interface between DOS and other applications (IBMDOS).

system integrator A computer consultant or vendor who tests available products and combines them into highly optimized systems.

target A device attached to a SCSI bus that receives and processes commands sent from another device (the initiator) on the SCSI bus. A SCSI hard disk is an example of a target.

TCM Trellis-Coded Modulation. An error-detection and correction technique employed by high-speed modems to enable higher-speed transmissions that are more resistant to line impairments. In TCM encoding, the first two data bits of an encoded group are used to generate a third TCM bit that is added to the group. For example, in V.32bis, the first two bits of a 6-bit group are used to generate the TCM bit, which then is placed as the first bit of a new 7-bit group. By reversing the encoding at the other end, the receiving modem can determine whether the received group is valid.

TCP/IP Transmission Control Protocol/Internet Protocol. A set of protocols developed by the Department of Defense to link dissimilar computers across many kinds of networks. This is the primary protocol used by the Internet. It was developed in the 1970s by the U.S. Department of Defense's Advanced Research Projects Agency (DARPA) as a military standard protocol. TCP/IP is supported by many manufacturers of minicomputers, personal computers, mainframes, technical workstations, and data communications equipment. It is also the protocol commonly used over Ethernet networks.

temporary backup A second copy of a work file, usually having the extension BAK. Created by application software so that you easily can return to a previous version of your work.

temporary file A file temporarily (and usually invisibly) created by a program for its own use.

tera A multiplier indicating 1 trillion (1,000,000,000,000) of some unit. Abbreviated as t or T. When used to indicate a number of bytes of memory storage, the multiplier definition changes to 1,099,511,627,776. One terabit, for example, equals 1,000,000,000,000 bits, and one terabyte equals 1,099,511,627,776 bytes.

terabyte A unit of information storage equal to 1,099,511,627,776 bytes.

terminal A device whose keyboard and display are used for sending and receiving data over a communications link. Differs from a microcomputer in that it has no internal processing capabilities. Used to enter data into or retrieve processed data from a system or network.

terminal mode An operational mode required for microcomputers to transmit data. In terminal mode, the computer acts as though it were a standard terminal such as a teletypewriter rather than a data processor. Keyboard entries go directly to the modem, whether the entry is a modem command or data to be transmitted over the phone lines. Received data is output directly to the screen. The more popular communications software products control terminal mode and enable more complex operations, including file transmission and saving received files.

terminator A piece of hardware that must be attached to both ends of an electrical bus. Functions to prevent the reflection or echoing of signals that reach the ends of the bus and to ensure that the correct impedance load is placed on the driver circuits on the bus.

thin-film media Hard disk platters that have a thin film (usually 3 millionths of an inch) of medium deposited on the aluminum substrate through a sputtering or plating process.

through-hole Chip carriers and sockets equipped with leads that extend through holes in a PC board.

throughput The amount of user data transmitted per second without the overhead of protocol information such as start and stop bits or frame headers and trailers.

TIFF Tagged Image File Format. A way of storing and exchanging digital image data. Developed by Aldus Corporation, Microsoft Corporation, and major scanner vendors to help link scanned images with the popular desktop publishing applications. Supports three main types of image data: black-and-white data, halftones or dithered data, and grayscale data.

token ring A type of local area network in which the workstations relay a packet of data called a token in a logical ring configuration. When a station wants to transmit, it takes possession of the token, attaches its data, and then frees the token after the data has made a complete circuit of the electrical ring. IBM's token ring system is a standard network hardware implementation supported by many manufacturers. It is currently the highest-performance-standard LAN system and transmits at speeds of 16 million bits per second. Because of the token-passing scheme, access to the network is controlled, unlike the slower Ethertet system, in which collisions of data can occur, which wastes time. The token ring network also uses twisted-pair wiring, which is cheaper than the coaxial cable used by Ethernet and ARCnet.

tower A personal computer that normally sits on the floor and that is mounted vertically rather than horizontally.

TPI Tracks Per Inch. Used as a measurement of magnetic track density. Standard 5 1/4-inch 360K floppy disks have a density of 48 TPI, and the 1.2M disks have a 96-TPI density. All 3 1/2-inch disks have a 135.4667-TPI density, and hard disks can have densities greater than 3,000 TPI.

track One of the many concentric circles that holds data on a disk surface. Consists of a single line of magnetic flux changes and is divided into some number of 512-byte sectors.

track density Expressed as Tracks Per Inch (TPI), track density defines how many tracks are recorded in one inch of space measured radially from the center of the disk. Sometimes also called radial density.

track-to-track seek time The time required for read/write heads to move between adjacent tracks.

transportable computer A computer system larger than a portable system, and similar in size and shape to a portable sewing machine. Most transportables conform to a design similar to the original Compaq portable, with a built-in CRT display. These systems are characteristically very heavy, and run only on AC power. Because of advances primarily in LCD and plasma-display technology, these systems are largely obsolete and have been replaced by portable systems.

troubleshooting The task of determining the cause of a problem.

true-color images True-color images are also called 24-bit color images because each pixel is represented by 24 bits of data, allowing for 16.7 million colors. The number of colors possible is based on the number of bits used to represent the color. If 8 bits are used, there are 256 possible color values (2 to the 8th power). To obtain 16.7 million colors, each of the primary colors (red, green, and blue) is represented by 8-bits per pixel, which allows for 256 possible shades for each of the primary red, green, and blue colors or 256×256×256 = 16.7 million total colors.

TSR Terminate-and-Stay-Resident. A program that remains in memory after being loaded. Because they remain in memory, TSR programs can be reactivated by a predefined keystroke sequence or other operation while another program is active. Usually called *resident programs*.

TTL Transistor-to-Transistor Logic. Digital signals often are called TTL signals. A TTL display is a monitor that accepts digital input at standardized signal voltage levels.

tweens Tweens are the name given to a series of animation or video frames between the key frames. When one object is transformed (morphed) into another, the initial object and the final object are set on the computer. Tweens are the frames that transpose the first object into the final image.

twisted pair A type of wire in which two small insulated copper wires are wrapped or twisted around each other to minimize interference from other wires in the cable. Two types of twisted-pair cables are available: unshielded and shielded. Unshielded twisted-pair wiring commonly is used in telephone cables and provides little protection against interference. Shielded twisted-pair wiring is used in some networks or any application in which immunity from electrical interference is more important. Twisted-pair wire is much easier to work with than coaxial cable and is cheaper as well.

UART Universal Asynchronous Receiver Transmitter. A chip device that controls the RS-232 serial port in a PC-compatible system. Originally developed by National Semi-conductor, several UART versions are in PC-compatible systems: the 8250B is used in PC- or XT-class systems, and the 16450 and 16550A are used in AT-class systems.

unformatted capacity The total number of bytes of data that can fit on a disk. The formatted capacity is lower because space is lost defining the boundaries between sectors.

uninterruptible power supply Also known as *UPS*. A device that supplies power to the computer from batteries so that power will not stop, even momentarily, during a power outage. The batteries are recharged constantly from a wall socket.

Universal Asynchronous Receiver Transmitter *See* UART.

UPC Universal Product Code. A ten-digit computer-readable bar code used in labeling retail products. The code in the form of vertical bars includes a five-digit manufacturer identification number and a five-digit product code number.

update To modify information already contained in a file or program with current information.

URL An acronym for Uniform Resource Locator. The primary naming scheme used to identify a particular site or file on the World Wide Web. URLs combine information about the protocol being used, the address of the site where the resource is located, the subdirectory location at the site, and the name of the particular file (or page) in question.

utility Programs that carry out routine procedures to make computer use easier.

UTP Unshielded Twisted Pair. A type of wire often used indoors to connect telephones or computer devices. Comes with two or four wires twisted inside a flexible plastic sheath or conduit and utilizes modular plugs and phone jacks.

V.21 A CCITT standard for modem communications at 300 bps. Modems made in the U.S. or Canada follow the Bell 103 standard but can be set to answer V.21 calls from overseas. The actual transmission rate is 300 baud and employs FSK (frequency shift keying) modulation, which encodes a single bit per baud.

V.22 A CCITT standard for modem communications at 1200 bps, with an optional fallback to 600 bps. V.22 is partially compatible with the Bell 212A standard observed in the U.S. and Canada. The actual transmission rate is 600 baud, using DPSK (differential-phase shift keying) to encode as much as 2 bits per baud.

V.22bis A CCITT standard for modem communications at 2400 bps. Includes an automatic link-negotiation fallback to 1200 bps and compatibility with Bell 212A/V.22 modems. The actual transmission rate is 600 baud, using QAM (quadrature amplitude modulation) to encode as much as 4 bits per baud.

V.23 A CCITT standard for modem communications at 1200 or 600 bps with a 75-bps back channel. Used in the United Kingdom for some videotext systems.

V.25 A CCITT standard for modem communications that specifies an answer tone different from the Bell answer tone used in the U.S. and Canada. Most intelligent modems can be set with an ATB0 command so that they use the V.25 2100 Hz tone when answering overseas calls.

V.32 A CCITT standard for modem communications at 9600 bps and 4800 bps. V.32 modems fall back to 4800 bps when line quality is impaired and fall forward again to 9600 bps when line quality improves. The actual transmission rate is 2400 baud using QAM (quadrature amplitude modulation) and optional TCM (trellis-coded modulation) to encode as much as 4 data bits per baud.

V.32bis A CCITT standard that extends the standard V.32 connection range and supports 4800-, 7200-, 9600-, 12000-, and 14400-bps transmission rates. V.32bis modems fall back to the next-lower speed when line quality is impaired, fall back further as necessary, and fall forward to the next-higher speed when line quality improves. The actual transmission rate is 2400 baud using QAM (quadrature amplitude modulation) and TCM (trellis-coded modulation) to encode as much as 6 data bits per baud.

V.32turbo A proprietary standard proposed by several modem manufacturers that will be cheaper to implement than the standard V.32 fast protocol, but which will only support transmission speeds of up to 18800 bps. Because it is not an industry standard, it is not likely to have widespread industry support.

V.34 A CCITT standard that extends the standard V.32bis connection range, supporting 28800 bps transmission rates as well as all the functions and rates of V.32bis. Products following this standard are now available. This was called V.32fast or V.fast while under development.

V.42 A CCITT standard for modem communications that defines a two-stage process of detection and negotiation for LAPM error control. Also supports MNP error-control protocol, Levels 1 through 4.

V.42bis An extension of CCITT V.42 that defines a specific data-compression scheme for use with V.42 and MNP error control.

vaccine A type of program used to locate and eradicate virus code from infected programs or systems.

VCPI Virtual Control Program Interface. A 386 and higher processor memory management standard created by Phar Lap software in conjunction with other software developers. VCPI provides an interface between applications using DOS extenders and 386 memory managers.

VESA Video Electronics Standards Association. Founded in the late 1980s by NEC Home Electronics and eight other leading video board manufacturers with the main goal of standardizing the electrical, timing, and programming issues surrounding 800×600 resolution video displays, commonly known as Super VGA. VESA has also developed the Video Local Bus (VL-Bus) standard for connecting high-speed adapters directly to the local processor bus.

VGA Video Graphics Array. A type of PC video display circuit (and adapter) first introduced by IBM on April 2, 1987, that supports text and graphics. Text is supported at a maximum resolution of 80×25 characters in 16 colors with a character box of 9×16 pixels. Graphics is supported at a maximum resolution of 320×200 pixels in 256 (from a palette of 262,144) colors or 640×480 pixels in 16 colors. The VGA outputs an analog signal with a horizontal scanning frequency of 31.5 KHz and supports analog color or analog monochrome displays.

video graphics array *See* VGA.

virtual disk A RAM disk or "phantom disk drive" in which a section of system memory (usually RAM) is set aside to hold data, just as though it were a number of disk sectors. To DOS, a virtual disk looks like and functions like any other "real" drive.

virtual memory A technique by which operating systems (including OS/2) load more programs and data into memory than they can hold. Parts of the programs and data are kept on disk and constantly swapped back and forth into system memory. The applications software programs are unaware of this setup and act as though a large amount of memory is available.

virtual real mode A mode available in all Intel 80386-compatible processors. In this mode, memory addressing is limited to 4,096 megabytes, restricted protection levels can be set to trap software crashes and control the system, and individual real mode-compatible sessions can be set up and maintained separately from one another.

virus A type of resident program designed to attach itself to other programs. Usually at some later time, when the virus is running, it causes an undesirable action to take place.

Visual Basic A high-level, graphically-oriented, fourth generation programming language used only in the Windows operating environment.

VMM Virtual Memory Manager. A facility in Windows enhanced mode that manages the task of swapping data in and out of 386 and higher processor virtual real mode memory space for multiple non-Windows applications running in virtual real mode.

voice-coil actuator A device that moves read/write heads across hard disk platters by magnetic interaction between coils of wire and a magnet. Functions somewhat like an audio speaker, from which the name originated.

voltage regulator A device that smoothes out voltage irregularities in the power fed to the computer.

volume A portion of a disk signified by a single drive specifier. Under DOS V3.3 and later, a single hard disk can be partitioned into several volumes, each with its own logical drive specifier (C:,D:,E:, and so on).

volume label An identifier or name of up to 11 characters that names a disk.

VRAM Video Random-Access Memory. VRAM chips are modified DRAMs on video boards that enable simultaneous access by the host system's processor and the processor on the video board. A large amount of information thus can be transferred quickly between the video board and the system processor. Sometimes also called *dual-ported* RAM.

VxD Virtual Device Driver. A special type of Windows driver for 386 enhanced mode. VxDs run at the most privileged CPU mode (ring 0) and allow low-level interaction with DOS and Windows programs running under Windows.

wait states Pause cycles during system operation that require the processor to wait one or more clock cycles until memory can respond to the processor's request. Enables the microprocessor to synchronize with lower-cost, slower memory. A system that runs with "zero wait states" requires none of these cycles because of the use of faster memory or a memory cache system.

Web browser An application that locates a document on the Internet using a URL (Uniform Resource Locator), retrieves it, and formats the document for display. Netscape's Navigator, Spyglass's Mosaic, and Microsoft's Internet Explorer are examples of Web browsers.

Web site An individual Web document collection named by a unique URL.

Whetstone A benchmark program developed in 1976 designed to simulate arithmetic-intensive programs used in scientific computing. Remains completely CPU-bound and performs no I/O or system calls. Originally written in ALGOL, although the C and Pascal versions became more popular by the late 1980s. The speed at which a system performs floating-point operations often is measured in units of Whetstones.

Whitney technology A term referring to a magnetic disk design that usually has oxide or thin film media, thin film read/write heads, low floating height sliders, and low mass actuator arms that together allow higher bit densities than the older Winchester technology. Whitney technology was first introduced with the IBM 3370 disk drive circa 1979.

Winchester drive Any ordinary, nonremovable (or fixed) hard disk drive. The name originates from a particular IBM drive in the 1960s that had 30M of fixed and 30M of removable storage. This 30-30 drive matched the caliber figure for a popular series of rifles made by Winchester, so the slang term Winchester was applied to any fixed platter hard disk.

Winchester technology The term "winchester" is loosely applied to mean any disk with a fixed or non-removable recording medium. More precisely, the term applies to a ferrite read/write head and slider design with oxide media that was first employed in the IBM 3340 disk drive, circa 1973. Most drives today actually use Whitney technology.

wire frames Wire frames are the most common technique used to construct a three-dimensional object for animation. A wire frame is given coordinates of length, height, and width. Wire frames are then filled with textures, colors, and movement. Transforming a wire frame into a textured object is called *rendering*.

word length The number of bits in a data character without parity, start, or stop bits.

World Wide Web Also called simply the Web. A graphical information system based on hypertext that enables a user to easily access documents located on the Internet.

WORM Write-Once, Read-Many (or multiple). An optical mass-storage device capable of storing many megabytes of information but that can be written to only once on any given area of the disk. A WORM disk typically holds more than 200M of data. Because a WORM drive cannot write over an old version of a file, new copies of files are made and stored on other parts of the disk whenever a file is revised. WORM disks are used to store information when a history of older versions must be maintained. Recording on a WORM disk is performed by a laser writer that burns pits in a thin metallic film (usually tellurium) embedded in the disk. This burning process is called *ablation*. WORM drives are frequently used for archiving data.

write precompensation A modification applied to write data by a controller in order to alleviate partially the problem of bit shift, which causes adjacent 1s written on magnetic media to read as though they were farther apart. When adjacent 1s are sensed by the controller, precompensation is used to write them closer together on the disk, thus enabling them to be read in the proper bit cell window. Drives with built-in controllers normally handle precompensation automatically. Precompensation normally is required for the inner cylinders of oxide media drives.

XGA eXtended Graphics Array. A type of PC video display circuit (and adapter) first introduced by IBM on October 30, 1990, that supports text and graphics. Text is supported at a maximum resolution of 132×60 characters in 16 colors with a character box of 8×6 pixels. Graphics is supported at a maximum resolution of 1024×768 pixels in 256 (from a palette of 262,144) colors or 640×480 pixels in 65,536 colors. The XGA outputs an analog signal with a horizontal scanning frequency of 31.5 or 35.52KHz and supports analog color or analog monochrome displays.

XMM eXtended Memory Manager. A driver that controls access to extended memory on 286 and higher processor systems. HIMEM.SYS is an example of an XMM that comes with DOS.

Xmodem A file-transfer protocol—with error checking—developed by Ward Christensen in the mid-1970s and placed in the public domain. Designed to transfer files between machines running the CP/M operating system and using 300- or 1200-bps modems. Until the late 1980s, because of its simplicity and public-domain status, Xmodem remained the most widely used microcomputer file-transfer protocol. In standard Xmodem, the transmitted blocks are 128 bytes. 1K-Xmodem is an extension to Xmodem that increases the block size to 1,024 bytes. Many newer file-transfer protocols that are much faster and more accurate than Xmodem have been developed, such as Ymodem and Zmodem.

XMS eXtended Memory Specification. A Microsoft-developed standard that provides a way for real mode applications to access extended memory in a controlled fashion. The XMS standard is available from Microsoft.

XON/XOFF Standard ASCII control characters used to tell an intelligent device to stop or resume transmitting data. In most systems, typing Ctrl-S sends the XOFF character. Most devices understand Ctrl-Q as XON; others interpret the pressing of any key after Ctrl-S as XON.

Y-connector A Y-shaped splitter cable that divides a source input into two output signals.

Yellow Book Yellow Book is the standard used by Compact Disc Read-Only Memory (CD-ROM). Multimedia applications most commonly use the Yellow Book standard, which specifies how digital information is to be stored on the CD-ROM and read by a computer. EXtended Architecture (XA) is currently an extension of the Yellow Book that allows for the combination of different data types (audio and video, for example) onto one track in a CD-ROM. Without XA, a CD-ROM can only access one data type at a time. Many CD-ROM drives are now XA-capable.

Ymodem A file-transfer protocol first released as part of Chuck Forsberg's YAM (yet another modem) program. An extension to Xmodem designed to overcome some of the limitations of the original. Enables information about the transmitted file, such as the file name and length, to be sent along with the file data and increases the size of a block from 128 to 1,024 bytes. Ymodem-batch adds the capability to transmit "batches" or groups of files without operator interruption. YmodemG is a variation that sends the entire file before waiting for an acknowledgment. If the receiving side detects an error in midstream, the transfer is aborted. YmodemG is designed for use with modems that have built-in error-correcting capabilities.

ZIF Zero Insertion Force. Sockets that require no force for the insertion of a chip carrier. Usually accomplished through movable contacts and used primarily in test devices in which chips will be inserted and removed many times.

ZIP Zigzag In-line Package. A DIP package that has all leads on one edge in a zigzag pattern and mounts in a vertical plane.

Zmodem A file-transfer protocol commissioned by Telenet and placed in the public domain. Like Ymodem, it was designed by Chuck Forsberg and developed as an extension to Xmodem to overcome some of that original protocol's limitations. Among the key features are a 32-bit CRC offering a degree of error detection many times greater than Xmodem CRC, a server facility, batch transfers, and fast error recovery. One feature of Zmodem is the capability to continue transmitting a file from where it left off if the connection has been broken. Zmodem also was engineered specifically to avoid sending certain sequences, such as ESCape-carriage return-ESCape, that the Telenet network uses to control the connection. Its speed, accuracy, and file-recovery capabilities make Zmodem the leading protocol for high-speed modem file transfers.

On the Web

These web sites may help you with terms that are not included in this chapter:

http://zeppo.cnet.com/Resources/Info/Glossary/

http://www-edlab.ucdavis.edu/ed180/hardwarepracticum.html

Index

Symbols

A

B

C

D

E

F

G

H

I

J

K

L

M

N

O

Q

R

S

T

U

V

X

Y

Z

Complete and Return this Card for a *FREE* Computer Book Catalog

Thank you for purchasing this book! You have purchased a superior computer book written expressly for your needs. To continue to provide the kind of up-to-date, pertinent coverage you've come to expect from us, we need to hear from you. Please take a minute to complete and return this self-addressed, postage-paid form. In return, we'll send you a free catalog of all our computer books on topics ranging from word processing to programming and the internet.

☐ Mrs. ☐ Ms. ☐ Dr. ☐

ne (first) ☐☐☐☐☐☐☐☐☐☐☐ (M.I.) ☐ (last) ☐☐☐☐☐☐☐☐☐☐☐☐☐☐☐

lress ☐☐☐☐☐☐☐☐☐☐☐☐☐☐☐☐☐☐☐☐☐☐☐☐☐☐☐☐☐☐☐☐☐☐☐☐

☐☐☐☐☐☐☐☐☐☐☐☐☐☐☐☐☐☐☐☐☐☐☐☐☐☐☐☐☐☐☐☐☐☐☐☐

☐☐☐☐☐☐☐☐☐☐☐☐☐☐☐ State ☐☐ Zip ☐☐☐☐☐ ☐☐☐☐

ne ☐☐☐ ☐☐☐ ☐☐☐☐ Fax ☐☐☐ ☐☐☐ ☐☐☐☐

npany Name ☐☐☐☐☐☐☐☐☐☐☐☐☐☐☐☐☐☐☐☐☐☐☐☐☐☐☐☐☐☐☐☐☐☐

ail address ☐☐☐☐☐☐☐☐☐☐☐☐☐☐☐☐☐☐☐☐☐☐☐☐☐☐☐☐☐☐☐☐☐☐

lease check at least (3) influencing factors for urchasing this book.

- nt or back cover information on book ☐
- cial approach to the content ☐
- npleteness of content ☐
- hor's reputation ☐
- lisher's reputation ☐
- k cover design or layout ☐
- x or table of contents of book ☐
- e of book ☐
- cial effects, graphics, illustrations ☐
- er (Please specify): ______ ☐

ow did you first learn about this book?

- in Macmillan Computer Publishing catalog ☐
- ommended by store personnel ☐
- the book on bookshelf at store ☐
- ommended by a friend ☐
- eived advertisement in the mail ☐
- an advertisement in: ______ ☐
- d book review in: ______ ☐
- er (Please specify): ______ ☐

ow many computer books have you urchased in the last six months?

- book only ☐
- oks ☐
- 3 to 5 books ☐
- More than 5 ☐

4. Where did you purchase this book?

- Bookstore ☐
- Computer Store ☐
- Consumer Electronics Store ☐
- Department Store ☐
- Office Club ☐
- Warehouse Club ☐
- Mail Order ☐
- Direct from Publisher ☐
- Internet site ☐
- Other (Please specify): ______ ☐

5. How long have you been using a computer?

- ☐ Less than 6 months
- ☐ 6 months to a year
- ☐ 1 to 3 years
- ☐ More than 3 years

6. What is your level of experience with personal computers and with the subject of this book?

	With PCs	With subject of book
New	☐	☐
Casual	☐	☐
Accomplished	☐	☐
Expert	☐	☐

Source Code ISBN: 0-7897-0825-6

7. Which of the following best describes your job title?

- Administrative Assistant ☐
- Coordinator ☐
- Manager/Supervisor ☐
- Director ☐
- Vice President ☐
- President/CEO/COO ☐
- Lawyer/Doctor/Medical Professional ☐
- Teacher/Educator/Trainer ☐
- Engineer/Technician ☐
- Consultant ☐
- Not employed/Student/Retired ☐
- Other (Please specify): ____________ ☐

8. Which of the following best describes the area of the company your job title falls under?

- Accounting ☐
- Engineering ☐
- Manufacturing ☐
- Operations ☐
- Marketing ☐
- Sales ☐
- Other (Please specify): ____________ ☐

9. What is your age?

- Under 20
- 21-29
- 30-39
- 40-49
- 50-59
- 60-over

10. Are you:

- Male
- Female

11. Which computer publications do you read regularly? (Please list)

____

Comments: ______________________________

Fold here and scotch-tape to

NO POSTAGE NECESSARY IF MAILED IN THE UNITED STATES

BUSINESS REPLY MAIL

FIRST-CLASS MAIL PERMIT NO. 9918 INDIANAPOLIS IN

POSTAGE WILL BE PAID BY THE ADDRESSEE

ATTN MARKETING
MACMILLAN COMPUTER PUBLISHING
MACMILLAN PUBLISHING USA
201 W 103RD ST
INDIANAPOLIS IN 46290-9042

The CD-Rom that accompanies this book will automatically start the install process using Windows 95's auto-play feature. If you have disabled this feature, or are using Windows 3.x, please see the README files in \ZDBENCH\WB96 (WinBench 96), \ZDBENCH\WS96 (Winstone 96), and ZDBENCH\WS32 (Winstone 32). If you have problems with this disc, please contact Macmillan Technical Support at (317) 581-3833. We can be reached by e-mail at **support@mcp.com** or on CompuServe at **GO QUEBOOKS**.

License Agreement

This package contains one CD-ROM that includes software described in this book. See applicable chapters for a description of these programs and instructions for their use.

By opening this package you are agreeing to be bound by the following:

This software is copyrighted and all rights are reserved by the publisher and its licensers. You are licensed to use this software on a single computer. You may copy the software for backup or archival purposes only. Making copies of the software for any other purpose is a violation of United States copyright laws. THIS SOFTWARE IS SOLD AS IS, WITHOUT WARRANTY OF ANY KIND, EITHER EXPRESSED OR IMPLIED, INCLUDING BUT NOT LIMITED TO THE IMPLIED WARRANTIES OF MERCHANTABILITY AND FITNESS FOR A PARTICULAR PURPOSE. Neither the publisher nor its licensers, dealers, or distributors assumes any liability for any alleged or actual damages arising from the use of this software. (Some states do not allow exclusion of implied warranties, so the exclusion may not apply to you.)

The entire contents of this disc and the compilation of the software are copyrighted and protected by United States copyright laws. The individual programs on this disc are copyrighted by the authors or owners of each program. Each program has its own use permissions and limitations. To use each program, you must follow the individual requirements and restrictions detailed for each. Do not use a program if you do not agree to follow its licensing agreement.